S0-AMQ-541

THE GREAT
CONTEMPORARY
ISSUES

BIG BUSINESS

THE GREAT

CONTEMPORARY

ISSUES

OTHER BOOKS IN THE SERIES

DRUGS
Introduction by J. Anthony Lukas
THE MASS MEDIA AND POLITICS
Introduction by Walter Cronkite
CHINA
O. Edmund Clubb, *Advisory Editor*
LABOR AND MANAGEMENT
Richard B. Morris, *Advisory Editor*
WOMEN: THEIR CHANGING ROLES
Elizabeth Janeway, *Advisory Editor*
BLACK AFRICA
Hollis Lynch, *Advisory Editor*
EDUCATION U.S.A.
James Cass, *Advisory Editor*
VALUES AMERICANS LIVE BY
Garry Wills, *Advisory Editor*
CRIME AND JUSTICE
Ramsey Clark, *Advisory Editor*
JAPAN
Edwin O. Reischauer, *Advisory Editor*
THE PRESIDENCY
George E. Reedy, *Advisory Editor*
FOOD AND POPULATION
George S. McGovern, *Advisory Editor*
THE U.S. AND WORLD ECONOMY
Leonard Silk, *Advisory Editor*
SCIENCE IN THE TWENTIETH CENTURY
Walter Sullivan, *Advisory Editor*
THE MIDDLE EAST
John C. Campbell, *Advisory Editor*
THE CITIES
Richard C. Wade, *Advisory Editor*
MEDICINE AND HEALTH CARE
Saul Jarcho, *Advisory Editor*
LOYALTY AND SECURITY IN A DEMOCRATIC STATE
Richard Rovere, *Advisory Editor*
RELIGION IN AMERICA
Gillian Lindt, *Advisory Editor*
POLITICAL PARTIES
William E. Leuchtenburg, *Advisory Editor*
ETHNIC GROUPS IN AMERICAN LIFE
James P. Shenton, *Advisory Editor*
THE ARTS
Richard McLanathan, *Advisory Editor*
ENERGY AND ENVIRONMENT
Stuart Bruchey, *Advisory Editor*

THE GREAT
CONTEMPORARY
ISSUES

BIG BUSINESS

The New York Times

ARNO PRESS

NEW YORK/1978

LEON STEIN
Advisory Editor

GENE BROWN
Editor

Library of Congress Cataloging in Publication Data

Main entry under title:

Big business.

(The Great contemporary issues)
Selections from the New York times.
Bibliography.
Includes index.
1. Big business—United States—History. 2. Corporations—United States—History. 3. Trusts, Industrial—United States—History. I. Stein, Leon, 1912- II. Brown, Gene. III. New York times. IV. Series.
HD2785.B495 338.6'44'0973 78-16236
ISBN 0-405-11196-7

Manufactured in the United States of America

The editors express special thanks to The Associated Press, United Press International, and Reuters for permission to include in this series of books a number of dispatches originally distributed by those news services.

Book design by Stephanie Rhodes

Contents

Publisher's Note About the Series

It would take even an accomplished speed-reader, moving at full throttle, some three and a half solid hours a day to work his way through all the news The New York Times prints. The sad irony, of course, is that even such indefatigable devotion to life's carnival would scarcely assure a decent understanding of what it was really all about. For even the most dutiful reader might easily overlook an occasional long-range trend of importance, or perhaps some of the fragile, elusive relationships between events that sometimes turn out to be more significant than the events themselves.

This is why "The Great Contemporary Issues" was created—to help make sense out of some of the major forces and counterforces at large in today's world. The philosophical conviction behind the series is a simple one: that the past not only can illuminate the present but must. ("Continuity with the past," declared Oliver Wendell Holmes, "is a necessity, not a duty.") Each book in the series, therefore has as its subject some central issue of our time that needs to be viewed in the context of its antecedents if it is to be fully understood. By showing, through a substantial selection of contemporary accounts from The New York Times, the evolution of a subject and its significance, each book in the series offers a perspective that is available in no other way. For while most books on contemporary affairs specialize, for excellent reasons, in predigested facts and neatly drawn conclusions, the books in this series allow the reader to draw his own conclusions on the basis of the facts as they appeared at virtually the moment of their occurrence. This is not to argue that there is no place for events recollected in tranquility; it is simply to say that when fresh, raw truths are allowed to speak for themselves, some quite distinct values often emerge.

For this reason, most of the articles in "The Great Contemporary Issues" are reprinted in their entirety, even in those cases where portions are not central to a given book's theme. Editing has been done only rarely, and in all such cases it is clearly indicated. (Such an excision occasionally occurs, for example, in the case of a Presidential State of the Union Message, where only brief portions are germane to a particular volume, and in the case of some names, where for legal reasons or reasons of taste it is preferable not to republish specific identifications.) Similarly, typographical errors, where they occur, have been allowed to stand as originally printed.

"The Great Contemporary Issues" inevitably encompasses a substantial amount of history. In order to explore their subjects fully, some of the books go back a century or more. Yet their fundamental theme is not the past but the present. In this series the past is of significance insofar as it suggests how we got where we are today. These books, therefore, do not always treat a subject in a purely chronological way. Rather, their material is arranged to point up trends and interrelationships that the editors believe are more illuminating than a chronological listing would be.

"The Great Contemporary Issues" series will ultimately constitute an encyclopedic library of today's major issues. Long before editorial work on the first volume had even begun, some fifty specific titles had already been either scheduled for definite publication or listed as candidates. Since then, events have prompted the inclusion of a number of additional titles, and the editors are, moreover, alert not only for new issues as they emerge but also for issues whose development may call for the publication of sequel volumes. We will, of course, also welcome readers' suggestions for future topics.

Introduction

Any attempt to understand the central role of business in the growth of our nation may very well begin with President Calvin Coolidge's incisive dictum that "the business of America is business." The historic root of that revelation lies in our colonial beginnings. Companies of investors, organized in England with the blessing of the Crown, were among the first to appreciate the "business" potential of the wilderness across the ocean. They raised the necessary capital and mobilized the venturers and agents sent westward to establish beachheads for future expansion. Their settlements along the eastern seaboard clung to the edge of a continent whose vast resources were only dimly perceived.

The purpose of their coming was clear. While others braved the wilderness to preserve freedoms of conscience and worship, English investors anticipated that the new land would yield, in time, huge quantities of raw materials that could keep England's mills and workshops humming. Across a bridge of ships, these would be exchanged for the finished goods produced in the homeland.

In the mercantilist faith that what was good for the Crown was good for America, Parliament enacted bans on production, shipping, exports and imports designed to keep the colonists on the low end of an imbalanced trade relationship. If, in the century before independence, British treasure grew as a result so too did resentment among colonial business leaders. Being Englishmen, they anguished over a loyalty to the Crown that denied them the exercise of rights with which they believed all Englishmen were endowed.

Moved by British traditions of representative government and the sanctity of private property and stirred by Protestant imperatives of work and thrift, colonial leaders first talked of independence and then openly declared their intentions. America was a new kind of political experience in the history of the world and the Divine Right of Kings had nothing to do with it. The Crown was an oppressor; free men had a natural right to preserve their freedoms - including the freedom of business enterprise.

In a predominantly agricultural society, many immediate needs were filled by household production. Trade in the young republic involved modest amounts of capital. Exchange between town and country could be close to barter. Aside from shipping, business was local with merchant and consumer confronting each other across the store counter; banker and borrower were neighbors; tradesmen knew the limits of their customers' credit. Supply and demand governed price determinations and the price of labor was skewed only by fluctuations in immigration and the fact that the far side of the new nation was open to the wilderness.

The greatest resource of the new nation was its spaciousness. The promise that lay beyond the horizon drew brave men and women westward. Paths turned into roads and then into turnpikes. Rivers became shipping highways. Half a century after independence a great canal was cut westward through the Empire State. Over mountains and across distant plains, peddlers and hawkers came on foot or by wagon, bringing pots, stoves, calico and pins from the east and in time opened stores where two roads crossed.

By mid-ninteenth century major technological changes were transforming the nation. The application of mechanical power to weaving and the production of arms with changeable parts marked a series of initiatives by the business community seeking new uses of energy and the further mechanization of production. In 1832, Baldwin opened its railroad shops and the manufacture of locomotives ceased to be a by-product of the production of iron. California entered the union in 1850; *The New York Times* began to publish in 1851. By 1859, U.S. industrial production for the first time exceeded the total value of its agricultural production.

The conquest of the continent required more than the exploits of hardy pioneers in covered wagons. Steam and steel were essential for the spanning of the nation with rails. For two decades in the middle of the eighteenth century money making men of vision vied with each other to link tracks to the Pacific coast. A generous government enabled them to cut a wide-swathed right of way across the continent, giving them the power of life or death over settlements, towns and rural areas by the fractional swing of the surveyor's scope.

The power required to finance the huge task was provided by the rapidly developing form of business organization that had its beginnings in the joint stock company. Aided by a series of Supreme Court decisions in the first half of the century, the corporation became the ideal means of great fortune making. By recognizing the separation of management from ownership, the new corporate "person" limited the personal liability of owners and opened the way for accumulating other people's money as capital.

After the Civil War, a corps of swashbuckling capitalists masterfully manipulated state legislatures stock, armies of laborers and values of land gifted to them by government. They filled the national scene with smoke-stacks, power-driven vehicles and a plethora of new products. For a time it seemed that Bernard Mandeville's dream in the infant days of capitalism would be fullfilled as the private vices of the masters of industry yielded public benefits.

But the dynamics of capitalist competition came to resemble Darwin's jungle rather than Mandeville's beehive. Corporate success demanded expansion and that meant the destruction or absorption of competitors. Giant corporations grew fewer as their size and power increased. In 1866, *The Times* cautioned against the tyranny of corporate giantism and foresaw a possible end of competition. A basic change was occurring in the nation's business life. It was no less than the diminishing potency of the self-correcting free market in the exchange of goods which, since Adam Smith, had been considered the foundation of the free enterprise system.

With the field narrowed, surviving giants reached out to each other. Joined through holding companies, combinations and merges or subtle understandings, they controlled supplies and administered prices. A *Times* editorial in 1882 castigated the masters of the trust who "trampled on the rights of citizens" and whose success kept pace with their ruthlessness. A lengthy review enclosed in *The Times* 1888 inventories the grip of the trusts on such diverse necessities as sugar, castor oil, school slates, linseed oil, steel rails, iron ore, plows, threshers and reapers and mowers, binders, beams, nails, pipes, iron nuts, stoves, paper bags, oilcloth, etc. etc.

* * *

From the start *The Times* reported the news authoritatively and thoroughly voluminously. Its responsibility to its readers was to provide fact and opinion. The separation is clear in the stained, antique pages of its early issues from which material has been drawn for this volume. The sense of outrage over legislative misconduct or the unrestrained use of economic power registers on its editorial pages and is documented in detail in its new columns.

For student and scholar alike, the fidelity with which *The Times* thus fullfilled its purpose provides a huge reservoir of the raw material of history. As the paper chronicled the evolution of anti-trust sentiment and its formal action into legislation in the final decade of the century, it sought both perpective and detail. In the public interest it spelled out the machinations of the Union Pacific malefactors but it also published, in 1898, Abram S. Hewitt's article castigating followers of William Jennings Bryan and the Socialists for deprecating the contributions of big business in bringing cheap goods and high wages to millions of Americans.

The record sampled in this volume provides an exciting kind of history - one devoid of the more sweeping generalizations of the text book but filled instead with the color, emotion and grittiness of accounts only a printer's day away from the event. It transmits the feeling of immediacy and contemporary concern that time tends to gloss over in later accounts.

The newspaper is history happening before historians are able to extrapolate theory and inevitability from events. When the focus of concern shifted from such prominent giants as Rockefeller, Carnegie and unorthodox types such as Daniel Drew to less conspicuous corporate management leaders, *The Times* provided support materials in its columns. As a newspaper of record, it published definitive statements by authorized spokesmen, official texts and documents, and excerpts from legislative records.

In 1909, *The Times* reviewed the long battle of the courts and legislatures against the trusts. In the same year it recorded in ample detail changes in management practices, product innovations and efforts being made by the business community to accomodate to changing law. It featured Henry Ford in a first-hand account of the techniques and significance of mass production and his philosophy of sales, low profit rates and higher wages. In its effort to clarify corporate and business conduct, the paper has published such distinguished analysts as Evans Clark, Stuart Chase, John Moody (predicting in 1929 further expansion of the economy), Alfred P. Sloan and Harold Ickes. The role of big business in American life has been depicted, for example, by Thurman Arnold, Sumner Slichter, Milton Friedman and now is covered on a regular basis by Leonard Silk.

While the nation sought at the turn of the century to reconcile private enterprise with public interest, business continued to push vigorously for new markets, new technology and a new image. Many who had climbed the ladder to success had followed stern dictums of God's calling and homage through good works. For them, the accumulation of wealth was evidence of righteousness. Long before Rockefeller invented public relations and corporate conscience by hiring Ivy Lee, gifts, endowments and, with Carnegie, the building of public libraries were meant to indicate a sense of stewardship.

Behind the public image, leaders of business and industry found a new arena for competition in the laboratory. Engineers studied variations in work flow, measured time and motion psychologists analyzed problems of mind and psyche at the work place; sophisticated machines replaced controls by workers setting the trend that led to automated and computerized factories All contributed to more speed and economy in production.

* * *

By the beginning of the twentieth century, the United States had become the richest and most powerful nation in the world. The resources of a continent, the backs and muscles of armies of workers, the drive of big business, the ingenuity of researchers, managers and merchandisers had scored the triumph.

The expanding role of business in national life led to major changes in the structure and organization of enterprise. Banking and finance provided the financial compost from which flowered multi-product corporations, conglomerates and, in time, multi-national intercontinental arrangements. While economies remained competitively national, finance capital moved toward internationalism, especially in basic materials, energy sources and the production of labor-intensive goods.

The first modern corporations in the land had turned to the burgeoning cities of the post-Civil War period to find their new mass markets. A major aspect of growth in the twentieth century has been the multiplication of markets through the creation of new goods and services. Vigorous advertising campaigns in the powerful mass media are employed to make these seem to be necessities of the good life. In chain store, supermarket, department store, mail order house or shopping mall the novelty, the bargain, the unique are hawked to arouse consumer anxieties.

* * *

Despite all its shortcomings, the free enterprise system remains triumphant. Nowhere else has an alternate system yielded greater social return. Others, with nationalized, controlled economies have had to banish freedoms that would target their faults. The problems of big business are testimony of our freedom. Indeed, our national character has been shaped by contending social forces - labor and capital, immigrant and "native," regional and national, private enterprise and public interest. Our safeguards have been a free press and an educational system that value the free market in ideas.

This volume provides the means for understanding and reassessment at a time when the spirit of business permeates every aspect of our lives: government, art, education, even sport. The genius and drive of business have expanded the volume of life, catering to need and the sense of status.

But have we improved the quality of life if in the midst of affluence, poverty of body and mind persist? What imperative of free enterprise commands the production of shoddy goods, bad taste and the corruption of the environment? In short, can the profit motive be channelled so as to enrich both the values and the material volume of American life? How, in spite of the comforts and anodynes it provides at a price, can business help rescue our nation from creeping spectator citizenship? Finally, how are we to curb administered pricing, preserve competition and profit-making and at the same time achieve equitable distribution and healthy circulation of the wealth of our nation?

If past is prologue, this compendium can aid in finding the answers and hint at the big business headlines of tomorrow.

LEON STEIN

Chapter 1

The Growth of American Industry

Two generations of Rockefellers, from left to right: John D. Jr., David, Nelson, Winthrop, Laurence and John D. 3rd.

NYT Pictures

The Tyranny of Corporations.

The recent union of the principal Express companies, by which they work in combination throughout the country, and the approaching entire consolidation of these associations which is rumored, with an immense capital and powerful machinery under one board of directors, calls attention anew to the *concentration of capital* which is going on in the United States.

The power which money gives in a commercial community, the reduplicating tendency of well managed capital, and the advantage in the "struggle for existence" which great organizing talent affords, have the tendency more and more to put the floating capital of the country into fewer hands, and to build up vast monopolies. We have only to look on the changes which have been in progress this very year to see this tendency.

Among railways, the Chicago and Northwestern has swallowed up a number of other lines, until it has become the greatest railroad corporation on this Continent; the Hudson River and Harlem roads are substantially in the control of one man, and, if report be true, the most vigorous efforts are being made to bring the enormous corporation of the New-York Central, with its thirty millions of capital, into the same hands.

The Pacific Mail Steamship Company has broken down all opposition, has increased its capital by ten millions, and will soon be a corporation like the old East India Company, holding undivided commercial control of the Pacific and of the sea-trade to California.

The Express monopoly is even more remarkable. Though the railroads ought to do their own "expressing," no road in the country would now venture to take it from these gigantic monopolies, or if they did, they would speedily be broken down by the enormous power of the capital and organization of the express companies. There will be speedily, we doubt not, in effect one express agency working like the Post-office from one end of the Union to the other, and able and ready to break down all opposition. In California, the Wells & Fargo, it is said, already drives the Government out of the Post-office business, at the same time paying the postage according to law.

One of our cotemporaries is so enamored with the effects of these private associations, that it proposes to place all the Post-office business of the country in the hands of the express companies.

If this be our tendency in America, the question arises what is to be the effect of these monopolies on public convenience. Thus far but few evils have been experienced from them. The Pacific Mail has reformed and improved the whole ocean service between New-York and San Francisco. The railroads have been fairly comfortable, and the express agencies have been marvels of efficiency and order. But the tendency of power—of the modern aristocracy of capital—is toward disregard of individuals and individual convenience and comfort. We already begin to feel the first grindings of the approaching tyranny of capitalists or corporations. Take our sufferings in New-York City from the street railroad corporations; the inconveniences, the crowding of passengers, the overcharging, the trifle they pay to the City for their valuable franchises, their superlative indifference and contempt for the rights or comforts of the people, and we can feebly discern what is before us when every public means of transit is in the hands of the tyrants of modern society—the capitalists. Again, let every traveler on the Hudson River and Harlem roads call to mind how entirely out of view has been any possible convenience or right of a passenger on those roads, as though the roads were built exclusively for the directors, and not for the public, and let him remember how utterly useless were any complaints or objections on his part or on the part of all the way passengers with regard to the practical management of the companies, and he will see what we are fast coming to under our modern aristocracy. Or let every housekeeper who receives from the express an enormous trunk at the basement steps, which no love or money can induce the agent to take up stairs; or every traveler who gets his valise at his hotel hours too late for his departure; or every merchant who pays exorbitantly for every small package sent, and who finds infinite trouble in securing restitution for any loss, say what they all think of the approaching blessed rule of private associations and monopolies, which so pleases the fancy of our evening cotemporary.

It may be said that competition can correct all this. But these companies reach such an extent of power, acquire such skill and possess such a capital, that competition is out of the question. What can competition do against Mr. VANDERBILT on the Hudson and Harlem Roads? Even the day-boats on the river only can compete with the roads by his sufferance.

What can any new company or set of individuals do against the express companies with fifty millions of capital, and all working together? They could buy out bodily any association which should venture to oppose them, or they could speedily ruin it. It is true that when an association is managed by such public spirited men as control the Pacific Mail, we do not need competition; but suppose them to abuse their trust and despoil the public as did the companies which preceded them on that route, what remedy have individuals? What competition can touch the City railroads or the gas monopolies? They are beyond the reach of even this remedy. Up to a certain limit—perhaps that of revolutions and vigilance committees—they can oppress and plunder the community without hindrance. Even the State Legislatures can barely hold their own against these powerful monopolies. They can bribe and bully and cajole, so as to squelch any bill directed against them.

It is no part of our present purpose to suggest a remedy. Indeed, we must frankly confess we see none. Nominally this is a free country and individual rights and personal immunities are supposed to be better protected than anywhere else in the world. But in point of fact there is no nation on earth where they are so utterly under the control and at the mercy of gigantic corporations and monopolies as in the United States.

November 10, 1866

The Insurrection Against the Railways.

During one-half the year the grain producers of the country are completely at the mercy of the railways. The great trunk lines from the West to the East exercise a despotic power over the fortunes of that agricultural empire known as the Northwest, embracing ten millions of people, and producing $1,000,000,000 a year. This power, far greater and more arbitrary than is known in any political organization of Western Europe, rests substantially without check in the hands of three men, and in the hands of those they choose to associate with them. This tyranny, oppressive and offensive as it is, is exercised with relentless severity. The farmer who raises his wheat or corn in the North-west, is taxed by it from fifty to seventy-five per cent. of his gross earnings. Of every four bushels he gathers, he is obliged to pay from two to three as tribute to this little band of rulers, who have almost imperceptibly been for years strength-ening their hold upon him. Corn which sold for seventy-three cents last month in Boston, netted the Illinois farmer only twenty-three. These exactions, ruinous in extent, are enforced with all the adjuncts that render taxation odious and intolerable. They are variable in form, uncertain in presentation, unequal in distribution, and collected often with insolence, and always with rigor. So galling are they in all their features, and so disastrous in their consequences, that no government could impose them to one-fourth the amount, or with one-half their aggravating incidents, without being surely and swiftly, and probably violently overthrown.

Though it is not the amount of the taxes which the railways levy that is their only oppressive feature, yet that is something which few people in the East realize. We are so largely engaged in the work of effecting exchanges only, and our transactions are made for the most part over an area relatively so small, that it is difficult for us **to understand the weight of the burden borne by the producers of the West in the expense of getting their products to market. We sell often at a loss, but we never find it more profitable to destroy our property than to try to sell it at all. But for months farmers in Iowa and Minnesota have been burning their corn for fuel, and many thousand bushels were allowed to rot on the ground rather than incur the expense of harvesting. When we remember the unexampled facilities the West enjoys for production—fertile soil, improved methods and machinery, and intelligent labor—this picture is nothing less than startling.**

But it is not the enormous cost of freight alone which makes the lot of the farmers a hard one. It is the manner in which this cost is imposed. Freights vary from month to month, and one-half the year are from one-third to double what they are during the other half. Corn, which can be sent from Chicago to New-York for sixteen cents in June, by water, and which the railways

will carry for twenty-five cents in August, the same railways charge thirty-six cents for carrying in January, and this is believed to be in one case twice, and in the other three times, what would fairly compensate the roads for carriage. Freights vary, too, with locality. Distances shorter by 200 miles are charged for at higher rates than longer ones. Between New-York City and the State of Indiana, 100 pounds of freight can be carried for twenty-five cents, and doubtless money is made by the operation. But between Rochester, N Y., and the same point in Indiana, a distance less by 400 miles, the charge is $1 25 for 100 pounds. Plainly more than four-fifths of this charge is profit. In other words, the profit is more than 400 per cent. These are but examples of facts, which the business community can furnish plenty of others to match.

Nor are these the only offensive characteristics of the present condition of affairs. The extortion, which every one can see are intolerably heavy and aggravating, are the work of a combination of men whose sole title to their profits comes from the free gift of the people. The public feel that they are being bound with bonds of their own forging. It is from the people that all railway franchises proceed. Moreover, in a large number of cases the people have actually taxed themselves to build the roads whose managers are now pressing them so sorely. This adds indignation to a sense of suffering and loss. Privileges which were given for public as well as private gain are perverted solely to private ends. The process partakes of robbery, or, at least, of swindling.

The secret of the course of the railways is not far to seek. Most of them are making apparently moderate dividends; but these dividends are the profits on an investment far smaller than their apparent capital, which is swollen by continual watering. This is equivalent to saying that the railway companies are greedy, and have the power within the forms of law to satisfy their greed. They are practically irresponsible. Legislation, so far, has been almost exclusively on their side. Everything has been done for encouragement, nothing for restriction. Now the tide is turning. There is a powerful reaction in the public mind, and especially in the West, which is taking the shape of widespread organization. What remedies will be finally devised it is too soon to say, but unless representative government is a delusion, the creatures of the law will, in the long run, be curbed by law.

March 28, 1873

RAILROAD COMBINATION.

THE "POOL" FORMED AT CHICAGO—ITS CHARACTER AND PROBABLE PERMANENCE—THE BALTIMORE AND OHIO NOT TO OPPOSE IT.

Special Dispatch to the New-York Times.

CHICAGO, Nov. 17.—Another conference of the Michigan Central, Lake Shore and Michigan Southern, and Pittsburg, Fort Wayne and Chicago Railroads was held at the general offices of the Pennsylvania Company, in this City, to-day, for the purpose of considering some further matters respecting the newly-formed pools of the Eastern lines. Mr. W. C. Quincy, General Superintendent of the Chicago Division of the Baltimore and Ohio Railroad, was present during the session, and was called upon to state the policy of the Baltimore and Ohio Railroad concerning freight and passenger rates. Mr. Quincy stated that although the Baltimore and Ohio had not joined the existing combination, it was the intention of its managers to act with it in endeavoring to maintain remunerative rates between this city and the East. His company proposed to secure fair rates, and could not be moved from this stand by any influence on the part of the press or the public.

From the remarks of Mr. Quincy it is to be inferred that, although not in the combination, the Baltimore and Ohio intends to operate with it. An effort was made at the meeting to reduce the existing passenger rates between this city and New-York from $22 to $20, which failed, beyond which no action of any public importance was taken.

The exact character of the present combination between the Eastern lines is as follows: The pool is composed of the Michigan Central from Chicago to Detroit, and all its connecting roads; the Lake Shore and Michigan Southern between Chicago and Buffalo, and all lines under its control; the Pittsburg, Fort Wayne and Chicago Railroad and all connecting lines under its control. One-half of the gross earnings from all business, local and otherwise, over each of the roads is to be retained to cover operating expenses, the remainder to be pooled on a basis of the comparative earnings of the various lines during the years 1873 and 1874. The compact under which the combination is made is to remain in force for two years, and any road desiring to withdraw will be compelled to give six months' notice of its intention to do so. It is the further intention of the pool to combine as far as possible the various agencies of roads into one, and in every manner possible reduce operating expenses.

The argument made in defense of the organization of this combination is that any further reckless competition between the lines cannot but result in bankruptcy. The compact sets forth that exorbitant rates cannot result in benefit to the people, but that moderate rates will alike benefit the public and the lines. In case of competition on the part of any outside line, like the Baltimore and Ohio, the pool roads will act conjointly in meeting any reduction that is made. In regard to the working of the pool, it may be stated that the railroad officials have thus far worked in unison, and that there is every prospect that the present combination will continue to exist for some time to come. With regard to an increase on the freight rates at present in force, it is announced officially that no increase will take place previous to Dec. 1.

November 18, 1875

WESTERN GRANGER LAWS.

CONSTITUTIONALITY AFFIRMED.

ACTION OF THE SUPREME COURT OF THE UNITED STATES IN THE ELEVATOR RATES AND RAILROAD CHARGES CASES—POWERS OF THE STATE OVER PUBLIC CARRIERS—ELEVATORS HELD TO BE A PORTION OF THE MEANS OF TRANSPORTATION—THE RAILROAD CASES.

WASHINGTON, March 1.—The Supreme Court of the United States to-day decided the so-called Granger cases; the first one being that of Ira Y. Munn and George L. Scott, plaintiffs in error against the people of the State of Illinois, in error to the Supreme Court of the State of Illinois. Mr. Chief Justice Waite delivered the opinion of the Court. The question to be determined in this case is whether the General Assembly of Illinois can, under the limitations upon the legislative power of the States imposed by the Constitution of the United States, fix by law the maximum of charges for the storage of grain in warehouses at Chicago and other places in the State having not less than 100,000 inhabitants, in which grain is stored in bulk, and in which the grain of different owners is mixed together, or in which grain is stored in such a manner that the identity of the different lots or parcels cannot be accurately preserved. It is claimed that such a law is repugnant: First, to that part of section 8, article 1, of the Constitution of the United States, which confers upon Congress the power "to regulate commerce with foreign nations and among the several States;" second, to that part of section 9 of the same article which provides that "no preference shall be given by any regulation of commerce or revenue to the ports of one State over those of another;" third, to that part of the fourteenth amendment which ordains that no State shall "deprive any person of life, liberty, or property, without due process of law; nor deny to any person within its jurisdiction the equal protection of the laws." We will consider the last of these objections first. Every statute is presumed to be constitutional. The courts ought not to declare one to be unconstitutional unless it is clearly so. If there is doubt, the expressed will of the Legislature should be sustained. The Constitution contains no definition of the word "deprive" as used in the fourteenth amendment. To determine its signification, therefore, it is necessary to ascertain the effect which usage has given it when employed in the same or a like connection. While this provision of the amendment is new in the Constitution of the United States as a limitation upon the powers of the States, it is old as a principle of civilized government. It is found in Magna Charta, and in substance if not in form, in nearly or quite all the constitutions that have been, from time to time, adopted by the several States of the Union. By the fifth amendment it was introduced into the Constitution of the United States as a limitation upon the powers of the National Government, and by the fourteenth, as a guarantee against any encroachment upon an acknowledged right of citizenship by the Legislatures of the States. When the people of the United colonies separated from Great Britain they changed the form, but not the substance, of their Government. They retained for the purposes of government all the powers of the British Parliament, and through their State constitutions, or other forms of social compact, undertook to give practical effect to such as they deemed necessary for the common good and the security of life and property. All the powers which they retained they committed to their respective States, unless in express terms or by implication reserved to themselves. Subsequently, when it was found necessary to establish a national Government for national purposes, a part of the powers of the States and of the people of the States was granted to the United States and the people of the United States. This grant operated as a further limitation upon the powers of the States, so that now the Governments of the States possess all the powers of the Parliament of England, except such as have been delegated to the United States or reserved by the people. The reservations of the people are shown in the prohibitions of the Constitution. When one becomes a member of a society he necessarily parts with some rights or privileges which, as an individual not affected by his relations to others, he might retain. "A body politic," as aptly defined in the preamble of the Constitution of Massachusetts, is a social compact by which the whole people covenants with each citizen, and each citizen with the whole people, that all shall be governed by certain laws for the common good. This does not confer power upon the whole people to control rights which are purely and exclusively private, (Thorpe vs. the R. and B. Railroad Company, 27th, 143;) but it does authorize the establishment of laws requiring each citizen to so conduct himself and so use his own property as not unnecessarily to injure another. This is the very essence of government, and has found expression in the maxim, "*Sic utere tuo ut alienum non laedas.*" From this source came the Police powers which, as was said by Chief Justice Taney in the license cases, (5 How., 583,) "are nothing more nor less than the powers of Government inherent in every sovereignty; * * * that is to say: * * * the power to govern men and things." Under these powers the Government regulates the conduct of its citizens, one toward another, and the manner in which each shall use his own property when such regulation becomes necessary for the public good. In their exercise it has been customary in England from time immemorial, and in this country from its first colonization, to regulate ferries, common carriers, hackmen, bakers, millers, wharfingers, inn-keepers, &c., and in so doing to fix a maximum of charge to be made for services rendered, accommodations furnished, and articles sold. To this day statutes are to be found in many of the States upon some or all these subjects, and we think it has never yet been successfully contended that such legislation came within any of the constitutional prohibitions against interference with private property. With the fifth amendment in force, Congress in 1870 conferred power upon the City of Washington to regulate * * * the rates of wharfage at private wharves, * * * the sweeping of chimneys, and to fix the rates of fees therefor * * * and the weight and quality of bread (3 Stat. 587, sec. 7;) and in 1848, to make all necessary regulations respecting hackney carriages and the rates of fare of the same, and the rates of hauling by cartmen, wagoners, carmen, and draymen, and the rates of commission of auctioneers. (9 Stat., 224, section 2.) From this it is apparent that down to the time of the adoption of the fourteenth amendment it was supposed that the statutes regulating the use or even the price of the use of private property necessarily deprived an owner of his property without due process of law. Under some circumstances they may, but not under all. The amendment does not change the law in this particular. It simply prevents the States from doing that which will operate as such a deprivation.

This brings us to inquire as to the principles upon which this power of regulation rests, in order that we may determine what is within and what without its operative effect. Looking then to common law, from whence come the rights which the Constitution protects? We find that when private property is affected with a public interest it ceases to be juris privati only. This was said by Lord Chief Justice Hale more than 200 years ago in his treatise, *De Portibus Maris*, (1 Harg law tracts, 68,) and has been accepted without objection as an essential element in the law of property ever since. Property does become clothed with a public interest when used in a manner to make it of public consequence and affect the community at large. When, therefore, one devotes his property to a use in which the public has an interest, he in effect grants to the public an interest in that use, and must submit to be controlled by the public for the common good, to the extent of the interest he has thus created. He may withdraw his grant by discontinuing the use, but so long as he maintains the use he must submit to the control. After quoting Lord Hale as to ferries, wharves, and wharfingers, and the decision of the Supreme Court of Alabama, because the Court thought they found in them the principle which supports the legislation they were examining, the opinion continues as follows:

"Enough has already been said to show that when private property is devoted to a public use it is subject to public regulation. It remains only to ascertain whether the warehouses of these plaintiffs in error and the business which is carried on there come within the operation of this principle. For this purpose we accept as true the statements of fact contained in the elaborate brief of one of the counsel of the plaintiffs in error. From these it appears that the great producing region of the West and North-west sends its grain by water and rail to Chicago, where the greater part of it is shipped by vessel for transportation to the seaboard by the great lakes, and some of it is forwarded by railway to the Eastern ports. * * * Vessels to some extent are loaded in the Chicago harbor, and sailed through the St. Lawrence directly to Europe. * * * The quantity [of grain] received in Chicago has made it the greatest grain market in the world. This business has created a demand for means by which this immense quantity of grain can be handled or stored, and these have been found in grain warehouses, which are commonly called elevators, because the grain is elevated from the boat or car by machinery operated by steam into the bins prepared for its reception, and elevated from the bins by a like process into the vessel or car which is to carry it on. * * * In this way the largest traffic between the citizens of the country north and west of Chicago and the citizens of the country lying on the Atlantic coast north of Washington is in grain which passes through the elevators of Chicago. In this way the trade in grain is carried on by the inhabitants of seven or eight of the great States of the West, with four or five of the States lying on the sea-shore, and forms the largest part of inter-State commerce in these States. The grain elevators or warehouses in Chicago are immense structures, holding from 300,000 to 1,000,000 bushels at one time, according to size. They are divided into bins of large capacity and great strength. * * * They are located with the river harbor on one side and the railway tracks on the other, and the grain is run through them from car to vessel or boat to car, as may be demanded in the course of business. It has been found impossible to preserve the owners' grain separate, and this has given rise to a system of inspection and grading, by which the grain of different owners is mixed, and receipts issued for the number of bushels which are negotiable and redeemable in like kind upon demand. This mode of conducting the business was inaugurated more than 20 years ago, and has grown to immense proportions. The railways have found it impracticable to own such elevators, and public policy forbids the transaction of such business by the carrier. The ownership has, therefore, been by private individuals, who have embarked their capital and devoted their industry to such business as a private pursuit. In this connection it must also be borne in mind that, although in 1874 there were in Chicago 14 warehouses adapted to this particular business, and owned by about 30 persons, nine business firms controlled them, and that the prices charged and received for storage were such as have been from year to year agreed upon and established by the different elevators or warehouses in the City of Chicago, and which rates have been annually published in one or more newspapers printed in said city in the month of January in each year, as the established rates for the year then next ensuing such publication. Thus it is apparent that all the elevating facilities through which these vast productions of seven or eight great States of the West must pass on the way to four or five of the States on the sea-shore may be a virtual monopoly. Under such circumstances it is difficult to see why, if the common carrier, or the miller, or the ferryman, or the inn-keeper, or the wharfinger, or the hackney coachman, pursues a public employment and exercises a sort of public office," these plaintiffs in error do not. They stand, to use again the language of their counsel, in the very "gateway of commerce," and take toll from all who pass. Their business, most certainly, "tends to a common charge, and is become a thing of public interest and use." Every bushel of grain for its passage "pays a toll, which is a common charge;" and therefore, according to Lord Hale, every such warehouseman ought to be under public regulation, viz.: That he take but reasonable toll. Certainly if any business can be clothed with a public interest and cease to be *juris privati*, only this has been. It may not be made so by the operation of the Constitution of Illinois, or this statute, but it is by the facts. We also are not permitted to overlook the fact that for some reason the people of Illinois, when they revised their Constitution in 1870, saw fit to make it the duty of the General Assembly to pass laws "for the protection of producers, shippers, and receivers of grain and produce," (article 13, section 7,) and, by section 5 of the same article, to require all railroad companies receiving and transporting grain in bulk, or otherwise, to deliver the same at any elevator to which it might be consigned, that could be reached by any track that was or could be used by such company; and that all railroad companies should permit connections to be made with their tracks, so that any public warehouse, &c., might be reached by the cars on their railroads.

This indicates very clearly that during the 20 years in which this peculiar business has been assuming its present "immense proportions" something had occurred which led the whole body of the people to suppose that remedies such as are usually employed to prevent abuses by virtual monopolies might not be inappropriate here. For our purposes we must assume that if a state of facts could exist that would justify such legislation, it actually did exist when the statute now under consideration was passed. For us the question is one of power, not of expediency. If no state of circumstances could exist to justify such a statute, then we may declare this one void, because in excess of the legislative power of the State; but if it could, we must presume it did. Of the propriety of legislative interference within the scope of legislative power the Legislature is the exclusive judge. Neither is it a matter of any moment that no precedent can be found for a statute precisely like this. It is conceded that the business is one of recent origin, that its growth has been rapid, and that it is already of great importance. And it must also be conceded that it is a business in which the whole public has a direct and positive interest. It presents, therefore, a case for the application of a long-known and well-established principle in social science, and this statute simply extends the law so as to meet this new development of commercial progress. There is no attempt to compel these owners to grant the public an interest in their property; but to declare their obligations if they use it in this particular manner. It matters not in this case that the plaintiffs in error had built their warehouses and established their business before the regulations complained of were adopted. What they did was from the beginning subject to the power of the body politic to require them to conform to such regulations as might be established by the proper authorities for the common good. They entered upon their business, and provided themselves with the means to carry it on, subject to this condition. If they did not wish to submit themselves to such interference, they should not have clothed the public with an interest in their concerns. The same principle applies to them that does to the proprietor of a hackney carriage, and as to him it has never been supposed that he was exempt from regulating statutes or ordinances because he had purchased his horses and carriage and established his business before the statute or the ordinance was adopted. It is insisted, however, that the owner of the property is entitled to a reasonable compensation for its use, even though it be clothed with a public interest, and that what is reasonable is a judicial, and not a legislative question. As has already been shown, the practice has been otherwise. In countries where the common law prevails it has been customary from time immemorial for the Legislature to declare what shall be a reasonable compensation under such circumstances; or, perhaps, more properly speaking, to fix a maximum, beyond which any charge made would be unreasonable. Undoubtedly in mere private contracts relating to matters in which the public has no interest, what is reasonable must be ascertained judicially. But this is because the Legislature has no control over such a contract. So, too, in matters which do affect the public interests, and as to which legislative control may be exercised; if there are no statutory regulations upon the subject the courts must determine what is reasonable. The controlling fact is the power to regulate at all. If that exists the right to establish the maximum of charge as one of the means of regulation is implied. In fact, the common law rule which requires the charge to be reasonable is itself a regulation as to price. Without it the owner could make his rates at will, and compel the public to yield to his terms or forego the use. But a mere common law regulation of trade or business may be changed by statute. A person has no property, no vested interest in any rule of the common law. That is only one of the forms of municipal law, and is no more sacred than any other. Rights of property which have been created by the common law cannot be taken away without due process, but the law itself, as a rule of conduct, may be changed at the will or even at the whim of the Legislature, unless prevented by constitutional limitations. Indeed, the great office of statutes is to remedy defects in the common law as they are developed, and to adapt it to the changes of time and circumstances.

To limit the rate of charge for services rendered in a public employment, or for the use of property in which the public has an interest, is only changing a regulation which existed before. It establishes no new principle in the law, but only gives a new effect to an old one. We know that this is a power which may be abused, but that is no argument against its existence. For protection against abuses by Legislatures the people must resort to the polls, not to the courts. After what has already been said, it is unnecessary to refer at length to the effect of the other provision of the fourteenth amendment which is relied upon, viz.: That no State shall "deny to any person within its jurisdiction the equal protection of the laws." Certainly it cannot be claimed that this prevents the State from regulating the fares of hackmen or the charges of draymen in Chicago, unless it does the same thing in every other place within its jurisdiction. But, as has been seen, the power to regulate the business of warehouses depends upon the same principle as the power to regulate hackmen and draymen, and what cannot be done in the one case in this particular cannot be done in the other. We come now to consider the effect upon this statute of the power of Congress to regulate commerce. It was very properly said in the case of the State tax on railway gross receipts, (15 Wall, 293,) that "It is not everything that affects commerce that amounts to a regulation of it within the meaning of the Constitution." The warehouses of these plaintiffs in error are situated and their business carried on exclusively within the limits of the State of Illinois. They are used as instruments by those engaged in State as well as those engaged in inter-State commerce, but they are no more necessarily a part of commerce itself than the dray or the cart by which, but for them, grain would be transferred from one railroad station to another. Incidentally they may become connected with an inter-State commerce, but not necessarily so. Their regulation is a thing of domestic concern, and certainly until Congress acts in reference to their inter-State relations, the State may exercise all the powers of government over them, even though in so doing it may indirectly operate upon commerce outside its immediate jurisdiction. We do not say that a case may not arise in which it will be found that a State, under the form of regulating its own affairs, has encroached upon the exclusive domain of Congress in respect to inter-State commerce, but we do say that upon the facts as they are presented to us in this record, that has not been done. The remaining objection, to wit: That the statute in its present form is repugnant to section 9, article 1, of the Constitution of the United States, because it gives preference to the ports of one State over those of another, may be disposed of by the single remark that this provision operates only as a limitation of the powers of Congress, and in no respect affects the States in the regulation of their domestic affairs. We conclude, therefore, that the statute in question is not repugnant to the Constitution of the United States, and that there is no error in the judgment.

In passing upon this case we have not been unmindful of the vast importance of the questions involved. This and cases of a kindred character were argued before us more than a year ago by the most eminent counsel and in a manner worthy of their well earned reputations. We have kept the case long under advisement in order that the decision might be the result of our mature deliberations.

The judgment is affirmed.

THE RAILROAD CASES.

The Supreme Court to-day, among others, also rendered the following decisions:

No. 27—*Pick et al. vs. Chicago and North-western Railroad Company et al.*, and No. 40—*Lawrence et al. vs. Paul et al. and The Chicago and North-western Railroad Company.*—Appeals from the Circuit Court for the Western District of Wisconsin.—These suits present the single question of the power of the Legislature of the State of Wisconsin to provide by law for a maximum of charge to be made by the Chicago and North-western Railroad Company, for fare and freight upon the transportation of persons and property carried within the State, or taken up outside and brought within it, or taken up inside and carried out. The decision is that until Congress acts in reference to the relations of the inter-State commerce, it is competent for the State to regulate the fares of the railroads so far as they are of domestic concern. This company, it is said, has domestic relations with the State, and incidentally these relations may reach beyond the State. Until Congress undertakes to legislate for those who are without the State, Wisconsin may provide for those within, even though it may indirectly affect those without. Affirmed. The Chief Justice delivered the opinion.

No. 324—*The Chicago, Burlington and Quincy Railroad Company vs. The Attorney General and State Treasurer of Iowa.*—An appeal from the Iowa Circuit.—In this case it is said railroad companies are carriers for hire. They are incorporated powers in order that they may the better serve the public in that capacity. They are, therefore, engaged in a public employment, affecting the public interests, and under the decision in Munn and Scott vs. the People of Illinois (the principal case) subject to legislative control as to their rates of fare and freight unless protected by their charters. In the absence of legislative regulation on the subject of fares the courts must decide for it, as they do for private persons when controversies arise, what is reasonable. But when the Legislature steps in and prescribes a maximum of charge, it operates upon this corporation the same as it does upon individuals engaged in a similar business. A uniform rate of charges for all railroad companies in the State might operate unjustly upon some. It was proper, therefore, to provide in some way for adaptation of the rates to the circumstances of the different roads, and the Legislature, in the exercise of its distinction, has seen fit to do this by a system of classification, and whether this was the best that could be done is not for the court to decide. Affirmed.

The Chief Justice delivered the opinion.

No. 352—*The Chicago, Milwaukee and St. Paul Railroad Company vs. Ackley et al.*—Error to the Circuit Court for Wisconsin.—The only question presented in this case is whether a railroad company in Wisconsin can recover for the transportation of property more than the maximum fixed by the statute by showing that the amount charged was no more than a reasonable compensation for the services rendered. The decision is that as between the company and a freighter, the maximum of the statute is the limit of the recovery for transportation actually performed. If the company should refuse to carry at the prices fixed, and an attempt should be made to forfeit its charter on that account, other questions might arise which will not be anticipated at this time. For goods actually carried, the limit of the statute is the limit of the recovery. Affirmed. The Chief Justice delivered the opinion.

No. 353—*Stowe vs. State of Wisconsin.*—Error to the Circuit Court for Wisconsin. The only question in this case, not decided in the case of the Chicago, Milwaukee and St. Paul Railroad Company against Ackley, just decided, is as to the effect upon the rights of these parties of the charter of the Milwaukee and Waukesha Railroad Company, passed by the Territorial Legislature of Wisconsin in 1847. This provides that on the completion of said railroad, or any portion of the track not less than 10 miles, it shall be lawful for the company to demand and receive such sum or sums of money for passage and freight of persons and property as they shall, from time to time, think reasonable. This, it was claimed, gave the company charter right to fix its own rates of fare and freight, subject only to a judicial determination as to whether they are reasonable. The court affirms the view of the Supreme Court of the State on this subject, that the charter was accepted and the corporation organized many months after the adoption of the Constitution and the admission of the State into the Union by Congress. Previous to that time it remained a naked proposition. For this reason it is held that its acceptance, after the organization of the State, so far as it is a contract, makes it manifestly a contract with the State. Affirmed.

The Chief Justice delivered the opinion.

No. 10—*The Winona and St. Peter Railroad Company vs. Blake et al.*—Error to the Supreme Court of Minnesota, and No. 74—*McGrath, Receiver, vs. Coleman.*—Error to the Circuit Court for the District of Minnesota. In the former case it is said that the road was by its charter bound to carry when called upon—as a common carrier—and charge only reasonable rates. These are incidents of the occupation in which it was authorized to engage. The case is held to fall within the decision in No. 99, decided at the same time, and stated above. In No. 74 it is held the question is the same, and the decision is affirmed in both cases. The Chief Justice delivered the opinion.

Mr. Justice Field dissented in all the Granger cases, and with permission of the court will hereafter file an opinion.

No. 170.—*Bayne et al. vs. The United States*—Appeal from the Maryland Circuit Court.—In this case the court affirms a decree below making the United States a preferred creditor of the insolvent firm of William Bayne & Co., of Baltimore. Mr. Justice Davis delivered the opinion.

The court then proceeded to hear rearguments in Nos. 58 and 59, municipal bond cases from the Southern District of Illinois, viz.: The Town of South Ottawa vs. Perkins, and the Board of Supervisors of Kendall County vs. Post. Mr. Justice Davis sits in the arguments and will participate in the decision.

March 2, 1877

RAILROAD SELF-CONTROL

A PROTEST AGAINST LEGISLATIVE INTERFERENCE.

LELAND STANFORD'S ANSWER TO THE BOARD OF TRADE QUESTIONS—ARGUING THAT SO-CALLED REGULATION OF RATES IS UNJUST AND PRACTICALLY A ROBBERY.

SAN FRANCISCO, Jan. 22.—Leland Stanford, President of the Central Pacific Railroad, publishes a three-column letter this morning to the special committee on fares and freights of the New-York Board of Trade, answering questions propounded by the committee, and also Judge Black's opinion.

Mr. Stanford says: "The general scope of the questions goes to the control, to a greater or less extent, of property which stockholders in railroad companies believe to be of right their own. Here it is pertinent, it seems to me, to call attention to the principles upon which our Government is founded. They are laid down in that great bill of rights known as the Declaration of Independence. There it is clearly enunciated that Governments are instituted to secure the people in their inalienable rights—life, liberty, and the pursuit of happiness." He continues: "Tariffs and the supervision of commerce and trade originated in a barbarous age, and were the direct offspring of robbery and rapine enforced by the hand of might. If the question of the control of railroads were to be threatened purely from a legal stand-point, I should have nothing to say, because it is *stare decis*. The essence of ownership is in control. The value of property consists in its use or the rents and profits to be derived. In the celebrated Granger cases, so called, the use of the profits and the control were declared to be the subject of legislation. The principle in these cases, especially as enunciated in the warehouse case, was that the right of the Legislature to control the use and the benefits of the property of private individuals in connection with their own personal services was to be determined by the nature of the business or the number of people with whom the business might be transacted. To sustain these decisions there was a violent assumption of fact. It does not follow that the warehouseman necessarily does business with a large number of people. A single individual might tax to the utmost the capacity of the warehouse, and, indeed, of several. In such a case, if one or more individuals may use the property and appropriate the services of one or more persons, there is no limit to which the power may be exercised over all kinds of business. Then, where is the harmony between a decision of the courts sustaining this doctrine and the fundamental principles of our Government, to which allusion has before been made. These decisions sustain Judge Black's assertion, but there can be no denying that they are a most flagrant violation of the principles of free government and are entirely in harmony with a theory of Government which rests its foundation on might and asserts the divine right of Kings. It was never intended that this should be a paternal Government; yet, does it not begin to assume that form when it is claimed that it should fix the term of contracts between independent parties by attempts at regulating the rates shippers shall pay and carriers shall receive for their services?"

Mr. Stanford adds: "But I proceed to treat the subject in its politico-economic aspects. In your first interrogatory you seem to beg the whole question, and assume that railroads are public highways and common carriers, and derive their franchise and existence from the public. I do not think the assumption is proper. Corporations are formed, I believe, throughout all the States of our Union under general incorporation laws, and they are formed by the individual corporators. The property of the incorporation is contributed by the stockholders, and the State no more creates the corporation or its property than it creates a joint partnership between individuals or the partnership property. The corporation obtains nothing which cannot be had by any set of individuals who choose to associate themselves together as a corporation for the same purpose.

"Your second question is, 'railroad managers justify the practice of giving low rates to some shippers and refusing them to others, on the ground of development of business in certain localities; is it consistent with the public welfare and the rights of citizens to allow railroad managers to decide what persons and places shall be thus developed?' I shall not say anything to justify discrimination against individuals and communities, but content myself on this head by simply stating that such has never been practiced by railroad companies with which I am connected. So far as they are concerned, they practice the same business principles that govern and regulate individuals in the management of their affairs. The primary consideration with railroad managers under the observance of the golden rule is their treasury. With this idea in view, and to meet competition, they often carry freight at less rates for a longer than for a shorter distance, and they accept the less rate because they cannot do better, and because a small profit is better than none. This is only in accordance with the principles of industry, thrift, and economy, which should ever be encouraged. To deny the companies the privileges of working for a small profit would be on a par with saying to an individual, 'Better be idle than take small earnings when larger cannot be had.' It is the policy of the Central Pacific and, I believe, of railroad companies of the United States generally, to accept a small profit where a larger cannot be obtained, as it is also its policy to encourage the development of the resources of the country. In doing so it practices no unjust discrimination; it charges nobody else more because of the rate it is compelled to accept from others, but it puts into practice a common and economic principle in fixing the charge for service by railroad companies. There are various things that may enter into the determination of rates, prominently among them the quality of the article carried and the quantity, the distance moved, the climatic and other difficulties to overcome in the transportation, the volume of business, whether the movement in either direction is about equal, and the question of competition.

"Your committee is undoubtedly aware that a very large portion of the coarse unmanufactured products of the country is moved below the average rate of the cost of transportation. Yet in so doing nobody is harmed. The railroad companies find the smallest profit better than none, and a rate barely sufficient to pay the expense of movement is better than idleness. Under this rule the country obtains a development; homes for the people are possible at remote distances from markets, and every industry finds encouragement. Under the substantially unlimited control of their own affairs which railroad companies have enjoyed, rates of transportation have steadily been reduced until at present their general rates are far below what even your committee would 10 years ago have deemed possible. Business can easily afford to pay about the average. The higher the maximum rate the lower the possible minimum. Given a certain amount to be earned, a reduction of the maximum necessarily increases the minimum. The minimum rates largely affect individuals and the question of the production and the general development of the country. The maximum charge, being upon manufactured and costly articles, is not felt by the producer or by the consumer, and a reduction of this rate of great convenience to the carrier and to the producers of cheap unmanufactured materials, and without which a very large portion of the latter commodities could not be produced or moved, would go substantially to the benefit of the middlemen, without making these articles any cheaper to the consumer. In other words, the great efforts made to reduce rates would not successfully be of any advantage to the laboring man who consumes. Reductions are sought by those engaged in business, and, if made, would inure almost solely to their benefit, and for this reason they are seeking to exercise a control over the property of others. There is not a principle of business exercised by the railroad companies in their management that is not deemed honorable, and which is not in constant practice by the merchant, the manufacturer, the lawyer, the doctor, and the farmer.

"As to the idea suggested by question five, that a court be established to determine, upon full inquiry, the questions of justice between the carrier and its patron, that is one matter; but so far as the establishment of a Board of Commissioners to exercise control over the property of others is concerned, that is another matter, and which I cannot be expected to approve.

"As to question six, I am not informed that competition is mainly supplanted by pooling arrangements. I believe that this pooling reaches only to the through business of a few roads, but if the Government is to equitably regulate railroads, the earnings of all will have to be pooled on the roads consolidated."

To the ninth question, referring to limiting earning, Mr. Stanford answers that there is no justice in limiting what may be earned by the exercises of sagacity and industry. Regarding increasing the capital of railroad companies, he says that is the concern of the companies themselves, and intimates that it is the business of nobody else.

As to question twelve, "What do you think of the practice of the railroad companies or railroad managers in contributing large sums to control elections or to influence legislation or to political campaign funds?" Mr. Stanford answers: "I think of that as I do of individuals doing the same thing—it is neither better nor worse in this case than in the other. I know, however, that the railroad companies do these things. It is invariably when they are compelled to do so to resist aggression and oftentime threatened confiscation of their property under the plea of regulation."

Question thirteen reads: "Do you think the uncontrolled power of large corporations and their subsequent violations of public rights, as developed in the late railroad investigation, is provocative of Communism and antagonism of capital and labor in this country?" "Leave the railroad industry uncrippled," says Mr. Stanford; "leave the control of railroad property as you leave that of other property, and you will never have reason to ask such a question. It seems to me that Communism does not come from the people who seek to control only their own property, but rather from those who wish not only to control and regulate properties in the creation of which they had no part or ownership, but also the labor of others bestowed in their management. What you propose in regard to railroad property is, to my mind, on a par with the principles contended for by the Communists, and the agitator Kearney advocated no doctrine in regard to property more atrocious than the principles embodied in the Granger cases and the laws which they sustain."

Mr. Stanford goes at length into the question of legislative control of railroads. He says: "In any scheme of Congressional legislation the mileage would have to be taken into consideration in order to be just, allowing to one company the same rates as allowed another for the same service. It would take into consideration the difficulties of operation, the different grades, the various climatic influences, the different cost prices of labor and supplies, the question of the movement of freight in different directions, the value of business, local and through, and the distance each moved, and soon, under such a system, it would be found that the advantages offered for transportation by the different companies would be unequal. The road having the least number of miles, were a mileage rate adopted, would move freights between two given points at a less rate than the other roads, and upon this basis it would command the entire business. If in distance the various roads were equal, the one having the easiest grades would have the advantage; and so on through all the various circumstances that probably would be taken into consideration by a legislative body in making up rates, it would be found that things that are unequal in

themselves cannot be made equal by any mere declaration of equality. The topography and the geography of the country are controlling factors in the regulation of rates, and they will remain unchanged. Business would seek the route offering the cheapest and best service between two points. To give a fair distribution of business, so that the different roads might live, would require a minimum as well as a maximum price to be established. Here you wou'd have an arbitrary system of regulation that would necessarily deny the privilege of competition, and disregard all those economic principles which should govern and regulate business.

"From the foregoing, my conclusion is inevitable that railroad property should be left to the management of its owners. The business is legitimate. Any interference by those who do not own it is a burden upon the property, and one which must eventually be borne by the people. If the people want to exercise a control over the road they must do as they have said to the corporation it must do when the State exercises the right of eminent domain: that is, to pay to the individual owners the full value of whatever is taken for public use, and to this it must come at last if the control is to be taken from the stockholders without confiscation. There is only one honest way to acquire control of property. Perhaps, since the wide circulation given to Judge Black's communication in answer to your questions, I may be pardoned if I refer to some of his statements. He finds authority to regulate charges upon railroads in that clause of the Constitution of the United States giving to Congress the authority to regulate commerce among the several States. Under this reading, the power of regulation is a power to regulate the carrier, whether that carrier be a corporation or an individual. The regulation of railroads upon this ground is entirely foreign to that which has heretofore engaged our attention, and the difficulties of regulation upon this theory are practically insurmountable, substantially for the same reasons, with the added difficulty that barriers would be erected to the commerce between individuals living in different States that would not exist between individuals living in the same State."

Referring to Judge Black's statement about Government aid to Pacific railroads, Mr. Stanford says: "So far from the aid of the Government being sufficient to build the Central Pacific Railroad, I can say, because I know whereof I speak, that every dollar derived from the loan of the Government credit went into the construction of the road, together with a much larger amount derived from the other resources of the company. It is susceptible of easy demonstration that the work of grading the first 150 miles of the Central Pacific Railroad from Sacramento eastward was more than would suffice to grade the road for a single track from the Rocky Mountains to the Hudson River. In conclusion, gentlemen, allow me to say that maximum rates determine the possibility of minimum rates; that maximum rates have enabled railroads to develop to the extent that they have the vast resources of the country; that the railroads in opening up new countries, adding new industries, conferring additional facilities for the interchange of commodities, and bringing the buyer and seller close together, have furnished and do furnish labor for the common welfare far beyond other agencies. The reduction of rates under the plea of regulation is a great blow to the laboring man who produces and to the laboring man who consumes. In my opinion any reduction scarcely goes to the benefit of the many, but to that of the comparatively few and comparatively wealthy, who occupy the positions of middlemen between the producer and the consumer. This question of transportation is of an importance that prevents its being settled excepting upon just and correct principles."

January 23, 1881

THE RAILROAD PROBLEM

IMPORTANT QUESTIONS DISCUSSED BY MR. NIMMO.

FIGURES SHOWING THE DECREASED COST OF TRANSPORTATION—POOLS AND THEIR BEARING UPON THE PUBLIC—GOVERNMENTAL RESTRAINT CONSIDERED.

WASHINGTON, Nov. 1.—The report of Mr. Joseph Nimmo, Jr., Chief of the Bureau of Statistics, relating to the railroad problem, and devoted particularly to the cost of transportation, confederations, or pooling arrangements and the governmental regulations of railroads, has been issued to the public. The reduction in the cost of transportation on the railroads of the country generally Mr. Nimmo finds is very clearly indicated by data relating to the following leading railroads, viz.: The Boston and Albany, New-York Central and Hudson River, New-York, Lake Erie and Western, Pennsylvania, Pittsburg, Fort Wayne and Chicago, Lake Shore and Michigan Southern, Michigan Central, Chicago and Alton, Chicago, Burlington and Quincy, Chicago, Milwaukee and St. Paul, Chicago, Rock Island and Pacific, and the Illinois Central. The number of tons of freight carried on these railroads increased from 45,557,002 tons during the year 1873 to 78,150,913 tons during the year 1880, an increase of about 71.5 per cent. The receipts from freight, however, increased from $112,004,648 in 1873 to $143,368,178 in 1880, an increase of $31,383,530, or only about 28 per cent. This small rate of increase of receipts in proportion to the increase of traffic was due to the fact that the average rate per ton charged on these railroads fell from 1.77 cents per ton per mile in 1873 to 1.07 cents per ton per mile in 1880, a decrease of 39.5 per cent. The following table indicates the increase of traffic and the decrease of freight charges on the New-York Central and Hudson River Railroad, the New-York, Lake Erie and Western Railroad, and the Pennsylvania Railroad from 1868 to 1880:

Year.	*Tons Transported.*	*Average Freight Charge per Ton per Mile. Cents.*
1868	11,193,120	2.153
1869	12,908,010	1.881[illegible]
1870	14,778,556	1.588[illegible]
1871	16,406,558	1.490[illegible]
1872	18,417,774	1.511[illegible]
1873	22,249,170	1.480[illegible]
1874	21,868,341	1.343
1875	22,231,172	1.180[illegible]
1876	23,599,239	1.014
1877	23,269,106	.983
1878	26,238,341	.935
1879	32,359,637	.792
1880	36,353,714	.836 3-5

The aggregate traffic on these three railroads was thus more than three times as great in 1880 as in 1868, while the average freight charges imposed in 1880, after making proper allowance for currency values in 1868, were 60 per cent. less than during 1868. From 1870 to 1880 there was a decrease of 39.45 per cent. in the freight charges on these railroads, a decrease of 32.51 per cent. in the charges on the New-York State canals, and a decrease of 12.32 per cent. in the average of the prices of those commodities commonly regarded as necessaries of life. In other words, the ratio of decrease in freight charges on railroads was somewhat greater than was the ratio of decrease in the freight charges on the New-York State canals, and more than three times as great as the average decrease in the prices of the necessaries of life. It is impossible, says Mr. Nimmo, to estimate the magnitude of the benefits which the reductions made in the charges for transportation on railroads have conferred upon the interests of agriculture, of mining, and of commerce. That the increase in the value of the domestic exports of the United States to foreign countries—from $442,820,178 during the year ended June 30, 1871, to $902,319,473 during the year ended June 30, 1881—has been largely due to such reductions is evident, he believes, from the fact that such exports are chiefly the products of the Western and North-western States, a large proportion of which is transported to the sea-board on railroads.

Regarding the restraints placed upon railroads by the Government, Mr. Nimmo says: "Few, and for the most part ineffectual, governmental restraints of a positive nature have been interposed in this country to the exclusive determination of freight charges by railroad officials. Freight charges are largely influenced by public sentiment, and by that comity which always prevails to a greater or less extent between the merchant and the transporter. But in the matter of railroad transportation, as in all other affairs affecting human interests, cupidity is sometimes stronger than that sense of right and justice which inclines men to the observance of reciprocal rights. The current history of railroad transportation in this country clearly indicates that there are evils connected with it which call for a public remedy; evils which affect not only the commercial and industrial interests of the country, but which also affect the railroads. Hence arises the demand for some sort of governmental intervention, either through the enforcement of specific provisions of law, or through the moral influence exerted by a well-grounded apprehension of such intervention, as a result of the scrutiny exercised by intelligent and faithful Boards of Railroad Commissioners. As the authority of the State Governments is circumscribed by State lines, State jurisdiction seems to be inadequate to dealing with the subject in its application to the great commercial movements of the country across State lines. The first practical step toward the settlement of this important question appears to be an intelligent investigation of it in all its bearings. The attention of this office is mainly directed toward the commercial and industrial aspects of the subject. The political or constitutional questions involved are especially subjects for the consideration of the national Congress. A better understanding of the relation of transportation to the public interests will undoubtedly tend to lead railroad managers to avoid just causes of complaint, and, besides, lead the people generally to more correct views as to the relations of the railroads to the commercial and industrial interests of the country.

"It is a source of encouragement that at the present time, intelligent and fair-minded men who differ widely as to the nature and extent of the controlling and restraining influence which should be exercised by State and national Governments agree that there should be no unfair discriminations in rates, either with respect to persons or to localities, that rates should be open and equal to all under like conditions; and also that any governmental regulations which may be established shall be both protective of the public interests and just to the proprietors of railroads."

Mr. Nimmo devotes a long chapter to the consideration of railroad pools, little of which, however, is not already familiar. Viewing pooling arrangements in their organic characteristics and from the stand-point of public interest, "it appears to be certain," he says, "that so long as their existence has no legal sanction and their edicts no binding authority under the laws of the land, they occupy a position of unstable equilibrium, since they are at all times liable to disruption as the result of changes in the conditions under which they are organized, and even as the result of changes of opinion on the part of the chief executive of any one of their constituent members as to the advantages which the organization affords to his particular road. Under the present order of things the disturbances in the commercial, industrial, and financial interests of the country resulting from railroad wars do not in any great degree influence the conduct of those who precipitate them. It appears evident, therefore, that before railroad confederations acquire stability they must have the prop of some external power, since not even any moral restraint ever tends to lead any member of such an organization to heed the opinions of any one, or even of all, of its competitors. In so far as relates to the public interests, other than those pertaining to the railroad companies, it is impossible at present to pass final judgment upon pooling organizations. As yet they are tentative and upon probation. Their beneficent features, or to speak more precisely, the fact that they tend to avert certain intolerable evils, and that there is no other known or immediately available instrumentality for effecting that object, commend them to toleration and to a degree of public favor while the experiment as to their utility is being fairly tried. But too little is known by the public in regard to their practical workings and the methods employed and the expedients resorted to in carrying them into effect to justify State Governments or the national Government in conferring upon them at once and unconditionally the attributes of legality. * * * To the minds of some of the most thoughtful and intelligent railroad managers and students of railroad affairs the prop of some external restraining influence appears now to be necessary in order to insure the maintenance of good faith between the different companies and the observance of rules which practice has proved to be necessary to the orderly management of the railroads of the country, both in their relations to each other and to the public. Apparently, the only available expedient of that nature is some sort of governmental regulation or control. * * * In view of the evils resulting from wars of rates, it appears to be not only desirable but feasible for the Government to require that all rates should be made public alike to all and not changed without due public notice. It is perhaps also advisable that a law should be passed requiring that railroad companies shall furnish cars to shippers equitably, in proportion to orders therefor, and that no preference in facilities shall be afforded to one shipper as against his competitor in trade. Preferences in the matter of supplying cars and furnishing other facilities for securing prompt and speedy transportation may prove in practice to be discriminations quite as unjust and injurious, even, as are considerable differences in freight charges. The enforcement of such rules as those above indicated would undoubtedly tend to correct very many of the most serious abuses which now exist in railroad transportation. If this much in the way of reform could be fully secured, it would probably be a matter of very much less difficulty to adjust differences as to the territorial limits of the traffic operations of competing lines, the relative rates which shall prevail over competing rail and water lines, and the relative rates which shall prevail with respect to the commercial interests of rival cities. * * * If the Government is to lend a helping hand in bringing about an adjustment of the difficulties which now exist, it must probably come about as the result of the formulation into positive enactments of practices in the dealings of railroads with each other and with the public, proved by experience to be just, proper, and necessary for mutual protection and the advancement of the interests of the country generally."

There are, Mr. Nimmo says, two vitally important questions confronting public attention: First—Are there evils connected with the railroad system of the United States which injuriously affect the public interests, and are those evils of such magnitude as to demand governmental interference? Second—By what means can such interference be exercised without subjecting the Government to a degree of responsibility and to difficulties of an administrative nature which would more than counterbalance the possible good results which might be expected to follow governmental interference for the purpose of correcting the evils referred to?

Mr. Nimmo believes that a thorough investigation of this whole question is imperative. Such an investigation should, he thinks, be conducted by a commission of experts fully competent to pass upon such subjects as the bearing of the transportation question upon the agricultural, industrial, and commercial interests of the country; the economic and practical questions connected with the actual conduct of the traffic interests of railroads, and the legal and constitutional questions involved in the solution of this complex and difficult problem.

November 12, 1881

GOULD AND HUNTINGTON AGREE.

Mr. Jay Gould and Mr. C. P. Huntington have concluded to end their Southern railroad war, and a compromise agreement is to be executed to-day. The Gould party signed the contract yesterday. The Huntington roads affected by the agreement are the Central Pacific and Southern Pacific. The Gould roads are the Texas Pacific, the New-Orleans Pacific, the Missouri Pacific and its old St. Louis, Iron Mountain and Southern, the Missouri, Kansas and Texas, with its old International and Great Northern. The bitterest of fights have been carried on between these interests competing, as the roads do, at important points. But by the terms of the agreement just reached all pending litigation is to cease and henceforth arbitration is to be the rule on all conflicting matters. The contract provides that the Texas Pacific shall stop construction at the present point of junction with the Southern Pacific, about 80 miles from El Paso. The road between this junction and El Paso is made subject to the perpetual joint use of each party to the contract, the cost of maintenance, repairs, &c., being equally divided between the two interests. Huntington acquires the right to intersect the Missouri Pacific 80 or 100 miles from New-Orleans, and thus secure a perpetual joint right of use to New-Orleans on terms the same as accorded to Gould on the other combination. It is set forth in the contract that all roads affected by the contract shall constitute one continuous line, with a pro rata mileage division of earnings. The business between New-Orleans and Galveston is to be divided between the companies.

November 17, 1881

CORPORATE WEALTH.

The great corporations which control the railroad property of this country are in danger of bringing themselves into direct antagonism with public sentiment and the power of the people. Mr. GALLAWAY, of the Manhattan Railway Company of this City, denies having said that that corporation has the Legislature on its side, and the courts on its side, and pays for its law by the year; but it matters very little whether he said it or not. Many of these great corporations have long acted on the assumption implied in the alleged remark. They have in past years, when public attention was not aroused on the subject or was otherwise occupied, succeeded very largely in shaping legislation to suit their purposes, and of late they have strenuously resisted, in this State at least, every effort to restrict their action within such limits as shall secure the rights of those who deal with them and conduce to the general interests of the public. The courts are compelled to interpret and apply the law as they find it, but much depends on the manner in which suits are brought and the way in which they are conducted. Unlimited wealth and the best legal skill can do much to secure judicial results against which narrow means and ordinary talent can contend with little avail. The resources of the former may multiply suits, vary their form, transfer them from one jurisdiction to another, and produce delays which are calculated to worry and wear out less powerful litigants. We are glad to believe that very few of our Judges are corrupt or subservient to the influences which corporations wield, but they must pass upon questions in the form in which they are brought before them and under the laws as they are, whether the latter adequately secure all rights and interests or not. Moreover, a single weak spot in the Judiciary is speedily found out. One pliable Judge may do mischief which all his associates cannot undo; or if the power is in their hands they cannot exercise it unless the case is brought before them in proper form and manner. Poor suitors have little chance in struggling against the money and legal skill at the command of the corporations, and most of them will give up the fight or keep out of it, submitting to wrong rather than encounter the difficulty and expense of obtaining redress.

Whether the corporations pay for their law by the year or by the "piece" is a matter of no consequence. It is notorious that they obtain the very best of legal service and pay the highest prices for it. Lawyers obtain princely incomes by attending to the legal business of these powerful clients. The learning and ability of the best equipped are at their command, and are sedulously applied to promoting their interests. They are, therefore, enabled to go to the very limits of the law in any direction that may suit their purposes, and to avoid, by ingenious indirection, a transgression of its requirements where such transgression cannot be regarded as safe. To make a legal contention with them is more than any ordinary citizen is willing to undertake. Even if he is sure the law is on his side, he shrinks from the expense, the worry, and the uncertainty of contending with such powerful adversaries. The consequence is that his rights and his protests are more and more disregarded, and he begins to doubt whether, indeed, the machinery of justice is not, to all intents and purposes, on the side of the wealth and power represented in the great corporations.

These vast aggregations of wealth certainly use their utmost power, wherever their interests are involved, to control the action of Legislatures. If any part of the Judiciary is susceptible to their influence it is brought to bear with its full force, and a Judge may do much to serve them without transcending the limits of the discretion necessarily left to him by the law. But what are these corporations? We are accustomed to attribute to them purposes and motives and to speak of them as unscrupulous, although they are proverbially without souls. This is because they are so largely under the control of a few men, who have acquired enormous wealth by directing their affairs. The circumstances under which the railways of this country have been developed and the extent to which they have been permitted to grow up without regulation or restriction, have enabled skillful and daring operators—the more unscrupulous the more successful—so to manipulate their business and the traffic in their shares as to bring into their own hands enormous wealth and power. The Vanderbilts and Goulds and Fields, rather than the corporations regarded merely as associations of numerous stockholders, exercise the sway under which the community shrinks. It is they who make war and peace among railroads, put rates up and down, control the tides of the stock market and profit by their rise and fall; and it is they who trample upon the rights of citizens and defy them to seek redress. Greed for wealth and power, and a lack of the scruples which deter other men, have given them their peculiar success, and these continue to control their action. Nobody questions the value of railroads to the public or the necessity of the corporate organizations by which they are owned, but unless they are brought under the wholesome control of law, whereby the rights of individual citizens and of the community at large can be secured, sooner or later a conflict will come between their power and the might of the people which will shake the very foundations of law and order.

January 15, 1882

SUPREME COURT DECISIONS.

AN INTER-STATE COMMERCE CASE—MOTIONS AND ARGUMENTS.

WASHINGTON, Oct. 25.—The Supreme Court rendered its decision to-day in the case of the Wabash, St. Louis and Pacific Railroad Company, plaintiffs in error, vs. the People of the State of Illinois. The specific allegation was that the railroad company charged Elder and McKinney 15 cents per 100 pounds for transporting goods from Peoria to New-York City and on the same day charged Isaac Bailey and F. O. Swannell 25 cents per 100 pounds for the same class of goods from Gilman, Ill., to New-York, Gilman being 86 miles nearer than Peoria to New-York. The discrimination, it was alleged, was in violation of the law of Illinois, which prohibits any charge for the transportation of passengers or freight within the State of Illinois proportionately greater than would be charged for the transportation of passengers or like classes of freight "over a greater distance of the same road." The gist of the decision is contained in the conclusion, as follows: "When it is attempted to apply to transportation through an entire series of States a principle of this kind, and each one of the States or of half a dozen States shall attempt to establish its own rates of transportation, its own methods to prevent discrimination in rates, or to permit it, the deleterious influence upon the freedom of commerce among the States and upon the transportation of goods through those States cannot be overestimated. That this species of regulation is one which must be, if established at all, of a general and national character, and cannot be safely and wisely remitted to local rules and local regulations, we think is clear from what has already been said. And if it be a regulation of commerce, as we think we have demonstrated it is, and as the Illinois court concedes it to be, it must be of that national character, and the regulation can only appropriately be by general rules and principles which demand that it should be done by the Congress of the United States under the commerce clause of the Constitution." The judgment of the Supreme Court of Illinois, which was adverse to the railroad, is reversed and the case is remanded to that court for further proceedings in conformity with the above opinion. Opinion by Justice Miller.

Justice Bradley delivered a dissenting opinion in which the Chief-Justice and Justice Gray concurred. In this opinion it is conceded that Congress might, if it saw fit, regulate the matter under consideration, but not having done so, it is held that the State does not lose its power to regulate the charges of its own railroads in its own territory simply because the goods or persons transported have been brought from or are destined to a point beyond the State borders.

October 26, 1886

SIGNED BY THE PRESIDENT.

THE INTER-STATE COMMERCE BILL BECOMES A LAW.

WASHINGTON, Feb. 4.—At 5 o'clock this afternoon the President signed the Inter-State Commerce Commission bill, and will send word of his action to the Capitol to-morrow without any memorandum of protest or explanation. He has given a good deal of attention to the subject since the bill came into his hands, and although he has been troubled by doubts as to the clearness of some of its provisions he has at no time hesitated to declare that some legislation was needed, and that a beginning should not be spoiled. A perfect law was not to be expected from a body in which many conflicting interests are represented by active and persistent men. If glaring difficulties become known before the next Congress meets the bill can be amended. A great deal will depend, the President knows, upon the men appointed as Commissioners. If they are men of integrity as well as ability they will proceed bravely but judiciously to carry out the provisions of the law, producing as little friction as possible. The problem presented of selecting the five Commissioners is greater than that of deciding upon what to do with the bill. There are several hundred applicants, very few of whom are at all fitted for the places. Several men whom the President would like to name are not inclined to accept. Mr. John D. Kernan, who is still spoken of, is regarded as one of the most promising candidates, for the reason that he has had experience on the New-York Commission. While it is not certain that he will be chosen and the names of Senators and Representatives have been used rather at the instigation of personal friends than by reason of any encouragement from the President, it is regarded as likely that he will be one of the Commissioners. The entire number will be sent in early enough to give the Senate time to confirm them before adjourning.

February 5, 1887

THE INDUSTRIAL CORPORATION

THE GREAT OIL MONOPOLY

HOW THE STANDARD COMPANY ROBS THE PUBLIC.

THE VIEWS OF AN EXPERIENCED OBSERVER ON THE SITUATION—A BRIEF REVIEW OF THE OPERATIONS OF MR. ROCKEFELLER'S CORPORATION—HOW IT GREW AND PROSPERED.

CLEVELAND, Nov. 17.—Very few men will ever know how much money was made by the Standard Oil Company in the recent flurry in the oil market, and the stockholder himself who obtains full knowledge of all the deals that have been made, and their results, must stand close to the inner door, of which John D. Rockefeller alone holds the key. While the Standard is, in the real meaning of the word, the greatest monopoly in America, as powerful in its own field as the Government itself, and holding the entire refined and crude oil market of the world in the hollow of its President's hand, its methods and dealings are the most securely covered up and hidden from the public eye of any corporation that anywhere approaches it in size or ramifications. It fears nothing in the world so much as to be talked about, and the last thing desired by its managers is the advertisement of the public press. Its business is all done by a few hands, although an army of executive officers carry out their decrees. No ray of information in the shape of an interview or otherwise ever shines out of the general offices, and Mr. Rockefeller or Col. Payne are the last men ever quoted as having opinions on the question of oil. The local press long since ceased calling at the Standard head-quarters for verification or denial of any of the numerous rumors and charges that have been afloat. A call met either with a refusal of admittance or a reference to some subordinate who was in the possession of no information, or who dare give nothing should he know ever so much. So the calls grew less frequent, and the Standard is never quoted as authority by the Cleveland press, and not often mentioned, except as the news comes in from outside sources. All departments of the Standard are kept distinct, and the most prominent and best trusted man in one branch knows nothing whatever of what may be occurring in another. A great many transactions never go on the books. The works are fenced in by high pickets to keep the public out; but a no less palpable and effectual reserve hedges the employes in, and causes them to keep their counsels to themselves. The giving of information even on trivial points is not encouraged, while the man who would do much talking about methods and results would soon find himself in need of a situation. When the employes are among themselves in public places or before outsiders, and have occasion to refer to business, they speak of parties only by initials, and end their conversation as soon as practicable. When information does leak out, a quiet effort is made to discover the channel, and if the offender is discovered he is quietly warned, or dismissed without warning. So far as skill, watchfulness, and an iron rule can secure it, the greatest possible silence is kept in Standard block, and about the business that is done therein.

A shrewd and experienced observer gives an opinion of the situation and the operations of the Standard as regards the present market. "In July last," said he, "crude oil was at 49¾ cents. Suppose the Standard then—as they no doubt did—bought 3,000,000 or 4,000,000 barrels, and had, we will say, 8,000,000 or 10,000,000 barrels by the time it had reached 65 cents. Then they turn in and commence to sell at that figure. They buy and sell, making a profit every time. With their inside knowledge, and their control of the market, I have no doubt that by the time oil reached 96 cents, the Standard manipulators had cleared for the company no less than $8,000,000. Following the same basis there is no reason for doubting that fully $50,000,000 would be made by the time the market touched $2—should it go there. These are large figures, I know, but it must be remembered that we are dealing with a large speculative field, and with a most gigantic monopoly. Another suggestion has been advanced in connection with the recent flurry that is worth glancing at. We will say that crude oil continues to go up; refined oil will, of course, bear a corresponding relation. On the 1st of last July all Europe had enough in store to last to January next. Now boom crude oil to $2, and when the present European supply gives out the Standard will be in shape to compel the Hollanders, the Belgians, and the English to buy at a fabulous price. There is no doubt that this is a part of the present deal, and no man could ask a better fortune than to have just as much money as will be made out of the European part of this present series of transactions.

"When the Standard was first incorporated as a company under the laws of Ohio its capital stock was placed at $1,000,000. In 1879 that stock was increased to $3,500,000. Within the last four months it has been expanded to $70,000,000, and the stock allowed to go into the market, although it has never got into the Street. It is now worth about 80 cents, which would give the company a value of some $56,000,000. When this increase of stock was made all the possessions and branches were turned into the common stock—the various works, pipe lines, and oil. It is surmised that this increase has been made with a view to unloading from the few on to the many, as against a possible coming day when the oil fields shall give out and the whole colossal business go to pieces. If that should happen the parties who held the stock of the Standard would have on hand a useless lot of assets, consisting of dry territory, rusting tanks, valueless machinery, buildings and stills, and miles of iron pipe under the sod. This suggestion is sketched here for what it is worth, and as an evidence of the opinions and theories that arise in oildom and float out over the country at large. When one measures this great monopoly as to wealth, power, and resources, it does not seem possible that the beginning was so small. In 1864–5, when the Pennsylvania oil excitement first commenced, the firm of Clark & Rockefeller was doing a commission business in the river section of Cleveland. The two partners were Morris P. Clark, a big Englishman, and John D. Rockefeller, a medium sized long-headed and cool Scotchman. Among thousands of others these gentlemen became interested in oil, and went into Pennsylvania and bought some territory. I do not know how they made out with it, but soon afterward their speculation took a new turn. Sam Andrews was a warehouse man who was shrewd and skillful in various ways, and Clark and Rockefeller made a deal with him by which the experiment of refining oil in Cleveland was to be tried. A still was erected and Andrews put in charge. He furnished the management and did the work while the firm put up the cash, and looked after the buying and the selling. All was at first done in a small way. After a time Andrews went to experimenting, and found a way by which oil could be refined better, and at less cost than by the old method. The business grew bit by bit, and some suggestions as to its possibilities began to dawn not only on these refining pioneers, but on other men whose minds had seen turned toward the subject of oil. About this time Messrs. Clark and Rockefeller had some difficulty as to a question about land, and the former sold out. Rockefeller and Andrews went on together, expanding their business and improving it. After a time Mr. H. M. Flagler, the present Secretary of the Standard, was taken into the partnership, and the firm became Rockefeller, Flagler & Co. Clark had seen enough of the business to know there was money in it, and a new firm was formed under the name of Clark, Payne & Co., the second partner being Col. Oliver H. Payne, the present Treasurer of the Standard.

"It is not known in whose mind first dawned the possibility of the scheme that has been so successfully put into operation, but Mr. Rockefeller has always been credited with its parentage. If he did not suggest it, his was the hand that put it into execution. Clark, Payne & Co. were approached by Rockefeller, Flagler & Co., and the idea that soon blossomed into the Standard was unfolded. These two went in on an equal footing. This combination gave them an advantage over any other one firm, and they were not the men to throw away that advantage. The next largest Cleveland firm was approached and allowed to come in, but on terms not quite so good as the two original firms had given each other. Then other firms were approached in turn, each one receiving less consideration than its predecessor at the hands of the then strong and determined combination. By the time the little fellows were reached the negotiation became practically a dictation: 'Here, your works are worth so much, your trade so much. We will allow you a share based thereon if you come in quietly, but if you don't agree to our terms we will knife you.' This is what their argument amounted to, and the careful outsiders who could see danger from afar accepted the terms and gained shelter. The foolish passed on and were punished with ruinous competition against odds that were too much for them, and under which they eventually went down. The Standard Oil Company was chartered into life, and its career was thus formally opened.

"The plan of monopoly and control was continually pushed forward. The Pennsylvania Legislature was at that time at the summit of its unenviable fame, and things were being carried with a high hand at Harrisburg. Charters for anything and everything were passed in batches, and any man who had on hand any scheme describable or undescribable, public or private, had only to select his charter, and pay the price of those who had it for sale. President Rockefeller saw one that was indefinite enough to suit his purpose in that of the South Improvement Company, and he soon had all its vague rights and privileges in his possession. The scheme that he had on hand was daring in its attempt, broad in its scope, and difficult in its accomplishment. He desired first to unite all the refiners in the country; then all the producers, and finally all the railroads doing business across the oil territory and between the oil fields and the markets. Oil was then very low; the producers and refiners were at war with themselves and everybody else, and nobody was gaining anything except the oil-buying public. It was the purpose of the South Improvement Company to make money for the producers, the refiners, and the railroads, and let the public look out for itself. But the scheme was more easily concocted than carried out. There were too many parties in interest, and all of them did not possess Mr. Rockefeller's admirable gift of silence. The plans were made public, and it requires no stretch of recollection to call up the row that ensued in Pennsylvania and Ohio. The public, that had been given no part in the South Improvement profits, took a hand in the matter, and eventually the scheme fell through, either by a repeal of the charter or an abandonment on the part of the manipulators, who saw that their programme could not be carried to a successful completion.

"The Standard returned to its legitimate business of refining and to the expansion of its market limits. It also continued its fight with the producers, who charged it with a purpose of combining the refiners for the purpose of getting the producers by the throat. In the end the Standard, of course, got about what it wanted. The deal with the railroads was made independent of the South Improvement machinery, and the Standard coined money and crushed rivals as it chose through its inside advantages of transportation. The railways were investigated, but the sum total of all the legislative investigations so far has been to establish the fact that oil when properly applied has the power to smother revelations that might not be pleasant. The railway companies implicated at first took the ground that no rebates had been given any one, but when that position was no longer tenable, fell back on the proposition that what they did for the Standard they would do for any one else. For any one who would send so many million barrels of oil over their lines they would allow so much rebate. But as the Standard was the only party that could furnish the business specified, the condition of the small refiners was just what it had been before. The monopoly is still at work in more directions than the mere manipulating of the market. It made a purchase of the Union Oil Company at Titusville, and gave in payment $2,000,000 worth of its present stock. The Empire Oil Works at Franklin cost $10,000 or $18,000 to build two years ago, and the Standard recently bought it out for $140,000 in stock. This price was given because the Empire had an advantage that most competing refineries do not have—it could send its oil to New-York on as good terms as the Standard could. This came about because its chief owner, Mr. Brundred, was the son of the General Manager of the Green Line Transportation Company, and could get as good figures as the Standard could. Unable to freeze him out, they bought him out, and kept him at work in his former refinery at a large salary. Another illustration of the methods pursued is found in the history of the Republic Oil Company, whose works were built some years ago on Willson-avenue, Cleveland. For a long time the Standard supplied it with oil through its pipe line, but after a time the manager of the Republic was called in and told that he could have no oil. Said the Standard agent: 'Go to work, Sir, and figure up what your land is worth, what your machinery and fixtures have cost, and add your good will at a fair sum. Then let us see the figures.' It was done, and the officers of the Republic estimated things at a reasonable sum, in their own favor to a small extent. When the total was shown, the Standard managers said: 'All right. We will give you a check for that amount and take the works off your hands. If this is declined, we cannot let you have any more oil.' Knowing what their fate would be were a dependence placed on the railroads, the offer was accepted, and the Republic Oil Company became a new branch of the Standard.

"There are at present in Cleveland some eight or nine oil refineries, independent of the Standard. They get their crude oil over the Cleveland and Pittsburg Road, operated by the Pennsylvania Company. The Standard has said to individuals among these refiners that they would buy all the concerns if they would all sell in one lump, but that they would not touch one of them alone, or any number of them without them all. The outsiders do not care to sell. They say that they can each make a little money refining, but that if they cannot make any they can shut down and lie idle. Most, if not all, of them are running now in a quiet way. The Standard is at present enlarging its carrying facilities. It owns one pipe line between Cleveland and the oil field, which cost $400,000, and a larger one is being laid at a cost $600,000. The present line cannot carry the oil needed when the temperature is less than 60°, and when it gets down to 45° it cannot furnish over 3,000 barr ls per day, whereas 14,000 are needed. The present line is held in the name of the Standard, and in some of the counties through which it runs it is listed in the Standard's name, while in others it goes on the tax-books in the name of the Cleveland Pipe Line Company. The opinion has been expressed that if the law officers at Columbus should do their duty they could shut the Standard off from all control of the pipe line and put it in the hands of other parties who would run it for the general benefit, as the Standard's charter does not authorize it to carry oil. But even though public policy should require it there is no danger of any official interference from Columbus."

November 19, 1882

A GREAT MONOPOLY'S WORK

AN INNER VIEW OF THE STAND ARD OIL COMPANY.

METHODS BY WHICH LEGISLATORS HAVE BEEN MANAGED, DISAGREEABLE COUNSEL-ORS THROWN OUT, AND FORTUNES MADE.

OIL CITY, Penn., Feb. 26.—When Mr. H. M. Flagler, Secretary of the Standard Oil Company, was testifying before a New-York committee a few weeks ago he was very careful not to go into details as to the workings of his company, nor could such information be obtained by any official scrutiny. There was a time when the Standard officers had reason to believe that an Ohio Legislative committee might suddenly demand the production of the records of the company, and it was far from the intention of Mr. John D. Rockefeller that even a body of men so distinguished as a sub committee of an Ohio Legislature should lay the skeleton of his business bare before the public eye. Orders were given to one or two trusted and responsible men. Two or three large packing cases were prepared and placed in a room at head-quarters. The books were laid out, or such of them as Mr. Rockefeller did not care to harbor in Ohio in case he thought any one was very anxious to see them, and their packing was left to the care of the man who was to accompany them East. The Standard agent at Columbus had orders to send on the instant the decision of the committee to issue an order for the production of the books. On the receipt of such information the books were to be hurried into the cases, carted to the depot, and sent to New-York City on the out-going of the first express train. Once there they would be beyond the jurisdiction of the State of Ohio, and Mr. Rockefeller could snap his fingers in the face of the Ohio Legislature. But the order did not come, whether because the committee were lobbied into quietness or bull-dozed out of an investigation that might investigate. THE TIMES's correspondent's informant—a Cleveland oil man who in past years has had intimate dealings with the Standard, but has not now—did not feel able to hazard an opinion.

"Inside of seven years," said this gentleman, "the Standard spent $325,000 in Harrisburg. In five years it spent over $60,000 in Columbus. In the same length of time, but covering different years, it spent $35,000 in Albany. Here are nearly $500,000 gone—to whom? Who knows? Does Mr. Rockefeller himself? Does Mr. Flagler or Mr. O. H. Payne? I suppose they know in general results just what legislation, direct and indirect, was had for their benefit, and can form some idea as to what further legislation and investigation that they did not desire was prevented. But no one supposes for a moment that any of these gentlemen could name the persons to whose pockets the money might be traced. Their dealing has all been with agents. The Standard plan has always been to select its agents and deal with them in general terms. 'Produce,' says Mr. Rockefeller, 'certain desired results that I shall name to you, and a certain named sum of money shall be yours. I do not want to know anything about your expense account. I do not want to know the name of a man with whom you have deal. Don't do anything that will involve you in trouble, or that will be in violation of law. If you do, the entire responsibility lies with you. This action that we fear is to the injury of our business, and we desire to prevent it. Now go and use your moral [*sic*] influence to prevent action, and when you have succeeded I will pay you the sum named for expenses and for your time.' The agent understands what all this means and goes to work. His profit lies between the price Mr. Rockefeller has agreed to pay and the sum that it will cost him to bribe, banquet, coax, and entrap the members of the designated Legislature into casting their votes and using their influence in the direction that the Standard agent desires. Sometimes in one State capital three or four paid agents have been at work, without any one of them knowing that the others were holding a Standard commission.

One Winter, when it was the desire of the Standard that a threatened or at least expected legislative investigation should not occur, or at least that in case it did the proper kind of a committee should be appointed, the company had in its direct employ a member of the House, a member of the Senate, an ex-member of the House, and three outsiders, one of the last named being a newspaper man. And of all this collection of agents only two, and they were the outsiders exclusive of the newspaper man, knew that they were not the only paid lobbyists on the ground. I may add that the committee was appointed, but it was composed of men of such moral and financial capacity as suited the Standard to a dot. Of course the whole thing ended in a farce, at the expense of the State that this thrifty committee represented.

"Mr. Rockefeller is an autocrat within his own sphere. He allows no interference with his plans, and although he reaches a gloved hand toward his associates and subordinates it does not need two grasps for them to learn that within is the grip of iron. Two or three slight differences of opinion as to matters that Mr. Rockefeller believed essential to his successful conduct of the Standard between that gentleman and Mr. Samuel Andrews, one of the original proprietors of the Standard, led to that gentleman's selling out and his quitting the business. Mr. Andrews believed that his interests demanded that he should know a little more of the details of the business. Mr. Rockefeller believed that Mr. Andrews knew enough. Mr. Andrews was opposed to any more expansion of the company. Mr. Rockefeller had other views. So Mr. Andrews sold out, his stock passing into the hands of the men who were then as now the real brain and bone of the Standard. When Mr. Andrews went out he was met by certain oil operators who believed that with him as a mentor a rival to the Standard could be built up. But Mr. Andrews could give little advantage to himself or to others by risking his now safe millions in a struggle the result of which could not but be doubtful at best, so the great opponent and rival to the Standard did not appear.

"Commodore Vanderbilt was in full control of the New-York Central when he first met John D. Rockefeller. By some means the latter gained a wonderful hold on the old man, and could get terms out of him that no other man would dare to ask. The story goes that Vanderbilt once said that Rockefeller was the only man in the world who could dictate to him. As that may be, the Standard had its way with the New-York Central and the Lake Shore from the start. William H. Vanderbilt has a suspicion of the Standard, and watches with an eagle eye every deal that is proposed to him from that direction. But year in and out the Standard has had chances in the way of low freight and rebates that no other concern in the country could dare to expect. Vanderbilt and the Standard President do not take each other into confidence to any great extent, and in their closest dealings are ever in a state of armed hostility. 'Oil is all right when one goes into it steadily and makes it a business,' said Mr. Vanderbilt to a gentleman one day, 'but I don't care to take much risk in that direction.' Mr. Rockefeller was once sounded as to his relations with Vanderbilt. 'Oh, yes,' he replied coolly, 'I believe we do ship some oil over his lines!' In fact, coolness of expression is one of Mr. Rockefeller's distinguishing characteristics. He had an employe whom he suspected of having given certain information that afterward appeared in print. He said to his private secretary: 'Suggest to Mr. Blank that he would do admirably as a newspaper man, and that we shall not need his services after the close of this month.' The Standard President was once at a watering-place suburb near Cleveland, when an ex-member of the Ohio Legislature came up and, introducing himself, said: 'I did what I could in that little matter at Columbus, and am glad that the Standard came to no harm.' 'I am glad to know you, Sir, personally,' said Mr. Rockefeller, 'but I have no idea what you have reference to in the matter of legislation,' and entering his carriage took up the reins and drove away."

"How much is Rockefeller worth?"

"I don't know. Some say five millions, and some say fifteen. No living man knows how much he does foot up, but six or seven millions will cover it. You see, his great investment is in the Standard, and a shift may come any day to run him up a million or down two. He never talks of his possessions, and I should not be surprised if he had a snug fortune laid away where he would find himself rich in case all of the Standard Trust property should be swept away from the face of the four States in which it is situated. You see, he is a Scotchman and comes of a thrifty stock. He was already rich before he gave any signs of it in his way of living. His house on the corner of Case and Euclid avenues is elegant inside, but not imposing outside. A company some years ago built a magnificent stone castle on the hills beyond Lake View Cemetery for the purpose of creating a gilt-edged sanatarium. The project failed, and the establishment fell into Rockefeller's hands at a sum less than the material of the house cost delivered on the ground. He lives up there in the Summer, overlooking the city, the lake, Wade Park, Lake View Cemetery, and the Northern Ohio Fair Grounds. He gives to the Church somewhat liberally, and is not counted parsimonious, although by no means free-handed."

"How much is Flagler worth?"

"I don't know. Perhaps four or five millions. He came in when Rockefeller, Clark, and Andrews had made a fair start in the refining of oil at Cleveland and had begun to see what opportunities were ahead of them in case they had the capital needed. He brought that capital, and things went with a dash."

"Who stands next?"

"Oliver H. Payne; I believe he is Treasurer, but I am not certain of that. He is worth three or four millions now, and will get a million more when his father's estate is divided—which won't be for some time, as Henry B. Payne is a very young old man. The executive work, or a good share of it, falls into the hands of Oliver Payne. He is the only one of the Standard people who has taken a hand in politics, and there are few men in with Rockefeller who would be allowed to go as far in that line as Payne has done. Every time the Standard's name is hitched to that of the Paynes and politics it makes Rockefeller unsasy. I don't believe Rockefeller would stand it very long. Col. Payne knows this, and this fact has had no little to do with keeping him out of politics personally."

"Who are some of the richest Standard stockholders?"

"S. V. Harkness is one. John Huntington has a small share or so that keeps him in good shape without any need of work. He got in with them years ago when he was a boss in the Cleveland City Council, and aided the Standard in getting some very valuable legislation through touching the dredging of the river and other improvements about their works. He used to be in with the Standard plans very deep, but of late years has done little more than draw his dividends and go to Columbus when some unusually delicate piece of work was to be done."

"A great deal of the public dislike of the Standard and distrust of its purposes in Western Pennsylvania—which at one time was at such a pitch that John D. Rockefeller would have been mobbed had he been found in the oil territory—was created and fostered by the newspapers of this region. Rockefeller called in a trusted and discreet agent, and told him what he wanted. The man came down into the oil region, making his first stop at Oil City. He represented himself as a capitalist, and through the proper channels opened negotiations for the purchase of the leading paper, perhaps the *Derrick* and perhaps some other, I could not find out which. It was not paying very well, and the sale was consummated. Gradual changes were made in the staff and in the tone, and finally the paper was willing to admit that perhaps all the villainies of the world were not commercially grouped under the head 'Standard Oil.' The same policy was carried out at Franklin, Titusville, Bradford, Meadville, and Erie. Sometimes it was successful, and sometimes it was not. The venture did not cost less than $60,000, but Mr. Rockefeller always felt that the money was well expended."

Here the Cleveland gentleman was asked as to the relations between the Standard and the Cleveland newspapers. "Some years ago," said he, "the Standard men held some stock in the *Herald*, but how much or in what shape I do not know. Col. Dick Parsons got them into it, and whether they are still in or not I cannot tell. But you can rest assured that no criticism of the great oil devil-fish will ever see its way into the columns of the *Herald* under its present management. The men who own it now are among the leading rich men of Cleveland, and they and the Standard people are all tied up in a sort of scratch-each-other's-back arrangement. The *Leader*, a few years ago, when a lot of small opposition refineries grew up along the Cleveland and Pittsburg Railroad track, did come out with a few anti-Standard attacks, but for some reason they died out, and nothing more was heard. The *Penny Press* has attacked the company a number of times in its espousal of the cause of the laboring classes. The relations between the *Plain Dealer* and the Paynes are such that, of course, no war would be expected from that direction. In fact, as a Cleveland man, I don't see any reason to war on the company to any great extent. Of course, it is a great and growing monopoly, its influence is as bad as its example, and its methods are demoralizing and corrupting. But it pays heavy taxes in Cleveland, with never a word of protest. It has covered one ward with business and keeps thousands of men at work. It has drawn population here, and pays out thousands of cash with every day that passes."

A gentleman from Western Pennsylvania, who has followed the course of events closely ever since oil was first discovered, gives an opinion on the future of the Standard as follows: "I had heard something of this Standard Trust arrangement before Mr. Flagler introduced it formally to the public some weeks ago to the Committee on Corners sitting in New-York. The Standard managers felt that something had to be done, as there was danger of their becoming involved in legal difficulties by doing a dozen lines of business under the charter that gave them the right to do only one—refine oil. You see they owned pipe lines and carried oil through them for other persons, and thus became common carriers. They owned railroad cars and carried oil in them for other persons. They owned the National Transit Company, the Lane Manufacturing Company, and a dozen other concerns which were cumbersome, to say the least, in handling as a part of the Standard Oil Company as first chartered. So the Standard Trust was created, with sufficiently wide powers to pave a road to the moon if the money could be raised, and with a capital stock of some $60,000,000. I am of the opinion that a shift of the present relation of affairs will not be a matter of the distant future. The present managers of the Standard have had a steady fight and a great weight of responsibility to carry for the past 20 years, and have been successful beyond the wildest dreams of any of them. I do not know as they intend to retire, but changes are liable to come at any time. And I believe that Mr. Rockefeller is getting affairs in such shape that he would get out well in case the Pennsylvania fields should give out, and no more oil be produced to speak of."

"What do you mean?"

"Simply that you will see Standard Trust stock on the street and among the quotations before 18 months go by. It can be put there at a greatly inflated figure—as the sixty-million issue of stock no doubt is—and then a large quantity be worked off on the public."

February 27, 1883

A NEW DISTILLERS' POOL

FORMING A HUGE MONOPOLY IN FRENCH SPIRITS.

THE FAR-REACHING PLANS OF THE LAST COMBINATION CALLED THE DISTILLERS AND CATTLE FEEDERS' TRUST.

What are known to the liquor trade as "high wines" are the products of the first distillation of corn mashed and fermented. When the high wines are run through charcoal a pure spirit is obtained. This is next passed through a still and column, and there results a product called finished goods, or French spirits. In the United States this is an immense industry. Out of the $118,000,000 collected by the United States Internal Revenue Department in the fiscal year ending June 30, 1887, some $70,000,000 was collected as taxes upon the American distillers of these French spirits. The principal distillers are in Ohio, Illinois, and Indiana, with Illinois as the chief section and Peoria as the headquarters of the business. Some 70 per cent. of the spirits produced are manufactured in the Fifth Collection District of Illinois.

These spirits are not drank "straight." When Saloon Keeper X, for example, buys one gallon of brandy at $5 50 he mixes it with four gallons of the French spirits at $1 30 a gallon, much to his profit. The French spirits which are so used to swell the profits of the retailers are mixed also with fine whiskies, gins, and rums. So it is evident that this French spirits business is one widely affecting the liquor trade. But in the past the distillers of these spirits have not worked together in harmony. There have been pools and pools among them, but they have been formed only to be broken. Distilleries turning out spirits were called "operating." Those not turning out anything were called "closed." The operating houses under one of the latest pools had to pay to closed houses an assessment to compensate the closed houses for remaining closed, and thus prevent an over-production. Some of these closed houses could not have distilled anything if their owners had wanted to. All there was to many was a chimney stack and a boiler. The legitimate trade call them not "closed" but "dead" houses. Their owners' policy was one of the causes that disrupted the pool. Another disrupting cause was the effort of some of the operating houses to make more than their share of the spirits needed by the trade. In the language of the distillers these firms were "stuffing their mash." By this the market often became overstocked, and the attempt to regulate supply and price failed. Consequently the distillers' profits often fell to a very low point.

Some of the distillers met several months ago to arrange for a new pool that could not be broken and whose obligations would be so strong that the members of it would be bound to respect them or else get out of the business. They wanted to form in the spirits industry an all-comprehending combination like the Standard Oil Company. But the exact plan of the Standard was a secret. After negotiating for a long time a quasi offer is said to have been made by some of the Standard officers to let the French spirits men know some of the policies and methods of the great oil trust in consideration of a promise of strict secrecy and a fee of $35,000. This offer was not fully accepted, but a little later the spirits men got hold of a scheme somewhat similar to the Standard. They engaged shrewd corporation lawyers and formulated their plan. Advances were then quietly made to distillers supposed to be willing to go into the proposed monopoly. As a result acceptances from 72 per cent. of all the houses in the business had been received last Saturday, with negotiations still being made with the others. The arrangements were kept from all persons except those interested and nothing was published hinting at the matter.

The new pool will aim to control the production and the regulation of prices something like the coal combination and the Standard Oil and Cottonseed Oil Trusts. It will also aim to govern directly the management of the entire business from the manufacture to the distribution. Much of the capital now invested in the Illinois section is owned or controlled in New-York. There are six houses here. Their share in the pool will be determined by a review of their business as shown by their books and adjudged pro rata by a committee of the trust's Directors. For an operating distillery scrip will be issued upon the basis, probably, of four to one. That is, for an operating distillery worth $100,000 the issue of scrip would be, as now contemplated, $400,000. In estimating the value of a distillery the earnings of each will be considered. A plant in Peoria, costing $350,000 and yielding a profit of $50,000 a year, would be counted worth more than a plant in St. Louis costing the same, but turning out a profit of only $20,000. The worth of all the distilleries may be estimated originally at $10,000,000, and with their earning capacity added at 25 per cent. more. Based on the worth of the distilleries, the scrip issued will be listed in New-York and Chicago. It is now expected that it will be put out at 25 cents on the dollar. Most of it of course, it is assumed, will be held, by the spirits men themselves, though even a total abstinence man may buy it freely and thus become a part owner or associate in the contemplated monopoly. It is calculated that the distillery business thus unified will make in the first year $10,000,000 as gross earnings, as against a much smaller sum for any previous year.

There are provisions for a fund to be used to buy up or crush out of trade any house that may be started after the new corporation has got down to work. Its policy toward rivals will be that followed by the Standard Oil Company. The capital represented in the association will aggregate $40,000,000. By its charter the company is styled "The Distillers and Cattle Feeders' Trust." Officers have been elected, and a Board of Directors has been chosen, and the details of the business, it is expected, will soon be so fully arranged that the power of the associated distillers will be felt, first upon the supply and prices of French spirits, and then upon the brandy, fine whisky, gin, and rum market generally.

The Kentucky whisky distillers have also organized a pool. One of their chief agreements is not to make any more whisky for a year.

August 20, 1887

THE FOES OF COMPETITION

TRUSTS AND OTHER TRADE COMBINATIONS.

THE GROWTH OF MONOPOLIES AND POOLS—GRADUATES OF THE STANDARD OIL SCHOOL OF POLITICAL ECONOMY—OPERATIONS OF THE SUGAR TRUST—THE STEEL RAIL RING—TRIBUTE EXACTED FROM THE FARMERS.

Some months ago THE TIMES began to direct attention to the formation of new conspiracies to throttle competition in many branches of industry. Combinations were coming into existence on all sides. The manufacture of oil from cottonseed had been monopolized by the formation of a trust like that of the Standard Oil speculators. Men who had learned the ways of monopoly in the Standard Oil school were reaching out for the control of gas supplies and transportation systems in great cities. The production of whisky was passing into the hands of a trust. Groups of manufacturers were striving to put an end to competition in many fields of production by means of alliances. THE TIMES collected, and presented from time to time, testimony concerning these combinations which was afforded by the current news and supplied from other sources of information. As our list of trusts, pools, and associations grew in length the subject became attractive to some of our contemporaries, notably to the Chicago *Tribune*, which undertook to assist in the work of laying bare the schemes by which greed was building the house of monopoly on the grave of competition. Later on certain journals of this city became interested and set before their readers the results of THE TIMES's inquiries, with some additions of their own. Consumers began to look for remedies and politicians consented to aid them. Bills for the suppression of trusts and similar combinations were introduced at Washington and in State Legislatures, and at last provision for investigations by Congress and by the Senate of this State was made.

We set forth below facts and suggestions relating to the war upon competition in several fields of industry. Some of these facts we have heretofore published, but it may be well to present them again now in connection with others of equal importance. We shall add to them hereafter. Some of the organizations in the list are Trusts, others are only associations, but the aim of all is to prevent competition and exact from consumers profits greater than can be obtained so long as competition exists. It will be seen that the protective tariff stimulates the growth of these combinations and enables them to take abnormal profits. Many a ring of producers has abused the privileges granted by the tariff. The protective policy has never had more dangerous foes than the monopolists who have been enriched by it. "If the sincere friends of American industry would protect protection," says the protectionist *Times* of Philadelphia, "they must promptly separate it from the extortion of trusts and monopolists. It can survive the hostility of open, manly foes; it cannot survive the suicidal blows of those who use protection only to abuse it by arbitrary oppression of consumers that would not be tolerated in despotic Russia." There are remedies which the people can use for the regulation or overthrow of monopolistic combinations. The state of public opinion and the action of legislative bodies indicate that some of these remedies will soon be applied.

TRUSTS AND COMBINATIONS.

Sugar.—The demand for sugar in this country is supplied by the refiners, in whose factories the raw sugars from abroad or from the plantations of Louisiana are prepared for use. The schedule of tariff duties on the several grades of sugar is so arranged that the rates on foreign sugar which would compete with the refiners' product are prohibitory. The duty on foreign raw sugars which are not above No. 13 Dutch standard in color ranges from 1.40 to 2.40 cents a pound, according to their comparative purity as determined by the polariscope. These are the sugars which pass through the refineries, and the duty collected upon them last year was more than $56,000,000. The grade most largely imported and refined is that which contains more than 94 but not more than 95 per cent. of pure sugar, and the rate of duty on it is 2.20 cents a pound. The rates of duty upon the grades above No. 13, Dutch standard, range from 2¾ to 3½ cents, but the value of such sugars imported last year was only $14,503. The country, then, depends upon the refiners for its supply.

The refiners have recently formed a Trust monopoly upon the plan used by the Standard Oil speculators. The Trust appears to have been completed in October last. "It may be considered a settled fact," said Messrs. Willett and Hamlen in their circular of Oct. 16, "that a combination has been completed, including all the New-York sugar refineries and the Boston refineries with one exception, thus bringing under the management and control of a committee of eleven refiners almost the entire consumption of raw sugar and production of refined sugar in the United States." At that time there were outside of the ring two refineries in Philadelphia, one in Boston, three small ones in New-Orleans, one in St. Louis, and two in San Francisco. A few days later the St. Louis and New-Orleans refineries were absorbed. It is reported that the Revere Refinery in Boston will soon cease to have an independent existence. Even if it should remain outside of the Trust its attitude would be entirely satisfactory to the ring. "The best possible relations exist between the Trust and the outside companies," said one of the owners of the refinery a few days ago. "Between us and the Trust there is no fight. Granulated sugar now brings 7⅛ cents a pound. Suppose we put the figures down to 6 cents? Why, it would simply be gobbled up by the Trust through its agents and would do the consumer no good. The prices rising are adopted by us, and as our small output does not threaten the Trust we arouse no antagonism and go on making money." At last accounts the two refineries in San Francisco had not come in, but their operations are a matter of little concern to the Trust. The monopolists have made their compact in secrecy. Even to this day prominent sugar men connected with the Trust do not admit that it exists. But it is understood that the value of the pooled property was about $15,000,000, for which Trust certificates were issued in the ratio of 4 to 1, so that the inflated certificate capital is $60,000,000. A sale of a block of these certificates has been made at 80, which would indicate a belief on the part of some one that the value of the property has been raised from $15,000,000 to $48,000,000 by the monopoly process. The Trust is governed by 10 Directors or Trustees. Three votes are cast, it is said, by Havemeyer & Elder, two by the Matthiessen & Weichers Company, one by the Brooklyn Refining Company, one by Dick & Meyer, one by the Boston Sugar Refining Company, one by the Standard Refining Company of Boston, and one by the refineries of New-Orleans. By common report, the President is Harry O. Havemeyer, and the Secretary and Treasurer is J. H. Searles. The Boston Trustees are Charles O. Foster and Capt. Thomas.

These 10 Trust magnates sitting in council can by one vote raise the price of sugar for more than 50,000,000 people. Nothing is required beyond a motion, the seconding of it, the calling of the roll, and the issuing of instructions to the Trust's agents. The people are powerless. They must pay the Trust's price or go without sugar. Even the refiners through whose mills in New-Orleans passes the sugar of the protected planters of Louisiana have conspired against them. The Trust exercises enormous power. The quantity of sugar consumed in the United States last year exceeded 3,000,000,000 pounds. An advance of half a cent per pound on this quantity is $15,000,000; 1 cent brings $30,000,000, 2 cents yield $60,000,000. Let us see what has happened in the sugar trade since the Trust was formed. The *Tribune* said a few days ago: "At present it [the Trust] is demanding 56 per cent. of the cost of raw sugar as its additional charge for refined; in January, 1887, the additional charge was 35 per cent., and in January, 1886, it was 32 per cent." The Trust has depressed the price of raw sugars brought to this country for sale to be refined, and at the same time has raised the price of the refined product. For example, a cargo of raw Manila sugar was sold in this port on Jan. 6 at the rate of 4⅜ cents a pound. Three weeks later a cargo of the same kind was sold at 4¼ cents, because there was and could be only one buyer and bidder—the Trust—and the Trust did not choose to pay any more. Just before these sales were made the *Tribune* said: "Since it [the Trust] became a fixed fact 'cut loaf' has gone up to 7¾ cents a pound, granulated to 6¾, and the soft sugars have all advanced. Raw sugar, on the contrary, has a downward tendency." Why? Simply because the protected Trust buys raw sugar and sells refined. A few days ago the price of crushed sugar had been pushed up to 8 cents; it has since been permitted to fall ¼

THE FOES OF COMPETITION

TRUSTS AND OTHER TRADE COMBINATIONS.

THE GROWTH OF MONOPOLIES AND POOLS—GRADUATES OF THE STANDARD OIL SCHOOL OF POLITICAL ECONOMY—OPERATIONS OF THE SUGAR TRUST—THE STEEL RAIL RING—TRIBUTE EXACTED FROM THE FARMERS.

Some months ago THE TIMES began to direct attention to the formation of new conspiracies to throttle competition in many branches of industry. Combinations were coming into existence on all sides. The manufacture of oil from cottonseed had been monopolized by the formation of a trust like that of the Standard Oil speculators. Men who had learned the ways of monopoly in the Standard Oil school were reaching out for the control of gas supplies and transportation systems in great cities. The production of whisky was passing into the hands of a trust. Groups of manufacturers were striving to put an end to competition in many fields of production by means of alliances. THE TIMES collected, and presented from time to time, testimony concerning these combinations which was afforded by the current news and supplied from other sources of information. As our list of trusts, pools, and associations grew in length the subject became attractive to some of our contemporaries, notably to the Chicago *Tribune*, which undertook to assist in the work of laying bare the schemes by which greed was building the house of monopoly on the grave of competition. Later on certain journals of this city became interested and set before their readers the results of THE TIMES's inquiries, with some additions of their own. Consumers began to look for remedies and politicians consented to aid them. Bills for the suppression of trusts and similar combinations were introduced at Washington and in State Legislatures, and at last provision for investigations by Congress and by the Senate of this State was made.

We set forth below facts and suggestions relating to the war upon competition in several fields of industry. Some of these facts we have heretofore published, but it may be well to present them again now in connection with others of equal importance. We shall add to them hereafter. Some of the organizations in the list are Trusts, others are only associations, but the aim of all is to prevent competition and exact from consumers profits greater than can be obtained so long as competition exists. It will be seen that the protective tariff stimulates the growth of these combinations and enables them to take abnormal profits. Many a ring of producers has abused the privileges granted by the tariff. The protective policy has never had more dangerous foes than the monopolists who have been enriched by it. "If the sincere friends of American industry would protect protection," says the protectionist *Times* of Philadelphia, "they must promptly separate it from the extortion of trusts and monopolists. It can survive the hostility of open, manly foes; it cannot survive the suicidal blows of those who use protection only to abuse it by arbitrary oppression of consumers that would not be tolerated in despotic Russia." There are remedies which the people can use for the regulation or overthrow of monopolistic combinations. The state of public opinion and the action of legislative bodies indicate that some of these remedies will soon be applied.

TRUSTS AND COMBINATIONS.

Sugar.—The demand for sugar in this country is supplied by the refiners, in whose factories the raw sugars from abroad or from the plantations of Louisiana are prepared for use. The schedule of tariff duties on the several grades of sugar is so arranged that the rates on foreign sugar which would compete with the refiners' product are prohibitory. The duty on foreign raw sugars which are not above No. 13 Dutch standard in color ranges from 1.40 to 2.40 cents a pound, according to their comparative purity as determined by the polariscope. These are the sugars which pass through the refineries, and the duty collected upon them last year was more than $56,000,000. The grade most largely imported and refined is that which contains more than 94 but not more than 95 per cent. of pure sugar, and the rate of duty on it is 2.20 cents a pound. The rates of duty upon the grades above No. 13, Dutch standard, range from 2¾ to 3½ cents, but the value of such sugars imported last year was only $14,503. The country, then, depends upon the refiners for its supply.

The refiners have recently formed a Trust monopoly upon the plan used by the Standard Oil speculators. The Trust appears to have been completed in October last. "It may be considered a settled fact," said Messrs. Willett and Hamlen in their circular of Oct. 16, "that a combination has been completed, including all the New-York sugar refineries and the Boston refineries with one exception, thus bringing under the management and control of a committee of eleven refiners almost the entire consumption of raw sugar and production of refined sugar in the United States." At that time there were outside of the ring two refineries in Philadelphia, one in Boston, three small ones in New-Orleans, one in St. Louis, and two in San Francisco. A few days later the St. Louis and New-Orleans refineries were absorbed. It is reported that the Revere Refinery in Boston will soon cease to have an independent existence. Even if it should remain outside of the Trust its attitude would be entirely satisfactory to the ring. "The best possible relations exist between the Trust and the outside companies," said one of the owners of the refinery a few days ago. "Between us and the Trust there is no fight. Granulated sugar now brings 7⅛ cents a pound. Suppose we put the figures down to 6 cents! Why, it would simply be gobbled up by the Trust through its agents and would do the consumer no good. The prices rising are adopted by us, and as our small output does not threaten the Trust we arouse no antagonism and go on making money." At last accounts the two refineries in San Francisco had not come in, but their operations are a matter of little concern to the Trust. The monopolists have made their compact in secrecy. Even to this day prominent sugar men connected with the Trust do not admit that it exists. But it is understood that the value of the pooled property was about $15,000,000, for which Trust certificates were issued in the ratio of 4 to 1, so that the inflated certificate capital is $60,000,000. A sale of a block of these certificates has been made at 80, which would indicate a belief on the part of some one that the value of the property has been raised from $15,000,000 to $48,000,000 by the monopoly process. The Trust is governed by 10 Directors or Trustees. Three votes are cast, it is said, by Havemeyer & Elder, two by the Matthiessen & Weichers Company, one by the Brooklyn Refining Company, one by Dick & Meyer, one by the Boston Sugar Refining Company, one by the Standard Refining Company of Boston, and one by the refineries of New-Orleans. By common report, the President is Harry O. Havemeyer, and the Secretary and Treasurer is J. H. Searles. The Boston Trustees are Charles O. Foster and Capt. Thomas.

These 10 Trust magnates sitting in council can by one vote raise the price of sugar for more than 50,000,000 people. Nothing is required beyond a motion, the seconding of it, the calling of the roll, and the issuing of instructions to the Trust's agents. The people are powerless. They must pay the Trust's price or go without sugar. Even the refiners through whose mills in New-Orleans passes the sugar of the protected planters of Louisiana have conspired against them. The Trust exercises enormous power. The quantity of sugar consumed in the United States last year exceeded 3,000,000,000 pounds. An advance of half a cent per pound on this quantity is $15,000,000; 1 cent brings $30,000,000, 2 cents yield $60,000,000. Let us see what has happened in the sugar trade since the Trust was formed. The *Tribune* said a few days ago: "At present it [the Trust] is demanding 56 per cent. of the cost of raw sugar as its additional charge for refined; in January, 1887, the additional charge was 35 per cent., and in January, 1886, it was 32 per cent." The Trust has depressed the price of raw sugars brought to this country for sale to be refined, and at the same time has raised the price of the refined product. For example, a cargo of raw Manila sugar was sold in this port on Jan. 6 at the rate of 4⅜ cents a pound. Three weeks later a cargo of the same kind was sold at 4¼ cents, because there was and could be only one buyer and bidder—the Trust—and the Trust did not choose to pay any more. Just before these sales were made the *Tribune* said: "Since it [the Trust] became a fixed fact 'cut loaf' has gone up to 7¾ cents a pound, granulated to 6¾, and the soft sugars have all advanced. Raw sugar, on the contrary, has a downward tendency." Why? Simply because the protected Trust buys raw sugar and sells refined. A few days ago the price of crushed sugar had been pushed up to 8 cents; it has since been permitted to fall ¼ cent, possibly because certain conservative Trustees saw that the pace was too hot.

An anonymous circular, written by some one familiar with the refining business, declares that the Trust has already made a profit of 12 per cent. on its inflated certificate capital, ($60,000,000,) or 48 per cent. on the estimated value of the property put into the ring. Is it probable that the operations of four months have yielded so much? Such a dividend would be $7,200,000. We have said that a profit of 1 cent a pound upon one year's consumption of sugar in the United States is more than $30,000,000. In the first week of October, when the Trust is said to have been completed, the price of cut loaf and of crushed sugar was from 6⅜ to 6½ cents and that of granulated was 6. Three weeks later the price of cut loaf and crushed had risen to 7 cents. At the beginning of January it was 7¾, while that of granulated was 7. In the second week of January and at the beginning of February the price of cut loaf and crushed was 8 cents; that of granulated was 7⅛. On the 17th inst., the price had receded to 7¾ for cut loaf and crushed and 6¾ for granulated. These quotations show that after the formation of the Trust prices were advanced from 1½ to 1⅝ cents for cut loaf and crushed, and 1 cent for granulated, and that of this advance 1¼ cents in one case and ¾ cent in the other are still maintained. And on the 17th inst., when the price of cut loaf and crushed was greater by 1¼ cents, and that of granulated by ⅝ cent, than on Oct. 10, the prices of "fair refining" and "centrifugal" sugars were even less than on that date. A profit of 1 cent a pound on the entire quantity consumed in four months would be more than $10,000,000. Has not the average additional profit of the trust in the last four months been nearly 1 cent a pound? The estimate of a 12 per cent. profit on $60,000,000, or $7,200,000, does not seem to be far out of the way after all.

While the Trust has the power to depress the price of raw sugar and raise the price of refined directly by its bid or decree, it also affects the market by reducing the supply. Since it was formed at least four of its refineries have been closed. Said one of the owners of the Revere Refinery (the independent but friendly factory in Boston) a few days ago: "Really, we are benefited by the Trust. It has, for instance, in this city four refineries. Now, to decrease production so as to raise the price they shut down three of these for the Winter." A special dispatch from Boston to the Chicago *Tribune*, dated the 3d inst., contains the following description of the work of the Trust there:

> "When the sugar Trust went into operation the public was assured that the combination would not close down any refineries and that the price of sugar would not be put up, the Trust being able to make a fair profit because of the decreased cost of manufacture. Careful inquiry, however, shows that the trade in this city is demoralized, that the majority of the refineries are shut down, and that a large number of men are thrown out of employment, with no hope of getting work this Winter. There are five sugar refineries in Boston—the Revere in East Cambridge, the Boston in Marshall-street, the Continental in Granite-street, the Standard in Granite-street, and the Bay State in Eastern-avenue. Last Summer all these refineries were running, employing 1,500 men, and incidentally giving employment to a large number of teamsters, freight handlers, and seamen. But the Continental Refinery, in anticipation of the Trust, shut down in November, and not a barrel of sugar has been turned out since that date. The men are discharged, with the exception of some of the expert workmen and the Superintendent. The Standard Refinery has a capacity of 2,000 barrels a day, and is now running on small capacity after a month of idleness. The force now employed there is not nearly so large as formerly. The Bay State Refinery, which has a capacity of 1,000 barrels a day, is shut down, and except, as in the case of the Continental that a few expert men are under half pay, has discharged its complement of workmen. The Boston Refinery, with a capacity of 2,000, is shut down and does no work whatever. The Revere Refinery is to be sold to the Boston and Maine Railroad soon, and then to be closed."

This shows how solicitous the managers of one protected industry are for the welfare of the workingman. The refining business is protected by duties on refined sugar that are prohibitory. In this region the Trust has shut up four of its factories. The fourth to be closed was that of Moller, Sierck & Co., at 502 Kent-avenue, Brooklyn. Fifteen hundred sugar workmen in that city were recently reported to be out of employment. Their wages had been low even when there was work for them, lower, some of them say, than wages for the same work in England, although refining here is protected by a duty of from 87 to 89 per cent. It is plain that a reduction of the tariff rate on raw sugars might not aid the consumer, but only increase the Trust's profits. The ring would get its raw material just so much cheaper and could maintain the price of the refined product of its factories. What the people should demand is such a change of the schedule and such a reduction of rates now prohibitory as will admit raw sugars of high grade and refined sugars in competition with the monopoly's product.

Castor Oil.—The duty on imported castor oil is one of the curiosities of the tariff. Last year upon the small quantity imported it was 194.77 per cent. The foreign oil is worth a little more than 40 cents a gallon and the duty on every gallon is 80 cents. The ad valorem rate mentioned above was exceeded last year by the rates upon only seven other articles—tannin, liqueurs distilled from grain, rum oil, œnanthic ether, and certain other poisonous fluids used in the adulteration and fraudulent "doctoring" of whisky and brandy. For so useful a medicinal agent the oil is in bad company. But the manufacturers do not complain. They have united in a kind of pool with the purpose of taking in the profits which can be piled up under the shelter of so high a wall as this duty of 194.77 per cent. When the last census was taken there were in this country 8 castor oil factories, but they employed only 108 persons. Now there are said to be 14, of which all but 1 are in the West, but there are only 5 of considerable size—3 in St. Louis, 1 in Belleville, Ill., and 1 in New-Jersey.

The Chicago *Tribune* recently published a history of the business in connection with a sketch of the pioneer mill at Belleville, in Col. Morrison's old district. The Belleville company's capital is $40,000, and the President is Herman G. Weber, United States Marshal for Southern Illinois. A pool to advance prices was formed by the factories three years ago, and the price was pushed up to 16¾ cents a pound, or about $1 34 a gallon. They overshot the mark, for although the duty is 80 cents, the cost of imported oil before the duty was collected was only 43 cents, and in 1886 more than 13,000 gallons were imported. For this reason and owing to the addition of three new mills to the list of producers, the price sagged and reached 12 cents at the end of 1887, (the year's importation having been only 1,507 gallons,) but then a new pool was made and the price was advanced. It is now from 14 to 15½ cents, with an upward tendency. The strength of the compact is shown by the Belleville company's treatment of its workmen some time ago when they threatened to strike. Marshal Weber assured them that a strike would only cause a transfer of the castor beans to "one of the other mills." It will be seen that the ring proposes to exact from the consumer all that the tariff barrier will permit. Foreign producers sell their oil for 40 cents, and the duty raises the price at the seaboard to $1 20. The ring price of the domestic oil is from $1 12 to $1 24. The pool also limits production. Any one of the four or five large mills can make enough oil, it it said, to supply the whole domestic market. The demand for the oil is not large, but upon what is sold the people are taxed heavily for the benefit of a "combine" of manufacturers who employ less than 100 persons. The farmers who raise the beans do not grow rich by selling them at $1 25 a bushel.

School Slates.—The manufacture and sale of school slates in the United States are controlled by a "combine." We again quote from the news columns of the *Tribune* of this city, because that paper in its editorial columns ignores the existence of tariff-sheltered combinations and asserts that protective duties cause "permanent cheapness through home competition." On or about Nov. 6, 1887, the *Tribune* said:

"The increase in the price of school slates that has just been ordered by the manufacturers' combination which controls the business in this country is the second advance that has been made within the last six months. Early in May prices were raised 12½ per cent. Last week this was increased about 5 per cent. more, and it is possible that prices may go still higher. The American slate is so far superior to anything produced abroad that there is little fear of foreign competition, even if there were no protective tariff of 35 per cent., as there is."

And then it is shown that large quantities of the slates, which are produced in Lehigh and Northampton Counties, Penn., were sold in foreign countries, in spite of German and Welsh competition. But were the prices for foreign buyers raised 1 ½ and 5 per cent.? Probably not. The tariff (which is not 35, but 30 per cent.) is not needed for protection, but it does serve to enable a ring of producers to exact high prices in the home market.

Linseed Oil.—The combination of linseed oil-makers is not an association or a pool, but a real trust, like the Sugar Trust and the Cottonseed Oil Trust. We quote from a review of the trade of 1887 published in the Chicago *Inter Ocean*:

"The annual production of linseed oil in the United States is 28,000,000 gallons, the West crushing about 20,000,000 gallons, and the mills of Chicago 3,750,000. The year 1887 will long be remembered because of the formation of the National Linseed Oil Trust, which was started in January and made such rapid progress that before six months had passed it virtually controlled and brought harmony among the crushers where chaos had reigned. There are now [Jan. 2, 1888.] 36 mills in the trust, representing over one-half the crushing capacity of the country. Certificates to the amount of $11,000,000 have been issued on the basis of $33⅓ a share, and are now salable in the open market at that price."

Accompanying tables show that in 1887 the jobbers' price of raw oil advanced from 38 to 52 cents (nearly 37 per cent.) and "closed firm at the top." Market reports in this city show that in October last the price here was 43 cents and that it is now 56 cents. The duty (25 cents a gallon) was equivalent last year to an ad valorem rate of 54.79 per cent. There were imported 5,277 gallons, worth 45 cents a gallon. The cost of imported linseed oil, duty paid is, then, about 70 cents. The trust can safely add 10 or 15 cents to the present price of its oil, and still hold the home market. But the duty may be reduced. Nothing but a reduction can save the people from this trust's exactions, if it be true that the purpose of the ring's projectors has been attained. At the close of the year the New-York crushers had not gone into the trust. The trust's prices seem to have been accepted since that time, however, without any audible protest.

Steel Rails.—The contest between the steel rail "combine" and the great railroad companies over the price of rails seems to have come to an end, for the companies have recently given to the railmakers orders for more than 500,000 tons of rails at the ruling price of $31 50. The companies were standing out for $30, and the makers were unwilling to take less than $34 or $35. All the old tales about the losses that must be incurred if rails should be sold for less than $32 or $33 were told again, but it appears that the "combine" has consented to make a quantity equal to one-quarter of the entire product of last year for $31 50. An attempt was made a few weeks ago in certain quarters to create the impression that the steel rail industry had been blighted by the President's tariff message; but the truth was that the railroad companies had become weary of paying exorbitant prices and had determined to bring the ring to terms. During the great development of the railroad system in the West last year they had been forced to pay even $40 a ton. They did not propose to do this again. The *Bulletin*, organ of the "combine," complained piteously early in December that the companies withheld their orders. It said:

"A few large contracts in October and early in November for rails which must in any event be bought before the middle of Winter would have helped wonderfully to arrest any tendency to dullness in the industries of the country. But instead of taking this course, which they could well have afforded to do, having plenty of money saved up from two years of prosperous business, these friends of ours virtually said to the steel rail manufacturers that they would wait until prices were lower."

And then the companies were warned that low prices for rails "mean also low freight rates" and ruin generally. But the companies had their way. Of course the members of the association would have the people believe that it is nothing more than a social organization, while in fact it fixes the price and regulates the output of a product through whose cost the nation can be taxed. "Harmony prevailed," said the *Tribune* in its report of the association's meeting of Nov. 15, "and it was agreed to leave the matter of output and other detail to the Board of Control. Prices are to be maintained at current rates." One month later the same paper gave publicity to the statement that the association would "order all steel rail mills closed if the price of rails should go below $32 a ton." When the ring finally made concessions and the orders were given the work was distributed. On the 1st inst. it was announced that the Lackawanna Iron and Coal Company had sold 30,000 tons of rails. At the same time the following statement was made:

"The Lackawanna Company has now sold its full proportion of the allotment to all companies of 800,000 tons, and can take no further orders at present. The Bethlehem Company is in the same condition."

This was published upon the authority of Mr. B. E. Clarke, President of the Thomas Iron Company. The "allotment!" The Board of Control regulates the output and distributes the work.

The present association was formed two years ago, when the price was $27, and it was enabled by the extraordinary demand of last year to push the price up to $40. There are about a dozen rail mills, and they are all in it. The demand for English steel rails increased last year 47 per cent., but in spite of this the price was raised only 4 per cent. This appears to have been the regulating effect of competition. Here, in the absence of competition, an increased demand was accompanied by a great advance in the price. While making a public address at Erie in October, 1886, the Hon. William L. Scott declared that he had bought 18 months earlier 10,000 tons of home-made steel rails at $25 50 per ton, and that the sellers were "perfectly satisfied with the price." There was no "combine" at that time. The association was formed some months after this purchase, and at the date of Mr. Scott's speech the price was $33. The advance in cost of production had not exceeded 10 per cent. Allowing for that, and assuming that at $25 50 there was a fair profit, the rate of $33 yielded an additional profit of $5. The price has since been $40; probably the average for last year was not less than $36, and upon the basis of Mr Scott's figures this price afforded a profit of $8 a ton in addition to a fair profit. Upon the year's production of 2,050,000 tons (for 1886 it was 1,562,000) this profit would be $16,400,000. The normal profit may have been $6,000,000 or $8,000,000 more. The 12,724 miles of new road laid last year required 1,300,000 tons of rails if the weight of those used was 65 pounds to the yard, so that the extra or ring profit on these was more than $10,000,000. The reduction of price to $31 50 shows that the profits yielded last Summer, when the price was $39 or $40, were extraordinary. All this excessive profit comes out of the people. As Mr. Scott said: "The railroads simply advance the money, and it is you who travel over the railroads, and who transport your merchandize and produce over them, who in the end pay this immense profit to the manufacturers." In the same speech Mr. Scott referred to the success of "a subject of the Queen" who had gone into the business of making iron and steel at Pittsburg. "I know positively," said he, "that although he did not own the entire works he drew out of that establishment during a period of 300 days profits amounting to $5,000 per day, or $1,500,000 in one year" Possibly he had in mind Mr. Carnegie, whose rail factory is in the "combine." He also said:

"Less than a year ago I was talking with a friend of mine on this question of steel rails. He probably purchases more steel rails than any man in the United States. I said to him: 'These mills are putting up rails pretty fast. Don't you think they ought to stop?' 'Yes,' said he, 'I think they ought to.' Said he: 'You know how the iron industries have been for the last few years—apparently hardly alive. But do you know one thing?' and then calling a certain iron and steel company in Pennsylvania by name he said: 'That company represents a capital of $10,000,000. You know how the iron and steel industries have been depressed, and yet I know that the principal bone of contention in the Board of Directors of that company for some time has been whether or not they should make an extra dividend of $10,000,000.'"

And at the time of that conversation the price of rails was below $30. The average for the year 1885 was only $28 50. Well might the Philadelphia *Times*, a protectionist journal, say a month ago: "Of these Trusts or combines which are now hanging like millstones around the neck of protection the Steel Rail Trust is the most defiant of common fairness, and most false to the protection that created it and gave millions of profits to its investors."

Iron Ore.—The President of the Western Iron Ore Association assures the Chicago *Tribune* that "there is no Iron Ore Trust or the semblance of one either in this association or to my knowledge elsewhere in the United States." Without questioning the truth of this assertion we may direct attention to certain transactions and conditions which show that great local combinations already exist, and that consolidations are taking place which will enable a few producers by and by to follow with ease what Trustmakers call the "tendency of the age;" and once more we shall quote from the New-York *Tribune*, which so frequently points to the benefits of free competition in the protected home market. On Aug. 9, 1887, the *Tribune* published a statement that ex-Senator Dorsey and other capitalists had arrived at Chicago "from Gogebic, where they had been consolidating the iron mines there into two trust schemes to control the output and the price." On or about July 17 it had published in its city news a description of Mr. Dorsey's "projected consolidation of iron mines in the Gogebic and Menominee regions." In company with certain capitalists he had "perfected a scheme" by which 14 iron mines, 12 of which were fully developed, were made the common property of one company with a capital of $10,000,000. There was also this statement:

"At the same time he has thrown together five other mines in a five-million-dollar syndicate, and it is said to be the purpose of the projectors of the consolidation to bring together all the iron-mining properties of the two ranges and create a common stock which can be listed on the Stock Exchange. The iron mines of the Marquette region in Michigan have been *under a combination arrangement for years*, and the mines of the Vermilion region, a few miles north of Duluth, are in the hands of two or three groups, so that with this arrangement with reference to the Gogebic and Menominee ranges perfected, the Bessemer iron ore supply from that region *will be in so few hands that it can be manipulated as a monopoly.*"

And on Aug. 14, Mr. Dorsey having returned to this city, the same paper published an account of this undertaking, from which we take the following:

"The operations in the iron field known as the Gogebic range have spread over into the Menominee range and assumed gigantic proportions. The consolidation perfected on Tuesday at Milwaukee, with a capitalization of $6,000,000, takes in five Gogebic mines, and is the second consolidation developed. The first one took in 12 mines on the Gogebic and Menominee ranges, capitalized at $10,000,000. A third corporation has been formed, with a capital of $[illegible],000,000, to construct a line of 15 iron freight steamers of 2,500 to 3,000 tons, to be confined to the ore shipping trade. Both the iron companies have entered into contracts with the steamship line for long periods. The consolidated companies, with the Wisconsin Central Railroad and Moore, Benjamin & Co., who own the big Colby and Aurora mines, *will control the Bessemer ore product of the region.*"

Trustmakers will see that these tales are not the inventions of their enemies. The financial embarrassment of Capt. Burton, one of the persons interested, seems to have caused some change in the plans of the consolidators. The mineral wealth of the Vermilion iron range and the methods by which a very powerful syndicate gained possession of Mr. Tower's interests there were described in THE TIMES of July 12, 1887. For his interests, the Chicago *Tribune* says, Mr. Tower received $6,000,000 and a quantity of stock. The same paper stated last August that among the members of the syndicate were J. D. Rockefeller of the Standard Oil Trust, D. O. Mills of this city, and J. C. Morse of the Union Steel Company. The entire range is not owned by this group, for there are five mines controlled by other groups, but the several groups appear to be connected. The Chicago *Tribune* says that J. C. Morse of the first syndicate is one of the owners of the neighboring Chandler mine. "The mine is a mate to the great Colby, on the Gogebic range, and its owners are practically the same." But we have quoted the statement that the Colby is owned by persons who are in the Dorsey Gogebic syndicate. The Chicago *Tribune* also points out that the same men, with others, are interested in the remaining Vermilion mines. Would it be difficult to consolidate all of these mines? Is it probable that there will be any competition among them? This seems to be an attractive field of inquiry for the House Committee on Manufactures. The Western Iron Ore Association, which includes the very prosperous gentlemen who have taken hold of these properties, has sent to Congress a memorial declaring that the present rate of duty, 75 cents per ton, is "insufficient for reasonable protection," and suggesting that it should be increased.

Steel.—In October the crucible and open-hearth manufacturers of steel formed an association and the Bessemer manufacturers another. The purpose of these associations, the Secretary of one of them says, is to "remedy irregularities in prices."

Plows.—There has been told in THE TIMES the story of a Western manufacturer of plows, as reported by Mr. P. J. Smalley of Minnesota. Briefly, it is as follows: This manufacturer until last year had been getting the steel parts of plows at 4½ cents a pound, and with this the steel mills seemed to be content. But the formation of a combination was followed by an advance to 10½ cents. To meet this the plowmakers formed an association and raised the price of plows. There was one plowmaker in Illinois who refused to enter the ring and accept its prices. The plowmakers in the association then induced the steelmakers to bring him to terms by compelling him to pay 2 cents a pound more for steel than members of the association were required to pay. In this way the farmers were forced to pay tribute.

The Commissioner is Horace W. Fowler of 257 Broadway, and the signers are Atha & Hughes, A. F. Buchanan & Sons, George W. Blabon & Co., Central Company, Thomas Potter, Sons & Co., and Joseph Wild & Co. A correspondent who directs attention to this circular or decree asserts that prices were advanced about 65 per cent. when the association was formed; that "all small mills have been crushed;" that there are 14 such mills closed and not allowed to do business. The tariff duty on oil cloths and upon oil cloth foundations or floor cloth is 40 per cent., a rate which seems to leave room for further additions to the price of the home product without inviting competition from abroad. F. D. R.

February 20, 1888

TRUSTS AND SOCIALISM.

At the annual banquet of the Boston Merchants' Association, in January last, the subject chosen for discussion was "Combination and Competition," and among the speakers was the well-known political economist, Prof. RICHARD T. ELY of Johns Hopkins University, from whose remarks at that time the following words are taken:

"It is, of course, only necessary for combinations to go forward to bring us to pure Socialism. Every Socialist knows this and rejoices in Trusts. One of the ablest political economists in the country told me a few days since that in conversation with a Socialist this Socialist said: 'Every time I hear of a new Trust I feel like throwing up my hat and shouting hurrah!' And the political economist added: 'If I were a Socialist I would say to our industrial leaders; "Keep right on, gentlemen. You are realizing for me my dreams. It is now only necessary for me to fold my hands."'"

It will not escape the attention of the Trust makers that the recent rapid growth of combinations not only has greatly encouraged those who for years have been advocates of State Socialism, but also has caused a new and interesting movement in New-England, looking to the operation of all industries by the Government. This movement especially deserves attention because those foremost in it are not immigrants who have brought to this country the ideas of Old World Communists, but representatives of old families in New-England, and men who have attained some reputation in literature, at the Bar, or in the pulpit. Among the Nationalists, as they call themselves, are EDWARD EVERETT HALE, THOMAS WENTWORTH HIGGINSON, Rabbi SOLOMON SCHINDLER, and other men whose names are known and whose influence has been felt far beyond the boundaries of the city in which they live.

It is a curious fact that the making of the first or parent club of Nationalists—the one formed in Boston last December—was due in great measure to the influence exerted by EDWARD BELLAMY's little book, "Looking Backward." The chief figure in this book is a rich young man who falls into a mesmeric trance in Boston in the year 1887 and is not awakened until the year 2000, when he discovers that all the Nation's industries and its commerce are carried on by the Government. The greater part of the volume is devoted to elaborate descriptions and explanations of the economic system resulting from the "nationalization" of all kinds of labor. The mind of the young man so strangely transported from the nineteenth century to the end of the twentieth is prepared for the new order of things by those who awaken him. The history of the great economic change is told to him briefly by his new friends, who say:

"The singular blindness of your contemporaries to the signs of the times is a phenomenon commented upon by many of our historians, but few facts of history are more difficult for us to realize, so obvious and unmistakable as we look back seem the indications, which must also have come under your eyes, of the transformation about to come to pass. The records of the period show that the outcry against the concentration of capital was furious. Men believed that it threatened society with a form of tyranny more abhorrent than it had ever endured. They believed that the great corporations were preparing for them the yoke of a baser servitude than had ever been imposed on the race, servitude not to men but to soulless machines, incapable of any motive but insatiable greed. Looking back, we cannot wonder at their desperation, for certainly humanity was never confronted with a fate more sordid and hideous than would have been the era of corporate tyranny which they anticipated.

"The movement toward the conduct of business by larger and larger aggregations of capital, the tendency toward monopolies which had been so desperately and vainly resisted, was recognized at last in its true significance as a process which only needed to complete its logical evolution to open a golden future to humanity. Early in the last [the twentieth] century the evolution was completed by the final consolidation of the entire capital of the Nation. The industry and commerce of the country, ceasing to be conducted by a set of irresponsible corporations and syndicates of private persons at their caprice and for their profit, were intrusted to a single syndicate rep-

resenting the people, to be conducted in the common interest for the common profit. The Nation, that is to say, organized as the one great business corporation in which all other corporations were absorbed; it became the one capitalist in the place of all other capitalists, the sole employer, the final monopoly in which all previous and lesser monopolies were swallowed up, a monopoly in the profits and economies of which all citizens shared."

The Rev. Dr. HALE, Col. HIGGINSON, and their fellow-Nationalists appear to expect that such a transformation will take place. In a recently-published collection of opinions expressed by members of the Boston Nationalist Club Col. HIGGINSON says: "It is my hope that the great ends sought by the scheme of nationalization may be attained, even though the progress be of an extremely slow nature. I believe that the essence of 'Nationalism' is for the very best interests of the people." The President of the club says: "We believe that it is the coming movement for the people, and that it will carry them more rapidly than the Republican Party did in 1855-6. We come out flat-footed and say that the Nation shall take charge of the business of the country; but, of course, we understand that it can only be done step by step." Rabbi SCHINDLER, who is translating Mr. BELLAMY'S book into the German language, is confident that the country's industries will "be thoroughly nationalized, so to speak, before the end of another century." Mr. BELLAMY expects that the Government will soon take the telegraph, telephone, railroad, and express systems and will extend "supervisory national control" over industries that supply the necessities of life and have fallen under the management of combinations, thus preparing the way for complete nationalization. "My fear," he says, "is rather that it is going to come too swiftly for the most judicious control than that it will keep us waiting too long." It is stated that about a dozen auxiliary clubs have been formed in the several States and that they are to be united in a national league.

The "Nationalists" have begun active work by supporting in the Massachusetts Legislature a movement in favor of the municipal control and ownership of gas supplies. So far as this work is concerned they are in accord with Prof. ELY and many others who urge that all industries and businesses that are "natural monopolies"—such as supplying gas, water, and electric light in cities, the railroad, street car, and ferry services, telegraphing and telephoning—should be carried on by the public authorities, but who at the same time draw the line sharply between the field of public industry and that of private industry, reserving for private activity all pursuits that are not "natural monopolies."

This movement, Quixotic as it is, silly as it is, deserves the attention of the makers and friends of Trusts. Those who have united in combinations have never supposed that they were hastening the coming of State Socialism, but we presume these gentlemen in Boston will undertake to convince them that this is just what they are doing. And in the effort to convince them they will use the very arguments by which the Trust makers themselves defend their schemes and seek to prove that competition is no longer beneficial and that Trusts are the instruments of philanthropy. It is unfortunate both for the "Nationalists" and the Trust makers that these arguments are not supported by the facts.

All accounts agree that the World's Fair at Paris resembles its predecessors in having been far from complete at the time of its opening, and that there is still much to be done before getting many of the exhibits in proper shape and place. Considering the long time during which this exposition has been in course of preparation and the great experience which Paris has had in these matters, we might be pardoned for concluding that failure to be ready at the appointed time is the normal and necessary condition of a Universal Exposition. But a most singular remedy, or rather compensation, has been suggested, that of reopening the fair next year, after a Winter recess, and inviting those monarchical countries that have boycotted it this year to take part in it then. This would seem extraordinary, because it would be a sort of admission that monarchical favor is a great element of success now lacking. Besides, the show next year would none the less be simply a continuation of the centennial exposition, precisely as the National Assembly sat through 1790 as well as through 1789. For that matter, the year 1789 was mild and moderate in its attitude toward the French monarchy compared with years that followed.

May 20, 1889

THE PEOPLE AND THE TRUSTS.

In the last six months the number of combinations designed to suppress competition has increased in this country, and the great Trusts almost without exception have become more powerful. The pecuniary gains of some of these have led manufacturers in other branches of industry to undertake the formation of similar "combines," and there is a decided and growing tendency toward the making of rings that shall increase the profits of manufacturing by preventing competitive sales of products. At the same time the movement of the people for the restraint or dissolution of these rings has gained force, and the results of it are beginning to appear in new legislation, crude, severe, and in some cases not well adapted to the purpose, but by its very severity indicating the intense hostility of the mass of consumers toward all schemes for the suppression of competition. It is also noticeable that the makers of the great Trusts, who not long ago sought only concealment and even refused to disclose their agreements to legislative committees, are now defending openly and with considerable skill the Trust plan, and even trying to convince the people that competition is the greatest evil of these days.

In spite of the victory won by the people in their attempt to punish certain corporations that violated the law by entering the Sugar Trust and surrendering control of their business to that association, this Trust controls the sugar market more effectively than it did when the suit was brought, and is making enormous profits out of its monopoly. Its dividends last year were equivalent to about 18 per cent. on a capital stock representing at par a sum that is about three times the actual value of the property put into the "combine." The outside companies exact a price only a shade lower than that of the Trust, and their profits are very large. The White Lead Trust has very recently absorbed the only formidable independent companies in the West, and is now striving to gain the adhesion of the only prominent independent company in the East. This recent development of its power is due to the fact that men who have for years been connected with the Standard Oil Trust have become pecuniarily interested in this combination. The White Lead Trust will soon rank with the Sugar Trust in capital and resources. At the present time capitalists from England are engaged with the salt manufacturers of this country in perfecting a scheme for uniting all of our salt-producers in a Trust that shall act in harmony with the Salt Trust of England. It is even suggested that the anthracite coal companies may be united in an actual Trust. The Trust plan is being introduced in large cities for the monopolizing of gas supplies and the watering of the capital on which consumers of gas must pay interest and dividends. These are some of the most striking symptoms of the Trust mania.

If the Trust-makers really believe that the people of the United States will consent that many of our leading industries shall be permanently monopolized in this way, they have been strangely misled. If they suppose that the people will be convinced by their arguments that competition ought to be suppressed, they have lost all power to measure the strength and drift of public opinion. For the solution of such problems as this which is presented by the growth of Trust schemes the people move slowly, but when they shall determine to apply a remedy for the disease, it will not be possible to oppose them successfully. They have no more liking for the doctrines of the Trust-makers than they have for the visionary schemes of the so-called Collectivists or Socialists, who hold that the multiplication of Trusts will inevitably and speedily lead to the operation of all manufacturing industries by the Government. They will have neither Monopoly nor Socialism, but will put down both.

At present they are dazed by the rapid growth of these organizations. But in the near future they will find weapons with which to assail them. They will make full use of existing laws. They will punish corporations that have obtained from them valuable privileges and powers only to use the same to the injury of those who granted them. Whenever it shall appear that a Trust or a similar combination has suppressed competition and practiced extortion under the shelter and with the aid of a tariff duty, that duty will be largely reduced or cut off altogether. In addition they will proceed against the combinations by means of new statutes that shall embody the common law with respect to the suppression of competition, that has been interpreted so many times and so clearly by our courts. If the laws recently enacted in three or four States shall prove to be inadequate or objectionable, other laws will be passed that will answer the purpose.

The idea that the American people will quietly submit to the loss of competition in manufactures and trade, that they will consent to come under the domination of rings of manufacturers, that they will permit such rings to fix the prices of staple products and necessaries of life and at the same time to exclude from the industries so controlled citizens who desire to use their capital and skill in those industries, that they will allow great confederations to tax them at pleasure for the enrichment of idle owners of decaying factories and antiquated machinery, and that they will submissively legislate for the protection and profit of such confederations, is one that cannot be entertained by honest and clear-headed men. The Trust-makers will try to commend it to the people, and will use in this work the resources of great money capital and social and political influence, but they will fail.

June 22, 1889

A NEW ANTI-TRUST BILL.

A MEASURE WHICH SENATOR SHERMAN THINKS CANNOT BE EVADED.

WASHINGTON, March 18.—Mr. Sherman, from the Senate Committee on Finance, reported to-day a substitute for his Anti-Trust bill. In the shape presented to-day Mr. Sherman thinks he has met and overcome all objections to the measure on the ground of unconstitutionality. The members of the committee reserve the right to express their opinion of the bill when it comes up for consideration.

The substitute provides that all arrangements, contracts, agreements, trusts, or combinations between two or more citizens or corporations, or both, of different States, or between two or more citizens or corporations, or both, of the United States and foreign States, or citizens or corporations thereof, made with a view or which tend to prevent full and free competition in the importation, transportation, or sale of articles imported into the United States, or with a view or which tend to prevent full and free competition in articles of growth, production, or manufacture of any State or Territory of the United States, with similar articles of the growth, production, or manufacture of any other State or Territory or in the transportation or sale of like articles the production of any State or Territory of the United States into or within any other State or Territory of the United States, and all arrangements, trusts, or combinations between such citizens or corporations, made with a view or which tend to advance the cost to the consumer of any such articles, are hereby declared to be against public policy, unlawful, and void.

The Circuit Court of the United States shall have original jurisdiction of all suits of a civil nature at common law or in equity arising under this section, and to issue all remedial process, orders, or writs proper and necessary to enforce its provisions. And the Attorney General and the several District Attorneys are hereby directed, in the name of the United States, to commence and prosecute all cases to final adjournment and execution.

Any person or corporation injured or damnified by such arrangement, contract, agreement, trust, or combination, defined above, may sue for and recover in any court of the United States of competent jurisdiction, without respect to the amount involved, of any person or corporation a party to a combination described in the first section of the act, twice the amount of damages sustained and the costs of the suit, together with a reasonable attorney's fee.

March 19, 1890

JAY GOULD'S LATEST DEAL

HE SECURES CONTROL OF THE UNION PACIFIC.

A SCHEME BY WHICH HE HOPES TO PRODUCE HARMONY AMONG ROADS IN THE WEST—MR. ADAMS TO RETIRE.

Jay Gould has got control of the Union Pacific Railway Company; at least that is what he himself says. Interested with him in the deal which has led to the acquisition of this property—to the re-establishment of his power in it rather—are, according to his own statement, William and John D. Rockefeller.

Mr. Gould said to a visitor yesterday: "The Union Pacific has come under our control. Mr. Charles Francis Adams will cease to be President. I will probably take the Presidency myself. Mr. Adams has been managing the property after a fashion which sets business control wholly at naught, and under his direction the Union Pacific, more than any other railroad in the West, has disturbed and upset harmony, knocked down rates, and forced the handling of business without profit. That sort of thing has gone so far that important interests in the company, including Sidney Dillon, Frederick Ames, and other prominent stockholders, have determined that his administration must end. I have become a large owner of the stock during the recent wholesale declines in its market value. Purchases of an important character have also been made by the Rockefellers. Mr. Dillon, Mr. Ames, and other old stockholders are anxious to co-operate with us, and, indeed, have invited us to assume th control, direction, and management of the property, and we accepted."

Mr. Gould, continuing what seemed to be a very frank declaration as to his Union Pacific acquisition and plans, said: "The Union Pacific hereafter will not be a disturber of Western railway peace. The Union Pacific-Northwest combination would be no longer able to prevent the maintenance of harmony among the leading Western railroads." Mr. Gould added that what he had in view was a new association for the Western railroads, including those of the Southwest and Northwest, which would be much more effective than had been any other association ever in the field. Rates would not be put up one day to be cut down secretly the next. He intimated that his old idea of a railway clearing house—practically a railway trust—would now be put in operation.

Mr. Gould spent much of yesterday in Wall Street in consultation with officers of the Atchison, Topeka and Santa Fé Railway. He declares that the Missouri Pacific and Atchison Railways have reached an agreement which is satisfactory to both and which will create lasting peace in Southwestern territory. There are even intimations that one of his sons may become an Atchison Director, and that a member of the firm of Kidder, Peabody & Co. may come into a like relation in the Atchison Directory.

Mr. Gould said yesterday that rates would be put up and kept up, and that the railroads of the West would earn double the amount of money that this year's figures show. He added that he believed the arrangement now in view would have an effect upon the investing public—reflecting in Wall Street quite as cheerfully as did the West Shore deal of half a dozen years ago.

November 12, 1890

A BIG MACHINERY TRUST.

A NEW HARVESTER COMPANY WITH A CAPITAL OF $35,000,000.

CHICAGO, Nov. 19.—There was organized in this city within the past few days one of the largest corporations in its line in the world. The charter was filed in Springfield to-day, and the name of the new company will be known as the American Harvester Company, for the manufacture of harvesting machinery. It will have a capital stock of $35,000,000. The Directors of the new company will be Cyrus H. McCormick, William Deering, Walter A. Wood, Lewis Miller, Col. A. L. Conger, and Gen. A. S. Bushnell.

"The purpose of the new company is the building of harvester machines," said Col. Conger, when questioned by an Associated Press reporter. "The present demoralization of the business necessitated the formation of a new company. I can recall over eighty different companies engaged in the business which have failed, entailing a loss upon farmers, laboring men, manufacturers, and others of between $35,000,000 and $40,000,000. While some companies have been successful, the general condition of the business was such that it became necessary to give the farmers better machines at lower prices, if possible, without disaster to the manufacturer. For several years manufacturers have been selling machines at so low a price as to give them no fairly-compensating profit. The cost of materials has been advancing, so that it has become necessary either to raise the price of machines to the farmer, or, through economy, produce and distribute them more cheaply, as it is the purpose and expectation of this new organization to do.

"It is no less to the interest of binder manufacturers than that of the farmers themselves that the latter should obtain binder twine at reasonable prices, and the hope of effecting this object is one of the important reasons for the formation of this new company. Freight will be saved by having machines made at factories situated so that there will be as few as possible of cross-shipments and unnecessary expenses, burdensome to both maker and user. There is no intention to raise the prices of the machines. We do not expect to check competition, but shall probably carry on the manufacture of the present machines at the several different works. The only way to accomplish this was by the formation of an entirely new company, and the names of the Directors whom I have mentioned will be a sufficient guarantee that the company will be successfully and conservatively managed. We have not decided upon all the officers, but it is understood that Mr. McCormick is to be President, Mr. Wood Vice President, and Mr. Deering Chairman of the Board of Directors."

November 20, 1890

TEN THOUSAND MEN TO GO.

EFFECT OF THE CONSOLIDATION OF THE HARVESTER COMPANIES.

ST. LOUIS, Dec. 30.—It was learned here to-day that the first official act of the American Harvester Company of Illinois, a consolidation of the eighteen harvester companies of the United States, with headquarters in Chicago, will discharge about 10,000 employes, whose services are rendered unnecessary by the consolidation of eighteen separate and distinct companies into one monopoly. Ten million dollars per annum is expected to be saved in wages alone through this consolidation. Three-fifths of the estimated savings in wages are said to be realized from the cutting down of the force of traveling men, and besides the general decapitation of the drummers there will be a sweeping discharge of office men, warehouse men, skilled workmen, and others, which it is acknowledged by the combination will throw at least 10,000 men out of employment at the beginning of the year. This is made possible by the fact that under consolidated management the output of harvest machinery will be limited to the great plants whose brands are standard all over the world, and that most of the small plants will be shut down.

The Minneapolis company has, it is said, already closed down and discharged its force, and after Jan. 1 many others will follow suit.

The formal notification from Chicago that the American Harvester Company has assumed the active management of affairs is expected this week. All the companies are waiting for it, and the moment it is issued the grand sweeping performance will begin and the books of every concern will be closed up to the date of the actual consolidation. Complete confirmation of the above statements was obtained to-day from Assistant Manager Kelso of M. M. Osborne & Co. of this city. He said the most sweeping discharge would be of traveling men. Of every ten now employed eight would be discharged on Jan. 1.

The new monopoly, which controls the output of harvesting machinery of the entire United States and a large European trade, has a capital of $35,000,000. It is incorporated under the laws of Illinois, the incorporators being Cyrus H. McCormick, William Deering, Walter A. Wood, George A. S. Bushnell, and Col. A. L. Conger. Cyrus H. McCormick is President of the consolidated company, Walter A. Wood is Vice President, and A. L. Conger is General Manager.

December 31, 1890

A GROWING INDUSTRY.

We hope it has not escaped the attention of Mr. JOHN SHERMAN that the enactment of his so-called Anti-Trust law has greatly stimulated the Trust-making industry. Possibly this has not been overlooked by the high-tariff journals that pointed during the campaign to this law as proof that their party had "kept its pledges" and made ample provision for the overthrow of every "combine" in the land. But they do not say anything about it. Some of them have published the news dispatches in which the proceedings of the new Trust-makers were reported, but have found no room for any editorial comment upon the interestings facts thus disclosed.

The list is one that certainly invites a little moralizing about the suppression of competition in large industries, if it does not call for some remarks about the law, which has been described by the New-York *Tribune* as a statute that "covers all the ground"; but those who so warmly commended the law during the campaign are silent now. We should except the Chicago *Inter Ocean*, which tells its readers that the combinations are fast dying out and that there are only two or three left. The manufacturers of reaping and mowing machines, the makers of thrashing machines, the manufacturers of window glass, the smelters of silver and lead ores—these are some of the gentlemen who have either recently completed great combinations or are now perfecting their plans. Ex-Gov. FOSTER of Ohio and many other Republicans are in the new Window-Glass Trust, and the member of the National Republican Committee from Ohio has become a prominent officer of the reaper and mower combination, which is called the American Harvester Company, and in which he represents, it is said, "the knife and sickle business." How Mr. SHERMAN'S heart must ache as he sees his party associates in Ohio defying his law!

We have not included in the list the so-called Wheel Trust, for this combination was made before the Anti-Trust law was passed. It cannot be used as an example of the manner in which the industry of Trust-making has been stimulated by the law, but it does appear that Mr. SHERMAN'S statute has given new life to it, for it has recently raised the price of wheels 70 per cent. It is curious that the law has had a similar effect upon the Axe and Tool Trust and the Starch Trust, as our readers will remember.

This exhibition of vigor was made by the "American Wheel Company," it seems, on the 2d inst. The central office is in Chicago, and the *Tribune* of that city says that the combination now controls 90 per cent. of the productive capacity of the industry. When a *Tribune* reporter called at the office for information, he found the gentlemen there strangely reticent. But the merchants and the manufacturers of carriages and wagons were more inclined to talk, as the following report from the *Tribune* shows:

"'Yes, I have just received news that wheels have advanced 70 per cent. in price,' said J. M. VAN NEST of the Michigan Buggy Company. 'This move, in conjunction with the increased cost of other materials, will cause an advance of from 10 to 20 per cent. on everything on wheels. The lighter vehicles will be advanced the most.

"'Sleighs will also be more expensive than heretofore. The plushes used as lining have risen 60 per cent. in the last two months, and the cloth goods from 10 to 20 per cent. Our leather costs us 15 per cent. more this year, and other materials have risen from 5 to 15 per cent. The least advance—5 per cent.—is in the iron work.'

"H. C. STAVER and the Abbott Buggy Company estimate the rise at from 5 to 20 per cent., according to the character of the vehicle. The same views are expressed all along the line except at C. P. KIMBALL & Co's."

At the house last mentioned it was explained that the advance would not increase the price of very expensive carriages.

Mr. SHERMAN asserted in a speech delivered during the campaign that his law had already begun to do the work for which it had been enacted. If the purpose of those who made it was to encourage Trust-makers it has already become effective.

December 10, 1890

WILL LOOK AFTER CORPORATIONS.

OBJECT AND PURPOSE OF A TRUST COMPANY IN NEW-JERSEY.

The organization of an odd sort of a company has been completed in New-Jersey. It will be known as the Corporation Trust Company of New-Jersey, and is designed to act for all those corporations which go over into that State for incorporation because of the peculiarly favorable laws there and the low tax rate. Its present offices will be at the corner of Greene and Grand Streets, Jersey City.

The offices will be about all there is to the new corporation. It will need no more extensive plant, for its object is simply to act as trustee of corporations organized under the laws of New-Jersey, but doing business outside of that State. Of these there are a great many. For them the new corporation will act as local agent, or, as it might be said, as a trustee for trusts, furnishing the office for them and acting as register and guarantee of their stock debentures.

Charles N. King will be the General Manager of the new concern. It has a capital of $100,000, which it is intended to increase to $1,000,000. The Directors are Gov. Leon Abbett, Henry C. Kelsey, Allan L. McDermott, Henry S. White, John McAnerny, James B. Dill, Charles N. King, Vincent H. La Marche of Brooklyn, and T. D. Jordan, Controller of the Equitable Life Assurance Society. Mr. McDermott is the President of the company, Mr. White the Vice President, Mr. McAnerny the Treasurer, and Mr. La Marche Secretary. It is stated that half a dozen other men prominent in New-Jersey politics are large stockholders.

The new company does not intend to stay in the offices it has now engaged at Greene and Grand Streets, Jersey City. It contemplates erecting a fine building for itself. Its prospective customers are all those corporations in New-Jersey which do most of their business in other States, and it will enable them to have an office in New-Jersey, as the law requires, and to have it open and doing business during the business hours of the day. It will even furnish the clerks if necessary. There will be proper rooms provided where these customers can hold their meetings, elections, &c., and transact all the business which the law requires that they should transact in New-Jersey. Safe deposit vaults will be provided for all customers.

The new corporation by its charter has the power to act as agent for non-resident corporations and to be designated as the person upon whom the service of papers may be made in the State. It is expected that it will do a large business in guaranteeing the regularity and legality of the issues of stocks, bonds, and mortgages of New-Jersey corporations. It will stand in the same relation to those securities as a title guarantee company does to the purchasers of real estate. The field that is open to the new company is shown by the fact that official figures show that there are more than 1,600 such companies organized under the laws of New-Jersey, with a capital stock of more than $600,000,000.

Dill, Chandler & Seymour are the counsel for the new company. Regarding its object and purpose the firm said yesterday:

"In the first place, in the very strictest sense it will enable such companies to comply with the laws of the State of New-Jersey as to having a local office, and in the second place it will financially guarantee the legality and non-liability of the stock. The company proposes to take such a stand that their guarantee of the legality and non-liability of the stock and debentures shall be as necessary to parties seeking to borrow money on such collateral as is the certificate of a title guarantee company as to the title to a piece of real estate in case a borrower wants to realize upon it. There is likely to be some legislation in New-Jersey the coming Winter more strictly enforcing the rule that corporations must maintain continuously an office in the State of New-Jersey, and have as well a person designated upon whom service of papers can be made within the State. All companies such as those referred to will therefore undoubtedly find it to their advantage to rent offices in the building of our company and take advantage of all the facilities afforded by it. The most profitable part of the business of our company, however, will probably be in guaranteeing the stocks of these foreign corporations, rather than in renting offices to them and providing them with a legal representative upon whom papers may be served, so that they may keep within the law of the State and the terms of their charters."

December 24, 1892

IRON HEEL OF MONOPOLY

HOW THE CIGARETTE TRUST CRUSHES OUT OPPOSITION.

DESPOTIC SCHEME PUT IN OPERATION TO DRIVE OUT COMPETING GOODS —A DEALER SELLING OTHER CIGARETTES THAN THE TRUST'S IS BLACKLISTED.

Of the 2,900,000,000 cigarettes of domestic make consumed in this country in the year ending June 30 about 98 per cent. were of the brands controlled by the trust known as the American Tobacco Company. There is great tribulation among all those cigarette manufacturers who are not in the trust and the jobbers on account of the way in which the market has been monopolized and because of the means by which the monopoly is maintained. There are fortunes of millions to be made in the manufacture of cigarettes. That is why the trust was formed.

Half a dozen manufacturers had the market to themselves until a few years ago. They had made and were continuing to make fortunes. They saw that others coveted their field and contemplated putting capital and labor into it.

So they conferred together and the conference resulted in combination, and the American Tobacco Company came into existence. The capital stock was fixed at $25,000,000. Of this $15,000,000 was common and $10,000,000 preferred. Almost all those manufacturers who did not go into the trust were eventually either driven from the field or forced to sell their plants to the trust. Then, by prodigal advertising of the brands manufactured in the trust factories and "freeze-out" methods not uncommon to industrial combinations, though in this case more stringent than usual and so more effective, was brought about the result of the last fiscal year when 98 per cent. of the consumption was controlled.

The trust's plan for putting out its product was at first under a system of rebates. This conflicted with the laws against trusts in many States, and in Texas President J. B. Duke of the American Tobacco Company was indicted. Nothing came of that proceeding, however. Now the trust has a method by which it believes that it brings itself within the law, and if not, does surely evade it, under the new scheme though the "iron heel of monopoly" crushes more ruthlessly than ever the rights of manufacturers outside of the trust and of the jobbers.

It is an ingenious scheme. The trust sells no goods. It just "consigns" its goods to dealers to be sold on commission. Just the same, the dealer has to pay the full value of the goods "consigned" to him ten days after they are received. Three months after delivery the trust balances its books with the dealer and pays him his "commission." It is, in other words, necessary for the dealer to wait three months for his profit on the goods he sells; but the trust gets the full amount of the purchase money, the "list price," as it is called, which means its price plus the profit of the dealer who sells the goods, ten days after delivery, and for the rest of the three months before the dealer gets his profit that profit can be used by the trust without the payment of interest or any other consideration.

But why should the dealers buy the trust goods under such a burdensome condition? Simply because if they buy any other goods they cannot buy trust goods except at the so-called "list price," which is the price for which they have themselves to sell them. The edict of the trust, not in words but in effect, is that any dealer who sells any other cigarettes than the cigarettes made by the trust cannot get any more trust goods except at a price which will make it profitless for him to handle them.

The trust has a regular detective service to see that its demand in this regard is carried out. A case in point is that of a very large Third Avenue jobber. Last July he received notice that no more goods would be "consigned" to him to sell on commission, but he might buy them at "list price"—the price for which he would have to sell. Inquiry as to the cause of the cutting off of this firm revealed that it was because it had been selling trust goods at prices lower than the trust had fixed to govern the jobbing trade. The dealer saw the downfall of his business, so far as cigarettes was concerned, unless he could get reinstated. Finally, the trust officers condescended to reinstate him on their lists; but as a penalty for his having seen fit to sell goods for any price he pleased, the sentence was pronounced upon him that for three months he would receive no commissions for handling trust goods. In a word, he simply had to handle trust goods for three months without making a cent of profit.

Now this same dealer has been blacklisted again. This time it is because one of the trust detectives went into his place and purchased 500 of a brand of cigarettes manufactured by a company that has started in opposition to the American Tobacco Company. He has been formally notified that no more goods will be "consigned" to him by the trust, but that he can buy them at "list price"—that is, the very price at which he would have to sell them. As the trust brands of cigarettes, through advertising, are those which consumers mostly call for, a jobber who has not got them to supply to his trade is in a bad way.

There is much chafing under the yoke and there is much talk as to what is going to be done. Many jobbers have been put under the ban by the trust for doing just what the Third Avenue jobber did. In several cases, one being that of a large dealer, the blacklisting has been the proverbial last straw, and the dealers have told the trust that they would get along without any more "consignments" of its cigarettes.

December 28, 1892

CHANGED IN NAME ONLY.

In Other Respects the Standard Oil Trust Remains the Same.

The plan for the dissolution of the Standard Oil Trust which has been developed by a committee of Trustees which began work in March of last year is now completed, and a meeting has been called to be held at the office of the trust, at 26 Broadway, next Wednesday. John D. Rockefeller, H. M. Flagler, J. D. Archbold, William Rockefeller, Benjamin Brewster, Henry H. Rogers, Wesley H. Tilford, and O. B. Jennings have had the matter in hand.

Acting under resolutions of the trust, the committee has been engaged in disposing of trust property at private sale, distributing the proceeds according to the respective interests. Next Wednesday the committee will submit a detailed statement of what it has done.

The dissolution of the trust is the result of litigation which was begun in 1890. An Ohio court issued an order requiring the officers of the trust to show reason why the trust should not be dissolved on the ground that it had forfeited its charter by an abuse of charter rights. At this time the trust was operated with a capital of $90,000,000, the property adjudged by the dividends that it produced being worth much more than the capital stock. The court decided that the dissolution of the trust ought to be confided to those who had managed its affairs, because thereby the chance of large losses would be avoided. Under this order the committee above named has been at work.

September 8, 1893

SENATOR ALDRICH AND SUGAR

THE REPUBLICAN TARIFF LEADER OWNED BY THE TRUST.

PROVIDENCE, R. I., June 19.—Never yet has the story been told of all the relations which the monster Sugar Trust bears to the lawmakers at Washington, who are charged with the making of laws affecting directly the cash account of that great monopoly. One chapter, which will startle all who have any interest in the progress of affairs at Washington, is furnished in some recent transactions in this city. It may be briefly and plainly told.

Senator Nelson W. Aldrich, the senior Senator from Rhode Island, the leader of the Republicans in the Senate when tariff matters are under discussion, is a business partner of John E. Searles, the Secretary and Treasurer of the Sugar Trust. Not only are Mr. Aldrich and Mr. Searles partners in an enterprise which involves millions of dollars, but the partnership was formed in such a way as to put Senator Aldrich under especial obligations to the Sugar Trust magnates.

It is startling to know that some of the Sugar Trust money, derived directly from the tariff on sugar imposed by the McKinley law, has been turned into a channel where it is helping bear on to fortune the Senator who led the fight to put that duty into the McKinley law, and thus contribute to the revenue which came to him almost as a relief measure, when he most needed it.

Within two years Senator Aldrich has been actively engaged in securing a monopoly of the street-railway system in Providence. It became necessary for him to have a large amount of money—more than he could himself control. The Sugar Trust came to his relief, and Treasurer Searles of the trust became a Director in Mr. Aldrich's company. He contributed, or he and his associates in the trust contributed, $1,500,000, which is but a trifle when compared with the $35,000,000 which the trust accumulated under the tariff duty to which Mr. Aldrich was so devoted.

The services of Mr. Aldrich in behalf of a high tariff were alike pleasing to Republican patriots and to the trust. The trust at any rate was grateful.

When the amendment which proposed to strike out of the now pending bill several millions of proposed Sugar Trust profits came up in the Senate at this session of Congress Mr. Aldrich was not there to vote for it. If he had desired to show his appreciation of the kindness done him by the Sugar Trust he could have done it in no other way so well.

Mr. Aldrich has explained his absence by saying he was "accidentally" away, not knowing the amendment was coming.

It was an accident which was most unfortunate for him, when considered in connection with the mutual obligations between himself and the Sugar Trust.

Their obligations, it will be seen, are mutual. Each has contributed largely to the prosperity of the other.

Their relations and dependency, the one upon the other, show either an unfortunate series of coincidences, or a most unwholesome mingling of a high public servant and a great private corporation. The leader of his party and the Sugar Trust each have obligations to the other.

Each has cast his bread upon the water, and it has come back after many days with Scriptural certainty.

June 20, 1894

A SUGAR TRUST VICTORY

Important Decision in Its Favor by the Supreme Court.

THE CONSOLIDATION WAS LAWFUL

Congress May Not Regulate Those Acts of Corporations Done Wholly Within a Single State.

WASHINGTON, Jan. 21.—The case of the United States vs. The E. C. Knight Company et al., appealed from the Court of Appeals for the Third Circuit, involving the constitutionality and validity of the Sherman anti-trust law, was decided in the Supreme Court of the United States to-day adversely to the contentions of the Government.

The suit was begun in the Circuit Court for the Eastern District of Pennsylvania and was brought to compel the defendant companies—the American Sugar Refining Company, the E. C. Knight Company, the Franklin Sugar Company, the Spreckels Sugar Refining Company, and the Delaware Sugar House—to cancel the contracts by which the stocks of the last four-named corporations were sold to the American Company, through John E. Searles, Jr., in exchange for American Company stock, on the ground that the transaction was in violation of the act of July 2, 1890, and that it effected a combination in restraint of inter-State commerce. The Circuit Court dismissed the bill, and the Court of Appeals affirmed that decision. Thereupon the United States prosecuted its appeal to the Supreme Court of the United States.

Chief Justice Fuller announced the opinion and decision of the court. After discussing the legal meaning and effect of the term "monopoly," the opinion proceeded:

The fundamental question is whether, conceding that the existence of a monopoly in manufacture is established by the evidence, that monopoly can be directly suppressed under the act of Congress in the mode attempted by this bill.

Under this head the scope of the duties and powers of the State to "protect the lives, health and property of its citizens, and to preserve good order and the public morals," and of Congress to regulate commerce among the several States, are discussed. The Chief Justice said:

The Constitution does not provide that inter-State commerce shall be free, but by the grant of the exclusive power to regulate it, it was left free except as Congress might impose restraints. Therefore it has been determined that the failure of Congress to exercise this exclusive power in any case is an expression of its will that the subject shall be free from restrictions or impositions upon it by the several States, and if a law passed by a State in the exercise of its acknowledged powers comes into conflict with that will, the Congress and the State cannot occupy the position of equal opposing sovereignties, because the Constitution declares its supremacy and that of the laws passed in pursuance thereof; and that which is not supreme must yield to that which is supreme.

The argument is that the power to control the manufacture of refined sugar is a monopoly over a necessary of life, to the enjoyment of which by a large part of the population of the United States inter-State commerce is indispensable, and that, therefore, the General Government, in the exercise of the power to regulate commerce, may repress such monopoly directly, and set aside the instruments which have created it. But this argument cannot be confined to necessaries of life merely, and must include all articles of general consumption. It is vital that the independence of the commercial power and of the police power and the delimitations between them should always be recognized and observed.

It was in the light of well-settled principles that the act of July 2, 1890, was framed. Congress did not attempt thereby to assert the power to deal with monopoly directly as such, or to limit and restrict the rights of corporations created by the States in the acquisition, control, or disposition of property; or to regulate or prescribe the price at which such property or the products thereof should be sold; or to make criminal the acts of persons in the acquisition and control of property which the States of their residence sanctioned. What the law struck at was combinations, contracts, and conspiracies to monopolize trade and commerce among the several States or with foreign nations; but the contracts and acts of the defendants related exclusively to the acquisition of the Philadelphia refineries and the business of sugar refining in Pennsylvania, and bore no direct relation to commerce between the States or with foreign nations. The object was manifestly private gain, but not through the control of inter-State or foreign commerce. It is true that the bill alleged that the products of these refineries were sold among the several States, and that all the companies were engaged in commerce with the several States and with foreign nations; but this was no more than to say that trade and commerce served manufacture to fulfill its function. There was nothing in the proofs to indicate any intention to put a restraint upon trade or commerce, and the fact, as we have seen, that trade or commerce might be indirectly affected, was not enough to entitle complainants to a decree.

The Circuit Court declined, upon the pleadings and proofs, to grant the relief prayed and dismissed the bill, and we are of opinion that the Circuit Court of Appeals did not err in affirming that decree. Decree affirmed.

January 22, 1895

MR. MORGAN TAKES HOLD

Railway Presidents Invited to Dine with the Financier.

FREIGHT RATE CUTTING TO CEASE

A Meeting at the Trunk Line Association Offices Settles the Question—Dinner at the Metropolitan Club.

Two or three days ago J. Pierpont Morgan sent invitations to the Presidents and some of the other chief executive officers of the railroads operating between New-York and Chicago to dine with him on his steam yacht Corsair, on Thursday evening, June 27. The implied object of this unusual social assembling of railway managers was to discuss the demoralized condition of freight rates both east bound and west bound.

By overzealous competition and the reckless cutting of rates some of the railroad companies were threatening a serious injury to the business interests of the country. Mr. Morgan, by virtue of his vast and diversified financial and railroad connections, was in a position to perceive and keenly appreciate the danger. The urgent need of pacificatory measures was apparent, and the distinguished financier, at the solicitation of parties interested, consented to exercise his influence in that direction.

The time designated for the yachting dinner party was purposely in unison with the date set for a meeting of the Presidents of the Trunk Line, and the Central Traffic Associations, in this city. The meeting was held yesterday, and it proved to be one of the largest and most satisfactory meetings of railroad men ever held to discuss rate troubles. Mr. Morgan's influence in behalf of harmony was potent. Contrary to expectation, there was an almost total absence of friction, and every question at issue was settled on the spot. All of the railway lines represented agreed to restore rates to the standard figures, and to hold them there rigidly.

The main action of the meeting, which was presided over by George B. Roberts, President of the Pennsylvania Railroad, was embodied in the following resolution:

"That from July 8, 1895, the Presidents or chief executive officers of the companies represented at this meeting pledge themselves to absolutely maintain the full published tariffs of east-bound and west-bound freight rates on all classes of traffic as now authorized by joint committee, until ten days after written notice is given the Commissioner of the Trunk Line or Central Traffic Association by any member of its withdrawal from the agreement; and, further, any contracts at rates below the authorized tariff shall be, on or before July 1, filed with said Commissioners.

"This resolution to be continued in effect so long as it is observed by all lines hereto, and which question of observance shall be determined promptly by the Commissioners on complaint made.

"That we also pledge ourselves that no contracts shall be made by our lines which will prevent the operation of the foregoing resolution, and we hereby agree to place our signatures to this resolution as a further evidence of our intent to faithfully observe its conditions."

Another resolution, proposed by Chauncey M. Depew, was adopted, providing that the power of fixing rates on east-bound freight traffic shall be vested in a permanent commission to be appointed by President Roberts. One of the effects of this step will be to do away with soliciting agents, who have in times past been largely responsible for the cutting of rates.

The matter of completing the much-discussed west-bound agreement in relation to freight traffic was left in the hands of a committee, with the expectation of a prompt report.

Passenger rates were taken up, and much to the gratification of all the representatives, the west-bound agreement of May 17 was signed by those Western roads which have, for one reason or another, heretofore failed to subscribe their signatures. This important agreement will become operative within a few days, just as soon as Commissioners Goddard and Blanchard can arrange the necessary details.

A very important outcome of this meeting was the formal enrollment, as a member of the Trunk Line Association, of the Chesapeake and Ohio Railroad. That road has long been an irritating outside influence, although its President, M. E. Ingalls, has all along been a member of the Board of Presidents in his capacity as President of the Big Four system.

The harmonious and conclusive action of the meeting naturally removed whatever business significance there might have been attached to Mr. Morgan's dinner party. The unpropitious weather rendered a trip on the yacht Corsair undesirable, and Mr. Morgan graciously changed the place of the dinner to the Metropolitan Club, where he entertained about fifty prominent railroad men last night. The affair was purely of a social character, and it assumed something of the nature of a jollification over the restoration of stable rates.

Following are the names of the gentlemen who attended both the meeting and the dinner: George B. Roberts, President of the Pennsylvania Road; Chauncey M. Depew, President of the New-York Central, and Horace J. Hayden, Second Vice President of the New-York Central; E. B. Thomas, President of the Erie Railway; M. E. Ingalls, President of the Cleveland, Cincinnati, Chicago and St. Louis and President of the Chesapeake and Ohio; Joseph S. Harris, President of the Reading; Charles F. Mayer, President of the Baltimore and Ohio; E. P. Wilbur, President of the Lehigh Valley; L. J. Seargeant, President of the Chicago and Grand Trunk and General Manager of the Grand Trunk; D. B. Caldwell, President of the Lake Shore; H. B. Ledyard, President of the Michigan Central; S. R. Calloway, President of the Nickel Plate; C. M. Hayes, General Manager of the Wabash; E. R. Bacon, President of the Baltimore and Ohio Southwestern; W. S. Sloan, Second Vice President of the Lackawanna; J. Lowrie Bell, General Manager of the Jersey Central; J. D. Layng, General Manager of the West Shore; J. E. Childs, General Manager of the Ontario and Western.

Referring to recent reports published about the originators of the rate cutting on east-bound freights, Mr. George B. Reeve, Traffic Manager of the Grand Trunk, has written as follows to General Agent O. S. Cockey in this city:

"The Grand Trunk was not the cause of the demoralization in east-bound rates. The facts are that for the last four months we have been almost starving for traffic on account of the other lines cutting the rates, and as we did not wish to evade the Inter-State commerce law we were compelled to reduce the tariff in order to meet the secret cuts made by our competitors."

June 28, 1895

ANTI-TRUST LAW DECISION

Agreement of the Trans-Missouri Freight Association Regarding Rates Deemed a Violation.

A SUPREME COURT DECREE.

Decision of the Circuit Court of Appeals in New York Erroneous—Can Manufacturing Trusts Be Reached?—Four Dissenting Justices.

WASHINGTON, March 22.—By a majority opinion, delivered by Justice Peckham, the Supreme Court of the United States to-day announced its decision that the agreement of the Trans-Missouri Freight Association to maintain rates within its territory was a violation of the anti-trust law of 1890, prohibiting contracts or combinations in restraint of trade, and must be abandoned. This reversed the decision of the courts below, which ordered a dismissal of the Government's bill. Justices Field, Gray, Shiras, and White dissented.

Justice Peckham, in giving the decision of the court, said the case presented two questions of importance:

Does the anti-trust act apply to and cover common carriers by railroads? If so, does the agreement complained of violate any provision of the act?

The Court finally holds: "The question is one of law in regard to the meaning and effect of the agreement itself, namely: Does the agreement restrain trade or commerce in any way so as to be a violation of the act? We have no doubt that it does. The agreement on its face recites that it is entered into 'for the purpose of mutual protection,' and a violation subjects the defaulting company to the payment of a penalty. While in force and assuming it to be lived up to there can be no doubt that its direct, immediate, and necessary effect is to put a restraint upon trade or commerce as described in the act. We think the fourth section of the act invests the Government with full power and authority to bring such an action as this, and if the facts be proved an injunction should issue.

"The decrees of the Court of Appeals of the Circuit Court must be reversed and the case remanded."

The dissent of Justices Field, Gray, Shiras, and White was announced by the latter. He said that the decision of the court followed the letter of the law, "which killeth rather than the spirit which giveth life." The ultimate analysis of that decision was that there must be no trade. An attorney who has been connected with the litigation in its progress through the Supreme Court of the United States, speaking of the effect of the decision, said:

"It settles that the Joint Traffic Association of the Eastern Trunk Lines is illegal and that the decision of the Circuit Court of Appeals in New York on Friday last, sustaining the lawfulness of that combination, was erroneous. It will also compel the dissolution of all similar combinations of railroads, holding, in effect, as it does, that the anti-pooling clause of the Inter-State Commerce act is very much widened by the Anti-Trust act of 1890. It leaves the question open whether manufacturing trusts can be reached practically under the anti-trust law."

March 23, 1897

THE INTER-STATE COMMERCE COMMISSION.

The powers of the Inter-State Commerce Commission fare badly at the hands of the courts. This, of course, is but another way of saying that the law under which the commission was created and operates was badly drawn for its purpose.

No one doubts that Congress intended to give the commission some substantial power in regulating the charges that may be made by the railroads. But if the commission can only pass on rates after they are adopted and put in effect; if then they can decide that they are too high or too low, but cannot decide how much too high or too low they are, and if any action of the commission as to rates can have no influence on the future, the commission comes perilously near to being reduced to a mere investigating committee. Undoubtedly a committee of investigation only may be very useful. But a commission supposed to have far greater powers is seriously hampered, and its usefulness impaired, if these powers are denied to it and investigation only is left.

The situation is very complex, confused, and, frankly, a little ridiculous. On the one hand the law, as interpreted by the courts in the recent Trans-Missouri decision, is cutting down the powers of the railroad companies in matters where every man of sense familiar with the facts knows that those powers should be larger rather than less. On the other hand, the law, as interpreted by the courts, is whittling away the powers of the Inter-State Commerce Commission, the only agency provided to supervise the use of such powers as the railroad companies have. The only hopeful element in such a case is that the very absurdity of it may compel action. What direction that action should take is, we believe, fairly clear as to its main lines. The powers of the railroad companies to fix rates, to agree among themselves as to these, and to adjust the business done should be enlarged, but they should be exercised solely with the assent, obtained beforehand, of the Inter-State Commerce Commission. We know of no other way in which the public interest and the interest of those engaged in the transportation business can be equitably determined and protected.

May 26, 1897

FOR HIGH WAGES AND CHEAP GOODS.

Men who write the history of this century will record the development of one great principle. It is the principle of association. It is finding expression in every phase of human life and in all directions. People are protesting against it under the form of trusts, great corporations, aggregations of wealth; but all forms of it are tending one day, to the supplying of all human wants at less cost, and at the same time to the increase of wages. The nineteenth century has done what seemed impossible—it has cheapened the necessaries of life and increased the wages of those who produced them.—Mr. ABRAM S. HEWITT, at the annual meeting of the University Settlement Society.

We are glad Mr. HEWITT has had the frankness and the courage to speak these plain, true words, and to speak them at a meeting of the University Settlement Society. We have of late been so flooded with the ignorant, undiscriminating talk of the half-baked about "predatory wealth," "culpable luxury," and the "octopus" that men of intelligence and wisdom have seemed to be intimidated into silence. They shrank from making themselves a target for the socialistic writers of Bryanite newspapers and the frothing demagogues of the stump. But Mr. HEWITT is too eminent as a philanthropist, he has by word and work and gift striven for too many years to make the poor happier and more comfortable to leave it open to any man to call him a plutocrat, predatory or otherwise. And the University Settlement was denounced during the recent campaign as a concern engaged in sowing the seeds of socialism. Mr. HEWITT was therefore just the man to make the bold declaration that some trusts and combinations are beneficent, and the University Settlement Society's meeting was just the place to make it. This double proof of sincerity and good faith heightens the effect of the declaration.

For trusts that buy tariff laws which enable them to establish baneful monopolies, abolish competition, and maintain high prices THE TIMES has an honest hatred. Mr. HEWITT had nothing to say in behalf of that kind of trusts. But when he said that there are combinations that cheapen the cost of the common necessaries of life and yet are able to increase the wages of their workmen, and that this principle of association is extending and has become the conspicuous industrial tendency of the time, he spoke from a knowledge of observed facts.

It will be largely through combinations that reduce cost of production while maintaining high wages that we shall be able, when we have become enlightened enough to tear down our tariff wall, to enter the markets of the world and sell goods in competition with the goods of England and Germany. We have become accustomed to a certain standard of wages that it is impracticable to lower very much. American workingmen live better and spend more money for food and clothes and rent and in recreation than foreign workingmen. They get high wages compared with either foreign wages or with American wages thirty years ago. But high wages, even though the high-paid operative turns out more units of product, may mean costly goods, and costly goods we cannot sell in China and South America in competition with the cheaper, or "pauper-made" goods of Germany and England. We cannot very well lower the standard of wages. We ought not to lower it. The cost of our goods must be reduced in some other way. Intelligent manufacturers are attempting to reduce the cost per yard and piece by resorting to what Mr. HEWITT calls the principle of association. Half a dozen mills making the same article maintain half a dozen offices in New York, half a dozen Presidents and Treasurers, half a dozen lawyers, half a dozen complete administrative outfits. They enter into association and get along with one New York office, one President, one Treasurer, one lawyer, and one administrative outfit. The economies effected by consolidation enable the concern to reduce prices a fraction of a dollar or a fraction of a cent. That fraction benefits the consumer. More than that, it brings the goods into competition with foreign goods in foreign markets, and now that our manufactories are every year producing a greater surplus over home demand, their prosperity and the prosperity of the country depend on building up a great export trade.

If we are to maintain wages we must reduce cost of production. The American workman will not be long in deciding whether the principle of association is a good thing for him. At present the declaimers against predatory wealth have his ear. He will presently listen to the calm and truthful expositions of men of wisdom like Mr. HEWITT.

Every American manufacturer who is an honest believer in the beneficence of the principle of association, however, ought to see and understand that the really predatory trust, the combination founded in Congressional bribery and maintained for iniquitous extortion, is his deadly enemy and the enemy of American prosperity. It is the genuine, undoubted octopus that is the whole stock in trade of the Socialistic agitators against all forms of combination, that gives plausibility to their harangues, and an example to illustrate their appeals.

January 29, 1898

ERA OF INCORPORATIONS

Remarkable Development in Organization of Capital.

SINCE PEACE WAS ASSURED

It Is Now a Question of Billions Instead of Millions — Present Figures Dwarf All Preceding.

The new corporation system of doing business, the result, mainly, of excessive competition and cheap money, is perhaps the most remarkable of the end-of-the-century phenomena. The centralizations of control, commonly and slangily called "trusts," have, since peace with Spain was assured, been on a gigantic scale.

The pace was set early last Fall by the incorporation at Trenton, N. J., of the Federal Steel Company, with an authorized capital of $200,000,000. This enormous capitalization has not yet been reached by any corporation chartered since then in the United States, but there is talk of combinations of capital and interests that will put this corporation in the shade. A Boston project is to promote a billion-dollar copper trust, there is a probability of amalgamating all iron, steel, wire, and tin-plate interests in a company with $800,000,000 capital, and a scheme in which many have faith is a fusion of anthracite coal interests with a capital of $200,000,000.

An idea of the development of the new form of doing business is had from the following tables, which give the most important incorporations last year after peace with Spain was assured and the incorporations of, with one or two exceptions, over a million dollars in New Jersey, New York, and other States up to March 31 this year, with the authorized capitalization, funded debt not being taken into account:

NEW JERSEY INCORPORATIONS—1898.

Title.	Stock Capital.
Standard Distilling and Distributing Company	$24,000,000
Federal Steel Company	200,000,000
International Silver Company, (silver and plated ware)	20,000,000
Otis Elevator Company	11,000,000
American Thread Company	12,000,000
American Linseed Oil Company	35,500,000
Continental Tobacco Company, (to take over plug business of Tobacco Trust)	75,000,000
American Tin Plate Company	50,000,000
American Potteries Company, (success in doubt)	27,000,000
International Paper Company	45,000,000
January, 1899.	
General Commercial Company	$1,000,000
Havana Electric Railway Company	10,000,000
Minneapolis General Electric Company	2,000,000
Rubber Goods Manufacturing Company	50,000,000
National Enameling and Stamping Company	30,000,000
Central Union Gas Company, (natural gas concern)	60,000,000
C. Rogers Brothers' Company, (silverware, private)	1,000,000
American Steel and Wire, (Western concern, former capital $24,000,000)	90,000,000
Standard Distilling and Distributing Company of New Jersey, (took over the Spirits Distributing Company of New Jersey; capital, $7,500,000)	24,000,000
Electric Company of America	25,000,000
United Lighting and Heating Company, (oil lighting)	12,000,000
International Air Power Company, (Leiter interests)	25,000,000
National Tin Plate and Stamped Ware Company	20,000,000
Cuban Land and Steamship Company	1,000,000
Diamond Wood Company	1,000,000
New York Auto-Truck Company	10,000,000
The O'Keefe Company	1,000,000
The Werner Company	3,500,000
National Carbon Company	10,000,000
Puerto Rico Company	1,000,000
Acheson Graphite Company	1,000,000
Penn Tobacco Company	1,000,000
Miners' Copper Company	2,000,000
Santa Fé Gold and Copper Company	2,500,000
February.	
Umbrella Hardware Company	$2,000,000
Auto-Electric Company	1,000,000
Mexican Copper Company	1,000,000
Anti-Brule Chemical Company	1,000,000
Florence Mining Company, (copper, Western mines)	3,000,000
Columbian Electric Car Lighting and Brake Company, (a development of a $2,000,000 corporation)	10,000,000
Walnitz Copper Company	1,000,000
Lanyon Zinc Company, (Kansas plants)	3,000,000
National Steel Company, (American Tin Plate interests. First incorporated Feb. 8 at $100,000)	59,000,000
Central New York Brewing Company	4,000,000
United Shoe Machinery Company, (Boston interests)	25,000,000
Kentucky Distilleries and Warehouse Company, (Bourbon whisky)	32,000,000
American Cereal Company, (not operative)	33,000,000
Pennsylvania Electric Vehicle Company, (formerly Philadelphia Motor Wagon Company, capital, $3,000,000)	6,000,000
American Linen and Fibre Company	2,000,000
United States Cast Iron Pipe and Foundry Company	30,000,000
New England Dairy Company	850,000
East Jersey Electric Company	1,000,000
Artificial Rubber Company	1,000,000
Merchants' Wire and Nail Company	1,000,000
American Copper Company	600,000
Pressed Steel Car Company	25,000,000
American Car and Foundry Company, (Michigan Peninsular Car Company foundation)	60,000,000
Union Bag and Paper Company	27,000,000
Electric Boat Company	10,000,000
American Felt Company	5,000,000
American Saddle Company, (bicycles)	1,500,000
Tacoma Railway and Power Company, (Tacoma interests)	2,000,000
American Beet Sugar Company, (Spencer Trask & Co.'s syndicate)	20,000,000
American Radiator Company, (withdrew charter of the Illinois Company)	10,000,000
Electric Vehicle Transportation Company	25,000,000
March.	
American Soda Company	$1,000,000
Royal Baking Powder Company	20,000,000
Arcadian Copper Company, (Michigan concern)	3,750,000
Columbia Refrigerating Company	3,000,000
United Pneumatic Fire Alarm Telegraph Company	1,100,000
Severy Process Company, (printing, lithographing, &c.)	7,500,000
Pacific American Fisheries Company, (salmon in Puget Sound waters)	5,000,000
International Docks Terminal Company, (local)	1,500,000
United States Dyewood and Extract Company	10,000,000
United Electric Company of New Jersey, (State operations)	20,000,000
American Brick Company	10,000,000
Park Steel Company, (Pittsburg interests)	10,000,000
Havana Commercial Company, (cigars, cigarettes, and tobacco)	20,000,000
Newport News Abattoir Company	1,500,000
Helvetia Copper Company	5,000,000
Continental Cement Company	10,000,000
Boston and Seven Devils Copper Company	7,000,000
American Shipbuilding Company, (great lakes interests)	30,000,000
American School Furniture Company	10,000,000
United States Publishing Company	2,000,000
Empire Steel and Iron Company	5,000,000
Nacozari Railroad Company	1,000,000
Flemington Coal and Coke Company	2,500,000
Easton Consolidated Electric Company	1,500,000
Egyptian Tobacco Company	1,500,000
American Ice Company, (refused charter in Maine)	60,000,000
White Motor Wagon Company, (Croker-Headley interests)	10,000,000
Metallic Rubber Tire Company, (Croker-Headley interests; capitalization nominally $100,000)	2,000,000
International Traction Company, (railroads, bridges, and railroad equipment; original capital, $85,000)	15,000,000
Isle Royale Copper Company, (Boston interests; part of a $65,000,000 consolidation)	3,750,000
National Salt Company, (takes over an old corporation)	12,000,000
International Steam Pump Company	27,500,000
Noonday Yeast Company	1,000,000
Welsh-Hackley Coal and Oil Company	1,000,000
Hamburg-Cordovan Leather Works	1,000,000
Columbia Automobile Company of New York	3,000,000
New England Electric Vehicle Transportation Company, (an offshoot of the Electric Vehicle Company)	25,000,000
Maritime Improvement Company	3,000,000
Sargent Automatic Railway Signal Company, (railway semaphores)	2,000,000
Investors' Co-operative Company	1,000,000
Philadelphia Fish and Game Company	1,000,000
United Fruit Company	20,000,000
American Woolen Company	65,000,000
United Zinc and Lead Company	6,000,000
American Steamship Company	1,000,000
Sutherland Construction and Improvement Company, (gas and electric construction, U. S. Grant promotion)	1,000,000
Compressed Gas Capsule Company (flasks for motors)	15,000,000
Consolidated Street Car Company	18,000,000
National Metallic Roofing Company (incorporated at $100,000)	12,000,000
Indo-Egyptian Compress Company (cotton handling)	17,000,000
National Cash Register Company	5,000,000
Brooklyn Gas and Electric Light Company	1,500,000
Boggs & Buhl Company (drapers and finishers)	2,000,000

NEW YORK INCORPORATIONS—1898.

Title.	Stock Capital.
National Biscuit Company	$55,000,000
International Paper Company	45,000,000
New York Gas and Electric Light, Heat and Power Company, (a Whitney-Ryan promotion. Capitalized at first at $25,000,000; bonded debt, $33,488,000)	36,000,000
Union Tobacco Company, (organized to fight Tobacco Trust, but absorbed by it February, 1899, capital originally $10,000,000)	24,000,000
International Tobacco Company, (in the interest of the Tobacco Trust. First incorporation $150,000)	25,000,000
North American Commercial Company, (to operate in the West Indies)	14,000,000
1899.	
Metropolitan Tobacco Company, (in the interest of Union Company to offset International)	$1,000,000
American Bond and Mortgage Guaranty Company, (for New York)	1,000,000
Buffalo Hump Mining Company	2,500,000
New York Suburban Gas Company	1,500,000
City Lighting Company of New York City	1,000,000
General Chemical Company of Phillipstown, N. Y.	25,000,000
Merchants' Distributing and Distilling Company	5,000,000

INCORPORATIONS, OTHER STATES—1898.

Title.	Stock Capital.
Cambria Steel Company	$16,000,000
United States Envelope Company	4,500,000
1899.	
Boston Transit Cab Company, (motor vehicles)	$1,000,000
American Ice Company	60,000,000
Federal Sewer Pipe Company	25,000,000
Borax Consolidated Company	12,000,000
Maryland Brewing Company	6,500,000
Pittsburg Brewing Company	13,000,000
Virginia Iron, Coal and Coke Company	7,500,000
Standard Sardine Company	5,000,000
American Brass Company	20,000,000
Spreckels Sugar Refining Company, (beet root sugar)	5,000,000

American Silk Manufacturing Company	12,500,000
American Last Company	3,500,000
Great Northern Paper Company	4,000,000
International Vehicle Company of New York	5,000,000
North Arkansas Mining and Investment Company	1,000,000
Philadelphia Company, (natural gas; original capital, $7,500,000)	21,000,000
American Warp-Drawing Machine Company, (Maine)	3,000,000
New River and Kanawha Consolidated Coal and Coke Company, (West Virginia)	10,000,000
Independent Light and Power Company (Spreckels's promotion, San Francisco)	10,000,000
National Fish Company	3,000,000
Superior Shipbuilding Company	1,000,000
Hartford Gold Extraction Company	5,000,000

These incorporations may be summarized as follows with other data for 1898:

Incorporations for United States, 1898	$900,000,000
Incorporations over $1,000,000 in New Jersey in 1898 after Santiago fell	499,500,000
Incorporations, New Jersey, January, 1899	384,000,000
Incorporations, New Jersey, February, 1899	463,250,000
Incorporations, New Jersey, March, 1899	521,600,000
Principal incorporations in New York, 1898	199,000,000
Principal incorporations in New York, 1899	37,000,000
Principal incorporations in all other States, 1898	20,500,000
Principal incorporations in all other States, 1899	234,000,000

INCORPORATIONS QUINTUPLED.

These figures establish that in the first quarter of this year the capitalization of the principal corporations which took their charters in New Jersey amounted to $1,308,850, and in New York and other States to $271,000,000, or an aggregate of $1,579,850,000. New Jersey's incorporations quintupled those of the rest of the United States. The monthly mean of New Jersey's charterings was $436,283,000, or at the rate of more than $5,235,000,000 annually, and that of those of the United States $526,617,000, or an annual trust output of $6,319,400,000. But these data do not take into account the minor incorporations of from $5,000 to hundreds of thousands of dollars. It is within the mark to estimate the capitalization of such new companies in New Jersey for the quarter ended March 31 last at $100,000,000. There were more than 400 of them, so that the average capitalization was $250,000.

To illustrate the magnitude of the incorporations of minor companies, the following transactions are taken at haphazard from the New Jersey incorporations of less than $1,000,000 of the past few weeks:

Cincinnati Axle Company	$25,000
Western Axle Company	25,000
National Graphite Company	250,000
Lyceum Publishing Company	50,000
Auditorium Pier Company	175,000
New York Steel and Wire Company	100,000
General Construction Company of New Jersey	200,000
Sewaren Company	125,000
Boston Envelope Company	25,000
L. M. Meeker & Co.	50,000
Monmouth Hotel Company	100,000
Clapp and Fowler Waste Company	25,000
Muncie Underwear Company	100,000
Continental Clay Products Company	500,000
F. G. Sutor Company	50,000
Seneca Lake Sale Company	100,000
Pocahontas Oil Company	100,000
Boston Zinc Company	250,000
Erie Construction Company	100,000
Columbia Theatre Stock Company	30,000
Haydenville Company	75,000
American Plaster Company	100,000
Ransome Concrete Company	250,000
Tabor Sash Company	250,000
McElroy-Grunow Electric Railway System	150,000
Manhattan Finance Company	100,000
Birmingham Cement Company	300,000
Empire Construction Company	50,000
Paramore Bleaching and Refining Company	100,000
Person & Riegel Company	50,000
Cuban Commercial Company	100,000
Art Manufacturing Company	500,000
International Zinc Mining and Smelting Company	280,000
Onward Construction Company	10,000
Conover Brothers' Company	650,000
Diamond Fly Paper Company	100,000
American Parquetry Company	100,000
Arnold-Levy-Morris Company	100,000
Majestic Velvet Mills	50,000
Warren Portland Cement Company	200,000
Wrightstown Water, Electric Light and Sewer Company	5,000
Baker Transportation Company	150,000
United States Sand Filtration Company	200,000
Citizens' Water Company of Cripple Creek	300,000
French Gelatine Company	20,000
Union Land and Construction Company	25,000
West New York Field Club	10,000
People's Real Estate Company	100,000
Newark Hygeia Ice Company	100,000
Burnham Food Company	10,000
Corona Compounding Company	100,000
Wonsononck Hotel Company	50,000
Cliffwood Brick Company	25,000
Eastern Water Power and Electric Power Company	100,000
Paxon's Island Water Power and Electric Power Company	100,000
Bonanza Chief Mining Company	150,000
Legal Rights Guaranty Company	150,000
Barker Mercantile Company	25,000
Cabana Company	500,000
Pennsylvania Window Glass Company	100,000
Glenwood Silk Mills	75,000
Registrar and Transfer Company	100,000
Buckley Machine Company	100,000
Co-operative Benefit Society of America	50,000

CONSOLIDATION SCHEMES.

Some of the schemes of consolidation and a few of the new incorporations have not fared well. In one or two instances projected combinations have been prudently halted by the promoters and underwriting syndicates; others were abandoned before any advanced stage was reached for a more propitious season for launching the ventures, and many plans hang between promotion and incorporation. Incorporated trusts have not all forged ahead to the test of dividend-paying. There has been a hitch in the acquisition by the International Air Power Company of the Rhode Island Locomotive Works, the Boston scheme to form a billion-dollar copper trust is dormant, and Thomas A. McIntyre's vast flour combination still lacks a charter. Affairs have not gone smoothly for the United Electric Company in New Jersey, there being a decided hitch in the deal to take over the People's Company in Newark. The exercise of the option on the twenty-million-dollar Liggett & Myers Tobacco Company of St. Louis by the Ryan syndicate has yet to be announced. The cereal, chewing gum, and potteries schemes languish, and there is talk of war on the combine of smelters, while hostility has developed between the New England leather manufacturers and the deal in which the Chicago capitalists are interested. Denial of rumors of trouble in the perfecting of the Kentucky Whisky Trust is met with affirmation from equally credible sources, and the project to unite glass-blowing and plate interests is in confusion. The promotion of a cotton mill consolidation has made no progress if it has not been abandoned, and Joseph Leiter's Chicago's milk-merging scheme may have a chance of revival in the remote future. Obstacles have been found in the advancement of the cast-iron pipe consolidation project. Other plans have encountered snags.

Projected incorporations whose capitalization has been named at more than $1,000,000 are found in the following table:

PROJECTED INCORPORATIONS.

(Imminent, probable, and possible.)

Steel and iron consolidation, including Federal Steel, American Steel and Wire, National Steel, American Tin Plate, and Carnegie, Cambria, Lackawanna, and other interests, hinging mainly on acceptance by Andrew Carnegie of an offer of $150,000,000 for his entire holdings and control in the Carnegie Steel Company and kindred equities	$800,000,000
Rival to Standard Oil Company, (Kansas promition for Indian Territory)	250,000,000
Flour mills consolidation, (T. A. McIntyre project)	125,000,000
Consolidation of anthracite coal operators	200,000,000
Clothing makers' consolidation	200,000,000
Whisky manufacturers, (to take in all rye and bourbon interests)	128,000,000
Bridge manufacturers	50,000,000
Yarn spinners, (Philadelphia promotion)	50,000,000
Plow manufacturers	6,000,000
Maine woolen mills, (on plan of American Woolen Company)	100,000,000
Ice manufacturers	2,000,000
American Hide and Leather Company	60,000,000
Pacific Coast Biscuit Company	10,000,000
American Edible Nut Company, (peanut interests of Virginia and North Carolina)	5,000,000
Realty Trust Company of Maryland, (increase of capital from $100,000)	2,000,000
Street railroads and electric light and gas concerns of Washington, D. C.	30,000,000
National Strawboard Company	6,000,000
Mutual Trust Company of New York	5,000,000
Boston Fruit Company, (bananas; M. C. Keith promotion)	3,000,000
*American Smelting and Refining Company	65,000,000
Soap manufacturers, (all concerns except Armour's)	27,000,000
Rolling mills consolidation, (Harry Rubens's promotion)	30,000,000
International Cement Company, (concerns outside of Ohio)	50,000,000
National Tube Company, (wrought iron pipe; not identified with corporation of same title)	60,000,000
Great Northern Paper Company	4,000,000
Crackers and biscuit manufacturers, (Pacific Coast; not hostile to American Biscuit Company)	10,000,000
Plumbers' supplies manufacturers	50,000,000
Bridge builders' consolidation, (said to be backed by Andrew Carnegie)	50,000,000
Stove manufacturers	75,000,000
Proprietary medicines	25,000,000
Burial Casket Company	28,000,000
British-American Brewing and Trading Company of Dawson, Northwest Territory, (Klondike breweries; New York and Brooklyn promotion)	5,000,000
Tobacco Jobbers' Protective Association, (local protection against the large companies)	1,000,000
Fine writing paper manufacturers	5,000,000
New York Livery Stable Company	7,000,000
Lithographers and engravers	50,000,000
Erie Preserving Company, (fruit and vegetables)	20,000,000
White vinegar manufacturers, (Niagara Vinegar Works promotion)	10,000,000
Federal Sewer Pipe Company	25,000,000
Federal Varnish Company, (C. R. Flint's promotion)	36,000,000
Bicycle manufacturers, (Spalding-Bidwell promotion)	10,000,000
Sheet steel manufacturers, (in harmony with American Tin Plate and National Steel Companies; W. H. Moore's promotion)	50,000,000
Federal Gas and Fuel Company, (Ohio)	2,000,000
Wine and Spirit Trading Company, (New York incorporation; co-operative, to fight whisky consolidation)	2,500,000
Five States Milk Producers' Association, (local)	17,500,000
American Sardine Company, (Maine packers)	3,000,000
Springfield Breweries Company, (Maine)	2,400,000
International Trust Company, (John E. Searles and other cotton interests)	5,000,000
Reed Tide Power Company, (energy from tidal action)	40,000,000
Pittsburg Laundries Company, (local)	3,500,000
Cincinnati Clothiers' Combination, (local)	1,000,000
Dairies consolidation, (all plants east of the Rockies)	50,000,000
Billiard, pool table, and bowling alley interests	4,500,000
Tanners of leather uppers	5,000,000
Copper, other minerals, and timber consolidation, (Michigan)	5,000,000
Gas and electric lighting fixtures	10,000,000
Glass tableware	15,000,000
Cocoanut manufacturers, (independent of Wetmore & Pride Company)	7,000,000
Bethlehem Steel Company	20,000,000
Monumental Ginger Ale and Mineral Water Company	1,000,000
Telephone apparatus consolidation, (Chicago promotion)	7,000,000
Lamp manufacturers, (decorated glass, china, and metal)	6,000,000
Coal mines in Pittsburg district	25,000,000
Combination of champagne houses	50,000,000
American Screw Company	10,000,000
Chewing gum manufacturers	6,000,000
Bar iron manufacturers	15,000,000
Connecticut and other oyster plants, including Southern interests	11,000,000
Paint manufacturers	12,000,000
Oil stove manufacturers	6,000,000
Pittsburg River Coal operators	20,000,000
Safe manufacturers	17,000,000
Vermont granite and quarrymen	2,000,000
Carded woolen mills	1,000,000
Car supplies manufacturers	50,000,000
General State Cab Company, (New York)	1,000,000
Cotton yarn mills consolidation, (English syndicate plan)	100,000,000
New England and Middle States jewelry manufacturers	25,000,000
Republic Iron and Steel Company, (Pennsylvania, Ohio, and West Virginia)	55,000,000
Greater New York breweries	50,000,000
Carpet mills	5,000,000
Baltimore brick manufacturers	4,000,000
Boston Auto-Truck Company, (J. H. Hoadley promotion)	10,000,000
Eastern jewelry manufacturers	25,000,000
*Boston Breweries Company	11,500,000
American Independent Telephone Company, (Chicago rival to Bell interests)	7,000,000
Total	$3,450,900,000

*Incorporated in April.

Even if these tremendous figures are scaled down to the reasonable limits of probability they furnish, with the data of accomplished incorporations for the current year, reason to believe that at the end of 1899 the trust idea will during the twelve months have expanded to the extent of at least $5,000,000,000.

STATISTICS THAT ASTONISH.

All these statistics dwarf many figures that have been regarded as colossal, hardly within the grasp of average understanding, but the popular tendency to placid consideration of immensities has been fostered during the present season of speculative riot by glib talk of billions. Not to multiply instances, the French war indemnity paid to Germany was $1,000,000,000, and it was regarded as an unparalleled financial scourge. The outstanding principal of the public debt of the United States reaches at the moment $1,433,548,76; the present tax valuation of New York City is $2,950,046,17; the national debts of France and Germany are, respectively, $6,200,000,000 and $580,000,000, while that of Great Britain is $,250,000,000. The available cash balance in the United States Treasury is only about $283,352,000, and the New York Clearing House banks' deposits less than $900,000,000.

Several publications devoted to economics have attempted to give an "approximate idea" of the march of industrial absorption or the advance of single control of competition. One of these computations places the total of new trust organizations in the whole of the United States for the year ended Feb. 28, 1899, at $5,200,000,000, with $715,000 funded debt, against new organizations with $3,290,000,000 stock and $379,000,000 bonds for the year ended same date in 1898. This should be read with the census statistics of 1890, which showed that the aggregate capital invested in manufacturing and mechanical industries in the whole of the United States was less than $6,530,000,000.

Schemes of consolidation which have not yet reached the stage where capitalization is mentioned include nearly every industry and all forms of manufacturing or employment of capital. A Texas scheme to raise prairie dogs for food is discussed seriously at Galveston. It is said of the hog that every part of the animal can be utilized from the end of its nose to the tip of its tail. Prairie dogs appear to merit the attention of economists in this regard. Ex-Lieut. Gov. Barnett Gibbs, in discussing the subject, pointed to the fact that not only the flesh, but the hide and lard of the little burrowing squirrel can be utilized, and sketched the profits of a prairie dog farm.

In the miscellaneous list of these yet undeveloped consolidations are found plans for cotton ties, glass factories—Cumberland and More Jonas basis, an ally of the American Woolen Company, for cheviots, cassimeres, &c., all matchmaking interests—not a matrimonial agency—animal glue, "shelf" hardware, flint-glass bottles, independent wholesale manufacturers of tobacco, oppositions to the Tin Plate Trust and the Biscuit Trust, a New England Finishing Company for dyeing, bleaching, and printing stuffs, and printing ink. Then there are trusts planned for meat, scrap iron, metallic paint, bronze manufactures, candy, pork, Chicago automobiles, thrashing machines, wall paper, sheet steel, flint-glass tableware, fertilizers, bricks and tiles, kitchen soap, pulleys, a scheme for a Southern banana exchange, gin distillers of Connecticut, rival shoe machinery and cotton compress combinations, a Western newspaper trust, a North Carolina and New Hampshire mica trust, a company to control tube transportation by compressed air, a New York scheme; a merger of wool hat manufacturers, a coffin hardware consolidation, a sash, door, and window-blind trust; a combine of worsted mills, of knitgoods, another of pad and papeterie interests, a union of toolmakers, one of wagon manufacturers, and another of carriage builders. Michigan is to have a Wolverine Fish Company, the Pacific Coast a Pacific Biscuit Company, Pittsburg one of lamp chimney manufacturers, and Buffalo is merging wire-cloth interests. There is to be a candy trust west of the Rocky Mountains.

CANADA GETTING INTO LINE.

There is to be a consolidation of coal elevator interests at Cincinnati, and Canada is getting into line with a combine of stove manufacturers, with American connections. One of the new schemes is to create a trust of wire cable manufacturers—rubber, not paper, insulation. Even the farmers have got together with a "hold-your-wheat" pact, and if some Wall Street predictions are true, the "sugar war" is to end by the Havemeyer interests sticking to sugar and the Arbuckle interests to coffee, which means that each side will consolidate the respective independent factories. The New York Clearing House banks and the banks cleared by them have not escaped attention in this regard. The recent adoption of rules for the collection of out-of-town checks has started a rumor of a bank trust, and another of Standard Oil or Rockefeller control of all the local banking institutions, including trust companies. The new trust idea has even reached the sale of the present Custom House and its site, and a rumor that there is to be a trust of trusts—a monopolistic Clearing House—has some foundation in fact. These possibilities might be considered with the official data of the new corporations. Those of the most important of them show that iron and steel lead with $585,000,000. Electric, gas, and natural gas, light, heat, and power combines follow with $186,000,000, tobacco with $171,000,000, traction with $147,000,000, and spirits with $85,000,000.

Not included in the summary of projections are local developments of passenger traffic projects, which will result in the consummation of mergers of vast importance and the increase of already large capitalization. Schemes of a like character in regard to gas and electric light, power, and heat corporations will lead to centralizations of control with enormous financial dealings. A few of the schemes are the Brooklyn passenger service consolidation, the bringing of such facilities in New York to an end-of-century conclusion in point of adequacy and speed; the merger of the various gas companies with the manufacturing basis relegated to extreme city limits where it will not constitute a nuisance, and the growth to the keenest activity of the New York Gas and Electric Light, Heat, and Power Company, a corporation of almost illimitable possibilities. Outside of New York the projects for centralizing anthracite and bituminous coal interests are making steady progress, and the capitalization in each case will reach into the hundred millions.

ATTORNEY GENERAL'S OPINION.

The opinion of Attorney General John W. Griggs, that the Sherman act does not operate against "trusts" unless their "restraint of trade" is inter-State or international, and that the remedy must be found or created in State enactments, has prompted action in many States. New York has various measures under consideration.

New Jersey law makers have acted according to their individual likes or political persuasion. When the story of a mammoth anthracite coal combine was sprung, some were up in arms and clamored for enactments to thwart it, but the Legislature expired in a general sentiment that a policy to still further promote the interests of incorporations was desirable. This was not extraordinary in view of the fact that New Jersey derives an annual income of between $2,000,000 and $2,500,000 from its friendliness to combinations of capital. Its rate is 1-10 of one per cent on $3,000,000; 1-20 on $5,000,000, and $50 for each $1,000,000 over this.

Kentucky has started in the Fiscal Court of Frankfort to indict all trusts operating in the district, this action being aimed at the Kentucky Distilleries & Warehouse Company. Arkansas has started an anti-trust movement. In Texas Attorney General Smith advised the Secretary of State to refuse a charter for the Eureka Banana and Development Company, a New Jersey corporation. Minnesota is framing laws for protection against trusts, a bill being in the Senate to declare forfeiture of charters of corporations combined "in restraint of trade."

The United States Circuit Court at Cincinnati is considering a petition against the Standard Distilling and Distributing Company. Attorney General Monnett, acting on Attorney General Griggs's opinion on the inadequacy and limitations of the Sherman act, suggests that all the State Attorney Generals unite in an action to control domestic corporations within the State, expressing the conviction that if such action was had the States would be rid of trusts in ninety days. Pennsylvania has started legislative action to have trusts investigated. At Washington the Industrial Commission has taken similar action.

INVITING CHARTER BUSINESS.

On the other hand, States are inviting trusts to make their home with them. West Virginia has amended her laws to invite charter business. Missouri is preparing to make itself as attractive to promoters as New Jersey, and on the other hand, to control trust combinations. In Virginia the futility of attacking trusts is being discussed. An article in The Richmond Times said: "We do not believe that such laws in any State are worth the paper they are printed on. We do not believe that the people of any State will submit to laws restraining trusts from doing business within their borders. Say what you please about trusts, the fact is that these organizations are making goods that the people want and that the people will have because they are making the cheapest and best goods in the world. The inevitable conclusion, therefore, is that, so long as the people are determined to patronize trusts, it will be impossible for any individual State successfully to legislate against them."

Delaware has passed a liberal and broad corporation law to attract promoters. The preliminary incorporation tax is 15 cents on every $1,000. The laws of Delaware allow all corporate meetings to be held out of the State and the transfer books of the corporation can also be preserved anywhere outside of the State of Delaware at the will of the corporation.

The American incorporation idea finds favor in England. Because of a ruling in a high English court, American companies having English owners will abandon British charters and reorganize as American corporations. Maine is examining the New Jersey system with a view to making changes in its laws to attract corporations, thus stultifying its recent action against the Ice Trust. Montana is evincing friendliness to the new corporate system of doing business. No action will be taken against trusts in North Carolina, Attorney General Walser being of opinion that its anti-trust law is inoperative.

The Illinois Legislature adjourned without passing its anti-corporation bill. As a test case United States Attorney General Griggs has sanctioned a proceeding in equity in the United States Circuit Court for the Southern District of Ohio against the Chesapeake and Ohio Fuel Company of Cincinnati, and fifteen other corporations with which it is allied, for violation of the Sherman act. The gist of the complaint is entering into a combination in restraint of trade and commerce.

April 17, 1899

BUSINESS MUST GO!

The efforts of the new socialism to put a stop to business are meeting with notable success in States nearer and older than Texas. In the State of Ohio, the home of the President, a law is on the statute book which declares it to be a crime to do business except by methods which are satisfactory to the believers in the new socialism. The Attorney General of that State has been diligent in hunting down persons and corporations that have attempted to do business, and has met with remarkable success in one conspicuous instance. We quote from The Chicago Inter Ocean an account of his triumph:

The withdrawal of the Standard Oil Company from Ohio is announced. The cause of the move is the series of onslaughts made on the corporation by the Attorney General of the State. The company has become tired of being treated as a public enemy. It will reorganize under the laws of New Jersey.

This withdrawal means a great deal more than the transfer of the corporate domicile. To be sure, such a transfer means that Cleveland, where the company has always had its headquarters, will lose a large office force and immense deposits of money; but these are small items compared with the great manufacturing plants which are to be abandoned. The refinery at Cleveland, the parent establishment, and the second largest of its kind in the world, is to be left idle. Its cooperage factory—the largest one ever operated—is already closed.

It is hardly too much to say that the Standard Oil Company is to Cleveland what the Union Stock Yards are to Chicago. Each concern is the head centre of one of the greatest industries of the times. There is a great deal of refining in other cities than Cleveland, as there is a great deal of packing outside of Chicago, but Cleveland is largely indebted to the manufacture of kerosene from petroleum for its extraordinary prosperity. It owes more to JOHN ROCKEFELLER than to any other dozen citizens.

The new socialists do not consider it a loss to a community to drive out of it a large employer of labor who pays out thousands of dollars every week and makes the place busy and prosperous. In their opinion these benefits are more than offset by that deadly but mysterious peril which none of them have ever yet satisfactorily defined of allowing business to be carried on on a large scale. They are determined to put a stop to business. They have won a great victory in Cleveland.

July 13, 1899

MANY HOLDERS OF STOCKS

Shares of Various Corporations Very Widely Distributed.

NUMBER STEADILY INCREASING

Comparatively Few Large Blocks of Stocks Held by Single Individuals —The Dividends Paid.

Inquiry among some of the largest corporations which do business in this country discloses the fact that the quarterly and semi-annual distributions of dividends are participated in by a vast and steadily increasing army of shareholders. In no case is it shown that concentration of control diminishes the number of shareholders in great business enterprises. The shares of stable, dividend-paying corporations are becoming more and more widely distributed each year, and in most cases the stock ledgers show that the majority of the stockholders are small investors. Although great capitalists control the properties, there are comparatively few large blocks of stocks held by single individuals.

Several years before he died William H. Vanderbilt sold about $50,000,000 worth of the stock of the New York Central Railroad because, as he then said, he believed it to be good policy to have railroad stocks as widely distributed as possible. Whether or not Mr. Vanderbilt's action stimulated the buying of railroad shares by persons of moderate means for investment, the fact is clear that in recent years there has been a constant and even rapid increase in the number of shareholders of dividend-paying corporations. Some of the big industrial corporations have increased the number of their shareholders 75 and 100 per cent. within a few years.

The payment of dividends by the large railroad and industrial corporations is not a matter that concerns the capitalist alone. By far the larger proportion of persons benefited by the distribution of dividends is men and women who are obliged to depend upon these dividends to meet, or help meet, their living expenses.

The Pennsylvania Railroad Company has the largest number of shareholders of any corporation in this country. There are about 30,000 holders of Pennsylvania Railroad stock, which is an increase of nearly 2,000 within five years. These holders are scattered over the United States and Europe, and since 1893 they have participated annually in the distribution of $6,465,250, being 5 per cent. on the outstanding capital stock of $129,305,000. In 1883 the Pennsylvania Railroad paid dividends at the rate of 8½ per cent. per annum. But that was only for one year.

WOMEN AS STOCKHOLDERS.

The stock of the Western Union Telegraph Company and its leased lines is distributed among 13,438 holders, according to the latest official record. The shareholders of the Western Union Telegraph Company proper number 9,182. One year ago they numbered 8,345. The shares of the Western Union's leased lines are held by 4,256 persons, the principal items of this aggregate being 1,768 holders of American Telegraph and Cable stock, 424 holders of Pacific and Atlantic stock, and 407 holders of the Northwestern Telegraph Company's stock. Dividends are paid quarterly on a capitalization of $97,370,000 at the rate of 5 per cent. per annum, making a distribution every three months of $1,217,000. On July 1 the Western Union Company declared its one hundred and twenty-third dividend. Since December, 1887, this company has paid dividends at the rate of 5 per cent. uninterruptedly.

Although large blocks of Western Union stock are held by George J. Gould and his brothers and sisters, Russell Sage, John Jacob Astor, John T. Terry, and other men of wealth, many thousands of shares are distributed among persons of moderate means, estates, savings banks, and trust companies. About one-half of the stockholders are women and the names of a large proportion of these have been on the company's books for twenty years and more.

When President Havemeyer of the American Sugar Refining Company publicly asserted a few days ago that the stock of that corporation was held by between eleven and twelve thousand persons, he stated a fact which the books of the company substantiate. The number of stockholders is nearer 12,000 than 11,000, and it is increasing constantly. Only a few years ago there were but 5,000 shareholders. In recent years this stock has become very widely distributed, there being holders in nearly every State in the Union. Dividends are paid quarterly on $73,900,000 of capital, the holders of the preferred stock receiving at the rate of 7 per cent. per annum and the holders of the common stock receiving at the rate of 12 per cent. per annum.

July 14, 1899

ULTIMATE RESULTS OF RAILROAD CONSOLIDATION.

The published reports of recent concentrations of railroad interests have been followed by the usual denials. These disclaimers have not removed from the public mind the very distinct impression that new relations of amity and alliance have been established between important trunk lines. It is quite possible to effect a practical consolidation of interests without a written bond. There may be no written bond in this case. Nevertheless, it appears to be true that the understandings that now exist between the Pennsylvania and the Baltimore and Ohio on the one hand, and between the New York Central and the Chesapeake and Ohio, with its Western connecting lines known as the "Big Four," on the other, are of a nature so close that they substitute the status of common interest for the old status of rivalry. If the further reports of a good understanding between the Central and the Pennsylvania rest upon a sound foundation, it is evident that all the important trunk lines leading from the Eastern seaboard to the interior and the West, excepting only the Erie, are now virtually under one control and have a common policy. This state of affairs, if completely established, would abolish competition in freight and passenger rates between the East and the West.

The first public comment upon this union of interests will be that it creates a giant railroad monopoly which constitutes a public peril. This is the superficial view. A virtual monopoly has perhaps been created, and conceivably this concentrated power might be used and abused to the public injury by the imposition of extortionate charges for carrying passengers and freight. Populists and the seekers after popular "issues" will be swift to view and describe this transaction as another sharp turn of the screw that is squeezing the life out of the toiling masses.

There are considerations of weight which make it seem improbable that the experienced and capable business men who are in control of these associated railroads will prove to be as shortsighted as the professional enemies of capital will believe them to be. The wisest and most successful business men of the present day, the really gifted captains of industry, do not favor the policy of discouraging business by high charges. The power of a monopoly is put to a very poor use when it is employed to extort "what the traffic will bear." The sound and wise rule of modern business is to impose such schedules of charges as will invite the largest volume of traffic, and then to employ men of such ability in management that the business is always carried on at the lowest possible cost, leaving a good return to capital after good wages have been paid to labor.

This, we say, is the rule with men of great ability at the head of great corporations. It is not yet the universal rule, for not all corporations are fortunate enough to have such men at the head of their affairs. But we are not ready to believe that the power which controls these associated railroads will be employed to burden the business of the country with extortionate rates, because that would be a foolish policy. More money is to be made by the wiser method, the modern method.

Another consideration which makes against the view that a dangerous monster has been created which will presently crush us is the present state of public opinion. The minds of the mass of the people are just now supersensitive on the subject of monopolies. It would not be a very wise or a very safe policy for a great master of railroads to begin an indiscriminate advance in rates determined only by his own greed and not by the cost of the service. Probably the most conscienceless monopolist in the land would admit that, with the people aroused against him and a Legislature at his heels, the outlook for a career of unmolested depredation would be highly unfavorable.

Mr. Bryan and all the politicians and newspapers that are tributary to the cause of Bryanism are clamoring against trusts and consolidations of capital. Every Legislature has not only its demagogues who are on the alert to seize upon material for popular agitation, but as well its sincere and able men wishing only the public good, who look upon the "aggressions" of capital as a public danger and seek by honest opposition to check them. Since the Granger agitation twenty years ago there has not been a time more unfavorable for the operations of a railroad monopoly that was really bent on enforcing a policy of extortion.

It must be remembered that the people will have their way in the end if the matter is serious enough to interest and arouse them. The inter-State commerce law has forced the railroads out of the status of independent competitors and into the status of business alliance. This last estate they may be permitted to enjoy indefinitely if in their use and enjoyment of it, they are guided by those enlightened principles of business management that make a corporation successful without making it unpopular.

December 4, 1899

IRON PIPE TRUST BROKEN

Declared Unlawful by the United States Supreme Court.

OPINION BY JUSTICE PECKHAM

Injunction Granted Under the Law of 1890 Is Upheld by the Highest Tribunal in the Country.

WASHINGTON, Dec. 4.—In the United States Supreme Court to-day the Addyston Pipe case was decided. This case involved the constitutionality of the combination of pipe manufacturers to manufacture pipe, which, it was charged, was a trust. The decision which was handed down by Justice Peckham was in opposition to the trust. The opinion of the Court of Appeals for the Sixth Circuit was affirmed.

In reviewing the case, Justice Peckham said that it had been brought under the Anti-Trust act of 1890, and that an injunction was asked to enjoin the six corporations engaged in the manufacture of water and gas pipe, which composed the combination, from continuing to do business under the agreement by which they had divided the territory of the United States among themselves, and by which they had arranged to fix prices.

Under this agreement members of the combination provided for auctioning off the right to make bids for supplying with pipe cities not in allotted territory, the successful bidder to meet no opposition from other members of the trust, or if other bids were made none of them should be higher than that of the company to which the award had been made by the combination. In cases in which bids were asked in territory allotted to members of the combination the agreement was that no bids should be made except under the supervision of the company in charge of that territory under the agreement.

The charge was that such a combination was a violation of the clause of the Constitution regulating inter-State commerce.

The district court in which the case was first heard refused to take this view of it, but it was reversed by the Court of Appeals of the Sixth Circuit, which held the combination to be antagonistic to the Constitution, ordering the issuance of the injunction prayed for. This latter decision was affirmed by the action to-day of the Supreme Court, with a modification that the decision should be construed as applying to inter-State business only.

The six companies composing the combination affected were the Addyston Pipe and Steel Company of Cincinnati, Dennis Long & Co. of Louisville, the Howard Harrison Iron Company of Bessemer, Ala.; the Anniston Pipe and Foundry Company of Anniston, Ala.; the South Pittsburg Pipe Works of South Pittsburg, Tenn., and the Chattanooga Foundry and Pipe Works of Chattanooga, Tenn. Their agreement provided that there should be no competition between the companies in thirty-six States, which were mentioned, in the manufacture and sale of cast-iron pipe.

In order that there might be no misunderstanding, an Executive Committee was named by the combination, the duties of whose members, among other things, was to determine to which member of the combination a given contract should be awarded. Once this were determined, a price was decided upon, and then the other members of the company made their fictitious bids above the price of the company selected for the work.

The case was brought and first tried in the Circuit Court for the Eastern District of Tennessee.

Passing upon the objection that the Constitutional provision could not be held applicable to individuals, Justice Peckham said:

" We conclude that the plain language of the grant to Congress of power to regulate commerce among the several States includes power to legislate upon the subject of these contracts in respect to inter-State or foreign commerce which directly offset and regulate that commerce, and we can find no reasonable ground for asserting that the Constitutional provision as to the liberty of the individual limits the extent of that power as claimed by the appellants. We therefore think the appellants have failed in their contention upon this branch of the subject." Further on the opinion held that "the direct and immediate result of the combination was necessarily a restraint upon inter-State commerce in respect of articles manufactured by any of the parties to it to be transported beyond the State in which they were made. The defendants by reason of this combination and agreement could only send their goods out of the State upon the terms and pursuant to the provisions of such combination. Was not this a direct restraint upon inter-State commerce in those goods? If dealers in any commodity agreed among themselves that any particular territory bounded by State lines should be furnished with such commodity by certain members only of the combination and the others would abstain from business in that territory would not such agreement be regarded as one in restraint of inter-State trade? If the price of the commodity was thereby enhanced, (as it necessarily would be,) the character of the agreement would be still more clearly in restraint of trade.

"Is there any substantial difference whereby agreement among themselves the parties choose one of their number to make a bid for the supply of the pipe for delivery in another State and agree that all the other bids shall be for a larger sum, thus practically restricting all but the member agreed upon from any attempt to supply the demand for the pipe or to enter into competition for the business? It is useless for the defendants to say they did not intend to regulate or affect inter-State commerce. They intended to make the very combination and agreement which they in fact did make, and they must be held to have intended the necessary and direct result of their agreement."

Remarking upon the general aspect of the case, Justice Peckham said: " We have no doubt that where the direct and immediate effect of a contract or combination among particular dealers in a commodity is to destroy competition between them and others, so that the parties to the contract or combine may obtain increased prices for themselves, such contract or combination amounts to a restraint of trade in the commodity, even though contracts to buy such commodity at the enhanced price are continually being made. Total suppression of the trade in the commodity is not necessary in order to render the combination one in restraint of trade. It is the effect of the combination in limiting and restricting the right of each of the members to transact business in the ordinary way as well as its effect upon the volume or extent of the dealing in the commodity that is regarded."

The opinion then adds:

" It is almost needless to add that we do not hold every private enterprise which may be carried on chiefly or in part by means of inter-State shipments is therefore to be regarded as relegated to inter-State commerce, so as to come within the regulating power of Congress. Such enterprises may be of the same nature as the manufacturing of refined sugar; that is, the parties may be engaged as manufacturers of a commodity which they thereafter intend at some time to sell, and possibly to sell in another State; but such sale we have already held is an incident to and not the direct result of the manufacture, and so is not a regulation of or an illegal interference with inter-State commerce. The principle is not affected by anything herein decided."

The decision draws a clear distinction between combinations affecting inter-State commerce and those applying to one State only. The opinion attracted very general attention because it is the first opinion on the subject of trusts which has been handed down since the subject of trusts has come into great prominence.

December 5, 1899

FOR REGULATION OF TRUSTS.

Industrial Commission Submits a Preliminary Report, with Recommendations, to Congress.

WASHINGTON, March 1.—The Industrial Commission to-day submitted to Congress a preliminary report on trusts and industrial combinations, together with testimony, review of evidence, charts showing effects of prices, &c. The commission makes the following recommendations, based on such information as it now has:

Promoters and organizers of corporations or industrial combinations which look to the public to purchase or deal in their stocks or securities should be required to furnish full details in regard to their business necessary for safe and intelligent investment. Any prospectus which fails to give this information, or which gives false information, should be held legally responsible. The nature of the business, together with the powers of the various officers, should be expressed in the certificate of incorporation, which should be open to inspection. The Directors or Trustees should be required to report to the members of such a corporation its financial condition in reasonable detail; to give members access to records of Directors' meetings or otherwise, and to furnish them before annual meetings with lists of members, with their addresses and their several holdings, and to provide in whatever other ways may be named in the certificate of incorporation means whereby the members may prevent the misuse of their property by Directors or Trustees.

It is recommended that the larger corporations should be required to publish annually a properly audited report showing in reasonable detail their assets and liabilities, with profit or loss; such report and audit to be under oath and to be subject to Government inspection.

With regard to the Inter-State Commerce Commission it is recommended that it receive authority not only to prescribe the methods of keeping accounts of the railroads and to demand reports in such detail as it may require, but also to inspect and audit such accounts; that the decisions of the commission be made operative at a day fixed in the decisions, and to remain so unless reversed by the United States courts on appeal; that the commission be authorized to prescribe classifications of freight articles and to make rules and regulations for freight transportation throughout the United States, and that penalties for violations of the Inter-State Commerce act should be appropriate fines against the carrier and not imprisonment of officials.

Commissioner Lorimer states that he concurs in all the recommendations, but withholds his judgment on transportation corporations until testimony now being compiled by the commission is submitted to Congress with recommendations.

Commissioner Clarke concurs in all recommendations except that he believes rates fixed by the Inter-State Commerce Commission should not go into effect in case of appeal until affirmed by the court, and that trial on appeal should be expedited.

March 2, 1900

GIANT STEEL TRUST LAUNCHED AT LAST

Under the name of the United States Steel Corporation, the "billion-dollar steel combine" which J. P. Morgan and his associates have for some time been perfecting, was formally launched yesterday when the articles of incorporation were filed in Jersey City with the County Clerk of Hudson County. Beyond the admitted fact, however, that this is actually the trust which for some time has been setting the financial and trade worlds agog, and that it is organized for the purpose of transacting such business as usually a well-regulated steel company does transact, little new is disclosed. Neither the real capital stock nor the concerns which will make up the company, nor the men who will be the controlling spirits in it figure in the articles of incorporation.

The new concern starts out modestly with a total authorized capital stock of $3,000, divided into 30 shares of $100 each—15 shares of 7 per cent. cumulative preferred stock, and fifteen shares of common stock, while the incorporators—Charles C. Cluff, William J Curtis, and Charles McVeagh—are merely the usual "dummy" incorporators. Mr. Cluff is a subordinate official of the Federal Steel Company, Mr. Curtis is a member of the firm of Sullivan & Cromwell, and Mr. MacVeagh is identified with the firm of Stetson, Jennings & Russell, the head of which, Francis Lynde Stetson, prepared the incorporation papers. It is explained, however, in the articles of incorporation, that "from time to time the preferred stock and the common stock may be increased according to law," so that Wall Street has little fear that the trust will be called upon to worry along for any considerable length of time on a $3,000 capital. Explanation for the failure to state the complete capital is given by a banker close to J. P. Morgan, who declares that, though the deal is practically completed, there were some few figures in the way of the capitalization, and earnings of some of the constituent companies that were still receiving consideration, and that for that reason it was deemed advisable at the outset to incorporate with merely a nominal capital.

As to the concerns to be included in the combine, there is still more or less press work. An official statement was expected yesterday from the office of J. P. Morgan & Co., setting out the companies and the plan of financing, but none was given out. Instead, after keeping the reporters waiting from 2:30 until 6:10 P. M., Robert Bacon, one of Mr. Morgan's partners, announced that he had expected to have a statement ready, but was very sorry that it had been delayed. "It may," he added, "be ready to-morrow, Tuesday." Generally, however, it is understood—and there is substantial basis for the understanding—that the new company will take over the control of the Carnegie, the Federal Steel, the American Steel and Wire, the American Tin Plate, the National Tube, the National Steel, the American Steel Hoop, and the American Sheet Steel Companies, by an exchange of stock. Trade arrangements may be made, also, with the Pennsylvania, the Cambria, and the Bethlehem Steel Companies, and with the American Bridge Company.

A WALL STREET ESTIMATE.

Upon what basis these concerns will be taken over—what valuation has been determined upon, the assets and earning powers of the respective companies considered, is a matter of much conjecture—necessarily so until an authoritative statement is forthcoming. One of the Wall Street reports had the figures as follows:

Carnegie Company—Minority stock, $73,621,000, divided into $1,000 shares. Each share to be paid for by $1,500 worth of preferred stock in the new company and an equal amount of common.

American Steel and Wire—$40,000,000 7 per cent. cumulative preferred stock taken in at 117½; $50,000,000 common stock taken in at 102.

Federal Steel—$58,586,900 7 per cent. preferred stock taken in at 110, and $46,484,300 common stock at 104.

National Tube—$40,000,000 7 per cent. cumulative preferred taken in at 120, and $40,000,000 common stock taken in at 140.

National Steel—$27,000,000 7 per cent. cumulative preferred taken in at 122, and $32,000,000 common stock taken in at par.

American Tin Plate—$18,325,000 7 per cent. cumulative preferred taken in at 120, and $28,-000,000 common stock at 132.

American Steel Hoop—$14,000,000 7 per cent. cumulative taken in at par, and $19,000,000 common stock taken in at 61.

American Sheet Steel—$24,500,000 preferred taken in at 97, and $24,500,000 common taken in at 60.

These figures, however, as has been pointed out, are not official or conclusive, though a Director of Steel and Wire is quoted as saying that they were substantially correct. On this estimate this would account for about $360,000,000 preferred and $360,000,000 common stock of the new company.

The saving to be effected by such a combination will, it is declared, be enormous. It is a fact that Mr. Morgan's figures as collated show that an expenditure of fully $250,000,000 would have been necessary on the part of the big companies taken in in order to safeguard each its own interest. Not one would have been able to go on operating successfully without having developed along much broader lines than at present—the Carnegie Company perhaps excepted, Federal Steel following next. It would have been necessary for each company, as competition grew keener, to own its own ore lands, mine its own ore—control, in fact, every intermediate product and process up to the turning out of the finest finished products. The so-called minor companies, too, would, it was demonstrated, be at great disadvantage because of the modern machines and mechanical appliances which the bigger companies possess.

Another item that looks big in Mr. Morgan's tabulated figures is a saving of over $80,000,000 per year by getting rid of the middlemen which competition makes necessary. In the language of a steel man, in fact, the deal is regarded as the "broadest, biggest, most gigantic, and most influential combination ever effected."

There is an understanding in Wall Street—founded on no one knows what—that the Directors of the company will be elected this week. The men said to be selected to enter this Directorate are J. Pierpont Morgan, Judge Gary of Federal Steel, Judge Moore of American Tin Plate, John W. Gates of Steel and Wire, and Charles M. Schwab and H. C. Frick—the incorporation papers stating that the Directors shall be three in number or, if more, multiples of three. It may be that only three will at first be named, in which event it is likely they would be J. P. Morgan, Judge Moore, and Mr. Schwab, or Mr. Frick.

STORY OF AN $800,000 SALARY.

One of the many stories afloat concerning the great deal has it that C. M. Schwab, who is slated to be the President and general manager of the new company, with H. C. Frick as Chairman, will receive a salary of $800,000 a year. Mr. Schwab, who was in conference for several hours yesterday with Mr. Morgan, was asked as to the report and as to the progress of the negotiations. He answered: "I have nothing to say."

"But about your salary?" ventured the reporter.

Mr. Schwab smiled.

"It's a lot of money—$800,000—isn't it?" he remarked, and was gone.

Besides Mr. Schwab, Mr. Morgan saw other steel men and lawyers from time to time during the day, including Judge Gary of Federal Steel and Francis Lynde Stetson. But what was discussed or done at these inner councils was zealously guarded.

John W. Gates, Chairman of Steel and Wire, who in a certain quarter not especially reliable is credited with having pleaded with Mr. Morgan not to give out the details of the combine until "the boys" had got a chance in the stock market, was in very good humor yesterday, but altogether uncommunicative. When seen he said, smilingly:

"I have nothing to say. Mr. Morgan will give you all the facts and figures. Go to his office."

"Well, are you satisfied with the terms?" asked the reporter.

"Oh, now—now," was the reply. "Didn't I tell you I had nothing to say?"

Max Pam, general counsel for the Steel and Wire Company, said:

"There's nothing for us to say."

Judge Moore of Chicago, the promoter of the National Steel, Tin Plate, and Steel Hoop Companies, seen at his offices at 71 Broadway, said:

"I never talk for publication."

President E. H. Gary of Federal Steel denied himself to reporters, sending out word that he would not have anything to say.

Francis Lynde Stetson, approached in the matter, said that as a lawyer, occupying a fiduciary position, he could not say anything even if he would.

"Will you tell how these various companies mentioned as being in the new concern are taken in?" he was asked.

"Should I tell you about these companies and they shouldn't come in that would place the matter in a very awkward position," was the answer.

"But the understanding is that all that matter has been arranged—what companies are to come in," persisted the reporter.

"There is nothing on which to base any such assumption," was the reply, the interview being closed at the same time.

Full light, however, is probable to-day, when it is understood a committee representing the constituent companies will hold a meeting, and when final details will be settled. Following this it is understood the respective Boards of Directors will issue letters to stockholders, stating the terms on which the companies are admitted and urging their acceptance.

THE FINANCING ARRANGEMENTS.

As for the arrangements for financing the corporation and for exchanging the securities of the participating companies, it is reported they have been practically completed. Prominent bank officers were quoted as saying that not more than $15,-000,000 will be needed to float the new company, and that this amount has already been set aside by the underwriters.

A more difficult problem deals with the sale of the new corporation's securities. Undoubtedly the securities will be listed on the New York Stock Exchange and probably on the London Stock Exchange. Morgan & Co.'s extensive connections abroad are likely to be used for the sale of large blocks of securities there. Reports have it that London, Paris, Berlin, and Frankfort will take at least $100,000,000 of them, but as to the truth of this nobody but insiders can say. It is also said that the underwriting syndicate will take $10,000,000 in bonds and $15,000,000 in stock.

Bankers discussing the matter yesterday said that they did not think the consolidation would have any immediate influence on the money market.

The reference in the articles of incorporation to the mining of copper led to a report that the Amalgamated Copper Company would be taken into the combine, but this is altogether lacking of confirmation.

Profiting by the trouble of the Federal Steel Company in respect to the question of the legality of its dividend payments on the common stock, it is noted as significant that the articles of incorporation of the new company provide that a full year's dividend on the preferred must be paid before any dividend on the common stock can be paid.

The Hudson Trust Company, which is named as the corporation's agent, last year became closely identified with the Morgan interests, and Mr. Morgan has been transacting much of his New Jersey business through that corporation. He is represented in the Board of Directors. The steel combine will have an entire floor of the Hudson Trust Company's new building in Jersey City.

February 26, 1901

WHAT LED TO THE COMBINATION.

Mr. Morgan Appealed To in Crisis Precipitated by Mr. Carnegie.

After having maintained silence on the subject of the new steel combination for many weeks and refusing to make any statement for publication, J. Pierpont Morgan yesterday gave an interview to a reporter for THE NEW YORK TIMES. Mr. Morgan was in his office at the time, and was reading a publication called Boston News Bureau Summary, which contained on its first page an article of some length entitled "The United States Steel Corporation—A Unification of Great Interests." Mr. Morgan said:

"The statement given out here to-day is all that there is to be said at present. There will be nothing else until our circular is issued, and that will not be until all the concerns have been brought in."

Then turning to the publication he was reading Mr. Morgan said:

"That is the best statement of the situation that has yet come to my notice. Had I written it myself I could not have stated the situation better."

Mr. Morgan then handed the paper to the reporter. The first statement in the article indorsed by Mr. Morgan is as follows:

The present operations should not be classed with promotions of industrial corporations for the purpose of converting existing manufacturing business into new securities to be floated upon the public. The proposed amalgamation means nothing more than a unification of existing security interests for the better protection and more harmonious operation of existing properties.

The article then makes the following statement, which is the first authentic admission of the questions which brought the consolidation about:

Mr. Andrew Carnegie recently threatened to duplicate the mills of various makers of finished productions because enough raw material was not being purchased from his mills. The companies making the finished productions threatened retaliation into the Carnegie field, with the result that a sort of industrial chaos was threatening in the steel and iron trades and in the security markets of this country.

The story then goes on to state practically the facts contained in THE NEW YORK TIMES of yesterday regarding the duplication and reduplication of plants which would have followed the carrying out of Mr. Carnegie's threat and tells how Mr. Morgan was brought into the matter as follows:

Mr. Carnegie said he must progress or go out of business. Other interests said they must do the same thing. Mr. J.P. Morgan was asked to furnish some plan of solution. With great reluctance he took hold of the situation. Before proceeding, however, Mr. Morgan demanded that $200,000,000 should be promised him by responsible banking and financial interests, should so much money be needed. The money was promised and Mr. Morgan set to work. Mr. Carnegie had the largest plant and the strongest position and named his terms of sale. He, however, signified his willingness to take securities in lieu of cash, and negotiations proceeded very rapidly.

The article states that two weeks ago the proposition was to take over only three companies with the Carnegie Company, viz., the Federal Steel, the National Tube, and the American Steel and Wire, but the Moore companies were taken into the consideration when it was found that, operating in unison, these companies were independent of every other company, from ore to finished product. This determination to take in the Moore companies was strengthened when it was found that the Moore companies were in a position to expand laterally into the fields of the four companies which it was proposed to consolidate.

The article makes the important statement that the new corporation is to be primarily a finance corporation, and the fact is set forth in the following terms:

This week a new company has been incorporated in New Jersey called the United States Steel corporation, which is backed by $200,000,000 of bankers' underwriting. This corporation will be primarily a finance corporation. It will purchase a majority of the Carnegie Company bonds and shares, and also a majority, if the stockholders elect to sell, of seven other leading steel and iron concerns, and by reason of such ownership insure the harmonious operation of the leading iron and steel plants of this country. In outline this is all there is of the so-called giant corporation. Not a dollar has been paid Mr. Carnegie, and in the end, Mr. Carnegie may receive no money except so far as he, in common with others, may elect to sell their securities at market prices hereafter.

In regarding the matter of underwriting, the article says:

Circulars will issue to the stockholders of the various companies, probably this week, offering an exchange of existing securities into United States Steel securities. Some part of the $200,000,000 subscribed will be called up to make organization and to furnish what new capital may be required, not for itself primarily, but for the companies for which it will be responsible when it takes majority control. The unification of these iron and steel interests through majority control in such a voluntary association as is the United States Steel Company, will make unnecessary the duplication of plants and the raising of a large amount of new capital.

Instead of $150,000,000 or $200,000,000 of new capital for the destruction of existing industries, $30,000,000 or $40,000,000 of capital may be paid in for their unification and harmonious operation, and whatever expansion may be necessary for the sub-companies each in its own field.

It is said that the underwriters who promised $200,000,000 have set aside for them $25,000,000 of preferred stock and $25,000,000 of common. We understand, however, that definite terms concerning this matter are not yet agreed upon, but that the bankers may get during the next eighteen months preferred stock at par for any money furnished, and a 100 per cent. bonus in common stock.

February 27, 1901

CONTROL OF WESTERN ROADS.

Chicago Accepts Report that the Morgan-Harriman "Community of Interest" Plan Has Been Adopted.

CHICAGO, June 16.—In railroad circles to-day the sudden departure of E. H. Harriman for the East, accompanied by John J. Mitchell, President of the Illinois Trust and Savings Bank, was accepted as support of the assertion that the Harriman combination has secured control of the Chicago, Milwaukee and St. Paul Road. The Tribune to-morrow will say:

"That a composite agreement has been made to perfect a community of interests among roads with tracks enough to twice belt the globe, is generally accepted in railroad circles.

"The meeting of the Western officials with Mr. Harriman is believed to have been the result of the recent controversy over control of Northern Pacific stock which drove short holders to cover at $1,000 a share. A few small roads out of Chicago are not parties to the agreement, but it is understood they will consent to anything that will maintain rates and end the squabble that has been kept up in the past among the various Western lines.

"It is asserted that all the roads West, Northwest, and Southwest from Chicago to the Pacific coast will be controlled in future by the following interests:

Lines west of Chicago to the Pacific Coast by Harriman, Kuhn, Loeb & Co., and the Rockefellers.

Lines northwest from Chicago, by Hill and Morgan.

Lines southwest from St. Louis by Gould and the Rockefellers.

Lines southwest from Chicago by the Atchison, Topeka and Santa Fé to which probably will be added before long the Chicago, Rock Island and Pacific.

"J. Pierpont Morgan and E. H. Harriman however, will be the real dictators and direct the policy to be pursued by these combinations, thus establishing the 'community of interest' which has been the dream of Mr. Morgan."

The railroads interested in the Harriman consolidation, with their mileage, are the following:

Road.	Total Mileage. June 30, 1900.
Atchison, Topeka and Santa Fé	6,946
Southern Pacific	7,614
Union Pacific	4,430
Northern Pacific	4,524
Chicago, Milwaukee and St. Paul	6,191
Chicago and Northwestern	5,077
Chicago, Burlington and Quincy	7,180
Missouri Pacific	5,324
Great Northern	5,127
Chicago and Alton	844
Wabash	2,326
Total	55,582

June 17, 1901

E. H. GARY AT HEAD OF ALLIS-CHALMERS COMPANY.

Chairman of Steel Trust's Directors Elected to Similar Position in Machinery Corporation.

CHICAGO, Jan. 25.—Elbert H. Gary, Chairman of the Board of Directors of the United States Steel Corporation, has been elected Chairman of the Board of Directors of the Allis-Chalmers Company, the largest machinery concern in the world, capitalized at $25,000,000. The announcement, it is said, has caused a sensation in commercial and financial circles, as it means that the Steel Trust intends reaching out into another line of business. William Allis, who retires with General Superintendent Edwin Reynolds, says ill-health is the principal cause, but refuses to give any information concerning the intentions of the company.

William J. Chalmers of Chicago is Chairman of the Executive Committee of the company and really has been its chief. The corporation was the result of the consolidation of the E. P. Allis Company of Milwaukee with the Frazer and Chalmers Company and the P. W. Gates Iron Works of Chicago, all manufacturers of mining machinery and all its products. Not long after the consolidation of the three concerns came the machinists' strike, which for a time involved many industrial plants throughout the country. From time to time various companies effected settlements with their men, but the Allis-Chalmers Company has held out against the strikers.

It it not known whether ex-Judge Gary's accession to the corporation will relieve Mr. Chalmers of some of his duties, but it is supposed the new Chairman's work will be largely on the financial side, leaving the operating of the factories in the hands of Mr. Chalmers.

Mr. Gary has been a leading official of the gradually expanding Steel Trust since it began to take form. He was one of the organizers of the American Steel and Wire Company. Later he became President of the $200,000,000 Federal Steel Company, and last year he was chosen Chairman of the Board of the United States Steel Corporation.

January 26, 1902

RISE OF THE SYNDICATE

Its Vast Profits In Launching The Modern Trust.

Steel and Northwestern Railway's Combinations Illustrations of the Underwriting Syndicate's Work—Mr. Morgan's Share In Its Development.

Criticism cabled over from London of the compensation to be awarded to the syndicate which is underwriting the securities of the new shipping combine has excited interest in the history of the development of these syndicates, and the extent of their profits in this country. The present criticism is over the fact that the underwriting syndicate for this consolidation is to receive a bonus of $25,000,000 in common stock and $2,500,000 preferred.

In spite of the extraordinary attention which has been attracted to this arrangement, it is pointed out by a prominent financial interest in Wall Street that this is not so large payment as was received by the underwriters of the Steel Trust organization. The Shipping Trust syndicate guarantees the sale of $50,000,000 bonds and about $120,000,000 in stock.

This syndicate has been called upon for $25,000,000 of its cash subscription. Interests connected with the new scheme admit, however, that most of the bonds of the new company have already been subscribed for outside of the syndicate. All that remains to be done, therefore, is to float the issue of $120,000,000 of stock. It is said that if the syndicate itself were to buy these bonds, its profit would amount to about 55 per cent., which would be reduced to some 80 per cent by the sale of the shares of stock at less than par value.

It has been figured by responsible persons that the profits of the syndicate will amount to about one-half the face value of the securities with which payment will be made to them, or some $13,000,000 or $14,000,000. Of this amount it is understood that J. P. Morgan & Co. will receive about $1,400,000 for managing the affair. This is considered a low estimate in Wall Street.

THE SYNDICATE'S DEVELOPMENT.

Since 1890 the underwriting syndicate has had a remarkable development in this country. It has made possible the formation of companies with hundreds of millions of dollars' capital; it has brought great banking houses into harmonious working agreements; it has brought American and foreign financial institutions into close co-operation, and it has fixed a very snug berth for the stock market manipulator—the man who acts as a sort of selling agent for underwriting syndicates.

Syndicates are paid usually in the securities of the companies they underwrite. The stock market operator turns those securities into cash. This is why underwriting syndicates often remain in existence long after the apparent use for them has expired.

Little is known outside of Wall Street banking houses of just what the part is which is played by these syndicates. The most remarkable illustration of the working of such a syndicate is found in that which underwrote the Steel Trust securities, and its operations will serve as a type of those of all the rest.

Attention was called by Prof. E. S. Meade of the University of Pennsylvania, in a lecture before the New York University on Wednesday night last, to the fact that the formation of the Steel Trust was brought about because New York banking houses still held a considerable amount of securities they had received as commissions for forming the smaller steel trusts—American Steel and Wire, Federal Steel, Steel Hoop, &c. There were six such corporations, aside from the Carnegie company.

These trusts had been organized on the height of the great demand for iron and steel products in the years 1898 and 1899. Many of them had been capitalized up to their fullest earning capacity, independent of any material assets. They had unified a vast number of miscellaneous companies, and many difficulties had been encountered by the bankers who guaranteed their securities. Messrs. J. P. Morgan & Co., for example, had underwritten the Steel Tube Company.

That is to say, the Morgan company had agreed to furnish the necessary capital for purchasing the securities of the subsidiary companies and to provide working capital for the Tube Company when fully organized. In return for this cash which was supplied, the Morgan company received a large amount of stocks in the new corporation. Likewise, a large amount of securities of the American Steel and Wire, Steel Hoop, Tin Plate, and other companies passed into the hands of Wall Street bankers.

So long as there was a great demand for steel products, says Prof. Meade, and the makers of the finished product bought their raw materials from Mr. Carnegie, there was no trouble. The bankers were gradually selling their stocks through operators, and there was no complaint from any source. In 1900 the market for the finished product fell off some, however, and the different steel trusts proposed producing their own raw materials.

Mr. Carnegie threatened that if this was done he would build large producing plants and compete with the product companies. This action on his part would have meant ruin for the other companies and the total loss of the holdings of the Wall Street bankers. To save their commissions, consequently, it was deemed necessary to buy out Mr. Carnegie and consolidate all of the steel-producing trusts.

To effect this consolidation, it was necessary to purchase securities amounting to about $1,000,000,000. Working capital had to be supplied to the new holding company, and cash had to be furnished for purchasing such of the necessary securities as must be bought in the open market. Messrs. J. P. Morgan & Co., therefore, organized a syndicate which agreed to supply $200,000,000 in cash upon its being demanded by the managers of the undertaking.

HOW TO GET THE MILLIONS.

It was obviously impossible for any one banking house to undertake to supply such a sum of money. Even had it been possible, the risk of loss would have been too great. Hence, while J. P. Morgan & Co. themselves subscribed a large amount of the sum, the major portion of it was distributed among a number of banking establishments.

The first and only call made for payment was for $25,000,000. This sum was paid to the Steel Trust, to be used when necessary to secure the securities of subsidiary corporations and to supply working capital. In return for this payment, the syndicate was paid 649,987 shares of the new common and an equal number of shares of the new preferred stock, (market value about $84,000,000.) It was expected that this payment of $25,000,000 would be returned, but the syndicate guaranteed the flotation of the entire issue of securities—some $1,410,000,000 in all.

It was never expected that the syndicate would be called upon to supply the total amount of money subscribed. In fact, such a call would have been decidedly embarrassing. Here is where the value of the guarantee came in, however. With such a guarantee as this, and with such a payment of stocks to operate with, the syndicate managers could go to trust companies and borrow money upon the securities received as commissions. With this cash the remainder of the deal could be financed. It could not have been possible without such guarantee.

The process is to gradually pay off the loans at the trust companies, sell the securities, and send dividends to the members of the syndicate. In the case of the Steel Trust, the $25,000,000 was returned within a short time, and it is expected that the total dividends upon the syndicate's subscriptions will amount to about $40,000,000. This will be 20 per cent. of the amount subscribed—about 160 per cent. of the amount paid in.

No such profit as this was ever before made by such a transaction in this country. It was explained by the managers, however, that the profit was not abnormal when the risk undertaken was considered. The risk might have been said theoretically to be epitomized as follows: The possibility that all of the subsidiary companies might not be secured, the possibility of panic conditions in the market, which would render the sale of the commission securities difficult—the possibility of impediments in the flotation of the company's securities. When it is realized that the capitalization of the Steel Trust was about $100,000,000 in excess of the aggregate capitalizations of the companies consolidated, the element of risk in this last possibility may be seen.

This, then, is the method of operation of the syndicate. Its theoretical purpose is to supply such cash as may be needed; its practical purpose is to furnish the necessary credit. When the necessities of the case make it essential to provide cash and credit, the scheme is not considered so successful. The profit of the syndicate is reckoned as a commission upon its liability, not upon the amount of cash paid in. It is an application of the same principle as that upon which bankers make loans. They agree to furnish money. As a matter of fact, they usually merely furnish a book credit, and upon that they charge interest. As in the case of syndicates, the collateral is very much more insecure, the interest charges are impliedly very much larger, although there is the possibility of there being no gain at all.

THE FIRST SYNDICATES.

Syndicates were first organized in England in about the year 1840, and in floating all large corporations and joint stock companies since that time, they have been extensively employed. The Bank of England itself, in its original organization, was planned upon very much the same lines as a bankers' syndicate of to-day. It was chartered primarily to guarantee a governmental loan in the latter part of the seventeenth century. The same plan has been utilized in nearly all large flotations of stock in England since then.

Strangely enough, this method of floating securities was not brought over to this country until 1890. Before that year, issues of capital had been floated by direct subscription. There had not existed the need for a syndicate to provide working capital or to buy up the securities of companies which it was desired to incorporate in a combination. The trust certificate plan had served the purposes now served by the great New Jersey trusts.

After 1890, when the trust certificate plan had been dislodged by the courts, it became necessary to combine corporations by purchasing their shares. This created the necessity for enormous capitalizations, and for great sums of working capital to acquire control of subsidiary corporations. The syndicate plan very naturally became ingrafted upon the financial machinery of this country.

Casuists figure upon other possibilities of the syndicate suggested by the proposed plan to convert 200,000,000 shares of the preferred stock of the United States Steel Corporation into bonds, and make an additional issue of $50,000,000 in bonds. An underwriting syndicate has been formed to guarantee this deal, and it is to be paid some $10,000,000. J. P. Morgan & Co., of course, get merely a commission, as managers, in addition to the profit upon the sum they subscribe to the total guarantee. Owing to the risk involved in these deals, it is always considered wisest to distribute the subscriptions as widely as possible.

It is said that the organizers of the Steel Trust have as yet not been able to sell their holdings of stock in the market. They still hold control, however, of the property, and can vote any action that may be desired. It is understood that it is this speculative interest which is principally concerned with the conversion. Two possibilities lay in the conversion, it is pointed out.

The first of these is that a 5 per cent. bond will be easier to sell in the market than a speculative stock, especially as the $300,000,000 of Steel first mortgage bonds are greatly inferior to the actual value of the material assets of the trust. Secondly, the control of $126,000,000 of the new second mortgage bonds will give their holders the power to force a foreclosure and reorganization of the company in case of a failure to meet fixed charges.

In case a large number of independent companies should grow out of the promise of profits now afforded by the great prosperity of the Steel Trust, and the gains of the trust should thereby be curtailed to the extent of rendering the corporation unable to pay the interest on the second mortgage bonds, a foreclosure could be brought about. The competing concerns could then be brought into the fold, the company entirely reorganized, new capital floated, and more profits secured for banking syndicates.

It is not argued that this is what promises to be the case with the Steel Trust, but that the possibilities of profit to underwriting syndicates have a conspicuous illusbut that the possibilities of profit to underwriters of the various securities floated by the United States Steel Corporation.

Syndicates as a rule feel that they should make about 20 per cent. on the amount of their subscriptions to these underwriting agreements. The amount of cash called in is ordinarily about 10 per cent., though this sometimes rises to 20, 30, and 40 per cent. Syndicates have been known as recently as 1890 to be in serious straits, and have to supply the full amount subscribed, and then be in doubt about a dividend. This does not happen often, however, as the managers of syndicates are usually houses of such standing that the success of the scheme is practically guaranteed before it is ever launched.

THE UNION PACIFIC DEAL.

Outside of the steel syndicate, the most profitable underwriting deal of recent years was that of the reorganization of the Union Pacific Railroad Company. Its profits were never publicly stated, but the circular containing the reorganization plan stated that the syndicate had pledged itself to supply $10,000,000, if needed. It was to receive $6,000,000 in preferred shares, of which Kuhn, Loeb & Co., as bankers, were to receive $1,000,000. The syndicate was never called upon to pay much cash, and Union Pacific shares are now selling at around 102 and 103.

The syndicate which underwrote the reorganization of the Erie Railroad received $15,000,000 in new prior lien 4 per cent. bonds, and contracted to furnish up to $14,000,000 in cash to the new company. In addition, the firm of J. P. Morgan & Co., as depositaries of the old securities which were to be exchanged for the new, were to receive $500,000 in cash as compensation.

Last October the Mexican National Railroad's affairs were readjusted. The syndicate which carried the scheme through bought for $12,967,000 cash the following securities, to which are added their present market quotations: Prior lien 4½ per cent. bonds, $9,221,000, (par value,) present quotation 102¾; first consolidated 4s, $3,595,312 par value, quotation 81¼, and preferred stock, $2,400,000 par value, present quotation 41.

In reorganizations the underwriting syndicates always assume responsibility for assessments not met by shareholders. This was a prominent feature of the Atchison reorganization plan which was made public on June 21, 1894. The Reorganization Committee, in a circular to the stockholders outlining the plan of rehabilitation, said:

"Syndicates may be formed on reasonable and usual terms to furnish the money needed in case of foreclosure to pay the non-assessments, pay bondholders their shares of the proceeds of the sale, and such syndicates by such payments and to the extent thereof shall be entitled to and shall represent and succeed to all the rights that the bondholders receiving such payments would have been entitled to if they had assented to this plan and deposited their bonds."

The assessments on the common stock of Atchison amounted to $10,000,000 when the company was reorganized, and a syndicate was organized in London and this country to supply the cash. This syndicate was to guarantee the exchange and flotation of the following securities: $120,000,000 general mortgage bonds, $87,000,000 second mortgage bonds, $12,000,000 prior lien bonds, and $102,000,000 of common stock. Just what sum was cleared by the syndicate in this reorganization was never announced, but the immense responsibility assumed justifies the statement that the profit was very large, $10,000,000 or $12,000,000 being regarded as a conservative estimate.

This matter of guaranteeing assessments was a very important one also in the reorganization of the Richmond and West Point Terminal Company—one of J. P. Morgan's great accomplishments. In the Richmond Terminal Company—which was a holding company, interested in the Richmond and Danville, East Tennessee, Virginia and Georgia, and other railroad properties in the South—were such interests as Gen. Samuel Thomas, Calvin S. Brice, Patrick Calhoun, John H. Inman, and Alfred Sully.

In the general crash of the 1893 panic period this company went to pieces, and J. P. Morgan & Co. reorganized the properties into the present prosperous Southern Railroad Company. The commission of the syndicate which floated the securities of this new company was in stock at that time valued at $7 a share, but is now selling at $39. It is supposed that the syndicate sold its holdings at about 25—thus bringing into its coffers a very comfortable number of millions of dollars upon its guarantee of some $10,000,000 or $15,000,000 of cash.

MR. MORGAN'S FIRST TRIUMPH.

The first great achievement of J. P. Morgan was his first reorganization of the Reading Railroad. It had been controlled for years by Franklin Gowen, who had done many spectacular things, such as floating the very elusive "deferred income bond." There was a contest between the Gowen interests and Drexel, Morgan & Co., which resulted in a readjustment of the company's affairs. Mr. Morgan is conceded in Wall Street to have made very large commissions by this deal.

The road was turned over to Austin Corbin, and very large net earnings were reported. A. A. McLeod attempted to combine the coal and carrying industries on the Reading lines, and the property went to smash. Following the panic of 1893, Mr. Morgan again reorganized the road, reaping large commissions once again.

The first of the large industrial companies to be reorganibed was the Sugar Trust. Its reorganization was forced by the fact that its charter under the laws of the State of New York had not been legally drawn, and it was forced to take refuge in New Jersey. The Cordage Trust was the first of the big industrials to be really reorganized after the modern fashion. Its troubles furnished one of the most picturesque incidents of the panic of 1893. Mr. Morgan was called into consultation in this readjustment, but the company nas had two reorganizations since its first disintegration.

In the formation of many large combinations, the underwriting agreement is private, and only the managers appear as financing the deal. In the Northern Securities combination, for example, no syndicate managers appeared at all. Control of the stocks to be consolidated was already secured, and that any consolidation was to be effected was ostensibly not one of the purposes of the company's formation. Shares of the Northern Pacific and Great Northern Railroads were deposited directly with the Northern Securities Company, without the intervention of bankers, and J. P. Morgan & Co. themselves secured the transfer of some $78,000,000 of Northern Pacific stock from the Union Pacific interests to the Northern Securities Company without one dollar of commission. Such was the testimony of Mr. Morgan before the United States commission in the Peter Power hearing.

Often a combination is brought about by inside interests entirely, bankers appearing merely as depositaries. This was the method used in the organization of the Glucose Trust, of Corn Products Company. The capitalization was $80,000,000, but no underwriting syndicate appeared to guarantee the flotation of the securities. All of this was done by "inside interests," who, of course, received a large commission.

To catalogue the profits which have been made by underwriting syndicates in Wall Street in recent years would be to make a list of all the important reorganizations and combinations which have been effected, record the amount of money guaranteed by the underwriting syndicates, and take 20 per cent. of the total sum. These syndicates have amounted to very much more within the last three years than ever before because of the custom which had grown up of not calling for more than a small percentage of the total. Previous to 1898 the total subscription was usually called for, but up to that year the two-hundred-million-dollar corporation was almost an entire stranger.

The profits to be derived from underwriting have grown to such an extent that many banks of considerable reputation in Wall Street rely almost entirely upon such profits for their incomes, letting the conventional banking business entirely alone. Sometimes the profits are not received in cash, but in bonds or stocks, and they have to be disposed of. This explains many sudden offerings of securities in the market.

THE OPERATOR'S PART.

If all the members of the syndicate receiving profit in such manner as this were to attempt to realize their cash values in the market there would be a general slaughter. It becomes necessary, therefore, to employ the skilled market operator. A well-known operator has been confessedly marketing the holdings of the steel underwriters for the year past, but the market so far has not responded as it had been hoped would be the case.

It is a very much simpler matter when syndicates undertake to guarantee the flotation of a single issue of bonds or stocks, such as the issue of $30,000,000 of Atchison debentures several months ago and of $10,000,000 of stock of the American Telephone and Telegraph Company a few weeks later. Such issues are turned over to syndicates, because the recommendation of certain bankers to the public of the gilt-edged quality of a security is worth to the corporation issuing the security very much more than the 2½ or greater per cent. paid as commission for the underwriting commitment. As such issues by strong corporations are ordinarily so easy to float, the commissions paid are compensatingly small.

Following the custom understood to have been inaugurated by J. P. Morgan & Co., houses which form syndicates and act as managers now usualy subtract a fifth of the net profits as compensation for their special services. A recent heavy bond issue by a very large system of railroads was made on a 5 per cent. basis to the railroad, with the payment in addition to the bankers of a flat $750,000, the bankers deciding on the selling price to the public, which, in this instance, allowed a commission of 1 per cent.

A well-known corporation lawyer in Wall Street was asked by a reporter for THE NEW YORK TIMES yesterday if the tremendous profits made by underwriting syndicates were not, in effect, abnormal tributes levied upon the public, if a return to the old system of direct subscription to the corporations themselves might not be quite as good in the end. To this question the lawyer replied:

"These syndicates are absolutely necessary. Without them the great corporations with tremendous capitalizations could not be organized. When such enterprises are launched, it is absolutely necessary to have money to guarantee that they shall be started without embarrassment. The money must be had at once. The syndicate supplies it, and sells the securities as there appears to be a demand in the market for them. If the corporation had to wait for such demand, it might never get on its feet at all."

May 4, 1902

PRESIDENT WOULD REGULATE TRUSTS

In Speech at Providence Says Government Should Control Capital.

MIGHT AMEND CONSTITUTION

If Step Were Necessary to Give Controlling Power—Ovations of Friday Repeated at All Places Visited on New England Tour.

THE SPEECH AT PROVIDENCE.

President's Views on the Industrial Problems of the Country.

PROVIDENCE, Aug. 23.—Not since the visit here of President Hayes, twenty-five years ago, has a Chief Executive been accorded so brilliant and thoroughly general a reception as that tendered here to-day to President Roosevelt. As representatives of the city, Acting Mayor Freeman, President of the Board of Aldermen, and City Clerk William E. Clarke met the President as he alighted, and extended to him the welcome of the people.

The party, which was joined by Senator Nelson W. Ardrich of this city; Senator George Peabody Wetmore of Newport, and Representative Melville Bulle of Newport, proceeded to the State House, Troop B, First Battalion of Cavalry escorting the carriages.

The streets on the way and the ground about the Capitol were lined with thousands of spectators. The residential and business sections of the city were gayly decorated with flags and bunting, and for the greater part of the way there were two solid lines of people who had come from every portion of the State to welcome the Chief Executive. Flags were waved, hats doffed, and cheer after cheer was given. The President bowed repeatedly in acknowledgment.

On arriving at the City Hall at the close of the drive, Gov. Kimball was in waiting in the reception room with members of the general and personal staffs. Luncheon was served, and the party then proceeded to the reception room, where the Lieutenant Governor, the General Assembly, general officers of the State, Justices of the courts, and other persons of note were in waiting.

Fully 15,000 persons were assembled to hear the President. On the platform which was beautifully decorated, stood nearly 1,000 of the most prominent citizens in the State, all of whom carried flags. Acting Mayor Freeman introduced President Roosevelt, who spoke as follows:

"We are passing through a period of great material prosperity and such a period is as sure as adversity itself to bring mutterings of discontent. At a time when most men prosper somewhat it always happens that a few men prosper greatly, and it is as true now as it was when the Tower of Siloam fell upon all who were under it that good fortune does not come only to the just, nor bad fortune only to the unjust. When the weather is good for crops it is also good for weeds. Moreover, not only do the wicked flourish when the times are such that most men flourish, but, what is worse, the spirit of envy and jealousy and hatred springs up in the breasts of those who, though they may be doing fairly well themselves, yet see others who are no more deserving doing far better.

ly well themselves, yet see others who are no more deserving doing far better.

"Wise laws and fearless and upright administration of the laws can give the opportunity for such prosperity as that we see about us. But this is all that they can do. When the conditions have been created which make prosperity possible then each individual man must achieve it for himself by his own thrift, intelligence, energy, industry, and resolute purpose. If when people wax fat they kick, as they have been prone to do since the days of Jeshurun, they will speedily destroy their own prosperity.

"If they go into wild speculation and lose their heads, they have lost that which no legislation can supply, and the business world will suffer in consequence. If in a spirit of sullen envy they insist upon pulling down those who have profited most by the years of fatness, they will bury themselves in the crash of the common disaster. It is difficult to make our material condition better by the best laws; but it is easy enough by bad laws to throw the whole Nation into an abyss of misery.

"Now, the upshot of all this is that it is peculiarly incumbent upon us in a time of such material well-being, both collectively as a Nation and individually, each on his own account, to show that we possess the qualities of prudence, self-knowledge, and self-restraint. In our Government we need above all things stability, fixity of economic policy, while remembering that this fixity must not be fossilization, that there must not be inability to shape our course anew to meet the shifting needs of the people as these needs arise.

"There are real and great evils in our social and economic life, and these evils stand out with ugly baldness during good times, for the wicked who prosper are never a pleasant sight. There is every need of striving in all possible ways, individually and collectively, by combinations among ourselves in private life and through the recognized organs of Government, for the cutting out of these evils. Only let us be sure that we do not use the knife with an ignorant zeal which would make it more dangerous to the patient than to the disease.

GROWTH OF INDUSTRIALISM.

"One of the features of the tremendous industrial growth of the last generation has been the very great increase in large private, and especially in large corporate, fortunes. We may like this or not, just as we please, but it is a fact, nevertheless, and as far as we can see it is an inevitable result of the working of various causes, prominent among which has been the immense importance steam and electricity have assumed in modern life.

"Urban population has grown in this country, as in all civilized countries, much faster than the population as a whole during the last century, and where men are gathered together in great masses it inevitably results that they must work far more largely by means of combinations among themselves than when they live isolated from one another.

"Now, I suppose that most of us prefer on many accounts the old conditions of life, under which the average man lived more to himself and by himself, when the average community was more self-dependent, and where, even though the standard of comfort was lower on the average, yet there was less of the glaring inequality in worldly conditions which we now see in our great cities.

"It is not true that the poor have grown poorer, but some of the rich have grown so very much richer, that where multitudes of men are herded together in a limited space the contrast strikes the onlooker as more violent than formerly. On the whole, our people earn more and live better than ever before, and the progress of which we are so proud could not have taken place had it not been for the great upbuilding of industrial centres, such as our commercial and manufacturing cities. But together with the good there has come a measure of evil. Life is not so simple as it was, and surely both for the individual and the community the simple life is normally the healthy life. There is not in the cities the same sense of common underlying brotherhood which there is still in country localities, and the lines of social cleavage are far more clearly marked.

"For some of the evils which have attended upon the good of the changed conditions we can at present see no complete remedy. For others the remedy must come by the action of men themselves in their private capacity, whether merely as individuals or by combination one with another. For yet others some remedy can be found in legislative and executive action, National, State, or municipal. Much of the complaint against combinations is entirely unwarranted. Under present-day conditions it is as necessary to have corporations in the business world as it is to have organization among wage workers.

THE VALUE OF GREAT WEALTH.

"But we have a right to ask in each case that they shall do good and not harm. Exactly as labor organizations, when managed intelligently and in a spirit of justice and fair play, are of very great service not only to the wage workers, but to the whole community, (as the history of many labor organizations has conclusively shown,) so wealth, not merely individual, but corporate, when used aright is not merely a benefit to the community as a whole, but indispensable to the upbuilding of the country, under the conditions, which at present the country has grown not only to accept, but to demand as normal. This is so obvious that it seems trite even to state it, and yet if we are to judge from some of the arguments advanced against, and attacks made upon, wealth, as such, it is a fact worth keeping in mind.

"A great fortune, if not used aright, makes its possessor in a peculiar sense a menace to the community as a whole, just as a great intellect does if it is unaccompanied by developed conscience, by character. But obviously this no more affords grounds for condemning wealth than it does for condemning intellect. Every man of power by the very fact of that power is capable of doing damage to his neighbors, but we cannot afford to discourage the development of such merely because it is possible they may use their power to wrong ends.

"If we did so we should leave our history a blank, for we should have no great statesmen, soldiers, or merchants, no great men of arts, of letters, or of science. Doubtless on the average the most useful men to his fellow-citizens is apt to be he to whom has been given what the Psalmist prayed for—neither poverty nor riches—but the great captain of industry, the man of wealth, who alone or in combination with his fellows drives through our great business enterprises, is a factor without which this country could not possibly maintain its present industrial position in the world.

"Good, not harm, normally comes from the piling up of wealth through business enterprises. Probably the most serious harm resulting to us, the people of moderate means, is when we harm ourselves by letting the dark and evil vices of envy and hatred toward our fellows eat into our natures.

"Still there is other harm of a more evident kind, and such harm it is our clear duty to try to eradicate if possible and in any event to minimize. The corporations—and therefore those great corporations containing some tendency to monopoly which we have grown to speak of rather loosely as trusts—are the creatures of the State, and the State not only has the right to control them, but is in duty bound to control them wherever the need for such control is shown.

TO REGULATE CORPORATIONS.

"There is clearly a need of supervision—need to exercise the power of regulation on the part of the representatives of the public—wherever in our own country at the present time business corporations become so very strong both for beneficent work and for work that is not always beneficent. It is idle to say that there is no need for such supervision. A sufficient warrant for it is to be found over and over again in any of the various evils resulting from the present system, or rather lack of system.

"There is in our country a peculiar difficulty in the way of exercising such supervision and control because of the peculiar division of governmental power. When the industrial conditions were simple, very little control was needed, and no trouble was caused by the doubt as to where power was lodged under the Constitution. Now the conditions are complicated, and we find it difficult to frame National legislation which shall be adequate, while as a matter of practical experience State action has proved entirely insufficient, and in all human probability can not or will not be made sufficient, to meet the needs of the case.

"Some of our States have excellent laws—laws which it would be well, indeed, to have enacted by the National Legislature. But the wide differences in these laws, even between adjacent States, and the uncertainty of the power of enforcement result practically in altogether insufficient control. I believe that the Nation must assume this power of control by legislation, and if it becomes evident that the Constitution will not permit needed legislation, then by Constitutional amendment.

"The immediate need in dealing with trusts is to place them under the real, not nominal, control of some sovereign to which, as its creature, the trusts shall owe allegiance, and in whose courts the sovereign's orders may with certainty be enforced. This is not the case with the ordinary so-called 'trust' to-day, for the trust is a large State corporation, generally doing business in other States also, and often with a tendency to monopoly.

"Such a trust is an artificial creature not wholly responsible to or controllable by any Legislature, nor wholly subject to the jurisdiction of any one court. Some governmental sovereign must be given full power over these artificial and very powerful corporate beings. In my judgment this sovereign must be the National Government. When it has been given full power then this full power can be used to control any evil influence, exactly as the Government is now using the power conferred upon it under the Sherman anti-trust law.

REMEDY MUST BE GRADUAL.

"Even when the full power has been conferred it would be highly undesirable to attempt too much or to begin by stringent legislation. The mechanism of modern business is as delicate and complicated as it is vast, and nothing would be more productive of evil to all of us, and especially to those least well off in this world's goods, than ignorant meddling with this mechanism, and above all, if the meddling was done in a spirit of class or sectional rancor.

"It is desirable that this power should be possessed by the Nation, but it is quite as desirable that the power should be exercised with moderation and self-restraint. The first exercise of that power should be the securing of publicity among all great corporations doing an inter-State business. The publicity, though non-inquisitorial, should be real and thorough as to all important facts with which the public has concern.

"The full light of day is a great discourage of evil. Such publicity would by itself tend to cure the evils of which there is just complaint, and where the alleged evils are imaginary it would tend to show that such was the case. When publicity is attained it would then be possible to see what further should be done in the way of regulation.

"Above all, it behooves us to remember not only that we ought to try to do what we can, but that our success in doing it depends very much upon our neither attempting nor expecting the impossible. Distrust the man who offers you a patent cure-all for the evils of the body politic just as you would distrust him who tries to sell you a medicine to cure all the diseases of your corporal bodies.

"Mankind has moved slowly upward through the ages, sometimes a little faster, sometimes a little slower; but rarely indeed by leaps and bounds. At times a great crisis comes in which a great people, perchance led by a great man, can at white heat strike some mighty blow for the right—make some long stride in advance along the path of orderly liberty and justice. But normally we must be content if each of us can do something, by no means all that we wish, but still something, for the advancement of those principles of righteousness which underlie all real National greatness, all real civilization.

"I see no promise of a complete solution for all the problems we group together when we speak of the trust question. But we can make a beginning in solving these problems, and a good beginning, if only we approach the subject with a sufficiency of resolution, of honesty, and of that hard common sense which is one of the most valuable and unfortunately not one of the most common assets in the equipment of any people.

CURE LIES WITH THE PEOPLE.

"I think the National Administration has shown its firm intention to enforce the laws as they now stand on the statute books, without regard to persons, and I think that good has come from this enforcement. I think, furthermore, that additional legislation should be had, and can be had, which will enable us to accomplish much more than has been accomplished along these same lines. No one can promise you a perfect solution, at least in the immediate future; but something has already been done, and much more can be done if our people temperately and determinedly will that it shall be done.

"In conclusion let me add one word. While we are not to be excused if we fail to do whatever is possible through the agency of Government we must ever keep in mind that no action by the Government, no action by any combination among ourselves, can take the place of the individual qualities to which in the long run each man must owe his success. There never has been devised, and there never will be devised, any law which will enable a man to succeed save by the exercise of those qualities which have always been the prerequisites of success—the qualities of hard work, of keen intelligence, of unflinching will.

"No action by the State in any form can do more than supplement the initiative of the individual, and ordinarily the action of the State can do no more than secure to each individual the chance to show, under as favorable conditions as possible, the stuff of which he is made.

August 24, 1902

ANTI-TRUST BILL INDORSED.

Elkins Measure Prohibiting Rate Discrimination Unanimously Approved by Senate Committee.

Special to The New York Times.

WASHINGTON, Jan. 26.—The Senate Committee on Inter-State Commerce to-day unanimously agreed to report the Elkins amendment to the Inter-State Commerce act. Only two members of the committee were absent, Patterson of Colorado and McLaurin of Mississippi, and both are in favor of the measure. The bill as prepared by Senator Elkins gives vital force to the original Inter-State Commerce act by imposing heavy penalties for violation of the law. The range of fines is from $1,000 to $20,000 for any such offense.

The essential part of the bill, which was to-day amended by the committee, so as to make it stronger than as drawn by its author, is as follows:

It shall be unlawful for any person, persons, or corporation to offer, grant, or give, or to solicit, accept, or receive any rebate, concession, or discrimination in respect of the transportation of any property in inter-State or foreign commerce by any common carrier subject to the acts to regulate commerce whereby any such property shall by any device whatever be transported at a less rate than that named in the tariffs published and filed by such carrier as is required by said acts to regulate commerce or whereby any other advantage is given or discrimination is practiced.

Every person or corporation who shall offer, grant, or give, or solicit, accept, or receive any such rebates, concession, or discrimination shall be deemed guilty of a misdemeanor, and on conviction thereof shall be punished by a fine of not less than $1,000 nor more than $20,000.

The committee put on an amendment providing that every violation of the law shall be prosecuted in any court of the United States having jurisdiction of crimes within the district in which such violation was committed or through which the transportation may have been conducted; and whenever the offense is begun in one jurisdiction and completed in another, it may be dealt with, inquired of, tried, determined, and punished in either jurisdiction in the same manner as if the offense had been actually and wholly committed therein.

Another amendment makes the act of the agent or officer the act of the corporation also. A third amendment, as follows, was adopted:

Whenever any carrier files with the Inter-State Commerce Commission or publishes a particular rate, or participates in any rates so filed or published, that rate as against such carrier, its officers, or agents in any prosecution, shall be conclusively deemed to be the legal rate, and any departure from such rate or any offer to depart therefrom shall be deemed to be an offense under this section of this act.

The fact that the Democrats on the committee were unanimously in favor of the bill is taken as significant of the merit of the measure and of the undivided support of the bill by the Democrats when it comes before the Senate. It is not unlikely that there will be a disposition to amend the bill in the House with a clause making its terms applicable to pooling as well as rebates.

January 27, 1903

Elkins Rebate Bill Is Signed.

WASHINGTON, Feb. 20.—The President late this afternoon signed the Elkins rebate bill. With the signing of this measure the Administration's anti-trust programme for this session of Congress is completed.

February 21, 1903

SUPREME COURT WRECKS MERGER

Northern Securities Company an Unlawful Combination.

DECISION BY CLOSE MARGIN

Minority of Four Declare the Doctrine Enunciated Might Lead to Interference With State and Personal Freedom.

Special to The New York Times.

WASHINGTON, March 14.—The United States Supreme Court to-day handed down an opinion in the merger case of the United States versus the Northern Securities Company, sustaining the contention of the Government that the railroad merger was illegal, and affirming the judgment of the United States Circuit Court of Appeals.

The decision was reached only by the narrowest possible margin, the alignment of the Justices being five to four. Justices Harlan, Brewer, Brown, McKenna, and Day formed the majority, while Chief Justice Fuller and Justices Holmes, White, and Peckham dissented. The narrowness of the Government's victory is accentuated by the fact that though Justice Brewer assents to the judgment of the majority, he reaches his conclusion by a different course of argument and writes a separate opinion to explain his views.

The Prevailing Opinion

The prevailing opinion was written by Justice Harlan and proceeded on the theory that Congress has a right under the Constitution to control inter-State commerce, no matter how conducted.

Justice Harlan holds that the evidence shows the Northern Securities Company to constitute such restraint of inter-State commerce as violates the Anti-Trust act and that the original purpose of the merger was to prevent competition between its constituent companies.

"The mere existence of such a combination," says Justice Harlan, "constitutes a menace to the freedom of commerce which the public is entitled to have protected.

Justice Harlan goes on to hold that the Anti-Trust act is not limited to application in unreasonable restraints on trade and commerce, but applies to all such restraints, reasonable or unreasonable, and declares that an act of Congress, constitutionally passed, "is binding upon all as much as if it were included in terms in the Constitution itself."

It is held that the court, having found an unlawful combination, has the power to end its existence.

Justice Brewer in his separate opinion expresses the view that recent anti-trust decisions have gone too far, and holds that the anti-trust act should not be interpreted as applying to reasonable restraints on commerce, but only to unreasonable ones. He is, however, persuaded that the formation of the Northern Securities Company constitutes such an unreasonable restraint.

Views of Dissenters.

Justice Holmes, in behalf of the minority, protested against the decision on the ground that it interfered with the exercise of powers incidental to the ownership of property. He declared that such a doctrine might be extended so that "the advice or mere existence of one man might be a crime."

Justice White declared that mere ownership of stock in a State corporation could in no sense be held to be an interference with traffic between States. Such a doctrine, he asserted, would give power to Congress to control the organization of all railroads doing an inter-State business, and to abrogate every charter and every consolidation of such lines. Such power might even extend to the prevention of organization of labor associations.

"Indeed," he said, "the doctrine must in reason lead to a concession of the right in Congress to regulate concerning the aptitude, the character, and capacity of persons."

The decree of the Circuit Court which was affirmed "enjoined the Securities Company, its officers and stockholders:

"From acquiring or attempting to acquire any more of such stock.

"From exercising or attempting to exercise any control, direction, supervision, or influence on the acts of either railway company by virtue of its holding of stock therein.

"From paying any dividends on such stock to the Securities Company.

"From permitting the Securities Company or its officers, &c., to exercise any control over the corporate acts of such railway companies."

An Expectant Audience.

An effort was made by the court to prevent knowledge of the fact that the opinion was to be rendered to-day from getting to the public, but when the members of the court filed into the chamber at noon they were awaited by an expectant crowd which filled every seat.

Attorney General Knox and Secretary Taft and an unusual number of Senators and members of the House of Representatives were present when Justice Harlan began the delivery of the opinion. The Justice read his opinion from a printed copy, which consumed about an hour and a quarter in its delivery.

All told, the court consumed two hours and three-quarters in disposing of the case. The fact was noted by several persons that the argument in the case was begun Dec. 14, just three months previous to the decision. For so important a case, this is considered a very brief interim between the arguments and the decision.

The case decided was originally brought by the United States against the Northern Securities Company, a corporation of New Jersey; the Great Northern Railway Company, a corporation of Minnesota; the Northern Pacific Railway Company, a corporation of Wisconsin; James J. Hill, a citizen of Minnesota, and William P. Clough, D. Willis James, John S. Kennedy, J. Pierpont Morgan, Robert Bacon, George F. Baker, and Daniel Lamont, citizens of New York.

THE PREVAILING OPINION.

Justice Harlan's Statement of the Majority's Views.

WASHINGTON, March 14.—Justice Harlan writes the opinion subscribed to by four out of the five Justices who constituted a majority. After announcing the origin and the purpose sought to be accomplished by the suit Justice Harlan reviews the facts as disclosed by the record in the case, showing that it had grown out of a combination of the Great Northern Railway Company and the Northern Pacific Railway Company into the Northern Securities Company. He then summarizes briefly the allegations of the Government and the defense of the Securities Company. Of the Government's case he says:

"The Government charges that if the combination was held not to be in violation of the act of Congress, then all efforts of the National Government to preserve to the people the benefit of free competition among carriers engaged in inter-State commerce will be wholly unavailing, and all transcontinental lines, indeed the entire railway systems of the country, may be absorbed, merged, and consolidated, thus placing the public at the absolute mercy of the holding corporation." Of the defendant's case Justice Harlan says:

"The several defendants denied all the allegations of the bill imputing to them a purpose to evade the provisions of the act of Congress or to form a combination or conspiracy having for its object either to restrain or to monopolize commerce or trade among the States or with foreign nations. They denied that any combination or conspiracy was formed in violation of the act."

Justice Harlan then comes immediately to the judicial consideration of the case and practically indicates the decision of the court in the first sentence of the opinion proper. In that sentence he says:

Act of Congress Violated.

"In our judgment the evidence fully sustains the material allegations of the bill, and shows a violation of the act of Congress, in so far as it declares illegal every combination or conspiracy in restraint of commerce among the several States and with foreign nations, and forbids attempts to monopolize such commerce."

He again recurs to the facts in the case and says that laying aside any minor things it is indisputable that upon the principal facts of the record under the leadership of Hill and Morgan the stockholders of the two railroad companies, having practically parallel lines of road, had combined under the laws of New Jersey by organizing a corporation for the holding of the shares of the two companies upon an agreed basis of value. Proceeding, he says:

"The stockholders of these two competing companies disappeared, as such, for the moment, but immediately reappeared as stockholders of the holding company, which was thereafter to guard the interests of both sets of stockholders as a unit, and to manage, or cause to be managed, both lines of railroad as if held in one ownership.

"Necessarily by this combination or arrangement the holding company in the fullest sense dominates the situation. Necessarily, also, the constituent companies ceased, under such a combination, to be in active competition for trade and commerce along their respective lines, and have become practically one powerful consolidated corporation, the principal, if not sole, object for the formation of which was to carry out the purpose of the original combination under which competition between the constituent companies would cease."

To Prevent Competition.

Justice Harlan says that the stockholders of the two old companies are now united in their interest in preventing all competition between the two lines, and that they would "take care that no persons are chosen Directors of the holding company who will permit competition between the constituent companies, the result being that all the earnings of the constituent companies make a common fund in the hands of the Securities Company upon the basis of the certificates of stock issued by the holding company. No scheme or device could more certainly come within the words of the act, 'combination in the form of a trust or otherwise * * * in restraint of commerce among the States or with foreign nations,' or could more effectively and certainly suppress free competition between the constituent companies.

"This combination is, within the meaning of the act, a 'trust'; but if not, it is a combination in restraint of inter-State and international commerce, and that is enough to bring it under the condemnation of the act. The mere existence of such a combination, and the power acquired by the holding company as trustee for the combination, constitute a menace to and a restraint upon that freedom of commerce which Congress intended to recognize and protect, and which the public is entitled to have protected.

"If not destroyed, all the advantages that would naturally come to the public under the operation of the general law of competition, as between the Great Northern and Northern Pacific Railway Companies, will be lost, and the entire commerce of the immense territory in the northern part of the United States between the great lakes and the Pacific at Puget Sound will be at the mercy of a single holding corporation, organized in a State distant from the people of that territory."

Justice Harlan agrees with the summing up by the Circuit Court of the results of the combination, which was that it places the control of the two roads in the hands of a single person, and, second, that it destroys every motive for competition between the two lines by pooling their earnings, notwithstanding both were engaged in inter-State traffic.

Anti-Trust Act's Application.

Entering upon an investigation of the authorities bearing upon the case, Justice Harlan deduces the following propositions as applied to the present case:

"That although the act of Congress known as the Anti-Trust act has no reference to the mere manufacture and production of articles or commodities within the limits of the several States, it embraces and declares to be illegal every contract, combination, or conspiracy, in whatever form, of whatever nature, and whoever may be parties to it, which directly or necessarily operates in restraint of trade or commerce among the several States or with foreign nations.

"That the act is not limited to restraints of inter-State and international trade or commerce that are unreasonable in their nature, but is directed against all direct restraints, reasonable or unreasonable, imposed by any combination, conspiracy, or monopoly upon such trade or commerce.

"That railroad carriers engaged in inter-State or international trade or commerce are embraced by the act.

"That combinations even among private manufacturers or dealers whereby inter-State or international commerce is restrained are equally embraced by the act.

"That Congress has the power to establish rules by which inter-State and international commerce shall be governed, and, by the Anti-Trust act, has prescribed the rule of free competition among those engaged in such commerce.

"That every combination or conspiracy which would extinguish competition between otherwise competing railroads engaged in inter-State trade or commerce is made illegal by the act.

"That the natural effect of competition is to increase commerce, and an agreement whose direct effect is to prevent this play of competition, restrains instead of promotes trade and commerce.

"That to vitiate a combination, such as the act of Congress condemns, it need not be shown that such combination results in a total suppression of trade or in a complete monopoly, but that by its necessary operation it tends to restrain inter-State or international trade or commerce or tends to create a monopoly in such trade or commerce and to deprive the public of the advantages that flow from free competition.

"That the constitutional guarantee of liberty of contract does not prevent Congress from prescribing the rule of free competition for those engaged in inter-State and international commerce.

The State's Rights View.

"That under its power to regulate commerce among the several States and foreign nations, Congress had authority to enact the statute in question."

Justice Harlan takes up the contentions of the counsel for the Securities Company, and in presenting them said that "underlying their argument is the idea that as the Northern Securities Company is a corporation, and as its acquisition of the stock of the railroad companies is not consistent with the powers conferred by its charter, the enforcement of the act of Congress as against these corporations will be in its operation an interference by the National Government with the internal commerce of the States creating those corporations." To this objection Justice Harlan replies:

"This view does not impress us. There is no reason to suppose that Congress had any purpose to interfere with the internal affairs of the States, nor is there any ground whatever for the contention that the Anti-Trust act regulates their domestic commerce. By its very terms the act regulates only commerce among the States and in the foreign States.

"Viewed in that light the act must be respected. By the explicit words of the Constitution that instrument and the laws enacted by Congress in pursuance of its provisions, are the supreme laws of the land, 'anything in the Constitution or the laws of any State to the contrary notwithstanding,' supreme over the States, over the courts, and even over the people of the United States, the source of all power under our governmental system in respect of the objects for which the Constitution was ordained.

Constitution and the Law.

"An act of Congress constitutionally passed under its power to regulate commerce among the States and with foreign States is binding upon all, as much as if it were embodied in terms in the Constitution itself. Every judicial officer, whether of a National or a State court, is under the obligations of an oath to so regard a lawful enactment of Congress. Not even a State, still less one of its artificial creatures, can stand in the way of its enforcement. If it were otherwise, the Government and its laws might be prostrated at the feet of local authority."

He brushes aside as scarcely worth mentioning the contention on the part of the securities company that the question involved is the right of an individual to dispose of his stock in a State corporation, saying:

"It is unnecessary in this case to consider such abstract general questions. They are not here to be examined and determined, and may as well be left for consideration in some cases necessarily involving their determination."

Justice Harlan also refers to the argument that the position of the Government amounts to declaring that the ownership of stock in a railroad corporation is in itself inter-State commerce, and to other similar declarations, and, commenting upon these, he says:

"We do not understand that the Government makes any such contentions or takes any such positions as those statements imply. It does not contend that Congress may control the mere ownership of stock in a State corporation engaged in inter-State commerce. It does not contend that Congress can control the organization or mere ownership of State corporations, authorized by their charters to engage in inter-State and international commerce, but it does contend that Congress may protect the freedom of inter-State commerce by any means that are appropriate and are lawful and not prohibited by the Constitution.

The Government's Case.

"It does contend that no State corporation can stand in the way of the enforcement of the National will, legally expressed. What the Government particularly complains of, indeed, all that it complains of here, is the existence of a combination among the stockholders of competing railroads which in violation of the act of Congress restrains inter-State commerce through the agency of a common corporate Trustee designated to act for both companies in repressing free competition between them."

The opinion then takes up the right of Congress to enact such legislation as the anti-trust law, and goes into an inquiry as to how far the courts may go in order to give effect to such an act and to remedy the evils designed to be suppressed by it. Quoting the famous declaration of the court in the case of McCulloch vs. Maryland, that the Government ordained and established by the Constitution is, within the limits of the powers granted to it, "the Government of all; that it represents and acts for all and is supreme within its sphere of action," Justice Harlan says it is the intention of legislation of this character to prescribe a rule for inter-State and international commerce which should prevent vexation by combinations, conspiracies, or monopolies which restrain commerce by destroying or restricting competition. He then adds:

"We say that Congress has prescribed such a rule, because in all the prior cases in this court the Anti-Trust act has been construed as forbidding any combination which by its necessary operation destroys or restricts free competition among those engaged in inter-State commerce; in other words, that to destroy or restrict free competition in inter-State commerce was to restrain such commerce. Now can this court, in reason, say that such a rule is prohibited by the Constitution, or is not one that Congress could appropriately prescribe when exerting its power under the commerce clause of the Constitution?

"Whether the free operation of the normal laws of competition is a wise and wholesome rule for trade and commerce is an economic question which this court need not consider or determine. Many persons we may judicially know of wisdom, experience, and learning believe that such a rule is more necessary in these days of enormous wealth than it ever was in any former period of our history; indeed, that the time has come when the public needs to be protected against the exactions of corporations wielding the power which attends the possession of unlimited capital.

Restraint of Trade.

"Be this as it may, Congress has, in effect, recognized the rule of free competition, when declaring illegal every combination or conspiracy in restraint of inter-State and international commerce. If in the judgment of Congress the public convenience or the general welfare will be best subserved when the natural laws of competition are left undisturbed by those engaged in inter-State commerce, that must be, for all, the end of the matter, if this is to remain a Government of laws and not of men."

Taking up the contention that railroad corporations created under the laws of a State can be consolidated only with the authority of that State, Justice Harlan says that he cannot understand why this suggestion was made in this case, "for," he goes on, "there is no pretense that the combination here in question was under the authority of the States under whose laws these railroad corporations were created." In the form of an interrogation he adds:

"But even if the State allowed consolidation would it not follow that the stockholders of two or more State corporations engaged in inter-State commerce could lawfully combine and form a distinct corporation to hold the stock of the constituent corporations, and, by destroying competition between them, restrain commerce among the States and with foreign nations?" Many citations were given in response to this inquiry, all bearing upon the right of States to control their own domestic commerce.

Justice Harlan then quotes the case of Gibbons vs. Ogden to the effect that "the power over commerce with foreign nations and among the several States is vested in Congress as absolutely as it would be in a single Government having in its constitution the same restrictions on the exercise of power as are found in the Constitution of the United States."

"If a State," he continues, "may strike down combinations that restrain its domestic commerce by destroying free competition among those engaged in such commerce, what power, except that of Congress, is competent to protect the freedom of inter-State and international commerce when assailed by a combination that restrains such commerce by stifling competition among those engaged in it?"

The Anti-Trust Act.

At this point Justice Harlan announces the inadvisability of the court's concurring in the view that the Anti-Trust act is repugnant to the Constitution of the United States. "The contention of the defendant," he says, "could not be sustained without in effect overruling the prior decisions of this court as to the scope and validity of the Anti-Trust act. If, as the court has held, Congress can strike down a combination between private persons or private corporations that restrain trade among the States, in iron pipe or in tiles, grates, and mantels, surely it ought not to be doubted that Congress has power to declare illegal a combination that restrains commerce among the States and with foreign nations as carried on over the lines of competing railroad companies in the exercise of public franchises and engaged in such commerce.

"Indeed, if the contentions of the defendants are sound why may not all the railway companies in the United States that are engaged, under State charters in inter-State and international commerce enter into a combination such as the one here in question and by the device of a holding corporation obtain the absolute control throughout the entire country of rates for passengers and freight, beyond the power of Congress to protect the public against their exactions?

"The argument in behalf of the defendants necessarily leads to such results, and places Congress, although invested by the people of the United States with full authority to regulate inter-State and international commerce, in a condition of utter helplessness, so far as the protection of the public against such combinations is concerned."

Coming again to the consideration of the contention that interference by the Federal Government with the affairs of a State corporation will prevent the Securities Company from exercising its functions and will be an invasion of the rights of the State under which the company was chartered, Justice Harlan says:

"We cannot conceive how it is possible for any one to seriously contemplate such a proposition." Continuing on this line, he adds:

"We reject any such view of the relations of the National Government and the States composing the Union. It cannot be given effect without destroying the just authority of the United States. Every corporation created by a State is necessarily subject to the supreme law of the land.

"And yet, the suggestion is made that to restrain a State corporation from interfering with the free course of trade and commerce among the States, in violation of an act of Congress, is hostile to the reserved rights of the States. The Federal court may not have power to forfeit the charter of the Securities Company; it may not declare how its shares of stock may be transferred on its books, nor prohibit it from acquiring real estate, nor diminish or increase its capital stock. All these and like matters are to be regulated by the State which created the company.

Powers of the Court.

"It would be extraordinary if the court, in executing the act of Congress, could not lay hands upon that company and prevent it from dong that which, if done, will defeat the act of Congress. Upon like grounds the court, without interfering with the rights of any State, can, by appropriate orders, prevent the two competing railroad companies here involved from co-operating with the Securities Company in restraining commerce among the States. In short, the court may make any order necessary to bring about the dissolution or suppression of an illegal combination that restrains inter-State commerce.

"All this can be done without infringing in any degree upon the just authority of States. The affirmance of the judgment below will only mean that no combination, however powerful, is stronger than the law or will be permitted to avail itself of the pretext that to prevent it doing that which, if done, would defeat a legal enactment of Congress, is to attack the reserved rights of the States.

"It would mean that no device in evasion of its provisions, however skillfully such device is contrived, and no combination, by whomsoever formed, is beyond the reach of the supreme law of the land, if such device or combination by its operation directly restrains commerce among the States or with foreign nations in violation of the act of Congress."

Discussing the question as to the effect of the Anti-Trust act on financial interests, Justice Harlan says the prediction had been made that disaster to business and widespread financial ruin would follow the execution of its provisions, and he adds that such predictions had been made in connection with all preceding cases under that act, "but," he says, "they have not been verified," and continues:

"It is the history of monopolies in this country and in England that predictions of ruin are habitually made by them when it is attempted, by legislation, to restrain their operations, and to protect the public against their exactions. In this, as in former cases, they seek shelter behind the reserved rights of the States, and the constitutional guarantee of liberty of contract. But this court has heretofore adjudged that the act of Congress did not touch the rights of the States and that liberty of contract did not involve a right to deprive the public of the advantages of free competition in trade and commerce.

"But even if the court shared the gloomy forebodings in which the defendants indulge it could not refuse to respect the action of the legislative branch of the Government if what it has done is within the limits of its constitutional power. The suggestions of disaster to business have, we apprehend, their origin in the zeal of parties who are opposed to the policy underlying the act of Congress or are interested in the result of this particular case.

"At any rate, the suggestions imply that the court may and ought to refuse the enforcement of the provisions of the act if, in its judgment, Congress was not wise in prescribing, as a rule by which the conduct of inter-State and international commerce is to be governed, that every combination, whatever its form, in restraint of such commerce and the monopolizing or attempting to monopolize such commerce, shall be illegal. These plainly are questions as to the policy of legislation, which belong to the legislative department, and this court has no function to supervise such legislation from the standpoint of wisdom or policy."

The Investment Claim.

Justice Harlan sets aside as fallacious the argument that the acquisition of stock by the Northern Securities Company was in the nature of an investment, saying that there had been no actual investment in any substantial sense. In this connection he refers to Mr. Morgan as authority for the statement that the stock had been transferred to the Securities Company merely for the purpose of suppressing competition, and in support of this statement quotes the testimony of Mr. Morgan in which he had said that the Securities Company had been created a custodian because it had no other alliances.

"This," says Justice Harlan, "disclosed the actual nature of the transaction, which was only to organize the Securities Company as a holding company in whose hands, not as a purchaser or absolute owner, but simply as custodian, were to be placed the stocks of the constituent companies."

Discussing the effectiveness of the relief at the hands of the court he quotes approvingly the disposal by the Circuit Court of that point and continues:

"The Circuit Court has done only what the actual situation demanded. It could not have done less without declaring its impotency in dealing with those who have violated the law. The decree, if executed, will destroy not the property interests of the original stockholders of the constituent companies, but the power of the holding corporation, as the instrument of an illegal combination, to do that which, if done, would restrain inter-State and international commerce. The exercise of that power being restrained, the object of Congress will be accomplished; left undisturbed, the act in question will be valueless for any practical purpose."

Attention also is given to the argument that the Anti-Trust act must be strictly construed in its criminal features. Quoting a number of authorities on this subject, Justice Harlan says:

"Guided by these long-established rules of construction, it is manifest that if the Anti-Trust act is held not to embrace a case such as is now before us, the plain intention of the legislative branch of the Government will be defeated. If Congress has not, by the words used in the act, described this and like cases, it would, we apprehend, be impossible to find words that would describe them. The defendants have no just cause to complain of the decree in matter of law, and it should be affirmed." Justice Harlan in conclusion says:

"The judgment of the court is that the decree below be and hereby is affirmed, with liberty to the Circuit Court to proceed in the execution of its decree as the circumstances may require."

March 15, 1904

MINORITY SEE PERIL IN MERGER DECISION

Dissenting Opinions Deprecate Court's View of Anti-Trust Act.

FOUR JUSTICES OPPOSED

Mr. Holmes Holds Sherman Law to be of a Criminal Nature—Rights of Property Declared Affected.

WASHINGTON, March 14.—Chief Justice Fuller and Justices White, Peckham, and Holmes, who dissent from the prevailing opinion in the Northern Securities case, present two opinions giving their reasons for not agreeing with the majority of the course in the decision reached. The first of these was delivered by Justice Holmes, and the second by Justice White. Justice Holmes in his opinion contends that the anti-trust statute is of a criminal nature, and says:

"It is vain to insist that this is not a criminal proceedings. The words cannot be read one way in a suit which is to end in fine and imprisonment, and another way in one which seeks an injunction.

"I am no friend of artificial interpretations because the statute is of one kind rather than another, but all agree that before a statute is to be taken to punish that which always has been lawful it must express its intent in clear words. So I say we must read the words before us as if the question were whether two small exporting grocers should go to jail."

Justice Holmes concedes, he says, for the purpose of discussion that Congress may take steps not only to regulate commerce but also to regulate instruments of commerce or contracts, the bearing of which upon commerce will be only indirect. But the mere fact of an indirect effect on commerce not shown to be certain, he argues would not justify such a law.

Referring to the contention as to the effect the acquisition of the stock of the Great Northern and Northern Pacific Railroad Companies would have in preventing competition between the two roads, Justice Holmes says:

"If such a remote result of the exercise of an ordinary incident of property and personal freedom is enough to make that exercise unlawful, there is hardly any transaction concerning commerce between the States that may not be made a crime by the finding of a jury or a court.

"The personal ascendency of one man may be such that it would give to his advice the effect of a command, if he owned but a single share in each road. The tendency of his presence in the stockholders' meetings might be certain to prevent competition, and thus his advice, if not his mere existence, become a crime."

Anti-Trust Act's Meaning.

Referring to the popular impression concerning the intention of the anti-trust law, Justice Holmes says:

"There is a natural feeling that some how or other the statute meant to strike at combinations great enough to cause just anxiety on the part of those who love their country more than money, while it viewed such little ones as I have supposed with just indifference.

"This notion, it may be said, somehow breathes from the pores of the act, although it seems to be contradicted in every way by the words in detail. And it has occurred to me that it might be that when a combination reached a certain size it might have attributed to it more of the character of a monopoly merely by virtue of its size than would be attributed to a smaller one.

"I am quite sure that it is only in connection with monopolies that size could play any part. In the first place size in the case of railroads is an inevitable incident, and if it were an objection under the act, the Great Northern and the Northern Pacific already were too great and encountered the law.

"In the next place, in the case of railroads, it is evident that the size of the combination is reached for other ends than those which would make themselves monopolies. The combinations are not formed for the purpose of excluding others from the field.

"Finally, even a small railroad will have the same tendency to exclude others from its narrow area that great ones have to exclude others from a greater one, and the statute attacks the small monopolies as well as the great. The very words of the act make such a distinction impossible in this case, and it has not been attempted in express terms."

He does not expect, he says, to hear it contended that Mr. Morgan could be sent to jail for buying in his individual capacity shares of stock of the two railroad companies, even if he bought them both at the same time and got more than half of the stock of each road.

"Yet," he says, "unless I am entirely wrong in my understanding of what a combination in restraint of trade means, then the same monopoly may be attempted and effected by an individual, and is made equally illegal in the case of Section 2.

"The law says nothing about competition, and only prevents its suppression by contracts or combinations in restraint of trade, and such contracts or combinations derive their character as restraining trade from other features than the suppression of competition alone."

JUSTICE WHITE'S OPINION.

Justice White's opinion was of considerable length. He bases it upon what he says are the two principal questions at issue. These, he says, are:

"Does the anti-trust act when rightly interpreted apply to the acquisition and ownership by the Northern Securities Company of the stock in the two railroads; and, second, if it does, had Congress the power to regulate or control such acquisition and ownership?"

In considering the question of power Justice White proceeds on the assumption that the anti-trust act forbids the acquisition of a majority of the stock of two competing railroads engaged in inter-State commerce by a corporation, but he holds that the point at issue really is whether Congressional supervision extends to the regulation of the ownership of stock in railroads, which is, he says, not commerce at all.

He dwells on the necessity for observing this distinction. "Does," he goes on, "the delegation of authority to Congress to regulate commerce among the States embrace the power to regulate the ownership of stock in State corporations because such corporations may be in part engaged in inter-State commerce? Certainly not, if such question is to be governed by the definition of commerce as given in the case of Gibbons vs. Ogden."

Justice White then holds that stock ownership in a State corporation cannot be said to be in any sense traffic between the States or intercourse between them. Power to control the ownership on inter-State railroads, he contends, necessarily would embrace their organization.

"Hence it would result," says the Justice, "that it would be in the power of Congress to abrogate every such railroad charter granted by the State from the beginning if Congress deemed that the rights conferred by such State charters tended to restrain commerce between the States or to create a monopoly concerning the same.

"Besides, if the principle be acceded to it must in reason be held to embrace every consolidation of State railroads which may do an inter-State commerce business, even though such consolidation may have been expressly authorized by the laws of the States creating the corporations."

Justice White says that the evil sought to be remedied in this case is the restraint of inter-State commerce. "Yet the decree," he says, "whilst forbidding the use of stock by the Northern Securities Company authorizes its return to the alleged conspirators, and does not restrain them from exercising the control resulting from the ownership.

"If the conspiracy and combination which existed was illegal, my mind falls to perceive why it should be left to produce its full force and effect in the hands of the individuals by whom it was charged the conspiracy was entered into."

Ownership by an Individual.

He contends that ownership by an individual is equally repugnant to the Anti-trust act with ownership by corporation.

Justice White takes issue with the proposition of the Government that Congressional power over inter-State commerce includes authority to regulate the instrumentalities of such commerce and to regulate the ownership and possession of property if the enjoyment of such rights would enable those who possess them, if they engaged in inter-State commerce, to exert a power over the same.

This proposition he asserts only states in another form that the right to acquire the stock is inter-State commerce, and therefore within the authority of Congress, and is refuted by the reasons and authorities already advanced to the effect that the proposition, if adopted, would extend the power of Congress to all subjects essentially local. He adds:

"Under this doctrine, the sum of property to be acquired by individuals or by corporations, the contracts which they would make, would be within the regulating power of Congress. If the wage-earner organized to better his condition, and Congress believed that the existence of such organization would give power if it were exerted, to effect inter-State commerce Congress could forbid the organization of all labor associations.

"Indeed, the doctrine must in reason lead to a concession of the right in Congress to regulate concerning the aptitude, the character, and capacity of persons."

March 15, 1904

THE TRUSTS AND THE PRESIDENT.

When MARK HANNA went up and down the Wall Street district in 1896 gathering funds for the McKinley campaign the motives of the men who responded to his appeals were very different from the motives of the chiefs of the Trusts who are now giving great sums to Chairman CORTELYOU or Senator ALDRICH to aid Mr. ROOSEVELT'S campaign. Then the Presidents or Treasurers of great corporations gave as a patriotic duty; in some cases Boards of Directors by formal vote authorized the expenditure as a contribution for the public defense. The country's business interests, its financial stability, its honor, were felt to be in peril. The threatened injury was the concern of all.

It is from no motive of patriotism, not even from motives of partisanship, that the Trusts, the industrial combinations, and the great railroad systems now contribute their tens of thousands of dollars to the Roosevelt campaign fund. There is no common danger. The body politic is not in peril. It is their own safety that these gentlemen are buying, as they think. In countless speeches—not in this campaign, much earlier—Mr. ROOSEVELT has portrayed to the people the ferocious features of the great and hungry trusts. He has insisted that they must be restrained, and in one notable instance he set in motion the machinery of the law to such good purpose that he not only restrained but destroyed. The Trusts stood in terror of him. They have not altogether got over their terror, but they are resolved to employ the most effective means at their command to secure, each for himself, immunity from pursuit and harassment by President ROOSEVELT should he be elected.

Accordingly, the checkbooks of the Trusts are opened and generous contributions are made, for the purpose, as they deem it, of buying the President. Mr. ROOSEVELT sends out Mr. CORTELYOU to make these collections from the Trusts. Instantly upon the appointment of Mr. CORTELYOU as Chairman of the Republican National Committee, the men of the Trusts perceived that the President was immediately, personally, and officially responsible for him. That a check given to CORTELYOU secures freedom from molestation by the President they firmly believe. The belief is natural, it is inevitable. The President's amazing course has made it so. Mr. CORTELYOU presents himself to these gentlemen as one who sells indulgences. Whenever he accepts a check from a Trust or from a railroad system made up of combined rival lines engaged in inter-State traffic he virtually and in effect grants a remission of Federal penance for any sins the contributor may have committed, or may in future commit, by way of restraint of trade. The President is put under obligations to the gentlemen into whose doings he might ask his Attorney General to make an official inquiry. Through his responsibility for Mr. CORTELYOU he pledges himself not to "run amuck," to begin no more terrifying proceedings against restrainers of trade or those having the power to restrain it.

These are the motives, this is the belief of the Trusts. They think they are buying the President. Mr. CORTELYOU is in all the land the most effectual campaign collector. Any corporation President who received his card would instinctively reach for his checkbook. He has been Secretary of Commerce, and officially has come into possession of a multitude of trust and corporation secrets. Even before this grave news from Washington, long before, it was understood that Mr. CORTELYOU would upon the near retirement of Mr. PAYNE be made Postmaster General. In that office he must pass upon the contracts of the railroad companies for carrying United States mails. Is any railroad President likely to overlook that probability and its implications? And this scandalous, corrupting, unspeakable business goes on every day in the week, not merely with the consent but by the authority and procurement of THEODORE ROOSEVELT.

October 3, 1904

HEPBURN RATE BILL IN.

Larger Powers for Inter-State Commission—A Court of Commerce.

Special to The New York Times.

WASHINGTON, Jan. 21.—Mr. Hepburn introduced in the House to-day his bill providing for the regulation of railroad rates. It was referred to the Inter-State Commerce Committee, of which Mr. Hepburn is Chairman, and undoubtedly will be brought from that committee within a few days with affirmative action.

The bill is regarded as a very conservative measure, and one which in the main is likely to receive general support in both houses. At the outset there is a declaration that rates shall be just, fair, and equitable, but no provision is made to fix rates except in cases where appeal is taken against alleged exorbitant charges or unjust discriminations.

Provision is made for appeal to the Inter-State Commerce Commission, which body is vested with authority to determine what shall be a just and reasonable rate. It is authorized during a judicial review of its order to modify or suspend the order under review. Carriers refusing to obey an order of the commission are subject to a penalty of $5,000 a day.

Against the decision of the commission either party may appeal to the Court of Commerce, which is established by the bill. This court is to consist of five Circuit Judges of the United States, to be designated on the first of each year by the Chief Justice of the United States Supreme Court. The President is authorized to appoint an additional Circuit Judge for each of the judicial districts of the United

States, who are authorized to perform the duties of the Judges of the Circuit Court.

An appeal from the Court of Commerce can only be taken to the Supreme Court of the United States.

The present Inter-State Commerce Commission is terminated, and provision made for a new commission to consist of seven members, each of whom is to receive an annual salary of $10,000. The commission now consists of five members, and the salary is $7,500.

The President is authorized to appoint an Assistant Attorney General for the enforcement of the act.

H. L. Bond, Jr., Vice President and general counsel of the Baltimore and Ohio Railroad, was again heard to-day by the House Committee on Inter-State and Foreign Commerce, and suggested among other things the establishment of a special court of equity, composed of circuit Judges; a larger Inter-State Commerce Commission, which when in a regular proceeding on petition finds any rate unlawful, shall find also what change is at that time necessary to make the rate lawful, and forthwith file a petition in the court praying for an adjudication of the matters embraced in the findings, as against the defendants.

January 22, 1905

PRESIDENT'S SIGNATURE AFFIXED TO RATE BILL

Special to The New York Times.

WASHINGTON, June 29.—The Senate to-day passed the Rate bill conference report and the joint resolution which makes the Rate bill go into effect sixty days after the President signs it. The President affixed his signature to the document at 11:15 to-night. Now that the bill has become a law, the House will pass the sixty-day joint resolution.

June 30, 1906

ETHICS AND ECONOMICS.

The Rev. CHARLES R. BROWN, lecturing in the Lyman Beecher course before the Yale Divinity School, declares sentiments which do his heart credit, and which will find a response in many quarters where, nevertheless, perplexity reigns regarding the practical remedy. Said Mr. BROWN: "We do not wish to wear shirts from the bargain counter if made by children who ought to have been studying or playing. We cannot consent to clothe ourselves upon the tears and blood of those who have been robbed and harmed by the effort to produce clothing cheap."

This is not a question of shirts alone. The questions raised go to the bottom of the social organization. Clergymen may dare to raise their voice against the frightful cost to humanity of competition, but no economist dare echo the cry in any legislation. Yet it is futile to demand competition and shrink from the result of competition. The wage earner who would survive must produce more or better than the incompetent. The employer who would survive must sell cheaper than his neighbor. The result is the survival of the unfittest ethically, although economically the most efficient. It is the savagery of competition which has resulted in the colossal trusts, which have wrought their own salvation only by crushing opposition. People demanded cheap products, and they got them, but at the cost of a Frankenstein whose features are only now being recognized.

Mr. BROWN'S voice is but one of the signs that the people are wearying of competition and may yet come to demand the regulation of competition. Thus in the railway rate debate nothing is clearer than the demand that rebates shall cease. Rebates are signs of competition. Abolition of rebates means so far the cessation of competition. Sentiment recognizes that a fair rate is better than an excessively low rate, which the exigencies of trade competition lead shippers to seek as a means of competing with their opponents. But how much of this economy of production and distribution will be allotted to wage earners? How much will those of Mr. BROWN'S way of thinking allow to be added to the price of what they buy? And if competition is to be abolished, what other way is there of settling what price shall be paid for anything?

In Congress they are considering fixing the price of railway service by legislation. Is this a step toward the goal fixed by Mr. BROWN? Are there enough of us of his way of thinking to embark upon experimentation in State regulation of commerce, thus giving to every producer a larger share of his product, and reducing profits of capital by forbidding "unfair" prices? Granting that ethical weariness with competition has arrived, is the community ready for the economic corollary? We ask a question which we will not undertake to answer, although the affirmative seems to be taken for granted by some newspapers which fail to perceive the distinction between aspiration and achievement, and by some legislators who pass too readily from buncombe to statute-making.

March 4, 1906

THE PACKING-HOUSE REPORT

The President in his message, and Mr. NEILL and Mr. REYNOLDS in their report upon which the message was based, set forth convincing reasons for the passage of the Beveridge amendment to the Agricultural Appropriation bill. In that part of the report made public yesterday—it appears that there is more to come if the President feels warranted in laying further installments before the people—Mr. NEILL and Mr. REYNOLDS put emphasis, not so much upon the passing of diseased meat into general consumption, as upon the almost indescribably filthy condition of the slaughter houses and the practice of the packers in preparing and canning for use as human food moldy scraps, half-putrid remnants, and other sweepings and cleanings of the slaughter houses, which, as if they were not already sufficiently offensive, are handled without any regard for decent cleanliness.

As the President points out, the inspection provided for by existing Federal laws is narrowly limited to passing upon the carcasses of slaughtered animals. No Federal Inspector examines the products prepared for canning either in respect to their fitness, or in respect to the use of chemicals and preservatives. Notwithstanding that, cans are delivered to the trade with false labels that deceive the purchaser into the belief that the contents of the can have been inspected by the Federal Government, and that their quality is "guaranteed." Over the general conditions of the slaughter houses as to cleanliness the Inspectors have no control whatever. The Beveridge bill provides for rigid inspection at all stages of the slaughtering process, and it authorizes inspection of products to be canned. More than that, it declares that "all slaughtering, canning, salting, packing, rendering, or similar establishments in which cattle, sheep, swine, and goats are slaughtered and the meat and meat-food products thereof are prepared for inter-State or foreign commerce, shall be maintained in a sanitary manner, according to the rules and regulations prescribed by the Secretary of Agriculture." It is made the duty of the Inspectors to see to the enforcing of this provision.

The enactment of the Beveridge amendment would protect the public against diseased beef, against canned stuff unfit for food, and against slaughter-house conditions judged by the Inspectors to be unclean, indecent, and dangerous to health. The President urges the immediate enactment into law of these safeguards, and the people, now that the official report upon slaughter-house conditions is before them, will resolutely support him. Upon a reform issue of this nature, which directly affects every breakfast-table and dinner-table in the land, the public will stand no trifling. President ROOSEVELT will not be trifled with, for in his message he serves notice that if adequate inspection is not secured by the passage of the legislation recommended he will "feel compelled to order that inspection labels and certificates on canned products shall not be used hereafter." That ought to bring the packers to their senses, for they must know that if the forged and false inspection label is stripped from their cans the products of their canneries will be unsalable. Indeed, the packers no less than the cattle-raisers are now in a position where they can be saved from yet more serious losses only by the passage of an amendment in the form recommended by the President. Speaker CANNON, Mr. LORIMER, and Mr. WADSWORTH will continue their opposition to the bill only at considerable peril to their political futures.

The Speaker seems to have sent the Pure Food bill to its death. Why is it that Mr. CANNON is so opposed to legislation intended to protect the people from being cheated and poisoned? We presume his constituents will take occasion to interrogate him upon this subject during the Congressional campaign.

The effect of the slaughter-house disclosures upon our export trade in meats and meat products has, of course, been seriously considered by the President. That it has been and will be disastrous cannot be doubted. The packers themselves have inflicted this loss upon the commerce of the country. The sure way to make it a permanent loss, to make certain that the meat export trade would never be built up again, is to palter with the inspection bill in the manner desired by the Speaker of the House and Mr. WADSWORTH and Mr. LORIMER. The enactment of the bill and the enforcement of its provisions will speedily restore confidence at home. The American people will go on eating meat knowing that it has been inspected, and that the slaughter houses have been put in a decent condition. Confidence abroad will be much more slowly restored, but in time, we feel sure, it will be restored. But we shall regain the lost ground only by an immediate and rigorous application of the remedies the President urges upon Congress. The meat question has become, suddenly, immeasurably the most important subject taken up by the Nation's legislators at this session. Their intelligence, their fidelity to public duty, and their regard to the public welfare will be measured by their action upon the Beveridge amendment.

June 5, 1906

WORKERS' BEST FRIENDS ARE CORPORATIONS---DAY

Chancellor of Syracuse University Denounces Meat Agitation.

ASSAILS THE PRESIDENT

Protests Against Coercion of Congress by Appeals to Popular Passion with Aid of Yellow Press.

SYRACUSE, N. Y., June 10.—Chancellor Day, in his annual baccalaureate sermon at Syracuse University to-day, reaffirmed his attitude toward large corporations, saying they were the logical result of the great stride the world is making. He again issued a warning against the assumption of too much power by the President, and in referring to the reports of conditions in Packingtown slaughter houses said that if one-hundredth part of what was printed was true people would be dying by the tens of thousands.

The sermon, in part, was as follows:

"The magnitude of our country and the immensity of its interests of about all kinds is both our glorious opportunity and our danger. We have come to our inheritance of large things, and we must take them in the proportion in which they have come to us. We must measure up to them. Great co-operative interests are not the product of human avarice nor of grinding indifference to popular rights. They are the result and the movements of a law with phenomena as unmistakable as any law in nature.

"The application and control of these mighty forces over such tremendous areas and for such amazing results is impossible to the individual. He may discover them, but men of supreme executive ability and capital must come in and develop them. The inventor is helpless until these men come to his relief.

"The economist of a century ago had no conception of times like these, and much of his philosophy is not applicable to such magnitudes and their forces.

Some Uses of Corporate Capital.

"No one can study our country, to say nothing of the world to every part of which we now are vitally and intimately related, and not see in vast corporate endeavors a simple and plain proportion. They belong to the logic of events. How could we have brought the iron from the mountains of Pennsylvania, wrought into the steel of a thousand utilities, or the oil from our valleys, or harvested the wheat and corn from Western prairies, or put a tracery of railways across the continent in every direction, or launched upon the seas steamships one of which costs millions of dollars, if men of mighty executive ability had not combined their genius and their fortunes in co-operative endeavor?

"If an individual had made your typewriter, it would have cost you $5,000. We buy it of corporations and companies representing millions of money in manufacturing machinery and skilled artisans and the amazing methods of promoting sales, for $100.

"Individuals once had the carrying trade of the country. Then you would have taken two days, traveling day and night, by stage coach from New York to Albany. And from Albany to Buffalo you would have passed over the railroads of six independent companies—one of them controlled from Utica to Syracuse and another from Syracuse to Auburn! You would have changed cars six times, and some time within the week, if you had kept on the tracks, you would have gotten from New York to Buffalo. A corporation takes you over the distance in palaces in eight hours and a quarter, with only four stops and no changes, for 2 cents a mile!

"The poor man owes more to the corporations than to any other commercial force for his opportunity to work at good wages, or to work at all, for that matter. The corporations which we sometimes thoughtlessly curse are the workingman's best friends. That there are evils to be guarded against and evils to be corrected, that there are some imperfect adjustments that fail of the largest results to the greatest number, and that do injustice to some interests, no one will dispute. But competition cannot be manufactured by legislation.

"Surely it must not be assumed that the hundreds of thousands of men of this country who represent its billions of investments and its corporate commerce are traitors to mankind upon whom war of extermination must be made. They are not buccaneers and marauders.

"And it is a thing altogether perilous at a time of such disturbed conditions with regard to Government and property and social state to sow carelessly to a whirlwind suspicion and hate, and the forming of which is already far above the horizon.

Safeguards of the Nation.

"If we cannot govern ourselves intelligently by our representatives, our Government will follow the slippery downward path of all oligarchies. Men who represent us in the judiciary and in legislative halls must be protected by public sentiment in absolute independence of their representative character which is secured to them by law, accountable to no one except to those who have sent them to be their representatives. And they must be protected in disagreement, sometimes, with the Executive and those whom they represent, as have some of the notable men of the past and present, until such time as they may be permitted to account to their constituents.

"A thousand times better continue a man in office who does not represent you upon some matters but who has the courage of his honest convictions, which compel him to differ and to so vote than a man whose agreement is servile either to the Executive or to you.

"To-day a great Congressman in Maine is threatened with defeat, and threats are muttered against a Congressman of this State and men of other States because they refuse to hand over their representative responsibility from the people to the Administration.

"They are the representatives of the people and not of the Executive, and by such representatives alone do the people have a voice in the Government. When Senators and representatives receive orders from the Executive, when appeals to popular passion are made to force them to action to which their sound judgment and honest convictions are opposed, the Government by the people and for the people becomes a misnomer and a deception. In that hour we are a monarchy without the name.

"It is to be hoped that we are not so dazed and daft by an office that has grown great with our greatness that it may be permitted to set aside courts, Senates, and Congresses.

"If it be thought by some of you that conditions do not justify our fears, I refer you to the threatened and openly threatened fate of Congressmen who have dared to be true and brave in their representative character. Why should our Senators be forced beyond their own convictions in a given case?

"Recently pressure was brought by a message, the purpose of which the Senators instantly understood and which evidently was intended to appeal to long prepared prejudices of the people. If we are a Republic, why should men of Senatorial dignity and long experience in both the House and Senate in most instances, be coerced by the arousing of popular passion, be forced to action which many of them condemned, by throwing among them the odors of a yellow press and turning upon them the riotous shouts of unreasoning hate and prejudice? This is a most dangerous stimulus. Is this the method of legislation to which this great nation has descended? Is this new way the best way to make our laws?

"The people should awaken to the danger that threatens representative government. Every man must set himself against the class and mass spirit. They are the words of the demagogue. Nothing promotes that spirit like attacks upon people in prosperous conditions by the denial of property rights or of those conditions which are made by the very law of human being. The rich must have the undisputed possession of their lawful wealth. And the man who toils with his hands must have a wage that will secure to him the sanitary comforts of his home, the education of his children, the self-respect of his family, and the courage and hope that make a man a useful member of society.

"We have fallen into a scandalmongering epoch. The foul harpies of slander have created a condition and all of the civilized world is nauseated at the thought of us. It has cost us tens of millions of money and the respect of mankind. It will and should cost us our self-respect if we do not burn out with the caustic of a hot indignation this sore of slander.

"The scandalmonger who drags the people through slaughter houses to exhibit in loathsome forms the food of their tables by exaggerations and Munchausen stories of things that always must be offensive at best are mistaken agitators and especially dangerous to us as a people at this time.

"A man writes a book or publishes a series of magazine articles and makes frantic effort to have a condition of frenzy created that will sell his foul-smelling pages to a people delirious with the fever of sensationalism. If what such a scandalmonger says were a hundredth part true the people would be dying by the tens of thousands from the poisons of the meats they eat, or the doctors all are mistaken about the toxic effect of such putrid things.

"But there are hundreds of thousands who never ask a question or apply the simplest analysis to any charge. A scare line in a yellow paper is equivalent to the verdict of a jury, and the people upon this verdict pronounce sentence of damnation.

"This is the epoch we are in. Nothing is right. Everything is wrong. Everybody is bad except the accusers. Everybody seems to be on the verge of being drawn into the filth and slime of defamation or the deadly fire damp of suspicion. Committees are sent out to bring back shocking things, and if they come back without them others are sent with more sensitive olfactories. Those whose judicial temperament unfits them for hysteria are threatened with dismissal or branded as remiss in duty. The people who wait for both sides of the case are tools of trusts.

"How long can a nation endure such a condition of things? They threaten the stability of all forms of business and create universal distrust. Shall we publish to the world that we have no courts for the correction of evils, but that we must leave such things to magazine writers and the makers of sensational literature, and the investigation of smelling committees who are seeking things to condemn, and to special executive message to be read by all nations, while the protesting voice of the accused for justice is overwhelmed and drowned in the roar of a popular frenzy and sentence is pronounced by the ex-parte verdict of the press?

"This epoch of scandalmongering will stand to our shame and to mark that strong spasmodic frenzy which arouses people in most unaccountable ways—something akin to that which causes panic when people throw aside will and reason and courage and destroy themselves when some danger is exaggerated by an excited shout of alarm.

"Our hope is in the solid, sober, Christian substratum of intelligent thinking which ever has been and ever will be the security of our institutions and the hope of our land.

"God has the making of us as a people, and in God we will put our trust, and we will, as we must, if this mighty fabric holds together, have confidence in men."

June 11, 1906

HOUSE DEFEATS SENATE ON MEAT INSPECTION

Upper House Surrenders and Government Foots the Bill.

SENATORS PROTEST IN VAIN

"We Have Been Whipped," Says Nelson, but Beveridge Says He's Satisfied—Wadsworth Gleeful.

Special to The New York Times.

WASHINGTON, June 29.—By coming into the Senate and asking permission to surrender to the House conferrees on the Meat Inspection bill Senator Proctor brought upon himself a storm of protests to-day, but in the end the Senate meekly surrendered and accepted the bill as insisted upon by the House conferrees.

As Chairman of the conferrees on the part of the Senate, Proctor's course was simply to report a disagreement or that the Senate conferrees had agreed to recede from the Beveridge amendment.

The Vermont Senator read a prepared speech, in which he declared it was surrender or nothing and the Agricultural Appropriation bill, carrying nearly $9,000,000, for one of the great departments of the Government, would stop stock still next Monday.

The announcement made a dozen Senators angry. Strangely enough, Senator Beveridge, who as the putative parent of the Meat Inspection bill for which the Senate conferrees were asking the privilege of a surrender, took a cheerful view of the disastrous situation. He congratulated the conferrees on the good fortune of surrendering under such favorable circumstances. He declared the House substitute had finally been changed in every particular except two, so that it was identically the Senate bill except as to these two particulars. The two amendments referred to were those putting the cost of the inspection on the Government and requiring packages of prepared and canned meats to be stamped with the date on which they were put up. Mr. Beveridge said he felt sure the packers were making a mistake when they objected to dating their goods, as this was the way to restore public confidence in their meats.

Believing it was better to gain the main object of the legislation than to imperil the bill by insisting on what was a minor detail, Mr. Beveridge closed by saying this inspection bill was the greatest legislative act of this end of the century and that when once it was on the statute books he would strive to secure the passage of another act requiring the packers to pay the cost and to date their packages of prepared meats.

Senator Nelson replied hotly to Beveridge that he was sorely disappointed at the surrender. "I shall go home like a licked dog. We have been whipped," said Nelson. "The packers simply got up on their hind legs and said to us, 'You shan't make us pay for this inspection.' If my young friend from Indiana thinks he will get any further legislation to bring the Meat Trust to obey the law he is mistaken. He will be a much grayer man than I am and a good deal older."

Senator Hansbrough contributed to the interest of the discussion by reading twenty telegrams from bankers, stockyard men, and cattle dealers, urging him to oppose putting the cost on the packers. Not one of them came from any beef men in his State. They were, he said, machine-made telegrams, inspired and ordered from Chicago.

Senator Simmons, speaking as the minority member of the Conference Committee on the part of the Senate, said he had been forced to agree to the report under protest because an appropriation bill was in jeopardy if he did not do so. He promised the Senate to introduce a bill next session, if no other Senator did so speedily, proposing to lay a tax on the packers, under the inter-State powers of Congress, by which the Meat Trust would be forced to reimburse the Government for every penny of the cost of inspection.

When Senator Proctor arose to ask a vote on his motion the point was made that he had presented no report, and he withdrew his motion and the conferrees retired, to report at the evening session. The House having in the meantime adopted the report of the conferrees, it was a foregone conclusion that the Senate would recede.

During the discussion of the "surrender" Mr. Wadsworth and his associate conferrees were in the Senate and listened smilingly to the denunciation of the defeat of the Senate bill.

June 30, 1906

TRUST BUSTING SINCE 1885.

Moody Shows Just What Was Done from Cleveland to Roosevelt.

WASHINGTON, June 29.—Attorney General Moody sent to the Senate to-day a statement of all suits that have been instituted by the Department of Justice under the Sherman Anti-Trust law, the Inter-State Commerce law, and the Elkins law, when brought, their character, and final disposition. The statement is divided into periods by Presidential Administrations, but attention is directed to the fact that neither the Sherman Anti-Trust law nor the Elkins law was enacted until after the close of the first Cleveland Administration and the act regulating inter-State commerce was in effect less than two years of that Administration. The Elkins law was enacted during the Administration of President Roosevelt.

Attached to the detailed statement is a summary which shows cases brought under the act to regulate commerce as follows:

Under Cleveland, 1885-1889, one indictment, which was nolle prossed.

Under Harrison, 1889-1893, 35 indictments, 5 convictions, 4 acquittals, 18 nolle prossed, 7 quashed, and 1 dismissed.

Cleveland's second term, 1893-1897, 19 indictments, 6 convictions, 1 acquittal, 8 nolle prossed, and 3 quashed.

Under McKinley, 1897, to Sept. 14, 1901, 22 indictments, 5 convictions, 1 acquittal, 4 nolle prossed, and 12 not prosecuted.

Under Roosevelt, Sept. 14, 1901, to June, 1906, 6 indictments, 5 nolle prossed, and 1 dismissed.

The cases brought under the Elkins act under Roosevelt's Administration were as follows:

Eleven indictments for receiving rebates, 19 for granting rebates, 6 for conspiring to grant rebates, a total of 36, of which 9 were convicted, 2 acquitted, 3 nolle prossed, and 22 are pending.

These figures do not include petitions to enjoin departure from published rates, actions to restrain railroads from giving preference, and minor infractions of the laws to regulate railroad rates.

Of the $500,000 appropriated to enforce these laws, $159,710 has been expended, $45,000 transferred to the Inter-State Commerce Commission, and $295,290 remains available.

June 30, 1906

HARRIMAN RAILROADS

Head of Union Pacific Now Controls 12% of Country's Mileage.

EARN $300,000,000 A YEAR

Besides the 25,000 Miles Which He Controls Harriman Has Important Voice in Other Roads.

The deposition this past week of Stuyvesant Fish from the Presidency of the Illinois Central was accomplished in a manner so characteristic of E. H. Harriman that it is not strange that the part played by the other Directors was almost ignored. It was Harriman that was pointed to as solely responsible for the defeat of Mr. Fish, despite his assertion, and that of the Directors who sided with him, that the fight was not between himself and Mr. Fish but between Mr. Fish and the Board of Directors of the road. It was all done in such obtrusive fashion that in the past week's comment on the incident the real object sought by Mr. Harriman in replacing Mr. Fish was more or less lost to sight.

While much that is personal crept into this controversy, the real motive that actuated Mr. Harriman can hardly have been a personal one. He wanted the Illinois Central, and he made up his mind that he would get it. President Fish opposed Harriman, and by doing so won his enmity. Then the fight became a personal one, and in the recriminations that passed the real meaning of the struggle was almost forgotten.

A few days before the eventful meeting of last Wednesday an intimate business associate of E. H. Harriman had this to say of the Illinois Central fight:

"I believe with Mr. Harriman that the Illinois Central and the Union Pacific ought to be in close partnership. The best interests of both roads demand that they co-operate to the fullest extent possible, and that is all that Harriman wants. There can now be no compromise in this fight, and I have not the slightest doubt that in the end Harriman will get the control of Illinois Central which he is seeking. If it does not come at next Wednesday's meeting it will at the next annual meeting."

Harriman did not wait for the annual meeting. He found himself in a position of vantage and profited by it. Another man might have done it with less disregard of conventionalities, but it is characteristic of Mr. Harriman that he does things in his own way, and then is at a loss to explain to himself why others fail to see things just as he sees them.

Control of the Illinois Central was not sought by Mr. Harriman because of any sudden whim. It had long been his fixed policy to add the Illinois Central to the already important list of Harriman roads, and he has now attained his object.

His success in this effort lends unusual interest at this time to the process of accumulation which has gathered together in the hands of Mr. Harriman by far the largest aggregation of railroad systems in the United States. It is only a few weeks ago that a very important if not a controlling voice in Baltimore & Ohio was obtained by Mr. Harriman and his associates, and now Illinois Central is added to the list.

There are in the United States, allowing for the increase in mileage during the current year, about 220,000 miles of railroads. Over 12 per cent. of this total, or approximately 25,000 miles, are now classed as Harriman roads, and the list apparently is not yet complete. For there is no reason to believe that Harriman, bold as he has been in acquiring railroads, will stop short in his policy of extending his influence in the railroad world.

Some idea of the importance of the position which Harriman has attained as a railroad leader may be had by a glance at these figures:

HARRIMAN ROADS.

	Mileage.	Capitalization.	Gross Earnings.
Union Pacific..	5,354	$457,000,000	$67,000,000
Southern Pac..	9,384	277,000,000	105,000,000
Illinois Central.	4,374	248,000,000	50,000,000
Balt. & Ohio...	4,481	211,000,000	75,000,000
Chi. & Alton...	915	104,000,000	13,000,000
Total	24,506	$1,327,000,000	$310,000,000

Large as is the percentage of these roads to the total mileage of the country, it does not tell the whole story. Harriman's influence in Chicago, Milwaukee & St. Paul is doubtless larger than has yet been openly admitted, and his and his associates' large holdings of Atchison are believed to make him by far the most important single interest in that property. Harriman's railroad interests are not always clearly distinguishable from those of the Standard Oil capitalists, but the view taken by some that Harriman is little more than an agent of the Standard Oil group apparently ignores Harriman's strong personality and his own great wealth. Were the Harriman railroads to be regarded merely as a part of what might be called Standard Oil roads, the total would represent nearer 25 per cent. than 12 per cent. of the total railroad mileage of the country. In that list St. Paul would certainly be included, and almost as surely New York Central.

It requires no effort of the imagination to realize the tremendous influence wielded by a man who personally controls the policies of corporations which together own 25,000 miles of railroads, having a combined capital in excess of $1,300,000,000 and earning in the course of a single year more than $300,000,000. That E. H. Harriman does dominate the roads that are grouped under his name few will question. Whether it is through subserviency on the part of his fellow-Directors or because of their complete confidence in Harriman's ability that Harriman is able to dictate the policy of the Union Pacific and the other roads of which he is the head is a matter apart from the present discussion. The fact remains that he does control this vast aggregation of railroads and that he is thus given a pre-eminent position in American railroad affairs.

It is not because of any result unfavorable to Mr. Harriman in a comparison between his ability as a railroad man and that of Stuyvesant Fish that apprehension was expressed in so many quarters over the passing of the Illinois Central into the control of Mr. Harriman. The explanation is found elsewhere. One reason is found in the very figures given above as an outline of Mr. Harriman's control of railroads. It is argued by Mr. Harriman's friends that he has done so well with the roads he had previously controlled that there can be no reason for uneasiness over his acquisition of another road. This, however, is not a valid argument against those who see a danger in the concentration of railroad control in a few hands. Indeed, the greater the prosperity of the roads controlled by Mr. Harriman the greater is his power.

His recent entrance into the Baltimore & Ohio and the control of Illinois Central, which he secured last week, give Mr. Harriman in connection with the roads he already controlled a line from the Pacific to the Atlantic, a line from Chicago to New Orleans, and from the latter point to the Pacific Coast. The Chicago & Alton is not, it is true, absolutely under Harriman control, but by his agreement with the Rock Island he enjoys alternately with that road the direction of Chicago & Alton affairs.

Mr. Harriman thus has two lines from the Mississippi Valley to the Pacific Coast, one in the North and the other in the South, and both joined by the newly acquired Illinois Central. The Baltimore & Ohio, over which Mr. Harriman is expected to exert still greater control in the future, supplies a line to the Atlantic Coast. It is a notable career of railroad acquisition, the latest step in which was taken at last Wednesday's meeting of the Illinois Central Directors.

November 12, 1906

TELEPHONE TRUST SERENE.

Bell Company Says Competition Has Nearly Ceased—Annual Report.

According to President Fish of the American Telephone and Telegraph Company in his annual report to the stockholders, the independent telephone companies have ceased to give serious concern to the trust, against which agitation was country-wide a few years ago.

"The so-called independent companies," says the report, "which are in competition with the Bell Companies throughout the United States have, so far as can be learned, except in a few localities, made no relative gain. It is a matter of common notoriety that many of them recognize that their situation is unstable. Comparatively few independent plants have been established in competition with the Bell during the last two years."

The report shows total earnings of $24,526,097, against $21,712,831 in 1905, and total expenses of $11,555,161, against $8,678,792 in the previous year. The payment of dividends of $10,195,233, against $9,866,355 in 1905, left a balance of $2,775,703, of which $1,773,736 was carried to reserves.

The surplus for the year was $1,001,967, against $1,424,388 in 1905. During the year the amount expended for maintenance and reconstruction by all the Bell telephone companies of the United States was $32,814,568, all of which was charged to expenses by the respective companies. "That plant," says the report, "could not be duplicated for $70,000,000. The scrap value of the lead and copper in the lines and cables alone is not less, at present prices, than $80,000,000. The amount contributed by the American Telephone Company in 1906 by way of investment in its own long-distance plant in telephones, in real estate, and in the purchase of stock and bonds and in loans to its operating companies was in all $61,141,000, an addition of almost 26 per cent. to its entire investment up to Jan. 1, 1906."

March 23, 1907

WHAT IS TO BE DONE WITH THE TRUSTS?

The Recent Decision Against Standard Oil Calls in Question $10,000,000,000 of Business. Duel Between Law and Industrial Progress.

FRANK FAYANT.

WHAT are we going to do with the trusts? For twenty years we have had on the Federal statute books a business law as drastic as any decree of the Middle Ages. It denounces all combinations—good or bad. That the law means just what it says has just been stated in very plain English by the United States Circuit Court at St. Paul, in the Government's suit against the Standard Oil Company. The Oil Trust must be destroyed. In even plainer language some months ago the Circuit Court at New York interpreted the law and ordered the dissolution of the Tobacco Trust.

All the Government now needs to do is to prepare bills of complaint against the hundreds of other trusts that have sprung up in recent years, and the courts will send to the financial scrap heap some $10,000,000,000 worth of big businesses. But is this going to happen? The wise men of old burned much midnight oil studying the problem: What happens when an irresistible force meets an immovable body? We have just such a problem now in this country. The Sherman Anti-Trust act of 1890 is an irresistible force; the big businesses of this country are an immovable body. That nearly a fifth of all the wealth of the country is in the form of corporate combinations is evidence that the Sherman act cannot be enforced.

LAW AND THE LAW BREAKER.

Features in the Tilt Between the Courts and the Trusts.

THERE'S no mistaking what the Sherman act says:

Section 1. Every contract, combination, in the form of trust or otherwise, or conspiracy in restraint of trade of commerce, among the several States or with foreign nations, is hereby declared to be illegal.

Section 2. Every person who shall monopolize, or attempt to monopolize, or combine or conspire with any other person or persons, to monopolize any part of trade or commerce among the several States, or with foreign nations, shall be deemed guilty of a misdemeanor.

Section 3. The word "person" or "persons" whenever used in this act shall be deemed to include corporations and associations.

The Government would have won its suit against the Standard Oil Company by making these two simple statements of fact:

1. The Standard Oil Company is a combination of oil companies.

2. It controls three-fourths of the oil-refining industry.

A similar bill of complaint could be made against every other industrial combination in the country, from the Steel Trust to the Chewing Gum Trust, and the courts would have to order them dissolved.

But the Government attorneys, in their attack on Standard Oil, went through its history with a fine-toothed comb and wrote a volume minutely detailing the story of its rise to power. Especially did they describe all the crimes it had committed in its forty years' rise. These crimes were chiefly:

1. Getting rebates from railroads.
2. Inducing competitors to limit output.
3. Running "fake" independent companies.
4. Stealing the secrets of their competitors' business.
5. Cutting prices at competitive points.

All this hard legal work was wasted because the court found it was "unnecessary to express any opinion" on these crimes. It made no difference to the court whether the Standard Oil Company had been burning its competitor's eyes out with hot irons or making candles by boiling babies in vats. It was a combination of competing companies, and therefore illegal.

Benefits from Trusts.

The Standard Oil lawyers likewise wasted much time telling the court of the varied economic benefits resulting from the combination—increased wealth production, command of the world's foreign trade, and low prices. But these things were of as little interest to the court as the catalogue of the company's crimes. If the Standard Oil Company had given all its profits to the poor it would have made no difference. The law denounced it for the crime of being big, and that was all there was to be said.

The Tobacco Trust had the same experience when the Government brought it into court. The court found it was a combination of competing companies and therefore illegal under the Sherman act. The court could not even find that it was a "bad trust." All its badness was in its bigness.

Judge Lacombe, who wrote the opinion, even went so far as to tell what a "good trust" it was. He said:

> The record in this case does not indicate that there has been any increase in the price of tobacco products to the consumer. There is an absence of persuasive evidence that by unfair competition or improper practices independent dealers have been dragooned into giving their individual enterprises and selling out to the principal defendant.
>
> During the existence of the American Tobacco Company new enterprises have been started—some with small capital—in competition with it, and have thriven. The price of leaf tobacco—the raw material—except for one brief period of abnormal conditions, has steadily increased until it has nearly doubled, while at the same time 150,000 additional acres have been devoted to tobacco crops and the consumption of the leaf has greatly increased. Through the enterprise of the defenants, and at large expense, new markets for American tobacco have been opened, or developed, in India, China, and elsewhere.

To Hear from Supreme Court.

The Supreme Court is yet to be heard from, for both the Oil and Tobacco Trusts will appeal to the court of last resort. The Tobacco Trust has been a near outlaw for more than a year, but this hasn't stopped it from paying $14,000,000 dividends this year on its common stock (nearly all owned by fifty shareholders) because the lower court granted a stay pending the appeal. The argument is set down for next month in Washington, and it is likely to be several months before the Supreme Court will render the final decision. That the Supreme Court will affirm the Circuit Court's decision there is little doubt. The Standard Oil appeal will follow along with the same result. Then we will be squarely facing the question, What are we going to do with the trusts?

A mere list of all the corporation "law breakers" in this country would fill several columns of THE TIMES, for nearly all the industrial companies that have been formed in recent years are combinations of competing companies. They have been organized for the purpose of restraining trade. A score of the largest of these combinations are appraised in the security markets at $5,000,000,000, and their yearly profits are running close to $500,000,000. These large "lawbreakers" are:

	Market Value.	Yearly Profits.
Steel	$1,500,000,000	$160,000,000
Telephone*	700,000,000	45,000,000
Oil	650,000,000	85,000,000
Tobacco*	500,000,000	40,000,000
Pullman Car.	190,000,000	11,000,000
[illegible]*	1[illegible]0,000,000	12,000,000
Copper	140,000,000	6,000,000
Harvester	130,000,000	13,000,000
Electric (General)	130,000,000	11,600,000
Telegraph (Western Union)	120,000,000	10,000,000
Sugar	100,000,000	8,000,000
Rubber	90,000,000	6,000,000
Leather	90,000,000	5,000,000
Meat Packing (Swifts)	80,000,000	18,000,000
Powder	75,000,000	5,000,000
Electric (Westinghouse)	70,000,000	4,000,000
Telegraph (Mackay)	70,000,000	7,000,000
Mercantile Marine	70,000,000	7,000,000
Biscuit	65,000,000	4,000,000
Car and Foundry	60,000,000	8,000,000
Total	$5,000,000,000	$465,000,000

*Combination, including controlled subsidiaries.

The popular hatred of monopolies is as old as trade itself. Away back in history you may read of drastic laws against men who conspired to control the trade in the necessities of life. That was before the days of public companies. The most drastic laws were directed against traders who attempted to monopolize the grain markets. And it is very curious to note that, alongside of these laws against monopolies, governments began to grant trading monopolies to companies formed for the purpose of extending commerce over seas.

The first great trading companies of the seventeenth and eighteenth centuries were monoplies granted by the Crown. The South Sea Company was a monopoly; so was John Law's Mississippi Company. Law's famous company, whose shares advanced in a violent bull market from 500 francs to 20,000 francs before the collapse, had a monopoly from the Crown for trading over a large part of the known world. While Governments granted many commercial monopolies, all monopolies without royal sanction were criminal.

Free competition was the very cornerstone of English industry when the factory system began to take the place of hand labor, with the introduction of steam power. It is this idea of free competition that runs through our common law, inherited from England, and which is the basis on which anti-trust legislation like the Sherman act is formed. In this country to-day we have four principal varieties of capitalistic monopoly—patents and copyrights; natural monopolies, due to the wealth or favorable location of lands, mines or waters; franchises, as railroads, telegraphs and telephones; and industrial monoplies.

Patents and Copyrights.

Here again it is interesting to observe how our Government, while seeking to destroy monopolies of one kind, grants and protects the most rigid and productive of monopolies in the form of patents and copyrights. Public sentiment favors monopolies of this character because they foster invention and the arts. Again, in franchise monopolies, public sentiment may be said to be in their favor, because unrestricted competition usually results in waste and confusion. The Government protects railroad monopolies, and there is a growing tendency to protect telephone monopolies. In St. Louis, for example, there are three telephone companies, and a business man is compelled to pay toll to all three; New York has but one company, and it probably would be impossible for a competing company to obtain the right to string its wires. Through a large part of Central New York the New York Central Railroad has an absolute monopoly, and recently the Public Service Commission refused to grant permission for the building of a competing road.

But the idea of industrial monopoly still arouses popular antagonism, especially in the agricultural sections of the country. In some of the Western States vigorous campaigns have been waged against all trusts, and the rigid enforcement of drastic laws has driven from these States untold millions of capital.

None of the big industrial combinations is a monopoly in the popular sense of the word, absolutely controlling its field of industry. The biggest trust of all—Steel—is so far from being a monopoly that, in the recent depression in the steel trade, it was powerless to prevent the demoralization of the trade through price-cutting by the independents. It tried to keep up prices, but in the end was forced to let the law of supply and demand fix them. Nor can the trust stifle competition; one of the biggest steel plants in the country was successfully organized to compete with it the year after the trust was formed. The Guggenheim Smelters Trust was popularly supposed to be a monopoly until a powerful competitor was launched this year.

Keeping Down Prices.

The Sugar Trust has been powerless to prevent the building of new refineries, as, for example, the Warner and Spreckels plants on the Hudson River, both young and prosperous. The only way the Rockefellers can hold their share of the oil trade is by keeping prices down to a narrow margin of profit. The Goulds have seen their monopoly of the telegraphs destroyed by the Mackays. The Amalgamated Copper clique attempted to run the copper market and failed utterly; the high prices they set for the metal flooded the world's market with the product of competing mines. The Tobacco Trust, attempting to monopolize the cigarette industry, opened the field for a host of competitors, and controls a smaller share of this trade today than it did some years ago. Even the packing-house capitalists could not prevent newcomers from building up businesses as big as theirs.

Mr. Roosevelt, during his "trust-busting" campaign, when he found that the war he was beginning, if followed to its logical end, would result in demoralizing a very large part of the industries of the country, thought there ought to be a way to draw the line between "good trusts" and "bad trusts." In his last year in the White House this was the idea uppermost

in his mind. Combinations were all right, he said, but the principle of combination in industry could be abused by unscrupulous men, and it was against this abuse that he believed the Government should make its fight.

He was particularly convinced that the Standard Oil Company was a very "bad trust," especially after one of the leading Directors of the company, in a carefully prepared public statement, called the President a liar. Of course, no one would be unkind enough to say that Mr. Roosevelt's attack on the Standard Oil Company was entirely due to his hatred for the managers of the trust, but there can be no doubt that Mr. Roosevelt's personal enmity made the Government attack more violent. Any one who talked with Mr. Roosevelt in the White House about the Standard Oil Company knows how he hated the company and all its works. He would pound the table and cry dramatically that they would all have to go to jail. But what Mr. Roosevelt thought about the crimes of Standard Oil was a matter of no importance to the courts. The Government's attorneys brought the company into the courts, and there was nothing else for the learned Judges to say than that the company was a violation of the law against all combinations.

Ever since the opening of the Government's "trust-busting" campaign, it has been a matter of interest in Wall Street why the biggest of all the trusts has been immune from attack. The Steel Trust, with a capitalization fifteen times as big as that of Standard Oil, has gone ahead untroubled by attacks from Washington. It was reported during the Roosevelt administration that the Steel Trust was being investigated by Chief Sleuth Herbert Knox Smith, and that a report similar to the oil and tobacco reports would be issued. But nothing has been heard of it since.

During the 1907 panic, when the manager of many large corporations were making violent attacks upon Mr. Roosevelt as a demagogue and a destroyer of property, the managers of the Steel Corporation were busily engaged in running back and forth between New York and Washington and keeping on the right side of the "trust-buster." Every few days some leading Steel man was a visitor at the White House. Even when the Steel Corporation negotiated for the purchase of its big Southern competitor, the Tennessee Coal and Iron Company, a plain violation of the Sherman act, Mr. Roosevelt and the Government "trust-busters" had not a word to say. Some of the radicals in Congress tried to stir up a row over this deal, but the Administration refused to take any notice of them.

Mr. Roosevelt, in his effort to destroy the "bad trusts," found the Sherman act just the weapon he needed. It was just as useful as the New York policeman's right to arrest any man "on suspicion." But the innocent man arrested as a suspicious character in the streets of New York goes free the instant he shows he isn't a criminal. Not so with the big corporation. Once the Government brings it into court, under the Sherman act, it is a criminal, no matter how clean its record. It is guilty of being big and must be destroyed.

As the courts read the law there are no "good trusts." All are bad. "The power to "restrict competition," says Judge Sanborn in the Standard Oil opinion, "is indicative of the character of the combination, because it is to the interest of the parties that such a power should be exercised, and the presumption is that it will be."

Changing Public Sentiment.

That there is a growing public sentiment in favor of the organization of industry on the big-scale plan, like the United States Steel Corporation or the American Telephone and Telegraph Company, is very plain. Radicals are still crying that all big businesses must be disintegrated, but serious-minded men, seeing the benefits that the country is deriving from big-scale organization, believe that the era of consolidation will go on. Leaders of economic thought in American universities, where have originated some of the most violent attacks on big businesses, are more and more coming to believe that the large corporation is permanently fixed in this country.

John Bates Clark of Columbia University, who was at the head of the commission appointed by Gov. Hughes to investigate speculation, says:

Almost all the legislation we have is designed to break up the trusts into smaller corporations. It is a natural reassertion of the old common-law principle that a combination in restraint of trade is contrary to the public interest and unlawful. It is based on common-law antagonism to monopoly and on a hasty inference that these big consolidations are necessarily monopolies. If we could break up a corporation that has a billion dollars worth of capital into a hundred companies with ten million dollars each, we would not solve the problem. There would still be ways by which the companies could come to an understanding with each other, and the new condition would not give to the producing companies as much efficiency in the way of serving the public as they might easily develop if they were united in a firm consolidation. The trust laws we have are a latter-day repetition of some laws that hundreds of years ago were in force in England, and were designed to prevent the formation of copartnerships in business. The time was when the public in England was as much afraid of the formation of business partnerships as the public to-day is afraid of the formation of trusts. But partnerships were formed in spite of the law, and it was discovered that the prices of goods did not go up.

The productive efficiency of the monster corporation should enable us to make goods more cheaply than we otherwise make them, and to export them to foreign markets. The trusts can help us to become a power in the commercial world. It is not comfortable for the owner of a small shop to be driven out of business by the big ones; but it is good for the public to have that shop survive which will sell the goods at the lowest rate.

Mr. Seligman's Opinion.

Edwin R. A. Seligman, an economist of the first rank, and one time President of the American Economic Association, says:

The methods of regulating a combination most promising of success are the maintenance of equality in transportation and the securing of a reasonable publicity in the formation and conduct of the enterprise. These objects as well as the removal of factitious advantages, once accomplished, the natural limits of combination will disclose themselves; the combination will turn into monopoly chiefly in those industries where monopoly itself is desirable. Evidently, however, in such cases the monopoly must be controlled, or, in last resort, managed by Government itself. Where the natural regulation of competition is completely shut out, it must be supplanted by the artificial regulation of Government. But where publicity and equality are preserved, the community may expect, in the vast mass of private industry, to reap the benefits of combination without suffering the burdens of monopoly.

Richard T. Ely of the University of Wisconsin, who is recognized in Europe as well as in America as an authority on the trust problem, says:

Concentration of production means large-scale production. It means the great factory and the mammoth department store. Large-scale production, when it comes about as the result of the free pay of economic forces, is justified by its efficiency. When it is able to maintain itself in a fair field without favors it gives a large return for expenditures of capital power and human labor power. It adds thus to the provision for human comfort, and should be no more antagonized than machinery should be. The so-called anti-trust legislation of the American commonwealths has produced harm and can produce nothing but harm.

One of the most ardent of the "trust busters," Mr. William R. Hearst, now comes out flat-footed in favor of business combinations. At the dinner given in New York a few nights ago to some of the leading street railway capitalists, Mr. Hearst said:

I do not oppose combination, but the abuse of it. The evil of monopoly, even, lies in the misuse of it. Intelligent and legitimate combination in business is merely a phase of higher organization, and invariably results in greater economy and greater efficiency. Such combination is therefore beneficial, and will benefit not only the creators of the combination but the

public generally whenever the public is allowed to participate in the advantages. To my mind, therefore, it is the duty of Government not to prevent the combination which is beneficial, but to insure public participation in the benefits.

Many good Americans who would have heartily supported a "trust-busting" campaign a few years ago, and who thought the Sherman act was needed, now look with favor on big businesses. One reason for this is the growing education of the public in business affairs.

Holders of Nation's Wealth.

The enormous increase in the army of American capitalists is a more potent reason. A few years ago a few thousand men owned the big industries of the country. Now they are owned, as THE TIMES recently showed, by hundreds of thousands. The transition from partnerships to great public companies has given every thrifty American opportunity to become a capitalist. Where three-score rich men owned the Carnegie Steel Works, a hundred thousand capitalists, big and little, now share in the profits of the industry. More steel workingmen are now owners of a share in the Carnegie Works than there were workingmen employed by Andrew Carnegie.

Since the era of huge industrial flotations opened in the '90s, after the dark days of the fiat-money campaigns, billions of dollars worth of industrial securities have been distributed broadcast over the land, and an army of wage-earners has become an army of capitalists. Investment has become a household word. Popular periodicals have turned from muckraking to instructing their readers in finance. Demagogues railing at the trusts find their audiences thinning out, and radical lawmakers who once used the word corporation as a synonym for crime, are now careful to distinguish between honest and dishonest corporations.

Bigness in American industry and commerce is coming to be popularly associated with honest American progress. The Steel Trust has done much to educate the public to the new view that it isn't a crime to be big. When the Steel Trust, with its unprecedented billion-dollar capital, was launched, it was the target of all the anti-trust attacks, but it weathered the storm, and a panic or two besides, and it now goes along as peacefully as a country bank. The thinking American is coming more and more to distinguish between right and wrong in trade, irrespective of the wealth of an individual or corporation.

It isn't because the Standard Oil Company is big that the public distrusts it. The popular belief is deep-rooted that the Oil Trust killed competition by underhand methods, and it is because of this belief that a good many good Americans, who firmly believe in the efficiency of big businesses, have a dislike for this particular big business. It is the same with the Sugar Trust. No reasonable man has any fault to find with the growth of this combination, so far as this growth has been due to business ability, but if the managers of the Sugar Trust are guilty of the ancient crime of theft, all reasonable men want to see the thieves punished. But these crimes charged against particular corporations have no bearing on the Sherman act, which simply denounces all combinations.

The Sherman act is on the statute books, and its enforcement depends largely on the policy of the Administration in power. A radical Administration at Washington, using the Sherman law as a cudgel, could run amuck over the land and create a reign of terror in industry.

Most of the industrial combinations now operating were formed in the McKinley Administrations. Their organizers knew they were violating the law, but they went ahead with their plans, believing that the law would never be enforced—at least not against corporations that did not attempt to squeeze the public or drive out competitors by underhand methods.

Mr. Taft's Problem.

Mr. Taft has a problem on his hands. He is a believer in big businesses, and he hasn't any liking for "trust busting." Within a few hours after his election a year ago he said:

> I hope that the business future has been made certain, and that investors may feel justified in investing capital and in putting out funds for railroad construction and for projecting and carrying forward great business enterprises. Every business man who is obeying the law may go ahead with all the energy in his possession, and every enterprise which is within the statutes may proceed without fear of interference from the Administration.

The "trust busting" now in the Federal courts is a heritage of the Roosevelt Administration. Mr. Taft hasn't sent his sleuths out after the trusts. But now he is face to face with the problem of enforcing the Sherman act—a law which doesn't appeal to his sense of justice, and which he knows doesn't embody American public sentiment.

December 5, 1909

PASS RAILROAD BILL IN SENATE, 50 TO 12

Republicans Solidly for It and Six Democrats Join Them—Night Session Is Held.

LA FOLLETTE VOTED DOWN

Special to The New York Times.

WASHINGTON, June 3.—Late to-night the Senate passed the Railroad bill by a vote of 50 to 12. All those who voted against it were Democrats, though six of the minority Senators voted with the Republicans. Every insurgent who was present—and that means practically all of them—voted with the regulars. The House has passed a bill different in many particulars and the measure will now go to conference.

The twelve Democrats who voted against the bill were Messrs. Bacon of Georgia, Fletcher of Florida, Frazier of Tennessee, Hughes of Colorado, Money of Mississippi, Newlands of Nevada, Percy of Mississippi, Purcell of North Dakota, Rayner of Maryland, Shively of Indiana, Smith of Maryland, and Smith of South Carolina. The six Democrats who voted for the measure were Messrs. Chamberlain of Oregon, Clay of Georgia, Gore of Oklahoma, Paynter of Kentucky, Simmons of North Carolina, and Stone of Missouri.

The day's session preceding the vote shortly before 10 o'clock had been dull in the extreme. Early in the morning an amendment by Senators Paynter and Sutherland had been adopted directing that the Inter-State Commerce Commission should complete its investigation of the pleas of roads for the suspension of the long and short haul clause within one year, though it might order that the suspension continue for a longer time to allow for the completion of the investigation.

That was the one positive change in the bill. The rest of the time went in consideration of a number of amendments, most of them offered by Mr. La Follette. Most of them had to do with the Court of Commerce and all were defeated.

The announcement of the vote on the bill was a signal for a fight as to what would be the next item on the programme to receive consideration. Mr. Beveridge, Chairman of the Committee on Territories, at once moved that the Statehood bill be made the unfinished business, and, in the face of personal requests from Mr. Aldrich and the leaders, refused to withdraw his motion. The Democrats and insurgents upheld him, but adjournment was taken until Monday morning without a vote.

What the Senate Bill Provides.

The Railroad bill, as it passed the Senate, provides for the creation of the Court of Commerce for the consideration exclusively of appeals from orders of the Inter-State Commerce Commission. The court is to consist of five Judges, whose powers are to be co-ordinate with the Judges of the Federal Circuit Court. They are to have five years' terms, first appointments to be made by the President, and others by the Chief Justice of the Supreme Court.

The Government, not the Inter-State Commerce Commission, is to be the defendant in all cases coming before the court, and the defense is placed under the direction of the Attorney General, but the commission and interested parties are permitted to intervene or carry on the suit in case of the failure of the Attorney General to do so. Appeal may be taken to the Supreme Court.

The long and short haul provision of the present law is amended so as to permit a greater charge for a short haul than for a long haul only with the consent of the Commerce Commission. Provision is made against the fixing of a lower rate to destroy water competition.

Railroad companies are required to furnish written statements of rates from one place to another upon the written application of a shipper.

Either upon complaint or upon its own initiative, the commission is authorized to determine the reasonableness of individual or joint rates or classification, and if such rates are found to be unreasonable, discriminatory, preferential, or prejudicial the commission may prescribe a proper maximum rate.

Unless set aside by a competent court of orders of the commission are to continue in force for two years.

Suspension of New Rates.

The commission has authority to investigate the propriety of any new rate, regulation, or classification, individual or joint, of any common carrier, and pending such hearing a suspension for ten months of the rate, classification, or regulation is provided for. The carrier is required to refund all charges found to be excessive.

Authority is also given the commission to establish through routes and joint classification or to prescribe maximum rates over the same, whenever the carriers themselves neglect to do so. This regulation also covers water lines which are connecting carriers.

Shippers have the right to designate a through route or part of a route over which their property shall be carried. A penalty of $5,000 is imposed upon carriers for disclosing any information concerning shipments. A like penalty is provided for violation of orders under Section 15 of the existing inter-State commerce law, and in this case each day that the violation continues is to be construed as a separate offense.

At intervals of six months the commission is required to make an analysis of tariffs and classification.

Telegraph and telephone lines are placed under the jurisdiction of the Commerce Commission. The commission is authorized to determine the reasonableness of rates and a penalty is imposed of from $100 to $2,000 against granting franks or passes for the transmission of messages. Special night and press report rates are authorized.

Federal courts are forbidden to suspend the operation of State laws except when the matter is presented to a Justice of the Supreme Court or a Circuit Judge and heard by three Judges, one of whom shall be a Supreme Court Justice or a Circuit Court Judge.

The law is to take effect sixty days from the date approved by the President.

June 4, 1910

TAFT QUICKLY SIGNS THE RAILROAD BILL

House Adopts the Conference Report and President Acts After Return at Night.

Special to The New York Times.

WASHINGTON, June 18.—Within three hours after the opening of to-day's session the House by two unanimous votes had adopted the conference report on the Administration Railroad bill and had accepted the Senate bill providing for statehood for Arizona and New Mexico. Both bills, with the signatures of Vice President Sherman and Speaker Cannon attached, were sent to the White House in order to receive the signature of President Taft upon his return to Washington after his few hours' stay in Villa Nova. Mr. Taft signed the Railroad bill at 10:26 o'clock to-night.

In addition to the passage of these two measures the House rushed the General Deficiency bill through with scarcely a change and sent it to the Senate, where it will in all probability be approved in short order.

It was so generally understood at the opening of the session that there would be no organized opposition to either the Railroad or the Statehood bill that the few speeches which were made on the former measure were listened to by only a handful of members. Most of the Republicans and Democrats were lounging in the cloak rooms waiting for the vote.

When the conference report on the Railroad bill was taken up an agreement limiting debate to an hour and fifty minutes was reached. Representative Mann of Illinois, Chairman of the Inter-State Commerce Committee, who headed the House conferrees, explained the provisions of the report, and declared that the compromise that had been effected had resulted in a satisfactory measure, especially the Commerce Court feature. He insisted that this provision was designed merely for political advantage. He deplored what he characterized as an effort to extend the powers of the Federal Government at the expense of that of the separate States.

Mr. Adamson announced that he would not vote for the conference report, although in the echoes of ayes which finally adopted it his voice could not be heard in the negative. Not a single amendment to the report was offered and not even Judge Adamson suggested that the House insist on a disagreement to the Senate amendments. Loud applause greeted the Speaker's announcement that the report had been adopted.

June 19, 1910

STANDARD OIL COMPANY MUST DISSOLVE IN 6 MONTHS; ONLY UNREASONABLE RESTRAINT OF TRADE FORBIDDEN

And of Such Unreasonable Restraint the Supreme Court Finds the Standard Guilty.

DECISION PLEASES TAFT

Decision Reads "Unreasonable" Into Law and Is What Trusts Wanted, Says La Follette.

Special to The New York Times.

WASHINGTON, May 15.—Final decision was returned late this afternoon by the Supreme Court of the United States in one of the two great trust cases which have been before it for so long—that of the Standard Oil Company. The decree of the Circuit Court for the Eighth Circuit directing the dissolution of the Oil Trust was affirmed, with minor modifications in two particulars. So far as the judgment of the court is concerned the action was unanimous, but Justice Harlan dissented from the argument on which the judgment was based.

The two modifications of the decree of the Circuit Court are that the period for execution of the decree is extended from thirty days to six months, and the injunction against engaging in inter-State commerce on petroleum and its products pending the execution of the decree is vacated. This letter modification is made distinctly in consideration of the serious injury to the public which might result from the absolute cessation of that business for such a time.

Broadly speaking, the court determines against the Standard Oil Company on the ground that it is a combination in unreasonable restraint of inter-State commerce. For the first time since it has been construing the Sherman Anti-Trust act the court takes that position, and thus definitely reads the word "unreasonable" into the law. It was on this ground that Justice Harlan dissented. This decision, therefore, is a practical reversal of the position taken by the court in the trans-Missouri case, one of the first cases under the Sherman law.

In that case Justice White joined with the late Justice Brewer in a dissenting opinion, while Justice Harlan was with the majority of the court. That decision held, as Justice Harlan now holds regarding the Standard Oil Company, that the combination complained of was in restraint of inter-State commerce and therefore under the inhibition of the statute. Justices White and Brewer then held that the combination complained of was an "unreasonable" restraint of commerce, and so brought itself under the ban of the law.

Justice Harlan sharply criticised the majority of the court for taking this position. He declared it to be a menace to the institutions of the country. He said it was amending the Constitution by judicial interpretation, and was unjustified. And he asserted that one of the greatest dangers to the country was the willingness of the courts to take such action.

How Decision Was Received.

The decision was received with varying emotion by the crowd in the little court room. Attorney General Wickersham hailed it as a victory for the Administration. Frank B. Kellogg, the Assistant "Trust Buster," who has had the chief management of the case from the Government from its inception, was of similar opinion. Progressive Senators like La Follette openly expressed distrust of the effect of the decision, and Senator Kenyon, who only a few weeks ago left the Department of Justice to enter the upper house of Congress, spoke of it as a "dangerous decision."

While in the Department of Justice, Mr. Kenyon was in charge of the prosecution of the Beef Trust, the members of which will be indicted individually on the criminal count. The department hopes to bring these cases to trial in the near future.

Trust lawyers who were in court did not display any willingness to comment on the decision. But among the lawyers who heard the Chief Justice deliver his epitome of the opinion, which he did without referring to the printed text of the decision and who were not connected with this case, the opinion prevailed that the decision was distinctly favorable to "big business." For a long time there has been open expression of the hope on the part of "big business" that when the decision in the oil and tobacco cases did finally come down, they would at least point a way under which the big corporations could continue to do business, and that the present general method would not be utterly destroyed.

President Taft himself, in messages to Congress and in public speeches, has declared himself earnestly in favor of retaining the economy and efficiency of combinations and of destroying merely those practices which unduly restrained inter-State commerce and stifled competition. There was a time when the President was in favor of some amendment to the Sherman law in the effort to reach this situation. But he finally came to the conclusion that it was impracticable to write the word "unreasonable" into the law, and pointed out that more and more the Supreme Court was tending toward the point where its decisions in trust cases would be based on that construction of the statute.

Way Out for Corporations.

Now it seems to have been done, and the forceful personality of Chief Justice White has so impressed itself upon the court that he has carried seven of the other Justices with him. Representatives of "big business" who heard him this afternoon did not hesitate to declare emphatically that the decision was all that the big corporations could ask. They regarded with especial favor the establishment of the proposition that a combination must be in "unreasonable" restraint of commerce to be unlawful.

This they believe points out the way by which the big corporations in the country can continue to exist. They recalled with satisfaction the fact that President Taft has specifically declared that it is not mere size which puts a corporation or combination under the ban of the law; it is not the breadth or scope of its operations, or the amount of its capitalization, but whether or not it does two things; fixes prices and controls output.

The representatives of corporations here to-day find in Chief Justice White's decision a practical agreement with the position of President Taft. They have been satisfied with that position and have realized for a long time that business must conform to such standard. Now they find relief in the decision of the highest court in the country, and some of them expressed the opinion this evening that the effect on the general business situation would be good.

There is very little difference in the views of the progressives and those of big business men here as to the effect of the decision. But whereas the corporation representatives regard it with favor, the progressives find in it cause for distrust and dissatisfaction. This view was especialy emphasized by Senators La Follette and Kenyon.

La Follette Not Satisfied.

"In the light of what Justice Harlan in his dissenting opinion said of the Chief Justice's decision," said Senator La Follette, I think that if it is true that the court holds that the law applies only to unreasonable restraint of trade it is a very dangerous decision. In that view of it I should say it is precisely what the trusts want, and they, more than any others, will be pleased with the decision. The court has amended the Sherman anti-trust law just as it was attempted over and over in the Senate to do it. What they did not get in the Senate they have now got from the court.

"If Justice Harlan interprets the decision correctly we shall have a plenty to do now with the law so amended. Every trust will now come into court and claim justification on a special set of facts going to support the claim that it is not restraining trade unreasonably, and it is to be expected that courts will make use of a sliding scale of reasonableness to apply to each case. I fear that the court has done just what the trusts have wanted it to do and what Congress has refused steadfastly to do."

Senator Kenyon of Iowa took a view similar to that of Senator La Follette. He said:

"I think the court has amended the anti-trust law, and it will lead to trouble. The courts will now be obliged to consider the reasonableness or unreasonableness of trust operations, and to-day's decision will prove to be only the beginning of a long and hard fight. It suggests that legislation will be demanded by the people to make good what has been taken from the law, but it is not easy to see just what legislation will fit the situation.

"I am inclined to feel that nothing short of jail sentences will accomplish any positive results. There has been discussion of the limitation of investments, with safeguards against stockholders being in more than one corporation, but all that is probably far in the future, and I do not care to talk about it. I do not hesitate to say, however, that there is danger in this decision."

On the other hand the decision was regarded by many as a great victory for the Government. Among these were Senator Cullom of Illinois, who sat through the greater part of the Chief Justice's delivery of the decision, and also through Justice Harlan's dissenting opinion. Senator Bailey of Texas manifested great pleasure in the decision. He went in and out of the court chamber several times in the afternoon, and after the adjournment of the court walked out through the Capitol and stood for several minutes talking with a group of Justices, including Chief Justice White, Justice Holmes, and Justice Van De Water.

"It is a correct interpretation of the law," said Senator Bailey, "and no corporation will be able under its operation to organize a trust or engage in business in violation of law. I think the Supreme Court has now made it impossible for a corporation to defy the law."

OPINIONS ON THE DECISION.

Attorney General Wickersham: "Substantially every proposition contended for by the Government is affirmed."

Frank B. Kellogg, counsel for Government: "It is a complete victory for the Government."

Senator Kenyon, formerly Assistant Attorney General: "I think the court has amended the antitrust law, and it will lead to trouble."

Senator La Follette: "I fear that the court has done what the trusts wanted it to do, and what Congress has steadily refused to do."

Alfred D. Eddy, Standard Oil counsel in Chicago: "The business of the Standard Oil Company will go on as usual, although changes will be made."

What Wickersham Says.

Attorney General Wickersham and Solicitor General Lehmann were surrounded as soon as the court adjourned by those who wanted to learn their views of the decision. Mr. Wickersham commented very briefly and then went to the Department of Justice, where he promptly withdrew into his private office and prepared a statement in which he formally expressed his view of the victory won by the Government. The statement says:

The Attorney General stated, with respect to the decision in the Standard Oil case rendered by the Supreme Court today, that the court unanimously affirms the decree rendered by the Circuit Court in favor of the Government in every particular save that it gives the defendants six months instead of thirty days' time in which to comply with the decree.

"Substantially every position contended for by the Government in this case is affirmed by the Supreme Court. In the reasoning by which the Chief Justice reaches the conclusion in which the whole court concurs he expresses the view that only contracts combination, &c, which in any way unreasonably or unduly restrain inter-State trade and commerce of which are unreasonably restrictive of competitive conditions are within the prohibition of the first section of the Sherman act. Justice Harlan, on the other hand, dissents from his view and contends that contract, &c., which does restrain trade and commerce is within the inhibition of the statute, but he concurs with the whole court in the decree of affirmance.

"The Chief Justice further holds that the second section of the act seeks, if possible, to make the prohibitions of the act all the more complete and perfect by embracing all attempts to reach the ends prohibited by the first section that is, restraint of trade by any attempt to monopolize or monopolization thereof, even though the acts by which such results are attempted to be brought about, be not embraced within the general enumeration of the first section. He further told that the criterion by which it is to be determined in all cases, whether a contract, combination, &c., is a restraint of trade within the meaning of the law, is the direct or indirect effect of the acts involved."

Chief Justice Reads Decision.

The Chief Justice did not read the long opinion, but, speaking extemporaneously, delivered a synopsis of the decision. He spoke, as usual, rapidly and with great variation in volume of voice, so that at times his words were distinctly audible in every part of the room and at other times even the stenographers directly in front of him were unable to catch a syllable. Several times Justice McKenna, who sits at his left hand, leaned over and suggested that he raise his voice so that he could be heard. Once or twice on such suggestions the Chief Justice repeated what he had said, and then for a time would speak forcibly, so that all could hear.

Always with earnestness and conviction the Chief Justice spoke, often accompanying his words with a gesture. When he discussed the motive of the men who enacted the Sherman law his voice rang through the courtroom as he said:

"The writers of that law were legislating for freedom."

It was just one minute to 4 o'clock when the Chief Justice began speaking in the

Standard Oil case. He was forty-nine minutes delivering his synopsis.

It was just twelve minutes of 5 o'clock when the Chief Justice concluded, and the audience gathered in the crowded court-room breathed a sigh of relief at the final gratification of a nation-wide curiosity in regard to the fate of one of the most gigantic business organizations known in the world's history. The Chief Justice gathered up his papers, flung his silken robe up over one shoulder and then over the other, and sank back in his chair and closed his eyes to rest. The other Justices, who had been craning around in their seats to listen to him, moved restlessly in their chairs, and seemed relieved that the mighty decision was at last out.

Justice Harlan Critical.

The next moment Justice Harlan was heard to speak and it was known that he had a dissenting opinion to deliver. The venerable Justice, like the Chief Justice, spoke off hand and with frequent gestures and decided animation. He launched at once into sharp criticism of the decision delivered by the Chief Justice and several times alluded sarcastically to the Chief Justice's reference to the application of the "light of reason" to the case. He then cited the decision of the court in the Hopkins case in 1896, later in the Trans-Missouri Traffic Association case and the Western Traffic Association case.

"Fifteen years ago," he said, "this court laid down the law and construed the Sherman Anti-Trust law and three times since the passage of the act the court has gone on record in regard to it. And in two of the cases the present Chief Justice dissented from the decision of the court."

Justice Harlan went on to urge that if laws were to be amended, those who seek that result should go to Congress, and not to the courts.

"I declare," he said, with emphasis, "without hesitation that to-day the greatest danger to our free institutions is the disposition of courts to encroach on the domain of the legislative branch."

The elaborate exposition given by the Chief Justice of the appication of the common law to the broad fundamental principle that every man should have his equal chance in the business world, Justice Harlan said, had no proper place in the decision of the case.

"Governments are entitled," he said, "to be judged by their statute laws rather than by the common law in a matter that goes like this case vitally to the welfare of the Nation."

controversy over the questions involved in the trans-Missouri case, and the decision made in that case by the late Justice Peckham, to which Chief Justice White dissented, Justice Harlan named over the eminent counsel who appeared for the defendant in that noted cause—John G. Johnson of Philadelphia, E. J. Phelps of Vermont, ex-Senator George F. Edmunds, and others—and declared that the court knew that those great lawyers went into every nook and cranny of the law in that case and failed to establish to the satisfaction of the court that there should read into the anti-trust the limitation as to unreasonable and reasonable restraint of trade.

He then pointed out that the court was reversing itself and that it was not only doing that, but was taking in the Standard Oil case opposition ground to that laid down in the case of the United States against the Chicago, Burlington & Quincy Railroad decided to-day, in which the Federal law requiring carriers engaged in inter-State commerce to provide safety appliainces on their cars to protect the life and limb of employes, was upheld. The court in that case had held that the carrier must make sure that every inter-State car before starting out was provided with the appliances required by the mandatory language of the law. It was not sufficient that these were reasonably calculated to accomplish the result sought; they must accomplish that result absolutely if the carrier desired to continue in the operation of an inter-State business.

Objects to Such Construction.

Justice Harlan then went on to say:

"The decision today means practically that the courts may by mere judicial construction amend the Constitution of the United States and the statutory laws. The anti-trust law of 1890 was passed when this country was in a crisis arising out of the accumulation of capital in a few hands and out of combinations which had their hands upon the throat of this country. The question before Congress at that time was what shall we do?

"Many things in this opinion may alarm the country. Who are the men moving about in darkness? And who have the light of reason? There was no doubt in the mind of the men who enacted the law of 1890 as to the meaning of the language they employed. They sought a remedy for the conditions then existing and thought they had found it. It has long been the contention of those who have questioned the meaning of the statute that Congress did not intend to restrain reasonable trade agreements, but only unreasonable restraint of trade.

"We have heard a good deal about common law, and it is not new to hear it asserted that common law did not restrict reasonable combinations in the business world. But it has been the uniform rule laid down in this court and followed until to-day that the law of 1890 prohibited all contracts in restraint of trade, and made no exceptions. The reading of the law is plain. It says, 'Every contract is declared to be illegal—every contract combination in the form of trust or conspiracy, in restraint of trade or commerce among the several States or with foreign nations, is hereby declared to be illegal.' Congress is the body to amend the law, and not the court by a process of judicial legislation wholly unjustifiable.

"Now, for another time the same arguments are employed by great men who come to us asking us to decide the same question in direct opposition to the conclusions reached on the trans-Missouri case.

"There has been no session of Congress since 1896 that somebody in the interest of opposite views to what this court has said in its decisions to date, has not applied to Congress to get the law amended. It has not been amended. There is probably no man in the country to-day who believes it will be amended. These people do not give up as long as they can fight. Whenever the chance offers, they raise the question and seek a construction of the law of 1890.

Criticises Judicial Delay.

"The most alarming tendency of this age, in my judgment, so far as institutions are concerned is the tendency of judicial delay. When men of vast interests are concerned and cannot get the law-making power to enact legislation they desire they bring up some case in an attempt to have the Constitution or the statutes construed to mean what they want them to mean. The courts are full of cases which involve attempts to have the laws reconstructed.

"We have announced our views of the act of 1890. They have been accepted and acted upon. And I suppose millions of property have changed hands under the decisions in 1890 and 1889. Prosecutions have been instituted and people have been sent to jain under these constructions of the law. Now the court in the opinion in this case says that this act of Congress applies to only those contracts in restraint of trade which are unreasonable. That is what the combinations said fifteen years ago.

In conclusion the venerable justice said that he had sought simply to review the reasoning laid down by the Chief Justice as to express his mind in opposition to the step taken by the court. Later he said he should commit his remarks to writing, with the exposition of the fundamental cases in which the court had during the last fifteen years made its record on the anti-trust law.

It was twenty-five minutes past 5 when Justice Harlan filed his opinion and gave way to the Chief Justice who proceeded immediately to entertain motions for the admission of candidates to the Supreme Court bar.

May 16, 1911

TOBACCO TRUST FOUND GUILTY AND MUST DISSOLVE; COURT IS TO FIX LEGAL FORM OF BIG BUSINESS

Special to The New York Times.

WASHINGTON, May 29.—In the long-awaited decision in the case of the Tobacco Trust, which was rendered by Chief Justice White in the Supreme Court this afternoon, the Government obtains an order for the dissolution of the concern, which is held to be a combination in restraint of inter-State trade, and the trust obtains opportunity to reorganize under the immediate supervision of the Circuit Court of the Second New York District, so that there may be recreated "out of the elements now composing it (the trust) a new condition, which shall be honestly in harmony with and not repugnant to the law."

Thus both the Government and the trust win. The Government obtains the dissolution of this particular offender against the Sherman law, but the Tobacco Trust and all the other big corporations and combinations which go collectively to make up what are usually denominated "the interests" get the very thing they have prayed for so long and so hard—they get not merely a direction by the Supreme

Court as to how they may proceed within the law but also a command to the Circuit Court actually to show them how to reorganize so as to "be in harmony with the law."

Corporations Have Sought a Rule.

Ever since these big trust cases—that of the Standard Oil Company and the one decided to-day—came before the Supreme Court the constant expression of corporation feeling about them has been one of hope that in some way the court would find or make opportunity to point out to big business how it might proceed within the law. The Supreme Court has heard that prayer. There can be no question that the reorganization of the tobacco company—for the readjustment ordered by the court will be nothing more or less than a reorganization—will be taken as the model set up by the courts of the form in which big business may proceed without fear of being in violation of the law.

From that point of view the tobacco company wins a victory quite as substantial and enduring as that of the Government. It was the immediate expression of corporation lawyers who heard the Chief Justice that this decision was a fitting successor and complement to that in the Standard Oil case rendered two weeks ago. The prediction was at once made that the stock market would open stronger on Wednesday, and that the basis for the long-awaited resumption of activity had now been achieved.

As in the Standard Oil case Justice Harlan delivered orally a separate opinion, in which he concurred in part with the opinion of the court and in part dissented. The Chief Justice was supported in what he said by seven of the other Justices, and Justice Harlan was alone in his position.

The Crime and the Remedy.

After an elaborate examination of the record in the case in which the Chief Justice declared with the utmost conviction that the tobacco company had been deliberately and wilfully guilty of violating the anti-trust law; that it had committed numerous acts with the intent and purpose of violating the anti-trust law, and that it had brought itself clearly under the ban of that statute, he proceeded to discuss the remedy which might be applied by the court. He said it might be one of two things, either an injunction ordering its dissolution, and prohibiting it from doing any further inter-State business; or the appointment of a receiver to take over its vast business and bring it within the law. Both of these remedies he dismissed upon consideration, chiefly because of the danger either would be almost certain to work upon innocent outsiders.

Then he delivered the decree of the court, which points out the way in which the reorganization is to be effected. The decree consists of four points, as follows:

"1. That the combination in and of itself as well as each and all of the elements composing it, whether corporate or individual, whether considered collectively or separately, be decreed to be in restraint of trade and an attempt to monopolize and a monoplization within the first and second sections of the Anti-Trust act.

"2. That the court below, in order to give effective force to our decree in this regard, be directed to hear the parties, by evidence or otherwise, as it may be deemed proper, for the purpose of ascertaining and determining upon some plan or method of dissolving the combination and of recreating out of the elements now composing it a new condition which shall be honestly in harmony with and not repugnant to the law.

"3. That for the accomplishment of these purposes, taking into view the difficulty of the situation, a period of six months is allowed from the receipt of our mandate, with leave, however, in the event, in the judgment of the court below, the necessities of the situation require, to extend such period to a further time not to exceed sixty days.

"4. That, in the event before the expiration of the period thus fixed a condition of disintegration in harmony with the law is not brought about, either as the consequence of the action of the court in determining an issue on the subject or in accepting a plan agreed upon, it shall be the duty of the court, either by way of an injunction restraining the movement of the products of the combination in the channels of inter-State or foreign commerce, or by the appointment of a receiver, to give effect to the requirements of the statute."

Model for Business Readjustment.

Thus the tobacco company gets eight months in which to complete a reorganization under the immediate supervision of the Circuit Court. It has full liberty to devise its own plan, but the plan must be satisfactory to the Circuit Court before it can be adopted, and the trust has warning that if a satisfactory plan is not found within eight months there may be issued an injunction stopping all its inter-State business or it may be thrown into the hands of a receiver.

Its new plan must be in full harmony with the law, but the Circut Court is there to tell it just how to obtain that harmony. The contention of big business that there was nowhere under the Government any agency that could tell it authoritatively what it could do under the law and what it could not do, finds its answer here.

The first impression in Washington is that the decision of to-day, following that of a fortnight ago, will result in a great readjustment of business and lead eventually to much less difficulty on the part of big concerns with the Sherman law.

Chief Justice White did not read his long, carefully prepared opinion, which approximates 18,000 words, and which appears in full in another part of THE NEW YORK TIMES, but spoke from notes as he did in the Standard Oil case. He took occasion to reply thus informally to some of the things Justice Harlan has said about the decision in the oil case. The Chief Justice declared that the Court had not read anything into the anti-trust act, but that it had "revivified" that statute.

Rule of Reason Reaffirmed.

The court reiterated its determination to follow the "rule of reason" in determining what restraints of trade violate the Sherman anti-trust law. Chief Justice White explained the decision of the court in the Standard Oil case, but did not qualify the reasoning in that case so as to harmonize it in any particular with the dissenting views expressed in that case by Associate Justice Harlan and other critics of the decision.

To-night it is regarded as settled that the "rule of reason" will prevail in the courts of the land in the interpretation of the Sherman anti-trust law until, at least, the personnel of the Supreme Court greatly changes or the Sherman anti-trust law is amended.

In reality the decision was nothing less than a deliberate exemplification of the application of the "rule of reason" to "undisputed facts." From the date of the organization of the first combination the Court found that there was a purpose to acquire dominion and control of the tobacco trade, not by the mere exertion of ordinary right to contract and trade, but by methods devised in order to monopolize the trade by driving competitors out of business.

This purpose was carried out ruthlessly, according to the Court, upon the assumption that to work upon the theory or play upon the cupidity of competitors would make success possible. Such action, viewed in the "light of reason," was regarded by the Court as violation of the law.

On practically every point on which the Government appealed from the decision of the lower court it scored a victory to-day. In the first place James B. Duke and the twenty-eight other individual defendants were held to be parties to the unlawful combination, instead of being freed from further responsibility in the case, as directed by the Court below.

Instead of dismissing the bill as to the Imperial Tobacco Company, the so-called British trust, and as to the British-American Tobacco Company, the creature of the two parent tobacco trusts, these two corporations were held to be co-operators in the unlawful combination.

So, too, was the United Cigar Stores Company, a retail organization, with stores throughout the country.

The attorneys for the Tobacco Company present in court took prompt advantage of the opportunity of the last day of the term to present a motion for leave to file a motion for rehearing and for stay of mandate for thirty days, and this motion was granted. That gives the trust at least an extra month in which to study its plan of reorganization, and possibly even longer.

Victory, Says Wickersham.

A statement from Attorney General Wickersham to-night characterizes the decision as a complete victory for the Government. The statement says:

"The decision in the tobacco case, in the most comprehensive and sweeping manner, sustains the position taken by the Government with respect to the decree below. It reverses the action of the Circuit Court in dismissing from the bill the individual defendants, the British-American Tobacco Company, Limited; the Imperial Tobacco Company, Limited, and the United Cigar Stores Company, holding that they are all parties to the unlawful combination which is condemned by the decree.

"The court gives an interpretation of its decision in the Standard Oil case, saying that it was there held 'that in view of the general language of the statute and the public policy which it manifested, there was no possibility of frustrating that policy by resorting to any disguise or subterfuge of form, since resort to reason rendered it impossible to escape by any indirection the prohibitions of the statute.'

"It then holds that the history of the tobacco combination, is so replete with the doing of acts which it was the obvious purpose of the statute to forbid, so demonstrative of the existence from the beginning of a purpose to acquire dominion and control of the tobacco trade, not by the mere exertion of the ordinary right to contract and to trade, but by methods devised in order to monopolize the trade by driving competitors out of business which were ruthlessly carried out upon the assumption that to work upon the fears or to play upon cupidity of competitors would make success possible.'

"Holding, therefore, that the combination as a whole and all its co-operating and associate parts, in whatever form clothed, constitutes a restraint of the trade within the first section of the Sherman act and an attempt to monopolize and a monopolization within the second section, the court remands the cause to the Circuit in New York for the purpose of working out some plan of disintegration of the combination which will recreate 'a new condition which shall be honestly in harmony with and not repugnant to the law.'

"It gives the defendants six months within which to work out that result with the right in the Circut Court to extend the right in the Circuit Court to extend it proper, and provides that during this period each and all of the defendants, individuals, as well as corporations, shall be enjoined from doing any act which might further extend or enlarge the power of the combination by any means or device whatsoever, and that if, at the end of the time so allowed, such a condition of disintegration in harmony with law is not brought about, it shall be the duty of the Circuit Court, either by way of injunction restraining the movement in inter-State or foreign commerce of the products of the combination or by the appointment of a receiver of the entire combination to give effect to the requirements of the statute.

"It is scarcely to be conceived that any more comprehensive and effective application of the statute to this vast combination could possibly have been decreed."

May 30, 1911

STANDARD OIL PLANS A GENERAL SPLIT-UP

Concludes Supreme Court Decision Means That It Shall Dissolve Into Subsidiaries.

NO OTHER WAY CONSIDERED

Intricate Work of Determining Pro Rata Shares of Stock Distributions May Take Longer Than Court Allows.

Plans of the Standard Oil, it was learned yesterday, are for a literal obedience of the decision of the Supreme Court and the division of the company into its multitudinous subsidiaries rather than the separation of the great business into parts representing its six general departments—crude oil, pipe lines, refineries, by-products, barrel and can factories, and transportation.

An active director declared yesterday that the company would be guided solely by the decision, which he explained had not yet been filed. "Of course," he said, "we know what the terms of the decision are and we have been studying the problem in the light of what we know."

Incidentally, he said that the work of arranging the details of the dissolution of the $100,000,000 holding company, far from being completed, as current reports have had it, would require many months of labor, and the company might finally ask for more time. "It may take six months and it may require eight," he said. The decision of the Supreme Court gave the company "at least six months," but the American Tobacco decision added a period of sixty days' grace, which it is to be presumed could be obtained by the Standard Oil Company should it be necessary.

Although the Director would not go into details, he explained that a literal observance of the Supreme Court's decree necessitated a complete separation of the company into its many subsidiaries, of which thirty-three were defendants in the appeal.

Contrary to the general opinion, he said, the company was not waiting for the court's opinion on the American Tobacco reorganization, which will be passed upon by the court before it is put into effect. "That has nothing to do with us," he said. "We must act according to the decision in our case."

When it is considered the separate capitalization of the companies named in the Government's case ranged from $50,000 to more than $25,000,000, with dividend rates and book values of the various stocks showing wide differences the magnitude of the task of making an equable distribution of their stocks may be appreciated.

One of the companies with a capital of $5,000,000 made profits of $5,506,237, and its stock had a book value of more than $20,000,000. Another, by contrast, with a capitalization of $10,000,000 showed profits in that year of $2,803,056, and its stock had a book value of $3,364,712.

The problem of dividing the properties among shareholders is further complicated by the fractional distributions which would be necessary to give stockholders in the $100,000,000 holding company a part in such subsidiaries for instance as have a capital of $100,000 or less.

During the four years since the suits were instituted there have been a number of substantial revisions upward in the capitalization of the Standard Oil subsidiaries which may materially simplify the problem of stock distribution. As has already been pointed out, an equable distribution of the shares of subsidiaries held by the Standard Oil Company of New Jersey would not affect the control of the various constituents. At the time the suit was under way the holdings of John D. Rockefeller in the Standard Oil Company of New Jersey were put at 247,-692 shares out of the $98,338,300 outstanding capitalization, a trifle over 25 per cent. The majority of the stock is contained in the holdings of twelve other individuals and estates, all closely associated with Mr. Rockefeller.

July 7, 1911

TOBACCO TRUST TELLS ITS PLAN

American Company to be Split Into Four Parts, Subsidiaries Into Ten More.

VOTE WITH PREFERRED STOCK

Each Company to be Independent; Stock Distribution to Sever Present Control.

The American Tobacco Company made public last night a summary of the plan for its disintegration which is to be filed with the United States Circuit Court tomorrow.

This official summary, Delancey Nicoll of counsel for the company said, was given out because "an incorrect statement of the plan had been put in circulation." It provides for the distribution of the property and business of the American Tobacco Company among three corporations besides itself. The five "accessory companies," which the Supreme Court found to constitute, in and of themselves, combinations in restraint of trade, are to be broken up into ten more companies. Other subsidiaries are to be separated from each and all these fourteen fragments.

Foreign business is to be made independent of the combination by cutting loose the British-American Tobacco Company, together with the Imperial Tobacco Company of Great Britain and Ireland, and the abrogration of agreements for the division of territory here and abroad.

The United Cigar Stores Company is to be freed of domination by the American Tobacco Company by the distribution of the two-thirds of the capital stock held by it among its common stockholders. The control of the United Cigar Stores Company, the summary says, "will pass to its present individual stockholders and the common stockholders of the American Tobacco Company, but in view of the fact that one-third of its stock is held by persons not connected with the American Tobacco Company it will not be in the hands of the twenty-nine individual defendants."

Of the $10,000,000 capital stock of the United Cigar Stores Company, the American Tobacco Company owns about $6,000,-000. Under the distribution plan the so-called insiders will receive only from $2,000,000 to $2,500,000 of it.

The companies into which the property and business of the American Tobacco Company as an operating concern are to be divided are the American Tobacco Company, the P. Lorillard Company, the Liggett & Myers Tobacco Company, and the R. J. Reynolds Tobacco Company. The Liggett Company will be a new concern and the Lorillard Company a reorganization of the present corporation of that name. For the factories and brands that these two take over they are to pay the American Tobacco Company $115,000,000. This will consist of 7 and 5 per cent. bonds, 7 per cent. preferred stock and common stock. These will be taken temporarily into the treasury of the American Tobacco Company, which will offer to exchange the bonds and preferred stock for its own securities.

Provision for Other Stocks.

The common stock is to be sold to common stockholders of the American Tobacco Company. The Reynolds Company is to be separated by distributing to the common stockholders of the American Tobacco Company the two-thirds of its stock now owned by the trust. In all these four companies voting power will be conferred on the preferred stock.

In the process of disintegration the American Tobacco Company is also to take into its treasury securities of its subsidiaries and sub-subsidiaries and distribute them among the common stockholders of the American Tobacco Company as dividends. They are not detailed in the summary, but are approximately as follows:

American Snuff Co. common stock..	$6,207,212
American Snuff Co. preferred stock..	2,373,913
McAndrews & Forbes Co. common stock ..	2,320,400
Conley Foil Co. stock.	528,750
R. J. Reynolds Co. stock	8,333,300
United Cigar Stores Co. stock	640,000
British-American ordinary shares...	11,481,890
Porto Rican-American Co. stock....	3,226,400
Total ..	$35,011,865

To these are to be added securities which the American Tobacco Company will receive as dividends on its stock in various subsidiaries which are to go through a similar process. These will be distributed by the subsidiaries among their common stockholders, including the American Tobacco Company.

Most of these are shares in new companies to be organized in order to disintegrate the business of some of the big subsidiaries, and no value can yet be placed on them.

The following securities, now owned by the American Tobacco Company, are to be disposed of, presumably for cash, within a time to be fixed by the court:

British-American Company non-voting preference shares	$6,805,113
Imperial Tobacco Co. shares	3,506,281
United Cigar Stores Co. bonds..	3,600,000
McAndrews & Forbes Co. preferred stock	750,000
Tota	$14,661,394

In all cases the American Tobacco Company is to be enjoined from voting the stock temporarily in its treasury or from exercising any control over the various companies."

As to the cost of the disintegration, the summary says:

"This plan involves the disposition by the American Tobacco Company of stocks, factories, brands, and other property earning a net annual income, based on actual results in 1910 of $22,593,312.

"The total cost to the common stockholders of the American Tobacco Company of putting into effect this plan of disintegration, including the increased interest and preferred dividend charges capitalized on a 5 per cent. basis, the payment of bonds at above par, the expenses of the disintegration itself, and the organization of new companies, will amount to at least $22,000,000. This amount is permanently taken from the common stockholders, in addition to the $36,651,925 in cash that they will pay and that will be used in paying off the bonds of the company in order to reduce its size."

October 15, 1911

FEW FAVOR REPEAL OF SHERMAN LAW

But Civic Federation Also Finds That Public Has No Wish to Destroy Large Corporations.

ANALYZES ITS LATEST VOTE

Federal Regulation Favored by 90 Per Cent. and Industrial Commission by 80 Per Cent.

The National Civic Federation made public yesterday an analysis of 16,000 answers received by it to a series of questions concerning the Sherman Law. The questions were sent to editors, political economists, lawyers, publicists, statisticians, manufacturers, merchants, bankers, and officials of commercial, labor, and other organizations.

"The replies," according to the federation, "indicate little sentiment in favor of the unconditional repeal of the Sherman law. On the other hand, it is shown that there is practically no desire to abolisih large combinations. The public have no desire for Government ownership on the one side, or unrestricted and unregulated private or corporate control on the other. They will accept large combinations adequately regulated."

Eighty-four per cent., according to the returns, pronounce the Sherman law neither workable nor clear, or workable without being clear; but only some 20 per cent. declare in favor of its repeal. Eighty per cent. of the replies favor Federal license or incorporation for companies engaged in inter-State commerce, about one-third of the eighty taking Federal licenses as an alternative. Seventy-five per cent. are opposed to holding companies, while the remainder nearly all want holding companies bound by restrictions that would prevent abuses.

Government regulation of capitalization is approved by 90 per cent., a few of the minority who disapprove suggesting that overcapitalization is not always an evil but sometimes brings capital into action that otherwise would remain idle. Three important advantages for those doing business on a large scale—economies in production, economies in distribution, and greater use of by-products—are admitted by all who answer that query. Thirty-five per cent. deny that such business brings steadier employment and better wages or better protection against industrial accidents, and 10 per cent. doubt that it brings more command of international trade.

Eighty per cent. favor an inter-State industrial commission, some qualifying this with the condition that it should be composed of business men only, and two labor representatives proposing that the commission should consist of one member from each State—a sort of inter-State business senate. A comparatively small proportion are in favor of control of prices by an industrial commission.

The federation attaches significance to the fact that the leaders of organized labor, representing 3,000,000 wage earners, are practically unanimous in demanding that the Sherman anti-trust law should be either repealed or amended to exempt from its operations organizations of labor and organizations of farmers. Many of them, however, urge its amendment from the standpoint of the business interests, saying that their experience and training in organization work and their contact with employers of the country have led them universally to the position that too much competition is the death of trade. Samuel Gompers, John Mitchell, James Duncan, Warren S. Stone, W. S. Carter, W. G. Lee, James M. Lynch, and A. B. Garretson all reflect this view.

"It is interesting to note," the federation's report adds, "that the manufacturers, bankers, wholesale and retail merchants, and also commercial organizations that took a membership vote, are strongly opposed to the repeal of the Sherman act, but just as strongly want it amended along lines that will permit regulation through an inter-State industrial commission of some kind."

January 31, 1912

STANDARD OIL MONEY IN VARIED BUSINESS

Great Surplus of the Old Controlling Group Has Sought Many Outlets for Profits.

TRACED IN 70 COMPANIES

Indications are increasing of the extended activity of Standard Oil money, not meaning the funds of the New Jersey Company or its old subsidiaries, but the surplus which John D. Rockefeller and his eight or ten close associates who share with him the dominant position in the "Oil Trust" have accumulated in the last score of years. How much the accumulations of this group have grown to could not be even remotely guessed, for while some of the old "Standard Oil crowd" added greatly to the huge sums they received annually in dividends on their oil shares, others have been less fortunate in outside investments. Some have died and have scattered their fortunes among many heirs, and others guard the secret of their wealth closely.

Since its organization and up to the time of its dissolution last year, the Standard Oil Company of New Jersey paid out more than $700,000,000 in dividends, the bulk of this sum being divided among the dozen men whose holdings constituted control. Their investments and surplus funds took greatly varied forms, the late H. H. Rogers and the Flaglers going in for the development of new railroad territory, others, among them the Bedford, Pratt and Tilford families, leaning particularly toward manufacturing companies. Others of the group, and here again H. H. Rogers was prominent, as is William Rockefeller, made commitments to established companies listed on the Stock Exchange which offered opportunities for stock market operations.

Less is known of the quiet drift of Standard Oil money into smaller enterprises, but it may safely be said that the recent large additions to the holdings of Standard Oil men in the Childs restaurants, as told in THE TIMES yesterday, is only a slight measure of the great sums which are being invested by this group in outside enterprises.

There is no clue in the Standard books of financial reference to the interests of this group in various corporations except where the names of some of the men themselves or of their known agents appear among officers or Directors. It is well known, however, that connections traceable in this way are only a small part of those actually held by Standard Oil men.

In the appended list of fifty-five corporations there does not appear, for instance, the Western Maryland Railroad, in which John D. Rockefeller is one of the largest holders of securities, nor the Missouri Pacific. Only those companies are named in which some of the old Standard Oil Directors appear themselves as Directors or members of their families. The same is true of the financial institutions named. Besides the sixteen printed below there are many others in which the Standord Oil voice is important if not dominant.

Railroad and Industrial Corporations.

Company.	Stock Capital.
Amalgamated Copper	$153,887,900
American Express	18,000,000
American-La France Fire Engine	2,000,000
American Light and Power	......
American Linseed	16,750,000
American Tobacco	118,931,500
Atlantic Coast Electric Railway	......
Atlas Tack	1,000,000
Boylston Manufacturing	650,000
Brooklyn City R. R.	12,000,000
Brooklyn Union Gas	17,898,500
Bush Terminal	8,500,000
Chelsea Fibre Mills	......
Coal Creek Mining and Mfg	......
Colorado Fuel and Iron	34,235,500
Consolidated Gas	99,738,400
Chic., Mil. & St. Paul Ry	232,623,100
Corn Products Refining	79,590,000
Cuba Company	8,000,000
D., L. & W. R. R.	30,147,200
Electric Bond & Share	4,000,000
Electric Utilities Corporation	4,410,700
Florida East Coast Railway	3,000,000
Great Western Power	25,000,000
International Cigar Machinery	10,000,000
Interlake Pulp & Paper	......
International Railway	16,320,500
International Traction	15,000,000
Long Island R. R.	12,000,000
Locke Steel Belt	......
Marsh Lumber	......
Morris Building	......
Matheson Lead	......
Millbrook Company	......
New York Central & Hudson River Railroad	222,729,300
New York, New Haven & Hartford Railroad	179,567,000
New York State Realty and Terminal Company	......
National Fuel Gas	14,723,000
Ohio Company of Associates	......
Portland Railway Light and Power	25,000,000
Peninsular & Occidental Steamship	......
Rosendale-Raddaway Belting and Hose	......
Richmond Light & Railroad	2,871,750
Southfield Beach R. R.	250,000
Southern Pacific	272,672,400
Staten Island Midland Railway	1,000,000
Self-winding Clock	......
Thompson-Starrett Company	1,500,000
Tintic Company	2,091,249
Virginian Railway	34,245,000
Virginia & Southwestern Railway	2,000,000
Union Pacific Railroad	316,215,600
V. & O. Press Company	......
Western Power	17,220,000
Western Union Telegraph	99,740,100

Financial Institutions, &c.

Atlantic Mutual Insurance Company.
Brooklyn Trust Company.
Farmers Loan & Trust Company.
Hanover National Bank.
Long Island Safe Deposit Company.
New York Trust Company.
Mechanics and Metals National Bank.
Merchants Fire Insurance Company.
Metropolitan Trust Company.
National City Bank.
New York Trust Company.
Plainfield Trust Company.
Southport Trust Company.
Title Guarantee and Trust Company.
Union Mortgage Company.
United States Trust Company.

Since the dissolution of the Standard Oil Company of New Jersey the mining industry particularly has attracted Rockefeller capital. The Amalgamated Copper Company has increased its field by buying out the United Metals Selling Company, which for years had been agent for the sale of its output. William Rockefeller personally has gone into a large number of new copper enterprises. He is said to have acquired recently an important share in the Tennessee Copper Company, and William G. Rockefeller appears as an officer of the Inspiration Consolidated, one of the important new copper properties, and has become interested in a number of others.

One of the important outlets for Standard Oil money is in enterprises which are seldom heard of, close corporations floated by organizers who have the confidence of the oil men. Many of these do not appear in any of the financial reference books.

June 7, 1912

FIND MODIFIED MONEY TRUST; PROPOSE CURE

Majority of House Committee Calls Morgan, Stillman, and Baker the "Inner Group."

THEIR CONTROL A MENACE

Drastic Measures to End Alleged Domination Over Credit and Stifling of Competition.

TO REGULATE EXCHANGES

Bill Drafted to Restrict Their Use of Mails, Telegraph, and Telephone.

MUST PROHIBIT WASH SALES

THE MONEY TRUST.
What It Is and Who Are In It, As Found by the Pujo Committee.
I. WHAT IT IS.

Your committee is satisfied from the proofs submitted ● ● ● that there is as established and well-defined identity and community of interest between a few leaders of finance, created and held together through stock ownership, interlocking Directorates, partnership and joint account transactions and other forms of domination over banks, trust companies, railroads and public services and industrial corporations, which has resulted in great and rapidly growing concentration of the control of money and credit in the hands of these few men.

If by such a trust is meant a combination or arrangement created and existing pursuant to a definite agreement between designated persons with the avowed and accomplished object of concentrating unto themselves the control of money and credit, we are unable to say that the existence of a money trust has been established in that broad, bald sense of the term.

II. WHO ARE IN IT.

Inner Circle.

J.P. Morgan & Co.,
George F. Baker,
James Stillman,
First National Bank,
National City Bank,
National Bank of Commerce,
Chase National Bank,
Guaranty Trust Company,
Bankers Trust Company.

Allies.

New York:

Kuhn, Loeb & Co.,
National City Bank,
National Bank of Commerce,
Kissel, Kinnicutt & Co.,
White, Weld & Co.,
Harvey Fisk & Sons.

BOSTON:

Lee, Higginson & Co.,
Kidder, Peabody & Co.,
National Shawmut Bank,
First National Bank,
Old Colony Trust Company.

CHICAGO:

First National Bank,
Illinois Trust and Savings Bank,
Continental and Commercial National Bank.

Special to The New York Times.

WASHINGTON, Feb. 28—A financial combination approximating what is popularly called a "Money Trust," but not formed in consequence of any definite agreement is asserted by the Democratic majority of the Pujo Committee to be in actual existence in the United States.

In an exhaustive report, presented to the House of Representative to-day, the seven Democratic members of the committee summarize and discuss the evidence presented before the body at its many sessions during the Winter.

They hold that the "most active agents" in bringing about the concentration of money and credit, alleged to have been disclosed, are J.P. Morgan & Co., the First National Bank of New York, the National City Bank of New York, Lee, Higginson & Co., and Kidder, Peabody & Co., of Boston, and Kuhn, Loeb & Co., of New York.

What the report describes as the "inner group" in this combination consists of J. P. Morgan & Co., "the recognized leaders, and George F. Baker and James Stillman in their individual capacities and in their joint administration and control of the First National Bank, the National City Bank, the National Bank of Commerce, the Chase National Bank, the Guaranty Trust Company, and the Bankers Trust Company, with total known resources in these corporations alone in excess of $1,300,000,000."

The firm of Kuhn, Loeb & Co., is described as being "only qualifiedly allied with the inner group."

How the Combination Controls.

The report, after asserting that the Money Trust existed, said that it had come about largely as follows:

"First-Through consolidations of petitive or potentially competitive banks and trust companies, which consolidations in turn, have recently been brought under sympathetic management.

"Second-Through the same powerful interests becoming large stockholders in potentially competitive banks and trust companies. This is the simplest way of acquiring control but since it requires the largest investment of capital, it is the least used, although the recent investments in that direction for that apparent purpose amount to tens of millions of dollars in present market values.

"Third-Through the confederation of potentially competitive banks and trust companies by means of the system of interlocking Directorates.

"Fourth-Through the influence which the more powerful banking houses, banks, and trust companies have secured in the management of insurance companies, railroads, producing and trading corporations, and public utility corporations, by means of stockholdings, voting trusts, fiscal agency and contracts, or representation upon their Boards of Directors, or through supplying the money requirements of railway, industrial and public utilities corporations, and thereby being enabled to participate in the determination of their financial and business policies.

"Fifth-Through partnership or joint-account arrangements between a few of the leading banking houses, banks, and trust companies in the purchase of security issues of the great inter-State corporations, accompanied by understandings of recent growth—sometimes called 'banking ethics'—which have had the effect of effectually destroying competition between such banking houses, banks, and trust companies in the struggle for business, or in the purchase and sale of large issues of such securities."

Two Reform Bills Proposed.

In order to carry out some of the many reforms suggested by the majority to end the alleged evils, the majority presents two bills. One proposes changes in the National banking laws for the regulation and restraint of concentration and control of money and credit.

The committee urges legislation affecting bank consolidation, interlocking directorates, interlocking stockholdings among banks, voting trusts, security companies as adjuncts to banks, fiscal agency agreements, bank investments in bonds, reform or railroad reorganization, limitation of borrowings by officers from their own banks, publicity of assets, and similar matters.

The committee advises that clearing houses be incorporated and seeks to accomplish this by prohibiting National banks from affiliation with an unincorporated clearing house, or any clearing house association tha adopts rules that infringe on the rights of National banks under their charters.

The report also recommends that National banks be barred from engaging in underwritings, and that the Inter-State Commerce Commission receive power to supervise the reorganization of inter-State railroads and control the security issues of such lines.

The other undertakes to compel the incorporation of Stock Exchanges by forcing them to make certain reforms before allowing them to use the mails. This is an indirect attempt to regulate the New York Stock Exchange. The committee does not recommend direct regulation of the affairs of the Exchange except through the application of a mail embargo.

Republicans Dissent.

None of the Republican members signed the majority report. Three of them—Hayes of California, Guernsey of Maine, and Heald of Delaware—filed the principal minority report. In it they deny the existence of a money trust, but admit that there is a dangerous concentration of credit. They recommend that more testimony be taken on the probable effect of the legislation proposed by Chairman Pujo and his Democratic associates.

Representative McMorran of Michigan, the fourth Republican member of the committee, refused to sign the Pujo or Hayes reports and submitted a report of his own, covering about 7,000 words, challenging the conclusions of the majority and paying a tribute to the New York financial world.

The failure of the Republicans and Democrats on the committee to unite upon a unanimous report is accepted as a sign of hard sledding for the proposed bills, if they are pressed in the new Congress. It means that they will be vigorously opposed by the Republican members of the committee.

ANALYSIS OF "MONEY TRUST."

Combination Is Pointed Out and Its Power Pictured.

WASHINGTON, Feb. 28.—In discussing the question of a combination of financial interests, having for its purpose the control of money and credit and thus constituting to all intents and purposes a real "money trust," the majority of the Pujo Committee reviews the evidence exhaustively and then says:

"Your committee is satisfied from the proofs submitted that there is an established and well-defined identity and community of interest between a few leaders of finance, created and held together through stock ownership, interlocking directorates, partnerships and joint-account transactions, and other forms of domination over banks, trust companies, railroads and public service and industrial corporations which has resulted in a great and rapidly growing concentration of the control of money and credit in the hands of these few men.

"If by the term 'money trust' is meant a combination or arrangement created and existing pursuant to a definite agreement between designated persons with the avowed and accomplished object of concentrating unto themselves the control of money and credit, we are unable to say that the existence of a money trust has been established in that broad, bald sense of the term, although the committee regrets to find that even adopting that extreme definition, surprisingly many of the elements of such a combination exist.

Form of the Combination.

"It would, of course, be absurd to suggest that control of the bulk of the widely distributed wealth of a great nation can be corralled by any set of men. If that is what is meant by gentlemen who deny the existence of a money trust your committee agrees with them. Such a thing would, of course, be impossible, and its suggestion is ridiculous. It is not, however, necessary that a group of men shall directly control the small savings in the banks nor the scattered resources of the country in order to monopolize the great financial transactions, or to be able to dictate the credits that shall be extended or withheld from the more important and conspicuous business enterprises. This is substantially what has been accomplished, and fairly represents the existing condition.

"Under our system of issuing and distributing corporate securities the investing public does not buy directly from the corporation. The securities travel from the issuing house through middlemen to the investor. It is only the great bank or banker with access to the mainsprings of the concentrated resources made up of other people's money in the banks, trust companies and life insurance companies, and with control of the machinery for creating markets and distributing securities who can underwrite or guarantee the sale of large scale security issues.

"If therefore, by a 'money trust' is meant 'an established and well-defined identity and community of interest between a few leaders of finance which has been created and is held together through stockholdings, interlocking Directorates, and other forms of domination over banks, trust companies, railroads, public service and industrial corporations, and which has resulted in a vast and growing concentration of the control of money and credit in the hands of a comparatively few men' your committee has no hesitation in asserting as the result of its investigation up to this time that the condition thus described exists in this country today.

Make-Up of the Trust.

"The parties to this combination or understanding or community of interest, by whatever name it may be called, may be conveniently classified, for the purpose of differentiation, into four separate groups.

"First—The first, which for convenience of statement we will call the inner group, consists of J. P. Morgan & Co., the recognized leaders, and George F. Baker and James Stillman in their individual capacities and in their joint administration and control of the First National Bank, the National City Bank, the National Bank of Commerce, the Chase National Bank, the Guaranty Trust Company, and the Bankers' Trust Company, with total known resources, in these corporations alone, in excess of $1,300,000,000, and of a number of smaller but important financial institutions. This takes no account of the personal fortunes of these gentlemen.

"Second—Closely allied with this inner or primary group and indeed related to them practically as partners in many of their larger financial enterprises, are the powerful international banking houses of Lee, Higginson & Co. and Kidder, Peabody & Co., with three affiliated banks in Boston—the National Shawmut Bank, the First National Bank, and the Old Colony Trust Company—having about two-thirds of the total resources of all the Boston banks; also with interests and representation in other important New England financial institutions.

"Third—In New York City the international banking house of Messrs. Kuhn, Loeb & Co., with its large foreign clientele and connections, while only qualifiedly allied with the inner group, yet through its close relations with the National City Bank and the National Bank of Commerce and other financial institutions, with which it has recently allied itself, has many interests in common, conducting large joint account transactions with them, especially in recent years, and having what virtually amounts to an understanding not to compete, which is defended as a principle of 'banking ethics.' Together they have with a few exceptions pre-empted the banking business of the important railways of the country.

"Fourth—In Chicago this inner group associates with and makes issue of securities in joint account, or through underwriting participations primarily with the First National Bank and the Illinois Trust and Savings Bank, and has more or less friendly business relations with the Continental and Commercial National Bank, which participates in the underwriting of security issues by the inner group. These are the three largest financial institutions in Chicago, with combined resources (including the two affiliated and controlled State institutions of the two National banks) of $561,000,000.

"Fifth—Radiating from these principal groups and closely affiliated with them are smaller but important banking houses, such as Kissel, Kinnicut & Co., White, Weld & Co., and Harvey Fisk & Sons, who receive large and lucrative patronage from the dominating groups and are used by the latter as jobbers or distributors of securities the issuing of which they control, but which, for reasons of their own, they prefer not to have issued or distributed under their own names. Lee, Higginson & Co., besides being partners with the inner group, are also frequently utilized in this service because of their facilities as distributors of securities.

A Maze of Co-operating Institutions.

"Sixth—Beyond these inner groups and subgroups are banks and bankers throughout the country who co-operate with them in underwriting or guaranteeing the sale of securities offered to the public, and who also act as distributors of such securities. It was impossible to learn the identity of these corporations owing to the unwillingness of the members of the inner group to disclose the names of their underwriters, but sufficient appears to justify the statement that there are at least hundreds of them and that they extend into the principal cities throughout this and foreign countries.

"The patronage thus proceeding from the inner group and its subgroups is of great value to these banks and bankers, who are thus tied by self-interest to the great issuing houses and may be regarded as a part of this vast financial organization. Such patronage yields no inconsiderable part of the income of these banks and bankers and without much risk on account of the facilities of the principal groups for placing issues of securities through their domination of great banks and trust companies and their other domestic affiliations and their foreign connections.

"The underwriting commissions on issues made by this inner group are usually easily earned and do not ordinarily involve the underwriters in the purchase of the underwritten securities. Their interest in the transaction is generally adjusted, unless they choose to purchase part of the securities by the payment to them of a commission. There are, however, occasions on which this is not the case. The underwriters are then required to take the securities. Bankers and brokers are so anxious to be permitted to participate in these transactions under the lead of the inner group that, as a rule, they join whenever invited to do so regardless of their approval of the particular business, lest by refusing they should thereafter cease to be invited."

The committee holds that the subway financing in New York, wherein 100 to 125 underwriters purpose to participate under the leadership of J. P. Morgan & Co., the First National Bank and the National City Bank as managers, is an illustration of this ability of the inner group to capitalize its financial power. The report continues:

"Your committee is convinced that however well founded may be the assurances of good intentions by those now holding the places of power which have been thus created, the situation is fraught with too great peril to our institutions o be tolerated."

Control of Security Market.

Turning to the character of the control exercised by the money trust, the report says:

"Through their power and domination over so many of the largest financial institutions, the inner group and its allies have drawn to themselves practically the sole marketing of the issues of the great-er railroad, producing and trading, and public-utility corporations, which in consequence have no open market to which to appeal; and from this position of vantage, fortified by the control exerted by them through voting trusts, representation in directorates, stock holdings, fiscal agencies, and other relations, they have been able in turn to direct the deposits and other patronage of such corporations to these same financial institutions, thereby strengthening the instruments through which they work.

"No railroad system or industrial corporation for which either of the houses named has acted as banker could shift its business from one to another. Where one has made an issue of securities for a corporation the others will not bid for subsequent issues of the same corporation. Their frequent and extensive relations in the joint issues of securities has made such a modus vivendi inevitable.

"This inner group and allies thus have no competition, either from others or amongst themselves, for these security issues, and are accordingly free to exact their own terms in most cases. Your committee has no evidence that this power is being used oppressively and no means of ascertaining the facts, so long as their profits are undisclosed.

"It should be noted, however, that issues of subsidiaries of the United States Steel Corporation within the past year amounting to $30,500,000 having been purchased by Messrs. Morgan & Co., were, the greater part of them, immediately resold at a profit to Lee, Higginson & Co. and Kissel, Kinnicut & Co., when, so far as appears, the corporation could readily have saved this intermediate profit or commission by being permitted to deal directly with the banking houses which purchased the securities for distribution.

"It is admitted that Messrs. Morgan reaped a profit on these issues. Yet they performed no service, so far as we have been able to learn. They neither formed the syndicate, nor did they lend their names to the issues. If they wanted to market the securities we assume that it was their privilege to do so as fiscal agents of the corporation. Otherwise, was it not their duty, situated as they were with regard to the Steel Corporation as the supreme power therein, without whose approval no Director could be named, to see to it that the best possible bargain for the corporation should be made, and not reserve to themselves a profit without risk or service?

"The suggestion that because these corporations have Boards of Directors composed of men of standing they are independent seems to us disingenuous. They and subject to removal by it at any election. They are not accountable to the shareholders, but to Messrs. Morgan and Baker, and are not free agents, no matter how eminently respectable and distinguished they may be.

"Not only does this domination of great banks and trust companies enable the inner group and their allies to control the disposition of new security issues through control of the main outlets therefor, but it also enables them to say what and whose securities shall not be bought and of enforcing the retention in these institutions of securities issued by them, which an independent management might consider it wise to dispose of.

Equitable Life an Object Lesson.

"The purchase of the Equitable Life stock by Mr. Ryan and Mr. Morgan in succession furnishes an object lesson of the value that leading financiers place on the control of corporate assets not belonging to the corporation but held in trust for other people, and a fair criterion from which to judge of the reasons why they have engaged so actively in buying into banks and trust companies and in securing control thereof through voting trusts.

"If the controlling stock of the Equitable Life, that yields only 7 per cent. on $51,000—$3,570 per year—was worth $2,-500,000 to Mr. Ryan and $3,000,000 to Mr. Morgan, why did it have that value? Was it because the life insurance company held in its treasury the majority stock of the Mercantile Trust Company, which was turned over to the Bankers' Trust Company, controlled by J. P. Morgan & Co. through a voting trust after Mr. Morgan bought Mr. Ryan's stock, and also the stocks of other banks and trust companies, including those of the National Bank of Commerce and the Fifth Avenue Trust Company? The Guaranty Trust Company, likewise controlled by Morgan & Co. through a voting trust, subsequently absorbed the Fifth Aveune Trust Company, and Messrs. Morgan, Baker, and Stillman took over one-half the holdings of the Equitable and Mutual Life Insurance Companies of the Bank of Commerce stock.

Baker Quoted Against Morgan.

Mr. Morgan's statement in evidence that group control of money and credit is impossible is called by the report "an obvious economic fallacy as the everyday transactions of business demonstrate." The report goes on:

"On the proposition that there is not and cannot be concentration of control of money or credit, it will be observed that Mr. Morgan is directly at variance with his associate, Mr. Baker, who deprecated further concentration in this regard, saying it has gone far enough, because in the hands of the wrong men 'it would be very bad'; that the safety of the situation lies in the personnel of the control. He evidently does not agree that the situation would correct itself.

"That such concentration is an existing condition and not a myth seems, indeed, to be agreed on all sides. Mr. Reynolds considers it a menace, while Mr. Schiff has been an interested observer of its rapid growth during the past few years, but is not worried because his firm is now so rich and powerful that it no longer requires credit. We note, however that he has been something more than a mere observer. His firm has acquired also within the past few years interests and representation in the National Bank of Commerce, Equitable Trust Company, United States Mortgage and Trust Company, and Fourth National Bank."

The question of interlocking Directorates and consolidations is next taken up. From the evidence the committee concludes:

"It is manifestly through the control of the leading New York institutions and their commanding position as the depositaries of the reserves of the country, and by reason of the fact that the New York Stock Exchange is the only public money market in the United States, that the money rates and the market for securities as affected by the money rates can be controlled.

Control of Loan Market.

"The evidence demonstrates that the inner group and the banks and trust companies with which they are affiliated through stock ownership, representation in Directorates, and otherwise, dominate the money market for loans on the Stock Exchange and on Stock Exchange securities. They lend not only their own money and the money of their depositors, including the depositors of the out-of-town banks, but that of their correspondents, on terms and security satisfactory to them, (the New York banks.) It is in their power by co-operation primarily to fix the call rate from day to day, and to determine what constitutes satisfactory collateral.

"This does not mean that all the loans thus made are controlled by them. Nor does it mean that loans may not be effected by other banks and bankers on collateral that the banks affiliated with the inner group would not accept. Such absolute domination is not necessary in order to control money rates or to influence security values. Nor does the proof show affirmatively that there is in fact any definite agreement or understanding pursuant to which the daily call rates for money are fixed. But the power and the opportunity are there and could be exercised without leaving proof or trace behind.

"Whenever the incentive is at hand the machinery is ready. It is made possible by this community of interest and family representation in the institutions that hold these resources. At best it is a dangerous situation, with its boundless temptations and opporunities, no matter how high or lofty may be the sense of responsibility of those who hold the power. It is too vast and perilous a power to be safely intrusted to the hands of any man or set of men, be he or they ever so patriotic or unselfish.

"At best it would require open, reckless, and long-continued abuse to cripple power thus intrenched. It could withstand many missteps even if they became known, which is quite unlikely. And after the man was crippled he would revive. If in the end the power should be destroyed, what is likely to happen to the credit and prosperity of the country while the edifice is crumbling?

"That argument does not appeal to us as an answer to the conclusion we have reached that such power is a menace.

"To us the peril is manifest. But the remedy is not so easily found or applied, having due regard, as we should, to the encouragement of enterprise."

Proposed Remedies for Evils.

As a first step to end the evils of financial concentration, the committee advises the prohibition of interlocking directorates. The argument that competent men would not be found to fill the directorates of banks if they were not permitted to be interlocked is met by an amendment to the law reducing the number of Directors to thirteen.

The report comments on the fact that in England and France there is no community of interest between the great institutions or interlocking of directorates, and hopes that state of healthful rivalry may be brought back in this country.

The committee would end the improper practices "that permit members of banking houses to sit on the boards and Executive Committee of inter-State corporations with which they are dealing in the purchase and sale of securities or on the Boards of Directors and Executive Committees of banks that are underwriting or buying securities issued by such banking houses."

In advising that inter-State corporations be prohibited from depositing with private banks, the report is apparently aiming straight at the Morgan firm. In fact, it says:

"It is not necessary to question the good faith or fair dealing of the bankers in their relations with these controlled corporations in order to realize the impropriety of permitting this condition to continue unchecked and without supervision."

Under the heading of "Concentration," the domination of railroad systems by this inner group, the way it has come about, and the extent thereof, are discussed in connection with the present method of reorganizing insolvent railroads and the constitution of voting trusts. The control of Messrs. Morgan over competing railroads is criticised thus:

"Your committee finds that vast systems of railroad in various parts of the country are in effect subject to the control of this inner group—a situation not conducive to geuine competition."

Here follows a description of the legal procedure on reorganization which is alleged to be responsible for much of the banking control over railroads, and in its place the English system of requiring that the plan of reorganization be put under the supervision of the court so as to prevent injustice to minority holders is recommended.

MAJORITY RECOMMENDATIONS.

What Pujo and His Associates Would Do to Curb "Money Trust."

WASHINGTON, Feb. 28.—Summed up, the recommendations of the majority of

the Pujo Committee for enactment into law are:

SECTION I.

As Regards Clearing House Associations.

A. Incorporation and Regulation.—National banks should not be permitted to be members of Clearing House Associations, which are not bodies corporate of the States in which they are respectively located, and every solvent and properly managed bank or trust company should have the right, enforceable at law, to become and remain a member: Provided, that no Clearing House Association should be required to admit a member, having a capital stock not less than that required of a National bank in the same locality

B. Examination of Members.—Regular periodical examinations of members by a committee of the association should be prohibited, and instead all such examinations should be conducted by public authorities.

C. Issuance of Clearing House Certificates.—Until other measures of relief are provided by Congress, such associations should be permitted to issue certificates on the security of their members' assets for circulation among members to pay balances owing to each other at the Clearing House, but only on condition that both the issuance and retirement of such certificates shall be under Governmental control.

D. Regulation of Rates for Collecting Out-of-Town Checks.—The practice now so general among such associations of compelling members, under pain of expulsion, to charge prescribed rates for collecting out-of-town checks should be prohibited.

E. Regulation of Rates of Discount and of Interest on Deposits, &c.—Such associations should be further prohibited from prescribing rates of interest or discount, rates of interest allowed on deposits, rates of exchange, or any other regulation not appropriate to their function of instrumentality for the collection of checks by banks of the same community one from another that interfere with competition.

SECTION II.

As Regards the New York Stock Exchange.

A. Conditions Precedent to Use of Mails, Telegraph, and Telephone.—That Congress prohibit the transmission by the mails or by telegraph or telephone from one State to another of orders to buy or sell or quotations or other information concerning transactions on any Stock Exchange, unless such Exchange shall—

1. Be a body corporate of the State or Territory in which it is located.

2. Require corporations whose securities it lists to make a complete disclosure of their affairs, in particular any commissions paid to promoters, middlemen, or bankers out of any such security issue or the proceeds thereof.

3. Require a margin of not less than 20 per cent. on all purchases of stock.

4. Prohibit as far as possible the execution of simultaneous or substantially simultaneous orders proceeding from the same person or persons to buy and sell the same security for the purpose of creating an appearance of activity therein, and any orders the purpose of which is to inflate or depress the price of any security.

5. Prohibit members from pledging securities purchased and carried for a customer for an amount greater than the unpaid portion of the purchase price, whether with or without the consent of such customer.

6. Prohibit members from lending to other members securities carried by the former for customers, whether with or without such customers' consent.

7. State in its charter the condition on which issues of securities shall be admitted or removed from the trading list, and provide for a judicial review of its action in this regard.

8. Keep books of account, showing the actual names and transactions of customers, and give access thereto to the Postmaster General.

SECTION III.

As Regards Concentration of Control of Money and Credit.

A. Consolidations of Banks.—Two or more banks should not be permitted to consolidate unless such consolidation shall have been approved by the Controller of the Currency as in the public interest. He should have plenary power to forbid it where it threatens to result in undue concentration of control.

B. Interlocking Bank Directorates.—No person should be permitted to be a Director in more than one National bank serving the same community or locality, nor should any person who is a Director of any State bank or trust company, or is a partner or associate of any private banker or banking firm, be eligible as a Director of any National bank serving the same community or locality, except that a Director in a National bank may have one partner who is a Director in a trust company.

C. Interlocking Stockholdings Among Banks.—No part of the stock of any National bank should be permitted to be owned or held directly or indirectly by any other bank or by any trust company or holding company; and no National bank should be permitted to own or hold any part of the stock of any other bank or trust company.

D. Voting Trusts in Banks.—The transfer of any part of the stock of National banks to Trustees solely or primarily in order that they may vote the same at annual elections and other stockholders' meetings—"voting trusts," as they are generally known—should be expressly prohibited.

E. Cumulative Voting.—Minority representation in the Directorates of National banks should be secured by adopting the system of cumulative voting, i. e., by providing that at elections for Directors each stockholder shall have as many votes as are equal to the number of his shares, multiplied by the number of Directors to be elected, which votes may be cast solidly for one Director or distributed among several, as the shareholder shall see fit. And no National bank should be permitted to purchase the obligations or lend upon the obligations or shares of any corporation whose Directors are not chosen at elections conducted under the cumulative system of voting.

F. Security-Holding Companies as Adjuncts to Banks.—The stockholders of a National bank should be expressly prohibited from becoming associated as stockholders in any other corporation under agreements or arrangements assuring that the stock of such other corporation shall always be owned by the same persons or substantially the same persons who own the stock of the bank or that the managements shall be substantially the same.

G. Fiscal Agency Agreements.—Inter-State corporations should not be permitted to enter into any agreements or other arrangements constituting any bank, banker, or trust company their sole fiscal agent, to dispose of their security issues.

H. Private Bankers as Depositaries.—Inter-State corporations should not be permitted to deposit their funds with unsupervised, unregulated private bankers who do not disclose their resources or liabilities, who keep no reserve, and are free to invest their depositors' money as they see fit.

I. Banks Not to Engage in Underwritings.—National banks should be prohibited from directly or indirectly engaging in any promotion, guaranty, or underwriting involving the purchase, sale, public offering, or issue, or other disposition of the securities of any corporation.

J. Investments of Banks in Bonds.—National banks should be expressly authorized to invest 25 per cent. of their capital and surplus in the obligations of States, cities, counties, or other municipal subdivisions and in mortgage bonds of corporations on which interest has been regularly paid for five years, or in case of new issues when the earnings of the corporation within the period were sufficient to have paid such interest.

K. Reform of Railroad Reorganization.—The method of reorganizing insolvent railroads should be reformed by adopting in substance the system provided by the Companies' act of Great Britain, whereby, briefly stated, the plan and procedure on reorganization are placed under the direction and control of the courts, the receiver is elected by the votes of those interested in the property, no sale is involved, a single shareholder can defeat an unjust plan.

L. Railroad Reorganization Under Supervision of Inter-State Commerce Commission.—The Inter-State Commerce Commission should be empowered, subject to review by the courts, to supervise and review plans for the reorganization of inter-State railroads and the issue of securities thereunder.

M. Inter-State Railroad Security Issues Under Supervision of Inter-State Commerce Commission.—The security issues generally of inter-State railroads should be placed under the supervision and control of the Inter-State Commerce Commission.

N. Competitive Bidding for Inter-State Security Issues.—It should also be required that in the disposition of such issues competitive bids, public or private, be invited.

O. Borrowings by Officers from Their Own Banks.—Borrowings, directly or indirectly, by an officer of a National bank from the bank of which he is such officer, and all other transactions between them of a financial character, should be rigidly prohibited.

P. Borrowings by Directors from Their Own Banks.—Borrowings, directly or indirectly, by a Director of a National bank or by any firm of which he is a member or any corporation of the stock of which he holds upward of 10 per cent., from the bank of which he is such Director, should only be permitted on condition that notice shall have been given to his co-Directors and that a full statement of the transaction shall be entered upon the minutes of the meeting at which such loan was authorized.

Q. Financial Transactions of Bank Officers to be in Their Own Names.—Loans or other transactions with a National bank in the interest of or for the eventual benefit of an officer or Director of a National bank, either alone or with others, should be required to be made or done in the name of such officer or Director.

R. Participations by Bank Officers and Directors in Underwritings.—Officers and Directors of National banks should be prohibited from participating in syndicates, promotions, or underwritings of securities in which their banks are or may become interested as underwriters or owners or as lenders thereon.

S. Accepting and Offering Rewards for Bank Loans.—It should be made a crime for officers or Directors of National banks to accept any compensation, commission, or other form of reward whatsoever, for making, directing, voting for, or otherwise promoting any loan of the bank's funds; and it should also be made a crime to offer any such inducement.

T. Limitation of Number of Directors of Bank.—The number of Directors of National banks should be limited to not less than five nor more than thirteen.

U. Publicity for Assets and Stockholders of Banks.—National banks should be required to open to public inspection schedules of their assets other than the names of borrowers, and to make lists of their stockholders public.

March 1, 1913

Trade Commission Bill Signed.

WASHINGTON, Sept. 26.—President Wilson today signed the Trade Commission bill. He announced several weeks ago that he would not appoint the members of the commission until the December session of Congress.

September 27, 1914

TRUST BILL READY TO GO TO SENATE

Conferees Agree on Clayton Measure, with Many Vital Points Modified.

KEEP INTERLOCKING CLAUSE

Price Discrimination Also Restored in Altered Form—Opponents Say It Is "Diluted."

Special to The New York Times.

WASHINGTON, Sept. 23.—The Senate and House conferees on the Clayton anti-trust bill reached an agreement late today, and Mr. Culberson notified the Senate that he would call up the bill at the earliest opportunity.

Opponents of the measure as it comes from the Conference Committee hold that it has been strongly "diluted," and that wherever teeth had been put into the bill in the Senate they had been withdrawn.

The price-discrimination section of the House bill, which was stricken out in the Senate, has been restored in a modified form. The House bill made it a misdemeanor for any person engaged in commerce to discriminate in price between different purchasers of commodities, "with the purpose or intent thereby to destroy or wrongfully injure the business of a competitor of either such purchaser or seller." It also provided as penalty a fine not to exceed $5,000, or imprisonment not to exceed one year, or both.

The conference report eliminates all reference to acts intended to destroy or injure the business of competitors and merely prohibits such acts "where the effect of such discrimination may be to substantially lessen competition or tend to create a monopoly in any line of commerce." Critics of the bill say this opens the door for endless litigation and that all reference to any penalty for violation of the section has been eliminated. The price discrimination section now reads:

> That it shall be unlawful for any person engaged in commerce in the course of such commerce, either directly or indirectly, to discriminate in price between different purchasers of commodities, which commodities are sold for use, consumption, or resale within the United States or any territory thereof or the District of Columbia or any insular possession or other place under the jurisdiction of the United States, where the effect of such discrimination may be to substantially lessen competition or tend to create a monopoly in any line of commerce.

Provisions are added which would prevent the section from applying to discriminations in price on account of differences in grade, quality or quantity and to prevent application of the law with respect to dealers selecting their own customers in "bona fide transactions and not in restraint of trade."

Bar Interlocking Directorates.

The House won out on its provision applying the prohibition of interlocking directorates to bank directors, but with an amendment as follows:

> That from and after two years from the date of approval of this act no person shall at the same time be a Director or other officer employe of more than one bank, banking association, or trust company organized or operating under the laws of the United States either of which has deposits capital and undivided profits aggregating more than $5,000,000; and no private banker or person who is a Director in any bank or trust company, organized and operated under the laws of a State having deposits, &c., aggregating more than $5,000,000 shall be eligible to be a Director in any bank or banking association organized or operating under the laws of the United States.

All banks, of whatever character operating under United States laws in cities of more than 200,000 inhabitants, are prohibited from having as Director or employe any private banker or any Director or any other officer or employe of any other banking association situated in the same place. This section does not prohibit a Director of Class A of the Federal Reserve Bank from being an officer or Director of one member bank.

Two years after the approval of the act no person shall be at the same time a Director in any two or more corporations any one of which has capital, surplus, and undivided profits aggregating more than $1,000,000 engaged in whole or in part in commerce other than banking, &c.

Applies to Railroads

This same provision applies to common carriers, if "such corporations are by virtue of their business and location of operation competitors, so that the elimination of competition by agreement between them would constitute a violation of any of the provisions of the anti-trust laws."

Railroad Directors also would be prohibited from serving as Directors of corporations dealing with securities or supplies in excess of $50,000 a year, except through competitive bidding under regulations by the Interstate Commerce Commission.

One provision was intended to meet the situation growing out of the New Haven developments. It was intended to make it a felony for any officer or Director of a corporation to misapply its funds or to permit them to be misapplied. This was made punishable by a fine of $500 or imprisonment for not less than one or more than ten years.

This embezzlement, however, only applies to every President, Director, officer, or manager of any firm, association or corporation "engaged in commerce as a common carrier," and only applies to the funds, credits, securities, and property "arising or accruing from or used in such commerce." Senators critical of the measure said the wording of the section restricted the felony to a very small proportion of the assets of any corporation engaged in commerce as a common carrier, and fell far short of reaching the evil at which it was aimed.

The penalty of $100 a day or imprisonment in the discretion of the Court, imposed by the House bill for violations of the sections relating to interlocking directorates was tricken out entirely by the conferees.

Little if any change was made in the provisions liberalizing the injunction laws. It s pointed cut, however, that in proceedings for contempt there is a discrimination. Where the United States is a party the court may try the contempt case, and where the Federal Government is not a party trial by jury may be demanded.

Alterations were made to Section 2 of the measure, which is the Senate amendment prohibiting "tying" or exclusive contracts The Senate absolutely prohibited contracts of this character, which prohibits or restricts the purchaser, lessee, or licensee from using any article, obtained under such a contract unless he purchased from the other party to the contract all his supplies, &c. This sort of contract was declared to be unlawful and contrary to public policy in the Senate amendment. Its violation was made punishable by a fine of not to exceed $5,000 or imprisonment not exceeding one year or both.

The conferees rewrote this section and prohibited such contracts only where the effect of such lease, sale, or contract might be to lessen competition or tend to create a monopoly in any line of commerce. No penalty is provided in the conference report. It was said tonight that this revised amendment would be contested in the Senate.

The labor exemption feature of the bill, inserted at the demand of organized labor, was retained in terms, although the conferees made several changes in the wording of the section. An introductory sentence was added, which provides:

"That the labor of a human being is not a commodity or article of commerce."

This section, which is No. 6 of the bill, then continues:

"Nothing contained in the anti-trust laws shall be construed to forbid the existence and operation of labor, agricultural, or horticultural organizations, instituted for the purposes of mutual help, and not having capital stock or conducted for profit, or to forbid or restrain individual members of such organizations from lawfully carrying out the legitimate objects thereof, be held or construed to be illegal combinations or conspiracies in restraint of trade, under the anti-trust laws."

Senator Reed of Missouri intends to fight the action of the conferees in eliminating his amendment making it mandatory for the courts to appoint receivers and sell the property of a corporation adjudged to be a monopoly or combination in restraint of trade.

September 24, 1914

CLAYTON BILL SIGNED.

President Approves Measure Completing Anti-Trust Programme.

WASHINGTON, Oct. 15.—President Wilson today signed the Clayton Anti-Trust bill, thus completing the Administration's trust programme. There were no ceremonies connected with the signing of the bill.

The Chicago Association of Commerce, in a telegram to President Wilson, today approved the Anti-Trust and Trade Commission bills.

"We believe that in the administration of these laws the opportunity afforded for a prompt hearing upon complaint will result in the speedy suppression of evil practices and in the promotion of honest business," the message said.

While railway securities legislation probably will be deferred until the next Congress, because no conclusion on the form of it has been reached and because President Wilson believes there is no pressing demand for it now, Mr. Wilson told callers today the question was still an open one.

October 16, 1914

Big Business as Seen by One of Its Leaders

Improved Relations of Corporations and Public—Member of the Rockefeller Group of Financiers Analyzes Industrial Situation

The author of this article is one of the veterans of big business in America. He was in the group associated with John D. Rockefeller in building the Standard Oil Company and is now President of the Corn Products Refining Company, a Director in many corporations, and a representative of industrial interests equaled in extent by those of few other capitalists.

By E. T. Bedford.

THE outbreak of war with a highly organized industrial nation wherein the Government has always given aid to the business interests, coming at the close of a long period of internal ferment when the attention of the American people has been largely occupied with consideration of the question of great corporations and their relation with the Government, should bring about a change in the attitude of the people and Government of this country toward legitimate businesses.

Size and efficiency should not be regarded as criminal in themselves. Government restriction of business abuses, not of legitimate activity, should be operated by simple machinery and based on laws which business men can understand.

In my opinion, the attitude of the American people toward the great corporations has changed very materially for the better in recent years, and the realization that large industrial units are required for the doing of large things is now very general. There have been excesses in public action against large corporations, but I think it is safe to rely on the essential fairness and the essential intelligence of the American people to see that the corporations which observe the law and the principles of fairness in business dealing shall receive fair treatment, both as a matter of principle and as a matter of national interest.

I do not believe in the theory that modern business organization tends inevitably, or even generally, to monopoly. My views on this subject, after many years of experience in businesses both large and small, operating with a capital of a very few thousands or many millions, might be summarized as follows:

1. Under modern economic conditions there is not only a place but a need for the large as well as the small business. The value of either to society depends entirely on the service which it gives, and the different kinds of service furnished by businesses of different size make the demand for the small as well as the large manufacturer, the corner grocery as well as the chain store.

2. Monopolies are possible in three ways—through patents, through control of the raw materials, and through unfair competition. The first two may be legitimate and permissible, for economic laws will regulate the price of their output and conditions of sale. The third is easily susceptible of regulation.

3. Unfair monopolies can and should be prevented by a Federal corporation act, which should be of such a sort as to be easily intelligible; which should do away with the present conditions under which things entirely legal in one State cannot be done by the same corporation in another State, and which should carry with it the penalty, to be exercised by the Federal Trade Commission, of withdrawal of the license to do interstate business.

Taking these points up one by one, I want to make it clear, first of all, that economic value, the thing that makes a business possible and profitable, depends on service to the public, but that this service may be of different kinds. The large corporation may produce and the large dealer may sell at a lower price than his smaller competitor; but the small manufacturer may produce near at hand, the small store may have the goods exactly when and where the customer wants them. Many people would rather pay 20 cents for something they want at once and can get at the next corner than to walk several blocks and get it for 18. Local and immediate service gives the small business a field in which the large one is not likely to be a successful competitor if its competition is fairly conducted.

However, it cannot be denied that the great efficiency that has been created in production in recent years is very largely to be credited to the big corporations which have been able to introduce the latest and most improved machinery and have had the courage to junk that which has been superseded. The excellence of the big corporation comes not so much from greater size as from greater efficiency. To a certain extent, of course, this efficiency is to be attributed to its size; it has more capital to finance improvement in methods and processes, its great extent enables it to operate more economically; and the men who are at the head of great businesses of international scope are more likely to have the courage and foresight which are required when valuable and new machinery, which is nevertheless not the newest and most efficient, must be thrown upon the scrap heap.

The large corporations have done wonders through skilled organizations, which their size has enabled them to maintain; through research work, which has improved quality, developed new processes, and created new products. But the small manufacturer gets the benefit of most of the pioneer work done by his large competitor. A great corporation can employ a man in research work for years, and when at last he has perfected his process the small competitor can buy him away at a price which the large producer cannot meet without displacing his entire scale of salary values.

Large corporations are obliged to maintain uniform prices, for they must issue their price lists, making known their maximum price to all buyers. While their competition has undoubtedly, as has been complained, limited the profit of the smaller manufacturer and forced him to a higher degree of efficiency in order to compete, it has frequently been stated on the witness stand in trust suits that the success of the small manufacturer may be attributed to the existence of the large corporations.

For they have blazed the way; the result of the research work which they have undertaken at great expense is nearly always shared by the small corporations which have had no share in the initial cost. And so it has often been found in the anti-trust suits that small competing manufacturers are the most important witnesses for the defense.

The fact is that the present necessities for big operations are proving the value of large agencies that can alone meet the requirements. No one can question the right of the Government to regulate large corporations, but it is imperative as a matter of national interest that this regulation be fairly and intelligently exercised. What is needed is a simple and intelligible law to prevent abuses, not legitimate uses, of capital.

Large corporations doing an interstate business are put to great trouble and expense by different laws in different States. Some States will not allow external corporations to own real estate; others will not allow corporations having more than a certain capital to do business at all; and the result is the necessary establishment of small subsidiary companies which serve no legitimate, economic purpose. Such matters as labels, in which State rules require the preparation of a number of different kinds of labels for the same product, sold all over the country, exhibit instances where there is no additional protection to the consumer but a greatly increased expense to the producer, a difference which the consumer must pay in the end.

A Federal Corporation act to be executed by the Federal Trade Commission would change all this and simplify the doing of legitimate business. But it is imperative that the law be simple and clear. When the Supreme Court of the United States differs by a five-to-four vote as to whether a man has broken the law or not, the business man is hardly to be blamed if he does not know whether a given practice is a legitimate and economical business procedure or a crime. This law should define clearly what constitutes unfair competition. It should require a Federal license for all concerns with more than a certain amount of capital; and it should make this license revoeable by the Trade Commission when it is proved that the corporation has violated the law. There would be no violations under an arrangement like that; the knowledge that illegal acts would result in the abolition of the permission to do business would make every man keep carefully within the law.

Further than this I do not believe Government regulation should or can profitably go, except in certain cases under conditions of great national emergency. Such conditions now exist on account of the war, and I think it proper and desirable that the Government should exercise some sort of regulation over the necessities of life and industry such as coal, flour, &c., under the competent advice and direction of such great men as are now serving on the Advisory Committees, for no business can be harmed and no serious wrong can be done by such great captains of industry as constitute these various committees if the Government will only heed their advice and counsel. The policies should be determined and enforced by the Government; the direction of the businesses under the proper regulation should be left to those business men. The Secretary of War is in charge of a department which includes many great hospitals; he has supervision of their general operation. But the Secretary of War would never dream of trying to superintend these hospitals in person. He knows that is a job for a medical expert. The Secretary of the Navy does not interfere in the technical management of a shipbuilding yard. And the heads of other departments are likewise unqualified for managing the very highly specialized technique of great modern businesses. Their function is that of control to the end that the interests of the nation may best be served; but there is no place for their interference except for that purpose and to the extent which will promote the attainment of that end.

This regulation should be only as a war measure; in time of peace the laws of supply and demand should and will supply sufficient check. High prices which have prevailed of late and have caused much complaint have been inevitable on account of the demand. The buyer who knows that the supply is limited and wants to get enough to meet his own needs makes the price. In the matter of coal, for instance, I know a buyer whose annual consumption is half a million tons. He must have coal, or his factories will shut down and thousands of men will be thrown out of work. He knows that conditions are such that there may be a shortage. He sends his buyers out with instructions to get coal at any price.

In a case like this the seller really has very little to say in the matter. He knows his competitors are getting this price and that if he does not get it he will, perhaps, be unfair to his shareholders. He knows, too, that if he names a lower price his production will quickly pass into the hands of a few buyers or speculators, and in the end the consumer will have to pay a price still higher. Here is a case where Government regulation is not only justifiable but advisable.

But this regulation of price, of distribution, carries with it an obligation on the part of the Government to supply the producer with the facilities for production. I talked recently with a very large coal producer, who said that he had plenty of coal but could not get it above ground. His miners would not work unless they were assured of a full day, and this necessitated having an adequate number of cars on the siding. This he frequently did not have, and the result was a great reduction in the amount of coal produced. So Government regulation of coal should imply Government regulation of the distribution of coal cars, to enable the producer to get his coal out efficiently and economically.

Much of the advice given recently as to how the consumer can fight the high prices and reduce the cost of living is rather uninformed, and much of the criticism of the increase in prices is unfair. For instance, the consumer is advised to make his purchases in bulk rather than in packages, in the belief that this is the most economical thing to do. It may be the most economical in the case of advertised products whose trade marks, because of advertising, demand a premium; but I doubt very much if it is the most economical method in the purchase of staple products.

During the recent period of high prices I have known of several staple products that were obtainable pound for pound at a less price from the manufacturers in sealed package than they cost in bulk. And this is not due to price cutting by retailers. That is a thing met with frequently, which, in my opinion, the manufacturer is powerless to stop, no matter how hard he may try to keep the price of his product uniform. But I know of many instances where these staples were sold by the manu-

E. T. Bedford, Capitalist, Who Has Turned to Authorship Long Enough to Discuss the Growing Amity of the Corporations, the Government and the Public.

facturer himself at a less price in the package than for the same goods in bulk.

Great economy has resulted to the manufacturer from improved machinery. A single machine packs, seals, and weighs a hundred or more packages a minute, and produces at a much lower cost than is possible when the goods are packed by hand in a paper bag. The average volume of business now done by the retailer would scarcely be possible if he were obliged to do the packing himself by hand, as was done less than a quarter of a century ago. The package business stands for economy, and there are a number of manufacturers packing more than a million packages a day who feel well paid if their margin of profit is as much as an eighth of a cent a pound.

Not only does the package mean economy, but the original container is a guarantee to the housewife of honest weight, quality, and sanitary condition. It was once a common occurrence for the consumer who now gets his syrup in a can sealed by the manufacturer to go to the corner store and have the syrup poured into the household jug from a large jug, with a corncob for a stopper, or from a barrel with its usual accompaniment of flies. Dried fruits come to him from the manufacturer in a package packed and sealed under conditions of the utmost possible cleanliness; he used to see them dug out of an incrusted mass with a fruit auger which sometimes, for convenience, was also used for poking embers in the store stove.

This improvement in sanitary conditions, this guarantee of honest weight, and this lower price are instances of the better service given by a single type of business through the development of great corporations which made heavy investments in research and which were not afraid to throw away pretty good machinery to install the best machinery. They consequently built up more efficient, more sanitary, and more economical processes. The benefit of their work is reaped not only by the public but by their smaller competitors, which have been able to acquire the same processes without the heavy expense, and which in their own field have an economic place because of their particular service—a place from which they should not be ousted, and cannot be without the employment of unfair methods.

These methods can be prohibited in the manner I have suggested above, with complete protection to the public and the small dealer and no interference with the legitimate function of the great corporation. And such sane, intelligible regulation, instead of the assaults on business merely because of its size, is what this nation needs to meet the economic competition of other countries which have already organised themselves as efficient economic bodies or are now in process of doing it.

July 1, 1917

WORLD WAR I

JOIN ALL INDUSTRIES IN AID OF DEFENSE

Wilson Mobilization Plan Will Enlist Every Factory That Can Make War Supplies.

RAILROADS ALSO A FACTOR

36,000 Scientific Engineers to Unite in Gigantic System Like That of Germany.

Special to The New York Times.

WASHINGTON, Jan. 16.—The Secretary of the Navy made public tonight details of the plans of President Wilson and himself for mobilizing the industrial resources of the country, including transportation, in time of war. That these plans were to be formulated was announced in New York yesterday through the medium of a letter from President Wilson to W. L. Saunders of New York, President of the American Institute of Mining Engineers, in which the society was asked to nominate a representative from its membership for each State of the Union to act in conjunction with representatives from four other technical societies to assist the Naval Consulting Board in the work of collecting data for use in organizing the manufacturing resources of the country for the public service in case of emergency. The four other technical organizations which are asked to cooperate are the American Society of Mechanical Engineers, the American Society of Civil Engineers, the American Institute of Electrical Engineers, and the American Chemical Society.

In his annual address to Congress on Dec. 7 President Wilson indicated that he might ask for a small appropriation to carry into effect the suggestion he made for arranging to mobilize our economic resources in any time of national necessity. The invitation to the five technical societies to co-operate with the Government to that end is the outcome of recent consideration given to the best means of adopting the plan which the President had in mind when he prepared his address.

Plan in Operation.

The details of the plans for industrial mobilization show that the movement has already been put into operation in part through the Committee on Production, Organization, Manufacture and Standardization of the Naval Consulting Board. Members of the five technical societies are serving on the Naval Consulting Board, and a representative of each society is a member of this committee. The committee has had several meetings, and after consulting with Secretary Daniels outlined the plans which were stated in President Wilson's letter to President Saunders, and the Presidents of other technical organizations.

Briefly, the plans contemplate the gathering of information that will enable the Government to know instantly in case of war just where it can obtain all the additional supplies that it will need to provide for its military and naval forces the sinews of war—munitions, clothing, foods, and the host of other things that would be required to equip and maintain an army. In addition, the number of locomotives and railroad cars, both passenger and freight, will be ascertained from the railroads, and to a certain extent the Government will have at hand information that will enable it to know in advance how it will be able to transport troops and supplies.

The plans approximate those which Germany has had in operation for many years. In his statement tonight Secretary Daniels said that "one of the belligerent countries now engaged in war," an apparent reference to Germany, "is utilizing about 80 per cent. of its industries in producing material for the army and navy." The United States Government, he said, would seek to do the same thing.

The plans provide for fulfilling, in part at least, the dream of military and naval officers in this country who were impressed for a long time prior to the European conflict with the advantage of the German system of making industrial resources capable of immediate mobilization in the event of hostilities.

Stride Toward Preparedness.

In the statement made tonight Secretary Daniels said:

"In a nutshell, the course proposed is to do in time of peace, quietly, efficiently, and thoroughly, the very things which all of us know must be done to achieve true preparedness, and thus prevent tremendous losses in lives and money possible if they are postponed until an outbreak of hostilities. In short, it is proposed, through the utilization of the membership of these societies, to oil up the great wheels of industry and keep them turning in the interest of the Government, prepared at any and all times to speed up in time of need. The plan is in substance as follows:

"These five engineering societies represent a membership of about 36,000 technical men scattered through every State. Their service is mainly in industrial plants, such as mines, mills, furnaces, factories, railroads, automobile plants, &c. The members of these technical societies are peculiarly fitted to perform this class of work in an intelligent and disinterested manner. They are men whose training and intelligence have fitted them to achieve results. As members of these societies their standing is assured and will inspire confidence. These men, not being Government employes—as the service will be rendered without salaries—will naturally act upon their own initiative as engineers, and in a truly patriotic manner. Such a body is strictly nonpartisan and not political.

"The plan involves a board of five engineers in each State of the Union, one from each of the societies. This will cover civil engineering, mining and metallurgical engineering, and mechanical, electrical and chemical work, which practically reaches the entire field. Each one of these men will be appointed at the request of the President of the United States, being first nominated by the society of which he is a member. On approval by the Secretary of the Navy he will receive his official appointment and become an associate member of the Naval Consulting Board, working through the committee of the board.

"These five men in each State will form the nucleus of an organization in each State. They will be asked to select members of their societies from all parts of the State and will furnish them with blank forms, on which will be made a true inventory of our country's producing and manufacturing resources, including transportation. The information given upon these forms will be used by the civilian consulting board and by the Government of the United States in perfecting the national industrial organization necessary to the plans for defense.

Work Started in New Jersey.

"To illustrate: The committee of the Naval Consulting Board has taken the State of New Jersey as a sample, it being essentially an industrial State. The official records of New Jersey show that there are about eight hundred plants there which might be useful in government service in case of war. Very small plants and also factories producing things that are not classed as munitions have been eliminated. The five societies mentioned have about 1,200 members in New Jersey, showing more than one man to a plant. What is true of New Jersey would be practically true of all other States, except that in the Western States the proportion of members to industrial plants would be larger.

"Once having the data, the purpose is to lay this before the Government and in this way bring the officials in touch with the industries, so that not only will the Government know the volume and extent to which these industries may render service, but it will be able to advise and direct the industries as to the requirements of such service, as, for instance, it is proposed to place small orders for certain munitions based upon conditions existing at the time. These orders will perhaps bring no profit to the manufacturers, but they will keep them in touch and tuned up for service in emergencies. They will, through such orders, have gauges on the shelves and at times in the shops, blue prints, specifications, and samples on hand. The men in each plant will have a working knowledge of Government requirements.

"One of the belligerent countries now engaged in war is utilizing about 80 per cent of its industries in producing army and navy materials. In case of war this Government would need to do the same thing, and in order to turn the wheels rapidly it is necessary in advance to know where to turn to obtain supplies, not only of munitions, but of everything needed to equip men in the service. And this practically means everything needed for the arming, clothing, transportation, sustenance and care of the men called to the colors. This would extend the influence of this work to all of the industries of the country, large and small, and it is particularly desirous in the case of plants of moderate size, the facilities of which might not otherwise be known to the Government, that they be maintained in condition to serve immediately. It would be possible, therefore, more generally to distribute orders for munitions which usually go to the big plants of the country, and through this organization of all industries to include a large number of smaller plants as well as those of the largest capacity.

"The preparedness of industrial plants is an important step in the protection of the country against attack, and is preliminary to successful resistance. It is not only the first step, but the most important one—a step which is less expensive than any other, and one which should excite less antagonism. It goes to the roots of the matter. While preparedness of plants to furnish supplies for war is the most important step, it is the one heretofore least thought of, as shown by the condition of certain countries at the beginning of the present European war."

January 17, 1916

WAR ORDERS' TOTAL NOW $3,000,000,000

Purchases in United States by Allies Have Reached Unprecedented Amount.

SCHWAB'S BIG OPERATIONS

His New $200,000 Plant to Make Only Boxes for Shrapnel—Secrecy in Deals.

Special to The New York Times.

PHILADELPHIA, July 16.—America, from Chicago east, is now on the shady side of $3,000,000,000 in all its war orders, counting blankets, machinery, locomotives, and other products not coming strictly under the head of munitions.

Twenty-four corporations alone account for more than $1,000,000,000 up to Feb. 1 of this year. This figure is said to be "highly conservative." In other words, this item, comprising scarcely one-third of the country's war receipts, is equal to the entire national debt of the United States, with 140 years of existence behind it during which it financed four wars of its own, innumerable Congressional "pork barrels," and satisfied the wants of a population of 100,000,000, or as many people as France and Germany have combined.

Official reports from the Bureau of Foreign and Domestic Commerce at Washington show that shipments of war munitions up to date have aggregated $446,000,000. These figures cover munitions in the strictest sense of the word. They do not include locomotives, blankets, rails, machines for gunmaking, or other materials of this class which are indispensable to the nations as part of their war supplies.

It must be remembered also that a tremendous amount of war orders already placed will not begin to run before the Fall and next year. Some of these contracts call for delivery as late as 1918.

The war has made millionaires and multi-millionaires of such Philadelphians as Alba B. Johnson and Samuel M. Vauclain, President and Vice President, respectively, of the Baldwin Locomotive Works; Roland L. Taylor, who laid the first stones of the Midvale Steel and Ordnance Company; E. T. Stotesbury, William H. Donner, former President of the Cambria Steel Company, and numerous bankers and industrial leaders close to the fountainhead of "big business" have seen wealth virtually pour into their pockets through merger transactions and stock market trading.

The Philadelphia district, taking in South Bethlehem and Wilmington, stands credited with $1,000,000,000 all by itself. As nearly as can be computed, for nothing can be learned accurately with the munitions makers tied lip and tongue by the Allies, fear of labor disturbances and other factors, including the Government, the Baldwin Locomotive Works have received, either directly or indirectly, for the Eddystone Munitions Company orders amounting to approximately $150,000,000. Beside this the company will participate in royalties of at least $2,000,000 from the Remington Arms Company plant at Eddystone, not to speak of two buildings which revert to it on the termination of the war.

The Midvale Steel and Ordnance Company, so William P. Barba, Vice President of the Nicetown plant, testified before the House Committee on Naval Affairs on March 23, was working on $60,000,000 worth of war contracts. At that time the Remington Arms plant had not started work on the second order for 2,000,000 rifles for the Allies, which, it is understood, the company took at $16.20 apiece, or a matter of $32,400,000 for the whole contract. In the Midvale business must be included the orders taken by the Cambria Steel Company, which, consolidated with the Midvale, brought a dower of rail contracts.

The war orders of the Bethlehem Steel Corporation at one time at least were an open book. They are placed at $300,000,000 up to February last. Charles M. Schwab, the salesman extraordinary of the war-order business, made no secret of scalping the cream of the Allies' business before J. P. Morgan made such a bargain as to be appointed the virtual representative of the foreign group. And to prove that his profits were not mere paper figuring, Schwab is reported to have gone so far as to distribute Christmas presents of anywhere from $100,000 to $1,000,000 to "deserving employes." One of these to receive the "cross of gold" to the extent of $1,000,000 as a bonus, it is said, was E. G. Grace, President of the company. Other "boys" fared proportionately well, depending on the way in which they had dug up their talents to further "getting out the stuff."

The Bethlehem Steel Corporation has produced munitions far in excess of any other plant in the country. Its payroll now equals 55,000 men. Only last week Schwab announced he had a war fund of $70,000,000 with which he intended to build his various units, the most recent acquisition to which was the Pennsylvania Steel, with its splendid Maryland Steel subsidiary at Sparrows Point, outside of Baltimore.

In many respects Bethlehem has surpassed the German-renowned Krupps. From Bethlehem to Redington, along the Lehigh River and south almost to Hellertown, the plant is so large that only a few officials really appreciate how extensive it is. And it is still growing. Only last week three large buildings were completed in which munitions will be manufactured for the Russian Government. These buildings represent an investment of $1,000,000 each. Close to Quakertown Schwab is having built the Victor Box Company at a cost of $200,000, simply to make boxes to transport shrapnel.

As an indication of the secrecy observed even in a proposition so simple as this, the agent intrusted with this work drew his laborers entirely from Philadelphia. Every one of them was a picked man who had worked in constructing buildings for war munitions, and who, above all, possessed the attribute of being able to keep his lips sealed. This box factory will be completed about Aug. 1. Here hundreds of thousands of boxes will be turned out weekly, and they will be painted inside and out. Thus the Allies will insure that shells will not rust, no matter how long they may be held behind the trenches.

Bethlehem's output averages 350,000 shells of all calibres a month. These include the English "three 29's," 60-pounders, 10-inch explosives, naval projectiles for England and a large order of the famous "75's." In addition to finished shells it is making accurately rolled bars out of which England and France will cut shrapnel billets. It is said that the price of an English 329 or a French 75 at Bethlehem is $12,000, while a 60-pound gun is reputed to bring $22,000.

It is also reported that Bethlehem is making rapid progress in the manufacture of its new siege guns of 42 centimeters, which are to outrival the Krupp "Big Berthas," the guns that pulverized the Belgian defenses. The American piece, it is asserted, will throw a shell twenty-four miles.

The du Pont Company, at Wilmington, next to Schwab, is said to be the big profit-maker with a foreign war account of more than $200,000,000. The profits arising from this business can be appreciated when it is known that powder brings $1.10 a pound. As given out it costs something in the neighborhood of 30 cents a pound to manufacture this explosive. In June 14,000,000 pounds went to Europe from Philadelphia alone.

Thus the Allies have fared in getting their munitions orders into the plants of this country. But not only have the Allies thrown business to America. Germany at the present time, indications here in Philadelphia show, is using America to further the conduct of its defense.

There is no question but that Norway and Sweden are acting as intermediaries for German purchases in this country. The last issue of the drug magazine, Weekly Drug Markets, dated July 10, published the shipment of 115,472 pounds of toluol from New York to Sweden. Toluol is one of the prime ingredients in the manufacture of high explosives, and this order, together with others in the past, is taken to be highly significant. It is known that Germany is carrying on a heavy trade with Sweden through the Baltic, and as such materials as this are indispensable to Germany's warfare, authorities here see the fulfillment of America's neutrality promise to Germany: "Anything we have is yours if you will pay the price and come and get it."

July 17, 1916

PRESIDENT NAMES DEFENSE ADVISERS

Board of Seven to Act with National Council Is Headed by Daniel Willard.

SAMUEL GOMPERS A MEMBER

Bernard Baruch and Julius Rosenwald Among Others Appointed—Executive Explains Their Duties.

Special to The New York Times.

ON BOARD THE PRESIDENT'S TRAIN, HARRISBURG, Penn., Oct. 11.—President Wilson made public tonight the names of seven men whom he has appointed members of an Advisory Commission to be associated with the Council of National Defense, created at the late session of Congress with an appropriation of $200,000. The men who make up the commission are distinguished in wholly different fields of activity, and it is known that the President had this in mind in naming them. The list follows:

Daniel Willard of Baltimore, President of the Baltimore and Ohio Railroad.

Samuel Gompers of Washington, President of the American Federation of Labor.

Dr. Franklin H. Martin of Chicago.

Howard E. Coffin of Detroit.

Bernard Baruch, the New York banker.

Dr. Hollis Godfrey of Philadelphia.

Julius Rosenwald of Chicago, President of Sears, Roebuck & Co.

Dr. Martin is a distinguished surgeon who was recommended by the Affiliated Medical Societies of the country. Howard E. Coffin has long been active in the American Automobile Association, and Mr. Wilson is known to regard him as a man who has done much toward co-ordinating the automobile industry for service in time of national emergency. Dr. Godfrey is a prominent engineer, who gave up his private practice to assume the Presidency of Drexel Institute in Philadelphia

In announcing the appointments, the President issued the following statement:

The Council of National Defense has been created because the Congress has realized that the country is best prepared for war when thoroughly prepared for peace. From an economic point of view there is now very little difference between the machinery required for commercial efficiency and that required for military purposes. In both cases the whole industrial mechanism must be organized in the most effective way. Upon this conception of the national welfare the Council is organized, in the words of the act, for "the creation of relations which will render possible in time of need the immediate concentration and utilization of the resources of the nation."

The organization of the Council likewise opens up a new and direct channel of communication and co-operation between business and scientific men and all departments of the Government, and it is hoped that it will, in addition, become a rallying point for civic bodies working for the national defense. The Council's chief functions are:

1. The co-ordination of all forms of transportation and the development of means of transportation to meet the military, industrial and commercial needs of the nation.

2. The extension of the industrial mobilization work of the Committee on Industrial Preparedness of the Naval Consulting Board. Complete information as to our present manufacturing and producing facilities adaptable to many-sided uses of modern warfare will be procured, analyzed and made use of.

One of the objects of the council will be to inform American manufacturers as to the part they can and must play in national emergency. It is empowered to establish at once and maintain through subordinate bodies of specially qualified persons an auxiliary organization composed of men of the best creative and administrative capacity, capable of mobilizing to the utmost the resources of the country.

The personnel of the council's advisory members, appointed without regard to party, marks the entrance of the non-partisan engineer and professional man into American governmental affairs on a wider scale than ever before. It is responsive to the increased demand for and need of business organization in public matters and for the presence there of the best specialists in their respective fields. In the present instance, the time of some of the members of the Advisory Board could not be purchased. They serve the Government without remuneration, efficiency being their sole object and Americanism their only motive.

October 12, 1916

GIVES 500 ENGINEERS TO THE SIGNAL CORPS

Experts in Telephone, Telegraph, and Wireless Work Provided by the A. T. & T.

The American Telephone and Telegraph Company has given to the United States what is perhaps the finest auxiliary signal corps possessed by any army. By arrangement with the War and Navy Departments the telephone officials will furnish picked engineers to the army and navy, paying them the difference between the army pay and their salaries with the telephone company. About five hundred engineers have been selected already for this work, and some of them have been sworn into the Government service. The work has been going on quietly for more than a week.

If the United States sends an army to the front, these men, the best engineers of the best telephone system in the world, will supply communication facilities. The corps will be made up of general engineers, plant engineers, and traffic engineers, to plan, set up and operate telephone, telegraph, and wireless plants. Also men will be supplied to assist in the wireless work of the navy if the regular force proves to be too small. The Bell system has a great many engineers —there are 3,000 in the Eastern division. It is estimated that 500 will be enough for the present needs of the military service.

Frank H. Bethell, Vice President of the New York Telephone Company, an auxiliary of the American Telephone and Telegraph Company, asserted last night that the Bell corps would be ready to supply any sort of communication facilities the army would need.

"The plan has been worked out in co-operation with the Signal Corps officers," he said. "We have raised a corps by asking for volunteers, and they have been studying the work the army and navy will require. I do not know the exact number that have been sworn into the Federal service. These men will be able to put up telephone, telegraph, and wireless systems, and maintain and operate them. I am confident they will prove an efficient force. The company will see that they do not suffer financially."

The American company perfected last year the wireless telephone system that made it possible to talk from Paris to Washington and from Washington to Honolulu. While Mr. Bethell did not go into details of the plans that are being made for the army service, it is more than likely that the army of the United States may be able to use wireless telephones in field operations. None of the European armies has this system.

April 9, 1917

PRESIDENT DENOUNCES PROFITEERS, SAYS FAIR PRICES MUST PREVAIL IN WAR, ASSAILS SHIP OWNERS FOR HIGH RATES

NATION'S FATE IN BALANCE

Prices Mean Efficiency or Inefficiency, Victory or Defeat.

OCEAN RATES EXACTING

President Asserts Marine Men Took Most Effective Means to Defeat Allies.

WANTS ONE PRICE FOR ALL

Public and Government Must Be Treated Alike—Steel Men Confer with Officials.

Special to The New York Times.

WASHINGTON, July 11.—In an open address teeming with sensational utterances President Wilson tonight served notice on mine operators, manufacturers, and shipping interests that the Government intended to fix prices of their products during the war period, and that the public must be served on the same basis as governmental agencies. Those who sought to avoid the rulings of the Government, he said, would be held guilty of an act favorable to the cause of the enemy. The price fixed, he said, must, of course, be a just one.

"We must make the prices to the public the same as the prices to the Government," the President declared. "Prices mean the same thing everywhere now. They mean the efficiency or the inefficiency of the nation, whether it is the Government that pays them or not. They mean victory or defeat. They mean that America will win her place once for all among the foremost free nations of the world, or that she will sink to defeat and become a second-rate power alike in thought or action. This is a day of her reckoning, and every man among us must personally face that reckoning along with her."

No Profits in Patriotism.

Patriotism and profits ought never in the present circumstances to be mentioned together, the President said, for patriotism leaves profits out of the question. No true man, he added, who stayed behind while others went to the front to risk their lives, would ask himself what he is going to make out of business.

"No true patriot," he said, speaking of the overseas expeditions, "will permit himself to take toll of their heroism in money or seek to grow rich by the shedding of their blood. When they are giving their lives, will he not at least give his money?"

The President said he could not believe that men living in easy and peaceful fashion would attempt to "exact a price, drive a bargain" while others were enduring the agony of this war on the battlefields and "bereaved women" and "pitiful children" were about them.

Special attention was directed to the ship owners who had raised freight rates because of the tremendous demand on shipping facilities.

"They," the President said, "are doing everything that high freight charges can do to make the war a failure, to make it impossible." He added that those who had raised freight rates had "taken the most effective means in their power to defeat the armies engaged against Germany." He took it for granted that they would reconsider the whole matter. In concluding his address he said:

"I shall expect every man who is not a slacker to be at my side throughout this great enterprise. In it no man can win honor who thinks of himself."

Reasonable Profit Plan.

The President's address was entirely in line with his whole attitude in regard to the prices which should be paid for essentials during the war period. He has stood behind Secretary Daniels of the navy and others who have demanded lower prices from certain interests than they were willing to give voluntarily. He recently decided that the Federal Trade Commission should be aked to determine the production cost and that Governmental agencies should then name an ultimate price based on the production plus a reasonable profit to make possible fair wages to the employes.

This program, while acquiesced in by some interests, it was stated, brought protests from others and promised to raise a price-fixing controversy which the President might find it difficult to adjust without asking Congress for legislation which would give him and his advisers absolute control of the industries affected.

The delay in the passage of the food legislation and the controversy over steel and coal prices were among the things which moved the President to break his silence. He felt that if the public was fully awakened to the crisis America faced, it would not countenance any selfish effort, and that American business men, once convinced of the judgment of his opinion, would co-operate to the full with the Government.

The address of the President came in a measure as an answer to the Administration advisers who have been in favor of granting more than the normal profit to various industries in order to speed up production.

Conference with Steel Men.

The President's address came as a complete surprise tonight to representatives of the great iron and steel interests who met here today with Secretary Baker, Secretary Daniels, William Denman, Chairman of the Shipping Board, and Bernard M. Baruch of the Council of National Defense to discuss steel prices and other questions involved in the shipbuilding program and other plans essential to the country.

It was freely predicted tonight that at least a tentative arrangement would be made today between the steel interests and the Government, partly as a result of the President's address, which would assure the delivery of steel at a price somewhere between the $56 a ton for plates suggested by Chairman Denman and the $95 a ton price quoted in the earlier conferences between the steel men and General George W. Goethals, general manager of the Emergency Fleet Corporation. The best advice tonight was that the ultimate price might be somewhere in the neighborhood of $65 a ton, the price fixed by Secretary of the Navy Daniels, but no official statement in regard to prices could be obtained.

One feature of the conference, it was said on high authority, was the clash between what Wall Street thought of prices in wartimes and the beliefs held by several of the Government officials. There was, as explained in statements by Secretary Baker and the representatives of the steel group, no definite effort to arrive at prices, but the question was uppermost in every mind. The conference will be continued tomorrow, and it is possible that the atmosphere will be considerably cleared, so far as prices are concerned, before final adjournment.

Two of the questions which were uppermost in the open discussions today were distribution and transportation. It is understood that the steel interests were given to understand that the Government must have all of the steel that it needs for the merchant ship building and navy requirements, and that it would find ways and means of obtaining it if it did not come voluntarily, even if it had to commandeer the output of the steel plants. Also it was stated that the answer of the steel men to this suggestion was:

"Tell us what you want us to do."

Told of President's Plan.

The steel men were told that the President was in favor of an investigation of production costs by the Federal Trade Commission to determine a fair price at which the Government as well as the public should obtain its steel, and that in fact the commission had been instructed by the President himself to undertake such an investigation, and probably would be prepared to make a report by Aug. 1, or a few days before that time.

Following the conference Secretary Baker made this statement:

"The conferences which have been held today between a committee of the American Iron and Steel Institute and the Secretary of War, the Secretary of the Navy, the Chairman of the Shipping Board, and Mr. Baruch of the Advisory Commission of the Council of National Defense were for the purpose of discussing the total steel production of the country and the advisability of its use for the purpose of carrying on the war. Pending the inquiries of the Federal Trade Commission, no consideration was given to the subject of price.

"The needs for the immediate future were estimated, and assurances of hearty co-operation on the part of the producers were given. The discussion took a wide range, involving statistics and estimates of production, and further estimates will be submitted by the manufacturers in the morning, when the conference will be continued."

It is understood that the steel men are still ready to furnish the Government with the 400,000 tons of steel a month for shipbuilding construction which they promised General Goethals some time ago when the $95 price was quoted as a tentative figure. There has been some gossip that the steel men were holding back since it became evident that the Government would strive for a price considerably under that level, and the Government has been urged again to take up a big wooden ship program.

It is also understood that the inclusion of steel in the President's proclamation restricting exports has had a decided effect, as it made possible the control of the sale of steel to Japan and other foreign countries which have been bidding the market up. The heads of a number of the largest steel and iron interests in the country were present at the conference, including the following: Elbert H. Gary, Chairman United States Steel Corporation; James A. Farrell, President United States Steel Corporation; Charles M. Schwab, Chairman Bethlehem Steel Corporation; E. G. Grace, President Bethlehem Steel Corporation; J. A. Burden, President Burden Iron and Steel Company; E. A. S. Clarke, President Lackawanna Steel Company; H. G. Dalton, President Pickands Mather & Co.; A. C. Dinkey, Vice President Midvale Steel and Ordnance Company; J. A. Topping, President Republic Iron and Steel Company, and James B. Bonner, representing American Iron and Steel Institute.

July 12, 1917

STEEL MEN ACCEPT PRICE FIXING BY THE GOVERNMENT

Trade Commission to Determine Costs and a Fair Profit to be Allowed.

PLANTS AT PUBLIC SERVICE

Orders Equitably Distributed—Public and Allies Probably to Get Same Rates.

OTHER PRICES TO BE FIXED

Will Cover All War Necessities in Spirit of Wilson's Appeal to Business Men.

Special to The New York Times.

WASHINGTON, July 12.—In line with the spirit of President Wilson's address to the country, in which he said that men were not patriots who talked of profits, based on war-time activities, while others sacrificed their lives, representatives of the big steel interests, in conference here today with Secretary of War Baker and other Government officials, agreed that the entire output of their plants should be at the disposal of the Government.

The price to be paid, they agreed, should be fixed after the Federal Trade Commission had completed its investigation of production costs. They asked that a reasonable profit be allowed in order to facilitate production and permit expansion, and this was assured. No definite statement was made as to the attitude of the steel interests toward consumers other than the Government, but it was understood that the same price would prevail.

Government officials, it is understood, undertook to aid the steel interests in carrying out this program by seeing to it that raw materials should be available to them at low prices. This matter will be taken up immediately. It was stated on high authority that the Government was in a mood to commandeer the raw material output if the producers did not consent to aid in carrying out the President's idea of universal service. The steel men said they could not produce steel at the prices quoted unofficially by Government agencies if raw materials cost from $40 to $50 a ton.

Commission Inquiry Wide.

The full import of the President's address was realized when information was obtained concerning the scope of the inquiry into production costs which the President asked the Federal Trade Commission to make. It is said that it is his intention to treat other war-time commodities in the same manner as steel, in order to prevent exorbitant prices.

The commodities on which the President has asked the commission to determine production costs are steel, iron, pig iron, lumber, coal, zinc, copper, lead, cement, aluminium, fuel oils, and gasoline. It was stated that the inquiry probably would be widened to include many other essentials.

The Trade Commission also is investigating food conditions, including the production costs of meat, flour, grain and dairy products. The cold storage and canning industries are also being investigated.

At present the efforts of the Trade Commission are being concentrated largely on steel, lumber, coal and fuel oils, and these will be among the first products made the subject of price-fixing. It is designed to place a comprehensive report at the disposal of the President by Aug. 1.

The President's address, made public last night, was accepted here as the final statement concerning the policy which he would adopt in the effort to stabilize the market and take the products necessary to the country out of the realm of speculation. It is believed, in official circles, that the big business interests of the country will adjust themselves to the rules laid down.

Prices to the Allies.

The question of prices to the allies of America, especially as affecting contracts already made, agitated some of the interests involved, today, and that angle of the matter will be the subject of negotiation. It is understood that the President is opposed to a policy that would impose unusual prices on the allies of America, but this was not made the subject of any official statement.

It was stated that the President was in a mood to make words good by acts if there was found any tendency to override the ethical standard which he set up for the business interests of the country, and that he would recommend legislation of the most effective order if conditions demanded it. Members of the official family at present, it can be said, do not believe such drastic steps will be necessary, and feel that big business will join in placing America on a sound military basis.

The President and his advisers, it is said, have no thought of hammering down prices to a point where production would be hampered and business embarrassed to a degree that would discourage expansion. A fair profit above production costs will be one of the cardinal principles of the price-fixing system.

The attitude of the steel men was taken as a good augury for the program adopted. There were present at the conference representatives of the United States Steel Corporation and practically all the other great steel concerns. With their approval this statement was made public by Secretary Baker:

The Official Announcement.

"At the conference this morning between the committee of the American Iron and Steel Institute and the Secretary of War, the Secretary of the Navy, the Chairman of the Shipping Board, and Bernard Baruch, further discussion was had of the prospective demand upon the steel industry of the country for supplies of various steel products for carrying on the war. The steel men repeated their assurance that their entire product would be available for the need and that they were doing everything possible to stimulate an increased production and speed deliveries.

"The price to be paid for the iron and steel products furnished was left to be determined after the inquiry by the Federal Trade Commission is completed, with the understanding that the price, when fixed would insure reasonable profits and be made with reference to the expanding needs of this vital and fundamental industry.

"The representatives of the Government assured the committee of the Steel Institute that it was the intention of the Government to distribute the war requirements over the entire iron and steel producing capacity of the country.

Reports that millions of dollars of contracts had been held up pending a price agreement were denied today with emphasis. It was stated, however, that the decision reached had done much to clear the atmosphere and to facilitate further construction, which demanded the essentials under immediate consideration.

No definite price has been fixed as yet for steel or any of the other commodities, and that will not be done under the President's program until the Federal Trade Commission has reported on its findings. In the meantime, however, in order not to delay any of the work necessary for America's preparation, money will be advanced on contracts for shipbuilding, aircraft production, and other activities, with the provision that final settlement is to be made on the basis of the prices which later may be fixed.

The President is awaiting now only the passage of the food administration legislation in order to put into full effect the policies he has decided upon to prepare the country for war conditions. He believes that through the Exports Council the food administration and the price-fixing system American business can be stabilized and the cost of living appreciably reduced.

Steel manufacturers, Secretary Redfield announced, have assured railroad car builders of enough steel to insure speedy construction. For some time builders have been having great difficulty in getting enough steel to keep their plants running. Mr. Redfield and Daniel Willard of the Defense Council's Advisory Commission made a personal appeal to producers to release steel for cars. There are now building in this country about 80,000 cars and 2,000 locomotives.

July 13, 1917

BOARD OF SEVEN NAMED TO GUIDE WAR PURCHASES

Scott Heads It, and Baruch, Brookings, and Lovett Comprise Buying Committee.

NO INTEREST IN CONTRACTS

Purchasing Dissociated from Personal Gain, Government Announces.

Special to The New York Times.

WASHINGTON, July 28.—The formation of a War Industries Board of seven members, which will supervise the actual expenditure of many millions of dollars, and a Central Purchasing Commission, to be composed of three of the members of this board and Herbert C. Hoover, was announced today as the program for the reorganization of the Council of National Defense, which has received the full approval of President Wilson.

Frank A. Scott of Cleveland, the present Chairman of the General Munitions Board, has been selected to head the War Industries Board, and associated with him will be Lieut. Col. Palmer E. Pierce, representing the army; Rear Admiral Frank F. Fletcher, representing the navy; Bernard M. Baruch, Robert S. Brookings of St. Louis; Robert S. Lovett, Chairman of the Executive Committee of the Union Pacific System, and Hugh Frayne, Chief Organizer of the American Federation of Labor in New York.

In the hands of this body of men will be placed unusual powers, as all purchases made by the Central Committee, on which Mr. Baruch, Mr. Brookings, and Mr. Lovett will serve, in association with Mr. Hoover when the question of foodstuffs is concerned, will be made in accordance with the general policies which the War Industries Board formulates and approves.

The plan of reorganization does not provide for the abolishment of the Council of National Defense, its Advisory Commission, or any of the subsidiary committees, which will be called upon from time to time to supply information and co-operate in any manner suggested.

Relations With the Allies.

No definite policy was announced as to the relations of the War Industries Board and its Purchasing Commission with representatives of the allies of America. It has been reported from time to time that Mr. Baruch or another might appear as the buyer for the allied nations as well as for the United States, but there is no such suggestion in the announcement made. It can be stated that there will be the closest co-operation with the buying interests of the Allies and that a definite policy will be reached which will avoid the danger of a competition in American markets which would tend to boost prices. Such a course, it is understood, is already being followed out in connection with the purchases of wheat and certain other grains.

It is the opinion here that the formation of the War Industries Board will prove one of the most important steps in the effort to bring about the stabilization of all American markets. It will provide also a definite body with which producers of the many war-time commodities may treat, and put an end to whatever confusion may have existed because of the cumbersome size of the Council of National Defense.

An official announcement issued by the Committee on Public Information shortly after the reorganization was put into effect contained this statement concerning the policy of the new administration:

The Official Announcement.

"The board will act as a clearing house for the war industry needs of the Government, determine the most effective ways of meeting them, and the best means and methods of increasing production, including the creation or extension of industries demanded by the emergency, the sequence and relative urgency of the needs of the different Government services, and consider price factors and, in the first instance, the industrial and labor aspects of problems involved and the general questions affecting the purchase of commodities.

"On this board Mr. Baruch will give his attention particularly to raw materials, Mr. Brookings to finished products, and Mr. Lovett to matters of priority. These three members, in association with Mr. Hoover, so far as foodstuffs are involved, will constitute a commission to arrange purchases in accordance with the general policies formulated and approved.

"The Council of National Defense and the Advisory Commission will continue unchanged, and will discharge the duties imposed upon them by law. The committees heretofore created immediately subordinate to the Council of National Defense; namely, Labor, Transportation and Communication, Shipping, Medicine and Surgery, Women's Defense Work, Co-operation with State Councils, Research and Inventions, Engineering and Education, Commercial Economy, Administration and Statistics, and Inland Transportation, will continue their activities under the direction and control of the council. Those whose work is related to the duties of the War Industries Board will co-operate with it. The sub-committees advising on particular industries and materials, both raw and finished, heretofore created, will also continue in existence and be available to furnish assistance to the War Industries Board.

"The purpose of this action is to expedite the work of the Government, to furnish needed assistance to the departments engaged in making war purchases, to devolve clearly and definitely the important tasks indicated upon direct representatives of the Government not interested in commercial and industrial activities with which they will be called upon to deal, and to make clear that there is total dissociation of industrial committees from the actual arrangement of purchases on behalf of the Government. It will lodge responsibility for effective action as definitely as is possible under existing laws. It does not minimize or dispense with the splendid service which representatives of industry and labor have so unselfishly placed at the disposal of the Government.

Acquisition of Mr. Scott.

"Frank A. Scott, Chairman of the new War Industries Board of the Council of National Defense, is a Republican. He has been serving as Chairman of the General Munitions Board of the council since April 9, when the board began its work. Mr. Scott is an acknowledged authority on the quantity production of munitions for modern war, and through his work the General Munitions Board is already in close touch with the exact munitions situation.

"When Secretary Baker telegraphed Mr. Scott to come to Washington to assist the Government in the munitions problem he was serving as Vice President, Treasurer, and Manager of the Warner & Swasey Company of Cleveland, a firm which had already made large quantities of machine tools, range-finders, gunsights, and other munitions for the Allies. After a series of conferences on the question of organizing industry to turn out in quantity the vast amounts of small arms, field guns, ammunition, explosives, and the many other varied requirements of a modern army, Mr. Scott was asked to remain in the capital indefinitely and undertake the work of correlating the needs of the army and the navy and developing sources of supply for the demands of the two in common.

"Mr. Scott was born in Cleveland March 22, 1873, the son of Robert Crozier and Sarah Ann (Warr) Scott. His father died when he was 10 years old, and since then he has paid his own way in the world. His first job was delivering newspapers, his second carrying messages for the Western Union Telegraph Company."

The Other Board Members.

Bernard M. Baruch, since the formation of the Advisory Commission of the Council of National Defense, has been Chairman of the Committee on Raw Materials. He was suggested for that position by Secretary Daniels, in accordance with the plan by which the President allowed each member of the Cabinet to select a member of the Advisory Commission.

The appointment was given to him, it was then stated, in recognition of his rare ability and success as a financier and organizer. He and his committee have adjusted the copper situation to the satisfaction of the purchasing departments of the Government, and recently, in the offices of the Secretary of War, aided in bringing about the complete co-operation of the special committee from the Iron and Steel Institute of America, with the result that the steel interests of the country agreed to supply their entire output to the Government on the basis of cost, to be determined by the Federal Trade Commission, plus a reasonable profit, to be determined by the Government. Mr. Baruch is 47 years old.

Robert Somers Brookings is a St. Louis merchant who also has gained prominence in educational circles through his active interest in the development of Washington University and the promotion of the Carnegie Institution and the Carnegie Peace Foundation, on the boards of both of which organizations he is serving as Trustee. Mr. Brookings was born in Cecil County, Md., Jan. 22, 1850. He is unmarried.

Lieut. Col. Palmer E. Pierce was graduated from the Military Academy at West Point in the early '90s, and was detailed to the Ninth Regiment of Infantry. He saw service in the Boxer rebellion, in Cuba during the Spanish war, and in the Philippine insurrection. He served several times as instructor at West Point, and recently was promoted to Lieutenant Colonel. At present he is serving with the War College Division of the General Staff. He is a graduate of both the School of the Line and the Staff class at Fort Leavenworth and of the Army War College.

Robert Scott Lovett is a national figure in American railway circles. Having served as President of both the Union Pacific and the Southern Pacific from September, 1909, to September, 1913, he has since held the position of Chairman of the Executive Committee of the Union Pacific system. In 1904 Mr. Lovett was made general counsel for the Union Pacific and the Southern Pacific—the Harriman lines—and continued to serve them in that capacity until 1909, when he was elected President and Chairman of the Executive Committee of both lines. Mr. Lovett was born at San Jacinto, Texas, June 22, 1860.

Hugh Frayne, labor representative on the new War Industries Board, is one of the prominent figures in the labor world. He is the official representative of Samuel Gompers in New York City, where he is chief organizer of the American Federation of Labor. In labor circles he is reputed to have proved one of the most successful of all labor organizers in dealing with employers. He has been in business for himself. He has also been successful as a harmonizer within the ranks of labor in New York City.

Admiral Frank Friday Fletcher was in command of the naval force on the west coast of Mexico that captured Vera Cruz, April 21, 1914, and was commander in chief of the Atlantic Fleet from September, 1914, to June, 1916. He is now a member of the General Board of the Navy, in which position he has served since June 20, 1916.

Admiral Fletcher was born in Oskaloosa, Iowa, Nov. 23, 1855. He was promoted to Rear Admiral Oct. 17, 1911, and served in command of the Fourth Division, Atlantic Fleet, from Aug. 1, 1912, to Jan. 4, 1913; of the second division from Jan. 4 to Nov. 6, 1913; of the Third Division from Nov. 6, 1913, to Feb. 18, 1914; of the First Division from Feb. 18, to Sept. 12, 1914, and as Commander in Chief of the Atlantic Fleet from Sept. 17, 1914, until June, 1916, when he was assigned to duty as a member of the General Board.

July 29, 1917

MAGIC GROWTH OF CHEMICAL INDUSTRY

$65,000,000 Has Been Contributed in First Eight Months of This Year for Manufacture of Chemicals.

NEVER was necessity more the mother of invention than that shown in the chemical industry in this country since the beginning of the war, and now that the United States is a participant, with chemical needs multiplied many times over, even more extraordinary results are expected. Last month more than $13,000,000 of new capital was authorized for enterprises for the manufacture of chemicals, drugs, and dye stuffs. In July the amount reported was $10,215,000. In these figures only companies with capital of $50,000 and over are included. Since January, 1915, the total new industrial investment in chemicals, dye stuffs, and drugs amounts to $280,670,000. Of this, $65,861,000 has been contributed in the first eight months of 1917.

Fumes from coke ovens, that went to waste in this country before the war, now are converted into valuable war products, such as toluol, benzol, and naphthaline, by methods improved by American ingenuity. New towns, growing like mining camps at the time of a big strike, have sprung up. The tables have been turned on Germany. The stopping of shipment of chemicals made there, instead of starving industries in this country dependent on them, as Germany expected, has forced the United States to manufacture chemicals which will now aid powerfully in our war against Germany.

At many points of attack Germany will encounter the skill of American chemists—on the battle front in France, in the air, under the water. Chemistry is a factor of increasing importance. Hundreds of Americans are at work on important unsolved problems in that field. Among these are neutralizing agents for poisonous gases; methods of guarding submarines against internal explosions; optical glass for range-finders; non-corrosive alloys for guns and submarines; fuel substitutes and combinations, and medicines formerly imported which must be produced on short notice. Chemical engineers are working literally night and day to discover materials which have become scarce or to find their substitutes.

"There is hardly a phase of modern warfare into which progress in chemistry does not enter as a factor of importance, from shells and munitions to the soldiers' clothing," said Dr. Charles E. Roth, Secretary of the American Chemical Society, from whom the above figures were obtained. "The American chemist is fighting the battles of democracy just as effectively as the soldier at the battle front. It is quiet work, in some isolated laboratory, and the public hears less of it, probably, than of almost anything that is being done in this war. The American chemist, with the aid of the financier, has accomplished within the last two years, in developing an industry, what it took Germany forty years to attain. Much has yet to be done permanently to place this country in a condition of chemical self-sufficiency, but we are now in good shape to take care of any problems that arise as to war needs and to hold and to extend after the war the ground we have gained in foreign markets since Germany was cut off from that trade.

"We base this expectation on what has already been done. The dye industry is only one instance, but it indicates in its way what has been achieved in others. In the early days of the European war our textile manufacturers could get only limited quantities of dyestuffs, if any, and threatened to close their mills or supply undyed goods. The public remembers well that scare. Today we have a dyestuff industry producing colors in sufficient quantity for all our needs, though not in a large or varied assortment. But time will place our nation on a better footing in this respect.

"Take an individual illustration of growth: Out in Cincinnati a firm had long been producing a few colors, mostly blacks and blues. For forty weeks now this same company has created a new dyestuff each week; also it has increased its capacity six times over its output before the war. In the early days of 1915 there were only seven companies actually producing colors in this country; now there are more than 100 making colors, intermediate or crude. Four or five companies made vegetable dyes and there are now nineteen. Since 1914 almost all manufacturers of coke have equipped their retort ovens with recovery apparatus to obtain the benzol, toluol, xylol, and naphthaline, or, as in the case of the larger steel companies, have installed the newer forms of by-product coke ovens.

"Synthetic indigo is one of our most recent additions. Until the world got this compound we were wholly dependent on the natural product grown in the fields of India. It required forty-one years of scientific research for European chemists to determine the constitution of indigo, and seven years for the industrial development of the process. It took German chemists seven years to develop indigo industrially. We have done it in less than one-third of the time. It must be remembered that our chemists had no industrial data to work upon, but only data on the first forty-one years of scientific research. The secrets of the commercial development in Germany were carefully guarded by patents.

"In its new development the chemical industry has profited by modern lessons in efficiency. It is noteworthy that new plants have been built at the source of supplies, frequently on the plain or in the wilderness. Around the first industry others gathered, so that a flourishing town appeared. In several instances sleeping villages have found themselves the centre of great industrial activity. Potash, the material used in so many industries and the famine in which caused the chemical industry in the United States to seize every possible source, elevated a mere railroad siding in Nebraska to the full-fledged town Hoffland: and Antioch, in Nebraska, also is coming into undreamed of prosperity as a potash centre. Maryvale, Utah, is on the map through chemical development of the native rock now furnishing potash at about $500 a ton. Formerly the rock was held to be worthless.

"All the progress in chemistry since the war will be exemplified at the National Exposition of Chemical Industries at the Grand Central Palace in New York City, beginning tomorrow. It will be the largest and most complete exhibition of these industries ever held, and more chemists will be assembled here than ever before were gathered together—say 14,000. The American Chemical Society, the American Electro-Chemical Society, and the American Institute of Chemical Engineers are among the organizations co-operating in this presentation of chemistry's advance. There will be conferences of national importance. Members of the Council of National Defense, at Washington, will attend some of the conferences when problems directly related to war production will be discussed. It will be study of the effort to make the world safe for democracy from the scientific viewpoint. The advantage that will result from this exchange and sifting out of ideas can hardly be estimated. This is our first war exposition and we expect it to have a popular appeal much stronger than that won by the previous ones."

September 23, 1917

Country's Industries Are Formally Mobilized To Help the Government Carry on the War

Special to The New York Times.

WASHINGTON, Dec. 12.—The industries of the United States were mobilized at the War Service Conference, to act in an advisory capacity to the Government, at a meeting at the Hotel Willard today, called by the Chamber of Commerce of the United States. Committees of business men from every part of the country made up the conference.

The captains of industry, it is announced, will have a committee of five to keep in close touch with the Government in all war affairs in which industry plays a part. The War Service Conference will take the place of the co-operative committees of the Council of National Defense, which were recently dissolved.

W. S. Gifford, Chairman of the Council of National Defense, said the War Service Conference would be of advantage to the Government in effecting a complete organization of industry throughout the country.

" It is not going to be an easy task to organize industry in the way we want it," said Mr. Gifford. " But we think it can be done effectively. It is obvious that some industries are more essential than others in war. Nevertheless, it is foolhardy to attempt to say that the time will not come when the so-called less essential industries may not be needed. We want to keep all the industries going that we possibly can."

December 13, 1917

WILSON TAKES OVER THE RAILROADS

RAIL CONTROL TOMORROW

Federal Direction to be Assumed at Noon Throughout Nation.

ALL EXECUTIVES TO STAY

EARNINGS ARE GUARANTEED

Special to The New York Times.

WASHINGTON, Dec. 26. — President Wilson formally announced tonight his decision to take possession and assume control of the railroads of the country at noon on Friday, Dec. 28. Action will be taken through the Secretary of War, but William G. McAdoo, Secretary of the Treasury, will be Director General of Railroads, and is so appointed in the proclamation issued by the President tonight.

In a statement accompanying his proclamation the President announced that as soon as Congress reassembled he would recommend legislation guaranteeing the maintenance of railroad properties in good repair and the payment of a net operating income equal to the average net operating income of each road for the three years ending June 30, 1917.

The President's proclamation contemplates the mobilization of the railroads of the country and all their appurtenances, and while it will give the Government possession of water lines that figure in rail-and-water transportation, it is not the intention to take over local water routes and those steamer lines which do not fit into the rail problem.

Through this action the President hopes to end the tangle of confusion into which the transportation facilities have been brought as a result of the war.

The President's decision to take over the operation of the railroads in advance of the reassembling of Congress was announced at 8 o'clock tonight, in a proclamation and the explanatory statement signed by himself.

About five hours before the President announced his determination to take over the railroads confidential messages went to the heads of the principal railroad systems of the country indicating that when possession had been taken of the transportation facilities a board of five or seven members would be appointed to advise with the Director General of Railways. The belief is that this board will be composed of representatives of the army and navy, the food and fuel administrations, because the executive departments of the administration mentioned are the chief Government shippers.

The President's action is based on the authority granted on Aug. 29, 1916, in the act which made appropriations for the support of the Army for the fiscal year 1917, and which provided that the President, in time of war, through the Secretary of War, might take possession and assume control of any or all systems of transportation and utilize them, to the exclusion, as far as may be necessary, of all other traffic, for the transportation of troops, war material, and equipment, and for such other purposes connected with the emergency as may be needful or desirable.

The President's Statement.

The President's statement follows:

I have exercised the powers over the transportation systems of the country which were granted me by the act of Congress of August, 1916, because it has become imperatively necessary for me to do so.

This is a war of resources no less than of men, perhaps even more than of men, and it is necessary for the complete mobilization of our resources that the transportation systems of the country should be organized and employed under a single authority and a simplified method of co-ordination which have not proved possible under private management and control.

The Committee of Railway Executives who have been co-operating with the Government in this all-important matter have done the utmost that it was possible for them to do; have done it with patriotic zeal and with great ability, but there were differences that they could neither escape nor neutralize. Complete unity of administration in the present circumstances involves upon occasion and at many points a serious dislocation of earnings, and the committee was, of course, without power or authority to rearrange charges or effect proper compensations and adjustments of earnings. Several roads which were willingly and with admirable public spirit accepting the orders of the commitee have already suffered from these circumstances, and should not be required to suffer further. In mere fairness to them the full authority of the Government must be substituted. The Government itself will thereby gain an immense increase of efficiency in the conduct of the war and of the innumerable activities upon which its successful conduct depends.

Public Interest First.

The public interest must be first served and, in addition, the financial interests of the Government and the financial interests of the railways must be brought under a common direction. The financial operations of the railways need not then interfere with the borrowings of the Government, and they themselves can be conducted at a great advantage. Investors in railway securities may rest assured that their rights and interests will be as scrupulously looked after by the Government as they could be by the directors of the several railway systems.

Immediately upon the reassembling of Congress I shall recommend that these definite guarantees be given. First, of course, that the railway properties will be maintained during the period of Federal control in as good repair and as complete equipment as when taken over by the Government, and, second, that the roads shall receive a net operating income equal in each case to the average net income of the three years preceding June 30, 1917; and I am entirely confident that the Congress will be disposed in this case, as in others, to see that justice is done and full security assured to the owners and creditors of the great systems which the Government must now use under its own direction or else suffer serious embarrassment.

Under McAdoo's Direction.

The Secretary of War and I are agreed that, all the circumstances being taken into consideration, the best results can be obtained under the immediate executive direction of the Hon. William G. McAdoo, whose practical experience peculiarly fits him for the service and whose authority as Secretary of the Treasury will enable him to co-ordinate as no other man could the many financial interests which will be involved and which might, unless systematically directed, suffer very embarrassing entanglements.

The Government of the United States is the only great Government now engaged in the war which has not already assumed control of this sort. It was thought to be in the spirit of American institutions to attempt to do everything that was necessary through private management, and if zeal and ability and patriotic motive could have accomplished the necessary unification of administration, it would certainly have been accomplished; but no zeal or ability could overcome insuperable obstacles, and I have deemed it my duty to recognize that fact in all candor now that it is demonstrated and to use without reserve the great authority reposed in me. A great national necessity dictated the action, and I was therefore not at liberty to abstain from it.

WOODROW WILSON.

The proclamation was issued by the President through Secretary Baker, being signed by the President and countersigned by Secretary Baker and Secretary Lansing. The act of Aug. 29, 1916, under which President Wilson acts, empowers the President, in time of war, "through the Secretary of War, to take possession and assume control." Therefore, the action embraced in its provisions is taken through Secretary Baker.

December 27, 1917

President Signs Exporters' Bill.

WASHINGTON, April 11.—The Webb Export bill, permitting American exporters to co-operate in export trade, was signed today by President Wilson.

April 12, 1918

WIDENING FIELDS FOR OUR BUSINESS

WHEN the War Industries Board passed out of existence on Jan. 1 it called attention to the unification of American business enterprise during the war and aroused speculation as to the vistas opening before it.

Owing to its international scope, the board could not end its duties abruptly. The allocation of raw materials, which has been one of its chief duties in agreement with the Allied Powers, will hereafter be made by the War Trade Board, which will also take over other details of the work relating exclusively to trade matters governed by these agreements. The Department of Commerce will also inherit from the board those affairs relating to future trade after peace is formally declared and commerce becomes normal again. But these changes make opportune an examination of the board's operations and of their probable effect.

On Jan. 1 the War Industries Board passed out of existence, and this fixes attention on what its operations, and those of the other great agencies with which it worked, mean to the future. First, as to what was accomplished after the colossal business machine got into full swing:

From factories whose materials were apportioned and promptly delivered under Government control, the manufactured war supplies were loaded into freight cars operated by the Government and thence taken to ships built and operated by the Government. On the other side, the ships discharged their cargoes on docks constructed by American engineers and thence on railroads built by the United States, the war supplies were conveyed to our armies at the front—one continuous unified operation.

As a detail, this machinery would take a pair of shoes made in Lynn, Mass., and through all these channels, and a series of warehouses, deliver the shoes, when needed, to the soldier in France. In the end the supplies moved forward, across a gap of 3,000 miles of sea, in practically complete order. Even a few months before success was attained many clear-headed judges, basing their conclusions on the great difficulties encountered in the past in transporting soldiers and supplies over great sea distances, predicted that no such accomplishment would be possible after such a short period of preparation.

That it was done is the real foundation for the confidence as to the future now felt by industrial leaders and business men. It was a new job for American industry, so much larger than any heretofore conceived, that no one could say just how it would come out; that it turned out as it did is the basis of confidence. These industrial leaders have proved in an immense operation what they knew to be true in operations of less extent—that is in great private enterprises. The principles of organization and production on a great private scale were taken to Washington and—after some delay at first in obtaining free swing—applied there. Methods of the national private enterprises were compared, and the best were selected for the centralized Government industrial machine.

Some lessons of primary importance were learned. One was a new comprehension of the industrial capacity of the country. There are various estimates as to how much the industrial capacity of the United States was increased in one year, and few of these are below 20 per cent. There are now in this country not less than 300,000 industrial establishments, some of them representing a score or more of individual factories, according to the estimate of the Department of Commerce. In 1914, at the opening of the war period, there were 275,000.

The value of the output of American industries last year, it is estimated, has been not less than $60,000,000,000. In 1914 the value was $24,000,000,000. Our total exports in 1914 amounted to $2,000,000,000; this year, on the basis of the eleven months' record, they will go above $6,000,000,000. In order to make the great industrial advance accomplished after we entered the war, not less than 4,000,000 new industrial workers had to be trained.

When in the War Industries Board the Conservation Section, in the war need of preventing waste, set out to reduce the number of patterns in different lines of manufacture, some remarkable discoveries were made, startling even to some of the manufacturers themselves. To illustrate, it was discovered that there were 1,100 different patterns of a buggy step and 232 of an article so lacking in individuality as a buggy wheel. The patterns of buggy steps were reduced to two and of wheels to four. There is an economy here not only in manufacture, but also in the prevention of the tying up of material in stock. One hundred and ninety-two different industries underwent this kind of scrutiny. In every one there were large reductions.

Sometimes human nature stayed the hand of efficiency. At a meeting of sweater manufacturers to cut to the bone the 100 colors in which sweaters were manufactured, one of the Conservation Section men said:

"There is pink. That certainly seems out of place in war time; let's cut that out."

Several sweater manufacturers sprang up.

"Don't do that," exclaimed one whose robust voice gained him precedence. "Take anything, but leave us pink and blue."

The conservation man wanted to know why.

"Because," said the sweater manufacturer, "pink stands for the boy baby and blue for the girl. It is as necessary to tell babies apart in wartime as it is in peace."

Pink and blue were left in.

A far-reaching benefit will result from this experience of the rigors of war. Since the signing of the armistice and the relaxation of the authority of the War Industries Board, manufacturers' organizations have taken steps to profit by the lessons of the war in guarding against the wasteful multiplication of patterns. The experience will be preserved for American industry by its transfer to the Department of Commerce.

New industries, forced by the necessity of war, when imports from Germany were cut off, open fresh horizons to American industry. There is a list of more than 300 new products sent to the Department of Commerce, but in some of these the variation is very slight or the same article, as a dye, bears a different name. Still the stride forward has been remarkable. At the head of the list in importance stand the dyes, medicines and potash. Before the war the United States was a large importer of dyes and other chemicals. This year the exports of chemicals from the United States will show a total of approximately $175,000,000. Before the outbreak of the war Germany, on account of her monopoly of the potash supply, had gradually extended her arm around the food supply of the world. The Chemical Division of the War Industries Board, which is to be preserved as a part of the Department of the Interior, went to work on this problem. This year it is estimated the output of potash will be 60,000 tons, nearly twice that of the preceding year. This is still far below our requirements, but with the extension of methods of extracting potash from waste products and the development of new beds in the West, we are on the way to becoming self-supporting in this fundamental of agriculture. To the layman some of the new methods read like magic. In one instance potash seems to be washed out of the air; fumes generated in the manufacture of cement are sprayed with water. Then the water is passed through [illegible] bags, which retain the potash. Behind what might appear to be boy's play is a chemical law, and the method has shown good results.

Before the war the farmer took more than 50 per cent. of our manufactured articles. The war has pressed the farmer to a new efficiency. This year the total crop acreage in this country was 355,895,722, an advance of more than 10,000,000 acres. In the staple, wheat, the gain was 14,000,000 acres. For these crops the farmer received the highest prices on record. His buying power has, therefore, been greatly augmented. Already there are many indications of this, in the purchase of new equipment to add to the efficiency of the farm. There are six times as many tractors on the farms now as there were at the beginning the war, probably close to 100,000 at this time. By the end of next year it is expected that this number will approach 500,000.

January 5, 1919

RAILROADS GO BACK TOMORROW WILSON SIGNS THE BILL

PROCLAIMS ROADS' CHANGE

President Also Sends a Letter Replying to Labor Demands.

TRUSTS BOARD UNDER BILL

Upholds Public Representation and Says Men Fair to Labor Must Be Named.

ROADS GAINED, HINES SAYS

He Declares That Operating Cost Was Cheaper Than if Owners Had Controlled.

Special to The New York Times.

WASHINGTON, Feb. 28.—President Wilson tonight signed the bill restoring the railroads to private ownership at 12:01 A. M. Monday. The President attached his signature in the face of determined opposition by organized labor, which had gone to such an extent that the American Federation of Labor, the four great railway brotherhoods and also the Farmers' National Council has asked him to veto the bill.

In a letter to the heads of the railway brotherhoods and unions the President refused to grant their request to appoint a special wage tribunal to pass upon the pending demands for increases in pay. Instead he declared that he believed the bi-partisan board as provided in the legislation just enacted by Congress, and which he signed tonight, would not only be fair and just, but would be "found to be particularly in the interest of railroad employes as a class."

In fact, the President said he found the bi-partisan board established by the bill "an appropriate" substitute for the committe of experts he had suggested to help settle the wage plan.

Backs Public Representation.

One of the main objections of the railroad unions to the labor board authorized in the bill was the assertion that the public representatives would be prejudiced against labor. President Wilson denied this suggestion with the statement that these public representatives should be men who would not entertain any antagonism toward workers.

The point was made by the President that the Labor Board was required to provide wages commensurate with standards paid for work in other industries and was also empowered to prescribe sufficient rates to pay for reasonable operating expenses of the railways, including wages. This last statement was taken to mean a hint of coming rate increases, particularly as a suggestion of that kind is included in the annual report of Director General Hines, made public today.

President Wilson's letter to the railway men was considered here as an absolute rejection of all the demands of labor in relation to the bill.

As usual, the President indicated in his letter a sympathy with the working man. He said he believed that the labor provisions of the bill would provide means for a better understanding between railroad management and employes, especially the employes. But labor has been so insistent that the railroad bill should not be enacted into law, and has made so many dire threats, that the President's letter is regarded as a flat refusal of labor's demands.

The letter was given out at the White House about 6:45 P. M. Accompanying it was a formal proclamation from the President restoring the roads to private ownership and, at the same time, authorizing Director General Hines and such portion of the Railroad Administration personnel as is necessary to continue in existence long enough to wind up the affairs of Government control.

Employes Going Back to Roads.

All the regional offices of the Railroad Administration pass out of existence with the going into effect of the railroad bill. This will affect about 1,400 employes of the service. There are another 1,400 here in Washington, and several hundred of these received their last pay checks today. It is expected that it will take from six months to a year to wind up the affairs of the Railroad Administration.

Director General Hines and his personal staff will remain in Washington and at once will begin the work of liquidation. It is said that Mr. Hines plans to leave the Government service about May 1.

It is expected that practically all of the employes who will leave the Railroad Administration will be absorbed by the railroads from which they came to the Government. The Interstate Commerce Commission, which will be enlarged, will take over others. Several technical bureaus may be absorbed en masse by other organizations.

A special board on wage adjustments, which has been working under the Railroad Administration, may be taken over by the wage boards provided in the new bill.

A statistical compilation by the Railroad Administration experts shows this comparison between 1918, the first year of Federal control, and 1917, when the roads were still in private hands.

TWELVE MONTHS ENDED DEC. 31.

	1918.	1917.
Oper. revenues ..	$4,842,695,884	$3,988,827,671
Oper. expenses...	3,939,315,122	2,808,544,956
Net oper. revs...	903,380,762	1,180,282,715
Operating ratio...	81.3	70.4
Net Federal income corresp'g to standard returns guaranteed by Government.	688,200,083	1,080,492,111

Standard return for the year, $890,335,685.

The "net Federal income" for the year, therefore, fell short by $202,135,602.

The operating costs for Class 1 railroads for 1914 were $2,140,000,000 and approximately $4,324,000,000 for 1919, being an increase of $2,184,000,000. This is the 102 per cent. increase to which Mr. Hines refers in his report.

February 29, 1920

AMERICAN INDUSTRY WON THE WORLD WAR

G. B. Clarkson, of National Defense Council, Tells in New Book How It Was Done.

ROLE OF STEEL AND NITRATES

Victorious Armies Could Not Have Conquered but for Workers' Support, Clemenceau Says.

The part played by the unheralded industrial soldiers of America in fighting the World War has been described vividly by Grosvenor B. Clarkson, a director of the United States Council of National Defense, in "Industrial America in the World War," a book of nearly 600 pages to be issued this week by Houghton Mifflin Company. Steel, nitrates and other industries have their rûle disclosed, with hitherto unpublished excerpts of conversation by big business men.

"It is certain," said Georges Clemenceau in a foreword to the book, "that none of the victorious armies could have conquered but for the support of its industries. It is no less clear that no European industry could have survived but for the support of American industry. Germany, which, living for the war, understood its requirements better than we did, had to pay dearly for unpreparedness. In the first quarter of 1915 she passed through a munitions crisis which was not far from being fatal. America, despite the power of her production, only escaped the danger by the magnificent effort of which Mr. Clarkson tells the story. As he rightly says, America was the 'last reservoir.'

M. Clemenceau reported that in eighteen months this countries sent the Allies about 5,000,000 tons of food and as much war material. He said that steel enough for 160,000,000 "75" shells and food for 12,000,000 Frenchmen for a year and a half were sent. "Mr. Clarkson," he commented, "is right: the men who won the war behind the lines—on which victory at the front depended—are entitled to the gratitude of the nations, and the nations do not even know their names. It is time justice should be done these men, and this book hastens that day."

Field Marshal von Hindenburg also pays tribute to what industry did to the German hosts.

Eulogy of B. M. Baruch.

Mr. Clarkson in his book tells of the evolution of the industrial mobilization under the direction of the Council of National Defense and kindred organizatoins, such as the Advisory Commission headed by Daniel Willard, President of the Baltimore & Ohio Railroad. He also spoke in praise of the nonpartisan attitude of Newton Baker, then Secretary of War, an attitude which he found reflected in the other Democratic Cabinet members. A striking eulogy of Bernard M. Baruch is incorporated in the book, Mr. Clarkson picturing the banker as energy personified. He tells a story of Baruch's methods when the time came to co-ordinate the voluntary co-operation of American manufacturers. One manufacturer, owner of a string of lumber mills, proved recalcitrant. He took the position that the Government could not conduct his mills efficiently.

"Quite true," remarked the unperturbed Mr. Baruch. "But by the time we commandeer those mills you will be such an object of contempt and scorn in your home town that you will not dare to show your face there. If you should, your fellow-citizens would call you a slacker, the boys would hoot you on the street and the draft men would likely run you out of town."

The critical situation in the late Fall of 1917 and the early Winter of 1918 is visaulized by the author, who said that the demands for ship transport were "stupefying."

"Yet," he writes, "within four months the sturdy divisions of the last reserves of fighting manhood of the white races were pouring through the neck of the bottle, now monstrously enlarged, at the rate of 225,000 men a month, and with an equipment of weapons and supplies, outside of artillery and projectiles, never surpassed or even equaled by much smaller armies so far from home. 'It can't be done, but here it is,' became the cool word of the hour."

The Role of Steel.

The major rôle of steel in the winning of the war comes in for much consideration from Mr. Clarkson.

"The world war was moved and fought on steel," he remarks, and a long and picturesque chapter recites how "business-as-usual" met its first set-back in the steel problem. He tells how for months the War Industries Board, the Fuel Administration, the Railway Administration and the captains of the steel industry tried to solve the problem of meeting an unlimited demand with a limited supply, with the steel men at first objecting to the low Government prices, but later coming whole-heartedly into line. Mr. Clarkson permits his readers a quick flash into a meeting of the War Industries Board, a meeting that took place when the air was full of uncertainty. Robert S. Lovett, Chairman of the Union Pacific Railroad, presided, and representatives of the steel industry were there, led by Judge Elbert H. Gary, Chairman of the Board of United States Steel.

"May I ask by what authority the War Industries Board has undertaken to fix these prices?" asked Judge Gary.

"A gentleman of your eminent qualifications in law," replied Judge Lovett after a moment of profound silence, "requires no information from me on that point."

From that point forward the two sides proceeded with much grimness to fight it out, the Lovett supporters finally winning.

The great task of moving freight and keeping it on the way to the overseas front is told in detail by Mr. Clarkson, the author paying special attention to the operation of priorities.

Nitrate, the base of nearly every high explosive, was a cardinal affair for the American industrial soldiers, Mr. Clarkson recalls, declaring that the destruction of a single nitrate carrier from Chile was a greater loss than the sinking of a battleship.

May 6, 1923

THE AGE OF MASS PRODUCTION

READY-TO-WEAR CLOTHING.

A Young Industry Which Has Rapidly Increased—Fair Profits for Manufacturer and Retailer.

The popularity and sale of ready-made, or "ready-to-wear," clothing, as the merchants now prefer to call it, has greatly increased in the last eight or ten years, according to good authorities. The cause is not hard to find. It is due to the greater care exercised in the making up and style of the goods. More pains are taken to make up the clothing in good style, and in such varieties of shapes and sizes, that it is rarely that a man cannot be fitted, and where alteration is necessary, it is no more than a custom-made suit usually needs. A man may decide some morning that his cutaway is a little shabby, and, as he may be going out that evening, he requires something better. It is only necessary to visit one of the large clothing houses in the city to find just what he wants, at almost any price, try it on, and have it sent home during the day; any necessary alteration is made in the course of a few hours, and he can comfortably pass the evening, confident that his appearance is all that can be desired.

The Origin of the Business.

Some ten years ago, at a time of panic in the money market, the clothing business was very far from what it is to-day. It was then the merchant tailors, with popular prices, began to undermine the "ready-made" business. They offered to make a suit to order for the same price charged for clothes ready made, using the best cloth and employing the best workmen. This naturally attracted the attention of many who had previously patronized expensive custom tailors, but who then realized the necessity for economy. These merchant tailors soon built up a large business. The first house of this kind, doing a mail-order business, was in Chicago. The fact that the promoters kept close to the latest styles was a great factor in the business, and that is where the competition helped the "ready-to-wear" dealers. It made the manufacturing clothiers pay more attention to style and cut, and to-day they have brought them both up to a high standard.

Clothing cut in large quantities is, of course, cheaper than where each suit is cut separately, and for the same priced suit will permit the use of a much better grade of cloth, and more care in the details of make-up. As a consequence, the two trades, for they are distinct, fill two important places in the mercantile world. During the past two or three years there has been a considerable increase in the number of clothing manufacturers in New York City. In 1895 there were 453, of whom 126 manufactured for boys and children exclusively. In 1896 there were 670, of which number 186 manufactured for boys and children. This year there are about 750 clothing manufacturers, a fact in itself significant.

The Cost of Manufacturing.

The cost and profits of the business make interesting reading. The fancy suit, everything except plain black, which retails for $15, is sold at wholesale for about $11. In small towns and out-of-the-way places, the retailer puts the price at whatever he thinks he can get, but in the larger places the profits are practically the same in the reliable stores. In addition, there is a discount of from 7 to 8 per cent. allowed by the wholesale dealer, which the retailer seldom fails to take advantage of.

The manufacturers' profit is, as a rule, about 15 per cent. It requires three and a fourth yards of cloth for a suit, which, at $1.50 per yard, makes the cost of the cloth $4.87½. The cutters are paid on an average $20 a week, and it is estimated that the cutting of a sack suit costs the manufacturer 35 cents. For making up the suit they pay $1 for the coat and 50 cents each for trousers and vest—$2 for the suit. The linings, buttons, canvas, padding, silk, stay-tape, &c., cost about $1.50 more. These items cannot be figured exactly, as they vary with different suits, being much cheaper for black clothes. The manufacturers purchase black buttons, linings, &c., in large quantities, and get them proportionately cheaper, whereas, for brown, gray, or other fancy suits, the buttons and trimmings must match the cloth, and the great variety of shades necessarily limits the quantity purchased. This makes the suit that the manufacturer sells for $11 cost him about $8.72½, and leaves him a profit of $2.27½, not including the discounts allowed to the retail merchant. But, to offset that discount, the manufacturer gets a discount on all the material that enters into the manufacture of a suit. Again, they have to pay salesmen on the road, and it is estimated that they receive about 5 per cent. of the sales, and their expenses will reach nearly 2 per cent. Some houses will make a larger profit by employing cheaper labor, paying $1.25 for the making up of a suit, and by using cheaper material, but the above figures are fair estimates.

Bicycle Suits Profitable.

As a comparison, it may be interesting to look at the cost of making cheap clothing, like bicycle suits, retailing for about $3.50. The cost of the cloth is about 30 cents a yard, and it would hardly be wise to dwell on the grade of the material. Two and three-quarter yards are used for the coat and short trousers, costing about 82½ cents. Ten cents is paid for cutting a suit; for making the breeches, $6 per dozen, and the coats, $10.50 per dozen, or $1.37½ for a suit. Trimmings are estimated at about 20 cents, including buttons, buckles, &c., and there is generally little or no lining used, so the suit would cost about $2.50 complete. These are sold at $3 each in good-sized lots. The retailer may sell them at $3.50, or he may offer them at cost as a leader for the purpose of attracting custom.

It must be remembered that many retailers often get better prices than those quoted above. If the wholesale price is $11, they may be able to get $16 or $18, if not too near a large city, while on the other hand where there is close competition, the profits are less than indicated. Manufacturers in taking advantage of certain styles may be able to reduce the cost materially in certain directions. A few inches difference in the length of the coat tails may mean many dollars in 5,000 suits. The cost of making the same style suits may vary a trifle each week. Where they are all machine made, from the cutting to the sewing on of the buttons, as is apt to be the case with cheap suits, the cost is less, and some apparently first-class suits are made in this way, selling at the regular price, and giving the manufacturers a better profit.

May 9, 1897

Automobile Industry's Advance.

WASHINGTON, May 5.—The automobile industry, according to a preliminary bulletin issued by the Census Bureau today, shows a very large increase for the calendar year 1904, as compared with 1900, the year of taking the twelfth census. In 1904 the amount of capital invested was $20,555,247, as against $5,768,857, or an increase of 256 per cent. The value of products increased 461 per cent., the amounts being stated at $26,645,064 in 1904, as against $4,748,011 in 1900.

May 6, 1906

SYSTEM THE SECRET OF FORD'S SUCCESS

By HENRY FORD (Ford.)

What system is employed? How is it possible to manufacture a high-grade car to sell at so low a price? In other words, to incorporate "high-priced quality in a low-priced car?" That is a big subject that has taken us five years to work out, and volumes could be filled without exhausting the ways and means employed. But the general principles involved are as follows:

First.—Cars must be built in large quantities, if the selling price is to be low—An output of 500 cars a year means a very considerably higher cost per car than when the output of that factory reaches 20,000 cars a year. The cost of designing, of special tools, experimentation, and exploitation are about equal in each case, but the cost per car is widely different, and in favor of the car built in quantity. Building in quantities means buying in quantities, and quantity buying gets the rock bottom price. This truth has within the last few days been forcibly illustrated to me. Last month we bought materials for 15,000 more cars, the largest order by far ever placed by any car manufacturer.

Second.—Making one piece do the work of nine—I recently witnessed the dissembling of a foreign-built car, and noted nine separate parts for a certain operation, which we accomplish with a single part. Each separate piece less lowers the cost of the complete car, and Ford cars have the minimum number of parts consistent with good practice.

Third.—Economy in shop practice—That means the installation of labor-saving machinery, the standardization of methods and products, and the employment of modern systematization. We put $250,000 into machinery for this new car, but by its use the output per machine has increased, with a proportionate decrease in the labor required. The cylinders, for instance, in the little runabout traveled 4,000 feet from the time they entered as rough castings until they reached the assembly room. New machinery for the T car has cut down this travel to 400 feet, and one man does the work of three on the former model. There are several operations where one man with the new machinery can do the work of five or six with the old, yet the old was new three years ago.

Fourth.—Economy in sale methods—By advertising and proving the merits of the car we have secured a big demand. Our dealers easily dispose of all their allotment without the usual expense, because we have built up a demand for them to supply. Because each dealer can readily sell a greater number of cars, he is willing to handle the Ford line on a smaller margin.

Fifth.—Large, well-trained selling organization—It is impossible to market a large output through a few dealers. A dealer with too large a territory hits the high spots only and sells no more cars than if he thoroughly canvassed a smaller field. With several thousand dealers we reach every corner of the globe, and by means of conventions, personal letters, courses in salesmanship, and educational house organ, The Ford Times, we increase the sales capacity of our entire selling force.

Sixth—Quantity sales necessitate a smaller profit per car to the manufacturer—When your annual output is 20,000 cars, it is not necessary to make a small fortune on each car in order to pay dividends.

Seventh.—Taking advantage of cash discounts on all bills payable, and keeping out of debt, by refraining from extravagance are important principles—High salaries for so-called star performers; extravagant expense accounts for entertainment; a costly sales method; lack of intelligent, systematic organization—all these must be eliminated to make possible and profitable a low-priced car.

After all, there is no secret about the low-priced car. It's all in the system employed. The material is the best that can be bought; the making and selling forces are ample and well-paid; nothing is skimped, except extravagance, and that is entirely eliminated.

January 3, 1909

AUTO ADVERTISING AND SALESMANSHIP

Hugh Chalmers Discusses Secret of Success in Influencing the Human Mind.

By Hugh Chalmers.

Automobile salesmanship is of two kinds—the sales of cars by the manufacturer to the dealer, and the sales of cars by the dealer to the public. Or, broadly speaking, wholesale and retail. So far as the wholesale side is concerned, automobiles have been bought rather than sold. The demand from dealers has been enormous. It has been too great for all of the factories in the country to fill, hence there has not been as careful application by many manufacturers of the principles of salesmanship in the distribution of automobiles as there has been in most other lines of commercial activity.

Many companies seem to go on the principle that as soon as the factory's output is spoken for by the dealers it is sold. This is far from true. Cars are not really sold until they are in the hands of users at a price that gives a fair profit to both dealer and manufacturer. Competition is strong among the dealers, and they know that it takes brains and hard work to sell cars, no matter what the man at the factory may think.

There are certain fundamental principles in salesmanship which apply in the distribution of clothing, farm machinery, pianos, talking machines, or any other line. Selling is simply the art of influencing the human mind, and the things which influence the human mind are pretty much the same all over the world in all lines of business. The problem, no matter what you may be selling, is to find out what these things are, and then use them.

The first potent factor in influencing the public is good goods. No possible amount of strenuous salesmanship and advertising will suffice to keep a poor article on the market. It is possible by strong salesmanship and clever advertising to sell a "first edition." Profitable business is a matter of repeat orders, and you can't have repeat orders when you put out poor goods. A salesman with good goods to offer always makes a better record in the long run than the salesman with inferior goods, even though the man with the poor goods may be superior to the other man in the practice of the arts of his profession.

The conditions, in quite recent years, in the automobile industry have been such that any factory that could turn out a car that had any merit at all could sell its output. The time is bound to come when only those factories which turn out cars of unusual and unquestioned merit will be able to sell their output.

When one stops to think of all the energy and all the brains concentrated now on the production end of the automobile business he is inevitably forced to the conclusion that sooner or later production will catch up with the demand. Then good salesmanship and good advertising will play a more prominent part in the automobile business than heretofore. It is playing a part now, but that part is not plain to every one. I have just been saying that the fundamental principle of salesmanship is good goods. When the time comes that production equals or passes demand, then the manufacturers who have maintained a high standard in spite of all temptations to lower the standard for the sake of turning out greater quantities will find that they have been much better salesmen than they knew. They will find themselves sitting on a solid rock of public confidence.

The second great fundamental principle in salesmanship and advertising is honest statement. This applies equally to salesmanship by word, and to all salesmanship in print, which is advertising. It is my observation that you can't fool the American public very long. You can't even fool a part of the people a part of the time. I have never known of a business to survive continual dishonest statement. There has been a tendency, I think, in automobile advertising to make extravagant statements. Automobile advertising has not been dishonest, but some of it undoubtedly has been careless. A great many people do not believe many of the extravagant claims that are made, and this has an unfortunate result on the industry as a whole.

I am a thorough believer in advertising. It is sometimes possible to market good products without very much advertising. But these are exceptions. There has been many a valuable invention or manufactured product which the world did not get the full benefit of simply because it was not advertised, and there has been many a good product utterly spoiled by poor advertising.

The automobile business more than any one I know lends itself to advertising. I am one of those who sincerely believe that the automobile business owes much of its present high move of prosperity to newspaper publicity. There is no business in the world right now which so fully occupies the mind of the general public as the automobile business. There is no business which receives so much favorable attention from the newspapers as the automobile business. I think we can credit the newspapers very largely for having worked up in the public mind so much interest in automobiles. It is largely owing to their attention that there is such an unusual demand for cars.

Automobile manufacturers, it seems to me, should do everything in their power to help keep alive this great public interest in automobiles. It is the most encouraging sign in our business. Every one talks about automobiles and knows something about automobiles, and wants to know more about them, whether they actually own cars or not. This is what we might call "mouth to mouth" advertising, and it is the best sort of advertising in the world. But this kind of advertising has to be started in the first place, and has to be kept going in the second place. It is started by publicity, and it is kept going by publicity. All the advertising that all of us do helps to keep alive the enthusiasm over automobiles.

February 27, 1910

BREAKING ALL RECORDS IN THE MAKING OF AUTOMOBILES.

IN his address before the Minnesota Hardware Association, at St. Paul, a few days ago, James J. Hill said:

"Four hundred thousand automobiles have been ordered for delivery within the present year. Averaging the cost of automobiles at one thousand dollars each, this means that there will have been paid for automobiles by the people of the United States four hundred million dollars in the year 1910. Not one cent of those four hundred millions is invested in anything that will produce one bushel of grain."

Mr. Hill's statistics are possibly of greater accuracy than is the political economy which he bases upon these statistics. His estimate does not differ from the one given at the meeting of the American Automobile Association held in Washington two weeks earlier than the date of Mr. Hill's address at St. Paul. A fairly accurate estimate of the number of automobiles ordered for delivery in the year 1910 in the United States fixes the number at about four hundred thousand. But

The Modern Method of Delivering Milk.

prolonged investigation and labor would be necessary if an approximately accurate average of the cost of the automobiles—that is to say, the cost of each one—were to be obtained. The best impression seems to be that the average would be found to be greater than one thousand dollars. For it has been observed that notwithstanding the attempt to produce automobiles at low cost, like runabouts, is constant and the output increasing that attempt has been coincident with a greater and greater demand for motor cars that are of very high grade, of as perfect construction as it is possible to make, with luxurious fittings and costly accessories. Many automobiles are now manufactured costing ten thousand dollars and more, and the tendency is to greater elaboration and luxury in construction.

But if we take Mr. Hill's estimate as approximately correct, then there are momentous, possibly portentous factors in the production of an article, at first almost exclusively designed for pleasure, for which the American people have been paying hundreds of thousands of dollars every year for the past eight years, and principally since 1906.

And as it is to be presumed that the demand for motor cars will not slacken, unless there be severe business demoralization, but instead will increase, then it might be computed that within the next ten years the people of the United States will have expended four billion dollars for motor cars.

The result of this diversion of capital and money toward a single industry, and that one whose product was first designed chiefly for recreation or pleasure, it is impossible to forecast, or even more than vaguely to surmise. But in order to get a fair appreciation of what this may mean financially and economically, it is the better part to trace briefly the history of this sudden and magnificent, in the sense of magnitude, diversion of capital and income from other fields to this one industry.

In the year 1892, Edison said to the present writer that at a rough estimate the American people were paying about three hundred millions a year for electric lighting service. About ten years earlier, Edison perfected his incandescent electric light, solving for commercial purposes the problem of the divisibility of the electric current.

So that what has been accomplished in the way of income to the manufacturers of automobiles in the United States within five or six years required more than ten years to accomplish in the marketing of electricity for lighting purposes.

But electric lights are no longer regarded as a luxury, but as a necessity, at least in well-populated communities. It required more than ten years to develop the highway trolley system that the yearly income from them would approximately equal the aggregate amount of money spent by the American people in one year for automobiles. In fact it would be difficult to compare favorably this stupendous yearly expenditure within five or six years after the manufacturing of automobiles in the United States assumed large proportions, excepting with the returns received by one or two of the greater coporations. The United States Steel Corporation in its income account might furnish a comparison in which the factors of the proposition are equal. That is to say, in the swiftness with which great income was received after organization. And, yet that comparison would not be wholly satisfactory, since the Steel Corporation represented nothing but the concentration under one control of many corporations which had been operating independently each of the other. In all probability there is no record of any manufactured product yielding in so short a time after manufacture was begun so great a yearly return as has been the case with the automobile industry. Certainly the mining of precious metals cannot be compared with it, since after sixty years of mining within the area of the United States and its territories, we have been able to make a record of approximately one hundred millions a year in gold.

The swiftness of the development of this industry has been so great that the record reads like the most fanciful and most romantic picture of a vivid imagination. It surpasses the highest flights of fancy of Jules Verne.

One example may be perhaps sufficient to illustrate the swiftness of this development. A corporation was organized a few years ago for the manufacture and marketing of automobiles. The original capital was one hundred thousand dollars. Yet the business increased so rapidly and the earnings were so large that it was possible to declare a stock dividend chiefly out of earnings of 1,900 per cent. In other words, **a capital of one hundred thousand dollars was increased to two million dollars, and paid for out of accumulated earnings secured in the course of three or four years.**

While it is not possible to obtain the details of a contemplated co-operation or combination, or some other form of corporate community of interest into which several corporations employed exclusively in the manufacture of automobiles have entered, yet it is a common understanding that this aggregation will represent some eighty millions of capital, not watered or in any way fictitious capital, nor to be exploited with the public.

Another illustration. There was perfectly accurate demonstration late in 1909, that from the automobile district of which Detroit, Mich., is the centre, specifications came for machinery of the kind used in the manufacture of automobiles to be manufactured and delivered in the year 1910, which would, if the orders could be filled, have kept in full operation every manufactory of machinery in the United States.

Of course, if the automobile industry, which is centered at Detroit, was of itself to occupy every machinery making plant in the United States for a full year, the manufacturers of automobiles in other parts of the United States would have found it practically impossible to secure even a small part of the machinery that they needed.

In the year 1898, the number of automobiles in the United States was so small that the occasional appearance of one on the streets was an event. And for a few years after 1898, all of the automobiles, with a few exceptions, were imported from Europe.

As recently as the year 1900, only one thousand automobiles were owned and driven on the streets of the United States. And yet the very accurate statistics collected for the Convention of the American Automobile Association, held two weeks ago at Washington, reported that at the present time in the United States there are a little under three hundred thousand automobiles. These have for the most part been paid for, and the estimated value of these machines is about four hundred and twenty-nine million dollars.

Therefore, if we include in these statistics the estimated money values of the automobiles ordered for delivery in the year 1910, the American people will have paid in ten years between eight hundred millions and nine hundred millions for their automobiles.

Again comparison may serve impressively to fix these stupendous figures representing actual cash outlays. There were paid for these machines in nine years more money than would have been received had all the land assessable for taxation in the States of Florida, Nevada, Oregon, Wyoming, and the Territories of New Mexico and Arizona been sold and cash paid for these lands.

The amount, including the estimate for 1910, is almost equivalent to one fifth of the property of greater New York as has been assessed for taxation purposes. But these assessed values in New York City represent the growth of what a hundred years ago was a little town to its present position of the second largest city in the world.

Edison said in 1892 that the commercial use of the electric light brought to him his first considerable fortune, about three million dollars, and the electric light works furnished a living directly and indirectly to about one million wage earners. That was a development which took ten years' time to reach. But in a like period of time the automobile manufactures of the United States have grown from nothing to an industry which is now paying approximately one hundred million dollars a year wages and salaries, and is furnishing their livelihood to three million persons.

The amazing swiftness with which the popularity of the motor car was developed is most suggestively shown in the records of the Customs House. It was stated to the American Automobile Association that within three years after the first importation of automobiles, the revenues received at the customs houses, principally that of New York, from this source, were more than sufficient to pay the entire cost of the diplomatic and consular service of the United States until the American manufacturers had so perfected the American automobiles as to command the home market.

The conditions are reversed now. Six years ago we were importing automobiles in such numbers that the customs revenues were sufficient to pay for our diplomatic service. To-day we are exporting automobiles in large numbers, the expectation being that in the year 1910 we will export five thousand machines.

A high officer of a banking institution which has maintained for four or five years large relations with some of the automobile interests, in speaking of Mr. Hill's estimate of four hundred millions as the sum the American people will pay in the year 1910 for automobiles, said that Mr. Hill was undoubtedly under rather than over the real figures, and that it was not improbable that as much as half a billion dollars would be paid next year for automobiles, since there will be many purchases of machines to take the place of used-up machines. The life of an automobile is not a very long one. So great an expenditure as a little under one billion dollars in two years for automobiles, and at last a billion and a half for ten years, is sure to be reflected in the number and magnitude of the manufacturing plants. There must be many plants, even if the capacity of each one is great, if it is to be possible to manufacture in a single year nearly three hundred thousand automobiles.

The estimate for the year 1909 was that two hundred and ninety thousand automobiles were made and marketed in the United States. This industry has required a capitalization of a little in excess of two hundred million dollars, absolutely new capitalization representing the creation of new wealth and the diversion of this money capital from other employments. In the State of Michigan there are thirty-seven automobile manufacturing plants; in Indiana twenty-eight, and in Ohio a like number, while Illinois has now twenty plants, and Wisconsin ten. It was regarded as a somewhat curious feature of this industrial development that it has been for the most part confined to the mid-West. That, doubtless, is in part explained by the fact that the carriage manufacturing industry, which for many years centred in New England and New York State, has shifted to the mid-West.

For instance, the City of New Haven, which some thirty years ago had forty carriage-making establishments, now has only two. And some of the larger factories in other years engaged in making carriages have abandoned that industry and devoted themselves to the manufacture of automobile bodies. Ten years ago there were only two or three automobile factories in the United States. The number this year is two hundred and twenty, including in that a few in the West still engaged partially in the manufacture of carriages and wagons.

It was stated at the recent meeting of the American Automobile Association that Detroit marketed in the year 1909 motor cars valued at one hundred million dollars in round numbers, and would receive this year about a hundred and twenty-five million dollars. The little town of Flint, Mich., marketed fifty million dollars' worth, and Cleveland approximately cars of a like value.

When it is said that the American people have and will have purchased in the years 1909 and 1910 automobiles for which the aggregate payment was three quarters of a billion dollars, the first thought invariably is that this is a stupendous amount of money to pay for what is a mere pleasure-giving product. It certainly requires no argument to show that the concentration of so great an amount of money into the manufacture and marketing of automobile cars must have a very important effect upon our economic condition, and especially that of the money market. But the majority of those who have given thought to the subject are wondering whether after all this is a symptom surely pointing to extravagance, which may have a very baneful influence.

For, in the first place, it has been within two or three years made clear that the motor car is surely playing an important part in the industrial, and even in the agricultural, development of the United States.

For instance, in the City of New York alone the use of motor cars for business purposes has so rapidly increased in the last two years as to make it certain that the availability and economy of them have now been perfectly demonstrated. Many of the great business houses rely upon them almost exclusively for the cartage of their merchandise. It is the opinion of the fire experts and those of the insurance companies that if an electric motor car could be perfected which would compare in low cost with the gasoline truck, then the use of animal power for trucking in New York City would in the course of a few years be abandoned. Many of the newspaper deliveries are now made exclusively by the motor truck.

Furthermore, with the expected development of highly improved farming within fifty miles of New York, it is regarded as certain that the automobile will play so important a part as to greatly reduce the cost of farm work and that of the conveyance of the products from the farms to the market. Mr. E. C. Converse, prominent with the Steel Corporation, and a banker as well, who has brought to maturity one of the most successful farms in the East, depends entirely on automobiles and motor trucks for transportation between his farm and the railway station. In the South, if the recently invented cotton picking apparatus meets the expectations which the inventors and men of capital now feel justified in entertaining, the motor car will be widely employed in cotton picking, although, of course, it is a special adaptation of the principle of the automobile to this purpose.

Mr. Hill is quoted as having said that not one dollar expended in buying automobiles in the year 1910 will be of service in raising a single bushel of grain. Others say that while this may be strictly accurate, yet it is after all no more than a half truth. For the great farmers of the West, who are year after year turning to the automobile, by no means rely on it for exclusive recreation. They find it is of great value and high economy, not so much in working the fields as in other ways contributing to the successful farm.

Again, this universal, or well-nigh universal, use of the automobile has, it is stated, done more to bring the attention of the American public to the economic importance of good roads than all the arguments and pleas of the past have been able to do. When Roswell P. Flower was Governor of New York he preached in season, and frequently out of season, what the economy was to farmers and business men in good roads. But Gov. Flower's pleas fell upon deaf ears. Not until the great use of the automobile did there come that good understanding of what perfect highways mean. It is to that more than to any other reason, probably, that New York has consented to the expenditure of fifty million dollars for the improvement of highways. In a few other States a like movement is in progress, so that if within the next four or five years the American people spend two or three thousand million dollars for automobiles, it is certain that gradually but surely our highways will be repaired and perfected until at last the two million miles of highways in the United States may be well compared with the admirable and highly economic highways that cobweb the entire Republic of France.

There is another economic aspect of this subject, which it is worth while to bear in mind. The four hundred million dollars which the automobile manufacturers of the United States are to receive for automobiles in the present year mean a widely diversified industrial demand. A considerable proportion of this money is of course paid out in wages and salaries, and the sum which is paid in the way of commissions to retailers must in the aggregate be large. Wages and salaries and commissions all mean industrial and commercial activity. The greater part goes to buy the necessaries of life. Some smaller part finds its way into the savings banks, and by that means is utilized into other industries, commerce, or in real estate improvement.

Then a very large part of the aggregate receipts must be expended by the automobile manufacturers for the purchase of iron and steel, and especially in the purchase of tools and machinery. It has already been stated in this article that if the specifications which came from the automobile district of which Detroit is the centre, for tools and machinery to be delivered in the year 1910 were accepted, then the fulfillment of the contracts would require the productive capacity of all the manufactories of tools and machinery in the United States.

There are other industries that have been greatly stimulated by this wonderful growth of the automobile market. The items of gasoline and rubber alone represent in the aggregate very large sums. So that it is easy to understand that the movement of four hundred millions of money from the American people to the automobile manufacturers does not mean the permanent concentration into the hands of these manufacturers of an amount of money about equivalent to one-half of the National debt of the United States, but the speedy distribution of the greater part of this money into various channels of industry, the scattering of it in the form of wages, and its return in that way to producers of the necessaries of life, as well as the collection of the surplus, which the wage earners are able to save, so that it may be deposited in the savings banks.

And yet there stands out the fact unparalleled in the entire record of industrial development in the United States in a hundred years, that within ten years at the most, and practically within six, there has been concentrated into one industry capital and money returns for the marketing of a single product which are in excess of the National debt of the United States, greater than the aggregate municipal debt of the city of New York, larger than the stupendous expenditures on bridges, subways, rapid transit, the Pennsylvania and McAdoo tubes in New York City, approximately at least one half of the railway capital of the United States, and greater than the assessed valuation for taxing purposes of the property of more than one half of the States of the Union.

Of course if it were not for the fact that this capital and vast investment in automobiles returns almost instantly through general industrial activity to the people, serving thereby to increase normally and healthfully our permanent National wealth, a phenomenon of this kind would mean in the course of a few years National bankruptcy. And it might mean speedy business demoralization and possibly panic were the automobiles exclusively used for pleasure. It is now realized that more and more they are becoming splendid instrumentalities for the economic advancement of industry. There is another phase of the subject not necessary to enter into at this time. It may be briefly alluded to by saying that with the development of the automobile for business purposes, it will surely come within the authority of the Inter-State Commerce Commission of the United States.

March 6, 1910

ROMANCE OF A $65,000,000 STORE THAT HAS NO SALESMEN

THERE is nothing new under the sun. There were astronomers, soothsayers, great warriors and decisive battles, and rich merchants five thousand years ago. When David sang he looked up unto the heavens and read in the stars the destiny of man, and through the pyramids the ancients calculated the procession of the Heavenly host. From the very ports about which the Balkans are now contending great ships went out and came in laden with the commerce of the East, while men fought for territory or spoil. Joseph was the first builder of Government warehouses down in Egypt.

But "the sun do move" and the world is "bettering the instructions" of the ancients; for whereas the tradesmen of the older times sold their wares in tents and stalls and for what would now be called "a debased currency," the merchants of our times do business in great palaces of steel and stone, and invite their customers by every pleasing art. Instead of the tents of sheepskins and goatskins and the caravans of camels loaded with merchandise, and the ships of inland seas and the rude craft of the coasting trade, there are now great fleets of steel ships and mammoth piles of many stories with moving stairways and massive hangings and amply endowed eating places, and the ever-young and always attractive salesladies to rake in the shekels and so swell the volume of trade and enhance the glory of living.

But there is nothing new under the sun. The department store of the day is the country store of yesterday, simply, adapted to the needs of urban life, the convenience of those who buy, and the success of those who sell. In the country store as it was known all over this land thirty or forty years ago and as it is still known in places far removed from the confusion of crowded populations, was the department store in embryo. In it everything was sold, from saleratus to shrouds, from calico to coffee, from saddles to sugar, from hymn books to harness, from plows to pickles, and in it the foundation was laid of many of the great fortunes of the present time. There has been a vast improvement in the style of doing business since the country store came to town in the department store; but after all it is the country store writ large and capable of still larger and closer touch with the buying public.

Many economists hold that the nearer the seller and buyer can be brought to each other the better for both; for the seller because he can sell at a lower profit and for the buyer because he will not have to pay so many profits on his purchases. It is with this idea that there has been established what are known as mail order houses, which sell directly to their customers without the aid of middlemen, from the producer to the consumer as nearly as it can be done in the present stage of doing business. It is claimed by some that these mail order houses are combinations in restraint of trade, but, per contra, it is contended that so long as it is lawful to sell bacon and broadcloth in the same establishment, and so long as the mails can be made to do the business of drummers, it cannot be argued successfully that such competition is other than beneficial.

This story is not to be considered, however, as in any sense controversial—it is intended to give simply an account of one of the most remarkable business enterprises of this remarkable age; the story of the founding, the growth, the character, the marvelous development of the house of Sears, Roebuck & Co. of Chicago, the largest and richest mail order house in the world.

Richard W. Sears, Founder of the Firm.

The business was established by Richard W. Sears in Chicago in 1895, only seventeen years ago. The beginning was small, but the growth of the concern has been little short of miraculous. It is not stated how much capital was invested in the original enterprise; but it has grown and grown and grown until the plant or establishment now covers four large city blocks with its great buildings, and two or three other blocks with its parks and playgrounds and other places provided for the pleasure and comfort of the army of people employed in its conduct. The buildings are of the most substantial construction of steel and brick and stone, and have been designed so as to give the most attractive and impressive ensemble.

There are merchandise, administration, printing, and manufacturing buildings, each designed especially for its particular work, and all equipped with the most modern conveniences for the transaction of business. There are many departments, of course, in such an establishment—a department where the daily mails are opened, a department where orders are entered for the merchandise department, a mammoth room where the files are kept and where the names of all the customers are kept, correspondence, mail addressing, house sales, shipping, health, clothing, and special departments; a "cafateria," where 3,300 have luncheon every day; kitchens and power plants and immense train sheds where thirty cars can be loaded with merchandise at the same time.

It takes a very large capital to manage a business like this. The general balance sheet of the house for Dec. 30, 1911, showed that the value of the real estate, buildings, plant, fixtures, machinery, patents, and investments in the securities of other corporations was $40,442,766.78. Added to this the advances to and investments in factories owned and whose output was taken by this company, $2,803,951.28; the advances to manufacturers whose output was chiefly taken by the company, $2,638,456.61; the value of the merchandise and supplies on hand, $9,381,-021.39; the cash in banks and on hand, $2,381,851.03; the market value of the municipal and railroad bonds held by the company, $2,173,011.65, and sundry other assets included in the balance sheet, the total assets of the concern a year ago was $60,768,948.80. Set against this was these liabilities: Preferred capital stock, 85,000 shares, at $100 each, 7 per cent. cumulative $8,500,000; common capital stock, 400,-000 shares, at $100 each, $40,000,000. Add to these liabilities for merchandise and other open accounts, for stockholders' dividend on preferred stock, payable Jan. 1, the retirement of 3,000 shares of preferred stock, and making the proper deductions for the dividends on preferred and common paid during the year, and the balance sheet showed that during the year the company made a profit of $6,984,966.96. The sales of the company, less returns, allowances, discounts, &c., amounted during the year to $64,423,035.91. That was for last year; it is estimated by I. S. Rosenfels, the publicity manager of the company, that the total profits for 1912 will approximate $8,000,000.

In August the number of employes on the payroll of the main plant at Chicago was 4,428 men and 4,040 women. During the busier days of the holiday trade it was expected that the force would be largely increased, and that it would then approximate 10,000, all well paid, all in love with their work, and all cared for with fine regard to their comfort and happiness.

The business of Sears, Roebuck & Co., as their immense catalogue, printed and illustrated in their own establishment shows, covers an immense range, embodying almost every article of possible use in the home, on the farm, in the factory or workshop. At present the firm does no business outside the limits of the United States. The theory upon which the business is conducted is set forth, in the catalogue, in which a guarantee is given that the customer is the sole judge of his own satisfaction, and that no transaction is considered closed until purchaser is satisfied.

No traveling men are employed by the company. It has no method of reaching purchasers other than by mail and through advertising. The business is entirely retail—no discounts being offered for quantity under any circumstances. The business is done strictly for cash and almost for cash in advance.

"If there is a distinguishing feature in the conduct of the business of Sears, Roebuck & Co., it is the absolute confidence of its customers, as shown by the fact that out of the $80,000,000 business which will be done in 1912 at least $75,000.000 is cash in advance."

A numerous corps of buyers is employed for the various lines of goods, and these buyers visit all American and European markets in making their purchases. Equal attention is given to all the various lines of goods carried in the catalogue, and the company cannot be said to make a specialty of any line. It owns, however, in whole or in part about twenty-five factories, and takes practically the entire output of as many more in such staple lines as furniture, hardware, harness and saddles, vehicles, clothing, shoes, millinery, bicycles, photographic goods, stoves, cream separators, sewing machines, paints, wall paper, agricultural implements, blumbing goods, lumber and millwork, and taking advantage of its manufacturing connections, it saves much of the middleman's profit. The company has about 5,000,000 regular customers in its index, representing more than 25 per cent. of all the families in the United States. Customers visiting the establishment receive every possible attention, the idea of the company being to make them feel that they are at home. Direct connection with the railroads for receiving and shipping goods reduces the expenses of teaming to a minimum. All the express companies have offices in the buildings of the concern.

One of the finest things about this establishment is the care with which it looks after its people. The civil service obtains in the management of its army of workers. Employes are promoted according to merit; a fair percentage of all the department managers started with the firm in clerical places. No pension system is in force for the benefit of employes, but a bonus is paid to all employes receiving less than $1,500 the year for length of service as follows: "On the fifth anniversary of the date of employment a check for 5 per cent. of the year's wages; 6 per cent. on the sixth anniversary, and so on up to 10 per cent. on the tenth anniversay and thereafter."

A savings department for the benefit of the employes is conducted by the company. More than a fourth of the employes deposit their savings in this department, upon which they are paid 5 per cent. interest, compounded quarterly. A discount is allowed employes on all goods bought for themselves or their families. A fully equipped branch of the Chicago Public Library is maintained in the merchandise building of the company, and adjoining the grounds of the company is a branch of the Young Men's Christian Association, which is maintained in part by the company and for the benefit of the people employed by it. The health of the employes is also cared for with special attention, and all the most modern appliances are used for the ventilation of the buildings. On the athletic field of the company, hard by the principal buildings, some great feats have been performed. There are tennis courts and diamonds and gridirons, and one of the most artistic and beautiful little parks in the city for the refreshment of those who work in the establishment. Among the employes there are eight baseball clubs, and among them there could be found, doubtless, many a Tyrus Cobb for the bat, and likewise many a Marquard for the pitcher's box.

The business is so well organized and covers so great a diversity of interests that it is not affected particularly by political conditions. Asked why there should be any antagonism to the mail order house by retailers or wholesalers generally, Mr. Rosenfels replied:

"The antagonism to mail order houses by retailers can be accounted for on the simple theory of competition, just as one retailer is antagonistic to another retailer. Antagonism by wholesalers is natural on the ground that all manufactured products supplied direct to the consumer without the assistance of a wholesaler or intermediate distributor naturally means a loss of business to those agencies."

Asked what was the economic value of the system built up by his company Mr. Rosenfels said:

"Generally speaking, the economy of selling by mail lies in the decreasing selling expense, which is absolutely saved by the purchaser, as the comparison of prices will show. It is generally assumed that the mail order business cuts out the middleman, but in a strict analysis this point will be found not peculiar to the mail order business, as manufacturers generally are now seeking to market their products without the assistance of the jobber."

This is the story. It is not controversial. It is merely descriptive of one of the most remarkable commercial undertakings in the country. J. C. H.

January 19, 1913

FORD SELLING AUTOS ON $5 CASH PAYMENT

Name Then Listed as Prospective Purchaser and Small Instalments Will Be Accepted.

WHOLE FAMILY CAN JOIN

Henry Ford has worked out a new plan, it was announced yesterday, by which, upon the initial payment of $5 any person in the United States will be listed by an authorized dealer as a prospective owner of a Ford motor car, and when the installments equal the price of the car, delivery will be made. In some cases it may take several months before the price of the car is fully paid.

Gaston Plantiff, who is Mr. Ford's Eastern representative, explained at the Ford Building, Broadway and Fifty-fourth Street, that the length of time in making the payments will make no difference. The prospective buyer's name will be kept on the list and after a substantial payment is made, it will be possible, provided satisfactory references are given, to obtain possession of the car, the balance being paid on the installment plan as is now the case with the deferred payment system in vogue with the Ford Motor Company as well as by many other automobile concerns.

This new play, which goes into effect tomorrow, is different from the customary deferred payment system, in that the small payments will be made at any local savings bank and will draw the regular interest of savings deposits. A special card for these payments is provided. It provides for weekly payments of a stated sum but the prospective owner may increase his weekly installments at will, thereby advancing the date when he will get possession of the car.

In the formal announcement, signed by Edsel B. Ford, as President of the Ford Motor Company, it is stated that this plan "extends to the whole family an opportunity to participate in the car purchase by permitting each member to contribute a small amount weekly to the plan with the wholesome effect of inculcating thrift and also demonstrating the benefits to be received from regular and consistent accumulation of funds to spend for things desired. The price reduction of Ford cars and trucks which went into effect last October, bringing them to the lowest level in the history of the Ford Motor Company, opened a market of unusual proportions and with the inauguration of the Ford weekly purchase plan this market now becomes even more comprehensive."

The regulations on the weekly purchase card specify that interest will be payable only on completion of all payments if made regularly, or when delivery can be made by the dealer through applying the total amount of the deposit as a first payment.

In the event of a condition arising whereby the prospective buyer should find it impossible to complete his payments for the car selected, the amount of money deposited in the bank may be withdrawn, entailing no loss to the depositor. It is stipulated, however, that this privilege of withdrawing deposits credited to the Ford weekly purchase plan will be permitted only in cases of extreme emergency at the discretion of the bank and the dealer.

April 8, 1923

TIME PAYMENT MANIA LAID TO AMERICANS

Clothiers' Paper Says That Most Wage Earners Have Mortgaged Their Incomes.

Special to The New York Times.

CHICAGO, Jan. 2.—A vast majority of the wage earners of the United States have mortgaged their incomes for years to come because of the trend of the people to buy luxuries and the necessities of life on the instalment plan, according to The National Retail Clothier, the official publication of the National Association of Retail Clothiers and Furnishers.

"Is this country going time-payment mad?" the article asks. It follows with this list of some of the things that are today being bought on time:

Buildings, life insurance, furniture, furnaces, vacuum cleaners, rugs, window shades, victrolas, pianos, radio outfits, washing machines, gas and electric stoves, electric fixtures and installation, jewelry, clothing, books, bonds, stocks, automobiles, magazines, band instruments and education.

One statistician has compiled a list of sixty-eight important commodities that are being sold on time payments.

Automobile and musical instrument sales are offered as examples of what is taking place all over the country. There are approximately 14,000,000 registered automobiles in the United States, of which 10.192,000 are passenger cars. Considering this with the fact that there are but 4,000,000 people who file income tax reports of over $2,000 a year with the Treasury Department, the deduction is made that there are two and a half times as many passenger cars registered as income tax reports of over $2,000. This is taken to mean that 6,000,000 persons earning less than $40 a week own an automobile each.

The article concludes with the statement that there were 300,000 pianos sold in America in 1923 for a total of $120,000,000, of which at least 75 per cent. were sold on time. Fifteen million dollars' worth of band and string instruments were bought during the year, over half of them on the partial payment plan, while 90 per cent. of the phonographs sold in America were sold on time.

January 3, 1924

ADHERING TO STANDARDS.

Benefits of It Shown in the Case of Women's Wear Goods.

The cry for the elimination of waste in industry is in all probability responsible for the growth of the standardization movement as a means of reducing the amount of chance in business. Groups in all lines of endeavor have taken steps in the last two years toward standardizing in one or another of the basic phases of each business, the United Women's Wear League points out in a statement issued yesterday.

In the waist, underwear, petticoat and other branches of business represented in the league the movement has been pronounced. Thousands of dollars have been saved for blouse manufacturers and retailers, and perhaps hundreds of thousands for silk houses, as a result of the first of the league's steps toward standardization, which was in regard to colors. This movement was started by the United Waist League nearly five years ago, and has produced with each new season, a standard color card containing the shades which are deemed by the leaders of the industry the most fashionable and adaptable for blouses for the ensuing seasons. In 1923, soon after the formation of the United Underwear League of America, standard colors were adopted for silk undergarments for the year, and these will be supplemented with new color selections during each succeeding year. At a meeting of the membership of the United Petticoat League of America during the past week standardization of colors was the principal subject discussed, and it is likely that at the next meeting of this organization a committee will be named to investigate and recommend standard colors for petticoats for the ensuing season.

Standardization of sizes by the adoption of sets of minimum measurements for the various articles of under apparel, which was accomplished by the United Unnderwear League of America about six months ago, has also resulted in huge savings to the apparel and silk manufacturrs, the organization reports.

Letters have been received from retail buyers of many of the country's most prominent stores stating that the standard minimum measurements have been of great benefit to them, in that they have given the buyer a definite standard with which to compare merchandise samples. If the samples do not conform with the standard minimum measurements, the buyers point out, no order is placed and the retailer is saved the costly embarrassment of having merchandise returned to his store by the consumer after she has tried it on, only to find that it is cut skimpily and under size.

The adoption of a set of minimum measurements for petticoats is another matter under consideration at this time by the United Petticoat League of America, and action on this will also probably be taken at the next meeting of the organization.

May 20, 1923

CORPORATIONS INVADE RETAIL SELLING TRADE

Million-Dollar Concerns, Doing Nation-Wide Business, Supplanting Corner and Neighborhood Shops—Observer Sees Big Future for Department Store Combines

By EVANS CLARK.

FIFTEEN years ago the groceries, shoes, clothing, drugs, cigars and other essentials that we buy from day to day were sold by corner stores, owned by men we knew or knew about, or else at department stores whose owners were still prominent citizens of the local community. Today we buy them from million-dollar corporations operating hundreds or seven thousands of stores just like ours in a hundred other cities. New names have sprung into national prominence—Woolworth, Kresge, United Cigars, Schulte, Atlantic and Pacific Tea—but few of the people who shop in these stores realize the titanic struggle that is going on among business strategists for the retail trade of the nation.

During the last ten years a revolution in retail selling has taken place, equaling in importance and in industrial drama the growth of the corporation and the trust in the manufacturing field during the close of the last century. It has been much the same story. The individual owner of the individual store has been swept aside before the greater economies, the larger profits and the increased efficiencies of large concerns owned by thousands of stockholders and operating on a national scale.

The battle of the big corporation against the little storekeeper is well under way to success. While the small stores still do business in great numbers, there is hardly a city, town or village in the country in which the corporation retailer has not at least a menacing foothold. The contest that has still to be decided is between the big corporations themselves. This struggle is not merely between rival concerns fighting for markets, but between different methods of selling goods represented by groups of big firms. The chain stores, the five and ten-cent group, the mail order houses, and the department stores are engaged in a battle royal for supremacy.

What the outcome will be no one can foretell with certainty. A point of view recently advanced by Paul M. Mazur, in an article published in The Harvard Business Review, has created wide attention among the strategists themselves. Mr. Mazur thinks that the old department stores have the strategic position, if they will only take advantage of it. The key to that position, he believes, is the key to every position of industrial power—combination.

"The past fifty years," he says, "have seen the growth of the single department store units; the next fifty years will see the consolidation of many units into large powerful groups."

Department Store Chain.

The process he foresees has already begun, although few realize how far it has gone. Already one corporation—the Associated Dry Goods Corporation—has secured control of eight large department stores and one big specialty shop. Three of these are New York houses—Lord & Taylor, James McCreery & Co. and C.G. Gunther's Sons, furs and coats.

Besides its New York holdings this corporation controls the following stores: Hahne & Co., Newark; J.N. Adams&Co. and William Hengerer, Buffalo; Stewart & Co., Baltimore; Powers Mercantile Company, Minneapolis, and the Stewart Dry Goods Company in Louisville.

The process of acquiring these concerns has been much the same as that followed in the manufacturing field—an exchange of stock of the company bought for that of the purchasing corporation on terms that seem advantageous to both. What the advantages are can be seen from the income statements of the parent corporation. In 1917 the net income of the Associated Dry Goods Corporation was $1,500,000. Last year it had grown to $3,900,000—an increase of 160 per cent. in five years.

Another corporation has been lately organized which expects to rival the Associated in the control of a string of big stores. This development is of particular interest because it is being undertaken by interests that have built up a nation-wide business in 5 and 10 cent stores—the S.S. Kresge Company. This is the only big corporation that operates in both fields. Apparently its strategy is to fight on both sides of the battle at once.

S.S. Kresge began his career in Detroit in 1897 with one store. In 1914 he had 118 of them and now he has 233—187 of these are 5 and 10 cent stores and forty-six are 25-cent to $1 stores. They are located in most of the more important cities north of Richmond, Va., and east of Lincoln, Neb. In the last ten years alone the profits of the S.S. Kresge Company have increased over 700 per cent. from $1,200,000 in 1914 to almost $10,000,000 last year. This concern did a business last year alone of $81,800,000.

Kresge Gets Big Stores.

Last year Kresge entered the department store field with a project of ambitious proportions. The S.S. Kresge Company formed the Kresge Department Stores, Inc., a Delaware corporation whose charter provides that it may enter the "chain department store business." Its purpose is states as follows: "To buy well-established stores to be operated by the S.S. Kresge Company and thus to enlarge their purchasing power, reduce prices and increase profits."

The first purchase was the L.S. Plaut store in Newark. This concern, established in 1870, still continues to do business under its own name. But the powers back of it have already made themselves felt. By the end of this year the floor space of the store will have been almost trebled. In March of this year the Kresge Corporation purchased the Palais Royal, a long-established Washington store. It is reported that $4,000,000 was involved in the transaction, and that the gross business of the store will grow this year from ten to fifteen millions of dollars.

The recent Gimbel-Saks merger in New York is another example of the process of consolidating department stores. The Gimbels first began business in Vincennes, Ind., in 1842. In 1887 they established a department store in Milwaukee, and in 1894 they opened one of the largest stores of its kind in Philadelphia. They expanded into New York in 1910. In May, 1923, they acquired ownership of Saks & Co., through an exchange of stock, and in the same month, announcement was made that Saks would open a new store on Fifth Avenue at Forty-ninth Street.

How successful the merger will be may be guessed from the sales figures of the two stores. In 1918 sales at the Gimbel stores were $45,000,000, while last year they were almost $78,000,000. In 1918 sales at Saks were a little over $7,000,000; last year they were $15,000,000. Net earnings of the Gimbel stores have increased in the five-year period from a little over $2,000,000 to $6,000,000.

Over against the growth of department store mergers must be set the amazing increase and success of the chain stores, the five and ten cent stores, and the mail order houses.

String of 10,000 Shops.

Chain grocery, drug and tobacco concerns have been the most spectacular in their rise. The Great Atlantic and Pacific Tea Company is by all odds the largest of them. That concern operates not less than 10,000 retail grocery stores today. Their sales this year will amount to over $300,000,000. Last year alone they had a surplus of over $6,000,000, after paying dividends to their stockholders. Besides their retail stores the A. and P. Company owns a can factory with an output of 20,000,000 cans a year and eleven bakeries which turn out 3,000,000 loaves every week. Only last March they bought one concern in Louisville, the Quaker Maid Company, which operates eighty-seven stores in that city alone. The total number of employes on their payroll is 65,000.

The Jones Brothers Tea Company is another rapidly rising concern in the chain store grocery business. This company represents a merger, effected in 1916, of two other companies incorporated in 1910. It controls the Globe Grocery Economy Stores, 281 of them; the Grand Union Tea Company with 193 stores in every State of the Union.; the Union Pacific Tea Company with 52 stores in Missouri and Kansas; the Progressive Grocery Stores, Inc., operating 115 stores in Westchester County, N. Y., and the John T. Tomich Company with 47 stores in New York and Westchester County. A novel feature of the Grand Union Company is a corps of 2,000 salesmen on regular routes, whom this company supplies with goods.

The Jones Company makes about half of the goods it distributes. It prepares also its own coffee, tea and spices for the market. The business of the corporation has grown from $13,000,000 to $31,000,000 in six years.

Another concern, the Jewell Tea Company, illustrates a variation in the methods of retail trade. This concern operates through wagons that serve regular routes. It buys or manufactures its products and distributes them to branch depots from which they are carried, as ordered, to their customers in the company's wagons. Sales last year amounted to $7,000,000—four times as much as they were six years ago.

The United Drug Company represents a merger of the Louis K. Liggett, William B. Riker and Jaynes Drug Company interests. This corporation does an annual business of $67,000,000, has almost 300 stores in the United States and controls the Booths Pure Drug Company of Great Britain, which operates 700 more stores in the British Isles. The United Cigar Stores, controlled by the Tobacco Products Corporation, operates 1,183 stores and 1,275 agencies in the United States, as well as the Service Tobacco Shops in Canada. In seven years the business of these stores has increased from $35,000,000 a year to almost $75,000,000. A. Schulte, a competing corporation, increased its sales from $672,000 in 1919 to $1,700,000 last year, a growth of over 150 per cent. in four years.

500 Per Cent. in Five Years.

Perhaps the rise of the Penney stores has been the most spectacular of all. J. C. Penney began business for himself in clothing, dry goods and shoes out in Kemmerer, Wyo., in 1902. He succeeded rapidly and looked around for more retail worlds to conquer. He conceived the idea of securing an interest in other stores by getting individuals in other places to go into partnership with him. He incorporated in 1912 and at that time he had thirty-four stores—thirty-one of them were not separately incorporated but were partnerships of this kind. The Penney stores now number 571. Last year they did a business of $68,000,000 and this year the total will come to $75,000,000. Last year the Penney company turned over a net income of $4,500,000. In 1918 its income was $700,000. This represents a growth of 540 per cent. in five years.

The five and ten-cent store development is more generally known. The F. W. Woolworth, Kresge, Kress and McCrory companies are leaders in this field in the order named. In 1912 the Woolworth Company did a business of $60,000,000; last year their sales were $193,000,000. In 1912 their net income was $7,500,000; last year it was $20,700,000. There are 1,260 Woolworth stores doing business now. Some thirty-two new stores have been opened this year and leases have been signed for fifty more.

The S. H. Kress Company operates over 150 stores, mostly in the South and Southwest. This business was started by Mr. Kress in Memphis in 1896. Last year his stores did a business of $34,000,000. The McCrory Stores Corporation operates 166 stores, mostly east of the Mississippi River, and do a business of $21,000,000. The founder, J. G. McCrory, began business in Scotsdale, Pa., in 1882.

Has 6,000,000 Customers.

The two leading mail-order houses of the United States are Sears, Roebuck & Co. and Montgomery Ward & Co. The sales of Sears-Roebuck alone were over $250,000,000 last year. Its headquarters are in Chicago, where it owns a plant covering thirty-seven acres of land.

Montgomery Ward has over 6,000,000 customers, located in every State in the Union, not to mention Canada, Mexico, South American countries and the Far East. Its business amounts to $124,000,000 a year. This concern has distributing centres in Chicago, Kansas City, Portland, Ore., St. Paul and New York City.

If the developments of the last five years are any criterion, the chain stores have a bigger future than either the department stores or the mail-order houses. The Department of Commerce at Washington publishes figures which show the growth from year to year of the three main groups of distributers. They show that the chain stores have increased considerably faster than the department stores, and that both have gone ahead of the mail-order houses.

Sales of 129 grocery chains show a growth in business of 87 per cent. from 1919 to 1923 and that of drug chains 44 per cent. in the same period. The business of 333 department stores in all parts of the country increased 24 per cent. Sales of the four leading mail-order houses during the same period, however, decreased slightly—about 1 per cent.

In predicting the future of retail distribution Mr. Mazur has made a thorough analysis of the comparative strength and weaknesses of the chain and department stores.

The weakness of the department store, says Mr. Mazur, in comparison with the chain specialty shop, is largely due to lack of concentration. This is felt in several directions. Take purchasing, for example. While a department store may do a total business of $10,000,000, this volume is split up into perhaps one hundred departments, each handling a different line of goods. This means that purchases of a single kind are reduced to $100,000 each. The chain specialty store concentrates its entire purchases in a narrow field of goods. The advantage is obvious—both in price concessions and overhead.

Combination Will Win.

Mr. Mazur contends, however, that in several directions the department store has an advantage over the specialty and chain store. The well-established department store, for instance, has built up a good-will and reputation that no chain or specialty shop can achieve in a long period of time. The latter must go through an expensive stage of development and operate in high-priced street-floor locations to obtain the good-will now held by the department store. Then, too, the department store has a relatively large volume of business, which permits advertising on a scale which the limited business of each city's chain or specialty shop cannot afford.

The relative strength and weakness of the various methods of retailing vary, according to Mr. Mazur, with the size of the city or town.

In this struggle, no matter what the size of the city, Mr. Mazur believes that the department stores must consolidate to function most effectively. He claims that the main disadvantages which the single store suffers from can be eliminated by such mergers.

"Consolidation," he says, "offers practically all the advantages of the chain store useful to the department store."

September 7, 1924

35 YEARS' GROWTH IN UTILITIES SHOWN

One Broadway Sign Gives More Illumination Now Than All Milwaukee Had in 1892.

A picture of thirty-five years of change and progress in the operation and management of public utilities was drawn yesterday by Frank L. Dame, President of the North American Company. The company, one of the largest of the utility holding companies, was organized in 1890.

Modern "big business" presents many difficult and trying situations, Mr. Dame said, "but I dare say that the North American system's business of more than $80,000,000 last year was done with far less wear and tear on official nervous systems than in 1891 when gross earnings were only about two per cent. of that amount.

"I have recently been re-reading the time-yellowed reports of my predecessors, including Henry Villard and C. W. Wetmore, who long since have passed away. Only thirty-three years ago today, in 1892, Mr. Villard stated in his annual report that 'incandescent lighting has shown a remarkably rapid growth, at this time more than 13,000 lamps being in service in Milwaukee.' These lamps were of the old sixteen-candlepower variety. Almost any one of the numerous large signs along Broadway now casts more illumination than the entire city of Milwaukee obtained from all of its electric lighting in 1892.

"In financing, too, conditions were vastly different in those early days. American business of 1925 has practically no trouble in getting here at home all the capital required for sound developments. Mr. Villard, however, spent many months of his North American Presidency in Europe, persuading foreign bankers that the power and light business in America offered investment opportunities.

"One of the greatest changes is in the field of public relations. Generally speaking, our national power and light companies of today are on excellent terms with their customers, who have invested hundreds of millions of dollars in the utilities that serve them. Such was not the case in the '90s. Not only were the utilities fighting among themselves in destructive competition but they often got into serious and costly controversies with customers and public officials. The sane, fair regulation that marks the conduct of the utility business today was undreamed of thirty-five years ago."

In reviewing the technical, social and financial advances made by the companies in thirty-five years, he said he was impressed by the possibilities of even greater progress in the next thirty-five years.

"Electricity has made life easier and happier for many millions of people. What will it be doing for them in 1960?" he asked.

June 16, 1925

VIEW ADVERTISING IN WRONG LIGHT

Tendency to Regard It a Luxury Limits Business of Many Manufacturers.

T LESSENS SALES COSTS

In Addition, Says Merchandising Expert, Publicity Helps Salesmen Increase Orders.

That many manufacturers are doing a much smaller annual business than they should because they persist in viewing advertising in the wrong light, was the contention put forward yesterday by a local business man who has an enviable reputation as an expert in the merchandising and advertising field. It is his feeling that these manufacturers are too prone to look upon advertising as a luxury that they cannot afford, especially advertising on a scale fully proportionate to their present annual sales volumes, instead of regarding appropriations for this purpose in the same light as investments in the physical sides of their businesses. Further than this, he holds, they underrate the power of advertising in lowering selling costs.

"While comparisons are never strictly accurate," the man in question said, "it seems that advertising might well be regarded in the same light as machinery and plant equipment. Just as a modern clothing factory can make 1.4 suits per man per day, against one suit a week made by hand by a tailor of the old school, so advertising makes it possible for the individual salesman to sell a larger volume at a lower cost.

"The suit of clothes is certainly made by the factory workman, just as the salesman gets the order signed but the plant equipment and machinery make it possible for the workman to reach his amazing efficiency just as advertising, properly planned, changes conditions and creates a new situation in which the salesman can obtain results that otherwise could only be had at higher cost or, in some cases, could not be obtained at all.

"When the tremendous enterprises that have been built up without a single salesman, but solely by advertising, are considered, it is apparent that advertising as a business force is not open to question. Consider, for instance, the well-known facial soap for which druggists disburse more money than for any other soap, although no personal sales pressure is used. Consider a well-known dentifrice which has reached a volume close to eight figures without salesmen, or a certain preparation for the fingernails which was in a weak position in 1915 after the salesmen had secured 75 per cent. distribution, but at once started to grow when the funds were used for newspaper advertising, and the goods moved out of the retail store.

"Scores of successful concerns might be cited which have built volume by mail or through the trade without salesmen or with a minimum of sales activity. Since advertising has proved itself, under certain conditions, as the direct source of volume and profits, the only question open in an individual business is how advertising can be engineered into the operations of that business and what results can be obtained.

"Fundamentally, advertising is a simple business force. It should be stripped of the complexities and exaggerations which at times have entered into advertising discussions. For, basically, advertising is simply selling—selling to the mass instead of selling to the individual. The factors entering into successful advertising are now well recognized. While there is much room for important advances in the science and art of advertising, the fund of facts and experience now in existence is considerable. More and more, advertising problems are being handled along engineering lines. Progressive advertising men, as well as business executives, consider the fact-finding work quite as important as the creative work. In case after case they have seen that facts can be of astonishing value in stimulating, guiding and improving the quality of creative work.

"Perhaps the most common objection raised by the business man who has not experienced the benefits of sound advertising is: 'Advertising may be all right for those concerns; my business is different and I do not see how advertising could possibly help me.' If this question is only approached with an open mind and a willingness to judge advertising by the results it has produced, it will be found that this objection in almost every case lacks validity.

Advertising Does Many Things.

"Two comparisons may illustrate that point. Engineers regard electricity as a force rather than a method, a force which can produce an almost unlimited variety of results from lighting a small lamp to driving a battleship or turning the machinery of a great industrial city. Obviously, a fundamental force such as electricity has many applications. Since scientific management is a group of principles and not a set of methods, it too, has an infinite number of applications, ranging from the organization of a small factory employing perhaps 25 people to the Ford industries employing

100,000, from the manufacture of a toilet product to the production of heavy machinery. So with advertising. It can serve many different uses, of which a few are:

"To do 100 per cent. of the sales job, as in selling by mail or selling products upon which no personal sales pressure is put.

"To create in the consumer's mind a desire for or interest in a product, the sale of which is completed by the dealer.

"To place a requirement on the salesman which will force him to increase his personal sales ability, and at the same time to interest and partially sell the buyer.

"To promote standardization and gain widespread recognition among the public and the trade for the advantages inherent in a standardized line of products as compared with a line offering almost unlimited variation, but a lesser value and other disadvantages.

"To develop good-will.

"To give general publicity to a product or an organization, as was done by many concerns during the over-sold period of 1919-20.

"Looked at in a slightly different way, advertising may be used for one of three general purposes:

"To create new users as, for example, the campaign of a rubber heel manufacturer, which featured freedom from fatigue and other evils caused by constant pounding on hard leather heels—a pioneer job in creating a great permanent market.

"To gain for one competitor a larger percentage of a total market; for example, the advertising of a certain brand of automobile lubricant and a well-known kind of gasoline.

"To cut into a new and rising market. Frequently social and economic conditions carry a new industry forward on a great wave of popular interest; for example, the amazing growth of the automobile industry from 1910 to date, and the astounding growth of the radio. In markets such as these advertising can be so built into a business as to insure it a permanently strong position in a new and rapidly growing industry."

August 17, 1925

AD MEN REAL 'RADICALS.'

William A. White Says They Change Life More Than Communists.

Advertising men have done more to revolutionize the daily life of the American public than Communists and all other radicals combined, William Allen White, publisher of The Emporia (Kan.) Gazette, said yesterday at a luncheon of members of the Advertising Club of New York at 23 Park Avenue. "The real revolutionist," he declared, "is the advertising man, whose stimulation of mass desire and demands results in mass production and buying. THE NEW YORK TIMES is the most dangerous newspaper in this respect in this city, much more so than the Fourteenth Street publications of the reds.

"If advertising should stop it would cause slow decay and ultimate collapse of the entire world. Could I control the advertising publications of this country I would control the entire land. More has been done by mass production, plus advertising, than all the legislation ever enacted. The wide distribution of wealth in the United States is directly due to the efforts of advertising men."

The other guest was Captain George Fried of the United States liner President Roosevelt, which saved twenty-eight of the crew of the Italian freighter Antinoe, which foundered in mid-Atlantic a year ago. Charles C. Green, President of the Advertising Club, presided.

January 13, 1927

CHAIN STORE PLAN FOR RENTING AUTOS

Yellow Truck & Coach Company Forms Hertz Drivurself Corporation.

TO ISSUE $14,000,000 STOCK

New Company Will Organize System of State and Local Concerns to Carry On Work.

What was said to be the first chain store plan transportation system in the world was announced yesterday, when it became known that the Yellow Truck and Coach Manufacturing Company had organized the Hertz Drivurself Corporation, with a view to instituting State and local companies throughout the country which will rent automobiles to individuals on a mileage basis.

John D. Hertz, Chairman of the board of directors of the Yellow Truck and Coach, who announced the project, said present plans called for an increase in the capital stock of the company to provide $14,000,000, of which $10,000,000 would be made immediately available for the new enterprise. The General Motors Corporation, of which Yellow Truck and Coach is a subsidiary, will purchase whatever portion of the new issue is not taken up by Yellow Truck & Coach stockholders at $20 a share.

A special meeting of Yellow Truck and Coach shareholders will be held on June 28, 1926, to approve the increase and to provide for the sale of 700,000 additional shares of Class B stock.

Hertz Heads Company.

Officers of the Hertz Drivurself Corporation are: Mr. Hertz, President; Irving B. Babcock and M. L. Ross, Vice Presidents; E. N. D'Ancona, Secretary; Mr. Hertz, Mr. Babcock, Mr. Ross, Fred J. Fisher and John L. Pratt, Executive Committee. Directors are the officers and Alfred P. Sloan Jr., John A. Ritchie, William Wrigley Jr., Pierre S. du Pont, John R. Thompson, Alfred H. Swayne, P. L. Emerson, Donaldson Brown, Charles A. McCulloch, John J. Raskob, Harold E. Foreman, Leonard S. Florsheim, Otto W. Lehman, Robert Lehman and D. G. Arnstein.

Commenting on the new enterprise yesterday Mr. Hertz said:

"This is the first time in history that a transportation system has been offered to the public on a chain store plan of operation. In the not distant future it will be possible to secure a luxurious private car on a mileage rental basis in any city in the United States, use it for either local or touring purposes and leave it in any other city where the individual renting the car may be when he finishes with it. For example, it will be possible to get a car in a New York City Hertz station and leave it in San Francisco or Portland, Ore., as the case might be.

System Already in Use.

"Several years ago the Hertz Drivurself System was organized with the object of licensing independent car renting companies in this country, and many of these companies are still operating under the name of 'Yellow Drivurself System.' The company was capitalized at $1,000,000, all of the stock being owned by Yellow Truck and Coach, and in about fifteen months we established in various cities some 300 stations. There are now about 6,500 automobiles in service in this rental corporation and we have been entirely unable to keep pace with the demand.

"The Hertz Drivurself Corporation has been organized in response to a great public demand. Its purpose is to make it possible to obtain the use of a Drivurself car anywhere in the United States, at any time, except perhaps in the most remote rural districts. Already we have fairly complete operations covering California, Florida, Illinois, Kentucky, Massachusetts, New Jersey, New York, Ohio, Oregon, Washington, Wisconsin and British Columbia. Surveys have been made of every other State in the Union, and the work of organizing these States as parts of the system is already under way."

June 9, 1926

MONTGOMERY WARD TO OPEN BRANCHES

Mail Order House Plans a Chain to Cover 1,000 or More Country Towns.

Special to The New York Times.

CHICAGO, Aug. 4.—An experiment in super-mail-order salesmanship, destined, if successful, to add a large volume of trade to the business of Montgomery Ward & Co., was announced tonight by Theodore F. Merseles President. The plan, it is expected, will virtually throw the company into the establishment of a chain store system with branches in a thousand or more country towns and villages.

The first step will be the opening of a merchandise display room on Aug. 14 in Marysville, Kan. This will be followed immediately with the opening of similar establishments in five other country hamlets. The initial purpose is to effect a direct personal contact with the customer, which heretofore has never been attempted.

"This experiment may show a new way of extending our mail order business," said Mr. Merseles. "Certainly the opportunity to talk with our customers and get their criticisms will be of great benefit to our business and materially improve our service to our customers."

August 5, 1926

NEW COMPETITION VEXES BUSINESS

Retailers Find Themselves Rivals of Wholesalers, Jobbers and Manufacturers in Struggle for Customers

By STUART CHASE.

ENTER the new competition. Competition, according to conventional ideas, takes place between businesses in the same horizontal plane, in the industrial flow from natural resource to consumer. Coal mine competed with coal mine, railroad with railroad, soap manufacturer with soap manufacturer, grocery wholesaler with grocery wholesaler, retail shoe store with retail shoe store.

All is changing. The horizontal lines are being disrupted in a hundred places. Competition between dealers in the same line of business continues, of course, but to this ancient warfare have been added all manner of new, turbulent and upsetting elements. Hustling chain stores, house-to-house canvassers, mail order campaigns, selling on the instalment plan, trade association drives, "naborhood" store publicity, resident buyers, "endless chain" operators, home town and regional boosting, foreign trade emergencies—are not only shattering the old concepts of competition, but are upsetting consumer-buying habits, making consumers call for strange products, carried on the spearpoint of national advertising and even shifting population as the "Southland calls."

Retailers find themselves competing with wholesalers, with jobbers, manufacturers, groups of farmers and vice versa. Once the business man knew who his competitor was, but today there is no telling from what hidden corner the blow will come.

The causes of this change lie in the changing current of our economic life. The very large returns to capital during the war and subsequently, together with the unprecedented amount of savings accumulated, have resulted in a substantial excess of industrial plant capacity over normal demand. The amazing growth in the technical arts has provided the machines and organization for turning out goods very much faster than purchasing power, as liberated under the going financial mechanism, can absorb them.

One cotton mill operator is now able to handle more looms than fifty operators could manage in 1870. One garment worker running six rib-cutting machines replaces twenty-five hand workers. Two men with an electric magnet can unload as much pig-iron as 128 men formerly could unload. One bottle-making machine operator replaces fifty-four handworkers and one cigarette rolling machine tender replaces 100 hand rollers.

These machines and this equipment cost money and represent a high capital investment. Whenever they stand idle the individual business has to bear a heavy burden of overhead expenses—depreciation, insurance, interest, taxes, maintenance, what not. And with purchasing power so often failing it is inevitable that they stand idle a very large fraction of the time.

In industry after industry the ratio of output to capacity averages in the neighborhood of 50 per cent., which means that equipment is idle half the time. There are, for instance, three times as many lumber mills as are needed to cut the annual demand for timber. Follow the current figures for capacity utilized in even such a well-established industry as iron and steel, and note how far capacity exceeds demand.

Thus the psychological stage is set for what O. H. Cheney, a New York banker, writing recently in The Nation's Business, has called "distributive pressure," the frenzied efforts of business men to find outlets and markets for their products, and so reduce the overhead cost of an idle plant. While it is undoubtedly impossible for all plants to be kept substantially at capacity under the prevailing financial system, each business man, following an old tradition, sees no reason why he should share in the national average of excess capacity.

By all the canons of successful self-help, it is up to him to advertise, break down sales resistance, devise new sales appeals, hustle generally. But the other fellows, most of them, are hustlers, too. And ever faster and more furious grows the game.

It is this pressure which has burst through the usually accepted ideas of competitive economics, turned the whole process upside down, and created the new competition. While the new elements weave and interweave, it is possible to recognize five more or less distinct tendencies.

Competition Between Groups.

With vertical competition thrusting in between the old orderly horizontal lines comes competition between manufacturers, wholesalers and retailers in the same industry. Manufacturers are competing more and more with wholesalers by selling direct to the retailer; they compete with the retailer by selling direct to the consumer. Retailers compete with wholesalers by organizing buying associations, and with manufacturers bent on direct selling through the mails, by the "patronize your neighborhood store" campaign. Wholesalers compete with retailers by organizing chain stores. Chain stores and wholesalers compete with manufacturers by organizing their own manufacturing plants.

Going a step further back toward the source of raw materials, dairymen compete with milk companies by forming their own distribution units; raisin growers, fruit growers and tobacco growers compete with old-line jobbers and wholesalers by organizing producers' cooperatives with up-to-date marketing departments, promoting trade names, labels, fancy packing and national advertising.

In this uproar distributers may find themselves with excess capacity, thus creating a "merchandising vacuum," which results in a clamor for more goods at a faster turnover. The stream turns and runs uphill. The pulling force to attract goods quickly leads the manufacturer back to his sources of raw material and supplies. He wants to control them; he does control them. And so out of the competitive welter comes what is beginning to be termed the "vertical trust"; the concern that owns the entire chain of processes from the gathering of the raw material, through its manufacturing and assembling stages, straight through to the distribution and sale of the finished product.

Next there is competition between alternative commodities. The man who is sick of paying rent and wants to build a house faces the problem: shall it be of wood, stone, brick or stucco? He begins to inquire into the relative merits of each. Instantly he will be bombarded by the propaganda of trade associations eager to impress him with the outstanding merit of their particular commodity; an associated lumber manufacturers' organization; closely followed by a face brick and a cement association. His roof develops into a struggle among a slate, a cedar shingle, a red tile, a copper and tar association.

Whoever heard in days past of a lumber dealer doing anything else than fight another lumber dealer? Now lumber dealers embrace one another and form a trade association with a ten million dollar fund to make American "lumber-conscious." The cotton men fight the woolen men and the silk men fight both. The oil men fight the coal men and the water-power men attack each.

Distributive pressure has become so strong that it has forced dealers in similar commodities into a unit, organized to attack alternative commodities. Competition among themselves still continues, but even more important is solidarity for the industry in the vastly greater struggle with other industries.

Then comes competition between all industries for the consumer's pocket-book. This is the most recent of the new forces and the most important. It is also the least understood. It is really competition of an industry for as much as it can get of the national income. Purchasing power being limited, it devolves upon each industry, even as it devolves upon each manufacturer, to engulf all the purchasing power possible before the supply runs out, and it has been found that in union there is strength.

The combined effects of all meat packers or of all flour millers or of all boot and shoe men will result in a larger slice of purchasing power than if each manufacturer struggled alone. The motive for the trade association with its organized publicity drive becomes even stronger.

This is not lumber against bricks, but lumber against every other industry in the country. Make the consumer lumber conscious, shoe conscious, straw hat conscious, white tooth conscious, silk shirt conscious, hollow tire conscious, aluminum conscious before his bank account runs out. If it is impossible to sell him on this year's wages take a mortgage on next year's wages, and behold!—$5,000,000,000 worth of instalment sales were recorded in 1925.

The flour millers have launched an "eat more bread" campaign. Their goal is 220 pounds per capita per annum. Not to be outdone, the meat packers implore us to "eat more meat." Their goal is 179 pounds per capita per annum. The milk men are organized to secure one quart per capita per diem; the butter men are bending their energies to have us equal the Australian average, which is ten pounds a year more than the American average; the cheese makers set their goal at the Swiss level, 22 pounds above the United States consumption.

Instalment selling is a direct result of distributive pressure. It is an attempt to enlarge the public's purchasing proclivity. It gives the industry organized to use the method a lien on purchasing power of the future, thus insuring a slice of next year's national income in advance of other industries.

But the new competition has jumped the bounds of separate industries and now involves entire communities. A few years ago a town was a town. Now it is the "livest little burg in the State"; the "fourth largest producer of suspender buttons in the country"; the "home of the Browns Potato Peeler." Signs greet the motorist as he enters the town and wish him farewell as he leaves, asking him to call again. Deadly rivalries develop between one community and its neighbor. Cases of infectious diseases are taboo in the local newspapers. Statistics of the increase in population are as optimistic as they are unreliable.

Nor is this competition confined to towns. States and whole regions pursue it actively with great treasure chests for publicity. Florida does battle with California. North Carolina asserts its difference from its neighbors. New England contends that its ancient prestige is by no means lost.

Out of the confusion have come concrete economic results. Population has actually shifted. Certain communities, together with their land values, go suddenly uphill. Others decline. Local trade booms and collapses. Local merchants go to Europe, or go into bankruptcy.

Finally competition has leaped national boundaries into frankly recognized international rivalries. This final classification is of course an old story. The only reason for mentioning it is the fact that it has become greatly intensified in recent years. Industrialists in every manufacturing country hope to keep overhead costs down by selling as much as possible of their output abroad. They are on the watch for purchasing power wherever it may show its wallet not only in their own country but in the entire world around. As invention and technical processes improve, the problem of idle plant grows, and the rivalry between industrial nations tends to become more intensive.

In the face of this competition, plans for world peace have, one fears, a difficult future before them. At the present time, due primarily to Europe's dislocation through war, the United States occupies a commanding position in world trade. But the very fact that purchasing power and wages are low in Europe makes for even greater efforts on the part of European industrialists to keep their plants going by capturing foreign markets. The struggle in the next decade promises to be a bitter one.

SAY INDUSTRY NEEDS ORGANIZED RESEARCH

Scientists at Syracuse Meeting Favor Experts Working on Their Own Initiative.

Special to The New York Times.

SYRACUSE, Oct. 20.—A modern industry must have a carefully organized and heavily financed research department, scientists of widely varying industries declared today at the intersectional meeting of up-State branches of the American Chemical Society at Syracuse University. The meeting was attended by 200 chemists and students, half of them from out of town.

An industry without a capable research department is in constant danger of losing its market to competitors, the chemists agreed. New uses for old products are discovered in laboratories every hour, it was said, and new products are being developed daily.

C. E. K. Mees, director of research for the Eastman Kodak Company, and Saul Dushman, chief physicist for the General Electric Company of Schenectady, were among the leaders in the discussion, with Charles M. A. Stine of the du Pont companies, G. W. Platt of the research department of Bordens, Syracuse; John Thompson of New York, director of research for Bordens; L. H. Cone of the National Aniline and Chemical Company, Buffalo, and S. C. Whitemore of the National Research Council, Washington.

On the subject of organized research, however, there was a decided difference of opinion. Some declared that gifted scientists should be allowed to pursue research as they wished, while others advocated control of research by the plant head or sales manager. Most of the chemists were of the opinion that the expert should be allowed "to work on his own."

G. Washington Platt, Chairman of the Syracuse section, presided. A. W. Burwell read a paper reporting that in his laboratory it was found possible to obtain fatty acids from crude oil by an oxidizing process.

Important papers were also read by Leopold Scheflan, Ernest F. Huff and A. W. Browne. The meeting was the largest and most successful the group has ever held.

The 1929 meeting, it was decided, will be held next Fall at Schenectady, with the Eastern New York section as hosts. The General Electric Works, Union College and Rensselaer Polytechnic Institute will be the gathering places.

The meeting closed with a luncheon in Slocum Hall. In the afternoon the chemists and students attended the Frosh football game at Archbold Stadium as guests of the university.

October 22, 1928

THE RISE OF A BILLION-DOLLAR CORPORATION

By R. L. DUFFUS.

A FEW days ago a board of directors, meeting in one of the newer buildings on West Fifty-seventh Street, ordered the payment of the largest bonus ever distributed to stockholders of any corporation in this or any other country. Its items were a 150 per cent. stock dividend, a cash dividend of $43,500,000 and an increase of $43,500,000 in the rate of the annual dividend. In short, Santa Claus came to the members of the General Motors Corporation. The occasion was all the more notable because General Motors was not organized until twenty years ago and because as late as eight years ago it was nip and tuck whether it should survive or dissolve itself into half a hundred bankrupt fragments.

General Motors—it was first the General Motors Company—came into existence under the ambitious hands of W. C. Durant. Durant got his start at a time when it was contended that the saturation point of the automobile-buying market might be close at hand. He refused to listen to this reasoning. He was as much of an optimist as Henry Ford himself. He had bought Dave Buick's primitive motor car, hammered it into a shape that Buick himself might not have recognized and started manufacturing it in his plant at Flint, Mich. Ford was getting on his feet—or wheels, rather—in Detroit. Wagon makers, gas engine manufacturers, manufacturers of bicycles and mechanics of an inventive turn of mind were being drawn, almost without planning, into an infant industry which drank gasoline, ate steel and grew like a hippopotamus. Durant saw the possibilities of growth and combination. His personal dream was not to be realized. Nevertheless, it was as ambitious as Ford's, whose first castings had been made in the same shop in which Dave Buick had worked.

Its Small Bebinnings.

The new company started off with a flourish. By the end of 1909 it had attained the then respectable total of more than $29,000,000 worth of sales for the twelve months, with net profits of more than $9,000,000. No one foresaw that the time would come when this company, or its direct successor, the General Motors Corporation, would do so vast a business that $29,000,000 would be mere pocket money. But such has been the case. If sales hold up for the last quarter of the present year as they did for the first three-quarters, the receipts from this source will be more than forty times what they were in 1909.

Emerging by a happy union of genius and good luck from the helter-skelter scramble of the automobile industry of twenty years ago, General Motors has ceased to be a private enterprise. It has become a phenomenon—a vast reservoir of capital and brains. More than $1,200,000,000 in assets, more than 200,000 employes, an output of more than 2,000,000 cars and trucks a year—such is the tremendous sequel to the modest beginnings of twenty and twenty-three years ago and to the threat of ruin which darkened the sky only eight years ago.

It has been said that if the owner of $10,000 worth of General Motors stock in 1913 had hung on to his certificates they would now be worth considerably more than $1,000,000. The illustration is purely theoretical. No individual, so far as known, did make $990,000 profit by the simple plan of hanging on. Some who tried to hang on lost their holds and their fortunes during the great deflation of 1920. But the figures do suggest what happened. To take a specific instance, General Motors stock was quoted in August, 1926, at 190 and rose within the year to 225. Within two years there have been dividends of stock and quotations climbed again to more than 224, a profit on each share of about $258.

General Motors has made, and been made by, at least eighty millionaires. It has spun riches out of molten metal and the brains of great executives. But its annals, when written, will not consist of the biographies of annoyingly gifted supermen. General Motors and Henry Ford together are the product of

Photograph by Brown Brothers.

An Automobile of 1894 Moves Up the Streets of Detroit.

gasoline and the American itch for speed. They are the children of the machine—as vastly different as children of the same parent can sometimes be. Ford used the methods of an absolute monarchy; General Motors, in its later stages, those of a decentralized republic. But both rode the wild horses of destiny.

The Magnetic Durant.

Durant was a fine figure of the Captain of Industry so much admired in the first years of the century. He was spectacular, dramatic and magnetic. He was a fighter and a dreamer—and is. For five years, from 1905 to 1910, he held first the Buick Company and then the General Motors Company under his fingers. In 1910 the net sales went nearly to $50,000,000, the profits to more than $10,000,000. Forced out in 1910 he came back to the presidency in 1915, after the du Ponts had invested heavily in the enterprise. The du Ponts then took it down to Delaware and in October, 1916, made a corporation of it.

The war brought prosperity. Sales soared to more than $172,000,000 in 1917, to nearly $270,000,000 in 1918, to more than $567,000,000 in 1920. In 1921 the crash came. The net profits had gone as high as $70,000,000. In the post-war year of doom and disillusionment they vanished altogether, leaving a net loss of $38,680,000. The future seemed to have vanished also. The house of Morgan had to step in to pick up the pieces. Out of this near-catastrophe was born the present gargantuan General Motors Corporation. Practically bankrupt, it had to remain in business because it was already too big for any one to buy. In order to survive at all it had to invent new methods, which revolutionized the automobile industry. It had been started as a holding company. Now it became an operating company. This was the first step.

It began to grow by acquiring or developing new units and by producing more cars for each unit. It would be pleasing to the romanticists to say that this growth had been foreseen and planned for in advance. But a company which began making bearings in the '80s or doorbells in the '70s obviously could not foresee, unless Mother Shipton was on its board of directors, that the horseless carriage was to turn transportation wrongside out. General Motors acquired in due season some eighty divisions or subsidiaries. It would be easy to play up the importance of the established companies that one by one were merged in the larger undertaking.

Power is Decentralized.

In many cases their roots went deep into the pre-automobile stage of American manufacturing—the pre-gasoline-engine, pre-electric, pre-almost-everything period. It is fascinating to trace the progress of a wagon-maker from horse-power to gas-power, from whip sockets to modern ignition systems. But the tradition of the wagon industry did more harm than good to the automobile industry. The most successful makers of automobiles were those who threw away or forgot all that had gone before and started a new science from scratch.

What General Motors assembled was not alone plants and businesses but men. For all practical purposes one plant was about as good as another. Most of the old machinery had to be scrapped in any case. What had really made the old machinery work was human energy, initiative and intelligence. The same qualities, plus a good deal of blind luck, made the new machinery work, too. Some of the blind luck was bad luck. Some important fractions of the automotive industry grew up by pure chance in spots which were not convenient to the sources of raw materials, or to the market, or to either. Once established in a certain spot they have usually had to stay there, because the cost of shifting was greater than the resulting advantages. But if some Napoleon had drawn the automobile map the dots which indicate motor factories would have been quite differently arranged.

However, since Mr. Durant stepped from the General Motors stage, that particular corporation has never had a Napoleon. It has had, more accurately, something like eighty Napoleons. It has been governed by conferences and committees. Almost the only orders given to executives, all the way down the line, were that they should get results. It is true that a good deal of the credit for the success of the corporation is given to Alfred P. Sloan Jr., who has been President since 1920. Mr. Sloan is a man with a record behind him. As a boy barely out of college he built up the Hyatt Roller Bearing Company, which is now a division of the corporation.

If the automobile had not arrived Mr. Sloan would certainly have been a business man of the first water, but probably never a President of a more-than-billion-dollar corporation. He rose to the top as inevitably as a cork in water. His qualities as an executive command admiration from all those who know about them. But they are not of the Napoleonic order.

He is as different from Mr. Ford as a man could be. He makes suggestions. He does not give commands. If he cannot persuade his associates that a certain policy is wise, that policy does not go through. The same principle applies to them in turn. They must persuade their own associates and immediate subordinates. Not that General Motors is bolshevistic. It is not yet governed by Soviets or shop committees. But management stands between the invested capital on the one hand and labor on the other, and within its own ranks management is thoroughly decentralized and democratic.

This system may be the next great step forward in American industry and business, particularly as large-scale operations become more and more common. But it was no one man's inspiration and it did not happen all at once on a particular morning of a particular year. Mr. Ford succeeded in running the Ford Motor Company almost single-handed because he had raised it from a pup. He had sat up with it nights and nursed it through the illnesses of childhood. But the General Motors Corporation was not one pup—it was a pound. It was full of orphans, some of them with tin cans tied on behind. It was full of individualities, local customs and traditions and conflicting problems and commitments. So baffling was the situation which it created that in 1920 and 1921 it was touch and go whether or not the aggregation should be allowed to break up into its constituent parts.

If this had occurred there would have been a crash that would have shaken the country. It was to prevent this calamity that the Morgans stepped in. Yet it seemed about as hard to make the corporation go as a unit as it was to make it go as eighty or more different sections. The job was too big for one man to handle. Sloan's stroke of genius was his decision not to try to handle it. He observed that private enterprises very often succeeded because the men at the head of them had a direct and personal interest in them. The usual corporation, on the other hand, tended to become autocratic and impersonal—in short, soulless. Sloan's idea for General Motors, therefore, was to give the management back to the men who had to produce the goods.

The result is that a senior executive of General Motors has at least as much leeway in producing and selling as he would have if he owned the business he directs. He may have more, for so long as his policies are profitable in the long run he does not have to take orders or accept conditions from the bankers. He gets all the capital he needs direct from the parent corporation. He may not even see any real money, except his own salary and dividends, for the proceeds from his sales are checked in at the central offices in New York and his payroll and monthly bills checked out.

Eighty subsidiaries or divisions means at least eighty senior executives, most of them entrusted with more power and responsibility than the management of the entire General Motors Corporation would have involved a few years ago. These men form the General Motors group of millionaires. Perhaps few or none of them could back a truck up to his favorite bank and come away with a million dollars in coin of the realm. Only those who make up their income tax returns know exactly what they are worth. But it is safe to say that all of them receive a yearly income which, if capitalized, would put them in the millionaire class. This is not because General Motors pays fabulous salaries, for compared with other great enterprises it does not.

The Eighty Managers.

The General Motors millionaires have been made by the operation of the Managers' Security Company, which was formed in 1923 to permit the important executives to buy part of the common stock. This stock was provided, not by the corporation itself but by the du Pont Company, which had and has a large minority interest. But what the managers bought was not so much marketable securities as a guarantee of personal rewards in case their future efforts should be profitable to the corporation. They received a blank check against a bank account yet to be filled. They have become rich by their own individual and united efforts. If you ask a General Motors spokesman if General Motors "made" these men he will tell you that the exact opposite is the truth. They made General Motors.

The progress sheet of the corporation shows what happened. Statistics are inevitable in presenting the story of a corporation. In this case it should be remembered that the figures symbolize not merely the rise of a great corporation but a vast increase in national wealth and a dramatic change in American habits of living. They stand for the spread of hard-surfaced roads into regions where only dust and mud had been known before. They stand for a revolution which has halved and quartered the farmer's distance from town. They represent the multiplication of the motor car until it has become a necessity for families far down in the economic scale, and until an allotment of two, three or even more cars to a moderately well-to-do family is not at all uncommon. For as General Motors grew the Ford Company and a score of smaller companies also grew.

Rivalry With Ford.

For a time, indeed, the struggle between the Ford Company and General Motors was as spectacular as the chariot race in "Ben-Hur." Mr. Ford's supremacy, for the first time in his later history, was seriously threatened. Temporarily, at least, General Motors won a victory over the single-handed and single-minded giant of the automobile industry, forcing him to drop the production of the old model Ford and to shut down his factories for many months while the new model was being developed.

In January, 1926, 44.43 per cent. of the new registrations were Ford cars, 22.07 per cent. General Motors cars. By October Ford had 31.64 per cent. to General Motors' 30.72. At the end of the year Ford made the swift decision to create the new model. Now he is coming back, but General Motors is still far ahead.

From 1921 on the business increased uninterruptedly. In 1923 total sales reached nearly $700,000,000. In 1926 they passed $1,000,000,000. In 1927 they were $1,269,519,673. This year they almost reached this huge figure in the first nine months—a total sale, at home and abroad, of more than 1,600,000 cars and trucks. That is to say, in nine months of a single year General Motors has made one automobile for every seventy-five men, women and children in the United States. Last year it was making about one in three of the motor cars turned out in the United States.

It employs about 210,000 men, ranking in that respect a little below the United States Steel Corporation, the Pennsylvania Railroad and the American Telephone and Telegraph Company. These three corporations, with General Motors and the Ford Company added, could muster more than 1,000,000 workers. The retail selling agents of the General Motors alone number 20,000.

After a period of swift expansion the automobile industry is reaching stabilization so far as the United States is concerned. The future can be guessed at by estimating the probable increase in population, the extent to which families now owning one or two cars will be able and willing to add to the number and the time it takes a car to wear out. This latter figure is now put at seven and a half years. The unknown factor is the extent to which American cars can be sold abroad. The General Motors Corporation is entering the foreign field like Julius Caesar marching into Gaul—only with considerably more tact. Its foreign trade is small only in proportion to its total trade. In 1926 its exports amounted to $98,000,000, in 1927 to $172,000,000, and this year, according to the estimates of Vice President J. D. Mooney, in charge of the export business, they will be more than $260,000,000—almost exactly the total output of the corporation in the banner year of 1918.

Its Huge Export Trade.

The corporation now has more than 6,000 distributers and dealers in more than 100 foreign countries. But this does not mean that it always ships abroad complete cars to compete with foreign cars in the native markets. Nothing is sent abroad that can be as cheaply made in the country where it is destined to be sold. Beginning with its first overseas plant in Copenhagen, established in 1924, General Motors has followed the policy of building its foreign plants into the economic structure of the country in which they are located. A visitor might go into the Copenhagen plant today and not find more than half a dozen men to whom English is a native language. All that is exported, in many cases, is the engine and the idea.

Each overseas company is an independent unit, with a manager who is as free and as responsible as the manager of an American division of the corporation. The General Motors world map now includes not only Copenhagen but London, Paris, Stockholm, Antwerp, Berlin, Madrid, Alexandria, Buenos Aires, Sao Paulo, Brisbane, Wellington, Osaka, Batavia and South Africa. The motor car habit and the motor car pocketbook are less common abroad than in the United States. But for precisely this reason the limits of the market are not yet in sight. As Europe regains its former prosperity and advances to new economic levels it will buy more American cars.

In China, Japan and India it will probably be many decades if not generations before the saturation point, measured by American standards, can be reached. Meanwhile American cars plough the deserts, wallow through the marshes and climb the mountains of the most remote regions of the globe. Men of all colors possible to the human epidermis, of all races, of all languages and of various previous conditions of servitude are learning how to put American automobiles together and how to operate them. The automobile is joining the sewing machine and the typewriter as a world missionary of American civilization.

November 18, 1928

SEES REVOLUTION IN BUSINESS HERE

John Moody Predicts Expansion of Present New Era in the Coming Decade.

EXPLAINS STOCKS' ACTIVITY

John Moody, President of Moody's Investors' Service, sees the eight years which have passed since the Presidential election of 1920 as "epochal years in the economic and financial history of the United States." Not only have they been years of progress and growing prosperity, he says in a current review, but a silent revolution has been going on in methods of production and distribution.

Among the favorable developments which have characterized the period since the World War, he says, are the introduction and development of new industries, the expansion in volume and output of older industries, the perfection of methods for developing efficiency, cutting out waste and speeding up deliveries of goods; the knitting together of business activities of every kind into larger and more harmonious units.

"More and more," he declared, "the corporate industries of the United States are becoming the property of the public; more and more are individual citizens investing their wealth and their savings in corporate securities. It is estimated that perhaps 15,000,000 men, women and children today own stocks or bonds of one type or another, while millions more are indirectly affected by such ownership."

"In my view," says Mr. Moody, "this new era in America is in its first stages only. The coming decade will witness its expansion and extension far beyond its present stage. It therefore behooves the American business man, the banker, the security dealer, the many who perform constructive services in these fields, to grow with the country, scan the future in the light of the present, and continuously develop new facilities for the larger business life which is looming in the years ahead.

"With the vast broadening of corporate activities, the machinery for carrying on the business of the country has grown in equal ratio. Banking facilities for the financing of this modern business giant have become immensely greater than ever before; investment banking for the mobilizing of capital has become one of the gigantic cogs in the wheel of American life. And all other activities necessary to serve this economic giant, such as engineering, auditing, research and statistical facilities, have been obliged steadily to expand their facilities.

"If there is any logical explanation for the unprecedented volume of sustained stock trading during the past year or two, it is wrapped up in the facts outlined above. It is being overdone, yes; but its basic causes are those which I have stated."

November 11, 1928

SEES ECONOMIC TREND TO FAVOR CONSUMERS

Emphasis on production, which has been a major factor in the United States for the past few years, is rapidly giving place to an economic structure based on increased attention to consumption and consumers' demands, according to Paul H. Nystrom, Professor of Marketing at Columbia University, who was a speaker last night at a meeting of the American Statistical Association in the Aldine Club, 200 Fifth Avenue.

Maximum production has led the nation to a saturation point in many of its greatest markets, he said, with the result that economists have begun preaching the doctrine of catering to and nurturing the consumers, studying their desires and fulfilling them and constantly devising new fashions in manufactures to please them.

"All consumption problems," said Professor Nystrom, "are problems of fads and fashions. Millinery and dresses are not the only things that change with passing days; we find fashions in houses, automobiles, kitchen utensils, home furnishings, foodstuffs and in the very habits of living. As this is to be an era of the economics of consumption, there must be study of consumption phases."

April 25, 1930

FINDS PUBLIC ACCEPTS ADVERTISING ON RADIO

W. S. Paley Says Listener Now Understands That Fine Programs Must Be Paid For.

America, through the influence of radio broadcasting, is learning to listen as unconsciously as it looks, William S. Paley, president of the Columbia Broadcasting System, declared in an interview yesterday.

Discussing the radio listener's attitude toward radio advertising, Mr. Paley said the listener had come to understand that without the advertiser, who foots the bill, there could be no such outpouring of fine radio programs as there is today.

"The listener," he said, "has accepted this just as he has accepted the fact that without the advertiser his newspaper could no be published. All he asks is that the advertiser comply with the dictates of the developing art of radio broadcasting. Fortunately, here we find a meeting of minds to the benefit of all concerned. The advertiser, too, has learned something, and today he is just as eager as the listener that what he pays to send out through the air shall so well represent him at his best that it must redound to his prestige and his profit."

September 24, 1930

PLASTICS INDUSTRY SERVES MANY NEEDS

Hundreds of Materials Made Here and in Japan Have a Wide Market.

DEVELOPED 60 YEARS AGO

Several Thousand Articles, From Billiard Balls to Radio Parts, Are Supplied.

The plastics industry is outstanding as an example of the resource and commercial value of industrial research. Sixty years ago this amazing industry did not exist at all. Very largely, as a matter of fact, it has been brought into existence since the World War, says a recent issue of The Index, publication of the New York Trust Company. Conjured achievement is to have created a out of laboratory test-tubes, its unique range of entirely new materials. industrial uses. These new materials generally cost less than natural materials or combine qualities which adaptable to a thousand and one natural materials do not provide.

The plastics industry is quite literally a creative contribution to the resources of civilization. Without its products, many great modern industries could not have progressed as they have either because materials essential for their development are not found in nature or because, when found, they are too rare or costly or are unsuitable for mass production.

Materials, for example, to provide satisfactory photographic films, radio and electrical parts at low cost or with the required qualities have had to be created. It has been the function of the plastics industry to create them and, after doing so, to develop additional uses for these new materials so that increased production thereof could be possible at progressively lower cost.

Diverse Uses and Properties.

"Plastics," sometimes called "composition," consist of a number of nonmetallic molded substances which, in their finished state, are by no means necessarily plastic: indeed, some of them are more like granite or steel in resistance to mechanical stress. On the other hand, clay products, Portland cement, glass, plaster of paris, rubber, rayon, cellophane, and even papier maché, all of which are plastics in the broad sense, are not regarded as products of the plastics industry.

As understood by the industry, its products comprise a variety of chemically dissimilar synthetic compounds and mixtures, most of them of organic nature and of resinous or horny character, which may be caused generally to assume definite shape when heated under pressure in a metal mold.

Several hundred different plastics, so termed, are made today in the United States, Europe and Japan; as many as six hundred trade names have been registered; and from one such plastic alone hundreds of different articles are made, a few taken at random being telephone receiver parts, billiard balls, radio receiver parts, door knobs and door plates, electric light switches, aircraft fittings, vacuum cleaner parts, knife and tool handles, bottle stoppers, desk and table tops, "silent" gears, typewriter parts, toys, tooth brush handles, fountain pens, pencils, armature and commutator parts, coat hangers, vases, automobile self-starter parts, and panels for interior decoration. In redesigning, beautifying and making modern containers more salable, plastic products are playing a leading rôle. It is possible to modify some plastic materials with respect to about thirty different properties, so that a single such material may sometimes be manufactured into as many as five hundred different articles.

May 8, 1932

THE CITY DEPARTMENT STORE: THE EVOLUTION OF 75 YEARS

The Macy Anniversary Directs Attention to the Development of The Great Institutions That Serve the American Shopper

From small and relatively recent beginnings, the department stores have become institutions of vast importance in present-day life. Hence the seventy-fifth anniversary this week of R. H. Macy & Co. has interest for the historian and for the student of business and social trends.

By L. H. ROBBINS.

FOR long after Captain Rowland H. Macy opened a fancy-goods shop in Sixth Avenue just below Fourteenth Street in 1858, seventy-five years ago, there was no department store in all the world. There were already merchant princes in New York, but they were specialists. The most illustrious of them sold dress goods and dress accessories only.

Historians are a little hazy as to the actual beginning of department stores. They mention the Bon Marché of Paris. But in the New York chapter they speak of the day in 1874 when the rising young firm of L. Straus & Son rented space in the basement of the little Macy store for a display of china, glassware and crockery. That was the first time in this country, they say, that dry goods and house furnishings were sold under one roof.

Before that year Captain Macy had acquired two small buildings adjoining his shop and had added stocks of haberdashery and toys. For a while he sold groceries also. He was a sturdy, bearded, picturesque figure. Some one has said that he resembled the poet Longfellow, except that he had tattoo designs on the backs of his hands; except also that he sometimes waited on customers in his shirt-sleeves, with a black cigar in his mouth. He had been a Nantucket whaling skipper; hence the tattooing, hence also the handle to his name, and the red star, his good-luck symbol, above his door. At first his family lived over the shop, in the time-honored way of merchant families.

The City of 1858.

In 1858 Manhattan town was mostly below Forty-second Street. Horse cars crept along the avenues and brought in the suburbanites from around Central Park, competing with half a thousand rumbling omnibuses. The El roads, with their smoky, puffy engines, and the cable-car lines had still to come. The trains of the Hudson River Railroad ran down the west side to Chambers Street. The New York & Harlem road and the New York & New Haven delivered their passengers near City Hall. Commuters from Newark and Elizabeth came all the way by boat. Union Square was becoming as fashionable a residence district as Washington Square. Tree-shaded Fourteenth Street, with its new Academy of Music at Irving Place, was a stylish promenade. Travelers gazed down upon the city from the spire of Trinity Church.

The woman shopper of 1858 visited almost as many stores as she had purchases to make. She bought gloves in one, perfume in another, bombazine in a third, a broom in a fourth. Her shopping list led her all over town. Wherever she went she was waited upon by men clerks. A little later hundreds of the men marched away to the Civil War and women clerks replaced them. The department stores today have few men behind the counters, and that circumstance dates back to the crisis of the 1860s.

Bargaining was the accepted rule in mercantile life. If the merchant asked a shilling and sixpence for cambric, the shopper bid a shilling and perhaps got the goods at her price after much haggling. Discounts were common, credit was demanded as a right by all respectable citizens and cash was long in coming forth. Captain Macy didn't care for that method. His system was to price-mark goods plainly, to hold to those prices and to insist on "terms strictly cash."

Another Innovation.

Captain Macy started also the custom of pricing goods in odd figures—$1.98 instead of $2, for instance. The world smiled, voiced the 1858 equivalent of "Oh, yeah?" and supposed that the object of such price-marking was illusion. Research shows, however, that the innovation was meant to be a check on the clerks, not all of whom in those days were above the suspicion of a Yankee shopkeeper. He reasoned that sales had a better chance of being recorded, and that the temptation to pocket a coin or a bill was less when the clerk had to visit the cashier's cage to make change.

Clerks in New York stores in 1858 served long hours for little pay, standing up from dawn till dark. The store was a dignified place, and their duty a solemn one. Conversation behind the counters was forbidden. Talk of what was on at the Eden Musée or at Barnum's had to wait until the sales force limped home on flat feet at night. There was no giggling among the little cash girls, red-ginghamed and pigtailed, who ran errands all day. Their lot was too serious for humor. There were no rest-rooms for weary helpers, no lockers for their coats, no hospital nurses for their ills.

There were no elevators, no escalators, naturally, when a store consisted only of ground floor and basement. Gas jets served for lighting. Arc lamps came in later, around 1878, and the first one was more a curiosity than a means of illumination. The first store telephone was a nuisance, so many customers flocked to use it for the exciting novelty of the thing. City delivery was a simple problem; a pushcart answered. Captain Macy's hand cart is still in existence, and the boy who pushed it about town in 1874 is still with the firm.

From such modest beginnings of long ago rose the department store of R. H. Macy & Co., which will observe, this week, its seventy-fifth anniversary. From such a beginning have risen all the great department stores, the most conspicuous mercantile phenomena of today.

Modern Developments.

They cover whole city blocks. They tower often to twenty stories in air and descend three or four levels below the street. They measure their floor space in millions of square feet. They count their employes in thousands. There are stores that can boast 150 departments. Such a store buys from 35,000 producers, uses the services, in the holiday season, of 14,000 persons and may do a yearly business running close to $80,000,000.

1858: Captain Macy's Store.

In variety they outrival the infinite Cleopatra. They sell motor-boats, and they sell rose-bushes. Any one of a dozen of the great New York stores deals in anagrams, aquariums, barometers, Bibles, cameras, clocks, divans, dolls, dumb-waiters, easels, flags, furs, golf clubs, gazing balls, humidors, hose for gardens and hose for legs, ice bags, ironing-boards, jar rings, jewelry, kapok, khaki, lingerie, lorgnettes, mail boxes, music, needles, nose masks, overalls, over-night bags, ponchos, punchbowls, road maps, rugs, samovars, spurs, tapestry, typewriters, ukuleles, umbrellas, vacuum bottles, Venetian blinds, weather vanes, window panes, yardsticks, lace yokes, young men's clothing, zwiebach and perhaps 800 other general classes of merchandise.

The separate items they carry need higher mathematics to enumerate. A typical New York store has made as many as 160,000 deliveries in a day. Its own trucks range over a territory 100 miles wide. Its mail delivery covers the earth and reaches even to Istanbul, Aden, Manila, Hongkong, Buenos Aires and Tanganyika.

The Crowds of Patrons.

Psychologists and sociologists wishing to study the largest cross-section of the American population possible to assemble in one spot would proceed to the metropolitan department store. On a dull day 125,000 people enter the doors, people enough to fill the Yale Bowl twice. In the holiday season their number approaches a quarter-million. More than one store in New York on an ordinary day is a city in itself as populous as Albany, Syracuse, Paterson or Hartford. The department store can claim the honor of being the biggest social centre of these times.

To prepare for this rush of trade requires a vast organism, a relatively small part of which is visible to the customers. On floor after floor which the public seldom sees the work of the sales force is thought out, planned, ordered and supported. The stock room that supplies a department is as ample and as active as the department itself. There is an air of aliveness and alertness in these important quarters behind the scenes, just as in the showiest of the show floors.

Store owners were their own buyers seventy-five years ago. Now they entrust that part of the work to highly paid experts, any one of them equipped with knowledge enough to be a complete merchant in his or her own right, but drafted by modern organization to play specialized parts. A store may have 100 buyers, and more than half of them will likely be women. Outside their offices the manufacturers' salesmen with sample cases sit waiting for audience, fifty at a time, like boys in a schoolroom. The total of salesmen calling in a day may reach to 600.

The old-time merchant depended on his five senses in selecting goods. The department store enlists science, and a busy testing laboratory takes the guess out of buying. **Ingenious machines grind and rub and pull and twist at the materials which the buyers have under consideration. They determine the tensile strength of paper.** thread, cloth and clothesline, the **bursting point of knitted and** woven goods, the heat transmission of garments and blankets, the resistance of textiles to fading in sunlight and shrinking in laundry tub.

They find out the wearing qualities of a hundred substances, from sole leather to silk; the bounciness of tennis balls and motor tires, the toughness of golf balls. There is even an incubator where moths are propagated to serve as living sacrifices in tests of the efficacy of moth-proofing products. One store laboratory in this city has made 79,000 tests in six years.

Deep below the basement selling floors, cataracts of parcels of every shape and size come pouring down the chutes from the sales floors and are swept along by the conveyor belts to be distributed for delivery. It is fast work there toward the close of the day, and the work continues far into the night.

Outgoing Purchases.

Fleets of odd-looking boxlike vehicles as big as livingrooms, rolling on wheels no bigger than a carpet-sweeper's, are trundled about by electric trucklets and gather in hampers of outgoing freight.' Such a vehicle, empty, rolls on to an elevator and vanishes upward. Later, from a floor high up under the roof, it comes down

These huge receptacles are the bodies of five-ton vans; they have been demounted and brought indoors. At night they are taken up to the street, lifted on their respective chassis and driven over the bridges, through the tunnels and away to suburban distribution depots. There they disgorge their freight into handsomer and smaller delivery trucks that whisk the shopper's purchase of yesterday to her door as she pours the breakfast coffee.

Incidentally, it was the Macy store, a little more than abreast of the times, that imported the first gasoline automobile from France. The machine astonished New York through the Summer of 1895, then started for Chicago. After sticking in 'the mud above Fordham Heights it reached Poughkeepsie the first day, six hours behind schedule. For another day or so it labored on, but at Schenectady it gave up the effort and took a freight train the rest of the way. Thirty years later that same store sold the last of its herd of 500 fine horses. Motorization had come.

Somewhere concealed in the labyrinths below the modern department store is a light and power plant of capacity to supply a community of 8,000 or 10,000 consumers. Somewhere higher up is the store hospital, commensurate in size with the power plant. And on the roof, perhaps, is a radio broadcasting station.

In the "Tube Rooms."

Behind the scenes also are the tube rooms, rooms that look at first sight like mammoth pipe organs—and very merry are the jingling tunes those pipe organs play. But do not think to walk right into a tube room. You have to be introduced.

Inside will be rows on rows of little desks. Girls at the desks work with the speed and the precision of machinery, opening cash carriers, making change, double-stamping the purchase slips, filing the stubs, returning the slips and popping the carrier into the pipe, all in one motion and all in a split second. They get a bonus for each mistake they catch, and they catch most of the errors, even at that speed.

Those are but sketchy outlines of a few of the details of the great thing that has come into the world within the memory of people not yet very old. The effects of the department-store movement on shopping are familiar enough. The stores draw crowds, and because people are gregarious by nature, the crowds draw greater crowds.

Throngs come not alone to buy, but also to see. The late John Cotton Dana called the department store the greatest of museums of modern art. He meant not the art that hangs in a golden frame on the wall, but the art that produces the things that life uses—chairs and carpets, dress fabrics, tableware, kitchenware, wallpaper, shoes—there is art, he said, in all things that man makes well.

Contrasts With Early Days.

The merchants of the 1860s would hardly know what to make of many things common in department-store conduct today. They would find continuation schools for junior clerks; dances, revues, Summer camps and rest farms for employes; linguists to act as interpreters for customers from foreign lands; special delivery hourly for travelers at hotels; personal service for people in haste; and psychology examinations for the drivers of the store trucks.

They would marvel at the air refrigeration on Summer days; at the ateliers of design in which skillful craftsmen create beauty while the crowd watches; at the trout pools in fishing-goods season, with brook and brown and rainbow trout at home in them. They would discover, somewhere on the premises, life-size dwellings completely and admirably furnished from cellar to attic. They would wonder at finding, in one large store, 400 college graduates in careers of merchandising.

No doubt they would be thunderstruck by it all. But the present-day public takes the department store for granted.

February 12, 1933

SEES TREND CHANGE IN MARKETING FIELD

3 to 5 Years Will Be Required to Eliminate Obstacles, F. R. Coutant Says.

NEED EDUCATIONAL WORK

Passing of 'Canned' Survey Era Will Usher in New Phase, Authority Declares.

By WILLIAM J. ENRIGHT

Another three to five years must elapse before scientific marketing emerges from its present state of "canned" research into an era of intelligent and economical effort, carried on by individual companies, Frank R. Coutant, director of reseach for Pedlar & Ryan and president of the American Marketing Society, told THE TIMES yesterday.

In the meanwhile, he added, a constant process of education must be carried on by marketing authorities to convince not only sales managers but higher executives of the value of scientific marketing. In addition to having been set back sharply by the depression, marketing research must overcome the obstacle of opposition from production and cost-minded business men, just as industrial research had to win over the objections of factory managers.

Present Surveys Inadequate

"In the beginning of industrial research," Mr. Coutant explained, "factory managers insisted that the laboratories clear all findings through them. They impeded progress. But eventually product research won through, in spite of the attitude of factory managers, and today it operates on a huge scale. Marketing science must conquer exactly the same obstacles to achieve its deserved place in the business world."

At present, Mr. Coutant observed, scientific marketing has made sufficient impression to create a great deal of mass or "canned" research. This usually takes the form of a study of an individual market by some group or seller of advertising and is made available to actual or potential advertisers. While marketing authorities do not object to such surveys, feeling that they will run their course within the next three to five years, he pointed out that very few of them are adequate. They contain certain elements of truth, he added, which, however, tend to make them more harmful from the standpoint of obtaining comprehensive facts about a market.

The passing of this phase of marketing science, Mr. Coutant continued, will usher in another era, in which the marketing activities of individual companies will be guided by one authority. He will not necessarily have to be surrounded by a huge and expensive staff but will be able to expand and contract his personnel to fit requirements. A growing body of "intermittent" research men is becoming available, and the judicious use of such talent in a flexible manner will achieve the best and most economical results. Today, Mr. Coutant declared, only about ten business organizations have been able to handle their marketing requirements in this manner.

Advertising agencies, he said, to whom must be given a great deal of credit for the development of scientific marketing, are handicapped by inadequate funds, inasmuch as few of them charge for their marketing services. When sales managers and other executives are sufficiently "sold" on marketing science to pay agencies for research studies, then the science should be able to make greater forward strides, Mr. Coutant felt.

Finds Plan Reducing Costs

Marketing research, he continued, must overcome many preconceived notions that business men hold. These include the belief that selling prices must be based absolutely on production costs, instead of on what the consumer will pay for a product; the feeling that executives can decide what the public will buy without adequate study of the subject, or the idea that what executives like will also be approved by consumers, and the practice of having sales figures analyzed by bookkeeping departments instead of by marketing authorities.

"While scientific marketing may not result in expanded sales volume," Mr. Coutant continued, "which is apparently the desired goal of all executives, however unsound it may be, it will generally reduce costs and increase profits. The fetish of greater and greater sales volume is being gradually abandoned, but a considerable number of executives still worship it."

In Mr. Coutant's opinion, the food industry has made the greatest strides in developing scientific marketing. Some of the automobile companies have also attained a degree of efficiency in marketing science, while the drug field has made but slow progress, he concluded.

March 29, 1936

BIG BUSINESS VS. BIG GOVERNMENT

SUPREME COURT HOLDS U. S. STEEL LEGAL; PUBLIC INTEREST DECLARED PARAMOUNT; MAY AFFECT MANY OTHER ANTI-TRUST SUITS

DIVIDE ON STEEL DECISION

Four Judges Give It, Three Dissent, Two Out of the Case

Special to The New York Times.

WASHINGTON, March 1.—In one of the most important opinions ever handed down by that body, the United States Supreme Court today held that the United States Steel Corporation is not a trust within the meaning of the Sherman anti-trust law.

The decision, opposite in effect to those of the court in the Standard Oil and American Tobacco Company cases, was concurred in by only four of the nine members of the court. Three dissented and two took no part in the consideration of the case or the decision.

The opinion was read by Justice McKenna and was concurred in by Chief Justice White and Justices Holmes and Vandevanter. Justice Day read the dissenting opinion, in which he was joined by Justice Clarke and Pitney. Justices McReynolds and Brandels did not have any part in the case.

The majority opinion held, in effect, that the Steel Corporation had committed no overt acts violative of the Sherman law since the Government's suit was filed; that although by its size and its control of equipment and resources in the steel business the corporation was in a position to dominate the trade, the mere fact that it was able to do so should not be taken as indicating that it did, in the absence of any evidence; and finally, that to order the dissolution of the corporation would involve the risk of great disturbance in the financial, commercial and economic structure, and thus would menace the public interest, which in this case the court held to be of paramount importance.

Day Holds Law Annulled.

In a vigorous dissenting opinion, Justice Day said that he could find no reason for the court's failure to apply to this case the same policy as was followed with respect to the Standard Oil and American Tobacco Company cases. The failure to follow that rule, he said, constituted an annulment of the Sherman act, making necessary some action by Congress indicating anew just what limitations were to be put upon trade combinations.

Justice Day said that he knew of no public interest that sanctioned the violation of law and no disturbance of foreign or domestic commerce that would justify the abrogation of statutes.

The dissenting opinion concerning the nullification of the Sherman law by reason of the alleged setting aside in this case of the precedents of the Standard Oil and Tobacco cases caused a great stir. The majority opinion justifies this setting aside of the heretofore usual rule in cases under the Sherman act on the ground that in this case there was no proof, as in the other two, that the corporation had from its inception been a law-breaker.

That the decision of the Supreme Court in the Steel Corporation litigation may have a far-reaching effect upon other anti-trust cases now pending or which may have been contemplated was the belief expressed tonight by more than one official. Attorney General Palmer and C. B. Ames, his assistant in charge of the anti-trust cases, withheld comment, but it was admitted that many vital points of law involved in other cases pending were dealt with in the court's findings.

Mr. Ames at once began a study of the decision and the minority report of the court and will make a statement to the Attorney General. In the meantime the status of other litigation must remain in doubt. The fact that the decision in favor of the Steel Corporation was rendered by a minority of the whole court may have some effect upon the program of the Department of Justice, but the intimation tonight was that a change of policy would not be surprising.

One expert, who has reviewed other anti-trust cases, expressed the belief that if the decision in regard to United States Steel remained effective a precedent would be established that would seem to settle, in favor of the corporate interests several methods of attach adopted by the Department of Justice.

For instance, the suit against the American Sugar Refining Company et al. was postponed "awaiting the decisions of the Supreme Court in the Harvester and Steel cases," according to the Attorney General's annual report. In the event, for example, that prosecution of the American Sugar case were to be continued, it would appear that the Attorney General would have to attempt to overthrow findings made by the Supreme Court in the Steel case in order to hope for success.

The circumstances surrounding the decision in the case of United States Steel may result in the whole program of anti-trust prosecutions being bought to the attention of President Wilson.

That the failure to obtain a decision against the Steel Corporation was a strong argument in support of the action of the Department of Justice in entering into a voluntary agreement with the packing interests was a point emphasized in some quarters today. At the time the agreement was made with the packers Attorney General Palmer expressed the belief that much better results had been obtained in the interests of the public than would have come out of a long suit in the courts.

Considering the decision rendered in the suit against the Steel Corporation, some hold that a case against the packers might have failed. Advocates of methods, other than the employment of anti-trust legislation to control the corporations, were using today's decision as an argument in favor of their contentions. The declaration of the minority of the court that the Sherman act is made void by the decision is likely to revive agitation for legislation looking to Federal chartering or Federal licensing systems.

The Federal licensing system, has been urged upon Congress by President Wilson. Attorney General Palmer has looked with favor upon this plan. The Trade Commission is also a supporter of Federal charters for great corporations, along the lines suggested to the Roosevelt administrations by the then Commissioner of Corporations James R. Garfield, whose views were indorsed by Roosevelt.

Important Cases That Are Pending.

Some of the important cases pending before the Supreme Court, which may be affected by the decisions rendered today, are as follows:

United States against Reading Company et al (anthracite coal combination). The decision of the district court in this case was favorable to the Government in substantial part. Reargument was heard at the beginning of the October term, 1919, and a decision is awaited.

United States against Lehigh Valley Railroad Company et al. The petition in this case charged that the Lehigh Valley's railroad, in combination with affiliated corporations, has monopolized trade and commerce in anthracite coal produced along and transported over its lines in violation of the anti-trust act. The district court dismissed the petition and appeal was taken to the Supreme Court. Decision is awaited.

United States against Eastman Kodak Company et al.—A decision favorable to the Government was handed down in August, 1915, and a decree granting the relief sought was entered in January, 1916. The defendants appealed to the United States Supreme Court. The case was prepared for argument during the present term.

United States against American Can Company et al.—The District Court handed down an opinion on Feb. 23, 1916, and on July 7, 1916, a decree was entered adjusting that the American Can Company was organized as a combination in restraint of trade. Considering the decree to be inadequate, the Government appealed to the Supreme Court. The case was prepared for argument during the present term.

United States against Southern Pacific-Central Pacific Railway Company et al.—This case was decided adversely in the District Court in March, 1917. The Government appealed to the Supreme Court, but hearings were adjourned during Federal control of the railroads.

United States against Quaker Oats Company et al.—This case was heard by three Circuit Judges under the expediting act. The decision of the majority was against the Government, one Judge dissenting. The Government appealed to the Supreme Court. The case was prepared for trial at the present term.

United States against Associated Bill-posters et al.—The defendants were charged with entering into a combination and conspiracy in restrain of trade and commerce in posters. A decision favorable to the Government was handed down in the district court in March, 1918, and a decree granting relief sought was entered in July, 1916. The defendants appealed to the Supreme Court. The case was prepared for argument during the present term.

United States against Keystone Watch Company et al.—The case is pending in the Supreme Court on cross-appeals from the decision of the lower court, which was in part favorable and in part adverse to the contentions of the Government. It was prepared for argument during the present term.

United States against American Sugar Refining Company et al.—This is a proceeding against an alleged combination in restraint of trade in the manufacture and sale of sugar. The case was ready for argument in October, 1915, when the court ordered the hearing postponed awaiting the decisions of the Supreme Court in the Harvester and Steel cases.

These civil actions, now pending in the Supreme Court, were brought before July 1, 1918. There are in addition several cases instituted before that date which are pending in the District Courts. Two cases, instituted in the lower courts since July 1, 1918, which may be affected by the Steel decision, follow:

United States against Sumatra Purchasing Corporation et al. (Sumatra leaf tobacco case). Southern District of New York—Indictments returned Oct. 7, 1918 (one under the Sherman act and one under Section 73 of the Wilson Tariff act), charging the defendants with conspiring to control the entire trade and commerce in the purchase of Sumatra leaf tobacco in foreign countries and the importation of same into and the sale thereof throughout the United States and to eliminate competition in and monopolize said trade and commerce and to increase the price of said tobacco in the United States.

United States against the Atlas Portland Cement Co., et al.—Petition filed Aug. 13, 1910, in the District Court, District of New Jersey, charging the defendants with combining and conspiring, through the instrumentality of the Cement Manufacturers' Protective Association, to curtail the production of cement, to reduce the quantity of cement sold under contract for future delivery at a fixed price and to bring about a uniform and materially increased price for cement regardless of the point of delivery.

Had Justices McReynolds and Brandeis taken part in the case and voted for dissolution, the court would have stood five to four in favor of dissolution, instead of four to three against it. It was under the regime of Justice McReynolds as Attorney General of the United States that the Government's dissolution suit was instituted.

Justice Brandeis, prior to his appointment to the Supreme bench, set forth his belief as to the status of the Steel Corporation under the Sherman Anti-Trust act when he appeared in 1911 as "counsel for the people" before a committee of the Senate, of which Senator Clapp was chairman, directed to investigate the whole subject of trusts. At that time Mr. Brandeis expressed an opinion to the effect that the Steel Corporation was in fact a trust.

In rendering its opinion the Court decreed that its findings were "without prejudice," which is construed to mean that the Government is entitled to reopen the case against the Steel Corporation. This qualification, "without prejudice," may also be construed to mean that the Government is not debarred from continuing its proceedings against other corporations which it is seeking to dissolve as combinations in restraint of trade.

How the case against the Steel Corporation could be reopened, however, unless there should be changes in the Court's personnel is not clear. It would be necessary for both Justice McReynolds and Justice Brandeis to retire before there would be an opportunity of trying the case on the possibility that an opinion rendered by an actual majority could be obtained.

It was pointed out that the Court today construed the law itself in an entirely new light. The majority opinion held that "any law does not make mere size an offense, or the existence of unexerted power an offense. It, we repeat, requires overt acts and trusts to its prohibition of them and its power to repress or punish them. It does not compel competition nor require all that is possible."

The Court drew a distinction "between acts done in violation of the statute and a condition brought about which 'in and of itself in not only a continued attempt to monopolize, but a monopolization.' " It was held that the Steel Corporation not only has not by overt acts dominated or monopolized the steel trade to the exclusion of competition, but it has not even created (by reason of its size and power) a condition which tends to create monopoly.

But the portion of the Court's opinion which more than any other caused remark was the statement, in effect, that the Steel Corporation is too big to be dissolved without involving the breaking up of other portions of the business structure. It was the Court's declaration that the paramountcy of the public interest was one of the grounds upon which the majority opinion was based that brought from the dissenting Justices the statement that they knew of no public interest which sanctioned the violation of a law.

March 2, 1920

BILLION CAPITAL VOTED BY A. T. & T.

Action of Shareholders Will Make Company Largest in America, if Not in World.

NO STOCK ISSUE THIS YEAR

The American Telephone & Telegraph Company yesterday stepped into the front rank as America's greatest corporation in point of size, and possibly the largest in the world, when stockholders at a special meeting ratified the proposal of the company's directors calling for an increase in authorized capital stock from $750,000,000 to $1,000,000,000. The corporations nearest in size are the United States Steel Corporation and the Standard Oil Company of New Jersey. The General Motors Corporation has also been mentioned as one of the near-billion dollar concerns, but in view of the fact that only a small percentage of its authorized capital stock of $1,347,500,000—based on the current price of General Motors common stock—has been actually issued, it is generally rated as below both American Telephone & Telegraph and the United States Steel Corportion in point of actual size.

A compilation based on latest available figures offers the following comparison of American corporations in and around the billion-dollar class:

	Authorized.	Outstandi'g.
American Tel. & Tel.	$1,000,000,000	$715,083,854
U. S. Steel Corp....	950,000,000	868,583,600
Stand. Oil of N. J..	825,000,000	707,902,800
Penn. R. R. Co.....	600,000,000	499,265,700
Gen. Motors Corp...	*1,347,500,000	*412,590,499

*Including 50,000,000 shares of common of no par value authorized and of which 20,557,581 shares have been issued on which valuation was figured at 14¾ per share.

Will Not Offer Stock This Year.

According to President H. B. Thayer, the American Telephone & Telegraph Company will not make any new offering of stock during 1923, in which case the outstanding total of the United States Steel Corporation will continue for at least another year ahead of the actual outstanding stock of the telephone corporation.

Through yesterday's action, the American Telephone & Telegraph Company has doubled its capital structure since March, 1920, when the authorized capital was increased from $500,000,000 to $750,000,000. The purpose was to have available an instrumentality for the raising of funds without increasing bonded indebtedness of the company, and through means of which the company has been able to show steady expansion. An indication of this growth was afforded in a record of earnings published in the company's annual report for 1922 which showed net income of $66,170,428 as against $5,486,058 in 1900—or a gain of 1,206 per cent. in twenty-two years.

Stock Is Widely Held.

In addition to being the largest corporation in point of capital structure, the company also has the distinction of having the greatest number of stockholders of any company on record. At the close of business on Dec. 31, 1922, according to the report of Mr. Thayer, there were listed on the corporation's books the names of 248,925 stockholders, a gain of 62,583 in a year. It was also indicated that the company is not a "pet" of the wealthy investors as the average number of holdings per person was only 28 shares and among the stockholders were 46,700 employes of the system.

At yesterday's meeting, the directors and officers were re-elected and Clarence L. Langridge was elected to the Board to fill the vacancy caused by the death of Charles D. Norton.

March 28, 1923

CORPORATION OWNERSHIP GROWING; NATION DEPENDS ON ITS PAYROLL

Americans have ceased to be so largely a nation of individualists, working for themselves, and have become a nation dependent upon their pay envelopes to a considerable degree. Back in 1899 the figures show that out of every 1,000 persons who worked for a living 182 were employed in manufacturing industries. But in 1919 the figures had become 260 in the thousand, or 43 per cent. increase. A much larger number of Americans are working for a proportionately smaller group of enterprises than ever before, and their ranks are being recruited faster than the total population. In 1919 the establishment hich employed more than 1,000 wage earners represented but one-third of 1 per cent. of America's fifty leading industries. They employed more than 26 per cent. of all industrial wage earners.

The extent of corporation ownership in 1919 was indicated by 86 per cent. of wage earners working for corporations. In other words, only 14 per cent. of industrial workers were employed by firms and partnerships. This was a drop of more than one-half in fifteen years. In 1919 there were 269,137 proprietors and firm members, against 273,265 ten years before.

April 1, 1923

HOLDING CONCERNS AIDS TO UTILITIES

Bulwarks of Strength to Operating Companies in Time of Stress, Experts Say.

GIVE IMPORTANT SERVICES

Have Helped Develop Electric, Gas, Telephone and Traction Properties—Investors Benefited.

The strength of public utility holding companies and the failure of many financial writers in the past to analyze them in accordance with the facts is made the subject of a special article by H. M. Byllesby & Co. in their weekly news bulletin. "The records of the older and better known companies of this kind speak for themselves and have fully upheld the confidence of investors," says the bulletin, which continues:

"Public utility holding companies not only have been financial successes, but they have made their way steadily in the face of discouraging circumstances and a lack of knowledge of the vital part they have played in the development of electric, gas, telephone and traction properties throughout the United States. Were it not for their instrumentality most cities and States would be far behind the present stage of utility development, and, after all, the basic reason for the financial success of any undertaking is the real need for its existence.

"During every period of business and financial stress the holding companies have proved veritable bulwarks of strength to the operating properties in which they owned investments. The bondholders and stockholders of the operating properties might often have had opportunity to regret their investments were it not for the financial, engineering and operating services of the holding organizations.

"This financial paradox is one to which the analysts of utility securities apparently have given scant attention. Usually they unhesitatingly recommend a bond or stock issued by a sound operating company in preference to the security of a successful holding company, on the ground that the investor's money is actually in the property and business itself and not once removed. The facts are, in numerous instances, that an acceptable investment in the property itself could not be made were it not for the holding company back of it. Moreover, it is next to impossible to provide a really first-class senior, direct property security without correspondingly enhancing the value of the junior securities owned by the holding company.

"The services rendered by the holding companies are many and important. By welding the financial interests of a number of properties they have succeeded in providing the essential commo.. stock equity money for the never-ceasing construction requirements. Customer-ownership financing has obtained large amounts of equity capital during the last few years, but usually only to the extent of the preferred stock portion of the total junior investment.

"By the character of their management the holding companies have established credit ability and reputations of the utmost value to the operated properties. They have been able to advance funds at critical financial periods and see the properties through to the success which depended only upon a proper supply of capital, at times when they could not obtain money individually and for themselves."

July 7, 1924

COOLIDGE DECLARES FOR COMMON SENSE TOWARD BUSINESS

He Asserts That There Will Be No Interference With Honest and Genuine Service.

SEES SENTIMENT SHIFTING

Once Fearing Monopoly, People Today Demand Rail Mergers, He Asserts.

INDUSTRY HELD WISER NOW

Public and Business Cooperating Is Government Ideal, He Tells Radio Audience.

Special to The New York Times.

WASHINGTON, Oct. 11.—President Coolidge delivered by radio tonight a speech that was listened to by 10,000 employes who celebrated the fifty-fifth anniversary of the founding of the H. J. Heinz Company. A great number of these employes and officers heard the speech at a banquet in Pittsburgh, but others who were dining in other parts of the country and in England also heard it.

Mr. Coolidge compared the relations between the Government and business and showed how public sentiment has changed toward big business in the last ten years due to a realization on the part of business that it owes a service to the public. The President said that twenty years ago the attitude of the American public was for the destruction of monopoly, while now public opinion was demanding consolidation, as evidenced in pending legislation for mergers in the transportation system of the country.

The text of his address was as follows:

The speakers who have preceded me in addressing this banquet will, of course, have left little for me to say about its unique aspects. Nevertheless, I cannot refrain from a reference to the fact that the thing we are doing tonight could only have been described a few years ago as a miracle.

Ten thousand employes and officers of a great business are celebrating the fifty-fifth anniversary of that business by dining together. Though they will sit down at boards in some seventy different cities in all parts of this country, as well as in Canada, England and Scotland, yet they will listen to the same addresses, by the same speakers, in all of these places, at the same moment of time. It tells us how wonderful are the achievements of science in our time. It emphasizes how completely the very destinies of the race are bound up with the progress of invention and discovery. We need day by day to gird ourselves for more speed merely to keep pace with our own progress.

Such an occasion as this always reminds me of the experience of Alice in Wonderland when she ran till she was tired out, and then found herself under the very same tree from which she had started. She appealed to the Red Queen, saying:

"In our country, you'd generally get to somewhere else—if you ran very fast for a long time."

The Red Queen was a bit contemptuous. She declared "A slow sort of country. Now, here, you see it takes all the running you can do to keep in the same place. If you want to get somewhere else, you must run at least twice as fast as that."

Your interstate and international dinner suggests that, like Alice, we must in these days run just as fast as we can if we would merely keep up with ourselves. In every department of human activity we see so rapid a procession of marvels that sometimes we wonder whether men will be able to keep control over the forces that are being developed. Because of the temptation to such misgivings, it is a good thing on this, the anniversary of a great business, to consider the progress that has been made in the organization and the administration of strictly practical concerns.

Says Man Still Keeps Control.

Let us consider your celebration of tonight from the viewpoint of a half century ago. In that light the wonder of radio will be hardly greater than the marvel of business expansion and development in the same period. We find that thus far, at any rate, social and political institutions have succeeded in maintaining control over all the strange new forces and formulas. Invention and industry and science and the new arts have been subordinated to the service of society.

There have been interesting speculations about the possibility that some evil genius of affairs might one day bring all mankind under the domination of a single political will. There has been conjecture that some extraordinary talent in organization might establish a financial or industrial overlordship of creation. Other fervid imaginations have pictured some super-chemist organizing a force powerful enough, whether by accident or design, to threaten the destruction of all life.

In the face of such fantasies we will find some reassurance in the fact that man has thus far contrived always to keep himself superior to his creations. Amazing as has been the development of science, it has not outrun our capacity to control its agencies. Business and industry have not developed into a menace to ordered society. Philosophy, speculation and scientific research have not destroyed the religious instinct that is fundamental in human nature.

On the other hand, the generation that has enlisted all these master forces of science, invention, discovery and industry is the best organized, the best governed, the best provided for and the happiest generation that has ever lived on this planet.

To say this is not by any means to insist that we have always dealt well or wisely with new forces and new forms of organizations. Mistakes have been made on the part of the public policy and periods of confusion have been experienced.

Says Business Must Protect the Public.

Early in the era of enormous organizations and quantity production and merchandising there was a period of hesitation and uncertainty about a proper public policy toward these great agencies. The laissez faire school of thought demanded complete freedom of individual business initiative, regardless of consequences. It assumed that uncurbed initiative and unrestrained competition could safely be set off against each other. It urged that free competition would prevent monopoly, while, on the other hand, the tendency to concentrated control would prevent the wasteful excesses of competition. It was somehow cheerfully assumed that the public interest, living in the no man's land between these two desperately hostile forces as the result of their contest, would get just what it wanted.

We know now that such a theory, under modern industrial and commercial conditions, could not succeed. Yet the old laissez faire philosophy was so strongly entrenched that it could not be dislodged until its program had been given a thorough trial. That trial came in the later half of the last century and the earlier years of the present. It resulted in a compromise, by whose terms the public interest was brought into the equation.

The details of that compromise are not yet entirely worked out. Its administrative processes are by no means perfected. But its theory is now definitely established and well understood. It is that neither concentration nor competition shall be permitted to the extent of injuring the public interest. Whether a business unit is good or bad is to be determined not by its size but by its practices. No business is allowed to set aside the law of supply and demand, the rules of open bargaining and fair competition.

The supervisory and regulatory power of society, exercised through the processes of government, is brought in as the supreme authority. No business may hold itself above consideration of the public interest and recognition of public authority. Business is required to adjust itself to this view of its public relations. If it will not fully and voluntarily adapt itself to these conditions, then they will be imposed upon it by the force of law.

That, it seems to me, is substantially the present-day attitude of society toward the relations of business and government. It is pretty generally accepted as a safe and proper rule, albeit there are infractions from time to time. But the policy is fixed, and both business and the people have generally acquiesced in it. Probably we shall never attain to perfection in its administration, but we are progressing.

Sees Change in Business Attitude.

Business itself has come to recognize the soundness of this rule and the absolute necessity of adherence to it. This attitude marks a long step toward industrial peace and economic stability. Powerful factors in the business world were for a time loath to abandon anything of their complete independence. They protested the whole theory of a right to interfere with their proceedings. Some of them made it necessary for the Government to invoke extreme measures before they would be convinced. But now at last they have accepted the doctrine that the public right must be considered and must be served.

Not only that, but business with quite impressive unanimity has admitted that the attitude of the public was correct and justifiable. I think we are warranted in feeling that the greatly preponderant share of business is entirely sincere in its conversion to the new view. A change has come over its entire attitude toward this set of questions. It has accepted the public's right of regulation, not grudgingly and with reservations, but frankly and openly.

On the other side, public authority as represented by the Government, has taken up an attitude of moderation and reasonableness in dealing with these difficult and complex problems. Laws aimed at curbing and regulating monopolies have been employed for control and regulation, not destruction. It is no part of public policy, as the American people now conceive it, to tear down legitimate and useful business. But it is their firm determination that business forms and methods shall be subordinated to the public interest.

Cites Railway Merger Legislation.

I cannot give a better illustration of this change of attitudes than by recalling that less than twenty years ago the Government was using all its power to prevent certain great consolidations of transportation systems, because it was believed these would be harmful to the general welfare. So far has public policy now swung in the opposite direction, that today we have legislation which opens the way to this same sort of transportation combinations.

But each plan, of course, is subject to Government approval. It goes even further. It contemplates compelling the consolidations, if they are not effected voluntarily. And there is gratifying indication that this new program is going to be accepted and put into effect without resort to compulsion.

The change in policy toward consolidation of railroads is warranted by the change in policy toward operation. The Government's power and its right to control and regulate the charges of public facilities is now fully recognized. Through the Interstate Commerce Commission the Government determines when and upon what terms securities of carrying corporations may be issued. Within the constitutional prohibition against confiscation it fixes their r[illegible] termines the income they may earn and demands from them for railroad use any surplus beyond the fixed rate of legal return. The public demands service of the railroads without confiscation, but at fair and reasonable rates fixed by the Government.

These are impressive accomplishments. They have been brought about chiefly because on both sides there was developed a new attitude toward all such problems. The men who have to do with determining large business policies have come to recognize their obligations to the public interest. They have realized, too, that their success as administrators of great affairs closely depends upon their admitting the public's right to be served rather than to be exploited.

In their new and more generous mood they have placed a liberal translation upon this formula of the public's right. They have set up in their business organizations agencies through which to learn what the public wants and how its wants may best be supplied. They have been prospered about in proportion as they have successfully appealed to the public along these lines. They have found that as they tried sincerely to give the public the best possible service at the lowest possible charge, the public in turn was willing to deal liberally with their necessities.

There is one main motive that has dominated the development of this entire policy. It is the supremacy of the Government. That Government must be free and independent of outside and private influences. It must be the servant of the public welfare and the creation of an informed and seasoned public opinion. It cannot be dominated by any privilege, it cannot be subservient to any private advantage. It must always represent the public.

Says Government Interferes Less.

Every effort in the past to bring about any other condition has ended in failure. The people of America have been and are determined to own and control exclusively their own Government. As a preliminary to the maintenance of their supremacy over their Government, they propose to keep the control and ownership of their own property. They know that when the Government begins to own the property it begins to own the people. They want all these powers in their own hands.

It is well worth while to look back over the relations between Government and business during the half century which spans the life of the great business you are celebrating tonight. Such a survey must impress upon you the fact that a great and fundamental change has come in the relations of business, the public and the Government.

It has been a change decidedly for the better. The rule of fair play, of square dealing, of giving honest treatment and full value in all transactions, whether they involve commodities, services or labor, has come to control most successful business organizations. The largest successes have rewarded those who have most frankly and fully accepted this rule.

Because of this new attitude there has been less of Government interference with business. There has been less need for it. The Government is not seeking justifications for annoying and disturbing business. It prefers to let business go its own way, so long as that is the right way; so long as it is the way of honest and genuine service to the real public interest.

You can be pretty sure that business which is so conducted as to deserve to be let alone will have few troubles with the Government. The Government wishes to see a true and practical ideal of working cooperation set up in the relation between business and the public in accord with the dictates of common sense. With the hearty sympathy of both business and the people we have made a long advance toward such a standard.

There are encouraging signs of readiness to go further on the same way. The Government will surely be prepared to give all encouragement in such a program. For by these methods only shall we bring about a proper balance, a secure and lasting adjustment of the supreme individual interest by bringing it into harmony with the highest consideration of the national welfare.

October 12, 1924

THE SUPER-TRUST ARRIVES IN AMERICA

By EVANS CLARK.

ENTER the super-trust, most highly developed form of industrial evolution, symbol of a new economic order, heavy-freighted with consequence—good or evil—for mankind. The simple trust, which aroused public opposition to the point of hysteria a generation or so ago, has now taken its place, along with other alarming developments, in the staid row of accepted institutions. The public thinks nothing today of a concern that operates a score of factories or retail stores that are numbered by the thousand. But now, as the American people have become vaguely aware of the Stinnes activity in Germany, comes the realization that what the name of Stinnes stands for in Europe has been accomplished in a score of directions here in the United States; that it has already set the mold for the reorganization of our entire economic life.

The trust is no longer simple, but exceedingly varied and complex. The United States Steel Corporation operates a dozen different industries contributory to the making of steel and steel products. The Ford Motor Company does not only make automobiles; it cuts trees, saws timber, mines coal and ore, runs a fleet of steamers, operates a railroad, blast furnices, steel plants, rolling mills and glass plants and owns whole towns, including the churches and the stores. The United Drug Company, organized primarily to dispense drugs, now makes them in prodigious quantities—along with candy, rubber goods and writing paper.

The du Pont Company, which started its life making explosives, now manufactures artificial silk, transparent wrapping paper, moving-picture films, paints and varnishes; owns and operates a metropolitan hotel and theatre and a great building construction enterprise; and dominates a merger of sixty-two concerns which manufacture five of the best-known m· of passenger automobiles, most of the taxicabs and a large number of the motor buses and trucks that we see in the streets today.

Not Necessarily a Monopoly.

The simple trust is organized horizontally, so to speak, on one plane of production or distribution—a string of shoe factories, a merger of railroad companies. The super-trust is organized vertically as well downward in the progress of manufacture toward the raw material and upward toward the sale of the finished product to the ultimate consumer. It is, in fact, often referred to as the "vertical trust." But its structure is often much more complex than these geometric phrases indicate. Some of the biggest super-trusts are highly organized horizontally—to the point of monopoly—on one or more planes at once; also vertically, and again diagonally, so to speak, in entirely separated industrial fields.

Neither sort of trust, it should be noted, is necessarily a monopoly; that depends on the proportion of the total national industrial activity on any one plane which it happens to control. As a matter of fact the super-trust tends less toward monopoly than the simple trust, for its success depends more on the number of industrial functions than upon the number of plants it controls.

The sweep and portent of the super-trust development as a whole is far more dramatic than the rise of the steel corporation, the du Pont or any other single concern. And not the least dramatic feature of it all is the fact that the public in general does not see the drama that is being played right before its eyes. It is the drama whose first act was the invention of the steam engine and whose last act has still to be written by its joint producers—man and the machine. Most people seem to think that the industrial revolution is over. The super-trust movement gives ground for the belief that it is hardly begun.

The first trusts were built in the glare of public interest. The super-trusts are being organized in the shadows of diverted public attention, but their effect on human welfare gives evidence of being fully as profound. Even the economists seem unaware of their significance. They have yet to measure the extent of this movement or thoroughly to analyze its implications. Apart from a thorough study of very inadequate census data by Dr. Willard L. Thorp and a few scattered papers by E. A. Filene, Lawrence K. Frank and others the field has never been really explored.

While few super-trusts can be classified as thoroughly organized—what limit can be set to the process, anyway?—there is hardly a big corporation in the country today that has not made decided progress along the road; and some have expanded in a number of industrial directions which would have seemed fantastic to the capitalist of thirty years ago.

Industry Enters New Stage.

In the absence of any thorough study of the subject the writer made a cursory investigation of some forty of the largest and best known American corporations. They fell into the following groups: Eight public utilities, eight oil companies, six steel companies, six combinations of retail stores, four mining concerns, four companies engaged in the manufacture of food stuffs and sixteen miscellaneous manufacturing concerns—machinery, paper and paper products, automobiles, rubber goods, tobacco, photographic supplies, shoes, electrical equipment, asphalt, building materials and glass products. Not one concern on the whole list confines itself exclusively to one plane of the productive process; every one has developed at least some of the attributes of the super-trust. Most of them are engaged in at least three to five separate industrial activities, while many showed ten and some over twenty.

Nor are these cases of isolated economic experiment. They are evidences of a changing economic order. The entire structure of our industrial life is entering a new stage of its development. As the process of organic evolution has been from the simple to the complex—from the single independent cell, with but one or two functions, to the more highly developed organism of many cells and many functions—so this economic change has been an evolution from the small independent factory, performing but one of the functions of production, toward the super-trust—a complete and self-sufficient industrial organism. The process is in fact sometimes called "industrial integration"—a good phrase, which gets the evolutionary meaning of the whole development.

It is fascinating to trace this latest advance of economic evolution—or the industrial revolution—as it took first one industry and then another by the force of inevitable logic. The first to fall in line were, of course, those to which its application was the most obvious. Steel led the way, with Andrew Carnegie at the head of the procession. As far back as 1897 Carnegie had got control of ore mines in Virginia, limestone in Pennsylvania and a half interest in the H. C. Frick Coke Company, which also operated coal mines; he had built blast furnaces and had tied into his organization the Edgar Thomson Works, manufacturing steel rails; the Homestead mills, making steel shapes, and the Hartman Steel Company which transformed these basic shapes into a number of finished products.

United States Steel Has 27 Railroads.

So when Judge Gary and the elder J. P. Morgan began to negotiate the formation of a great new steel merger Carnegie could afford to invite their emissary into his library, take out blue prints and maps, describe his whole organization in minute detail and make it plain that the information "need not be considered confidential." He had proved that he could make tubes more cheaply than the National Tube Company, structural steel at a lower cost than the American Bridge Company, and wire at less cost than the American Steel and Wire. Today the Carnegie works, along with these other plants, are among the strongest units of one of the country's most highly developed super-trusts—the United States Steel Corporation.

The Steel Corporation is certainly—as Judge Gary is fond of calling it—a "well-rounded proposition." However well rounded, it often eludes attention because its constituent parts operate under their own original names—are, in fact, continued as separate corporate entities and controlled, usually through stock ownership, by the parent corporation. Only a familiarity with the Steel Corporation's organization would lead the average man to link the operations of the Oliver Iron Mining Company out in the Missabe Range, Minn.; the Duluth, Missabe & Northern Railroad, the Pittsburgh Steamship Company, the Illinois Steel Company, the Tennessee Coal and Iron Company or the Federal Shipbuilding Company with the offices on the upper floors of 71 Broadway, where Judge Gary and his associates lay down the broad lines of policy which knit all these concerns—and about sixty others—into the great coordinated business of steel making. The companies controlled by the Steel Corporation now have between them a total of 152 works engaged in the process of making steel, not to mention all the auxiliary forces which include, among others, 27 different railroad companies owning more than 2,000 miles of track.

Carnegie and Gary have set the type for the steel industry. All the other large steel concerns are now organized—more or less completely—on super-trust lines. The Bethlehem Steel Company shows almost as impressive a list of subsidiary operations, and it has reached out further even than the Gary concern at both ends of the industrial scale.

Bethlehem's Ramifications.

Bethlehem has secured part ownership of a large number of iron ore companies in Cuba, Chile and Mexico, and it has gone more extensively into the manufacture of finished steel products—gas and oil engines, hydraulic presses, pumps and boilers. It operates eight shipbuilding and repairing plants, including Fore River, Sparrow's Point and other famous yards. The Pittsburgh Steel Company, the Inland Steel Company, the Colorado Fuel and Iron Company and other leading independents have all of them followed suit.

Other metal manufactures also tend more and more toward the super-trust. The process has gone especially far in copper. The Anaconda Copper Company, for example, is one of the most highly developed, a well-knit combination of lumbering and mining—mining both the ore and the coal needed for manufacture—transportation by rail and water, smelting and refining, and the transformation of the raw copper by the controlled American Brass Company into half a hundred products—wire, rods, tubes, cable, shingles and so on.

Ford and General Motors.

While its assets are not as large as those of the Steel Corporation, the Ford Motor Company is probably the most highly developed super-trust in the country today. Ford begins as far down vertically as Gary does—with the ore and the timber—but he carries the process of manufacture into more intricate refinements. An atmosphere of pioneering hangs about Mr. Ford's undertakings, too, which is still fresh and to which no one can set the limit of accomplishment. The visitor can stand on the roof of the Ford power house at his River Rouge plant today and see the iron ore, limestone and coal coming in on his boats and railroad at one end of the plant and at the other see that crude dirt emerging as parts of the finished Ford automobile packed away in freight cars ready to be assembled when they reach their destination — to put them together there would unnecessarily increase the shipping costs.

The General Motors Corporation has reached the super-trust stage by a very different route from the Ford organization. The Ford Motor Company is a one-man achievement, built from the ground up, step by step. General Motors is a gigantic merger of existing concerns into an aggregation of coordinating parts. Some sixty-two companies have been linked in a chain of production that does not reach down as far as Mr. Ford's—they buy most of their raw material and steel—but ties up the thousand and one subsidiary processes in the making of an automobile and carries them through to the finished Buick, Cadillac, Oakland, Olds or Chevrolet. In a different field the International Harvester Company rivals Ford and the steel companies in the functional development of its organization, and the oil companies, following the lead of Rockefeller, carry the industrial process through from the oil well in Mexico to the filling station on Broadway.

In all these instances the drive toward super-trust expansion has been **primarily a desire to knit together the process of manufacture; but other motives have produced somewhat different forms of organization. Six are easily distinguished:**

1. The utilization of by-products. The great Chicago meat-packing concerns are the classic example of this sort of expansion. Armour & Co., for example, originally threw away most of the slaughtered carcass that was not used for meat. Today this waste has been reduced to the vanishing point. In its place are thriving subsidiary industries—leather, glue, soap, curled hair, tennis racket strings.

2. Making different products from the same basic materials. The Du Pont Company's expansion into the fields of fiber-silk, movie films and viscoloid followed an increasing knowledge of the use of cellulose, the basic substance from which explosives are made. The tendency among electric light and power companies to operate electric railroads follows the same principle.

3. Varied demands of the same market. Often a large concern which has developed a market for certain products finds it advantageous to manufacture other kinds of articles. The Pittsburgh Plate Glass Company, for example, a highly developed super-trust, has taken to manufacturing paints, oils and varnishes, painters' supplies, brushes, &c. The General Asphalt Company makes paving, plants and road rollers.

4. The use of idle plant. An interesting illustration of this motive is the entrance of Armour & Co. into the produce field. In order to utilize empty space in refrigerator cars during slack meat seasons the company has gone extensively into the butter, cheese and egg business.

5. The need for auxiliary products. In the manufacturing process it is often necessary to utilize various products which do not appear at all in the finished article—which are outside of the main stream of production. Large concerns are more and more finding it to their advantage to control these auxiliaries directly. The Steel Corporation owns huge tracts of timber in Minnesota, for use in shoring up the underground ore mines along the Iron Range, and it controls coal mines in Illinois, Kentucky and West Virginia to supply the fuel for its blast furnaces and power plants. Public utility companies are rapidly gathering up coal properties.

6. Investment of surplus capital. This motive accounts for some combinations among super-trusts that could not be explained on any other ground. The enormous investment of the du Pont Company in the General Motors Corporation and in real estate —both unrelated to the manufacture of explosives—may be explained this way.

But back of all these explanations and classifications lie profits. The super-trust is here because it is profitable—more so than the simple trust, just as the simple trust proved more effective in this direction than the individual unit of production. The super-trust is more profitable because it is more efficient; and its efficiency is both positive and negative. Compared with the simple trust, the super-trust can turn out a better product and at the same time reduce its cost.

Pooled resources of capital, brains, muscle and machinery make possible an accelerated improvement in the manufacturing process. The Ford concern in one vast interlocking self-improvement organization. A new wrinkle here is applied there and everywhere; a kink untied in the rolling mill unties a kink in the body shop—and the atmosphere in Ford plants is electric with inquiry and experiment. Undreamed-of standardization becomes possible: bolts always fit nuts and parts are readily interchangeable.

But even more impressive e the wastes, the lost motions, which are sloughed out of the process of manufacture. In the first place, the entire business of production is geared, as one great interconnecting machine, to the demand for the finished product. Iron ore is mined in Minnesota and blast furnaces are tapped in Gary, not blindly or with eye to speculative **profit, but in direct proportion to the market for rails and wire fences. And each step fits into the next with calculated precision. The South Chicago blast furnace does not have to wait on an uncertain supply or the haggling of the market for its meed of ore, nor is there any reason why the chemical content of that ore should not be exactly what it ought to be to meet the requirements of that particular charge. The activity of that furnace, in turn, is no greater or less than the rolling mills require to fill the orders in sight, or just around the corner. And when the demand does swing from heavy to light and back again the whole concern is substantial enough to take up the slack with much less of the jolts and jars of overwork and underwork.**

Miracle of Better Wages.

Not only is there coordination about the super-trust, but also balance, stability. It does not carry the eggs of its existence in the basket of one plant or process. It divides them among a score of plants producing a dozen products. Damage to one does not break them all. Then, too, the mere weight of its cash reserves steadies it and the whole ship of finance in panic seas. It would be difficult to measure the public service which the Steel Corporation, for example, has rendered as a business stabilizer.

And finally, consider its economies. Industry tends to get topheavy with too much overhead. The super-trust reduces the overhead weight. If five separate industries in the same chain of production are combined in one concern, five separate advertising, sales and insurance departments—to pick out the most obvious examples—can be consolidated into one and its total activity cut in half or even less. Only the final product then needs advertising copy and a corps of salesmen. And, more important yet, four profits may be merged in one. In an unorganized economic world the toll of profit is collected at each station on the road of manufacture. The super-trust at least "keeps all the profit in the family," and even the most voracious corporation can wax fat on a final profit far less than the sum of what otherwise would be taken.

It is the super-trust that has made possible the great economic miracle—the expansion of profits with reduced prices and increased wages. Take the reports of the Ford organization and list the figures in three parallel columns. They will demonstrate the unbelievable. The price of the car has gone down further and further, while wages have gone up. And yet Mr. Ford now pays the largest income tax in the United States, not excepting John D. Rockefeller Jr. It is a joyous, not a vicious, circle that waxes fatter by the simple process of nourishing itself.

Question Marks.

The super-trust—at least as Mr. Ford administers it—puts a question mark beside a good many cherished beliefs. It suggests to the statesman that "big business" may not be an unmitigated evil. Short of a monopoly on any plane of its productive process, closely coordinated big business may mean lower prices, more prosperity all around and the progressive elimination of the extremes of the business cycle.

It suggests to the labor leader that if the employer himself voluntarily continues to raise wages and improve working conditions, the union must find some more constructive reason for its existence.

It suggests to the business man that the time-honored policy of paying as little as possible to labor and charging the consumer as much as the traffic will bear is precisely the reverse of the modern formula for business success.

And, finally, the super-trust puts a question mark squarely in front of itself. The risks to the public in its existence are profound in proportion to the enormity of the power lodged in the hands of its executives. How far they may be permitted to remain unrestricted overlords of their newly acquired domain will depend largely, of course, upon their statesmanship and human understanding.

December 13, 1925

NEW RIPLEY ATTACK STIRS WALL STREET

Break in the Stock Market Follows Demand for More Light on Corporations.

Advance copies of an article by Professor William Z. Ripley of Harvard University, a noted economist, to be published in the September issue of The Atlantic Monthly, found their way into Wall Street yesterday and produced a sensation almost as profound as that created by his utterances several months ago on the subject of non-voting stocks. His latest article, urging fuller publicity in the financial affairs of corporations and suggesting that the Federal Trade Commission exercise the powers already vested in it to compel the submission of more complete and comprehensible reports was partly responsible, in the opinion of Wall Street, for the sharp reaction which took place in the stock market in the final hour of trading yesterday. Many stocks which have been leaders in recent upward movements broke violently under the pressure of a heavy concentration of selling orders.

General Motors and United States Steel, which have consistently held the leadership in recent advances, were among the first to sag in yesterday's decline. The former closed at 207 after selling as high as 214¾, while the latter ended the day at 149⅛ after touching a high of 153. The du Pont shares closed with a net loss of 8 points. Other wide breaks were recorded by Allied Chemical and Dye, down 3½ on the day; American Ice Company, with a net loss of 3¾; Atlantic Coast Line, with a net loss of 2⅞; Case Threshing, with a net loss of 5¾; United States Cast Iron Pipe, off 11 points on the day; General Asphalt, down 5¼, and Air Reduction, down 3.

Comment by Brokers.

Earlier in the day leading brokerage houses had directed attention in their market comments to the article by Professor Ripley and its possible effect on price movements. The fact that individual companies were severely criticized in the article for their failure to keep their stockholders and the public intelligently informed concerning their affairs was emphasized for the bearish influence which such strictures were likely to have.

One prominent firm referred to the excitement caused by Professor Ripley's previous comments on non-voting stocks and the resultant change in the New York Stock Exchange's policy in the listing of such stocks, and inquired whether it was not reasonable to expect some similar public reaction from the latest comments from this source.

The article by Professor Ripley, which is entitled "Stop, Look, Listen," draws attention to the little-realized fact that the Federal Trade Commission already has it in its power to require corporations to submit both annual and special reports in such form as the commission might prescribe, such reports to be rendered under oath. The record of debate on the subject at the time that Congress gave the Commission the authority makes it clear, according to Professor Ripley, that the law-making body intended this work to constitute one of the chief activities of the Commission.

Professor Ripley recalls that comprehensive and ambitious proposals for Federal incorporation or Federal license to engage in interstate commerce have been put forward before. It is not necessary, he says, to consider these proposals in connection with the question of adequate publicity. Whether or not, on the ground of corporate shortcomings or abuses, such a proposal should be advocated need not concern us at the time, he says, adding that the far-reaching proposal of President Taft, by special message to Congress on Jan. 7, 1910, recommending Federal incorporation, turned out to be politically impracticable on the one hand and economically inexpedient on the other.

Adequate Power in Act of 1914.

The immediate impulse, he recalls, was the decisive dissolution decrees of the United States Supreme Court in the Standard Oil and the American Tobacco decisions. But these developments, he shows, led forward logically to the enactment of the Federal Trade Commission law of 1914, which is still in force and effect, as an amendment of the Sherman anti-trust law. This statute, which is usually thought of in connection with unfair trade practices and the regulation of monopoly, contains, in Section 6, Professor Ripley discovers, a positive delegation of authority to this body which is entirely adequate, he says, to the performance of the service so greatly needed at the present time.

The Federal Trade Commission, had it chosen to exercise these powers, says Professor Ripley, might since 1914 have gathered and compiled information—to paraphrase the statute—concerning the organization, business and management of any large corporation engaged in commerce, except banks and common carriers. No additional legislation is necessary, he finds, and the most effective of all conceivable remedies awaits application. He contends that there is nothing revolutionary or paternalistic about the plan and that the President can find no economic objection to the declaration of a policy which would commit the Administration to the carrying out of the law.

Safeguarding Investments.

He believes that nothing will more surely conduce to popular thrift than to throw all possible safeguards about the investments of the people, and that if the word goes forth that the Federal Trade Commission is henceforward to address itself vigorously to the matter of adequate and intelligent corporate publicity the desired end will be speedily accomplished.

Professor Ripley takes particular exception in his article to the inadequacy of the balance sheets published by many corporations. He points out that they are prone to be inadequate or misleading in two principal respects; one is the downright omission of important items in the property account, and another is the failure to disclose the method of the valuation, whether it be of property or stock in trade.

He cites the leaflet report of one large oil company as setting forth that its investments in stocks of other corporations amount to so-and-so much. He also refers to the statement of the President of a large railway equipment company as giving the actual value of a plant as in excess of a total at which the entire property and equipment of the company are carried in the accounts. He wonders that no obligation seems to have been recognized to explain the matter further.

He mentions cases of "enigmatic accounting" in many instances and dissects the balance sheets and income statements of a number of prominent concerns to support his contention that stockholders are not receiving the right kind of information concerning the corporations in which they are interested.

Rights of the Public.

Professor Ripley argues that stockholders are entitled to adequate information and th the State and the general public have a right to the same privilege. First of all, he points out, one must remember that incorporation is a privilege. The people grant to a private body the ineffable enjoyment of immortality, of succession, of impersonality, and of limited liability, he says. Under partnerships or other purely private forms of organization, he says, trading is carried on without limitation upon the personal liability of those who engage therein, and certain obvious safeguards for creditors and the public arise from the purely personal attributes of the concern. The grant, by public act, of limitation upon this personal liability for debts or other obligations abrogates many of these formerly existent safeguards, which must of course be offset by new provisions at law.

Professor Ripley contends that the nation has had too many examples of downright deception in regard to the current valuations as carried on balance sheets. As at present conducted, he says, such appraisals, whether in prospectuses or in annual reports, are invariably made up not by experts of independent status, but by those whose prospects and emoluments are directly dependent upon the existing management. It is inevitable under such circumstances, he says, that these valuations should be biased by the wish to please.

Quite irrespective of artificial stimulation or suggestion, says Professor Ripley, the impulse nine times out of ten is toward overstatement. Shareholders have a right, he says, not only to an independent appraisal by engineers at the time of issuance of a prospectus, but also to a current check by independent engineers from time to time.

Professor Ripley gives credit to the New York Stock Exchange for the efforts it has made to encourage wider publicity of corporate affairs. He cites the United States Steel Corporation and the General Motors Corporation as two outstanding pioneers in the movement to recognize the need of complete public information relating to large corporations.

SAYS CORPORATIONS MUST HAVE SECRETS

Alfred P. Sloan Jr., President of the General Motors Corporation, in an interview in the current number of World's Work on "Modern Ideals of Big Business" meets many of the points raised by Professor Ripley in his recent criticism of the failure of corporations to give the public more information regarding the conduct of their affairs.

After pointing out that he frequently sends letters to all General Motors stockholders, informing them of the operations of the company and explaining in detail the policies of financial control, Mr. Sloan says:

"It is obvious, too, that there are limits to what the public should be told, even to what the stockholder should be told. If the management is dealing with a serious problem of personnel, for example, such as the question of which of two men should be chosen for a desirable vacancy, no conceivable good could be attained by discussing the matter in public and serious harm might be done. In general the current details of management are not matters that are of legitimate public interest.

"Even general policies sometimes depend for their success upon the assurance that they should not be prematurely made public, and in such cases clearly the stockholder's own interest is best protected by the management refraining from any announcement."

There are two fields, he declares, into which the modern corporation realizes it must not enter. One is religion. The other is politics.

"No corporation," he says, "has a right to concern itself with the political faith of its employes or with the ordinary political activities of the community.

"There is one tendency in the development of modern corporations that should receive serious public consideration. This is the tendency to diffuse stock ownership to a point where there ceases to be a responsible and consistent control of ownership and management. Just how far this process can go with safety to the public, on the one hand, and with efficiency of management on the other, is worth thoughtful study.

"Considerable diffusion is inevitable, because as corporations grow in size they must more and more appeal to the general public for the enormous sums necessary to finance the needed additions to capital investment in new plant and equipment. But it seems to me that there is a point beyond which diffusion of stock ownership must enfeeble a corporation by depriving it of virile interest in management upon the part of some one man or group of men to whom its success is a matter of personal and vital interest. And conversely, at that same point, the public interest becomes involved when the public can no longer locate some tangible personality within the ownership which it may hold responsible for the corporation's conduct."

September 27, 1926

THE DOLLAR NOW ENCIRCLES THE GLOBE

By STUART CHASE.

THAT the great Stinnes interests of Germany should recently have come to the United States for the funds to finance a reorganization of their far-flung operations and that American capital will hereafter have a first lien on the property is merely an unusually dramatic example of what has been going on for the past few years. The United States not only sends its manufactured goods into the four corners of the earth but American financial interests are now active factors in the domestic business life of all the leading nations.

To say that America is buying out Europe, Canada and South America is, of course, too strong a statement, although it is constantly made by those who speak both in praise and blame. But the expansion of American corporations into other lands and the purchase by Americans of an interest in foreign concerns are major economic developments of the post-war era, the significance of which has yet to be fully understood.

Staggering sums have been invested in the industries of other countries, not only in Europe but throughout the world, and almost every large American concern also operates plants abroad. American telephone interests are reaching out for Government systems in Spain, France, Belgium and Italy; American construction companies are lending foreign Governments money wherewith to pay for constructing public works; American manufacturers are establishing branch plants in Europe, Japan, the Argentine, Australia and South Africa; the Standard Oil Company gives away lamps in China to promote the sale of kerosene; the General Motors Company is sending twice as many cars abroad in 1926 as it did in 1924; American tobacco interests control Turkish and Greek crops and have acquired some British cigarette firms; vast holding companies are acquiring an ever-extending control of foreign enterprises. Month by month the map of the world shows additional locations where American enterprise, American engineers, American capital are digging in, consolidating, strengthening their position.

Up to July 1, 1925, the total investment by American capital abroad was estimated at $9,522,000,000 by the United States Department of Commerce. Of this $4,147,000,000 was in the form of loans guaranteed by foreign Governments, and the balance, $5,375,000,000, in the form of industrial securities and direct investments. The distribution was as follows:

Latin America	$4,140,000,000
Canada	2,545,000,000
Europe	2,115,000,000
Asia and Oceania.......	722,000,000
Total	$9,522,000,000

Flow of Dollars Grows.

During 1924 the increase in private capital abroad was little short of $1,000,000,000; in 1925 it was estimated at $2,500,000,000. All signs point to a steady increment in 1926. Many economists predict a total of $25,000,000,000 of private capital abroad by 1935; $25,000,000,000 it will certainly be if the present rate of expansion is maintained.

The heaviest investments are in the Americas, Canada and the lands south of the Rio Grande. All of Europe has absorbed less than Canada; Asia's portion is a third that of Europe. Africa is still a garden comparatively unwatered with dollars, but there are a few American investments in South Africa, the best known being the majority of the shares of the Diamond Syndicate, and in Liberia Mr. Firestone's $100,000,000 project to turn large sections of Liberia into rubber plantations has begun its harbor constructions.

In 1900 a bare $500,000,000 of American capital was invested abroad. By 1910 the total had grown to only $2,000,000,000. The vast shift which has turned us from a debtor into a creditor nation was the result of the World War, and has come about almost entirely in the last ten years. In 1910 our investment in Canada was only $300,000,000, while England's was $1,825,000,000—six times as much. In 1923 our investments in Canada had leaped to $2,400,000,000, passing England's, which remained at $2,000,000,000. In Argentina the Chicago beef companies control the cattle output. It may be that today our world total of foreign investments of private capital are actually greater than England's, and if not greater the margin is being closed with incredible rapidity.

Consider the Standard Oil Company of New York as an example of how American corporations are functioning abroad. In 1914 it entered into a sixty-year agreement with the Republic of China to explore for oil and exploit such fields as might be found. For this a corporation was formed, of which 55 per cent. of the capital stock should be owned by the American Company and 37 per cent. by the Chinese Government, leaving 8 per cent. in the treasury. When the Standard Oil Company entered China it gave away kerosene lamps—on the safety-razor principle. Now it sells lamps at cost, 2,000,000 of them annually. And these free or low-priced lamps have helped to increase the sale of kerosene in China from 13,500,000 gallons in 1908 to 200,000,000 gallons today. At Tientsin the company—with an eye to competitive commodities—has built a candle factory with an output of 600,000 cases a year.

The Standard Oil Company of New York is the "dominating oil marketing agent throughout the Orient," and it is the principal agent in Greece, Turkey and the Balkans. It has a large storage and distribution plant at Athens. Its sales in India are growing steadily. It is one of the five American companies in the Iraq concession, covering the oil of the Mosul fields. It has a great plant at Yokohama. And last July it bought 15,000 tons of kerosene from the Soviet Government.

Meanwhile the Standard Oil Company of California controls 900,000 acres of oil lands in Colombia, the Argentine, Ecuador, Venezuela and Mexico. It is organizing a distribution service throughout Mexico. The Standard Oil Company of Indiana, through subsidiary corporations—one of them lately bought from Edward L. Doheny—is interested in oil lands in Colombia, Mexico, New Guinea and Venezuela. The Vacuum Oil Company, influential in Egypt and the Levant, has entered into a contract with the Russian Government to purchase a minimum of 130,000 tons of kerosene in the next two years. And the Vacuum is negotiating for shares in the coal mines of Lower Austria. All of which gives a scant, but authentic, picture of American oil dollars as they swing from Mexico to China.

Consider also telephones and radios. Here is the International Telephone and Telegraph Company, closely affiliated with the American Telephone and Telegraph Company. It is one of those latest developments of superfinance—a holding and a managing company. It not only holds the shares of the subsidiary corporations, but it sends out managers, engineers, accountants, experts of all kinds to operate or help to operate them. This company has, through a subsidiary, taken over the whole telephone service of Spain from the Spanish Government, where it is introducing the dial system. After twenty years the Government may take it back by paying a premium of 15 per cent. The company owns the Thompson-Houston telephone equipment plants of France, employing 2,200 operatives. This plant supplies much of the equipment for the French telephone system.

The International also operates the foreign business of the Western Electric Company through another subsidiary, with manufacturing plants in England, Belgium, France, Spain, Italy, Japan, China, Australia and South America, employing 17,000 workers and selling $30,000,000 worth of products a year. It controls the telephone systems of Cuba and Porto Rica and owns the Mexican Telephone and Telegraph Company. Rumors persist that it is negotiating for the Government telephone systems of various other European countries—particularly France, Belgium and Italy. It recently sold $20,000,000 of equipment to the Italian Government.

The Radio in China.

Meanwhile the Radio Corporation of America operates the American end of radio services in England, Norway, France, Germany, Sweden, Italy, Poland, Holland, Japan, the Argentine and the Dutch East Indies. Through a subsidiary, the Federal Telegraph Company, it is developing the radio possibilities of China.

Here is the Foundation Company, which has sent sand hogs down to blast and burrow for the underpinning of many of the skyscrapers of downtown New York. But from Manhattan it looks east and south over the Atlantic. With branches in London, Paris, Mexico City, Lima, in Brazil, Columbia, and Montreal, it sends sand hogs and engineers to construct harbors, power dams, railroads, sanitation systems, public works, around half the world. It operates in fourteen foreign countries.

It is banker as well as engineer. It lends the Peruvian Government $15,000,000, taking bonds in exchange, and then builds public works in Peru, being paid therefor by its own money. It does the same thing for the Government of Greece, amounting to $2,500,000 for drainage work in Macedonia. To Cordoba, in Spain, it lent 2,500,000 pesos for construction work. Recently the Foundation Company has been bidding on the 500-mile Central highway development for Cuba, a system of roads to cost $50,000,000.

The General Motors Company has export and assembly plants in the Argentine, Brazil, Belgium, France, Germany, Denmark, England, Ireland, New Zealand, Spain, South Africa, Canada. Its overseas selling organization covers the world. Shipments of cars abroad have actually doubled in the past two years—64,000 went over in the first six months of 1926. It is considering the purchase of 800,000 acres of rubber land in Cuba.

The International Harvester Company has manufacturing plants in Canada, France, Germany and Sweden, making binders, reapers, mowers, rakes, tedders and twine. It has selling agencies and distributing posts the world around; sisal plantations in Cuba and Manila; fiber plants in the Philippines; timber and pulpwood holdings in Canada. And the same sort of far flung and expanding organization is maintained by the Eastman Kodak Company, the American Radiator Company, the United Shoe Machinery Company, the Ford Company and many other American manufacturing enterprises. United Fruit owns extensive sugar and fruit plantations in Costa Rica and Jamaica, besides hotels, railways and docks.

Investments Far Afield.

Let us turn to organizations concerned more with investment than with primary manufacturing. The American International Corporation for example, was chartered in 1915 under the laws of New York, with a capital stock of $50,000,000. Its charter gives it very broad powers to deal in almost anything at home or abroad. The principal business and objects of the corporation are "the development of export and import trade, the use of American materials and manufactures abroad, the employment of American capital and American engineers in the construction of foreign enterprises, the enlargement of the system of ocean transportation under the American flag; and the encouragement of American business men in undertaking projects abroad and extending other domestic opportunities to foreign countries."

It has sent many expeditions and commissions to South America, Europe, Asia and other parts of the world to report on definite proposals as well as upon the possibilities of assisting development of these regions with more American dollars. It holds stock in many subsidiary companies—banks, finance companies, steamship lines, the China corporation, engineering concerns, manufacturing companies, export agencies. One of its subsidiaries, Ulen & Co., recently lent $10,000,000 to ten Polish cities and $3,000,000 to Lisbon, Portugal, for municipal works. Another of its subsidiaries carries on a coffee trade, another sells boots and shoes around the seven seas.

There is almost no end to the examples which might be cited of American dollars going to function in other lands. In transportation, manufacturing, mining, engineering, public works, branch banking, marketing, in nearly every conceivable type of economic activity they are engaged outside the boundaries of their homeland. The few instances mentioned have paid very well to date—in manufacturing, trading and finance. A casual survey by geographical areas may help to round out the picture. Take, say, a large country such as Germany, and a small country such as Bolivia. The inventory of major investments in them was largely compiled in 1925, and the golden stream has been rising steadily since that time.

Private loans to the German dye, sugar, coal, potash and shipping industry and to German banks totaled about $50,000,000 on Oct. 15, 1924. Soon afterward came the Dawes plan loan of $110,000,000, which was oversubscribed by American investors; also came new loans to the Ruhr Coal Syndicate, the Rhone-Main-Danube, the Rhenish-Westphalian Syndicate totaling some $10,000,000, and $25,000,000 to the German Gold Rediscount Bank. The Equitable Trust Company, the Chase National Bank, Dillon, Read & Co., and the International Acceptance Bank, a subsidiary of the American International Corporation, have taken the lead in German industrial financing. And there is the new Stinnes loan of $25,000,000.

America in Germany.

For direct investments, the Berlin Karlsruher Industry Company, formerly the German Arms Company, with a capital of 30,000,000 gold marks, is reported to be under American control; the Botany Mills of New Jersey has acquired a $4,000,000 interest in German textile plants; the Hamburg-American Line is now controlled by the United States Line under a twenty-year agreement. The International Agricultural Corporation owns 50 per cent. of the large Sollstedt potash property, including mines and chemical plants. Dillon, Read & Co. have a holding in eleven coal mines, formerly controlled by Stinnes.

The largest German chain-store system has been financed by American capital. Among the American companies operating plants in Germany are the Ford Company, Singer Sewing Machine, Quaker Oats, Standard Varnish, Torrington Company, International Harvester, American Radiator (three plants), B. F. Goodrich Rubber plant with 12,000 men, Chicago Pneumatic Tool, Standard Oil, International Mercantile Marine, Radio Corporation, Otis Elevator, Eastman Kodak and various film companies.

In one fortnight a New York banking house received 100 letters from German firms asking for a total of $500,000,000 in loans. Meanwhile such great firms as Krupps, August Thyssen, Siemens & Halske and Electric Power Company have been floating loans running into the tens of millions on the American market. Dozens of loans have been made to German municipalities, like the famous loan to the City of Coblenz.

In 1912 the total American investment in Bolivia was $10,000,000; today it is over $80,000,000. American citizens and corporations have lent $30,000,000 to the Bolivian Government. Another $50,000,000 is invested in tin and oil. The Standard Oil Company of New Jersey has a concession covering 7,400,000 acres of oil lands for a period of fifty-five years. The concession includes the right to operate railways, trams, harbors, telephone and telegraph lines and other public utilities. The Sinclair Company is also competing for petroleum lands.

Controls Bolivia's Tin.

One-quarter of the world's output of tin comes from Bolivia. The National Lead Company has invested $50,000,000 in tin mines, including a railroad, and controls 80 per cent. of Bolivian production. The Guggenheims own six tin mines in the Inquisivi Province. W. R. Grace & Co. have 3,500 acres of mining properties. Three other large American companies have mining interests in Bolivia.

Meanwhile American engineers constructed the Bolivian Railway, and securities of the company are held in America. The Equitable Trust Company has handled government loans. Ulen & Co., the subsidiary of the American International Corporation, have recently been engaged in public works construction, including the financing and building of the sewer systems of the cities of La Paz and Cochabamba. The same company is building a $10,000,000 railway for the Government. An American firm acquired in 1922 about 300,000 hectares of land in eastern Bolivia for colonization purposes. American capital is behind the National Match Factory of Bolivia.

What is true of Germany and Bolivia is true to a greater or less extent of every country. Similar report could be made regarding most other political subdivisions of the earth's surface—leaving out some deserts, jungles, ice caps and mountain wildernesses. Wherever men have settled into civilized communities, and wherever the treasures of minerals outcrop in marketable quantities, American dollars have gone, American engineers are at work. American methods, American practices, are penetrating the economic structure. The process accelerates at an unheard-of rate. Where it will end, no man has the hardihood to forecast.

December 12, 1926

MERGERS CONTINUE IN TRADE AND INDUSTRY

Economy and Elimination of Competition the Chief Reasons—Recent Combinations.

Strong competition which has developed in many lines is mainly responsible for the large number of mergers which have developed during the year. In fact, 1928 will probably go down in financial history as the "year of mergers" and all of them are not yet concluded. Negotiations are now under way for further combinations in such important lines as motors, oil, chain stores, dairy products and railroads.

In the main these mergers have been effected by the exchange of stocks, but in a few cases there have been outright purchases. The main advantages to the purchasing company are the elimination of superfluous sales agencies, economies in manufacturing, and in many cases, the acquisition of strategic sales locations and nationally known trade marks.

The most recent combinations have been as follows:

CHAIN STORES—American Department Stores Corporation, acquiring Wright, Metzler Company, Uniontown, Pa.; Wright, Metzler Company, Bronxville, Pa.; Caldwell Stores, Inc., Washington, Pa.; J. M. Hartley and Son Company, Fairmont, W. Va., and Hartley-Rownd Company, Clarksburg, W. Va., Kroger Grocery and Baking Company has purchased fifty-seven Piggly-Wiggly Stores in Memphis and all Piggly-Wiggly Stores in Louisville and Cleveland. Sanitary Grocery Company, Inc., and Safeway Stores, Inc., have consolidated. The Capital Stores, Inc., New Bedford, Mass., has merged with the Puritan Grocery Stores, Inc., Fall River, Mass.

MAIL ORDER HOUSES—The National Bellas Hess Company, Inc., has purchased the Charles William Stores, Inc.

BAKERIES—The Purity Bakery Corporation and Cushman's Sons, Inc., will merge. United Biscuit Company of America has absorbed the Ontario Biscuit Company. The Purity Bakery Corporation has acquired the Tip Top Baking Company of Louisville, Ky.

ADVERTISING—The George Batten Company of Baltimore has purchased control-Inc. have combined.

CHEMICALS—The Davison Chemical Company of Baltimore has purchased controlling interest in the Read Phosphate Company, Savannah, Ga.; the Welch Chemical Company, Columbus, Ohio; the Porter Fertilizer Works, Atlanta, and the Gulfport Fertilizer Company, Gulfport, Miss.

DAIRY PRODUCTS—The Borden Company has acquired Thompson's Malted Milk Company, Wisconsin; the Kennedy Dairy Company, Madison, Wis., and the Clover Leaf Milk Company, Chicago.

IRON AND STEEL—Joseph T. Ryerson, Inc. of Boston has acquired E. P. Sanderson & Co. of Cambridge, Mass.

PUBLIC UTILITIES—The Inland Telephone Company has been incorporated in Delaware to combine twenty-six independent telephone companies in Ohio, Wisconsin, Minnesota and Pennsylvania.

AUTOMOBILE EQUIPMENT—The Electric Auto Light Company of Toledo has purchased a substantial interest in the Eclipse Machine Company at Elmira, N. Y., manufacturers of bendix dry mechanism.

PAINT—A merger is nearing completion of nine paint companies on the Coast, including the California Paint Company, Hill, Hubbell & Co., Jones & Dillingham, Rasmussen & Co., Seattle Paint Company, Magner Bros. Paint Company, Bridley Wise Paint Company, Brininstool Paint Company and Technical Oil and Paint Company.

PUBLISHERS—The Bragdon, Lord & Nagle Co., publishers of Textile World will merge with the McGraw, Hill Publishing Company. The Outlook Company has purchased the Independent of Boston.

FINANCE—Merger of the Union Commerce Investment Company and the Griswold First State Bank of Detroit has been approved. The Standard Mortgage Corporation of Los Angeles has merged with the California-United States Bond and Mortgage Company, affiliated with the United States Bond and Mortgage Company of New York.

SHOE MANUFACTURING—The Ground Gripper Shoes Company, Inc., has acquired the Kahler Shoe Company and the Powers Realty Trust Company.

RAILROADS—O. P. and M. J. Van Sweringen have acquired by purchase control of the Buffalo, Rochester & Pittsburgh Railroad.

AMUSEMENT—Warner Brothers Picture, the Vitaphone Corporation, the Stanley Company of America and the First National Pictures, Inc., have been brought together in one group.

LAUNDRIES—The Mid-Continent Laundries, Inc., has been formed by bankers to acquire the business and assets of nineteen laundry and dry cleaning concerns in Chicago and the Middle West.

PUMP COMPANIES—The Wayne Pump Company has acquired the Boyle-Dayton Company.

October 14, 1928

TRADE BOARD REPORT ON DU PONT DEALS

Finds Relations With Steel and Motors Cut Company's Selling Costs.

NAMES NO LAW VIOLATION

Humphrey, in Minority Report, Attacks the Inquiry as "Bureaucracy Gone Insane."

SEES END OF SUCH CASES

Commissioner Says Investments by du Ponts Are of No Concern to the Commission.

Special to The New York Times.

WASHINGTON, Feb. 2.—The relations that exist or formerly existed between the du Pont interests of Delaware, the United States Steel Corporation and the General Motors Corporation were held today in a report by the Federal Trade Commission as having assured the du Pont company "an outlet for a considerable portion of its important products at little or no selling cost." At the same time Commissioner Humphrey filed a dissenting opinion, asserting that the report was "an illuminating illustration of bureaucracy gone insane" and that no such inquiry would ever again be undertaken by the commission.

Mr. Humphrey declared that in investigating the relationship of the three interests concerned the commission had departed from the sphere in which it was placed by Congress. He described the investigation as in the nature of a "fanatical inquisition."

Summing up his conclusions, Mr. Humphrey contended that all that the commission had disclosed was the method by which the du Ponts had invested their surplus earnings, and this, he declared, was no concern of the Federal Trade Commission.

Beyond the statement regarding an outlet for the du Pont products, the report so bitterly assailed by Mr. Humphrey presented only what were alleged to be facts. It did not impute a violation of the law to any of the three interests whose activities were investigated.

Recalls Reason for Inquiry.

The commission stated that it began its inquiry by reason of an announcement of E. I. du Pont de Nemours & Co. on July 27, 1927, that it had bought 114,000 shares of the common stock of United States Steel and the circulation of press reports that the chairman of the du Pont company was to succeed the chairman of the Steel Corporation, who was ill, or that the du Ponts would have representation on the Steel Corporation's board of directors.

"This was regarded the more probable," said the report, "because of the dominance through stock ownership of the du Pont company over the General Motors Corporation, which, in turn, is one of the largest buyers of the Steel Corporation's product. There also was the well-known connection between J. P. Morgan & Co. and the Steel Corporation on the one hand and on the other the Morgan important financial relations with the du Pont company and their representation on the General Motors board."

The report went on to say that "this apparent community of interest of such magnitude called for an inquiry into the facts and their significance."

In pursuance of this authority the correspondence files of the du Ponts were examined, and this was one of the phases of the matter severely attacked by Commissioner Humphrey.

After tracing the earlier history of the du Pont company, the report referred to proposals made within the company by John J. Raskob, then treasurer, to turn its wartime investment into peace-time channels.

"It had, at the close of 1917," the report said, "an outside investment of $40,000,000, including $12,500,000 in the dye industry, leaving a balance of $50,000,000 capital which would be without employment at the close of the war. 'It is imperative,' the treasurer of the company reported to the finance commission on Dec. 19, 1917, 'that this amount be employed, otherwise the earnings of our company after the war will be insufficient to support the dividend policy and the matter of properly employing this money in a way that will result in a proper return to our company is one of most serious consequence.' "

Tells of Stock Purchases.

The company treasurer decided, according to the commission report, that the motor industry, as represented by the affiliated General Motors, United Motors and Chevrolet, appeared to be the most attractive field for investment. Accordingly, stocks were purchased.

"The real object of this stock purchase," the report said, "was, in the view of the company's treasurer, not the employment of the du Pont company's surplus for the purposes of an emergency reserve to be drawn upon by the company in case of unusual need but the branching out into a new and permanent business by the du Pont company and the ultimate control of the company in which the investment was being made."

The report said that "in 1920 the du Pont company, with the backing of J. P. Morgan & Co., bought from Mr. Durant, who was in financial difficulties, common stock of General Motors Corporation amounting to about $33,750,000. Mr. Durant, resigning as president and director and retiring from the management of the corporation, Pierre S. du Pont became president."

Purchases for du Pont interests of $14,000,000 of United States Steel stock was recommended by Irenee du Pont, chairman of the board and chairman of the finance committee, on May 7, 1927, according to the commission report.

"Because several interests were joined in the purchase of this stock it was rumored in financial circles that a huge steel stock pool was being formed and that corporate interests were to be merged. The total number of shares purchased by the three interests was 201,044. No evidence was found to indicate that control over the stock was thereafter exercised jointly. The du Pont block amounted to about 1.6 per cent of the outstanding common stock of the

United States Steel Corporation and 1 per cent of the total outstanding voting stock.

"According to the statement of officials of the United States Steel Corporation, it holds no stock of the du Pont or General Motors company, and officials of the General Motors Corporation state that it holds no stock of the United States Steel Corporation.

"No member of the board of directors or individual holding an important office in either the du Pont Company or General Motors is a member of the board of directors or holds an important office in the United States Steel Corporation, as disclosed by the most recent published statements of the three companies, except George F. Baker Jr., who is director for both the Steel Corporation and General Motors.

Relation With Morgan.

"On the other hand, the interests of the three companies are loosely connected by J. P. Morgan & Co., who have been the fiscal agents of the Steel Corporation and have had important financial relations with the other two for many years, two partners (Junius S. Morgan Jr. and George Whitney) of which are members of the General Motors board, and one partner (J. P. Morgan) of which is chairman of the Steel Corporation board.

"A letter to the commission, dated March 19, 1928, and signed by Irenée du Pont, stated that E. I. du Pont de Nemours & Co. have sold their entire holdings of United States Steel Corporation common stock. The stock was reported to have been sold at a profit of $2,2?0,000."

Discussing the question of possible sales between the du Pont and General Motors Corporation as a result of the financial interest of the du Pont company in General Motors, the report said:

"Nevertheless, the net results of the financial relationship existing between the du Pont company and General Motors, as shown by the sales of the former company to the latter, is what the treasurer of the du Pont company suggested as one reason for his company's purchase of General Motors stock, viz., to assure an outlet for a considerable portion of several of the company's most important products at little or no selling cost. This, however, is only one reason for this financial relationship, and not necessarily the most important one."

Humphrey's Dissenting Views.

In his dissenting view Commissioner Humphrey said that "this is the only case in the history of the country where the government, when no wrongdoing was alleged, put a concern to the cost, the annoyance and the discredit of an investigation. I doubt if a parallel case can be furnished in any civilized country. If obeying the law is no protection from such outrageous usurpation of power by a creature of Congress, then it means that the citizen is helpless and the end of free government."

Mr. Humphrey said that no complaint had been made to the commission. He then went on:

"The resolution itself says that the investigation is not made to ascertain if there has been any violation of the anti-trust law—the statutory limit of the commission's power—but to see what is the effect of the respondent's action from an economic standpoint. Suppose the action was uneconomical? Suppose the investment was unsound? Of what concern is it to the Federal Trade Commission? From a legal standpoint there would be just as much sense in the Federal Trade Commission investigating the moral effect of the female Sunday school teacher on the Einstein theory.

"It is utterly unthinkable that Congress would do a thing so insanely contrary to all principles of government as to create a body with power which it could exercise at its own volition to investigate corporations to see if they were wisely investing their earnings, so long as it was admitted that they were obeying the law.

"When the great corporations comply with the anti-trust laws will be time enough to see whether they observe economic laws. Our duty is to see if corporations make their money honestly, not that they invest wisely. Our duty is to prevent violation of the law, not to exert parental control over those who obey it.

"This is an ex parte proceeding. Any other corporation than the respondent might just as well have been selected for this excursion into State socialism at government expense, illegally incurred. Such proceedings might easily have destroyed a weaker concern.

"While many complaints against corporations were awaiting investigation, alleging fraud, attempting to destroy competition and creating monopoly, and in other ways violating the anti-trust laws, the commission was wasting its time and money trying to find out whether the respondents needed a guardian to tell them how to wisely invest their surplus earnings."

Mr. Humphreys asserted that a mere majority of the commission was present when the resolution of warning was adopted, and this, he said, was "not by accident."

Says Two Were Lawyers.

"Two of the three commissioners who voted for it were lawyers," he added. "Neither is on the commission now. The three constituting the majority at that time had strange and startling ideas about the government control of corporations and still stranger and more erratic ideas about the powers and duties of the commission."

The two lawyers mentioned by Mr. Humphreys who are no longer connected with the commission are John F. Nugent of Iowa, a Democrat, and Abram F. Myers of New York, a Republican. The name of the third member could not be deduced from anything Mr. Humphrey said.

"It is beyond all reasonable probability," said Mr. Humphreys, "that the President will ever appoint, and the Senate confirm, a majority of the commission who hold such irrational opinions of the powers and duties of the commission. The history of this case furnishes most an instructive instance of how men clothed with a little brief authority become drunk with their own greatness and lose all sense of proportion and become entirely blinded to the rights of the citizen."

February 3, 1929

BLOOMINGDALE JOINS HUGE STORE MERGER

To Be Linked With Abraham & Straus, Filene, White and Lazarus Concerns.

SALES $106,000,000 A YEAR

Three Brothers Agree to Trade Control for Stock in Holding Company.

Bloomingdale Brothers, Inc., is to enter a department store merger which represents annual net sales totaling $106,000,000, it was learned yesterday.

The other members of the merger were announced last March as Abraham & Straus, Inc., of Brooklyn, with annual net sales of $25,000,000; William Filene's Sons Company of Boston, controlling R. H. White Company, with combined annual sales in Boston of $46,000,000, and F. R. Lazarus & Co. of Columbus, Ohio, with annual sales of $12,000,000. The Bloomingdale store's annual sales are $23,000,000.

The merger has been under negotiation since February, principally through Lehman Brothers, investment bankers, for the declared purpose of "bringing under unified control successful retail stores through their acquisition, affiliation or consolidation."

It was through Lehman Brothers that the purchase by R. H. Macy & Co. of L. Bamberger & Co. of Newark was arranged in June, combining annual sales totaling $125,000,000.

The prospective relations between the Macy-Bamberger merger and the Bloomingdale-Filene-Lazarus-Abraham & Straus merger could not be learned yesterday, nor where in the process of consolidating successful department stores it is proposed to put Arnold, Constable & Co. of New York and the Namm store of Brooklyn, which are now also understood to be the object of negotiations not yet completed.

Holding Company Formed.

The mechanism of the merger in which the Bloomingdale corporation has agreed to join is a holding company in which stock control of the participating store corporations will be exchanged for stock in the holding company.

Details of the exchange are to be announced formally within a month. It was explained that the merger would not result in any change in the individual character or local identity of the stores involved. Upon this condition, the three Bloomingdale brothers, Samuel J., Hiram C. and Irving I., whose father founded the store in 1872, decided to join the merger, after deliberating since last February. Samuel J. Bloomingdale, who is president, is understood to have agreed with his brothers that the merger was a step in the direction of more satisfactory and economical distribution of goods to the store's steadily growing number of customers.

The unification of operations on the production side of the business, it was pointed out, has already led to group buying by department stores, enabling manufacturers to plan their production more definitely and thereby lessening the cost of selling all the way to the consumer.

The ownership of the Bloomingdale store in New York and of the Abraham & Straus store in Brooklyn has remained more than fifty years in the families of the men who started them as small enterprises and put their own names over the doors. Both of these department stores were big businesses before the founders died or retired, but it was only during the past decade that their children converted them into corporations and allowed the public to purchase a minor interest—principally through Lehman Brothers and Goldman, Sachs & Co.

Bloomingdale's Opened in 1872.

The founder of the Bloomingdale store was Lyman Bloomingdale, who was an expert assembler of hoopskirts until they went out of fashion in 1872 and left him out of a job. With his brother, Joseph, he immediately opened a small dry goods store. The first day's net sales were $3.63.

On the way to the total net sales of $23,000,000 last year, at a 6.62 per cent margin of profit, many of the common practices of the large department stores of today were first introduced by the Bloomingdales and played an important part in the growth of their establishment. According to Samuel Bloomingdale, who is now president of the corporation, the Bloomingdale store was the first to install a passenger elevator, an escalator, and to deliver parcels in automobiles at a time when they still frightened horses, as well as the first to institute feature sales and to advertise extensively in the daily newspapers.

Bloomingdale Brothers, Inc., now employs about 2,500 persons and owns the entire block on which it is located between Fifty-ninth and Sixtieth Streets and Third and Lexington Avenues. Plans for the erection of a new eleven-story building, by sectional replacement of the old building without interrupting business, have been filed and work is to be started by the end of the year.

According to the announcements, it will be "a completely modern store, containing every known device for improving and speeding up service and sales." It will be topped by an architectural tower to be known as the Lyman G. Bloomingdale Memorial.

Brooklyn Store Older.

In Brooklyn a similar sectional replacement of the Abraham & Straus store by a new ten-floor establishment is under way, without interruption of its annual sales of $25,000,000. The store was founded in 1865 by Abraham Abraham and his partner, Joseph Wechsler, just before the collapse of inflated war prices and in a section of Brooklyn which was then regarded as too far uptown, but the business survived.

Nathan and Isidor Straus soon joined Mr. Abraham with a chinaware department, and in 1893 they bought out Mr. Wechsler and changed the firm name to Abraham & Straus. Nathan Straus, who had not been active in the management for some time, retired four years ago to a career of philanthropy. Simon F. Rothschild, president of Abraham & Straus, Inc., and Edward C. Blum, first vice president, are both sons-in-law of the founder, Mr. Abraham.

Both Abraham Abraham and Lyman Bloomingdale, whose great establishments are now to be linked, started their careers as apprentices in the same dry goods shop in Newark before the Civil War.

September 17, 1929

BIGGER COMPANIES TESTED BY SLUMP

Large Industrials Have Fared Better Than Small Rivals, Bankers Assert.

DIVERSIFICATION A FACTOR

Better Management and Caution in Dividend Policy Also Cited as Reasons.

The theory that large industrial units can pass through a period of business depression without sustaining the drastic contraction of earnings that small industrial companies experience has received a severe test during the current recession in commercial activity, according to bankers in Wall Street. While most of the leading industrial units have made a favorable showing in comparison with the earnings of smaller companies in the same industries, several of the large companies have also made disappointing showings in the face of depression, the bankers report.

While a few economists believe it is still too early, after a year of depression, to conclude whether the large companies have done better than the small ones, most experts feel that as a group the standard industrial leaders, such as United States Steel, General Motors and General Electric, have withstood adverse trade conditions in a far more satisfactory manner than most of the small companies in their respective fields.

The theory that large units could withstand depression better than small units was based on several arguments. First, it was contended, the largest companies in the country are usually engaged in several lines of business, and their greater diversification would render them less vulnerable to a sharp drop in activity in any one line. During the last year, bankers declare, diversification of output has been extremely valuable to many industrial companies. The United States Steel Corporation, for example, earned almost its year's dividend requirements in the first half of 1930, largely because of its diversified production, it is contended.

Large Orders for Pipe.

While small steel firms whose activities were confined to automobile steel were reporting a sharp contraction of earnings, owing to the depression in the automobile industry, the Steel Corporation was receiving large orders for pipe from the natural gas and oil industries, and was thus able to make a satisfactory showing.

Diversification of output also assisted the General Motors Corporation in earning more than two-thirds of its annual dividend requirements during the first half of 1930, bankers declare. Smaller companies, manufacturing high-priced automobiles only, were in many cases unable to earn their dividend requirements, it is held, while General Motors, largely through its activity in the low-priced car field, was able to earn its dividend requirements by a safe margin. If General Motors had specialized in high-priced automobiles it would have been almost as vulnerable to business depression as the small companies, bankers believe.

Good Management a Factor.

Another advantage which many large corporations hold over smaller units, it is contended, is superior management. The large company usually can afford to pay more for management than the small company, it is held, and can therefore obtain more capable officers.

As a result of better management and the advice of a conservative board of directors, the large companies usually maintain smaller inventories and larger cash positions than most of the smaller companies do, in proportion, many bankers believe. Consequently, when a period of declining commodity prices appears, the large units may be expected to sustain smaller inventory losses than the minor companies.

By maintaining a liquid position, the large units would also be able to make advantageous purchases of materials and could embark on plant extensions at the most economical time.

Conservative Policies Cited.

Owing to the conservative policies followed by the directors of most of the leading industrial companies with regard to dividends, not as many of the important units have had to reduce their disbursements to stockholders as of the smaller companies, which have generally been more liberal in their distributions, according to bankers in Wall Street. During the boom period of 1929 the industrial leaders rarely based dividend distributions on the exceptional earnings of that period. In many cases the large firms paid to shareholders less than one-half of the net profit for the year. By conserving their cash, these companies were enabled to withstand the succeeding months of depression in a satisfactory manner, it is stated.

The number of large industrial firms which have had to sacrifice inventories has been much smaller than the number that had to adopt these drastic measures during the depression of 1920-21, it is held. Better management was responsible for the more conservative policies of the large companies in 1929, bankers believe.

September 7, 1930

200 Corporations Had 40% Of Nation's Net Income in 1930

The great extent to which large corporations are participating in the nation's business is indicated in the income tax returns filed for last year, showing that 200 corporations, representing less than one-sixteenth of 1 per cent of the 303,000 companies filing returns, reported more than 40 per cent of all net income and 45 per cent of all gross assets.

These companies include forty-five railroads, fifty-eight public utilities and ninety-seven industrial corporations, according to the report of a survey prepared by Dominick & Dominick. The firm has carried its survey further, and quotes the National Industrial Conference Board to the effect that only 3.4 per cent of all manufacturing companies in this country employ more than 250 wage-earners and only 1.4 per cent employ more than 500.

June 14, 1931

EASING TRUST LAWS URGED BY CHAMBER

Program to Take Country Out of Depression Is Based on Nation-Wide Referenda.

FOR AN ECONOMIC COUNCIL

But One Voluntarily Set Up by Business Itself—Private Job Insurance Proposed.

Special to The New York Times.

WASHINGTON, Dec. 17.—**A program designed to lead the country out of depression was offered today by the Chamber of Commerce of the United States. Its four main recommendations, dealing with long-range problems as well as the immediate situation, were as follows:**

"The setting up by business itself of a national economic council to aid all fields of industry, finance and commerce in their planning.

"Modification of the anti-trust laws to make clear lawfulness of agreements intended to relate production to consumption.

"Relief in emergencies for the natural resource industries, such as coal, oil and lumber, by the creation of a government tribunal which would permit agreements for curtailment of production when in the public interest.

"Establishment of privately sustained systems of unemployment benefits as well as other similar benefits based upon definite reserves previously established."

The program was based on referenda on eleven recommendations submitted to its membership, the proposals on which the vote was taken having been prepared by a committee on continuity of business and employment, headed by Henry I. Harriman, vice chairman of the board of the New England Power Association, and a natural resource committee, with Matthew S. Sloan, president of the New York Edison Company, as its chairman.

"The subject matter of the two referenda, the chamber said, "takes on particular importance at this time by reason of the fact that in the present session of Congress virtually all of the proposals advanced will be under consideration in one form or another."

Pointing out that a Senate committee has been holding hearings on a proposed economic council, the announcement said, the chamber would favor a voluntary council, not under government control.

Another point voted was that employers collectively and individually should provide adequate reserves for unemployment and other benefits and, through trade associations, should make such reserves and benefits uniform throughout each field. It was voted also that unemployment which now exists or may occur should be dealt with upon an individual base locally through organization to that end.

On the question of the "dole" the

chamber membership adopted this suggestion:

"Needed relief should be provided through private contributions, supplemented by State and local governments, and without any Federal appropriations for such purposes."

HAYS FOR EASING BAN.

Says Legislative "Strait-Jacket" Dwarfs Industries.

Special to The New York Times.

BOSTON, Dec. 17.—Calling for revision of the Sherman anti-trust law and Clayton act, Will Hays, president of Motion Picture Producers and Distributers of America, today denounced "straightjacket" legislation which, he said, threatened to dwarf and distort "many of our soundest and most essential industries."

Mr. Hays, addressing the Boston Chamber of Commerce, declared that "in the era of ruthless competion these now antiquated statutes were necessary."

"But," he continued, "business has progressed in spirit as well as method, in conscience as well as complexity. The American business man today is entitled, on the basis of his proved intelligence and recognition of community interests, to reasonable freedom at the hands of government—freedom to work out the problems which are equally germane to the legitimate successful operation of business and to the welfare and prosperity of every workingman and every workingman's family.

"There is a healthy disposition on the part of our national legislators to consider the revision of the Sherman anti-trust law and the Clayton act. This is well.

"No one, of course, would suggest that legislation yield its right to interpose upon business reasonable conditions, clearly in the public interest. I only urge that the method employed shall be such as to cause the result to coincide with the intent. I ask for reasonable freedom for American business to keep itself abreast of changing conditions and to erect a more stable edifice of prosperity.

December 18, 1931

Text of President Hoover's Announcement Of His Signing of Finance Reconstruction Bill

Special to The New York Times.

WASHINGTON, Jan. 22.—The text of President Hoover's announcement today that he had signed the Reconstruction Finance Corporation bill follows:

I have signed the Reconstruction Finance Corporation act.

It brings into being a powerful organization with adequate resources, able to strengthen weaknesses that may develop in our credit, banking and railway structure, in order to permit business and industry to carry on normal activities free from the fear of unexpected shocks and retarding influences.

Its purpose is to stop deflation in agriculture and industry and thus to increase employment by the restoration of men to their normal jobs.

It is not created for the aid of big industries or big banks. Such institutions are amply able to take care of themselves. It is created for the support of the smaller banks and financial institutions and, through rendering their resources liquid, to give renewed support to business, industry and agriculture. It should give opportunity to mobilize the gigantic strength of our country for recovery.

In attaching my signature to this extremely important legislation, I wish to pay tribute to the patriotism of the men in both houses of Congress who have given proof of their devotion to the welfare of their country, irrespective of political affiliation.

January 23, 1932

POWER BOARD HITS HOLDING COMPANIES

Declares the Public Interest Demands Government Supervise Big Utility Concerns.

FINDS CONTROL INTERLOCKS

Report Covering Year's Inquiry Says 10 'Top Companies' Are Dominant in Industry.

SERVICE CONTRACTS CITED

Regulation of the Arrangements Between Operating and Holding Corporations Is Recommended.

Special to THE NEW YORK TIMES.

WASHINGTON, July 17.—The public interest requires government control over the holding companies as well as over public utilities in the opinion of the Federal Power Commission which published today a preliminary report on the results of a year's study of this type of company.

The commission found that ten "top companies" control as many groups of power utility groups serving 12,437 communities with a population in excess of 42,000,000. These ten groups, including ninety-one companies, are said to control forty-eight major power projects under license to public utilities.

"The companies of these groups," the preliminary report, a "foreword" to a 150-page unpublished report, states, "distribute over 49,000,000,000 kilowatt hours of current of which 8,000,000,000 is received from the licensed plants already operating.

"The degree of community of interest between the ten groups is indicated by a table showing that nineteen directors were directors or officers in the top company or a subsidiary company of at least two groups, one director thus being connected with four groups. A dozen charts show graphically the ramifications of control in all its complexity for each group, although the extent of existing financial relationship was found to be beyond the scope of this inquiry."

Recommends Supervising Contracts.

The commission recommends that public control over holding companies include the "service organizations of these holding companies" with supervision of all contracts between holding companies and their operating companies, as well as "regulation of accounts with requirements providing specifically for the filing of financial and other reports on prescribed forms for full publicity."

The study of holding company relationships was undertaken primarily for the purpose of instructing the commission on how to deal best with power licensees and touched hardly at all on the financial relationships between companies, the foreword states.

However, the study disclosed, the commission said, "the dominance of the holding company in that portion of the power field covered by projects licensed under the Federal Water Power act."

"Even though the holding companies and their affiliated companies," the foreword says, "should grant to the Federal Power Commission free and unrestricted access to all of their records, the commission, in order to obtain information and data necessary for determining the cost of services furnished, or for passing upon the reasonableness and propriety of fees and charges for services, etc., or perhaps for passing upon the propriety of the services themselves, would, perforce, have to become involved in and consider matters and transactions not having direct relation to any licensee or to any licensed project.

As to Charges Made for Salaries.

"For example, certain service organizations charge licensees with the salaries of their employes at headquarters who perform services for the licensees. To this salary charge is added a percentage for 'office overhead,' said to be on an actual or approximate cost basis.

"To verify this overhead charge and to determine whether it represented a cost to the service organization properly chargeable against a certain licensee or a particular project would mean an audit of a large part of its accounts, a consideration of the items going to make up the total overhead cost, the allocation thereof among the departments of the service organization and the various operating and other companies to which services were furnished, &c.

"The commission would be confronted also with the fact that the holding companies, their service organizations and certain of their controlled and affiliated companies are not subject to regulation by any public agency, that they are not required to keep their accounts in any particular manner or under any prescribed rule, with the result that the correctness and propriety of the accounts themselves are subject to question."

The power commission found that an increasing amount of power is being transmitted across State boundaries, with 98 per cent of the power from one unnamed licensed power project entering into interstate commerce.

"In this investigation of the ownership and, control of its licensees," the report went on, "the commission has sought the control to the ultimate or top dominant company. It appears that in most instances the last company in the chain of control of the licensees to report is the company in which is centred the ownership and power of control of all the operating companies of the system. It is known, however, that in certain instances other companies may be superimposed upon these so-called top holding companies.

"It is to be noted that since the beginning of this study of the holding companies, as they affect the licensees under the Federal Water Power act, a rather kaleidoscopic change in the picture of the holding company plan is being brought about.

To Wait on House Inquiry.

"Also, during the time the study

was being prosecuted, the House of Representatives, under Resolution 59, Seventy-second Congress, first session, undertook an inquiry of a broader scope, which developed recommendations governing the entire scope of holding companies. In deference to that investigation, and for the other reasons stated, the commission has decided to await the result of the Congressional study and submit any further recommendations in the light of the additional information thus to be disclosed.

"In general, the companies cooperated heartily with the staff of the commission in the laborious assembling of the information desired. The issue of legal authority or statutory jurisdiction with regard to several of the items included in the questionnaire was not raised, and in only one instance was there a failure to receive a full return from the holding company controlling the operation of major projects.

"Therefore, one top company is omitted from all the tables, namely, the Associated Gas and Electric System which failed to make the requested return although its two operating companies holding licenses answered the questionnaire. This exception alike brings into contrast the cooperative spirit of the other top companies and proves the necessity for unquestioned authority being vested in some public agency."

July 18, 1932

TRADE GROUPS HAVE WIDE ACTIVITIES

By GEORGE H. COPELAND.

THE national industrial recovery bill, now being framed by Congress, which proposes Federal supervision over industrial production, prices, wages and hours of work, directs attention to the progress which business has already made toward self-regulation. Little by little it has learned the value of cooperation, and now the individual units of practically every important industry in the country are joined together for the exchange of vital information and the solving of common problems. The organizations which direct these activities are the trade associations.

The trade association is not engaged in the actual transaction of business for profit. It is, according to the American Trade Association Executives, "an organization of producers or distributers of a commodity or service upon a mutual basis for the purpose of promoting the business of their branch of industry and improving their service to the public through the compilation and distribution of information, the establishment of trade standards and the cooperative handling common to the production or distribution of the commodity or service with which they are concerned."

Development of Associations.

Probably the first trade association to be formed in the country was the Writing Paper Manufacturers Association, organized in 1861. With the growth of industry the associations multiplied until in 1925 the National Industrial Conference Board estimated that there were about 1,000 such groups in the country. In the boom days that followed, this number undoubtedly increased, with encouragement from Herbert Hoover as Secretary of Commerce, but after 1929 the withdrawal of members whose finances were depleted probably brought their number back near the 1925 figure.

Most trade associations are national in scope; a few are international. They deal with all sorts of business, from the manufacturing of macaroni or toys to wood turning and mining. Some typical associations, with their enrolment a few years ago, are: The American Petroleum Institute, 4,000; the Associated General Contractors, 2,080; the National Association of Builders Exchanges, 6,000; the American Iron and Steel Institute, 2,200; the National Association of Ice Industries, 1,700; the Motion Picture Theatre Owners of America, 8,000; the American Bankers Association, 20,000, and the Oil, Paint and Varnish Association, 1,400.

Certain trade associations which have tried to regulate their industry by cutting production and thus keeping prices up have at times run afoul of the law. Competition has always been the cornerstone of American business and our courts have always held that nothing must be done to prevent a free and open market. Common-law doctrines thus forbade restraint of trade, conspiracy to monopolize and unfair competition, and these were incorporated in the Sherman law.

A Fine Legal Question.

The line between legitimate regulation and restraint of trade has always been a fine one. In discussing trade agreements Justice Brandeis gave the test of legality as "whether the restraint imposed is such as merely regulates and perhaps thereby promotes competition, or whether it is such as may suppress or even destroy competition."

The collection of statistics is an important activity of trade associations. They may relate to production, quantity produced, shipments, sales, orders, stocks and employment. These statistics are spread abroad for members of the association, and for the public as well.

In many industries the development of uniform cost-accounting has been accomplished by trade associations. This assures all manufacturers in that business that others have included the same items in their costs, that there is a common understanding of overhead and cost records, control of raw materials, and so on.

It is estimated that, in normal years trade associations spend about $35,000,000 in industrial research. They also support several hundred fellowships in universities, and maintain about sixty research associates in the United States Bureau of Standards. Associations may maintain their own laboratories for research or they may cooperate with commercial laboratories.

Simplified practice—the collective effort of an industry to reduce waste in the production and distribution of its products, through eliminating unnecessary varieties in sizes, dimensions, grades or qualities—is a well-established trade-association activity, interest in it having been aroused out of the wartime contact with the War Industries Board. In a survey made in 1927 it was found that 243 associations had accepted sixty simplified-practice recommendations. This meant more economical manufacture, more efficient labor, less capital tied up, less overhead and increased turnover. American industry is saving, it is estimated, $300,000,000 a year by means of simplification alone.

Standardization in the mining, electrical, mechanical and other engineering fields has been achieved partly through trade-association activities. Efforts of the National Electrical Manufacturers Association, for example, resulted in a series of standards covering the manufacture, test and performance of all kinds of electrical generators and motors, electric tools and grinders, balance coils, transformers and other electric equipment.

Relations between business and the public have become more important each year. The trade associations have recognized this trend and have spent time and money to engender public confidence in business. They spent, in addition, about $10,000,000 a year on commercial advertising.

Building Up of a Market.

Certain industries run up against particular problems which can be solved only by concerted effort under the direction of trade associations. An example was that faced by the Associated Salmon Packers in 1926. For years the red varieties of salmon had preference in the market because the public knew no other kind. But more than half the entire pack each year is of the "pink" and "chum" (white) varieties of salmon. By advertising the prestige of pink salmon was advanced. A three months' campaign was carried, on at a cost of $200,000, featuring a contest for dishes prepared from pink salmon. Sales jumped 500 per cent.

The trade association has proved of great value to its members and to the public by doing away with trade abuses and unethical practices. Commercial arbitration has aided in this purpose, while some associations have expelled members who refused to arbitrate disputes.

Most trade associations have credit and insurance bureaus, which help one another to solve problems met in those fields. They have also been active in attempts to reduce industrial accidents and labor turnover, to encourage the training of workers and understudies and to develop teamwork and morale in industry.

May 21, 1933

ROOSEVELT SIGNS THE SECURITIES BILL

Special to THE NEW YORK TIMES.

WASHINGTON, May 27.—The administration Securities Bill, designed to protect the investing public by means of publicity concerning stock issues, was signed today by President Roosevelt.

Senators Fletcher and Robinson of Arkansas, Representative Rayburn of Texas, chairman of the Interstate and Foreign Commerce Committee, and officials of the Federal Trade Commission were grouped about the President when he affixed his signature early this afternoon. The pen he used was presented to Mr. Rayburn.

President Roosevelt, on signing the bill, hailed it as at last translating "some elementary standards of right and wrong into law."

In a statement he said:

"It gives me much satisfaction to sign the Rayburn-Fletcher Securities Bill, and I know I express national feeling in congratulating Congress on its passage. For this measure at last translates some elementary standards of right and wrong into law.

"Events have made it abundantly clear that the merchandising of securities is really traffic in the economic and social welfare of our people. Such traffic demands the utmost good faith and fair dealing on the part of those engaged in it.

"If the country is to flourish, capital must be invested in enterprise. But those who seek to draw upon other people's money must be wholly candid regarding the facts on which the investor's judgment is asked.

Bill Is "No Insurance."

"To that end this bill requires the publicity necessary for sound investment. It is, of course, no insurance against errors of judgment. That is the function of no government. It does give assurance, however, that, within the limits of its powers, the Federal Government will insist upon knowledge of the facts on which alone judgment can be based.

"The new law will also safeguard against the abuses of high-pressure salesmanship in security flotations. It will require full disclosure of all the private interests on the part of those who seek to sell securities to the public.

"The act is thus intended to correct some of the evils which have been so glaringly revealed in the private exploitation of the public's money. This law and its effective administration are steps in a program to restore some old-fashioned standards of rectitude. Without such an ethical foundation economic well-being cannot be achieved."

Machinery to Be Rushed.

Machinery to supervise the sale of securities will be ready to be set in motion when the law becomes effective ten days from today. The Federal Trade Commission announced that it expected to have formulated the rules and regulations and to have worked out forms for registration before the law became operative. Despite the short time, it was said, the commission believed that examinations of brokerage house statements could be concluded within the time set.

"This act," the commission said, "is probably the most important piece of legislation that has been passed by the present Congress.

"It is not an emergency measure but is a permanent addition to our regulatory legislation. It will bring together for the first time accurate and detailed information about the various concerns engaged in interstate commerce. It will make available to the public for the first time accurate information as to the operation and conduct of the business enterprises of the country.

"From the information required by this bill a great deal may be learned about business trends, and information may be obtained that will enable the prediction of the approach of economic depressions and the taking of steps to prevent them.

"The publicity of this information will undoubtedly exert a great stabilizing influence.

To Prevent "Exploitation."

"The basic policy of the act is that of informing investors of the facts concerning securities to be offered for sale in interstate and foreign commerce and providing protection against fraud and misrepresentation.

"It will be the aim and purpose of the Federal Trade Commission under the authority of the act to prevent further exploitation of the public by the sale of fraudulent and worthless securities through misrepresentation, to place adequate and true information before investors, and to protect honest enterprise seeking capital by honest representations against the competition afforded by securities offered through crooked promotion and misrepresentation.

"Statistics indicate that the sale of worthless securities through misrepresentation and fraud has amounted to the colossal sum of $25,000,000,000 during the last ten years. This means $250 for every man, woman and child in the United States."

Chairman March said the commission intended to administer the act so as to give purchasers of securities full and accurate information and at the same time interfere as little as possible with the legitimate financing of legitimate business.

The statement declared that the commission was fully aware of the magnitude and importance of the responsibility imposed upon it by the act.

Many Problems Expected.

"The commission," it added, "to a large extent is familiar with many of the problems that will be presented as a result of its investigations into blue sky activities. Mr. Huston Thompson, a former chairman of the Federal Trade Commission, was largely responsible for the draft of the bill as presented to Congress and had a large part in presenting the bill to the committees of both houses.

"The public should thoroughly understand that the commission is not authorized to pass in any sense upon the value or soundness of any security. Its sole function is to see that full and accurate information as to the security is made available to purchasers and the public, and that no fraud is practiced in connection with the sale of the security.

"Speculative securities may still be offered and the public is as free to buy them as ever.

"The commission's duty is to see that the security is truthfully presented to prospective purchasers. The fact that a description of the security and of the concern issuing the security is filed with the commission is in no sense and must not be regarded as an endorsement or approval of the security or the concern by the commission.

"The commission believes that a proper and efficient administration of the act will prevent a large part of the frauds that have heretofore been practiced upon the public through the sale of securities. It will be the commission's endeavor to so administer the act."

May 28, 1933

PRESIDENT STARTS RECOVERY PROGRAM, SIGNS BANK, RAIL AND INDUSTRY BILLS

ROOSEVELT HAILS GOAL

He Calls Recovery Act Most Sweeping Law in Nation's History

JOHNSON ADMINISTRATOR

Col. Sawyer Is Named to Direct Public Works, Eastman as Railway Coordinator.

'MILLION JOBS BY OCT. 1

Special to THE NEW YORK TIMES.

WASHINGTON, June 16.—Assuming unprecedented peacetime control over the nation's economic life, President Roosevelt placed in operation today his sweeping program for recovery from the depression.

Within two hours he signed acts of Congress giving him control over industry, power to coordinate the railroads, and authority to start work on a $3,300,000,000 public works program, and then began the active administration of these and other major measures.

In signing the National Industrial Recovery Act the President declared that it was "the most important and far-reaching legislation ever enacted by the American Congress," and said that it "represents a supreme effort to stabilize for all time the many factors which make for the prosperity of the nation and the preservation of American standards."

The Glass-Steagall Banking Reform Act, which the President described as "the second most important banking legislation enacted in the history of the country"; the long-disputed Independent Offices Act, including the veterans legislation; the Deficiency Act, the Taxation Act, and the Farm Credits Act received the President's signature during the day.

Administrators Are Named.

Turning to the administrative side of the industrial recovery program, the President appointed General Hugh S. Johnson, former soldier and manufacturer, as administrator of industry; made available $400,000,000 under the public works title for State roads, and allotted $238,000,000 to the Navy Department for laying down thirty-two new war vessels under the terms of the London treaty.

A special recovery board was named by Mr. Roosevelt to work with General Johnson. It consists of Secretary of Commerce Roper, chairman; Attorney General Cummings, Secretaries Wallace, Perkins and Ickes, Budget Director Douglas and Chairman March of the Federal Trade Commission.

General Johnson also will have an advisory council of business and labor leaders, the personnel of which has not yet been announced. Among those reported under consideration, however, are Myron C. Taylor, Alfred P. Sloan, Walter C. Teagle, Gerard Swope and Will Vereen.

Colonel Donald H. Sawyer was named temporary administrator of public works and was directed, with a special Cabinet board consisting of Secretary Ickes, chairman; Secretaries Wallace, Roper and Perkins, Assistant Secretary of the Treasury Robert, Colonel George R. Spaulding, and Budget Director Douglas, to submit to the President without delay the works on which construction can be undertaken promptly and to outline a program for future work.

Eastman Rail Coordinator.

Joseph B. Eastman, a member of the Interstate Commerce Commission, was appointed coordinator of railroads and was directed to begin his work at once. His most important immediate concern will be the railway wage scale negotiations, following which, savings by the reduction of duplicating facilities will be undertaken.

General Johnson conferred with the President late today and then left by airplane for Chicago to meet with leaders of the bituminous coal industry. He said that he would return late tomorrow night, and that he hoped to name a large group of men to aid him in perfecting trade codes. Most of the ten major industries, he said, had made rapid progress in this respect, and he hoped to see final agreements reached by the big trade associations within a very short time.

Expressing hope that unemployment would be decreased by at least 1,000,000 men by Oct. 1, President Roosevelt took an optimistic view of the industrial situation in a long statement on the Industrial Recovery Act. He called upon industry to cooperate by hiring more men to do existing work, at shortened working hours and a living wage.

Roosevelt Pledges Government Aid.

The President said that the act was a challenge to industry and labor, and pledged the protection of the government to both against unfair practices, if they would assist in raising price levels, increasing wages and reducing work hours. He promised that "this is not a law to foment discord, and it will not be administered as such."

While the anti-trust laws will be relaxed by the new legislation, the public will be protected against the abuses which led to their enactment, the President promised in his statement. He said that they would still be enforced against "monopolies that restrain trade and price fixing which allows inordinate profits or unfairly high prices."

The whole spirit of the act, he declared, would be to protect industry that cooperates completely and endeavors to raise prices justly, and at the same time keeps up wages and shortens the working hours so as to increase employment.

Happy as He Signs Enactments.

Mr. Roosevelt appeared to be in a happy frame of mind this morning as he affixed his signature to the new measures. The first be signed during the day was the Banking Reform Act, which was carried through perseveringly by Senator Glass of Virginia in the face of many obstacles.

As Senator Glass, accompanied by Senator Bulkley, Representative Steagall and others, appeared in the circular office of the President to be photographed during the ceremonies the President addressed Mr. Glass affectionately, saying:

"You old warrior! If it had not been for the veterans, Congress would have adjourned last Saturday and you would not have had your pet measure on the statute books."

Describing the measure as having had more lives than a cat, he declared it had been killed "fourteen times in this session," to be revived in the final days.

The President's Statement.

Senators Wagner and Robinson of Arkansas and Representatives Doughton and Ragon were present at the signing of the Industrial Recovery Act. President Roosevelt's statement follows:

History probably will record the National Industrial Recovery Act as the most important and far-reaching legislation ever enacted by the American Congress. It represents a supreme effort to stabilize for all time the many factors which make for the prosperity of the nation and the preservation of American standards.

Its goal is the assurance of a reasonable profit to industry and living wages for labor, with the elimination of the piratical methods and practices which have not only harassed honest business but also contributed to the ills of labor.

While we are engaged in establishing new foundations for business which ultimately should open a return to work for large numbers of men, it is our hope through the so-called public works section of the law to speedily initiate a program of public construction that should early reemploy additional hundreds of thousands of men.

Obviously, if this project is to succeed, it demands the whole-hearted cooperation of industry, labor and every citizen of the nation.

Many Pens as Souvenirs.

Senator Dill and Representative Rayburn attended the ceremonies incident to the signing of the Railroad Control Act. The President used many pens in attaching his signatures, and each of the sponsors left with one of them as a souvenir.

The last of the bills was signed at 12:05 P. M., following which the President devoted two hours to seeing departing members of Congress and in discussing patronage. The seekers of patronage for their constituents were told that jobs such as postmasterships and deputy internal revenue collectorships would be filled without delay.

Late in the afternoon, before calling his last conference with the press prior to going on his vacation, the President signed the Independent Offices Appropriation Bill containing the veterans' allotment plan which caused the controversy in the closing days of the session of Congress, the Deficiency Bill with its appropriation for the public works section of the Recovery Act and several other measures. Among the acts signed to wipe the slate clean were those on taxes and farm credits.

The Taxation Act continues for an additional year the current levies on gasoline and on electric current, but provides that after Sept. 1 the electric power tax will be levied on power companies instead of consumers. Total revenue from this act is expected to be $165,000,000.

The Farm Credit Act establishes a new organization for the purpose of centralizing farm credit extensions. The amount of money to be at the disposal of this agency is indefinite, as into it is to be paid the remainder of the revolving fund of the Federal Farm Board. Its resources are estimated at $175,000,000.

Fatigued by the Session.

The men who had sponsored the bills that became law today were happy, although most of them seemed tired and nerve-wracked by the turmoil through which they had passed in the closing days of Congress.

Senator Glass, who was co-author of the Federal Reserve Act, admitted that he had almost sent himself to the hospital in behalf of the banking reform legislation. He said that he would do it again, and declared he experienced a great thrill when the President signed it.

"The bank reforms provided in the act," Senator Glass said, "are almost as important to the banks and the public as the Federal Reserve Act itself. It supplements and strengthens the Federal Reserve Law."

The Glass-Steagall Act is directed toward a unified banking system, provides a limited deposit guarantee, requires divorcement of security affiliates from banks under government supervision, compels private bankers to give up either the deposit or security business, and requires stricter regulation of national banks.

Wagner Hails Recovery Act.

Senator Wagner of New York, who helped frame the Industrial Recovery Act and direct its passage, hailed that law as the greatest achievement of the administration in an economic and industrial way.

"It will bring us on the road to recovery," he said. "Ultimately, if it is intelligently administered, as I know it will be, it will bring this country out of the depression."

The most far-reaching of the administration's legislation, the Recovery Act gives the President, through administrators, wide power to promote the self-regulation of industry under Federal supervision as a means of curtailing overproduction, improving wages, shortening hours of labor and, thereby, increasing prices and employment. A bond issue of $3,300,000,000 is authorized to finance the construction of Federal, State and local public projects.

Representative Sam Rayburn of Texas, chairman of the House Interstate Commerce Committee, thought the Railroad Bill would go a long way toward affording financial aid to the carriers by permitting them to reduce expenses, under the supervision of the Federal coordinator, and through the repeal of the recapture clause.

"They will not be required to continue payments under the recapture clause, and will be returned about $14,000,000 in interest and payments already made," he said.

June 17, 1933

400 Industrial Concerns Raise Income To $558,000,000 From $69,000,000 in Year

Four hundred leading industrial corporations had last year an aggregate net income of $558,000,000, against only $69,000,000 in 1932, according to an analysis of annual statements by the Standard Statistics Company reported by The Associated Press.

As in the previous year, these companies, as a whole, paid out more in dividends than they earned, although disbursements to stockholders were reduced. The total deficit to surplus, after dividends, was only $16,000,000, compared with $646,000,000 in 1932. Total common and preferred dividends paid were $574,000,000, reduced from $715,000,000 in 1932.

A composite balance sheet for the 400 corporations shows total invested capital of $19,958,000,000 for 1932, and a net return on that capital of only 1.1 per cent, while for 1933 total invested capital was $19,455,000,000 and the return was 3.5 per cent.

Total cash and equivalents held in the corporate treasuries at the end of 1933 was $2,609,000,000, off 5.4 per cent from a year earlier, but inventories, valued at $3,364,000,000, were 13.3 per cent higher. Much of the reduction in cash went to finance the expanded inventory accounts, apparently.

Despite the fact that industry was forced to contend with new problems of code operations in the last half of 1933, says Standard Statistics Company, in analyzing the reports, almost every group succeeded in bettering its margin of profit for the year as a whole.

May 5, 1934

Business and Democracy

Our progressive friends tell us repeatedly that we should remember that the little business of a hundred years ago has become the big business of today. The advice is excellent. Industrial democracy was possible a hundred years ago because each man could own his own tools and work with them. Industrial autocracy, under a limited State supervision, is necessary today because we have big business. Very few men possess the qualities necessary to conduct a big business efficiently. Men with these qualities would not be elected by popular vote, because popular vote is sentimental. Business leaders must fight their way to the top and be selected by the survival-of-the-fittest method. They do not always make pleasant leaders, but in the long run they are better than the squawky kind that would be elected by popular vote. This is the age of big business and therefore it is the age of undemocratic business, whether it be conducted under capitalist, Fascist or Communist principles.—LLOYD M. CROSGRAVE, Muncie, Ind.

January 20, 1935

PRESIDENT HITS BACK AS CHAMBER REVOLTS

Strong Big Business Minority Stands By Roosevelt Despite Commerce Body's Break With New Deal

HOW 'PARTNERSHIP' DISSOLVED

By ARTHUR KROCK.

WASHINGTON, May 4.—The rather incongruous partnership between certain conservative business and banking groups and the New Deal was publicly dissolved this week, the mists of fear in which it was formed having been absorbed by the sunlight of recovery. A majority of the delegates of the Chamber of Commerce of the United States decided to go back to their economic home.

But, if the critical resolutions of the chamber speak for a majority of the employing classes (the President does not believe they do), Mr. Roosevelt still has an influential minority in the capital community behind him, and the new attitude of the chamber instantly brought from organized labor a pledge of firm support for the rest of the recovery program of the President now in Congress.

In the sense that most large enterprises in the field of industry are represented in the chamber membership, its majority's voice may properly be termed that of Big Business. But it speaks with authority for intermediate and small business as well. Certainly, with the National Association of Manufacturers and the American Bankers Association, the chamber mirrors the composite thought of a large section of employers and their bankers in this country. Therefore a review of the relations between these organizations and the government since March, 1933, may fairly be said to be a survey of the partnership movement between business and the administration since the President was inaugurated.

The Public Enemy Period.

As every one remembers, the tendency of capital as well as labor, finance and private citizenship in the dark times that surrounded the inauguration was to urge that unprecedented power over everything be placed in the hands of Mr. Roosevelt. Congress was urged to lend its authority over many functions of government. Criticism was frowned upon, and persons and newspapers expressing it were attacked as public enemies by many who had voted for Mr. Hoover and who, as late as November, 1932, had expressed distrust of the Democratic candidate.

In such an atmosphere, in May, the chamber held its 1933 convention. Representatives of industry who spoke were full of praise and hope for the President. The resolutions greedily swallowed the NRA, tolerated the AAA and were almost timid in proposing certain modifications of the Securities Act, then pending. The double budget—emergency and ordinary—came in for polite criticism, and there was uttered a gentle warning about monetary devaluation. But, on the whole, the partnership was going strong. The President had an ovation when he addressed the convention, and its officers, under Henry I. Harriman, were pledged to the policy of coc eration.

Doubts Assailed.

By the time for assemblage in May, 1934, the administration's banking and securities reform theories were beginning to disturb the chamber seriously, although the resolutions endorsed the President's silver policy, as then revealed, and refrained from any broad attack on his program. This time Mr. Roosevelt did not address the members, but he sent a friendly message, and Mr. Harriman was able to prevent the expression of any real unpleasantness.

This was the year of the Congressional elections, however, and in the campaign criticisms of the New Deal from the hustings helped to impel members of the chamber to demand a more aggressive policy from the directors. Accordingly, these met in September and publicly sought from the President a dated pledge to balance the budget and stabilize the dollar, though manifestly he was not in a position to do either. He resented the move and ignored it. The elections, which in the President's name gave the New Deal an unprecedented majority, directly sustained Mr. Roosevelt's attitude toward the directors of the Chamber.

Bankers' Olive Branch.

Meanwhile, in October, the ruling spirits of the American Bankers Association succeeded in growing in the financial community an olive branch acceptable to the White House. After much preliminary manoeuvring (which was kept secret from militant members who opposed the administration's banking policy) and several drafts, Jackson E. Reynolds of the First National Bank of New York, "a Morgan bank," framed a tender of peace which the President was willing to receive in person.

Mr. Reynolds told his brethren in Mr. Roosevelt's presence that no reasonable person could expect the dated pledges sought by the directors of the chamber in September. The President made a grateful response, asking bankers, business men and others for an "all-American recovery team," and he and the bankers were temporarily and officially at peace.

Having viewed this performance, and concluded from the elections of November that the President was boss of the nation until 1940, the guiding forces of the chamber decided again to surrender. They met in mid-November and published the statement that "the President's utterances encourage the belief he is receptive of suggestions for promotion of the common welfare." Mr. Harriman hailed the arrival of recovery and became a joint scout and mascot for the all-American team.

The team was never formed, however, and some members of the uncompleted squad quit as early as December, 1934. All through the periods of panic fear, growing anxiety, faint criticism, acute criticism, surrender and peace, the National Association of Manufacturers had been restless. Its membership spoke scornfully of the "pussyfooting and kowtowing" of the chamber at a joint business conference at White Sulphur Springs, dominated by the NAM. Secretary Ickes's interviews about spending 105 billions on work relief in twenty years had alarmed and angered many business representatives.

At this point, cool, wise and smooth, Owen D. Young appeared at White Sulphur and poured quantities of oil. He induced the conference to strike out all harshness. He changed the resolutions so that every possible concession to the administration was made. The President had said he welcomed constructive suggestions from all groups, and in that spirit the conference document was prepared.

Parting of the Ways.

But it opposed relief supervision by a political power and urged that private agencies conduct the dole. It deplored work relief. It called for a balanced budget in 1937; asked that social security legislation be deferred for longer study; that credit control be relinquished by the government; that the Securities Act of 1933 be modified; that, if work relief were put through, lower than the prevailing wage be paid.

The latter point the President accepted. But the others were irritating to him, as his entourage revealed when Judge Ames, of the Texas Company, a Southern Democrat of gentle mien, brought the resolutions to the White House. A secretary suggested that the paper be left with him. The President could not see Judge Ames that day, but if he would wait around, Mr. Roosevelt might find a few minutes the day following. Judge Ames left his paper and departed.

Immediately after publication of the resolutions of the conference, and the cool reception of Judge Ames, Secretary Ickes and Administrator Hopkins led an administration chorus of satire and attack on the document. The President answered a question at his press conference by saying with deliberate nonchalance he had "five or six" similar petitions and would try to read them all on Sunday.

The peace was over and hostility to the pending reform measures so spread among members of the chamber that Mr. Harriman was unable longer to hold a majority against sharp criticism. Informed of the situation, the President not only made no address; he did not send a message.

Partnership Ends.

The majority of the chamber expressed its long-pent up feelings about social security, the NRA, government control of trade associations, utilities and banking reforms, the AAA and the Wagner and other measures in the interest of organized labor. Mr. Harriman was succeeded by Mr. Sibley, who himself had thought when the convention began that the attacks would be fewer and more moderate. The partnership was severed.

But where before a defeated minority had nowhere to go, this time a defeated minority found a very excellent lodging. That was the White House. Headed by Mr. Harriman, Gerard Swope, Winthrop Aldrich and others, a very eminent industrial and financial group resolved itself into the Business Advisory and Planning Council of the Department of Commerce, called on the President and endorsed the objectives of his program.

Thus the record proclaims that a substantial section of very big business believes that advancing national recovery requires and can absorb the remainder of the New Deal reforms, with certain modifications, even though a majority is on record to the contrary. Like the Republicans in Congress, big business gives many votes to administration measures.

With a Congress majority, a powerful big business minority and unestimatable millions of people behind him, the President can be expected to continue to link recovery and reform until he has obtained all he can in 1935 from Congress and then let recovery have the field for the remainder of his term.

May 5, 1935

ALL NRA ENFORCEMENT IS ENDED BY PRESIDENT AS SUPREME COURT RULES ACT AND CODES VOID

COURT IS UNANIMOUS

President Cannot Have 'Roving Commission' to Make Laws by Code.

NO INTRASTATE WAGE PACT

Indirect Effect of an Activity on Interstate Commerce Is Held to Be Insufficient.

PARLEY AT WHITE HOUSE

AAA Officials Also Plunge Into Study of Effect of Opinion on Farm Legislation.

By ARTHUR KROCK.
Special to THE NEW YORK TIMES.

WASHINGTON, May 27.—By a unanimous decision in the Schechter poultry case the Supreme Court today held unconstitutional the National Industrial Recovery Act, due to expire by limitation on June 16, and, by voiding the 750 codes which are the heart of the National Recovery Administration and denying the right of Congress or its agents to fix wages and hours in intrastate trade activities, demolished the chief administrative recovery weapon of the New Deal.

Immediate cessation of NRA code enforcement was announced by Chairman Richberg of the National Industrial Recovery Board following a conference at the White House in which President Roosevelt, Attorney General Cummings, Solicitor General Reed and Mr. Richberg participated. Mr. Richberg coupled with his announcement a plea to employers not to scrap the achievements in the field of fair practice and labor relations which had flowed from the Recovery Act.

The court, speaking through the Chief Justice, who read the passages vehemently, once more declared that Congress cannot give to the President or to private persons what Justice Cardozo, in a separate assenting opinion, called "a roving commission" to make laws in the form of codes or otherwise. Congress must specify standards and list objectives and provide a definite range of action.

But even when Congress has done that, said the court, its delegation of authority cannot apply to those engaged in intrastate industry, which was defined as any not "directly" affecting the current or flow of interstate commerce. The court specifically included mining, agriculture and manufacture.

Hour and Wage Rules Collapse.

Justice Cardozo pointed out that the attempted regulation of wages and hours was "the bone and sinew of the codes," and that therefore by the decision of the court they "collapse utterly." Since industry directly affecting interstate commerce is too small a group on which to base the NRA recovery plan, the theory and practice of NRA were killed by the decision, even though Congress should rewrite the law.

Realizing this, Congressional leaders at once took steps to substitute for the fallen code system such interstate trade regulations as those contained in the Black Thirty-Hour Bill and the Guffey coal legislation, and such labor wage-bargaining as is provided in the Wagner bill.

Government attorneys had been optimistic about the Schechter case and to them the decision was a bombshell. Donald R. Richberg and Solicitor General Reed, who had defended NIRA, left the court room with downcast faces. The Attorney General in his office stopped chewing a ham sandwich. The argument between the House and Senate over the time extension of NIRA and the terms thereof was temporarily laid aside. At the headquarters of Triple-A, which is administering some of the codes, the opinions were studied to determine whether they foreshadow the doom of that recovery experiment also.

Conferences were held at the Department of Justice, and then the Attorney General, the Solicitor General and Mr. Richberg were summoned to a late afternoon conference at the White House—the first of many—to ascertain what could be salvaged in the brief time remaining between today and June 16.

Regret was heard on all sides that the administration had taken the advice of those, among whom Professor Felix Frankfurter is prominently mentioned, who counseled delay in testing the constitutionality of NIRA until it was too late to reform ranks before the June doomsday. The once-despised "chicken-killing" case had taken rank with McCulloch v. Maryland. General satisfaction was expressed that at last, in a grave matter, the court had been united in its opinion.

Foes in Congress Rejoice.

The many foes of NRA in Congress rejoiced. Senator Borah welcomed the new proclamation of the Constitution and Senator King "thanked God for the Supreme Court." Republicans pointed happily to what they called the vindication of Herbert Hoover's recent attacks on the recovery methods of the New Deal. At NRA headquarters officials and employes sat in gloom, wondering what is to become of them, and Washington landlords and restaurateurs, who have prospered from the influx of government workers, sadly examined their scales of prices.

Politicians noted with deep interest that on this same day the Supreme Court overthrew the Huey Long radicals who forced the Frazier-Lemke farm debt cancellation through Congress by declaring it unconstitutional, and reasserted the judicial independence of government commissions by holding that the President acted improperly in removing a Federal Trade Commissioner for causes not listed by Congress as bases of dismissal in the act creating the commission.

Labor was shocked, but rallied instantly behind the Black, Guffey and Wagner bills, determined to rescue some of its protections from the recent adverse decisions of the Supreme Court.

FACA Sends Up Cry for Help.

At FACA and the office of the special adviser to the President on foreign trade, as well as in other agencies set up by NIRA, the cry went to Congress, "Save us quickly or we sink." Simultaneously a band was forming in the Senate to let the hair go with the hide and, by obstruction and delay until June 16, to make of NIRA and all its works only a memory.

Conservatives in the administration recalled how they had opposed NIRA on two grounds when Senator Wagner, Raymond Moley and certain industrial groups proposed it: that economically from the viewpoint of recovery, it defeated its own ends by putting the cart before the horse in fixing higher wages and shorter hours before business had the increases to absorb their costs; and that the delegation of law-making to code authorities was unconstitutional. In this opposing group at the time were notably Secretary of State Hull and Lewis W. Douglas, former Director of the Budget.

The NIRB held a meeting. There was desultory discussion of what to do. Remedial legislation was proposed to meet the flaws discovered by the Supreme Court. Some one thought it might be well to press for a constitutional amendment. Then everybody agreed there was no use in talking until the White House conferences were concluded. The meeting broke up without any clear program. It reflected the devastation wrought by the accurate aim and propulsive force behind the judicial cannonade today.

Two Sections to the Opinion.

The unanimous opinion of the court—for the addendum by Justice Cardozo, with the concurrence of Justice Stone, was only an expansion of the theme on the point of intrastate wages and hours—was divided into two sections.

In the first the National Industrial Recovery Act was held invalid through the unconstitutionality of Section 3 on the ground that this section turned over actual law-making to individuals outside Congress without specifying conditions or setting metes and bounds. In the second section the court reiterated that the indirect effect of an industrial activity on interstate commerce does not bring it within the purview of the Federal Government; that the effect must be direct to validate Federal regulation.

At the outset of the opinion it was to be seen that the dictum of the Circuit Court of Appeals, in reversing the conviction of Schechters on wages and hours violations, had the attention of the Supreme Court. After reviewing the nature of the Schechter business, the opinion curtly remarked: "Defendants do not sell poultry in interstate commerce." The Supreme Court then devoted a thousand words or so to the history of the Live Poultry Code of Fair Competition and held in passing that "the requirement of 'straight-killing' (prescribing that a customer must take the run of the coop) was really one of 'straight selling.' "

The government, continued the court, had stressed the point that consideration of the code statutes "must be viewed in the light of the grave national crisis with which Congress was confronted." This is a tenable request, said the court, but the argument "cannot justify action which lies without the sphere of constitutional authority." As on previous occasions, the court pointed out that "extraordinary conditions do not create or enlarge constitutional power."

Holds Codes "Are Codes of Law."

The NIRA was not a device for voluntary effort, said the court. It did not merely offer privileges or immunities to trade groups, voluntary or otherwise. It was coercive law-making, for "the codes of fair competition which the statute attempts to authorize are codes of law." They are imposed both on those who approve and those who object to them and they carry penalties.

In the "hot oil" case, the court reminded the government it had recognized the need to adapt legislation to cover details of industrial activity with which Congress could not specifically deal. That Congress could lay down policies and leave to individuals the making of rules within these limits, and the determining of facts, the court agreed. But this recognition "cannot be allowed to obscure the limitations of the authority to delegate, if our constitutional system is to be maintained."

The NIRA case is distinct from the oil case, said the court, because in the former statute the subject of the prohibition—oil—was defined, and the only question was whether Congress had bounded the range of action delegated to the President. But in this case the question was whether Congress had adequately defined the subject itself from which the codes depended. The NIRA, from which flowed the codes of "fair competition," did not define what fair competition means. But the widest definition of that phrase in the law does not reach the objective of the codes. The very concept of NIRA took the codes far afield from that.

Trade Board Powers Defined.

In the law setting up the Federal Trade Commission, the expression 'unfair methods of competition" was carefully written into the statute as within the commission's purview, and an accepted judicial process of determination was set up.

The NRA dispenses with this procedure and the subject matter of review and action as well. The government, said the court, had repeatedly referred it to Title I of the NIRA for definitions. But justification for the codes was not to be found there. "Rather the purpose [of Section 3] is clearly disclosed to authorize new and controlling prohibitions through codes of laws which would embrace what the formulators would propose, and what the President would approve, or prescribe, as wise and beneficent measures for the government of trades and industries in order to bring about their rehabilitation, correction and development," according to the policy of Section 1.

There is no dispute that the goal of NIRA was national recovery, and that was the purpose of each code, including the one before the court. But, asked the Justices, can any one contend that Congress can delegate its authority to trade groups so that they may enact any laws they consider essential to the recovery of their trade? Do they become legislative bodies because they know intimately the details of their own business?

"Such a delegation of powers," wrote the court, "is unknown to our law and is utterly inconsistent with the constitutional prerogatives and duties of Congress * * * Congress cannot delegate legislative power to the President to exercise an unfettered discretion to make whatever laws he thinks may be needed or advisable for the rehabilitation and expansion of trade or industry."

Groups Could "Roam at Will."

What fetters were there in NIRA? asked the court. Trade groups must be truly representative. They must not promote or permit monopolies. But they may "roam at will," under Section 1 and make into law "what is really only a statement of opinion as to the general effect upon the promotion of trade or industry of a scheme of laws." And the President may impose his own conditions in addition.

The court cited with approval the statutes creating the Interstate Commerce Commission, the Communications Commission and the flexible tariff powers of the President as properly-devised delegations of power, and approved the methods by which the statutes are carried out. "But Section 3 * * * is without precedent. It supplied no standards for any trade, industry, or activity." It permits code-making to prescribe them. The discretion of the President is unfettered. It is "an unconstitutional delegation of legislative power."

This ended the first division of the opinion, and the remainder was devoted to a discussion of what activities affecting interstate commerce fall within the right of Congress to regulate. In the Schechter case, interstate transactions ended when the poultry was trucked to the Brooklyn slaughter-houses for local disposition. Facts not disputed repel the argument that the poultry was in a "current" or "flow" of interstate commerce and therefore within the regulatory power of Congress. The poultry came to "a permanent rest within the State."

There must, said the court, be a distinction between the direct and indirect effect of transactions on interstate commerce. Each case must be settled on the basis of the facts, but the principle is clear. For instance, the negligence of an intrastate railroad employe with a safety device used in interstate commerce has direct effect. But when effects are indirect "such transactions remain within the domain of State power." Otherwise the Federal Government through the commerce clause would control all the activities of the people and the States would have no authority, save by Federal sufferance.

The hours and wages of the Schechter employes, said the court, were imposed on persons with no direct relation to interstate commerce. The government argued that these conditions affect prices generally. "But the government proves too much." If it can regulate intrastate wages and hours because of their indirect effect on interstate commerce, "it would seem that a similar control might be exerted over other elements of cost, also affecting prices, such as the number of employes, rents, advertising, methods of doing business, &c."

Once more the court emphasized the dictum of the Minnesota moratorium decision. "It is not our province to consider the economic advantages or disadvantages of such a centralized system. It is sufficient to say that the Federal Constitution does not provide for it * * *. Without in any way disparaging this motive [to effect recovery] it is enough to say that the recuperative efforts of the Federal Government must be made in a manner consistent with the authority granted by the Constitution."

On both points, therefore, the court reversed the convictions of the Schechters.

Cardozo Amplifies Opinion.

Justice Cardozo in the amplifying opinion said that NIRA gave the President "a roving commission to inquire into evils and on discovery correct them." This, he and Justice Stone agreed with the rest of the court, was unconstitutional. But Justice Cardozo recalled that he had dissented from the "hot oil" decision because there, in his belief, "no roving commission" had been granted.

The two justices concurred that codes of fair competition would be lawful which sought to eliminate unfair methods of competition, "ascertained upon inquiry to prevail in one industry or another," if the President is told to inquire into and denounce such practices. But under the NIRA code conception, when a code includes "whatever ordinances may be desirable or helpful for the well-being or prosperity of the industry affected," its function is not merely negative but positive, and this is "delegation running riot." Such power cannot be transferred. "The licit and illicit sections [of NIRA] are so combined and welded as to be incapable of severance without destructive mutilation."

But even if the Poultry Code had been adopted by Congress and not the President, said Justices Cardozo and Stone, it would be void because the defendants' employes were engaged in intrastate activity, and there is no Congressional authority over those. Since wages and hours are the very "bone and sinew" of the NIRA plan, to take these from a code is to destroy it.

"There is no opportunity in such circumstances for the severance of the infected parts in the hope of saving the remainder," wrote Justice Cardozo. "A code collapses utterly with bone and sinew gone."

May 28, 1935

UTILITIES BILL MADE LAW

Roosevelt Aides in Congress Battle Watch Him Sign Measure.

VIRTUAL 'DEATH SENTENCE'

Will Break Up Most of Big Holding Company Networks Within Three Years.

INVESTOR GROUP 'TO FIGHT'

Special to THE NEW YORK TIMES.

WASHINGTON, Aug. 26.—The Utilities Bill, providing for the eventual elimination of holding companies except those essential to the operation of single integrated systems, became a law at 3:10 P. M. today when President Roosevelt signed it in the presence of those who led his fight for the bill through Congressional committees and on the floors of the House and Senate.

Final approval of the bill took place as the result of a breaking of a jam in Congress which only a week ago threatened to stifle the bill.

Newspaper correspondents were not permitted to witness the signing of the measure, but the President was quoted by those in his office as having remarked that this was the "biggest" bill he had ever signed.

A primary result of the measure will be elimination within three years of most of the great utility holding companies which now extend their operations through networks of operating companies. It will make impossible the future formation of an organization such as that built up by Samuel Insull.

Wheeler and Barkley at Signing.

Foremost among the smiling members of Congress who witnessed the signing of the act, and who received one of the souvenir pens distributed on such occasions, was Senator Wheeler. Beside him stood Senator Barkley, author of a compromise plan which resulted in acceptance by the House of a virtual "death sentence" provision after that body had declined repeatedly to agree to such a proposal.

The principal result of the compromise plan has been the delegation of authority to administrative officials to carry out the President's plan for the elimination of the medium-size holding companies rather than the elimination of them by fiat along with the quite large ones.

Also present at the ceremonies in the President's office were Senator Brown, Chairman Rayburn of the House Interstate and Foreign Commerce Committee; Dozier A. de Vane, Solicitor for the Federal Power Commission; Benjamin V. Cohen, General Counsel to the National Power Policy Commission, and Thomas G. Corcoran, counsel for the Reconstruction Finance Corporation, who with Mr. Cohen had a large part in shaping the bill.

Operations Are Restricted.

The act generally gives the Federal Government the same control over public utility holding companies as is exercised over operating companies by State authorities, and it requires Federal sanction for issuance of securities by holding companies, acquisition of properties and the handling of other types of business.

The term "death sentence," coined by the opposition, was applied to the provision that after three years holding companies must limit their operations to single integrated systems and business directly connected with the supply of power service to consumers. The only exception to this rule consists of discretionary authority granted to officials to exempt holding companies controlling a group of power systems, all in the same region, which may be too small to operate economically independently.

In any event holding companies beyond the second degree are prohibited, and all holding companies must distribute voting power "equitably" among stockholders.

Profits are forbidden in intra-system service and the Federal Power Commission received authority to regulate rates, facilities and business practices by utilities doing an interstate business.

Joseph P. Kennedy, chairman of the Securities and Exchange Commission, who would have to direct the registration of public utility holding companies and pass upon which ones must dissolve after 1938, refused to discuss rumors of his resignation. Mr. Kennedy denied, however, that he opposed the appointment of J. D. Ross, advocate of public ownership of utilities, as a member of the SEC.

Mr. Kennedy recalled that he had accepted his official position for one year, which has expired, and added that family considerations made him desirous of leaving Washington. The Utilities Act did not appreciably complicate his problem, he explained, since the question of dissolutions would not arise until 1938. Registration of the companies could be handled without much trouble and may be stopped entirely by injunction if companies throw the act into court.

Dr. H. S. Magill Predicts Fight.

The signing of the bill prompted a statement tonight by Dr. Hugh S. Magill, president of the American Federation of Utility Investors, predicting a continued fight against its operation by "the 10,000,000 investors in the stocks and bonds of American industries."

"Investors in the stocks and bonds of all companies, particularly investors in securities, are deeply disappointed by the passage, under tremendous pressure, of the utility bill with its hastily rewritten 'death sentence' clause," Dr. Magill said. "This action, taken by a tired, worn-out Congress in the closing hours of the session, at the demand of the President, and in utter disregard of the recommendations of the House committee that had carefully considered the bill for months, is one more example of autocratic dictatorship which seeks complete political control and bureaucratic domination of all industry.

Charges 'Confiscation.'

"The long, hard-fought battle in support of the rights of the investor, and against the ruthless destruction of investor-owned property, had been won. Three times the House voted down the 'death sentence.' Then, by a political coup, backed by the four billion dollar White House lobby fund, an amended bill was put over without any opportunity for consideration of its provisions.

"That this action is regarded by investors as an attack on all investor-owned and privately managed business is evidenced by the immediate decline in the market value of stocks and bonds amounting to hundreds of millions of dollars.

"If the President and those who helped him put over this piece of high-handed partisanship think they have succeeded in keeping this subject out of the next campaign, they are mistaken. The 10,000,000 investors in the stocks and bonds of American industries, comprising that great body of thrifty, industrious citizens who ask nothing more than the right to possess and enjoy the fruits of their labor and their savings, will continue to fight in defense of their constitutional rights and against greedy political control and unconstitutional confiscation of private property."

August 27, 1935

U.S. STEEL PROGRAM SEEN AS TAX SAVER

In announcing plans for the consolidation of several of its operating subsidiaries, the United States Steel Corporation gave impetus last week to the movement for simplification of corporate structures that was begun more than a year ago, according to industrial leaders in Wall Street.

This trend toward simplification, it was said, is designed not only to make possible greater operating efficiency but also to enable huge concerns to avoid at least a part of the heavy taxation that is inherent in the administration's "anti-bigness" and anti-holding company policies.

Already several laws have been enacted which hit huge holding companies, such as United States Steel, and industrialists state that they expect further efforts will be made in Washington to break up such companies or to tax them severely. Among the laws affecting holding companies that have been approved in the last two years are one taxing inter-company dividends and one prohibiting holding companies from deducting, in their consolidated tax returns, losses of one operating subsidiary from the profits of another.

These laws have impelled the big industrial companies to consider merging their operating subsidiaries and have raised also the question in some of them whether it would not be desirable to change the status of the parent company from that of a holding unit to an operating unit.

Steel and Motor Set-Up Differ.

The United States Steel Corporation's set-up is that of a holding company, controlling, by ownership of stock, numerous operating subsidiary corporations. This structure contrasts with that of the General Motors Corporation, which is essentially an operating company, owning directly the plants and assets of its principal manufacturing divisions which are not corporations themselves.

A clue to the difference between the set-up of the United States Steel Corporation and that of General Motors is found in the designation of heads of their component parts. The former gives the title of "president" to the head of each operating subsidiary; General Motors, on the other hand, calls the heads of the Chevrolet division, Fisher Body division and other operating departments, general managers.

The set-up of United States Steel, and similarly constituted companies, executives believe, made them vulnerable to the various tax measures aimed at holding companies. This situation is being corrected by United States Steel through the amalgamation of Illinois Steel and Carnegie Steel, and by the projected consolidation of other subsidiaries. Not only will these steps place the corporation in a better position with respect to tax legislation, it is said, but it will enable it to present a closely welded front to any effort to break down large corporations into their original component parts.

Principal Units of U. S. Steel.

The United States Steel Corporation does not operate directly any iron or steel works. Its principal subsidiaries, through which it indirectly carries on its operations, include the following companies:

Carnegie Steel, Illinois Steel, American Steel and Wire, Cyclone Fence, Standard Fence, American Sheet and Tin Plate, National Tube, Oil Well Supply, Tennessee Coal, Iron and Railroad, Columbia Steel, American Bridge, Canadian Bridge, Ltd.; Minnesota Steel, Lorain Steel, Scully Steel Products, United States Steel Products, Federal Shipbuilding and Dry Dock, Universal-Atlas Cement, H. C. Frick Coke, Duluth, Missabe & Northern Railway and leased lines; Elgin, Joliet & Eastern Railway and leased lines; Bessemer & Lake Erie Railroad, and Pittsburgh Steamship Company.

Moves taken toward unification of this vast industrial empire include the amalgamation of Carnegie and Illinois Steel, through the formation of the Carnegie-Illinois Steel Corporation. Steps are being taken also to weld more closely the component units of each important operating subsidiary. Thus it is reported that American Sheet and Tin Plate plans to merge with Sharon Tin Plate.

One of the first large industrial units to rationalize its structure recently was the United States Rubber Company. Of its sixty-two wholly owned subsidiaries at the end of 1933, sixteen were eliminated in 1934, and fifteen more were in process of dissolution early this year.

September 22, 1935

THE FUNCTION OF GOVERNMENT

The New Deal View

By HAROLD L. ICKES.
Federal Administrator of Public Works.

The debate between the spokesmen of the administration and the spokesmen of business grows sharper. The issue involved will be a leading one in the campaign now opening. What should be the relationship between government and business? There is wide divergence between the two views, as the accompanying articles reveal.

GOVERNMENT has never been an end in itself, but only a means to an end, that end being the highest possible welfare of the people. The government of the United States was organized and is maintained not for the particular and exclusive benefit of any one class, but for self-protection from foes from without and from exploitation from within by the selfish and the ruthless.

Unfortunately, government can be subtly perverted from the purposes for which it was established. Unless we are constantly on guard, we are likely to discover, to our shocked surprise, that as the result of penetration from within the people are left with only the indicia of power, while the actual power rests in the hands of that very class which government was established to restrain.

A race of pioneers experienced in exploiting nature, we turned, when the physical frontiers no longer existed, to the industrial exploitation of human labor—men, women and children. Then the industrial Simon Legrees, fearing that the economic and social system they were erecting might some day tumble about their ears, set out to secure control of government. Putting a sufficient number of their friends in the seats of power, they discovered ways of circumventing the democratic process.

Shouting the slogan "less government in business" these rugged individualists finally took complete possession of the United States Government. We were in a new economic era. Then came the falling of the skies in September of 1929. Our common purpose under the leadership which the nation chose for itself in 1932 has been to repair the dikes in order to hold back the floods that were threatening to overwhelm us.

This administration has been accused of starting out in March of 1933 with preconceived, dogmatic conceptions about the superiority of public over private enterprise. Nothing could be more untrue. We have been bespattered alternatively with Communist and Fascist mud, we have been charged with desiring to regiment all and everything. Let us begin by disclosing the record.

Ever since Alexander Hamilton wrote his report on manufactures, the government of the United States has recognized that it had duties to perform in connection with private industry. But the line which separates the sphere of private business from public activity has never been easy to draw.

We are still often challenged as to our attitude toward private business. From the beginning we offered no opposition to any private efforts to reinvigorate the economic life of the country, but we were confronted with the confessed helplessness of private business. Our intervention was demanded by these apostles of private enterprise.

In response to their demand, the National Recovery Administration was set to work. Business asked us to remove the "unnecessary restraints of the Sherman Anti-Trust Laws," and pleaded with us to allow it to impose rules and regulations for the conduct of private business. Such price-fixing and production-control regulations as found their way into the codes got there almost exclusively at the demand of business men themselves. The disappointing results of NRA cannot be laid at the door of the government; the responsibility lies with business. The government failed only to the extent to which it misjudged the ability of business to govern itself.

* * *

DURING the past twelve months a legend has grown up, and has been repeated so often that its authors are beginning to believe it, that recovery had started "naturally" in June of 1932, and that it has been retarded by the "artificial" actions of the New Deal. I should like to remark that if recovery had started in 1932 it would not have been a result of natural causes. The Republican administration under Mr. Hoover did not put its faith in any theoretical "natural" recovery. His administration encroached directly on the sphere of private business, although accomplishing little good. He spent millions of dollars in attempts to maintain the prices of agricultural products, he tried to inflate credit by open-market operations with government securities and finally he organized the Reconstruction Finance Corporation with the express object of preventing the depression from taking its natural course in so far as this was leading to the ruin of a number of favored individuals and corporations.

No responsible thinker continues to believe in the natural recovery of our modern economic system; direct governmental action of one sort or another is demanded on all sides. The doctors disagree not about the necessity for medicine but about the type of remedy which is necessary.

Every few days some self-appointed dictator of private business pretends to lay down the terms on which the government of the United States should be carried on. We deny that such spokesmen have the authority to which they lay claim. The term "business" includes not only the trust magnates, the Stock Exchange speculators, but thousands of hard-working Americans dotted across the continent.

These self-elected spokesmen demand that we balance the budget. That is the goal which this administration has set itself and which it is now approaching. But what of the national balance sheet showing national expenditure and national income? This is more nearly balanced today than it has been for six years, and that is the true measure of the prosperity of our people.

Associated Press.
Harold L. Ickes.

"A nation, like an individual, must live within its income," say these would-be economists. Save for a comparatively few exceptions, our people have no incomes if they do no work. In the same way a nation's income is measured by the work it does. Our efforts have been devoted to restoring the national income from the catastrophic level to which it fell in 1932. A recent report issued by the Department of Commerce shows our success. The national income produced is at last within striking distance of the income paid out.

This rising national income means that without additional taxes, governmental receipts will rise, while at the same time governmental expenditure on relief will fall as unemployment falls. This road of rising receipts from an increased national income is the only one that leads to a balanced budget and it is the road we are on.

* * *

TODAY, as on the day it went into office, this administration seeks less, not more, regimentation. It is only the sophist who interprets every new law as an addition to regimentation. Most of our liberties derive not from the absence but from the presence of laws, and this is as true of the liberties of business men as it is of our personal liberties as citizens.

Throughout our history our government has acknowledged the duty to concern itself with business. Hundreds of printed pages of hearings before Senate and House committees bear witness to the fact that business men are continually asking the government to interfere with the conditions under which they operate.

The extension of governmental activity has been a characteristic of American growth. Fire departments, highway systems, education services, public health and sanitation all tend to become public enterprises, and the regulation of private utilities is accepted. Governmental activity in one form or another has always been called in when private enterprise has failed to meet the need. That is still the test.

This administration is not driven by dogma to encroach on private business. But while we are not fatalistic believers in the virtues of State action neither are we under the illusion that rugged individualist enterprise is sacred. It must meet the historic test. Does it provide for our national needs? Is it producing the goods?

* * *

WHAT of the future? Is our vision so limited and so uninspired that we see nothing ahead except a return to those conditions that we called prosperous prior to 1929? Or shall we, chastened in spirit by our narrow escape from a social and economic cataclysm that seemed to engulf all of us in a common disaster, really set to work to build on this continent such a nation as the humane and socially minded of our Founding Fathers saw in their dreams—a nation consisting not of a numerically small class holding most of the wealth of the country, with 60 per cent or more lacking adequate food and clothing and shelter, but a nation which, except for that mere handful of misfits and derelicts that are constantly being sloughed off every social group, shall be composed of citizens who are economically free because they possess the means of supplying themselves with those things that make life worth while and who are therefore truly politically free?

May we have the courage and the wisdom, we the people of the United States, to avoid the shoals and the rending reefs that imperil us and continue on the true course that was set for us by those wide-visioned men of heroic mold who launched the good ship America. Just as they dared to defy the power and might of Great Britain in order to set a people free, so let us prove ourselves to be their not unworthy descendants by daring in our turn to save and improve what they wrought for us.

February 2, 1936

The Business View

By HARPER SIBLEY,
President Chamber of Commerce of the United States.

BUSINESS is not something which stands apart. It is not a particular group or class which can be segregated or isolated as a detached segment of society. On the contrary, it is the sum total of all those activities involved in the production of goods and commodities and the performance of services which have to do with the material side of human existence. As such it is the concern not only of corporations or industrialists but of all those who work for a living, whether employer or wage-earner, producer or consumer, farmer or manufacturer. It is the source of tangible wealth in which we all hope to share.

Considered from this viewpoint, business has shown and is showing a surprising vitality. It is slowly bringing order out of the confusion of depression. Under the impetus of individual planning, and in spite of serious handicaps, the parts of production, distribution and construction are falling back into place. While attention has been fixed upon unemployment the fact has been generally overlooked that even in the depths of depression business provided employment for more than 40,000,000 workers. Feeling its responsibility, it carried on its payrolls several million who were not then needed to maintain its decreased rate of production.

Industry is now showing signs of gathering momentum. Needs long suppressed are clamoring for fulfillment. Following the usual course of the business cycle a period of low and hesitant production has been succeeded by a more insistent demand for goods of all kinds, and the wheels are turning more rapidly as the volume of production is stepped up.

There is much reason to believe that this recovery is due to natural rather than to artificial causes. The patient, if we may so regard business, is responding to its inherent powers of recuperation, rather than to the feverish stimulus of government spending. But more rapid recovery is checked by too much medicine. Business manages to meet the more immediate demands made upon it, but it is not yet allowed to exert its potential energies in building for the future and in pushing to higher levels that condition of well-being which we term the standard of living.

When times are normal approximately one-half of industrial employment is absorbed in the production of goods for immediate needs, while an equal number of workers is required for the construction of the producing plant and equipment itself. This second group builds for the future rather than for the present. It is in this field that employment still lags and the retarding effects of depression most persistently linger.

* * *

IT goes without saying that one cannot build for the future when there is no way of anticipating with a reasonable degree of certainty what that future will be—what risks must be run and what obstacles must be overcome. Ways have been devised of guarding against natural risks, which can be reduced to an actuarial basis. There is no way of guarding against artificial risks created by political action. As long as they may be encountered capital will be reluctant to invest, industry will hesitate to expand and buying of durable goods will be governed by unavoidable present needs.

Economists have made much of the fact that government has stepped out of the field of administration into the field of business management. The destinies of business are accordingly shaped not only by the natural succession of events but in increasing measure by political decree. National policy bears more directly upon the conduct of business than heretofore. Individual activities involved in trade and industry fall to a much greater extent under the shadow of legislation.

This adds to the uncertainties which business faces, makes long-range planning more difficult, halts investment and retards the industrial momentum. An indeterminate or vague public policy, coupled with governmental experimenting in the economic field, intensifies the retarding influences.

Stability and definiteness in public policy, therefore, may be regarded as constituting one of the most important conditions for recovery. Artificially created uncertainties, whether legislative or administrative in origin, should be reduced to an unavoidable minimum consistent with the protection of the public interest and the achievement of legitimate governmental ends.

If business is to bear the burden of creating employment and meeting the expenses of government, it has the right to as clear an understanding as possible of the difficulties with which it must contend, the risks it must take and the limitations to be imposed upon it. If it is to go forward, it must be able to chart the road ahead which it is to follow.

As it is, business is now forced to deal with a number of indeterminate political factors. Some of these are:

Public expenditures in excess of public revenues, foreshadowing a substantial but indefinite increase in taxation.

The use of the taxing power as a method of enforcing compulsory control of business activities.

The employment of regulatory power, not primarily to prevent clearly defined abuses, but to determine business policy.

The expenditures of tax receipts to launch or finance enterprises in competition with private business.

The use of Federal power to manage private relationships between employers and employes within the States.

An unstable monetary base which may be changed by administrative action.

The decisions of the Supreme Court of the United States reaffirming constitutional limitations upon the exercise of legislative powers by Congress have been reassuring. They have brought into clearer perspective the conditions under which business may be carried on. But they set only broad limits to public policy. Within the sphere of legislation and administrative action many serious uncertainties are still to be encountered.

Power delegated to administrative agencies lacks definition. Business management, which must take the initiative in industrial enterprise, finds itself in the uncomfortable predicament of not knowing how much it is to be taxed to sustain public spending, what wages it may be called upon to pay employes, to what extent assets and liabilities may be affected by monetary changes and whether government will enter into competition with it.

* * *

IN more positive form, therefore, some of the needs of business are:

The curtailment of public spending and the balancing of the budget at the earliest possible moment.

The adoption of an equitable and stable system of taxation and the restriction of the use of the taxing power to the raising of general revenue.

The establishment of a sound and stable monetary base as soon as circumstances will permit.

The limitation of administrative authority and the clearer definition of the purposes to which it is to be directed.

The assurance that experimentation in governmental projects is not to be continued as a permanent policy.

The withdrawal of government from competition with private enterprise.

The first approach to confidence would be the abandonment of those generalizations which distort the truth and lead to prejudice and animosity. Business is not all greedy and rapacious, any more than public officials are all unscrupulous politicians. Business men are as much concerned with the advancement of the public welfare as are government servants. That is particularly true today when the well-being of the largest of corporations runs parallel with the well-being of the public upon which it relies to purchase its goods or services. Neither large nor small business enterprise can prosper in an impoverished country.

Good government and good business must face in the same direction! There is nothing to be gained and much may be lost by their working at cross purposes. Together they can solve the very grave problems which still stand in the way of recovery!

February 2, 1936

CONGRESS PASSES CHAIN STORE BILL

Anti-PriceDiscriminationMeasure Is Sent to President for Signature.

REBATES ARE FORBIDDEN

Federal Trade Commission Is Empowered to Fix Maximum Point for Discounts.

WASHINGTON, June 18 (AP).—Far-reaching legislation intended to protect the independent merchant from price advantages allowed large competitors was passed tonight by Congress and sent to President Roosevelt.

Congressional action was completed when the Senate agreed to a conference report, already approved by the House, on the Robinson-Patman bill to tighten the anti-trust laws.

Primarily the bill is designed to prevent unfair price discriminations through the use of false discounts and rebates for services not actually performed.

It would permit the Federal Trade Commission to fix the point beyond which discounts for quantity purchases could not go. The commission would be instructed to prevent discounts for purchases so large that competitors would be unable to match them, thus creating monopoly.

A business man, feeling he had been the victim of unfair price discrimination, would be able to take his case into Federal Court in his own State instead of coming to Washington and working through the Federal Trade Commission.

Exemptions from the operation of the law would be granted in the handling of perishable foods and in other emergencies.

June 19, 1936

Text of Roosevelt Address

Special to THE NEW YORK TIMES.

PHILADELPHIA, June 27.—The text of President Roosevelt's speech of acceptance was as follows:

Senator Robinson, members of the Democratic convention, my friends:

We meet at a time of great moment to the future of the nation. It is an occasion to be dedicated to the simple and sincere expression of an attitude toward problems, the determination of which will profoundly affect America.

I come not only as the leader of a party—not only as a candidate for high office, but as one upon whom many critical hours have imposed and still impose a grave responsibility.

For the sympathy, help and confidence with which Americans have sustained me in my task I am grateful. For their loyalty I salute the members of our great party, in and out of official life in every part of the Union. I salute those of other parties, especially those in the Congress who on so many occasions put partisanship aside. I thank the Governors of the several States, their Legislatures, their State and local officials who participated unselfishly and regardless of party in our efforts to achieve recovery and destroy abuses. Above all, I thank the millions of Americans who have borne disaster bravely and have dared to smile through the storm.

Declares Nation Has Conquered Fear

America will not forget these recent years—will not forget that the rescue was not a mere party task—it was the concern of all of us. In our strength we rose together, rallied our energies together, applied the old rules of common sense, and together survived.

In those days we feared fear. That was why we fought fear. And today, my friends, we have won against the most dangerous of our foes—we have conquered fear.

But I cannot, with candor, tell you that all is well with the world. Clouds of suspicion, tides of ill-will and intolerance gather darkly in many places. In our own land we enjoy, indeed, a fullness of life greater than that of most nations. But the rush of modern civilization itself has raised for us new difficulties, new problems which must be solved if we are to preserve to the United States the political and economic freedom for which Washington and Jefferson planned and fought.

Philadelphia is a good city in which to write American history. This is fitting ground on which to reaffirm the faith of our fathers; to pledge ourselves to restore to the people a wider freedom—to give to 1936 as the founders gave to 1776—an American way of life.

'Economic Royalists' Carve New Dynasties

The very word freedom, in itself and of necessity, suggests freedom from some restraining power. In 1776, we sought freedom from the tyranny of a political autocracy—from the eighteenth century royalists who held special privileges from the crown. It was to perpetuate their privilege that they governed without the consent of the governed; that they denied the right of free assembly and free speech; that they restricted the worship of God; that they put the average man's property and the average man's life in pawn to the mercenaries of dynastic power—that they regimented the people.

And so it was to win freedom from the tyranny of political autocracy that the American Revolution was fought. That victory gave the business of governing into the hands of the average man, who won the right with his neighbors to make and order his own destiny through his own government. Political tyranny was wiped out at Philadelphia on July 4, 1776.

Since that struggle, however, man's inventive genius released new forces in our land which reordered the lives of our people. The age of machinery, of railroads, of steam and electricity; the telegraph and the radio; mass production, mass distribution—all of these combined to bring forward a new civilization and with it a new problem for those who would remain free.

For out of this modern civilization economic royalists carved new dynasties. New kingdoms were built upon concentration of control over material things. Through new uses of corporations, banks and securities, new machinery of industry and agriculture, of labor and capital—all undreamed of by the fathers—the whole structure of modern life was impressed into this royal service.

Sees a New Despotism, New Mercenaries

There was no place among this royalty for our many thousands of small business men and merchants who sought to make a worthy use of the American system of initiative and profit. They were no more free than the worker or the farmer. Even honest and progressive-minded men of wealth, aware of their obligation to their generation, could never know just where they fitted into this dynastic scheme of things.

It was natural and perhaps human that the privileged princes of these new economic dynasties, thirsting for power, reached out for control over government itself. They created a new despotism and wrapped it in the robes of legal sanction. In its service, new mercenaries sought to regiment the people, their labor and their properties. And as a result the average man once more confronts the problem that faced the Minute Man.

The hours men and women worked, the wages they received, the conditions of their labor—these had passed beyond the control of the people, and were imposed by this new industrial dictatorship. The savings of the average family, the capital of the small business man, the investments set aside for old age—other people's money—these were tools which the new economic royalty used to dig itself in.

Says Liberty Requires a Decent Living

Those who tilled the soil no longer reaped the rewards which were their right. The small measure of their gains was decreed by men in distant cities.

Throughout the nation, opportunity was limited by monopoly. Individual initiative was crushed in the cogs of a great machine. The field open for free business was more and more restricted. Private enterprise became too private. It became privileged enterprise, not free enterprise.

An old English judge once said: "Necessitous men are not free men." Liberty requires opportunity to make a living—a living decent according to the standard of the time, a living which gives man not only enough to live by, but something to live for.

For too many of us the political equality we once had won was meaningless in the face of economic inequality. A small group had concentrated into their own hands an almost complete control over other people's property, other people's money, other people's labor—other people's lives. For too many of us life was no longer free; liberty no longer real; men could no longer follow the pursuit of happiness.

Against economic tyranny such as this the citizen could only appeal to the organized power of government. The collapse of 1929 showed up the despotism for what it was. The election of 1932 was the people's mandate to end it. Under that mandate it is being ended.

As to the Vote and 'Economic Slavery'

The royalists of the economic order have conceded that political freedom was the business of the government, but they have maintained that economic slavery was nobody's business. They granted that the government could protect the citizen in his right to vote but they denied that the government could do anything to protect the citizen in his right to work and live.

Today we stand committed to the proposition that freedom is no half-and-half affair. If the average citizen is guaranteed equal opportunity in the polling place, he must have equal opportunity in the market place.

The economic royalists complain that we seek to overthrow the institutions of America. What they really complain of is that we seek to take away their power. Our allegiance to American institutions requires the overthrow of this kind of power. In vain they seek to hide behind the flag and the Constitution. In their blindness they forget what the flag and the Constitution stand for. Now, as always, the flag and the Constitution stand for democracy, not tyranny; for freedom, not subjection, and against a dictatorship by mob rule and the overprivileged alike.

The brave and clear platform adopted by this convention, to which I heartily subscribe, sets forth that government in a modern civilization has certain inescapable obligations to its citizens, among which are protection of the family and the home, the establishment of a democracy of opportunity, and aid to those overtaken by disaster.

But the resolute enemy within our gates is ever ready to beat down our words unless in greater courage we will fight for them.

For more than three years we have fought for them. This convention in every word and deed has pledged that that fight will go on.

The defeats and victories of these years have given to us as a people a new understanding of our government and of ourselves. Never since the early days of the New England town meeting have the affairs of government been so widely discussed and so clearly appreciated. It has been brought home to us that the only effective guide for the safety of this most worldly of worlds is moral principle.

We do not see faith, hope and charity as unattainable ideals, but we use them as stout supports of a nation fighting the fight for freedom in a modern civilization.

Faith—In the soundness of democracy in the midst of dictatorships.

Hope—Renewed because we know so well the progress we have made.

Charity—In the true spirit of that grand old word. For charity literally translated from the original means love, the love that understands, that does not merely share the wealth of the giver, but in true sympathy and wisdom helps men to help themselves.

We seek not merely to make government a mechanical implement, but to give it the vibrant personal character that is the embodiment of human charity.

We are poor indeed if this nation cannot afford to lift from every recess of American life the dread fear of the unemployed that they are not needed in the world. We cannot afford to accumulate a deficit in the books of human fortitude.

In the place of the palace of privilege we seek to build a temple out of faith and hope and charity.

It is a sobering thing to be a servant of this great cause. We try in our daily work to remember that the cause belongs not to us but to the people. The standard is not in the hands of you and me alone. It is carried by America. We seek daily to profit from experience, to learn to do better as our task proceeds.

Governments can err—Presidents do make mistakes, but the immortal Dante tells us that divine justice weighs the sins of the cold-blooded and the sins of the warm-hearted in different scales.

Better the occasional faults of a government that lives in a spirit of charity than the consistent omissions of a government frozen in the ice of its own indifference.

There is a mysterious cycle in human events. To some generations much is given. Of others much is expected. This generation of Americans has a rendezvous with destiny.

In this world of ours in other lands, there are some people who, in times past, have lived and fought for freedom, and seem to have grown too weary to carry on the fight. They have sold their heritage of freedom for the illusion of a living. They have yielded their democracy.

I believe in my heart that only our success can stir their ancient hope. They begin to know that here in America we are waging a great war. It is not alone a war against want and destitution and economic demoralization. It is a war for the survival of democracy. We are fighting to save a great and precious form of government for ourselves and for the world.

I accept the commission you have tendered me. I join with you. I am enlisted for the duration of the war.

June 28, 1936

INDUSTRY GIVES UP FIGHT ON NEW DEAL; TO AID UNEMPLOYED

Manufacturers Association to Cooperate With Government in Relieving the Idle.

CHESTER SOUNDS KEYNOTE

Advises Leaders Meeting Here to Back Federal Agencies for Social Progress.

MOULTON CITES SOLUTION

Sees Expansion of Production Absorbing Jobless—Weir for Human Approach.

Fight by Industry Ended

Leading industrialists who have been severe critics of the New Deal called for a constructive program by industry to cooperate in solving unemployment and other social problems growing out of the depression and in seeking means to prevent or alleviate future crises at the opening sessions yesterday of the Congress of American Industry, the forty-first annual convention of the National Association of Manufacturers, at the Waldorf-Astoria Hotel.

The gathering was the largest in the history of the association. About 1,800 persons attended the annual dinner held last night in the grand ballroom of the hotel. The convention will end with morning and afternoon sessions and a luncheon today.

The keynote of the convention, as expressed in the opening address of Colby M. Chester, chairman of the General Foods Corporation and president of the association, was one of cooperation with the government in social and economic progress instead of the bitter attacks against the Roosevelt administration which have characterized the conventions of the association in the last few years.

Weir Stresses Human Problems

Speaking at the dinner last night, E. T. Weir, chairman of the National Steel Corporation, said that industry should undertake the solution of human problems arising out of the depression because it was best equipped to do so. It is up to industrial leaders today, he went on, to "develop industry so that its efficiency as an exchange will equal its efficiency as a maker of goods, and thereby improve industry's social function as they have already improved its technological function."

Lewis H. Brown, president of the Johns-Manville Corporation, also a speaker at the dinner, advocated "a wider appreciation and understanding of the social responsibilities of business" on the part of business men. He said that Americans want "work, more money, still more leisure, security against unemployment now and against poverty in old age, and more and better goods at lower prices." It was the duty of business and industry to help supply those wants, he asserted.

Mr. Chester opened the convention yesterday morning with an address in which he put forward a proposed twelve-point program acknowledging industry's obligations to the public. He recommended that industry join in the creation of a "National Depression Study Committee" to analyze the causes of the depression in an effort to eliminate or minimize business cycles. He urged industry to "absorb all the unemployed possible" and to "bend every effort of science and management to create still more jobs and more of the comforts of life for the American people."

Employment Figures High

Mr. Chester revealed that employment among members of the association was 106 per cent of 1929 figures instead of 90 to 95 per cent as generally estimated. He said this estimate was based on a canvass of firms employing 1,500,000 persons or one-sixth of the workers in manufacturing.

At the luncheon meeting Dr. Harold G. Moulton, president of the Brookings Institution, said that expansion of production and not a shorter working week was the cure for unemployment. Dr. Moulton predicted that eight or nine million more men could be put to work by a program of increased production, especially in the heavy industries.

Both Dr. Moulton and Mr. Chester opposed an arbitrary thirty-hour week as likely to impede recovery. Following the keynote set by Mr. Chester, various other speakers at the morning and afternoon sessions urged constructive efforts by industry to help solve the country's social problems.

Nearly 2,000 men and women attended last night's dinner. They represented industrial organizations in all parts of the country. The two balconies as well as the main floor of the ballroom were crowded to capacity. The dais was arranged with five rows of tables, at which sat nearly 100 of the most prominent American business and industrial leaders. All were introduced by Mr. Chester to the audience at the beginning of the speech-making, which was broadcast over a national hook-up by NBC.

In his speech at the dinner last night, Mr. Weir asserted that the public's state of mind would continue to have an unfavorable effect upon business until it was changed.

Urged to Drop Resentments

"Mere resentment on the part of business will not change it," he said. "It presents a practical problem. It should be handled in a practical manner—which means action and words, not just words.

"Several steps suggest themselves. First, whatever is wrong in the present actions and policies of industry, industry should be the first to recognize and correct. Second, whatever is right in industrial action and policy should be retained and defended against all odds. Third, within industry's limits and in accordance with sound principles, industrial leadership should now attempt to constructively influence human conditions surrounding production. Fourth, industry should keep the public fully informed of its actions and policies. It should speak constructively.

"This attack," he continued, "would be conducted by thorough research and by the methods of the workshop—which certainly would hold more hope of success than naive attempts to bring Utopia by the writing of books or the passage of laws.

"Industry is more cohesive than other groups. It intermeshes with more divisions of our economic system than any other group. Its policies and actions directly and immediately affect the great majority of our people. Its leaders, with their responsibility to employes, stockholders and consumers, are already trained to reconcile diverse interests, to act in broad spheres, and to aim for ultimate rather than immediate objectives. It commands the resources and the manpower to undertake a vast project. Its plants are the best laboratory for the study of the human and economic problems under discussion. If industry united on any constructive program, it would inevitably encourage emulation and cooperation in other groups.

"As a fundamental it should be accepted that the primary function of industry must continue to be the increase of total wealth through increase in the volume and quality and decrease in the cost of goods.

Warns of Unsound Gains

"Another objective should be control of the processes which increase real income. Of course, real income increases only as the volume of goods increases. But the volume of goods is regulated ultimately by the demand for them. Demand can be increased not only by increase in the total national income, but also by distribution of the increase through the whole population. Increases that are gained by certain groups at the expense of the entire population add nothing to total buying power and aggravate economic troubles. Similarly, wage increases or investment returns that are paid solely through price increases are only apparent gains which add nothing to buying power and lead first to inflated values, then again to depression.

"It is probable that work on this problem will indicate that special attention should be given to low-income groups. This would have human value because these groups are most in need. It would have economic value because any increase of income to these groups would be largely and quickly converted into increased demands for goods, increased production and increased total wealth.

"Hand in hand with the problem of increasing real income will go the problem of retaining the increase. The effect of even greatly increased income would be nullified if the income were to be stopped or reduced and the savings from it wiped out by the extremes of uncontrolled economic fluctuations. This problem, of course, is largely the problem of unemployment—which must be a major objective in any program of industry.

"Industry should spare no effort to make it clearly understood that the aims of industry and the aims of the great body of people are mutual—not opposed.

"At present we have the paradoxical situation of industry going to any lengths to give the public complete information about its products, while it makes little effort to give information concerning the policies and conditions surrounding the making of those products. Thus we have the equally paradoxical situation of the public accepting without question anything that a manufacturer says about his product and doubting many of the things he says about himself or his methods."

Service Seen as Business Aim

Mr. Brown said that the demands of the American people for a higher standard of living constituted "a challenge and a new opportunity for service to the nation."

"Sometimes," he went on, "we forget that the sole purpose of business is service. Profits must not be the end of business, but merely a measure of a service that has been well rendered."

If private business is permitted to function unhampered, he said, the country can anticipate "a new era of abundance such as would have been undreamed of only a few years ago."

He urged leaders of business and industry to "find out what your customers want and deliver it to them."

"Prove to them," he continued, "that the American system of private enterprise can deliver more for less than any system of social economics the world has yet seen. Make your employes and stockholders realize they are partners in this enterprise. Sell these ideas as well as products to them and to your customers. Make them proud of its accomplishments—proud to be a part of the American system—happy in helping to build the bigger theatre. That is your task. It must be done."

Wages cannot be any higher than is economically possible, said Mr. Brown, adding that industry wanted to pay as much as possible because high wages result in increased purchasing power which in turn means more business. Real wages in industry in the past years, he said, have increased steadily not only in dollars, but also as a portion of the national income and "they will continue to do so as the result of the free functioning of our American economic system."

Backs Minimum Wage Laws

He urged support of State minimum wage laws to make it easier to adjust them to local conditions and to wipe out sweat shops which, he said, existed only in a few industries in a few States and could be more quickly abolished by State than by national legislation. He predicted that the five-day week would come about naturally.

He said that steadily increasing employment will bring a decrease in relief loads. If there is a prospect of a balanced budget, cooperation by management and labor "discussing questions of mutual interest rather than grievances, greater utilization of horse power to make possible higher wages and shorter hours, stabilization of the internal price structure on a basis of fair balance between producing and consuming groups which would follow an international currency stabilization, and opening of capital markets which will encourage development of new industries to absorb the technological unemployment of older ones," he foresaw a further development of mass production and a "real economy of abundance" for the American people.

He said there would then be a fulfillment of "our economic philosophy of more value for less money and a gradual increase in the real purchasing power of our citizens."

Mr. Brown said that industry would do its share in paying the cost of unemployment relief, but that it asked that "the cost of production shall not be burdened with an undue proportion of such costs, as this reacts against the general welfare." He said that industry wanted a "pay-as-you-go" system for old-age pensions for all citizens, not merely factory workers, with the costs borne by general taxation on the basis of ability to pay. He urged an end to child labor.

He advocated modification of the surplus and capital gains taxes and amendment of the income tax regulations so that money spent for capital assets, "thus providing jobs," be reasonably exempted. He favored "governmental protection of the investor against dishonest financial mismanagement, but a free opportunity for capital to obtain legitimate investment in productive enterprise."

In his address yesterday morning Mr. Chester said that industry should make its studies of the causes of depression available to the government "to the end that another period of business disruption and consequent human suffering may be eliminated or at least mitigated.

Study of Depression Urged

"Industry," he added, "cannot just sit back and enjoy the fruits of prosperity. We must understand better what has been happening since 1929. Now that the course of depression lies behind us, lending itself in its entirety to analysis, it is the job for industry, general business and all affected sectors of our economic life to join in creating a national depression study committee."

He urged that the natural processes of recovery should now be allowed to operate and warned that this would be interrupted by any such arbitrary legislation as the thirty-hour week.

"We cannot get more by producing less," he said. "We cannot get more by dividing the same amount of work. Multiplying products, creating more things—that is the American formula for prosperity."

Mr. Chester put his twelve points of industry's public responsibility in the following form:

"1. Industry must accept its responsibility for the national welfare as being an even higher duty than the successful operation of private business.

"2. Industry must continue to fulfill its obligations to the public in making better goods at lower costs, thus raising the standard of living and keeping the door of personal opportunity open.

"3. Put every possible employable in manufacturing industry back to work.

"4. Keep its own house in order, exposing its policies at all times to public scrutiny.

"5. Stand four-square against monopoly.

"6. By its actions engender growing confidence on the part of workers.

"7. Invite increasing public understanding of industry by telling the facts.

"8. See that workers, management and investor, according to their contribution, share fairly in the proceeds of manufacturing.

"9. Help to create economic security for all, preserving as well the opportunity for the individual to attain his own greater security.

"10. Zealously live up to its responsibilities and insist that all other factors of our economic life, including labor organizations, be made equally responsible.

"11. Make its cooperation available to government in a constructive manner at all times.

"12. Join other business groups in studying the depression in order to avoid or minimize another one."

Average Wage Not Cut

Mr. Chester said that industry had kept its word not to cut wages or increase hours after the NRA was declared unconstitutional.

"Business gains since NRA went out have been among the most pronounced in history," he continued. "The record shows that on the average there were no wage reductions.

"The average weekly earnings, which mean more than the hourly rate to the worker, have increased 15 per cent. Under the NRA the high point of employment in all occupations was 85.9 per cent of the 1929 figure. Today the gainfully employed in all occupations is 92.8 per cent of 1929.

"It is evident that if the average company today is employing more men than it did before the depression, the only possible explanation for a smaller total employment is that less companies are now in business. And this is actually the case.

"Full and increasing employment will be stimulated by the better flow of capital into development of necessary new industries. Since total employment is so closely related to the number of employing companies, these figures emphasize the need for sufficient reserves to see our factories through bad times."

Arthur Kudner, advertising man, said that business faced the job of "selling itself to the country."

"In this task," he went on, "it will be well to remember that business is less in a battle than in a courtship. The object of the courtship is to win the fickle public's favor.

"You will do better as a lover if you exhibit charm, good humor, tolerance, gallantry, thoughtfulness, daring and romance than if you exhibit stubbornness, pomposity, fatuousness, bad temper and fault-finding.

"So let your personality, if you would beat your rival, be more in the guise of Clark Gable, say, than of Scrooge. In other words, 'say it with flowers,' and not with spinach. Above all, say it! Say what business honestly has to say in its own behalf. Nowadays the rôle of the strong, silent man is of doubtful virtue, so rare is the discrimination which can distinguish between being silent from simply being dumb."

At the afternoon session Charles R. Hook, president of the American Rolling Mill Company, and vice president of the association, said that much of the labor trouble in industry could be averted if employers and employes exchanged information in a spirit of cooperation. He asserted that business men should "take the mystery out of business," and explain just why they could not raise wages or improve working conditions if such changes were impossible. He added that one of the greatest problems confronting industry was to help provide good housing for the masses, especially in the field of houses selling at $2,500 to $5,000 each.

Outlook Viewed as Rosy

Walter D. Fuller, president of the Curtis Publishing Company, said that American business men faced a future brighter than anything in the past if they took full advantage of their opportunities to let the public know and understand industry and management.

"Looking at our 127 million fellow-Americans from their viewpoint," he added, "not from ours, are we doing a good job? It's the way they think of us that counts, not what we think or what we say. There are plenty of illustrations of where the public's thumbs are up. I'm sorry to say there are other places where the thumbs are definitely down. Wages that are not fair, hours that are too long, bad working conditions, unreasonable supervision are things for us to correct. It's our job to so conduct ourselves and our industries that thumbs are up for all of us and then, when and where we know we are right, let's shout it from the housetops. It isn't the American way to 'hide our light under a bushel' and when we are right let's be sure this American public knows about it.

"Our publicity must be honest and sincere and well done for it has got to penetrate inside the little private world that is each one of us. If it doesn't get inside it won't last. And then in this publicity let's be sure we look at things from the other fellow's viewpoint. Look at it from the angle of the one-third of our population who earn their living by common labor, or the 15 per cent in agriculture, or the 27 per cent in skilled labor, or the 25 per cent in executive and white-collar jobs.

"The immediate job we have, as I see it, is about like this: Unity of our associations and of industries toward a common objective. Coordinated effort on the part of all of us to see that our industries are worthy of the respect we want America to feel toward them. Cooperative effort to carry convincingly to this American public and to its leaders the story of American industry, its problems and its accomplishments."

December 10, 1936

69 CONCERNS NET $5,000,000 AND UP

They Earned Nearly a Third of All Corporate Income in U. S. in 1933, Study Shows

Sixty-nine corporations with net incomes of $5,000,000 or more in 1933 received nearly a third of the total income of all corporations in the country, according to a report made public yesterday by the Twentieth Century Fund, Inc.

Corporations with assets of $50,000,000 or more in that year received 36 per cent of all corporate profits, the report disclosed, and those with assets of $1,000,000 or more received 79 per cent of the total.

The report showed also that in 1933 there were 375 corporations, excluding financial corporations, that owned 56.2 per cent of the country's total corporate wealth.

At the other end of the scale, according to the report, were 211,586 corporations, or 54.5 per cent of the total number, with assets of less than $50,000 each and owning only 1.4 per cent of the total corporate. assets.

Of corporations with assets of $50,000,000 or more, all but forty-nine were engaged in manufacturing, transportation and other public utility operations and finance. Large corporations, the report indicated, were relatively less predominant in agriculture, mining, construction, trade and service industries.

"It must not be assumed," the report said, "that the prevalence of large corporations in an industry indicates the extent of control, if any, which these corporations are able to exert over prices, wages, output or trade practices in the industry.

"Moreover, size has a different significance in different industries. In the public utility and transportation fields, which are to a considerable extent under public regulation, it has a very different meaning from what it has in manufacturing, where problems of competition and monopoly are of pressing importance. Public utilities are monopolies by design, while the creation of larger railroad units has been the deliberate aim of Federal legislation."

Officials of the fund pointed out that while the number of corporations earning profits and also the aggregate of profits had probably increased since 1933, the degree of concentration of assets and of profits was probably approximately the same.

The figures made public by the fund were taken from a report on "big business" in the United States that the organization has been preparing for two years and that will be made public soon.

January 25, 1937

GIANTS OF BUSINESS UNCERTAIN RISKS

20th Century Fund Reports on Study of 200 Big Concerns of the Early 1900s

SIZE NO INDEX OF PROFITS

While Some Trusts Yielded Rich Returns to Investors, Others Caused Losses

A two-year factual study of big business has convinced the Twentieth Century Fund that mere size is not synonymous with immense profits, the fund announced yesterday.

An analysis of the earnings of the huge trusts of the early Ninteen Hundreds, which were popularly supposed to have reaped swollen profits, has disclosed, according to the fund's report, that the big corporations were uncertain profit-makers.

Some of the trusts yielded rich returns and others heavy losses to investors, the study shows. The first installment of the report shows that ninety-three large industrial corporations, each with a capitalization of $10,000,000 or more, organized during the trust movement prior to 1904, were included in the analysis.

"For only thirty-four of these corporations, however," the report says, "was information available on stated capital and earnings, as well as on dividends and stock prices.

Range of Average Earnings

"For these thirty-four corporations, the average ratio of net earnings to stated capital (bonds, stocks and surplus) over a period varying from seven to fourteen years for the separate companies ranged from 1.6 to 12.3 per cent.

"The best results for the thirty-four companies as a whole were in 1902, 1906 and 1907, in each of which years about 7.25 per cent was earned on total capitalization.

"On their common stock issues, nine of the thirty-four companies paid no dividends for periods ranging up to fourteen years. * * * The average dividend paid by the thirty-four companies was 2.7 per cent on the par value of their common stock.

"If a supplementary list of fifty-nine large industrial corporations (for which data on earnings or capitalization were lacking) is added to the thirty-four * * * the ninety-three corporations, as a whole, paid common stock dividends between 1900 and 1914 averaging 4.3 per cent, with twenty-four paying nothing.

"The usual rate promised on the preferred stock of the seventy-three companies that had preferred stock outstanding was 7 per cent. Only thirty-nine of the companies, however, paid at the promised rate, including some that postponed their payments or paid in scrip. The average rate actually paid was 5.3 per cent.

"An investor who in 1900 bought 100 shares of each of the ninety-three companies at the average price of the year would have paid about $499,000. In 1914 his investment would have been worth approximately $704,000."

Cites Failure of Big Concerns

The report cites sixteen large corporations that failed before 1914 and concludes that "the majority of large corporations existing between 1900 and 1903 had not been profitable up to 1914 for the investors in common stock."

Passing on to the period from 1909 to 1924 the report discusses 200 corporations that in 1909, a year of normal business, had the greatest amount of stocks and bonds outstanding.

"Of the 46 railroads in the list of 200," the report says, "14 dropped out before the end of 1924. Of these, 12 went into receivership.

"Of the 55 utilities included among the 200, 28 disappeared from the roster before the end of 1924.

"Of 99 industrials included in the list of 200 * * * 47 dropped out before the end of 1924.

"Of the entire 99 industrials not more than 74 were successful enough to make their common stocks good investments. In 40 instances, however, the common stock rose more than 100 per cent in value. Only about 120 of the 200 giant corporations of 1909 proved profitable for the investors in their common stocks over the following fifteen-year period, but 48 of them were very profitable. It is likely, however, that the capital lost in the unsuccessful stocks amounted to a larger sum than the capital gains and dividends received from the successful ones."

June 15, 1937

SHOWS BIG BUSINESS SURVIVED DEPRESSION

Survey Made by Twentieth Century Fund Reveals Little Fellow Suffered More

The two-year survey of American business profits made by the Twentieth Century Fund discloses that big business survived the depression better than did the "little fellow," the organization announced yesterday. Sheer size, however, was not responsible for this, according to the findings reported.

Chief structural differences between the two categories of companies, the Fund says, are that big business borrows comparatively less money than does smaller business, and that the money big business does owe is largely in the form of fixed debts which fall due at stated times; the small business owes money in the form of notes and accounts payable, which are subject to call by creditors.

The bigger the business, the more stable its set-up becomes, according to a tabulation made by the fund, showing a steady progression in the decrease of percentage of floating debt to all debt, and in the increase of percentage of fixed debt to total debt, as the companies increase in size. There is also a decreasing tendency in percentage of borrowed capital to total capitalization as the corporations increased in size.

"On the whole," the survey says, "the corporations with assets of more than $500,000 get a greater proportion of their capital from stockholders and a smaller proportion from lenders than do the smaller ones. On this score, the larger corporations are 'safer' than the smaller ones."

June 18, 1937

ROOSEVELT SCORES BUT SIGNS PRICE ACT

President Hits at Use of Rider, Hoping Bill Will Not Lift Prices to Consumers

WASHINGTON, Aug. 18 (AP).—President Roosevelt scolded Congress today for what he termed its "vicious" action in tacking a price-bolstering rider on an essential tax bill.

Nevertheless, he signed the legislation, expressing hope that the rider known as the Tydings-Miller Price Maintenance Bill would not boost prices to consumers as much as some of his advisers feared. He pointed out that to kill the Price Bill he would have had to veto the tax measure, carrying funds for the District of Columbia. The country, he said, will "recognize the unfairness" of placing any President in such a position.

Backers of the Tydings-Miller measure said its purpose was to eliminate price-slashing of nationally advertised products—cosmetics and other drug store goods, for example. One of the sponsors, Representative Miller (D.-Ark.), said it would help stop "predatory price-cutting as a weapon of monopolistic large distributors to crush small business men."

The measure would permit manufacturers throughout most of the country to contract for minimum retail prices on their goods. It effectuates State "fair trade acts" and exempts them from Federal anti-trust laws. Such acts are now in force in forty-two States—all except Delaware, Mississippi, Missouri, Alabama, New Hampshire and Texas.

The State acts make lawful contracts between manufacturers and distributors whereby retail prices are set up for trade-mark or identified merchandise sold in open competition with other merchandise of the same general class.

Early in the session Mr. Roosevelt wrote Vice President Garner that he thought the legislation unwise. He said it would tend to raise prices at a time when the cost of living was advancing too rapidly.

Attacks Rider System

Mr. Roosevelt said he hesitated to approve the measure because it "weakens the anti-trust laws." In signing it he expressed the hope "that future sessions of the Congress of the United States will forego the practice of attaching unrelated riders to important and specific bills."

His statement said in part:

"This is the first instance during my term of office that this vicious practice of attaching unrelated riders to tax or appropriations bills has occurred."

The President said that during discussion in the Senate "a wholly unrelated amendment pertaining to existing anti-trust laws in so far as they affect retail sales" was attached.

August 19, 1937

DISSENT BY BLACK HITS CORPORATIONS

WASHINGTON, Jan. 31 (AP).—Justice Black urged today that the Supreme Court abandon a fifty-two-year-old interpretation of the Constitution giving corporations the protection of the Fourteenth Amendment.

The amendment provides that no State may "deprive any person of life, liberty or property without due process of law."

The court has long held that "person" means corporations as well as individuals. Mr. Black suggested that this had wrongly subjected State laws regulating corporations to "censorship of the United States courts." He expressed his views in dissenting from the opinion of seven of his colleagues that California may not tax premiums received by the Connecticut General Life Insurance Company from other insurance companies doing business in California.

Urges Overruling of Precedent

"A constitutional interpretation that is wrong should not stand," Mr. Black said. "I believe this court should now overrule previous decisions which interpreted the Fourteenth Amendment to include corporations.

"The States did not adopt the amendment with knowledge of its sweeping meaning under its present construction.

"'No section of the amendment gave notice to the people that, if adopted, it would subject every State law and municipal ordinance affecting corporations (and all administrative options under them) to censorship of the United States courts.

"No word in all this amendment gave any hint that its adoption would deprive the States of their long recognized power to regulate corporations."

February 1, 1938

ROOSEVELT ASKS INQUIRY ON MONOPOLY; SAYS PRIVATE POWER LEADS TO FASCISM

LEGAL CURB SOUGHT

President Would End Practices Which He Says Menace Democracy

STUDY TO PRECEDE LAWS

Only Bank Holding Unit Control Is Urged This Session —Borah Hails Aims

By FELIX BELAIR Jr.

Special to THE NEW YORK TIMES.

WASHINGTON, April 29.—President Roosevelt sent his long-awaited message on monopolies to Congress today. In it he called for "a thorough study of the concentration of economic power in American industry and the effect of that concentration upon the decline of competition," and an extensive investigation by Congress directed toward remedial legislation.

The President recommended that the study be conducted by the Federal Trade Commission, Department of Justice and the Federal Securities and Exchange Commission. For this he asked $500,000. And he requested $200,000 more for the Department of Justice "to provide for the proper and fair enforcement of the existing anti-trust laws."

There is a growing "concentration of private power without equal in history" in the country today, Mr. Roosevelt asserted, and he warned that this power, when its strength exceeded that of the government, was "fascism."

Program Is Presented

"The power of a few," he declared, "to manage the economic life of the nation must be diffused among the many or transferred to the public and its democratically responsible government."

The investigation by Congress would embrace a seven-point program designed to bring laws for breaking up price-fixing and other monopolistic practices, which, he said, restricted competition and threatened both political democracy and free enterprises for profit. Democracy and free enterprise, he added, should operate for the protection of each other.

At the same time, President Roosevelt declared that he had no intention of starting any ill-considered campaign of "trust-busting" which lacked proper consideration for economic results. It was his main purpose, he said, "to stop the progress of collectivism in business and turn business back to the democratic competitive order."

Would Curb Bank Holding Units

He limited his recommendations for action during the present session of Congress, except for the two appropriations, to the field of bank holding companies. Legislation was proposed to control their operations, prevent their acquisition of any more banks or establishment of new branches by holding company controlled institutions and make it illegal for bank holding companies to borrow from or sell stock to a subsidiary or affiliated company.

The President referred to "unhappy events abroad" as having retaught Americans two simple truths about the liberty of a democratic people:

"1. Liberty of democracy is not safe if the people tolerate the growth of private power to a point where it becomes stronger than their democratic state itself. That, in its essence, is fascism—ownership of government by an individual, by a group, or by any other controlling private power.

"2. The liberty of a democracy is not safe if its business system does not provide employment and produce and distribute goods in such a way as to sustain an acceptable standard of living. Both lessons hit home."

Subjects for Investigation

The subjects suggested for investigation and ultimate action by Congress and the President's observations on each were as follows:

Improvement of anti-trust procedure: Anti-trust laws should be revised to make them "susceptible for practical enforcement" by placing the burden of proof of innocence on those charged with violations. Such practices as identical bids, uniform price increases, price leadership and other specified signs of rigidities would be prima facie evidence of violation.

Mergers and interlocking directorates: Provision of effective methods for breaking up interlocking directorates and more rigid scrutiny by the Federal Trade and Security and Exchange Commissions of corporate mergers, consolidations and acquisitions than is now authorized by the Clayton act.

Financial control: Enactment of legislation directing financial institutions to serve the interests of independent business and restrictions against abuses promotive of concentrated power over American industry. In this connection investment trusts should be brought under strict supervision.

Bank holding companies: Legislation should be enacted providing for ultimate separation of banks from holding company ownership or control.

Trade associations: Provision for supervision and effective publicity of trade association activities, with a clarification of their legitimate spheres of activity to enable them to combat unfair competitive practices and prevent interference with legitimate competitive methods.

Patent laws: Amendment of existing laws to prevent use of patents to suppress inventions and create industrial monopolies, with provision for the encouragement of so-called open patent pools.

Tax Corrections: Modification of existing tax laws to encourage competitive enterprise, with retention of the undistributed profits tax in principle both to prevent further concentration of economic power and encourage distribution of dividends for reinvestment in a free market. Also graduate corporate income tax so as to make business bigness demonstrate its superior efficiency.

Bureau of Economics Urged

The President proposed that a Bureau of Industrial Economics be created to do for business what the Bureau of Agricultural Economics now does for farmers, by keeping the business community constantly advised on supply and demand conditions.

The broad objectives set forth in the President's message received an enthusiastic reception from Senators Borah and O'Mahoney, sponsors of the Federal Licensing Bill, although the former expressed misgivings as to the advisability of the lengthy investigation.

"I have no objection to the investigation proposed, in view of the fact that it will be very difficult to legislate before next session," said Senator Borah.

"The great fear I have is that the investigation will string along and finally reach the dust of the upper shelf in the form of ten or twenty volumes which few will ever consult. We know now that monopoly exists in this country; that it is undermining our whole economic and social structure.

"But both of the old parties have for years adopted the policy of procrastination; thus actually betraying the interests of the people, until we are right now in the midst of this long-continued depression paying for this criminal delay.

Borah for Limiting Inquiry

"We ought certainly to be ready by next session to act.

"The President's statement of facts leaves really only one question for study — that is how to deal with the subject.

"If the investigation is confined to the question of remedy and the form of legislation, all very well and good."

Senator O'Mahoney said:

"I welcome the message as the beginning of a positive Administration program to meet the greatest problem of our day—the domination of the economic life of the nation by concentrated wealth, and I shall cooperate in every possible way to secure immediate Congressional authorization for the proposed study.

"The result of these studies will, I am confident, only serve to strengthen the position of Senator Borah and myself that a national law defining the powers, duties and responsibilities of all corporations engaged in interstate and foreign commerce is essential."

April 30, 1938

CALLS BIG CONCERNS COMPETITION AIDS

Brookings Report Says They Foster Useful Policies Rather Than Harmful Monopoly

PICTURES WIDE BENEFITS

Struggle Between 'Big Three' in Autos Cited as Showing High Mark of Economy

WASHINGTON, July 13 (AP).—A Brookings Institution report contended today that giant corporations had fostered "useful competition" rather than harmful monopoly.

"The persistent dissolution of large corporations," it said, "would bring us to the point where we had not the power to make the industrial advances which would progressively lower prices. 'Pure competition' is not the path to economic progress in an industrial age."

Other conclusions contained in the report were:

Even if a concern has a monopoly of a product, it is likely to meet keen competition from companies whose products, though different, are almost equally satisfactory to consumers.

Efforts to maintain artificially high prices under modern competitive conditions have little chance of success over a period of years. The price-fixing power of so-called monopolies "has clearly diminished."

The study, "Industrial Price Policies and Economic Progress," was made for the private research agency by Dr. Edwin G. Nourse and Dr. Horace B. Drury. They disagreed with those who have argued that bigness in business is a curse and who have yearned for a society made up largely of competing "little fellows."

Drs. Nourse and Drury said, for instance:

"Competition is quite as keen and much more productive of results when we find industrial giants marshaling their mighty resources to perfect new techniques and new schemes of organization through whose use more and better goods may be put within the reach of the masses.

"The battle between the three giants in the automobile field sets the high mark of economically useful competition that our system has thus far presented.

"But the competitive struggle among the leading chemical companies, the great mail order houses, the leading food chains, the principal electrical concerns, and many others is of the same general order."

About 40 per cent of the nation's industrial production is controlled by huge corporations, they said, and that is the approximate percentage found in 1900.

The economists drew a definite line, however, between big combinations of today and those of a generation ago. Present day combinations, they said, were formed largely to effect economies and promote efficiency, and "most of them actively seek to broaden their market by giving to the consumer more for his money."

Formerly, they said, the combinations tried chiefly to control markets, suppress competition and raise prices.

In the field of price determination, the report held that the old theories based on supply and demand or cost plus profit must be scrapped for the sake of economic progress and stability.

There is, it said, a more constructive attack on pricing which "starts from the consumer's wants and purchasing power and courageously accepts the task of finding a means of satisfying these wants within the limitations of this purchasing power."

Accordingly, it asserted, "far-seeing and courageous price-making has made the enlightened business executive the most important factor in the functioning of the modern economic system."

The study contrasted what it called the economically useful competition in the automobile industry with the competition of many small firms in home-building and asked:

"If we could get home-building giants competing with each other, might we not get a similar lowering of prices of basic materials by supplying an assured quantity market which would make possible the long-delayed liaison between low-cost fabrication and cheap materials in that field?

"Local builders have shown themselves incapable of developing either operative efficiency on the modern industrial plane or the pressure toward mass supply and rock-bottom prices for materials."

Although calling the big business concern "the most effective agency for originating and carrying out a consistent program of progress through price reduction," the economists said "it must not be supposed that we conceive of such an organization as making prices or itself solving the pricing problem."

"The 'administered prices' of the big corporations," they continued, "are the expressions of the thinking of particular men who occupy executive positions. They reflect the way in which these individuals suppose that the economic process works.

"A big corporation is a potent instrument in the hands of a stupid man to carry into effect a price policy which may stunt its growth or lead to its actual death. It is in the hands of one who understands the laws of economic growth, an equally powerful instrument for carrying out a price program which will stimulate and develop the market, lead to capacity operations and thereby contribute to that general prosperity on which the given business itself will feed in the future.

"What does seem evident is that there must be opportunity for effective leadership brought to focus at the proper points to give it maximum effectiveness. In this connection we have considered not merely the policy role of the giant corporation, but also that of the trade association in which many corporations and even small companies are joined, and the way in which policy may be exercised through governmental agencies acting as regulatory bodies or as participants in some operating organization made up of private concerns.

"While experience is not as yet sufficient to demonstrate fully what powers these democratic schemes of group organization might in the long run have in the way of industrial leadership, it does point clearly to a serious dilemma. Either they tend to keep their activities on the level of the debating society with no actual control over members, or else they tend toward the path of regimentation which leads to authoritarian control.

"So far as present experience goes, these organizations have not yet proved their ability to avoid such compromise as (we have) called the 'triumph of mediocrity.' Even though unable to bring up the laggards, the group solidarities show a disquieting power to exert a retarding influence on those who could and would be pacemakers."

July 14, 1938

MONOPOLY IS HELD MINOR PRICE CLUE

Book by H. S. Dennison, Manufacturer, and J. K. Galbraith Offers Plan for Business

ASKS 'ART' OF REGULATION

Scientific Controls Declared Necessary if Socialization Is to Be Avoided

Special to THE NEW YORK TI...

WASHINGTON, July 17.—"Monopoly," as defined by the Sherman and Clayton acts, is but "an insignificant part" of the problem of keeping prices right for the consumer, according to H. S. Dennison, president of the Dennison Manufacturing Company, and J. K. Galbraith of Harvard University, whose book, "Modern Competition and Business Policy," has just been published by the Oxford University Press.

The anti-trust policy of the government, they write, "deals with monopolies, and the monopolies which come within the definition of the Supreme Court are of very narrow importance; their restraint on the country's whole production of wealth is fractional in comparison with the perfectly legal restraints which business judgment imposes on the producer who has reached the size where he must plan his production with regard for its effect upon price."

"Even when the courts succeeded in dissolving a 'trust'—at best they only replace monopoly restraint with that dictated by business judgment without being able to give any assurance that the prices under the latter will be lower than the monopoly price," the authors add.

Production Goal Stated

The writers refer frequently to a goal of "socially optimum production" and state that "there is no question of reproach in any of this discussion of below optimum production.

"The individual business man in supporting prices at the best expense of production," they write, "is but following the course that must be taken by any intelligent man in pursuit of his own interests, or the interests of the stockholders to whom he is legally accountable.

"What does concern us is that aside from extreme business fluctuations (which may be a somewhat related matter) we have in price jurisdiction and the attendant curb on potential output one significant explanation of the failure of the American economy to achieve the standards of abundance which all with a gleam of imagination know are possible."

At a time when the Administration, through its "Monopoly Committee," is starting an investigation into the fundamental ills of the country's business and industrial economy, these writers offer a plan for business regulation as "a substitute for anti-trust prosecution."

They assert that socialization, atomization or scientific regulation are the only choices if American industry is to operate in a socially desirable way and advocate scientific regulation.

Warn of "Atomization"

A sort of "atomization" of big business, the writers contend, would be involved in any attempt to return to the automatic self-regulation under natural competitive conditions which may have existed in simpler eras.

The authors argue that to attempt to reinstitute regulative competition "would be to impose upon much of American industry a wholly new and untried form of organization." They add that "to achieve self-regulative competition, American industry would have to undergo major surgery."

Declaring that in "a business structure as varied and complex as that of the United States there can be no simple formula," the authors urge more studious attention to the subject of regulation, with industry itself participating in the planning.

"The device we recommend," they declare, "is not regulation per se but exploration of the art or technique of regulation. We must do some rational experimental work in the art of industrial regulation."

They suggest that Congress set up a commission "to identify and make the necessary study of industries with a low social performance." The commission would cooperate with representatives of the industries in working out plans which would be finally passed upon by "a technically qualified semi-judicial Board of Review."

July 18, 1938

AN INQUIRY INTO THE MONOPOLY ISSUE

Thurman Arnold Holds That Concentration of Industrial Power Is a Tax on the Public and a Threat to Democracy

A Congressional committee, a Presidential commission and the Department of Justice are at present concerned with the question of monopolies in American business life. The problem, as the Administration law enforcement agency views it, is presented in the article below. The author, formerly Professor of Law at Yale University, is Assistant Attorney General in charge of anti-trust activities.

By THURMAN ARNOLD,
Assistant Attorney General

MONOPOLIES with varying degrees of control, inflexible price structures, coercion of independent business men, and private control of what might be termed "economic toll bridges" have been familiar features of American life since Ida Tarbell wrote the history of the Rockefeller dynasty. The power of great organizations to levy what are in effect taxes is commonplace. It may sometimes be exercised benevolently, but, nevertheless, it is a dictatorial power subject to no public responsibility, which is the antithesis of our democratic tradition. The exercise of that sort of power today is nevertheless one of our national problems.

Because we have felt this conflict between dictatorial industrial power and democracy without openly recognizing it, our thinking on the monopoly problem has been more confused than on any other national problem. We have believed that monopolies were bad and should be prosecuted and at the same time insisted that business should be let alone to expand as it wished. We have resented equally attempts to modify or repeal the Sherman Act and attempts to enforce it. We have been enthusiastically in favor of an anti-monopoly policy in general and against it in particular cases. Practically all of the complaints against monopoly practices have come from business men who happen to suffer from the particular practices complained of. At the same time, most of the criticisms against the Department of Justice for taking steps to enforce the Sherman Act come from the same class.

The commentators in the press demand anti-trust enforcement in general and criticize almost every prosecution in which respectable business men are involved. The grounds, following a stereotyped pattern, usually take the following form:

(1) The department is interfering with legitimate business at times when business needs confidence.

(2) The department is ungrateful for the achievements and benefactions of defendants.

(3) The department has no right to prosecute one case instead of another unless it prosecutes every case at once.

(4) The prosecution is dictated by political reasons.

Thus, any vigorous prosecution policy on the part of the anti-trust division must be conducted under a constant barrage of charges indicating inconsistency and bad faith. This barrage in the past has often been very potent in reducing the enforcement of the anti-trust laws to a mere ritual.

NO realist should complain about this. It arises not out of malice but out of a conflict between two contradictory attitudes h d simultaneously by the same persons. The situation is similar to that in the days of prohibition when men wanted liquor and moral observance of the prohibition law at the same time. The result has been forty years of ritualistic anti-trust enforcement which has preserved the ideal while at the same time it permitted sub rosa acquiescence in industrial empire building. Taking the period of the

The two Roosevelts as trust-busters: Above, a recent comment on F. D. R.—"Who left the gate open?" and at the left, T. R. in action—"No mollycoddling here."

R. A. Lewis in The Milwaukee Journal and The New York Globe.

last forty years as a whole, it can be said that the practical activities relating to the Sherman Act have been a series of illogical compromises.

For this condition the courts have often been blamed because they have put obstacles in the way of enforcement. Yet the root of the difficulty is found elsewhere. By its failure to stick to any consistent enforcement policy over any long period of time, the government has so accustomed the public to lack of enforcement that any change is immediately resented. This has not been the fault of the Department of Justice. No organization can act beyond the limits of its funds and personnel.

To illustrate this we have only to look at the type of organization to which the duty of enforcement of the Sherman Act has been delegated. One reading the history of the administration of Theodore Roosevelt might get the impression that "trust busting" was one of its major activities and that the crusade failed for reasons which lie somehow deep in the nature of our economic organization. Yet, such histories seldom point out that the actual number of people engaged in the anti-trust division during Theodore Roosevelt's crusade consisted of only five lawyers and four stenographers. Suppose that the supervision conducted by the Securities and Exchange Commission today had to be handled by nine people. Granted that the laws were continued, their effect would sink into insignificance. Stock Exchanges would run as they pleased and the Securities and Exchange Act would be as incomprehensible to business men as the Sherman Act is now.

The business activities which the Anti-Trust Division is supposed to supervise and curb are of far greater extent and much less localized even than the conduct of our securities markets. Yet, prior to the increase of government activities of all kinds, there has been no corresponding development in the organization devoted to anti-trust enforcement. Judge Stephens, the first head of the Anti-Trust Division appointed by the present Administration, took over an organization of only fifteen men. He increased it to forty. When I took office there were fifty-eight attorneys engaged in a task which covered every city, small and large, in the nation and practically every business activity. In the meantime, the Securities and Exchange Commission, where real results were being accomplished, had expanded to about 1,200 men with regional offices scattered over the country.

NOTHING can be more indicative of the purely ritualistic enforcement of the anti-trust laws than the size of the personnel devoted to enforcing them. The Anti-Trust Division has constantly been in the public eye because of the emotional importance of the ideal which it represented. Yet the fact that nothing more was desired of it than the celebration of the ideal of competition is evidenced by its limited personnel and its small budget. The Lands Division of the Department of Justice has averaged three times the budget of the Anti-Trust Division.

In general it may be said that the problem of enforcement of the Sherman Act has been treated in the past as a moral and not as an economic problem. An occasional dramatic example is all that is required to keep a purely moral light shining. Once a week is enough to go to church. In demonstrating that moral problem, the will-o'-the-wisp "corporate intent" has been pursued through endless pages of testimony and legal argument. To a large extent, the *fact* of monopoly control has been regarded as less important that the *mental state* of those who acquire it. In prohibition times we wanted the moral comfort of the prohibition ideal dramatized without interfering with our liquor supply. In anti-trust enforcement we have wanted the moral comfort of the ideal of free and unrestricted competition without interfering with the expansion of our great business empires. At least the organization of anti-trust enforcement agencies has been adapted only for that general purpose.

IT is my belief that the period of easy acquiescence in industrial empire building is coming to an end. A different policy is being forced on us by the failure of our great industrial organizations to adapt their price policies so that they can employ labor and run their plants to capacity. The tragedy of prices made higher and profits made lower because of the overhead costs of the idle machinery made necessary by these higher prices has been brought home to us so dramatically in the recent depression that we are not likely to forget it. In the depression of 1933 financial organization seemed to be our most outstanding weakness. It was followed by the passage of the Securities and Exchange Act and the development of the highly efficient organization which now administers that act. In the last recession we appeared to be choked with inventories which could not be distributed. Men were discharged by great organizations at a scale new in our history. Prices controlled by small groups appeared to have no relation to purchasing power. There was no real understanding that price policy and increase of productive capacity are inextricably linked together in a successful distribution system. The present recession has been followed by a recession has been followed by a demand for an investigation of monopoly practices and price policies just as the depression of 1933 was followed by a demand for control of the marketing of securities. There is reason to believe that in the enforcement of an anti-monopoly practice we are today in the same stage comparatively that we were in 1933 with relation to policies relating to financing and marketing of securities.

MY guess is that present conditions will lead us to the development of more effective supervision of inflexible price structures and restraints of trade than we have ever had before. I hope this prediction is correct, because if it is not we are moving inevitably toward a highly centralized industrial State like Germany and Italy rather than the model of a more competitive economy like Sweden. A highly centralized industrial State cannot be avoided by preaching against fascism and invoking the symbols of freedom any more than the diseases of the human body can be cured by preaching against the evil spirits which were supposed to have caused them. Practical remedies consist in curbing growing power to fix prices because such power is in its essence a power to tax without public responsibility. Once it is acquired and once the possibility of competition is removed, there is no final alternative except State control.

In the brief space allotted to me in THE TIMES, I cannot discuss detailed suggestions for legislation or for an enforcement program that would be adequate. I will therefore attempt only to outline the problem in general. For this purpose, a figure of speech may be useful.

When we look over the economic system today, we see two worlds. In one world concentrated industrial power maintains high prices, no matter how much the demand for the product falls off. The result is that production drops, men are laid off, and heavy deflationary pressure is put on the rest of the system. Examples of this differing in degree are found in nearly all the highly organized industries today.

In our second world almost unlimited competition still prevails and cannot be controlled, or is controlled only with difficulty. This is the world of farmers, retailers, small business men supplying consumers both goods and labor. In this world, when supply increases or demand falls off, prices drop, but people go right on producing as much as the conditions of the market will permit. The first world is one of concentrated control, of high and rigid prices, restriction of production, and wholesale discharge of labor. The second world is one of competition, low flexible prices, large production, and labor standards often at the starvation level.

THE trouble with our economic system is that the first of these worlds works at cross-purposes with the second. In the first world, capital works to keep up prices and lay off labor. Unemployed labor has no power to purchase the consumer goods furnished by the second world.

Now, everybody knows by this time that we are in this country capable of producing an abundance for everybody. We have the materials, the factories, the men and the money. The problem is how to unleash productive forces. The New Deal has tried to do so up to date by providing our competitive world with increased purchasing power. It has spent money on relief, on new construction, to aid home owners and so on. It has raised wages and helped farmers to try to restrict excessive output and raise crop prices that were unfairly low. But all this effort is blocked as long as the first world will not march in the procession, as long as by maintaining high inflexible prices it drains the money away from those who receive it from the government, and then stops the circulation of money by failing to produce goods and by laying off men who should be consuming what the competitive world produces.

Administrative objectives have been misrepresented as if they were an attempt to raise all prices or to lower all prices. One is called inflation, the other deflation. This is not the purpose. Instead, it is to lower the prices which are too high and interfere with production without lowering prices and wages that are too low. In fact, we must raise all the starvation prices and the starvation wages.

WE have not yet solved the difficulties created by the first economic world, the world of high inflexible prices and low production. Productive capacity and price policy are not yet linked together. We are building plants for a ten-year period and fixing prices on what the market may be expected to bear for the next three months. Some sort of pressure is necessary to get the executives of this first economic world to understand their responsibility toward the evils of prices which leave their plants idle and their men unemployed. Adjustments will have to be made.

During the period of such adjustments, the government must aid by sustaining purchasing power with its present recovery measures. However, if the executives do not do their part, present measures may not succeed. The government can and will prevent suffering in an unemployment spiral with the full force of its credit. It cannot, however, produce prosperity without cooperation from big business along the lines indicated. The question is what moderate pressure from the government is required to bring inflexible prices into a new alignment so that the present recovery measures will furnish sufficient purchasing power to bridge the adjustment period.

The first step in exerting such pressure is to get the public to realize what the monopoly problem is. Without public support, no program of anti-trust enforcement or legislative reform of conditions which cannot be reached by the anti-trust laws can be successful because both legislative remedies and anti-trust enforcement involve interfering with plans of expansion of respectable business men and great organizers whom the public admires. Every one is afraid of taxes but prices are not ordinarily considered as taxes. If the picture could be brought home to the American people in small groups that the determination of the prices which they must pay for the things which they need to buy, or the things which they want to buy, is a taxing power subject to no public responsibility we would be half way on the road to a solution. The public will insist either that competitive conditions be restored or that prices be regulated.

LET us see how this power to tax operates. Suppose that the entire product is in the hands of a few sellers who desire to make all the profit that they can out of that product. When the purchasing power expands, they raise the prices in order to get the lion's share of that expansion instead of lowering them in order to distribute the most goods possible. They are able to do this because there is no effective competition and because the principle aimed at is not distribution but profit.

Temporary profits enable them to accumulate a surplus to protect the security owner. When the purchasing power drops in times of depression, they do not lower the prices to meet the drop in purchasing power. Instead, they lay off their employes. The government then has to take care of the employes by relief or other means. This is really a subsidy to industry by the government because it keeps the employes fed and clothed until business picks up again and the small group who control the product are willing to take them back. Most people do not consider unemployment relief to persons discharged by a great industry as a subsidy to that industry, but, nevertheless, that is exactly what it is. Thus, monopoly control works out in such a way that the public is taxed not only by way of prices in times of expansion but also by way of relief in times of unemployment.

I will refrain from giving statistics about the enormous concentration of industrial power which has occurred since the war and its effect on small business. One can get a better and more human picture out of a single example which I think is typical of much of the coercive force over industrial organization today. It presents in concrete form an important aspect of the monopoly problem.

A FEW weeks ago representatives of the wastepaper industry in a large city called on me. They claimed that about 6,000 people were dependent on collecting wastepaper in their particular area. The technique of this industry consists in skill and experience in establishing routes and forming an organization capable of collecting a steady supply. Those men told me that there was only one buyer in a great area of the country to whom they could sell their product. He was a sort of a toll bridge over which every one had to pass.

The reason for his power was that the ultimate consumers of wastepaper in that large area would only buy from him. The collectors of wastepaper told me that he had reduced the price a ton so much below the cost of gathering it that they were actually paying for the privilege of collecting paper. I asked the question, "Well, if it costs you money to collect paper, why don't you quit?" "We can't quit," a collector replied simply. "Everything we know how to do is the wastepaper business. We go on and on until the little bit we have saved is gone, hoping for something to happen. If we give up our routes and lose our organization, we can't get them back. They are all we have. So, we go on and on, exhausting our credit, spending our savings. Doing something is bad, but it's a lot better than doing nothing these days."

I have picked this example because it is the reverse of the ordinary situation. These men were in trouble because a monopolistic power was lowering prices instead of raising them. A buyer controlled instead of a seller. Yet, the arbitrary exercise of the power to fix the price, without public responsibility, was just as much of a tax as if it had been levied by a central government. Indeed, it went further than any public body can go in a democracy. It was a capital levy.

MOST people do not realize how typical this situation is. Yet automobile dealers, independent moving picture theatres, independent oil companies, farmers, in fact all unorganized business finds itself subjected to a greater or lesser degree to similar arbitrary power to tax by fixing prices. The instances of exercise of this sort of power do not get into the press. No one can be connected with the administration who does not feel the force of this enormous, persistent, bottled-up pressure. As typical of this, I quote from Senator Borah in addressing the Senate on May 26:

"I have in my files over a thousand letters the writers of some of which, in great detail, tell me how they have been crushed and destroyed by the large combines. They have been really deprived of a livelihood along lines they had chosen to follow for life. They simply could not contend with these great combinations, any more than a small army could contend with an army of a million."

You can't solve this problem by preaching. Suppose you were the president of a corrugated box company. If you could get your paper cheaper because some one was making a capital levy on the collectors of that commodity, would your directors or stockholders let you pay more somewhere else? Of course not. The pressure would all be the other way just as those who control the market find all the pressure tends to make them raise prices for temporary profit. In a fight without a referee a man with brass knuckles will win. This will be true no matter how much preaching goes on to the effect that in the long run such practices will ruin the game.

In the past, so far as the exercise of monopoly power is concerned, the referee has been absent. We have kept alive the anti-monopoly ideal by an occasional prosecution. We have encouraged the growth of monopoly power by refusing to build up an effective enforcement organization. The resulting condition has not been the fault of our great organizers. They have played the game according to the rules as they found them as all good players must. They have gone as far as the imposition of penalties permitted. This is what every hard playing football team has to do, or lose to its rivals.

If a single one of the bodies in an industry turns buccaneer, all the decent ones must follow in his steps in the absence of proper rules of the game. For example, we find the government today prosecuting the movies for obtaining an arbitrary monopoly power over theatres. Yet, in 1921, Mr. Zukor, with prophetic vision, predicted all the evil results which would follow the acquisition of theatres. After his predictions Mr. Zukor became one of the leaders in the organization of theatres which are now the subject of a pending anti-trust prosecution. Is it fair to criticize him? Under the circumstances, with an acquiescent government from 1920 to 1930, if he had not acquired control, some one else would have. You cannot refuse to penalize infractions of the rules in a competitive game and then complain because the more gentle team does not win.

The answer is not a question of breaking up large businesses into small ones regardless of their efficiency. This is neither the ideal of the policy of the Sherman Act nor should it be the ideal of further anti-monopoly legislation. No government group that I know of desires to break up efficient mass production. We only desire to condemn combinations going beyond efficient mass production which have become instruments arbitrarily affixing inflexible prices or exercising coercive power.

The line between efficient mass production and industrial empire building cannot be drawn in the abstract. It can only be clarified with respect to particular industries. Both the application of the Sherman Act and the decision as to what legislation is required to supplement the act require the exercise of judgment on two questions. The first is this: Does the particular combination go beyond the necessities of efficient mass production and become an instrument of arbitrary price control? The second question is: Does any particular arrangement affecting marketing practices tend merely to create orderly marketing conditions in which competitors can exist, or is it an instrument to maintain rigid prices. Obviously, the answer to these questions can only be a question of controlled judgment made after factual investigation of the particular industry.

The need, therefore, of more definite application of the anti-trust laws can only be met by prosecution coupled with public statements giving the reason for the exercise of these judgments in each case. A series of statements of the grounds for prosecution in particular cases should furnish a link between the courts and Congress so that the one may interpret and the other supplement the law. This policy of public statements to clarify the act and to be a guide to business men was announced by Attorney General Cummings in a release dated May 18, 1938.

In the meantime, the Anti-Trust Division is attempting to outline a consistent policy for the use of the tools which Congress has given it. Whether this policy is liked by business or not, it will at least be understood. That is the first step toward sensible amendment.

The other step toward amendment is to survey the whole problem of the various laws, many of them expressing inconsistent policies and philosophies. The effect of this total mass of legislation, decisions and practices must be studied. That is the function of the Temporary National Economic Committee set up by President Roosevelt to study the entire monopoly problem.

August 21, 1938

'MONOPOLY' INQUIRY IS TOLD IT HUNTS A BUSINESS RARITY

Thorp Clashes With Arnold, Trust Prosecutor, Over Effect of the Anti-Trust Laws

CONCENTRATIONS CHARTED

Aluminum Corporation Is Held Sole Instance of a Company Dominating a Field

Special to The New York Times.

WASHINGTON, Dec. 2.—The actual rarity of "monopoly" in American business as surveyed by a government economist was emphasized today before the Temporary National Economic Committee.

While the committee endeavored to reduce to a statistical picture the much-disputed problem of concentration of wealth, Dr. Willard L. Thorp said that where monopolistic practice tends to exist, this consists more generally of control of industries by relatively small groups of unrelated houses than by what is generally considered to be "monopoly."

Thus the committee learned by Dr. Thorp's showing that while the Aluminum Corporation of America is an isolated example of dominance in a single field by a single corporation, the women's clothing industry is a field where the four largest companies control only 2 per cent of the business.

A Clash of Personalities

The hearings turned from a dry presentation of statistical summaries into a clash of personalities when Assistant Attorney General Thurman Arnold, who has charge of enforcement of the anti-trust laws, challenged Dr. Thorp's statement that the Sherman act had been "in considerable part responsible" for the growth of concentrated enterprise in the United States.

Dr. Thorp's presentation, combined with the differences of viewpoint, indicated clearly on this, the second day of the committee's hearings, the intricate problems faced by the committee in carrying out its mandate to recommend revisions in the laws controlling competition.

While the twelve-man committee, composed equally of legislative and departmental representatives of the Administration, would from time to time ask questions or make statements showing the divergence of their personal views, the witness

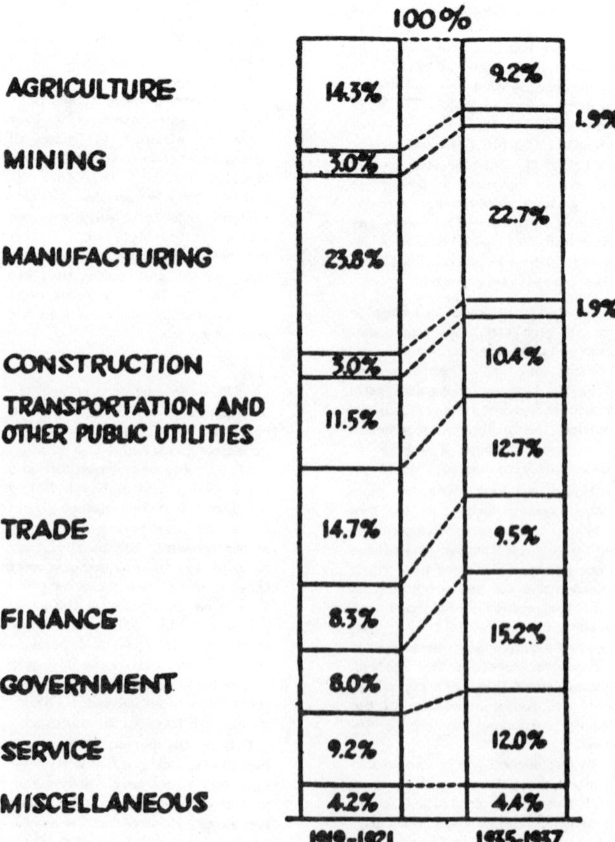

outlined variations in the pattern of American business which make generalities impossible.

Dr. Thorp, who is chief economist for Dun & Bradstreet, is on leave from his New York office to head the Commerce Department's research for the inquiry.

He told the committee that while one-tenth of 1 per cent of the nation's employers employ 12.3 per cent of all employes in manufacturing and business, exclusive of the railroads, 76 per cent of the employers—those having one to nine in each of their establishments—employ an aggregate of only 11 per cent of the workers.

Although there were some 6,000 chain store companies with 140,000 outlets in 1935, they did only 22 per cent of the total volume of business, he said.

In outlining the structure of the nation's "economic machine," he referred to the concentration of corporate enterprise. Assistant Attorney General Arnold shot forward in his chair, showing undisguised annoyance when Dr. Thorp, standing with pointer in hand before some of his charts, said that he would "like to advance the suggestion that the Sherman Act or Anti-Trust Law is in considerable part responsible for the development of these large enterprises."

"I don't think that is the position which the anti-trust division is taking, and I don't think it is one that they are in a position to take," Mr. Arnold asserted emphatically.

Frank and Oliphant Intervene

Jerome Frank, member of the Securities and Exchange Commission, said, in the role of peace maker, that he knew of cases in which attorneys had advised their clients that by merging their competitive corporations they could escape the anti-trust laws.

Herman Oliphant, the Treasury's general counsel, intervened, only to be interrupted by Mr. Arnold, who asserted that the view of the anti-trust laws expressed by Dr. Thorp was "a common interpretation, newspaper interpretation of the anti-trust law."

"We will get a specific decision on that, I think, in the Aluminum case," the former Yale professor added.

Mr. Arnold left the hearing room for the day at the moment that Dr. Thorp, himself a former Amherst professor, was observing that "there is actually no manner in which you can measure the extent of unlawful agreements and combinations."

O'Mahoney Notes Interest Shown

It was "unusual" for a large audience to pay such close attention for five hours to "testimony of such a highly technical character," Senator O'Mahoney, chairman of the committee, remarked. He said that the testimony of Dr. Thorp illustreated the transformation of our economy from one confined to a restricted geographical area and with small agencies to one covering a large area and carried on by big agencies."

"The shift of employment from one type to the other raises the question as to what industry should do to give stability to its operations," the chairman continued. "We now face a problem of marketing. To be properly produced, goods must be properly distributed. And as Dr. Lubin said yesterday, the big markets are to be found

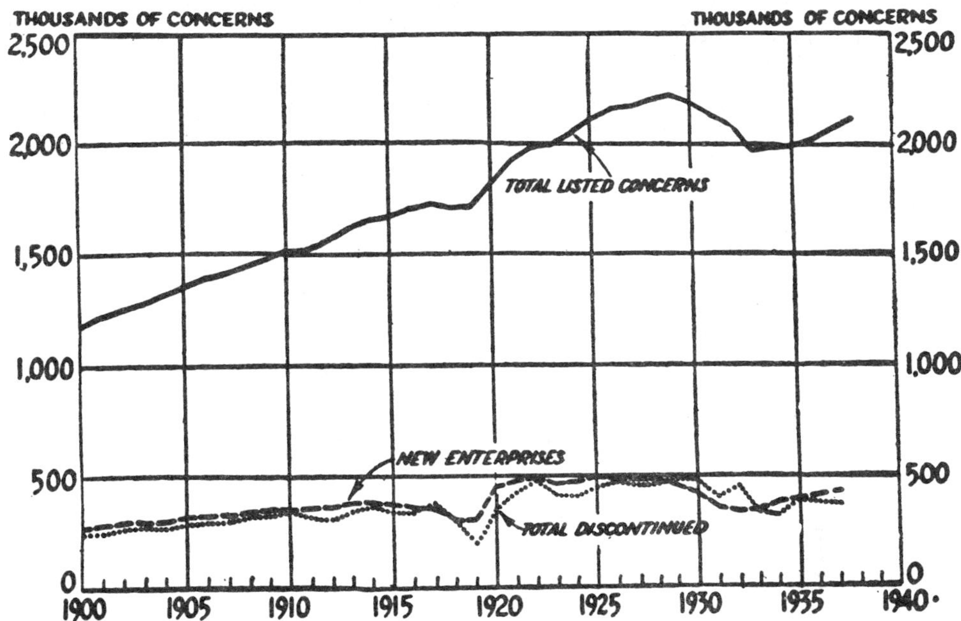

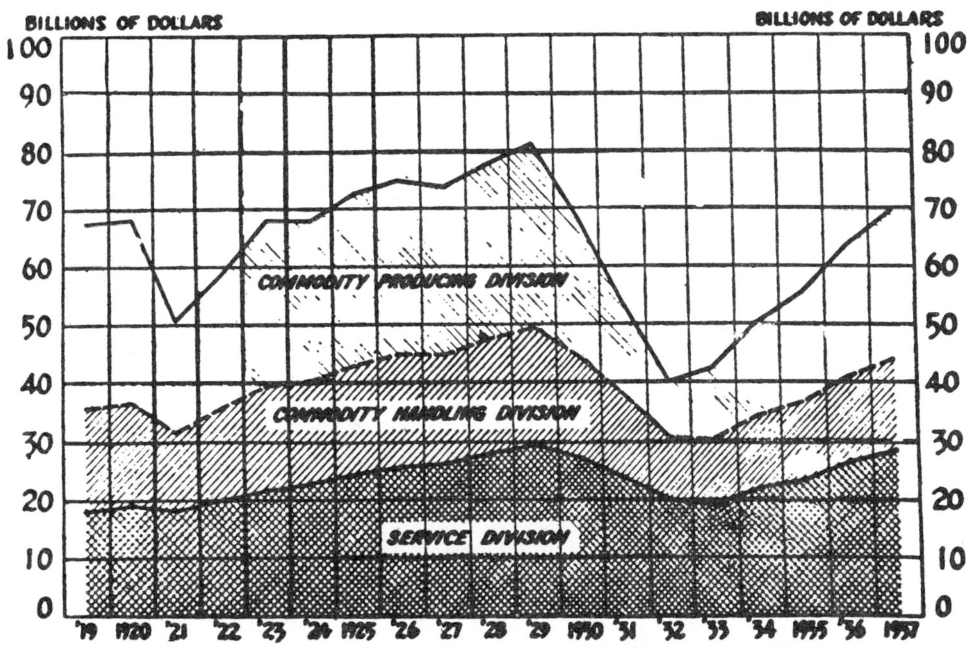

The number of business concerns in the United States showed a steady increase from 1900 to 1929 with only minor fluctuations. Between 1929 and 1933 the number of concerns dropped from 2,213,000 to 1,961,000 in 1933. The upturn has been slow since that date. The data for this chart, obtained from Dun & Bradstreet, cover industrial and commercial enterprises, but excludes financial institutions, railroads, professional enterprises and farmers. This was one of the more than a score of charts on the national economy which figured in Dr. Willard L. Thorp's testimony yesterday before the "Monopoly" Committee's inquiry in Washington.

From 1929 to 1932 the national income decreased by more than 50 per cent. There was a subsequent recovery to $70,000,000,000 in 1937. The commodity producing division of the economy shows the largest fluctuations and appears to have declined over the period 1919-37. The service division tended to increase over this period and has shown the smallest fluctuations. These data were obtained from the Bureau of Foreign and Domestic Commerce and the National Bureau of Economic Research.

Substantial shifts have occurred in the industrial origin of the national income since the World War. The contribution of the commodity producing division of our economy has declined relatively whereas the contribution of the service division has increased. The relative decline was most pronounced in agriculture, mining and construction. Agriculture accounted for one-seventh of the national income in 1919-21 and less than one-tenth in the years 1935-37. Government's contribution increased from 8 per cent in the earlier period to 15.2 per cent in the most recent years. These data were obtained from the Bureau of Foreign and Domestic Commerce and the National Bureau of Economic Research.

among the thousands of the working people."

Dr. Isador Lubin, the Labor Department's Commissioner of Statistics, yesterday was the committee's first "prologue" witness. He testified on the actual flow of goods and services in the national economy.

Dr. Thorp today gave a picture in sharp contrast to many popular conceptions of the organization of industry, the concentration of industry and the factors involved in industrial development in this country. In dismissing "monopoly" as a rarity, he stated that the more common form of concentration was where two, three, four or more corporations blanketed a given field of activity.

Other Kinds of Competition

Among other points in Dr. Thorp's testimony were these: There were other important types of competition than price competition, such as competition of the products of competing industries like rayon and silk. New enterprises have been established in recent years at a faster rate than old enterprises collapsed. It was virtually impossible to define "industry." The individual business man has many problems, including changing government policies. But there still is ample freedom of opportunity to enter business in this country, despite certain restricting factors.

The interchange between Mr. Arnold and Dr. Thorp focused attention on the government's attitude under the anti-trust laws. The official transcript read:

Dr. Thorp—I should like to advance the suggestion that the Sherman act, or Anti-Trust Law, is in considerable part responsible for the development of these large enterprises. The reason for that is that through the process of interpretation we have arrived at a state of law where five enterprises, each of which, let us say, represents 10 per cent of an industry, cannot have collective action with regard to the prices or markets or allocation of production without running afoul of the anti-trust laws. That becomes a combination or conspiracy in restraint of trade. If, however, those five enterprises should merge into a single enterprise, then that single enterprise has no problem of conspiracy or combination; it is only a single enterprise.

Mr. Arnold—I don't think that is the position which the anti-trust division is taking, and I don't think it is one that they are in a position to take. We have the identical problem in the aluminum case.

Mr. Oliphant—Do you know of any combinations or mergers dictated solely by the consideration that you enumerated? That would be the best way of putting it.

Mr. Arnold—That is a common interpretation, newspaper interpretation of the Anti-Trust Law, but without arguing the point, I wish to make the record clear that we made no such distinction, and we will get a specific decision on that, I think, in the aluminum case.

Dr. Thorp—I am merely citing this in terms of business motivation, and I am afraid business is not always motivated in a perfect understanding of the meaning of the laws.

Mr. Arnold—I would question that statement very seriously.

Mr. Frank—Isn't it possible, Mr. Arnold, that some lawyers heretofore have given their clients the interpretation of the anti-trust laws to which Mr. Thorp refers, and while they may have been in error, that, nevertheless, would account for the motivation for which he directs attention. I have some reason to believe that there has been such advice given by counsel.

As to the Lack of Enforcement

Mr. Arnold, who is enlarging the anti-trust enforcement staff of the Department of Justice, later asked Dr. Thorp if he "would not say that lack of enforcement" had been an important contributory factor in the concentration of industry.

Dr. Thorp smiled, in apparent assent. Representative Sumners, vice chairman of the committee, observed: "That is, until very recently." This statement seemed to amuse the committee, but not Mr. Arnold.

Dr. Thorp at another point noted the great variation in problems of industry as illustrated by the relief sought through the NRA codes.

"Did not those agreements make for monopoly?" asked Senator King. "Wasn't that their purpose?"

"I wish you'd just accept my testimony as showing the variety of these problems," Dr. Thorp replied.

"Well, they wanted relief from the anti-trust laws, didn't they?" Senator King asked.

"Yes, that's true, all right," Dr. Thorp agreed.

Mr. Arnold observed that "had the code agreements been reasonably consistent with orderly marketing they probably would have come within the rule of reason."

When freedom of opportunity was under discussion Mr. Oliphant observed that "the door to opportunity seems largely an opportunity to fail."

"This shows," Dr. Thorp said of a chart illustrating the rate of business failures, "that people are free to lose their own or their mother-in-law's money in business."

Chairman O'Mahoney observed that "we can't put up safeguards against incompetence," but Dr. Thorp said an effort to do so had been made through education.

Borah Says "Half a Dozen" Rule

Senator King declared that hope was "the mainspring of business." The hope, Senator Borah observed, was that the government would pass no restrictive laws.

"You must expect that under democratic government," said Senator King.

"But it isn't democratic government when half a dozen men run it," Senator Borah replied.

While his data showed "there is a continuous flow of enthusiastic and hopeful individuals, many somewhat too optimistic, and the doors of free enterprise are open," Dr. Thorp pointed out there were certain limitations to freedom to enter certain fields of business.

These included fields covered by closely held patents; those in which natural resources are already privately owned; instances in which wide public acceptance of a product makes competition virtually impossible; the high cost of production in some fields, with the necessity for large amounts of capital; and the cost of marketing.

He said that 400,000 new enterprises opened business in 1937, while 350,000 closed their doors, but the total number of listed firms, other than in farming or railroading, dropped from 2,213,000 at the 1929 peak, to 1,900,000 at the bottom of the depression.

Dr. Thorp went into detail to show the great difference in performance of industries under similar economic conditions.

As to chain stores, he showed that chains in 1935 made only 4.3 per cent of total retail sales in the hardware business, 14.5 per cent in restaurants, 23.8 per cent in drug stores with fountains, 38.2 per cent in grocery stores, 50 per cent in shoe stores and 90.8 per cent in variety stores.

Inter-industrial competition was a competitive factor strongly emphasized by the witness. The manufacture of buggies dropped to zero by 1931. Wagon manufactures amounted to 100,000 units in 1935, compared with 600,000 in 1900, a period in which the truck started from zero and by 1936 reached 4,000,000 units.

Coal has suffered in the competition with other fuels; domestic and imported sugar compete; and rayon has risen in the textile field since 1912 to the point where, by 1937, it exceeded sales of silk and climbed far above cotton.

Mere bigness of a corporation did not necessarily imply concentration, or even monopoly, Dr. Thorp made clear. He told of great corporations with largely decentralized plants and of tremendous corporations which covered only a small part of a given field.

Says Some Mergers Make 2+2=5

Representative Sumners asked whether mergers were largely motivated by the desire of "somebody to make money on new securities."

"You take two companies," Dr. Thorp said, "and give each a value of 2. You put them together and give the new corporation a value of 5. You distribute the capitalization by giving two parts to each of the merged concerns, and the fifth you sell to the public. That's all there is to it. I don't know how they sometimes make two and two equal five, but they do."

He added, however, that bigness had certain advantages which might account in some instances for the added value.

Leon Henderson, executive secretary of the committee and former WPA economist, will sum up the "prologue" material presented by Dr. Lubin and Dr. Thorp at a session of the committee called for tomorrow morning. It had been expected that the "prologue" would be concluded today.

Gives Examples of Concentration

By The Associated Press.

WASHINGTON, Dec. 2.—The much-disputed question of how rigidly American business and industry is concentrated in the hands of a controlling few was reduced to statistics today and added to the record of the monopoly committee.

Dr. Willard Thorp, in a classroom lecture to the Senators, House members and departmental executives who comprise the investigating group, told them that two-tenths of 1 per cent of the corporations hold 52 per cent of corporate assets.

Dr. Thorp traced the number of new business enterprises which appeared and old enterprises which disappeared annually. A study made in Poughkeepsie, N. Y., showed that only 46.9 per cent of new firms lasted more than three years, 21.4 per cent ten years and 9.7 per cent twenty years. Poughkeepsie being a "relatively stable community," he said, he thought that other towns would show an even lower rate of survival.

The growth of many corporations, he said, was a matter of "internal growth" through the reinvestment of profits, but there have also been many mergers, particularly at two periods—from 1898 to 1902 and in the Nineteen Twenties. A total of 1,245 manufacturing and mining companies had been absorbed by mergers by 1929, he said.

The periods in question, he continued, were periods in which "the desire to have new securities made available for flotation" was a foremost consideration and the "promoters largely were people interested in investment banks."

He gave the following figures on concentration within specific industries:

Aluminum—One company, 100 per cent.
Automobiles—Three companies, 86 per cent.
Beef Products—Two companies, 47 per cent.
Bread and Bakery Products—Three companies, 20 per cent.
Cans—Three companies, 90 per cent.
Cement—Five companies, 40 per cent.
Cigarettes—Three companies, 80 per cent.
Bituminous Coal—Four companies, 10 per cent.
Copper—Four companies, 78 per cent.
Corn Binders—Four companies, 100 per cent.
Corn Planters—Six companies, 91 per cent.
Flour—Three companies, 29 per cent.
Plate Glass—Two companies. 95 per cent.
Safety Glass—Two companies, 60 per cent.
Iron Ore—Four companies, 64 per cent.
Lead—Four companies, 60 per cent.
Oil Wells—Four companies, 20 per cent.
Steel—Three companies, 60.5 per cent.
Whisky—Four companies, 58 per cent.
Women's Clothes—Four companies, 2 per cent.
Wood Pulp—Four companies, 35 per cent.
Zinc—Four companies, 46 per cent.

While some companies might do large proportions of the business in particular lines, Dr. Thorp said there was a high degree of competition between some industries, mentioning types of transportation, types of fuels and types of textiles.

December 3, 1938

FIND IDENTICAL BIDS IN FEDERAL BUYING

By LUTHER A. HUSTON
Special to THE NEW YORK TIMES.

WASHINGTON, Jan. 1—Identical bids were submitted on nearly 25 per cent of the items upon which the Federal Government invited bids during the twelve months' period from December, 1937, to November, 1938, inclusive, the Temporary National Economic Committee disclosed today in making public a summary of a report of the Treasury Department subcommittee on its study of government purchasing activities. In dollar value the report said, more than 10 per cent of Federal purchases in this period were of items upon which identical bids were submitted.

"Of the $860,044,970 expended under competitive bidding by both the service and the civil branches of the government $87,326,426 worth of supplies were purchased in instances where identical bids were received," the committee reported. "In the twelve-month period there were 331,851 bid openings, of which 76,705, or 24.1 per cent, were in instances where identical bids were received. From the 76,705 instances of identical bids, there were chosen 25,610 transactions as indicative of conditions in specific industry groups."

Table of Bids Presented

The report contained the following table showing the number of identical bids per industrial grouping and the percentage which that number is of the total selected identical bids:

Industry Group.	No. of Bids.	P.C. of Total.
Iron and steel and their products (not incl. machinery)	6,693	26.1
Stone, clay and glass prods.	3,275	12.8
Machinery, exclusive of transportation equipment	2,988	11.7
Food and kindred products	2,623	10.2
Chemicals and allied products	1,576	6.2
Printing, publishing and allied industries	1,405	5.5
Forest products	1,104	4.3
Paper and allied products	719	2.8
Coal and petroleum products	669	2.6
Nonferrous metals and their products	641	2.5
Textiles	423	1.7
Rubber	309	1.2
Transportation equipment (air, land, water)	311	1.2
Leather	87	0.3
Miscellaneous and unclassified industries	2,787	10.9

In a discussion of factors which "tend to encourage the practice of identical bidding," the report summarized comments made by agencies which contributed to the study as follows:

"(a) The adoption of industrial standards relating chiefly to quality, size, finish and performance, and the utilization of standardized manufacturing machinery and materials have the effect of reducing variations in production costs.

"(b) Legislation of whatever sort, which provides for market agreements or for minimum resale prices, tends to result in identical prices. Illustrative among these laws were mentioned State milk control laws, the Agricultural Marketing Act and the National Bituminous Coal Act.

"(c) Fair practice agreements in industries tend to produce identical prices.

"(d) Price control or leadership by a single or by a few leading manufacturers in any given industry tend to cause identical prices. If in existence, outright price agreements between producers would produce the same result.

"(e) Trade associations are believed to have a tendency to foster practices which bring about identical prices. Among such practices may be mentioned (1) the adoption of price schedules, (2) the allotment of sales territory among the members of the association based on production facilities, geographical restrictions, transportation limitations or other basis."

Bidder Certificates Suggested

Out of twenty-four replies to a request for comment on the advantages of identical bidding, the report stated, only four suggested limited conditions under which such bidding might be advantageous.

Among many suggestions that were made in response to a request for comment as to what might be done to bring about "the abolition of identical bidding and preserve the principle of open and unrestricted competition" was one that bidders be required to certify that the prices bid were not the result of any agreement with any other bidder. It was also suggested that a designated authority might be established to which cases of identical bids or suspicions of collusion in bidding might be reported for investigation.

Other suggestions along this line included:

"When there is evidence of collusive bidding and the tie bids are relatively lower than the untied bids, reject all bids and place a mandatory order with one of the tie bidders (the allocation to be decided by lot or other equally satisfactory plan), with the provision for the payment of 75 per cent (or other fixed percentage) of the tie bid price, the final payment price to be the 'fair price' for the material determined by a cost investigation. The 'fair price' might be determined by various methods. Appropriate legislation would be required to make this plan effective."

"When there is evidence of collusive bidding in an industry, investigate the cost of production throughout the industry, and by public declaration establish a 'fair trade' for the product. This investigation would give wide publicity to the disclosure of any evidence of excessive profits earned by a member of the industry or by the industry as a whole."

"If in repeated purchases of a particular commodity, the government as a rule received identical bids, would it not be well for the government to make all of its awards to one bidder in the expectation that this practice would cause other bidders to lower their prices and bid competitively?"

January 2, 1940

Fewer Curbs on Business and More on Unions Favored by U. S. Voters, Gallup Survey Finds

A majority of voters favor more regulation of labor unions and less regulation of business at the present time, a survey by the American Institute of Public Opinion, of which Dr. George Gallup is director, has indicated.

"Leaders of the A. F. of L. and the C. I. O., whose conventions were being held early this week, may well ponder the state of public opinion in the nation regarding labor," Dr. Gallup says.

"The survey indicates that labor unions face a much more serious public relations problem than business, which was for many years the target of New Deal reform. The study shows that business stands far higher in public favor today.

"In conducting the study the institute was not concerned with the merits or demerits of either business or labor, or their respective rights. As a fact-finding agency, it simply sought to measure the nation's attitude toward further regulation of business and of labor in the months ahead.

"The study put two questions to a cross-section of voters the nation over. The first was: 'During the next four years do you think there should be more or less regulation of business by the Federal Government than at present?'

"The vote of those with opinions was as follows:

More 27%
Less 51
Same 22

"One voter in five, 20 per cent, was undecided or without an opinion.

"The second question dealt with regulation of labor unions. 'During the next four years do you think there should be more or less regulation of labor unions by the Federal Government than at present?'

"The returns show that more than twice as many people favor more regulation of labor unions as favor more regulation of business.

More 60%
Less 21
Same 19

"Approximately one voter in five, 27 per cent, expressed no opinion.

"One discovery made by the poll is that desire for greater labor union regulation is not confined to the upper and middle income groups. These groups are for such regulation by over 60 per cent, but even in the low income group, among people earning $20 a week or less, a substantial majority—57 per cent—is for union regulation.

"The low income group is, however, much more in favor of business regulation than the middle and upper group."

November 22, 1940

TNEC ASKS U.S. LAW ON TRADE CHARTERS

By JOHN MacCORMAC

Special to THE NEW YORK TIMES.

WASHINGTON, March 31—A national charter law for corporations, repeal of the Miller-Tydings Enabling Act permitting resale price maintenance contracts, abolition of basing-point systems for calculating prices, reform of the patent laws, control of mergers and improvement of State regulation of insurance companies are among the principal recommendations made to Congress by the Temporary National Economic Committee after its two years of investigation into the concentration of economic power in the United States. It heard 552 witnesses, took 20,000 pages of testimony and cost $1,062,000.

The committee suggests that the Federal Trade Commission and the Department of Justice receive more adequate funds with which to administer the anti-trust laws and that penalties for their infraction be stiffly increased.

It declares that the corporation has been the principal instrument of the concentration of the economic power and proposes, therefore, that under its suggested national charter law, interlocking directorates be prohibited and corporation directors be made personally liable for anti-trust offenses.

Patent Law Changes Urged

The patent law changes which it recommends are also designed to prevent monopoly by providing for unrestricted licensing of patents at reasonable prices, limitation of the life of patents and of suits for their infringement.

Because of "the control exercised by foreign governments and their dependent agencies over American concerns through the patent system," the committee further recommends that no application for a patent be permitted to be filed abroad until specific permission has been obtained from the proper American government agency.

In presenting the report to the Senate today Senator O'Mahoney, chairman, said that "within the compass of these volumes is to be found the substance for reorganization of democracy which must come after the war."

Senator Shipstead asked him whether he thought the United States would ever have an administration with courage enough to enforce the anti-trust laws.

Senator O'Mahoney pointed out that a substantial total in fines was now collected by the anti-trust branch of the Justice Department. Senator La Follette said that Thurman Arnold, Assistant Attorney General, would present many more cases which he has prepared against monopolies if he had adequate appropriations.

Effects of Centralism Told

The committee stated that political centralism was the product of economic centralism. It argued that laws made for individuals or "natural persons" were unable to control "the huge collective groups which use the tools of the twentieth century."

The report, commenting on the results of government attempts to control monopolistic industry, reported germs of fascism in the Bituminous Coal Act and "aspects of socialism" in the TVA.

As the latest example of "amazing" economic concentration, the report pointed out that 45 per cent, or $13,000,000,000 worth, of defense contracts were awarded to six closely inter-related corporate groups.

Not all the recommendations were unanimous. Senator O'Mahoney, chairman of the committee, Representatives Sumners and Reece and Wayne C. Taylor, Under-Secretary of Commerce, dissented from the recommendation for repeal of the Miller-Tydings Enabling Act. Representatives Sumners and Reece, Joseph J. O'Connell Jr. and Sumner T. Pike, Commissioner of the Securities and Exchange Commission, dissented from the recommendation for a national charter law mainly, they said, because its intent "was not clear."

Isador Lubin, Commissioner of Labor Statistics, and Leon Henderson, SEC official, said that the program presented in the report of the committee would not have prevented the last depression and will not meet the problems of tomorrow.

The committee continues:

"Like government organization, business organization has no right or function to control the activities and the lives of men. In the modern world these two organizations, in principle designed only to serve men, have instead undertaken to order the lives of all for their own selfish interests. It is this basic fact which is the cause of the terrible disorder that now threatens to wreck the world.

Restrictive Practices Charged

"No person who with an open mind reviews the material gathered by this committee can fail to conclude that the rise of political centralism is largely the product of economic centralism. The records of this committee prove that restrictive practices are used by some business organizations not only to destroy competition but to regiment men.

"We know that the patent system, created by Congress for the purpose of fostering trade and industry, has been used to suppress trade and industry and to exact tribute from those who were permitted by the holders of patents to stay in business.

"We know that large collective enterprise in this country has entered into league with large enterprises in other nations to commit those abuses which, throughout our growth as a nation, have been universally condemned as contrary to public interest.

"Modern economic organizations have attained such power and size that they make international compacts in a field from which the States which create them are barred by the Constitution."

After urging decentralization of industry and the allocation of funds by Congress to eliminate monopoly control and stimulate competition, the committee declared:

"The principal instrument of the concentration of economic power and wealth has been the corporate charter with unlimited powers, charters which afforded a detour around every principle of fiduciary responsibility; which permitted promoters and managers to use the property of others for their own enrichment and to the detriment of the real owners; which made possible the violation of law without personal liability; which omitted every safeguard of individual and public welfare which common sense and experience alike have taught are necessary."

The committee recommended that the Miller-Tydings Enabling Act, which permits legalizing resale of price maintenance contracts in interstate commerce, be repealed. It proposed that Congress enact legislation declaring that pricing systems founded on basing-points were illegal. It suggested a continuing Congressional committee on interstate trade barriers.

It recommended that government puchasing functions be centralized in one agency.

Regarding patents the committee recommended the following:

The owner of any patent on pain of forfeiture would be required to grant only unrestricted licenses and not be permitted to impose restrictions upon the buyer in sales of patented articles.

The sale, license or assignment or other disposition of any patent would be filed with the Federal Trade Commission thirty days after execution, on pain of forfeiture.

A single court of patent appeals would be created, with jurisdiction coextensive with the United States and its Territories.

The life of a patent monopoly would expire not more than twenty years from the filing of the application.

Noting that there were more than 1,500 national and regional trade associations and about 6,000 State and local associations, the committee recommended that all trade associations whose members were engaged in interstate commerce be required to register with an appropriate Federal agency and file reports of their activities.

The committee recommended that the Federal Trade Commission be authorized to forbid the acquisition of the capital assets of large corporations unless the effect of the merger would be desirable. It is suggested to Congress that such mergers be forbidden unless the acquisition would result in greater efficiency and economy and would not lessen competition or create monopoly.

April 1, 1941

WORLD WAR II

DEFENSE CONTRACTS CLOSE TO 1939 SALES

113 Concerns Have Work Equal to 97% of Volume That Year

Defense contracts awarded to 113 industrial companies to May 31 are equal to 97 per cent of their entire 1939 sales, according to a survey by THE NEW YORK TIMES. Contracts awarded these companies amount to $7,201,465,000, as shown in the table, or almost half of all defense contracts awarded by the government, compared with 1939 sales of $7,426,289,000. Both plant expansion awards and subcontracts received from other concerns are excluded from the company figures.

The forty-eight shipbuilding, aircraft, iron and steel and automobile companies included in the 113 concerns alone account for more than 42 per cent of all defense awards.

Their contracts are equal to 136 per cent of their 1939 sales. If subcontracts and plant expansion awards could also be included, these percentages would be considerably higher.

DEFENSE CONTRACTS AWARDED

June 13, 1940 to May 31, 1941

(In thousands of dollars; excluding plant expansion contracts)

No. of Cos.	Total Contracts.	1939 Sales.	P. C. of Sales.
7 Shipbuilding	$1,662,080	1503.2	$110,573
18 Aircraft	2,305,255	900.9	244,791
2 Arms	119,801	562.9	21,281
3 Aircraft Parts	159,946	291.8	54,821
11 Iron & Steel*	1,563,302	82.4	1,897,299
8 Railroad Eq..	199,153	80.3	248,053
6 Textile	98,915	61.9	159,686
5 Machine Tool	10,492	43.1	24,329
11 M. & Ind. Eq.	80,053	42.6	187,942
1 Auto Access..	109,913	37.1	296,258
12 Automobile .	761,211	33.1	2,298,627
4 Elect. Eq....	128,988	25.8	492,103
4 Cop. & Brass	43,336	16.4	264,443
3 Building Sup.	7,974	7.7	103,822
3 Farm Equip..	21,790	7.1	306,944
5 Rubber	31,247	4.4	715,317
113 Companies ..	$7,201,465	97.0	$7,426,289

*Including shipbuilding operations.

June 10, 1941

NELSON MADE HEAD OF ARMS PROGRAM WITH SOLE CONTROL

President Puts Him Over OPM, SPAB and Other Agencies, for All-Out Production

ROLE LIKE BARUCH'S IN '17

Making of Planes, Tanks, Guns Issue — Final Decision Given Him in Dealing With Britain

By FRANK L. KLUCKHOHN
Special to THE NEW YORK TIMES.

WASHINGTON, Jan. 13—Donald M. Nelson was named by the President today to head the entire armaments production program with power to make "final" decisions on procurement and production.

The President stated that he was giving Mr. Nelson, who has been serving concurrently as executive director of the Supply Priorities and Allocations Board and priorities director of the Office of Production Management, authority over Vice President Wallace and William S. Knudsen and Sidney Hillman, OPM co-directors. It was Mr. Roosevelt's greatest delegation of power since 1933, when he made Brig. Gen. Hugh S. Johnson administrator of the National Recovery Act and director of the recovery effort.

Although the executive order legally defining the duties of Mr. Nelson has not yet been drafted and although Vice President Wallace indicated that Mr. Roosevelt would remain active, the President's statement seemed to indicate that Mr. Nelson would have powers and responsibilities as great as those given to Bernard M. Baruch as director of the War Industries Board, by President Wilson in the first World War.

In his statement President Roosevelt indicated that he was prepared to adopt the system for producing enough planes, tanks and guns to beat Germany, Japan and Italy as outlined in the war mobilization plan.

Text of President's Statement

The President's statement, which was read to reporters by Stephen Early, his secretary, said:

"By Executive Order I will establish the War Production Board, which will be granted the powers now exercised by the Supply Priorities and Allocations Board.

"I will appoint Donald Nelson as chairman of the War Production Board. In addition to being chairman of the board, he will be charged with the direction of the production program and have general supervision over all production agencies. His decision as to questions of procurement and production will be final.

"Mr. Nelson will report to the President as to the progress of the program. He will no longer serve as director of the Priorities Division but will devote his entire time to directing the production program.

"Vice President Wallace, as chairman of the Economic Defense Board, will serve as a member of the War Production Board, as will the other members of SPAB."

Under this arrangement Mr. Nelson would have authority over not only the industrialists and labor leaders who are in Washington to harness American production to a victory program but also over the Army and Navy, although they would legally still have contracting authority. He will be able to deal in final decisions with Lord Beaverbrook, British Minister of Supplies, it was said.

For the President's statement said that Mr. Nelson would have the last word on procurement and production, which would subordinate the military and naval procurement sections, and asserted that it was Mr. Nelson, and not the new War Production Board, he was equipping with "final" authority.

On the new super-board, as the Executive outlined it, there will be Mr. Wallace, Secretaries Stimson, Knox and Jones, Harry L. Hopkins, Leon Henderson, Price Control Chief, and Messrs. Knudsen and Hillman.

In his press conference at 4 P. M. President Roosevelt told reporters that there would be nothing on production reorganization today. Mr. Nelson and Vice President Wallace were called out of a SPAB meeting to see Mr. Roosevelt at the White House at 5 P. M.

Prior to the start of the war the President refused to accept the war mobilization plan, despite the urging of Mr. Baruch and the outline for American mobilization of industrial power given in the war mobilization plan which the armed services revised each year. Instead he first formed an Advisory Defense Board with little authority and later the Office of Production Management with authority split between an industrialist, Mr. Knudsen, and a labor leader, Mr. Hillman.

Now that the United States is at war as a result of attack, the President seemingly has decided to make one man responsible for production this year of 60,000 airplanes, 45,000 tanks, 20,000 anti-aircraft guns and 8,000,000 deadweight tons of merchant shipping. Mr. Nelson will make ready for even greater production next year.

British officials, members of the Cabinet and of Congress have been urging production control by one man. Announcement of the President's step came two hours before Wendell L. Willkie was scheduled to make a radio appeal for one-man control.

Advance copies of his speech, featuring this demand, were available early today. When the speech was broadcast, Mr. Willkie deleted his reference to one-man control of war production.

The executive order revealing how large Mr. Nelson's legal authority will be remains to be issued. Mr. Wallace, leaving the White House, said somewhat cryptically:

"It gives Mr. Nelson a direct channel."

This was taken in some quarters to mean to and from the President. In the first World War, Mr. Wilson, while retaining ultimate authority and responsibility, in practice left production matters largely to Mr. Baruch.

Mr. Early said that SPAB was automatically "replaced" by the new organization. SPAB was headed by Vice President Wallace, who, according to authority, was told that he was put in the position as a stop-gap when he assumed authority Aug. 28. There was no indication how much OPM and the Office of Emergency Management, under which production and procurement agencies were grouped, would be affected.

The habit of tall, husky Mr. Nelson of looking mildly through his spectacles in talking to visitors, while smoking a large cigar, at first misled official Washington, which finally recognized that he has tremendous abilities. After his dealings with the ticklish priorities problem, the opinion was expressed that he might be the hope of the production program.

Coining the slogan "double or nothing," Mr. Nelson has held an unalterable conviction from the time he arrived in Washington that everything must be subordinated to the war effort.

On the day the Vice President and Mr. Nelson jointly held the first SPAB press conference, a reporter asked whether business should not be "better than usual."

"That is a fine slogan," Mr. Wallace agreed, "don't you think so, Mr. Nelson?"

"No, business as usual must go to hell, Mr. Vice President," Mr. Nelson snapped.

For many years a protégé of Julius Rosenwald, head of Sears Roebuck, Mr. Nelson is one of the few business executives in Washington used to dealing in astronomical figures such as 40,000,000 gross. The main thing of interest to him is getting the job done.

He came to Washington in the first place as an aide to Secretary Morgenthau on airplane procurement. In the late Spring of 1940 he was made a member of the original National Defense Advisory Commission, having charge of purchases. When the OPM was formed in the Winter of 1941 he performed work judged officially to be so good that he was named administrative officer in SPAB when it was formed by the President Aug. 28 of the same year.

WAR PRODUCTION HEAD

Donald M. Nelson
Harris & Ewing

In April, 1941, friends say, he went to President Roosevelt intending to resign. They say that the President told so many anecdotes that he could not get a word in edgewise.

Finally, according to this story, Mr. Nelson said as he left:

"I'm leaving, Mr. President."

"See you in a few days," the President is said to have replied.

Mr. Nelson is still here.

Move Praised in Congress

Some of the comments at the Capitol were these:

"I think the President's action will bring about greater and speedier procurement of ships, planes, tanks and guns," said Senator Barkley, majority leader. "Mr. Nelson is eminently qualified to head the new board."

Senator Taft of Ohio stated: "The new organization should prove a great advance in production activities."

Senator Brewster of Maine, a member of the committee investigating defense contracts, said:

"Mr. Nelson is the best possible choice for the position that could have been made, particularly if he will exercise all the powers granted him and some more to boot."

Representative Earl Michener of Michigan, Assistant Minority Leader, said:

"I very much approve of giving one individual the power to act. I hope Mr. Nelson is the proper man."

January 14, 1942

INDUSTRIAL PROFITS IN 1941 NEAR 1929

By KENNETH L. AUSTIN

Industrial profits in 1941 were second only to those of 1929 and, for some groups, exceeded the records of that boom year by a comfortable margin, a survey of the first seventy-one principal corporations to report last year's results shows. Twenty-two of these companies earned more in 1941 than in 1929 or any other year in the last fourteen years. Five others bested 1929 results but earned slightly less than in one or two intervening years.

Combined net profits of the seventy-one companies for 1941 were $426,114,500, in comparison with $364,906,900 in 1940 and with $526,-302,400, the only better year, in 1929. This decline of $110,000,000 from the 1929 peak, however, consists mainly of a $90,000,000 shrinkage in the combined profits of five steel companies.

Sixty-six companies other than steel earned $236,031,800 in 1941, against $183,634,900 in 1940 and $255,900,500, the peak year, in 1929. The profits thus came within 7.7 per cent of the record results.

Earnings Cut in Taxes

There is no doubt that 1941 earnings would have exceeded those of any prior year substantially had the same rates and principles of taxation applied. As it is, industry needed a far greater volume of business than in 1929 to produce the results achieved last year, for the following principal reasons:

1. Income taxes in 1929 were negligible in contrast with the heavy income and excess profits taxes applicable to 1941 results.

2. No social security taxes existed in 1929; in addition to meeting such charges in 1941, a great many companies provided additional contributory retirement assistance for salaries in excess of $3,000 per annum.

3. Wage rates were substantially higher. At the close of 1941 factory payrolls were at about 165 against 107.7 for 1929, with the 1923-1925 average as par. The cost of living, incidentally, rose from 101 in January to 110 in December, against 122.5 in 1929.

4. Total employment was substantially higher, reflecting production at near capacity and limited work weeks for labor. At the close of 1941 factory employment was about 135, against 101.1 for 1929, based on the 1923-25 average as par.

5. Income from investments was sharply lower. In 1929 many industrial companies enjoyed substantial returns on their investments in stocks and bonds of other companies and the placement of funds in the call loan market. By 1941 the bulk of such investments had been liquidated, and interest received on bank balances and funds invested in Government bonds produced a small return on cash assets, although these were very large.

6. Higher rates of depreciation were established and appropriations for contingency, inventory, self insurance and other reserves were considerably higher than in 1929. Many companies were setting up reserves to cover eventual return to peace-time operations.

Mitigating Factors Cited

On the other hand, there were in effect during 1941 certain mitigating factors, such as improved efficiency of operation, both from the standpoint of raised standards of health and safety and general improvement in working conditions, and from that of savings attributable to new inventions, processes and methods. A general amelioration in the capital structures of industrial corporations including the retirement or refunding at lower interest rates of senior obligations, also contributed to a higher return per dollar of business volume.

Midway in position among factors affecting earnings were costs of materials. Generally speaking, the prices of most commodities had not quite attained the average 1929 level by the end of last year. The general commodity index rose from 80.8 in January to 92.5 in November, against 96.5 for 1929, but this included farm products, which rose from 71.6 to 90.6 (104.9 in 1929) and foods, which rose from 73.7 to 89.3 (101.0 in 1929).

Other commodities began 1941 at 84.3 and reached 93.5 in November, against 92.6 in 1929, reflecting mainly the rise in building materials from 99.6 to 107.5 ((97.1 in 1929) and in hide and leather products from 102.4 to 114.1 (109.2 in 1929). Metals and metal products in November were 103.3 against 104.4 in 1929; chemicals were 89.8, against 94.4, and fuel and lighting materials were 78.8, against 81.6.

For the steel industry, which as a whole produced 65,261,688 net tons of semi-finished and finished steel products in 1941, against 45,997,746 net tons in 1929, costs and taxes appear to have been predominant factors in the relatively poor showing. While steel mill employment reached 140, against 98.9 in 1929, steel payrolls attained 172, against 106 in 1929. Income taxes of the companies reviewed were in excess of the net profits shown for 1929.

While contrasting figures for the World War years are not available for all steel companies, United States Steel earned a peak of $271,531,730 in 1916, when wages were $263,400,000 and accrued taxes were $26,600,000, against $197,592,060 in 1929, when wages were $420,100,000 and taxes were $51,000,000, and $116,019,518 in 1941, when payrolls were $601,-117,053 and taxes were $191,496,-332. Similar conditions relate to Bethlehem Steel's results for the same years.

Table Showing Profits

The following table gives the combined results of certain groups, with the number of companies in each, and all seventy-one companies by fiscal years for fourteen years:

(Figures Are Thousands of Dollars)

Year.	Steel (5).	Foods, Beverages, Tobacco (13).	Textiles, Apparel, Leather (14).	Total Includ. Other Mfg. (71).
1928 ..	164,106	101,284	29,949	385,571
1929 ..	280,402	117,798	22,854	536,302
1930 ..	146,508	114,984	12,481	335,240
1931 ..	8,795	76,721	1,900	96,609
1932 ..	*106,062	65,396	*2,936	*64,986
1933 ..	*50,366	69,243	11,650	24,497
1934 ..	*19,658	80,681	8,626	92,056
1935 ..	17,955	82,426	11,388	155,859
1936 ..	85,530	97,092	15,913	279,298
1937 ..	148,934	82,451	11,259	337,444
1938 ..	*2,938	53,270	1,304	84,075
1939 ..	85,561	61,792	10,346	240,958
1940 ..	181,272	86,193	11,021	364,907
1941 ..	190,083	104,742	16,058	426,114

*Net loss.

The table shows the severity of the 1938 recession and the sharp climb that resulted from the outbreak of the war in Europe. Combined earnings of thirty-nine "other" industrial companies, not shown separately in the foregoing table, were $115,231,000 for 1941 compared with $115,238,000 for 1929, and it was principally in the mechanical industries that new high records were set last year. The meat packing industry also reached a new peak in 1941.

February 1, 1942

ROOSEVELT BACKS BAN ON TRUST SUITS DELAYING WAR JOB

By FRANK L. KLUCKHOHN

Special to THE NEW YORK TIMES.

WASHINGTON, March 28—President Roosevelt has accepted the decision of his official aides that pending anti-trust suits deemed capable of interfering with war production be dropped and that such suits be avoided as far as possible during the conflict, it was revealed at the White House today.

In thus emphasizing the important part which big business is playing in the war, the President, in letters to the Attorney General and the Secretaries of War and Navy, called for Congressional action to extend the statute of limitations so that violators of the anti-trust laws might be punished after the war. At the White House it was said that Congressional leaders already had agreed to push through such legislation.

President Roosevelt acted upon the basis of a memorandum recommending such a course of action, dated March 20, and signed by Attorney General Biddle, Secretaries Stimson and Knox and Thurman Arnold, Assistant Attorney General in charge of the Anti-Trust Division.

These officials took the position that some of the pending investigations, suits and prosecutions undertaken in accordance with the anti-trust laws would, if continued, "interfere with the production of war materials."

For Action in Fraud Cases

They insisted, however, that violators of this law should not escape ultimate prosecution; that prosecution should not be avoided unless war production would be affected and, finally, that no entity which had sought to defraud the government should in any event obtain postponement of investigation and subsequent action.

A procedure was suggested to Mr. Roosevelt and accepted, by which pending and future anti-trust cases would be rapidly examined by the Attorney General and the Secretaries of War or Navy, who would decide whether war production would be interfered with if the government proceeded. In case of difference among these officials, the decision of the Secretary of War or Navy would prevail, subject to final review by the President.

This policy was approved by the Executive in letters, also dated March 20, in which it was stated that, unless the war were won, "the anti-trust laws, as indeed all American institutions, will become quite academic."

"While every precaution will be taken to prevent any one from escaping prosecution if he has violated the anti-trust statutes, whether he is now engaged in war work or not, we must keep our eyes fixed upon the one all-important primary task—to produce more materials at greater speed," the President said. "In other words, we shall give our at-

tention to first things first."

The President's decision was regarded as of far-reaching importance in official Washington, not only because of the immediate issue involved, but because of assertions that the action provided one of the first major indications that the Chief Executive was prepared to subordinate internal social struggles to the prosecution of the war.

His decision was made public at a time when the Truman Committee is investigating the alleged withholding of war patents up to this last midweek by the Standard Oil Company and the alleged cartel arrangements of the corporation in connection with the German chemical trust, I. G. Farbenindustrie. Mr. Arnold testified Thursday and Friday before the committee that other American companies, operating in cartels, had restricted production of magnesium, aluminum, drugs, dyestuffs and other war materials. He suggested vigorous enforcement of the anti-trust laws.

It was noted in official circles today, however, that under his war powers, inherent and voted by Congress, the President could force the freeing of essential war patents without recourse to lengthy court actions which, as his aides pointed out in their memorandum, "unavoidably consume the time of executives and employes of those corporations which are engaged in war work."

Mr. Roosevelt emphasized in his letter that "the crisis of war should not be used as a means of avoiding just penalties for wrongdoing," adding that "in other words, it must be made very clear that the war effort is being impeded."

The Executive remarked that no right-minded person should use the country's extremities as an excuse to violate any statute.

The President stressed especially the need for carrying out the suggestion that only those industries actually engaged in war work should be exempted under the new procedure, and also the need for taking steps to assure that guilty corporations should not run over the statute of limitations. He further favored immediate prosecution where fraud against the government was involved. He praised the decision of his aides to publicize each decision to forego prosecution which would be made under the procedure outlined.

Reporters were informed that Mr. Roosevelt had taken up the issue with the Attorney General and that the memorandum outlining a new policy was a result of his initiative.

The President, it was said, had discussed the matter of legislation to extend the statute of limitations with Vice President Wallace, Senate Majority Leader Barkley, Speaker Rayburn, House Majority Leader McCormack and the chairmen of the Senate and House Judiciary Committees — Senator Van Nuys of Indiana and Representative Hatton W. Sumners of Texas. There was unanimous approval by them of this plan, it was said.

March 29, 1942

Questionnaires Strangle Business And Bring Demand for an Inquiry

Special to THE NEW YORK TIMES.

WASHINGTON, Dec. 1—Testimony that government red tape, particularly the flooding of industries with questionnaires, was strangling business, increasing consumer and taxpayer costs and hampering war production prompted the Joint Committee on Reduction of Non-essential Federal Expenditures to report out unanimously today a resolution calling for a Congressional investigation and legislative remedies.

Secretary Morgenthau and Harold D. Smith, Director of the Budget Bureau, who are members of the committee, joined in the voting. Further testimony is scheduled for Thursday.

According to witnesses and exhibits, 495,480 man-hours were spent during a single quarter by companies of a manufacturer's organization filling out questionnaires for the OPA and other agencies. Questionnaires, the representative of a drug company testified, cost his firm $100,000 a year. The managing director of a contractors' association, whose membership is engaged almost 100 per cent in war work, asserted that while executives used to spend 80 per cent of their time supervising construction and 20 per cent answering government questions, the situation now was just the reverse.

Overhead costs in the contracting industry, H. E. Foreman, representing the Association of General Contractors of America, said had been increased 50 per cent by question answering and construction costs 10 per cent. Contractors were required to fill out from forty-seven to fifty-two questionnaires at quarterly or monthly intervals, some bulking twenty-six pages.

The National Association of Manufacturers reported that eighty-nine of its member companies were required to file 3,479 reports to governmental agencies, or an average of 164 for each company. Surveys indicated that 64 per cent of the questionnaires contained duplications by various agencies and 34 per cent were almost entirely duplications.

Complaints against delays encountered in agencies were also cited.

C. M. Van Kirk, vice president of E. R. Squibbs & Sons, told the committee that an anti-whooping cough serum was withheld from the market for six weeks awaiting the establishment of a price ceiling by OPA.

"After about six weeks," he said, "I called up the responsible official in Washington and reviewed just what had happened. I told him that if we were not authorized to release this serum within forty-eight hours, I thought I could prove that infants had died while they had been pussyfooting around. The product was released the next day."

The filling out of questionnaires from the OPA and other agencies was costing his company $100,000 a year, he added.

The committee took especial interest in an OPA regulation identified as No. 1-1071-PLOF-5-NOBU-COS-WP, which requires special reports in the drug and cosmetic fields whenever a product or a container is changed.

Reports on 800 Changes

His company, Mr. Van Kirk said, had been required to make perhaps 800 such changes since last March and that an entire day was consumed in making a report on each change. The company was behind schedule in making reports on changes, he went on, exclaiming:

"And we don't propose to discontinue our war effort work in order to make out these reports."

Efforts by committee members to find out what was done with the reports and questionnaires after they reached the agencies were unavailing.

Senator Byrd announced after the hearing that the committee would require all Federal agencies to produce copies of all their questionnaires and explain what use was made of the answers.

"Further, we will insist that when information is required from industry and business the questionnaires shall be standardized by the departments and agencies."

Senator Vandenberg, co-sponsor of the investigation resolution, was the first witness today.

"The burden of paper work, the enervating enmeshments of red tape, which has descended upon American business and the individual American citizen as result of rationing," he said, "is a deadly menace to national morale and a serious threat to the war itself. It is costing manpower and it is costing money which ought to be dedicated to more productive purposes."

He had received "literally thousands" of letters begging for relief. A farmer complained that he was required to fill out a two-page questionnaire to get a pair of boots.

A farmer needing a truck receives with his application blank a booklet containing 24,000 words of instructions, the Senator said. He is called upon not only to give the correct mileage each of his tires has made during a stated past-period, but how far each will travel during the next six months.

December 2, 1942

War 'Compulsives,' Not New Dealers, Force Industry Concentration, Cherne Says

War "compulsives" rather than long-haired New Dealers are forcing the concentration of industry, the growth of monopoly, the death of small enterprise and the rationalization of business, Leo M. Cherne, executive secretary of the Research Institute of America, declared yesterday at the weely luncheon meeting of the Sales Executives Club of New York at the Hotel Roosevelt.

In his talk Mr. Cherne took issue with B. C. Forbes, publisher, who had introduced him and who had observed that if Washington continues to attempt to supply the deficiency caused by the drying up of venture capital "it will become one big owner, one big boss of American industry and we will be heading inescapably into socialism."

If this country can turn out $135,000,000,000 of goods each year and pay workers enough to buy them, it need not worry about labels, such as fascism, communism or socialism, Mr. Cherne said.

With men like Ferdinand Eberstadt of Wall Street, Charles Wilson of General Electric and the War Department running the war production effort, "the last New Dealer died of an inferiority complex," he declared.

"How much longer will you delude yourself that the rationalization of industry is the result of machinations by David Ginsburg of the OPA?" Mr. Cherne asked. "These patterns cannot be turned back. There have been miracles in part on the production line, but behind them were twelve months of paper work and blue printing by business men called to Washington. They are regulating your business much more than any long-haired group."

Mr. Cherne predicted that within sixty days industry would be classified into "essential," "useful" and "non-essential" categories. The government is working on a master limitation order which will specify what products can be made and is trying to get up enough courage to issue it, he added.

January 6, 1943

SMALL INDUSTRIES AND POST-WAR ILLS

By J. H. CARMICAL

Although the country does not yet fully realize it, the United States, under the stress of war, is undergoing a most important industrial change. By the aid of war contracts and other assistance from the Federal Government, the large companies in virtually every industry are assuming greater importance, while the small units are being forced gradually out of business or assuming a lesser role.

Whether we like this trend or not does not matter, for there is not much that can be done about it. To fight the war, the United States Government had to have enormous quantities of finished materials, and quickly. Because of their research and engineering staffs and their experience in quantity production, the government of necessity had to turn to the large companies.

Under the exigency of the post-war period, there is some doubt that this trend can be stopped. For some time after the war there will be a heavy demand for civilian supplies, and the big companies, by converting their war plant facilities to this object, will be in the best position to meet it. For this reason, it is argued, the reconstruction period will be just as effective in continuing the trend as the war was in starting it.

An illustration of the change that is taking place in industry generally is demonstrated by what is happening in the oil companies. At the time of the dissolution of the Standard Oil Company in 1911 by a Supreme Court decision, that organization controlled about 90 per cent of the petroleum business in the United States.

With the advent of the motor car, the petroleum industry expanded by leaps and bounds and now ranks among the first few important groups. The Standard Oil companies that were set adrift expanded sharply, and several of them now are larger than the parent concern was at the time of the dissolution. However, their portion of the domestic business is considerably less, most of these companies doing only about 30 per cent of the oil business in their respective territories. There is some overlapping of territories resulting from the purchase of marketing companies, and it is quite probable that the volume of business done by these companies and their subsidiaries now is between 35 and 40 per cent of the total for the country.

The remainder of the domestic oil business is divided among a few large independent companies, several of which operate on a nationwide basis, and hundreds of small refineries and distributors. Although no survey has been made to show how this business is divided, it is estimated that the large independent companies get, roughly, one-half the remainder of 60 to 65 per cent of the domestic business.

The so-called independent group of companies never became particularly active in the foreign field, although from time to time a few of these companies did branch out in that direction. At the time of the outbreak of the war in Europe in 1939, it was estimated that the Standard Oil group, including the production that its members had developed abroad, controlled 90 per cent of the foreign business of the United States companies.

When the United States entered the war it was necessary that production of aviation gasoline be increased enormously and that large quantities of other oil products, of superior quality be supplied to the armed forces. In addition, some special products were needed to meet various conditions of a global war. While the twelve to fifteen large oil companies were able partly to meet the requirements, it was necessary that producing facilities be expanded enormously. The Federal Government in most instances supplied the necessary funds for these facilities and at the same time gave priority ratings to the raw materials needed for their construction. Contracts also were entered into for the purchase of their production.

The small refiner, for the most part, has confined his activities to the production of gasoline, kerosene, light and heavy fuel oils. With the rationing of gasoline, he has lost a substantial part of his market for that product. Since this commanded a higher price than did other products which he produced, gasoline was his "money crop." Now to supply the demand for fuel oils, the prices of which are fixed, he must produce less gasoline and a substantial part of this he is compelled to run to storage. To complicate his position fur[illegible], there has been no change in p[illegible]s of crude oil and costs of refinery operating have increased.

Even if the small refiner is able to weather the war period, his position after the war will be just as difficult, if not more so. So far, he has not been able to get any materials to expand operations or to improve the quality of his product. In fact, it is not necessary to make improvements now, for the motorist is willing to take almost any gasoline which is offered to him. However, when the government no longer needs the entire output of the big refiners and they are in position to supply domestic needs, the situation of the small refiner will become untenable.

The products of the large refiner are not confined to gasoline, kerosene and fuel oil. His plant is equipped to produces high-octane aviation gasoline, many grades of lubricants and many specialty items. At present he is producing some butadiene for synthetic rubber, and when the present rubber program is completed he will be making enough to supply the nation's normal rubber requirements of about 600,000 tons annually. Also, he is producing toluene for explosives and is doing this on such an efficient basis that he will have no difficulty in keeping this field after the war. If he found a change was necessary, the plants probably could be converted easily to the production of other high-grade petroleum products.

Under the defense program prior to Pearl Harbor and the war effort since, the United States Government has expended billions of dollars on the construction of plants and the expansion of existing facilities of almost every large industrial company in the country. The proportion expended in the oil industry probably is no greater than in any other great manufacturing group.

Of course, it is not known what disposition will be made of these plants after the war. That will depend upon the vagary of politics. However, in most instances the plants are so constructed that they are an integral part of a large company, and it will be most difficult to segregate them and place them under separate management.

January 24, 1943

SEC Surveys the War Industries To Speed Contract Renegotiation

Special to The New York Times.

PHILADELPHIA, April 10—A cross-section of leading American war industries, reporting for 1941 final net profits of as much as 133 per cent of invested capital, was made public today by the Securities and Exchange Commission for use in renegotiation of war contracts that carried excessive profits.

One of the most comprehensive surveys ever prepared by the SEC, the study discloses in detail profits of 864 industrial corporations and the relationship of such profits to net invested capital for the five years, 1936-41.

Following the recent renegotiation procedures on war contracts, brought about as a result of Congressional committee hearings and under which considerable war profits have been turned back to the Federal Government, the SEC survey is considered to be highly significant and is expected to be of prime importance in the letting of future war contracts to the companies involved.

The survey was prepared by the staff of the commission for use by the Price Adjustment Boards of the Army, Navy and Maritime Commission, as well as the Military and Naval Affairs Committees of the House and the War Production Board.

The first compilation of its kind ever assembled, the SEC survey was based upon the latest available figures in the annual reports of the companies, which had a total invested capital in 1941 of more than $28,000,000,000, on file with the commission. It will be brought up to date each year.

Civilian as well as military production was reflected in the annual reports, but no attempt was made in the SEC survey to show what portion of the net profits of any of the companies was derived from execution of war contracts. All the companies, however, were selected because of their participation in the war effort.

The two extremes in the survey were the Cessna Aircraft Company, which had a final net profit in 1941 that was 133.1 per cent of the total invested capital, and the twenty-six companies among the 864 that reported deficits for the year. All the companies in the report are listed on one or more of the national securities exchanges.

In the survey, invested capital was computed as at the close of the periods covered and comprised the following: Funded debt, non-current debt to affiliates, other long-term debt (including such classifications as serial notes, mortgages, notes with a maturity longer than one year, long-term purchase contract liabilities or purchase money obligations), minority interest, preferred stock, common stock and surplus.

In a few instances where a "reserve" was considered as part of surplus by the registrant, it was included in invested capital, otherwise it was excluded. Bonds, notes and mortgage installments due in one year and Treasury stock or bonds carried as an asset by the registrant were excluded from the computation of invested capital.

A number of major war industries, such as the Higgins and the Kaiser organizations and Sun Shipbuilding and Dry Dock Corporation, which are not listed on any exchange, were not included in the report.

It was pointed out, too, that in several of the cases reported, renegotiations have already been started and some completed. From the end of April, 1942, until the end of January, 1943, the War Department alone effected savings of $1,045,000,000 on war contracts, such savings being represented by cash refunds or price reductions. The average overcharge was found t[illegible] be about 12 cents on the dollar.

Aircraft and aircraft equipment, with a total of twenty-eight companies showing an average net profit after all deductions that was 30.68 per cent of the total invested capital, was the group with the highest combined percentage. Total invested capital was $394,367,000 and net profit after all charges was $118,065,000.

The net profit of the Cessna Air-

craft Company, of course, led all those in the aeronautical group, the company, with an invested capital of $1,205,000 in 1941, having a final net profit of $1,604,000, or 133.11 per cent on invested capital. Earlier figures for Cessna were not included, since it did not become a listed corporation until 1941.

The Consolidated Aircraft Corporation, with invested capital of $9,243,000 in the same year, had a net profit of $8,025,000 after all charges, or 94.72 per cent, a figure that compared with 28.39 per cent in 1940 and with 12.11 per cent in 1937.

The Bell Aircraft Corporation's net profit after all charges as a per cent of invested capital in 1941 was 36.24 per cent, compared with 11.22 per cent in 1940 and 4.68 in 1937. Bell's invested capital in 1941 was $5,438,000, and its net profit after all charges was $1,971,000.

Net profit of the Curtiss-Wright Corporation, with invested capital of $61,378,000, was $25,718,000 in 1941, or 41.90 per cent of the invested capital. Its corresponding percentage in 1940 was 35.11 per cent, and in 1937 6.80 per cent.

The Douglas Aircraft Company had in 1941 a net profit after all charges that was 51.03 per cent of its invested capital. The Fairchild Aviation Corporation, 45.36 per cent; North American Aviation, Inc., 51.06 per cent; Ryan Aeronautical Company, 38.10 per cent, and Wright Aeronautical Corporation, 45.76 per cent were among the others.

Metal Working Group

The metal working machinery group, with eighteen registrants having total invested capital of $101,440,000, had the second highest net profit after all charges as a per cent of invested capital in 1941—27.89 per cent.

The South Bend Lathe Works, with an invested capital of $2,149,000 and a final net profit of $17,000 after all charges, or 46.53 per cent of the larger figure, led the list of metal machinery concerns in that respect. Its net profit as a percentage of invested capital in 1940 was 34.59 per cent and in 1937 28.88 per cent.

South Bend's record, like that of the metal working machinery group as a whole, however, was much more consistent with peacetime performances than many of the other war industry groups. The eighteen registrants' net profit after all charges as a per cent of invested capital in 1937 was 26.21 per cent and in 1940 25.89 per cent, compared with 27.89 per cent in 1941.

Turning in a total net profit after all charges that was 25.15 per cent of the invested capital, the five companies in the shipbuilding group had the third highest return in that respect. The combined average in 1940, when our naval and merchant marine expansion got under way, was 22.93 per cent, compared with a minus 1.63 per cent in 1937.

The New York Shipbuilding Corporation, with a net profit of $3,075,000 in 1941 representing 37.21 per cent of total invested capital of $8,265,000, led the shipbuilding group. In 1940 the percentage was 25.09, while in 1937 it was a minus 15.56 per cent.

The Bath Iron Works Corporation's net profit in 1941 was 24.73 per cent of invested capital, while that of the Newport News Shipbuilding and Dry Dock Company was 27.05 per cent.

The only two other groups of companies, the final net profits of which were greater than 20 per cent of invested capital in 1941, were the engine and turbine manufacturers and the rolling mills without steel-making facilities, with 23.30 per cent and 21.26 per cent, respectively.

The Continental Motors Corporation, having a final net profit of $3,232,000, or 33.35 per cent of invested capital of $9,691,000 in 1941, and the Briggs & Stratton Corporation, having a final net profit of $1,155,000, or 32.88 per cent of invested capital of $3,513,000, had the highest such percentages in the engines and turbines group of eight companies.

Not the highest percentage but the most startling change among the five rolling mills without steel-making facilities was the Eastern Rolling Mill Company, which had a deficit of $134,000 in 1940 but turned in a net profit of $341,000, or 21.41 per cent of $1,593,000 of invested capital in 1941.

The other four in this group, Acme Steel Company, Detroit Steel Corporation, Bliss & Laughlin, Inc., **and Superior Steel Corporation, all had final net profits in 1941 that were between 20.08 and 23.51 per cent of invested capital; Bliss & Laughlin, Inc., having the highest figure.**

Steel Producers

One of the largest groups from the standpoint of invested capital and importance in war work, the steel producers with blast furnace facilities, had one of the lowest net profit returns, 7.01 per cent of invested capital for 1941.

The Bethlehem Steel Corporation, for example, had invested capital of $665,644,000 in 1941 and received net profit of $34,458,000, or 5.18 per cent.

The United States Steel Corporation, with invested capital of $1,599,917,000, had a net profit of $116,171,000, or 7.26 per cent, while the Republic Steel Corporation, with invested capital of $350,909,000, had a net profit of $24,038,000, or 5.18 per cent, after all charges.

Comparable records were established by the Alan Wood and Steel Company, the American Rolling Mill Company, the Colorado Fuel and Iron Corporation, the Crucible Steel Company of America, the Inland Steel Company, the Jones & Laughlin Steel Corporation, the National Steel Corporation and others in the group, the percentage in no case reaching 10 per cent.

Oil Refineries

The oil refining group, with thirty-five registrants having total invested capital of $7,214,625,000, had a slightly better record, taken collectively. The total net profit of all thirty-five was $493,104,000, or 6.84 per cent of invested capital in 1941.

The net profits as a per cent of invested capital of some of the larger refining companies were: Standard Oil Company (N. J.), 7.58; Texas Company, 8.54; Tide Water Associated Oil Company, 6.66; Sun Oil Company, 11.67; Standard Oil Company (Ind.), 6.59; Socony-Vacuum Oil Company, Inc., 5.72.

Following is a partial list of other companies covered in the survey, together with, first, their invested capital; second, their final net profit in 1941, and, third, the net profit as a per cent of invested capital:

Corporation.	Invest. Cap. (000 Omitted)	Net Profit. (000 Omitted)	PC. of Cap.
Automobile Parts and Accessories			
Bendix Aviation...	$37,303	$13,268	35.57
Borg-Warner	44,765	7,475	16.70
Briggs Manufactur	34,115	5,511	16.15
Electric Auto-Lite	32,744	5,866	17.91
Libbey-O-F Glass.	41,271	8,821	21.37
Reynolds Spring...	2,343	804	34.31
Timken-Det Axle.	14,707	4,972	33.81
Timken Roller B..	44,220	9,477	21.43
United Specialties.	1,772	760	42.89
Automobiles			
Chrysler	$177,391	$40,114	22.61
General Motors...	1,129,391	201,653	17.86
Hupp Motor Car..	1,413	316	22.36
Chemicals			
Air Reduction.....	$41.398	$7,117	17.19
Clorox Chemical..	1,528	390	25.52
Novadel-Agene ...	3,535	989	27.98
Parker Rust Proof	2,692	749	37.11
Electrical Supplies and Equipment			
Clark Controller...	$1,570	$641	40.83
Conn. Tel & Elec..	723	351	48.55
Master Electric...	3,030	965	31.85
Square D	7,265	3,104	42.73
Miscellaneous Iron and Steel Products			
Van Dorn Iron Wk	$1,140	$527	46.23
Steel Producers Without Blast Furnace Facilities			
Carpenter Steel...	$8,780	$2,012	22.89
Rustless Ir and Stl	10,056	2,335	23.22
Universal-Cyc S..	6,472	1,753	27.09
General Industrial Machinery			
Hein-Werner M P.	$585	$174	29.74
Hoover Ball and B	2,091	568	27.16
Ind Pneumatic T..	5,065	1,555	30.70
Ingersoll-Rand ...	41,606	9,340	22.45
Locke Steel Chain.	883	261	29.56
F E Myers & Bro.	4,468	1,090	24.40
Neptune Meter....	3,958	1,052	26.58
Pierce Governor...	652	182	27.81
Torrington	10,905	3,385	31.04
Victor Equipment.	857	203	23.69
Special-Industry Machinery			
Lynch	$1,781	$519	29.14
Meyer-Blanke	568	127	22.36
Non-Ferrous Metals			
Illinois Zinc.......	$1,266	$396	31.28
Producers and Fabricators of Non-Ferrous Metals			
Akron Brass Mfg.	$256	$117	45.70
Hoskins Manufact.	1,780	604	33.93
Udylite	955	307	32.15
Radio and Radio Equipment			
Belmont Radio....	$1,122	$281	25.04
Crosley	6,021	1,493	24.80
Magnavox	754	185	24.54
Solar Manufactur.	461	147	31.89
Railroad Equipment			
Pittsburgh Forg...	$3,039	$743	24.45
Youngstown Stl D	4,939	1,374	27.82
Screw Machine Products			
Aero Supply Mfg..	$1,692	$806	47.64
Tires and Other Rubber Products			
Baldwin Rubber...	$2,572	$612	23.79

The survey, which required ninety days to complete, was made under the direction of Ralph H. Krapp of the Trading and Exchange Division of the SEC. The original suggestion that such a survey would be helpful in renegotiating proceedings came from the SEC, Mr. Krapp said, and was followed immediately by requests for its preparation from various government agencies active in that field.

April 11, 1943

ARMY SEIZES RAILROADS ON PRESIDENT'S ORDER

By LOUIS STARK
Special to THE NEW YORK TIMES.

WASHINGTON, Dec. 27—President Roosevelt ordered Secretary of War Henry L. Stimson at 6 P. M. today to take over all railroads in the continental United States at 7 P. M., despite assurances at 5 P. M. that the fifteen nonoperating unions were canceling their notices for a strike Dec. 30 and were ready to have him arbitrate the amount they were to receive for overtime pay.

The President, however, declared that he could not wait "until the last moment to take action to see that the supplies to our fighting men are not interrupted."

He said that he was taking over the railroads because the nonoperating employes, numbering 1,100,000, did not agree with the carriers "upon the scope of the issues to be arbitrated by the President." Strike orders of three operating brotherhoods, the firemen, conductors and switchmen, were still in force.

Lieut. Gen. Brehon B. Somervell, commanding the Army Service Forces, was designated by Secretary Stimson to take over the railroads in conformity with the Presidential order.

Directly responsible for operating the roads under General Somervell will be Maj. Gen. C. P. Gross, Chief of Transportation, Army Service Forces.

Mr. Stimson also announced that the Army officials would have the advice of Martin W. Clement, president of the Pennsylvania Railroad, as well as the staff of the Association of American Railroads.

An offer to act as labor consultants is being made by Mr. Stimson to A. F. Whitney, president of the Brotherhood of Railroad Trainmen, and Alvanley Johnston, president of the Brotherhood of Locomotive Engineers. These two brotherhoods accepted President Roosevelt's wage arbitration offe last week and canceled their str.ke orders.

The President's arbitration award was announced today. It granted to the trainmen and engineers 5 cents an hour for work in excess of forty hours a week, or in lieu of claims for expenses while away from home.

Increase Is 9 Cents an Hour

Added to the 4 cents an hour previously awarded to the operating unions by a Presidential board, the President's award makes a total wage increase of 9 cents an hour, which gives to the trainmen and engineers increases aggregating $81,000,000 a year.

The President also ruled that these two unions were entitled to a vacation of one week a year with pay at the basic hourly rate of employment. The wage increases, according to the Presidential announcement, shall remain in effect until the end of the war.

Seizure of the railroads appeared to have been averted when the fifteen nonoperating unions sent a letter to the President advising him they were ready to abandon their repeated refusal to accept a sliding scale of wage increases of 4 to 10 cents an hour and were willing to have him arbitrate what they were entitled to for overtime after forty hours a week.

The President had stated on June 16 at a press conference and had repeated several times that there was no justification for railroad workers not being paid time and a half after forty hours.

The heads of the brotherhoods of firemen, conductors and switchmen, who rejected the Presidential arbitration proposal last week, announced tonight that they would reconsider their attitude tomorrow. It was expected that they would follow the lead of the seventeen other unions and accept Presidential arbitration.

Informed Federal sources expressed the opinion tonight that Government operation would be brief, with Presidential arbitration awards covering all the wage disputes and enabling return of the roads to private management.

It is estimated in management circles that if the overtime award is extended to the other three operating unions the total wage advance for the operating unions would be about $100,000,000. The four-to-ten cents sliding scale increase for the nonoperating unions was estimated at $182,000,000. An award of five cents for overtime would cost an additional $125,000,000.

In signing the executive order taking over the railroads, the President said:

"Railroad strikes by three brotherhoods have been ordered for next Thursday. I cannot wait until the last moment to take action to see that the supplies to our fighting men are not interrupted. I am, accordingly, obliged to take over at once temporary possession and control of the railroads to ensure their continued operation.

"The Government will expect every railroad man to continue at his post of duty. The major military offensives now planned must not be delayed by the interruption of vital transportation facilities. If any employes of the railroads now strike, they will be striking against the Government of the United States."

Non-Operating Group's Letter

The text of the letter from the non-operating unions was as follows:

"Dear Mr. President:

"On Nov. 4, Hon. Fred M. Vinson, Director of Economic Stabilization, approved a sliding scale of wage adjustments for the non-operating group and provided these increases should become effective on Nov. 19. We protested against these increases because we did not feel they were sufficient to meet the problem.

"We have now concluded to abandon any further objections to Judge Vinson's order making these increases effective retroactive to Feb. 1, 1943.

"However, in view of recent offers by the railroads to grant to the operating group the benefits of the Fair Labor Standards Act in respect to overtime for the sixth day in any work week, we feel that the equities of the situation require that this consideration be extended to the nonoperating group.

"While we prefer the benefits of this overtime be distributed in a pro rata amount to all employes, if that is not agreeable to you we will accept the literal application of the Fair Labor Standards Act provisions on overtime.

"Therefore, there is no longer any dispute over the amount of wage increase to be granted to our group. The only remaining question in dispute is 'shall the non-operating group receive the benefits of overtime after forty hours per week offered to the operating group.' We agree to leave decision on this single question in dispute to the President of the United States and agree to accept the decision.

"Having, with your assistance, accommodated our immediate difficulties, we are withdrawing approval heretofore granted to the employes to stop work at 6 A. M. on Dec. 30, 1943.

"We thank you for your assistance in this disposition of our difficulties."

Signers for the Unions

Signers were George M. Harrison, J. J. Duffy, J. A. Franklin, Felix H. Knight, V. O. Gardner, S. J. Hogan, James J. Delaney, George Wright, Roy Horn, E. E. Milliman, A. E. Iyon, Edward Flore, I. M. Wicklein, Joseph P. Ryan, H. J. Carr and B. M. Jewell, chairman.

In the executive order taking over possession and operation of the railroads, the Secretary of War was authorized to terminate operation "as soon as he determines that such possession, control and operation are no longer required to prevent interruption of transportation service."

Secretary Stimson was not authorized to make a contract with the railroad labor organizations. In this respect, the order differed from the one which the President signed in the most recent seizure of the soft-coal mines as the result of a strike by the United Mine Workers. On that occasion, he authorized Secretary of the Interior Harold L. Ickes to make an agreement with the union.

In today's order, however, the Secretary of War was authorized to prescribe compensation of employes subject to any approval which may be required by law, by executive orders or by regulations relating to economic stabilization.

The Secretary was also authorized to recognize the right of employes to continue their membership in labor organizations and to bargain collectively with the representatives of the carriers' owners, subject to existing statutes and executive orders.

Restrictions on Bargaining

Such collective bargaining, however, under the executive order, is to cover only matters "pertaining to wages to be paid or conditions to prevail after termination of possession, control and operation under this order."

Significance was attached to the President's statement that his seizure order was predicated on the fact that the nonoperating employes and carriers did not agree on the scope of the issues to be arbitrated by him.

The carriers had offered the unions 4 cents an hour in lieu of overtime. The unions demanded 6 cents.

The unions wanted the President to arbitrate the overtime issue after they had been assured of the 4-to-10 cents an hour sliding scale increase. The railroads wanted the President to arbitrate the entire wage issue, including the straight "across-the-board" wage demand as well as overtime. The unions thus wanted to have only the issues in dispute arbitrated while the carriers wanted to have the wage picture considered as a whole.

No official statement was available tonight from the three carrier negotiating committees.

On their behalf it was said that they had not been supplied by the nonoperating unions with a copy of the statement sent to the President, and it was pointed out unofficially that they had made a contract with the nonoperating unions on Aug. 7 for an increase of 8 cents an hour.

Pay Stand of Carriers

The carriers had expressed readiness last week to divide this 8 cents increase into 4 cents an hour for a general wage increase and 4 cents an hour for overtime. Previously, the carriers had offered to the operating unions 4 cents an hour in lieu of overtime and away-from-home expenses, an offer that was increased by the President today by 1 cent.

Surprise was expressed in Congressional circles over the failure of the President to assign the task of operating the railroads to Joseph B. Eastman, director of the Office of Defense Transportation.

Senator Clyde M. Reed, Republican, of Kansas, said that it was "unfortunate" that the job was not given to Mr. Eastman, as he was "the natural man and most capable man for handling the situation."

Senator Reed added:

"The President has terribly messed up this whole labor thing. This is a regrettable but natural outcome of an uncertain and vacillating labor policy."

Behind-the-scene developments today disclosed that the President's action was the culmination of a protracted duel between James F. Byrnes, Mobilization Director, and Stabilization Director Vinson on one side and the non-operating unions on the other for President Roosevelt's ear.

Debate With Non-Operating Unions

Messrs. Byrnes and Vinson insisted that the non-operating unions abandon their demand for 8 cents an hour, which had been recommended by a Presidential emergency board on May 24 last and which the President had also asked these unions to accept. The carriers had made a contract to put the increase into effect, but Mr. Vinson insisted that the 4-to-10 cents an hour sliding scale conformed to stabilization standards he had enunciated, while the 8 cents "across-the-board" increase violated the Little Steel wage stabilization formula.

The non-operating unions prevented the railroads from putting the 4-to-10 cents increase into effect by filing a protest with the National Mediation Board. This protest was made after Mr. Vinson had informed the carriers that it was mandatory for them to pay the 4-to-10 cents increase.

Shortly after the non-operating unions sent their letter to the President, they also informed the National Mediation Board that they were canceling their protest against immediate payment by the roads of the 4 to 10 cents sliding scale wage increase.

The non-operating unions then announced that they were waiting for word from the White House in response to their offer to have the President arbitrate the overtime dispute. It was at this time, late in the afternoon, that these unions were advised by White House sources that Mr. Byrnes was insisting to the President that they had not called off the strike. They sent word to Mr. Roosevelt through a White House official that their letter, sent by messenger about 4:30 P. M., contained notice of the strike's cancellation.

Difference of Views Expressed

It was reported today that the President and Mr. Byrnes expressed two viewpoints at the conferences with the carriers and the non-operating unions last week. The President is understood to have agreed that 6 cents an hour was a fair concession for overtime beyond forty hours to the non-operating group. This payment would be in addition to the 4 to 10 cents an hour increase which Mr. Vinson had approved. In other words, the total amount of wage increase was to be from 10 to 16 cents an hour if the President had his way.

"You cannot do that," Mr. Byrnes is said to have advised the President in the presence of the other parties.

Subsequently the President is understood to have indicated rea l-ness to concede 4 cents an hour beyond the 4 to 10 cent sliding scale.

The President left for Hyde Park after this conference, and the following day, when the carriers and the non-operating unions conferred in Mr. Byrnes' office, the carriers slashed the wage concessions to a total of 8 cents an hour. Of this sum, 4 cents was to be a general wage increase and 4 cents was to cover overtime.

The conference adjourned with the understanding that the non-operating group was to give its formal answer to the President today. However, Mr. Roosevelt took over the roads, and now that he has allowed the two operating unions 5 cents an hour for overtime, it is expected that he will make a similar allowance to the nonoperating unions.

What is in doubt is whether the President will side with the carriers and reduce the 4 to 10 cents an hour sliding scale to 4 cents or whether he will approve the sliding scale and add the 5 cents for overtime to it.

December 28, 1943

Rail Wage Dispute Is Ended And Lines Go Back to Owners

Stimson Set Return at Midnight on Word From President—Non-Operating Men Get 9 to 11 Cent Rise—Vinson Agrees

By JOHN H. CRIDER

Special to THE NEW YORK TIMES.

WASHINGTON, Wednesday, Jan. 19—President Roosevelt announced final settlement of the railway wage case yesterday afternoon and Secretary Stimson returned the railroads to their owners at midnight.

The settlement was disclosed by the President at his press conference a few minutes after 4 P. M. The Secretary of War set the machinery in motion when he received a letter from the President reminding him that the executive order of Dec. 27 to take over the railways authorized him to return them when he was satisfied that the possibility of traffic interruptions had passed.

The final agreement in the wage dispute was reached between the Carriers Conference Committee and the fifteen non-operating unions. Since the operating brotherhoods and the roads had previously come to terms, all possibility of a railroad strike ended with the acceptance of the non-operating agreement by Fred M. Vinson, the Economic Stabilization Director.

Increases of 1 to 5 cents an hour were added to the sliding scale increase of from 4 to 10 cents approved by the Shaw emergency board for the non-operating unions, making total increases of from 9 to 11 cents an hour. For workers earning less than 47 cents an hour the settlement in lieu of overtime calls for 11 cents an hour more; from 47 to 57 cents, 10 cents more; from 57 cents an hour up, 9 cents more.

President Roosevelt said that there was no objection to the terms of settlement from the operating brotherhoods, since their scales were generally more than 80 cents an hour and there was no discrimination. The operating workers got a flat five-cent per hour increase in lieu of overtime and expenses away from home.

The President said that settlements also would be made for express company workers and employes of short line railroads.

Word of the agreement with the unions was conveyed to the President in a letter from John J. Pelley, president of the Association of American Railroads. While Mr. Roosevelt was reading the letter to the press conference, he paused to say that Mr. Vinson had just informed him the agreement was acceptable.

Likewise, when he read an expression of hope by Mr. Pelley that the increase granted in lieu of overtime would be made effective as of Dec. 27, as in the case of the operating brotherhoods, Mr. Roosevelt declared that he would so instruct Secretary Stimson.

A few hours later Secretary Stimson issued an order that "continued possession, operation and control by the United States of the carriers" should end at midnight.

"The expeditious termination of Government possession, operation and control of the carriers, with the minimum imposition of administrative burdens on the War Department and on the carriers which is consistent with proper protection of the Government's interests, will facilitate the prosecution of the war," he declared.

The Secretary provided that the Government would waive all rights to an accounting provided the railroads executed a release indemnifying the Government against claims by third parties and foregoing any claims which they themselves might have against the Government.

The express companies, which also were taken over by the Government, have about 35,000 employes, compared with around 1,000,000 for the Class I railroads. The short lines have another 20,000 workers.

It was understood last night that the short line agreement, containing increases similar to those approved for the Class I workers, had gone to Mr. Vinson. The express workers are expected to get from one to two and a half cents an hour increases in lieu of overtime, because thy work a forty-hour instead of forty-eight-hour week.

LETTER TO STIMSON

President Roosevelt's letter to Secretary Stimson urging return of the railroad properties was as follows:

"I am advised by Mr. J. J. Pelley that the Carriers' Conference Committees have reached an agreement with the fifteen non-operating employes organizations and I am also advised that the agreement is approved by Stabilization Director Vinson as being consistent with the stabilization program.

"The agreement contains a provision that the allowance agreed in lieu of overtime shall become effective as of Dec. 27, 1943.

"When you took charge of the railroads on Dec. 27, 1943, you announced that wages were frozen as of that date. The allowance for overtime now agreed upon can be made effective as of Dec. 27, 1943, only by a modification of your order freezing wages of that date. order freezing wages as of that date.

"Mr. A. F. Whitney and Mr. Alvanley Johnston, who represent the trainmen and engineers, were appointed by you as Labor Consultants when you took charge of the railroads. They have communicated with me recommending **that the allowance now agreed upon be made effective as of Dec. 27, 1943.**

"The order was modified in the case of the three brotherhoods that reached an agreement on Jan. 14, and I think that the nonoperating brotherhoods who have now reached an agreement should be treated like the other employes. I, therefore, request you to modify your order of Dec. 27, 1943, making effective as of that date the agreement reached today.

"As this settlement brings to an end the wage controversy between the carriers and their employes, I hope as soon as you have satisfied yourself that the provisions of the Executive Order have been complied with, that you will promptly return the railroads to the owners."

THE PELLEY LETTER

The text of Mr. Pelley's letter to the President follows:

"Supplementing my letter to you of Jan. 14, in which I advised you of the successful result of negotiations between the carriers' conference committees and the firemen's, conductors' and switchmen's organizations, I beg now to advise that the carriers' conference committees have reached an agreement with the fifteen nonoperating employes' organizations.
tions.

"This agreement ratifies the graduated scale increases which were recommended by the Special Emergency Board and not disapproved by the Stabilization Director, and also disposes of the issue of time and one-half for work performed in excess of forty hours per week. The agreement was submitted to Judge Vinson this morning for his consideration, and we are hopeful that he will find it consistent with the stabilization program.

"The agreement contains provision that the allowance which has been agreed upon in lieu of overtime shall become effective as of Dec. 27, 1943, and like other provisions of the agreement is, of course, subject to governmental approval.

"You addressed a letter to the Secretary of War in which you **asked him to make the overtime provision in the case of the conductors, firemen and switchmen effective as of Dec. 27, and it is respectfully suggested that you may find it appropriate similarly to advise the Secretary as to the effective date of the supplementary increase in lieu of overtime in the case of the fifteen non-operating organizations.**

"Should this agreement with the non-operating organizations receive Governmental approval it will dispose of the entire wage controversy between the carriers represented by the Eastern, Western and Southeastern Carriers' Conference Committees and their operating and non-operating organizations.

"We are deeply appreciative of the invaluable assistance which you have personally rendered to the parties."

January 19, 1944

Army Seizes Ward Stores; Avery Still Defies WLB

Plants in Seven Cities Are Taken Over on President's Order—No Trouble Arises and Government Files Test Suit

Special to THE NEW YORK TIMES.

CHICAGO, Dec. 28—For the second time in eight months and for the same reason, defiance of the National War Labor Board, the Government, acting this time through the Army, seized today the executive offices and other Chicago facilities of Montgomery Ward & Co., the country's second largest mail order organization.

At the same time the Army seized other war properties in Detroit, where four of the company's stores have been strike bound since Dec. 9, and in Jamaica, L. I.; St. Paul, Denver, San Rafael, Calif., and Portland, Ore.

Soon after Maj. Gen. Joseph W. Byron and his staff of fourteen officers took possession of Ward's properties in Chicago, on the North Side, a Government suit was filed in the Federal District Court here to test "once and for all" the right of the President and of various other Federal agencies to adjudicate labor disputes.

Army personnel posted copies of the statement in the various departments to inform the public and the employes that the properties were being operated by the Army.

Both the seizure and the court action were taken under the guise of war-time necessity, based on Ward's refusal to obey certain directives of the War Labor Board dealing with a dispute between the company and the United Mail Order, Warehouse and Retail Store Employes Union (CIO). The company has refused to comply with the agency's orders calling for maintenance of membership, arbitration, check-off of union dues, seniority and back wages.

When the war business day ended, Sewell Avery, the company's militant chairman, was still challenging the legality of the seizure. This was a repetition of his stand when troops first took possession of Montgomery Ward's Chicago plant in April. At that time, he resisted Government action until soldiers carried him bodily from his office to the street.

Mr. Avery was quoted tonight as saying that he planned to be at his desk as usual tomorrow "unless I am thrown out or fenced in."

At 5:26 P. M., General Byron, accompanied by an aide, left their temporary office on the eighth floor, supposedly to meet elsewhere with CIO union agents concerning enforcement of certain War Labor Board orders. At 5:30 P. M. Mr. Avery left his private office, still, as far as he was concerned, running the company's business.

Neither Gen. Byron nor Mr. Avery commented on the impasse.

How far Mr. Avery might carry his defiance this time was problematical. Lawyers expect the issue to develop into a historical legal battle over constitutional rights and powers, with its destination the United States Supreme Court.

"Ward's cannot in good citizenship accept or obey the commands of those who have no legal power to give them, and who are seeking to deprive Ward's of its constitutional rights and liberties," Mr. Avery said in a statement which he personally read to Gen. Byron.

President Roosevelt, in ordering seizure of the Ward properties in seven cities, accused Mr. Avery of "consistent and wilfull defiance" of WLB decisions, and declared that "the Government cannot and will not tolerate any interference with war production in this critical hour."

Indications were that the Government wanted not only a peaceful seizure for now, but also a judicial settlement of the case, which would avert recurrence of the widespread criticism of the action against Ward's in April. At that time Attorney General Biddle took possession through the medium of the Department of Commerce.

Pickets on Duty Since Dawn

At dawn, hours before Mr. Avery and General Byron and his staff arrived at the Ward offices, the union's local, Number 20, threw a picket line around the company's main properties in carrying out strike orders decided upon last night.

Except for picketing and occasional jeering calls of "scab" at employes who went to work, no further action occurred until Mr. Avery arrived at 9:45 A. M.

Five or six minutes later four Army staff cars, bearing General Byron and his staff, drove up. The general and some of his aides went at once to Mr. Avery's office on the eighth floor. Mr. Avery's secretary escorted the general into the chairman's office.

Then General Byron read President Roosevelt's seizure order. This order recited a long list of alleged grievances of the United States vs. Montgomery Ward and particularly Sewell Avery. It recited that nearly 12,000 workers were being affected by Ward's refusal to heed WLB directives. Work interruptions had occurred, war production was impaired, and therefore, the order read, the War Department had been instructed to take over Ward's properties.

Mr. Avery maintained a stony visage. After the reading of the order he said he would give his answer later. The Army officers retired to an office nearby.

About three hours later Mr. Avery issued a reply in which he gave notice of his defiance of the WLB, called the President's seizure order a violation of the Constitution and asserted that Congress "had given the President no power to seize the non-war business of Ward's."

Soon after his arrival at the Ward offices, Gen Byron issued a statement in which he asked the cooperation "of every executive and employe" and expressed the hope that "it will be possible in the near future to relinquish control of this enterprise."

Meanwhile, with the nominal military seizure, the union's picket lines were withdrawn, the union hailing the Government action as a victory.

Earlier in the day, the Government's suit, filed in Federal Court soon after General Byron took over, was assigned to Judge Philip L. Sullivan. All immediate technicalities as to service were amicably settled by the Ward lawyers. Neither side appeared before Judge Sullivan, and it was explained that Ward's had twenty days in which to answer.

The complaint was thirty-two pages long, and contained eight affidavits. In essence it asked judicial approval of the fait accompli, the Army seizure. It also asked a temporary injunction to restrain Mr. Avery and fifteen other Ward officials from interfering with Army management of the Ward plants.

The complaint described Ward's as a war business. Mr. Avery contends it is not.

The bill recited that the company maintains facilities in many cities, including 600 stores, that it employs 70,000 persons, that it distributes or manufactures supplies vital to war needs.

Then the suit went into a list of grievances, in substance that Ward's had failed to obey directives of the War Labor Board concerning CIO labor disputes. In conclusion it sought to portray what ill effects Ward's successful disobedience of WLB orders might mean.

"Persistent refusal of Ward's to accept determination by WLB or to settle its labor disputes peacefully," the suit declared, "has led other parties to labor disputes to refuse to accept the determinations of the board, threatens the maintenance of the no-strike-no-lockout pledge, and threatens to break down the procedure established by Congress for the peaceful adjustments of labor disputes in time of war, and to disrupt the national price and wage stabilization act."

December 29, 1944

INDUSTRIAL PROFIT IS CHARTED BY SEC

Drop of 1.6 Per Cent in 1943 From Preceding Year Found for Seventeen Groups

PHILADELPHIA, Jan. 21 (AP)—Net profit on sales after taxes decreased 1.6 per cent in 1943 from the 1942 level for seventeen heavy industry groups, Part 3 of a Securities and Exchange Commission study on profits and operations of 1,530 listed corporations disclosed today.

The survey, released in five parts and covering 118 industry groups with total assets of $62,000,000,000, was made at the request of Government agencies from annual reports filed with the commission.

The 280 companies in Part 3 had assets of $16,060,302,000 in 1943. Their net sales amounted to $18,044,430,000 in 1942 and increased to $22,972,374,000 in 1943. Net profit after income taxes in 1942 amounted to $837,567,000, compared with $823,904,000 in 1943. Net profit before taxes was reported at $2,383,282,000 in 1942 and $2,571,158,000 in 1943, an increase of 7.3 per cent.

The complete effect of renegotiation on the 1942 financial statements of 202 companies was shown. For these companies net sales before deductions for renegotiation were $13,950,921,000 and voluntary deductions from net sales amounted to $173,874,000. Further deductions from net sales as a result of renegotiation amounted to $184,104,000. These deductions reduced net profit after taxes $21,493,000 and reduced reserves set up for renegotiation $23,169,000.

Of the seventeen industry groups, steel producers with blast furnace facilities reported the largest sales volume. Fourteen companies in this group had in 1943 net sales of $6,105,940,000, net profit on sales after taxes of 2.7 per cent and net profit as a percentage of net worth of 5.3.

The sixteen companies in the miscellaneous iron and steel products group reported the highest percentage of profit after taxes as a per cent of net worth—23.8 per cent in 1943—and the twenty-three nonferrous metal companies reported the highest 1943 net profit on sales after taxes, 9.2 per cent. Other groups' profits ranged down to 2.1 per cent.

January 22, 1945

180,000 CANNON PRODUCED BY G.M.

DETROIT, Feb. 9 (AP)—The General Motors Corporation has turned out 1,000,000 machine guns, 2,400,000 carbines and 180,000 cannon since 1940, it stated today in a report on its wartime production.

Since 1940, the company said, it has also produced 140,000,000 shells and shell casings, 180,000 aircraft engines, 9,000 complete planes, 31,000 tanks, tank destroyers and armored cars and 740,000 trucks.

General Motors added that because of military restrictions it had not been possible heretofore to describe the company's war production except in terms of dollar value.

Difficult Jobs Sought

C. E. Wilson, company president, said that the firm had deliberately sought "the more difficult jobs because it was felt that through these its engineering and production experience would be of most service to the country."

He asserted that the items mentioned were only a few of the 3,600 different products the company makes for war, and listed among new programs "new types of tanks, radar equipment, high-explosive rocket shells, rocket bombs and jet-propulsion engines."

February 10, 1945

SAYS GOVERNMENT FAVORS MONOPOLIES

Report to House Group Asserts 'Giant Corporations' Have Bought 70% of War Plants

WASHINGTON, Dec. 25—A secret report now in the hands of the House subcommittee on monopoly charges that the Government itself is greatly accelerating and strengthening monopolistic control in the country by turning over to big business the bulk of plants built during the war at the taxpayers' expense.

Up to June 30, the report estimates, 70.1 per cent of the sales of wartime plants had been made to "giant corporations" and they also had acquired 72.8 per cent of the leases of such plants.

"The proportion of the value of these facilities going to giant corporations was higher than their ownership of manufacturing facilities in 1939," it adds, "and not only had the big surplus plants gone to the giant corporations, but they also had obtained a significant number of the small and medium-sized plants which were apparently well suited to smaller businesses."

All the 18 plants sold for more than $5,000,000 went to "giant corporations." Also, they obtained 15 of the 54 plants sold for $500,000 to $1,000,000 and 14 of the 143 plants sold for $100,000 to $500,000.

"Should the 250 largest corporations acquire the Federal facilities on which they generally hold purchase options, their plant and equipment would aggregate nearly $38,500,000,000," the report continues. "Thus they would hold 65 per cent of the country's production facilities.

"Of greater importance, however, the facilities of the 250 industrial giants alone would total almost as much as the entire facilities owned by all manufacturing corporations in the country in 1939."

The attack on the Government's war-plants-disposal policy is contained in the third section of the 200-page report. The document is a comprehensive study of economic concentration in the United States. In the two other voluminous sections, the report recommends eighteen drastic trust-busting proposals and severely criticizes several Government agencies for failure to enforce existing anti-trust laws.

Prepared by a staff of experts, the report has been under hot debate within the committee for several weeks. The three Democratic members want to make it public, but the two Republican members are insisting on open hearings before official action is taken on the report.

A final showdown on the issue is planned by the Democrats after the Christmas holiday. They want to get approval of the report before the new Republican-controlled Congress convenes Jan. 3.

"If concentration is to be reduced," the report states, "there must be a concerted effort involving all phases of Government. In some agencies there is not only lack of interest (in enforcement of anti-trust laws), but there are policies which actually promote concentration. This kind of working at cross-purposes not only limits the effectiveness of Government efforts to prevent concentration, but constitutes the most serious kind of waste of Government funds—since anti-trust activity must be increased to combat the concentration resulting from other Governmental activity."

According to the report, the sixty-three largest manufacturing corporations in the country had increased their net working capital to nearly $10,000,000,000 as the end of 1946 approached.

"With this capital," it adds, these sixty-three giants could purchase all of the usable Government-owned facilities at their option price, or they could purchase the assets of 71,700 smaller manufacturing corporations with assets of less than $3,000,000 each, which represents 94 per cent of the total manufacturing corporations in the United States.

"Large firms are, in fact, now using their wartime financial gains to buy up small firms, as is indicated by the current sharp increase in mergers and acquisitions."

December 26, 1946

Chapter 2

Coping With Industrial Giants

Harold Geneen, president of I.T.T.,
about to testify before
the Senate Judiciary Committee.

NYT Pictures/George Tames

Drawing by Carl Rose

Is Madison Avenue a Svengali mesmerizing innocents into a nightmare of buy-now-pay-later, or a Santa Claus channeling the plenty of a free economy?

In Defense of Madison Avenue

The Main Street of advertising, an inhabitant says, is wrongly pictured as a primrose path leading consumers astray. Where, he asks, would we or our standard of living be without it?

By JAMES KELLY

LIKE Hollywood, Wall Street and Broadway, Madison Avenue is known by the companies it keeps. Like them also, Madison Avenue has been dreamed about, written about, lied about—and become a label. It is, *last* of all, a narrow thoroughfare running from Twenty-third Street to the Harlem River on the east side of Manhattan and peopled during the daylight hours by messenger boys, chic office girls, and level-eyed executives with undented hats and shiny shoes. *First* of all, it is the accepted capital of a community of 45,000 advertising people (about 25,000 of them in New York City alone) who have been entrusted by hard-headed big and little business men with the spending of an estimated $10,000,000,000 in 1956. By popular consent, it is the voice, image and brandmark of our own free enterprise. Or by not-so-popular consent.

Madison Avenue these days is under sharp indictment. Advertising is America's pagan religion, the Account Executive for Indictments says, and it forces a fantastically false way of life through expert use of its own Golden Rule: "We have something to sell and we can make you buy it." Tantalized and tempted by dream-world pictures dangled before them, the victims of Madison Avenue have an itchy urge to buy now and pay later. They mortgage their futures in installment buying.

Beware the amoral power now loose in the land (the indictment goes on). Look out for the euphoric products that may lead you down the primrose path to puffy overweight and cancer. Bert Piel, Harry Piel and Snooky Lanson are paid by the smile, and no questions asked.

IT is shocking (the indictment goes on *and* on) that nobody seems to care whether an advertising campaign is good or bad for the country. It is all a numbers game, with virtuoso agency men playing the public like a piano. Headlines with a benefit twist, short copy and shorter ideas designed to fit the reader's attention span, illustrations that people can identify themselves with—the tired old one-two-three pitch for the mass audience.

And here's that bright new medium, television, operating in exactly the same way. On behalf of a television client, an agency will prepare hard-sell commercials and frame them in an elaborate show supplied full-blown by one of the super-specialist television package companies. And success or failure depends upon how many people saw the show (reported by hocus-pocus ratings), not upon how many enjoyed it. The same success or failure applies to politics as well as products. Madison Avenue sells ideologies and candidates just as it sells soap, in quantity and by advertised brands. All right.

Fuzzy thinking, stoutly replies Madison Avenue. In the first place, the American consumer is a beneficiary, not a victim, of our so-called commercialism. He is better housed, dressed, fed, entertained and catered to than anybody living anywhere else in the world. Solely because of mass production and multiple distribution, his standard of living is higher. If he has the dollars to installment-buy a car or TV set, he is supposed to have the sense of what to buy and how much. Credit is a privilege, not an opiate—a vote of confidence in a land of plenty with an abundant future. Don't forget that the extreme opposite of credit is barter. That even General Motors expands by borrowing. That everybody who owns an insurance policy is buying future security on the installment plan. And that every business house, including banks, steel companies and utilities, is at least partly made of glass.

A second line of defense is to imagine what it would be like to live without Madison Avenue. A knowing merchant from Gallipolis, Ohio, thinks he could live without it very readily. Instead of paying for gimmicked-up advertisements with eye-patches, white horses, and thin but sexy models trying to look like housewives, let's just save the $10,000,000,000 and lower prices all the way along the line. The way he figures it, 15 per cent of that staggering sum goes to advertising agencies to sell things the public never missed and doesn't want now.

IT is true that no other force besides advertising pushes the philosophy of obsolescence so hard or spreads the frontiers of human requirements so far. It wins acceptance for new products before their time and sets the wheels of technology in motion. But what is wrong with that? Without Madison Avenue, mass production would stop in its tracks. Unit costs of consumer goods would shoot up through the ceiling and out the roof. A ranking officer of the Ted Bates agency (founded in 1941 and billing an estimated $100,000,000 annually among just sixteen clients) declared that the American standard of *(Continued)*

JAMES KELLY, a literary critic among other things, was once a "no-account executive" (as he puts it) on Madison Avenue, and is now a vice president of an agency on Fifth.

living as we recognize it would go out of existence without the forced distribution of advertising.

He believes that the staggering billions of dollars spent for advertising in America actually cost the consumer little or nothing when one considers the low unit costs made possible by mass production. "Advertising sells superiority, after superiority has come into its own," this adman firmly stated. "You can't sell it if the product hasn't got it."

Advertising must be on the scene to create a consumer unrest that will make a monopolistic manufacturer improve his product and lower his price. Otherwise, the kitchen mixer which could weigh six pounds and sell for $16 would continue to weigh 150 pounds and sell for $128.50. Q. E. D. Free countries can expand their economies through advertising; controlled countries cannot.

Without advertising, our entire mass communications network would turn into a non-network: a real body blow for the 626 magazines of general circulation, 1,700 daily newspapers, 9,000 weekly newspapers, 2,947 radio stations and 465 television stations with over 38,000,000 television homes. Newspapers would become four or six-page handbills on cheap paper, without illustrations. Our popular magazines and trade and professional publications would be eliminated.

AMERICAN business requires a maximum audience, and it is up to Madison Avenue to deliver. If the system didn't work, the shrewd, cold-blooded management men who are paid to give their investors the best of it would find another system. The fact is that never in the economic history of civilization have so many (160,000,000) depended upon so few (45,000) and entrusted them with so much money ($10 billion).

The few, of course, get their rewards, but they are just enough by ordinary corporate standards: an average of 7 per cent profit received on net income, or 1 per cent on gross billing.

For this modest percentage Madison Avenue, to phrase its key defense with a flourish, serves as alarm clock for America's sleeping desires. It quarterbacks our way of life, operates as custodian of our enthusiasms, and keeps those dollars in streamlined circulation. It accepts the heavy responsibility for who we are and for the shape of our collective personality in the world at large.

PUTTING America's urge for self-improvement back to back with the equally strong urge to do-it-yourself, Madison Avenue has breathed new life into the 97-pound weakling and the girl whose friends wouldn't tell her. It shows mother how to get the kids to eat their cereal (Snap! Crackle! Pop!), and it shows grandfather how to set up a little extra security for himself and grandmother during the greater number of retirement years they can now look forward to together. It builds the showcase, fills it with alluringly styled and priced products, and shills for the sale.

Human nature is the force we are dealing with. The publisher of Printers' Ink has observed that advertising holds a mirror in front of basic human needs—and then adds the wish-fulfillment images. But the wish-fulfillment images will change, and possibly improve, only as human nature allows it. Soap opera will give way to singing opera when the audience is ready.

ADVERTISING is not a hungry predator on the prowl nor is it a fey branch of show business; it is an integral part of society and should be judged as such. It is naive to be surprised that dependable techniques, used to sell goods and services, are used to sell *desire* for goods, services—and the desirability of one particular candidate over another. This is a free economy, isn't it?, with the freedom of the individual to choose a way of life and the amenities that go with it.

Maybe the men of Madison Avenue think of these great Moral Questions or maybe they don't, but they get pretty

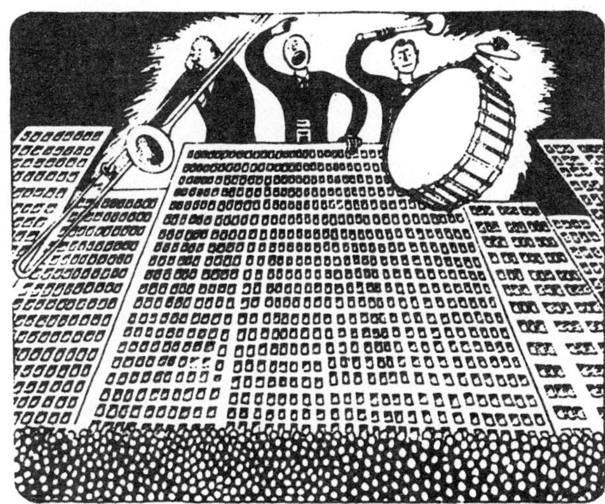

tired of snapping into the same old conditioned responses when a person from some other avenue lowers his head and begins to raise cocktail-party questions. Sometimes, too, they may try the jocular evasion gambit and identify themselves as foot doctors or piano players in houses of ill repute. But cocktail queries can have a lemon twist of truth that draws out the serious adman, if he can concentrate under the circumstances.

Is advertising a profession, a business, or a game of wits in which anybody can join if he has any? A consensus on Madison Avenue gives it the business label. One prominent agency president put it this way:

"A good advertising agency today is a collection of trained specialists with performance standards not exceeded in any profession. Guesswork moves out when knowledge of product, market and sales moves in. No client can be served in present competitive conditions by an agency which tries to fly by the seat of its pants or use intuition in place of informed judgment. When you are paying $50,000 for three minutes of commercial time on a half-hour show, it had better be good."

Advertising accounts and advertising people seem to be bounced around from agency to agency all the time. Is this what causes the tensions, ulcers and drinking after work? When an agency loses an important account, it is a spectacular performance held (in a manner of speaking) in Macy's window and duly celebrated by the communications media directly affected. Most of the wholesale firings, however, occur in smallish tent-show agencies.

AS for tensions and ulcers, they certainly exist. Especially among peripheral copywriters, art directors and account executives who would be doing something loftier "if it weren't for the money." These are the colorful ones whose goings-on are most celebrated in fiction and in fact. It is of course possible that some of the admen one sees having a martini or two at the Biltmore Men's Bar may *not* be tense or insecure. They are really eating peanuts, not tranquillizer pills. And they are drinking with clients.

Why do they dress and talk like that? Not many of them do. The men of Madison Avenue most aware of the flair of the clothes they wear are usually new Princetons and Yales starting out in the mailroom, or smart operators who believe that there is an official dress for the road to success. As for the colorful jargon by which advertising men are alleged to address one another, dismiss it as a word game started by bright satiric minds and caricatured by dull ones who never quite caught the joke (but know hepness when they hear it). Madison Avenue-ese is used with the same frequency in direct communication as Elizabethan verse.

SO, the defense of Advertising Row and its inhabitants can be summed up quickly: *it* functions and *they* do. The plot is orderly, with a climax at the point of sale. After all, we made you what you are today, says Madison Avenue modestly to critics and friends—but don't get too satisfied! Let's just skim *this* idea on the pond and see whether it reaches the other side.

December 23, 1956

The MR Boys Are Out to Make You Buy and Buy and Buy

THE HIDDEN PERSUADERS. By Vance Packard. 275 pp. New York: David McKay Company. $4.

By A. C. SPECTORSKY

IF Vance Packard is to be believed—and on the evidence of his book there's no reason to doubt him—1984 is obsolete. Big Brother isn't watching you at all, for the simple reason that he has no need to do so. For, with the probes and prescriptions of applied psychology and psychiatry, Big Brother (or Big Business, or Big Government) is manipulating your daily life so the surveillance is unnecessary; puppet-like, you do as you're told and, puppet-like, you yourself don't know you're being manipulated.

"The Hidden Persuaders" is all about MR, or Motivation Research. It is about those technicians, the MR men (or depth boys, as they're called) who plumb our psyches, our hidden anxieties, aspirations, frustrations and aggressions, not to find ways in which to relieve them of their unserviceable aspects and to channel usefully their positive ones, but to play on our total subconscious for pelf. These are the new breed of merchandising brainwashers who wield an invisible club-like baton of applied depth psychology over the secret, silent symphony of our discontents, hopes, strivings. For every tranquilizer we buy to calm us down, they wage a calculated campaign to stir us up, to find and expose the raw nerve and saw away at it until it sings in agony the sponsor's commercial—convincing us that only his product will bring surcease.

Machiavelli (a piker by current standards) prescribed, in his way, for the comparatively simple problems of princes. Today's Machiavellian MR boys face more challenging chores, such as solving the problem of getting us all to spend, at once, the discretionary dollar, the one we don't need for necessities but might save for a dull day or a better buy. They have two other major problems: to accelerate consumption beyond reason, and to stimulate brand loyalties among mass-produced products and services which are virtually identical.

THE omnibus solution they have hit upon is to educate the public in semantic dysfunction; that is, to teach irrational responses to symbols (rather than sane responses to the things the symbols stand for) and to make of each consumer a walking repository of unthinking signal reactions, like those Pavlovian dogs which salivate at the sound of a bell.

The MR technique is not employed merely for the moving of goods, however; it has served and is serving in politics as well as packaging, in the packaging of the Organization Man as well as the products and way-of-life he'll buy, in the molding of team players and the team spirit, in the purveying of baseless optimism. Such is Vance Packard's assertion. Let's see how he supports it with data—of which he has amassed an impressive amount.

Among the lessons taught by MR is the exploitation of eight hidden needs. Thus, to sell freezers, forget their function and play on the need for emotional security: the freezer as bountiful mother should be your message. Play on the need for reassurance of worth: to sell detergents forget about cleanliness—stress, instead, the dignity of housework. Pander to ego gratification. If, for example, you want to sell a bulldozer, it's all right to picture the machine as a mighty monster, but be sure to feature a man as its potent master. Work on the need for a creative outlet, *viz.*, if you're selling cake mix hold out one ingredient which the housewife can add, fresh. To sell a new car annually, equate it with a renewal of potency. Exploit man's need for a sense of power, for a sense of roots, for a feeling of immortality. Apropos the last: in selling life insurance stress the fact that the lives of legatees will be dominated by the insured after his death.

Shall we proceed? Gear your product and your pitch for the built-in sexual overtone. Don't sell cosmetics, sell hope. Don't sell shoes, sell pretty feet. More important, if you want to sell beer, employ a singing commercial that will appeal to children—they'll sing it all day, at no cost to you, and they can't be turned off like TV.

Are you among those who decry the level of mass entertainment? Put yourself in the seller's shoes and consider: "Mrs. Middle Majority"—with her limited outlook and pallid personality—does 80 per cent of all purchasing for 65 per cent of the population. She's the prime target of MR, not you. But you're there, too: If a TV show is "too good" you'll talk about it during the commercial, so be prepared to have the MR boys downgrade it. And be prepared to have your social strivings exploited by three MR-devised means to give your purchases status symbolism: bigness (see the '57 cars), high price, the testimonial (lucky you—you can share the best with men of distinction).

The proliferation of this book's examples of MR at work is both frightening and entertaining. And the range is wide: from specifics, like the foregoing, to such general considerations as the promulgation of "psychological obsolescence," or the technique of making people replace durable goods before they're worn out—goods which used to be sold on the basis of their longevity, at that. It's a one-two punch: first, make the public style conscious; second, switch styles.

MR. PACKARD is not merely an accumulator of data, however. He attempts two evaluations of considerable import. The first is of rather intramural interest and concerns the actual newness and validity of MR. The conclusion is that it *is* quite new; though many of its principles were intuitively employed in the past, a lot has been added and the whole somewhat systematized; and that it is, in the main, valid if too much reliance is not placed on it.

The second evaluation is more in the nature of a questioning about the morality and social ethics of MR. These are tricky waters to navigate. Can we demand of men of science, for example, that—like members of holy orders—they dedicate (or doom) themselves to forswear the fruits of worldliness? Where do intelligent applications of new techniques and the seized opportunity stop and corruption begin? Is an expanding economy such a desirable goal that the means to it can legitimately include the knowing (if not downright cynical) tailoring of the human animal via procedures initially developed for therapeutic purposes?

Wisely, Mr. Packard, who is a writer and teacher, does not attempt didactic answers. He reveals the MR men themselves in the act of agonized self-appraisal (a rare posture), and comes up with a few personal, tentative answers, but some basic questions remain unresolved. And that is one of the strengths of this fascinating book—it is frightening, entertaining and thought-stimulating to boot.

Mr. Spectorsky is author of "The Exurbanites."

April 28, 1957

M'CRACKEN ATTACKS AD AGENCIES' ROLE

Advertising agencies were charged yesterday with enslaving the American public as they assertedly flattened out the nation's ideal of independence. Here, said the Rev. Dr. Robert J. McCracken, minister of Riverside Church, "is one of the most pernicious and vulgarizing influences on our manners and morals."

Dr. McCracken made the attack in an address at the graduation exercises of Pratt Institute at 215 Ryerson Street, Brooklyn. He received an honorary degree of Doctor of Humane Letters.

The concept of character is changing in this country, and hardly for the better, Dr. McCracken observed. Individuals are no longer rugged, but are conforming to patterns set by "hidden and irresponsible persuaders" in gray flannel suits who, he said, are the major elements of social control.

June 7, 1958

Powerful Consumer

An Appraisal of the Need for Studies Of Buying Habits at the Grass Roots

By ELIZABETH M. FOWLER

The American consumer showed his strength last year—and it is possible that he changed the course of economics. As a result, what he does this year will be scrutinized more closely than ever before.

Economists say his spending eased the effects of the recession. He demonstrated his power in other ways as well.

For example, the consumer cold-shouldered the big, sleek cars offered him by the Big Three auto makers, and their sales tumbled sharply. Yet, he showed great interest in the small economy cars put out by American Motors Corporation (its stock rose 416 per cent last year on booming sales) and by foreign car makers. While he dashed the big auto makers' hopes, the consumer bought in record volume from retailers in 1958.

Economics has become a highly statistical art, with its practitioners talking in aggregates of national income, capital expenditures, tax receipts, retail prices and such. Yet the economists have paid little attention to the consumer and what he wanted, what he planned to buy, and how he had changed his mind over any period of time.

True, every sizable, wide-awake company has a marketing research department devoted to estimating market potentials and testing products. But little has been done in the realm of what might be called psychological economics. Much more emphasis has been placed on production—on what businessmen planned to do and did—than on consumption, perhaps with the idea that what is produced must somehow be consumed at a price.

The grandfather of modern economics, aptly named Adam Smith (1723-1790), had a higher regard for the consumer: "Consumption is the sole end and purpose of all production; and the interest of the producer ought to be attended only so far as it may be necessary for promoting that of the consumer. The maxim is so perfectly self-evident that it would be absurd to attempt to prove it."

Absurd or not, the fact remains that the consumer's point of view has been much neglected. Possibly a major reason is that it costs so much to find out his plans, and overnight he may change them. Perhaps, too, producers have relied too much on the theory that if "I make a better mousetrap someone will buy it." Yet the consumer may not really need a better mousetrap.

Back in 1935 William H. Lough and Martin R. Gainsbrugh, economists, wrote a book on the subject called "High-Level Consumption," deploring the dearth of interest in consumer economics. They pointed out that "popular demands are apt to shift suddenly, undermining whole industries." The auto makers discovered that last year. The makers of sack and chemise dresses last year found plenty of sales resistance, too. Also, consumers were evidently saturated with home appliances because sales were off substantially.

Little Progress Made

In the fifteen years after that book, economists made little progress in detecting consumer attitudes, although marketing research men were busier than ever establishing their relatively new field. Then along came George Katona, of the Survey Research Center at the University of Michigan. He had long argued that the economists should take more interest in psychology. In a book called "Psychological Analysis of Economic Behavior" published in 1951, he wrote:

"There have been until very recently but few psychological investigations into such common forms of everyday behavior as buying, selling, investing, going into business, increasing production and the like." He insisted that "economics without psychology" had not succeeded in explaining economic processes and "psychology without economics" had no chance of explaining basics of human behavior. "Very little has been done that has made use [of both]" he declared.

Survey Started

Putting his ideas into action he launched a periodic survey of consumer attitudes and actions, the results of which have been published two or three times a year since then. It is called "Consumer Attitudes and Inclinations to Buy." It has won support of the Federal Reserve Board. It summarizes the results of interviews with about 1,350 adults, representing a nationwide cross-section.

Just last October the National Industrial Conference Board announced that it, too, planned to enter the field with a continuing survey of consumer buying plans, under the sponsorship of Newsweek Magazine. The man behind this is none other than Martin Gainsbrugh, now chief economist of N. I. C. B.

In its announcement N. I. C. B. paid tribute to the pioneering efforts of George Katona and also Mr. Katona's joint efforts with Rensis Likert to determine the public's bond-buying motivations during World War II. It paid tribute, too, to the National Bureau of Economic Research which has been conducting a mail survey on buying intentions among subscribers to a consumer magazine.

N. I. C. B. says that its survey stresses consumer buying plans with only "incidental reference" to psychological aspects. It interviews consumers more frequently than the other surveys and concentrates on short-run buying plans ("next six months"). Thus it hopes to provide a "foreshadowing tool."

Few Refuse to Answer

The interviews are conducted by phone, last for about twenty minutes, and the incidence of refusal to cooperate has been very low. Over 5,000 interviews are conducted monthly, and every three months N. I. C. B. and Newsweek publish the results.

To concentrate its talents on the new project, N. I. C. B. said recently it would abandon its retail price survey, compiled since 1918. The final report was made a few weeks ago.

The Government's Census Bureau has just begun a survey of consumer buying intentions, too. On their rounds the census enumerators ask buying questions, covering about 18,000 households every three months, it is reported. However, the project will be experimental for about a year, while the Federal Reserve Board, the sponsor, weighs the results and decides whether the figures are useful. Economists are far from unanimous as to whether the changing attitudes of consumers can be gauged and results used constructively to help both industry and the Government.

However there is no doubt that the American consumer, who fooled many economists last year, has awakened their interest in him. By so doing he has changed the course of economics. At least, that is what the sponsors of consumer buying surveys believe. As a result, tomorrow's economist may have to add psychology to the basic tools of his trade.

February 13, 1959

Giving Birth to New Products

Doting Corporations Give Tender Care and Feeding

By CARL SPIELVOGEL

The increasing tempo of technological obsolescence is allowing marketing men little chance to rest.

Products that used to have a profit-life of twenty-five years, may now often count on no more than five years. In the volatile pharmaceutical and electronic fields, the period is often as short as six months.

However, the realization that 85 to 90 per cent of all new products fail, places managements generally on the spot. Usually, the failure of a company to introduce products leads to stagnation. But the introduction of wrong products can be equally damaging and result in severe loss of capital and prestige.

A Real Job Now

At many companies, a new box is being added to the ever-present organization chart: vice president in charge of the future. There was a time when such a post was considered perfect for the boss' nephew, a fellow he wanted on the payroll, but did not know what to do with.

Now the post is going to men with vision and marketing know-how who are willing to fight for the things they believe are good for the company. As a top marketing man put it:

"No new product can succeed without one guy who believes with all his heart in this thing and is willing to work to ram it through."

Statistics do not have much meaning in this area, but if there can be such a thing as a typical new product, it will probably take at least five years in the laboratory and at least two years for market development.

Investing in Research

Many companies have invested heavily in research facilities and staffs. Sharing the work load in this area are outside organizations, some of whom do the sole development work carried on by companies, or augment a company's efforts.

A leading outside organization is Arthur D. Little, Inc., whose clients include many of the nation's "blue chip" companies. And although new product development is only one phase of their extensive operation, it is one of the more interesting phases of an operation where rocket development is carried on along with work on food product tastes and aromas.

"Many companies are still overly concerned with static functions, selling more of what they have," contends Richard J. Coveney, vice president in charge of operations here for Little.

"But let's face it. You must have new products whether you want them or not. Call research and new product development a Frankenstein around your neck if you wish, but you can't escape it."

Most clients interested in putting out a product, do not know in which direction to move when they approach Little. Sometimes they manifest nothing more than "a general anxiety" about their business. Other times a company president comes to the consulting company and says, "I would rather go down with a big mistake than preside at a bankruptcy."

In surveying a company's over-all needs the counsel from Little might be that certain products should be earmarked for immediate development. Others should be gotten into quickly through the acquisition of another company. And finally, Little might suggest that it undertake the development of some new products for a client.

A Thinking Man

If it is a matter of engineering work to improve a specific product, the assignment is turned over to Little's engineering department. If it involves "blue sky" then it goes to a special think group headed by William J. J. Gordon, a bearded, motion-picture casting director's dream of the way a thinking man should look.

In his native habitat, the company's research quarters in Cambridge, Mass., Mr. Gordon was encountered wearing chino pants, a red sport shirt open at the neck, tennis shoes, and a red, work handkerchief protruding from a back pocket.

He presides over a seven-man group in the company's invention design group. There are no women in this circle.

Experiment Abandoned

"We've tried using women," Mr. Gordon said, "but it didn't work. They tend to introduce to our discussions an element of competition."

The group's thinking is done in a sound-proof room that has three tape recorders. Large pads are on all walls and on easels, so that wandering thinkers may quickly jot down their thoughts. The floor is used by smokers as a large ash tray. Anything that might disturb thought processes is eliminated.

Mr. Coveney reported that "a study of the results and procedures of many group sessions has shown that the most important element is to keep group thinking on a general plane. For example, in a group meeting focused on inventing a new egg beater, the emphasis should be on force, rather than beating eggs.

"After the speculative implications of the general notion of force have been explored by the group, specific ideas about actually beating eggs will evolve naturally, but these ideas will be more basically novel due to the fundamental nature of their source."

Not all of the inventions result because of a client's interest. Recently, a member of the group became incensed after reading a newspaper account that a child had died from accidentally taking an overdose of aspirins.

The group got busy and in a near-record period of four days developed an additive that could be put into aspirins. It makes it impossible for a child to tolerate more than two aspirins at one time.

Roadblocks Encountered

A major problem in new product development, according to Mr. Gordon, is that their introduction to a company's line "is not rational. There is a tremendous amount of inertia in the way of launching a new product.

"For one thing, you come to a sales vice president who has his budgets and products all in shape and through the introduction of a new product you threaten to disrupt the status quo. He is naturally going to resist.

"Another problem is that companies do not want a new product to be anything like any product they are already marketing. They are always afraid that their marketing people will lose their enthusiasm and say that is too much like the old one.

"Another major block is that a client often says, 'we are afraid to put our name on the new product, because if it is a lemon, we are going to get a black eye.'

We suggest that companies set up a pilot company and test market their items under a different name. This has been done successfully by some major organizations.

"Then they can put a large enough sample into a particular city, let's say 30,000 pieces of a new saw. If the reaction is to their liking they can then swing it into their regular line."

Suspicious of Signs

Mr. Gordon, who works with many companies, contends that there are dangerous signs of "organization man" thinking filtering down to research levels.

"Research people should be walking around with a perennial harried and anxious look. Instead I go into many company research departments where everyone walks around with a smile. Either that, or the first thing they want to do is show me their organization chart. These are bad signs."

April 5, 1959

Advertising: Industry's Men in High Posts

By PETER BART

An interesting change has quietly been talking place in the corporate status of advertising and public relations men.

Two decades ago the men who handled these responsibilities usually occupied a low niche in the corporate hierarchy and took their orders from the sales department.

Today, however, the man in charge of advertising at many companies is a full-fledged corporate officer. "It is not at all uncommon these days for a company to have a vice president in charge of advertising or even an executive vice president in charge of marketing," notes Peter W. Allport, president of the Associaton of National Advertisers. "This change is a clear reflection of the growing importance of advertising."

Back in 1932, Mr. Allport says, only about four of the 250 member companies in A. N. A. had advertising vice presidents, while today nearly 100 of the group's 700 members have such officers.

Public Relations Affected

A similar change apparently has taken place in public relations. Robert W. Miller, chairman of the Program in Public Relations at Columbia University's School of General Studies, recently surveyed 253 corporate presidents on their public relations policies. Of the 182 responses, 34 per cent said that the man in charge of public relations was a vice president at their companies; 84 per cent said the function of public relations was "growing in importance" within their companies, and 77 per cent said thus the chief public relations man had access to management policy discussions.

"This represents a significant change in the role of corporate public relations," Mr. Miller concluded. "The acceptance of public relations at the policy level within the corporation has come about largely within the past five years."

The rising corporate status of the advertising and public relations man should have important policy implications, in the view of some Madison Avenue observers.

Some of these observers, in fact, suggest that there is a clear relationship between the quality of a company's advertising and the corporate standing of its top advertising executive.

If a product manager supervises advertising and must report directly to the sales department, the resulting ads are often "hard sell" and tasteless. However, at companies where advertising decisions are made at the top echelon, the advertising may reflect quite a different tone. Executives at this level usually don't have to concentrate on meeting sales quotas, and are mindful of general corporate advertising objectives. They thus carefully stay away from advertising that may undermine their company's over-all image-building objectives.

"At many companies advertising has become one of the major costs," the A. N. A.'s Mr. Allport says. "It's inevitable, therefore, that top management would want to take a hand in advertising decisions—a development that is good both for the company and for advertising."

July 9, 1962

Newness of a Product Held Inducement to Buy

The word "new" attached to a product is an inducement to buy it, a reversal of thinking of some years ago, when many potential consumers preferred to wait until a new item was proved in the marketplace.

A view to this effect was expressed last week by Kenneth Van Dyck of the Van Dyck Corporation, Westport, Conn., a product planning and design organization. He suggested that consumer reluctance to buy an item until it was tested by someone else had been overcome by today's better engineering and design work.

"Old-fashioned reasoning called for smart buyers to wait until the manufacturer 'debugged' a new product," he said, "but it's not that way any more. Customers who wait just lose months of benefit or enjoyment, and wind up buying the same thing a year late. Newness and uniqueness now add that extra sparkle and buy-urge to a product, whereas in the past newness sometimes acted as a deterrent."

November 17, 1963

Advertising: Impact of Facts Called Fiction

By PETER BART

A prominent market researcher has come to the conclusion that "facts" aren't really of much importance in advertising.

Some advertisers, he says, go to great pains to explain the facts about their brands in the hope of convincing consumers to buy the product and there has been a trend lately toward factual, "long-copy" advertisements.

All this may bring praise from those consumer groups that believe that advertising should be more informative and less emotional. But, in the opinion of the researcher, Jack B. Haskins, "facts" don't necessarily sell goods.

Mr. Haskins, former manager of advertising research for the Ford Motor Company and now a professor at Indiana University, made his observations in the March issue of The Journal of Advertising Research, published by the Advertising Foundation.

In his article, Mr. Haskins reviewed 13 studies that related changes in attitude with learning, and found that there was no clear correlation between factual recall on the part of consumers and intent to buy.

Some ads, he said, seemed to change consumers' attitudes and arouse a determination to buy the products, yet the consumers could not recall any particular facts conveyed to them in the ads. In other cases the factual recall was high, but there was no will to buy.

In one confidential study, Mr. Haskins said, a company ran controlled experiments in two media using two different campaigns. Follow-up surveys found that advertising in one medium had little impact on sales or awareness, but consumers were able to recall a remarkable amount of factual content from the ads. Ads in another medium, however, had "a significant effect on sales and awareness," but consumers could recall few facts.

Said Mr. Haskins: "We must conclude that changes in brand preferences were accompanied most strongly by changes in brand awareness, and that the learning of product features and slogans gave no clue at all to a person's brand-buying preference."

Though it is "easy" for an ad man to turn out factual ads and then measure factual recall, he observed, it is fallacious to assume that facts change minds and thereby sell products.

March 24, 1964

Job Figures Reflect Shift to an Economy Based on Services

By WILL LISSNER

The shift in the nation's employment from goods manufacturing to services has become so pronounced that it is no longer correct to call the United States economy an "industrial economy." It is a "service economy."

Research at the National Bureau of Economic Research, a private nonprofit agency in New York controlled by leading universities and professional organizations, has established the preponderance of the service industries, the bureau reported yesterday.

This preponderance is expected to become even more significant as automation and other technological advances are adopted more widely throughout the economy.

Decline Began in '53

It means that substantially less than half the working population is now needed to turn out the cornucopia of goods the United States people consume and share with the rest of the world, and that the numbers of goods producers will get fewer and fewer. At the same time, fewer workers will turn out more and more goods.

The number of workers in the industries that make tangible goods began declining in 1953, when the United States Office of Business Economics estimated their total at 33.3 million. Since then the total has declined to 31.4 million.

The proportion of total employment in the goods-producing industries began falling below 50 per cent in 1955, and now it is 45 per cent and still declining.

So far this decline has failed to produce the mass unemployment that was expected, because

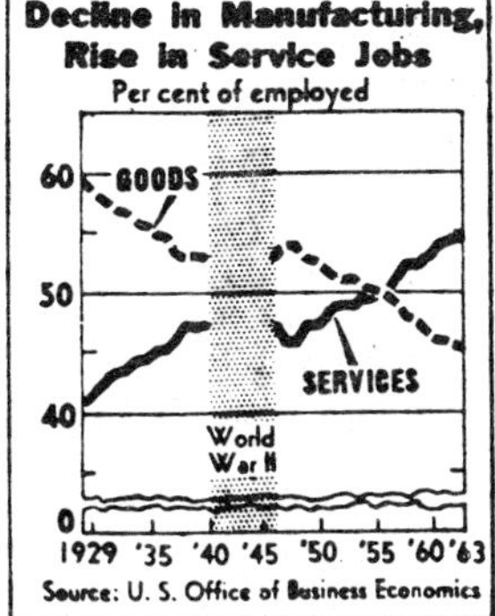

Chart illustrates changed pattern for jobholders.

the industries providing services have grown so phenomenally, Dr. Victor R. Fuchs, associate director of research at the bureau, finds. Dr. Fuchs is directing a research project on the service industries.

There is a higher rate of unemployment for the goods-producing industries, but very largely this is accounted for by greater seasonal unemployment in that sector, he says.

The service industries consist of trade, finance, insurance and real estate; Personal, professional, business and repair services, and general government. Workers in them have doubled since 1929, when total employment in the service industries was 18.6 million. Now it is about 38 million.

Between 1870 and 1920 the shift to services could be explained by the relative decline of the agricultural sector of the goods-producing industries. Since 1920, however, the nonagricultural goods sector has been in relative decline, and in the last decade it has shown an absolute decline in jobs. This has produced important differences in the kind of work forces employed, Dr. Fuchs says.

Many service occupations do not make special demands for physical strength, so women can compete on more nearly equal terms with men, he says. Thus, women hold nearly half the jobs in the service industries, but only a fifth of those in goods-producing industries.

Proportionately, Dr. Fuchs continues, more older workers are employed in the service industries; more part-time workers also.

A continued shift in service-industry employment will tend to favor self-employment, he believes, but this may be offset by the influx of young workers and women into the labor force, as these groups are predominantly wage and salary workers.

However, with the employment of women, part - time workers and the self - employed rising with the rise of services, the threat of a decline in union influence appears, he says, because unions are less important in the service industries than in the goods industries.

On the other hand, Dr. Fuchs reports, members of the National Bureau staff—Danel Creamer and Geoffrey H. Moore — have shown that the service industries have greater stability in income and employment. Thus, they may tend to moderate the swings to boom and slump in business.

Dr. Moore, who is director of research, reported at a meeting last week on research made by Dr. Victor Zarnowitz and others on the accuracy of short-term forecasts in economics.

He said that several hundred forecasts in the postwar period, when analyzed, showed that forecasters, including Government forecasters, did fairly well on the first quarter ahead and moderately well on the second quarter ahead.

However, for three or four quarters ahead, he said, "the advantage of forecasting over some simple method of carrying forward past changes is very small." For the past two quarters the errors get larger and larger, he said, and annual forecasts have an average error of $10 billion, which is 40 per cent of average yearly changes in total output.

June 28, 1965

WARD AND SEARS ARE MANY THINGS

Mail-Order Field Includes Insurance, Travel, Fine Art and Rentals

STORES ARE IMPORTANT

2 Big Companies Now Offer Special Foreign Fashions in Their Catalogues

By LEONARD SLOANE

If Richard W. Sears or Aaron Montgomery Ward could return to life today, they would never recognize what has happened to the mail-order companies they founded.

For both Sears, Roebuck & Co. and Montgomery Ward & Co., along with the smaller mail-order houses, are a far cry from what they were in the late nineteenth century. Not only are their catalogues, or "wish books" as they were once called, markedly different from the original versions, but the companies themselves have also diversified into a plethora of activities that were undreamed of earlier. Today, the companies no longer consider themselves mail-order concerns.

The first break from strictly mail-order operations came in the nineteen-twenties when Sears and Ward opened their first retail stores. Store sales have grown so fast that today they are the major portion of the business for both companies. At present, catalogue sales account for less than 30 per cent of total volume, with the rest derived from store and telephone sales.

Later, the companies branched into ownership, both partial and complete, of some of the manufacturing corporations that supplied them with merchandise. They also instituted an extensive variety of private brands, many of which have today become widely popular.

Move Into Service Field

These private brands are often manufactured to specifications and standards established by Sears and Ward. They have become so important that at Ward, for example, merchandise accounting for 80 per cent of total volume is expected to have a private brand by the end of this year.

In recent years, however, the two mail order giants have moved briskly into an area that can be broadly termed consumer services, which are quite dissimilar from the sale of basic merchandise.

Activities such as insurance, travel, fine art, dry cleaning and rentals are now being carried on as important segments of the business of the two leading mail-order companies.

In the world of fashion, Ward announced a few weeks ago that it was joining forces with some of the top names in fashion to offer haute couture to mass markets through its catalogues. Leading designers from Italy, France and the United States created a special collection of dresses, suits, coats, sportswear and accessories that will be displayed in Ward's fall catalogue to be published on July 1.

The designers participating in the Ward "couture-by-mail" collection are Emilia Pucci, Laura Aponte, Nina Ricci, Jacques Heim, Vin Draddy and Melba Hobson. Through the efforts of these experts and others who design fashion merchandise for the company, Ward expects to top last year's volume of $150,000,000 in fashion sales in 1963.

Sears, too, presents couture clothing by European designers. It sells coats, suits and dresses at popular prices under the label of Claude Riviere, who designs two collections a year for Sears. The company also merchandises a wide variety of other fashionable clothing both in its retail stores and in its catalogues.

Sears's casualty and fire insurance subsidiary, the Allstate Insurance Company, has become an important revenue producer for the parent corporation. In addition, Allstate is now a well-known company in the highly competitive insurance industry. It sells insurance by mail, at retail stores and at catalogue sales offices throughout the country.

Total net income and realized capital gains of Allstate last year amounted to $48,109,522, or 63 cents a share of Sears common stock. The entire Sears operation reported combined net income of $264,683,794, or $3.50 a share, in its latest fiscal year.

Another insurance affiliate, the Allstate Life Insurance Company, completed its fifth year of operation in 1962. Allstate Life and an associated life insurance company had $2,250,600,000 worth of life insurance in force and assets of $32,471,019 at the end of the year.

In the Travel Market

Both Ward and Sears have pushed into the booming travel market by sponsoring mail-order trips and tours. Ward instituted its packaged travel tour service in 1961, with all types of tours and excursions offered in its mail-order catalogues.

Sears has a recently formed, wholly owned organization known as Allstate Enterprises designed to participate in many service fields, of which travel is an important one. Through this organization, it formed the Allstate Motor Club in 1961 to offer travel information as well as emergency road service to its members.

The motor club also presents both independent and escorted tours and travel throughout the United States and the rest of the world.

Two dry-cleaning centers were opened by Sears in 1961, at which homemakers have the opportunity to do their own dry cleaning in automatic machines. These centers are near Sears' stores.

Sears moved into the art world last year by commissioning the actor and art expert, Vincent Price, to collect original works of art for sale at selected stores. The Vincent Price collection has been praised not only by the public but also by many art critics.

Also in 1962, Sears began an experimental rental service whereby it offers a wide range of merchandise for rent by the hour, day, week or month. Some Sears retail stores are now operating rental services, aimed especially at do-it-yourself workers and hobbyists. Among the items that can be rented: floor sanders, power tools, plumbing tools, moving equipment and painting equipment.

Both Sears and Ward have wholly owned subsidiaries to finance their rapidly growing credit operations, which now present a substantial part of total sales. Sears has the Sears Roebuck Acceptance Corporation, while Ward owns the Montgomery Ward Credit Corporation. These subsidiaries each have more than $400,000,000 worth of customer installment contracts purchased from the parent companies.

To service the major and minor appliances sold by the mail-order companies, large-scale and complete service organizations have been established. Ward alone has 1,800 men in its repair service force and makes 5,000 home service calls a day.

Another service presented by the companies is the availability of outside salesmen who call on customers directly in their homes. Working out of catalogue offices and retail stores, these salesmen sell items such as home furnishings, appliances and home modernization programs. Estimating, installing and financing are part of the total package they offer.

In 1962, Sears announced another first—the opening of a 12,500 - square - foot drug store at a Fort Worth, Tex., shopping center owned by its Homart Development Company subsidiary. The drug store contains a variety of general merchandise in addition to drugs and prescriptions and a catalogue sales department. A full-size Sears department store also is at the same shopping center.

As these recent innovations indicate, the history of mail-order companies has been one of continuous development. Ward was founded in 1872 by Aaron Montgomery Ward and his brother-in-law, George R. Thorne. Its first catalogue was a single-page price list 8⅞ inches wide and 20 inches long, on which the names and prices of more than 100 items of merchandise were printed.

Ward's first sale was a $14 order from a postmaster in Effingham, Ill.

A charge of 15 cents was made for each catalogue distributed to customers until 1902. The company entered the retail field in 1926 with the opening of three display stores and its first catalogue store was opened in 1934.

Sears originated in 1886 when

Richard W. Sears began selling watches, to supplement his income as a station agent in North Redwood, Minn., for the Minneapolis & St. Louis Railway. He moved to Chicago the next year and hired a watchmaker named Alvah C. Roebuck. The company's earliest catalogue was issued in 1888 and included only watches.

The first Sears retail store was opened in 1925 at its mail-order plant in Chicago. The Allstate Insurance Company was formed six years later.

Financial Figures

The extent of the mail-order industry today can be quickly noted by looking at the financial statements. Sears and Ward are billion-dollar corporations and nationwide leaders in the merchandising field.

Sears's sales in the year ended Jan. 31, 1963, were $4,603,318,-710 and combined earnings, as noted, topped $264,000,000. Ward reported sales in the same fiscal year of $1,425,187,840 and earnings of $20,415,681.

At the end of the last fiscal year, Sears had 748 retail stores and 969 catalogue sales offices in operation. In Central and South America it had another 41 stores and 15 sales offices, and in Canda it is a 49 per cent partner in the ownership of Simpsons-Sears, Ltd. (Canada). Ward had 512 retail stores and 691 catalogue stores at the end of the fiscal year.

What next for the mail-order companies? They now sell via the mail, the store and the telephone. The services they offer have also expanded tremendously in recent years.

Although the companies are making careful plans for the future, the eventual end to their development is anyone's guess. The only thing certain is that changes will continue to be made as the erstwhile strictly mail-order concerns—merchants first, last and always—strive to develop new ways to provide for the needs of the consumer.

May 19, 1963

The Knowledge Industry: Ideas and Profits

Students in a teacherless classroom in the Weber School District, Ogden, Utah, use teaching machine made by the education science division of U. S. Industries, Inc. The students read material and answer questions on devices.

Business Runs From School to Machines

By DOUGLAS W. CRAY

The United States is still largely a production-oriented economy in which factories, assembly lines and material output are the familiar industrial landmarks—the nuts and bolts of an expanding gross national product.

Often overlooked in this mix, however, has been the astonishing growth, within it, of what has come to be known as the "knowledge industry." It is an idea-oriented industry that by now, according to some measurements, represents a multibillion-dollar business in itself.

Fritz Machlup, a professor at Princeton University, is generally credited with being the first to attempt to pin down just what the generation, dissemination and assimilation of knowledge in the United States adds up to. His book, "The Production and Distribution of Knowledge in the United States," has become a kind of industry bible.

The Cost of Knowledge

According to his calculations, $136 billion, or 26 per cent, of the gross national product was spent in the United States in 1958 for the production and distribution of all kinds of knowledge. His total covered $60 billion for education, $11 billion for research and development, $38 billion for all media of communication, $9 billion for information machines and $18 billion for information services.

Bringing his figures up to date last year, Fortune magazine estimated that the nation's total outlay for knowledge in 1963 amounted to $195 billion.

Whether or not one agrees with these sweeping estimates, there is little question that the knowledge business has attained authentic and imposing industry status.

Measuring the Impact

Clark Kerr, president of the University of California, has observed: "What the railroads did for the second half of the last century and the automobile for the first half of this century, may be done for the second half of this century by the knowledge industry."

No longer the sole province of educators and school systems, the knowledge industry today encompasses almost

Westinghouse has developed a record that broadcasts both sound and television pictures from its grooves. A standard turntable and television set can be used in system. Special equipment is built in beneath the turntable.

every nook and cranny of business, education and government. Its scope will be reflected here this week when the American Management Association sponsors a week-long conference with "The Impact of Educational Technology" as its theme.

According to Charles F. Schwep, educational consultant for the association and conference director, the gathering is "designed to help educators communicate their needs and requirements to industry—and to permit industry to define its needs for the world of work. . . . It will be a search for **answers, a major effort to stimulate practical school-industry-government cooperation on national and local levels."**

A "search for answers"—or simply for new techniques and then new applications and markets for these techniques—has characterized the expanding knowledge industry in recent years.

It has led to the development of "programed instruction" courses, now widely used **in schools, as well as industrial training programs and the introduction of a vast array of audio-visual teaching aids that constitute the "hardware" of the knowledge industry.**

In programed instruction, a learning system that only came into its own about four years ago, the subject matter is broken down into a large number of small steps, or frames, organized into an instructional sequence. The student, working at his own pace, masters these steps one at a time.

The Equitable Life Assurance Society, the American Telephone and Telegraph Company, International Business Machines, the First National City Bank and a host of other major corporations have adopted the "programed learning" technique for teaching everything from the fundamentals of life insurance to the properties of a new drug.

At the Warner-Chilcott Laboratories, for example, drug salesmen were given a 40-hour programed instruction course about a new weight-control drug.

I.B.M. has used the technique to train customer-engineers and has been able to reduce training time by 27 per cent and increase grade scores markedly.

Training Time

Gordon Rhodes, director of training for the First National City Bank, estimates that programed instruction reduces average training time by 20 to 25 per cent, but it can range up to 50 per cent.

Some companies, such as Equitable, have assigned company personnel to develop programed courses internally. Others have turned to the increasing number of companies that specialize in writing programs. Costs for these custom-made programs can run as high as $60,000.

Scott B. Parry, president of Scott B. Parry and Associates, estimates that government and industry currently contract for about $15 million a year in custom-made programed instruction.

The expanding interest in and the use of programed instruction has led a number of large companies to enter the field. I.B.M., for example, acquired Science Research Associates, a Chicago concern specializing in modern learning systems.

The Xerox Corporation has acquired Basic Systems, Inc., and more recently American Education Publications, a publisher of classroom periodicals

C. Peter McColough, executive vice president of operations for Xerox, made clear his company's plans in a talk to the Los Angeles Society of Financial Analysts last month.

"We view," he said, "education as one of the major paths of our future growth, and as a wonderful opportunity to contribute something of value to a pressing and compounding human problem.

"It is, therefore, Xerox's intention to devote significant financial and human resources toward studying the needs of education—in the United States and throughout the world—and toward evolving new services that help meet some of those needs."

July 11, 1965

The Franchising Dollar and the $70-Billion Debate

By GEORGE ROOD

Franchising, with volume of $70-billion last year, is no longer an industry of scattered snack bars and frozen-custard stands.

It's a thriving industry that now accounts for about one of every four retail sales dollars.

An estimated 100 new franchised outlets—ranging from shoe-repair shops and drive-in dairies to English-style pubs and golf driving ranges—are being opened every day. But at whose expense?

One side in the dollars-and-cents debate contends that the opening of a nationally franchised business in a community cuts into the sales of the local independent small-business man.

The other side argues that a franchise creates more local jobs and tax dollars, while helping to generate heavier customer traffic. And, after all, isn't a franchisee a small-business man himself?

Maybe so, but this doesn't seem to lessen the fervor of the debate.

A spot check with several small-business men in communities in upstate New York, New Jersey and sections of New England, where new franchise operations have recently been opened, indicated that many look upon the franchisee as "an added competitor." One independent hamburger-stand operator, who asked not to be named, went so far as to say that the new franchised business in his town was "squeezing out the little guy."

National and regional groups that deal with small-business men are reluctant to get involved in the debate because they represent both the small independent and the franchisee. But they do readily acknowledge the problems raised by unscrupulous "fringe franchisers" that license units in conflicting territories and misrepresent the capital needed and the potential profit.

What does a franchise entail? Primarily, it is a license to sell the specific goods or services offered by a franchising company. The man who is said to have started it all was Louis K. Liggett, who began franchising Liggett-Rexall retail drug stores in 1902.

Impact Emphasized

The impact of franchising on the national economy is being emphasized this week, which has been designated National Franchise Week. The somewhat poetic theme for the event is "On Our Own, But Not Alone."

The International Franchise Association, a Chicago-based trade group, estimates that today there are some 750 substantial franchising concerns with about 450,000 franchised outlets.

The average local franchise operation employs about five persons, but some, such as Holiday Inns or Howard Johnson's restaurants have some 40 to 60 employes on the average payroll.

The scope of franchising includes gasoline stations, automobile dealerships, car-rental outlets (Hertz and its No. 2 friend, Avis) and some cola bottlers (500 of Pepsi-Cola's 520 bottling plants are franchises). Service stations have the most outlets (more than 200,000), followed by franchised car dealers (about 35,000). But the industries most commonly identified with the postwar proliferation of franchising are motels, restaurants, doughnut shops and frozen-custard and snack stands.

A New Concept

Franchising has even entered the bar business. The Watney Mann Group announced plans in London this year to set up a franchise network that "will lead to the creation of a chain of pubs right across America."

The English-style bars will be specially designed and will sell Watney's beer and ale (what else?), which is already being marketed in 100 United States outlets.

One of the newest concepts in the field is multiple franchising. Two years ago, a group of businessmen formed Franchises International, which now has 130 sales centers **with an average net worth of $250,000.** The centers, which **themselves** are run under franchises, **sign up franchisees for three chains:** Edie Adams Cut & Curl **beauty shops (50 open, 50 more franchised), Mary's Drive-Thru Dairies (50 open, 75 others licensed) and Heap Big Beef roast-beef sandwich restaurants (100 under lease or under construction).**

Leonard Saffir, vice president for marketing of the franchising company, which is being acquired by the City Investing Company, comments that "we have about a dozen other franchise programs under development, including recreation units and nursing homes."

As franchising continues to spread, more and more American communities and businessmen are facing a complex ques-

George Falls, left, in charge of franchise sales for Holiday Inns, looks over sketches with Philip Snyder, who plans Holiday Inn in Torrington, Conn. This advertisement appeared recently in newspapers.

tion: What is the economic impact on a community when a nationally franchised business moves in?

Holiday Inns of America, which is typical of the large franchising concerns, has just completed a study designed to help answer that question.

On a national basis, the 819 Holiday Inns in operation as of March 31 were providing a total payroll of $98.28-million a year and were paying $1.32-million in local and state taxes. With 104,263 rooms on the books, this means that each room is adding $1,051 to the gross national product.

William Walter, executive vice president of Holiday Inns, stresses that "every time a new Holiday Inn opens its doors in a town, some 60 new jobs are created." The average 100-room inn has an annual payroll of $120,000. The restaurant manager for a typical 100-room inn spends close to $8,000 on his basic inventory of food, with dairy products, meat, fresh produce and frozen foods all purchased from local suppliers.

Once opened, an average Holiday Inn restaurant pays out about $200 a day in expenses, or $73,000 a year.

Of course, it's not a one-way street. Much of the equipment and furnishings comes from the motel chain's headquarters in Memphis. Generally, however, area contractors are hired to build new Holiday Inns, based on specifications drawn up by the company.

Among the pioneers in the franchising business is the Howard Johnson Company, which began in 1926 with home-made ice cream in a Wollaston, Mass., patent-medicine store. The company now has about 800 restaurants, with almost half of them run as franchises and the rest company-operated. of nearly 300 Howard Johnson's motor lodges, more than 280 are franchises.

According to Howard B. Johnson, president, the average restaurant in the chain employs 40 to 50 workers. Restaurant operators buy some food locally, such as fresh vegetables, eggs and bakery products, but they are also supplied with a broad line of food and other products through the company's commissaries and distribution centers.

"Through the years," Mr. Johnson observes, "we have noticed that when a widely recognized national company enters a community through a franchise operation, it often draws the attention of travelers and outsiders to the community. A franchised business may also stimulate other business endeavors in the same area. For example, when a Howard Johnson's restaurant or motor lodge opens, it may be followed by construction of a gasoline station, gift shop and other retail outlets in the same area."

Lucrative Line

Among the food lines that have proved lucrative for franchisers is doughnuts. One of the first to turn doughnuts into dollars was William Rosenberg, now chairman of Universal Food Systems, Inc., parent company of Dunkin' Donuts of America. Starting with a factory-to-factory coffee-truck run in Boston, he built up a $50-million-a-year business that franchises some 300 Dunkin' Donut shops' and 40 Howdy Beefburger stands.

It was a dozen years ago that Mister Donut of America was begun by Harry Winokur, now chairman, with his first doughnut shop in Revere, Mass. Today, it's a 252-shop chain, with about 80 per cent of the shops run by franchises and the rest by the company.

The average Mister Donut shop employs 10 to 15 persons and has sales of about $175,000 a year. It buys some food products such as soft drinks, locally, although the doughnut mixes and equipment come from the parent company's headquarters in Westwood, Mass.

Others among the leaders in the food end of franchising include Pancake Houses, McDonald's hamburger stands, Chicken Delight and Kentucky Fried Chicken, Barton's candy stores and a myriad of frozen-custard companies.

Outside the food and lodging business, there are franchises for everything from shoe repair shops to golf driving ranges.

The Auto-Soler Company of Atlanta has franchised more than 100 Heel Bars, equipped to put a new pair of heels on shoes automatically in three minutes. Meanwhile, the National Broadcasting Company has been negotiating to acquire Arnold Palmer Enterprises, Inc., which franchises golf driving ranges, putting courses and indoor golf schools bearing the professional golfer's name.

Most franchisees are in the black now that the industry has come of age, but some still have complaints. A few franchisees object to having to "buy too much from the company store" (contract purchases from the company, rather than from local sources). Others say they get "too many orders" from the parent franchising concern.

The Small Business Administration found in a recent study that the purchaser of a franchise could generally expect to be obligated to "a minimum investment of money; a standardized inventory and/or equipment package; the standard quality level, operating procedures and promotional efforts of the system, and royalty or franchise fees."

Cost Varies

How much does it cost to buy a franchise? A University of Minnesota research project states that "requirements for initial capital vary from $1,000 or less to $100,000 or more, depending largely on the type of business. Variations within a franchise organization depend on the scale of operations the franchisee wishes to establish."

Payment is usually made through the charging of an initial fee and royalty payments based on the franchisee's sales or purchases of operating materials from the franchising concern.

Let's say you're a retired executive of a small company

with life savings of about $25,-000 and you want to go into business for yourself. You hear from a friend that he has been making out well as his "own boss," running a doughnut shop in a neighboring town, so you decide to look into it.

You find that you can get a franchise from Mister Donut for your town with $20,000 to $25,-000 in cash required to cover the purchase of equipment and exclusive rights for about a two mile area for 20 years. The franchising company pays for the construction of the shop, and you will have to pay rent of between $800 and $1,000 a month based on the Mister Donut average. In addition, you'll have to finance about $20,000 for other equipment needed. The majority of the Mister Donut shops bring in earnings of $15,000 to $20,000 a year, and after the first year your investment is considered worth about three times earnings, or $45,000 to $60,000.

Under the franchise agreement5 of course, you have to buy your doughnut mixes, coffee, paper products and certain other items from the company. But other products, such as dairy goods, can be purchased locally. The company usually buys the land for the shop (average cost: $60,000) and hires an area contractor to build the shop (average outlay including on-site improvements: $50,000).

Both franchisers and franchisees are generally aware that they share as a basic problem the legal status of the franchising method of distribution, which has been challenged in the courts when it has been allegedly used to restrain trade. The Supreme Court, however, ruled last month that although companies cannot impose selling restraints on dealers who purchase their goods outright, they can set conditions for sales made on consignment. The ruling stemmed from the marketing operations of Arnold Schwinn & Co., a bicycle maker.

But the Court has also ruled illegal the arrangements under which 30 small producers of mattresses shared the expenses and benefits of advertising the Sealy label and agreed not to encroach on each other's sales territories.

The Better Business Bureau reports it has received protests from franchisees who say they were given conflicting territories, thinking the areas would be exclusive. J. R. Hoffman, vice president of the B. B. B., said, "We have also gotten complaints about misrepresentation on capitalization in which an operator was told he could get started with x number of dollars but found it impossible. Or he was given a misleading idea of how much profit he could expect to make. But this is contrary to the usual practice. Most franchisers are perfectly respectable."

Despite scattered complaints from franchises and intermittent grumbling by some small-business men, the franchising industry had its best year in history in 1966 reaching $70-billion in sales, or about 10 per cent of the gross national product.

Customer is served in his car at the grand opening of a new Mary's Dairies franchise in Belleville, Ill.

Growth Continues

And this growth is continuing.

A new Holiday Inn has just been completed in Winona, Minn. Donald L. Stone, manager of the Winona Chamber of Commerce, says, "It's been only a few weeks since the inn opened, but I've noticed a marked increase in traffic in our town already. It's a little bit like bringing a big national department store into a small town."

Howard Johnson's is busy developing a 50-unit franchise chain of self-service, drive-in snack bars, known as Hojo Junctions, with the first opened last September in Troy, Ohio. The operator of the Troy unit estimates that it is now serving 350 to 400 customers a day, or a weekly customer total that is equivalent to 20 per cent of the community's population.

Franchisers obviously are keeping up with the competition.

On a recent hot and muggy day in Manhattan, Howard D. Johnson, founder of the chain now headed by his son, encountered an independent vendor selling ice cream bars at the corner of Fifth Avenue and 59th Street. He bought one, then turned to a friend and quipped with a grin: "I always have to see what the competition's like."

July 9, 1967

THE GIANTS GROW BIGGER

DIRECTORS TO FACE ANTI-TRUST SUITS

Attorney General Clark Says 'a Few' Disagree With His View of the Clayton Act

Special to The New York Times.

WASHINGTON, Oct. 10—Crusading against interlocking directorates, the Department of Justice has found that 1,500 men hold directorships in more than one leading industrial concern and that sixty of these men are on the boards of two or more competing companies.

In announcing the data today, Attorney General Tom C. Clark said twenty directors already had resigned or agreed to resign from the boards of fourteen corporations, but that "a few have disagreed with our view of the Clayton Act." These men, serving on boards of competing corporations, will wait to see what happens in the courts. The department soon will file civil suits against them.

The data on interlocking directorates were obtained in a five-month survey conducted by John J. Sonnett, assistant attorney general in charge of the anti-trust division. The Clayton Act makes illegal the holding of directorships by the same person in two or more corporations if one has capital, surplus and undivided profits above $1,000,000.

Since May 1 directorships of 10,000 persons in 1,600 leading corporations have been investigated. The directors were informed of the Government's attitude and invited in for discussions.

Mr. Sonnett declared that Congress, in passing Section 8 of the Clayton Act, showed a desire to prevent potential restraints of trade.

"As a result of our inquiries," he commented, "we found that a number of large corporations have on their boards men who are also representatives of their competitors. While a number of these directors have resigned, a few have disagreed with our view of the law and have decided to await court proceedings. Accordingly, the Government will in the near future file civil suits against such directors."

October 11, 1947

DU PONT HEAD CITES AID TO 'LITTLE MAN'

Pointing to Cellophane, He Tells House Inquiry Big Business Helps Small to Prosper

By H. WALTON CLOKE

Special to THE NEW YORK TIMES.

WASHINGTON, Nov. 15—Declaring that the best opportunity for little business "lies in the horizons opened for them by the basic new developments offered by big business," Crawford H. Greenewalt, president of E. I. du Pont de Nemours & Co., disclosed today that his company would spend $35,000,000 for research in 1950.

Testifying before a House Judiciary subcommittee that for the last month has been investigating monopoly and "bigness" in business, he declared that the development of nylon, cellophane and other products had helped little business prosper. "Here," he added, "are opportunities by thousands and hundred thousands."

To clarify his point, Mr. Greenewalt told the subcommittee, headed by Representative Emanuel Celler, Democrat, of New York, that only 60 per cent of du Pont's cellophane film is used in the form in which it is shipped.

The other 40 per cent is "converted," Mr. Greenewalt testified, into various articles such as tape, bags, envelopes, tubes and other items. "There are 300 firms in this field," he told the subcommittee, "all of whom have built up prosperous businesses of their own, based on cellophane."

The relationship between big and little business is the same in the nylon industry, according to Mr. Greenewalt.

Calls Most Customers Small

Du Pont, he said, has about 6,000 cellophane customers, of which less than 100 are big companies.

It has been estimated, he asserted, that the cellophane industry in America now provides 40,000 jobs, with an annual payroll of $120,000,000. Seven thousand of these employes are in the direct production end of the industry and 33,000 in supply, distribution and converting.

Mr. Greenewalt criticized a "thought-pattern" that holds "bigness per se to be in violation of the anti-trust laws." "It is the customer, and the customer alone," he added, "who casts the vote that determines how big any company should be."

"The only power corporations have, whether they be large or small," the witness said, "is the right to stand in the market place and cry their wares. If the customers find those wares good, they will buy and the corporations will prosper. If they do not, the proprietor soon will be sitting on the curbstone, whether we are talking about a large manufacturer or a roadside market."

Asserting that size in business does not in itself create monopoly, Mr. Greenewalt told the subcommittee that du Pont did not enter a business "to which we can make no technical contribution," nor does it seek to dominate a particular market.

Asked by Representative Kenneth B. Keating, Republican, of New York, if he thought the size of businesses should be limited, Mr. Greenewalt said that, assuming the present anti-trust laws were being enforced, any limitation would mean fewer industrial research developments and less opportunity for small business.

Representative Celler took issue with a statement of the witness that he also assumed that the anti-trust laws were being obeyed. Mr. Celler cited nineteen anti-trust actions filed against du Pont in recent years and $65,000 in fines paid by du Pont in 1942 as the result of suits charging restraint of trade and price-fixing. He also called attention to a suit now pending against the company to force it to divorce itself from General Motors and other companies.

Earl Bunting, managing director of the National Association of Manufacturers, testified that labor monopolies as well as business monopolies should be subject to anti-trust laws. He argued that industry-wide bargaining, exercised through international unions, represents a monopolistic practice in restraint of trade.

"The danger arises from the fact that centralized control enables the international union to take action affecting an entire industry," he continued. "Thus the consumer is deprived of liberty of choice between competing producers. The small business man is particularly helpless in such industry-wide power manipulation."

Business size, the NAM director said, was only one factor in competition, and a few producers selling nationally are more competitive than a large number operating in different and limited localities. Artificial limitation of size would impair or destroy incentives for business to become more efficient, he asserted.

November 16, 1949

TRUMAN SIGNS BILL ADDING TRUST BAN

Approves Measure Curbnig Corporations on Buying Up Assets of a Competitor

Special to THE NEW YORK TIMES.

WASHINGTON, Dec. 29—President Truman signed "with great satisfaction" today a bill designed to tighten the anti-trust laws governing mergers of corporations.

The measure would forbid any corporation from purchasing the assets of another if the transaction would reduce competition substantially. It could have far-reaching effects, depending on how it is interpreted by the courts.

The bill became law at a White House ceremony attended by several of its principal supporters in Congress and members of the Federal Trade Commission. The President gave out the following prepared statement:

"I have today signed H. R. 2734, which amends the Clayton Act, relative to the prevention of monopolies.

"I have signed this act with great satisfaction, because it closes a gap in our anti-monopoly laws that has existed since 1914. Under the Clayton Act, enacted in that year, corporations have been prohibited from destroying competition through buying up the stock of their competitors. But until now, corporations have been able to defeat the purpose of the law by buying up the assets, rather than the stock, of competitors. Now, under this new law, the same principle will apply to the purchase of corporate assets as to the purchase of stock.

Expects F. T. C. to Be Alert

"Much of the concentration of economic power which has taken place since 1914 has been due to this gap in the law. The closing of the gap is an important step in preventing the growth of monopolies and thus assuring the survival and health of free competitive enterprise.

"I have repeatedly recommended the enactment of this legislation to the Congress, as a major element in the program of this Administration to prevent the growth of monopoly and greater concentration of economic power and to create conditions favorable to small and independent business. I am very glad that this major piece of legislation has at last become law. I shall expect the Federal Trade Commission to be alert and vigorous in its enforcement."

Representative Emanuel Celler Democrat of New York, principal sponsor of the bill in the House, issued a statement declaring that the "loophole" closed by its enactment "has been largely responsible for the spectacular mergers which have whittled away at the foundation of a truly competitive system."

"Armed with this new and salutary statutory authority," he said, "the Federal law enforcement agencies will be able to prevent in the future those competition-stifling mergers of the past which have led to a serious degree of concentration of economic power today."

Senator Joseph C. O'Mahoney, Democrat of Wyoming, who first proposed such a law as chairman of the Temporary National Economic Committee in 1941, made public two letters he had written in connection with the legislation.

Says Merger Was Called Off

In one, addressed to James M. Mead, chairman of the Federal Trade Commission, he said that passage of the bill already had resulted in the abandonment of plans for a merger of the two largest companies in the coated abrasives industry. He identified them as the Carborundum Company of Niagara Falls, N. Y., and the Minnesota Mining and Manufacturing Company of St. Paul. The merger plans were called off two days ago, Mr. O'Mahoney said.

"The new law which goes on the statute books today will give the Federal Trade Commission the legal basis for proceeding by preventive action if any attempt should hereafter be made to revive the merger plan," the Senator wrote.

In a letter to Attorney General J. Howard McGrath, Mr. O'Mahoney said that enactment of the bill would doubtless "make your department most anxious to see that nothing is left undone" to complete the prosecution of a pending antitrust case involving the two companies.

"Some of those who resisted the passage of the bill amending the Clayton Act contend that it was unnecessary because the department had the power to prosecute monopolistic practices under the Sherman Anti-Trust Law," he added.

"The fact that the Carborundum Company and the Minnesota Mining and Manufacturing Company were planning their merger was an indication of belief that the merger could not be prevented."

December 30, 1950

BIG BUSINESS LOSES IN INCOME SLICING

Proportion of Total Earnings in U. S. Has Dropped Since 1929, Economist Finds

By WILL LISSNER

In the period since 1929 that has been marked by rapid expansion of all segments of national income, the profits of the largest corporations represented a declining share of that income, Dr. A. D. H. Kaplan of the Brookings Institution reported last night.

While big business, measured by the record of the largest corporations, earned a declining share of national income, the medium-size and smaller corporations received an increasing share of national income as profits, Dr. Kaplan said.

The Washington economist presented a preview of the findings of a five-year study of big business before executives of companies that had cooperated in the investigation. They met at a dinner given by Alfred P. Sloan Jr. and Ernest T. Weir at the Waldorf-Astoria Hotel which was attended by 275 men from nearly 100 large companies. The Brookings study was made possible by grants from the Maurice and Laura Falk Foundatoin and the Alfred P. Sloan Foundation.

One of the main issues of the studies, Dr. Kaplan said, was how big business had affected the balance of competitive opportunities for risk-takers and employes.

From 1929 to 1948, the economist reported, national income grew in current dollars from $87,000,000,000 to $223,000,000,000, or nearly three times, and meanwhile corporations consistently produced about half of it. Unincorporated businesses produced about one third and Government the remainder.

The main block of national income produced by corporations was received by rank-and-file employes in the form of wages and salaries, Dr. Kaplan continued. These payments rose from 34.6 per cent of total national income in 1929 to 37.3 per cent in 1948. Compensation to management and corporate officers receded percentagewise from 1929 to 1948. Interest payments declined sharply. Profits before corporation income taxes increased from 11.5 per cent to 13.8 per cent, but profits after such taxes declined from 10 to 8 per cent.

"To the extent that distribution of national income represents a measure of income opportunities," Dr. Kaplan declared, "it is apparent that rank-and-file employes of corporations constitute the chief factor in the enlarged share of the national income produced in recent years by corporations."

Unincorporated enterprises produced 36.5 per cent of national income in 1929 and 33.6 per cent in 1948. Despite this decline, the shares of national income received as income by the employes and by the owners of these enterprises increased in the period. Noncorporate profits rose from 15.9 per cent of national income to 17.8 per cent, Dr. Kaplan found.

The profits before taxes of the 100 largest industrial corporations declined from 3.7 per cent to 3.3 per cent of the national income between 1929 and 1949, the economist reported. Those of other large corporations, including utilities and financial institutions, dropped from 2.4 per cent to 2.0 per cent. However, profits of medium-sized corporations rose from 4.8 per cent to 7.0 per cent and those of small corporations from 0.6 per cent to 1.5 per cent.

Another issue to which the investigation was addressed was, "Are the giants secure?" Dr. Kaplan found that both the industries and the individual corporations represented among the 100 largest industrial corporations in 1909 had undergone profound changes by 1948.

The iron and steel industry dominated the big-business sector in 1909. However, its share of the total assets of the 100 largest industrial corporations dropped from 30 per cent to 11 per cent. Transportation equipment and petroleum rose phenomenally in rank. Private transport and the leather industry dropped out of the group. Coal mining sagged to last place.

The United States Steel Corporation has grown with the economy, but whereas its assets were 22 per cent of the total assets of the 100 largest industrial corporations in 1909, they now represent only 5 per cent, Dr. Kaplan said. Of thirteen other steel companies among the giants in 1909, only three survived in the list of 1948, along with five newcomers. Of the 100 giants of 1909, only thirty-six were among the 100 largest of 1948.

"The top is a slippery place," Dr. Kaplan declared.

January 29, 1953

DIVERSIFICATION HELD RECENT MERGERS' AIM

Science Service

CAMBRIDGE, Mass., July 25—American industry has diversified its activities in the post-war years, a suvey by Arthur D. Litle, Inc., here shows.

Many companies have gotten into some other business by merging with other companies. Such mergers, mostly seeking product or market diversification, have been proceeding at the rate of two a day for the past seven years.

Instead of seeking to control markets, as was the case in many earlier business combinations, the present trend of diversification increases competition, the survey notes. The diversifying concern seeks to avoid a narrow market and the sharp swings in demand of a single field.

A leading producer of railroad air-brake systems formerly relied entirely on the undependable demand of the nation's railroads. It recently purchased another company making road-building machinery and industrial engines. Other railway equipment companies now manufacture aircraft equipment, electronic devices, oil-field pumping equipment, jet engine parts, vacuum pumps, farm machinery castings, heat exchangers and plastics.

One company, formerly selling six related products to one industry, now makes twenty-eight products for nine industries and has reduced its dependence on the original market by 40 per cent.

July 26, 1953

Brownell Wants Trust Laws To Aid, Not Stifle, Business

By RUSSELL PORTER

Attorney General Herbert Brownell Jr. contrasted yesterday the Eisenhower Administration's approach to anti-trust law enforcement with that of the Roosevelt and Truman Administrations. He said the new Administration had borne out the expectations of those who predicted it would "again become primarily interested in promoting competition rather than in attacking industry."

At the annual meeting of the New York State Bar Association, Mr. Brownell approvingly quoted a prophecy from an unidentified source a year ago. This said the new Administration might give the country "a better defense against monopoly than the Democrats, for all their crusading zeal, were ever able to achieve."

Mr. Brownell announced that criminal anti-trust proceedings were being limited to "clear-cut" violations, such as price-fixing, allocation of territories or customers, and boycotts.

Promises Report in Fall

He said the Department of Justice would issue a report by this fall to show business men how they can keep within the law, and to guide the department in selecting anti-trust cases.

This report will be made by the National Committee to Study the Anti-trust Laws, composed of sixty lawyers, law professors and economists appointed by the Attorney General.

Mr. Brownell said the Administration had not aimed at "mere doctrinal perambulation" but at "making real strides toward either cracking restraints on market entry or controls over price." It has been trying to remove barriers to competition in both production and distribution of goods and services, he added.

In the year after Jan. 20, 1953, when the Eisenhower Administration took office, the Attorney General went on, the anti-trust division of the Department of Justice has brought eighteen criminal and eleven civil cases.

"This case volume approaches the pace of like periods in the recent past," he said. He added that this record had belied forecasts that the new Administration "would trouble big business no more."

He said the division had made real progress in solving the problem of delay in anti-trust cases. "From May 1, 1953, to Jan. 20, 1954," he said, "60 per cent more cases were terminated than during the corresponding nine months of the preceding years. This amounted to forty-two cases; twelve by court decision, three by dismissals and twenty-seven by consent judgments and nolo pleas."

The division also has started to wind up cases pending an undue length of time, he added. "From May, 1953, to January, 1954," he said, "one-third of the division's old cases—eighteen out of fifty-six — were terminated. Eight were filed between 1941 and 1946 and were among the twelve oldest in the division."

In addition, he declared, the division is trying to cut the length of trials by the use of stipulations. In one case it reduced the time from an expected three or four weeks to a little more than a day.

Mr. Brownell said the new policy as a whole was based on

the Eisenhower Administration's philosophy that the anti-trust laws comprise a charter for economic freedom on which our political and social freedoms depend. He said the Administration was trying to preserve freedom for initiative, opportunity to advance, and the chance to enter the business or profession of one's choice.

"During the international crisis for a number of years," he continued, "all of us have acquired a new realization of the values and principles upon which our American society is based.

"For democracy to survive and be strong, its economic liberty must be safeguarded and maintained."

He then quoted approvingly a statement by Dr. Carl L. Becker that the primary aim of all governmental regulation of the economy should be "not to supplant the system of private enterprise but to make it work."

Basis of Prosecutions

Stanley N. Barnes, assistant Attorney General in charge of the anti-trust division, told the same meeting that any criminal prosecutions outside the "clear-cut" violations mentioned by Mr. Brownell would be based on "recent Congressional mandates" not on "sociological theories."

He said he would not have recommended the filing of some cases he found pending when he took office. He added that he was reviewing all pending cases to determine whether further action was warranted.

"No suit will be filed that is not legally sound and in the public interest," he asserted. "Law-abiding businessmen should not fear the strong arm of justice. I do not conceive that the anti-trust laws aim to place restrictions upon industry or to impose regulations upon economic initiative.

"On the contrary they seek to relieve business from arbitrary types of restrictions which arise from unreasonable restraints and monopolistic conditions created by entrenched individual firms or combinations. To uphold freedom to compete and to remove artificial obstacles to competition are the goals we seek.

"I view the anti-trust laws as strong legal instruments to shore up our system of free enterprise by insuring to all who wish to enter any field or start any new industry, that they may do so without fear of arbitrary restraints and predatory practices by those already established. In this spirit I will continue to carry out my duties."

He said the division was experimenting with a new procedure in civil complaints by negotiating consent judgments before filing complaints. This, he said, might save much time and expense in the trial of civil cases.

January 29, 1954

DISCOUNT VOLUME PUT AT $50 BILLION

Cut-Rate Outlets Are Said to Account for $25 Billion, or 18% of All Retail Trade

STEADY RISE IS REPORTED

Business Executives Divided on Remedies, Survey by U. S. Chamber Finds

By CHARLES E. EGAN

Special to The New York Times.

WASHINGTON, Nov. 4—Retail discount outlets now account for an annual volume of $25,000,000,000, or 18 per cent of all retail trade, and the volume is steadily rising, according to the United States Chamber of Commerce.

Total discount volume throughout the country, including that done in the wholesale field, has reached $50,000,000,000 a year, the report said.

The chamber's figures, made available today, were based on reports from top executives in the retail, wholesale and service fields. The executives supplied information on the comparatively new "discount" type of competition for study by a national distribution panel set up by the chamber's domestic distribution department.

Generally, retail discount houses are outlets operating in low-rent premises, where customers select their own merchandise, pay cash and carry their purchases away, the report said. Because of the low operating costs, it added, the discount retailers boast they can undersell the more orthodox type of retailer by a wide margin.

Wholesale discount houses were described as jobbing establishments specializing in getting merchandise from manufacturers and reselling to retail outlets on an extremely narrow profit margin.

For Information Purposes

The report, released by the national business men's group today, is merely informative, officials said. They explained that the chamber had taken no position on the matter of discount houses but had simply gathered the data for interested members.

Approximately 70 per cent of those questioned in the distribution and service fields said that they were faced with competition from retail or wholesale discount concerns, with the share that such concerns took of available business ranging from 10 to more than 50 per cent.

Although agreed upon the difficulties of discount competition, those responding to the panel's questions were sharply divided as to the remedies. About half of them said that they were adopting more aggressive competitive merchandising tactics and about 40 per cent said that they expected to press suppliers for the same price treatment accorded discount houses.

About 15 per cent of the retailers said that they were "fighting fire with fire" by cutting their own prices.

Disagree on Legislation

There was a divergence of opinion also as to whether Federal legislation was desirable. Replies from 15 per cent indicated they felt that there was no need for any change, but others said that some action amending the Robinson-Patman Act was in order.

Those urging legislative action, however, also were divided, with half of them advocating the strengthening and the rest pressing for modification of the anti-trust laws as they affect pricing.

One group of executives would like to see the Robinson-Patman Act clarified to permit them to meet competitive price offers. A substantial group, however, including one-third of all the wholesalers, believes the act should be modified in the opposite direction to prohibit any form of price discrimination regardless of volume, type of business or other factors involved.

The panel's report said:

"A rough-weighted average of all replies pegs the discount volume at 14 per cent of the total.

"Service businesses, as would be expected, show less price cutting than either wholesale or retail. Retail replies show a higher percentage than any other group. Of these, 18 per cent say more than 50 per cent of the volume is through discount channels and only 23 per cent indicate no competition of this type.

[illegible] weighted average for retail alone is 18 per cent. The average for wholesale is 15 per cent."

November 5, 1954

MERGERS PLAGUE U. S. AND BUSINESS

Rise in Combinations Offers Legal Problems to Both—3 Basic Laws Rule

By LUTHER A. HUSTON

Special to The New York Times.

WASHINGTON, May 29—One of the livest and most perplexing problems currently besetting business and antitrust law enforcement agencies is that of mergers of industrial corporations.

In some industries mergers seem to be almost the order of the day. Where combinations are proposed business faces the problem of whether merger plans might run afoul of the antimonopoly laws.

The enforcement agencies, charged with the responsibility of guarding the economy from possible harmful effects of mergers on our competitive system of free enterprise, are concerned over what has been described as the current "wave of merger activity."

Not all amalgamations of business and capital are illegal. The courts, the enforcement agencies and industry have found many of them to be in the interest of the national economy.

However, there is a "shadowland" of statutory interpretation wherein neither business nor enforcement has the benefit of precisely stated law or clear judicial rulings. There business seeks to find out what it can do and enforcement tries to halt harmful combinations in their incipiency.

Three Basic Laws

The basic antitrust laws are the Sherman Act of 1890, the Clayton Act of 1914 and the Robinson-Patman Act of 1936.

The Sherman Act made all forms of combination or conspiracy in restraint of trade illegal.

The Clayton Act outlawed price discrimination and made unlawful the acquisition by one corporation of the stock of another where the effect would be to "substantially lessen competition, or tend to create a monopoly."

The Robinson-Patman Act expanded the Clayton Act by banning discounts, rebates, allowances or advertising service charges more favorable to one purchaser than to his competitors.

Mergers come principally under the Clayton Act. Stock acquisitions were barred by Section 7 of that law. What is known as the Celler Act of 1950, amended Section 7 to prohibit acquisition of assets, as well as stock, where the effect would be to lessen competition.

Herbert Brownell Jr., the Attorney General, has described Section 7 as "furnishing a legal tool to cope with monopolistic tendencies in their incipiency."

One of the problems Mr. Brownell now is pondering is whether to recommend to Congress changes in Section 7. It has been the position of the Department of Justice that no changes should be proposed until the courts have ruled on pending cases to test the Celler Amendment. Judicial interpretation of the assets acquisition provision now are lacking.

In the meantime, the Department of Justice seeks to halt mergers "in their incipiency" where it encounters proposals that might be illegal or not in the public interest. The Justice Department however, has ways of finding out about them. They are:

¶The group contemplating the merger comes in and asks for an opinion.

This is a voluntary action. There is no law that requires business to notify the Government or ask its advice when mergers are contemplated. It has been a practice, however, for many years for corporations desiring to amalgamate to ask for what is known as a "railroad release."

This procedure provides that if the merger plan submitted meets with the approval of the Department of Justice, the corporations are told they may proceed without fear of criminal prosecution under the Sherman Act. They might still face civil action, however, if the manner in which the merger plan was carried out subsequently was found to contravene the anti-monopoly laws.

¶The Justice Department finds out about proposed mergers by watching the newspapers.

If stories are printed that one or more corporations contemplate uniting the department may decide to take a look at it.

In that case, letters are sent to the parties involved asking certain information. The corporations may comply with, or ignore the request.

¶A competitor complains that an amalgamation was in process that will damage his business.

If the complainant could make a showing sufficient to warrant his charges, the department would undertake an investigation.

Factors to Be Weighed

Under the circumstances the information reached the Justice Department, these were some of the factors that would be weighed in determining whether the proposed merger ran afoul of the Sherman or Clayton acts:

¶The location, physical and financial size, past acquisitions, products, and activities of the merging companies, individually and in combination.

¶The structure and size of the industy in terms of production and capacity.

¶The relative position in the industry of the two companies individually and combined.

¶The ease by which new competitors may enter the industry.

¶The number of companies active in the industry, their respective size and relative standing in sales and total assets.

¶The sales, relative standing and like factors of the two companies and their competitors in definable market areas, if relevant.

¶The nature of the industry—that is, whether infant, dynamic or declining.

May 30, 1955

FORD STOCK TO GO ON SALE TO THE PUBLIC IN JANUARY, ENDING FAMILY'S SOLE RULE

FOUNDATION GAINS

Fords to Retain 40% of Control in Deal, Market's Biggest

By A. H. RASKIN

Common stock of the Ford Motor Company, the world's largest family-owned industrial empire, will go on public sale in January for the first time.

The way was cleared for the biggest stock offering in financial history by an announcement yesterday that the Ford family would relinquish majority control over the company founded by Henry Ford fifty-two years ago.

Sixty per cent of the voting power will go to holders of the new common stock; 40 per cent will stay with the family. The decision to let the public share the wheel with the Ford heirs means that industry's richest and most tightly held "closed corporation" will have to lift the blinds that have concealed its profits from outside scrutiny. How much the company earned always has been closely guarded.

The initial sale of 6,952,293 Ford shares is expected to bring in $400,000,000 to $500,000,000.

YIELDS FULL CONTROL: Henry Ford 2d, president of the Ford Motor Company.

This would indicate a price of $60 to $70 a share, although no official determination has yet been made.

Offered by Foundation

The stock will not be offered by the company, but by the Ford Foundation, which made the announcement. This is the giant philanthropic trust the family set up in 1936 to make grants for the promotion of human welfare in a broad area of national and world affairs.

The foundation owns 88 per cent of all Ford stock, but none of it has voting power. Under the present stock arrangement, full voting power resides in 172,645 shares of family-owned stock. The stock-sale plan involves an intricate shift in the whole financial base of the company. The total number of shares will rise from 3,495,040 to 53,461,470, and the family will surrender three-fifths of its control.

The desire of the foundation trustees to diversify their investment portfolio was a major factor in the decision of the Ford family to permit public sale of the Ford stock. The family shared the trustees' belief that it was unsound for the foundation to put all its eggs in one basket.

With the money the fund gets from its sale of Ford stock it will invest in other corporations. However, a spokesman said it was unlikely to buy the stock of other automobile manufacturers.

After the initial stock distribution, Ford will join General Motors, Chrysler and 1,100 other corporations whose securities are listed for trading on the New York Stock Exchange. Keith Funston, president of the exchange, hailed the Ford decision as "a landmark in the history of public ownership" of American business.

Ford, with 193,000 employes and assets that a year ago totaled more than $2,000,000,000, is operating at a profit rate that exceeds the company's total earnings for all the twenty-one years preceding World War II. It expects to produce 2,500,000 automobiles and trucks this year, more than one-quarter of the national total.

The decision to let the public share in the company's ownership and control reversed a policy its founder set when he and eleven associates started the enterprise in 1903 with an actual cash investment of only $28,000.

Sixteen years later, after some of his fellow stockholders had questioned the wisdom of his expansion plans, Mr. Ford and his son, Edsel, bought the others out and full control passed into the hands of the family.

The policy shift in favor of public sale was made by agreement of the Ford heirs and the foundation trustees after more than two years of negotiation. Charles E. Wilson, former president of the General Electric Company, chairman of the foundation's finance committee, and Sidney J. Weinberg, banker and director in a dozen large corporations, were reported principally responsible for persuading the family to let the public share the driver's seat.

The plan calls for a basic recapitalization of the company. At present, the family holds all the 172,645 shares of voting stock. In addition, there are 3,322,395 shares of Ford stock with no voting rights. Of these, the foundation owns 3,089,908, the family owns 190,347 and 108 Ford executives and key employes own 42,140.

Employes Get Role

The refinancing program calls for splitting the 3,322,395 shares of nonvoting stock on a fifteen-for-one basis. The family-owned voting stock would be split on a twenty-one for one basis. The difference was intended to compensate the family for its willingness to give up its sole right to vote on management affairs.

Under the new arrangement, the old nonvoting stock would acquire voting rights as it was issued to the public. This also would apply to shares owned by the 108 key employes and to 101,000 additional shares they are entitled to buy on an installment basis over the next three years.

The new common stock would go into a pool that would hold 60 per cent of the company's voting stock, no matter how many shares actually were released by the foundation. What the foundation kept would have no voting rights until it put the stock on public sale.

Thus, after the first sale, 60 per cent of the voting rights in the company would be exercised by the owners of the 6,952,293 shares to be sold in January and the Ford employes who would hold 632,100 shares of the split stock.

This 60 per cent control would not be diminished by the fact that the total number of shares outstanding after the split would be 53,461,470. The foundation at this point would be holding 39,396,327 shares on a nonvoting basis. These shares would draw dividends but would have no weight in management affairs.

If the foundation, in the interest of further diversifying its own holdings, decided later to sell more of its stock, the shares it released would become part of the pool that participated in the 60 per cent voting control.

After the conversion of their original 172,645 shares of voting stock and their 190,347 shares of nonvoting stock, the Ford family will own 6,480,750 shares of a new voting "B" stock. Whenever any of these shares are sold or transferred outside the family, they will have to be converted into regular voting common stock on a straight one-for-one basis.

So long as the total family holdings do not fall below 2,700,000 shares, they will be entitled to an aggregate vote of 40 per cent in the company's destinies. If they go under that figure, the ratio will drop to 30 per cent.

If the total continues to fall until it drops below 1,500,000, the "B" stock will lose its special status and the family shares will vote on the same basis as the common stock. No fixed percentage of control will be reserved to the family.

Wall Street experts noted that effective control of the company was virtually certain to remain with the family, even after the transfer of 60 per cent of the voting rights to outsiders. In practice, the holders of 5 to 10 per cent of the stock usually are able to exert a controlling voice in the affairs of a corporation that has large numbers of stockholders.

Financial observers said they expected no change in the company's basic policies. Ford plans

MODEL T OF 1915: This is how old "tin lizzie" looked after the body was enclosed

MODEL A OF 1928: It featured nickeled headlights, four-wheel brakes and bumpers

to spend $1,000,000,000 in the next three years on modernizing and expanding its facilities. Foundation spokesmen said the spreading of their financial base would not mean any change in either the scope or direction of the foundation's activities.

One unusual aspect of the Ford stock program is that all the money to be realized from sales to the public will go for charitable purposes. None will be used to help pay for the company's expansion program or to provide working capital for current operations.

Ordinarily, companies going to the public with new stock flotations are seeking capital to permit an improvement in their operations or to enable them to take on additional responsibilities.

In expressing his gratification at the Ford decision to sell stock, Mr. Funston of the Stock Exchange said:

"I am highly gratified that ownership of another of this country's industrial pioneers will be made available to investors across the nation. In my opinion this development is a landmark in the history of public ownership."

Will Urge Approval

"It is my intention to recommend to the Board of Governors of the New York Stock Exchange that they approve the new common shares for listing and trading on the exchange upon completion of distribution."

The biggest previous piece of industrial financing involved the sale last February of 4,380,683 shares of General Motors stock for $325,773,903. The transaction was handled by an underwriting syndicate of 330 houses headed by Morgan Stanley & Co.

It was believed likely that as many as 500 brokerage houses would be involved in the Ford sale. The demand for shares is likely to be so strong that many Wall Street analysts predicted that an allocation system would have to be devised to guarantee that the distribution would be handled equitably. Some said they were sure that the issue would be oversubscribed on the first day.

November 7, 1955

G.M.'s 1955 Profit Exceeds a Billion, Setting U. S. Mark

Special to The New York Times.

MIAMI, Fla., Feb. 2—The General Motors Corporation, which has a long record of firsts, took another in 1955. It became the first company in American history to earn more than a billion dollars in a year.

More precisely, net profits after taxes were $1,189,000,000. G. M. cleared that much on record sales of $12,443,000,000. In 1954, when volume was $9,284,000,000, the company had a net profit of $806,000,000.

Harlow H. Curtice, president, disclosed the company's 1955 operating results at a press conference here today, preceding the opening Saturday of the Miami phase of the G. M. Motorama of 1956. He told newsmen that in 1955:

¶G. M.'s payroll rose to $3,127,000,000, a new high, from $2,610,000,000 in 1954.

¶Its world-wide employment averaged 624,000 persons, up 47,000 from the 1954 average.

¶Its total tax bill would be in the area of $1,600,000,000.

"More than $2,180,000,000 in payrolls went to 410,000 hourly rate employes in the United States in 1955," Mr. Curtice said. "In 1954, a total of $1,747,000,000 in payrolls was paid to 367,000 hourly rate employes."

Among the many other firsts held by the giant automotive concern are: first in size in its industry: first with respect to the amount of stock in the hands of shareholders; first manufacturing enterprise to push sales above the $10,000,000,000 level in a single year; first company to make available a successful electric self-starter for an automobile (1911), and the first manufacturer to have produced a total of 50,000,000 passenger cars (reached in 1954).

In response to questions, Mr. Curtice indicated he was dead set against imposition of any controls that might touch his industry.

As for proposed laws controlling auto makers' relations with their dealers: "We don't need them—whenever we develop better terms, we pass them right on to our dealers." On proposals to limit automobiles' top speed: "They'd just make cars more dangerous."

On consumer credit controls, Mr. Curtice held that the increase in consumer debt last year merely reflected the rapid climb in consumer spending, and installment credit now was proportionately no higher than it should be.

"Down payments are 40 per cent, which is historic," he said. "Installments run only twenty-eight months. Repossessions are at a subnormal rate. So why this concern?"

He said G. M. A. C., the G. M. credit arm, was "fully satisfied" with current credit conditions and had no policy changes in mind.

Ivan Wiles, vice president of G. M. and Buick division general manager, reported that in Flint, Mich., where five G. M. divisions employ 90,000 persons, average earnings in 1955 were $5,460, compared with $4,200 in 1950.

"The employe in our shops can —and does—buy a Buick," he said. "For the first time, it's gotten so the man on the auto assembly line can buy what he makes."

General Motors' profit last year was equal to $4.30 each on 275,140,965 common shares outstanding. This compares with $3.03 a share earned in 1954, as adjusted to reflect the 3-for-1 split last September.

Stockholders received $2.17 a share in dividends in 1955. The balance was retained by the corporation for use in the business.

Discussing the General Motors tax bill, Mr. Curtice said:

"Provisions for United States and foreign income taxes last year are estimated in the area of $1,350,000,000, compared to $839,000,000 in 1954. The total 1955 G. M. tax bill, including provisions for state and local taxes, will be in the area of $1,600,000,000. The comparable 1954 figure was $1,035,000,000."

The corporation's record sales of $12,443,000,000 last year were 27 per cent above the 1954 volume of $9,824,000,000 and 24 per cent greater than the 1953 total of $10,028,000,000, the former peak.

Mr. Curtice said the sales record in 1955 had been achieved "despite a decline in defense deliveries to 7 per cent of the total sales, compared with 14 per cent in the preceding year."

February 3, 1956

HIGH COURT HOLDS DU PONT VIOLATES ANTITRUST LAWS BY G. M. STOCK OWNERSHIP

By EDWIN L. DALE Jr.
Special to The New York Times.

WASHINGTON, June 3—The Supreme Court ruled today, 4 to 2, that E. I. du Pont de Nemours & Co. was in violation of the antitrust laws by holding 23 per cent of the stock of General Motors Corporation.

The ruling was based on a finding that this stock ownership gave du Pont a preference with General Motors in the market for automotive finishes and fabrics.

The majority overruled District Court Judge Walter La-Buy of Chicago. It sent the case back to him for determination of the "equitable relief necessary." The court did not specify the relief. Presumably it would involve at least some divestment by du Pont of its General Motors stock.

[Within an hour of the decision, du Pont stock rose 8 points to 202½ on the New York Stock Exchange. But, at the end of the day's trading it had declined to 197½, a net gain of 1 point over Friday's close. Sales totaled 9,800 shares. General Motors stock showed little reaction, declining only ¼ to 42½ on a heavy volume of 33,700 shares.]

The majority opinion was written by Associate Justice William J. Brennan Jr. and was concurred in by Chief Justice Earl Warren and Justices Hugo L. Black and William O. Douglas.

A long and strongly worded dissent was written by Justice Harold H. Burton. It was concurred in by Justice Felix Frankfurter.

Justice Tom C. Clark disqualified himself because he had been Attorney General when the Government first brought the case. Justice John Marshall Harlan did so because he had acted as an attorney representing du Pont. Justice Charles E. Whittaker was not on the court when the case was argued.

Although the Government had brought the case under several provisions of two antitrust laws, it was decided today solely under Section 7 of the Clayton Act. This bars stock acquisitions or mergers where the effect may be, among other things, to "tend to create a monopoly in any line of commerce."

The case, as the Supreme Court majority and minority opinions viewed it, turned chiefly on four points—two of law and two of interpretation of the evidence. The majority established these two precedents on points of law:

1. Section 7 of the 1914 Clayton Act was meant all along to affect "vertical" as well as "horizontal" mergers, or stock acquisitions. In a vertical merger a corporation acquires control of a potential customer or supplier; in a horizontal merger a corporation acquires a competitor.
2. The Government, to prove a violation of the Clayton Act, must only prove that there will be a "probable" lessening of competition or tendency to monopoly when it brings its suit, not that this condition existed when the stock acquisition was made. The du Pont acquisition of General Motors stock took place in 1918, 1919, after a recommendation of the du Pont Board in 1917.

This apparently means that the Government can bring suit against past stock acquisitions if it can prove that probable anticompetitive effects now exist. Justice Burton's dissent said this meant that the Clayton Act had been a "sleeping giant all along" and that all corporations that had acquired stock in other corporations since 1914 were exposed now "to the bite of the newly discovered teeth."

Amended in 1950

The act was amended in 1950 to make clear that it did apply to vertical mergers. Never until this case had the Government even alleged that vertical mergers were affected by the original act. This case, agreed to be a vertical case, was brought in 1949.

By far the greatest portion of both arguments, however, was related to one of the two points of evidence—whether in fact du Pont's ownership of 23 per cent of General Motors stock gave it a preferential position as a supplier.

The majority, citing extensively from the evidence at the original trial before Judge La Buy, concluded that "du Pont purposely employed its stock to pry open the General Motors market to entrench itself as the primary supplier of General Motors' requirements for automotive finishes and fabrics." The majority asserted:

"The fire that was kindled in 1917 continues to smolder. It burned briskly to forge the ties that bind the General Motors market to du Pont, and if it has quieted down, it remains hot, and, from past performances, is likely at any time to blaze and make the fusion complete."

The minority, quoting even more extensively from the evidence, rejected this conclusion completely. It argued that in many products other than finishes and fabrics du Pont had little success in selling to General Motors; that some G. M. divisions used du Pont finishes while others used competitive finishes, and in general that what success du Pont had was based on superior "quality, service and price."

The second issue centering on the evidence was whether the General Motors market for fabrics and finishes was "substantial" enough to matter.

The majority decided that this was a special market, and a large one, and thus clearly was "substantial." The minority said sales to General Motors were only a small portion of total sales of finishes and fabrics.

Although the original Government case revolved in considerable part around the size of the two corporations, today's ruling did not touch on that issue.

The two Supreme Court opinions today diverged more completely than anything else on the evidence of whether du Pont had in fact become a favored supplier of General Motors. The majority, for example, cited a letter written in 1926 by J. L. Pratt, a G. M. vice president, to the general manager of G. M.'s Delco Light Division. Mr. Pratt urged that du Pont be given preference "on those items that du Pont can take on the basis of quality, service and price."

The minority asserted that "du Pont never did receive the business to which the correspondence related," even though the du Pont product was offered at a lower price and "the technical staff at Delco thought the du Pont product superior."

June 4, 1957

A Defense of Bigness In Business

It is in fact, says an observer, desirable because it promotes research and competition.

By SUMNER H. SLICHTER

THE recent decision of the Supreme Court in the du Pont-General Motors case suggests the desirability of a review and an appraisal of American policy toward competition, monopoly, and bigness in business. The decision reveals the strong determination of the court to prevent competition from being weakened and the court's willingness to resort to controversial interpretations of the law in order to implement the public policy of preventing restraints on competition.

But the decision also reminds us that much thinking on the relation of bigness to competition is out of date and unrealistic. Hence, the adaptation of traditional American anti-trust policy to the facts of modern industry requires that we take a fresh look at the role of large enterprises in American business—particularly the role of large enterprises as a source of vigorous and dynamic competition.

When one compares the economy of the United States with the economies of other advanced industrial countries, four characteristics stand out conspicuously.

(1) The Government of the United States endeavors through broad and drastic laws to prevent restraints on competition and to forestall the growth of monopoly. Most other advanced industrial countries either tolerate considerable restraint on competition or even encourage organizations of business men that are designed to control competition.

(2) Competition in American industry is far more vigorous and pervasive than in the industries of any other advanced industrial country. Indeed, the vigor of competition in the United States almost invariably attracted comment from the European productivity teams that visited this country in the years following the war.

(3) The United States has many more huge business enterprises than any other country. Several years ago this country had more than 100 corporations (exclusive of purely financial ones) with assets of more than $250 million each. General Motors produces far more cars than the combined British, German and French automobile industries, and the United States Steel Corporation produces more steel than the entire British steel industry.

(4) Production in many American industries (especially those requiring large capital investment) is highly concentrated in the hands of a few large concerns. As a general rule, the concentration of production in other industrial countries is far less than here.

These four characteristics of the American economy are not unrelated. It would be wrong to ascribe the widespread and intense competition in American industry *solely* to the strong public policy against restraint of trade, monopolization and interference with competition. Conditions in the United States—the absence of class lines, the abundance of opportunity, the weakness of tradition—have long made life here highly competitive in all its aspects and competition in business is just one manifestation of this general competitive spirit. But America's unique and firm public policy against restraints on competition has undoubtedly helped greatly to keep industry here strongly competitive.

THIS strong policy, however, has paradoxically encouraged the development of giant industrial corporations and the concentration of production in many industries among a few large concerns. The growth of enterprises in Europe has been limited by the practice of forming cartels—a practice which governments have tolerated and even encouraged. The cartel or trade association divides markets among its members, limits the growth of the most efficient concerns, and assures the weak, high-cost concern a share of the market.

In the United States, where cartels are illegal, each concern is pretty completely exposed to competition from all other firms, and business goes to the firms that can get it. This means that in many industries production is gradually concentrated in the hands of a few industrial giants, and only a small part of the business is left for small firms.

The trend toward corporate bigness in industry has led many students of anti-monopoly policy to believe that the American policy of encouraging competition and discouraging monopoly is turning out to be a failure and to conclude that steps need to be taken to limit the influences of large enterprises in American industry. Of many proposals that have been made, two principal ones are of particular interest.

ONE proposal is that new restrictions be placed on mergers. Some have urged that no merger be permitted which cannot be justified by technological reasons. Some have proposed that mergers involving a corporation above a given size be prohibited unless found by the Federal Trade Commission to be in the public interest.

The second proposal deals with the concentration of production in various industries into a few enterprises. It is urged that the Government undertake a com-

SUMNER H. SLICHTER, Lamont University Professor at Harvard, has been writing on American and world economics for 30 years.

GIANT—"We need to take a fresh look at the role of large enterprises in American business—particularly the role of large enterprises as a source of vigorous and dynamic competition." This is part of a new du Pont orlon fiber plant in South Carolina.

LARGE-SCALE—One alone of America's "Big Three" in the automotive industry makes more cars than the combined British, French and German industries. Above, power lines at a Detroit automobile plant.

prehensive survey of American industry to determine whether enterprises exceed the size required by modern technology and that the Government be authorized to break up firms that are unnecessarily large.

Both of these proposals are based on fallacy. They rest upon a mistaken conception of the role of large corporations in American business and particularly upon the relation of large corporations to competition. Each, if put into effect, would weaken rather than strengthen competition. In fact, in order to stimulate competition, existing restrictions on mergers should be relaxed, not tightened, and large enterprises, instead of being threatened with break-up, should be given a clear mandate to grow, provided they use fair means. Let us examine more completely each of these two proposals to restrict the growth of enterprises.

I

The proposal that new restrictions be placed on mergers arises from the fact that the United States in recent years has been experiencing a great wave of mergers. But recent mergers have not weakened competition. On the contrary, they have indirectly strengthened it because they have enabled managements to build more diversified and better-integrated enterprises — enterprises which are more capable of reaching all parts of the vast domestic market, of adapting themselves to market shifts and changes in technology, of riding out the ups and downs of business, and of supporting technological research and development. Many large firms and firms of moderate size have acquired small firms, but the acquisitions by the very largest firms have not been numerous.

The specific circumstances surrounding each merger are unique, but a case-by-case examination shows how mergers are helping to build stronger enterprises, better able to compete and to hold their own in competition.

Let us consider a few examples. A maker of cans bought a concern manufacturing plastic pipe in order to get a foothold in the plastic pipe business. A maker of railroad freight cars bought companies making electrical equipment, truck trailers and dairy supplies in order to shift from a declining business to expanding businesses. A food manufacturer bought a West Coast manufacturer of salad seasoning in order to give nation-wide distribution to its product. A maker of household ware bought a supplier in order to have a source of pressed wood handles for its appliances.

Unusually competent managements often buy other concerns so that they can spread good administrative methods to less efficiently operated enterprises.

THE many advantages produced by mergers show that the proposal that mergers be prohibited unless they can be justified by technological reasons does not make sense. There are good reasons for mergers that have nothing to do with technology.

Moreover, it would be unwise to require Government approval of all mergers involving an enterprise above a specified size. That would be substituting the decision of Government officials for the decision of business men on matters that the business men are better able to understand. The public interest is amply protected by the present drastic provision of Section 7 of the Clayton Act.

Indeed, the fact that mergers often make for more vigorous competition by helping managements build stronger and more efficient business enterprises indicates the need for relaxing the present severe restrictions on mergers contained in Section 7 of the Clayton Act. This section prohibits any merger which is likely to lessen competition substantially in *any* line of commerce. The fact that the merger may increase the intensity of competition in *other* lines of commerce makes no difference. As Section 7 now reads, the *total effect* of the merger on competition is irrelevant. If it is likely to lessen competition substantially in any one line of commerce, it is illegal.

Obviously, the section as it now reads, conflicts with the national policy of encouraging competition. It should be rewritten to make the legality of mergers depend upon the *total* effect on competition, thus permitting any merger that has the net effect of increasing competition.

II

The second proposal — to remake the structure of American industry by breaking up the largest enterprises—rests upon the mistaken view that, where output is concentrated among a few concerns, effective competition does not occur. The error of this view is shown by the vigorous competition in various industries in which most of the output is made by a few firms—in such industries as the automobile, tire, refrigerator, soap, cigarette, paper products, television and many others.

There are two principal reasons why competition tends to be vigorous when production is concentrated among a few large concerns. One is that such enterprises keep close track of their rank in sales and fight hard to move ahead of rivals or to avoid being surpassed by rivals. The second reason, and one that is rapidly gaining in importance, is the fact that competition among large firms is being stimulated by the growth of technological research.

It is only within the last several decades that managements have generally discovered the big returns yielded by technological research. As a result, the outlays by private industry on research and development increased nearly six-fold between 1940 and 1953. In 1957, the total research and development expenditures of private industry, exclusive of the aircraft industry, which is a special case, are running about 71 per cent greater than they were in 1953. By 1960 outlays on research are expected to be 21 per cent above 1957.

No expenditures are more competitive than outlays on research, for the purpose of these expenditures is to improve products, develop new products and cut costs. More than 70 per cent of the outlays on research and development are made by firms with 5,000 or more employes because concerns with large sales can best afford this overhead expense. Hence the rapidly mounting outlays on research indicate both the growing competitiveness of American industry and the increasingly important role large enterprises are playing in making competition more intense.

Incidentally, competition among large firms is superior in quality to competition among small firms and serves consumers more effectively. This is because the greater research by the large firms gives the consumers a wider range of choice over a period of years than competition among a much larger number of small firms that can afford little or no research. The large firms are constantly experimenting with new features in their products which they hope will win the favor of consumers. Sometimes consumers like the new features, sometimes they do not, but at any rate they have been given a choice. In general, the wider the range of choice open to consumers, the more effectively is the welfare of consumers advanced.

IN view of the growing importance of large enterprises as a source of competition and the superior quality of this competition, a move to break up large concerns would be a blunder. There is much to be said, however, in favor of incentives for enterprises to split themselves voluntarily, if the managements consider a split desirable. The resulting increase in the number of top managements with independent authority to make policies and to try experiments would be favorable to technological progress — provided the concerns are large enough to support extensive research. A good incentive for voluntary splits would be created by relieving stockholders from liability for the capital gains tax on the appreciation in their holdings from the time they purchased the stock up to the date of the split.

But enforced splitting of enterprises, except as a remedy for flagrant monopolizing of trade by unscrupulous methods, would be another matter. It would be demoralizing to managements to be penalized for winning customers by having to submit to an enforced disruption of their organizations.

In fact, the present law needs to be clarified in order to encourage a few of the very largest concerns to strive harder for a bigger share of the market. The Sherman Act forbids monopolization of commerce or attempts to monopolize it. In general, successful growth, due to superior efficiency and not aided by illegal practices, does not violate the law provided there is no deliberate attempt to acquire monopoly power. But what practices are evidence of "deliberate attempts" to achieve monopoly power?

The managements of a few very large and efficient con-rns apparently fear that efforts to get more business by cutting prices will be held to be attempts to monopolize. There is need to make clear that efforts to win business by giving consumers the benefits of low costs will not be regarded as monopolistic.

III.

Americans should hold fast to their traditional views of the importance of vigorous competition in industry. This philosophy and the actual practice of vigorous competition have been un·que and invaluable nation assets which have contributed immensely to the progressiveness and efficiency of industry in the United States.

But Americans need to discard some widely held but out-of-date views concerning the relationship between bigness and competition. They need to grasp the fact that when production is concentrated among a few large concerns, rivalries become peculiarly intense and the additional fact that in an age of technological research the large enterprise is an increasingly important source of competition.

AMERICANS need to understand that a variety of conditions — rapidly changing technology, the growing importance of industrial research, the growing strength of trade unions—tend to increase in many industries the size of the enterprise that is able both to compete and to survive in competition. Hence, we are likely to see a spread of the tendency for production to be concentrated in a few large or fairly large firms.

But this trend, if it occurs, should not disturb us. It will simply represent an adaptation of industry to the conditions of the time.

The strength of competition in American industry will to an increasing extent be determined by the scale of technological research and development. Research will grow as rapidly as engineers and scientists can be found to man the laboratories. Hence, one can predict with confidence that competition in American industry will continue to gain in intensity. And large enterprices, far from being a menace, will, to a growing extent, be the instruments by which the country is given the benefit of large-scale technological research and of increasingly vigorous competition.

August 4, 1957

AUTOS AND SMOKES

TO THE EDITOR:

Sumner Slichter ("A Defense of Bigness in Business," Aug. 4) argues that there is "vigorous competition in various industries in which most of the output is made by a few firms. . . ." One wonders, however, precisely what Professor Slichter means by "vigorous competition" in two of the industries he cites.

Rivalry in the automobile industry in recent years has not been marked by competition in prices but rather by a race for greater horsepower (accompanied by lower engine efficiency) and "sleek, slick and sassy" styling innovations.

As for the tobacco industry, the chief manifestation of its competitive situation seems to be highly ingenious and imaginative, though not too enlightening, advertising copy.

PAUL GOODMAN.
New York.

CONCENTRATED POWER

TO THE EDITOR:

Mr. Slichter has given a carefully reasoned defense of oligopoly in industry. Surely it is true that attempts to encourage competition by an enforced break-up of large corporations are, under certain conditions, ill-advised and blundering. But is it also true, as Mr. Slichter argues, that oligopolistic competition is superior to small firm competition? Mr. Slichter's defense of his rather startling thesis involves an interesting tour de force. I was so fascinated by it that it took some time for me to realize that I was in a blind alley.

In reality Mr. Slichter is jousting at windmills. Economists do not oppose bigness per se, whatever the lawyers may interpret their recommendations to mean. Rather, is it not relative size and the concentration of economic power that is the issue? They have been afraid that such concentration deterred economic progress. In this context excellence of management and the "high quality" of competition are beside the point.

The fear of the classical economist and the modern liberal was and is that the absence of active competition and the resultant barriers to free entry of new firms ultimately would short-change an economy. The genius and dynamic of capitalism has seemed to these economists to consist in the recurrent ability of the economy to produce new (and better) goods with new men using new resources.

CHARLES J. STOKES,
Professor of Economics,
Atlantic Union College.
South Lancaster, Mass.

August 18, 1957

ECONOMY ALTERED BY PENSION FUNDS

20th Century Fund Reports 'Socializing' of Wealth

By CHARLES GRUTZNER

Private pension funds are growing faster than any other form of investment and are a major factor changing the nature of the capitalist system in this country, the Twentieth Century Fund reported yesterday.

Such funds now total nearly forty billion dollars and are increasing by more than four billion dollars a year. This wealth, along with other vast accumulations of trust money such as mutual investment funds and insurance, is being put to work as capital by trust officers.

Decisions as to how and where it is invested are made in most cases, the report says, by bankers and other trust officers rather than by the actual investors.

The Rev. Paul P. Harbrecht, author of the report, said in an interview that this "rapid institutionalization of the ownership of property" posed a challenge "to find a rational framework to accommodate it."

"This is socializing the wealth of capitalism," Father Harbrecht declared. "This is not socialism by a long shot, but it is nothing like the capitalism defined by Karl Marx and Adam Smith."

Father Harbrecht is a member of the Institute of Social Order, the national Jesuit social science center in St. Louis. He is a lawyer and holds the degree of Doctor of the Science of Law from Columbia University. He has studied and lectured on the impact of the corporation as an instrument of social change.

The report is in a 328-page book titled "Pension Funds and Economic Power." Father Harbrecht calls the emerging system "the paraproprietal society" and defines it as "the society beyond property."

The Twentieth Century Fund is a nonprofit, nonpartisan research foundation that was endowed by Edward A. Filene of Boston.

The report makes the point that pension funds are neither public nor private property, except in the sense that they are not controlled by the state. The report notes that this vast working wealth is "owned by no one in the meaningful sense of the term." This, it says, is a new phenomenon in a capitalist society that has traditionally considered the distinction between public and private ownership to be adequate and complete.

Possible Danger Noted

Father Harbrecht said that a possible danger existed because "these pension funds are not supervised by any public authority as to how they are invested." He qualified this by adding: "Of course, the Securities and Exchange Commission would jump on anyone who tried to rig the market."

A fruitful field for further study, according to Father Harbrecht, is how these vast trust funds can best be invested.

"It is important to invest these funds properly," he said, "but we are not yet too clear just what we want these pension funds to do beyond providing the needed payments to the employes on retirement."

In most pension systems, Father Harbrecht reported, the unions had no voice on how the trust funds were to be invested. Employers generally turned this responsibility over to financial institutions, whose sole concern in most cases was to obtain the highest possible yield consistent with safe investment.

He said there had been a swing in such investments from bonds and Government securities to stocks of corporations, mostly blue-chip stocks. While this is inflationary, he said, it enables pension funds to keep pace with the general inflation.

Annual stock purchases on the part of pension funds are larger than those of any other group of major buyers. Father Harbrecht said pension funds were currently buying stocks equivalent to about 30 per cent of the total annual net additions to stocks outstanding. He said 86 per cent of these purchases were on the New York Stock Exchange.

The report noted efforts by some unions to have pension funds invested in housing construction or other community facilities that might benefit employes during their working years as well as after retirement. Such proposals have generally gone unheeded.

Report Discusses Impact

The report concerns itself particularly with the impact on the capital market of non-insured pension funds called pension trusts. This type of fund, with more than half of all the assets in private pension funds, is administered by a bank, trust company or group of individuals.

In the "insured plans," which in effect use the contributions to buy retirement insurance from an insurance company, the pension assets are not segregated, but are made part of the undivided assets of the insurance company.

Father Harbrecht said that the possible influence of the pension trusts on corporate control and on the nation's economy was "of first significance."

Advance findings on part of Father Harbrecht's study, which were made public by the Twentieth Century Fund two weeks ago, dealt with the inadequacies of present laws and practices. That report said that a fourth of all American workers were covered by pension plans in private industry, but that no more than half of them would ever receive a cash benefit from the plans as they were now constituted.

Fund Growth Listed

The report made public yesterday shows that private pension funds are growing faster than public pension funds although they have not yet overcome the early lead of the public pension funds.

A table based on S. E. C. statistics shows that the assets of all public and private pension and retirement funds grew from $36,500,000,000 in 1950 to $80,600,000,000 in 1957. Of the 1957 total, $33,300,000,000 was in private pension funds, a gain of $4,300,000,000 over the previous year. Corporate non-insured funds accounted for $19,300,000,000, and insured pension funds amounted to $14,000,000,000.

Public funds in 1957 totaled $47,200,000,000, an increase of $2,200,000,000 over 1956. The public funds included railroad retirement, civil service retirement, state and local retirement, and old-age and survivors insurance.

Father Harbrecht estimated that the total for private pension funds was now near $40,000,000,000. He said the growth of private funds could not be expected to level off until 1975, by which time the total might be between $126,000,000,000 and $134,000,000,000. Non-insured trust funds might account for between $75,000,000,000 and $86,000,000,000 of the 1975 total.

Pointing out that non-insured private pensions had assets of $5,500,000,000 in 1950, the report said they would have more than quadrupled by early 1960, when their assets are estimated to reach about $25,000,000,000. It predicted that "it is quite probable that at least by 1975 the non-insured funds will comprise two-thirds of all funds invested for pension plans."

The report said pension fund investments in corporation stocks produced a greater concentration of control than even these figures showed, because a single trustee—usually a large bank—often had investment control over many different pension funds.

It cited findings of the New York State Banking Department that more than 98 per cent of the pension fund assets held by all banks in the state were in the hands of the thirteen largest banks. Less than 2 per cent was held by thirty-eight other banks.

Noting that nearly a third of all shares outstanding in the stock market were now held by all types of financial institutions, the report said:

"It is quite likely that certain New York banks will soon approach a point where their combined holdings of stock for pension funds could give their opinions considerable weight in the councils of the larger corporations.

"While it is the policy of many large corporations to include provisions in their pension plans to prevent their funds from gaining control of other corporations, no such restrictive policy has yet been announced by the banks.

"Unquestionably, they will seek to spread their stock investments widely to stave off acquiring the responsibility of corporate direction as long as possible. But as the stock purchases of the pension funds continue to grow, we can anticipate that at some time in the not-too-distant future the banker-trustees are going to be faced with an uncomfortable choice.

"They will have to buy into a position of authority in the larger corporations or reject profitable investments in order to avoid the responsibilities that accompany large shareholdings."

November 30, 1959

HIGH COURT LIMITS PRICE-FIXING ROLE OF MANUFACTURER

Finds Parke, Davis Violated Antitrust Act in Move to Enforce Controls

Special to The New York Times.

WASHINGTON, Feb. 29—A manufacturer's right to fix the retail price of his product and then to enforce that price was sharply restricted today by the Supreme Court in an important antitrust decision.

By a vote of 6 to 3, the court held that Parke, Davis & Co. violated the Sherman Antitrust Act when it attempted, in 1956, to maintain fixed retail prices for its drugs in Richmond, Va., and the District of Columbia.

Justice William J. Brennan Jr., writing for the majority, was joined by Chief Justice Earl Warren and Justices Hugo L. Black, William O. Douglas and Tom C. Clark. Justice Potter Stewart concurred in the result.

The dissent, by Justice John Marshall Harlan, was joined by Justices Felix Frankfurter and Charles E. Whittaker.

Vital Change Cited

The dissenters said that the court had made a vital change in antitrust law by sending "to its demise" a doctrine first established in 1919, in the case of United States V. Colgate.

The Colgate case held that the Sherman act left manufacturers free to chose their customers. Thus it was legal, the court said, for a company unilaterally to announce retail prices and then to refuse to sell to dealers who would not abide by them.

The Colgate doctrine was limited to unilateral retail price-fixing. It did not cover contracts or agreements between manufacturers and wholesalers or retailers to maintain resale prices.

Subsequently, Congress enacted statutes permitting such resale price maintenance by agreement wherever legal under so-called fair trade laws.

Many Void Law

But in a growing number of states, now about sixteen, fair trade laws have been held invalid. In some others, and the District of Columbia, there have been no fair trade laws. In these areas manufacturers desiring to fix retail prices have had to rely on unilateral action under the Colgate doctrine, and today's decision is significant in these areas.

The Parke, Davis activities involved in the case stemmed from price-cutting by some drugstores. To stop the price-cutting Parke, Davis took the following steps:

¶Representatives visited each of the cut-rate retailers and warned him that, if the cutting continued, Parke, Davis would refuse to deal with him.

¶Representatives visited all the wholesalers in the area and warned them that if they sold to offending retailers their supplies would be cut off.

¶When some retailers refused to go along with the fixed prices despite the warning, they were unable to get Parke, Davis supplies from either the wholesalers or the company direct.

Non-Advertising Agreement

When these tactics proved ineffectual, the company got one cut-rate retailer to agree that he would stop advertising his reduced prices—though continuing to sell at those levels—if he could get supplies again. Parke, Davis told the other retailers about this, any they agreed to do the same.

This non-advertising agreement lasted only a month, when

the price was started again. Parke, Davis, then gave up trying to enforce retail prices, because Justice Brennan said, the Justice Department had begun looking into the matter.

Justice Brennan intimated that it might be time to overrule the Colgate decision if the Government requested such an overruling, as it did not in this case. It was this intimation that caused Justice Stewart not to join the majority opinion.

But in any case, Justice Brennan found, Parke, Davis had gone beyond "mere announcement" of prices "and the simple refusal to deal" and had employed "other means to effect adherence to resale prices."

The Colgate rule does not mean, he said, that the Government must prove an actual agreement to fix prices to show a Sherman act violation. Pressures of various kinds by the manufacturer may take the case outside the Colgate exemption, he said.

"If a manufacturer is unwilling to rely on individual self-interest to bring about general voluntary acquiescence [in his prices]," Justice Brennan wrote, "and takes affirmative action to achieve uniform adherence by inducing each customer to adhere to avoid such price competition, the customers' acquiescence is not then a matter of individual free choice prompted alone by the desirability of the product."

All this, Justice Harlan said, left the Colgate rule a hollow shell, giving manufacturers a theoretical right that they had no legal way to enforce.

He said the few activities carried on by Parke, Davis did not go beyond unilateral action. He analyzed other cases in which price-fixing activities had been held unprotected by the Colgate rule and concluded that in all of them the manufacturers were vastly more aggressive than Parke, Davis had been here.

The case was argued for the Government by Daniel M. Friedman and for the company by Gerhard A. Gesell of Washington.

March 1, 1964

The Merchant's View

An Appraisal of Outlook for Small Retailers as the Giants Grow Bigger

By HERBERT KOSHETZ

Retailing can easily set records in the year ahead. All the factors are in its favor. The market, based on population, is growing. But, more important, the average consumer has the means to buy, and, according to the latest surveys, he appears to be more inclined to make purchases than he was, for example, in late 1959 or early 1960.

But despite the optimism, many small independent merchants will find the year difficult to survive. For them it again will be a year of attrition in which they must somehow overcome increasing competition from the burgeoning growth of discount stores, chains and the expansion aims of the giant operators of variety and department stores.

If it's any comfort, many competitors of the small independents also will fall by the wayside. The fiercest competition will be among the large operators. Unfortunately, the dutsraised in the bone-breaking struggle of the goliaths often obscures the plight of the man on the fringe of the battle.

Independents Seek Help

Many independents are not willing to admit it, but there is a growing sentiment for a concerted plea to the Government to get additional assistance in their fight to stay alive. The antitrust laws apparently are not strong enough to insure the continued existence of small business as it is known in the country today.

Cynical as it may be, the argument is often advanced that it would be better for all concerned if the small independent who cannot stand on his own feet were to go under. The implications of such thinking are much deeper than they appear on the surface. Those who accept the idea have resigned themselves to the eventual taking over of all business by large operators. Automation, they say, will win over completely, not only in production but also in distribution.

This will mean, among other things, that giant retail distributors will own not only their outlets but also sources of production. It is envisioned, for instance, that distribution costs will be much lower, and that these savings can be passed on to the consumer.

This is good, as far as it goes. What no one has satisfactorily explained, however, is how diligently consumers are going to buy these goods in an economy that has successfully eliminated the middle man and his retinue of service people and all the employment provided in blanketing a market consisting of many small as well as large outlets.

Price Discrimination Rampant

Despite existing statutes such as the Robinson-Patman Act, which seeks to insure fair competitive prices among large and small wholesale buyers, it is generally conceded that price discrimination is fairly rampant and that the syndicate buyer has a distinct advantage over his smaller counterpart. Admittedly, enforcement is difficult, and the problem is further complicated by the fact that those who are hurt as a result of violations are reluctant to press complaints for fear that they will antagonize some customers.

If the small merchant becomes an insignificant factor in the economy, it will mark the end of an era. And there are troubled conjectures as to what will emerge.

Half of the more than 4,000,000 business concerns in the United States are retail outlets. Yet it is estimated that in the food field 15 per cent of total sales originate in stores operated by fewer than 100 companies. Supermarkets now account for more than 50 per cent of all grocery sales.

Concentration Grows

E. B. Weiss, vice president of Doyle, Dane, Bernbach, Inc., advertising agency, wrote recently that by 1970 forty giant retail organizations would control 60 per cent of the nation's total retail volume in practically all major merchandise classifications. He points out that two large retailers, Sears, Roebuck & Co. and the Great Atlantic and Pacific Tea Company, have chalked up $5,000,000,000 each in sales in the year now ending.

By 1970, he said, there may be several large retailers with sales of $8,500,000,000 each a year and shortly thereafter some retailers will be doing as much as $10,000,000,000. Pointing up the competitive battle of the giants, Mr. Weiss makes one point that may prove significant in the retail picture. He points out that at present more and more chain stores are doing 50 per cent of their total volume in 25 per cent of their store units. He predicts that soon these chains will be accounting for 75 per cent of their total volume in 25 per cent of the units.

He is alluding to the fact that among giant retailers the trend is definitely toward larger and fewer units. If such is the case, it would appear that the type of legislation small retailers will be insisting upon for their protection will be laws limiting the size of any given retail unit. This, of course, could be governed by existing population growth, number of retail concerns already doing business in the area and other factors.

Is there any precedent for this type of legislation? The retailers might well point to the laws, national and state, that govern the establishment and conduct of branch banks and insurance companies.

In the light of the fact that the largest retail operations are publicly owned, some limitation on the size of individual units might prove a boon to stockholders who, by themselves, have no way of controlling the over-ambitious plans of operating personnel.

December 24, 1961

Centralizing Government

TO THE EDITOR OF THE NEW YORK TIMES:

Big Business has for years been outspoken in its opposition to "creeping socialism." But what are the mergers which are becoming increasingly common in industry, banking and now railroads but a form of business socialism that more than ever will concentrate control over the nation's economy in the hands of an "increasing" few?

I am hardly a socialist, but if "creeping socialism" is inevitable—and to a certain extent I think it is—I prefer it in the hands of the Government and Congressionally approved executives, merely as the lesser of two evils. I prefer bureaucratic waste to efficiency, if efficiency means a concentration of power for ultimately private advantage. Mussolini, you will recall, made the trains run on time.

SIDNEY TILLMAN.

New York, Jan. 29, 1962.

February 5, 1962

STEEL GIVES IN, RESCINDS RISES UNDER PRESSURE BY PRESIDENT

KENNEDY IS VICTOR

Uses His Full Powers for 72 Hours to Subdue Industry

By RICHARD E. MOONEY

Special to The New York Times.

WASHINGTON, April 13 — President Kennedy triumphed today over the titans of the steel industry.

Almost precisely seventy-two hours after the United States Steel Corporation's abrupt announcement of a price increase, the corporation backed down and rescinded the increase late this afternoon.

The action by United States Steel, the nation's largest steel producer, followed announcements by the Inland Steel Company and the Kaiser Steel Corporation that they would not increase their prices, and a statement by Bethlehem Steel Corporation, the nation's second largest producer, that it was canceling its rises.

By early evening seven of the eight companies that had raised their prices in the last three days had canceled them. The eighth, Wheeling Steel Corporation, said it would announce its decision tomorrow.

Many Forms of Pressure

For three days the great forces at the command of the President of the United States had been brought to bear on the steel industry.

Some of the effort was exerted in the open—the President's open denunciation of the companies, calculated to arouse public opinion against them; the opening of grand jury proceedings leading to possible antitrust action, and the threat to divert orders to companies that had not raised prices.

But privately as well, the President and his advisers were bringing every form of persuasion to bear on the industry, trying to hold back the companies that had not yet raised prices and induce the others to roll back the price increase.

Kennedy's Statement

President Kennedy was informed of the actions by United States Steel and Bethlehem off Norfolk, Va., where he was aboard a cruiser observing naval maneuvers. He issued this statement:

"The people of the United States are most gratified by the announcements of Bethlehem and United States Steel Company that their proposed price increases are being rescinded.

"In taking the action at this time, they are serving the public interest and their actions will assist our common objective of strengthening our country and our economy."

Even during this dramatic day, as the steel industry started to weaken, the Administration pressed on with the actions that the price increase had started.

Secretary of Defense Robert S. McNamara announced that defense business would be channeled, if possible, to companies that had not raised steel prices. Grand jury subpoenas were served on some of the companies that had raised their prices. And the Labor Department issued a new set of statistics designed to prove the Administration's case that the price increase was not warranted.

Tonight it was evident that President Kennedy had scored a great personal success such as few Presidents had experienced in their relations with American industry.

He had strengthened his position for dealing with the business community. He had regained stature in the eyes of labor leaders. He had aroused a resounding chorus of popular support that would do his party no harm in next fall's elections.

The conflict between Government and the leading steel companies was set off Tuesday when United States Steel announced that it would raise the price of steel about $6 a ton.

White House Incensed

This announcement, which was quickly followed by similar announcements from seven other big companies, was received almost as a declaration of war at the White House.

Only a few weeks previously, the companies and the steel union had negotiated a new contract, to take effect July 1. The Administration had kept the two sides under pressure to reach an agreement that would not set off a new wage-price spiral, and it hailed the agreement, which contained no direct wage increase but only fringe-benefit improvements, as noninflationary.

President Keenedy was furious at the price increase, regarding it as a "double cross" of the Administration. Immediately he and the highest officials of the Administration set to work to counter the steel companies' move.

The objective of the Administration was to prevent the nation's third largest industry — its sales are exceeded only by those in autos and petroleum — from setting off an upward spiral of prices and wages.

The strategy was to divide and conquer. If two big companies could be persuaded to hold the line, the rest would have to retreat.

The key target in the strategy was Inland Steel, eighth largest in the industry. A secondary target was Armco Steel Corporation, the sixth largest.

Behind all the public declaiming and swinging of clubs, Administration officials were engaged in intense personal campaigns to persuade these two not to follow the lead of United States Steel, and to persuade other companies to retreat if possible.

By long-distance telephone the ranking powers of the Federal Government called the ranking powers of the steel industry—management, directors and stockholders. Edward Gudeman Jr., the Under Secretary of Commerce, was a central figure. He knew Inland Steel well as a lifetime Chicagoan, and he handled the dealings there.

President Kennedy turned to the long-distance telephone too.

This morning, in Chicago, the industry began to crumble. The Chicago Daily News published an interview with Joseph L. Block Inland's chairman, who is vacationing in Japan.

"We do not feel that an advance in steel prices at this time would be in the national interest," Mr. Block said.

Less than an hour after the paper hit the streets, Inland announced its position. It was made public by Philip D. Block,

Jr., vice chairman of Inland, a cousin of Joseph Block.

President Kennedy heard the news on the steps of the White House as he bade farewell to Mohammed Riza Pahlevi, Shah of Iran. "Good, good," the President said. "Very good."

At 12:15 P.M. he held a final strategy conference with the officials who were working on the steel campaign in its many aspects.

An hour later, Secretary McNamara announced the Pentagon order on steel buying. He told a news conference that he believed, both as a Cabinet officer and former president of a big business, the Ford Motor Company, that the price increase was not justified.

Forty-five minutes later, news bulletins said Kaiser Steel Corporation had announced that it, too, would hold the line.

Kaiser was the company that broke with the industry in the 1959 strike and was first to make peace with the United Steelworkers of America. Its action today was just as welcome to the White House.

The President, at Andrews Air Force Base preparing to take off for Norfolk, took a last-minute telephone call on board his plane from Dr. Walter W. Heller, his chief economic adviser.

He was airborne when the big news came. At 3:20, Bethlehem Steel retracted the price increase. The game was won, though the big one, United States Steel, had yet to make its concession of defeat.

At Norfolk, the President went straight to a motorcade and missed the Bethlehem development. Andrew T. Hatcher, his associate press secretary, caught up with the announcement by telephone from Washington about an hour after the event and passed a note to Mr. Kennedy.

Meanwhile, Secretary of Labor Arthur J. Goldberg had gone to New York City to talk to the men at 71 Broadway, headquarters of United States Steel, including the chairman, Roger M. Blough. About 5 P.M., word sped around Washington that the end was at hand. Mr. Hatcher was on the phone again with Washington, this time from dockside as the President prepared to sail.

United States Steel's announcement, according to one report, was to come from the White House. Another report said it would come from Mr. Kennedy himself. It came from 71 Broadway at 5:25 P.M.

April 14, 1962

TRIBUNAL WIDENS CURBS ON TRUSTS IN 2 KEY RULINGS

Voids Merger and Upholds Prosecution of Officers Acting for Companies

Special to The New York Times.

WASHINGTON, June 25—In two of its most important antitrust decisions in years, the Supreme Court today gave Government trust busters powerful weapons to enforce competitive conditions in business.

First, the court gave a broad reading to Section 7 of the Clayton Act, which is aimed at corporate mergers. It said that Congress had intended to curb "in their incipience" any tendencies toward concentration in industry."

And second, the court rejected an argument that individual corporate officers could not be prosecuted under the Sherman Act for actions taken in their companies' behalf. Six lower Federal courts had accepted this argument.

The question of individual prosecutions has had special interest since the great electrical cases of 1961, which ended with seven business executives in jail. Today's case involved Raymond J. Wise, vice president of the National Dairy Products Corporation.

Warren Writes Opinions

Chief Justice Earl Warrer wrote both opinions. The court reached both results unanimously, although with some differences of view in part along the way.

The merger case was the first big legal test of what Congress meant when it amended the Clayton Act's Section 7 in 1950. The amendment was sponsored by two long-time antitrust advocates, Representative Emanuel Celler of Brooklyn and Senator Estes Kefauver of Tennessee, both Democrats.

As amended, the section prohibits corporate acquisitions whose effect "in any line of commerce in any section of the country . . . may be substantially to lessen competition, or to tend to create a monopoly."

Lawyers have inevitably argued over what such words as "line of commerce" and "substantially" mean. In today's decision, interpreting them for the first time, the court read them broadly in favor of Government contentions.

Brown Company Involved

The case arose from an acquisition in 1955 by the Brown Shoe Company of St. Louis, fourth largest American shoe manufacturer. Brown accounts, however, for only about 4 per cent of the annual national shoe production.

Brown acquired the G. R. Kinney Company, which operates the country's largest retail family style of shoe chain. Kinney had about 400 stores in 270 cities, accounting for 1.2 per cent of national retail sales in dollar volume.

A Federal District Court in St. Louis found the merger a violation of Section 7 and told Brown to submit a plan for divestiture of Kinney. While the case was pending Brown had operated Kinney as a separate entity so that they could be split easily if required.

On appeal in the Supreme Court, Brown Shoe argued that the combined concern did not account for enough of the country's shoe production and sales to meet the Clayton Act test of a "substantial" effect on competition. It said the shoe business was composed of highly competitive small units.

But Chief Justice Warren said the Justice Department had demonstrated a recent trend toward concentration in the shoe industry, with other acquisitions by Brown and other companies.

He noted that Congress had used the word "may" lessen competition and said that that indicated a concern "with probabilities, not certainties."

He said Congress had seen a "rising tide of economic concentration" and had wanted to "arrest mergers at a time when the trend to lessening of competition in a line of commerce was still in its incipiency."

'Mandate' of Congress

"We cannot avoid the mandate of Congress," he said, particularly when tendencies toward concentration "are being accelerated through giant steps striding across a hundred cities at a time."

This was apparently a reference to the widespread outlets of both Brown and Kinney.

The Chief Justice found both vertical and horizontal injury to competition.

The vertical effect, he said, would be to cut smaller manufacturers off from the business of supplying Kinney stores, which might tend to buy Brown's products. The horizontal effect would be to end competition between Kinney stores and Brown's fewer retail outlets.

The Brown company had argued that these effects could not happen because Brown and Kinney sold shoes in different price brackets—Kinney "popular price," or cheaper than Brown's "medium price."

The Chief Justice agreed with the District Court in rejecting this argument. And he agreed in defining the lines of commerce in this case as three—men's, women's and children's shoes.

Justice Tom C. Clark, in a concurring opinion, said he would find just one "line of commerce," shoes of all kinds.

Justice John Marshall Harlan said the Supreme Court should not review the case now, since it was not a "final" antitrust judgment subject to direct appeal in the Supreme Court. He relied on the fact that Brown Shoe must still present to the lower court its divestiture plan.

But since that jurisdictional argument did not prevail, Justice Harlan went on to the merits and agreed that Brown must lose.

The case was argued by the Solicitor General, Archibald Cox, for the Government, and by Arthur H. Dean of New York for Brown Shoe.

In today's other case, Mr. Wise and his employer were accused of conspiring to eliminate price competition on milk sales in the Kansas City area. Mr. Wise was charged with acting solely in his "capacity as an officer" of national dairy products.

Federal District Judge R. Jasper Smith dismissed the indictment on the ground that the Sherman Antitrust Act did not apply to individuals acting for their companies. He said they were covered by Section 14 of the Clayton Act.

The Clayton Act provision has never been successfully invoked by the Government. Like the Sherman Act, it provides for a jail term of up to a year for violators. But it sets the maximum fine at $5,000, while Congress raised the maximum under the Sherman Act to $50,000 in 1955.

The first assistant in the Justice Department's Antitrust Division, Robert L. Wright, argued the case for the Government and John T. Chadwell of Chicago for Mr. Wise.

June 26, 1962

What 17 Million Shareholders Share

More Americans own stock in U.S. corporations today than ever before. But is that sufficient to justify the claim of a 'people's capitalism'?

By MICHAEL D. REAGAN

THE year 1963 may go down in the annals of Wall Street as the Year of the Stock Split. The Columbia Broadcasting System, Chrysler Corporation and Radio Corporation of America announced splits entitling a holder of one existing share to receive two or three shares instead. The biggest was a two-for-one split by the American Telephone and Telegraph Company. And, in the largest corporate financing effort on record, A. T. & T. offered stockholders the rights to purchase $1,225,000,000 of new stock. Recently these rights set off an unprecedented trading scramble.

A. T. & T. with 2.25 million shareowners holding 244 million shares, epitomizes "people's capitalism," a term popularized by the New York Stock Exchange in recent years to suggest widespread participation of the general public in the ownership of American industry and, implicitly, popular participation in the operation of big businesses. "People's capitalism" conveys an image of economic togetherness, the little fellows and the big, the stockholders and the presidents and directors of corporations. But is the image accurate?

Drawings by James Flora

"CAPITALISTS ALL"—Among occupational groups, professional men have the highest percentage of stockholders—farmers the lowest.

First, some 15 billion shares of publicly held corporations are now in circulation. According to a recent report by Jean Crockett and Irwin Friend, of the Wharton School of the University of Pennsylvania, the value of stocks held by individuals is approximately $400 billion; another $100 billion is owned by domestic corporations.

The striking fact about stock dis-

CONCENTRATION—Some 80% of all stock is owned by 1.6% of the people.

tribution, on which rests the claim of a "people's capitalism," is the substantial increase in the number of shareholders that has occurred since 1952. In that year, there were 6.5 million stockholders—somewhat less than the estimated total for 1929, before the crash. By 1962 the New York Stock Exchange reported 17 million owners.

Part of this increase is attributable to employe-participation plans, part to the increased popularity of investment companies, which permit a purchaser to spread his risks while buying only one issue. Nearly a quarter of a million holders have been attracted by the widely publicized Monthly Investment Plan—the application of installment buying to stock ownership. But most of the increase must be credited to greater affluence (more families with savings to invest) and, apparently, to a belief that the market can only go up.

ON the basis of the New York Exchange's studies, the average shareholder bears little resemblance to the bloated cigar-smoking capitalist of the old cartoons. He—or, more likely, she, since 51 per cent of shareholders are women—is 48 years of age, has finished high school, has had some college training and has a family income of $8,600.

The average stockholder lives in a middle-sized city. If his home is a metropolis, however, it is more likely to be San Francisco than New York or Chicago (26.6 per cent of San Francisco's residents hold stock, as against 14.4 per cent in New York, and 13.8 per cent in Chicago). As for states, Connecticut has the highest proportion of shareholders—18.1 per cent—while Alaska, Hawaii, Mississippi and South Carolina have no more than 3 per cent.

Stockholders are to be found in every occupational category, but the percentages vary decidedly. Thus while 36 per cent of the nation's professional men and 32 per cent of its proprietors and managers own stock, only 6 per cent of service workers, 3 per cent of laborers and 1.4 per cent of farmers are shareholders. In between are clerical and sales workers—nearly 25 per cent—and housewives—15 per cent. Considering these occupational categories from another angle, the housewives make up the largest group among the country's stockholders: with 5.4 million of them, they account for about 33 per cent of the total. They are about equaled by the professionals and managers together, with clerical and sales workers next in line.

The relationship of the small stockholder to the corporation whose shares he owns is generally minimal: he signs an annual proxy approving the management-selected slate of directors, looks for the dividend checks in the mail, and, if they stop coming, sells the stock.

DISTRIBUTION—Stock held by individuals is valued at $400 billion; another $100 billion is owned by corporations.

As Prof. Bayless Manning of the Yale Law School has said, "It is the corporation as an institution which is permanent and the shareholders who are transitory." The average stockholder is not a proprietor, but an investor or speculator. When hundreds of thousands of individuals share the "ownership" of a company, what each of them owns is really the stock certificate—a claim to dividends or capital appreciation—rather than the corporation. The exceptions are the small number of individuals who may own a substantial percentage of the shares of a particular corporation, enough to demand a representative on the board of directors. The Mellon family's position in Gulf Oil, the McCormick family and International Harvester, and the Watson family and I.B.M. are examples.

EVEN among small holders, however, there are some who use their ownership rights for purposes other than investment. Perhaps the best known are those champions of "corporate democracy," Lewis D. Gilbert and Wilma Soss, the latter the president of the Federation of Women Shareholders in American Business. These very individualistic individuals appear at hundreds of annual meetings a year—on the basis sometimes of hundreds of shares, sometimes a single share—to demand more accessible

MICHAEL D. REAGAN is an associate professor of political science at Syracuse University's Maxwell Graduate School of Citizenship and Public Affairs. He is author of the recently published "The Managed Economy."

BOOM—The notion of a "people's capitalism" is based on the sharp gain in the investor total since 1952.

meetings, more information for the stockholders, limitations on executive compensation and stock options, and other asserted reforms based on the assumption that managements will shortchange the small shareholder unless closely watched and subjected to periodic criticism.

IN the last five years, stockholding has also been taken up, on a single-share basis, by members of CORE and other race-relations groups, who then use their rights acquired by shareholding to urge integrated employment or integrated lunch counters. This has been done at annual meetings of some of the major variety-store chains.

Another minority group of small shareowners consists of trade-union members. Some are long-time employes proud to own a piece of the company to which they have devoted their lives. Some are union leaders. In the case of James B. Carey's electrical workers, the union owns shares of each company with which it bargains. In recent years, executive stock options have been a favorite target for Carey at annual meetings.

While these minority stockholders buy stock in order to voice criticisms, the vast majority of stockholders apparently cares little how the firm is run so long as it is financially successful. When some stockholders rose to demand the ousting of top officials at General Electric's meeting following the price-fixing scandal of 1961, they were roundly booed by the majority, which usually comes for the box lunch served after the polite speeches.

In our picture of the average stockholder, "average" refers to characteristics of the people who own shares, but *not* to the dollar value of their holdings. On this crucial matter, the New York Stock Exchange does not collect current figures, but a 1952 report prepared by the Brookings Institution for the Exchange suggested a very uneven distribution. It found that security holders who had more than 1,000 shares accounted for 58 per cent of the total shares, although they made up only 2.1 per cent of total shareholders.

Other sources confirm this pattern and do devastating damage to the picture of a "people's capitalism." For example, according to income tax records used in the Wharton School study of stock ownership, as of 1960 those families with incomes over $25,000—constituting only 1 per cent of all tax filers—owned 48 per cent of all the stock held by individuals.

(It is pertinent that, according to figures developed by the Conference on Economic Progress, more than 20 million families—almost half the nation's total—had incomes of $6,000 or less in 1960. One would not expect the amount of stock held by families at this income level to be substantial, even when they are shareholders.)

THE most striking estimate of the concentration of stock ownership is by Robert J. Lampman in a National Bureau of Economic Research study, "The Share of Top Wealth-Holders in National Wealth"; he reports that 80 per cent of all personally held stock in 1953 was in the hands of 1.6 per cent of the adult population. Because of this, and because stock prices have risen several times in recent years, these top wealth-holders accounted for 26 per cent of all personal wealth as of 1956. This figure was lower than it was in 1929, but noticeably higher than it was in 1949, when this group's share had reached a post-1929 low of 20.8 per cent.

Thus, while optimists may point to 17 million shareholders in the nation, pessimists **will note that most of these shareholders hold very few shares. "People's capitalism" may mean a large number of stockholders, but it does not mean an equal sharing of industrial ownership.**

Concentrated ownership has a direct effect upon participation in the elections of corporate boards and other matters, like mergers and executive stock option plans, which shareholders may vote on. Such elections, unlike Presidential elections, are not on the basis of one-man-one-vote; they operate on the principle of one-*share*-one-vote. One shareholder with many shares outweighs many shareholders with a few shares each.

HERE a significant paradox emerges. Along with the idea of "people's capitalism" has gone the notion of "corporate democracy": That the more shareholders there are, the more democratic will become the control of large corporations. Bayless Manning has pointed out, however, that diffusion of ownership in fact produces a concentration of control—either in the hands of directing groups (a high proportion of whom are managing officers as well as directors) or stockholders having the largest single blocks of stock (even though far below a majority of shares) in a given corporation. (Not all corporations are like A. T. & T., in which no individual holds even half of 1 per cent of the shares.)

Why should this be so? The answer lies in the nature of the corporate election. The board of directors nominates a single set of candidates for the shareholders to vote on. A few vote personally at the annual meeting; most vote by proxy. No organized alternative slate is presented.

In effect, the "choice" is to vote for the official slate or not at all, for neither the 2.25 million stockholders of A. T. & T. nor the 200,000 in each of many other corporations possess any mechanism for getting together to promote a write-in substitute. Corporate elections are not a vehicle for the effective participation of average stockholders in major corporate decisions.

WHAT then are the consequences of a substantial increase in the number of persons holding equity shares? One effect may be psychological. Those who have a stake in a corporation—even to the extent of a single share—may feel an increased sense of involvement in the business system. The owning of shares may thus be a minor impulse toward political conservatism in economic matters.

Another effect may be to unstabilize the stock markets to some degree because amateurs are easily scared and few of the 17 million consider themselves to be experts in market analysis. Wall Street columnists often distinguish between **professional and small-stockholder reactions and rates of participation in the market. One tangible effect is to increase the sales of market analysis newsletters. The cynic might also suggest that the more popular the stock market becomes, the less need there will be for race tracks to satisfy the gambling urge.**

The real consequence for the economic system of 17 million shareholders may be, as was suggested by Adolf A. Berle Jr. and Gardiner C. Means in their 1932 classic, "The Modern Corporation and Private Property," to divorce ownership from control in large, publicly held corporations.

THE logic of this position is that the function of the corporation changes from the delegated task of making a profit for the owners to self-perpetuation of the firm as an autonomous entity with responsibilities to employes, customers, suppliers, distributors—perhaps even the community at large—as well as to shareholders. So, too, corporations talk of themselves as "balancing the best interests" of these various claimant groups.

Thus the rise of the corporate-conscience doctrine, with its emphasis on good works rather than high profits—though the more down-to-earth proponents will point out that good profits are a prerequisite to expenditures on good works.

The Berle-Means theme, taken up by business spokesmen as well as by a host of social scientists and law-school writers, has come to dominate sophisticated thinking about the shareholder-corporation relationship in the 30 years since its first publication, and the evidence of "people's capitalism" does not dispute it. There is one development, however, that may require modification. This is the rapid growth of the executive stock-option plan since it was first made possible by changes in the tax

regulations of 1950.

The executive stock option sets aside shares of stock, as of a given date and market price, for later purchase by selected executives. If the price rises, the option is exercised and a sizable no-risk profit may be secured. Previously, if the optioned stock was held by the executive for at least six months, the profit secured was taxable at the capital-gains rate, with a maximum of 25 per cent. The new 1964 tax legislation requires that such stock be held for three years before sale if it is to qualify for the capital gains privilege. The rationale for the option plan is that hired managers are in this way encouraged to take a proprietary, not just an employe, interest in the firm.

Almost all the larger firms now have such plans, and they do indeed create a profit interest for the executive. It was announced in December, for example, that Chrysler executives had recently obtained gains in the neighborhood of $4 million by the sale after six months of stock obtained through options. The option price was, in some cases, $20, while the sale price was $85.

The option plan certainly provides a strong personal incentive for large-corporation executives to increase profits. To this extent, it seems to undercut assertions about the loss of the profit motive that were derived from the Berle and Means thesis and may mean more emphasis on short-run profit, less on intangible restraints in the name of future goodwill.

On the other hand, the stock option does nothing to compel distribution of a larger proportion of profit to ordinary shareholders, nor does it affect the use of corporate profit for charitable, educational or quasi-political purposes. If anything, higher profits may simply provide that much more revenue which directors and officers can apply to whatever purposes they deem suitable, within the broad boundaries set, not by nonexistent stockholder control but by the rather permissive attitudes of the courts toward directorial decision-making. "Executives' capitalism" may be a more apt name for our corporate system than the overworked, largely unsupported slogan of "people's capitalism."

February 23, 1964

Bell Grows Two Billion Dollars Bigger

Everyone depends on it, everyone must do business with it, everyone is affected by it: that's A. T. & T. and its affiliates, for which the only word is colossal.

By HAYES B. JACOBS

THE business that sprang from young Alexander Graham Bell's invention of the telephone in 1876 is now a Communications Colossus, towering over any other privately owned corporate enterprise on earth. It is so big, important, all-pervasive and "necessary" that attitudes toward it, like those toward other giant organizations, such as armies, navies and governments, inevitably range the full scale from respect to scorn, from love to hate. It has been satirized by novelists as a greedy, monopolistic "empire." It has been hailed for superior business methods, technological achievements and employe heroism. It has been cited for its contributions to the nation's economy, defense and social welfare. And it has been hacked at by antitrust lawyers as a ravenous, overfed ogre.

Admire it or not, there it stands, the mighty Bell System—cautious, conservative, fabulously successful. On the land, under the sea, in the air, beside the bed—and lately even in outer space. Everyone is dependent on it, everyone must do business with it, everyone is affected by it.

The System is composed of the parent, management unit, American Telephone and Telegraph Company; a manufacture and supply unit, Western Electric Company; a research and development unit, Bell Telephone Laboratories, and twenty-odd operating telephone companies. As a colossal entity it can all be described, but only partly, in colossal figures. It has more assets (more than $28 billion) and more customers (it operates 68,650,000 telephones) than any other United States business. It employs 733,000 people—more than the respective populations of eleven states —and 27,000 of them do nothing but sit and give out "Information." Its annual payroll runs to $4.5 billion. The ever-mounting demand for its services brings more than $9.5 billion a year into its coffers.

A.T.&T. (head, shoulders, best foot and wallet of the Colossus) is owned by 2.25 million investors, foreign and American—the latter representing 1 out of every 95 of our population, only some of them, contrary to a Wall Street myth, being widows and orphans. To keep up with the demand for its services it has recently announced plans to spend $3.25 billion in 1964. Of that sum, $2,012,000,000 is for growth, $423 million for modernization and $815 million for what it calls "just standing still." To help raise the money it will soon offer 12.25 million shares of additional common stock ("the stock that acts like a bond") to its investors. To give them added buying incentive it will increase its quarterly dividend from 90 cents to $1 in April and, "if it meets share owners' approval" at the next annual meeting, split its stock two-for-one in June. (Hot market tip: it will probably meet their approval unless, as could happen, the earth ceases to rotate.)

Since World War II, the System has had to raise about $21 billion in new capital—enough to buy the entire United States gold stock and have $5 billion for a rainy day. What kind of business is it that spends that kind of money; that looks around for still more; that needs $815 million a year in order to "stand still"?

THE Bell System is not only big, but self-conscious about its size. However, to those who have suggested that there should be "lots of telephone companies," it asks, "Would you want several dozen telephones in your house?" (Several *extension* phones now—that's another matter.) A question could also be put to those who have suggested that the Government should run such a basic service for the People. That question is: "How do you, the People, like the United States postal service?"

Big, rich and undeniably monopolistic (it calls itself, but not very often, a "natural" monopoly), the Bell System, through its operating companies, nevertheless provides what is indisputably the best, most reliable communication service on the face of the globe. And it is a fact, overlooked by many of its critics, that it is very closely regulated by the Government, which controls its rates, quality of service and earnings. Considering all this, then, still another question can be asked: "Why shouldn't its 2.25 million investors reap a good profit?" Under its system, the System claims, everyone benefits.

"WE'VE striven by words and by works," says Frederick R. Kappel, chairman of the board of A.T.&T., "to convince the country that a good profit is in everybody's interest." And he adds: "By this, we certainly do not mean all the profit we can get."

Another fact, not well known, is that there are still some 2,650 independent telephone companies. (In the early nineteen-hundreds there were about 20,000.) They are owned by 600,000 investors, employ 100,000 people and serve over half the nation's geographical area. All of them, of course, use the System for interconnecting service. And it is the System that carries all major national radio and TV network programs over its facilities, provides most A.P. and U.P.I. news wires, and thousands of private-line and teletypewriter networks.

A.T.&T.'s president is Eugene J. McNeely, an earnest, unassuming 63-year-old Missourian who started as a $25-a-week student engineer and now earns about $200,000

HAYES B. JACOBS is a freelance whose work appears regularly in several magazines.

a year. (Kappel, as chairman and chief executive, also started at $25 a week and makes more than $250,000.) One of McNeely's dicta to employes is: "We must not throw our weight around, and we must not provide service just by rote and rule." His office is in the A.T.&T. headquarters building at 195 Broadway; his residence (two phones) is uptown, on Madison Avenue, and he has a 70-acre country place (three phones) near Kingston, N. Y.

SYSTEM executives are eager to make one point: they hope nobody gains the impression, from the increasingly large sums sought for "improvement," that the business they manage is worn out or run down. It is, they point out, not so much run down as run ragged—by a rapidly multiplying public that clamors for more and more service.

The volume of long-distance traffic, for example, doubles every six to eight years. That has forced the System, at huge cost, to provide such innovations as D.D.D. (direct distance dialing). Kappel's edict was that D.D.D. service should be so good that people would "swear by it and not at it." Because it further depersonalizes phone service and is wiping out exchange prefixes, for which many people have sentimental or status-oriented attachments, there has been considerable swearing. D.D.D. gives good swift service, routing calls in an average of 10 seconds, an impressive figure considering that there are 251,425,000 conversations, including local calls, buzzing daily over the nationwide network. But as demands for service mount, the System can see that it must build a still larger, more flexible network, keep down still bigger traffic jams and, with the help of electronics, cut the routing time drastically.

In a single year, the System puts in, takes out or rearranges some 15 million telephones, and whereas a phone used to be just a phone, a million of these are now complex, six-button junior robots each requiring up to 50 special wire arrangements, and so popular that by 1970 twice as many are expected to be requested every year. Today, the United States has about 84 million phones; by 1980 the System will have had to provide the major share of 235 million. It is partly that kind of activity, plus ever-increasing maintenance programs, that the System calls "just standing still."

Western Electric Company, with 13 manufacturing plants and 35 distributing houses, turns out more than 50,000 items of communications equipment annually and buys, for a billion dollars, 150,000 others. Last year it sold $2,278,000,000 worth of equipment to the Bell operating companies and $492 million worth of defense gear to the Government. It has 150,000 employes, and two large subsidiaries, the Teletype Corporation and the Nassau Smelting and Refining Company.

In 1949 the Justice Department attempted to separate Western from A.T.&T. Ironically—as System officials quickly pointed out—at the same time the Justice Department was trying to break up the System, the Defense Department was turning to it for a staggering array of military projects.

THE suit was settled in 1956 by a consent decree, limiting Western to the manufacture of equipment for the Bell System and defense-contractor use. Western also agreed to get out of the movie sound system business, and to make some 8,000 communications items, including the Bell-invented transistor, available to anyone royalty-free. It is still a major defense and "government adjunct" industry; one of its key projects right now is providing planning and engineering support for the landing of men on the moon.

Bell Laboratories, owned jointly by Western and A.T.&T. and generally acknowledged as the world's greatest industrial research and development center, is made up of 14,500 scientists, engineers and supporting staff. Its 1964 budget is about $350 million, divided almost equally for System and Government work. But dollar signs give only a partial clue to the reasons for its prowess.

OTHER important factors have been foresight and imagination, and a remarkable "looseness" of management's grip on personnel. Bell Labs hires brilliant men, reminds them that the basic Labs job is "improving communications," then almost literally leaves them alone.

Dr. James B. Fisk, the tall, wiry, M.I.T.-trained physicist who heads the Labs, sees his domain as "a community of gifted people," an "institution of men, working together intimately but independently, each free to follow his own mind." Such men must have a goal, he adds, "that is sufficiently important, broad and technically meaningful that gifted people will be inspired, challenged and rewarded."

The idea is amplified by Dr. W. O. Baker, vice president for research, who pictures the special community as being "big enough and good enough to have a culture of its own." Baker scowls at the mention of words such as "teamwork"; he favors a mildly unified group of strong-minded individuals. "Teamwork," he says wryly, "is a kind of dirty word around here."

Bell Labs' many contributions in its broad field have often overturned established science and technology. From its "gifted people" have come the "negative-feedback amplifier" that has resulted in distortion-free long-distance circuits; information theory; investigations in electron diffraction and the wave nature of matter, and the transistor. The last two have brought Nobel Prizes to their discoverers.

Other achievements are the coaxial cable system, the fundamental discoveries leading to the science of radio astronomy, long-life vacuum tubes, automatic error correctors for computers, sound movies, hi-fi recording, the first intercity TV transmission and the solar battery.

NOW emerging from the Labs are major advances of the last decade. One of these is Touch-Tone service. In the next ten years dial phones will be converted to ten-pushbutton sets, with which calls can be made more than twice as fast as with dialing.

Another is conversion to E.S.S., an electronic switching system that will make the nation's telephone network a super-brain-and-muscle machine with faster and more sophisticated memory and performance capabilities than any yet devised by man. Customers will be able to reach frequently called numbers, local or long distance, by dialing (or pushing) only two digits instead of seven or ten. They will dial a code so incoming calls will reach them automatically when they are visiting a friend. They will add, without operator help, a third person to an existing conversation, and they can get immediate connection to a busy line as soon as it becomes available.

Also on the way is a coin phone with only a single slot; the phone tallies the money, and no operator will have to count all of the "bings" and "bongs." This will lead to direct dialing of long-distance calls from pay stations.

SINCE it is one of the largest organizations in the world, the Bell System is open to the criticism that it is made up of Organization Men, and to the extent that that loosely defined term has any validity, the criticism is valid—though not throughout the System. On executive and management levels the tendency toward conformity, "group-think" and committee decision-making on trifling as well as important matters is often evident. (Six executives, including a highly paid medical director, once sat for four hours considering the design, colors and wording of some Blood Bank posters, pledge cards and leaflets.)

EXCEPT for the technical staff at Bell Labs, the System offers uncomfortable quarters to most individualistic, "inner-directed" workers. Its personnel departments, where as many as 100 applicants may be interviewed before a single low-level administrative va-

Drawing by Stevenson; © 1964 The New Yorker Magazine, Inc.

"To me, it isn't just installing a 'phone, Lou. It's giving one human being a means of reaching out to other human beings."

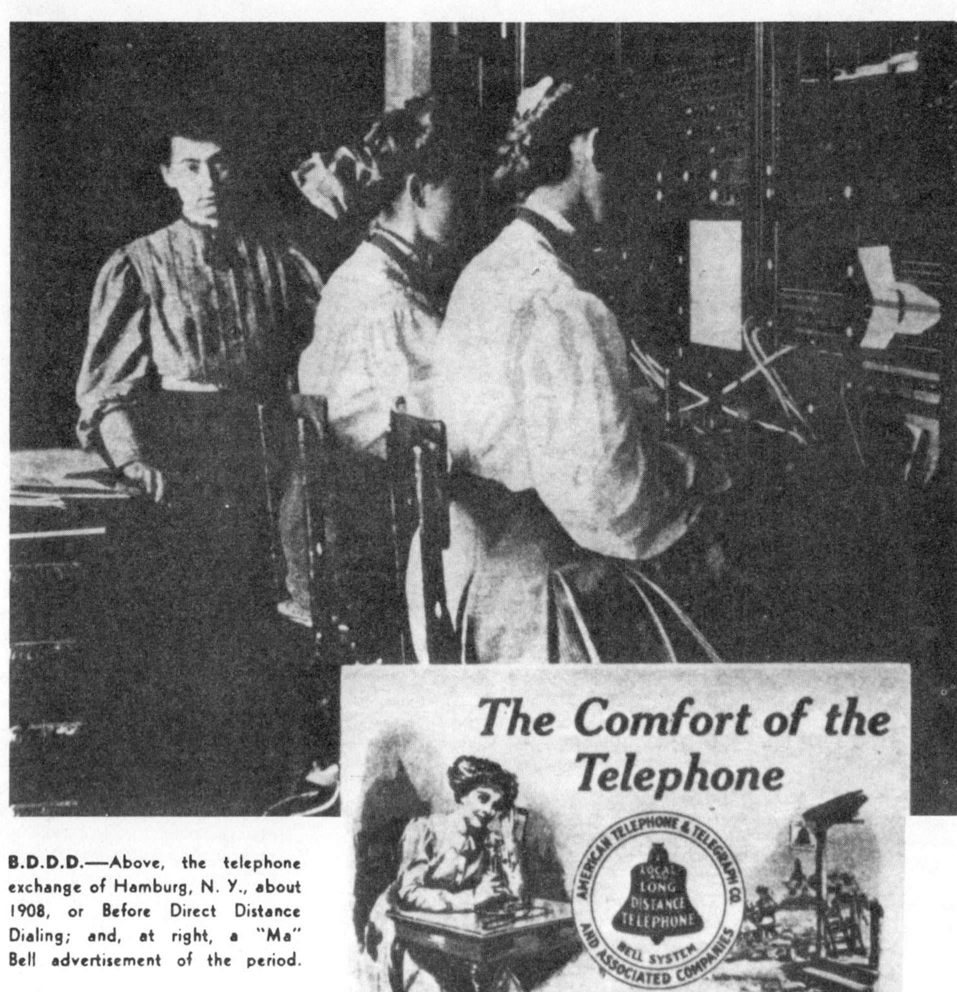

B.D.D.D.—Above, the telephone exchange of Hamburg, N. Y., about 1908, or Before Direct Distance Dialing; and, at right, a "Ma" Bell advertisement of the period.

cancy is filled, are unusually adept at spotting the nonconformist, the man who is not likely to become a good "System man."

The System has even been known to scrutinize an applicant's wife—or at least her geographical origin. A Western-born applicant at one of its East Coast units once cleared all the interview hurdles up to the executive vice-president, who asked if his wife was from California. Told she was not, he said:

"Good! We're not prejudiced, but we *have* found that a lot of good men come here and like us fine, and then their wives get homesick for California and urge them to move back."

Conformity to System mores is subtly, sometimes openly, urged in matters of dress ("Won't you *please* think about buying a hat?" a department head once asked a subordinate), of participation in civic and community affairs, and even of place of abode. A man who worked in a Manhattan office, and lived within walking distance, was once told by his boss, a commuter from New Jersey, that he was "the last man in this department who's going to be allowed to live in New York."

Insistence on uniformity, on "the System way," has extended down even to matters of punctuation. A new young junior executive who questioned the punctuation in a letter typed by a spinster secretary (with 32 years of Bell System service) received her patient explanation: "You see, sir, we don't use many commas in the Bell System."

Rewards for the faithful employe are many; the Colossus offers the same job security as the Government, gives generous sickness and retirement benefits, reviews salaries annually, and in general takes a paternal interest in its employes. (*Maternal*, some say, referring to the system as "Ma" Bell.)

MOST employes respond with loyalty and outspoken pride. A recent New Yorker cartoon touched a near truth when it depicted a phone installer addressing an associate. "To me," he said, "it isn't just installing a phone, Lou. It's giving one human being a means of reaching out to other human beings."

The System is extraordinarily sensitive about its public image and has spent millions on public relations and publicity to promote such ideas as "The voice with a smile" and "The best possible service at the lowest possible cost." More millions go into advertising, aimed at selling service, service "extras," acquainting customers with changes and maintaining institutional prestige.

The watchword throughout is quiet dignity and conservatism. A. T. & T.'s ads, prepared for the last 55 years by the staid old N. W. Ayer agency of Philadelphia (sometimes called "the Bell System of the advertising world") tend toward the friendly-folksy, all-is-well, bless-our-native-land theme.

A STARRY-EYED, ever-dependable operator ("Close by if you need her") gazes out of the page, looking for emergencies—a fire to summon firemen to, or a hurricane to stay right on the job during. Family groups are depicted, with glowingly healthy, apple-cheeked youngsters and beaming, silver-topped grandmas and grandpas. Everyone keeps in constant long-distance touch with everyone else, smilingly remembering all birthdays, graduations and anniversaries. And everyone's steps are saved with those extension phones. Contentment, in Telephone Ad-land, is a conversation, and happiness is a warm receiver.

Striving for the preservation of its image has made the System intensely press-relations conscious. In no other business or industry are P.R. and publicity activities so closely coordinated and controlled. A brief press release from one unit of the System may be circulated for approval to as many as 50 executives in that and other units before it is issued. The wording of a single clause may stir up what a harried P.R. executive once called a "tempest in an A. T. & T. pot."

A timely story with real news value may thus be held up for weeks. "I guess you'd say we'd rather be coordinated than hit the front pages," a Bell publicity man explained. "It's frustrating, but at least no one can ever call us publicity hounds."

THE result of all the caution is an almost wholly favorable climate of press and public opinion, which the System checks on regularly with elaborate surveys and analyzes with the help of sociologists and psychologists.

It is easy to predict, too, that A. T. & T. will get a favorable press when it splits its stock next June, even though some of its own share owners may not know precisely what is going on. At the meeting at which the last split was accomplished, one share owner, an elderly lady, approached the dais and asked in a whisper: "When are you going to bring in the stock?"

"Bring it *in?*" asked a baffled System official.

"Yes," she said. "I want to watch you split it."

Industries Will Get Merger Guidelines

By EILEEN SHANAHAN
Special to The New York Times

WASHINGTON, May 15 — An entirely new approach to the enforcement of the antitrust laws is about to be attempted by the Federal Trade Commission.

Under the new program, the commission will conduct studies of the competitive situation in specific industries and, upon completion of its inquiries, issue broad rules that will indicate to business, in advance, whether or not certain types of mergers would be prosecuted by the Federal agency.

The first such industrywide study was ordered by the F.T.C. today. It will involve the development of standards for the approval or disapproval of mergers of cement producers with their customers and suppliers —so-called vertical mergers,

The commission's decision to order the cement industry study was an outgrowth of a merger case involving the Permanente Cement Company of Oakland, Calif.

The commission ruled today that Permanente's acquisition of a direct competitor in the cement business, the Olympic Portland Cement Company of Seattle, had violated the antitrust provisions of the Clayton Act.

However, the agency said it did not have enough information on which to base a decision concerning the legality of Permanente's acquisition of two producers of ready-mixed concrete that had been customers of Permanente.

Commissioner's Proposal

The idea of conducting basic economic studies of various industries in order to develop standards to guide the F. T. C. in ruling on mergers was largely conceived by Commissioner Philip Elman, who wrote the agency's opinion in today's case.

The new approach appears certain to raise some anxieties in the business community, simply because of its newness. But it also appears possible that it may ultimately win considerable business support for several reasons.

For one thing, publication of standards by which mergers in specific industries would be judged by the commission would remove many of the uncertainties that now surround almost any proposed merger.

Mergers of a type that the commission may find to pose no threat to competition would not be deterred by fears of subsequent challenge in the courts.

The F.T.C. presumably would be ready and willing to give prompt answers as to whether or not it would let pass without challenge any merger in an industry it had studied.

Positive Approach

In addition, in Mr. Elman's opinion, at least, the new standards would be designed to take into account economic reasons why certain mergers should be permitted instead of concentrating entirely on reasons why they should be blocked.

In a recent little noticed speech in which he outlined the commission's new antitrust approach, Mr. Elman said:

"While we want to discourage merger activity that has the effect of fostering or entrenching monopoly power, at the same time we should not discourage merger activity by small firms aimed at building them up into effective competitors or mergers and joint ventures that are necessary for new entry into noncompetitive markets."

Business complaints that Government antitrust activities have prevented the buildup of new competitive units have been widespread in recent years.

The rules the commission plans to develop in the industries selected for antitrust study would cover, among other things, the following points:

¶Whether there are particular products markets in which economic concentration is so great that future mergers should be prohibited entirely.

¶Whether there are certain product lines in which future mergers should be forbidden to companies beyond a certain size but should be encouraged for concerns of smaller size.

Scope of New Rules

¶What the permissible limits are of mergers not only between direct competitors but also between suppliers and customers and between businesses in wholly unrelated lines of activity.

In his opinion in the Permanente Cement case, Mr. Elman said that vertical integration of suppliers and customers in the cement industry "is of growing importance and urgency and has apparently assumed industrywide dimensions.

"Where a problem involves an entire industry made up of a large number of firms, it may be uneconomical, inefficient and inequitable to proceed exclusively on the basis of individual adjudicative proceedings.

"Industrywide problems require, so far as is practicable, industry-wide solutions."

The commission therefore ordered a study "appraising the general economic facts and market structure" in the cement industry.

The opinion made clear that antitrust suits in the cement industry would not be suspended pending the outcome of the study.

The question of the legality of the specific acquisitions by Permanente Cement of customer concerns was ordered remanded to a commission hearing examiner, who would take additional evidence and make a new decision to recommend to the agency.

Today's action set aside a ruling by Walter K. Bennett, a hearing examiner, that Permanente had illegally acquired two Portland concerns—the Pacific Building Materials Company and the Readymix Concrete Company.

However, the commission upheld Mr. Bennett's ruling that Permanente's acquisition of Olympic in 1958 violated the antitrust laws. Permanente was ordered to take action to divest itself of Olympic within one year.

May 16, 1964

Clayton Antitrust Law 50 Years Old and Strong

Anti-Merger Section Shows Its Bite to Businessmen

By ANTHONY LEWIS
Special to The New York Times

WASHINGTON, Oct. 24 — Fifty years ago last week President Woodrow Wilson signed into law a bill whose short title said its purpose was "to supplement existing laws against unlawful restraints and monopolies."

It was the Clayton Act, second of this country's basic antitrust statutes. The first was the Sherman Act, dating back to 1890.

The Clayton Act was a sprawling piece of legislation, about 6,000 words long. It dealt with such subjects as price discrimination and tie-in agreements. It made embezzlement of corporation funds in interstate commerce a Federal crime. It prohibited railroads from buying supplies from companies in which their directors had a substantial interest.

But the section of the act that turned out to have the real bite in the long run — the one that is on businessmen's minds today — was the anti-merger provision. That is Section 7.

William H. Orrick Jr., the Justice Department's antitrust chief, has indicated that Section 7 may be used even more vigorously in the future.

Curiously, Section 7 was virtually a dead letter for many years. It was weakened by interpretations holding that it applied only to acquisitions of another company's stock, not its assets, and only where the result might be to lessen direct competition between the acquiring and acquired corporations.

In 1950, in the Celler-Kefauver Act, Congress removed these doubts. It made clear that both stock and asset acquisitions were covered. (The Supreme Court held in 1957, in the du Pont-General Motors case, that the statute had always covered both.)

And Congress in the 1950 amendment demonstrated the intention to deal not only with horizontal mergers, between competitors. Also covered were vertical acquisitions—of a supplier or customer — and conglomerate mergers, between makers of differing products.

Section 7 as it stands condemns any merger whose effect, "in any line of commerce in any section of the country . . . may be substantially to lessen competition, or to tend to create a monopoly."

As always, it is up to the courts to give meaning to those vague words in concrete cases. A rundown of just a few recent cases demonstrates why business planners today are bound to have Section 7 on their minds.

Just two months ago an agreement by the Chrysler Corporation to acquire Mack Trucks, Inc., smashed on the rocks of the Clayton Act's anti-merger proviso.

Chrysler contended that the deal would enable it to compete more effectively with bigger makers of heavy-duty trucks. But Federal District Judge Reynier J. Wortendyke Jr. of New Jersey said the merger would stop planned Chrysler expansion of its own

Associated Press
William H. Orrick Jr.
U.S. antitrust chief

truck efforts and eliminate an independent competitor.

Judge Wortendyke temporarily enjoined the merger, and Chrysler and Mack then called it off. Few doubted that the judge was correctly reading the Supreme Court's recent opinions, for their trend has unmistakably been to deal strictly with mergers.

Last June 22 the Supreme Court for the first time held that Section 7 applied to joint ventures — agreements by competing companies to set up a joint corporation for certain purposes. On the same day the court upset a decision that a merger of glass and metal container manufacturers could not be anti-competitive.

On April 6 the court applied in stringent terms to a Lexington, Ky., bank merger the prohibition in Section 1 of the Sherman Act against combinations in restraint of trade.

In that case Justice William O. Douglas said any horizontal merger of companies that were "major competitive factors" in a market violated the Sherman Act. Thus the court seemed to take a broad view of the anti-merger effects of both antitrust statutes.

Proposal Dropped

One moral spun out of the recent cases is that the largest American companies can no longer safely expand by merger. Under Justice Department attack the Humble Oil and Refining Company thus gave up its attempt to acquire the Western facilities of the Tidewater Oil Company. Humble had only a tiny share of the West Coast market, but its national economic power was so great that the department felt any acquisition would hurt competition.

Another point that has been emphasized in recent opinions is that actual proof of injury need not be shown. It is enough to prove a tendency—economic concentration "in its incipiency," as Chief Justice Earl Warren put it in 1962.

Beyond that, the thrust is toward simplifying standards of proof generally — toward eliminating the mounds of economic data that characterize antitrust trials. Justice Byron R. White said last June:

"Where a merger is of such a size as to be inherently suspect, elaborate proof of market structure, market behavior and probable anti-competitive effects may be dispensed with in view of Section 7's design to prevent undue concentration."

The importance of merger policing by the Justice Department lies partly in the fact that it is so difficult t reach situations where concentration is already a fact. It has been years since a large-scale attack on monopolization was brought successfully under Section 2 of the Sherman Act.

Department Determined

The department is determined to prevent any movements toward significant new economic concentration by merger. It will use both Section 7 and the Sherman Act's Section 1, as expounded in the Lexington bank case last April, toward that end.

The Government's watchfulness on mergers was indicated again this week. The department brought suit under Section 7 to block acquisition by the Standard Oil Company (New Jersey) of the Potash Company of America.

Mr. Orrick, the antitrust chief, has also raised the interesting possibility of using Section 7 more often and more vigorously to attack long-past mergers by companies that are now giants. He did so last May in a speech celebrating the forthcoming anniversary of the Clayton Act.

"Surely the pervasively negative impact which undue concentration has on our economic, political and social life justifies using all legal tools available," Mr. Orrick said.

"Although we are planning no broad-gauge inquiry into past [merger] transactions, in appropriate hard-core cases of economic concentration we will give serious consideration to its [Section 7's] use. Where anti-competitive overconcentration exists, Congress has made it my duty to act to maintain the free, competitive economy so vital to our national welfare."

It is clear that any executive of a large business has plenty to think about as he contemplates the Clayton Act today. No shifts in the future emphasis of antitrust policy seem likely at the moment, but Election Day is still ahead.

October 25, 1964

PENNSY AND N.Y. CENTRAL WIN APPROVAL OF MERGER; THE NEW HAVEN INCLUDED

I. C. C. UNANIMOUS

Commission, 6-5, Also Rejects Bid to Unite 3 Western Roads

By ROBERT E. BEDINGFIELD
Special to The New York Times

WASHINGTON, April 27 — The Interstate Commerce Commission authorized the Pennsylvania and the New York Central Railroads today to effect the biggest merger in corporate history.

The new enterprise, to be known as the Pennsylvania New York Central Transportation Company, will have total assets of more than $4-billion, placing it among the 10 largest nonfinancial corporations in the country. It will operate over 19,000 miles of road and handle about one-eighth of the nation's railroad freight.

As a condition for its unanimous approval of the Pennsy-Central merger, the I.C.C. required the combined system to take over all the passenger and freight operations of the bankrupt New Haven Railroad.

Western Bid Rejected

In another action, the commission rejected by a 6-to-5 vote a merger of the prosperous Northern Pacific, Great Northern, and Chicago, Burlington & Quincy Railroads. It said the benefits of such a consolidation would be outweighed by the value of maintaining rail competition in the West.

[In New York, Alfred E. Perlman, president of the Central, and Stuart T. Saunders, chairman of the Pennsy, said at a news conference that they did not anticipate any problems in absorbing the New Haven or in completing their merger.]

The commission conceded that the Pennsy-Central unification "will, without a doubt, lessen railroad competition to some degree." But it also stressed that rail traffic in the East "does not adequately support the existing railroad plant" of the territory served.

In giving its approval to the merger, the commission said its purpose was to open the way for the development of a modernized railroad system "trimmed of unnecessary plant, unencumbered by service obligations no longer responsive to the public needs, and free and able to grow as and where the nation's transportation requirements dictate."

The agency said it believed the consolidated system would be in a better position to compete not only with motor-carrier and water-carrier competition, but also with two other "great rail systems" recently formed in the East. These are the Chesapeake & Ohio Railway, which in 1963 was granted control of the Baltimore & Ohio Railroad, and the Norfolk & Western Railway, which in 1964 acquired the New York, Chicago & St. Louis (Nickel Plate) and four other railroads.

The I.C.C.'s decision may be appealed directly to the commission for 30 days or at any time in the courts. Unless legal action is taken to prevent the merger, the two railroads are free to begin their unified operation within 35 days, or starting June 1.

While the Justice Department probably was the most vociferous opponent of the merger plan, its arguments failed to impress the commissioners. Whether the department will now appeal the case to the courts is unpredictable—as is how the United States Supreme Court would rule if an appeal is made.

Historically, the Supreme Court has upheld the I.C.C. on the grounds that it is an "expert" body and—under provisions of the Transportation Acts of 1920 and 1940—is not bound to observe antitrust provisions with respect to mergers, so long as its decisions are consistent with "the public interest."

Conditions Imposed

In addition to its stipulation that the New Haven be taken in by the merging railroads, the commission imposed several other conditions. These include the following:

¶The payment of indemnities by the merged company to the Erie-Lackawanna,

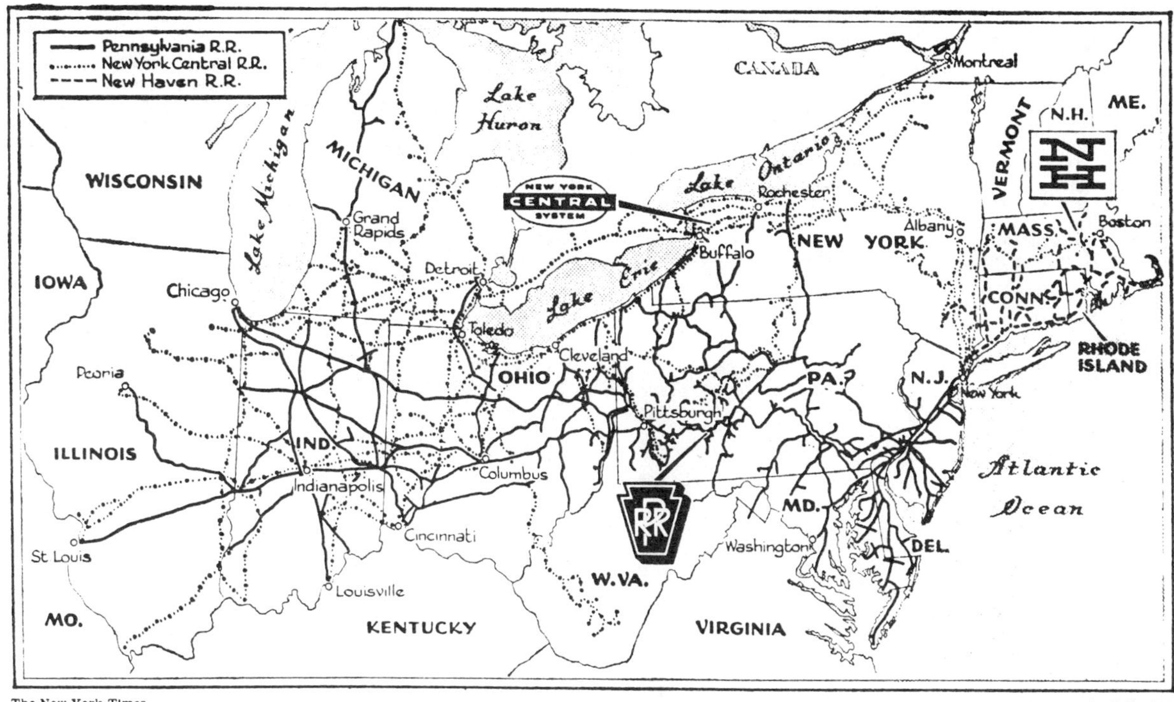

The New York Times April 28, 1966

APPROVED: The Interstate Commerce Commission has authorized merger of the Pennsylvania and New York Central Railroads. New company will have to take over all passenger and freight operations of bankrupt New Haven line.

the Delaware & Hudson and the Boston & Maine Railroads in any year the revenues of those carriers are less than a standard based on their revenues of 1964.

¶In the event that the Erie-Lackawanna, Delaware & Hudson and Boston & Maine are unsuccessful in their current efforts to be included in the Norfolk & Western Railway system — hearings on this now are under way before the commission — those three roads will have a year to ask to be included in the Pennsy-Central system.

¶Acceptance of the New York, Susquehanna & Western Railroad in the consolidated system. The terms under which this will be done have yet to be worked out by the three lines.

¶The Lehigh Valley Railroad, now controlled by the Pennsylvania, must be made available for merger to the Chesapeake & Ohio or the Norfolk & Western Railways. If neither of those lines are willing to absorb it, the Lehigh Valley must also be merged into the Pennsy-Central.

Curb on Layoffs

Te Pennsylvania Railroad at the end of 1965 had 61,943 employes and the Central had 44,-371. All of them are protected under the merger, whether they are union members or not. The consolidated carrier will not be permitted to reduce the work force unless business drops 5 per cent or more in any 30-day period. The staff may be reduced only then, and the reduction must be limited to 1 per cent for each 1 per cent decline in excess of the 5 per cent drop.

The I.C.C. noted that this extensive protection for employes was worked out by the railroads and the unions in May, 1964. The commission said that with normal attrition and voluntary resignations by employes who are unwilling to move to new locations, the consolidated carrier should be able "to maximize the proficient utilization of its retained work force."

The two railroads estimate that after eight years of merger, they will realize savings amounting to $81-million a year based on their operating costs in 1961.

Much of this saving is expected to result from rerouting traffic, operating fewer and heavier freight trains, making more intensive use of each other's freight yards and eliminating about 80 to 170 "interchanges," or junctions, where 600,000 cars a year are now transferred from one of the two lines to the other.

Faster Service Seen

Transit time over 33 routes is expected to be reduced by as much as 38 per cent and the average reduction will be about 15 per cent. The I.C.C. emphasized that it will be feasible for the consolidated system to conduct almost "nonstop" freight service between principal cities served while "locals" serve multiple-stop routes and branch lines.

The commission said that from Boston to Cincinnati the transit time would be cut more than 27 per cent from the time of either road's fastest train today. From Buffalo to St. Louis, the time savings will be 36 per cent; Cleveland to New York City, 25 per cent; Chicago to New York 11 per cent. and Detroit to Jersey City, 26 per cent.

Little has been said publicly as to what is in store for the Pennsylvania's and the Central's long-distance passengers, or what may be the future of the Pennsy's crack streamliner, the Broadway Limited, and the Central's famed 20th-Century Limited.

It is expected that all Central trains, except commuter runs, now terminating at Grand Central in Manhattan will move to the new Pennsylvania Station being built at 33d Street in Manhattan, where the old station has been pulled down. In Chicago, the Central trains that have long rolled into LaSalle Street Station in the Loop are due to be shifted to the Union Station several blocks north of LaSalle Street.

Stuart T. Saunders, now chairman of the Pennsylvania Railroad, will be chairman and chief executive officer of the merged system; Alfred E. Perlman, president of the New York Central, will be president and chief operating officer. There will be two vice chairmen, on to be designated by the Pennsylvania's directors and one by the Central's directors.

What psition Allen J. Greenough, vice president of the Pennsylvania, will hold is not known. He is expected to be a director of the consolidated carrier, which will have 25 board members, 14 of them to be nominated by the present Pennsylvania board and 11 by the Central board.

Terms Outlined

The terms of the merger agreement were worked out for the two railroads by three of Wall Street's biggest brokerage concerns, Morgan Stanley, the First Boston Corporation and Glore Forgan & Co.

Central stockholders will receive 1.3 shares in the new company for every Centra lshare they now hold; Pennsylvania stockholders will receive one share for each share they now hold. Pennsy stockholders will thus receive about a 61 per cent stock interest in the consolidated company on the basis of the 13.8 million shares of Pennsy and the 6.9 million shares of Central outstanding at the colse of 1965.

The Pennsylvania has 97,424 shareholders, while the Central has 26,118.

The largest individual stockholder of the Central is Allan P. Kirby, who owns 300,100 shares.

Mr. Kirby is chairman of the Alleghany Corporation, which until earlier this month owned nearly one million shares of Central, or about a 15 per cent interest. Alleghany exchanged all but about 150,000 shares of its Central stock for its own preferred and common stock.

Although the Mellon family of Pittsburgh long has been regarded as among the Pennsylvania's largest stockholders, the extent of its holdings is not known.

One of the Pennsylvania's biggest acknowledge stockholders is Howard Butcher 3d, senior partner of the stock brokerage firm of Butcher & Sherred in Philadelphia. Mr. Butcher, in an interview a few years ago, said he had sold to friends, associates and clients of his firm more than 1.3 million shares of Pennsylvania stock.

In approving the merger of the Central into the Pennsylvania, the commission took full note of the erratic financial performance of both lines and of

Eastern railroads in general in recent years. The Central last year had operating revenues of $661.5-million and a net income of $41.5-million. The Pennsylvania had gross revenues of $892.5-million in 1965 and earnings of $33.9-million.

For both roads, 1965 results were the best for many years. Back in 1961, when the two roads agreed on their merger plan, the Pennsy operated at a profit of only $3.5- million and the Central at a net loss of $12.5-million.

The case is probably the most gigantic ever undertaken by the I.C.C. since its organization in 1887. The commission's actual written opinion, prepared by Commissioner Kenneth H. Tuggle, is printed in a 92-page single-space legal document.

Hearings in the merger spanned 130 days and testimony taken from 450 witnesses filled 40,000 pages. The hearings were conducted for the commission by two of its key examiners, Jerome K. Lyle and Henry C. Darmstadter Jr. In recommending the merger to the I.C.C. on March 29, last year Mr. Lyle and Mr. Darmstadter presented the commissioners with a 586-page document.

In its ruling today, the commission said: "Operations under the merger will allow the movement of the largest amount of freight as far as possible without stopping. Terminals will be consolidated, interchanges between the applicants' systems will eventually be eliminated and the most efficient yards and facilities of the individual applicants will be used."

April 28, 1966

COURT TOUGHENS RULE ON MERGERS

Voids Chain Move Despite Lack of Competition Curb

By FRED P. GRAHAM
Special to The New York Times

WASHINGTON, May 31—The Supreme Court gave the Government broad authority yesterday to bar mergers between competing companies in industries experiencing rapid concentration, even if no adverse affect upon competition could be proved.

In a decision hailed as "very important" by the head of the Justice Departmet's Antitrust Division, the high court overturned a lower court ruling that had refused to block the 1960 merger of two grocery store chains in Los Angeles.

The 6-to-2 decision, written by Justice Hugo L. Black, emphasized that the number of store owners in the area had been declining rapidly while the size of the chains had increased.

This alone was sufficient to bar the acquisition of Shopping Bag Food Stores by Von's Grocery Company, Justice Black said.

Third and Eighth

He pointed out that in 1958 Von's sales ranked third in the area and Shopping Bag's sales ranked eighth. Together, they sold 7.5 per cent of the area's groceries in 1960, and the merged chain of 66 stores became the second largest in Los Angeles. The largest was Safeway Stores.

Associated Press

VIEWS MERGER BAR: Donald F. Turner, the head of the Antitrust Division of the Justice Department.

Pointing out that Congress wrote the antitrust laws "to preserve competition among many small businesses," Justice Black said the "rapid decline" in owner-operated groceries justified a court ban against the merger, even though there was no proof that it would lessen competition.

He directed the lower court to order an immediate divestiture of Shopping Bag by Von's Grocery.

Ruling on the same facts, which were agreed between the parties, Federal District Judge Charles H. Carr had ruled that the Government had failed to prove its case.

He said the main reason for the decrease in the number of stores was the change from the small corner grocery to the supermarket, and he cited evidence that experienced men could still open successful single stores and small chains in the area.

Donald F. Turner, head of the Antitrust Division, said this afternoon that the majority's adoption of the Justice Department's position on so-called "horizontal" mergers should virtually end mergers between healthy competitors in circumstances analogous to the Los Angeles grocery stores situation.

Horizontal mergers involve companies competing directly with one another in the manufacture or distribution of similar products.

Observing that today's case laid down a "pretty tough line on horizontal mergers," Mr. Turner said:

"Whenever we find any merger between healthy substantial competitors, with 4 per cent or so of the market each, in an industry that tends toward competition, we'll sue."

Today's decision was the first time the high court had applied the Celler-Kefauver antimerger law to retail concerns in a local market. Its strong decision meant that local retail mergers that might have passed unnoticed in past years might now precipitate Justice Department counteraction.

Tart Dissenting Opionion

In a tart dissenting opinion, Justice Potter Stewart charged that the Court had relied upon "a simple exercise in sums" and "substituted bare conjecture" for proof of lessened competition.

"The Court's opinion is hardly more than a requiem for the so-called 'mom and pop' grocery stores—the bakery and butcher shops, the vegetable and fish markets—that are now economically and technologically obsolete in many parts of this country," he said.

"No action by this Court can resurrect the old single-line Los Angeles food stores that have been run over by the automobile or obliterated by the freeway."

Quoting from Mr. Turner's writings as a Harvard law professor before he joined the Government, Justice Stewart concluded that the case presented only "an ephemeral possibility" that the merger would lessen competition.

He said the only consistency in the high court's antimerger decisions was "the Government always wins."

Justice John Marshall Harlan joined in the dissent. Justice Byron R. White wrote a separate concurring opinion. Justice Abe Fortas did not participate.

Richard A. Posner of the Solicitor General's office argued for the Government. William W. Alsup of Los Angeles argued for the grocery chains.

June 1, 1966

Conglomerate Merger Spreads Its Diversified Wings

By JOHN J. ABELE

They laughed when the cigarette company bought the distributor of Scotch whisky.

"Cigarettes and whisky?" asked one Wall Street observer. "What next?"

Among the things that came next: an airplane manufacturer bought a sausage-maker; a distributor of automobile parts bought a motion-picture company, and an oil and gas company proposed to take over a truck manufacturer.

Highly diversified consolidations of this sort have puzzled many casual observers of the business scene who had been reared on the adage that shoemakers were supposed to stick to their lasts.

The growing trend of mergers of companies in entirely different fields of endeavor also has unleashed a new stream of jargon into the vocabulary of the financial community.

Any security analyst worth his sliderule these days has to be able to toss off with aplomb such terms as multi-industry company, free-form management and synergism. He also has to know that a conglomerate is a collection of companies, not rocks.

The conglomerate merger is the thing in business today. Some studies indicate that conglomerate mergers—the fusing of companies in different industries—account for about 70 per cent of all recent mergers.

In the situations referred to above, the American Tobacco Company proposed a merger with the Buckingham Corporation, a distributor of Scotch whisky; Ling-Temco-Vought, Inc., a producer of aerospace and electronic products, merged with Wilson & Co., Inc., the meat packer; Gulf and Western Industries, a producer of auto

James L. Ling, left, of Ling-Temco-Vought, Inc., maker of aerospace and electronic products, which merged with Wilson & Co., Inc., meat packer. Charles G. Bluhdorn, in center, established Gulf and Western Industries by joining Michigan Plating and Stamping Company with other makers of auto parts and then with concerns in movies and other fields. Roy L. Ash, right, is president of Litton Industries, which started in electronics and branched out.

parts, zinc products and fertilizers, acquired Paramount Pictures and also proposed a union with Desilu Productions, and Signal Oil and Gas Company announced plans to acquire Mack Trucks, Inc.

The conglomerate form of merger has raised a variety of questions in appraising the progress of industrial companies. It has involved some dazzling displays of financial legerdemain, set off fireworks in the stock market, and produced some new questions about the course of antitrust policy.

The conglomerate merger is a basic departure from the traditional forms of corporate consolidations that have usually been described as either horizontal or vertical in nature.

In a horizontal merger, one company acquires another in the same industry. A chemical company buys another chemical company, for example, or a department store buys another department store.

The basic objective of such a merger is to expand or extend an existing line of products, to acquire distribution in new marketing areas, or to achieve economies in production or distribution.

In a vertical merger, the acquiring company takes over a company that involves some sort of supplier or customer relationship.

A paper producer, for example, would acquire a producer of timber or wood pulp or a manufacturer of finished paper products, such as packaging materials.

The basic purpose of the vertical type of merger is to assure a supply of raw materials for the basic manufacturing operation or to provide markets for end products.

The ultimate effect of such mergers, however, has been to concentrate production and distribution resources in a small group of very large companies.

This development has drawn increasing attention and legal action from the antitrust division of the Justice Department and from the Federal Trade Commission on the basis that such moves tend to reduce competition within industry.

The impact of various antitrust moves by the Justice Department and the F.T.C. has been strong enough so that most legal authorities consider the prospects of any future large-scale horizontal or vertical mergers to be practicall, nil.

But the conglomerate merger in which a company acquires another concern in a completely different field has presented interesting new vistas for many corporate managers.

The conglomerate structure is hardly new. Many of the nation's largest corporations have some elements of conglomerate operations.

The General Motors Corporation, for example, is the nation's largest producer of automobiles but it is also a major producer of refrigerators, other household appliances and locomotives.

The Standard Oil Company (New Jersey) is not only the nation's largest oil company but one of the largest producers of chemical products as well.

The General Electric Company serves over 100 different markets, ranging from small light bulbs to giant electrical generators and aircraft engines.

New Companies Emerge

But the bulk of the recent interest in the conglomerate movement has been devoted to the emergence of a relatively new crop of companies, which have leaped into the ranks of the nation's largest corporations through rapid-fire series of acquisitions and mergers.

The success of some of the leading practitioners of this process has spawned a number of imitators and would-be imitators.

The two companies cited most frequently as the most successful examples of the conglomerate approach to rapid growth are Textron, Inc., and Litton Industries.

Textron, originally a New England textile manufacturer, has grown into an enterprise with annual sales of more than $1-billion derived from some 28 separate divisions that formerly were independent companies.

It long ago abandoned the textile business and acquired operations that range from helicopters to eyeglasses. Over the last 10 years, its net income has climbed to $44-million from $6.5-million.

Litton's History

Litton started out as a relatively small California electronics company. From that base, it branched out into an array of activities that includes office machines, communications equipment, paper manufacturing, shipbuilding, book publishing and food-service operations.

Litton had sales of $1.2-billion last year, compared with $28-million in 1956. During the same period, its net income soared to $55.6-million from $6.7-million.

Among the more notable recent entries into the conglomerate derby have been Ling-Temco-Vought, Inc., and Gulf and Western Industries.

As its three-ply name implies, Ling-Temco-Vought was formed through a consolidation of three companies in the aerospace and electronics fields.

Over the last year, it has compounded this diversification through the acquisitions of the Okonite Company, a fabricator of metal products; the Rome Cable Company; and, most recently, Wilson & Co., Inc., the Chicago-based producer of meats, sporting goods and chemicals.

Less than a decade ago, Gulf and Western was a completely unheralded producer of auto parts known as the Michigan Plating and Stamping Company.

Its metamorphosis into a corporate giant has been due to the efforts of Charles G. Bluhdorn, an Austrian-born security analyst who first acquired control of Michigan Plating and then added to it a long list of other auto-parts manufacturers and distributors.

Gulf and Western's growth accelerated sharply early last year when it acquired the New Jersey Zinc Company and took another big leap forward later in the year when it merged with Paramount Pictures, the motion-picture producer.

Other Acquisition Plans

Since then, Gulf and Western also has disclosed plans to acquire Desilu Productions, a leading producer of television films; Famous Players Canadian Corporation, a Canadian motion-picture theater chain; South Puerto Rico Sugar Corporation, and North & Judd Manufacturing Company, a hardware producer.

The pell-mell pace of acquisitions by Ling-Temco-Vought and Gulf and Western has brought both companies a great deal of publicity and attracted great interest in their stocks.

But many other companies also have been following a strong acquisition course, which has taken them into a variety of fields far from their original businesses.

A recent survey of multi-industry companies by Roland B. Williams of the investment research department of E. F. Hutton & Co., Inc., listed some 24 companies in the multi-industry category.

In addition to the companies already mentioned, the list included Automatic Sprinkler Corporation, Bangor Punta Corporation, City Investing Company, Eltra Corporation, FMC Corporation, W. R. Grace & Co., Houdaille Industries, Walter Kidde & Co., Inc., Ogden Corporation, and Philadelphia and Reading Corporation.

Other entries were C.I.T. Financial Corporation, General Electric, Glidden Company, International Telephone and Telegraph, Lear-Siegler, Inc., National Distillers and Chemical Corporation, Olin Mathieson Corporation, Pittsburgh Plate Glass Company, and Teledyne, Inc.

Other followers of the conglomerate movement mention such companies as Singer Corporation, Indian Head, Inc., TRW, Inc., and United Fruit Company and Tran-america Corporation.

The reasons why these companies have diversified so widely are almost as diverse as the extent of their operations.

Four Key Factors

In a recent discussion of the conglomerate form of organization, Standard & Poor's Corporation, a leading investment advisory service, listed four principal factors:

"Desire for diversification to offset seasonal or cyclical factors, or because prospects within its original industry were limited.

"Entry into a new field to avoid possible antitrust problems that might result from acquisitions within a company's original area.

"Realization by astute and ambitious professional corporate managers of the equity enhancement possible through well-selected acquisitions.

"Important tax or cash-flow advantages that can accrue from certain types of mergers, particularly those involving a natural resource company."

Standard & Poor's noted that the boom in acquisitions had been aided in recent years by the steady upward movement in the general economy.

Most of the conglomerate companies, it pointed out, "have not had to face a serious recession or even a protracted period of business stability in which their growth might be stalled or reverses posted."

Mr. Williams of E. F. Hutton makes a similar point. "The soundness of these organizations," he says, "may not be revealed with certainty until tested by a setback in the general economy. Some of the entrepreneurs in this movement may prove to have more ambition than talent."

The frequent acquisitions by the conglomerate companies is a factor that complicates investment appraisals of the stocks of these companies.

The acquisitions make it difficult to make meaningful comparisons of year-to-year results. Further complications are caused by the varying accounting practices of the different companies.

"Under such volatile conditions," Mr. Williams declares, "it is virtually impossible for investors or even trained security analysts to make accurate earnings projections."

The conglomerate companies follow a variety of systems of management philosophy. The general trend, however, is to decentralize operating control to the various units, which become individual "profit centers" that are expected to reach a prescribed rate of profitability.

The progress of the various units toward these goals is monitored by a central corporate headquarters, frequently quite small in size, which handles general corporate functions such as finance, legal work, tax problems, public relations and industrial relations.

In some cases, the corporate headquarters will have a team of experts available to assist the operating units with special problems.

The rise of the conglomerates has sparked a continuing debate in the financial community as to their relative merits as opposed to more traditional forms of business organization.

One Strong Critic

One of the strongest critics of some of the conglomerates has been Barron's, the financial weekly. In an article last month by Barton M. Biggs, the magazine took aim at the "synergistic" approach of the conglomerates; the concept that the combined efforts of two companies can produce better results than the sum of the efforts of the two companies operating independently.

"Two and two cannot indefinitely continue to make five," the Barron's article declared.

A prime defender of the conglomerate approach, on the other hand, is Equity Research Associates, an investment-advisory service that has been one of the key verbalizers of the "free-form" concept of management.

According to Equity Research, the hallmarks of "free-form" management are flexibility, initiative, creativity and adaptability.

It holds that managements that follow this philosophy are more disposed to respond quickly to new challenges and opportunities and therefore are likely to reap greater rewards—in the stock market as well as in the statement of profits.

Equity Research contrasts this approach to the more traditional concepts of management, such as that espoused by Alfred P. Sloan Jr., former chairman of the General Motors Corporation.

The "General Motors school," according to Equity Research, emphasizes a systematic management with defined responsibilities and highly organized means of communication and decision making to accomplish specific tasks.

The manager who follows this concept, it argues, "is not interested in individual people but tasks to be done. He has neither general ideas or fundamental convictions, but is strictly a pragmatist who effectively reacts to events as they occur. He is affected by change but does not stimulate it."

In addition to these basic questions about the relative merits of the conglomerate or free-form management, a new question has arisen in recent weeks, the old problem of antitrust considerations that became a stumbling block for horizontal and vertical mergers.

The antitrust aspect of conglomerate mergers arose when the Supreme Court upheld a decision by the Federal Trade Commission upsetting the acquisition of the Clorox Company by the Procter & Gamble Company.

Acquisition Turned Down

Clorox, a producer of household bleaches, was acquired by Procter & Gamble in 1957. Although P. & G. is a leading producer of soaps, detergents and other household products—and one of the nation's major merchandising companies—it did not have bleaches in its product line at the time of the acquisition.

The F.T.C., in ordering P. & G. to divest itself of Clorox, argued that the acquisition threatened to reduce competition in the bleach field because P. & G. eventually might have entered the field with a product of its own.

Some legal authorities regarded the Supreme Court decision as a signal to antitrust agencies to take a tougher stance on conglomerate mergers.

Others have taken a narrower view of the decision, largely because of the similarity of P. & G.'s existing products and those produced by Clorox.

But the decision undoubtedly will make many corporations take a closer look at the possible antitrust implications of future conglomerate mergers.

It may have been a coincidence but, within days of the Supreme Court decision, the National Biscuit Company and the Colgate-Palmolive Company, two other merchandising giants, called off their proposed merger.

May 15, 1967

MERGER GROWTH AT HISTORIC HIGH

F.T.C. Says 1967 Spurt Put Total Above 1929 Level

Special to The New York Times

WASHINGTON, March 18—Corporate mergers showed the largest increase in modern industrial history in 1967, whether measured by number of mergers or number of acquisitions of sizable companies, the Federal Trade Commission reported today.

In all, there were 1,496 mergers of manufacturing and mining companies during the year, a substantial rise from the 995 mergers of 1966.

The number of mergers last year exceeded the number recorded in 1929 for the first time ever.

As for mergers involving large companies, which the trade commission defines as those in which the acquired company has assets of $10-million or more, there were 155 of these in 1967.

The aggregate assets involved in these large acquisitions, which the commission said totaled $8-billion, were double those of the large companies that merged in 1966.

Trend Continuing

The trend toward mergers of large companies is continuing this year, the commission said.

During the first two months of this year, "some 19 large mergers, with aggregate assets of $1.3-billion, were consummated, while 20 other announced mergers, involving a total of $2.3-billion of assets, were pending."

Most of the large mergers in 1967 were of the "product extension" type, the commission said. These involved the acquisition of a company whose product or service bears some market relationship to the product or function of the acquiring company.

Eighty-three per cent of the total number of large mergers in 1967 and 80 per cent of the assets involved in large company mergers were of this variety, the commission said.

March 19, 1968

Conglomerate Tale: Transamerica Corp.

By ROBERT E. BEDINGFIELD

If a textbook is ever written on how to conglomerate successfully, a thick chapter will need to be devoted to the Transamerica Corporation.

It has been 10 years since Transamerica, under terms of the Bank Holding Company Act of 1956, was required to divest itself of its banking entities and it has been steadily expanding into non-banking businesses all that time.

Today it is one of the largest holding companies in the country. Its more than $3-billion of assets are invested in 32 major subsidiaries with more than 1,000 offices in all 50 states and five Canadian provinces as well as a score of foreign countries.

Its largest single asset is the wholly owned Occidental Life Insurance Company, which with $19-billion of insurance in force is ninth largest in the industry and one of the fastest growing. It also owns several smaller life companies and property and casualty companies.

2d to King Ranch

Transamerica is second only to the King Ranch as a real estate empire in the West. The United Artists Corporation, the big movie distributor, and Trans International Airlines, Inc., the nation's second largest supplemental air carrier, both are Transamerica properties.

Other major subsidiaries include De Laval Turbine, Inc., Transamerica Financial Corporation, which is the former Pacific Finance Corporation; Transamerica Computer Company; Transamerica Investment Counselors, Inc.; Transamerica Capital Fund; Transamerica Fund Management Company, and the Transamerica Title Insurance Group.

John R. Beckett, Transamerica's president, describes his company as "a major service organization."

In an interview here the other day in Transamerica's suite at the Essex House on Central Park South, Mr. Beckett said that in his eight years as president of the company he has endeavored to direct its activities as much as possible "into the service area rather than into manufacturing."

He noted that since 1960 Transamerica has tripled its per share earnings and now derives more than 94 per cent of its $65-million (1967) net profits from "service-oriented business." He continued:

"We think the service business has a great future and is subject to fewer ups and downs in the economy than manufacturing. In the capital goods field you can hold off buying when things turn bad. You don't, however, see the service business going down as fast.

"Our concept is based on a few simple things. One, the population is getting richer; two, as a man becomes more affluent he spends a greater amount of his money on services rather than goods. Three, most everyone has more leisure time and can look forward to still more of it in the next few years. And, four, the population is showing a greater number of young people while at the other end the older person is retiring earlier and living longer."

All those points, Mr. Beckett said, should result in Transamerica's reporting a 10 to 15 per cent gain in earnings this year—with the 10 per cent surtax already taken into account—and, if the market continues to value Transamerica's earnings as high as it does now, a split of the stock, which last week sold up to 68¾.

"We try to keep the value of the stock within the reach of the average investor," Mr. Beckett said, "because there are so many of him. The average investor likes to buy 100 shares of stock at a time. Usually he has only about $3,000 to invest and once you get above $30 a share for your stock you limit your market.

"With more than 140,000 shareholders we are among the top 30 companies in the United States from the standpoint of the number of stockholders. So we are getting a really broad following from the average citizen and in our business, which is service, that's the man we want."

Transamerica has increased its cash dividend every year since 1962 and has distributed a stock dividend in six of the last seven years. In 1968 the stock dividend was 4 per cent. "We find the majority of our stockholders like stock dividends," Mr. Beckett said.

"My own feeling," he remarked, "is to give a small stock dividend periodically. And as long as you do it all the time and as long as the dividend is not too big you are okay. Our goal is to have the dividend increase faster than inflation."

John R. Beckett, president of Transamerica Corporation

Transamerica's newest venture is the Transamerica Capital Fund. This is a fully managed investment company organized two months ago whose assets will be invested for capital appreciation. Mr. Beckett said that when Transamerica decided to start the fund, its original goal was to start the operation with assets of at least $10-million.

"Evidently people think highly of our investment acumen," Mr. Beckett said. He added that the initial solicitation, which ended yesterday, had far surpassed his management's greatest hopes. With the solicitation confined largely to Transmerica's own shareholders and employes, the fund will start out tomorrow with more than 18,000 shareholders and assets of more than $70-million.

Transamerica's emphasis on service-oriented business probably will soon extend it into the educational and medical service fields.

"We haven't figured out how to get into either of those operations yet, but we are working on it," Mr. Beckett said. He added that Transamerica was using United Artists' facilities to determine the best way to go about entering the education field.

Mr. Beckett said that it was his belief that "over the years ahead business will start giving its employes three-and four-month sabbaticals to attend school. We feel a lot of money will be spent on employe education," he said.

As far as the medical-service field is concerned, Transamerica has gained some experience already through Occidental Life, which has been handling the Medicare program for half of the people living in California. Occidental has been processing doctor bills of people on Medicare, checking the claims out with Government computers, and making payments directly to the doctors.

"We are doing it more cheaply than the Government could do it," Mr. Beckett said.

He conceded that Transamerica's real estate operation is not now profitable. Even so, he said the company has absolutely no plans of getting out of it. The net worth of the real-estate operation, which includes the Diamond Bar in Los Angeles and several other projects in California, Arizona, Colorado and Washington, is between $15-million and $20-million, Mr. Beckett said, "but we could liquidate it for an awful lot of money.

"But there is no reason to liquidate it. We've been in the business for over 35 years and it's a great inflation hedge."

Mr. Beckett is a firm believer in letting one thing lead to another and he told how Transamerica's title insurance business was getting the company deeper into real estate in another direction.

"You know every five years the average person moves and that generally requires two title searches. Meanwhile, we have started a home-for-home selling business in cooperation with companies whose employes move frequently."

A logical next step, Mr. Beckett figures, would for Transamerica to go into the moving business.

Mr. Beckett, 50 years old, is a securities analyst, who left his ivory tower where he scanned data on corporate activities for Blyth & Co., Inc., to move out in the field and do what corporations do and do it very well. Prior to joining Blyth & Co. in 1944 he was a senior securities analyst for the Securities and Exchange Commission. Associates call him shy and introspective, but he smiles easily and is described as "a great guy."

September 1, 1968

U.S. ACCUSES I.B.M. OF MONOPOLIZING COMPUTER MARKET

Suit Charges Company With Preventing Competition In Digital Equipment Field

BREAKUP MAY BE ASKED

Action Is 3d Major Antitrust Move in Final Days of the Johnson Administration

By EDWIN L. DALE Jr.

Special to The New York Times

WASHINGTON, Jan. 17—The Justice Department announced today that it had filed suit against the giant International Business Machines Corporation, alleging it monopolizes the $3-billion general purpose digital computer market. It indicated that it would seek at least a partial breakup of the company.

The suit against I.B.M. was the Government's third major antitrust action in a week and part of an enormous flurry of last-minute activity on the part of officials of the Johnson Administration. These included:

¶Recommendation by the Justice Department today that the Government end price-fixing of sales commission charges in stock transactions.

¶Release of a report by a Presidential committee proposing changes in the way the Government deals with its employes.

¶Announcement that the Interior Department is planning to set aside more land for parks.

¶Issuance of regulations by the Department of Transportation requiring that social considerations be taken into account in the location of highways.

¶Release of a large number of studies, long in preparation by a number of agencies and committees, on subjects ranging from urban housing to beautification of public utility lines and installations.

The antitrust suit against I. B. M., filed in Federal District Court in New York, followed the filing last week of antitrust suits against major auto manufacturers, charging a conspiracy to delay development of anti-pollution devices and a legal move against the merger of Atlantic Richfield Oil Company and Sinclair.

The suit alleged that I. B. M. had engaged in a number of selling and marketing practices that were said to prevent "competing manufacturers of general purpose digital computers from having an adequate opportunity effectively to compete for business."

Sales and leases of general my introduction dealing with intergroup relations, I would I.B.M.'s $5.3-billion gross sales in 1967. The suit said I.B.M. held 74 per cent of the market for this product.

It asked the court to order the company to cease the practices complained of and added a vague request for "relief by way of divorcement, divestiture and reorganization with respect to the business and properties of the defendant as the court may consider necessary or appropriate to dissipate the effects of the defendant's unlawful activities."

Presumably, the Justice Department will detail what it has in mind by way of breaking up the company when the case comes to trial.

The suit was filed at the direction of Attorney General Ramsey Clark in the waning hours of the Johnson Administration. Today was the last full business day of the outgoing Administration.

Ironically, Nicholas deB. Katzenbach, Under Secretary of State and a former Attorney General, is to become I.B.M.'s general counsel.

And Burke Marshall, an I.B.M. vice president, was a key Justice Department official during the Kennedy Administration.

Inquiry Began in 1967

I.B.M., however, has been under Justice Department investigation since at least the beginning of 1967. Last month, one competitor and one customer—the Control Data Corporation and the Data Processing Financial and General Corporation—filed antitrust suits against I.B.M.

The Justice Department complaint said that beginning in 1961 I.B.M. "has attempted to monopolize and has monopolized" the general purpose digital computer market. Digital computers, the suit said, represent "over 95 per cent of all computer sales and leases."

The suit was filed under Section 2 of the Sherman Act, covering monopolization, which is used relatively seldom. Most Sherman Act suits are for price fixing and other conspiracies in restraint of trade, among competitors, under Section 1.

I.B.M. has already indicated that by the middle of this year it will change some of its pricing practices — probably including those complained of in today's suit. But whether this would be enough to satisfy the Government cannot be known now.

Neither is it known what attitude the new Attorney General, John N. Mitchell, and his still unnamed Antitrust Division chief, will take to the suit. If the case goes to trial it could last for years, including almost inevitable appeals.

The practices complained of today included the following:

The company quotes a single price for the computer itself, related "software" and supporting services. The Justice Department said that this device was used to discriminate among customers "by providing certain customers with extensive software and related support in a manner that unreasonably inhibited the entry or growth of competitors."

This pricing system was also used, the complaint said, to limit "the development and scope of activities of an independent software and computer support industry."

The company, according to the complaint, also "used its accumulated software and related support to preclude its competitors from effectively competing for various customer accounts."

Software is the program, or instructions, that makes the machine perform the desired task.

Next, the company was charged with introducing new models of computers "with unusually low profit expectations, in those segments of the market where competitors had or appeared likely to have unusual competitive success."

The company was also said to have announced "future production of new models for such markets when it knew that it was unlikely to be able to complete production within the announced time."

Finally, the company was charged with having "dominated the educational market" for these computers "by granting exceptional discriminatory allowances in favor of universities and other educational institutions."

The digital computer, the kind that Americans have become familiar with in the last 10 years, basically counts at a fantastic speed through its ability to identify positive and negative electrical charges.

This ability, in addition, enables the machines to make decisions by sensing the simple presence or absence of a charge. These are the machines that send out utility bills, and pay checks, and that played a major role in sending Apollo 8 to the moon.

Analog machines, much simpler affairs, are not exact devices, and show only an analogous relationship between what is to be measured and a reading device, and include such instruments as the slide rule, thermometer, and water meter.

Statement From I.B.M.

I.B.M. said yesterday it would defend itself forcefully against charges by the Justice Department that it was monopolizing the data processing industry.

The company said it believed the Government's action was "unwarranted and without foundation."

"This lawsuit is the outgrowth of previously reported discussions going on for nearly three years between the Justice Department and various companies in the data processing industry. I.B.M. has cooperated fully in this review.

"One of the key issues in these discussions has been whether there is sufficient competition in the data processing industry or whether I.B.M. has such monopolistic power that fully effective competition does nat exist.

"Evidence of the open and strongly competitive nature of the computer business is abundant. Virtually nonexistent 20 years ago, it has grown into a multi-billion-dollar industry that has attracted more than 60 manufacturers of computer systems and some 4,000 companies dealing in related equipment support and services.

"I.B.M. will defend itself forcefully against this action, which it believes is unwarranted and without foundation. The company believes furthermore that the highly competitive data processing industry will remain a growing and dynamic one."

January 18, 1969

Letters

to the Editor of The Times

Conglomerates vs. Monopoly

To the Editor:

A student of competitive processes in the economy, I have watched with fascination the switch during the last year from tolerance of conglomerate mergers to a feverish general condemnation of them. The closest parallel to this is the resentment which take-overs in Britain during the last ten years have aroused from conservative and sluggish managements ripe for take-over.

I detect the same strain in the present excitement, as conglomerates have at long last begun to touch really large and well-established firms.

No doubt some conglomerate mergers do pose problems for competition, particularly those which unite and thus may tend to entrench firms with leading positions in their industries. Others of these mergers may lead to inefficiency or financial guttings. Moreover, anything which increases the over-all concentration of the economy should cause concern on social and political grounds.

But the current agitation now seems to have lost perspective on what is, compared to the scope of the entire economy, a problem of modest dimensions. Hardly any of the new conglomerates come close to the size or security at such long-standing conglomerates as General Motors, General Electric, du Pont, and RCA, to name but the most obvious examples. None of them is within hailing distance of the market power long held by these firms and quite a few others.

The same newness and unpredictability about the new conglomerates which distress the more traditional industrial and financial spokesman also make them not only more vulnerable but also more potentially valuable as independent competitors (again excepting leading-firm mergers such as International Telephone and Telegraph specializes in).

Recent take-over threats have brought out with embarrassing clarity that many eminent corporations have indeed been performing well below their potential for efficiency and innovation. This economy, like Britain's, can ill afford the luxury of shielding soft managements from the discipline of possible take-over.

In this light, the current round of blanket condemnations will in retrospect be seen as primarily an attempt to protect well-placed but inefficient firms rather than to preserve competition.

Winnowing out the true chaff among conglomerate mergers will require far more discernment than is now being displayed. Moreover the tempest in this teapot is diverting attention from the real unfinished business of antitrust policy: to reduce the degree of monopoly now prevailing in a series of major industries. For this, the recent IBM case should be merely the first step.

The antitrust agencies and the Congress need to reassess their priorities and move to reduce market power, rather than rush to its defense.

WILLIAM G. SHEPHERD
Associate Professor
of Economics
University of Michigan
Ann Arbor, March 25, 1969

March 30, 1969

U.S. SERVES NOTICE CURBS ARE LIKELY ON GIANT MERGERS

Attorney General Cautions on Links of Any 2 of 200 Biggest Manufacturers

NEW GUIDELINES SET

By EILEEN SHANAHAN
Special to The New York Times

WASHINGTON, June 6—Attorney General John N. Mitchell served notice today that the Justice Department was likely, in the future, to take legal action to block any merger between two companies that are among the 200 largest manufacturing corporations.

Mergers among nonmanufacturing companies of a size similar to the top 200 in manufacturing also face challenges.

Such corporations include major retailers, transportation and communications companies, banks and insurance companies.

They are likely to be called to account if they try to merge with each other or with one of the top 200 in manufacturing, Mr. Mitchell said.

In addition, he said, the Justice Department will probably oppose any acquisition by one of the top 200 of a concern that is a leader in its own industry, regardless of its size, if that industry is dominated by a relatively small number of companies.

Stricter Standards Listed

Mr. Mitchell outlined the strong antimerger policies the Justice Department will follow under his leadership in a speech to the Georgia Bar Association at Savannah. His office made the text of his remarks available here.

The antitrust standards enunciated by Mr. Mitchell are stricter than any that have been followed by any Attorney General in the past.

Mr. Mitchell's Assistant Attorney General for Antitrust, Richard W. McLaren, has indicated previously that his thoughts were trending in this direction, but had not flatly committed himself to a policy of probable opposition to all of the types of mergers mentioned by Mr. Mitchell.

The antimerger guidelines published by the Justice Department's Antitrust division in the final months of the Johnson Administration fell considerably short of the Mitchell standards.

They did not suggest any attack on mergers simply because of size. Rather, they relied on demonstrable damage to competition as the basis for antitrust suits.

Mr. Mitchell said he believed "the future vitality of our free economy may be in danger because of the increasing threat of economic concentration."

He said he believed the suits the department would bring under these new standards "are clearly authorized by present antitrust law"—a point that is vigorously disputed at present.

Attorney General Mitchell

"By halting the trend toward concentration," Mr. Mitchell continued, "we remove what we believe is an inadvisable alternative of outright Government regulation as is now applied to public utilities, communications and other highly concentrated industries. We will stimulate our most reliable economic regulator—free competition."

Mr. Mitchell said that "superconcentration" exists in the manufacturing sector of the American economy today, as a result of mergers that have brought 58 per cent of all manufacturing assets into the hands of the 200 largest industrial corporations and 75 per cent into the hands of the top 500.

The move toward ever-larger companies, through mergers, does not bring most of the benefits that are claimed for mergers, Mr. Mitchell said.

Studies show that big companies are not necessarily the most efficient or profitable, he said.

Nor does corporate bigness necessarily stimulate "the most imaginative scientific research. Recent studies show that the medium-size firm tends to be more productive in its scientific research precisely because it is not in a dominant position."

"It has also been argued that the large firm, because of its concentration of talent and other resources, is better able to market goods and services that the public wants. But this, too, is not proven by the facts.

"For example, leading firms in two of our most highly concentrated industries—automobiles and razor blades—only offered the American consumer important new products in response to aggressive foreign competition.

"Thus, our experience has been that the American consumer has not always benefited by the very large corporation."

Conglomerates Cited

While Mr. Mitchell's warning against mergers by the largest corporations would apply to old, established corporate giants, such as General Motors, that are in only a few lines of business, he also argued that there were some additional dangers in the growth of conglomerate corporations, which are in many different lines of business.

Conglomerate companies are more likely than others, he said, to engage in mandatory reciprocal arrangements with their suppliers; that is, to use their purchasing power to insist that the supplier fill his own needs, wherever possible, by buying from the conglomerate.

Conglomerates also pose the danger that they may act out of "community of interest," he said.

This, he explained, "is not a formal agreement but merely the recognition of common goals by large diversified corporations."

June 7, 1969

200 Biggest Manufacturers Listed

Following is a list of the 200 largest manufacturing corporations, as compiled by Fortune magazine. The threat of anti-trust action against mergers by the largest companies, announced yesterday by Attorney General Mitchell, applies not only to these manufacturing companies but also to an unspecified number of the largest companies in transportation, communications, finance, retailing and other nonmanufacturing areas.

1. General Motors
2. Std. Oil (N.J.)
3. Ford Motor
4. Gen. Electric
5. Chrysler
6. I.B.M.
7. Mobil Oil
8. Texaco
9. Gulf Oil
10. U.S. Steel
11. International Tel.
12. West. Electric
13. Std. Oil of Calif.
14. McDonnell Doug.
15. DuPont
16. Shell Oil
17. Westinghouse
18. Boeing
19. Std. Oil (Ind.)
20. R.C.A. Corp.
21. Gen. Telephone
22. Goodyear Tire
23. Bethlehem Steel
24. Swift
25. Ling-Temco-Vought
26. Union Carbide
27. Gen. Dynamics
28. Eastman Kodak
29. North Amer. Rockwell
30. Procter & Gamble
31. Int'l Harvester
32. National Dairy
33. United Aircarft
34. Continental Oil
35. Lockheed Aircraft
36. Firestone Tire
37. Phillips Pet.
38. Armour
39. Tenneco
40. Litton Ind.
41. Monsanto
42. Sun Oil
43. Singer
44. General Foods
45. Grace (W.R.)
46. Caterpillar Tractor
47. Textron
48. Occidental Petrol.
49. Borden
50. Dow Chemical
51. American Can
52. Burlington Indus.
53. Sperry Rand
54. Int'l Paper
55. Union Oil of Calif.
56. Continental Can
57. TRW
58. Sinclair Oil
59. Cities Service
60. Uniroyal
61. Atlantic Richfield
62. Minnesota Mining
63. Republic Steel
64. Bendix
65. FMC
66. Armco Steel
67. Alcoa
68. Signal Companies
69. Gulf & Western
70. U.S. Plywood-Champion
71. Ralston Purina
72. Honeywell
73. Allied Chemical
74. Reynolds (R.J.)
75. Celanese
76. Consolidated Foods
77. Coca-Cola
78. Avco
79. Raytheon
80. Grumman Aircraft
81. Owens-Illinois
82. Goodrich (B.F.)
83. National Steel
84. Corn Products
85. Amer. Tobacco
86. Nat'l Cash Register
87. Colgate-Palmolive
88. Getty Oil
89. Amer. Home Products
90. Amer. Standard
91. Inland Steel
92. Ashland Oil
93. Beatrice Foods
94. Ogden
95. Anaconda
96. PPG Industries
97. General Tire
98. Weyerhaeuser
99. Deere
100. Boise Cascade
101. Georgia-Pacific
102. Amer. Cyanamid
103. Genesco
104. Olin Mathieson
105. Borg-Warner
106. Stevens (J.P.)
107. Carnation
108. Mead
109. Xerox
110. Norton Simon
111. Eaton Yale & Towne
112. Crown Zellerbach
113. AMK
114. National Lead
115. Standard Brands
116. White Motor
117. Kaiser Alum.
118. Campbell Soup
119. Pepsico
120. Reynolds Metals
121. Bristol-Myers
122. Whirlpool
123. Kaiser Industries
124. Teledyne
125. Marathon Oil
126. Youngstown Sheet
127. St. Regis Paper
128. Motorola
129. National Biscuit
130. Allis-Chalmers
131. Amer. Motors
132. SCM
133. Heinz (H.J.)
134. Pfizer (Chas.)
135. Kennecott Copper
136. Kimberly-Clark
137. Hercules
138. Warner-Lambert
139. Std. Oil (Ohio)
140. Studebaker-Worthington
141. Zenith Radio
142. Northwest Industries
143. White Consolidated
144. Glen Alden
145. Martin Marietta
146. Scott Paper
147. Philip Morris
148. Tex. Instruments
149. Pullman
150. Interco
151. General Mills
152. Combustion Engineering
153. Colt Industries
154. Anheuser-Busch
155. United Merchants
156. Burroughs
157. Babcock & Wilcox
158. Rexall Drug
159. Ingersoll-Rand
160. Amer. Smelting
161. Dresser Ind.
162. Squibb Beech-Nut
163. U.S. Industries
164. Del Monte
165. Johnson & Johnson
166. Hormel (Geo. A.)
167. International Utilities
168. Merck
169. A.M.F.
170. Nat. Distillers
171. Amer. Metal Climax
172. Armstrong Cork
173. GAF
174. McGraw-Edison
175. Time Inc.
176. Kidde (Walter)
177. Magnavox
178. Avon Products
179. Johns-Manville
180. Gillette
181. Phelps Dodge
182. Quaker Oats
183. Pet Inc.
184. Dana Corp.
185. Iowa Beef Packers
186. Pillsbury
187. Emerson Elec.
188. Agway
189. Whittaker
190. Central Soya
191. Diamond Shamrock
192. Ethyl
193. Clark Equipment
194. I.M.C.
195. No. Amer. Phillips
196. Otis Elevator
197. Sterling Drug
198. Hess Oil
199. Northrop
200. Carrier

June 7, 1969

Antitrust Drive Dims Enthusiasm on Mergers

By JOHN J. ABELE

Thomas Watson's old formula for successful business conduct—"Think"—has been revised by the Department of Justice. It now reads: "Think Antitrust."

That is the message the department's antitrust division has been beaming out to the business world this year in a series of lawsuits and speeches.

The actions and the words have indicated not only a tougher stance on antitrust matters but a major effort to broaden the dimensions of antitrust law.

The campaign has been led by Richard W. McLaren, Assistant Attorney General in charge of the antitrust division. Before taking office early this year, Mr. McLaren was a Chicago lawyer who specialized in defending companies against antitrust charges.

In the business world, Mr. McLaren's vigorous offensive has produced some applause, some criticism and a considerable amount of uncertainty over what sort of mergers will be countenanced by antitrust authorities in the future.

Not incidentally, the growing possibility of antitrust suits has diminished the enthusiasm of some merger-minded companies and contributed to a percentible slackening in the pace of big mergers.

Although smaller mergers have continued at a brisk pace, there have been few deals of the blockbuster proportions that were so frequent last year.

In some situations, the mere threat of possible antitrust action has been enough to dissuade companies from going ahead with projected combinations.

Two weeks ago, for example, the First National City Corporation called off its proposed acquisition of the Chubb Corporation, a big insurance organization, within hours of learning that the Justice Department would seek to block the deal.

Antitrust considerations are not the only reasons for slowing the record merger wave of recent years. The slide in the stock market this year has reduced the attractiveness of stock as a medium of exchange for acquisitions. This has been particularly true of conglomerate companies, whose stocks have been among the hardest hit in the general decline.

The steady upward spiral of interest rates also has made it more difficult and more expensive to borrow money and to issue debt securities for acquisition purposes.

The attractiveness of debt securities also has diminished by the proposal of Representative Wilbur D. Mills, chairman of the House Ways and Means Committee, to limit tax advantages of debt securities used in acquisitions and by the stiffer attitude of the New York Stock Exchange toward the ability of listed companies to meet interest charges on debt securities issued in acquisitions.

But the big guns in the antitrust arsenal are suits filed to block or undo mergers and these have been firing rapidly in recent months.

Last week, the Justice Department announced that it planned to oppose the projected merger of the International Telephone and Telegraph Corporation with the Hartford Fire Insurance Company, one of the nation's largest casualty insurers.

The suit would be the second brought against I.T.T. in recent months. In April, the department filed a suit against the big conglomerate's acquisition of the Canteen Corporation three days after the deal had been completed.

In other major actions, the department has sought to block the take-over of the Jones & Laughlin Steel Corporation by Ling-Temco-Vought, another major conglomerate, and to stop Northwest Industries, a railroad-based conglomerate from continuing with its efforts to take over the B. F. Goodrich Company.

F.T.C. Also Active

The Federal Trade Commission, the other arm of the Federal Government's antitrust enforcement, has been trying to block White Consolidated Industries, another conglomerate, from taking over the Allis-Chalmers Manufacturing Company.

Further evidence of the Justice Department's heightened interest in antitrust matters was provided earlier this month when Attorney General John N. Mitchell, in a speech before the Georgia Bar Association, said the department was likely to take action against any merger move involving companies that rank among the nation's 200 largest manufacturing companies or 200 largest nonmanufacturing companies.

This standard would apply to mergers of manufacturing and nonmanufacturing companies, he said, and would also affect proposed acquisitions by these companies of smaller concerns that are leaders in their particular industry.

Under these standards, several of the large mergers that have taken place in recent years presumably would have been challenged.

Perils Are Noted

In his speech, Mr. Mitchell said he believed "the future vitality of our free economy may be in danger because of the increasing threat of economic concentration."

This view is disputed by a number of business observers who contend that the degree of concentration has not increased significantly in recent years, despite the high level of merger activity.

These critics also contend that Mr. Mitchell's standards would protect the status of giant corporations such as American Telephone, General Motors and Standard Oil (New Jersey), whose present size is due in part to acquisitions they have made in the past, while inhibiting other large corporations from making acquistions.

The preponderance of conglomerate companies among antitrust targets has prompted some business observers to charge that antitrust officials appear to be biased against the newer conglomerate-type companies and in favor of older industrial giants who are, or might become, the object of takeover bids.

'Pro-Establishment'

"It looks to me as if antitrust is pro-Establishment," is the way one of these critics puts it.

Mr. McLaren has rejected the charge, saying he is neither for nor against conglomerates, or mergers for that matter, but that he is interested in achieving the traditional objectives of antitrust legislation—maintaining and increasing competition.

Some of the edge was taken off the pro-Establishment charges two weeks ago, when the Justice Department announced that the United States Steel Corporation had been charged with violations of antitrust laws by engaging in reciprocal buying practices with other corporations. At the same time, Big Steel agreed to a consent judgment to settle the the suit.

The New York Times

Richard W. McLaren, the head of antitrust division in the Justice Department.

Reciprocity—in which one company buys goods and services from another, provided the second company buys goods and services from the first company—has been a particular target of Mr. McLaren's campaign.

The argument against reprocity is that by creating artificial conditions for the purchase and sale of goods and service, the practice has the effect of limiting competition.

Potential for reciprocity was one of the factors in the Justice Department's suit against the I.T.T.-Canteen merger. The suit contends that I.T.T. would be inclined to use Canteen's food service operations in its far-flung industrial operations and could induce its customers to also use Canteen's services.

Other suits filed by the Justice Department have also adopted traditional antitrust arguments, such as actual or potential threats to cmpetition, in attempting to ward off large mergers, particularly those of the conglomerate variety.

In the suit against Ling-Temco-Vought and Jones & Laughlin Steel, for example, the department cited expansion plans of the two companies that covered some of the same fields. A merger, it argued, would reduce the possibility of the companies' entering the same field, thereby limiting future competition.

In attacking mergers on these bases, the department has departed from its erstwhile reluctance to prosecute conglomerate mergers, which, by definition, involve companies engaged in different lines of commerce.

With this barrier gone, conglomerate companies are more likely to be subject to antitrust attack. To avoid that possibility, they are planning vigorous defenses to win their cases in court.

In announcing last week that it planned to proceed with a stockholder vote on the contested merger with I.T.T., Hartford Fire said it had been advised by its legal counsel that the Justice Department action "involved uncharted legal areas and that the outcome of any Justice Department action is extremely problematical."

In an earlier comment, I.T.T. described the basis of the suit as "novel and untried, without legislative mandate from Congress and unsanctioned by previous court cases."

The statement added: "The proposed litigation appears to be part of the announced effort by the Justice Department to bend the antitrust laws to stop mergers among large companies regardless of the fact that there is no discernible adverse impact on competition."

Other observers have been critical of the Justice Department's emphasis on potential threats to competition rather than actual threats.

"It's like hanging a man for an imaginary crime," declares one of these observers.

June 29, 1969

Curb on Mergers Is Suggested By a Staff Study for the F.T.C.

By EILEEN SHANAHAN

Special to The New York Times

WASHINGTON, Nov. 4—The recent wave of mergers among American companies is concentrating business decision-making in "a few vast corporations," a staff study for the Federal Trade Commission warned today.

The study added that the trend was threatening to create what amounted to "closed circuit" markets, from which small and middle-size concerns would be excluded.

The study proposed a number of changes in the law, aimed both at discouraging mergers and at protecting the public from harmful consequences of concentration of economic power that it said already existed.

In the latter category were proposals that much more detailed financial reports be required from large, diversified companies and that the law covering interlocking directorates be greatly expanded. At present, the ban on such interlocks merely prohibits officers and directors of one company from sitting on the board of another company that is its direct competitor.

The study by the F.T.C. staff, which was 17 months in the making and is more than 700 pages long, analyzed in scores of different ways the extent to which mergers have concentrated economic power in fewer and fewer hands over recent years.

It noted, for example, that the 200 largest manufacturing corporations in 1968 controlled almost two-thirds of all manufacturing industry assets — a proportion of total assets that was equal to the share held by the 1,000 largest corporations in 1941. And this increase in power in the hands of the 200 largest manufacturing companies came at a time, the report noted, when the actual volume of industrial assets was, itself, growing very rapidly.

The staff report was prepared mainly under the direction of Dr. Willard F. Mueller, who is now a professor of economics at the University of Wisconsin at Madison, but was for many years chief economist of the F.T.C.

He presented the report to the Senate Antitrust and Monopoly Subcommittee at a hearing.

Dr. Mueller's own conclusion was that vigorous anti-merger action was needed now to avoid the "danger that the economy may become cartelized and centralized in a fashion that cannot be reversed."

He said the nation could not wait for further studies to determine what actual harm increased concentration was doing.

This conclusion was disputed by one of the five members of the F.T.C., Mary Gardiner Jones. The commission itself took no position on the staff study, but merely submitted the study to Congress for its consideration.

Miss Jones, in a statement accompanying the report, said that the report "relies essentially on hypothesis and theorization" to reach its conclusion that concentration is actually producing injurious, anti-competitive effects.

She said the legislative proposals made in the study were premature and should await completion of the second part of the commission's merger study, which is to examine the actual impact of mergers, economically, socially and otherwise.

Sound Basis Seen

Another member of the commission, Philip Elman, said that the recommendations of the report appeared "soundly based" but also emphasized the importance of the second phase of the merger study.

The statistical analysis contained in the report showed, contrary to general belief, that what were commonly referred to as "conglomerate" companies—that is, those engaged in a large number of different lines of business — have not dominated the merger wave of the nineteen-sixties.

It said:

"During 1961-1968, the most active acquiring corporations made acquisitions totaling $20-billion, or almost 60 per cent of all acquisitions of the top 200 during the period.

"Only 11 of these 25 were among the so-called new conglomerates, and even some of these were not, strictly speaking, new companies, for example, the International Telephone and Telegraph Corporation. Eight of the most active acquirers were petroleum companies and six others covered a variety of industries."

The report noted that its analysis of the dangers of creation of large conglomerate companies specifically included highly diversified companies — the General Electric Company might be an example — that have been in existence for many years, but are not usually called conglomerates.

Such conglomerates, whether old or new, tend to behave toward one another with what the report called "forbearance." That is, they do not tend to compete vigorously in a market where they might do so successfully because of fears of retaliation by another conglomerate in another market.

In addition, the study said, interlocking directorates, intercorporate stockholding and joint ventures "extend traditional 'communities of interest' among key industrial decision-makers."

Dr. Mueller, in his presentation to the committee, concluded that "conglomerate interdependence and forbearance represents the most serious threat to competition resulting from the growing merger-achieved centralization of economic resources among a relatively few conglomerate enterprises that meet as actual or potential competitors in many markets."

The F.T.C.'s study criticized the Securities and Exchange Commission for not going far enough in its recent revision of its rules covering the financial reports of diversified companies. It said that "profit information by product line," among other things, should be required to be reported. Otherwise, there is no way of analyzing whether the competitive process is functioning, the report said.

It proposed that the S.E.C. and the F.T.C. itself jointly frame new reporting requirements for conglomerates.

The report also criticized the accounting profession for sanctioning the development of accounting practices that "have granted merger-minded companies broad opportunities to mislead investors and to obtain unwarranted support in the securities market for their aggressive programs of expansion."

"Present accounting practices impose stricter accounting tests on firms that grow internally, creating new productive capacity, than those that grow primarily through acquisition," Dr. Mueller added.

November 5, 1969

F.T.C. MAPS CHANGE TO AID CONSUMER

Major Reorganization Set by Chairman—Agency Was Nader Target

Special to The New York Times

WASHINGTON, June 8—The Federal Trade Commission, which has been accused in recent years of being lax in protecting consumer interests, announced today a major reorganization of its staff to "increase the consumer's faith in the market place."

The commission's chairman, Caspar W. Weinberger, said that President Nixon might have had the charges of inefficiency in mind when he asked Mr. Weinberger to "revitalize" the agency.

Many of the commission's staff positions will be abolished in the reorganization. Mr. Weinberger would not discuss individuals who would be replaced, but he said that "several personnel changes" would be announced soon.

The reorganization, which becomes effective July 1, creates two major areas of activity—antitrust investigation and consumer protection.

Bureaus Abolished

Under the changes, the commission's Bureaus of Field Operations, Textiles and Furs, and Industry Guidance will be abolished and their responsibilities shifted to other bureaus. The Bureau of Restraint of Trade will be replaced by the Bureau of Competition, with seven divisions, and the Bureau of Deceptive Practices by a Bureau of Consumer Protection with nine divisions.

The trade commission has the primary responsibility within the Federal Government for protecting the consumer from deceptive business practices.

The commission also shares with the Justice Department the responsibility for preventing corporate mergers and other business arrangements that might lessen competition or tend toward monopoly.

In the summer of 1968, a group of law students headed by the consumer advocate, Ralph Nader, issued a massive report charging the agency with complete inefficiency and its staff with incompetence and indolence.

The Nader report accused the F.T.C. of relying too heavily on voluntary enforcement tools, of lacking aggressiveness in seeking out abuses and of concentrating on petty problems.

Last fall, a study group of the American Bar Association reported to President Nixon that the commission wasted too much of its time and money on "trivial matters"; that its staff was characterized by "incompetence," particularly at the top; that it did less work with more staff now than it did 10 years ago, and that it should be abolished if reforms were not carried out.

Expanded Field Offices

Mr. Weinberger said that in a major part of the reorganization the commission would expand its field offices outside of Washington. The commission, he said, hoped to begin initiating cases in the field rather than going through a complicated bureaucracy before filing suit.

The chairman said that a new economic adviser would be appointed to help educate the staff and that a new Congressional relations office would work with Congress to press for legislation.

The commission, he said, will ask Congress to give it injunctive powers to enable it to force an immediate end to an allegedly illegal practice so the F.T.C. will not have to go through the slow process of obtaining a cease and desist order.

"Organizational changes aren't going to solve all the problems," Mr. Weinberger said. "But I hope this will mean people will regain and have increased trust in the market place. There is a growing awareness that the American public will not accept second-rate performances or second-rate goods."

June 9, 1970

A Switching Point for Rails?

Future Uncertain As Amtrak Takes Charge

By ROBERT E. BEDINGFIELD

An era that began in 1825, when a small locomotive built by John Stevens chugged around on a circular track in Hoboken, N.J., came to an end yesterday. The National Railroad Passenger Corporation, or Amtrak, set up by the Congress to take over the unprofitable duties of hauling passengers from the private railroads, came into being.

In the nearly 150 years since the Stevens locomotive, the railroad industry has rarely been free of problems — and growth. Now, however, with the problems still remaining in the wake of the Penn Central Transportation Company's bankruptcy last June 21, the future course of the railroads is a matter for conjecture.

The family automobile, the bus and the airline rendered the intercity rail passenger virtually obsolete, and whether Amtrak can make him viable again remains to be seen.

But probably he will be extinct by 1985.

Nevertheless, even though most railroads have turned over their deficit-ridden passenger service to Amtrak, the lines are confronted with these urgent questions about the next decade:

¶Will they be able to increase their share of freight traffic? Will doing this require new techniques? More trackage? Less trackage? Where will they get the money to finance new equipment?

¶Will the Government relax its strangling regulation of the industry? Help it with massive injections of yearly credit?

¶Will the labor unions cooperate in the attempts to change the course of the industry?

¶Will Wall Street help in financing the railroads?

¶What about suburban transit? Will the railroads continue to turn over their functions to various metropolitan transit authorities, or will they set about improving their service and increasing the number of their riders?

¶If mergers among themselves are apparently not the solution for ailing lines — as witness the Penn Central debacle — what about allowing the railroads to enter the trucking, waterway and airline businesses to form integrated transportation systems?

These questions were put to railroad men, truckers, Government officials, union people and Wall Street analysts. Their answers ranged from hopeful to pessimistic.

Regarding freight, the general opinion is that the railroads probably will have to handle one third more traffic in a decade hence than they do now. That assumes their share of the market — now about 41 per cent of all intercity movement — will stand still and that the total economy will grow only at a modest pace.

Certain categories of freight will never move overland except by railroad — coal, iron ore, sand and gravel and stone. In other categories the railroads can hold their own with highway or waterway traffic, if they are allowed to use their natural advantages. Those categories include trailer-on-flat-car movements of commodities of all types, but particularly manufactured goods, new automobiles and automobile parts, furniture, meat, fruit and vegetables and hundreds of other high-rated goods.

Some new trackage may be needed for some facilities — millions of tons of freight now originate at points that don't have switching tracks —but a strong contention of railroad executives is that with today's good highways, the present rail network of 207,000 miles is too large, by as much as 60 per cent.

The Penn Central's trustees have told the Congress that their bankrupt system's 20,000-mile plant could be reduced by about 40 per cent.

As far as suburban transit is concerned, railroad men are known to unanimously agree that carrying of large numbers of people to and from urban centers is more properly a function to be served by local transportation authorities than by private industry.

"It's a matter of economic realism," said a former executive of the now-bankrupt

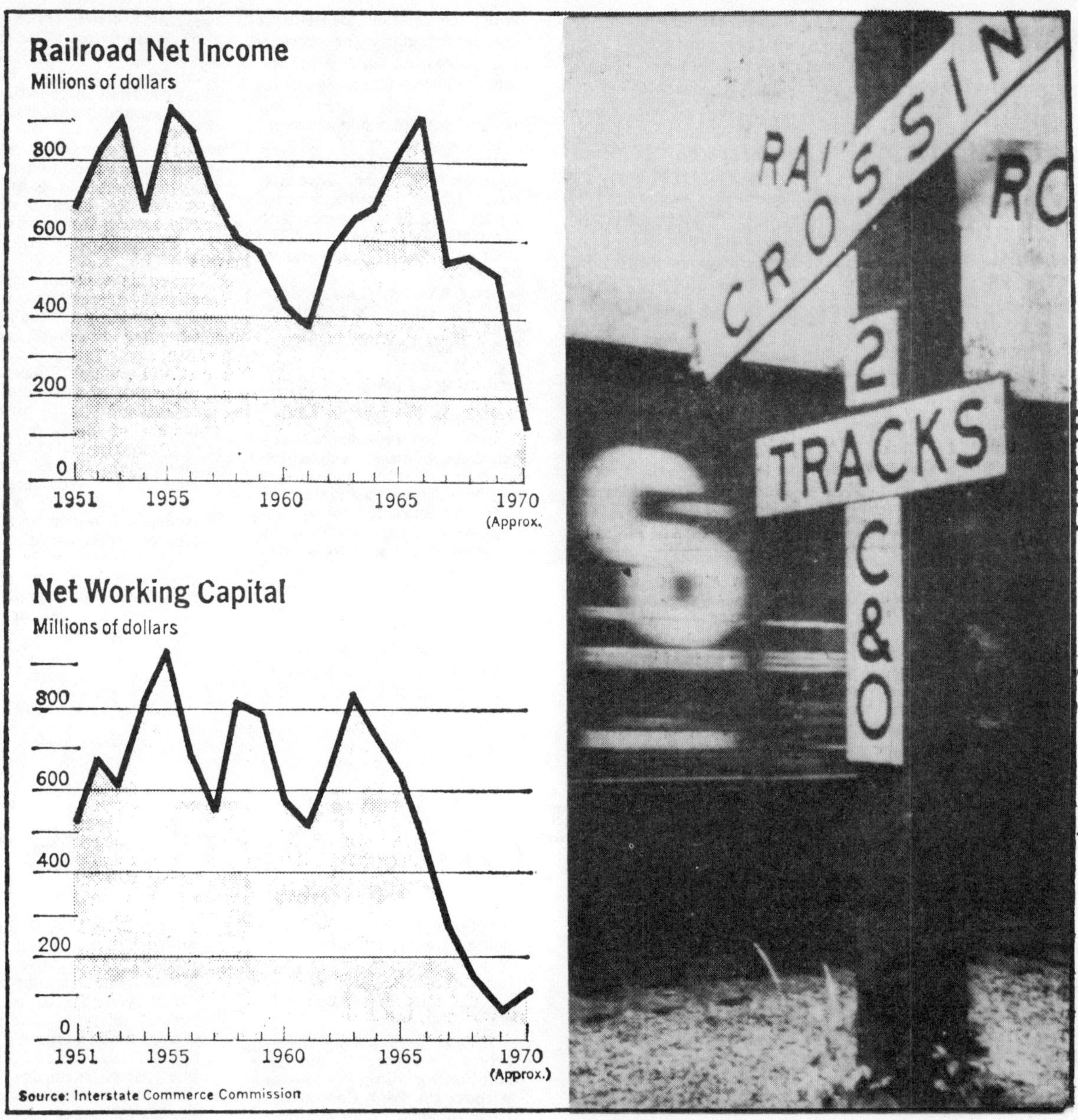

Boston & Maine Railroad, that the traditional passenger-carrying railroad can no longer perform commuter transportation services without sustaining substantial losses, because of steadily increasing operating costs and limitations of the fare structure.

Railroad old-timers declare that the commuter never paid his way — an assertion the jampacked night - and - morning rider will find hard to believe. There can be no argument, however, that off-hour traffic at full fares, and express and mail revenue, all have vanished with good roads and automobiles.

The B.&M. official cited one of the first Federal-state commuter passenger experiments, conducted in Massachusetts over an 18-month period between 1963 and 1964. Frequent service at reasonable fares got the motorist out of his car and into the commuter railroad coach — but at a cost that the B.&M. and the New Haven railroads could never have hoped to cover without substantial subsidies.

•

As a result of the experiment the state of Massachusetts formed the Massachusetts Bay Transportation Authority which provides rapid transit service in Boston and more than 60 other towns and villages throughout the state. The formation of the Metropolitan Transportation Authority in New York, with the purchase of the Long Island Rail Road and the acquisition for commuter-moving purposes of the New Haven and the Penn Central was a logical sequel.

Can railroads become fully integrated transportation companies—on the road, rail and sea? Right now, that can't happen unless the Congress changes existing regulations. Even over the longer term, that seems unlikely because of the political power of the competing forms of transportation, particularly the trucks.

In the early years of this century there were several jointly owned rail and steamship lines, and competitors in each field complained they were whipsawed. Finally, the Southern Pacific Railroad, at the outbreak of World War I disgorged the Mallory Line, which had operated between New Orleans and New York.

Back in 1924, the Association of Railroad Security Holders, alarmed that the infant trucking industry had begun long-haul movements, proposed that the railroads provide shippers with store-door service themselves. To the disgust of some railroad executives several carriers decided to do so, and today among the biggest trucking lines in the country are a dozen or so that are railroad-owned. Those lines, however, all pre-date 1935, when the trucking industry came under the Interstate Commerce Act.

Like the Civil Aeronautics Act, which prohibits railroads from being in the airline business, the Interstate Commerce Act specifically prevents a railroad from acquiring a trucking company or entering the business by acquiring a trucker's routes. There is nothing within the act to prevent a trucking operator from going into the railroad business, but so far, none has indicated an active interest in doing so.

But it is this and other

"unbelievable" disparities in the Government's promotion of transportation modes other than the railroads, "outmoded regulations" and labor's unyielding position with respect to work rules that railroad executives insist must be changed if they are going to avoid recurring financial crises.

There is no disputing the carriers' current financial plight. Of the 71 major lines, 34 began the year with deficits in working capital. In 1970, while railroad revenues reached a record $12-billion, a 5 per cent increase over the 1969 total of $11.4-billion, ordinary net income fell from $504-million to $126.8-million.

Last year's results were the worst since 1939. Twenty-one lines operated at a loss, with the Penn Central deficit reaching a massive $431-million. Even if Penn Central's results were eliminated, the industry's net income last year still would have been lower than at any time since World War II.

Notwithstanding the industry's tenuous financial state, about two-thirds of the plant and equipment has been new since the end of World War II. From 1946 to 1970 the railroads spent $25-billion on improvements. It hasn't been enough, and to make up for past deficiencies and to expand for the future, the lines estimate they will have to increase capital expenditures to an annual rate of $3.3-billion for the next 11 years.

The railroads have gone heavily into debt to pay for the improvements they have already made. Their equipment obligations in the last 10 years have soared to a record $4.3-billion, an increase of $1.5-billion. The roads' inability to generate cash, the fact that they have been unable to earn as much as a 6 per cent return on investment in any year since the nineteen-twenties except the war year 1943, and the unusually cyclical nature of their business, have made the financial community unwilling to undertake more than two or three new equity offerings for the railroads since the Great Depression.

•

"It will take a period of steady earnings and growth, before Wall Street will be willing to sell new railroad equities," says Isabel Benham, first vice president of Shearson Hammill, Inc. Miss Benham, like railroad management, is hopeful that the Congress will put the Government's credit behind the industry.

This is one of the key suggestions of ASTRO, an acronym for America's Sound Transportation Review Organization, an arm of the railroad's public relations division, the Association of American Railroads. George Smathers, former Democratic senator from Florida, now general counsel for ASTRO, testified before the Senate Commerce Committee last month that the Government at a cost of about $600-million a year could enable the industry to meet its annual capital needs of $3.3-billion.

As examples of the aid that the rails believe the Government could provide, Mr. Smathers enumerated the various ASTRO recommendations, including not only loan guarantees, but also direct Federal loans to financially weak roads and the establishment of a railroad trust fund of $400-million for road improvements, for which there is a precedent in the Highway Trust Fund. The railroads would pay a user tax into the fund. Other ASTRO recommendations include a Federally aided, quasi-public organization to operate an emergency freight car fleet, allocation of Highway Trust Fund monies for grade crossing improvements and an expanded Federal research program.

•

Another issue — winning the cooperation of labor in making the railroads' productivity curve a little steeper—is not as simple as it is often made to seem. William H. Moore, president of the Penn Central, told a conference in Bloomington, Ind., last week that "labor and legislative intransigence" block the industry's attempts to bridge a desperate productivity gap. He warned that "the industry will drown in this sea of inequities unless changes are made—and made very soon."

Mr. Moore was speaking particularly of the Indiana Assembly's recent refusal to repeal that state's so-called full-crew laws, which provides that any freight train of 70 cars or more must have a six-man crew—an engineer, a fireman (even though there is no firebox on a Diesel), a conductor, a flag man and two brakemen.

Donald Beattie of the Congress of Railway Unions has made it plain that his members are not going to give up their so-called featherbedding unless the host of hourly workers on the railroads get something in return.

The rail negotiators are just as insistent that the general wage level on the railroads will be held—to the extent the roads can hold them—until the dual bases (hours and miles) of pay for railroad workers are done away with.

In that impasse, mutual confidence in each other's good will, on the part of labor and management, would be of invaluable help in reaching an accord. Unfortunately, mutual good will is just what the negotiators on both sides lack.

May 2, 1971

The root of all evil—concentrated economic power

By ROBERT C. TOWNSEND

America, Inc.

Who Owns and Operates the United States. By Morton Mintz and Jerry S. Cohen. 424 pp. New York: The Dial Press. $10.

"The management of power in a complex society," writes Ralph Nader in his introduction to this relentless book, "is built around institutions. In our country, the most enduring, coordinated and generic power is the corporate institution. . . . Historically, many of our country's struggles have been challenges of the corporate power to define the area of its accountability. This was true of the Populist and Progressive movements as well as the challenges of organized labor and the regulatory state of the New Deal. Against these and lesser buffetings, the corporation with its peerless resiliency of bending now and consolidating later, prevailed only to increase its power. . . .

"Corporate fraud and other economic crimes . . . escape the normative perception that would be applied, for example, to a pickpocket by most people. From educational to media systems, people are not afforded adequate opportunities to learn about and ethically evaluate price-fixing, adulterated citrus juices, hams and poultry, deliberately fragile bumpers, unperformed but billed-for services, suppression of life-giving innovations and many other crimes which bilk the consumer, in Senator Philip Hart's estimate, of some $200 billion yearly. . . . These depredations are part of a raging corporate radicalism which generates technological violence, undermines the integrity of government, breaks laws, blocks needed reforms and repudiates a quality-competitive system with substantial consumer sovereignty. If radicalism is defined as a force against basic value systems of a society, then the corporate state is the chief protagonist."

"America, Inc." is an important book by Morton Mintz, an investigative reporter for The Washington Post, and Jerry S. Cohen, a lawyer who was chief counsel and staff director of the Senate Anti-Trust and Monopoly Subcommittee. The 522 chapter notes alone, pointing more often than not to obscure but valuable source documents, are worth the price. High-school and university economics courses all around the country should find it valuable. Lest Spiro worry, the book is all for making the American system work rather than replacing it: "The root of evil is concentrated economic power. It cannot be entrusted to either private or public hands."

This is the central thesis of the book: that too great a concentration of economic power (three companies for example, make 83 per cent of the autos in the United States) leads to all sorts of anti-competitive behavior (reduced innovation, high costs and prices, competitors frozen out), that is bad for the consumer, bad for the concentrated industry in the longer run, and ultimately bad for the United States, which attracts lower cost imports and sees its exports decline to the detriment of its balance of payments. "In most cases," the authors write, "such economic goals as better products and service at lower prices and such social goals as maximum individual freedom and initiative, can best be achieved in a society in which competition is the regulator of the economy."

A recent issue of the Yale Law Journal (Vol. 8, No. 3) contains an important study by Bradford C. Snell, a third-year law student, that makes a good companion piece to "America, Inc." He argues that the annual model-year style change practiced by the American automobile industry is an "unfair" trade practice, and Ralph Nader has joined with the editors of The Journal in a petition to the F.T.C. requesting an immediate investigation. Thus the number of independent auto producers reached a peak of 88 in 1921. By 1935 only 10 were left and today four producers remain. What happened? According to the study, General Motors in 1923 introduced annual change and that did it.

As an example of how style change works, the study shows that the Big Three spent $1.5-billion to change their 1969 models; yet the Bureau of Labor Statistics reported a net reduction in performance improvements of $3 per 1969 automobile. In other words, the Big Three "spent more than a billion and a half dollars *(Continued)*

Robert C. Townsend is the author of "Up the Organization."

to make their 1969 models seem 'new and different' in appearance."

The effect of this massive annual snow job has been to lock out competitors. "In 1970, it would cost a company $779 million to enter the automobile industry. The costs of annual style change capability, it is estimated, account for fully $724 million, or more than 90 per cent of this figure. . . . By contrast, had the industry not been restructured by annual style change, it is estimated that entry in 1970 could have been achieved for $55 million. . . .

"It has been noted that the innovative characteristics of the industry began to decline shortly after annual restyling was introduced in the 1920's. . By introducing a 'new' model each year, they provide customers with the illusion of progress, and yet avoid the necessity of adopting technological improvements which would lower maintenance or initial purchase cost. It has been argued, for instance, that application of known metallurgical processes would permit doubling the life of an automobile for an additional cost of $36 per year. Crash-absorption bumpers have been developed which could save the public $1 billion a year. . . . Pollution - free electric and steam vehicles can now be produced which would cost half as much to own and even less to operate than conventional gasoline automobiles.

"These developments, however, would increase automobile durability and thereby reduce demand, price and profits on new car sales. It is suspected, therefore, that the Big Three have repressed these cost-savings advances while offering consumers instead an annual restyling policy designed to bolster replacement demand through planned obsolescence." Those of us who have had a car repaired recently may suspect that they are repressing something else in order to feed their dealers' service departments. The Insurance Institute for Highway Safety released test data in March (Status Report Vol. 6 No. 5) showing that a 5 mile per hour impact on the front bumper of your 1971 Chevy Impala will produce $367 of damage, while the same impact on the rear bumper will produce $447. William Haddon, president of the Institute, told a Congressional subcommittee that the 1971 car models show a pattern of damage that "on balance appears to have worsened" from 1970 models.

It must be clear by now that the competitive system of free enterprise has long been dead and buried in the American automobile industry. "America, Inc." comes to the only possible conclusion: "Diffusion of economic power is indispensable to a society that aspires to be responsive to the rightful social and economic claims of free citizens. This does not mean a return to the backyard foundry, any more than diffusion of political power contemplates a return to the township as the ideal unit of government. But it does mean that the giant corporation must be broken up." Don't panic, stockholders. Your G.M. and your U.S. Steel will be worth substantially more to you when they are broken up into 20 or 30 well-financed, well-managed companies each.

The evils of concentration are not confined to the auto industry. Senator Gaylord Nelson is quoted in the book as saying, "Americans, ever suspicious of concentrated political power, have permitted concentrations of economic power to develop substantially unchallenged, that would make a Roman emperor gasp."

How concentrated economic power is translated into concentrated political power is found in the authors' treatment of the oil industry. Here is an overquick summary.

Fact: Using 1968 as an example, a mere 12 oil companies got one fifth of the after-tax profits of the 2,250 largest American companies surveyed by the First National City Bank of New York.

Fact: Because of special tax privileges (un-American?), oil companies pay Federal income taxes at a rate of about 8 per cent (about the same rate as a migrant worker) compared with 40 per cent for all corporations.

This is concentrated economic power; watch it become political power.

Fact: A majority of a White House Task Force appointed by Mr. Nixon in 1969 recommended *abolition* of the oil import quota system.

Fact: The Chairman, George P. Schultz, an economist and at the time a Cabinet member, testified to the effect that the quota system was a $5.2-billion dollar-a-year gouge out of the hides of American consumers, serving no purpose but to inflate the coffers of the major oil companies (heavy contributors to Mr. Nixon's 1968 campaign).

Fact: Mr. Nixon buried the reports, never referred to the majority recommendation, and reconstituted the committee with his ex-campaign chairman and Attorney General John Mitchell, replacing Schultz.

Fact: The new Oil Policy Committee, six months later, reached its decision to retain the oil import quota system "without any formal discussions or working papers by the responsible officials involved," according to Bernard Nossiter in The Washington Post.

The concentrated power of the oil industry is well known and resented. Mintz and Cohen note that "An extraordinary assessment of the role of oil appeared on June 25, 1969, in Ted Brooks's 'From the Oil Desk' column in The Wichita Eagle. In 'A Letter to Major Firms,' signed 'The Independent Independents,' Brooks said: We are writing to ask you to remove yourselves, your membership, your people and your influence from our trade associations and political groups . . . By our nature we are tied to local and regional economic communities. The proceeds of our small achievements stay with us. In one way or another they are almost entirely spread among our neighbors and business associates. The harvest you reap goes elsewhere. And when the harvest ends you go with it.

"Please do not tell us again about your contributions . . . in taxes, public works and doing good. We are grateful. But on the corporate level you clog our courts with your reluctance to pay taxes. You subvert the interests of our politicians with contributions we cannot hope to match. Your money warps our legislative process. Our officialdom is constantly reminded that those who play your game go on to greater awards than those who act only in the public interest. And this they do. . . .

"Wherever power, money and threats will obtain allegiance, you obtain it. The conventions and pronouncements of the American Association of Petroleum Geologists, a great scientific body, are beginning to sound like waterfront precinct meetings. The American Association of Petroleum Landsmen is dedicated to proving your worth. You have terrorized almost all of the marketing and jobbing associations into rubber-stamping your doctrines. The National Petroleum Council serves as your point of government infiltration and outright government-industry job-swapping. The American Petroleum Institute seeds our civic organizations with its propaganda. Shockingly, you even extend this to our schools, where our children are exposed to indoctrination in the beliefs that could insure the acceptability of your domination forever." Remember, now, these are small oil companies talking to big oil companies.

"America, Inc." has an ingenious solution: "To overthrow the government of oil, the legitimate government should establish a corporation of the TVA type to develop, exploit and sell oil shale, the black rock that, under heat, yields oil . . . ." They go on to explain that we have enough shale in parts of Colorado, Utah and Wyoming to supply oil for the whole country, at its present rate of consumption, for 2,000 years. With our oil reserves inside the country, we would not only be independent of Arabian potentates but could eliminate the hazards of salt water and beach pollution from offshore drilling and tanker spillage. And here's the best part: 80 per cent of the oil shale land belongs to the public — you and me.

Problem: How do you elect a President and a Congress with the guts to give up all those oil industry campaign contributions?

The book's other proposals make sense, too, to the extent that any proposals can make sense without the names of the people who are supposed to carry them out.

Recommendation: Corporations now pick one of the 50 states as their legal home—usually Delaware is picked for its lack of legal strictures (for example, a Delaware-chartered-company can now get away without having any annual meeting at all). To replace this system, the authors recommend that "Federal chartering of corporations . . . subject to safeguards such as a special court of appeals . . . would allow the legitimate government to recapture its proper role as the quarterback of the economy without new bureaucracy and without that meddling which is rightly condemned [they should have explained how this was to be accomplished] . . . it could be used to restructure certain concentrated industries . . . limit the business activities in which a business could engage . . . halt and reverse the conglomerate tide . . . The government would do this by utilizing its power to grant, modify and implement or revoke charters to achieve adherence to national goals and priorities as set forth in Federal statutes, such as those intended to preserve the environment. Yet the day-to-day implementing of national goals would be in private hands."

Recommendation: Reform the Federal crime laws so that penalties are felt by the responsible individuals behind the corporate veil. As Nader says in his introduction to "America, Inc.": "Suspension of corporate managers and board members, temporary bans on corporate advertising because of deceptive practices, requiring publication of convictions to inform consumers who have been harmed or deceived by culpable conduct, and imposing the sanction of environmental bankruptcy for a company continually contaminating its neighbors' environment are some suggestions that may effectively deter illegal behavior."

Recommendation: Enforce the antitrust laws against anti-competitive behavior.

Mintz and Cohen make other sensible recommendations, but it all gets down to this: break up the concentration of economic power. Until that is done, "we can fiddle with this and that, but true progress will elude us."

So what's new? Milton Friedman, the conservative economist, is quoted as saying that no form of government can be devised "which will not be taken over by vested economic interests and exploited for the preservation and enhancement of their own wealth." Most historians would surely agree.

I can see one slender chance that would prove all the experts wrong. Suppose there is a flood of people like those young Yale law students. Suppose they realize how big the stakes are; that in fact they are trying to save the two most hopeful systems the world has come up with yet—the democratic political system and the economic system of competitive free enterprise.

Suppose they are encouraged by the knowledge that privilege and corruption are not an inherent part of either system, but a cancerous illness.

Suppose they are tough enough not to fold when the establishment turns the full power of its propaganda to proving that these young challengers are un-American subversives in the employ of foreigners?

Suppose they are smart enough to realize that time is their enemy. They feel young and strong. The custodians of privilege look old. But privilege belongs to immortal corporations who have always been able to outlive their challengers.

Finally, and most important, suppose they are disciplined enough to resist the natural appeal of love, marriage and children so they can work like Nader — 20 hours a day, 7 days a week. Nader knows it's more fun to be thin and strong and uncomfortable and hungry and poor and alive working for his fellow man. But can enough of these bright young people try it for long enough to find out? How many will take the easy way and settle for being fat and weak and comfortable and satiated and rich and half-dead working for privilege?

It's getting late. The time to start is now. In the Consciousness Zero land of the corporate giants, competition where it counts is a joke, the market place where it matters is a myth, and what's left of free America is being eaten alive by a few hundred monster corporations while government branches, departments, bureaus and agencies serve as chefs, waiters and busboys. For would-be Naderites with the will to attempt the liberation of the country from its vampire-organizations, "America, Inc." is the manual and the manifesto to begin with. I wish I'd written it. ■

May 30, 1971

Nader Asserts Monopolies Mulct the Public of Billions

Report Charges Political Power Aids Giants in Blocking Antitrust Suits

By EILEEN SHANAHAN

Special to The New York Times

WASHINGTON, June 5—Ralph Nader and a team of his young investigators charged today that the American public was paying billions of dollars annually in higher prices, lost production, excessive pollution and lack of innovation because of the practices of monopolies that they said no one was trying to break up.

The nation is also paying in many ways for the political power that these economic giants have, not the least important aspect of which is the power to block antitrust suits against themselves, according to the report of Mr. Nader's study group.

Existing monopolies and "shared monopolies"—where a few companies control half or more of the production of an industry—must be broken up if competition and its benefits to the public are to be restored, the study said.

United Press International

Ralph Nader announcing study results yesterday.

It recommended new legislation to authorize the breaking up of most corporations with assets in excess of $2-billion but proposed that suits against "shared monopolies" be attempted under existing law.

The report of Mr. Nader's study group, entitled "The Closed Enterprise System," was prepared by a team of eight lawyers and economists under Mark J. Green, a 1970 graduate of the Harvard Law School.

It covers 1,148 typed pages and is based, among other things, on interviews with more than 500 past and present antitrust officials and others familiar with antitrust enforcement.

The report dwells at length on what is alleged to be politically motivated interference with antitrust cases. It details dozens of purported incidents in the last 20 years of intervention by members of Congress and of the White House staff—by no means all of which it said were successful, however.

To minimize the prospects of successful political intervention, the study group proposes requiring public disclosure of all contacts between business executives and top officials of the Justice Department "or anyone in the White House, including the President."

Recommended Rules

"The public officials involved would be under an affirmative obligation to match up their calendars with the filed reports to insure that none were omitted," it says. "The filings would be kept on public record for perusal by interested parties. Any meeting unreported by businessmen would be a Federal offense. Any meeting knowingly unconfirmed by the public official involved would be malfeasance of office, making him subject to removal."

As another deterrent to political influence on antitrust cases, the study recommends that the Assistant Attorney General in charge of the Antitrust Division be permitted to file civil antitrust suits and to convene grand juries to bring criminal cases, without the specific approval of the Attorney General in every instance. Other kinds of suits brought by the Justice Department—for example, tax evasion cases—do not have to be signed by the Attorney General, the report says.

If the Attorney General wishes to continue to review antitrust cases before they are filed, he should be required to state, in writing, his reasons for refusing to bring a case that the antitrust division recommended, the study proposes. The Attorney General's memorandum would be made public, except in cases where he overruled the filing of a criminal suit in which individuals were to be named as defendants.

Among the many other recommendations made by the study were the following:

¶An increase in the penalties for criminal violations of the antitrust laws, which cover such offenses as price fixing, to provide, among other things, minimum jail sentences, which do not exist now. Also an increase in the fines for criminal violations, which are now set at flat rates, to as much as 1 per cent of a guilty company's sales during the period of criminal activity.

¶A fivefold increase in the budget for antitrust enforcement to a total of $100-million annually. The present $20-million budget of the Justice Department's Antitrust Division and the Federal Trade Commission combined amounts to only two-thirds of this year's increase in the budget for the Federal Bureau of Investigation or one-fifth of the cost of one C-5A military plane.

¶An outright ban, by legislation, on any further mergers by the 500 largest industrial corporations, unless they simultaneously divest themselves of assets of the same value as those they are acquiring through a new merger.

¶A breakup of "shared monopolies," sometimes also called oligopolies, so that no industry would have four concerns accounting for more than 50 per cent of total output or eight companies for more than 70 per cent. Studies have demonstrated that these are the points "where competition stops," the study says.

¶Repeal of the Federal laws that permit states to enact so-called fair trade laws, which allow manufacturers to dictate the prices at which retailers sell their products.

¶A merger of the Justice Department's Antitrust Division and the Federal Trade Commission into a single Competing Protection Agency, because having two agencies now "unwittingly divides and conquers."

Large portions of the study dealt with the effectiveness of of antitrust enforcement under the different officials who have held the various key jobs during the last 20 years.

Kitzenbach Criticized

The worst marks were given to the Johnson Administration; the first Attorney General appointed by Mr. Johnson, Nicholas deB. Katzenbach, and the man who was head of the Antitrust division during most of Mr. Katzenbach's time as Attorney General, Donald F. Turner, who has returned to his professorship at the Harvard Law School.

Mr. Katzenbach was accused of not being interested in antitrust matters and of being easily swayed by political pressures. Mr. Turner was accused of not having the courage of the strong antitrust convictions that he expressed in extensive writings, both before and after he was Assistant Attorney General.

The present head of the antitrust division, Richard W. McLaren, was given a mixed grade. He was praised for filing suits against conglomerate mergers —those having companies in completely different industries —but was criticized for his belief that there was no need to attempt to break up existing concentrations of business power, because changing technology would bring in new competitors.

Mr. McLaren was also inferentially praised for fighting hard, reportedly to the point of threatening resignation, for two anti-merger cases he wanted to file, which Deputy Attorney General Richard G. Kleindienst allegedly attempted to block.

2 Merger Cases

One attacked the acquisition of Canteen Corporation by International Telephone and Telegraph Corporation and the other sought to block the merger of two drug concerns—the Warner-Lambert Company and Parke Davis and Company. The I.T.T.-Canteen case was filed by the Justice Department and the Warner-Lambert matter was turned over to the Federal Trade Commission, which subsequently filed suit.

A Justice Department spokesman issued a statement denying that Mr. McLaren had threatened to resign over either of these cases.

The statement did not deny assertions that Mr. McLaren had been overruled in other cases—for example, that he had wanted to investigate allegedly illegal reciprocal buying arrangements in the oil industry but had been overruled by Attorney General John N. Mitchell.

Mr. Katzenbach denied that he had yielded to political pressures in any of his decisions against bringing specific antitrust cases. The decisions were always made on the merits of the case, he said.

But he added that Mr. Nader's "muckraking" approach had "proved successful in calling public attention to such problems as auto safety and environmental pollution." He added: "If this report results in more public interest in antitrust enforcement, then I think it relatively unimportant that many of its facts are wrong and its judgments biased."

Mr. Turner, who conceded the accuracy of many of the study's statements about cases that were not brought, quarreled with the conclusion that the reasons were political.

For example, he said that he thought then and thinks now that it would have been a good idea to bring suit to force the American Telephone and Telegraph Company to divest itself of its manufacturing subsidiary. But, he said, there were "perfectly legitimate reasons" why Mr. Katzenbach said no — among them, that there was some doubt of the legality of attacking a corporate relationship that had been sanctioned by a decree signed by the Justice Department in the Eisenhower Administration.

Mr. Turner and others also contested the interpretation made by the Nader study group of the failure of a series of Attorneys General to file suits to break up the General Motors Corporation. The reply boiled down to assertions that the various cases proposed by the antitrust division staff at various times were never solid enough.

The charges of attempted interference in antitrust cases by members of Congress included allegations involving Representative Emanuel Celler, Democrat of Brooklyn, the chairman of the House Antitrust Subcommittee, who is said to have intervened on behalf of clients of his law firm.

Mr. Celler could not be reached for comment on the charges, which have been made publicly before, nor could former Senator Eugene J. McCarthy, Democrat of Minnesota, who reportedly succeeded in blocking a criminal case against some bankers in Minnesota, although a civil suit was brought.

In about half the cases of alleged intervention by members of Congress that were detailed in the report, the reported attempts to influence the Justice Department were unsuccessful.

The study group did not make any new economic analysis of its own to determine what the public was losing because of monopolies. It relied on previously published studies by several economists to reach its conclusion that the costs of monopoly were running between $48-billion and $60-billion a year.

The report also assailed the widely held idea that larger companies were the most efficient. It said that it was not the intent of anti-trust advocates to fragment big companies into units so small they would not be efficient but into units of the most effective size.

The study named 12 industries that it said the antitrust divisions staff, under Mr. Turner, had found "promising" targets for suits against "shared monopolies" of two or three companies. They were: electric lamps, tires and tubes, flat glass, steel ingots, automobiles, metal containers, explosives, sulphur, primary batteries, carbon and graphite, cereals, and auto rentals. Less likely prospects for successful shared monopoly cases were found in the transformer, copper, truck and gypsum industries.

June 6, 1971

Nader Antitrust Report

Study Offers Cases Showing the Cost To Consumers of Market Concentration

By LEONARD S. SILK

The massive report on antitrust policy just released by Ralph Nader, the consumer advocate, and his team of young investigators is full of cases to beguile businessmen and students of industrial economics. Here are some examples:

¶Between 1953 and 1961, 100 tablets of the antibiotic drug tetracycline retailed for about $51. This price was set by an illegal conspiracy of some of the nation's biggest pharmaceutical companies. Ten years later, after the exposure of Congressional hearings and indictment under the antitrust laws, the price of tetracycline for the same quantity was about $5, a 90 per cent decrease.

¶In the early nineteen-sixties, an international cartel cornered the world market in quinine, which is taken mostly by older people to restore their natural heart rhythm. The price of quinine was raised from 37 cents an ounce to $2.13 an ounce.

¶In 1964, the price of bread in the United States averaged 20 cents a loaf. In Seattle, a local price-fixing conspiracy set the price of bread at 24 cents a loaf. When a Federal Trade Commission ruling ended the conspiracy, the Seattle price began to decline and reached the national average in 1966. During the 10 years of the price conspiracy, however, consumers in the Seattle-Tacoma area paid an estimated $35-million extra for bread.

¶In the early nineteen-sixties, nearly all of the country's manufacturers of plumbing fixtures met secretly and decided to produce only the most expensive sinks and toilets, charging uniformly high prices. Consumers had to purchase these "Cadillacs" of plumbing fixtures.

None of these cases cited by the Nader group would have surprised Adam Smith, the founding father of modern economics. Smith disliked cooperation among businessmen as much as he did Government regulation of business.

Few American businessmen would attempt to justify price fixing—at least publicly — or would attack the antitrust laws in principle.

Hofstadter's View

As the late Richard Hofstadter, the historian, put it, "Visitations by the Department of Justice are a nuisance, lawsuits are expensive and prosecution carries an unpleasant stigma, but the anti-trust procedures can be considered an alternative to more obtrusive regulation, such as outright controls on prices. At any rate, big business has never found it necessary or expedient to launch a public compaign against antitrust enforcement; the pieties at stake are too deep to risk touching."

However, where concentration of industry is concerned, rather than a price conspiracy, most businessmen refuse to accept the idea that antitrust and anti-merger actions serve consumer interests.

The Nader report seeks to offer cases to show the costs to consumers of market concentration. For instance, it mentions a case of market concentration in the Duluth-Superior area of Minnesota, where three big milk companies accounted for more than 90 per cent of all the milk sold. By contrast, in the Minneapolis-St. Paul area there was a large number of competing milk companies and it was easy for new concerns to enter the market.

A 33% Difference

Despite similar production and distribution costs for milk in the two markts, the wholesale price for a half gallon of milk in 1967 was 33.8 cents in Minneapolis-St. Paul and 45 cents in Duluth-Superior, a 33 per cent difference.

The report also noted that in the mid-nineteen-sixties most university students were paying 25 cents a page to have their papers copied by machine. As competition among copying services grew, the price fell to between 2 cents and 5 cents a page. The service became faster and the machines more conveniently located.

But champions of highly concentrated markets argue that the great size of corporations produces many efficiencies and encourages technological innovation.

The Nader group maintains that the reputed efficiencies of large-scale operations are overrated and become inefficiencies when the scale grows too large. The fact is, however, hat economists lack careful quantitative evidence on the ptimal size of companies.

Little detailed work has been done since the reports in the nineteen-thirties of the Temporary National Economic Committee. That study found considerable variations of efficiency among companies of different size in different industries.

Most economists now contend that economies of size are frequently outweighed by the greater efficiency that results from sharp market competition. Their view is that competition is also a spur to technological innovation.

Brookings Study

This position is documented in a study done for the Brookings Institution, "Technological Change in Regulated Industries," edited by Associate Dean William M. Capron of the John Fitzgerald Kennedy School of Government at Harvard University. The study reached the over-all conclusion that competition should be increased even in the regulated industries as a stimulant to technological advancement.

In the Brookings study, Prof. William G. Shepherd of the University of Michigan urges the Federal Communications Commission to seek ways to introduce competition into certain parts of the telecommunications industry — for instance, in the large-scale transmission of date, use of domestic satellites, alternatives to land-based transmission and the supply of equipment.

Prof. Almarin Phillips of the University of Pennsylvania finds that the Civil Aeronautics Board, by legalizing a price-fixing monopoly, has diverted competition in the airlines to nonprice factors, including not only speed or convenience but in-flight amenities. Regulation of the airlines has bred excess capacity and low profits, according to Professor Phillips.

Aaron J. Gellman of the Budd Company and the University of Pennsylvania concludes that the Interstate Commerce Commission, through minimum rate regulation, has stifled innovation in surface freight transportation by denying carriers the right to reduce rates when new low-cost equipment is introduced. Mr. Gellman argues that innovative performance in the transport industry can best be improved by gradually eliminating regulation and by encouraging intermodal transport concerns to develop.

Reportedly, the Nixon Administration is toying with the idea of deregulating transportation. But some economists are worried that the Administration might deregulate only transportation prices and rates, but not entry.

Economists' Fear

The economists fear that if tight and highly concentrated market structures are preserved, the deregulation of prices would hurt rather than benefit consumers and transportation users.

It is significant that, as the economists—both liberal and conservative — move back toward Adam Smith in their respect for competition, the young lawyers are heading back toward Teddy Roosevelt and the trust-busting movement.

This combination of trends is one that big business cannot ignore.

June 16, 1971

I. T. T. Under Fire

Growth Produces Criticism Of Power, Tactics

By MICHAEL C. JENSEN

Harold S. Geneen, the 61-year-old president, chairman and chief executive of the International Telephone & Telegraph Corporation, listened carefully as Representative Emanuel Celler, chairman of the House Antitrust subcommittee, spelled out in earthy terms his opinion of the giant, Geneen-built conglomerate.

"Having this great economic concentration in your company," said Rep. Celler, Democrat of Brooklyn, "you remind me of what somebody said before this committee some years ago: 'Every man for himself, said the elephant as he danced amongst the chickens.' "

Mr. Geneen, who last year was the country's highest-paid executive at $766,000, responded that he sometimes felt more like the chicken than the elephant, but he quite clearly was unable to generate any great feeling of sympathy in the Washington, hearing room.

That exchange took place nearly two years ago, and in the intervening months the nation's eighth largest industrial concern has been almost steadily under fire for its concentration of industrial power and its business tactics.

In the last 10 years, under Mr. Geneen's rigid control, I.T.T. has grown from a modest $811-million, foreign-oriented communications company with telephone subsidiaries in South America and Europe, to a $6.4-billion conglomerate with a balanced mix between United States and European sales in a variety of fields.

By virtue of its acquisitions, I.T.T. is a major factor in the rental-car business (Avis), hotels (Sheraton), bread and cakes (Continental Baking) and life insurance (Hartford).

Partly as a result of all this merger activity, the company has been investigated or criticized by Ralph Nader, the Justice Department, the Securities and Exchange Commission, the Federal Trade Commission and the American Institute of Certified Public Accountants, to name a few.

In the most dramatic development to occur during the last few years, I.T.T. agreed in July to divest itself of some of its largest subsidiaries and to sharply limit its future United States acquisitions.

Notwithstanding the barrage of criticism aimed at the company, however, Mr. Geneen has been able to put together an impressive record of consistent earnings growth, and in the process has given I.T.T. a solid standing with Wall Street.

In fact, so successful has he been in building I.T.T. sales, and profits that many analysts feel the most serious problem facing the company is not whether the Government will allow it to grow domestically but what will

Net Income by Groups

Millions of dollars

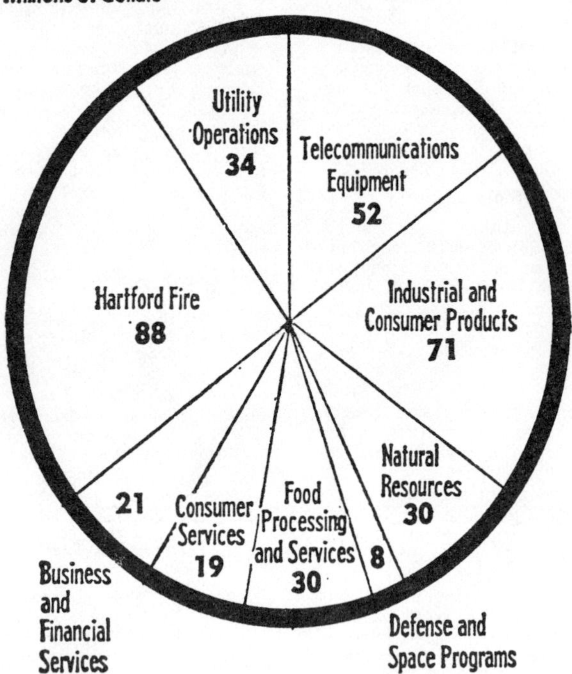

happen when Mr. Geneen reaches retirement age four years from now.

Certainly he has overshadowed the company in a way that is seldom seen today but was characteristic of an earlier generation of industrial titans like Alfred P. Sloan Jr. of General Motors and Andrew Carnegie, the steel magnate.

Mr. Geneen is known as a tough-talking, demanding, sometimes 20-hour-a-day executive who has virtually sacrificed his personal life to build I.T.T. to its present position, and he expects nothing less from his top lieutenants.

"He doesn't mess around," said one former I.T.T. vice president who worked for Mr. Geneen during his early days with the company. "I remember one meeting he started off by saying: 'Gentlemen, I've been thinking. Bull times zero is zero bull. Bull divided by zero is infinity bull. And I'm sick and tired of the bull you've been feeding me.' "

Very little bull is fed to Mr. Geneen these days. His "red-flag" system of spotting disasters before they happen, his marathon monthly meetings of top management and his midnight telephone calls and late-night conferences with key operating and staff executives have been well publicized.

The highlight of the Geneen career at I.T.T. was the country's biggest merger in history—the $1.5-billion acquisition of the Hartford Fire Insurance Company.

Challenged by the Federal Government and a host of other agencies and consumer advocates, the deal finally was allowed by the Justice Department provided Mr. Geneen would give up other assets, including Avis, Levitt and some other lesser operations.

The consent agreement is still before the courts, so for the moment, on the advice of his lawyers, neither Mr. Geneen nor any of his executives is talking to the press. For that matter I.T.T. relations with the press have frequently been stormy, and the company has been accused of using excessive zeal in getting its point across.

It is possible to paint a reasonably comprehensive picture of the company's prospects and operating methods by interviewing former I.T.T. officers, executives who worked for Mr. Geneen at other companies, security analysts, Government officials, competitors, friends and critics.

Although life at I.T.T. under Harold Geneen has never been placid, it has been hitting an unusually frenetic pace in recent months.

Overhanging the company are a report scheduled to be issued almost any day by the House subcommittee on Antitrust and an investigation by the Securities and Exchange Commission into (1) the tactics used by I.T.T. in its merger with Hartford Fire Insurance and (2) some alleged insider trading of stock by company officers and directors that took place within weeks of the announcement of the consent agreement.

The House report, which is 703 pages long, will include on analysis of the problems stemming from concentration of industry, with separate chapters devoted to I.T.T. and five other conglomerates: Litton Industries, Ling-Temco-Vought, Gulf & Western, Leasco and National General.

And while the S.E.C. would not discuss its investigation, it is understood that the commission is taking a close look at the circumstances surrounding the insurance company merger and at the sale of stock by five I.T.T. vice presidents, the company's secretary and the chairman of Hartford Fire Insurance in advance of I.T.T.'s agreement with the Justice Department.

The announcement of the agreement sent I.T.T. common stock down seven points to 55 on the New York Stock Exchange during the first trading day after the consent announcement. The stock has since recovered to about the 60-level, but continues below its 1971 high of 67.375 recorded earlier this year.

Two I.T.T. executives failed to report their stock sales within 10 days after the month in which they were transacted, as required by S.E.C. rules, an omission which an I.T.T. spokesman attributed to an "oversight." The company has denied any wrongdoing and said the officers involved were either unaware of the consent discussions, or sold their stock well before any sign of an agreement was visible.

Although the insider stock-trading topic is controversial at the moment, defended by some of the company's alumni as innocent and viewed more skeptically by others, there is little doubt that the company's stock is well regarded by the public and by Wall Street analysts.

Most of the security analysts who follow I.T.T. closely are convinced that the consent agreement will help the company rather than hurt it, and are recommending either retention or purchase of its shares.

"We are convinced that I.T.T. will be able to accom-

What If He Didn't Work?

"What does Hal Geneen do when he isn't working? Well for a start I'd have to say that he hardly ever doesn't work. There were many nights when I'd leave the office at 10 or 11 P.M., and he was still there working. Then he'd take three or four briefcases home with him."

The speaker was Henry E. Bowes, executive vice president of the Bell & Howell Company, and a former senior vice president at I.T.T. during the early and mid-nineteen-sixties.

What Mr. Bowes said was reinforced by other acquaintances of Mr. Geneen. Despite a deep enjoyment of hunting quail and partridge, of fishing and an occasional golf match, the I.T.T. head almost never forgets business.

"He does let down on the golf course, sometimes," said Mr. Bowes. "One time he went a whole nine holes without asking a question."

Although Mr. Geneen is often portrayed as a man with simple tastes, he maintains a Fifth Avenue apartment in Manhattan, and homes in Key Biscayne, Fla., and Oyster Harbors on Cape Cod. He is driven about in a chauffeured limousine and wears expensive tailored suits, friends say.

"The thing he doesn't go in for," said one associate, "is the social thing. I don't know that he's ever thrown a really big social party."

Mr. Geneen's first marriage ended in divorce, and at present he is married to his former secretary from Bell & Howell. He has no children, and, acquaintances say, he has little family life.

"He just never lets up," said one old business associate. "You look behind those glasses and the wheels are going around about 100 miles an hour."

What would make Mr. Geneen leave I.T.T., largely his creation, and certainly his monument?

"I have a feeling," said one friend, "that if he had the chance to go to Washington as Secretary of Commerce or Treasury, something like that, he might consider it to be an appropriate high point in his career."

plish its growth objectives [10 to 12 per cent annually] with Hartford Fire, which already has profits three times that of all the areas being divested combined," said one analyst.

"As for limitations on future acquisitions, it should be noted that I.T.T. has really not made any major acquisitions for the past couple of years and . . . acquisitions can still be made abroad."

Not every investor, of course, is totally enchanted with the company. Dr. John N. Stone, a Michigan optometrist, complained that he was uneasy over the I.T.T. takeover of Europe Fund International, in which he said his 1,400 shares of Eurofund were converted into 497 shares of I.T.T.

"With Eurofund," he said, "I felt I was an investor, with I.T.T. a speculator."

Perhaps the most fascinating and talked-about factor in I.T.T.'s remarkable growth story is Harold Geneen, who proudly boasts about the company's unbroken string of 48 consecutive quarters in which earnings were higher than the equivalent quarter the year before.

The hard-driving chief executive's most obvious characteristic is his toughness and his refusal to accept failure, or even a slowing down of accomplishment.

"When he wants to shave expenses, he just does it," said one executive who worked for Mr. Geneen in his pre-I.T.T. days. "I remember one time I got an order from Geneen that said 'get rid of two bodies, one male and one female.' Those were his exact words.

"I fired the girl, but I had just hired a young man, who moved his family from another state and quit his job to join us. So I took him off the payroll and moved him to a remote office. I paid him for three months out of my expense account. Then Geneen moved to another company, and I brought this fellow back out into the open."

A self-made man, the British born Mr. Geneen, now a naturalized citizen, attended New York University at night and started his business career as a runner on Wall Street.

After a succession of executive jobs with Bell & Howell, Jones & Laughlin Steel and the Raytheon Company, he was hired to head I.T.T. This was reportedly after a series of disputes with Charles F. Adams, Raytheon's chief executive, who allegedly refused to make Mr. Geneen president of the company.

At I.T.T. Mr. Geneen has surrounded himself with executives who, like himself, are willing to subordinate their personal lives to the success of the company, associates say.

"He's got them by their limousines," said one alumnus who is a fan of Mr. Geneen but was not willing to maintain the pace.

Certainly the pay is excellent. In addition to his salary and bonus of $766,000 last year, Mr. Geneen exercised stock options worth $795,000 on paper at the time of exercise between Jan. 1, 1970, and March 10, 1971.

His top managers are also paid better than most chief executives in the world. Last year his five top officers were paid more than $200,000 each in salary and bonus.

"I'll tell you how he got me in there," said one man who worked for Mr. Geneen during his early years at I.T.T.

"He asked me what I was earning, and I said $40,000 in salary and $10,000 in bonus. 'I'll give you $80,000, plus $20,000,' he said.

"Then he asked me if I liked to travel, and I said yes, so he said he'd put me on the international board and guarantee me a trip to Europe every quarter.

"He asked me if I was on the board of directors at my company, and I said no, so he said that although he couldn't promise anything, he'd try to get me on at I.T.T., and he did. Then he asked me if I had stock options and I said no, so he said he'd get them for me. Let me ask you, how can you resist that kind of thing?"

Among the executives who have resisted are some who headed companies acquired by Mr. Geneen.

"What you have to adapt to," said one former company president who decided not to stay under the Geneen umbrella, "is a total loss of independence.

"Everything has to be cleared by his staff—every press release, every man you hire at a salary over $30,000. I just found it was asinine and refused to do it.

"But you know the guy has put together 48 consecutive quarters and when he says 'march,' you march."

One former Geneen executive who served with him both on his headquarters staff and as an operating official said: "Geneen has

1960

Sales $811.4-million

Profits $30.6-million

1970

Sales $6.4-billion

Profits $353.3-million

In a little more than a decade Harold S. Geneen has built I.T.T. into the nation's eighth largest concern through an aggressive acquisition program. But in recent years the giant has come under increasing scrutiny by Government agencies, consumer groups and accountants for its concentration of industrial power and business tactics.

been accused of chewing people up and spitting them out. Thats not true. He attracts achievers, people who like to get things done.

"Some guys get tired and feel they don't want to live in that environment of driving themselves so hard. The name of the game is to get profits up more than 10 per cent every quarter."

When Mr. Geneen joined I.T.T. in 1959 he inherited a company that had most of its sales abroad, and had suffered badly from expropriations during World War II.

He immediately embarked on a program to diversify the concern both geographically and by activity. Domestic sales now account for about 58 per cent of the company's business, a ratio Mr. Geneen feels is right for I.T.T.

The company has slightly more than 200 subsidiaries in North America, Europe, Africa, the Middle East, Latin America, the Far East and the Pacific.

Only about 19 per cent of the concern's sales are now in telecommunications equipment, I.T.T.'s original franchise.

Some 29 per cent are in industrial and consumer products, 19 per cent in food processing and services, 13 per cent in consumer services and the rest scattered in natural resources, defense and space programs, business and financial services and utility operations.

To cope with this diversity, Mr. Geneen has developed a highly structured system of management meetings and reports, and he keeps more than a dozen brief cases stuffed with reports for reading at home, on planes and during other recesses from the office.

Much of this is designed to prevent unpleasant surprises. "Hardly a year went by," said one former I.T.T. executive, "without some manager saying everything was rosy all year, and then you'd go into the December meeting and he'd be losing a couple of million dollars. When that happened, the key people involved were either fired or transferred to Outer Siberia."

"He's tough," said one former manger. "Geneen himself will walk right up to the ragged edge. But he has a fantastic feeling for the use of money. He foresaw the trend toward service industries, for example."

One area in which Mr. Geneen has been accused of getting a bit too close to the "ragged edge" is in accounting procedures. And although his former managers defend his accounting as imaginative but relatively conservative, compared with other free-wheeling conglomerates, not all observers feel that way.

One advisory firm recently questioned whether "the market [will] continue to accept at face value I.T.T.'s apparent earnings growth? Or will it begin to look more deeply behind reported earnings and assign a lower price-earnings ratio?"

Although I.T.T. earns high marks in most categories, particularly in consistent earnings performance, it has not been at the top of the list in return on equity. A study by Forbes magazine early this year said I.T.T. ranked only 26th among 40 conglomerates in five-year return on equity, and was 317th among all companies.

Furthermore, the study said, I.T.T. ranked 17th among 43 conglomerates in five-year annual sales growth (29.8 per cent) and 12th of the 43 in five-year annual growth of earnings per share (10.8 per cent).

One of the most widely discussed questions among I.T.T.-watchers these days is who will replace Mr. Geneen when he reaches the mandatory retirement age of 65. The most frequently mentioned candidates are the obvious ones: Executive vice presidents Richard E. Bennett, Francis J. Dunleavy, James V. Lester, Hart Perry and Ted B. Westfall.

Most observers, however, feel that no matter who is picked, the company will change its operating techniques once Mr. Geneen steps down, if, in fact, he does — there is a school of thought that says he might continue in the chief executive's slot for many years, first having gotten the mandatory retirement rule changed.

Perhaps the most appropriate quotation regarding a Geneen retirement is the answer given by Thomas Jefferson when he was asked whether he was replacing Benjamin Franklin as envoy to Paris.

"I succeed him," said Mr. Jefferson. "No one could replace him."

September 5, 1971

G.M. Said to View Antitrust Efforts

By JERRY M. FLINT
Special to The New York Times

DETROIT, Sept. 21—The centralization of the General Motors Corporation is tied at least in part to an effort to make the company more difficult to break up in antitrust actions, according to Automotive News, a trade publication.

There is no question that the centralizing of General Motors is under way and is being pushed by its president, Edward N. Cole.

The change in management direction is particularly noteworthy because the auto maker grew to be the largest manufacturer in the world under a system of decentralized operating divisions, and the management theories were created by Alfred P. Sloan Jr., who led G.M. as president or chairman from 1923 to 1956.

Market Growth Cited

Mr. Cole's own explanation for the drive to centralize G.M. operations has been tied to the growth of the market, the proliferation of vehicle types, the pressure for safety and pollution controls that need central direction and increasing costs.

The heart of G.M. operations is its car divisions. At one time

United Press International
Edward N. Cole

these five divisions controlled the design, manufacture and sales of their vehicles, within guidelines set by the General Motors organization. Now, said Automotive News in an article in its Sept. 20 issue, these divisions appear to be turning into mere sales organizations.

For years G.M.'s competitors, the Ford Motor Company and the Chrysler Corporation, tried to imitate the G.M. divisional pattern, but both gave up, finally setting up product-design, engineering and manufacturing units distinct from the car divisions, which became sales and service organizations. Now General Motors appears to be creating an organization more like its competitors.

Mr. Sloan, in his book, "My Years With General Motors," called the G.M. organization "a happy medium in industrial organization between the extremes of pure centralization and pure decentralization."

The General Motors Corporation had no comment on the Automotive News story or on questions about the centralizing process within the concern.

The article noted that the Chevrolet division of G.M. as of Oct. 1 would be out of the car-building business, turning its last car assembly plants over to the G.M. assembly division. This will give the assembly division control of 18 of 24 G.M. assembly plants, and more are expected to follow.

In putting at least part of the reason for this change to an effort to stymie antitrust, Automotive News said that Mr. Cole "reportedly told a conclave of G.M. executives, some 10 years ago, that he would like to centralize operations to make it tougher for the Justice Department to break up the corporation," although the Government has never attempted to break up General Motors.

Mr. Cole, who became president in 1967, has often talked about changes in General Motors that would lead to centralization, but he has not mentioned antitrust. For example, in a lengthy speech to the G.M. middle management in 1966, before he was president, he called for more coordination of the total corporate effort, a stronger role for centralized engineering and styling teams and stronger leadership for the G.M. Technical Center.

These ideas were aimed at holding down the costs and problems caused by product proliferation and duplicated efforts.

Mr. Sloan in his book said, "General Motors' long-term survival depends upon its being operated in both the spirit and the substance of decentralization."

September 22, 1971

Advance Publicity In Antitrust Case Ordered by Judge

By EILEEN SHANAHAN
Special to The New York Times

WASHINGTON, June 13—In the first such order ever issued, a Federal judge is requiring the Government to publicize widely the terms of settlement of an antitrust case before the settlement becomes final.

The case involves two trade groups that were accused of having conspired to block the sale of foreign-made steam boilers in the United States by denying the foreign products the safety certifications that are required by law in many localities.

The idea behind the judge's order was that persons other than those directly involved in the case should have an opportunity to learn of the settlement and have time to file a protest if they found the terms of the settlement inadequate.

The order was issued yesterday by David N. Edelstein, chief judge of the United States District Court for the Southern District of New York. Details of the settlement and of the judge's requirement for publicizing it were announced today.

In issuing the order, to which

The New York Times
Judge David N. Edelstein

the parties in the case agreed, Judge Edelstein called it "a historic first."

The order requires that an advertisement, detailing the terms of the proposed settlement, be published in seven consecutive issues of The New York Times, as a paper of general circulation, and of The New York Law Journal, as a paper seen by lawyers.

The advertisement will specifically invite comments on the settlement from interested members of the public and tell them where they may obtain or inspect copies of the basic documents in the case.

Anyone who wishes to comment on the settlement has 60 days from today in which to do so.

Under ordinary procedures for settling antitrust cases, the settlements become final within 30 days after being filed with a court. Judge Edelstein proposed the extension of time.

Procedures Criticized

The judge's action, which did not appear to imply that he saw anything wrong with the settlement of this specific case, followed mounting criticism of the procedures for settling antitrust cases from antitrust lawyers and from such organizations as Ralph Nader's antitrust study group.

The criticism intensified following disclosure of the involvement of a White House staff member in the settlement last year of cases against the International Telephone and Telegraph Corporation.

The basic thrust of the criticism has been that parties other than the defendants and the Justice Department should have a greater opportunity than they do now to challenge antitrust settlements that they believe are not in the public interest.

Up until the early nineteen-sixties, there was no opportunity for participation by third parties in antitrust settlements, which were announced and made final simultaneously.

Attorney General Robert F. Kennedy, heeding criticism that had been heaped on his predecessors,, adopted the procedure of announcing settlements 30 days before they became final. Dissatisfied parties could then ask for changes in the settlements, and n a few cases they have been successful. But no procedures for publicizing the settlements, beyond issuance of a Justice Department press release, were employed.

The current case involves the American Society of Mechanical Engineers, Inc., and the National Board of Boiler and Pressure Vessel Inspectors.

According to the Justice Department's original complaint, which was filed in July, 1970, the two organizations conspired illegally to deny certain safety certifications and stamps to foreign-made boilers and pressure vessels. Forty-two states and many local governments require such certifications of boilers.

The complaint said that a majority of the members of the committees of the two organizations that dealt with the safety certifications were officers or employes of domestic manufacturers of boilers or pressure vessels or their suppliers or insurers.

As is true in all settlements of antitrust cases, the accused parties did not admit that they had engaged in the illegal conduct that was alleged. But they agreed to take a number of steps aimed at making such illegal behavior impossible in the future.

Among other things, they agreed to inaugurate within 90 days "a fair, reasonable and nondiscriminatory procedure enabling foreign manufacturers who meet the requirements" to receive safety certifications and stamps "on an equal basis with domestic manufacturers."

Provisions involving licensing of inspectors on a nondiscriminatory basis are also included in the settlement.

June 14, 1972

The Companies We Keep

By NOEL PERRIN

THETFORD CENTER, Vt.—In the last ten years a good many Americans have begun to feel surrounded by a few monster corporations. I.T.T. is only one example. It is quite an example, I admit. I.T.T. owns Sheraton Hotels, Avis cars, Morton Frozen Foods, "Who's Who in America," the City Window Cleaning Company of Central Ohio, Bobbs Merrill, Levitt and Sons, and something over four hundred other companies. You almost can't live in the United States and not too easily in Europe without sooner or later being an I.T.T. customer.

But I.T.T. is not the only company with tentacles. Another conglomerate, Litton Industries, sells you Stouffer foods when you're hungry, Rust furnaces when you're cold, books (seven different companies) when you're bored. Should you want to build a house, it has two real estate companies to sell you land; and if instead you decide to build a cabin in the woods, a company (New Britain Machine) to sell you the hand tools. Charge any of these purchases, and you will use a plastic credit card made by still another Litton company. On the other hand, if you pay by check, you can expect to use one made by its Checkmaster subsidiary, or perhaps by its quite separate Check Printers of America. Not bad for a company only nineteen years old. Think what it will be like at thirty.

The whole economy is like this. The New Yorker who gets tired of Sealtest ice cream with all its adulterants and buys a quart of Breyer's to try a brand with natural ingredients may be amused—or may feel slightly paranoid—when he discovers in the fine print on the carton that he has merely moved from one division of Kraft to another. Serious paranoids tend to think that if they write a letter to one of the monsters, say a letter protesting its involvement in war manufactures, the very stationery they write on will turn out to be made by the company. Nor is this simply paranoia.

If you did write to Litton about the destroyers and bombers it makes, you might perfectly well sit at a desk it also makes (Lehigh-Leopold Furniture and Standard Desk are both Litton companies), type with one of its Royal typewriters, use its Valentine or Fitchbury paper.

Then there is the slightly smaller monster called Textron. If you write to Textron about its helicopters or target location systems, you could use your Shaeffer pen to write on your fashionable Eaton stationery, or perhaps type on Berkshire or Camp typing paper. You'd have been Textron all the way. Later you could go into bathroom, put up a new soap dish, rub on a little British Sterling after-shave lotion, pull up your Talon zipper, adjust your Maico hearing aid, and still never have left Textron. The bride who choose Gorham sterling is a Textron girl. Quite possibly anybody who picketed Textron would find they had made his picket sign.

Is there no escaping the tentacles? I think there is. At least there's something small companies could do, so we would know who they are. It's a device adopted long ago by English pubs.

Anyone who has been to England knows that most pubs are like Avis and Gorham, that is, wholly owned subsidiaries. The giant English beer companies own strings of hundreds each. Visit a picturesque little pub in Cambridgeshire called The Volunteer, and you will find from the quaint wooden sign out front that it is a wholly owned subsidiary of Greene, King & Co. Stop in at The Star and Garter, and you see it belongs to Tolly Ales.

But a few pubs are not like that. I can remember on my first day in England being taken to one in London called The Spaniard. It isn't anybody's subsidiary, and the sign out front read proudly, "The Spaniard. FREE HOUSE." I found the phrase as stirring as a bugle call.

Those American companies which have not yet been swallowed by some conglomerate could easily take over the device, and I think it would bring them a host of new customers. Suppose, for example, there were two brands of strawberry jam on a supermarket shelf, one called Aunt Ruth's and the other called Aunt Sally's. Suppose the small print on one said Aunt Ruth's Home Foods, Los Angeles, Cal., a division of the Minnesota Mining & Manufacturing Co., and on the other it said Aunt Sally's Preserves, Canton, Ohio, A Free Company. I wonder which would sell better, especially to people under thirty.

In fact, I wonder if even so small a change as that might not begin to deconglomerate the conglomerates.

Noel Perrin is professor of English at Dartmouth College.

September 18, 1972

New Challenges in Antitrust

Companies Increasingly File Their Own Suits

By ERNEST HOLSENDOLPH

In 1968 when the Control Data Corporation filed its private antitrust suit against the International Business Machines Corporation the move was a momentous one.

Private antitrust suits were not common at that time, but they were quietly on the rise. There had been Trans World Airlines' suit against the Hughes Tool Company, which was filed in 1961, but rarely had two such prominent corporate names been involved in this type of litigation.

In times past, when an executive felt abused by "monopolistic" competition, he took his medicine quietly, if not altogether sportingly. There was always the chance that one of the big brothers —the Federal Trade Commission or the Justice Department's antitrust division —just might charge out of Washington to the rescue.

But times change. In a quiet but almost inexorable way, corporate behavior in this area has changed in the last decade. When the Bell & Howell Company took the initiative the other day and filed an antitrust action against the giant Eastman Kodak Company, it was just the latest action underlining the trend.

Companies are now willing to use private initiative —and their own dollars — to get relief from alleged monopolistic practices.

Laws previously used to punish are now being used affirmatively. For instance, Control Data, which settled its suit with I.B.M. out of court last week, substantially changed its mix of activities when it gained the right to acquire I.B.M.'s Service Bureau Corporation. The accord, however, has since been challenged in court by the Telex Corporation.

"Use of the laws has become respectable and we're viewing them a different way," said Harvey J. Goldschmid, who teaches antitrust law at Columbia University's School of Law.

Other upcoming private antitrust cases will pit Litton Industries, Inc., against the Xerox Corporation. Litton alleges that Xerox has monopolized the office-copier market. Also, a host of copper fabricators are taking on the Anaconda Company and the Kennecott Copper Corporation because of these giants' own fabricating activities.

A local case has the Rheingold Corporation, a regional brewer, charging Anheuser-Busch, Inc., and its distributors with predatory pricing under the Robinson-Patman amendment to the Clayton Antitrust Act. Rheingold says the St. Louis company has installed special low prices just in New York to eliminate local competition.

And I.B.M., while girding for a battle with the Government because of a suit filed by the Justice Department in 1969, also faces another private antitrust suit filed by the Telex Corporation. The suit is slated to be heard soon.

These prominent cases and others are just the tip of a spiral that took off about 10 years ago, most legal observers believe. It began when the Government won price - fixing convictions against electrical manufacturers and, drawn like bees to honey, utilities fell over themselves filing 1,700 damage claims.

"Subsequent to that set of developments, many of the depradations taken for granted in business simply ceased to be taken for granted," said Harold E. Kohn, a prominent Philadelphia lawyer who worked on the electrical cases.

The dramatic growth in cases is outlined in the annual reports of the Administrative Office of United States Courts and the United States Judicial Conference. In 1961, a total of 420 antitrust cases were filed by Government and private parties. By 1972, a total of 1,299 cases were filed by private petitioners alone.

Partly because of the growing volume and the near-saturation of the judicial system, there is a mounting backlog of these cases. In 1968 there were 1,360 cases on hand; in 1970 there were 1,933, and last year there were 2,563 cases waiting for disposition. Although the numbers are somewhat inflated because of simultaneous filings in separate districts, the trend is nonetheless unmistakable.

A number of reasons are given for the burst of activity in the private antitrust field, despite the staggering costs in legal fees and executive time.

Traditionally it has been felt that the Government was in the best position to suggest a rational and fair remedy in antitrust cases.

"Baloney," said Howard O'Leary Jr., general counsel and staff director of the Senate Antitrust subcommittee. "No one knows market conditions better than the companies involved in a given industry—and they are the best qualified to talk about remedies."

The Bell & Howell suit probably illustrates the point. Kodak, Bell & Howell alleges, uses its dominant position in the marketing of film to undercut competition from other manufacturers of amateur photographic equipment.

The way it is done, according to Bell & Howell's complaint, is that Kodak secretly designs and comes out with special films that are compatible only with Kodak cameras, thereby weakening the sales of equipment from competitors.

Bell & Howell wants the courts to force Kodak to forewarn its competitors about new films and also seeks triple damages for previous injuries.

A substantial advantage to a complaining company in a private action is that the company has control of its suit and can specify the kind of relief it needs.

"A victim could die waiting for the politics of Washington to make his case a

Oliver Williams

priority," said John E. Haigney, chairman and chief executive of Rheingold. "The Government has superior subpoena powers and more manpower, but they can't do everything."

He explained that the New York beer-buying public was not likely to complain so long as the major brewers were underselling local brewers. Only after the local brands are killed off and the prices are jacked up, he claims, will the outcry come—and at that point it would be too late for meaningful relief.

The sale of Rheingold, to Pepsico, Inc., which is now being held up, at least temporarily, because of an F.T.C. challenge, ironically was brought about partly because of the weakness in Rheingold's brewing operations.

The cost of private antitrust suits can be astronomical. The discovery process, where the complaining company sifts through thousands of documents supplied by the defendent, can cost hundreds of thousands of dollars in staff time as executives are diverted from regular duties, according to Mr. Kohn, the Philadelphia lawyer.

Tens of thousands of dollars in legal fees mount over months and sometimes years. Lawyers in some prestigious Manhattan law firms charge as much as $150 to $200 an hour for their time.

•

In the Hughes-T.W.A. battle the courts arrived at a $7.5-million legal fee for one side alone, but lawyers say the over-all cost may well have been twice that amount. In the Control Data-I.B.M. settlement, I.B.M. agreed to pay $15-million in legal costs.

And the relief, if it comes, may be delayed for years. The records of the Administrative Office of the United States Courts in Washington show that in 1972 nearly 500 private antitrust suits were pending for three years or more.

The job of locking horns with I.B.M. involved such high cost that some antitrust lawyers feel the Justice Department brought its own challenge only because Control Data, the private complainant, had offset much of the cost.

Certain kinds of antitrust action became more practical in 1966, when a court ruling made class actions a more viable tool.

In an indirect way the consumerism movement of the nineteen - sixties is thought to have influenced the new antitrust activity. The decision by the Purex Corporation, Ltd., to sue the General Foods Corporation, Purex acknowledges, was reached partly because Purex feared the possibility of shareholder suits for not being aggressive in defending corporate interests.

The prospect is for the spiral in private antitrust suits to continue. A Federal judge recently held in Washington that international steel quotas on exports from Western Europe and Japan to the United States are subject to antitrust challenge.

Federal District Court Judge Gerhard Gesell held that private parties in the United States might, at some point, seek triple damages in a civil action if they could find a basis to claim injury resulting from quota arrangements.

•

Nothing can be more encouraging than success, of course. And the startling victory of the International Telephone and Telegraph Corporation last year, when it succeeded in having the courts order the General Telephone and Electronics Corporation to divest itself of the Hawaiian Telephone Company, caught the eye of many corporations. Control Data's apparent success in forcing I.B.M.'s divestiture of the Service Bureau Corportion, a $63-million operation, will also be a factor in future cases.

Professor Goldschmid of Columbia Law School, and others, see some danger in the growing popularity of private antitrust suits, though they feel that the cause of fair competition is well served by the development to a point.

A rash of "ambulance-chasing" by antitrust lawyers may have broken out. The flood of suits could overwhelm the courts, Professor Goldschmid said, and certain carefully constructed licensing systems may be upset.

Antitrust has become a new game, and evidently everyone wants his innings.

January 21, 1973

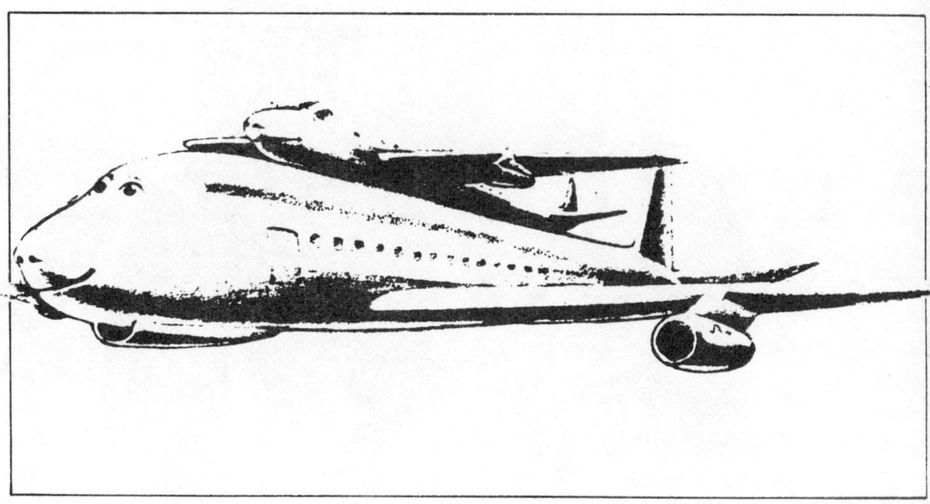

On these pages, a sampler of multinationals and what they do: T.W.A. manages Ethiopian Airlines.

The multinationals

Giants beyond flag and country

By Harvey D. Shapiro

The meeting at the Palace of Versailles last March had all the trappings of a diplomatic congress. For three days the 90-odd delegates from nine nations held closed-door meetings to discuss international monetary problems, tariffs and foreign-investment restrictions, and they concluded with a joint communiqué setting forth their views. The delegates did not represent any governments, however. The participants included David Rockefeller, chairman of Chase Manhattan Bank, J. Kenneth Jamieson, chairman of Exxon Corporation, and Giovanni Agnelli of Fiat, as well as the top executives from such giant firms as I.B.M., Caterpillar Tractor and Imperial Chemical Industries. Altogether, the 50 European and 40 American executives represented multinational corporations with assets well over $300-billion.

Both the setting and the substance of this meeting may be a commentary on the growing importance of multinational corporations and the questions they raise about the existing system of nation-states. A multinational corporation is one which not only sells in more than one country but also obtains its raw materials and capital, and produces its goods, in several countries. Most important, it is, in some sense, managed from a global point of view.

According to recent estimates, the gross world product is valued at $3-trillion, of which some $450-billion, or 15 per cent, is produced by multinational corporations. This sector is growing at the rate of 10 per cent a year, faster than the economies of many nations, and Prof. Howard V. Perlmutter of the Wharton School has estimated that by 1985 some 300 giant multinational firms will produce more than half of the world's goods and services.

About 200 giant U.S.-based corporations are regarded as multinational, while some 3,600 additional American firms already have at least one foreign subsidiary. American-based firms account for nearly half of total multinational output, but many multinational corporations are based in Europe and Japan, including giants like Unilever and British Petroleum, and 500 or so smaller foreign firms have plants in the U.S.

This month the Senate Finance Subcommittee on International Trade, headed by Senator Abraham Ribicoff, is holding hearings to assess the impact of multinational corporations on the troubled American economy. Multinational firms have been accused of deepening the nation's trade deficit and participating in the currency speculations which helped produce two devaluations of the dollar. According to Burton Teague, a senior research associate at the business-sponsored Conference Board, "Many businessmen look at multinationals as a means of distributing the fruits of technology and managerial expertise throughout the globe, but American labor views them as exporting jobs, while some less developed countries see them as a new generation of exploiters." Political leaders aren't sure what to make of them, but this much seems certain: For the first time since the clash between the emerging nations and the medieval church was settled in favor of the nation-state, a powerful and unique new international entity has emerged in the world that is raising important political, social and legal questions.

ALMOST everybody knows Hershey bars come from Hershey, Pa., but where do Nestlé's chocolate bars come from? Well, these days they're made in Pereira, Colombia; Tempelhof, West Germany; Caçapava, Brazil, and Fulton, N.Y., as well as dozens of other places around the world. Though many U.S. shoppers think of Nestlé's as another little American chocolate maker, the Nestlé Company of White Plains, N.Y., is actually a subsidiary of Nestlé Alimentana, S.A. The name does not evoke an image of massive, many-tentacled power like that of I.B.M. or ITT. Nonetheless, the corporation is the 29th largest in the world in terms of sales, and ranks with Unilever as the largest of the food processors.

The firm had total income of $4.2-billion last year, of which 53 per cent came from Europe, 33 per cent from the Americas, 11 per cent from Asia and 3 per cent from Africa. At headquarters in Vevey, Switzerland, on Lake Geneva, a cosmopolitan group of Nestlé executives orchestrates the activities of the firm's hundreds of subsidiaries, which operate 300 factories, maintain 677 sales offices and employ 110,000 people in 60 countries.

Nestlé Alimentana, a direct descendant of the baby-food business launched by Henri Nestlé in 1866, is now a holding company sitting atop a mind-boggling array of subsidiary companies which it has formed or acquired. It controls two other holding companies, Unilac, Inc., of Panama and Nestlé Holdings Ltd. of Nassau, and beneath this

Harvey D. Shapiro, a writer and consultant on governmental affairs, is currently a fellow at the Russell Sage Foundation.

superstructure operates dozens of companies using the Nestlé name and selling Nestlé products such as Nescafé and Nesquik cocoa all over the world. It also controls, or is allied with, dozens of other firms which don't fly the Nestlé flag, like Libby, McNeil & Libby, the giant American canner, Bachmann Bakeries of the Netherlands and the United Milk Company of Thailand. These firms sell their products under hundreds of brand names, including such popular labels as Crosse & Blackwell soups and Deer Park Mountain Spring Water.

The actual production of the firm's coffees, chocolates, baby foods, dairy products and frozen foods is highly decentralized. Cocoa, coffee beans and other raw materials are bought in local markets by individual subsidiaries, and "we vary each product according to local tastes," says Gerard J. Gogniat, chairman of Nestlé's in White Plains. Nestlé companies make their soups thick and creamy in West Germany and thin, like bouillon, in Latin America.

While the products may be adapted locally, the recipes for marketing and operations are written in Vevey. Headquarters receives regular projections on sales and profits from the subsidiaries, along with plans on how they will achieve their goals, and the parent company takes an active part in developing marketing strategies, brand names and even packages to insure success in each market. Some 25 million foreigners visited Spain last year, and while many may have been mystified by the local food, Nestlé Alimentana made sure they could find their old friend Nescafé in a familiar package.

When new products, marketing techniques or technologies prove successful in one country, they are transmitted via the parent organization to other subsidiaries. And if a Nestlé affiliate should falter, the trouble shooters at Nestlé Products Technical Assistance Co. Ltd. (Nestec) will parachute onto the scene to straighten things out. Headquarters also keeps an eye on coffee and cocoa markets, where Nestlé is among the world's largest customers, and it scans global political and social developments. Are there threats in Chile? New markets opening in China? A shift to consumer goods in Eastern Europe? A bad cocoa crop in Ghana? A new taste for wine in the U.S.? From listening posts all over the world, reports flow into Vevey. Ultimately, headquarters also coordi-

DRAWINGS BY FRED MARCELLINO

Europeans make Good Humors and Ovaltine.

Honeywell runs France's Machines Bull.

nates the massive flow of funds among the subsidiaries, lending money to some, drawing down profits from others, always keeping abreast of impending changes in currency exchange rates, and, some say, manipulating the over-all flow of funds to minimize the firm's worldwide tax burden and maximize profits.

Nestlé's top executives come from several countries, but they all seem to regard nation-states more like sales territories than sacred ties of blood and history. For example, Nestlé's U.S. chairman, Gerard Gogniat, who is also a director of Libby's, is a native of Switzerland who joined Nestlé Alimentana in 1946. He moved 12 times over the next 20 years, rising through various executive positions with Nestlé affiliates in Canada, Latin America, Stamford, Conn., Vevey and Paris before coming to White Plains in 1966. This summer, the 47-year-old executive, who speaks softly—in five languages—will return to Vevey to become one of the parent company's seven top-level "general managers."

When Gogniat leaves White Plains, Nestlé president David E. Guerrant, an American, will become chief executive of the corporation while remaining chairman of Libby's. His successor as chief executive officer at Libby's was Douglas B. Wells, an American who joined Nestlé's in White Plains in 1949 and served tours of duty with Nestlé affiliates in New Zealand and South Africa before Vevey installed him as president of Libby's last July. To insure a steady crop of good Nestlé men, last fall the parent company converted an old hotel in Rive-Reine to house its International Training Center, at which Nestlé executives from around the world come to prepare for senior management roles. After a little postgraduate training there, one suspects, they go forth to sell chocolates to the world with passports stamped "Swiss" or "French" or "American," but with an outlook marked simply "Nestlé."

THE rise of multinational corporations like Nestlé Alimentana is rooted in the logic of economics. Growth is the *sine qua non* of capitalism: As firms saturate their local markets, they broaden their horizons and seek new markets. Instead of expanding existing plants to supply these new markets, it is often more economical to open new factories near them and to buy raw materials in the area. When a new market is in another country, political concerns may require this choice. There are often political dangers for a product labeled "imported," as the Japanese are finding out, but tariffs and quotas on imported goods don't apply to the same goods if they are produced domestically by foreign-owned corporations. So, as the Japanese economist Chiaki Nishiyama notes, "The higher trade barriers become, the more attractive it will be for foreign capital to go into that country for investment." And once a corporation invests in another country, like a person who buys a house in a community, the firm begins an involvement that broadens its interests and its outlook. In contrast to a firm which simply ships in some goods to be sold, a company which makes a direct investment in plant and equipment in another nation becomes an employer and taxpayer, citizen and political participant. It brings in not only goods, but technology and a way of life.

The extractive industries had no choice but to invest wherever natural resources were to be found; so firms like Anaconda, Exxon, British Petroleum and United Fruit were becoming multinational in the 19th century. Rising tariffs after World War I led many manufacturing companies abroad for the first time, but this movement was slowed by the Depression and World War II. The development of truly multinational corporations began on a broad front in the late nineteen-forties. The movement was led by American corporations which saw lucrative new markets in countries rebuilding their war-torn economies, as well as opportunities to produce cheaply abroad for sale at home. U.S. overseas direct investment increased from $11.8-billion in 1950 to $32-billion in 1960 and $86-billion in 1971. Two-thirds of this postwar growth was in Western Europe, and most of that was concentrated in such fast-growing, nonextractive industries as chemicals, electronics, autos and

And McDonald's spreads across the globe.

computers. The number of foreign subsidiaries of U.S. firms increased from 2,300 in 1950 to more than 8,000 in 1970, while total foreign assets controlled reached $125-billion.

In his 1967 book "The American Challenge," J. J. Servan-Schreiber warned of an impending takeover of the European economy by American-based multinationals.* However, Servan-Schreiber sketched only part of the picture. The rise of the Common Market since 1958 has reduced European trade and investment barriers and permitted American-sized economies of scale, while government-encouraged mergers have created a number of trans-European firms that can generate surpus capital. As a result, an impressive number of European firms have been quietly expanding foreign operations recently.

In contrast to the early European investments in raw materials in colonial areas, the recent European foreign investment has been in the U.S.,

*"The American Challenge" was foreshadowed by Fred McKenzie's "The American Invaders," which warned "The most serious aspect of the American industrial invasion lies in the fact that these newcomers have acquired control of every new industry created during the past 15 years." McKenzie's book was a best seller when it was published in London in 1902.

primarily in technologically sophisticated industries such as chemicals and synthetic fibers, as well as consumer goods. These days, the manufacturers of such "all-American" products as 20-Mule Team Borax, Bic pens, Librium, Ovaltine and even Good Humor ice cream are owned by European companies. Two devaluations of the dollar, which have made investments in the U. S. relatively less expensive, serve to accelerate the trend.

Not only are European firms pulled here by the world's largest and richest market and by the sophisticated R. and D. community, they are also being forced to become multinational by competition from American-based multinational companies. Joseph Rubin of the international accounting firm of Alexander Grant, Tansley, Witt, explains: "In order to remain competitive, European firms in multinational industries have had to obtain a foothold in the world's largest market in order to dilute their over-all costs over a greater sales base and lower their per-unit costs."

Japanese companies are also belatedly becoming multinational. Despite its success as an exporter, Japan has only $4.5-billion in overseas direct investments, mainly in raw materials in nearby, less-developed countries. Now that the Japanese Government has eased its stiff controls on the export of capital, however, foreign investment is likely to rise to $10-billion by 1977. Some of this will flow to the U.S., but a significant amount is being directed toward Europe, where Japan's mushrooming export sales totaled $1.6-billion last year and where the kind of protectionist rumblings that have endangered her American markets are beginning to be heard.

Dr. Peter Gabriel, the new dean of Boston University's College of Business Administration, predicts: "The L.D.C.'s [less developed countries] and the Eastern bloc [the Soviet Union, China and Eastern Europe] represent the biggest single growth area for multinational corporations in the remainder of this century." Gabriel, a former partner in McKinsey & Co., an international consulting firm, argues, "The needs of the Third World and the Eastern bloc countries for the resources and capabilities the multinationals possess are almost infinite, but the multinational involvement will be very different from that in the West."

Rising nationalism in the former colonial areas has fostered a suspicion of any new exploitation Billions of dollars of investments have been expropriated in such countries as Algeria, Argentina, Indonesia and, most recently, Chile. The oil-producing nations have been demanding not only a larger share of profits, but of ownership as well. And in 1970, the Andean Common Market countries stipulated that foreign companies had to turn over ownership of their operations to local control within 15 to 20 years.

"The era of the multinational corporation as a traditional direct investor in the L.D.C.'s is coming to an end," Gabriel says. Instead, firms which once sought 100 per cent ownership of foreign subsidiaries are becoming more flexible. For example, du Pont and American Cyanamid have accepted minority interests in Mexican ventures. Gabriel sees the management contract, in which firms "invest" their skills instead of their money, as an even more likely model for the future. T.W.A. has managed Ethiopian Airlines since World War II, for example, while Goodyear has agreed to operate two state-owned tire companies in Indonesia for a fee based on sales and profits.

Nestle companies make their soups thick and creamy in West Germany, and thin like bouillon in Latin America.

Multinationals don't have any opportunities to acquire ownership interests in Eastern bloc countries, except for Rumania and Yugoslavia, but Dr. Gabriel argues these countries will increasingly seek management contracts with multinational firms to obtain the technology, managerial skills and capital they need to compete in the growing East-West trade. These days, a variety of firms have management contracts with the Soviet Union, among them Fiat, which built the Togliatti auto factory in Russia for a reported $50-million, as well as International Harvester and Renault, which have similar arrangements in Eastern Europe.

Some Eastern bloc countries are even developing their own state-owned multinational enterprises. The Soviet Union has a group of eight banks in Western Europe. In a joint venture with Belgian interests called Society Scaldia-Volga, the Russians have opened a small plant near Brussels where Volgas and Moskvitches are assembled largely for the Belgian market. Meanwhile, in October several oil-rich sheikdoms began talking about "downstream" investments in refineries or even gas stations; perhaps Europeans will soon be filling up with Faisal Supreme or Saudi Ethyl.

Whether as owners or managers, as senior or junior partners, multinational enterprises seem destined to continue expanding their role. Only such giants, or major governments, can now afford to develop new technologies and new products. Few institutions in the world, public or private, for example, could have mustered the $5-billion I.B.M. spent to develop its 360 series of computers. Moreover, as multinational firms operate in more and more markets, Joseph Rubin points out, firms in one country must either acquire, or be acquired by, competitors in other nations, just as local and regional industries in the U.S. gradually were consolidated into a nationwide economy earlier in this century.

Earlier this year Carl A. Gerstacker, chairman of Dow Chemical, told the White House Conference on the Industrial World Ahead, "We appear to be moving in the direction of what will not really be multinational or international companies as we know them today, but what we might call 'anational' companies — companies without any nationality, belonging to all nationalities." European firms are leading the way in this. S.K.F., a Swedish ball-bearing manufacturer changed its "official language" on all memos and even conversations in its headquarters from Swedish to English, the *lingua franca* of multinational business. Royal Dutch-Shell and Unilever operate companies which, in each case, are controlled by a pair of holding companies, one based in England and the other in the Netherlands; their executives and employes are even more polyglot than their shareholders. Most American-based multinationals still tend to do 70 per cent of their business at home, but a few American firms are also submerging their nationalities. More and more firms are staffing overseas subsidiaries with local citizens, and foreigners have become executives and directors of such corporations as I.B.M., H. J. Heinz and Xerox; in addition, shares of G.E., du Pont, Ford, Kodak and Goodyear are sold on stock exchanges in Paris, Amsterdam, Brussels, and Frankfurt or Düsseldorf.

"McDonald's golden arches will soon be everywhere . . ." The multinationals foster a growing sameness.

Paralleling the rise of more "anational" firms, the world's major banks have divided themselves into multinational consortia. The largest, Orion Bank Ltd., was founded in October, 1979, by Chase Manhattan, Royal Bank of Canada, Britain's National Westminster Bank, Westdeutsche Landesbank Girozentrale, Credito Italiano and Mitsubishi

Bank. Orion is represented in more than 100 countries and headquartered in London, but it has no real "nationality."

Instantaneous global communications, the computer and the rise of professionally trained managers have made control of these far-flung enterprises feasible, though managerial styles vary from tightly controlled empires to loose confederations. When the Cummins Engine Company of Columbus, Ind., launched Kirloskar-Cummins Ltd. as a joint venture in India a decade ago, Cummins vice president George Thurston recalls, "All the machinery we brought in was based on the concept of a man standing at a machine while doing his work. But we learned the Indian is much more content if he can squat, so we had to re-engineer the machinery and lower the controls so a guy could work squatting." Like many multinationals, Cummins has adopted Nestlé's approach of defining goals but leaving local managers some discretion in how to achieve them. However, the multinational headquarters almost always reserves for itself the tasks of long-range planning, research and development, and finance.

Because they introduce advanced technology and management on a large scale, the corporations have been telescoping the process of development in many countries. In the Third World, Nestlé is teaching new agricultural methods to its suppliers and new child-rearing and health-care practices to mothers to whom it hopes to sell baby food and dairy products. Ultimately, multinational companies "may be a more effective device than foreign trade in improvir~ the standard of living in the L.D.C.'s," says Charles P. Kindleberger, professor of economics at M.I.T. He explains, "You didn't get an equalized standard of living and wage scale in the U.S. until capital moved out through the country, and national companies helped do this, though the populists hated these companies, especially the chain stores." Although multinational firms may move to an area because of its low wages, the firm's payroll may increase local income dramatically. When Cummins opened its Poona, India, plant, George Thurston recalls, "We used to have three buses to pick up the workers. Now our biggest problem is parking space for their cars and bicycles. People have reached that economic level."

A free flow of goods, investments and technology may heighten worldwide productivity and economic efficiency in the long run, but such free movements could also lead to instability and painful dislocations. Higher living standards, moreover, require new styles of living. For instance, when Sears helped introduce mass merchandising in Mexico, its retail stores provided more varied goods and created new jobs and industries to supply the stores. But these stores, with their impersonal cash-and-carry operations, also replaced the social life that surrounded local markets. Thus, multinational corporations hasten and exacerbate the social changes that accompany development, and sometimes sow tensions which lead to their own expropriation.

While Third World nations would like to acquire the managerial expertise, capital markets and research facilities that come along with multinational headquarters, they are more likely—with their uneducated labor force, low wages and uncluttered land—to attract chemical plants, oil refineries and sprawling, messy, labor-intensive industries. This is particularly so, says Dr. John Hackett, executive vice president at Cummins Engine Company, because "countries like Brazil aren't nearly as concerned about ecology as the U.S. and Japan." Thus, as pollution legislation grows more stringent in the developed countries, multinational corporations are likely to tempt the less-developed nations with incomes approaching New York or Chicago—at the cost of looking and smelling like northern New Jersey or South Chicago.

Trade unions in the industrialized nations are, of course, concerned that the movement of plants to other countries will mean loss of jobs. However, American labor's claim that multinationals "export jobs" from the U.S. is challenged by Prof. Robert B. Stobaugh in a study financed by the U.S. Department of Commerce. Stobaugh and his associates at the Harvard Business School examined nine major overseas investments and concluded they created more jobs for U.S. workers than they eliminated; if these investments hadn't been made, the study asserted, America would have lost 600,000 jobs, since the firms would have been unable to compete successfully. However, the study noted that these investments tended to "displace" production workers, while increasing managerial, research and service jobs.

Union leaders also worry that multinational companies can undermine collective bargaining by threatening to move rather than meet union demands. Henry Ford II, for example, told Prime Minister Edward Heath in 1971 that if striking workers at Ford's Dagenham, England, plant weren't tamed, the company might abandon the factory.

"International bargaining doesn't exist anyplace and I don't see how it can," says Gus Tyler, assistant president of the International Ladies Garment Workers. Garment workers making $3 an hour in the U.S. and 16 cents an hour on Taiwan have little common ground for negotiating with an employer, Tyler says, so to help stanch the flow of jobs abroad American labor is relying for the present on legislation. The A.F.L.-C.I.O. supports the Burke-Hartke bill, which seeks to tighten controls on foreign investment and restrict imports. "In the long run," Tyler admits, "we have to hope wage levels elsewhere will come up."

Perhaps they will, for in an economy dominated by multinational companies, all roads are supposed to lead to equilibrium. In theory, industry would gradually be moved from high-rent, cluttered areas to cheap, vacant land, thus evening out global land use, and global wages, interest and prices would all tend to become more equal. However, the uniformity resulting from thus tying together various national economies is a double-edged sword. Multinationals are making the world's business procedures, measures and standards more uniform, as goods are being made and used in widely varied settings. But they are also fostering a growing sameness in the world's major cities. "It's sad, but work habits are going to become the same everywhere," says Giorgio Della Seta, a vice president of the Pirelli Tire Corporation, who bemoans the decline of the long Italian lunch break. All the typewriters and radios and toys and underwear in the world sometimes seem to be made in the same Hong Kong factory. An effective marketing program demands that all British Petroleum stations look pretty much alike. McDonald's golden arches will soon be everywhere. And a Hilton is a Hilton is a Hilton.

This growing sameness applies to people as well. Professor Kindleberger sees multinationals as creating a new cadre of international managers who will be committed to the aggrandizement of their firms and to their own salaries and stock options, but to little else. Like the mobile American executives who shuttle among the bedroom suburbs outside U.S. industrial centers, these international managers will be efficient and useful to be sure, but bland and interchangeable as well. They will be the merchants in the Global Village they're helping to create. They will, that is, unless they are checked by political forces.

The sovereignty of the state requires that it be responsible for all that occurs within its borders. But the multina-

Which is to govern: the law of the land, or the law of supply and demand?

tional corporation requires a free flow of capital, goods, and labor as if there were no borders. Which is to govern: the law of the land or the law of supply and demand? Prof. Raymond Vernon, the director of Harvard's Center for International Affairs, argues this "asymmetry" between multinational corporations and nations can be tolerated only up to a point; the threat, as he sees it, is reflected in the title of his recent book about multinationals, "Sovereignty at Bay."

Business spokesmen often deny there any conflict. Burton Teague of the Conference Board says, "I'm not convinced by any means that the multinational corporations are exercising political power. They make their decisions on the basis of hard, cold business facts." True enough. The treasurers of many multinational firms acted like textbook examples of profit-maximizing managers when they began speculating in currencies in 1971. By all accounts, their movement out of dollars helped set off the worldwide monetary crisis that became a political issue in several countries and led to the first devaluation of the dollar and the revaluation of the yen. They also are said to have joined in the speculation that led to the second devaluation, though it is impossible to say which of the various types of currency speculators was most responsible for our recent troubles. Whatever their monetary role, it is clear that multinational corporations have economic power, and economic power is political power.

Multinational companies might have caused fewer problems in a 19th-century night-watchman state concerned only with maintaining order, but modern governments have assumed the obligation of managing the economy and promoting the general welfare. "How can a national government operate a domestic financial and economic policy when it can't control the decisions of all the factors within the economy?" George Ball, a senior partner at Lehman Brothers and a former Under Secretary of State, asks. In a democratic society, the government manipulates the environment in which economic decisions are made. But multinational companies inhabit a different environment. A central bank may raise interest rates to slow inflation, but a multinational corporation may borrow funds in a low-interest country. The Canadian Government may attempt to change its unemployment rate, but the nearly 50 per cent of Canada's manufacturing and mining companies controlled by U.S. firms may determine their hiring policies in response to American rather than Canadian economic policies. The U.S. seeks to maintain its military superiority on the basis of its sophisticated weaponry, yet companies like G.E. that build those weapons want to export their military technology through their subsidiaries in other nations.

One alternative is for a nation to lock the door on movements of capital and goods. By taking such a step, however, a country risks falling behind in economic and technological progress in the rest of the world. Despite General de Gaulle's opposition to the American challenge, the French Government found it had to permit G.E. to take over troubled Machines Bull, the principal French computer company. (Honeywell recently acquired it from G.E.) Although the auto industry is often a matter of national pride, France permitted Chrysler to acquire a 77 per cent interest in Simca. After U. S. investment was restricted by France in 1963, U.S. companies set up shop in other Common Market countries, ultimately forcing the Pompidou government to relax the restrictions in order to share in the jobs and income gained by its neighbors.

Whatever their benefits, though, multinational corporations cannot simply be left to their own devices. What's good for General Motors is not always good for the U.S., and even when it is, it may not also be good for the people of Norway, Brazil or other countries. Under chairman Harold Geneen, ITT has become a model of efficiency and "good management," but it has been accused of manipulating governments for its own purposes from Santiago to San Diego. The important decisions about the world's resources cannot be left solely to the profit-maximizing managers of multinational corporations because their calculations leave out the social costs of their actions. They won't pay for cleaning up their pollution or supporting their discarded workers unless someone makes them. The 19th-century experience with laissez-faire economics demonstrated that there must be a social and legal framework to insure that corporations ultimately serve the public interest.

But multinational corporations have shaken off the traditional sources of countervailing power. They've outgrown trade unions, consumer groups, local and state governments. Currently, multinational corporations are responsible to both their home country and their host countries, and the jurisdictions are sometimes overlapping but often absent. The host governments' fear of losing the benefits of multinational operations leaves the companies with sufficient bargaining power to forestall regulation in many areas.

The traditional, good liberal, common-sense solution is clear: Global corporations should be responsible to a global regulatory authority. Despite the United Nations' impotence, many still call for a multinational solution. George Ball, for example, proposes a treaty creating a supernational regulatory authority to charter multinational corporations and specify their rights and obligations, while also standardizing host government regulations and taxes. Such a treaty would begin with the developed nations—"The less-developed countries are too concerned with their nationalism right now," Ball says — and, like the International Monetary Fund or the General Agreement on Tariffs and Trade, it would gain signatories over time.

However, even if the dislocations caused by multinational companies were to be regulated by international agreement and cushioned by some form of financial assistance, many nations might still may be reluctant to shift part of their economic fate out of their own hands. The less-developed countries may lead rather than follow the industrialized nations in dealing with multinationals, for the Third World is demonstrating that it can obtain many of the benefits multinational firms offer while retaining national control of its economy. Dr. Gabriel of Boston University foresees a growth in "bilateral relationships" in which corporations and governments will bargain over new and existing investments one by one. "Such a situation would resemble nothing so much as true capitalists in a free market, each seeking his own self-interest," he says. The result would be an untidy and uneven process, as corporations sought outlets for their capital and products and nations looked for corporations to fulfill their plans for national development. When those national aspirations didn't accord with the multinationals' plans—if India wants a steel industry or Norway wants fishermen—then the nation might create *ad hoc* or permanent subsidies and penalties to change the economic landscape and persuade the multinational corporation to do its bidding.

Economic rationality demands that a nation be what it is best equipped to be, but politics holds the promise of being what a nation wants to be. There need not be a conflict, of course, but the nations of managers and researchers and financiers are more likely to accept their lot than those who seem destined to be the world's factory workers and hewers of wood and haulers of water. They may not maximize global economic efficiency that way, but as Professor Kindleberger says: "The political solution to the question of multinational corporations depends on what it is that people want to maximize." ■

March 18, 1973

THINK, SELL, GROW

I.B.M. and all the dwarfs

... but their real strength has been in marketing.

RANDY ENOS

By Harvey D. Shapiro

ARMONK, N. Y. Recently Dr. Ralph Gomery, the boyish-looking Princeton Ph.D. who is director of research at the bucolic I.B.M. laboratories a few miles from here, sat down to lunch with two secretaries, a scientist studying laser beams and a maintenance man to talk about their jobs. At about the same time, several hundred employes of the I.B.M. World Trade Corporation filed into a Manhattan hotel ballroom for a two-hour discussion of the company's global problems and prospects.

Meanwhile, at I.B.M.'s headquarters in Armonk, amid the apple orchards and parking lots, Frank T. Cary, the $400,000-a-year chairman of this giant corporation, was hearing an employe's grievance under I.B.M.'s "open-door policy," and Ralph A. Pfeiffer Jr., president of I.B.M.'s Data Processing Group, was preparing to leave for another of his weekly visits to one of I.B.M.'s more than 200 domestic field offices.

"All of this is characteristic of our efforts to keep in touch with our people and maintain a small-company atmosphere," Cary explains. It doesn't seem at all ironic to Cary that I.B.M., the company that has produced the bulk of the world's electronic data-processing equipment and punch cards is now working diligently to keep its own people from feeling as if they are only numbers. This attempt to avoid being hoist with its own petard has become a major preoccupation at the I.B.M. Corporation, as it seeks to remain what Fortune called "the supergrowth company of the century."

In 1911, financier Charles R. Flint merged three little firms into the Computing-Tabulating-Recording Company, and 13 years later, when this producer of scales and time clocks had sales of $4-million, it was rather grandiosely renamed the International Business Machines Corporation. By last year, the company had swept past such giants as U.S. Steel and Texaco to rank as the sixth largest industrial corporation in the United States and the seventh largest in the world, with sales of $9.53-billion (including $5-billion abroad) and profits of $1.28-billion. Its 265,000 employees in 117 countries have produced an estimated 70 per cent of the 145,000 computers in the world, and each year I.B.M. continues to sell $500-million worth of typewriters, dictating machines and other office equipment. It has been so far ahead of its competitors that the electronic data-processing industry was often described as I.B.M. and the Seven Dwarfs, until two of the dwarfs—actually corporate giants G.E. and RCA—quit competing with the I.B.M. juggernaut, whose uninterrupted spiral of prosperity has made its stock a legend.

I.B.M.'s almost unparalleled record of growth has brought problems, of course, and high among them these days is the Federal Government's antitrust suit seeking to break I.B.M. into several separate companies in order to enhance competition. Some legal experts consider the case, which is inching toward trial, to be the most important antitrust suit since Standard Oil in 1911.

But I.B.M. is more than another big company and more than an interesting legal exercise. It is the dominant force in what economists say will become the world's largest industry in the nineteen-eighties, and it is in many ways intimately intertwined with the way we live. Its electronic data-processing machines, which perform relatively simple computations but do so with mind-boggling speed, have made it possible to increase vastly the sweep of administration, to centralize and control from remote points the minutiae of human existence. And this marvelous efficiency has taken its toll in human interchange, as all activities from rapid transit in San Francisco to welfare in New York must be redesigned to suit the pleasure of the computer.

Virtually all major organizations now use computers for bookkeeping activities, such as billing and making out payrolls, yet I.B.M. is constantly developing new applications for its equipment, and computers are increasingly moving into the central activities of the world's institutions, producing goods, managing money, educating students. Nowhere is this involvement more extensive than at I.B.M. itself, where computers now sit out on the production floor at I.B.M.'s plant in East Fishkill, N. Y., for example, directing the flow of material and checking the quality of production. Througnout I.B.M. some portion of nearly everybody's work is organized around computers.

Moreover, as one Harvard University researcher who is studying I.B.M. notes, "More and more all companies and governmental organizations are finding themselves in a situation where technological innovations and changing conditions make it necessary to organize large numbers of creative, thinking people in a way which wasn't true in the past. And I.B.M., where more than half the employes are college graduates, is really a model for this. It's saying that you can be both very big and remain dynamic. It's something that's going to be copied a great deal."

Consequently, I.B.M. is important not only for what it makes, but also for what it is like. Yet to many of those who fear that a computerized world will ease our labor at the cost of folding, spindling and mutilating our humanity, I.B.M.—like the computers it makes—is a black box whose bulky presence is obvious but whose contents remain only vaguely understood.

In the hopes of looking inside I.B.M., I called James B. O'Connell, its director of external information, and asked him for assistance in writing an article. After spending several weeks trying to convince me and this magazine to drop or delay the article, I.B.M. finally offered to let me interview top executives—but no lower-level employes—if I would agree not to use a tape recorder and to check all direct quotes with the company. In return, I.B.M. provided me with a carefully prepared tour of various operations, complete with typed schedules, multimedia presentations and, on two occasions, a chauffeured limousine from Manhattan to Armonk and back.

At each of the half-dozen I.B.M. facilities I

Harvey D. Shapiro is a writer, consultant on government affairs and a fellow at the Russell Sage Foundation.

"If the top 25 executives were dropped into the Atlantic Ocean, the average customer would never know."

visited, while I took notes on my interviews, Mr. O'Connell took notes on me. Big Brother assumes a primitive form at I.B.M., for never was I left alone; even when I went to the bathroom, someone invariably accompanied me. Nonetheless, while I talked to the I.B.M. Establishment on some days, on others I interviewed lower-level employes (without company clearance) and I also talked to a variety of former employes to find out what life is like at the pre-eminent suburban white-collar advanced-technology corporation.

Like chairman Cary, the I.B.M. executives I met are clean-cut, with sideburns precisely to mid-ear. Though formal and polite, they are good-natured, outgoing, pure of thought and word, and articulate until the conversation turns controversial; then there are furtive glances in the direction of Mr. O'Connell. Whatever seething passions, emphatic opinions, or strong emotions may lurk below the surface, the I.B.M.'ers I met appeared as bland as an ulcer diet and as placid as the suburban meadows outside their windows.

IRONICALLY, I.B.M.'s gray regiments were put together by one of American industry's classic managers, Thomas J. Watson Sr., who was I.B.M.'s chief executive from 1914 until his death at age 82 in 1956, when his son Thomas Jr. succeeded him. Though Watson Sr. was an authoritarian and arbitrary manager, he took a warm personal interest in the well-being of his employes, save those who drank or womanized, and he elevated those who caught his fancy. Once he promoted a young man in Texas largely because he was a namesake of President Eisenhower's, whom Watson admired, says former I.B.M.'er Charles Smith, now a vice president of Bankers Trust Company.

Because of Watson's notions of decorum, I.B.M.'ers who met the public were directed to stick to white shirts and dark suits; even the repairmen still dress that way and many carry briefcases, in which they keep their tools and lunch. Watson also savored a rah-rah atmosphere, and for years I.B.M. gatherings were replete with slogans, epigrams and above all company fight songs, like "Ever Onward," or "Hail to the I.B.M." Sample lyrics:

Our voices swell in admiration;
Of T. J. Watson proudly sing;
He'll ever be our inspiration,
To him our voices loudly ring.

Though Watson chose "Think" as the company slogan, a more apt motto for I.B.M. would have been "Sell." While many assume I.B.M. has built a better mousetrap, James Bochnowski, a 16-year veteran of I.B.M. and now a vice president and computer analyst for the brokerage house of Donaldson, Lufkin & Jenrette, Inc., says, "In many cases, I.B.M. hasn't been that much of an innovator in terms of new ideas and products—though they're certainly competent in those areas—but their real strength has been in marketing." Watson had begun his career as a traveling salesman, and "in the early days Mr. Watson felt a salesman could do anything. Thirty years ago he used to promote successful salesmen into jobs as plant managers, personnel men or anything else," recalls Robert McGrath, who spent 16 years in marketing at I.B.M. McGrath, now a vice president of Recognition Equipment in Dallas, edits a directory of former I.B.M.'ers, a publication popular among executive recruiters as well as I.B.M. alumni.

I.B.M. emphasized marketing existing products rather than inventing new ones, when the digital computer was looming on the scientific horizon after World War II. "UNIVAC was the place where people who were interested in the scientific new world were located and where the real push to enter that new world seemed to come from," says Prof. Martin Shubik, an economist at Yale and another former I.B.M.'er.

I.B.M. soon jumped on the computer bandwagon, however. By the mid-nineteen-fifties, while Thomas J. Watson Jr. was assuming greater and greater responsibilities, he committed the company to a massive research and development effort in electronic data processing. Meanwhile, I.B.M. salesmen were using their experience in the punch-card and office-equipment field to swamp their less marketing-oriented rivals. Because I.B.M. computers quickly became predominant, those who were creating the computer languages and programs and those who were training programers and systems analysts often geared their work to I.B.M. products. And since everything and everybody seemed to be geared to I.B.M. products, this only reinforced the inclinations of many data processing customers to buy I.B.M. equipment. "If you knew 70 per cent of the world's people spoke English, what language would you choose to learn?" asks George Sadowsky, a computer expert at the Urban Institute.

Though I.B.M. itself is often slow in innovating because of its size, nothing really happens in the computer industry until it happens at I.B.M. Several years ago Burroughs introduced "virtual memory," which increased the information storage capacity of its computers, but few customers were interested until I.B.M. added it to its System/370 in 1972. Similarly, after Control Data Corporation introduced its 6000 model, which had an enlarged capacity for computing, orders slowed as soon as I.B.M. announced that it planned to introduce its own large economy-size computer, the 360-90. (The model numbers, like those in Oldsmobile 98, mean nothing.)

I.B.M. has operated across the entire spectrum of the industry, producing small, medium and large capacity computers and providing programs, servicing and training for customers. Until 1970, I.B.M. offered its products as part of a "bundle" of "hardware," peripheral equipment, programs and servicing, which left little room for those seeking to operate in only certain segments of the computer industry. Peripheral-equipment makers often found a change in I.B.M. equipment rendered their products incompatible or obsolete. Yet few firms could muster the large sums of money needed to compete head to head with I.B.M., because I.B.M. had set the pattern of leasing rather than selling computers. Leasing means the costs of producing a computer aren't recouped at the time of sale but rather over several years, so it is often difficult to finance services equal to those offered by a giant like I.B.M., says Dan L. McGurk, president of the Computer Industry Association, which represents several smaller companies. Many of I.B.M.'s competitors have been forced to quit. RCA took a $400-

(Continued)

million loss in abandoning its electronic data-processing operations, and the general dropout rate has only prompted even more customers to heed the admonitions of the I.B.M. salesmen to sign up with the company that will be around for a while.

I.B.M. now spends more than $500-million a year on research and development, including $50-million to support wide-ranging basic research on everything from laser beams to cryptography (to shield data banks from unauthorized users) at its laboratories in Yorktown Heights, N. Y.; San Jose, Calif., and Zurich, Switzerland. The Research Division is now ranked by some observers with the Bell Labs among the world's foremost scientific facilities, but Professor Shubik says, "While consideration for technology has shot up considerably, I.B.M.'s thinking about research scientists has been, well, these are like giant pandas in a zoo. You don't really quite know what a giant panda is, but you sure as hell know (1) you paid a lot of money for it, and (2) other people want it; therefore it is valuable and therefore it's got to be well-fed."

The Harvard researcher, who asked to remain unidentified because he is still studying I.B.M. and other companies, agrees: "The regular scientist is like a resource at I.B.M. He doesn't have the status at the center of the company, which is still reserved for the marketing men." Frank Cary and about two-thirds of I.B.M.'s top executives started out as salesmen, and the care and feeding of the 10,000-member sales force still occupies a great deal of executive time.

The man in charge of molding these salesmen is Ralph A. Pfeiffer Jr., 46, a burly former football player (at Cleveland's John Carroll University) who has spent his entire career (24 years) at I.B.M. Pfeiffer is a salesman more in the tradition of Oral Roberts than Willy Loman. His handshake is as firm as the gaze he fixes on whomever he is talking to, and as he speaks he nods gravely and frequently interjects your first name into his sentences, to let you know he's sincerely relating to you.

I.B.M.'s "marketing representatives" aren't fast-talking peddlers by any means, Pfeiffer says, since the typical computer customer may sign an agreement to buy or lease upwards of a million dollars' worth of equipment, for which I.B.M. may well design or adapt special programs and provide regular servicing. I.B.M. teaches its sales trainees all they need to know about computers during the company's 53-week training program, so educational background isn't as important as personality. "We're interested in people who see the positive side of life, who look at things as opportunities, not problems. We want people who will work well with others, develop rapport and have a self-initiating mode of being and will be winners. We want that Jack Armstrong, the all-American boy," Pfeiffer says.

On the wall of Pfeiffer's large, airy, corner office in Harrison, N. Y., next to his I.B.M. achievement awards and a picture of John F. Kennedy, there is a framed quotation from football coach Vince Lombardi: "Winning is not a sometime thing." Not at I.B.M. it isn't.

In the last 15 years, though, the salesmen who run I.B.M. have been challenged internally by the firm's spectacular growth (averaging 14 per cent per year) and its increasingly complex technology. When Thomas J. Watson Jr. became chief executive in 1956, he saw a need not only to create a research division, but also to tranform his father's one-man show into a coherent organization. For the first time, an organization chart was drawn up and executives were assigned specific duties to replace Mr. Watson Sr.'s whimsies, while a corporate staff was created to coordinate the firm's increasingly global activities.

At the same time, Watson *fils* phased out the songbooks, and while he kept the Hundred Per Cent Club for salesmen who met their quotas, their annual gatherings became less evangelical and more educational. When Thomas J. Watson Jr. vacated the chairmanship after a heart attack in 1971 (he's now chairman of the executive committee), his successor, T. Vincent Learson, accelerated the professionalization of I.B.M.'s management. Learson, at 6-foot-5, was an awesome presence with piercing blue eyes. He joined I.B.M. as a salesman after graduating from Harvard in 1935. In 1964, he managed the introduction of the wildly successful System/360 computers and did the same with System/370 in 1970, while gaining a reputation as a tough-minded manager who showed little interest in employes' personal foibles as long as they delivered the goods; those who didn't disappeared, and some say that during the 1970 recession, he considered dropping I.B.M.'s long-standing policy of never laying off anybody.

While Thomas J. Watson Jr. describes himself and Learson as "emotional managers," Frank T. Cary, 52, who became chairman in January, has been called "the antithesis of impulsive," and securities analyst James Bochnowski says, "He's certainly cautious and believes in having the staff work done and the alternatives explored." The short, cherubic-looking Cary's elevation at I.B.M. symbolizes the company's complete transition from charismatic leadership to organized bureaucracy, with rules and plans rather than personality now the governing force. These days, says William Moore, chairman of Bankers Trust and a long-time director of I.B.M., "You just always have the feeling that the planning is beautifully done. Their planning is just incredible."

Even at the top of I.B.M., corporate components, like circuits in a computer, have their own back-ups. I.B.M. is now run by a three-man "corporate office," consisting of Cary, senior vice president Gilbert E. Jones and Thomas J. Watson Jr. Thus, although he has reached the peak of American corporate life, Frank Cary, who joined I.B.M. in 1948, says of his new position, "As a member of the corporate office, I shared in the total responsibility for the performance of the I.B.M. Corporation, so it's not really all that much of a change. We don't change as dramatically as an enterprise that has one fellow at the top."

In fact, Robert McGrath says, "If the top 25 [I.B.M.] executives were dropped into the Atlantic Ocean, the average customer would never know." He adds that the bureaucratic overlapping is even greater at lower levels of I.B.M.: "The boxes are so small the average individual can't do much one way or another to change the corporation. Today it's like a West Point parade where a man could faint and nobody would know until it was all over."

Paradoxically, while blue-collar workers elsewhere show signs of mushrooming discontent, I.B.M.'s production workers seem relatively contented, and the firm has had few labor problems. "I.B.M. has been very careful to keep trade unions out by paying its people very well," says Dan McGurk of the Computer Industry Association. Moreover, the nation's largest nonunion employer transferred its blue-collar workers from an hourly wage to straight salaries in 1958, and I.B.M. has been a pioneer in offering employes free insurance, paid holidays, education and recreation. Its products are made in relatively small work areas rather than on impersonal assembly lines. Instead of breaking jobs into monotonous little tasks, I.B.M. keeps enlarging them, so a worker usually has something he can say he made, microscopic though it often is. And since technology has produced a new generation of computers every half-dozen years, the blue-collar worker has less opportunity to become bored because he is always adding new skills and learning new jobs.

However, the same technology that has made the blue-collar jobs at I.B.M. relatively interesting is "proletarianizing" the work of the college-educated managers and engineers who constitute a majority at I.B.M. The complexity of contemporary computer technology requires massive working groups in which each member has only a small role. The result is sometimes frustration and alienation.

A recent American Management Association survey found: "Today's manager reports that his opportunities for direct participation in the decision-making process seem to be rapidly decreasing in the highly bureaucratic and authoritarian structure of the technocorporation of the nineteen-sixties." And Dr. Michael Maccoby of Washington's Institute for Policy Studies found that the typical middle manager in advanced technology companies "considers his work to be technically interesting, creative and important to the company, and not exceedingly supervised. Yet he is nagged by thoughts of being merely part of a huge machine, of becoming technically obsolete, or of being bypassed for promotion. He doesn't think he has much power to affect the policies of the company."

At I.B.M., Frank Cary admits, "a great deal of what we do really requires team kinds of operations. We're a very task-force-oriented company." Yet I.B.M. has succeeded in effectively organizing and motivating its massive numbers of educated white-collar workers by persuading many of them to look beyond themselves, to see themselves as part of some noble undertaking and, consequently, to do I.B.M.'s bidding rather cheerfully. "The message here is that it is O.K. to be a buck private, because you're a soldier in the army of the Lord," one Westchester engineer explains. To instill that message, Thomas J. Watson Jr. says, "we try to get the individual to recognize he is a greatly appreciated part of I.B.M."

The company has scattered its employes throughout Westchester, for example, instead of concentrating them in one big I.B.M. campus or office tower, in part to keep its facilities small and more intimate. At each installation, there are endless rounds of meetings between employes of one level and those a couple of levels above them, meetings designed to tell everyone how his job fits into the organization and how he's doing at it. "We work very hard at getting our people to understand the 'why' of things," Ralph Pfeiffer explains.

Moreover, at each installation, executives are encouraged to know every employe's first name and his problems. As Halvan J. Lieteau, general manager of I.B.M.'s Bedford-Stuyvesant assembly plant, points out, "It helps if you can say, 'Happy birthday,' 'How's the family?' It shows we're all in this together." Top management sets the tone: "Vin" Learson was known for such grand gestures as visiting a hospitalized employe, attending the retirement dinner of the lady who taught him key punching and speeding aid to I.B.M.'ers caught in natural disasters. Cary has inspired similar stories. Dinners with employes and their families are still held at all I.B.M. field offices, but the chairman can't attend all of them, so Learson took to videotaping a set of general remarks and then recording dozens of comments with a local flavor which were spliced into the basic videotape.

To hear I.B.M. executives talk about the company, it seems to rank in historical importance somewhere between the Renaissance and the discovery of America. Internally, perhaps even more than for public consumption, I.B.M. leaders like to talk about the company's role in "easing mankind's burden" and "being central to a lot of the world's work." After describing the I.B.M. World Trade Corporation's operations in 116 foreign countries, I.B.M. senior vice president Jones quickly points out that "trade is a great way to break down the barriers between one political institution and another." (The I.B.M. World Trade Corporation's slogan is "World peace through world trade.") Think, I.B.M.'s house organ, is full of stories and pictures showing I.B.M. products helping medical researchers save lives, or aiding urban planners, or dealing with pollution, or performing assorted other good deeds.

The company also makes much of its efforts to help minority groups, whose members compose 6 per cent of I.B.M.'s professional employes in the United States and 4 per cent of its managers. I.B.M. is the only major corporation with a manufacturing plant in the Bedford-Stuyvesant section of Brooklyn; it does have operations in South Africa, but it pays its black workers very well and treats them better than the Government there would like; it has provided a good deal of financial aid to black colleges and it gives employes paid leaves to teach minority students or help manage poverty programs. Such activities are duly recorded for internal as well as external consumption.

Thus I.B.M. is presented to its employes as a benevolent and beneficial institution of crucial importance to the world, and if that isn't sufficient to make it the focal point of the employes' lives, I.B.M. has structured the work environment to help achieve that goal. At headquarters in Armonk and at the many other suburban and exurban offices and plants, the cars pour up the driveway each morning just before 8:30, and from then until 4:30 there is seldom anyone to see or talk to save I.B.M.'ers. There is nowhere to go at lunchtime except the company cafeteria, nothing to do except utilize the company's recreation facilities, and nowhere to escape to except the company's nature trails.

After hours, since I.B.M.'s managers and engineers may compose the bulk of the educated, professional middle class in surrounding semi-rural towns, they tend to get together socially, sometimes at the company's dollar-a-year country clubs or at the family picnics, awards luncheons and dances run by their local I.B.M. Club, employes say.

Among I.B.M.'s 8,000 employes in Westchester, civic involvement seems to be limited mainly to the local school boards. This is not surprising, according to Dr. Michael Maccoby, because "the demands of technology have tended to liberalize the political ideology" of advanced-technology managers at companies like I.B.M.; yet they are "oriented toward personal success, interesting work and a comfortable family life. Few are active in bettering their community. Few worry about the social effects of the products they create, even though a majority believe that advanced technology contributes to 'dehumanization.' "

For many I.B.M.'ers life is often confined to *Kinder, Küche* and computer. While Henry Ford offered an honest day's wages for an honest day's work, I.B.M. offers something only slightly short of an organic social system out of medieval Catholic social theory. When I.B.M. executives talk about "commitment" and "dedication" and "the I.B.M. family," one doesn't know whether to feel better or worse when it becomes clear they really believe it.

Frank Cary's priorities were revealed not long ago when The New York Times asked a variety of economic leaders what they regarded as the nation's most pressing problems. While others in this pre-Watergate period listed war, crime or pollution, Cary worried most about "the nation's lack of belief in its own institutions and in the leadership of those institutions." Cary need have little concern about his institution, particularly among the older I.B.M.'ers. Typically they've spent their entire careers at the company, and for them there is no God but I.B.M. and Frank Cary is now its prophet. Younger employes often have fewer loyalties and a different view. "All this family-dinner stuff, this togetherness crap, is a pain in the butt," says one engineer. Cary admits, "There is a tendency on the part of younger people to have less faith in the management of the enterprise," but so far I.B.M. has been successfully assimilating a new generation of I.B.M.'ers, both male and female.

For years I.B.M. has treated women with courtly gentility,

putting them on pedestals but not into high-level jobs. Now women are demanding more, and I.B.M. has promoted one woman to vice president and put another on the board of directors. (The director is former Ambassador Patricia Roberts Harris, who is a black, a woman and a highly competent lawyer—and soon may be on more corporate boards than anyone since J. P. Morgan.) According to company figures, women hold 8 per cent of the professional jobs at I.B.M. and only 3 per cent of the managerial jobs, but Thomas J. Watson Jr. notes, "I wouldn't say Women's Lib is an issue around here."

As George Sadowsky of the Urban Institute says, "I.B.M. is a religion, a very successful religion, more so than most. It really indoctrinates its people." Sadowsky adds, "Those who can't stand the discipline leave," and there has been a stream of I.B.M.'ers who've left the company, generally to set up or join small firms in and around the computer industry. (And while some have built successful businesses, McGrath says a high percentage of them fail because their narrow functional responsibilities at I.B.M. leave them ill-prepared for more general managerial tasks.)

Ultimately, the vast majority of I.B.M.'ers stay put, giving the company a low turnover rate, a high *esprit de corps* and lots of people who will say they're "proud to be a small part of I.B.M." It's no wonder, then, that I.B.M.'ers got on so well with their recent visitors from the People's Republic of China. The Chinese technicians, with their Mao jackets and little red books, had a good deal in common with the I.B.M.'ers, attired in their Watsonian dark suits and white shirts and guided by the precepts of chairmen Watson, Learson and Cary. Like the Chinese, the I.B.M.'ers see themselves as part of a glorious revolution, one which is not only changing the world but giving meaning, purpose and direction to their lives. (And while there are few Maoists in Armonk, the Chinese are said to be fairly eager to bring a few I.B.M.'ers into their midst.)

At the Research Division, Dr. Ralph Gomery says, "We do science here. It's kind of our life." But the salesmen who run I.B.M. have managed to envelop many of the employes in an organization and a life-style which develops individuals who are as efficient as they are interchangeable and dull. At the same time they have created a corporation of such dynamism and power that it is generally agreed it could put all of its competitors out of business anytime it might choose to do so.

Not surprisingly, then, the biggest threat to this smoothly running machine right now is the Justice Department, whose antitrust suit seeks to dismember I.B.M. The Government's suit, which follows several civil antitrust suits filed by I.B.M. competitors, was filed quietly on Jan. 17, 1969—the last business day of the Johnson Administration—and it dropped out of sight until last year when Federal District Judge David Edelstein began nudging it toward resolution.

There is widespread speculation on Wall Street that the Justice Department may have demanded radical surgery largely to persuade I.B.M. to settle out of court for a more modest divestiture of certain operations. That was the result of the Federal Government's 1933 and 1952 antitrust suits against I.B.M. The Justice Department has so far failed to specify just how it would break up I.B.M., but the specter of antitrust was sufficient, some say, to persuade I.B.M. to "unbundle"—i.e., sell separately—a variety of products in 1970 and to settle out of court with Control Data Corporation to keep the evidence in that company's antitrust suit from being used in the Government's suit. On June 20 the Government asked a Federal judge to hold I.B.M. in contempt and fine it up to $1-million for failure to produce some 12,000 documents from the Control Data suit.

Prof. Charles H. Berry, an economist at Princeton University, says if the Government's antitrust case ever comes to trial, "it is entirely likely that it's going to rewrite antitrust law and refine it still further." Berry notes that, unlike the classic turn-of-the-century monopolies, I.B.M. didn't achieve its market position through a combination or conspiracy in restraint of trade, which is prohibited under Section I of the Sherman Antitrust Act. Instead, I.B.M. grew internally, so the Justice Department must go after it under Section II of the Sherman Act, which prohibits maintaining a monopoly position in an industry, and Berry notes, "There have been very few Section II cases."

In dismissing the Greyhound Computer Corporation's antitrust suit against I.B.M. last July, Judge Walter E. Craig noted that size alone isn't illegal, nor is the mere possession of monopoly power. "It is the wrongful use and exercise of monopoly power which is proscribed" by Section II, the judge pointed out. To win its case, the Justice Department will have to prove, first, that I.B.M. possesses monopoly power in a particular market, and, second, that it has maintained this power through willful action, such as anticompetitive pricing practices, rather than through the excellence of its products or management. Both questions are very complicated. "Unlike copper or steel, a computer is a very complex system of instruments in which the various pieces can all come from I.B.M. or from a variety of manufacturers, so the way a market is defined and measured will yield a significantly different extent of I.B.M.'s dominance," Professor Berry notes, while even more subtlety is needed to differentiate excellence of management from willful exclusion of competitors.

As Professor Shubik says, "The economics of the case are incredibly difficult to specify. A simple empirical test is that if you were to offer me a high enough per diem consulting fee, I would be willing to work for either side in the I.B.M. antitrust suit in perfect comfort and utter objectivity." On balance, Shubik says it might be socially and economically beneficial to break up I.B.M. but it's not clear.

I.B.M. has approached the suit in characteristic fashion. Board member William H. Moore notes, "They built the best legal staff so that when D-Day came, they were ready." I.B.M.'s contingent of lawyers is directed by vice president and general counsel Nicholas deB. Katzenbach, no stranger to antitrust, since he was once Attorney General in the Johnson Administration. Nor is I.B.M. without friends in Washington, although Thomas J. Watson Jr. was on the White House "enemies" list, a fact that may well have surprised him since he was a member of Democrats for Nixon and his brother Arthur, the former chairman of I.B.M. World Trade Corporation, was the President's Ambassador to France. The two contributed a reported $300,000 to President Nixon's re-election campaign. Then too, I.B.M. has 580,000 shareholders, and the Justice Department, like the Supreme Court, has been known to follow the election returns.

If and when the case is tried, whatever the District Court decides is likely to be appealed to the Supreme Court, and if I.B.M. ultimately loses, Berry notes, "the dissolution remedy is one alternative, but it is not one which has been at all characteristic of the courts."

T. Vincent Learson has confidently predicted the breakup of I.B.M. "will never happen," and the pace of the courts suggests that the enterprise Thomas J. Watson Sr. built is likely to be around for a while yet. In any case, its style and its procedures, as well as its products, are likely to make the company increasingly important throughout the nation and the world. For looming behind I.B.M. are scores of other high-technology companies whose rapid growth suggests that an increasing share of industrial power, jobs and life-styles will be molded in places like Route 128 outside of Boston, Princeton and Hightstown in New Jersey, Palo Alto, Calif., and Armonk, instead of the old industrial centers like Detroit and Pittsburgh.

Many of these advanced-technology companies will be directed by the same dictates, and perhaps some of the same men, that have guided I.B.M. Perhaps Fred W. Tappe was right when he wrote the words to the rouser that used to be *de rigueur* at I.B.M. rallies:

March on with I.B.M. We lead the way!
Onward we'll ever go, in strong array;
Our thousands to the fore, nothing can stem
Our march forevermore, with I.B.M. ■

July 29, 1973

Kresge's Discounting Success

8 Inventory Turnovers Is K Marts' Yearly Goal

By ISADORE BARMASH

TROY, Mich.—The S. S. Kresge Company executive carefully studied the highway traffic outside his company's modernistic citadel-like headquarters in this Detroit suburb. "We are," he said quietly, "a company in a hurry."

This comment, coming from a man who earns $160,000 a year, surprised a visitor last week. Why should a company that in the last six years leapfrogged over F. W. Woolworth, W. T. Grant, McCrory, R. H. Macy, Federated Department Stores and others to become the nation's third largest nonfood retailer still be in a hurry?

Kresge achieved an enviable 20.8 per cent sales increase in its fiscal year, ended Jan. 30, to $4.63-billion from $3.83-billion the year before. Net income rose 18.1 per cent to $138.2-million, or $1.15 a share, from $117-million, or $1 a share. But Kresge acknowledges it is drawing a bead on the No. 2 chain, the J. C. Penney Company (which had sales last year of $6.2-billion). So Kresge, despite its sharp gains, still has a long way to go.

Over the last decade, Kresge has dazzled security analysts with a compound annual growth rate of 28 per cent in net income. However, that remarkable achievement faded in the fourth quarter of last year when net income rose only 4.6 per cent from a year earlier. Company executives blamed the slower earnings growth on price controls and a less favorable sales mix, with sales gains coming mostly in lower-profit hard goods.

By opening more than 600 K Mart discount stores, the 100-year-old Kresge concern has shown the most dramatic growth of any American retailer in the last dozen years. One reason it's in a hurry is that it has targeted a goal of $12-billion in sales by 1980—about two and a half times its present volume.

•

This ambitious goal means that the company must add something like an average $1.23-billion in sales in each of the next six fiscal years. This would be a larger increment than Kresge has put on during any of its peak years—and all its last dozen have been peaks. Thus the 1980 target will require even more aggressive efforts by a company that has already dazzled its rivals. But some tongues have started wagging over Kresge's ability to digest such huge gains.

The company's pensive, diffident-appearing chairman and chief executive officer, Robert E. Dewar, seems almost at odds with the corporate penchant for haste. But his words dispel that impression.

"In the last five years," he said, "we have critically examined the United States as to retailing competition and demographics to determine what our goal should be by 1980. We think our potential is tremendous.

"We are already in 196 of the country's 261 standard metropolitan districts. Within the next two years we will be in 25 more."

Kresge's sales goal, however, is only a surface reason for its haste. The real reasons are a race against time, inflation, competition and perhaps some adverse change in consumer psychology.

Wall Street's appraisal of Kresge's performance is generally high. Says David C. Taylor, partner of Coleman & Co., an institutional research firm, "More than the establishment of specific goals, Kresge's success is due to its dogged determination to stick to operating priorities which they have set for themselves."

Recent interviews with 10 of Kresge's top executives showed that:

¶The 100-a-year store expansion rate, which left many competitive retailers with their mouths wide open, will be continued and even accelerated. In the next few years as many as 160 new stores a year are projected. Kresge executives believe they can capitalize on the company's 2 per cent profit margin only by constantly increasing its sales.

¶Costs of construction and therefore of leases (Kresge leases all its stores) are rising so fast that every week that goes by without a new K Mart delays Kresge's objective of reaching its desired return by the end of a new store's third year. Each store's goals include eight complete turnovers of inventory each year (against six for the rest of the discount industry) and a 25 per cent return on investment. Its fast turnover, Kresge insists, means that only 35 to 40 per cent of its funds have to be tied up in inventory at any one time.

¶Having aimed its K Mart stores at the large urban-suburban centers and at medium-sized cities, Kresge is now reaching out to a new market, the smaller city of 12,000 to 15,000 population. The company has devised a new K Mart, which it calls "Group 9," of only 40,000 square feet, compared with other K Marts that range from 64,000 to 93,500 square feet. As many as 200 or 300 of the new small stores are to be opened by 1980.

¶While it is not easy to jar an outright admission from the organization-conscious, straight-laced men who run Kresge, it is likely that their haste also arises from the realization that they made a late start in the discount industry and from an underlying fear that the attraction of low-margin merchandising may disappear as quietly as it began in the United States in the late nineteen-forties.

•

The closest any of the executives came to conceding such a possibility was Walter H. Teninga, vice chairman.

"We're certainly aware that the K Mart vehicle as such may not necessarily be good forever," he said. "But we believe that the concept of low-margin retailing, especially as we have been practicing it, will be around for a long time."

He said that, until the recent economic pinch abroad, Kresge had been eyeing Europe, especially West Germany, as well as Mexico for likely K Mart developments like those it already has in Canada and Australia.

The concept of haste was handed down by a man whom most of those who now run the company consider the architect of its success.

In 1957 Harry B. Cunningham, who had been sales director, was named to the new post of general vice president. He was instructed by Franklin P. Williams, then president, to find some way out of the profit squeeze on the Kresge variety stores.

Shift in Retail Rankings

Sales of nonfood retail stores, 12 largest in order (millions of dollars)

1973		1963	
1. Sears, Roebuck	$12,306	1. Sears, Roebuck	$5,115
2. J. C. Penney	6,244	2. J. C. Penney	1,834
3. S. S. Kresge	**4,633**	3. Montgomery Ward	1,500
4. F. W. Woolworth	3,722	4. F. W. Woolworth	1,183
5. Montgomery Ward	3,230	5. Federated	933
6. Federated	2,962*	6. Allied Stores	830
7. W. T. Grant	1,850	7. May Dept. Stores	724
8. City Products	1,642	8. W. T. Grant	699
9. Allied Stores	1,598	9. R. H. Macy	583
10. May Dept. Stores	1,555	10. McCrory	569
11. Dayton-Hudson	1,407	**11. S. S. Kresge**	**511**
12. Gamble-Skogmo	1,395	12. Gimbel Brothers	492

*preliminary

Specializing in fast-moving, basic goods sold mostly at list price, Kresge variety stores were getting only three and a half turnovers in their inventory each year while discount stores were achieving six.

Mr. Cunningham toured the country for two years, studying various forms of retailing as well as mergers and other forms of affiliation. When he became president in 1959, he decided that discount stores offered the best potential.

What happened then has become company lore. Mr. Dewar, Kresge's chairman and a former assistant to Mr. Cunningham, recalls: "Harry was a very infectious man. He had a habit of 'listening constructively' and then moving quickly. He advised his co-workers, 'We'll have to move fast—and not just put a toe in the water.'" (Mr. Cunningham retired as chairman last year but remains a director.)

After winning the board's approval, Mr. Cunningham, as Kresge's president, moved quickly in the face of some criticism. He allocated $80-million for the entry into discounting before even one K Mart had opened its doors and reduced the dividend.

"You're always asking us for suggestions," a stockholder told him at the 1962 annual meeting. "I have one for you: Why don't you resign?"

Under the Cunningham thrust and the development of a prototype store by C. L. Yohe, a regional manager noted for his meticulousness, the program was put into effect. In 1962 the first K Mart was opened in Garden City, Mich., a 64,500-square-foot unit that became the model for all the rest.

Since that beginning, the K Marts have remained largely unchanged — clearly defined traffic flow, wide, maintained aisles and departments identical in location whether the stores are in Michigan or Florida.

A careful watcher of other discounters, the Kresge team learned from their mistakes and tribulations.

In the early nineteen-sixties, for example, E. J. Korvette, which had been widely heralded for its expansion prowess, was already having growing pains, operating on a layer of thin management. Interstate Stores was aggressively expanding on both coasts but was a decade away from its real financial troubles.

The closed-membership chains were beginning to falter because their customer base wasn't strong enough.

As for the variety chains like Kresge's, all of them, including Woolworth's, Grant's, Newberry's and McCrory's, were diversifying into discounting, department-store or specialty chains. For retailers, it was clearly a time for making major moves.

In shifting its thrust to discounting, the Cunningham team made several basic decisions:

¶All resources and assets of the company were to be put behind the K Mart program. This meant that every function of the business was to be geared to produce maximum results for the new venture.

¶Convinced that the plan needed total support from the staff, Kresge brought in no outsiders except trainees and used its approximate 700 managers of Kresge variety stores as its cadre of managers for the new chain. (Kresge still has 360 variety stores and makes a profit on them but it isn't opening any new ones.)

As Ervin E. Wardlow, Kresge's president, expressed it:

"I think Mr. Cunningham's most important decision was to use his variety-store managers. Can a high-gross manager of a variety store change into a low-margin manager? He convinced them to stop thinking of standard percentages and to concentrate on dollars and to look at the R.O.I.—return on investment.

"And it worked just fine. Each man had the experience and knew how to handle people, all of which helped in managing K Mart stores. Some of our biggest K Marts are being run by 55-year-old men."

¶Finally, recruitment was sharply stepped up in the colleges. In the last few years, Kresge has been topped only by the Federal Government as the largest recruiter of college graduates in the country. More than 3,000 are currently in executive training at Kresge.

An average of about 1,500 are hired every year to participate in the five- to six-year program, which starts everyone as a stockman and graduates him as a store manager.

Trainees normally begin at $8,400 and get $9,000 within a year. K Mart store managers earn about $27,000 a year, and buyers at corporate headquarters earn $35,000 to $60,000 a year.

As the trainees approach store-manager status, Kresge each year plucks out the best for special 12- to 18-month duty at headquarters.

The point, according to Richard H. Falck, senior vice president-sales and general merchandise manager, is: "We want those with outstanding performance to obtain new insights into our company by working with top management. It will give them a broader base when they become store managers."

The store managers help Kresge maintain its profit margin: Company earnings are 6 per cent of sales before taxes and approximately 2 per cent of sales after taxes.

Some outsiders ask whether the K Mart system is based on a die stamped out of Troy, Mich., and sent out all over the country. They note the identical stores in 600 communities, the detailed manuals on how to stock, how to display and when and how to promote and the approved lists of merchandise.

Mr. Falck, for one, bristles at such a suggestion.

"Our store managers order

Kresge at a Glance

[In Thousands of Dollars]

Year ended	Jan. 30, 1974	Jan. 31, 1973
Sales*	$4,633,223	$3,836,826
Net Income*	138,251	117,075
Earnings per share	1.15	1.00
Avg. number of common shares outstanding	119,661,367	119,210,445

by far the bulk of the goods they need and feel they run their own show," he declared.

The inescapable conclusion, however, is that Kresge's is highly "manualized." This is probably the reason the chain has been able to make great strides at a time when other discounters have run into problems of either overexpansion or financial distress.

"It's been a magnificent thing for people who work in Kresge," sums up Mr. Teninga.

Last year 600 of the 1,700 trainees hired dropped out. Carl Darnell, personnel director, said it was a normal ratio.

"After all, when we hire 21- to 24-year-olds, we are asking them to make a career here," he said. "Not everyone likes retailing. You have to get excitement out of selling. But we've been lucky, both with new and staff people. Going with a winner builds pride."

In merchandising, Kresge concedes that it is a fashion follower rather than leader, often waiting to see what moves at Sears and Penney before it jumps in with both feet. Sometimes, Kresge steals an advance.

"We beat both Sears and Penney to double-knits," brags Mr. Wardlow. Apparel and other soft lines are made to K Mart specifications and bear its own label.

The Metropolitan New York market has so far failed to attract a major entry by K Mart, but there are a number of Kresge variety stores there.

A K Mart that recently opened on Staten Island is said to be "doing well," after some initial parking problems.

Kresge has more interest in the area, and sees opportunities for K Mart in northern New Jersey, the Jersey coast and upstate New York.

Chances are that both the extreme standardization and the aggressive recruitment will continue to provide an effective metabolism for Kresge's hearty appetite for new stores.

New departments, such as pharmaceuticals, auto accessories and building materials, are adding to the over-all volume at the same time that the relatively recent push in apparel has effectively built this category in ratio of sales. Currently, "soft goods" account for about 48 per cent of volume.

A "troika" that has been appointed to succeed Mr. Cunningham consists of Mr. Dewar, chairman and chief executive officer; Mr. Wardlow, president and chief operating officer, and Mr. Teninga, vice chairman and chief financial and development officer. Mr. Dewar earned $244,400 in 1972, while Mr. Wardlow and Mr. Teninga each got $163,300.

Despite the troika setup, however, it is clear that Mr. Dewar call the shots.

The soft-spoken, articulate chairman, a 51-year-old lawyer who has been at Kresge for 25 years, has amassed a great deal of merchandising and operational knowledge to add to his legal background. He appears mild on the surface, but a colleague says he can be "tougher than a junkyard dog" if it seems necessary.

April 7, 1974

Bell Report Offers Strategy on Rulings

By DAVID BURNHAM
Special to The New York Times

WASHINGTON, June 18—A confidential research report for the Bell System has recommended a national public relations strategy to counter what the report calls "the knee jerk reaction of most of the public" that economic competition means lower prices and better service.

The report is an outline of how the Bell System proposes to guide public opinion against two important decisions by the Federal Communications Commission that have exposed the American Telephone and Telegraph Company and its subsidiaries to increased competition for the first time in several decades.

One of the commission decisions has permitted concerns other than the telephone company to manufacture and market such equipment as switchboards and dialing equipment that are "interconnected" with the national telephone system.

The other commission decision allows companies other than those associated with the Bell System—what are known as "specialized common carriers"—to provide point-to-point communications for large industrial customers.

The unusually candid research report outlining the telephone company's proposed strategy to mold public opinion, a copy of which has been obtained by The New York Times, appeared to have been written by the Planning Division of the Illinois Bell Telephone Company.

The report said that a major obstacle to the company's counterattack against the F.C.C.'s decisions was the public's "deeply held beliefs about the 'American way-of-life' namely, the inherent benefits of competition or 'free enterprise'. . ."

To meet this obstacle, the report called for "the intelligent exploitation of every avenue of communication available to us, the careful targeting of specific points in unique approaches and all part of an over-all and systematic development of our case before the public."

The report said the purpose of the research on which it had based its conclusions was not to find the one best answer, but rather to "sharpen the focus and presentation elements of a selected set of 'facts.'"

The research report did not explain the precise objectives of the proposed public relations program. But the program appeared to be a broad effort to persuade the F.C.C. through the public to reverse its earlier rulings or at least go no further in adopting rules that force the telephone company to compete for certain kinds of business.

Allegations of anticompetitive business practices by A.T.&T. will be the subject of a hearing by the Senate Antitrust and Monopoly Subcommittee on Thursday.

The hearings are part of a series aimed at collecting information to support a bill introduced by Senator Philip A. Hart, the subcommittee's chairman, to outlaw monopoly power in seven industrial sectors.

"Competition and the belief system surrounding it and the 'free enterprise system' is the fulcrum on which our case and that proposed by the F.C.C. teeters," the report concluded.

"The knee-jerk reaction of most of the public is that 'competition' among companies providing products or services is inherently and always 'good' —resulting in the lowest prices and highest quality and choice in the marketplace," the report states.

Noting that "our argument asks the public to accept the antithesis of what they have been encultured to believe," the report said there were potential dangers in the proposed public relations program.

"Thus, in pursuing our objectives," the report continued, "we stand to alter forever key elements of our image that we are not sufficiently innovative or technologically competent to overcome the challenges of competition [from the specialized common carriers] and interconnection."

June 19, 1974

Exxon Displaces G.M. as No. 1 in Sales

By PETER T. KILBORN

Fortune magazine has just issued its list of the nation's 500 biggest corporations, and never in the 20 years that it has tracked their performance have the rankings been so changed. The reason, the May issue of the magazine reports, is oil.

Fortune's new list of the biggest publicly held industrial corporations for 1974 introduces a new No. 1: the Exxon Corporation. It displaced the General Motors Corporation, which had been America's biggest industrial company for 40 years. Exxon was No. 2 in 1973.

Propelled by soaring prices for oil, Exxon's sales — the gauge by which Fortune determines size — surged from $25.7-billion in 1973 to $35.8-billion last year.

G.M., meanwhile, languished in the face of an acute decline in automobile sales, much of it brought on by consumers' reluctance to pay higher prices for petroleum products. The auto manufacturer's sales dropped from $35.8-billion in 1973 to $31.5-billion last year.

Similar situations recurred

Largest US Industrial Corporations
(Ranked by sales. Figures in the millions.)

RANK '74	'73	COMPANY	SALES	ASSETS	NET INCOME
1	2	Exxon	$42,061	$31,332	$3,142
2	1	General Motors	31,550	20,468	950
3	3	Ford Motor	23,621	14,174	361
4	6	Texaco	23,255	17,176	1,586
5	7	Mobil Oil	18,929	14,074	1,047
6	11	Standard of Calif.	17,191	11,640	970
7	10	Gulf Oil	16,458	12,503	1,065
8	5	General Electric	13,413	9,369	608
9	8	I.B.M.	12,675	14,027	1,838
10	9	I.T.T.	11,154	10,697	451
11	4	Chrysler	10,971	6,733	(52)
12	13	U.S. Steel	9,186	7,717	635
13	15	Standard Oil (Ind)	9,085	8,915	970
14	18	Shell Oil	7,633	6,129	621
15	12	Western Electric	7,382	5,240	311
16	21	Continental Oil	7,041	4,673	328
17	16	E. I. du Pont	6,910	5,980	404
18	26	Atlantic Richfield	6,740	6,152	475
19	14	Westinghouse	6,466	4,302	28
20	36	Occidental Petroleum	5,719	3,325	281

Source: Fortune Magazine. (Loss)

The New York Times/May 5, 1975

throughout the list. Ten of the 20 biggest companies in sales last year were oil companies, up from seven a year earlier.

Texaco, Inc., moved up from sixth place in 1973 to fourth place in 1974. The Mobil Oil Corporation moved up from seventh to fifth, the Standard Oil Company of California from 11th to sixth and the Gulf Oil Corporation from 10th to seventh. The Occidental Oil Corporation leaped from 36th to 20th.

Where oil companies rose, automobile companies fell. General Motors is now No. 2. The Chrysler Corporation fell most—from fourth largest in 1973 to 11th in 1974, American Motors dropped from 38th to 93d. Ford held on to third place, but its sales barely budged, from $23-billion in 1973 to $23.6-billion last year. Sales of the oil companies, meanwhile, were soaring.

There were other dislocations. The International Business Machines Corporation, for years synonymous with growth, emerged as the ninth biggest company, down from 8th in 1973. The General Electric company, down from fifth to eighth.

In net income, a better test of a company's performance than sales growth, the oil companies again led all other industries. Exxon was first with earnings of $3.1-billion. But several companies in other industries held their own.

I.B.M. recorded American industry's second highest profit, $1.8-billion. And the Eastman Kodak Company, while 32d biggest in sales last year, ranked 10th in earnings.

Two years ago, Chrysler was Fortune's fifth most profitable company. Last year, Chrysler's rank was 493, the consequence of a $52-million loss, the biggest deficit among the 500.

Oil companies recorded the greatest sales gains last year, an industry average of 80.4 per cent. But their profit growth, 39.6 per cent, was exceeded by that of the mining companies, 100.8 per cent; metal manufacturing companies, 78.6 per cent, and chemical companies, 40.5 per cent.

Fortune observed that, in absolute terms, the big industrial companies reported extraordinary growth. Sales of all 500 companies rose 25 per cent. In uninflated dollars, however, they rose only 5.7 per cent.

If oil companies were excluded from the group, sales in real dollars actually fell 4.7 per cent. The 12.8 per cent profit growth of the 500 companies would have been only 4.1 percent without the oil companies' contribution. Thus, in real dollars, profits of the nonoil sector actually declined.

May 5, 1975

17-STATE RAIL NET SET IN NORTHEAST

A Federal Plan to Absorb 7 Bankrupt Roads in Freight System Becomes Law

By RALPH BLUMENTHAL

By not acting, Congress sealed into law last night a sweeping Federal plan to absorb seven bankrupt Northeast railroads into a cut-down, semi-nationalized rail system.

The multi-billion-dollar plan, embodying the largest corporate reorganization in American history, provides for a federally financed Consolidated Rail Corporation, known as Conrail, and a Government-created private railroad competitor to take over from the bankrupt private lines next year most of the rail freight-hauling in a populous 17-state region.

Commuter Lines Affected

Conrail will also take over almost all the 90,000 employees of the absorbed railroads and run the New York metropolitan area commuter rail lines, although intercity trains will continue to be operated by the National Railroad Passenger Corporation, known as Amtrak.

The plan must now be implemented with legislation. Conrail is scheduled to start rolling on or shortly after Feb. 27, 1976.

Under the unusual enactment procedure, Congress had until midnight last night to reject the final reorganization plan submitted 60 working days ago by the United States Railway Association, the Government agency charge with restructuring the bankrupt lines.

However, it was clear long before Friday's weekend adjournment that the urgency of the Northeast rail crisis made any veto of the only viable salvage plan unthinkable.

The bankrupt railroads are now losing more than $1 million a day, or about $500 million a year.

The last possibility that either house might block the plan all but vanished Thursday with a long-awaited agreement giving the Chessie System a major part in the restructuring.

Basing his remarks on the expected acceptance, Arthur D. Lewis, chairman of the railway association, Friday hailed Congress's enactment of the plan.

"The acceptance is a major step forward in the reorganization process," he said through a spokesman, adding, "It is essential now that implementing legislation be adopted as soon as possible."

With the plan adopted, attention focused on emerging House and Senate bills to grant Conrail the $2.5-billion start-up funding the railway association called for and to otherwise flesh out the skeletal Conrail structure. In addition, the legislation was aimed at reshaping some regulatory powers of the Interstate Commerce Commission to give the new railroads more flexibility to adjust rates.

Approval Not Needed

Under an implementation bill currently undergoing revision in the House Transportation and Commerce Subcommittee, railroads would be free to raise and lower their rates each year by up to 7 percent without prior approval of the commission.

The proposed bill also contains a controversial provision to grant all solvent railroads participating in the reorganization immunity from deficiency judgments. That is, if a creditor of a bankrupt railroad should file suit claiming the property was sold too cheaply, not the purchaser but the Government would be liable for any award. Conrail itself was originally granted this protection.

The Senate Transportation Subcommittee is due to start considering its Conrail bill this week. Passage in both houses however, is not expected before early next year.

"This is the 'bill,' at this point," said Tom Allison, transportation expert on the staff of the Senate Commerce Committee, gesturing over a pile of papers and memorandums strewn over his desk last week.

Some Criticism Voiced

Meanwhile, critics of the plan continued to circulate their objections. Pennsylvania and New Jersey expressed concern over the survival of their rail commuter lines under Conrail, and Pennsylvania questioned the terms of the deal with Chessie.

The Penn-Central complained that its properties were being grossly undervalued by the railway association, and the First National City Bank, which recently analysed financial needs of the rail industry, saw far greater Conrail expenses than had been anticipated.

Basically, the reorganization plan provides for stripping 5,750 light-density miles from the current 21,000 miles of track operated by the seven bankrupt lines—Penn Central, Erie-Lackawanna, Ann Arbor, Reading, Lehigh Valley, Central of New Jersey and Lehigh and Hudson River.

The more lucrative 15,000 remaining route miles will be divided between a new Government-created, profit-making corporation, Conrail, and an expanded private Chessie System. Thus, the railway association felt, it is not creating a Government rail monopoly.

Under the plan, Conrail will account for about 37 percent of the region's net ton miles annually; Chessie, 32 percent; the Norfolk & Western, 21 percent; and smaller solvent lines, 10 percent.

Conrail will purchase rights of way and rolling stock from the bankrupts with Conrail stock and certificates of value. However, the railway association's decision to rate the bankrupts' properties at their net liquidation value — that is, scrap value — of $621 million has provoked outrage by the bankrupts. Penn-Central's trustees have valued their own property alone at $7.4 billion.

The dispute really involves different ways of looking at the liquidation and is likely to be resolved only by the United States Court of Claims after years of litigation.

Chessie's projected purchase of some of bankrupt lines has also become controversial. After recently offering the eqivalent of $62.5 million for the proerties, Chessie on Wednesday toughened its terms to $54.5 million, plus other demands. The railway association, however, facing little choice, agreed the next day to charges by the Pennsylvania Department of Transportation that the public was being shortchanged.

Financial forecasts of the railway association are that Conrail will initially run large deficits but will begin realizing income from operations and generate a positive cash flow from 1979 on.

The $2.5 billion funding request, which the plan maintains will represent the total Federal cash commitment, includes a $250 million Conrail contingency fund and a $100 million discretionary fund for the Secretary of Transportation for projects related to but not exclusively limited to Conrail.

In addition, the plan forsees a $4.2 billion expenditure from Conrail revenues and investors 1976 to 1980 for right-of-way improvements.

November 9, 1975

The Case for Federal Corporate Charters

The following is excerpted from "Constitutionalizing the Corporation: The Case for the Chartering of Giant Corporations," by Ralph Nader, Mark Green and Joel Seligman, published by the Corporate Accountability Research Group, Washington, D.C.

The genius of our Constitution is that it guaranteed rights to powerless individuals against the powerful collective called government so the people would control the government, rather than the reverse.

But after two centuries, nongovernmental organizations have managed to escape the kind of accountability that a democracy imposes on its centers of power. These are our giant corporations. They are effectively private governments with vast direct and indirect impact on communities, citizens, taxpayers, workers, investors, small businesses and future generations.

The existing system of state chartering for these corporations is a farce. The control of national and multinational corporations requires national authority. Who would not be embarrassed to defend the proposition that only a state—and not the Federal Government—can charter a General Motors or an International Telephone and Telegraph? Also, our current economic crisis and corporate crime wave underscore the failure of the old corporate law system. To put it simply, if big business today is so good, why are things so bad?

The problem is ultimately one of power: how can we limit unaccountable power and how can we ensure that those who do exercise managerial power are the best managers feasible? Federal chartering of the nation's 700 largest corporations seems the most logical and workable mechanism.

In the early 1800's, charters were selectively granted by the states, and contained limitations on how large a company could grow, where it could do business, and what business it could engage in. After the Civil War, the growth of railroads and the introduction of the trust device enabled industrialists like John D. Rockefeller to dominate not merely a local market, nor even a regional market, but a national one.

State corporation laws began to retaliate against such abusive activity; New Jersey went into the chartermongering business in the 1890's. New Jersey effectively legalized the trust by allowing one company to control the stock of another; it ended all size constraints, allowed nonvoting stock and stock watering, and gave chartered firms perpetual life. The result: while New Jersey granted 834 charters and earned $857,000 in chartering tax revenues in 1896, it granted 2,093 charters and earned $3.2 million by 1906.

Then came Delaware, which drastically reduced shareholder rights, enhanced management prerogative and allowed a corporation to conduct business in any way it chose as long as the state did not explicitly forbid it—and Delaware forbade very little. As a consequence, corporate franchise fees averaged 31 percent of its total state revenues from 1913 to 1934.

By 1963, other states had begun to catch up, or come down, to Delaware's corporate law standards. Delaware's state legislature then created a commission, comprised of a few top corporate lawyers, to draft further liberalizations of the state corporation law. The legislature unanimously ratified the revisions in 1967. Incorporations soon doubled. By 1974, 76,000 corporations were chartered in Delaware, including 52 of the top 100 corporations and 251 of the largest 500—the successful result of a law for sale.

The Constitution's silence about giant cor-

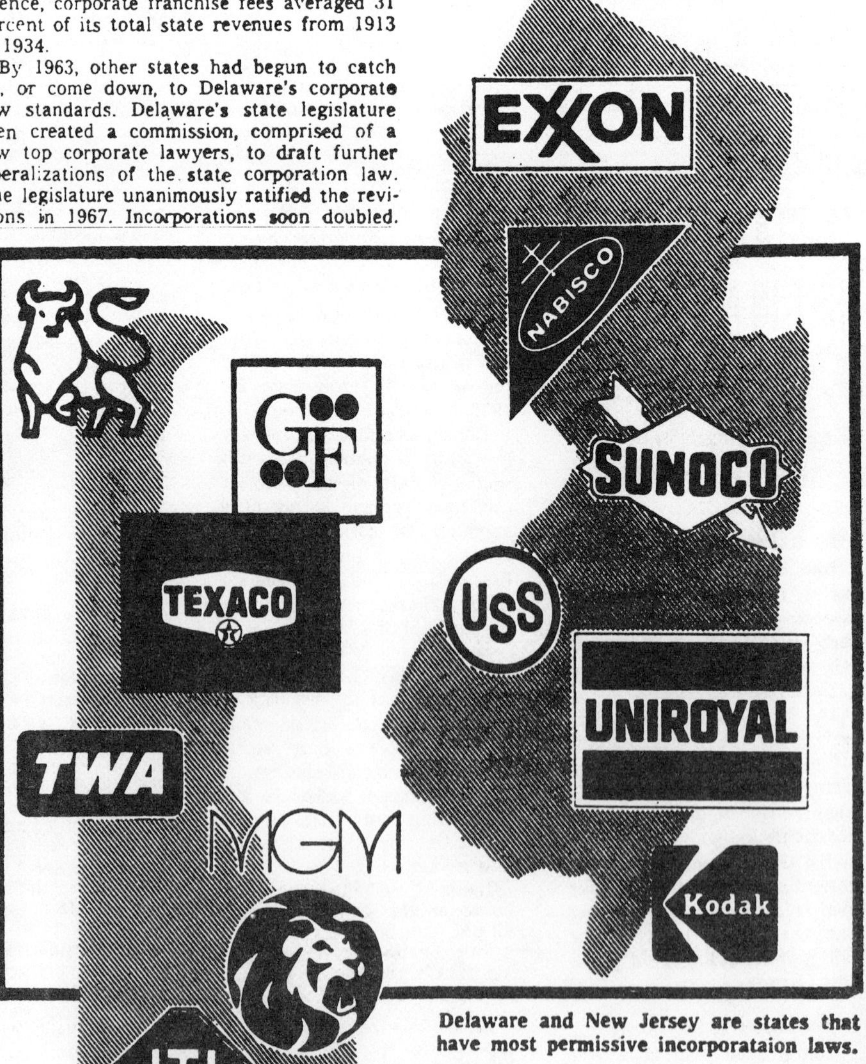

Delaware and New Jersey are states that have most permissive incorporataion laws.

porations was perhaps understandable for an agrarian economy in 1789, but it is anomalous in 1976. It is time to "constitutionalize" the corporation, to provide checks and balances between shareholders, the board and executives; decentralized decision-making; the limitation of powers; rights to free speech, disclosure and privacy, and freedom from monopoly, surveillance, and managerial tyranny; self-help and private property, and an informed corporate constituency.

A Federal Chartering Act would have several aims:

¶To avoid executive oligarchy and to promote more corporate democracy. Managers must surrender some of their authority to the board of directors and to shareholders. Victims must have direct rights of relief against corporate perpetrators. So in certain situations communities could vote to require a plant to stop polluting, or workers could buy stock and, with cumulative voting, elect directors, or employees will be free to speak and free from invasions of privacy by their controlling employers.

¶To increase disclosure by these corporapower. Because giant monopolies and oligopolies frustrate the pro-consumer benefits of government. This will not be a mere academic exercise—along the Hudson River, political candidates can not now avoid talking about General Electric's highly publicized PCB (polychlorinated biphenyls) contamination of the river.

¶To impose the discipline of competition on managers who want to exploit their market polies frustrate the pro-consumer benefits of economic competition—lower prices, less waste, more innovation, greater variety of goods, less centralized power—a program of deconcentration is essential.

¶To enable affected interests—consumers, workers, shareholders—to appeal directly to court to vindicate their rights. Liberalized standing and class action rules would facilitate this direct self-help against unresponsive corporate or governmental bureaucracies.

If enacted, the Federal chartering legislation would provide that all corporations continue to incorporate in a state; the Federal Government would additionally require the largest of them to charter in Washington. This dual system fully appreciates the constitutional principle of Federalism.

The act would cover all industrial, retail and transporation corporations which sold more than $250 million in goods or services in the United States in any one of the previous three years, or employed more than 10,000 persons here in one of those years and, in either case, were listed on a national securities exchange or held of record at least 2,000 shareholders. The reforms could be tailored to the operations of the largest financial corporations in subsequent proposals.

It is probable that some United States corporations will consider fleeing abroad rather than complying with an effective Federal chartering law. The exchange listing and 2,000 American shareholder provisions would ensure they cannot. Delisting and elimination of all but 1,999 United States shareholders would be a practical impossibility for most domestic giants.

The Securities and Exchange Commission would enforce most of the act's provisions—although the Federal Trade Commission could handle the disclosure sections and the Justice Department's antitrust division, the antimonopoly provisions. Corporate officers convicted of a willful violation of the act would not be allowed to serve as an officer or director in an American corporation or partnership for five years. Fines should be calibrated to annual corporate sales—a violation by G.M. should not be penalized as though perpetrated by Mrs. Smith's Pie—and should increase for repeated violations.

These serious penalties recognize that, unlike, say, the impetuous murder of a spouse, corporate crime is committed by sophisticated and deliberative business persons who carefully weigh the costs and benefits.

In few aspects does state corporation law fail quite so completely as the state's inability —or unwillingness—to enforce the law. Enforcement of prohibition seemed vigorous by comparison.

Delaware has no enforcement wing. In fact, of the 22 states that responded to a survey on the subject last year, 18 acknowledged that they did not employ a single person to enforce the substantive provisions of their corporation laws. Not one could point to a single instance of punishing a corporation in 1972, 1973 or 1974, other that for failing to pay franchise taxes or file an annual report. Most had no idea whether the corporations they did penalize subsequently complied with sanctions.

The enforcement record of the Securities and Exchange Commission — the existing agency we believe best suited to enforce most of the Federal Chartering Act—shines by comparison.

In another problem area, while on paper giant corporations may appear to be expressions of democracy, with shareholder-owners electing directors who "manage the corporation" and who select and oversee the corporate officers.

But because management controls the nominating and proxy machinery, the expenditure of corporate funds and the use of corporate personnel in election contests, its directorial candidates and its resolutions almost invariably prevail—99.7 percent of all directors' elections in our largest corporations are uncontested. And under Delaware law, there are very few management activities which actually trigger a shareholder vote. G.M. could sell off its Buick division and not need to get shareholder approval.

Of an average 14.49 directors on the boards of the top 200 industrial companies, 6.56 are "inside directors" employed by or beholden to the chief executive, while 69 percent of the "outsiders" are simpatico fellow corporate executives. Said one executive, "I can't think of a single time when the board has failed to support a proposed policy of management." Thus the Penn-Central board, like most cuckolds, was among the last to discover the truth.

Secrecy often seems the first rule of corporate bureaucracies—whether they are dealing with citizens, Congress or the regulatory agencies. Indeed, the Federal government often promotes this secrecy by its "rule of confidentiality," whereby only aggregate industry data can be released, not company-by-company data. And the S.E.C.'s failure to promote uniform accounting rules has worked to keep the investing public often uninformed about a firm's true performance.

Even at the Federal level, it has been argued, governments are often "so woefully uninformed of corporate affairs that even honest and well-intentioned men cannot effectively execute public policy."

As for employee relations, while the Constitution carefully restrains all levels of government from invading the rights of citizens, it effectively allows every business corporation to do so. A 1974 Senate study estimated that between 200,000 and 300,000 private business polygraph tests are administered each year; two surveys estimated that companies eavesdrop on or investigate the loyalty of one-fifth of all American workers.

"We complain about government and business, we stress the advantages of the free enterprise system, we complain aobut the totalitarian state," said General Robert E. Wood, former chairman of the board of Sears, Roebuck & Compnay, "but in our individual organizations . . . we have created more or less of a totalitarian system in industry, particularly in large industry."

Federally chartered corporations would be required to observe First Amendment requirements of free speech and assembly, which would prohibit retaliation against employees who in good faith communicate apparent corporate violations of law to directors, legislatures or law enforcement agencies. These giant companies would also respect the privacy of its employees: for example, the use of hidden microphones or television cameras, which violate the privacy of numerous innocent employees, would be proscribed; employees would be able to examine their corporate personnel files.

While the states were gutting their laws, three major merger waves—in 1898-1902, 1925-1929 and 1967-1969—led to a concentration of industrial assets in this country: nearly two-thirds of our manufacturing sector is now controlled by oligopolies and the largest 200 industrial firms own about two-thirds of all industrial assets.

More competition is an important antidote to corporate power. Thus, no Federally chartered corporation should be allow to acquire any company among the eight largest in any industry where four or fewer concerns control 50 percent or more of the market. And to the extent such corporations do make acquisitions in unconcentrated industries, they must within three months divest themselves of an approximately equal amount of assets. There would be a presumption of illegal monopoly power if four or fewer corporations accounted for 50 percent or more of a market for any two consecutive years among the most recent five. An Antimonopoly Court would determine appropriate relief, which would usually entail divestiture.

Several counter-arguments to Federal chartering can be, and have been, made, including the following.

¶Isn't it just more regulation?

¶Won't Federal chartering be a costly burden on business?

¶Will it lead to a Federal take-over of business, to socialism?

In answer to the first, a reinforced S.E.C. and Justice's antitrust division would enforce the law. Historically, these two agencies have made the market process work better, rather than substituted for it. Indeed, it is when the market fails to perform as expected and when such agencies fail to take corrective action that we get truly burdensome regulation, like wage and price controls.

As for the cost burden, it would fall not on the approximately 1.8 million small and moderate size businesses in this country, but only on those 700 giants who, given their size and impact, can best afford and deserve it.

Finally, Federal chartering is approximately as socialistic a concept as Federal charters for banks, which have existed since 1864, or the Justice Department's proposal in 1975 to shift regulation of insurance companies from the states to Washington.

If anything, the precise reverse of Federal chartering leading to a Federal take-over might be true. As business grows bigger, less accountable and less law-abiding, government will be compelled to extend its authority over this rogue elephant in our midst.

May 9, 1976

The Editorial Notebook

No-Fault Antitrust

In January 1969, the Justice Department filed an antitrust complaint against the I.B.M. Corporation. Eight years later, the Government completed court presentation of its case. It will take another five to seven years for I.B.M. to argue its side, for a Government rebuttal and a court verdict. Final resolution will then await appeals through the Federal courts. Now the lawyers say they are confident the case can be cleaned up by 1987!

No one knows precisely how much all this will cost. But it is known that over one hundred million pages of documents have been circulated among the interested parties, and 45,000 pages of court testimony have been offered so far. The ultimate number of witnesses is expected to exceed 450. I.B.M. alone is said to be spending $20 million a year on legal costs.

•

The circumstances in *U.S. vs. I.B.M.* are obviously unusual: The case is extremely complex, the Government's presentation has been tardy, the judge has been poorly equipped for the issues. And despite protestations to the contrary, I.B.M. appears in no hurry to finish. But typically, any major civil suit under the Sherman Antitrust Act takes years to adjudicate, at a cost of millions.

Is there no better way? Some procedural changes could make a difference and prevent difficult cases like *U.S. vs. I.B.M.* from deteriorating into a generation-long farce. A few experienced judges might be designated in each Federal district to handle such complex suits; they could be given funds to hire expert economists and engineers to help them with technical issues. The Justice Department might be encouraged to engage private trial lawyers when its own staff seems inadequate. And judges might insist that the Government prepare its cases thoroughly before filing a complaint, instead of searching for evidence for years thereafter.

But a more fundamental reform of antitrust law is needed. The Sherman Act forbids monopoly control of a market without reference to how the monopoly came about. Yet the Supreme Court and the Justice Department have been reluctant to condemn unless it can be shown that a company "willfully" acquired such dominance. Hence vast amounts of time and effort are spent in cases like I.B.M. to find clues about a company's past conduct. If the courts were to interpret the Sherman Act more literally, or—better yet—if Congress changed the act cases could be decided solely on the economic issue of whether monopoly power exists. This would greatly streamline proceedings.

Some contend that this so-called "no-fault" approach to civil antitrust actions would unfairly penalize innovative firms. Few deny, for example, that I.B.M. and Kodak have won their shares in the market largely by doing their jobs very well. Thus one might question the wisdom of a policy that discourages overwhelming success in free enterprise merely for the sake of tidiness in antitrust procedure.

One of the original proponents of "no-fault," Professor Donald Turner of the Harvard Law School, accepts the point. Mr. Turner, a former head of the antitrust division of the Justice Department, would apply the law only when a company's monopoly position persists for a long time and when there are large prospective benefits to consumers to be gained from ending its market domination. This would reward firms for their efficiency, yet place a reasonable limit on those rewards.

Antitrust policy, which may have seemed simple enough in the trust-busting days of Teddy Roosevelt, must be adjusted to suit the times. When companies are alleged to have committed antitrust crimes—fixing prices, unfairly burying competitors—they must be tried for their conduct. But when the real issue is whether markets work well enough to match efficient production with consumer needs, the pattern of conduct is irrelevant and only gets in the way. If the public stands to gain from the break-up of a huge corporation, then five or fifteen years is too long a time to wait. If the public is to gain little or nothing, the company should be spared the cost and diversion of a lengthy defense. The time for "no-fault" antitrust has arrived.

June 12, 1977

Corporations: 'The Antitrust Artichoke'

To the Editor:

There is already a no-fault concept inherent in the antitrust laws. Monopoly, or a tendency to monopolize, or any attempt to monopolize, is a "per se" violation, and nothing further need be shown to convict. The difficulty comes in attempting to define what it is which is being monopolized, i.e., the "market" affected.

In the specific case of I.B.M., what you see is not a legal defense but more a legal offense. By overwhelming the system with documents, testimony, rebuttal, discovery and so forth, I.B.M. has found a way to confound the law by sheer volume of response. The realistic expectation is that the outcome of the entire process, some 20 years long, will be moot since the computer industry in 1980 will only remotely resemble the 1969 version.

However, all of this, though close to the "heart," is nonetheless merely a leaf on the antitrust artichoke. There are other tender leaves — Federal judges who prefer intellectual gymnastics and highly complex, sophisticated legal theories (i.e., "specific intent," "causation," etc.) to the common-sense application of the law in the real world, where most of us, if not the judges, live.

The very heart of the artichoke is the thoroughly nonsensical concept of the corporation as a "being," entitled to all of the legal protections afforded human beings under the Constitution. Since major corporations routinely maintain legal departments, augmented as necessary by outside counsel, they have become quite adept at "evolving" the complex legal theories beloved of judges, and to their favor.

Since such legal costs are passed on to the consumer in product costs, at least that portion not subsidized by the taxpayers through deduction, the intended ultimate beneficiary of the law pays when it is not enforced, when enforcement is attempted, and for the corporate "moulding" process.

The only substantive answer, both in respect to antitrust laws and others aimed at corporate activities, is to rid American jurisprudence of the myth that corporations are beings subject to the same civil codes and procedures as are afforded human beings.

We require a civil code applicable solely to corporate and other commercial entities, starting with the assumption that such are not necessarily innocent until proved guilty, and a recognition of the fact that the financial resources of major corporations make "equality before the law" and "equal justice" a fallacy.

Given what you know of the current Justice Department effort vis-à-vis I.B.M., imagine if you will what chance any private individual or small company would have trying to press an antitrust claim against a major corporation. With respect to major corporations, the antitrust laws—and any others, for that matter—will not be fully effective until small businesses and/or private individuals are able to avail themselves of remedies under such laws as a practical matter. Such is not the case today.

LEONARD J. PALMER
Rego Park, N.Y., June 13, 1977

The writer is an executive at two computer data processing companies.

June 18, 1977

Who Owns U.S. Business? Slowly the Word Comes Out

A new set of regulations, designed to provide more information on who really owns American corporations, was scheduled to take effect at the end of this month, but it has been postponed for eight months by the Securities and Exchange Commission. The proposed rules came under intense attack from institutional investors, including insurance companies, banks, pension funds and investment houses. All of them complained that the reporting requirements would be too burdensome.

The S.E.C. now requires that a "beneficial owner" of at least 5 percent of a company's outstanding shares, or anyone seeking to acquire 5 percent, register with the commission. Beneficial owners are defined narrowly as those receiving a financial benefit from the stock ownership. Thus the large institutional investors, which often hold the largest blocks of public-held stock in American corporations, are not required at present to report on their holdings.

"We don't know who owns and controls the stock of American corporations," says Michael Locker, president of Corporate Data Exchange, a New York-based nonprofit research foundation devoted to matters of corporate disclosure. "I don't think we can have effective accountability of the major corporations until we have that information."

Last week Corporate Data Exchange (which is also working on a study for a Senate subcommittee to document the stock ownership of the 125 largest industrial, financial, transport and utility corporations) issued the first of a series of reports on specific industries, presenting detailed information on the principal voting shareholders of major corporations in the industry.

The first of these "Stock Ownership Directories," which the foundation says shows for the first time the principal stockholders of many of the country's largest corporations, deals with the transportation industry. The findings offer some insight into the fund of information that could be made available if key voting shareholders had to report their holdings. For example, the report discloses that:

¶A single investment company, the Dreyfus Fund, ranks among the top three voting shareholders in all 11 major United States airlines. Dreyfus is the largest identifiable voting interest in five of these airlines — Pan American, Eastern, Delta, Braniff and Continental — with the size of the Dreyfus block varying from 3.27 percent of the voting shares of Delta to 4.71 percent of those of Braniff .

¶A Liechtenstein resident and former owner of the West German magazine Stern, Richard Gruner, is one of the largest identifiable stock voters in three of the nation's major airlines—American, Pan American and Continental.

¶Rockefeller family interests, including the Rockefeller Foundation, the Rockefeller Brothers Fund, Descendants of John D. Rockefeller Jr. and Rockefeller University, still hold 2.27 percent of the voting stock of the Standard Oil Company of California, 2.23 percent of the Mobil Corporation, 1.97 percent of the Exxon Corporation and 1.2 percent of the Standard Oil Company (Indiana).

¶The Morgan Guaranty Trust Company, which recently argued before a Senate subcommittee considering pension fund legislation that its trading has a minimal effect on stock prices, is the largest identifiable shareholder of Pepsico Inc. (with 8.64 percent of the voting stock), and the fifth largest shareholder in American Airlines (with 2.43 percent of the voting stock).

¶The Newmont Mining Corporation, a leading member of the consortium that recently acquired the Peabody Coal Company, is the largest identifiable stockholder in the Continental Oil Company, whose Consolidated Coal subsidiary is another major coal producer.

¶Twenty-seven of the 52 companies involved in transportation with annual sales of more than $1 billion have at least one shareholder who votes 5 percent or more of the stock. Fourteen of these major shareholders are employee thrift and savings plans. The companies in this category include Mobil, T.W.A., Tenneco, Standard Oil of California and United States Steel.

Corporate Data Exchange obtained most of its information during a six-month examination of the security portfolios of 2,000 institutional investors and by examining reports filed with five Federal regulatory agencies. Its next major reports will look at agribusiness companies and the banking industry, including information on the major corporate relationships of the leading banks. The transportation study was funded by grants from the Transnational Institute, a project of the Institute for Policy Studies, the World Council of Churches and the United Methodist Church, among others.

Much of the information gathered and published in the first report would have been required under the rules just postponed by the S.E.C. These will broaden the definition of "beneficial owner" to include any person or institution who has the right to vote or dispose of securities, or who shares in such powers, as well as anyone who has the right (through an option, for example) to bring his total acquisition to more than 5 percent within 60 days.

When these requirements were approved last February the commission ruled that certain institutional investors—including banks, brokerage firms and pension funds—could report on a short form, telling how many shares were held (with changes in those holdings in each quarter), the number of accounts represented by the holdings, whether the voting and trading powers were shared with anyone else and, if so, with whom.

Individuals and insurance companies will be required to report on a longer form, giving additional information on the sources of funds used in making stock purchases and the purpose of purchases, particularly any intent to acquire control of a corporation.

The new rules will exempt firms from having to report on any share holdings that had no voting or trading powers associated with them, such as shares held by a brokerage house for an owner who retains the right to vote or dispose of them.

The delay in implementing the new reporting requirements, S.E.C. officials said, will enable interested parties to comment, between now and mid-October on how the rules might be changed.

ANN CRITTENDEN

August 14, 1977

In The Nation

Playing It Both Ways With Business

By ARTHUR KROCK

WASHINGTON, Oct. 26—The choice by the Atomic Energy Commission of E. I. du Pont de Nemours & Co. to design, construct and operate the new and vast facilities for the production of the H-bomb is another instance of the fact that, when the Government needs skills and organizations to do big jobs, especially in the area of security, it must call upon those which often at the same time it is attempting to disperse by anti-trust prosecutions. The instance of the du Pont Company is striking because of the current litigation with the Department of Justice in which it is involved.

Washington also, as always in times of national emergency, is filling up with men drafted from industry because of their unique abilities to put the nation in an effective state of economic and military preparedness. Among those in the present list are executives of companies which are under anti-trust arraignment by the Department of Justice or the Federal Trade Commission for developing organizations which other arms of the Government find indispensable to effect industrial mobilization. This is the two-policy anomaly of recent Democratic Administrations which steadily attempt to break up the facilities on which they must depend in a crisis.

As explained by Crawford H. Greenwalt, president of du Pont, the company accepted the new Government assignment it did not seek "only upon assurances from the highest sources that the project is of vital importance to the security and defense of the United States and that, in their opinion, the du Pont Company is peculiarly well equipped in technical personnel and resources as well as by experience to undertake this great task."

One of its "resources" is to be found in its relation to General Motors, which the Government is also asking to undertake contracts of vital importance that no lesser organization could carry out. But one purpose of the anti-trust suit against du Pont is to divest it of its interest in General Motors on the ground that this effects an empire of monopoly.

The A. E. C. Contract

The arrangement between du Pont and the A. E. C., as Mr. Greenwalt explained to his stockholders, "provides that the Government pay all costs, that du Pont receive a fee of one dollar, and that any patents growing out of du Pont's work become the property of the Government of the United States. You will recall that the Hanford Project [the huge atomic energy production in World War II] was undertaken on the same basis * * * The new project will entail the detachment from present duties of a number of the company's ablest management and technical personnel. The compensation of those individuals will, of course, be paid by the Government, but their withdrawal from normal commercial operations will constitute a substantial contribution by the company."

The president of du Pont did not add, though he might have, that a considerable section of its management has been diverted from regular duties for periods of great and recurring length by the anti-trust suits. And the same point could be made by many other industrial units from which the Administration is drafting executives and on whose technical organizations a large part of the success of the present mobilization will depend.

The three pending anti-trust actions against du Pont emphasize the anomaly of policy. First, an arrangement of the company with Imperial Chemicals, Ltd., a British concern, to exchange technical information and patents, is attacked as having impeded others in industry from getting information to which they are entitled. And association with British interests in forming companies abroad—Canada, Brazil, etc.—is assailed as having adversely affected American commerce. Second, the Government asks the du Pont Company to divest itself of its interest in General Motors, and members of the du Pont family to relinquish their holdings in the United States Rubber Company. Third, the Government seeks to require the du Ponts to open to all their cellophane patents on the ground that this is a monopoly in violation of the Sherman Act.

"Bigness" Pro and Con

Part of the first charge seems to attack procedures which the President is asking American industry to follow under Point Four. The second suit appears to reflect Government objection to "bigness" (though the department denies this), but "bigness" is what helped to qualify the company to do the Hanford job and the new one on the H-bomb. The third suit is more in character with the construction of the Sherman Act which has been made by most Democratic Administrations.

The Department of Justice, of course, has impressive arguments to support its claim that anti-trust suits are no part of a policy to harass big business on ideological grounds and/or with the platforms in mind of certain important groups allied politically to the Administration. It can give many examples of abuse of industrial power.

But the fact remains that some of these actions are directed against the very organizations which could not meet the needs of public emergencies if the suits are successful. Among these needs are individual talents in industry, such as those possessed by W. H. Harrison, K. T. Keller and M. W. Boyer, who have just been drafted for important defense assignments, but all of whose companies, or companies closely related, one way or another, are being prosecuted under the anti-trust laws.

October 27, 1950

PERMANENT WORK ON ARMS SET BY G. E.

Division Created to Function in War or Peace to Assure Quick Weapon Source

Special to THE NEW YORK TIMES.

SCHENECTADY, N. Y., Nov. 22—A move that will set aside part of its physical plant, tools and equipment and technical personnel as a permanent source of weapons for defense has been made by the General Electric Company.

The new set-up, which will be known as the Defense Products Division will be headed by John W. Belanger, who has been promoted from general manager of the company's large apparatus division to vice president.

The new division will include the aircraft gas turbine department, with headquarters at Lockland, Ohio, and the aeronautics and ordnance systems department here. The former plant develops and produces turbojet engines and turbo-superchargers for aircraft and the latter turns out gunfire and jet engine control systems.

Mr. Belanger said that the arrangement centered responsibility in one spot and in one person and would save much time in getting production for defense from a low to high rate of output. The division will provide the plans and other facilities needed by sub-contractors once General Electric has to expand or step up its rate of output.

He predicted that the new set-up would become more or less routine "for a long period of time." He described it as a step in the direction of "stand-by plants," saying that the country could no longer afford to have defense plants spring up during a war, then die with a period of peace.

G. E. Needs Machine Tools

The process of building plants, acquiring machine tools and other equipment to go into large-scale production at a time of national danger is very costly, Mr. Belanger stressed. By keeping a greatly reduced defense production unit in being at all times with additional buildings and equipment ready for any emergency, the country would be in a much stronger position, he asserted.

Discussing some of the bottlenecks in the production of jet aircraft engines now, Mr. Belanger put the shortage of machine tools high on the list. General Electric has a team of engineers scouring Europe for machine tools and has picked up "a good quantity" in Germany, Switzerland and Italy, he declared.

Some of the tools bought in Europe will go to subcontractors of General Electric who are working on the jet engines ordered by the United States Air Force and Navy, he said.

General Electric's decision to maintain a part of its production facilities and experienced personnel as a stand-by plant ready to go into immediate operations on defense orders follows one line of recent reasoning in both Washington and in industry.

Some companies with large defense orders are finding that the "brick and mortar" part of the problem of turning out weapons is much more difficult than during the expansion period of World War II. Plants that could be put up in less than a year at that time are now taking a year and a half or more.

Loss of Personnel Cited

Many of the plants built for the production of aircraft engines, airframes and even tanks during World War II have been turned over to other users since the end of hostilities and not all of them can be recaptured by the Federal Government.

Machine tools stored at the close of that conflict have been found to be either not in the best of shape or of a type not so widely in demand for today's job. A lot of them can be used to advantage, but by no means all of them.

The dispersal of experienced personnel is another great loss when a plant closes down at the end of a war. Many such workers can be brought back in an emergency, but those who cannot be found must be replaced by newly trained workers, and the training process takes valuable time.

With a plant functioning in peacetime, even at a low level, a part of it could be used for other purposes, but the hard core of workers and machines could be kept in place and ready for a large expansion program when needed.

The announcement by General Electric follows a statement on Nov. 10 by Charles E. Wilson, president of General Motors, that his corporation had drafted plans for a "dual purpose" factory to be erected near Arlington, Tex.

Mr. Wilson, who has urged planning for prolonged military production, said that the Texas factory would be completed in 1953. He added that it was designed so it could be used for total war production, for combined civilian and military output, or for total output of automobiles.

In a speech at the annual dinner of the American Ordnance Association in Cincinnati, Mr. Wilson asserted that it was time the country realized the need of a permanent defense program if the shift from peace to war production were to be made smoothly and quickly and without uprooting thousands of workers.

November 23, 1951

100 Big Corporations Got 64% of Defense Contracts

Analysis of Awards Over 3 Years Shows Clear Trend Toward Concentration —G.M.'s 7.2% Share Tops List

Special to THE NEW YORK TIMES.

WASHINGTON, Jan. 18—One hundred large corporations, with General Motors in first place, received 64 per cent of the defense contracts awarded during the three-year period that ended on last June 30.

A semi-annual analysis available today—the last to be issued by the Defense Department—showed a clear trend toward further concentration of war contracts and a diminishing share for small business.

The compilation credited the 100 top-ranking corporations with 61.2 per cent of the defense contracts awarded up to the end of June, 1951, 62.4 per cent a year later and 64 per cent at the middle of last year. All the calculations are based on dollar value of the contracts.

In releasing its report, the Defense Department said that "for economy reasons" no further semi-annual listings would be compiled.

General Motors was unchallenged in first place with 7.2 per ecnt of the total, followed by Boeing Airplane Company, with 4.4 per cent and General Electric Company, 3.6 per cent.

G. M. defense contracts were valued at $7,095,800,000, against a country-wide total of $98,723,000,000 for the three-year period, which roughly coincided with the Korean war.

The report, compiled by the office of Charles S. Thomas, Assistant Secretary of Defense for Supply and Logistics, acknowledged that many small business concerns were handicapped in bidding for large defense contracts.

"Prime contractors for aircraft, tanks, weapons, electronics and other complex equipment or specialized types of military supplies are of necessity selected on the basis of their ability to manu facture and assemble the matériel in quantities and on schedules required by the armed forces," the report said.

"Small firms usually are not able to act as prime contractors for the heavy equipment that represents a very large part of the total value of military purchases, because they are unable to provide the necessary engineering, research, managerial and production resources that are required."

The report pointed out, however, that small business played an important role through subcontracting and through prime contracts for items it was equipped to supply.

During the three years, the report said, concerns employing fewer than 500 workers received prime contracts worth more than $18,000,000,000, nearly one-fifth of the value of all defense work placed in the United States.

Reflecting cutbacks in tank and vehicle output and a continued build-up in procurement of airplanes, the report showed that the dollar value of contracts held by two aircraft companies—Boeing and Consolidated Vultee—had been more than double in the first six months of 1953.

As a result, Boeing moved from eighth to second place in the rankings and Convair from sixteenth to eighth place.

The top ten contracts, in order of their rank, are as follows: General Motors, Boeing Airplane Company, General Electric Company, Douglas Aircraft Company, United Aircraft Corporation, Chrysler Corporation, Lockheed Aircraft Company, Consolidated Vultee Aircraft Corporation, North American Aviation, Inc. and Republic Aviation Corporation.

January 19, 1954

Defense Is the Biggest Business; Pattern Shifts on West Coast

49.7 Billion Is Sought

By RICHARD RUTTER

There's no business like big business and the biggest of all is defense business. This has evolved under the heat of the "cold war" into the biggest single economic activity, not only in the United States but in the world.

For the fiscal year that begins next July 1 and ends June 30, 1963, the Kennedy Administration is asking Congress for $49,700,000,000 in defense funds. That represents almost 10 per cent of the gross national product—the total of all goods and services.

The importance of defense business in the nation's over-all economy can hardly be exaggerated. It affects scores of industries, involves jobs in the millions and payrolls in the billions.

Actually, no exact measurement of the part defense business plays in the national economy has ever been made. But a few striking statistics are evidence in themselves of how big this activity is.

80% of Volume

The aerospace industry, for instance, depends heavily on defense business—to the extent of about 80 per cent of its volume. In 1961, sales of aircraft, space vehicles, missiles and components to the Government alone amounted to $11,501,000,000. By contrast, other customers accounted for $3,372,000,000 in sales. The aerospace industry employs some 700,000 workers. The backlog of Government orders stood at $11,045,000,000 on last Dec. 31.

In the present fiscal year purchases by the Pentagon of space, military and other electronic gear and services are estimated by the Electronic Industries Association at $7,800,000,000. In fiscal 1963 this figure is expected to rise to about $9,000,000,000 and account for 55 per cent of the total sales of the electronic industry. Ten years ago Government expenditures for electronics were less than one-eighth that amount. The electronics content of the defense budget has risen from 7 to 17.5 per cent.

In the present fiscal year prime defense contracts awarded will amount to some $29,000,000,000, a peacetime record by far.

Where is the money going?

That is a question every taxpayer has a right to ask and the Kennedy Administration has supplied a detailed answer, albeit somewhat buried in the 1,171 pages of the 1963 budget. The Defense Department has introduced a major innovation in outlining military expenditure plans. It consists of "program packages" (or "Hitch packages" named for the innovator, Charles A. Hitch, Assistant Secretary of Defense, Controller). Put together are all similar functions, regardless of service, agency or previous budgetary status and placed under a definitive heading. This is the way the "packages" are listed in the coming 1963 fiscal budget:

¶Strategic Retailatory Forces—$9,400,000,000. In this category falls the Polaris program involving submarines, missiles and support activity. Also, the Atlas and Titan missiles and manned bombers.

¶Continental Air and Missile Defense Forces—$2,000,000,000. Here are included manned interceptor aircraft and their support, surface-to-air missile, detection gear.

¶General Purpose Forces—$18,400,000,000. The category covers tactical air and aircraft procurement, ordnance and related equipment, tactical communications.

¶Sealift-Airlift Forces—$1,300,000,000. This program is for the Military Air Transport Service, the Military Sea Transport Service and the procurement of aircraft and ships for transporting personnel.

¶Reserve and National Guard Forces—$1,900,000,000.

¶Research and Development $5,700,000,000. The Federal

Government is the biggest single spender in the field of research, which includes applied research, weapons development, advanced technology and the like.

¶General Support—$12,800,000,000. This is a catch-all category covering miscellaneous aircraft procurement, oceanographic research ships, operating costs of defense agencies and other noncombat activities.

¶Civil Defense—$7,000,000.

¶Military Assistance—$1,500,000,000. This is the part of foreign aid that is designated strictly for military purposes as distinguished from the much larger sum earmarked for economic support overseas.

The Defense Department believes that the new "package" method will be more meaningful than the former budget method. All parts of a program, Polaris, for example, are tied together and the total cost of a program is readily identifiable.

The real crux of Mr. Hitch's "program package," as the electronic trade group points out, is that there is a five-year projection for all major programs and categories. Through this technique, the Pentagon is able to detail all related costs of a program—such as the Minuteman missile or the RS-70 bomber—over a five-year period, maintaining close control and also enabling the Administration to keep Congress informed of exact plans and expenses.

A more detailed breakdown of the new defense budget gives a good idea of the type of equipment for which these huge sums are being spent.

B-52 Build-up

Take manned bombers, for instance. The build-up of the B-52 force of military planes to fourteen wings will be completed by the end of this year. Several B-52 squadrons are being equipped with the Hound Dog air-to-ground missile. The Skybolt air-to-ground missile in time also will be part of B-52 equipment. This year some B-52 squadrons will be equipped with Quail decoy missiles.

The defense program as of now calls for a steady increase in the potent intercontinental missiles. Envisioned is a thirteen-squadron Atlas missile program and a twelve-squadron Titan program. Twelve squadrons of 600 dispersed Minuteman missiles have been funded through the present fiscal year. Funds for four more squadrons are included in the 1963 budget and additional squadrons will be procured in later years.

Twenty-nine Polaris submarines have been funded to date. To this force, the Pentagon plans to add six more submarines in fiscal 1963 and six in fiscal 1964, bringing the total to forty-one. The first six Polaris submarines are equipped with the A-1 missile with an effective range of 1,200 nautical miles. The seventh to nineteenth submarines will be equipped with the A-2 missile, which has a range of 1,500 nautical miles. The twentieth and all subsequent submarines will carry the A-3 missile with a range of 2,500 nautical miles.

Defense against missile attack is also a key part of the military program. It encompasses the Ballistic Missile Early Warning System, well on the way to completion, a Missile Defense Alarm System (orbiting satellites) and a Bomb Alarm System. Under advanced development is the Nike-Zeus defense system. Incoming targets are detected and tracked by radar, the Zeus missile is launched and steered to an intercept point and then its nuclear warhead is detonated by ground command — thus destroying the target toward the end of its ballistic trajectory.

No More Procurement

Significantly, no additional procurement of manned interceptor aircraft is contemplated this year. The active force consists of F-101, F-102 and F-106 all-weather interceptors.

The man in uniform, of course, still is an integral part of the defense program. Accordingly, the Pentagon will be spending large sums for small arms, combat vehicles, portable communications gear, ammunition, protective field masks and so on.

Then, there is the man at sea. The Kennedy Administration plans an active fleet of 824 ships by the end of fiscal 1963. This will include attack carriers, anti-submarine warfare carriers, cruisers, command ships, destroyer-type vessels, submarines, and amphibious, mine warfare and auxiliary ships. The Navy missile program provides for substantial quantities of air defense missiles including Sparrow III, Sidewinder IC, Terrier, Talos, Tartar and Bullpup. Also budgeted are Shrike antiradar missiles, Subroc antisubmarine rockets, ZUNI air-to-surface rockets, new type bombs and torpedoes.

In the area of manned aircraft, more than $1,000,000,000 has been earmarked for procurement of the F4H-F-110 fighter plane in fiscal 1963. This will be followed by development of the TFX, an interservice tactical fighter. Defense Department expenditures for aircraft electronics during fiscal 1963 is estimated alone at some $1,500,000,000.

The 1963 defense budget continues a trend toward increased emphasis on research and development. Funds requested for research, development, test and evaluation are put at $6,650,000,000 in the next fiscal year, compared with $6,000,000,000 in fiscal 1962.

Aside from all this, there is the nation's burgeoning space program — another major factor in the economy. The budget of the National Aeronautics and Space Administration has risen from $95,000,000 in 1961 to $3,800,000,000 in fiscal 1963. In fiscal 1964 it is expected to reach $5,000,000,000 and by 1970 the figure may be about $10,000,000,000. Most of the N. A. S. A.'s spending is for research, development and operation. The rest goes for construction of facilities.

The advent of the Space Age, it is apparent, has brought about a sharp shift in the pattern of defense spending. In the fiscal year that ended June 30, 1956, almost 33 per cent of the Defense Department's prime contract awards went for manned aircraft, against 5.6 per cent for missiles. By fiscal 1961, missiles accounted for 25.6 per cent of military spending, aircraft only 21.5 per cent. Electronic equipment of various kinds accounted for 13.7 per cent of prime contract awards.

The New York Stock Exchange has taken a close look at the fifty largest defense suppliers listed on the Big Board. The study shows that these fifty in fiscal 1961 garnered 65.4 per cent of prime contracts, compared with 57.1 per cent in 1957. A five-year analysis reveals further that these con-

Defense Companies Listed With Prime Contracts

Company	Total Prime Contracts 1957-81 (millions)	% of All Prime Contracts 1957-61	Prime Contracts Annually (a) (millions)					Rank Among 100 Leading Military Prime Contractors				
			1961	1960	1958	1958	1957	'61	'60	'59	'58	'57
General Dynamics	$ 7,199	6.7	$ 1,920	$ 1,260	$ 1,616	$ 1,383	$ 1,019	1	1	1	2	1
Boeing	6,133	5.7	920	1,009	1,167	2,131	907	4	3	2	1	2
Lockheed Aircraft	4,435	4.1	1,175	1,071	899	755	536	3	2	5	4	6
General Elec. Co.	4,412	4.1	875	963	914	783	877	5	4	4	3	3
No. Am. Aviation	4,271	4.0	1,197	908	1,018	648	500	2	5	3	7	7
United Aircraft	3,048	2.8	626	517	538	661	706	7	7	7	5	4
Amer. Tel. & Tel.	2,746	2.6	551	467	477	660	592	8	8	10	6	5
Martin-Marietta	2,579	2.4	692	597	524	400	366	6	6	8	10	9
Douglas Aircraft	2,151	2.0	307	405	676	513	249	14	10	6	8	14
Sperry Rand	1,692	1.6	408	296	403	370	215	9	13	12	11	17
Int'l Busin's Mach.	1,576	1.5	330	290	277	317	362	12	14	17	14	10
Raytheon	1,475	1.4	305	323	393	237	218	15	12	13	22	16
McConnell Aircraft	1,464	1.4	220	195	404	352	294	23	22	11	13	11
Radio Corp. of Am.	1,420	1.3	392	405	200	288	133	10	9	22	15	24
Republic Aviation	1,296	1.2	296	265	281	265	190	16	15	16	19	21
Westinghouse Elec.	1,255	1.2	308	258	238	269	182	13	16	19	18	22
General Motors	1,251	1.2	282	219	211	281	259	19	20	20	17	12
Bendix Corp.	1,236	1.2	267	239	271	208	251	20	18	18	24	13
Chrysler	1,026	1.0	158	187	323	259	99	27	24	14	20	29
Gruman Aircraft	1,023	1.0	238	239	300	245	..	22	19	15	21	..
Gen'l Tire & Rub.	996	0.9	290	243	207	160	96	17	17	21	26	31
Northrop	931	0.9	156	140	145	284	207	28	28	25	16	18
Standard Oil (N.J.)	892	0.8	168	174	172	187	192	26	25	24	25	20
Avco Corp.	857	0.8	252	157	184	87	178	21	26	23	31	23
Chance Vought*	840	0.8	103	142	...	360	235	36	27	..	12	15
Int'l Tel. & Tel.	723	0.7	202	189	139	97	97	25	23	26	30	30
Newp't News Shpg.	694	0.6	290	215	99	54	36	18	21	36	53	69
Curtiss-Wright	613	0.6	70	70	67	211	195	47	45	53	23	19
St'dard Oil of Cal.	576	0.5	109	111	123	117	115	34	32	28	28	27
Thiokol Chemical	536	0.5	210	131	102	57	36	24	29	34	51	67
Burroughs	495	0.5	112	125	121	72	66	33	30	29	35	40
Am. Bosch Arma	479	0.4	108	71	102	71	128	35	44	35	36	25
Collins Radio	437	0.4	94	103	115	61	63	37	33	30	44	42
Philco†	434	0.4	119	95	96	66	58	31	36	37	38	46
Ford Motor	427	0.4	81	31	89	157	69	43	81	39	27	39
Bethlehem Steel	417	0.4	79	62	124	42	109	44	49	27	60	28
Pan Am. Airways	410	0.4	127	96	80	61	46	29	35	42	45	55
Minn.-Honeywell	408	0.4	86	98	105	47	74	40	34	32	55	38
Thomp. R. W'dbrg.	400	0.4	77	121	103	64	36	45	31	33	41	68
Texico	393	0.4	86	77	80	75	76	39	40	43	33	37
Goodyear Tire & R.	385	0.4	63	85	90	58	90	53	39	38	50	33
Continental Motors	338	0.3	53	65	72	73	87	49	48	44	34	35
Socony Mobil Oil	338	0.3	53	54	72	67	82	58	47	49	37	36
General Precision	327	0.3	81	72	73	53	48	42	42	47	54	53
Hercules Powder	319	0.3	117	92	55	27	28	32	37	56	88	81
Bell Interconti'ntl‡	318	0.3	..	61	56	82	119	..	51	55	32	26
Garrett Corp.	314	0.3	60	72	77	47	59	56	43	46	56	44
Merritt-Chp., Scott.	288	0.3	..	89	106	..	93	..	38	31	..	32
Bath Iron Works	283	0.3	73	..	85	36	89	46	..	40	67	34
Olin Mathieson	278	0.3	53	38	67	58	62	59	69	52	48	43
Totals	$66,864	62.5	$14,850	$13,199	$14,139	$13,854	$10,823					

* Merged into Ling-Temco-Vought in Aug., 1961.

† Philco became a subsidiary of Ford Motor in Dec., 1961.

‡ Formerly Bell Aircraft Corp., sold defense business to Textron, Inc. in July, 1960.

a Fiscal years ended June 30.

Source: The Exchange, publication of the New York Stock Exchange.

cerns accounted for almost $67,-000,000,000, or 62.5 per cent, of all Defense Department contract awards from fiscal 1957 through 1961.

Thirty-three of the companies were among the top fifty prime contractors in each of the five years and all but four of them ranked among the 100 leading contractors in each of the five years. The top five companies for the 1957-61 period were General Dynamics, Boeing, Lockheed, General Electric and North American Aviation. These five accounted for 24.6 per cent of all prime contracts.

Contract figures do not represent all the military work done by the leading contractors. About 50 per cent of all prime contracts are subcontracted to other companies. And about a third of the subcontract work goes to small business concerns, according to the Defense Department. In addition, small business concerns received directly 15.9 per cent of prime contract awards in fiscal 1961.

There is another significant trend within the changing pattern of defense business. It hits home to many Americans, since it concerns employment.

The ratio of hourly production workers in the vast aerospace industry has fallen to slightly more than 40 per cent. During World War II nine out of ten employes in the field were on production lines. Meanwhile, technical personnel, including scientists and engineers and the semi-technical group of draftsmen and engineering aides, now account for 25 per cent of the total. Every fourth employe in the aerospace industry has a technical skill of some kind.

This trend toward increasing employment of technical personnel and declining production jobs is certain to continue in the years ahead, because of the highly complicated weapons systems, spacecraft and related equipment that are needed for the national military effort.

The aerospace industry already has the highest percentage of research and development technicians among all industries. Some 63 per cent of aerospace scientists and engineers are engaged in research and development.

Defense business is not only very big business but also a deadly serious business. Robert S. McNamara, Secretary of Defense, put it into perspective when explaining the military budget last winter to the House Committee on Armed Services:

"Our policy is not merely defensive. We need not and are not merely reacting to the Communist initiative. Our ultimate objective is a peaceful world in which every nation, large and small, is free to determine its own destiny. . . . We shall not hesitate to take up arms to defend freedom and our own vital interests. We are resolved to continue the struggle in all its forms until such time as the Communist leaders, both Soviet and Chinese, are convinced that their aggressive policies, motivated by their desire to communize the world, endanger their security as well as ours."

April 29, 1962

Aid to Business:

Some Big Companies Have Their Hands Out

Long before the concept of the "welfare state" emerged under Franklin D. Roosevelt, conservative industrialists coined the term "welfare capitalism" to sum up corporate benevolence in protecting both workers and society. Last week the country got repeated reminders that a new form of "welfare capitalism" is emerging—one in which giant corporations go on public welfare to stave off liquidation.

The luckless leaders in this industrial tin-cup brigade are the Penn Central Railroad and the Lockheed Aircraft Corporation. Under strong urging from the Pentagon, Congress has voted Lockheed $200-million as the first installment in a financial rescue operation that is likely to cost the taxpayers at least three times that much.

The ailing Penn Central is on its way to a Federal guarantee of $125-million in loans to keep its commuter, passenger and freight trains running after New Year's Day. Nearly $50-million of the Government help is needed to pay the Penn Central's share of the retroactive wage increases Congress ordered all the nation's railroads to put into effect as part of the stay-on-the-job law prohibiting a rail strike until March 1.

Boundaries Blurred

Uncle Sam's two direct bailout moves for indigent corporations are by no means the only things Washington has been doing this year to blur the traditional boundaries of private enterprise. Congress is still stewing over whether to go along with House-Senate conferees on a scaled-down grant of $210-million for the supersonic transport, a project of primary benefit to Boeing and the commercial airlines. A new quasi-governmental corporation was brought into being by the Administration and Congress to take over the running of all intercity passenger trains, thus relieving the railroads of an unwanted loss-leader. And that most venerable of Federal wards, the merchant marine, got a big new infusion of Government cash through a subsidy program designed to underwrite the building of 300 ships in American yards.

Critics of the proliferating Federal role in the care and feeding of industry have two main lines of worry. One is that it erodes the notion that businesses must pay some penalty for mismanagement and inefficiency. The result, in the words of Dr. John M. Blair, chief economist for the old Kefauver committee in its studies of price-fixing in drugs, oil, steel and other industries, is to deaden "the normal cost-pruning effect of competition."

"Without the brutality of competition," says Dr. Blair, "managements tend to get fat and complacent, confident that the Government won't let them go under. And that is especially true in transportation, where every branch of service says it is up to the Government to equalize subsidies so it gets as much as any other—highways, airports, whatever."

The other worry about the fail-safe approach that shields corporations from the financial consequences of failure is the improbability of ever being able to turn off the flow of Federal support. "It is sort of like Cambodia, the first bundle of money is not the last," comments Senator Philip A. Hart, Democrat of Michigan, chairman of the Senate Antitrust subcommittee.

"Those who urge aid of the type we are giving the Penn Central or Lockheed are usually the most apt to mouth the old self-reliance maxims," Senator Hart adds. "When some welfare applicant named John Jones comes along, the argument is made that if he only would work he wouldn't have this problem, that we will be making him dependent, dampening his initiative. But with a railroad you assume it is sincere, that it is in a jam for no fault of its own and that it is important to society as a whole that it be rescued."

The antitrust laws offer no remedy, in his judgment. On the contrary, the very fact that a company is in trouble makes it easier to escape Justice Department challenge if it seeks to merge with a more robust competitor.

'Incestuous' Relations

A quarter-century of intimate ties between the Pentagon and major defense contractors, operating in plants built and equipped at Government expense, has had a pervasive influence on the new trend. "Industry and the Pentagon are so in cahoots it is almost incestuous," says one Senate investigator of Lockheed's difficulties in building the C-5A jumbo jet transport. "The Air Force wants its plaything so badly it cares about nothing else. In Britain a civilian Ministry of Technology does the procurement for the military. In the Pentagon it is the military who dominate the civilians on procurement."

Professor Roger Murray of the Columbia School of Business finds no parallel between what the Government is now doing and the $10-billion in loans the Reconstruction Finance Corporation made available during the great Depression to prevent mass bankruptcies of banks, railroads and other businesses. One difference was that the economic downturn of the 1930's was so catastrophic it defied the control of any single industry or enterprise. The other was that Jesse H. Jones, the Texas banker, who headed the R.F.C., drove a much harder bargain than is being demanded now.

"If we take the extraordinary step of bailing out the Penn Central on the basis of its importance to the total economic system," says Professor Murray, "we should be sure it doesn't become an Operation Rathole. What made the R.F.C. work so well was that Jesse Jones insisted on a senior credit position for every Government advance. Banks had to struggle to meet the onerous conditions he wrote into every loan. Where you merely put a guarantee on things that are already pledged, it is hard to see what incentive you are creating to make management want to get the Government advance out."

—A. H. RASKIN

December 20, 1970

Government 'Generosity'

To the Editor:

When the Lockheed Corporation developed money trouble, it went to the Federal Government and got money to stay in business.

When I.T.T. discovered some pending antitrust legislation, it went to the Federal Government and asked it to play monopoly.

In return for playing the game, I.T.T. graciously offered to buy the Government a present—the 1972 Republican convention.

Ford, according to The Times, recently conducted faulty antipollution tests that raised the possibility that it might be barred from selling its 1973 cars on schedule.

So Ford is going to the Government with the request that, since Ford can't comply with the law, would the Government mind changing the law?

Since we live in a democracy, I think it's only logical for me to assume that if I went to the Government, I too would receive money to stay in business and immunity from laws which caused me hardship.

I could understand being refused if we lived in, say, a plutocracy.

But we don't. Do we?

W. Robert Weiss
New York, May 25, 1972

June 7, 1972

G.O.P. Discloses Corporate Aid on Convention

By BEN A. FRANKLIN
Special to The New York Times

WASHINGTON, Oct. 18—Nearly half the $1.8-million reported cost of the Republican National Convention earlier this year was paid for by defense contractors, other large corporations doing business with the Government, and businesses regulated by Federal agencies, according to a financial disclosure statement required by law and filed here by the Republicans today.

The $860,000 in contributions, made by a total of 60 corporations, was in the form of payments for advertising space in the Republican National Committee's convention program book, at $10,000 or more a page, a practice also pursued by the Democratic National Committee, but with far less success.

According to less complete financial data filed last month with the Government by the Democratic National Committee, the Democrats netted only about $700,000 from the sale of ads in their convention program, about half of it remitted by corporations with major Government contracts or under Federal regulation. The Democratic Convention, held in Miami Beach last July, was reported to have cost $2-million.

The financial report filed today by the treasurer of the Republicans' Convention arrangements Committee, Mrs. J. Willard Marriott, said that the sale of all ads in the program book had brought in a total of $1,664,601, less the $218,386 reported production costs of the magazine-style program. The net was $1,446,115, or 78 per cent of the party's cash outlay for the Miami Beach convention from Aug. 21 to Aug. 24.

A separate group, the Finance Committee to Re-elect the President, Mr. Nixon's chief campaign finance organization, has been fighting an attempt in Federal Court here to force disclosure of donors who made contributions before April 7, the effective date of the new Federal Election Campaign Act.

But the Republican National Committee's convention report today included a letter from Mrs. Marion Marriott, the wife of the hotel and restaurant chain owner, saying that all convention transactions back to last Jan. 1 were being voluntarily disclosed.

In an interview, Mrs. Marriott said that no policy conflict with the Finance Committee to Re-elect the President had been intended. "I didn't check it out with them," she said. "We did our report this way for our own bookkeeping convenience."

A spokesman for the Finance Committee to Re-elect the President declined to comment, saying that the committee's position on pre-April 7 disclosure had been given in court. The committee's lawyers have contended that such disclosure, if required by the court, would impinge on the constitutional rights of Republican donors.

The Republican convention statement itemized expenditures of from $10,000 to $11,500 a page for program ads placed by such companies as General Motors, Ford, Chrysler, International Telephone and Telegraph, the Aluminum Company of America, North American Rockwell, Ingersoll-Rand, Todd Shipyards, the McDonnell Douglas Corporation and a long list of electronics, basic manufacturing, heavy construction, airline, railway, petroleum and communications companies.

The Republicans said that they would close the books on their 1972 convention with a surplus of about $100,000, to be transferred to a fund for planning the 1976 convention. The Democratic National Committee, already carrying more than $9-million in debts from the 1968 campaign, said last month that their convention this year had added $127,000 to the outstanding debt.

October 19, 1972

Musical Chairs in Business and Government

By MICHAEL C. JENSEN

Hundreds of generals, high-level civil servants, commissioners and Congressmen each year switch from government jobs to closely related careers in private industry.

Some of them live in two worlds, moving easily back and forth between government and industry—a pool of skilled professionals who alternate between sensitive political posts and high-salaried positions in business.

Only last week, for example, Clark MacGregor, who served as President Nixon's campaign director, was named a vice president in the Washington office of the United Aircraft Corporation, a major defense contractor.

Occasionally influential job switchers are caught up in a swirl of controversy, as the ethics of their dual existence is questioned.

But generally there is little sense of outrage at their behavior and, indeed, few proven cases of outright impropriety—perhaps because influence peddling is accepted as part of an old American tradition that says: "I can get it for you wholesale."

The moral question continues to be raised, however, each time these officials trade their military hats, spartan government offices and modest salaries for plush, carpeted suites and quantum jumps in pay. Are they simply fostering a smoother relationship between business and government, as some suggest?

Or are they taking unfair advantage of a system that allows them to misuse their expertise and former contacts on behalf of a private corporate interest?

Ralph Nader, the consumer advocate, scoffs at the practice as "deferred bribes" and suggests that too often there is a cozy relationship between regulators and regulatees, between buyers and vendors.

Stewart L. Udall, a former Secretary of the Interior, adds that the abuses fostered by such mobility make it "incestuous and corrupting."

Most of the government officials who switch, however, Republicans and Democrats alike, defend their action as both legally and morally proper and deny that they are capitalizing on their former government connections.

Indeed, many of them question whether the Government could operate effectively without such an infusion of talent from private industry.

"The Government needs businessmen, and business needs the people who leave the Government," said Robert N. Anthony, Assistant Secretary of Defense from 1965 to 1968. Professor Anthony returned to Harvard University's Graduate School of Business Administration after leaving the Defense Department.

Whenever administrations in Washington change, even when a party remains in power in an election year, there are massive shifts at high levels. This year, for example, a number of President Nixon's staff and Cabinet officers are expected to return to private life, despite the Republican victory last Tuesday.

During such turnover periods, the propriety of government officers moving into closely related jobs in private industry generally comes under increased scrutiny and the question of the public interest arises.

Is it morally proper for the former Commissioner of a Federal regulatory agency to reappear before his fellow Commissioners as a high-paid lobbyist on the other side of the table?

What are the ethical connotations of former Administration aides, who are now representing corporate interests, still holding broad powers within the party in office, and maintaining close links with the White House?

There are myriad examples of high-level job switches, some of them controversial, and others little publicized. Representative cases include:

¶Bryce N. Harlow is vice president of governmental relations and chief lobbyist for the Procter & Gamble Company, reportedly at a six-figure salary. He has served on the White House staff as a $42,500 counselor to President Nixon and is considered a power in the Republican party. Mr. Harlow played a major role writing the last three Republican party platform while he was employed by P. & G.

¶Nicholas deB. Katzenbach is vice president, general counsel and a director of the International Business Machines Corporation, with earnings last year of $189,000. He is overseeing the company's defense against a United States Justice Department antitrust suit that was filed in 1969 after an extended period of preparation. Mr. Katzenbach formerly served as Attorney General, the top job in the Justice Department, from 1965 to 1966 at $35,000 a year.

¶Clarence D. Palmby is vice president of the Continental Grain Company. He reportedly doubled his $38,000 salary last June, when he resigned as Assistant Secretary of Agriculture to join Continental. Mr. Palmby is being investigated by the Federal Bureau of Investigation for a possible conflict of interest in the controversial $1-billion grain deal with the Soviet Union. He has denied any such conflict.

¶James J. Needham is chairman of the New York Stock Exchange at a salary reportedly exceeding $150,000. Until he won the job last August, he was a $38,000-a-year Commissioner of the Securities and Exchange Commission, the Federal agency that regulates the New York Stock Exchange.

●

¶Gen. James Ferguson is vice president of the United Aircraft Corporation, a major aerospace manufacturer that does nearly half its business with the Government. Before joining United Aircraft, General Ferguson was commander of the Air Force Systems Command, which buys aircraft and jet engines.

¶Carl E. Bagge is president of the National Coal Association in Washington. He doubled his $38,000 salary when he resigned as a Commissioner of the Federal Power Commission to join the coal industry group. Mr. Bagge has since submitted pleadings for consideration by the F.P.C.

So vast is the movement of government officials to closely allied fields that such shifts must be considered typical rather than atypical. Indeed, some government officials estimate that as many as 200,000 Federal employes at all levels leave their jobs each year.

Furthermore, such shifts are not limited to the Federal level. Last week, for example, the Detroit Edison Company, the object of several lawsuits filed by Michigan's Attorney General, hired Leon S. Cohan, the No. 2 man in the Attorney General's office, as its vice president for legal affairs.

Some of the job switchers, the "influentials" as they are sometimes called, function mainly in private life, moving only occasionally and sometimes reluctantly into public affairs. These men take government salaries of $30,000 or $40,000 at a considerable sacrifice. They do, however, recharge their Washington batteries and develop contacts with new arrivals during their periodic forays into Washington life.

Many investment bankers fall into this category. Among them are George W. Ball, a partner of Lehman Brothers, Inc., who served as Under Secretary of State from 1961 to 1966, and Henry H. Fowler, a partner of Goldman, Sachs & Co., who was Secretary of the Treasury under President Johnson. Another is Nathaniel Samuels, a partner of Kuhn, Loeb & Co., who was Deputy Under Secretary of State for Economic Affairs under President Nixon.

Most such officials are well aware of the law governing conflicts of interest and according to the Justice Department, existing regulations are generally effective in forestalling flagrant cases of influence peddling or misuse of old friendships.

Not everyone is so sure, however, that the law goes far enough or, indeed, that it even comes to grips with the basic problem — creation of an aura of cooperation between high officials in government departments and in industry.

Nicholas Johnson, a member of the Federal Communications Commission, thinks the problem goes far beyond the government employe who takes a related job in private industry.

"It is a thousand times bigger and is called the subgovernment," he said.

What the Law Says

Some 200,000 Federal employes depart from Government service each year, but they provoke fewer than two dozen allegations of conflict of interest, according to Stephen M. Weglian, an attorney for the United States Department of Justice.

As far as Mr. Weglian is concerned, the statutes serve a "prophylactic" purpose and effectively forestall conflicts of interest.

"Occasionally someone walks the thin line," he said, "but for the most part, they're scrupulous."

There have been fewer than a dozen prosecutions for such violations in the last five years, Mr. Weglian said, and none have been major.

The Justice Department official said his unit, which is called Protection of Government Integrity, monitors the Government for conflict of interest situations, keeping a close eye on Sections 207 and 208 of the United States Criminal Code.

The laws throw up a lifetime barrier against former officers or employes of the executive branch acting as an agent for anyone in a governmental proceeding relating to a matter in which they participated "personally and substantially" while in the Government.

Furthermore, they erect a one-year barrier against personal appearances before a Government agency, when a former employe has had the subject matter at hand "under his official responsibility" during his last year of employment by the Government.

As far as negotiating for new jobs is concerned, the criminal code says it is a violation of the law for an officer or employe of the executive branch to participate "personally and substantially" in a Government proceeding if it involves a person or organization with whom he is negotiating for a job, unless he first advises his superiors of the matter.

On their face, these laws may seem strict, but critics of the system point out that they do not prevent former Government officers from advising new employers on matters in which they were once involved, so long as they do not make a pleading themselves before a Government body.

"That's the intimate and continuing relationship between industry, the trade press, the bar, government agencies and Congressional subcommittees."

Ralph Nader says people take jobs in government because they know they will increase their employment prospects in private life. Furthermore, he says, much of their behavior in government is shaped toward that end.

Referring to Mr. Harlow of Procter & Gamble as an example, Mr. Nader said: "He capitalized himself with on-the-job training."

Mr. Harlow happily acknowledges that he served as a close personal aide for President Eisenhower and Nixon. Since leaving the Government, he has on occasion participated in Presidential missions abroad, sometimes as the only industrialist on the trip.

The P. & G. official was willing to talk about his movement between the White House and the big soap-manufacturing company, but asked not to be quoted directly.

Mr. Harlow has been credited in Washington with helping kill legislation that would have created a consumer protection agency and for helping secure for his employer favorable rulings on the use of phosphates in detergents.

Regarding stories that he still maintains a close link to the White House, Mr. Harlow is outspoken about the fact that he is paid for being persuasive and influential. He feels that if he can't perform that task effectively, P. & G. should have someone else as its chief lobbyist.

Nicholas Katzenbach, on the other hand, is sensitive about the fact that he formerly headed the Justice Department and now is overseeing the defense of I.B.M. against a highly publicized Justice Department antitrust suit.

•

Mr. Katzenbach left his job as head of the Justice Department in 1966 for a post as Under Secretary of State. He joined I.B.M. in 1969.

He said in a telephone interview that he took the precaution in January, 1969, of obtaining from Baddia J. Rashid, director of operations for the antitrust division of the Justice Department, a memorandum stating that a search of the division's files had not turned up evidence of "any direct decision-making involvement" on his part, in the I.B.M. investigation.

One of the most controversial government departments is Agriculture and Stewart Udall is especially critical of "the swinging door at the top level."

"They come out of the agribusiness and they go right back into it," he said in a telephone interview.

Mr. Udall noted that Secretary of Agriculture Earl L. Butz and his predecessor, Clifford M. Hardin, virtually switched jobs at the Ralston-Purina Company and the Agriculture Department.

The case of Clarence Palmby has contributed substantially to the controversy surrounding the Agriculture Department. Mr. Palmby led a trade delegation to Moscow last April to discuss with the Russians credit terms for a grain deal with the United States. At the time he was an Assistant Secretary of Agriculture.

It was later disclosed that a few days before the trip to the Soviet Union, Mr. Palmby signed a purchase agreement for an apartment in New York, listing four Continental Grain Company officials as credit references.

Early in June he left the Department of Agriculture for a vice presidency at Continental Grain. Less than a month later, he personally escorted some members of a Soviet buying team on a sightseeing tour of Washington.

The Soviet team soon after bought 5 million tons of wheat from Continental Grain, by far the largest single purchase in its record-breaking $1-billion grain deal last spring.

•

Mr. Palmby, in an interview in which he was accompanied by Continental Grain's counsel, said his role in Moscow had been confined to explaining the United States credit program.

He asserted that he had never before met the Russians he later escorted around Washington and claimed that he had played no role in Continental Grain's negotiations with the Russians. On advice of counsel, he declined to discuss the timing of his employment with Continental Grain, but said he had spelled it out fully to the F.B.I.

A Justice Department spokesman declined to comment on the status of its investigation of Mr. Palmby.

Although the Agriculture Department is currently in the spotlight, military job switches probably have been the subject of more controversy than those in any other branch of government.

Early this year, a Pentagon survey compiled for Congress identified 993 officers above the rank of major and 108 high-level civilian Pentagon employes, who had moved into defense-industry jobs in the previous three fiscal years.

Senator William Proxmire, a Wisconsin Democrat, and a frequent critic of the flow of military officers to the defense industry, pointed out as early as 1969 that more than 2,000 retired military officers of the rank of colonel or Navy captain and above, were employed by 100 defense contractors.

One military officer who made such a job switch was retired Gen. James Ferguson, who soon after stepping down as commander of the Air Force Systems Command in 1970 became a vice president of United Aircraft.

Formerly an Air Force Deputy Chief of Staff for Research and Development, General Ferguson was responsible for the advancement of aerospace technology when he retired from the Air Force as a four-star general.

About 48 per cent of United Aircraft's sales in 1971 consisted of prime contracts with the United States Government and subcontracts with other aerospace manufacturers who are prime contractors to the Government, according to documents filed with the Securities and Exchange Commission.

General Ferguson declined to be interviewed, but a United Aircraft spokesman said he submits a written report each year to the Secretary of the Air Force and disclaims any conflict of interest in his present job.

One example of an official who left a regulatory agency for private life is Carl Bagge, the head of the National Coal Association.

Until December, 1970, Mr. Bagge had been a Commissioner of the Federal Power Commission, the body that regulates such major coal customers as the electric utility industry.

Last summer, acting on behalf of the coal group, Mr. Bagge entered two pleas to his old employer, the F.P.C., opposing a requirement that was being fought by the electric utilities.

"Sure, I filed our views," Mr. Bagge said in an interview, "but they were turned down five to nothing."

Defending the practice of regulatory officials taking jobs in the industries they regulate, Mr. Bagge said: "You couldn't get people, except élitists, on regulatory bodies if they couldn't utilize the knowledge and insights they've acquired about how a system operates. If that's a deferred bribe, then so be it."

One individual whose Washington exposure helped propel him into one of the most important jobs on Wall Street is James Needham, now chairman of the New York Stock Exchange.

Clark MacGregor, President Nixon's 1972 campaign director, was named last week as vice president of United Aircraft.

A largely unknown New York accountant in 1969, working for the certified public accounting firm of A. M. Pullen, he was picked by President Nixon for the prestigious, if not particularly high paying job of Commissioner of the S.E.C.

Speaking at a conference in New York in late 1970, Mr. Needham suggested that the New York Stock Exchange had not been completely effective in dealing with the industry's problems and called for greater responsibility on the part of the national stock exchanges.

Less than two years later, at the age of 45, he was tapped for the top job at the Big Board, although industry insiders say he was well down on a shopping list of prospective candidates. One of his primary jobs is to guide the exchange through a period of accommodation with various turbulent forces in and out of Wall Street, including the S.E.C.

Some of the job switches are more surprising than others. When Albert Gore, the former Democratic Senator from Tennessee and a long-time battler of industrial pollution, was named as chairman of the Island Creek Coal Company last September, some Washingtonians cocked an eyebrow.

However, there was little surprise when the name of Herbert Brownell, former adviser to President Nixon and a long line of Republican politicians, surfaced in a massive natural-gas deal being negotiated with the Soviet Union. Mr. Brownell has successfully combined his law practice and politics for the last 40 years.

Nor was it surprising when Frank Ikard, a former Congressman from Texas, showed up as head of the American Petroleum Institute, which represents the nation's major petroleum companies.

A few names crop up time and again in Washington. Among them are Arthur H. Dean, a prominent Wall Street lawyer, who served as Ambassador to Korea and United States disarmament negotiator, and W. Averell Harriman, a limited partner in the banking house of Brown Brothers Harriman & Co., who was Ambassador to the Soviet Union and Britain, as well as negotiator at the Paris peace talks.

Sometimes the "influentials" who move between the two worlds find themselves in the midst of heated controversy. Roswell L. Gilpatric, former Deputy Secretary of Defense under Robert S. McNamara, was charged by the Senate Permanent Subcommittee on Investigations in 1970 with "flagrant conflict of interest" in the awarding of an F-111 airframe contract to the General Dynamics Corporation.

The committee said he had been a "top-level policy counselor" to the company for two and a half years before going to the Pentagon and "should have disqualified himself" from decision making on the contract.

Mr. Gilpatric, a New York attorney, denied that he had been a top-level counselor to General Dynamics.

Despite the controversy over job switches, they will continue, and in the weeks ahead as President Nixon reshapes his staff and cabinet, attention will be focused both on the new arrivals and on the departing officials.

Nor will the changes and switches be confined to his office. Even as they take place, a body called the President's Commission on Personnel Interchange will continue to recruit business executives for temporary service in government jobs and will place career government officials in temporary jobs in private industry.

And at high levels, business officials from the nation's limited pool of executive talent will be recruited to help run the Government, lending their specialized brand of expertise.

November 12, 1972

3 I.B.M. Directors Appointed by Carter

Businessmen who are looking for winners in the incoming Carter Administration might well conclude that the International Business Machines Corpo- computer company's directors have been appointed by President-elect Jimmy Carter to Cabinet jobs.

They are Patricia Roberts Harris, a Washington attorney; Dr. Harold Brown, president of the California Institute of Technology; and Cyrus Vance, a Manhattan attorney. They have been designated to fill the jobs of Secretary of Housing and Urban Development, Secretary of Defense and Secretary of State, respectively.

The resignation of the three directors would present no problem for I.B.M., according to a spokesman. "Should Mrs. Harris, Dr. Brown and Mr. Vance be confirmed by the Senate in Cabinet posts and decide to leave the I.B.M. board, there is no requiremnt in the by-laws that we replace them," he said.

December 22, 1976

MANAGEMENT TECHNIQUES REFINED

EFFICIENCY SOCIETY A WASTE PREVENTER

Not Only That, but It Would Let All Humanity Share in the Benefits of Its Savings.

PUTS ITS BAN ON FAKERS

Seeks to Standardize the Men Who Offer to Apply Efficiency Methods to Big Business.

When Louis D. Brandeis of Boston appeared before the Interstate Commerce Commission and in behalf of the shippers fought against an increase of freight rates he said that the railroads of the country could save a million dollars a day by increased efficiency of operation. This statement attracted so much attention that Mr. Brandeis was asked to say something more about the matter. Then it developed that he had only quoted Harrington Emerson, whose profession is called "efficiency engineering." Then it came out that Mr. Emerson was only one of a group of men whose business it was to show big industries how to make more money by improving their business methods. The business of these men is described in any article written for The Survey by Boyd Fisher, who says:

"These men specialize in different kinds of business. Like glorified auditors or accountants, they go from client to client, criticising, standardizing, and systematizing well-established enterprises." The chief feature of the work of these experts is a careful timing, with a stop watch, of the motions of specialized workmen, mainly the unskilled, and the establishment, for the benefit of foremen and workmen, of uniform instructions on the basis of the economical motions of the most expert and efficient workmen on the job. Among the other features of their work are cost accounting, stores keeping, planning and routing of work, and organization charting.

After the statement of Mr. Brandeis the business of these efficiency men got a big boost. The interest of all big business men was greatly excited, and they naturally concluded that, if greater efficiency was good for railroads, it was just as good for all other kinds of big business. The business of these experts grew, and as it grew a great many men crowded into it.

Many of them were not efficiency men at all, but just the other thing. So it became necessary to clear up the business, and this was done by the creation of the Efficiency Society, which drew together more than a thousand men of accomplishment in almost every line of work and industry. Early in the year it effected an organization to study and furnish the standards for judging the various methods of efficiency and scientific management and for appraising the industrial engineers who were anxious to install them. Included in the membership of this society are railroad men and Deans of colleges, heads of manufacturing corporations and progressive workmen in mills, newspaper men, Government officials, and a surprisingly varied list of other men who know how to do things for bettering conditions in certain industries, to increase the percentage of result for a given expenditure of cash and human effort.

"Especially at the start the society expects both to help establish a professional standing for and to apply professional checks upon the efficiency engineer," Mr. Fisher says. "It wishes to make him more careful in his claims, and to prevent him from discrediting the new calling by attempting jobs too big for him. It will attempt the difficult work of eliminating fakers without unduly judging individuals."

But this is merely the superficially obvious work of the society. Its real function is much more fundamental. Printers' Ink magazine, in a recent appraisal of the new society, said:

"Organized only last March by some of the biggest men in industry and commerce, the Efficiency Society is already more than 1,000 strong in membership, and is fairly on its way to realize its ambition to become the great National 'how' society. It's President is James G. Cannon, President of the Fourth National Bank, New York City.

"The plans of the society have been

taking form ever since Spring. If they can be carried out in any considerable measure—and there is no apparent reason why they should not, and many reasons why they should—they will constitute the society an influence in business comparable to the Government and second only to it in power."

The Secretary of the society, H. F. J. Porter, has withdrawn from active work as an industrial engineer to devote his time wholly to the work of the society at its headquarters, 29 West Thirty-ninth Street, New York City. The society does not hope to obtain its great power as a strong fighting organization, but as a "get-together" organization. In this respect it differs from some of the great organizations dealing with industry, such as the National Manufacturers' Association and the American Federation of Labor. It hopes to acquire a genuine mediating influence. It expects to represent and champion the interest of industry as a whole, and not the special interests of either of the contracting parties.

"It is interested," says Mr. Fisher, "in securing by scientific methods bigger and better results. It is reasonably expected that the benefits of these results will accrue to three parties—to capital, in the form of increased output from the same investment and working force; to labor, in the shape of less fatiguing work and markedly higher wages; to the consuming public, in the guise of cheaper wares. It will regard any increases of results which are not willingly and equitably shared between these three parties as highly detrimental to the efficiency movement.

"In this connection the society considers the objections raised by laboring men and others to some forms of scientific management, which in practice simply speed them up without their getting any return benefit, as being objections well taken.

"The efficiency movement is and should be a human movement. In the future it will, in all probability, be rated a development of industry on the human side as important in its effects as the introduction in the eighteenth century of machinery was on the mechanical side. At least that is the aim of its founders, and some of the results achieved in industries which, like bricklaying, had scarcely changed in the methods used in 2,000 years give promise of making the prophecy come true."

November 6, 1912

WANT SOCIOLOGISTS IN THE BIG STORES

Percy S. Straus Says They Are as Necessary as the Scientific Managers.

WELFARE WORK DEVELOPED

Supervision of Detail, He Maintains, Requires Training as Thorough as a Professional Education.

A thorough education is not only an aid but an actual necessity in running a department store, according to Percy S. Straus, head of R. H. Macy & Co. and President of the New York Dry Goods Association. The largest of retail mercantile institutions he compares to a community, and its successful operation requires sociological as well as merchandise experts and scientific managers.

"Those of us who are active in the management of department stores," says Mr. Straus, "are at the throttle of one of the most delicate machines that has been developed by modern commerce. By virtue of the number of differing daily transactions, each one of which involves the independent activity of many employes, the proper supervision of its detail requires as much study and training as the professions whose followers are expected to hold university degrees. And, as each of the transactions involves a number of points of contact with the store's patrons, each presents many possible points of friction, to avoid which is a scientific study.

"In fact, the conduct of a department store has developed from old-time storekeeping to a point at which a thorough education is not only an aid but an actual necessity. Today we must be, among other things, merchandise experts, scientific managers, and sociologists."

The Welfare Work.

Scientific knowledge of social conditions is required in dealing with the community of employes of a department store no less than in serving the public. Mr. Straus points out that welfare work, now organized in most department stores, is not a discovery but a development of good management, just as are the parcel conveyors which collect purchased articles by departments, and automobiles used in delivery. He says:

"I dislike the term 'welfare work' on account of its patronizing ring. I have tried to devise a substitute, but so far unsuccessfully. It is the result of the same ethical awakening that has brought with it the new sense of responsibility of Boards of Directors. It is an expression of a realizing sense on the part of employers that good business requires a more personal relationship between themselves and their employes than can be expressed in dollars and cents on the payroll. In its first development it showed itself in pleasant lunchrooms and sanitary locker rooms. Since then it has grown to include many of the activities of a well-equipped Y. M. C. A., improved by the personal touch of sympathetic workers.

"Personally I am a firm believer in its beneficent effect not only on the employe but on the employer as well. It leads to a realization that both have much to learn, and that each can learn a good deal from the other. As is the case in nearly all new movements it has been allowed to exceed the limits of wisdom in some directions, and in none more than when it has been used as a means of advertisement. I think that the only setback that the development of welfare work has received has been from those institutions that have on the surface appeared to be its best friends. Flowery pamphlets, profusely illustrated, calling attention to such work, are apt to be resented by those employes who do not want to be patronized. And representatives of labor have been quick to object when it has been called philanthropy instead of what it is—good business.

"The New York Dry Goods Association has formed a Trade Welfare Committee. That committee has enlisted the trained workers in the stores in a board for the purpose of co-ordinating that work in the different stores. The purpose is to enable those that have not kept pace with the movement to learn from the experience of those who have been more progressive. We hope for good results from this new attempt at co-operation.

Attacks Unjustified.

"Just as the village store is the centre in which the dwellers in small communities foregather in largest numbers, so is the department store the place which, in the course of a day, week, month, and year, attracts the biggest crowds of any institution in the larger cities. The department store stands for big business, and is subject to the attacks of both the well-meaning enthusiast and the muckraker. Most of such attacks are unjustified. Some are based on conditions that crop up in any rapidly developing industry. Criticism is the penalty of prominence, and being prominent, we must anticipate this criticism by study, and an active desire to correct where we find it necessary. If we discover a fault we must not fear to admit it. To emulate the ostrich is to be dishonest to ourselves, and honesty is without doubt the best policy.

Mr. Straus describes coupon distributing agencies as "the opening guns of a campaign to spread a new gospel of giving something for nothing." Then he adds:

"They also signalize an attempt to induce manufacturers to try another method of stepping in between the retail distributor and his patrons. Why should a retailer sell merchandise that contains as an inducement to the consumer a slip of paper that is claimed to represent an actual discount of 4 per cent. or the equivalent of an 8 per cent. discount in merchandise? If there be a real margin of profit to justify such a gift from the manufacturer to the consumer, would it not be better from any square dealing point of view to reduce the price to the retailer correspondingly and enable him to pass the advantage to the consumer?

"It is merely another attempt to befog the direct appeal for patronage on the basis of quality and value. As retail distributors, we department store men must combat this questionable attempt to put us in the class of mere manufacturers' agents, who are to hand out branded merchandise to a clientele created by unbusinesslike methods that are sure to be short-lived in their appeal. As soon as the public realize that they have been betrayed, the innocent merchant will be made to suffer with the guilty manufacturer."

May 22, 1915

IDEAL BUSINESS HEAD.

Qualities Needed for the Post and the Reasons Therefor.

The question of who makes the best head for a business was brought up by the Secretary for an association who has held that position for a number of years and has had good opportunity to see how various types of men are suited to control large organizations.

"The factory man's chief drawback," he pointed out in his remarks, "is his unfamiliarity with actual selling conditions and what the retail trade will take in the way of new styles. I remember one organization that lost $20,000 in one season. The financial man happened to take in a musical show that was starring a famous French actress. She was wearing several hats that had been designed especially for her in Paris. He sent the factory man to the show, much against the latter's desire because he was of strictly Puritan stock, and arranged to have samples made of the hats worn by the star. In a short time these new hats came along and proved to be the highest sellers the house ever had. A $20,000 loss was converted into a profit of $40,000 for the season.

"The point I wish to bring out is that if the mill or factory man is left to his own devices and he happens to be of the usual staid, conservative sort, any ideas he may get will prove away behind the times. So it seems necessary to hook him up with the salesman.

"On the other hand the salesman is apt to forget all factory or mill problems. All he can usually see is that a certain style is good and ought to be produced at once. The changes necessary in equipment or processing do not bear the least weight in his mind. He regards the factory merely as a necessary evil.

"As the head of a business the salesman is weak in two points, the actual manufacturing and the financial end of the business.

"So that it seems to me that unless a man is well up on all three phases of the modern business organization, he does not make the ideal head. The better plan, where the business permits, is to have men at the head of these special departments and an executive well trained in all of them to keep each branch hooked up with the other. The ideal head, then, should be no more salesman than he is a manufacturer and he should be acquainted with the financial problems of both."

May 11, 1919

TEACH PSYCHOLOGY FOR THE ADVERTISER

Columbia Increases Courses in the New Science—Extension Registrations Heavy.

The third day of registration at Columbia University yesterday showed a big increase in the University Extension courses. It was pointed out yesterday that this was due to the tendency since the war of older people to go back to college for more intensive training or simply to improve their general culture.

A marked increase also was shown in the number of students who want to study psychology. This new science is in the midst of a great expansion at Columbia, and announcement was made of a much larger program of courses this year. Advertising is a field to which the university will now apply its psychological work on a broad scale. The course in the psychology of advertising deals with human behavior as it may be excited and controlled through advertising. The devices and methods of advertising will be illustrated and analyzed to determine their value in arousing attention and interest and creating belief.

The announcement of the course stresses that psychological laws will be applied to make advertisements readily understood and remembered, and that the human motives that may be appealed to in advertisements will be studied in detail.

September 20, 1924

THE NEW BUSINESS TYPE.

The business world of New York has been left poorer by the death within a short period of Mr. HENRY DAVISON, Mr. STETTINIUS and now Mr. A. C. BEDFORD. All of them men comparatively young, as age is now reckoned, all of them men of large affairs, they had strikingly illustrated the possibility of adjusting a high and flexible talent for business to changed modern conditions. They belonged to a new type of business man of which there are happily multiplying examples. Their distinctive characteristic is that they unite great ability with a sense of great responsibility. They feel themselves responsible, first of all, to the interests represented in the large enterprises over which they preside. These they labor to make as efficient and successful as possible. But they also feel their responsibility to the public. This they show in seeking to do away with as many as may be of the old features of corporation management which became both offensive and dangerous in the popular mind. The main thing has been the aim to establish franker relations. Open books and fully published accounts of financial transactions are now the rule. Complaints are not contemptuously ignored in the ancient fashion, but are actually welcomed for the sake of looking into them to discover if there is anything in the conduct of the business which ought to be corrected. The lines of an altered corporation policy are slowly being framed, a d the men mentioned above, with many others, have been doing their best to complete the work.

It is not contended that this attitude is a mark of superior virtue. Such men as Mr. BEDFORD would be the first to repudiate any such idea. They would simply call the changed methods which they have advocated and practiced good business. Such it undoubtedly is. Today an exceptional genius for affairs must have a grasp of the whole environment in which its work is to be done. It will demonstrate unusual capability by seeking to understand all the elements of life, by studying the impulses and reactions of the common mind, by appreciating the just demands which the new publicity may make upon companies affected with a public interest—in short, by thoroughly realizing the world of the present in which it moves about. These are the ways in which marked business capacity survives and triumphs under shifting conditions. A changing world requires changing methods of doing the great business. And in no way have men such as Mr. BEDFORD exhibited their peculiar powers more clearly than in this development of a fresh type, able to face unexpected obstacles and to surmount them by native sagacity joined to an acute perception of what must be done in order to fit old business to new needs.

September 23, 1925

SCIENTIFIC MANAGEMENT.

The United States Department of Commerce Suggests Eight Rules.

The April News Bulletin of the Department of Commerce contains the following item on scientific management:

"If we follow the eight rules on 'How to Manage,' by W. H. Leffingwell, many of our problems on the elimination of waste will be solved. Continually putting these into practice and always having them in mind when establishing our procedures and work controls will assure us of progress in eliminating waste. They are:

"Define your purpose. You must know what is to be done before you can know how. This is your master task.

"Analyze your problem. Your master task will then break up into many detail tasks. Consider them all—neglect none.

"Seek the facts. Study every condition governing each task and the undesirable element to be eliminated and the desirable element to be retained. Then standardize right conditions.

"Devise the one best method. Aim to conserve energy, time, space, material. Determine relation of details to master task.

"Find the person best fitted. For each task certain personal qualities are essential. In each person certain qualities predominate. Find the person best fitted.

"Teach the person best fitted the one best method. Not by driving, but by thorough, patient teaching are understanding and skill developed.

"Plan carefully. Right planning of arrangement and sequence of work will enable you to accomplish tasks in logical orer, accurately, quickly, economically.

"Win cooperation. Cooperation means working together. It cannot be demanded; it must be won. Accept your share of the responsibility. Respect the rights and aspirations of others.

"This is scientific management, and through scientific management may we expect to eliminate waste."

May 8, 1927

MANAGERIALABILITY RARE, SAYS RASKOB

Capital and Labor Plentiful, but Brains Must Be Sought—Carnegie's Method.

GENERAL MOTORS SYSTEM

"The three governing factors in industrial production are capital, labor and management," John J. Raskob, Chairman of the Finance Committee of the General Motors Corporation, writes in Industrial Management. "Each is essential to the successful conduct of a manufacturing business.

"It might be possible to operate a business with capital and labor under indifferent management, and, in the absence of competition, to conduct it at a profit," Mr. Raskob continues. "American business knows no such Utopian condition. Competition is keen. Interested capital and competent labor are plentiful and relatively easy to secure. But management, that is, the brains necessary to direct sales and production effort to show a profit in competition with other capable minds, must be more diligently sought. It is difficult to measure managerial ability except by performance. In fact, native ability can be developed only by giving its fortunate possessor an opportunity to exercise it.

"The great industrial and business enterprises of this country have in the past been built up by men who had the managerial gift and knew it. Coupled with it they also had ambition and initiative. It seems strange now, in view of the co-ordination of talent required for the conduct of the business of a great manufacturing corporation, that the foundations of many of them were in each case the work of one man.

"The far-sighted ironmaster Carnegie, was among the first of the organizers of a corporation in world-wide trade to recognize that there was a limit to the inducement offered by salary. He knew that the kind of executives he was developing would be quite able to organize and operate companies of their own. Consequently he made them his partners, so that their combined ability would continue to be concentrated more effectively upon the development of his steel business. He was able to show them that they could profit more certainly and extensively as his partners than in any other way.

"I hold this to be a sound principle of organization, but I would go further. In a corporation like General Motors, owned by 50,000 stockholders, the opportunity to profit by the prosperity of the business should be extended to every member of the organization, according to the importance of the part he plays in producing effective results. This is exactly what General Motors Corporation is doing.

"Each of the divisions (of the corporation) is conducted as a business in itself. The responsible head operates the business with no other limitation than that which has been established by the policy of the corporation, expressed through its Advertising Committee. For example, each make of car is intended to satisfy a certain class of consumer demand. The only limitation placed upon the executive in charge of a car division is that he produce the best car possible between certain established cost limits.

"To complete the picture of the extensive plant system, whose specialized products go into the finished cars, it may be added that the thirteen accessories divisions are operated by so many independent factories, also in widely separated localities. Each is operated on the basis of maximun efficiency, so that the price of the output will be such as to induce the heads of the car divisions to purchase from G. M. C. accessories divisions instead of buying outside. They are free to do so, however, if they find it advantageous. Hence, it is the aim of each accessories division to outstrip competition both in quality and price.

"The Fisher body division maintains a body-making plant adjoining that of the car-assembly plants where the bodies for that particular make of car are turned out. Incidentally, the subsidiaries of this division manufacture plate glass, lumber, automobile hardware and other material entering into the construction of the bodies.

"The coordination of the activities of all these divisions must be such that there will be no undue conflict, competitively, between the product of one division and that of another. General policies must be determined from the standpoint of the corporation as a whole rather than from that of any one division. This is done through the interdivisional relations committees of the corporation."

September 11, 1927

Harsh Boss Found Mental Hazard to Worker; Fear of Scolding Said to Impair Efficiency

Experiments in the elimination of "the boss," at least as that individual has been traditionally regarded by the industrial worker, carried out at the Hawthorne plant of the Western Electric Company, have convinced officials of the company that the traditional relationship of the individual worker to his or her immediate superior has been the greatest single obstacle in the way of increasing the welfare both of the worker and of the corporation. Reports on experiments which have already been conducted for two years at the plant were made yesterday at the Personal Research Federation Conference at the Engineering Societies Building by G. A. Pennock and M. L. Putnam of the company and Professor Elton Mayo of the Harvard School of Business Administration.

The experiments started out to discover the relative influence of various tangible factors on the character of work done by shop employes. The emotional upset and consequent loss of efficiency resulting from fear of a "bawling out" was first discovered largely by accident. It has now resulted in a revolutionary change in methods of training subordinate supervisors throughout the plant, which employs 40,000 men and women.

Mr. Pennock described experiments made with small groups of workers whose attitude and production were carefully checked, while their personal feelings and health were likewise carefully charted. Both their happiness at work and their efficiency of performance, the tests indicate, are far more influenced by mental hazards than by all the physical factors involved. The tests also indicated that a short rest period, both morning and afternoon, tended to more than compensate in increased efficiency for the time consumed by the rests.

Mr. Putnam described in detail the "supervisory training methods" that have been evolved in consequence of the conclusions reached in the tests. A staff of "interviewers," selected from the rank and file of the employes, is devoted to discussing their problems with the individual workers. The results, anonymously presented, are used in conferences with the "supervisors." In addition, it is planned to recruit future supervisors from the ranks of the interviewers.

Dr. Mayo in his address declared that the work being done by the Western Electric Company was of the greatest significance. Particularly, he declared that it would be difficult to realize today what the potentialities of the interviewing system might be in the field of public health and in increasing the happiness and welfare of workers in industry.

November 16, 1929

APPLY NEW THEORY TO CONTROL OUTPUT

Engineers See Cost Reduction and Improved Standards by Using Statistics.

GROUPS PROMOTE PLAN

Three Countries Analyze Project to Broaden Its Use—Assures Uniformity of Quality.

Application of statistical theory to the control of manufacturing operations, in order to reduce costs and to simplify standardization problems, is spreading rapidly through American industry and will have a far-reaching effect upon every branch of industrial operations, engineers predicted here last week. Originating on the Continent, this new concept of approach has stirred world-wide interest in the last few months, and committees have been formed in this country, England and Germany to promote development of the project and to broaden its field of application to as many industries as possible.

General adoption of the plan by industry would mean greater uniformity of quality in products, a speeding up of production, fewer rejections and a reduction in the cost of inspection, it was held.

Technical authorities agreed yesterday that the engineering field of greatest economic significance for the application of the statistical method is in the establishment of economic standards of quality and of procedures for effecting economic control of the quality of a manufactured product. Broadly speaking, statistical methodology makes it possible to establish limits within which variation in any quantity, of interest to management, should be left to chance. Only when variation extends beyond these limits is it economical to take action.

Principal Use in Steel Industry.

At the present time the principal applications of the statistical method continue to be in the steel industry. Its use, however, is being rapidly extended to the glass, mining, electrical and ceramic trades.

The latest theory on which to base the practical technique for industry to use in establishing economic tolerances and methods of inspection was outlined by Dr. W. A. Shewart of the Bell Telephone Laboratories, who returned recently from an extensive tour of European laboratories and plants. He declared that the final quality of a manufactured product is dependent upon two types of causes, which arise either from the manufacturing process or from the state of the raw materials used; namely, assignable causes and chance causes.

Dr. Shewart's theory depends upon the fact that when it is possible to detect and eliminate all assignable causes of quality variation, the quality of the final product can be assumed to be definitely within control. This condition can only exist when quality is under the sole influence of a constant system of chance causes, in which no one cause predominates and where the total effects of all the chance causes, regardless of which ones are present, will at no time exceed natural limits of quality variation.

As a constant check on the quality of a product in its various stages, random sampling is employed. The theory of such sampling is first used to enable engineers to plan a rational procedure to determine the proper sample sizes and to make the most efficient use of engineering data. Another stage requires the use of the statistical method to develop economic standards of quality. It is applied to ascertain the desired characteristics of quality, so as to be of greatest usefulness from the viewpoint of design, production and inspection, and in the establishment of efficient sampling procedure to obtain adequate assurance that the quality specified is, in fact, being attained under the manufacturing conditions.

By obtaining economic quality control of manufactured products, five advantages can be obtained: reduction in the cost of inspection, reduction in the cost of rejections, attainment of maximum benefits from quantity production, attainment of uniform quality and a reduction in tolerance limits where quality measurement is indirect.

At the present time a committee composed of members of the American Society of Mechanical Engineers, the American Society for Testing Materials and the American Statistical Association has under way **several studies of various phases of the subject. In England and France similar committees were created recently to analyze the method of operation.**

The American group believes that statistical methods constitute the best means for correcting data for errors of measurement; detecting assignable causes for variation in any phenomenon; choosing the best functional forms for the expression of distributions and relationships, and laying out efficient research programs.

A great deal remains to be done, however, on the theoretical sides, it was agreed yesterday. One of the problems being considered is that of efficient specifications of materials from the viewpoint of the latest developments in the mathematical theories of statistics.

September 11, 1932

Mathematical Theory of Poker Is Applied to Business Problems

By WILL LISSNER

A new approach to economic analysis that seeks to solve hitherto insoluble problems of business strategy by developing and applying to them a new mathematical theory of games of strategy like poker, chess and solitaire has caused a sensation among professional economists.

The theory has been worked out in its beginnings by Dr. John Von Neumann, Professor of Mathematics at the Institute for Advanced Study, Princeton, N. J., and Dr. Oskar Morgenstern, Professor of Economics at Princeton University. In its present form the theory represents fifteen years of research, apart from the years spent by Dr. Von Neumann before 1928 in working out the basic theory of games.

Dr. Von Neumann, a collaborator of Albert Einstein, who did mathematical work important in the development of the atomic bomb, is recognized by his colleagues as one of the great original workers of the day in mathematics. He is the author of "Mathematical Foundations of Quantum Mechanics." Dr. Morgenstern, former director of the Austrian Institute for Business Cycle Research at the University of Vienna, is considered one of the world's leading mathematical economists. He is the author of "Economic Forecasting."

They published the results of their years of reasearch in a 625-page book, "Theory of Games and Economic Behavior," with nearly every page studded with formulae, mainly in the theory of sets and groups and in linear geometry.

The book was issued by the Princeton University Press in September, 1944.

Because the book was so "formidable" intellectually, as one professional critic put it, involving, as the authors admitted, "mathematical deductions" that "are frequently intricate," with "the logical possibilities" extensively exploited, the work went unnoticed for nearly a year and a half by the technical economic journals, with the exception of the Annals of the American Academy of Political and Social Science.

The current issue of the American Economic Review, journal of the American Economic Association, devotes a full-length article to the book hailing it as "indeed a rare event," and the critics of other professional journals have pronounced the work an outstanding contribution.

Big Potentialities Seen

Prof. Leonid Hurwicz of Iowa State College, now on leave to the Cowles Commission for Research in Economics at the University of Chicago, writes in the American Economic Review that "the potentialities of Von Neumann's and Morgenstern's new approach seem tremendous and may, one hopes, lead to revamping and enriching in realism a good deal of economic theory."

Professor Hurwicz says "it would be doing the authors an injustice to say that theirs is a contribution to economics only."

"The scope of the book is much broader," he adds. "The techniques applied by the authors in tackling economic problems are of sufficient generality to be valid in political science, sociology, or even military strategy."

In mathematics as well as in economics the Neumann-Morgenstern approach represents a break with the traditional development. The mathematical theory of games was based on the calculus of probabilities. Thus it was concerned with the probable distribution of cards at any stage of the game.

It was shown, for example, that the odds against any individual poker player's holding any one of the forty classes of straight flushes before the draw are 64,973 to 1; that drawing to two pairs, the chances are 11 to 1 against getting the third to either pair. In the eighteenth century classic, "Hoyle's Games," the bible of the card and the horse player, many of these probabilities are given for card games and races, although the calculus then was in its infancy.

However, the present mathematical methods, essentially those of the differential and integral calculus, were not adequate for solving some of the problems of games. One unsolved problem, cited by Prof. E. J. Gumbel of the New School for Social Research, is that of a game with several participants, each trying to maximize his gain without being able to control the activity of the other participants.

To solve these problems Professor Von Neumann, in his preliminary work, "Zur Theorie der Gesellschaftspiele," published in the Annals of Mathematics in 1928, and in the present work developed with Dr. Morgenstern a novel analytical apparatus drawn mostly from mathematical logic, set theory and functional analysis.

Strategies Analyzed

Using these new mathematical tools, they analyzed the strategies open to players in games of chance like dice-throwing and matching pennies and in games of strategy like poker, bridge and chess. They proved that there might be no best strategy for a player to employ, or there might be several equally good ones.

In matching pennies, for example, where the opponent shakes up his pennies and lets them fall into an order fixed by chance, the best strategy is to adopt none. For Professors Von Neumann and Morgenstern have proved that if the opponent "stacks" his pennies according to any preconceived plan, one can win by matching chance against strategy; that is, by shaking up the pennies and letting chance determine their order.

In chess, however, he proved that a good strategy existed because this is a game of perfect information, each player knowing at every stage of the game all the moves made previously.

Similarly for games of mixed strategies, where information is imperfect, they proved that a good strategy was possible. Each game, they showed, has its own characteristic function. Thus, as Louis Weisner of Hunter College has pointed out, for games of more than two players like poker, where the players may form coalitions that are decisive to the strategies, "all questions relating to coalitions such as the forces which impel the formation of coalitions, the desertion of some members of a coalition to another, mergers or fights between coalitions, the division of profits or losses among members of a coalition are answerable in terms of the characteristic function."

Practical Use in Games

The solutions are too technical for brief exposition and cannot be given here. A brief exposition of a few takes seventeen pages in The American Economic Review. They will be of practical use in games of chance and strategy, however, to experts in higher mathematics.

How Drs. von Neumann and Morgenstern discovered that the theory of games of chance could be used to analyze economic situations is not reported in their book. In a letter to this writer while the book was in preparation, Dr. Morgenstern explained that in carrying on his work in mathematical economics, he encountered many problems that could not be handled by the traditional tools drawn from the calculus, and hence he reached the conclusion that economics was following a blind alley in depending mainly on them.

They explain in the book, however, that they are not making a mere analogy between games and economics but seek to establish "that the typical problems of economic behavior become strictly identical with the mathematical notions of suitable games of strategy." Their aim is the development of a theory that is mathematically rigorous and conceptually general, so that the science can go on, as all sciences have gone on, to genuine prediction by theory.

Five-sixths of the book is devoted to the mathematical theory, one-sixth to the economic applications. Among the latter are situations characterized by duopolistic and oligopolistic competition, where the market is dominated by two or a few sellers; the formation of coalitions, where buyers or sellers combine against other groups of buyers or sellers; and by organization of cartels. Not only "rational" but "irrational" economic behavior is comprehended by the theory.

Professor Hurwicz holds that reading the book will be a new **stage in their education for the great majority of economists; the others may not be able to follow it.**

Reader's Views Seen Affected

He says that because the noneconomic results are more specific, mathematical readers "interested in the nature of determinacy of chess, in the theory of 'bluffing' in poker, or in the proper strategy for Sherlock Holmes in his famous encounter with Professor Moriarty" will enjoy the sections on strategic games proper. He adds, "the reader's views on optimum military or diplomatic strategies are also likely to be affected."

One defect of the theory is that it applies to capitalist economics only. This was pointed out by Mr. Gumbel in The Annals, and by Mr. Weisner in Science and Society. This criticism applies to the economic interpretation in terms of marginal utility economics, however, and not to the mathematics, the foundations of which Mr. Weisner found "firmly laid," arousing his admiration.

In sociological circles opinion was divided. The reviewer of The American Journal of Sociology "found the 'Theory of Games' at all times a model of clear and careful exposition." The reviewer of Social Forces reported "this may be an extremely valuable new direction or it may be an interesting but useless development." While very few problems of a strictly sociological nature were attempted, Drs. von Neumann and Morgenstern believe that sociometric problems are best approached from this direction.

EXAMPLE OF ANALYSIS OF BUSINESS STRATEGY

A's Profits

A's choice of strategies \ B's choice of strategies	B_1	B_2	B_3
A_1	2	8	1
A_2	4	3	9
A_3	5	6	7

B's Profits

A's choice of strategies \ B's choice of strategies	B_1	B_2	B_3
A_1	11	2	20
A_2	9	15	3
A_3	8	7	6

To make the mathematical thinking of Dr. John Von Neumann and Dr. Oskar Morgenstern more easily understandable, Leonid Hurwicz of the Cowles Commission for Research in Economics, with the aid of Mrs. D. Friedlander of the University of Chicago, has converted several of the mathematical formulae into numerical examples. These tables are one of them, as presented in The American Economic Review.

They illustrate a duopolistic situation, one in which the market is dominated by two sellers, A and B, where each one of the duopolists is trying to make the largest profits. The first table shows the profits seller A will make, depending on his own and B's choice of strategies. The strategies open to seller A are denoted by A subscript 1, etc.; the columns correspond to the strategies of seller B and are denoted by B subscript 1, etc. Analogous information regarding B's profits is given in the other table.

A will notice that by choosing strategy A subscript 3 he will be sure that his profits cannot go down below 5, while either of the remaining alternatives would expose him to the danger of going down to 3 or even to 1. Another reason for choosing A subscript 3 is that if there is a danger of a "leak," that B might learn his decision, and if A had chosen strategy A subscript 1, B obviously would choose strategy B subscript 3 to maximize his own profits, and this would leave A with a profit of only one. Had A chosen strategy A subscript 2, B would respond by selecting B subscript 2, leaving A with less than the 5 he would get by choosing A subscript 3.

Similar reasoning on B's part would make him choose strategy B subscript 1 as the optimal strategy. Thus, Neumann and Morgenstern reason, the outcome of duopolistic competition is determinate, A will choose strategy A subscript 3, B will choose strategy B subscript 1, and neither would be inclined to alter his decision even if he found out what the other's strategy was. The illustration, of course, loses the generality and the rigor of the formula.

MORE COMPANIES TRAIN EXECUTIVES

New Concentrated Programs Adopted by Many Concerns Complete Job in One Year

By ALFRED R. ZIPSER JR.

First progress reports from more than 100 companies on results of concentrated executive training programs instituted shortly after the war indicate that top caliber executives can be developed in much shorter periods than was possible up to the end of 1941, Lawrence A. Appley, president of the American Management Association, declared last week. In an interview following the association's annual personnel conference here he said that many companies have reduced training time for executives from five years to one.

Reporting companies, Mr. Appley pointed out, cover manufacturing, distribution and virtually every other field of economic activity. A good number, he added, had executive training programs before the war but speeded them up by intensive planning and organization to build up the war-depleted executive reservoir in the shortest period possible. Many companies instituted training plans for the first time to achieve the same objective.

The whole field of executive training is now meeting with more interest by both large and small companies of every type than ever before because of the uniform success of concentrated programs, Mr. Appley reported.

"While there has been no decrease in efforts of business organizations to develop and set up more rapid and efficient training systems for middle and line management," he declared, "training officials are at last beginning to give the same attention to executive development that they have been giving for years to foremen and other supervisors."

Pattern Is Universal

Methods for accelerating executive training vary from company tc company, Mr. Appley explained, but there is a general pattern which is followed almost universally. By scientific tests, it is determined exactly what training and experience the potential executive must have and this is given to him in an organized and concentrated manner. Periodic evaluation of his progress is made.

This contrasts with the common pre-war method of hiring many potentially good executives and letting them go through normal processes of becoming an executive in a haphazard way, Mr. Appley said.

Companies which have adopted organized training say they never will return to the unplanned pre-war approach to keeping an adequate executive reservoir, he declared.

The most formidable problem in accelerated executive training is proper selection of candidates who will be able to absorb it, Mr. Appley said. In general, each candidate must demonstrate that he has a potential for further development and must have satisfactory training and experience in lower management echelons prior to his selection.

Although executive training experts throughout industry are not intentionally picking veterans for training, Mr. Appley pointed out that the greatest number of candidates are veterans.

An indication of the interest in executive training now shown by most management was the enthusiastic reception at the conference itself to an address by William E. Henry, assistant Professor of Psychology of the University of Chicago. Professor Henry delivered the only talk on executive training at the conference, which featured lengthy discussions on wages and productivity, pension plans and other employe benefits and the growing importance of human relations in personnel administration.

A study of 300 executives in companies with diversified operations recently completed by the University of Chicago's committee on human development shows that desirable personality traits rather than specific skills make a successful executive, Professor Henry reported.

September 26, 1948

'BRAIN' TO PILOT AIRLINE'S BOOKS

By JOHN STUART

A man who has saved dollars by ignoring pennies finds his business growing so big he has had to hire an electronic brain to keep track of the money.

He is John S. Woodbridge, controller of Pan American World Airways. A year ago he perfected an accounting system that left out odd cents in all dollar tabulations. He devised a system for averaging out the results. He figured then it saved Pan American thousands of dollars a day. It has since been widely adopted by controllers of other big corporations.

But he made known last week that even simplified records can become unmanageable. In airline metaphor, he said:

"Visualize a billion and a half cards, each seven and three-eights inches long. That's the number we process annually. If laid end to end it would take a jet plane, at 550 miles an hour, thirteen days of continous flight just to pass over them."

Rent: $1,000 a Day

So Mr. Woodbridge has ordered from Thomas B. Watson Jr., president of International Business Machines, one of his Type 705 electronic data processing systems. It will cost the penny-wise Mr. Woodbridge some $30,000 a month rent. But in saving of time on present accounting and in "Mining" rapidly for new results from existent data, he believes it well worth it.

Pan American serves all six inhabited continents with eight types of planes and 1,264 pilots on 62,757 route miles. It now handles 7,000 air waybills a day. It has been possible so far to obtain only the most general idea of trade trends from them. With the new machine Mr. Woodbridge expects to give his traffic department a quick answer when it asks "What is the pharmaceutical trade between Uruguay and the rest of the world?"

That and hundreds of other details will be at his fingertips through the system that does 750 hours of machine tabulation in fifteen hours, by making 8,400 additions and 1,200 multiplications a second.

Crew scheduling is another headache. Pilots may, by law, fly only eighty-five hours a month. Both they and the company want to fly as close to the limit as possible.

Crews are scheduled from bases in New York, Miami and San Francisco. Their time cards, the planes they are qualified to fly, special assignments, sick leaves, increases or decreases in schedules, can all be fed by transceivers on leased wires from all bases into the head offices in Long Island City.

There, from the electronic brain's specially air-conditioned and humidity-controlled room, a list of qualified names can be flashed back almost instantly for flights to any corner of the earth.

Electronic Clearance

Pan American clears some $49,000,000 of billings with other airlines every year through the clearing houses of the national and international air transport associations. The bills are paid promptly when rendered. But it has been taking Pan American two weeks to prepare them from around the world.

The new system will enable presentation within twenty-four hours. Mr. Woodbridge believes this will add some $4,000,000 to the company's bank accounts.

It will simplify inventory control of some 110,000 items from simple bolts to whole wing assemblies on the far flung system. Records that now require 366 file trays with 1,250,000 cards will be kept on ten reels of magnetic tape.

Mr. Woodbridge thinks his $1,000 a day for the brain will be not only penny-wise but also pound-and-dollar-wise.

October 9, 1955

NEW MAGAZINE DUE

Dr. Herman B. Wells, president at the University of Indiana, announced yesterday that Indiana's School of Business will publish a new quarterly magazine, Business Horizons, beginning in December. Speaking at the University Club here, he pointed out that business management is approaching the status of a profession. "Roughly one out of every seven students enrolled in American colleges and universities is majoring in business.

"Modern business management is, in the main too complex, too difficult and too important to be left to amateurs and hunch players. It is a game for professionals — for professional business managers."

The new publication will be edited by Indiana's School of Business under the guidance of its dean, Dr. A. M. Weimer, and S. F. Otteson, director of the Bureau of Business Research.

Single issues of Business Horizons will cost $1.50.

October 8, 1957

COSTS OF OUTPUT CUT BY RESEARCH

New Techniques Streamline Operations—Companies Cite Huge Savings

By WILLIAM M. FREEMAN

A scientific way to cut costs and speed output is gaining greater acceptance among business men.

The technique is used to solve business problems being handled in a certain way because they always were or because the man at the top is positive that he has devised the best way possible.

The method is called operations research. Many companies that have tried it report dramatic successes.

George W. Chane of Ernst & Ernst, management consultants, commended the technique last week to two dozen company presidents and chairmen attending a five-day management course for top executives.

"Many business men have an obsolete view of what internal cost improvement really involves," he said. "They have an equally obsolete view of how great the benefits are.

"Modern programs include far more than good plant layout, sound organization and a specific plan for business growth. Well-integrated inventory and production control, for example, could very quickly increase machine utilization from 10 to 25 per cent in many instances and reduce in-process inventory from 10 to 40 per cent. And this is only one phase of modern cost control."

Mr. Chane, who spoke at the American Management Association's Academy of Advanced Management at Saranac Lake, N. Y., cited three instances of how operations research was combined with automation to lower internal costs:

An airline cut the time needed to get a new work shift on the job from thirty-five to five minutes.

A wire and cable company was able for the first time to measure accurately the effectiveness of new inventory procedures.

A big music publisher was able to use automation to tackle the job of determining royalty payments to composers of music played on radio and television.

A recent conference at the Case Institute of Technology, Cleveland, reviewed operations research advances linked to computers and management decisions generally.

The installation of an integrated process control system at the Cummins Engine Company of Columbus, Ind., was studied at the conference. The new system for receiving and processing orders was found to eliminate many steps that had caused delay and extra expense. The older method required sixteen working days and the new system took five and a half. Major changes in making the original orders more complete and accurate were credited with the saving.

Reorganized methods of material and production control also were studied. These changes created a need for a central point at which data could be processed. An electronic digital computer was bought to control data on 20,000 out of 25,000 parts and to make decisions on reordering. This permitted more efficient production planning.

The entire process of control, from raw materials to finished parts and engines, was broken down into several well-defined steps. Formulas were computed that permitted more economical control of each step.

Another study reported on at Case was on the use of electronic computers in the railroad industry to speed the distribution of empty freight cars. The computers were called on to process information on the cars, which produce no profit when they are idle. It has been estimated that 10,000 empty boxcars a day, which is not uncommon on the larger roads, can cost a railroad $10,000,000 a year.

Dr. David B. Hertz, manager of operations research of Arthur Andersen & Co., accounting concern of this city, said the method was being used more and more widely by business men.

He made the comment in reporting findings of an American Management Association survey of how widely the technique was being used. As recently as 1951, he said, there was "virtually no recognition or understanding of industrial operations research by American management," whereas today it is making rapid advances.

Of 631 companies questioned by the association, 324, or 51.3 per cent, are using the method. Of 307 not using it, 144 indicated that they were considering it. Not one of the companies using operations research said they intended to discontinue it.

The association said that of the 288 companies that offered evaluations of their operations research programs, fifty-five said they had realized appreciable savings. Considerable improvement in operations was reported by seventy-five companies, and 167 said it was too early to tell.

Improvements were reported by aircraft companies, utilities and transportation concerns more often than by companies in other industry categories.

Survey participants also were asked whether they could identify dollar savings, actual or future or both, attributable to operations research activities. The number of answers to the question was too small to be significant, but some of the amounts were impressive.

Seventeen companies reported savings of more than $100,000, and five cited savings of more than $1,000,000. A chemical company and a petroleum concern each noted a saving of more than $2,000,000. Twenty-three companies looked for savings of more than $100,000 and eighteen expected to save more than $300,000. Five expected to save more than $1,000,000.

Some of the replies emphasized that the dollar savings were a small part of the gains.

January 12, 1958

Junior Executives Star in New Business Game

One of the teams in a McKinsey & Co. competition simulates operation of a business

By WILLIAM M. FREEMAN

Job experience is as difficult for the would-be top executive to get as it is for employes farther down the scale, and one company is doing something about it.

Because business concerns, like theatrical producers, are unwilling to hire star performers without previous star experience, McKinsey & Co., one of the country's oldest management consulting firms, is simulating such experience in a business game.

McKinsey's method does not involve a costly electronic computer to figure out complicated decisions and their effects. It uses nothing more complicated than a board marked off in squares and some printed sheets for scorekeeping.

Staff members gather regularly on Saturdays, normally a day off, in the concern's offices in this city, Washington, Chicago, San Francisco and Los Angeles to play the game, which was invented by Gerhard R. Andlinger of the McKinsey staff.

Mr. Andlinger, a 26-year-old graduate of Princeton and Harvard Graduate School of Business Administration, worked out the details based on ideas he obtained in studying operations research and war gaming at the Army electronic proving ground at Fort Huachuca, Ariz.

In his version, three teams, four or five men to each, compete with each other in simulating business situations and manipulating the real-life elements of a business—marketing, advertising, production, research and development and finance.

Every fifteen or twenty minutes, which represents three months in terms of reality, the teams come up with decisions on various factors. Umpires calculate the impact of one company's actions on its rivals, according to predetermined rules and report operating figures to each team. The teams then make new decisions for the next quarter.

One side of the board supplied to each team represents the market, rural and urban, with each square a customer. The other side records the decisions made, backed by a form that summarizes the company's course. Expenditures for research, market studies, salesmen and advertising are recorded and evaluated. The trick is to make the proper decisions and come out ahead of a competitor while "learning by doing."

March 28, 1958

Company Economists Playing Bigger Role

Company economists had more to say and were listened to more carefully by management in its decision-making last year than at any other time in business history.

That is the substance of the findings of Socony Mobil Oil Company, Inc., which surveyed 309 of the country's largest corporations to ascertain the role of the economist in private business. The study is reported on by Clark S. Teitsworth, Socony Mobil director, in the January issue of the Harvard Business Review.

One of the directions in which economists were found to be exerting influence was in getting management to make allowances for trends developing in the national economy. Some concerns have made their economists directors, others have put them on the capital budget committees and some use the economics department to train young executives.

January 12, 1959

BIG JOB IS OPEN: 'LOOKING AHEAD'

More Companies Find They Need Full-Time Officer for Forward Planning

By WILLIAM M. FREEMAN

A big job is open in American industry. Here is how the specifications read:

"Director of corporate planning, reporting directly to the president, responsible for all aspects of short-range and long-range forward planning, corporate, marketing, production, engineering, economic and manpower, among others. He will have access to all elements of the company and its divisions, but will take no part in actual operations. He and his group will serve strictly in a staff capacity."

More and more companies are adding this job, defined more or less this way, to their executive roster. The premise is that industry must look ahead for the reason that competition demands it and that research and development workers are striving every day to feed new products and new selling techniques to the factory-consumer assembly line.

Any company interested in staying in the race must look ahead, in the view of top management. That is why the planner has been taking an honored position.

Westinghouse Air Brake Company has an assistant vice president in charge of planning and marketing. Lockheed Aircraft Corporation calls the job that of director, diversification task force. Continental Copper and Steel Industries contents itself with director of corporate planning.

The Stanley Works uses the title of head of forward planning. The Radio Corporation of America electron tube division likes manager of planning. The parent company likes director of marketing research and development. Chain Belt Company of Milwaukee calls the post director of commercial development. The Food Machinery and Chemical Corporation of San Jose, Calif., leans to manager, systems development department. International Business Machines Corporation has the title of director of long-range planning. The Carrier Corporation, air-conditioning manufacturer of Syracuse, N. Y., likes head of planning. The Monroe Calculating Machine Company of Orange, N. J., calls the job director of planning.

Many companies have such positions, under one title or another. In some, the work is a function, often secondary, of the director of marketing. The primary responsibility, of course, still rests with the chief executive officer — the president, the chairman, the executive vice president or whatever title he might have. The job of forward planning in every case is a "staff" or thinking position, whereas carrying it out is a "line" post.

However, while the concept of looking ahead is made up of company goals and profit potentials, only a few industrialists have "a working-horse conception" of realistic forward planning as a dynamic and organized function supported in line with its importance, in the view of J. F. Sorzano, head of J. F. Sorzano Associates, a specialists and a pioneer in the field.

"The rest simply do not understand the subject sufficiently to formalize full-time corporate planning programs," he commented. "To be sure, the head of every company no matter how small, engages in some form of forward planning. It might be nothing more than deciding to open up a new sales territory next year, or to raise prices. He is planning ahead, but in bits and pieces.

"To be effective, forward planning must be short-range and long-range, and it must span all phases of a company's business. Above everything else, it must not be done by bits and pieces."

Mr. Sorzano has prepared what amounts to the first concise blueprint on the subject, covering, on a broad basis designed for easy adaptability, the duties, the responsibilities and the qualifications of the modern full-time director of corporate planning, whatever his actual title.

The blueprint he has worked out is this:

"He should report directly to the president and be responsible for all aspects of short and long-range activities. He should have access to all elements of the company and its divisions, but, generally speaking, he should preferably play no part in operations. It would be best for the director and his group to function in a staff capacity, leaving it to the president of the company or his designee to do the implementation. This keeps the planning director and his people out of the hair of the operating executives."

The work covers every phase of a company's business, taking in marketing, distribution and service, manufacturing and engineering, finance, accounting and statistical controls, cash flow and capital finance requirements, personnel, labor and executive manpower, scientific research and development, new product development and process improvement, diversification and vertical expansion and public, community and shareholder relations.

Mr. Sorzano's study describes a qualified prospect for such a post as 40 to 55 years old, with a technical university degree and perhaps with some post-graduate work behind him in economics, business administration or management.

As for experience, the candidate should have served several years in line managerial capacities.

August 7, 1960

Conference Room Gains Status In Era of Business-by-Committee

By GLENN FOWLER

Just as Parkinson's Law posits the proliferation of committees to carry on the work of the modern business corporation, today's manual of office planning dictates the allocation of ever increasing amounts of space to conference rooms.

Only in recent years has the corporate conference room come into its own. Its predecessor was the "board room"—a closed-off area that lay undisturbed in most executive suites between infrequent meetings of the company's directors. Lesser lights in the business were rarely permitted to enter the sacred confines of the board room.

But today not only the directors meet for mutual pursuit of whatever the company is pursuing. At every level, from the company's officers down to its office boys, conferences are held, whether to set high policy or to induct the newest recruits to a training regimen.

Time-Consuming Meetings

Many executives, in particular, complain that an inordinate amount of their time is consumed in conference. Frequently one-third or more of a middle-range executive's working hours are taken up by meetings.

Whether he likes it or not, however, the typical executive bows to today's corporate togetherness. And the planners of office space, who deem it their duty to provide suitable areas for whatever activities their client companies consider important, are giving increased attention to the design of conference rooms.

One architectural firm that specializes in office planning, Freidin-Studley Associates, finds that the conference room in today's business suite must perform a variety of activities. Jack Freidin, a member of the firm, likens the evolution of the conference room from the board room of yesteryear to the evolution of the "family room" from the old-fashioned parlor in residential architecture.

"The board room was a smoke-filled, oak-paneled area shaped primarily to contain a long table of polished mahogany and an aura of hushed silence," Mr. Freidin says. "But it went out of style with the rolltop desk. So many new activities that call for meetings have become a normal part of modern business procedure that companies today must have an area specially designed for flexible use by groups of people."

Another factor is the high cost of floor space in today's office skyscrapers. Because they must pay high rentals for prime space, companies are anxious to use their floor area as intensively as possible. This usually rules out reserving the conference room only for directors' meetings.

The versatile conference room, according to Mr. Freidin, is created most effectively through the use of movable partitions, sectioned or folding furniture, and a variety of built-in or portable equipment. Typically, it can be converted in a few minutes from a small auditorium into a dining room.

Dining facilities, bars and equipment for entertaining have become almost standard conference room fixtures. Built-in television sets, film projection booths and screens, display panels and the like are becoming increasingly common as more visual aids are used for employe training, for advertising presentations and for other group activities.

In some offices, Mr. Freidin says, an executive might attend a meeting of the board of directors in the morning, have lunch in the executive dining room, deliver a talk to a group of trainees in a small lecture hall, view a television film commercial, and attend a cocktail party after office hours—all without leaving the conference room.

The well-designed conference room usually has all the specialized equipment for these activities concealed in cabinets, in the ceiling and in the floor, making it possible to preserve an uncluttered appearance when the various devices are not in use.

Because the company president probably spends more time in conference than do most of his subordinates, the conference room frequently is attached to the president's office. A movable partition can be used to separate the two spaces, which can then be combined to form either a larger conference room or a huge office.

The decor and furnishings of conference rooms vary as widely as do the types of business that use them. The main thing, says Mr. Freidin, is that a conference room should be designed to put its occupants at ease—though not so much at ease that they fall asleep.

"Wall treatment, for instance, must be interesting but not distracting. Lighting must be adequate but not glearing. The furnishings must harmonize but not be over-designed so that they preclude a businesslike atmosphere."

Mr. Freidin has observed lately a trend among many companies toward cutting down the number of meetings their executives must attend. But he does not see any possibility that, in the office of the future, the conference room will be done away with. Instead, he believes, companies will seek new ways to make their conference rooms more conducive to efficient and productive work.

April 1, 1962

MANAGEMENT SHIFTS TOWARD TECHNOLOGY

The United States is not only in a period of accelerating technological change. It is also going through a scientific industrial revolution in terms of the nature of the top management of leading corporations. That is the finding of a recent study made by Scientific American, the magazine.

Since 1940, it is pointed out, the nation's total manpower in science and technology has grown faster than either the population or the total labor force. The average annual rate of increase has been about 5 per cent, nearly four times that of the labor force as a whole. In 1940, manpower in science and technology accounted for 1.5 per cent of the total labor force. By 1960 it had increased to 3.2 per cent and, according to a projection by the National Science Foundation, it will rise to 4.7 per cent by 1970.

Meanwhile, the participation of scientists and engineers in top industrial management has also steadily increased, the magazine says. In 1900, only 7 per cent of the top business leaders had a technical background. This proportion grew to 13 per cent in 1925, to 20 per cent in 1950 and, in 1963, to 36 per cent. In the first 50 years of this century, the percentage rose 1.3 points every five years. In the last 13 years the percentage of technical men in top positions has increased five points every five years as the trend has become more marked.

Scientific American comments:

"Clearly then, a new type of business executive, one whose background is heavily oriented to science and engineering, is emerging at an ever-faster rate. Within a short time—by 1980—he will represent a majority in the top management of leading American firms. The plain conclusion to be drawn is that United States industry is coming under new management."

The study also showed that almost three-quarters of all scientists and engineers are in private industry and research, the others working for government and universities. Further, a very high proportion of scientists and engineers are young, with about 74 per cent under the age of 45, compared with 61 per cent in that age category for the labor force as a whole.

February 9, 1964

THE RICH MAN'S SON---HOW HE IS BEING TRAINED TO SUCCEED HIS FATHER

OFTEN the question is asked in these days of great corporations and greater financial interests dominating them, not singly, or in twos or threes, but by the scores and hundreds, whence are coming the men who in the next generation shall man and officer the mighty ship of finance. Most people answer it by saying that the law of the survival of the fittest will determine—by pointing to the vast number of successful men of to-day who have forced their way out of the ruck of the toilers into the positions of prominence that they now hold. So they look for this generation of captains of industry to give way to another that shall spring up unheralded and one day make itself known only by demonstrating its fitness to rule and its ability to maintain its supremacy once attained.

This is the natural and, in the main, probably the correct view. It accords with the American theory of opportunity, harmonizes with the apparent testimony of current events as recorded in the daily press and magazines. So much attention is paid to the doings of the class commonly termed the "Idle Rich"—their likes and dislikes, their clothes, their amusements, and the things which annoy them, that one is disposed to conclude that these folk must constitute the entire generation of sons and daughters of modern American finance.

It is not a rare theory, indeed, that looks to the eventual creation of trust estates, handling through institutions or through salaried officials the accumulations of wealth that have been piled up by the great financial men of the nineteenth and early twentieth centuries. Behind it lies the belief that if such does not happen, the "spenders" speedily will redistribute the fortunes with a disregard for consequences that will produce all sorts of undesirable corporate complications.

An idea as extreme as this does not, however, appear justified by the facts. If an American theory of opportunity applies to the poor and to people of moderate wealth, so also it must apply to those who have the exceptional advantages that come with important financial affiliations, provided only the individual seeks to utilize them. And if he does, it necessarily follows that for various years after he has attained his majority he will be little heard of in public—in fact, appearing hardly at all until the time comes for him to assume his father's responsibilities and justify before the financial world the claim of genuine attainment that they entail. Thus the daily papers and magazines will be left to recount the doings of the "spenders" which, as a matter of fact, are a whole lot more interesting than those of the workers.

+ + +

Within the domains of "Standard Oil" may be found perhaps the most notable illustration of many sons being trained up to fill the places of their fathers, and the fact is particularly interesting because the elders are men drawn together by the varied circumstances of business competition, and for the most part quite unrelated. Indeed, "Standard Oil" is primarily an institution of families. Beginning with the Rockefellers, one goes down the list of Flaglers and Pratts and Bedfords in the oil business proper, and the Stillmans in the larger circle of financial influence. Henry H. Rogers, recognized as the virtual head of the "system," has been always something of a solitary figure, and John D. Archbold another. So, to a certain extent, has been James Stillman President of the National City Bank, the principal institution of its kind within the Standard's bailiwick.

It is interesting to see how this family institution is being maintained. In the first place there is John D. Rockefeller, Jr., who has already assumed many of his father's interests outside of the inner circle of Standard Oil affairs. In fact, it has always been a hobby of the elder Rockefeller not to be in many Directorates and at the present time the corporation Directory gives his name only in the board of the Standard Oil Company of New Jersey, of which he is President.

John D. Rockefeller, Jr., started a daily grind at 26 Broadway as soon as he was graduated from Brown University in 1898. A year ago he succeeded to his father's place in the Directorate of the United States Steel Corporation, the Delaware, Lackawanna and Western and Missouri Pacific Railroads, and as a Trustee of the University of Chicago. He is, of course, a Director of the Standard Oil Company, and also represents his father's personal interests in the Colorado Fuel and Iron Company, which is one of the many corporations ruled from 26 Broadway.

It had always been supposed until recently that "Young John D.," as he has become known, would eventually become the commanding general of the Standard Oil forces, and men who have come into contact with him in a business way have believed that he had the stuff in him for the task. But the younger Rockefeller's health is such that it is taken for granted downtown now that the successor to William Rockefeller and Henry H. Rogers will be William G. Rockefeller, a son of the former and nephew of the present titular head of Standard Oil.

+ + +

William G. Rockefeller, like most of the other young men in the Standard coterie, has been heard of but little, and it is only recently that he has been pushed to the front. Whereas his father is a Director in forty-one of the largest corporations in the land, he is in the boards only of the Brooklyn Union Gas, the National Fuel Gas, and the New York Transit Companies, together with that of the Union Pacific Railroad. Of H. H. Rogers, Jr., little has been heard in the financial district. Just now he is spending the Winter on a yacht his father has hired for him down in the West Indies somewhere.

A very interesting Standard Oil family is the house of Pratt, a name that is known in educational circles as well as financial, and is perpetuated in Brooklyn by many monuments of generosity. Charles M. Pratt the elder was one of the earlier associates of the Rockefellers in the oil business, coming into the system through an inevitable amalgamation and making himself a power in it from that time until his death a few years ago. He was succeeded by his son, Charles M. Pratt, who is now Secretary of the Standard Oil Company, and several other sons have collateral connections that make them a part of the larger institution. The third generation of Pratts have hardly attained an age yet sufficient to indicate their business trend in any particular.

Coupled with the name of Pratt in the Standard Oil is that of Bedford. E. T. Bedford the elder was many years ago a member of the oil firm of Thompson & Bedford, which, like the Pratt concern, underwent an amalgamation. With Mr. Bedford are his two sons, Charles and Fred T., Jr., the former in the Standard Oil Company proper and the latter Treasurer and General Manager of the New York Glucose Company, of which his father also is President. It is assumed that the Bedfords will hold similar positions in the New Glucose Company, which is to include not only the New York Glucose, but the Corn Products Company as well.

+ + +

Like the name of H. H. Rogers, that of James Stillman has stood out by itself, even among the many able men in the upper ranks of the Standard Oil party. As President of the National City Bank and a representative of the vast Rockefeller interests in fifty-eight other corporations, Mr. Stillman has held a place of power hardly second to that of H. H. Rogers and William Rockefeller. Like them, he has sons coming up in the business. James A. Stillman, the old Yale football tackle, went into the National City Bank as soon as he was graduated from college, in the later nineties, and has now become assistant cashier of the institution, as well as one of its Directors. Charles C. Stillman, the other son, is learning the railroad business in the West, and works daily in the shops of one of the great transcontinental systems like a common laborer.

+ + +

A different kind of a family institution from the Standard Oil Company, yet no less unique in its way, is the American Smelting and Refining Company with its many allied corporations. In this case there is but one family, and that one of the most remarkable that the country has ever produced. The sons of Meyer Guggenheim, seven of them, are the men who direct the affairs of Smelters and its various constituent companies. They occupy all a single office at 71 Broadway—an office which appears more like the library of a private residence than the fountainhead of a great business enterprise. About the wall of one great room which stretches across the entire rear side of the building are the desks of the seven brothers—Isaac, the eldest; Daniel, Murray, Solomon R., Benjamin, Simon, and William Guggenheim.

It is an interesting tradition that underlies this family combination, and while it has been written many times before the present no account of this nature would be complete without mention of it. Meyer Guggenheim, the father, came over from Switzerland in the middle of the last century. Settling in Philadelphia, he became an itinerant vendor, going from place to place with his wagon and trading in the multitude of things that were thus dealt in from house to house a half century or more ago. In some one of these trips he met a man who had invented a brand of stove polish, and became interested in the undertaking. Eventually he embarked in this business, and with his headquarters in Philadelphia built up a comfortable fortune, taking his eldest son, Isaac, with him.

+ + +

Not many years later a relative came to this country from Switzerland with some samples of finely made lace, and it occurred to Meyer Guggenheim that there was an opportunity to build up a lace business along with that in which he had already made a success. He tried the experiment, and it proved no less profitable than his first one. Subsequently he became interested in mining properties through a loan made to a Western mining promoter, and eventually turned the major portion of his attention into this direction. The details of the story how the great Guggenheim fortune was built up from this point would make too long a tale for this telling. The important fact is that Meyer Guggenheim lived and worked not for himself, but that Meyer Guggenheim's sons should be able to take their place among the financial powers of the country.

As soon as the boys were able to assume the management of the business, the father laid plans for his own retirement, and undertook no longer the investment of his money directly, but loaned it without restriction to the boys, requiring only a 6 per cent. interest return. Now there is another generation coming up, Robert M., the son of Daniel, who is having his first years of experience in the harness; his brother, Harry F. Guggenheim, and his cousin, Edmond Guggenheim, the son of Murray, who is taking a mining and engineering course in Columbia University as a preliminary to his life work in the Guggenheim properties.

Outside of great industrial enterprises, it is hardly as common a thing to find sons being trained up to follow in their fathers' footsteps. There are some notable instances of it, however, and among the best known of these is that of J. P. Morgan, Jr., who has been for some years the head of the English house of Morgan & Co. He is by no means an unfamiliar figure in Wall Street, and the financial world would look forward to the time when he will succeed his father as head of the banking firm in this country. Another instance in which a banker's son has been taken into his father's firm early in life is that of Mortimer L. Schiff, son of Jacob H. Schiff, who is the senior partner in the firm of Kuhn, Loeb & Co. In Kuhn, Loeb & Co. also are Paul M. and Felix Warburg, the first of whom married a sister of Mrs. Schiff and the second Mr. Schiff's daughter.

In the railroad world the Vanderbilt family has long stood by itself in this respect. William K. and Frederick Vanderbilt, the sons of William H. Vanderbilt, have been familiar figures in American railroad affairs for a quarter of a century, as their father and grandfather were before them. Within the last few years William K. Vanderbilt, Jr., who is best known to the American public perhaps as a patron of automobiling and many other forms of sport, has been in harness at the Grand Central Station most business days during the year. He is now the financial head of the extensive electric traction interests of the Vanderbilt railroad systems, a position that is bound to grow in importance as the electrification of suburban railroad lines throughout the State progresses.

+ + +

James J. Hill, for the purposes of American finance, is the first in his line. Readers of THE TIMES are familiar with the fascinating story of his career, how he undertook to build a railroad on a basis so honest that his freights could be lower than any one else's freights and still the road would make money. Helping Mr. Hill, at least during the latter years of his great task, have been his two sons, one of whom, James N. Hill, is now Vice President of the Northern Pacific Railroad, succeeding the late Daniel Lamont, during his life Mr. Hill's most trusted friend and adviser. The other son, Lewis W. Hill, is Vice President of the Great Northern. Both are the active men in their properties, and it is a question that Wall Street discusses with some interest as to which one will be the successor of his father as the head of the Hill railroads when the gray old veteran retires, whose motto has been, "Let 'em all build to the coast if they want to. It will develop the country, and I guess there is enough in it for all of us."

January 14, 1906

THE SELF-MADE RULERS OF OUR RAILROADS

Notable Examples Which Show That Success In Railroad Leadership Necessitates Experience in All Branches of the Service.

By EDWIN WILDMAN.

THE popular conception of the railroad President as a corpulent, lethargic gentleman of ponderous mien, enjoying the fruits of others' labors, drawing an immense salary, and spending his time in wheeled palaces or easy chairs in gilded offices, is hardly borne out in the lives of these responsible factors in the country's growth and finance.

Habit is such a tenacious vice that once acquired it is not easy to escape its tentacles. Men who have learned to rise by candlelight and hustle off to a yard switch, a signal station, a baggage room, or a telegrapher's key, and by force of circumstances have closeted themselves with a ten or sixteen hour job in which a single mistake might cost a score of lives and wreck a $500,000 investment, find it difficult, if they would in the mellow years, to release the clutch of early environment and training.

When a great railroad President dies and the trains and operating force stand attention the five minutes that his body is lowered into its final resting place, it is fair to assume that it is a just tribute to an erstwhile co-laborer in every grade of work through which he has during his lifetime passed in order to reach the apex of power.

PRACTICAL EXPERIENCE OF TWO RAILROAD MEN.

REMARKABLY inspiring and significant is the fact that to-day there is hardly a railroad President at the lever of America's great transportation systems who has not served a long apprenticeship in the lowest round of line work. Observe James McCrea, President of the Pennsylvania Railroad, jumping off his private car at a wreck near Christiana, some years ago, offering his services to his foreman. "There's nothing you can do," says the burly foreman in charge of the wreck. "Nothing I can do?" McCrea retorted. "Do you mean to tell me there is nothing a fellow can do with a road blocked with wreckage and trains on both sides? Well, let me tell you there are ties down there in the ditch that we can carry up to replace this track," and forthwith McCrea, stripping off his coat, flung a heavy timber to his shoulder, the while taking charge and directing action that put the boss wrecker into the shadow.

Could and would McCrea have done this if he had not in his youth been a rodman on the line and worked up through the grades as faithfully as any other employe and obviously with greater intelligence? It is a way with these railroading giants—they are never above their job. McCrea's chance

was no greater than that of hundreds of other rodmen and engineers. He simply made himself felt in the business. He started at 17 years of age, put on heavy cowhides, and went at his work with all the force that was in his huge 6 feet 2 inches of bones and brawn. He learned every foot of trackage and studied the possibilities of every curve and level of the road.

He went through the grades, from rodman, conductor, assistant, engineer, Vice President, to the Presidency so rapidly that he became the logical successor to A. J. Cassatt, who in his youthful days was a co-rodman with him. A man who has charge of 12,000 miles of railways and the responsibility of 130,000,000 passengers annually and 400,000,000 tons of freight must know his job. There can be no guesswork, no theory, no idealism about it—and it took him less than half a century to climb the ladder.

"That's Jim McCrea," they say down in Pittsburg, when he enters the Duquesne Club, "the man who can't be beat at billiards, for the man who can beat him doesn't dare to." It's a man's tribute to the dominant personality of a masterful mind.

Railroading is masterful work. You can't inherit a railroad Presidency and hope to hold the job. The Vanderbilts and Goulds of to-day and Stuyvesant Fish "inherited" ownership, but not one of them actually presidented a road—to use that term, and all that it implies. In this country we have a way of expecting the man who holds the office to deliver the goods. Dummy Presidents and dummy Directors soon get found out. The American spirit puts it squarely up to the man who wears the shoulder straps.

Now, take the case of Louis W. Hill, President of the Great Northern. A railroad property was his for the earning, but he didn't "inherit" the Presidency. His elder brother Jim inherited the Presidency, but it slipped from his grasp quicker than you can say Jack Robinson. Jim was not masterful. Louis is. He commenced at the bottom. He began like any other employe, as a freight checker. He worked in a far Western flag station. He took a course in the shops, and was as literally subject to the rules and regulations as any other man. He took a turn in the engine barn. He found out what it meant to have the responsibility of a station. After fifteen years of hard work in railroading Louis W. Hill was elected by the Directors President of the Great Northern, and James J. Hill, his father, stepped out. "Accurate and ample information is the first step toward success," is the recipe of James J. Hill. "Make the most of yourself. Some opportunity comes to every man."

At 14 years of age this colossal figure in American railroading was clerking in a village store. The West was his opportunity. He went to St. Paul and took a position as a clerk in a packet line. Nine years later he owned his own business, and twenty-five years later he had spanned the continent from St. Paul to Seattle with a new trans-continental line, and a few short years later had crossed the Pacific with the finest line of freight and passenger steamships afloat on the waters of our Western ocean, invading and capturing a large share of the Oriental trade. And this is a man who peeled potatoes for his board in the Merchants' Hotel in St. Paul half a century back.

SOME PECULIARITIES OF JAMES T. HARAHAN.

THERE'S no college that fits a youth for the job of brakeman. The job is a course in itself. James T. Harahan found it so. His primary education began forty-five years ago in the school of car wheels, rails, and engines. At the outbreak of the civil war Harahan was a switchman in Alexandria, Va. The switchman's job didn't satisfy him. He wanted to move, and his wants soon reached the ears of his superiors. They promoted him to brakeman. The two positions qualified him for a boost. The old Nashville & Decatur road needed a roadmaster, and Jim Harahan got the job. In fact, he always had his eye on the job just beyond his immediate reach.

No one liked to be Jim Harahan's boss—Jim was sure to get the job away from him. He finally got Stuyvesant Fish's job. Mr. Fish was President of the Illinois Central, President by "inheritance," and he couldn't hang on. Harahan knew every tie and engine, every switchman and station master on the road. He was virtually its President before E. H. Harriman dropped the mantle of power on his shoulders.

It wasn't an easy thing either to get Jim Harahan to take the responsibility. He had his "terms," and one of them was that he wouldn't live in New York. "You couldn't hire me to take his job if I had to live in New York," he said. "I won't consent to have the headquarters of the Illinois Central anywhere but in Illinois. You can't manage a railroad 1,000 miles away. You have to be on the spot." Harahan, as every man on the road knows, is everlastingly on the spot. His farmer-like face, large bold head, and shrewd, genial eyes are familiar to his army of employes. The lives of passengers as well as the opportunities of employes are vouchsafed under the Harahan type.

B. F. YOAKUM, TEXAN BUILDER OF RAILROADS.

HE IS, however, not a glittering exception in the galaxy of railroad Presidents who have carried dinner pails and have done their ten hours a day. There's chain bearer and rodman Yoakum—Benjamin Franklin by given name. B. F. Yoakum shot up like one of his namesake's kites. In some of his dreams he has been as bold as the veritable and original B. F. himself. Yoakum is to the Southwest what James J. Hill is to the Northwest—a "constructive genius" some fine phraseologist has called him, and, mayhap, the name is worthily placed, for Yoakum, erstwhile rodman, has corralled 17,500 miles of railway in our Texan country and its feeders.

Yoakum is a Simon-pure Texan, big, brawny, breezy. His father was a country physician, and wanted Ben to become the Rev. Ben, but the boy's blood was filled with iron, and he took to railroading as a duck takes to water. There weren't any railroads in Texas worth mentioning in those days, so Yoakum got a job as boss of a surveying gang on the Great Northern. Surveying was an opening wedge to construction—and that end of the work found in him an enthusiast. He saw what Jim Hill was doing in the Northwest, and his heart warmed for his native plains in the South.

He dreamed one night of the gleam of steel from Waco to the Gulf, and set about materializing things. The Vice Presidency came as naturally to him as did later the Presidency of the Frisco lines. Yoakum has been called an empire builder, and so he is. First he extended the trackage in the Southwest and then sang the siren song to hundreds of thousands of emigrants from Italy who came via the Gulf of Mexico to develop and populate his empire. Its a big one now, and Benjamin Franklin Yoakum is capable of meeting every responsibility of the game. It is told of Gen. "Phil" Sheridan that he once said: "If I owned hell and Texas, I'd rent Texas and live in hell." In answer to which Yoakum replies: "He wouldn't say so to-day. Texas has society enough now, and water, too."

C. S. MELLEN, "SHIRT SLEEVE RAILROADER."

THEN there's Mellen, who at eighteen was happy on $25 a month as a clerk in the office of a tiny railroad up in New Hampshire—where he stayed for eleven years. Mellen, Charles S., who now, at sixty years of age, is the man whose eye is figuratively upon you and whose ticket agent collects your fare if you want to travel in Massachusetts, Connecticut, Rhode Island, by steam or trolley; who transports you by water along the coasts of three States, and whose rails even penetrate New York, New Jersey, and Pennsylvania.

Charles S. Mellen is a masterful railroader. He was so busy learning his job as a youth that college was passed up and "education" was left to percolate by contact. Mellen learned so much about railroading from switch to cash box that when Mr. Morgan determined to give James J. Hill a turn in the Northwest he took Mellen and sat him down in St. Paul to reorganize the Northern Pacific. Mellen is a "shirt-sleeve railroader," and he got so busy with Western traffic and Western railroads that one day Wall Street heard of a merger, and the Great Northern, the Burlington, and the Northern Pacific were rolled into one and the Northern Securities Company came to life.

There wasn't any more work for Mellen out West, so Mr. Morgan wired him to come East at his expense, and things began to happen in New England. He drove Cassatt and the Vanderbilts out of New England, checkmated Charles W. Morse on the Sound, and bought up the trolley lines to boot. The Presidency of the whole aggregation fell into his lap. Charles S. Mellen is sometimes called the human iceberg. He is a New Englander born and bred.

He doesn't go in for "society," and he isn't at all a chatty person. It is said that he isn't even rich. But he is dogged and aggressive; he knew his mind at eighteen, and he knows it at sixty. He is just a plain railroader and knows tracks and men.

He is as "hard" as George F. Baer, with whom he matched prowess in the Pennsylvania field. Baer is a man of iron jaw: a set, steely man, who would have been an Iron Duke if he had been born in Bismarck's skin.

G. F. BAER'S SCHOOL WAS THE CIVIL WAR.

BAER is a man who knows no compromise when right is on his side, and right is usually right as interpreted by the man who is called the master mind of the coal regions of America. George F. Baer is a German. He didn't learn railroading in that little typesetting shop where he served as a printer's "devil" fifty years ago; nor as an amateur surveyor in Central Pennsylvania; but he learned some things about engines during the civil war, through which he fought, starting as Captain of a volunteer company, and emerging as Adjutant General of the Second Brigade of the Army of the Potomac. He learned about railroading as a humble attorney for a wee railroad in Berks County, Pennsylvania.

It was the eagle eye of J. P. Morgan that discovered Baer. The obscure attorney became conspicuous in the defense of corporate rights, and Mr. Morgan put his tag on him at once and made him his representative in Pennsylvania. That was Mr. Baer's opportunity. Mr. Morgan wanted to get one of his roads into Pittsburg. "Can you do it?" he asked Baer. "I believe it can be done," Baer replied. "You're it—I want men who can do things," and Baer was slapped on the back by Morgan, and the railroad got into Pittsburg, and Charles F. Baer became President of the Philadelphia & Reading.

It was Baer who said during the famous coal strike "that the rights and interests of the laboring men will be looked after and cared for, not by agitators, but by Christian men to whom God in His infinite wisdom has given control of the property interests of the country." It made some people smile, but Baer didn't care—he doesn't do much smiling himself—he's too busy—with railroading, with history, horticulture, chess playing, and farming. He is an organizer and a chief, watchful and ambitious, coldly just, austere and terse to a point of brusqueness, not possessing much in common with men of the type of erstwhile section hand W. C. Brown, not unknown to the traveling public who pay their fares over the New York Central lines, of which he happens to be President.

W. C. BROWN STARTED AS A SECTION HAND

BROWN is more to the point. Baer is masterful, perhaps intolerant; but Brown is commanding and a general of rails as Chaffee was of soldiers. He trusts his subordinates as long as he keeps them—or they part company sine die. W. C. Brown knows what the duty is of every one of his 150,000 men on the system, and it is a big one, extending its tentacles like a spider web over several States, fairly veiling the face of New York. Brown knows what a job calls for, because he has been on it himself. When Mellen went West, Fireman Brown came East. He wasn't on the box this time, but in his private car.

Back in the seventies Bill Brown was a section hand, not an experimental one, but the real thing. He and his wife lived in a little lean-to in Waterloo, Iowa, and Bill had to bring home the envelope every Saturday night. But, pshaw! the section hand job was a big lift for Brown. At sixteen years of age he had a job compared with which section work was loafing—his splintered hands and toughened knuckles told the story—Bill was an engine wooder, heaving six-footers into the locomotive's tinder box on a jerk-water road. That was the beginning of President Brown of the Vanderbilt lines. Between heaves he picked up the Morse alphabet on station telegraph keys, and before he knew it he found himself a train dispatcher on the Chicago, Burlington & Quincy, the youngest on record in those days.

Brown got his "slap on the shoulder" one stormy night when he stuck to his post and straightened things out in a way that made his superiors sit up and take notice, and incidentally saved the road large sums of money. He was made chief train dispatcher of the road. Brown was intelligent, he was faithful, he was diligent—he was masterful. The rest of Brown's career is not interesting. It's just a repetition of promotions, an account of energetic action at the right moment, a story of settling strikes, running his own engine, mending his own track, bossing his own gangs, and doing the whole job from track to station and station to general offices, of this, that, or the other railroad.

Brown is a New York Stater born, Herkimer County nourished, and Iowa bred and risen, yeast self-generated. He knows the Western roads, the Rock Island, Burlington, the Iowa and Missouri lines—he knows the universal language of rail and tie, and engine and boss, from A to Z, and is an eternal inspiration to any boy, poor, obscure, humble but energetic and intelligent, who is willing to put up a good fight and a long one for something worth while.

T. P. SHONTS'S CAREER A VARIED ONE.

TO look at him to-day you wouldn't suspect the embryonic wood-heaver of Iowa days any more than you could imagine the Chesterfieldian, smooth, and polished Shonts, a water boy on a construction train out in that same State. They are both products of the Iowa idea, or rather are Iowa ideals. T. P. Shonts is still a railroad President as well as a Subway President. Shonts didn't get as many hard knocks as some of his contemporaries. He branched off into law and married a banker's daughter. It didn't interfere with his being a good construction man, however, and as a personal conductor who knew his business he attracted the attention of Theodore Roosevelt. The rest is too well known to recite. Shonts is a man of strong will and daring. He has a broad grasp and never lets loose of one good thing until he's got his hooks upon another, and then he still hangs on to the last. That's the reason he's still President of one Western road and Director of several, besides his present occupation with New York City's transportation problems.

It takes early training to do these things. You can't acquire them after an adolescence of college clubs and afternoon teas.

HOW MR. TRUMBULL MADE HIS START.

THE man who started "cross lots" from Kansas City to Topolobampo Bay, on the Pacific Coast of Mexico, is neither a society man nor did he begin life in a lean-to; he commenced his race for supremacy in the railroad world as a bookkeeper in a general store at Pleasant Hill, Mo., and landed in the Empire Building, New York. Frank Trumbull, President of the Colorado Midland, the Colorado Southern, and several other roads streaking off sou' by sou'east, had a brother, in the bookkeeping days, who said: "Frank, you are too young to be wasting your brilliancy on Pleasant Hill folk. Come out to Sedalia and I'll get you a job where the real thing is appreciated."

Frank balanced up the books and started for a town on the railroad. He got his job in the Missouri, Kansas & Texas Railroad offices at $45 a month, and all at the age of sixteen years. At twenty-one he was chief clerk at $175 a month. For fourteen years he rose steadily, but mighty slowly. Jay Gould was gathering in roads around Texas, and Trumbull was one of the assets he figured on, but Trumbull slipped the noose—he wasn't going fast enough, under the Jay Gould system, and opened up a coal business for himself.

There's where he got the other man's point of view—and he says it taught him more about railroading than did his previous experience on the inside. So after five years Trumbull was called back to the job as receiver of the Colorado & Southern. He became General Manager and President, and has never let it get away from him.

"There wasn't even the impression of a cent in the treasury when I took it over in 1893," said Mr. Trumbull. To-day it yawps from Kansas City to Galveston on the southeast and toward the Pacific on the southwest. But though Frank Trumbull has mastered the railroad business out West, he is qualified for afternoon teas in New York—he was born in Massachusetts, and his mother is a lineal descendant of Gov. William Randolph of Virginia. The reflection, however, never seems to have obsessed him, and he is still on the job.

SOME CANADIAN RAILROAD BUILDERS.

UP in Canada American railroad blood has been doing big stunts, too. In fact Canada couldn't get along without telegraph operator Sir William Van Horn, K. C. M. G., builder and ex-President of the Canadian Pacific, owner of the railway business in Cuba, and incidentally in Guatemala; nor Thomas Shaughnessy, K. C. B., erstwhile purchasing agent of a Western road, as well as former clerk in the Atlantic & Pacific Railroad at St. Louis; Charles M. Hayes, now President of the Grand Trunk and a lot of other railroads—all Yankees bred and born, who came from little towns, commenced on the track or in the office, and won the highest offices in the service and the titular recognition of their adopted sovereign.

All these men are peculiarly fitted for masterful tasks unique in railroading. Canada is such a vast, partially peopled area that the railroad President becomes a sort of land baron as well. The Canadian Pacific owned 25,000,000 acres of uninhabited territory; it still offers 10,000,000 to prospective passengers—settlers. Last year nearly 100,000 Americans were lured across the border, and the year before 65,000. Canada has 75,000,000 acres awaiting settlers, and it's up to these three ex-American railroad Presidents to do their share in fitting up the country. Shaughnessy is 53, Hayes is 53, and Van Horn is 66 years of age, all working like nailers at the railroad business since they were in their teens.

E. H. HARRIMAN TEACHER, NOT LEARNER.

NOW Harriman is an anachronism, upside down. He never learned railroading; he taught it. Harriman is the little Napoleon, the No. 1, I am, the man who railroaded all the railroads together. E. H. Harriman is a great railroader. The greatest of the great, for he has empirized the railroads of America. What Morgan and the men he slapped on the back built, Harriman watered and made to bear fruit. Harriman began at fourteen as an errand clerk in a broker's house less than half a century since, down on Wall Street, where railroads are simply checkers and chips. Harriman's career is an inspiration to boys with an itching palm for power and money, but I take it from Harriman himself: "It is not everything to make money, boys; it's something to live and do something lasting for your country, and that's my ambition—to do good in the world, and to do it so that it will stand"—and I believe he meant it, little villages that were molested, large cities that were upset, broad plains that were disturbed, big mountains that were bored, and you and I and others who have lost and made money on the ebb and flow of Harriman stock to the contrary notwithstanding.

Harriman was a broker, Brown a section hand, Shonts a water carrier, McCrea and Cassatt rodmen, Hill a freight handler on a packet boat, Thomas of the Lehigh a telegrapher, Baer a railway attorney, Underwood of the Erie a switchman, Ripley of the Sante Fé a clerk, Harahan a switchman, Truesdale of the Lackawanna a clerk, Mellen a clerk, Yoakum a brakeman, Earling of the Chicago, Milwaukee & St. Paul a telegraph operator, Murray of the Baltimore & Ohio a ticket agent, Hughitt of the Chicago & Northwestern a telegrapher, Harris of the Chicago, Burlington & Quincy an office boy, Trumbull a clerk—and there you have it—now Presidents all.

Young America can take its choice, begin where you will; the opportunities are as great in the actual business end of a railroad as ever; in fact, they were never so big, for there were never so many railroads, and there are several little hamlets in Texas, Colorado, Missouri—even in Pennsylvania and New York—that have never heard the screech of an engine whistle.

April 18, 1909

TRAINED MEN NEED OF BUSINESS WORLD

School of "Hard Knocks" a Thing of the Past, Says Dean Johnson of N. Y. U.

RESEARCH WORK VALUABLE

It Will Locate and Destroy Germs of Business Depression and Lessen Poverty, He Says.

The days of the school of "hard knocks" is over, in the opinion of Dean Joseph Francis Johnson of the New York University School of Commerce, who predicts that the Andrew Carnegies, Marshall Fields and James J. Hills of the future will have had in their early manhood the training that is being given by such schools of commerce as are now established at Harvard, New York University and a few other colleges.

"The time is near," declared Dean Johnson, "when our leading bankers will be the graduates of the university schools of commerce, and when the appointment of an untrained man to membership of the Federal Reserve Board at Washington will be as unlikely as the elevation of a shyster lawyer to a seat in the Supreme Court of the United States. A banker will then be thought of as a professional man as today we think of the lawyer, the physician, the architect, the engineer, the certified public accountant.

"Other business callings will also be gradually lifted to a professional status, such as advertising, insurance, management, industrial engineering, journalism, secretaryships of chambers of commerce, brokerage, especially in investment securities, railroad and steamship transportation, and I am also inclined to include book publishing, merchandising, the management of large hotels and restaurants, city management and the conduct of the multiform business activities of the nation, the State and the municipality."

One of the great handicaps confronting university schools of commerce, said the Dean, has been that universities in their search for teachers have had to compete with big business for the services of such men.

"The best teachers of such a faculty," he said, "are constantly tempted by the offer of salaries in business positions many times larger than the university can afford to pay. This doubtless will always be the case, but schools of commerce in the future will not suffer greatly from the dearth of good teachers. There are men who love the science underlying commerce, just as there are men who love the natural sciences, and many of these men love to teach. Such men are and always will be our best teachers."

Dean Johnson said that when he first began teaching at New York University the functions of a school of commerce were so poorly understood that an old classmate at Harvard asked him what kind of a "business college" he was teaching in.

"The knowledge is gradually gaining ground," said the Dean, "that the university school of commerce is aiming not primarily to show young men how to make money, but to make men so thoroughly understand the laws governing business that society as a whole will be benefited. The primary aim of the agricultural college is not merely to make its graduates scientific and successful farmers, but to increase the country's crops, to kill the pests which now make farming a most uncertain occupation, to put science into agriculture and make it a real art and not merely a gamble between soil and climate.

"Our schools of medicine have as their ultimate goal not merely the cure of disease, but the prevention of disease, and in the last twenty years, by the aid of the Roentgen ray and the microscope, they have made giant strides toward that goal. The high aim of our veterinary colleges is the safeguarding of a large part of the country's food supply, and it is the high aim of our colleges of arts and science to see that society shall be ennobled by knowledge of what is choicest in the culture and learning of all time.

"In like manner, university schools of commerce are actuated by a fine ideal of social service. They seek not merely to equip their students for success in business, but by the instruction they give, by their bureaus of business research and through the scientific and impartial investigations of members of their faculties, to put all business on a scientific basis, lessen poverty and unemployment, destroy the germs of panic and depression, and promote the happiness and welfare of all the people."

March 15, 1922

AUTO CO. MANAGERS TO GET STOCK BONUS

General Motors Announces Plan to Make Partners of Its Principal Executives.

PUT UP TO STOCKHOLDERS

Announcement was made last night of the proposed formation of the Managers' Securities Company, by means of which about seventy of the principal executives of the General Motors Corporation will get a block of shares of General Motors common stock, or 12 per cent. of the amount outstanding, which has a present value of more than $33,000,000.

The plan as announced by President Alfred P. Sloan Jr. in a letter to stockholders involves the payment by the corporation to the Securities Company of 5 per cent. of its net earnings in excess of 7 per cent. on the invested capital employed each year as a bonus. The plan is subject to the approval of the stockholders, who will meet in Wilmington, Del., Nov. 23 to act upon it.

The plan, according to Mr. Sloan, is "to interest the men occupying important positions of management in the company as partners with the stockholders in this corporation."

"In a great structure such as the General Motors Corporation," said Mr. Sloan, "where our problems and our operations are so diversified and where capital must be employed and plants operated in the best interests of the corporation as a whole, as against any separate part or division, and where new capital supplied should be injected where it will accomplish the greatest good, it is important to find, develop and retain men to occupy important managerial positions who are capable of assuming great authority and responsibilities that make these positions important. Not only is it necessary that these managers be capable of handling efficiently the immediate problems of their respective divisions, but it is essential that they view broadly and understand the policies necessary to coordinate the various ramifications of this vast business and thus secure proper return to the stockholders on upward of $500,000,000 of capital employed."

October 29, 1923

YOUNG MEN COME TO FORE IN WORLD AFFAIRS

New Leaders in Industry and Statecraft Make Up in Genius What They Lack in Years

By JAMES C. YOUNG.

YOUNG men in increasing numbers are taking important parts in running the business, the statecraft and the science of the world. A man of 40 has just been selected by one of the three largest American industries to direct its activities. A man of 32 has charge of the working out of reparation problems on which the immediate future welfare of Europe largely depends. A third, still in his early thirties, has contributed one of the big developments in radio communication. Young men stand forth in every field of endeavor, wherever inquiry may be directed. The premium on enthusiasm is as high today as on experience. When both are combined, the product comes near to genius.

The election of Walter S. Gifford to be President of the American Telephone and Telegraph Company and to direct its 15,000,000 telephones and its $2,000,000,000 of capital brings into power a man who possesses these two elements of experience and enthusiasm in an uncommon degree. The achievements crowded into his career of a comparatively few years represent a sum of experience that falls to few men. As for his enthusiasm, it is the stuff that made his career and produced the experience.

Men inside the big telephone company point to a recent bond issue as one example of what Gifford enthusiasm has accomplished. Back in 1919 he was Vice President in charge of finance, and the matter of raising some $90,000,000 came to his attention. The market was not particularly favorable to new utility issues. A sale of these securities through the accepted channels would mean heavy charges by an underwriting syndicate and by bond dealers and other middlemen.

A Man of Ideas and Courage.

Mr. Gifford decided to sell that issue to the public direct without anybody's intervention. Doubtless his decision caused a gasp, within the company and without. The idea was not distinctly new. The thing had been done on a limited scale. But the distributing of $90,000,000 in securities over the counter without any shaving of principal was an innovation in corporate finance. Naturally, there were many persons who said that it couldn't be done. But Mr. Gifford went ahead and presently turned in the $90,000,000. Not long afterward he was promoted to Executive Vice President. The world of communication has expected for some time that he would be called upon to undertake the Presidency, the biggest job of its kind.

This is an instance of the Gifford career. He has been known, since his first steps upward, as a man having ideas and willing to risk his job in carrying them out. During the war he was called the mobilizer-in-chief of the Committee of Industrial Preparedness, which he served as secretary. That committee carried on one of the tasks that won the war, because it was largely instrumental in making available the things needed.

Mr. Gifford began his career with an excellent preparation. Born in Salem, Mass., of well-to-do parents, he attended Harvard and was graduated no longer ago than 1905, having completed the four-year course in three years. It seems but yesterday a scant twenty years from sheepskin to control of an industry greater than many a Government. Incidentally, Mr. Gifford got his first job as a payroll clerk and won his first promotions because he showed a head for figures. In ten years he was chief statistician.

Ideas and statistics are not ordinarily associated. But the quality of his imagination extended beyond figures. It is said by some of his fellow-workers that he first conceived the idea of the night letter by telegraph, and thus added millions to the company's revenues.

Up the Financial Ladder.

In the field of finance one of the first personalities that comes to view in the group of young men who are running affairs is Harvey D. Gibson, President of the New York Trust Company, who is not yet 43. Mr. Gibson first emerged in his middle thirties as President of the Liberty National Bank. He was probably the youngest bank executive of that rank ever selected. Later the Liberty National was merged with the New York Trust, with Mr. Gibson in command of the new institution.

One of his biggest jobs came to him in war times, when he was called upon by the late Henry P. Davison to run the American Red Cross in the capacity of general manager. That job involved the directing of expenditures representing some $280,000,000, and demanded administrative ability of the first degree. As President of the New York Trust Mr. Gibson has guided its operation along steadily broadening lines. He now has additional interests of other kinds.

Mr. Gibson, like Mr. Gifford, is a college man and comes from New England. He was born in North Conway, N. H., and attended Bowdoin College. Then he got a job in the financial department of the American Express Company. To put it a little more accurately, the company was experimenting with college men and decided to see if he could sweep floors. He swept, and there his career began.

Presently he was carrying parcels; then, in the natural order of things, he was graduated to a junior clerkship. The process was not so easy nor so simple as the description might indicate. There was the bitter day when he decided that the job of carrying parcels was a poor one for a man of his education and his ambitions. He could do a lot better than that, and he meant to do it. So he went off to get another job with another company, where his merit might be understood a little better. He actually got into the second office before it occurred to him that this was quitting in the face of difficulty. He went back and tried again, and after a time the junior clerkship was his reward.

About the next thing that the future banker did was to get married on $75 a month. Then an examination came along for every employe of the financial department, and the young bridegroom passed at the head of 1,000 men. But his abilities were to find other outlet soon. The chance arose to participate in business building, and he did things in that direction that brought him to New York headquarters at 26 in an executive job. At 28 he was part owner in the biggest tourist agency of the country. Soon followed his entry into finance and his steady progress to be one of the notable men of Wall Street.

Copy Boy to Millionaire.

The field of transportation recently presented a shining example of how far and how fast a young fellow may go in this hustling country of ours. The two big motor bus companies of America, operating the New York and the Chicago lines, were brought together in a $25,000,000 consolidation by John Hertz, aged 42. To show that success in this land does not depend upon a college degree or a distinctly American background, it may be said that Hertz was the son of Austrian immigrants and had no prospects. He ran away from his home in Chicago at 11, after a whipping, and became a copy boy in a newspaper office.

That is an interesting sort of job. Young Hertz took note. He learned that items contributed to the sporting page were worth 25 cents each, and thereupon he became a reporter. Frequently his bits of information were used, after some editor had arranged the material. Thus Hertz began an education which he continued later in night classes and topped off in the broad school of experience.

It required time for him to find his proper medium. He managed a pugilist. He did many other odd jobs. He became part owner of three motor cars that were hired out by the hour. He went to Europe and saw how cheaply light, fast taxicabs were operated there. He came home and went into the taxicab business, reducing Chicago rates by half. Instead of the bankruptcy that so many predicted, he acquired money faster than most men would conceive possible. Soon he had a hand in the taxicab enterprises of other cities. New York owes John Hertz thanks for the reduction in taxi rates.

Taxicabs led logically to motor buses, and now the head of the $25,000,000 combination is entitled to rank with the big transportation men of the country. This corporation is expected to do a business surpassing that of many railroads. Conceivably it may become a most important factor in the rapid transit of America's two largest cities. Such is the progress in thirty-one years of a boy who went out in the world to get ahead or sink.

Once a Water Boy.

Another Chicago man whose success proves that the poor boy can rise to the top as fast as the college-bred youth is Charles M. Kittle, President of Sears, Roebuck & Co. Mr. Kittle at 44 directs the greatest business of its kind in the world, a superdepartment store conducted by mail. He was not especially trained for this business, but made his mark in a distinctly different field, beginning as water boy for a section gang on the Illinois Central Railroad.

Mr. Kittle was 14 when he carried his first pail of water to the thirsty fellows working on the Central's track not far from his home. It wasn't much of a job, as jobs go, but it seemed to be the only one handy, so he took it and carried water with a right good-will. Meanwhile he cast about for opportunity and decided to be a telegrapher. There must be some special destiny that attracts men to the telegraph key. It has proved the upward lever for many a successful graduate.

There is nothing to show that Kittle was an exceptional telegrapher, but he doubtless applied himself to the job with the same sort of energy that had helped in the water-carrying days. He went to night school and began to read big, heavy-looking books that told about the science of freight management and such matters.

A boy with a taste like that was bound to get ahead. Opportunity soon provided Mr. Kittle with an empty place at the elbow of his superintendent. He had the impressive title of chief clerk and enough responsibilities to have bent many backs. His own held out very well and he advanced with the years until his office door bore the legend in big black letters, "Vice President."

There opportunity again entered. Mr. Kittle was persuaded to join the Sears-Roebuck organization. It might appear at first glance that a rail executive would be out of place in wholesale merchandising. But experience and enthusiasm—that magical combination mentioned before—stood him in good stead. He has reached the biggest job in the company and is numbered among the representative men of Chicago.

Romance of the Rail.

Railroading has always been a field of high adventure and great achievement. It is a business that begets big men. We used to hear that the days of individuality had passed by in railroading; that the whole order of things was regulated and established. It was said, for instance, that the last of the race of railroad kings had dropped their sceptres because there never would be any new systems of the same extent as the old.

That sounded logical enough, in a way, with national regulation going far to make railroading almost a governmental function. In spite of all these conditions, however, a new dynasty has risen in this field. It bears the name of Van Sweringen. None of the earlier reigns ever had a beginning more romantic, according to the American way of thinking, and certainly no other railroad epic has been written in bolder strokes.

"O. P.," at 44, is the man who leads off in the combination of the Van Sweringen brothers, ably followed by "M. J.," the other brother. They began life selling newspapers. After some years they came to be known as factors in Cleveland real estate.

That was in the earlier years of the century, when suburban developments were the order of the day all over the country. Smart promoters had discovered that city air was bad for everybody who possibly could afford a home on the outskirts. Particularly that was the place for the children, the woman who stayed at home, and the tired business man. The Van Sweringens were active in suburban promotion. They acquired a plot of ground near Cleveland known as Shaker Heights. No finer site for a development could have been picked out. There was a single difficulty. The spot lay some miles from any transportation line.

Anybody would have said that the nearest electric line would perceive the advisability of building a spur track over to Shaker Heights, thus starting the wheel of progress. But the electric line did not think much of Shaker Heights. The officials merely smiled at the Van Sweringens.

It was the turn of the Van Sweringens to show independence. If the electric line wouldn't build, well, the brothers would lay their own tracks. In the end they had to build their spur and pay the electric line for running cars to carry their commuters. That spur track proved the magnet that drew them into railroading. Now they have acquired the Erie, the Nickel Plate, the Chesapeake & Ohio and the Pere Marquette, and are said to be planning a system stretching to the Pacific. They are the youngest men who have ever made so big a mark in American railroading.

Statecraft and Radio.

While young men are thus dominating communication, banking, motor transportation, the mail-order business and railroading, another young man has undertaken to settle the troubles of Europe. He is Seymour Parker Gilbert Jr., Agent General for Reparations at 32. He will control the practical application of the widely heralded Dawes plan, which is expected to restore a large measure of stability in Europe and avoid some of the international bickering over the damages Germany must pay. This also is the biggest job of its kind in the world, one requiring acumen of the highest sort and experience far broader than might be looked for in a man of his years.

Mr. Gilbert is the outstanding figure of his day among young men who have entered public affairs. He was Assistant Secretary of the Treasury before he had turned 30, and has financial knowledge that frequently causes comparisons between his career and that of Alexander Hamilton, who retired a Secretary of the Treasury at 38.

Mr. Gilbert is another of the college-bred class. He was born in Bloomfield, N. J., and was graduated from Harvard Law School. He took up practice in his early twenties. He had not pleaded long before the bar when the war broke. Delicate health kept him from becoming a soldier. He went to Washington, joined the Treasury Department on a war job, and before long had shouldered so big a part of the work on financing the war preparations that he won a title and standing of the first rank.

It is a huge job that Mr. Gilbert has tackled in Europe. Early indications point this success in it. He is known for a quiet temperament that gets things done by straight thinking and prompt application of ideas. Of all the representatives that we have sent to Europe on errands official and unofficial, Mr. Gilbert is the youngest to fill such an important post.

Another young man, Edwin H. Armstrong, has made possible the recent amazing advance in radio. At 15 he caught the inventive fever common to many boys interested in radio. That inclination led him into long and complicated experiments. He entered Columbia University and brought out the first of his three primary inventions at the age of 22. At 27 the second followed, and the third at 31. The amplifying bulb that has made radio practicable for common use is his great contribution to the science. He is now 33. The radio world expects that he will do other notable things, perhaps in eliminating static, a problem occupying the attention of inventors the world around.

February 1, 1925

AN IMMIGRANT BOY CLIMBS TO THE TOP

Sarnoff Steps Ahead as Radio President of R. C. A. to Make His Dreams Come True—Foresees Bright Future for Radio

By RICHARD B. O'BRIEN.

THE story of David Sarnoff, who at the age of 39 is now president of the Radio Corporation of America after starting life here as a penniless Russian immigrant thirty years ago, reads like one of the tales which Alger might have fashioned and titled "From Newsboy to Riches, or the Rise of David Sarnoff." Mr. Sarnoff, who spends much more time in planning for the future than in contemplating the past, would tell you that Alger is out of date and a relic of a less progressive and enlightened era than the present. But the fact remains that he has been chosen to succeed Major Gen. James G. Harbord in guiding the future destinies of the R. C. A.

David Sarnoff understood not a word of English when he walked down the gangplank of the ship that carried him from his native Russia to the sidewalks of New York. Today he sits behind a glass-topped desk in one of the world's tallest skyscrapers as head of a gigantic organization whose world-wide influence is a byword on two continents. Between the boy and the executive lies a quarter of a century filled with years of struggle in the face of great odds, of obstacles surmounted, of enormous energy, tremendous perseverance and hardships endured before the heights of success were scaled.

Father Led the Way.

Sarnoff's father had come to this country a few years before his family. He had worked hard and saved so as to bring them over, but the effort had proved too much for him and when they arrived they found him an invalid. Conditions were such at home that the boy immediately had to help the family income. Selling papers, delivering meat, singing in the choir, and doing odd jobs, all outside of school hours, occupied the most of his working hours. It was a childhood devoid of all the pleasant, fleeting days that should not be denied to youth. While others played in the streets, David toiled tirelessly so that those dependent upon him might eat. While others slept he worked and studied far into the night that he might improve his mind. It was a childhood spent in the ghetto of a big city with no time to play. He was a boy carrying the burden of a man. When he was 15 his father died and young Sarnoff left school to get a steady job. Since he had been selling newspapers most of his life, it was not strange that the first place to which he turned was a newspaper office.

A Turning Point.

"I went up to the old Herald plant at Thirty-fifth Street and Broadway," he said. "In the entrance of the building was the office of the Commercial Cable Company, and I stopped there and asked the manager where to apply for a job on The Herald. Instead he offered me a job as a messenger boy at $5 per week. Beyond him were the telegraph operators and I thought that while working as an office boy I could learn to become an operator. So I took the job, and the first $2 I saved I spent for a telegraph instrument and started to study the Morse code. I studied diligently during every spare moment and practiced on the instrument for an hour or two every night. The manager was good enough to let me practice on the office instrument when it was not in use. Within six months I had learned the code and was able to operate with a fair degree of efficiency."

Within a year Sarnoff had advanced sufficiently to be made a junior operator with the Marconi company. From then on radio **gripped him and he became a real enthusiast. He sensed its wonderful future. He plumbed its depths. He read many technical books on the subject. He spent his week-ends in the experimental laboratory which the company had on Front Street.**

In those days radio was a mere babe squawking to make itself heard. There were only four seagoing vessels equipped with wireless and the Marconi company had but four coastal stations. But Sarnoff was confident that the indispensable man of the future was the one who understood all about radio from the practical standpoint. So he continued to apply himself diligently and the marvel of this new science he soon made his own. When Wanamaker decided to equip his New York and Philadelphia stores with wireless stations, Sarnoff applied for the operator's job. It was while he was at the Wanamaker station that his big chance came. On April 14, 1912, the steamship Titanic was sunk. For seventy-two consecutive hours he snatched from the air the tragic story of the sea and the list of those who went down to a watery grave and the survivors of the awful disaster. This was the turning point in his life.

In 1917 he had become commercial manager of the Marconi company, and when the organization was taken over by the Radio Corporation he kept the same post with the new company. Since then he has advanced step by step, finally becoming general manager and vice president several years ago. And now that he has ascended to the presidency of the corporation and reached the summit he looks into the horizon of the future for new worlds to conquer.

The Future Outlook.

"It is the peculiar gift of wireless communications," said Mr. Sarnoff, "that radio should be the strange bedfellow of so many arts, industries and services. It bears definite blood relationship to the communications family. It is related by marriage to the phonograph, the motion picture and the theatre. Its principles have been adopted in the technique of other industries.

"Beyond the needs of wireless telegraphic and telephonic service which called the new art into being, perhaps the most natural kinship to radio is in the field of entertainment. Entertainment is built upon the arts of communication. Every dramatic performance, every scene or picture visualized upon the screen is an act of communication. The phonograph, the player piano, the radio set, all are instruments of musical or speech communication.

"Modern electrical and radio development has made possible the synchronization of sight and sound on the same film, has brought a new art and a new promise to the motion-picture industry. The shackles of silence have been struck from the screen. Motion-picture presentation has been completely revolutionized. This development in the motion-picture industry has created a new vista for the motion-picture art. It has inspired technical achievement in other details of picture production. Color photography has come to add new values to the screen. Wide-screen projection promises to reproduce scenes and spectacles in true size and perspective. Stereoscopic or three-dimensional effects are being developed in motion-picture photography.

"All in all, it is apparent that the rôle which radio is destined to play in entertainment is limited only by its possibilities as a communications force. In that respect we have not yet plumbed the depths of radio development."

January 12, 1930

CASTE TREND SEEN IN TRADE LEADERS

Survey Finds Well-to-Do Types Becoming Preponderant at Current Rate of Increase.

SOCIAL ORIGINS STUDIED

Lack of Native Ability Rather Than Lack of Opportunity Blamed for Failures to Rise.

The business leaders of America are likely to become fixed in a caste-like group, similar to the hereditary aristocracies of Europe, if present trends continue, according to statistics presented by F. W. Taussig and C. S. Joslyn of Harvard University in "American Business Leaders," published today by Macmillan.

The group could not at present be fairly characterized as a "caste," the authors say, but "there is clear evidence that the representation of the well-to-do classes among American business leaders is increasing at a rapid rate and is likely to become preponderant if the present rate of increase is maintained during the next few decades."

The book is subtitled "A Study in Social Origins and Social Stratifications" and contains the results obtained from 7,371 complete returns to questionnaires sent to 15,000 business leaders in America.

The immediate objects of the inquiry were to ascertain from what social classes American business leaders are recruited; to determine whether the proportionate contribution of each social class to the supply of business leaders is less than, equal to or greater than the proportion of that class in the population at large; to throw light, as far as possible, on the relative influence of heredity and of environmental factors in causing such disparities as may exist between the representation of the several classes among business leaders and their representation in the population at large.

"The fundamental problem in which we are interested," the authors write, "is that of economic inequality. The particular kind of inequality with which we are concerned is that arising from differences in the representative earnings of individuals engaged in different occupations. It is the kind of inequality typified by the $25,000 a year salary of the chief executive of a business, the $2,500 salary of the bookkeeper or clerk, and the $1,500 a year wages of the factory operative."

The general conclusions reached by the authors on this problem and set forth clear of the limitations is that "lack of native ability rather than lack of opportunity is primarily responsible for the failure of the lower occupational classes to be as well represented (among business leaders) as the higher classes."

F. W. Taussig is the Henry Lee Professor of Economics at Harvard University, and C. S. Joslyn is an instructor and tutor in sociology at Harvard. The inquiry was made possible by a grant from the Milton Fund of Harvard.

September 26, 1932

INQUIRY INTO HIGH SALARIES PRESSED BY THE GOVERNMENT

Examples of Lavish Stipends and Bonuses That Are Challenged By the New Deal—Many Big Pay Checks Have Already Shrunk

By L. H. ROBBINS.

ONE aim of the New Deal, it becomes plainer, is to question high salaries and high bonuses of Big Business. Since last May the Federal Reserve Board has inquired into possibly excessive compensation paid to officers of member banks. The Reconstruction Finance Corporation has made note of similar lavishness among non-member banks and also among insurance companies seeking government loans.

At the same time the Power Commission has been looking over public utilities for untimely bounteousness toward their higher-ups, and the Federal Coordinator of Transportation, Joseph B. Eastman, has addressed the railroads so pointedly that no railroad president in the country is now drawing more than $60,000 a year, though some of them had more than twice that pay in 1932. A Senate resolution authorized all this activity.

This month the scrutiny widens. The Federal Trade Commission has sent a questionnaire to 2,000 corporations engaged in interstate commerce, listed on the New York Stock Exchange or the Curb Market and having capital and assets of more than $1,000,000. These corporations are asked to report salaries, bonuses, commissions and fees paid to their executives. If they find it difficult to supply the desired information, the Trade Commission cheerfully offers to send its own agents to go over their books. There is "a storm of protest," attended by talk of "unheard-of meddling."

The Era of Big Salaries.

The princely salary and the regal bonus for business management are fairly new in the world. They came in after the McKinley era, along with consolidations and the expansion of business to national scope. A century ago the president of a now great New York bank received $2,000 a year. A generation ago the bank president who got $25,000 was doing well. As late as 1900 such executives as the president of a New York City elevated railroad made out with salaries of $5,000 and no bonuses, and were envied, at that. Observers present today can remember when $5,000 a year in almost any calling was eminence.

By comparison, the president of the B. M. T, last year received $135,000—incidentally, he has taken a cut this year to $40,000; and another New Yorker when chairman of a bank got in one year a salary of $75,000 from the bank, plus $25,000 from affiliates of the bank, plus $1,160,000 in bonus checks, a year's total of $1,700,000. Another former executive of a New York bank had a retirement allowance of $100,000 a year, but voluntarily gave it up last week. Bank heads whose yearly pay reaches that figure are common.

When Big Pay Began.

The general counsel of a great express company in 1900 drew $12,000 a year, which was deemed "a terrific salary" in those days. The president of one of the most important industrial companies in 1910 received $17,500. Heads of certain important industrials today are said to get $75,000 or better.

In the early days of the Steel Trust the country gasped at the salary of $100,000 paid to Elbert H. Gary and at the bonuses that brought his compensation close to $500,000 a year. Amid the discussion John D. Rockefeller declared Judge Gary's services worth $1,000,000 a year and expressed willingness to pay him that sum if he should ever wish to join Standard Oil. Mr. Rockefeller voiced the feeling that has prevailed in big business until the present time toward men of superior directing ability. It became an accepted doctrine that a man who can keep a vast industrial organization going, with steady profits for its owners and steady employment for its workers, is never overpaid at any salary.

During the war period and in the halcyon days of the Coolidge boom so much money was made that few stockholders and fewer statesmen felt disposed to stint the remuneration of the managers who brought in the flood of dividends. Salaries skyrocketed all over the land. The heavy surtaxes of the early Twenties, designed to levy on the super-fortunate, gave compensations another push upward, for companies doubled salaries of their responsible officers to make up to them for what the revenue collector took away.

Rise of a New Class.

By 1929 there had grown up in the United States a new and resplendent class of workers whose emoluments exceeded those of most great owners of earlier days. There were $50,000 men enough in the country to make a fair-sized army, and $100,000 men enough to officer it. Put the grand total vaguely, thus, for their number is not known for certain. Salaries, except those of people employed by the public, have been, up to now, private matters, to inquire into which is, under the existing code of ethics, bad taste. It has not been considered any business of the public's how much a private concern pays its leaders.

The income-tax returns in the years when they were visible gave some inkling of the fortunes that a host of men were getting at the pay window, but the reports lumped salaries, bonuses and all other income, and salaries remain more or less a mystery. Occasional lawsuits and legislative investigations give the public its best glimpses into the region of high pay. Since the depression set in, stockholders have increasingly lost their old contented docility, and the glimpses have become more frequent. Now, too, the Federal Government is apparently out with a lantern, and more may be learned as time and the New Deal go on.

Bonuses in Six Figures.

Judge Gary's compensation seems only moderately large now, for numerous men have passed him in annual pay. Eugene R. Grace, head of Bethlehem Steel, got a bonus of $1,623,753 in 1929 and a salary of $12,000 besides. His compensation in five years totaled $5,497,684. The company has since modified the system whereby fifteen high men shared in bonuses amounting in a good year to about $5,000,000.

And there is George W. Hill, president of the American Tobacco Company, whose salary and commissions have at times exceeded a million a year and might in 1930 have reached $2,200,000 if a stockholder had not brought court action. The controversy had to do with a stock subscription plan under which 13,440 shares of company stock were allotted to Mr. Hill as a reward for his skill in directing the company to dividends. It raged through the courts, including the highest in the land, and in the end Mr. Hill declined the allotment.

Executives in all kinds of business representing large accumulations of capital shared in the big money of the late Twenties. If salaries remained modest, bonuses became enormous. Insurance, public utilities, transportation, industrials and banking led in rewarding leadership. The movies and baseball were not far behind. The movies had, in fact, created a Croesus class of their own before the golden decade began. Chain merchandising added its quota to the glittering pageant of the prosperous.

No longer to ambitious American youth did it seem the height of achievement to become President of the United States. With enterprise and luck, a boy could be making Presidential pay at 30 in staple groceries or any one of a dozen other lines. The President had to be satisfied with a mere $75,000, the Vice President or a Cabinet member with only $15,000. The Chief Justice of the Supreme Court received but $20,500 and the associate justices $500 less, and all that the Governor of New York State got out of it was $25,000 a year and his house rent.

Hollywood Salaries Curbed.

President Roosevelt has lately called attention to the inequalities that have arisen in rewards for service in Hollywood, where directors often get five or six times the pay of the Chief Executive of the nation, and one child actor, still lisping, may draw more money in salary and royalties than the entire Supreme Court. Presidential pressure has put a provision into the moving-picture code, imposing heavy fines on companies paying unreasonable salaries.

Some examples of weekly salaries in the picture business, reported on reliable authority, are: Greta Garbo, $9,000; Will Rogers, $7,500; Maurice Chevalier, $7,500; Constance Bennett, $7,000; John Barrymore, $6,500; Norma Shearer, $6,000; Richard Barthelmess, $6,000; Wallace Beery, $5,000. One child actor **has lately "accepted a cut" of $76,000 a year, which leaves him with only $42,000. It will be seen that national leaders are quite outclassed by the Hollywood celebrities. President Roosevelt's weekly pay is only $1,440. Chief Justice Hughes gets less than $400.**

In some lines of business the upward surge of salaries continued after the depression had laid off millions of workers and cut the pay of millions of others. Between 1929 and 1932 the salaries of the presidents of four of the five largest insurance companies rose $23,000 per man, in one case putting the beneficiary up to $200,000. The average pay of the presidents of the five companies was $135,000, and of the vice presidents a little more than $43,000, before general cuts of from 5 to 25 per cent were taken this year. Insurance in 1928 paid eighty of its high officers an average of $55,000 apiece.

As to public utilities, a Public Service Commission hearing this year brought out that one electric company in New York City had raised the pay of its principal officers by about $40,000 between 1931 and 1932, in a period when the payroll dropped $2,000,000. Another such company, while its payroll was shrinking $1,500,000, raised its executive staff from $149,700 to $230,300. This year the executives of most public utility companies have taken cuts. At least one corporation of this class, the New York Telephone Company, has not raised salaries since 1929, and its heads have taken cuts besides.

The Purpose of Washington.

Just what Washington has in mind concerning the superlatively salaried folk is not yet clear. It is suggested that the purposes may be: (1) to find out whether high salaries at the top tend to curtail wages at the bottom; (2) whether, in the case of public utilities, heavy-salary expenditures tend to maintain high rates to the consumers; (3) whether the investment public should not be informed to what extent funds of the corporations are paid out in excessive salaries, and (4) whether the government is losing large sums in taxes by the payment of excessive salaries by corporations that have reported no net income for taxation.

The questionnaire now circulating in Wall Street may be used, it is said, as the basis of legislation equipping the government with power to impose extra taxation on corporations paying such salaries. The cry of "unconstitutional prying" is raised, nevertheless the corporations concerned are advised by their legal staffs to fill out the blanks.

Salaries and Borrowing.

Railroads, insurance companies and other corporations appealing for government loans to tide them over the evil years have had no choice but to lop salaries. The government is in the creditor position and can dictate. President Daniel Willard of the B. & O. accepted a salary cut of $15,000 after he had already taken a still larger cut, and at the same time the government reduced its interest from 6 per cent to 5 per cent on the B. & O.'s $71,000,000 loan. The Southern Pacific, to obtain a loan of $23,000,000, had to cut the pay of its chairman, Hale Holden, 60 per cent, from $150,000 to $60,000, the most unkindest cut any big railroader has suffered. General Atterbury of the Pennsylvania, though his company is not now a borrower from the government, voluntarily cut his pay from $121,000 to $109,000 and then to the maximum of $60,000 "suggested" by Mr. Eastman.

Administering the Emergency Railroad Transportation Act, Mr. Eastman found salaries of some outstanding railroad presidents to be as follows: Willard, B. & O., $120,000; Shoup, Southern Pacific; Gray, Union Pacific; Bernet, Pere Marquette and C. & O.; Loree, D. & H.; Downs, Illinois Central, and Pelley, New Haven, $90,000 each, and Williamson, New York Central, $80,000.

A Question of Psychology.

Observers of these activities of the government wonder if, in the background, there may not be a purpose not yet stated. There are distinct signs that the administration regards conspicuous examples of exceptional prosperity in the midst of hard times as not conducive to the general morale. Mr. Eastman, in telling the railroad heads it might be desirable for them to be content with modest stipends for a while, admitted that the big money paid to them was an insignificant item compared to the sum total of railroad expenditures. "Nevertheless," he added, "it has a psychological importance which much exceeds its money significance, and consideration of it cannot and should not be avoided."

Again, Mr. Eastman said: **"My belief is that a danger now exists in the fixing of high salaries for executives in private business which did not once exist, and which grows out of the fact that great corporations with widely held stock are controlled not really by the legal owners of their properties but rather by boards of directors who tend to become self-perpetuating and who may have a comparatively small stake in the industry. Nor do I know of any reason to believe that the competency of executives can be safely judged by the salaries they receive."**

What further steps the New Deal may have in mind for protecting the public interest against "avoidable expense and preventable waste" remains for the future to reveal. Will huge incomes of all sorts be questioned next? Nobody knows—and nobody knows what the Supreme Court will say about these new proposals for restraining "rugged individualism."

THE HIGH SALARY ISSUE

From The St. Paul Pioneer Press.

YOUNG AND SWOPE GIVE UP G.E. POSTS

Chairman and President at Retirement Age Step Aside for Younger Men

TO REMAIN AS DIRECTORS

C. E. Wilson, Who Joined Company in 1919, Succeeds Swope —P. D. Reed Heads Board

Two of the country's outstanding industrial leaders, Gerard Swope and Owen D. Young, who have served for seventeen years as president and chairman of the board, respectively, of the General Electric Company, announced yesterday their retirement, effective at the end of the year, from active participation in the management of the company.

They will be succeeded by Charles E. Wilson, executive vice president of General Electric, who is to take over the position of President, and Philip D. Reed, assistant to the president, who will become chairman of the board. Both were elected by the directors yesterday and will take office on Jan. 1.

Both Mr. Swope and Mr. Young, who in announcing their retirement stated that they did so "with no reservations because there are younger men whose experience and capacity have been demonstrated," will remain, however, as directors of General Electric, and also will be available to the company in an advisory capacity as honorary president and honorary chairman of the board, respectively.

Mr. Swope will be 67 years old on Dec. 1 and Mr. Young reached his sixty-fifth birthday on Oct. 27 last. Thus, in line with the company's policy, whereby individuals occupying important administrative positions consider retirement when they have reached the age of 65, the two top executives, who have played an important role in the development of the company to the point where today it enjoys the ranking of the nation's No. 1 electrical equipment organization, are stepping aside in favor of younger men.

Joined Company in 1893

Mr. Swope, the son of a St. Louis watchmaker, was born in St. Louis in 1872. He joined the General Electric Company in the Summer of 1893 as a "dollar-a-day" helper in the Chicago service shop, while still an undergraduate at the Massachusetts Institute of Technology. He was graduated with an electrical engineering degree in 1895 and returned to Chicago, this time in the shops of the Western Electric Company. After working his way up to the vice presidency of Western Electric, Mr. Swope returned to General Electric in 1918 and in 1922 was made president.

A native of Van Hornesville, N. Y., where he was born in 1874, Mr. Young, after being graduated from St. Lawrence University decided upon a law career, and in 1913 was appointed general counsel for General Electric. In addition to his legal activities Mr. Young also was appointed vice president in charge of policy and when the late Charles A. Coffin resigned in 1922, was chosen chairman of the board to succeed him.

Mr. Young is a director of many corporations, including General Motors and the National Broadcasting Company. He was chairman of the board of the Radio Corporation of America until 1929.

His work on the Reparations Commission in Paris in 1923, when he unofficially represented the United States along with Charles G. Dawes, resulted in the Dawes Plan. Later, Mr. Young became agent general of the Reparations Commission and put the Dawes Plan into actual operation.

Wilson Began as Office Boy

General Electric's new president, Mr. Wilson, started with the Sprague Electric Company as an office boy in 1899 at the age of 13. He went from office boy to shipping clerk and was made assistant superintendent of factory in 1914. In 1918, the year following transfer of the conduit business from Sprague Electric to General Electric, he became assistant general superintendent of the company's Maspeth, L. I., and New Kensington, Pa., works.

In 1923 he went to Bridgeport, Conn., as managing engineer in charge of the conduit and wire business, and two years later he was appointed assistant manager of General Electric's Bridgeport plant. In December, 1930, he was elected a vice president of General Electric and was one of the original members of the organization's newly formed appliance sales committee.

Mr. Wilson, who celebrates his fifty-third birthday today, also is chairman of the board of General Electric Contracts Corporation, a director of the Edison General Electric Appliance Company, Inc., of Chicago, a director of the Trumbull Electric Manufacturing Company, and numerous other electrical equipment companies.

Mr. Reed was born in Milwaukee on Nov. 16, 1899. He joined the General Electric Company in its law department in 1926, holding degrees both in electrical engineering and law. In 1928, Mr. Reed was transferred to the incandescent lamp department of General Electric and from July, 1934, until his appointment as assistant to the president in December, 1937, he was general counsel for the lamp department. In addition to holding directorships in various General Electric affiliated companies, Mr. Reed also is a director of the Bankers Trust Company.

The Letter of Retirement

In a letter to General Electric's directors announcing their retirement, Mr. Young and Mr. Swope wrote:

"On May 16, 1922, we undertook, at your election, the offices of chairman and president, respectively, of the General Electric Company, and as a result of your annual designation we have held those offices ever since.

"When we took office we indicated our view that it would contribute to the morale and effectiveness of the organization if as a general rule men in important administrative positions would consider retirement when they reached the age of 65. We realize that there have been, are and probably always will be exceptions, where it is desirable in the company's interest for men to continue in their place beyond that age.

"Having adopted that policy of retirement during our administration, we now apply it to ourselves. We do so with no reservation, because there are younger men whose experience and capacity have been demonstrated to you who are now available for those offices.

"Accordingly, we now ask for retirement from the offices of chairman and president, respectively, at the expiration of the present calendar year. We took up these offices together and we wish to lay them down together. We will remain as directors and make ourselves available for such service as you and our successors may deem helpful to the company.

"May we express to you and through you to the organization our appreciation of the privilege of working so happily with you and them for these many years."

Following the meeting yesterday the directors also announced that a dividend of 65 cents a share on the company's common stock had been declared for the fourth quarter of this year, payable on Dec. 20 to holders of record of Nov. 24. This payment, together with 75 cents a share for the first nine months of the year, makes a total of $1.40 a share in dividends to stockholders for 1939, compared with 90 cents paid in 1938.

November 18, 1939

LAND OF OPPORTUNITY

Somehow the delusion persists that the era of great opportunities for humble people in this country has ended. There is talk that the time is over when a boy starting at the foot of the ladder could expect, with reasonable care of his health, his morals and his manners, to arrive anywhere near the top. We are gloomily told that the work-and-win, strive-and-succeed days passed beyond recall when the romantic Horatio Alger laid down his pen. But the pessimists who propagate this nonsense don't take the trouble to look up the facts.

The Bell Telephone System has been doing some fact-finding in this field. It has studied the biographies of the presidents of its eighteen operating companies that cover this opportunity-bereft country. It discovers that all eighteen of them, including President Walter S. Gifford of the American Telephone and Telegraph Company, began at the bottom. And they can hardly be holdovers from some bygone golden age in America, for they all are still young enough to be exceedingly vigorous.

Mr. Gifford and four others on the list started as clerks. Of these, President James W. Hubbell of the New York Telephone Company drew $8 a week, and Chester I. Barnard, head of the New Jersey Bell Company, got $50 a month. Two of the eighteen were night operators. A third was an engineer, and Allerton F. Brooks of the Southern New England Company was only an engineer's assistant. Others were collectors, stenographers, draftsmen, service inspectors.

Very likely they were warned by croakers and crêpehangers that America was no longer a land of opportunity; that all the big openings had been seized and the big jobs filled. But they didn't believe it.

July 4, 1944

Henry Ford 2d, at 28, Takes Helm Of Firm With Billion in Assets

DETROIT, Sept. 21 (AP)—Henry Ford 2d, 28 years old, today was named president of the billion-dollar Ford Motor Company.

He took over the top post in the far-flung Ford enterprises simultaneously with the announcement of the resignation of his grandfather, Henry Ford, who founded the family-owned company in 1903.

Announcing his desire to again withdraw from the presidency, the elder Ford, who was 82 years old last July 30, told the company's board of directors:

"I feel free to take this step at this time because the critical period during which I again assumed office has passed. As you know, I have many personal interests to which I now desire to devote most of my time."

The elder Ford turned the presidency over to his son, Edsel B. Ford, on Dec. 31, 1918. He took over the helm again on June 1, 1943, a few days after Edsel Ford's death.

Interested in Sociology

Unlike his father and his grandfather, young Henry Ford is of robust physique. He brings to his post a tremendous capacity for work and an intense interest in economics and sociology. At Yale, where he completed his formal education, he majored in sociology after a year in engineering, which he frankly admitted he did not like.

Asked once what was his main objective as executive vice president of the Ford Company (a post he held for nearly two years), he replied:

"To put the Ford Company back into first place in production and sales." (The Ford Company was second to Chevrolet throughout most of the decade immediately preceding the war.)

With this objective in mind, young Ford got away to a flying start last July 2 by showing the new 1946 Ford car, less than two days after the date authorized by the War Production Board for resumption of civilian car production.

After turning out nearly 1,000 vehicles, however, Ford was forced to close down the assembly plants because of strikes among nearly a score of supplier firms. The shutdown sent 50,000 workers in Ford plants into idleness.

The youthful president of the greatest family-owned industrial enterprise in the world is engagingly informal. He writes with his left hand and rarely wears a hat.

Born in Detroit on Sept. 4, 1917, he was educated at Detroit University School, Hotchkiss and Yale. He was married on July 13, 1940, to Miss Anne McDonnell at Southampton, L. I. They have two daughters.

At the outbreak of the war he enlisted in the Navy and was discharged with a lieutenant's commission in 1943 following the death of his father. Still in the armed services are his brothers, Benson and William Ford. There is also a sister, Josephine.

Young Ford is interested in aviation, but he does not believe its development will cut into the automobile business. Learning to fly a plane he was tutored by his lifelong friend, Harry Bennett, long the elder Ford's chief lieutenant in company affairs. Bennett himself was taught by Charles A. Lindbergh.

In one of his first public addresses as executive vice president of the Ford company, young Ford, addressing automobile dealers, said:

"Our post-war plans must not only be of a product nature but of a social nature. It seems to me the job of the automobile industry after the war is not only to build a worth-while product but also to provide its employes with a secure existence and to educate them to further progress."

Young Ford's close associates credit him with a broad knowledge of the history, background and aspirations of organized labor and add that he regards money as only a basic essential of industrial production and human welfare.

In a recent interview he said: "No wage is too high if it is earned; $50 a day would not be too high—provided it was earned, but $1 a day is too high if it isn't earned."

The elder Ford said he planned to remain on the Ford board of directors "and to assist in an advisory way." The "other personal interests" he referred to presumably have to do with further developing the product of the soil for use in industry—an almost lifetime obsession with Ford.

The 82-year-old Ford has appeared little in public during the last year, but at his offices it was said his health was "all right" and was not a factor in his decision to again relinquish the company presidency.

NEW AND RESIGNING FORD COMPANY HEADS

Henry Ford 2d and his grandfather, whom he succeeded as president of the concern, look over a model of the Ford Rouge plant.

Associated Press Wirephoto

September 22, 1945

GRANDSON SCRAPS FORD'S PROJECTS

Also Gets Rid of Aides of the Founder in Reorganization of Automotive Empire

DETROIT (AP) — A far-reaching reorganization program rapidly is nearing completion in the great family-owned Ford Motor Company.

For more than a generation the far-flung industrial empire was ruled by its founder, Henry Ford, who alone determined its policies. Today Henry Ford II, his grandson, directs the destinies of the company. To it he has brought many new ideas.

Whether for better or worse still must be determined, but in less than three years he has revamped the administrative and much of the production personnel.

Where his grandfather named only such officers as corporate law required, Henry Ford II has surrounded himself with ten vice presidents, each a working executive.

Gone—by retirement, resignation or dismissal—are virtually all the old-timers who formed the group, largely without title, that worked close to the elder Ford. Gone, too, are virtually all the pet projects of the founder.

Founder Approaching 84

The elder Ford, who is in retirement, will be 84 next July. One after another such projects as his great multi-million-dollar rubber plantation in Brazil and many of his farm undertakings have been disposed of.

"We are in business to make automobiles and automobiles only," explained young Henry Ford. He apparently includes farm tractors, for their large-scale manufacture is proceeding.

According to most recent information the elder Ford and his wife, Mrs. Clara Bryant Ford, still own a majority of the company's voting stock. The remainder is divided among the widow and children of his only son, Edsel B. Ford, who died in 1943.

But the elder Ford takes no part whatever in the affairs of the company. He resigned the presidency in favor of his grandson and namesake on Sept. 21, 1945, explaining only that he desired to devote his time to "many personal interests."

At the time the resignation caused no great comment; it was assumed the elder Ford would continue to dominate company affairs, as he had ever since the Ford family, in 1919, came into sole ownership of the vast properties.

But this time there apparently was more behind the resignation than appeared on the surface. He dropped entirely out of the picture. His 28-year-old grandson, whom he brought into the company only two years earlic , following his release from the Navy, began to make things hum.

Figures in "Palace Revr'-tion"

His first major act was to replace the almost legendary Harry H. Bennett, long known as "Henry Ford's Man." Bennett followed into retirement such figures as Charles E. Sorensen, production expert, thirty-nine years with Ford; R. R. Rausch, also a production expert; P. E. Martin, a vice president who joir-d Fc l soon after the company was formed;

A. M. Wibel, long time purchasing agent; Laurence Sheldrick, chief engineer for many years; William J. Cameron, for two decades Ford "spokesman," and others associated with the earlier regime.

Because of the known sharp differences of opinion among some of the old-timers the upheaval that saw many of them retired was referred to at the time as a "palace revolution."

The personnel retired by young Ford represented upward of a million dollars a year in salaries. It soon became evident, however, that the reorganization was not just an economy move. Young Ford wanted, he said, to regain for his company the first-place honors in production and distribution which it held for many years prior to 1930.

To help in this objective he has created a highly efficient—and high salaried—policy committee, consisting of himself, his brother, Benson Ford, and these vice presidents: Ernest R. Breech, executive; H. L. Moekle, in charge of finances; Del S. Harder, operations; John S. Bugas, industrial relations; Lewis D. Crusoe, planning and control; Albert J. Browning, purchasing; Harold T. Youngren, engineering; J. R. Davis, sales and advertising; M. L. Bricker, manufacturing, and William T. Gossett, general counsel.

Certainly, Benson Ford, a director as well as a policy committee member, and another brother, William, will have high posts in the great empire Henry Ford founded in 1903 with a paid-in capital of only $28,000.

His fellow car manufacturers credit Henry Ford II with tremendous progress in the short time he has headed the big industrial organization. They say he also has set up an entirely new idea of labor relationship between the Ford management and its 104,000 hourly-rated workers. One of his favorite assertions is that "no wage is too high as long as it is earned."

Yet to be learned definitely are the exact circumstances attending the complete retirement of the elder Ford and the turning over of full authority to his grandson. It has been reported, but without confirmation that the widow of Edsel Ford insisted upon the reorganization and demanded that her son be president in fact as well as in name. The stockholdings she controlled and the possibility she might put them up for sale are said to have given weight to her demands.

March 23, 1947

TESTS TO SELECT BEST EXECUTIVES

University of Chicago Reports Surest Way to Pick Bosses by Laboratory Methods

CHICAGO, March 6 (AP) — Laboratory tests now are being used to tell whether a person has the makings of a business executive.

The tests were developed by a group of University of Chicago psychologists headed by Dr. Burleigh B. Gardner. They say they may solve an ancient problem of business—how to select potential executives without first investing costly training that may prove to be useless.

The tests make use of a series of pictures, and the person being tested merely tells a story suggested to him by each picture. This takes about forty minutes. Then another person, who has never seen the subject of the tests, spends seven hours interpreting the verbal replies.

The results, Dr. Gardner said, determine whether a person warrants training to be an executive. A good boss, he declares, is one who needs achievement to be happy, one who is not still dominated by his parents, and who can accept authority. Those are among the qualities looked for in the tests.

Says Dr. Gardner:

Ordinary Tests Inadequate

"The ordinary battery of ability tests are quite adequate for routine hiring. However, a more extensive and complete analysis of the person seeking the higher executive positions is necessary, since it is insufficient to know only his level of intelligence and basic abilities.

"Every now and then a young man, because of technical abilities, has been promoted upstairs and soon afterward his department begins to divide itself into a group of snarling individuals, with organizational harmony dead or dying and the work of the office degenerating into costly inefficiency.

"The root of the trouble—a bad choice of executives—can be spotted, and moreover it can be spotted in advance."

Dr. Garner and his associates assert on the basis of experience with such corporations as International Harvester, Container Corporation, General Mills and others, that their tests can aid a company in its executive selection—and save considerable money and time.

Terms of Personality

The interpretation of the tests for executives is made in terms of their total personality — mental abilities, emotional difficulties and so on. In addition the expert looks for eleven qualities of executiveship. These were determined by testing 103 of the topmost executives in the business world, although Dr. Gardner declined to give their names.

Of the executives tested—other than the original 103—all but three reports jibed with company estimates, Dr. Gardner reported. The three were "startlingly" at variance "but within four months all three came a cropper that validated test results."

Those instrumental in developing the tests along with Dr. Gardner were Prof. W. Lloyd Warner, anthropologist and chairman of the university's committee on human development, and Dr. William E. Henry of the Department of Psychology.

March 7, 1948

Portrait of 'Decontrol Charlie' Wilson

As the next Secretary of Defense, the former head of General Motors brings an engineer's approach to his Pentagon job.

By ELIE ABEL

DETROIT.

CHARLES ERWIN WILSON welcomed the confusion a few weeks ago when some newspaper readers—and not a few editors—got the impression that the C. E. Wilson about to be tapped for Secretary of Defense by President-elect Eisenhower was Charles Edward Wilson, former Director of Defense Mobilization. "He has been quite a protection to me," said Charles Erwin, speaking of Charles Edward. "When anybody did start a rumor about me, people thought it was the other guy."

The two Wilsons, both captains of industry, had in recent years both been concerned with the problems of American defense. When Charles Edward, former president of General Electric, was defense production chief in Washington, Charles Erwin as president of General Motors was dogging the Government for more steel, aluminum and copper with which to build automobiles. The Wilsons, who are not related, were frequently at odds.

It was Charles Erwin of General Motors, seeking to establish his separate identity, who coined the quip: "He's Control Charlie. I'm Decontrol Charlie."

Official Washington may well be puzzled by Decontrol Charlie, the next Secretary of Defense. A late-blooming social conscience and an efficiency expert's determination to take the economic waste out of old-fashioned collective bargaining have set him apart from most industrialists of his generation. He is an introspective tycoon, a conservative who finds the future far more exciting than the past.

He thinks fast, but takes action only after days or weeks of chewing over a decision and discussing it with his associates. He has no flair for oratory, yet acquits himself well in the give-and-take of a press conference.

A BLUE-EYED, white-haired engineer of 62, Mr. Wilson was working a double shift between Nov. 20, when General Eisenhower designated him to take charge of the Defense Department, and his departure from General Motors on Dec. 1. (That final day he actually spent in flight over the Pacific with the President-elect, to see for himself what the Korean front looked like and to collect some of the facts

ELIE ABEL, head of The Times bureau in Detroit, knows Mr. Wilson's story from on-the-scene observation and many talks with him.

he would need in re-assessing America's defense policies.)

His fourteenth-floor office, on a Saturday afternoon, was alive with sound and movement. Two secretaries struggled to skim and sort the letters and telegrams that drifted like snow over desks and tabletops. Most of the messages were congratulations, some suggested quick, painless solutions for the military stalemate in Korea. A larger number from job seekers.

General Eisenhower telephoned from New York to discuss the appointment of Secretaries for the Army, Navy and Air Force. Mr. Wilson called J. Edgar Hoover in Washington to request that the Federal Bureau of Investigation look into his personal record. Mr. Hoover was not at his desk. The F. B. I. promised to find him.

The telephone was seldom silent. More letters and telegrams arrived. The incoming Defense Secretary was chain-smoking furiously. "He swears off every other week," said one of his aides. Finding time at last for the promised interview, Mr. Wilson talked of his training as an engineer, how it had served him well as head of the industrial empire called General Motors.

"Engineers are trained to have a great respect for truth and facts," he said, speaking slowly. "You don't hunch an engineering problem. Engineering, basically, is an excellent background for whatever job you may be called to do. I am hoping it will serve me as well in government."

HE spoke of the five-year escalator contract between General Motors and the United Automobile Workers, C. I. O., as an engineer's approach to the problem of determining fair wages. (The agreement hitches hourly wage rates to the cost of living, so that employes have a measure of protection against the cheapening of the dollar. But the automobile worker's purchasing power is not stationary. Wages are increased automatically each year by 4 cents an hour. This is regarded as labor's share in the increasing productivity of General Motors and the country.)

For this agreement, now standard in the automobile industry, Mr. Wilson gets much of the blame or credit. He began to think it through during the winter of 1941-42, when he broke his hip while ice skating and had ample time for reflection. The formula, first introduced in 1948, has been denounced from the left and the right. John L. Lewis, president of the United Mine Workers of America, called it a "broken leg contract." Others have described it as "built-in inflation." Mr. Wilson said the critics might do well to look at the wage charts as an engineer would do.

"We tried to analyze the facts of the struggle over wages," he said. "When a union asks for more than it really wants, or is entitled to get, and when management automatically says 'no' to every union proposal, that is the wrong approach.

"We are trying to give labor, without strikes and interruptions of production, the gains they would have made just the same the hard way. These people who think you can stop inflation by holding down the workingman give me an awful pain. Some of them think I am a terrible left-winger. But I feel I understand the difference between being social-minded and socialistic. I'm too liberal to be a Socialist."

POINTING to a framed quotation that hangs on the wall of his office, Mr. Wilson said: "That pretty well sums up my personal philosophy." The quotation reads:

"Individual freedom alone can make a man voluntarily surrender himself completely to the service of society. If it is wrested from him, he becomes an automaton and society is ruined. No society can possibly be built on a denial of individual freedom. It is contrary to the very nature of man, and just as a man will not grow horns or a tail, so he will not exist as man if he has no mind of his own. In reality, even those who do not believe in the liberty of the individual believe in their own."

The text, by Mohandas K. Gandhi, was a gift to Mr. Wilson from his closest personal friend, the radio and television entertainer, Arthur Godfrey. The two met at a party in New York four years ago. Mr. Godfrey persuaded Mr. Wilson to appear on his morning radio program and the banter they exchanged became the foundation of a warm friendship.

This sample gives the flavor of their repartee:

Godfrey—What do you think of that jet power? Where do you think we're going with it?

Wilson—Well, it certainly is a wonderful thing for an airplane. But when it comes to try to move a train or an automobile or truck with a blast of hot air you can't do it. Some people think our sales departments are pretty good at giving them a little extra speed with that hot air.

Mr. Wilson's reputation for earnestness and industry goes back to his boyhood in Minerva, Ohio. Both his parents had been teachers and he developed as a child a reverence for education. Having been graduated from the Carnegie Institute of Technology at the age of 18 (by completing a four-year engineering course in three) he joined the Westinghouse Company in Pittsburgh as a student apprentice, at a wage of 18 cents an hour.

The Wilsons at home.

At 22, on a salary of $80 a month, young Erwin Wilson married Jessie Ann Curtis of Costello, Pa., and designed the first automobile starting motor produced by Westinghouse. He did not own an automobile at the time; he could not afford one. During World War I he designed and developed radio generators for the Army and Navy.

Joining General Motors in 1919 as chief engineer and sales manager of the Remy Electric Company, one of its Detroit subsidiaries, he rose rapidly in the organization. He became a vice president nine years later and in 1941 succeeded William S. Knudsen as head of the corporation. His engineering background had been broadened by sales and production experience.

HE was less well prepared for the problem of labor relations that faced him in the new job. Long, costly strikes were almost the rule in Detroit during that period, as the young and vigorous Automobile Workers Union buckled to the task of organizing all the giants of the industry.

Throwing himself into this struggle, Wilson came up against Walter P. Reuther, then director of the G. M. department for the U. A. W., later its international president and now president of the C. I. O. He was overmatched at the start, for the union leader was a resourceful debater and a tough, imaginative strategist. The industry was stunned when the president of General Motors consented to a six-hour public debate with Reuther on the merits of the so-called Reuther plan for building warplanes in existing automobile plants.

The plan, Wilson said, was "just a publicity trick." Reuther belabored the industry for bringing out 1942 model automobiles "filled with gadgets" when the armed forces were hard pressed for weapons. The argument grew increasingly technical as the two debated whether this machine tool or that could be converted for defense production. Some reporters say the debate ended in a draw; a large number feel that Reuther won the day.

In subsequent engagements they took off the gloves. But as the combat phase continued, through it all, union officials now concede, Wilson was learning and "growing."

THE corporation, after V-J Day, was preparing to roll new automobiles from its assembly lines when the U. A. W. served a demand for a 30 per cent wage increase. The demand was rejected, and General Motors entered upon a 119-day strike, one of the most expensive in history.

It was this strike that encouraged Wilson to apply the "engineer's approach" he had sketched in a hospital bed five years earlier. In 1948 G. M. proposed, and the union accepted, his plan for an escalator contract with an annual improvement factor. The first contract ran for two years. It was modified and extended to five years in 1950.

He recognized that cost-of-living adjustment by itself would have been rejected because it would have frozen the employe's real wage. The answer that Wilson came up with was a permanent, annual "productivity" increase. This he described as giving the employes their rightful share in the improved efficiency of the industry.

A devout believer in the gospel of an expanding economy, he contends that real wages must be increased progressively, as workers are consumers as well as producers.

Since the first escalator contract was signed more than four years ago, General Motors has not been troubled by a single, significant work stoppage. Producing cars steadily for the lush post-war market, it went on to establish record earnings. Wilson's personal salary and bonuses in 1951 amounted to $626,300, the highest income reported by any company executive in the United States.

HIS decisions at General Motors were not unanimously applauded, nor did the board of directors always give Wilson his head. His stubborn insistence on the development of a light, inexpensive car for the low-income market was vetoed after many months of preparation. He was widely criticized for taking too much responsibility into his own hands, and poking a finger into decisions that might have been left to subordinates. It was not until 1948, with the appointment of Harlow H. Curtice as executive vice president, that Wilson delegated many of his responsibilities.

ONE admiring G. M. man said that Decontrol Charlie's achievements could not be measured in physical terms, although the corporation's manufacturing space had been doubled since 1941 and its gross sales stood at $7.5 billion in 1950 and 1951. "You might say," he remarked, "that Alfred P. Sloan developed the concept of the G. M. organization. C. E. Wilson made it work."

Others, including several board members, have made clear their opposition to his works in the labor field. They feel that he has yielded too much in exchange for continuous production, that the whole auto industry may be in a precarious position if the nation should slide into a period of deflation, since the escalator provides that wages cannot fall below the level of 1948.

The critics within G. M. are embarrassed by Wilson's articulate defense of the contract in speeches and magazine articles, and even more by his high regard for Walter Reuther. Between the two men there has developed a relationship of friendly antagonism, based on mutual respect.

If their attitudes are also tinged with personal affection, neither man will admit to it. They have enjoyed meeting from time to time to discuss matters of mutual interest. "I don't want to praise Walter too highly," Mr. Wilson said recently, "because my praise wouldn't do him any good."

MR. WILSON refuses to discuss at this stage the policies that he and General Eisenhower would institute at the

Mr. Wilson and foreman at his farm inspect a prized assembly line.

Pentagon. As head of General Motors, the nation's largest defense contractor, he has outlined definite ideas on several aspects of the program. Whether he will now be able to carry them out depends to a large extent on the foreign and budgetary policies of the incoming Republican administration. He has, for example, expressed concern over two dangers: That the United States might help to precipitate a third world war by overarming and that the American people might lose their essential liberties if Government were granted excessive power in the name of defending freedom.

"The military program must not be expanded beyond the minimum needed to defend the country," he said in one speech. Defining that "minimum" will now be his responsibility.

He advocated pay-as-you-go financing of defense expenditures with tax rates being set sufficiently high to meet current costs. He also favored a review of the stockpiling program and a careful reappraisal of the amounts of critical materials that should be allotted for defense.

In October, 1951, Mr. Wilson said the time had come for the nation to realize the need of a permanent defense program, based on dual-purpose plants that could shift easily from civilian to military production as the need arose. Stockpiling of arms and equipment was a doubtful measure, he contended, because of the constant changes in design. Instead, he proposed that pilot assembly lines for defense goods be set up and maintained indefinitely in dual-purpose plants.

LOOKING ahead to the new assignment, Mr. Wilson shows a good deal of humility. "I hope the people don't expect too much of me," he said. "Actually, I can't deliver the General Motors efficiency and organization—I am only one man."

He recalls an occasion in 1945 when he came to believe that wartime manpower restrictions should be eased to facilitate reconversion from military to civilian production. He went to Washington to seek the support of Bernard M. Baruch. Mr. Baruch felt the timing of Mr. Wilson's proposal was wrong.

"You engineers and mechanics don't understand political leaders."

Mr. Baruch added.

"Political leaders must keep looking over their shoulders all the time to see if the boys are still there. If the boys are not still there, they are no longer political leaders."

Decontrol Charlie was still chewing on that thought as he cleared his desk in Detroit.

December 14, 1952

A Girl's Hope For a Tycoon Still Flickers

By CYNTHIA KELLOGG

A GIRL'S chances today to marry tomorrow's millionaire are as good as they were in the Twenties. For the American Dream that the poor farm boy can rise to the top of the great corporation is still a fact.

Although men born to business or a profession predominate in the group of business and industrial leaders in this country, at least a third of them have made their way up from the farm, laborer, white collar or other occupations.

This was the happy finding of two University of Chicago men who set out to discover whether the prediction in 1928 of two Harvard University men — that by mid-century the Horatio Alger opportunities would have disappeared in this country — had come true.

In fact, they found that more men from the lower occupation levels had risen than in 1928 and that the largest concerns were those that were most often led by the man who had risen.

The American business man gets to the top not through marrying a woman of position or one who works single-heartedly to help him, but on his own, according to Prof. W. Lloyd Warner and James Abegglen of the University of Chicago.

If he marries the boss's daughter, they say in their new book, "Big Business Leaders in America" (Harper, $3.75), it usually takes him longer to rise. Like the boss's son, they say, he has to work harder to prove himself.

Few Cinderella Stories

The authors found few Cinderella stories in their study of 8,000 "tycoons" throughout the country, on which their book is based. The men who were born laborer's sons usually married laborer's daughters, the big business men's scions tended to marry in their own set. The sons of white-collar workers often married above themselves, perhaps the daughter of a professional man or of a business executive.

These were the types of wives the men had:

¶The family-centered woman, concerned with managing the home and raising the children.

¶The civic-minded-social-minded wife. By taking an interest in the affairs of the community and society, she demonstrated to the world her husband's successful position in business. This was the most common role, with the family-centered role second. However, the authors added, the women who combined both roles were likely to be the most helpful to their husband's careers.

¶The valued consultant and, perhaps, partner, in business. She was a rare wife, for the majority of these men tend to divorce utterly their home and business lives.

¶The career woman. She was even rarer, for the demands of her husband's career made a separate career for her difficult.

How can a girl tell if a man is going to the top? If he is not born into it, the average one enters business just before his twenty-second birthday. By the time he is 29, after shifting jobs and companies, he is generally associated with the concern in which he will rise. He will be 45 or 46 when he becomes a top executive.

His chances are best in rapidly expanding fields—the petroleum and chemical industries, trucking, aircraft, radio and television. Utilities, mining, railroads and electrical machinery manufacturing are also good.

If he is born into the business he will come from the North; if he rises in it he comes from the Middle West. He probably will move his family from the region he was born in and finally settle in the Middle Atlantic states.

He has had an unhappy home life. His mother has been, perhaps still is, the strong force in his life to better and improve himself.

December 3, 1955

Crawling To the Top

THE ORGANIZATION MAN. By William H. Whyte Jr. 429 pp. New York: Simon & Schuster. $5.

By C. WRIGHT MILLS

IN his new book, "The Organization Man," William H. Whyte explores some of the ideologies that have accompanied the growth of large-scale organizations. This is now a very old theme—"the bureaucratization of modern society"—and so far as fundamental ideas about it are concerned Mr. Whyte provides nothing new. But he is an energetic reporter. Working with the ample resources of Fortune magazine, of which he is assistant managing editor, he has fleshed out the well-known bones with up-to-the-minute detail from the white-collar worlds of office, laboratory and suburb. He has the patience carefully to analyze malarkey; the writing skill to make details so fascinating the reader overlooks his inattention to their fuller meaning. His belief in the value of the individual mind lends an edge to his work, and makes his description of the ethos of the technician in America today among the best available.

He understands that the work-and-thrift ethic of success has grievously declined—except in the rhetoric of top executives; that the entrepreneurial scramble to success has been largely replaced by the organizational crawl. He sees that education, in particular higher education, has been adapted to this trend and is now actively furthering it. He provides frightening statistics on the decline of the liberal arts and the basic sciences and indicates clearly the mediocrity of the types of mind that are selected and formed by the corporate realms. He demonstrates that these same corporate norms now prevail widely in academic and scientific institutions of America, as well as how they are supported by everyday life in the packaged suburbs of white-collar men and women.

His real worry is about the declarations of dependence he hears everywhere in America today; his real theme is the expressions of these declarations. This mythology, which Mr. Whyte believes now dominant in the organizational world, includes the faith that human salvation lies in the use of physical science techniques in some kind of "social engineering"; the faith that, with such techniques, politically neutral "experts in human relations" will "guide men back, benevolently, to group belongingness," and the curious notion that the properly "administered group," and not the individual, is the best means of decision and creativity.

Painting by Georgia O'Keefe. Courtesy Stieglitz Collection, Fisk University.

MR. WHYTE makes short shrift of each of these notions. He is against them because morally they are a denial of all that is meant by the creative and independent individual, and because intellectually they are, after all, nonsense. That his own analysis stands out so powerfully testifies, for one thing, to the fact that most "applied social science" does not. Mr. Whyte has taken most practical "social science" in just the way it ought to be taken by any detached student: not as knowledge but as a phenomenon to be analyzed. As a result, his account of the organization of the social studies today, with their absurd pretensions, their fetish of "methodology," their acceptance of the unintelligent policies of the big foundations—is first rate.

> **Conflict**
>
> **IN our attention to making organization work we have come close to deifying it. We are describing its defects as virtues and denying that there is—or should be—a conflict between the individual and organization. This denial is bad for the organization. It is worse for the individual. What it does, in soothing him, is to rob him of the intellectual armor he so badly needs.**
>
> **—"The Organization Man."**

So far as the facts and trends he so adroitly reports are concerned, Mr. Whyte's book is uniformly pessimistic. But he doesn't seem able to leave it at that. With truly great skill, he manages to keep the tone of his book that of an earnest, optimistic Boy Scout. The trouble is he really isn't prepared.

The only general advice he offers his white-collar men is: "Fight the organization. But not self-destructively." "I write," he proclaims, "with the optimistic premise that individualism is as possible in our times as in others. I speak of individualism *within* organizational life." He believes that you can't go back to the old entrepreneurial way, and he refuses to be nostalgic about that. But he doesn't want to go forward either; he doesn't seem able to imagine any organization that is structurally different from those which he describes. So he sticks to ideology and attitude. He writes, as if in conclusion, "the fault is not in organization, in short; it is in our worship of it." Not, please note, even in the *kind* of organization that prevails—just in "our" attitude toward "it."

He does offer one specific piece of advice: cheat on any "personality test" you're given. In short, deceive your corporate superiors. Well, I agree with Mr. Whyte that the tests are themselves a cheat of the independent mind and an intellectual fraud as well. But his own analysis of the corporate man, in education as in business, makes it seem most unlikely that in the near future many will feel any need to cheat in order to pass these moral tests with ease and comfort. In the meantime, such deception as he recommends is quite in line with the ethos that already prevails in much of the corporate world. Moreover, wouldn't the truly independent man, whom Mr. Whyte professes to admire, "fight the organization" rather than deceive it? Wouldn't it be better to refuse—if possible as a group—to take the silly things? And wouldn't it be still better if Mr. Whyte would shelve his earnest optimism just long enough to explore the economic basis and the political meaning of the white-collar ideologies he so intelligently describes?

His unsturdy little mood of earnest optimism is based on the illusion that, by a mere act of personal will, white-collar men can change their world—or at least overcome the complacency with which they often accept it. The truth would seem to be that although the corporate way may not be inevitable, still its power is now such that the area of willful—and effective—action open to the white-collar man is small indeed. Moreover, as Mr. Whyte well knows, personal will itself is now the prime object of "The Organization's" control. In fact, the moral problem of social control in America today is less the explicit domination of men than their manipulation into self-coordinated and altogether cheerful subordinates.

Mr. Mills, author of "The Power Elite" and other books, is lecturing this year at the University of Copenhagen.

December 9, 1956

M'NAMARA NAMED FORD'S PRESIDENT

Will Be Head of Operations —Henry Ford 2d Still Is Chief Executive

CHANGE AT FORD: Robert Strange McNamara, left, new president of Ford Motor Company, confers with Henry Ford 2d, chairman and chief executive of the company, at Dearborn, Mich. Mr. McNamara, 44, was chosen for position yesterday by Ford directors.

The Ford Motor Company yesterday named a scholarly looking 44-year-old one-time professor of accounting as its fifth president.

He is Robert S. McNamara, who has been Ford's vice president and group executive in charge of the car and truck divisions since 1957. Previously, he had been controller and had served in the company's planning and financial analysis offices.

Mr. McNamara succeeds Henry Ford 2d, who had been both president and chairman. Mr. Ford remains as chairman and chief executive officer of the company founded by his grandfather.

In announcing the appointment of the new president, the company emphasized that Mr. Ford would continue to have full responsibility for the general management of the company, with special attention to corporate policy and planning. Mr. McNamara's responsibility will be mainly in operations, it was declared.

Division of Duties

Thus, staff vice presidents for finance, legal affairs, industrial relations, product planning, engineering and research, manufacturing and public relations will report directly to Mr. Ford. Vice presidents and group executives in charge of the car and truck divisions, Ford International, general products and defense products will report directly to Mr. McNamara.

In other management changes, James O. Wright, 48 years old, a vice president and former general manager of the Ford division, was named to succeed Mr. McNamara as vice president and group executive in charge of the car and truck divisións. In recent months, Mr. Wright frequently had been mentioned as a possible new president of the Chrysler Corporation.

Lee A. Iacocca, 36 years old, former vehicle marketing manager of the Ford division, was named a vice president and general manager of the Ford division, succeeding Mr. Wright.

New Post Created

Charles R. Beacham, vice president and former assistant general manager of the Ford division, was appointed to the new central staff position of vice president in charge of marketing.

Since the retirement last July of Ernest R. Breech as chairman, Mr. Ford, president and chief executive officer since 1945, has been both chairman and president. Mr. McNamara's appointment as president had been rumored for some time in auto circles.

Mr. McNamara is the first Ford president since Henry Ford began his reign in 1906 who has not been a member of the Ford family. Henry Ford was president from 1906 to 1919 and again from 1943 to 1945. His son, Edsel Ford, was president from 1919 until his death in 1943. Henry Ford 2d was elected president on Sept. 21, 1945.

Mr. McNamara joined Ford in 1946 after service in World War II as an Air Force officer. He managed the company's planning and financial analysis offices until 1949, when he was promoted to controller. In August, 1953, he was appointed assistant general manager of the Ford division, and in January, 1955, was elected a vice president and general manager of the division.

On Aug. 8, 1957, he was elected a director of the company.

Mr. McNamara was born in San Francisco in 1916. He was graduated from the University of California and took a graduate degree at the Harvard Graduate School of Business Administration. He was an assistant professor of accounting for three years at Harvard before going into the Air Force in 1943.

At a press conference yesterday, Mr. Ford announced that the company would spend $138,000,000 on foreign facilities and tooling this year and $220,000,000 in 1961.

Mr. Ford said the company planned to maintain production at present rates for the rest of the year. He predicted that automobile sales for the entire industry this year would aggregate about 6,650,000 units.

Mr. McNamara said that dealer stocks of Ford cars were lower than the average for the industry. But he acknowledged that the company may have overestimated the auto sales potential last summer when dealer stocks in the industry were exceptionally high.

November 10, 1960

EDUCATION: A PROFILE OF THE BUSINESS EXECUTIVE

By FRED M. HECHINGER

Education rather than a wealthy father is the new American key to managerial success. The Horatio Alger story of the poor boy making good enjoyed its greatest popularity in the days when top business posts remained largely in the hands of the rich and well-born, but the real triumph of the open society has been achieved in the past ten years. Statistics indicating dramatic change were provided by a study of "The Big Business Executive" last week.

In 1950, about 36 per cent of the nation's big business executives were identified as sons of wealthy families; in the current generation of business leaders—15 years later—only 11 per cent come from such a background.

Even more conclusive, because less subject to varying interpretations of wealth, is the fact that two-thirds of the business leaders at the turn of the century had fathers who were heads of the same corporation or were independent businessmen; fewer than half of the present men at the summit fit into that category.

At the same time, there has been

NATION'S EXECUTIVES: CHANGES IN BACKGROUND AND EDUCATION

FAMILY BACKGROUND

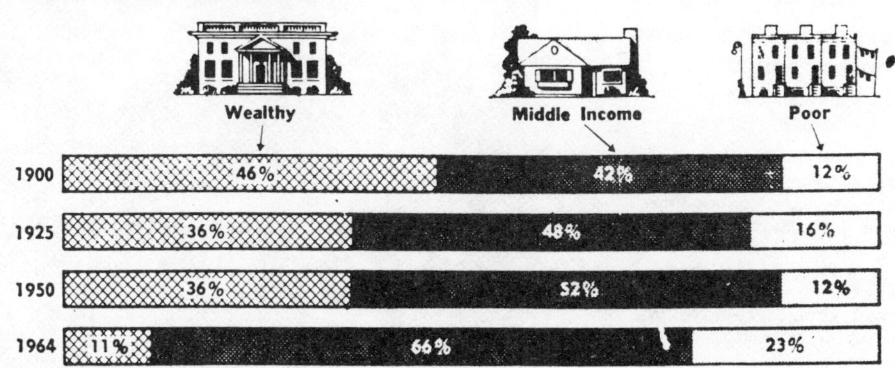

EDUCATION

More college graduates

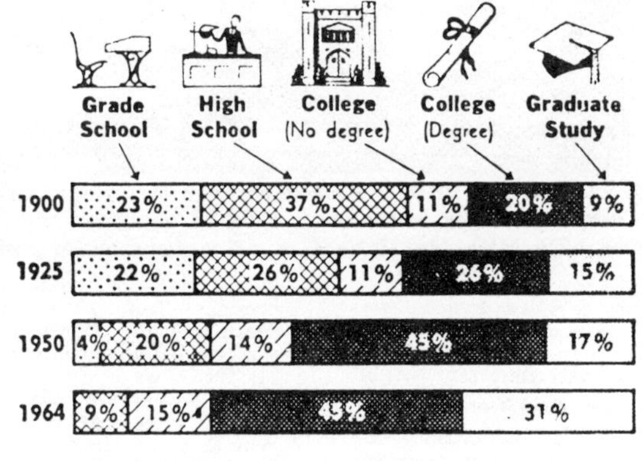

More technical degrees

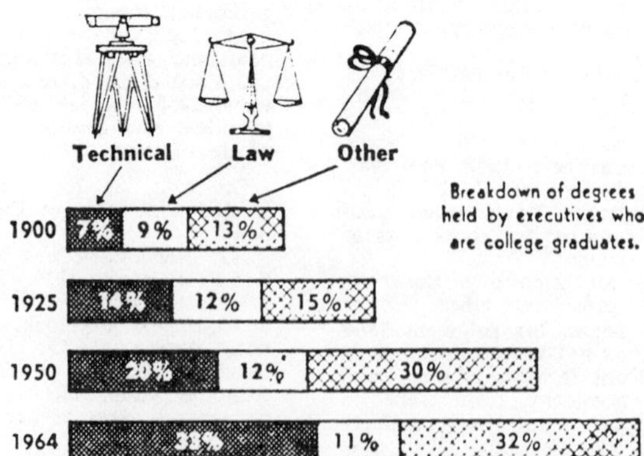

Education has replaced wealth and family background as key to industrial leadership. Study of 1,000 top executives of 600 largest U.S. corporations, undertaken by "Scientific American," shows (top chart) the growing success of men from poor and middle-income families; the increasing importance of higher education (center) for top management people; and rise in technically trained leaders (bottom).

a remarkable shift toward technological-scientific training in the educational backgrounds of those who run the nation's business and industry. As of 1964, some 38 per cent of the big business executives had such education—degrees in engineering or natural sciences.

The study of the social and educational background of approximately 1,000 top officers—presidents, chairmen or executive vice presidents—of the 600 largest non-financial corporations was sponsored by the magazine, Scientific American. It was conducted by Market Statistics Inc., in collaboration with Dr. Mabel Newcomer, a former head of the department of economics at Vassar College. A major purpose was to update Dr. Newcomer's important sociological study, "The Big Business Executive—The Factors that Made Him: 1900 to 1950."

It would be a sentimentalized distortion to suggest that wealth is a handicap or that the poor boy has a high chance to rise to the top. The real shift has been toward dominance by the middle-income groups, another way of saying that the controlling force is that of the middle class, with a college or university education. Taken together, middle-class and poor families have provided the overwhelming majority of today's corporate leadership.

Moreover, the shift toward engineering-science education among the managerial class mirrors a trend that has gone even further—some feel to excess—in the Soviet Union, where even the younger echelons in public administration and politics are increasingly recruited among engineering graduates.

Quite apart from such specialization, higher education in general is the ladder to success: in 1964, 91 per cent of the big business executives had some college education, and many had received graduate degrees. Among the younger members of the current leadership 35 per cent had graduate education, compared with 20 per cent in the same group in 1950 and 10 per cent in 1900.

In the course of this century, the proportion of executives with higher education has more than doubled. But the percentage of executives with degrees in science and engineering has increased nearly five times over—from 7 per cent in 1900 to 20 per cent in 1950 and 33 per cent today.

The trend will continue. A different study, conducted by the Harvard Graduate School of Public Administration, found that among the younger executives in the 35 to 45 year age group, among whom most top officers of the future will be recruited, more than 50 per cent have science or engineering degrees.

Moreover, science-engineering education seems in large part responsible for opening society's gates. Of the 1964 generation of top executives who rose from humble origins, 40 per cent had technical training, while only 20 per cent of those from wealthy families had such specialized education. Thus, the general education background appears to be more satisfactory to the rich, who have natural connections with top leadership, whereas those who must make the uphill journey on their own are more readily propelled by technological competence.

Most revealing is the revolutionary broadening of the base of the colleges and universities at which succeeding generations of top executives were educated.

In the 1900 group, the overwhelming majority of those who attended college at all went to Harvard, followed by Yale and Columbia, with a few from M.I.T. and the University of Michigan.

In 1925, Columbia had moved to the head of the parade, followed very closely by M.I.T., Harvard, Yale and Princeton. Lehigh, Michigan and Amherst had also made the list.

By 1950, Harvard was considerably in the lead, with Yale a fairly close second, followed (but with a steep drop) by Princeton, Cornell, Michigan, Columbia and M.I.T., and with Wisconsin, the University of Pennsylvania and the University of California coming up rapidly.

All this diversification was merely a prelude, however, to the 1964 listing. Not only has the number of the college-trained skyrocketed—from 53 among the top leaders in 1900 to 791 today; more important, these leaders emerged from a total of 45 colleges and universities. Harvard and Yale are in an easy lead, followed by M.I.T., Princeton, Cornell, the University of Illinois, Stanford, Columbia, Michigan, Pennsylvania, Wisconsin, California and Dartmouth. The rest of the extensive list includes new additions ranging from Chicago, Ohio State and New York University to the University of Oklahoma and Clemson College.

Even the graduate education of today's top executives was provided by a highly diverse list of institutions—a total of 35. Here Harvard was far and away in the lead, with 52 of the top executives, while Yale was ahead in undergraduate alumni. Next in line as graduate schools for 1964's top management were M.I.T. (16), Columbia (15), Michigan (13) and Yale and Cornell (12).

Lest the rise in the importance of technological-scientific education be misinterpreted to mean that general education is no longer considered essential, some typical comments by the respondents to the study must be cited. An arts major said: "I feel my lack of technical knowledge is a distinct handicap." But typical for a number of engineers was this comment: "Engineering education should provide wider exposure in the arts and humanities." Another engineering graduate credited much of his success to his high school studies in Latin, Greek, history and English. Better grounding in economics was demanded.

The search continues for the best of both worlds—the humanities and technology. And a laconic captain of industry, asked to list "pivotal factors" in his career, wrote: "Hard work. Ability to organize and delegate. Ability to handle people. Sense of humor. Divine discontent. Innovation."

May 30, 1965

Alfred P. Sloan Jr. Dead at 90; G.M. Leader and Philanthropist

Alfred P. Sloan Jr., who shaped the General Motors Corporation into one of the world's largest manufacturing enterprises, died of a heart attack yesterday afternoon at Memorial Sloan-Kettering Center here. He was 90 years old.

Mr. Sloan had been in excellent health until Tuesday, when he complained of not feeling well. He was taken to the hospital, which his philanthropy helped to establish, on Wednesday afternoon from his home at 820 Fifth Avenue. He succumbed yesterday at 2:35 P.M.

With him at the hospital was his brother, Raymond P., special lecturer in the School of Public Health and Hospital Administration of Columbia University.

Mr. Sloan was acclaimed last night as one of the great captains of industry of his age, not alone for his managerial skills but also for the pioneering automotive advances that he oversaw. These included four-wheel brakes, ethyl gasoline, crankcase ventilation and knee-action front springs.

In a joint statement Frederic G. Donner, chairman of General Motors, and James W. Roche, its president, said:

"His contributions to science and education and those of the foundation that bears his name were matched only by his accomplishments in business and industry."

Mr. Sloan made his mark, his associates said, "as a planner, organizer and administrator."

Roy Abernathy, president of the American Motors Corporation, called Mr. Sloan "the most advanced practitioner of modern management of our time."

A friend in the industry, Lynn A. Townsend, president of the Chrysler Corporation, said last night that Mr. Sloan's "services to our nation and our industry cannot be measured."

Associated Press
Alfred P. Sloan Jr.

In Detroit, Henry Ford 2d, chairman of the Ford Motor Company, extolled Mr. Sloan as "one of the small handful of men who actually made automotive history."

"Under his leadership," Mr. Ford said, "General Motors developed from a loosely organized group of companies into the present highly efficient giant corporation."

At his death Mr. Sloan was honorary chairman of General Motors, and in this capacity he had attended a board of directors meeting here last month. Associates who talked with him then said yesterday that he participated in the session with his usual acuity.

Mr. Sloan headed General Motors as president and then chairman from 1923 to 1956.

His Work, His Hobby, His Love

In the nineteen-thirties when Alfred Pritchard Sloan Jr. was chief executive officer of the General Motors Corporation a friend told him that a man of his position ought to own a yacht. After some hesitation, the slim, dandily dressed industrialist agreed and bought a 236-footer for $1 million.

He incorporated it, christened it René, hired a crew of 43 at an annual cost of $119,609 and embarked on a few cruises. But life afloat quickly bored him, and the yacht was virtually laid up until he sold it in 1941 to the Maritime Commission for $175,000.

This nautical fling was notable in Mr. Sloan's life because it was one of the few ventures that did not turn a handsome profit and because it was a leisure-time caper. Indeed, it was perhaps his only frivolity, for Mr. Sloan did not smoke, rarely drank, read little for pleasure and never engaged in golf or any other sport. A functional, frill-less man, he was convinced that sports were a waste of a man's time.

Such dissipations, moreover, interfered with his work, his hobby, his love — the running of General Motors. Even in retirement, when Mr. Sloan was administering his multimillion dollar medical and educational benefactions, his sole relaxation was an evening's television watching.

When Mr. Sloan became vice president of operations of General Motors in 1920 the company accounted for less than 12 per cent of motor vehicle sales in the nation; when he stepped down as chairman in 1956 its share was 52 per cent. Moreover, General Motors had expanded into one of the world's largest companies. It was also among the most profitable and, operationally, one of the smoothest.

These accomplishments were credited to Mr. Sloan's management policies. He centralized administration and decentralized operations, grouping together those that had a common relationship. He also realigned the company's products so that one brand of automobiles did not conflict with another. Each product — cars, electric iceboxes or whatever— was set apart in its own division. It was part of Mr. Sloan's genius that he was familiar with every detail of each division.

Along Staff Lines

In his 14 years as president of General Motors (1923-37) and in almost 20 years as chairman of the board (1937-56) Mr. Sloan ran the company on the staff principle, with himself as chief. But despite the eminence of his position he did not comport himself like an autocrat, nor did he hoot and holler. (He was known throughout the organization as "Silent Sloan.") He also refrained from ordering underlings about.

"I never give orders," Mr. Sloan once said. "I sell my ideas to my associates if I can. I accept their judgment if they convince me, as they frequently do, that I am wrong. I prefer to appeal to the intelligence of a man rather than attempt to exercise authority over him."

An associate likened him to a roller bearing — "self-lubricating, smooth, eliminates friction and carries the load." A typical workday bore out this portrayal.

Mr. Sloan arrived at his office in the General Motors Building, 1775 Broadway (at 57th Street) at 9:30 A.M. (In winter he drove from his 14-room apartment on Fifth Avenue; in summer he commuted to Pennsylvania Station from his 25 acres in Great Neck, L.I., and rode the subway to West 59th Street.)

Father Was Well-to-Do

With metronomic precision he ticked off the day's conferences. He was restless, squirming in his chair, gesturing, putting his small, well-shod feet on the table. When he talked, it was in a quiet voice that curled out of the side of his mouth with a trace of a Brooklyn accent. When he listened, it was with the extra intentness of the deaf.

By 5:30 he was ready to depart for home with a briefcase under his arm; and after dinner with his wife he usually worked for a few hours and was in bed at 10 o'clock. Two weeks a month he spent in Detroit, where he rarely stirred out of the gray G.M. building, not even to a hotel.

Summarizing his recipe for success, Mr. Sloan said:

"Get the facts. Recognize the equities of all concerned. Realize the necessity of doing a better job every day. Keep an open mind and work hard. The last is most important of all. There is no short cut."

He was born in New Haven on May 23, 1875. His father was a well-to-do coffee and tea importer, and later a wholesale grocer. The Sloans moved to 240 Garfield Place, Brooklyn, when Alfred Jr., was 10. He attended public school until he was 11, when he entered Brooklyn Polytechnic Institute where he established a reputation as a prodigy in mechanics and engineering. At 17 he enrolled in the Massachusetts Institute of

Technology in Cambridge, and by grinding away every possible minute he graduated in three years.

With his father's help Alfred got a draftsman's job in the Hyatt Roller Bearing Company at Harrison, N.J. The company was not doing very well, but Alfred had confidence that it could be made to show a profit. He persuaded his father and another man to put up $5,000 and place him in control. In the first six months the business yielded $12,000 in profits.

It was the automotive industry, however, that made the company's fortune. Automakers had been using a heavily greased wagon axle until Mr. Sloan persuaded the Olds Motors Company to try his bearings. Henry Ford and the other manufacturers soon followed suit, and Hyatt Bearing started making money hand over fist.

By 1916 the company was doing a gross business of $10-million a year and making profits as high as $4-million. Of equal importance, Mr. Sloan had made a name for himself in Detroit as a knowledgeable and reliable business man with keen insights into the auto industry.

His First $5-Million

By that year General Motors, replacing Ford, had become Mr. Sloan's largest customer, and there was some hint that it might make its own bearings. Instead, General Motors, which had been stitched together from several independent auto concerns by the mercurial William Crapo Durant, bought Hyatt for $13.5-million.

He promptly merged it with some other parts and accessory companies into the United Motors Corporation and installed Mr. Sloan as president. In the process Mr. Sloan pocketed his first $5-million, a start on a fortune that was to rise to $250-million.

Late in 1918, through the initiative of John J. Raskob, General Motors took over United Motors as its own parts division, and Mr. Sloan went along as its executive head. Successively, he was named a member of the G.M. board of directors and a vice president.

Meanwhile, Mr. Durant, his backer and sponsor, was swept out of the company through stock purchases by the du Pont interests. Two and a half million shares passed to them in a single day.

Pierre S. du Pont thereupon became president of General Motors, but being unfamiliar with the motor-car business he leaned on Mr. Sloan, who became vice president of operations in 1920. Three years later Mr. du Pont left the presidency and put Mr. Sloan in the chair.

The corporation's net sales were then $698-million; six years later there were $1.5-billion. In the process, General Motors' Chevrolet displaced Ford as sales leader in the low-price field, and the market price of its stock was up 480 per cent.

This growth cost Mr. Sloan much leg work. "It may surprise you to know," he said at the time, "that I have personally visited, with many of my associates, practically every city in the United States, from the Atlantic to the Pacific and from Canada to Mexico.

"On these trips I visit from 5 to 10 dealers a day. I meet them in their own places of business, talk with them across their own desks and solicit from them suggestions and criticisms as to their relations with the corporation."

And a Sloan visit was not soon forgotten, for Mr. Sloan was 6 feet tall and weighed 130 pounds. He arrived dressed in what was then the height of fashion — a dark, double-breasted suit, a high starch collar, conservative tie fixed with a pearl stickpin, a handkerchief cascading out of his breast pocket and spats. It was enough to awe any dealer.

When Franklin D. Roosevelt took office in 1933 Mr. Sloan at first cooperated with the New Administration, becoming a member of the Industrial Advisory Board of the National Recovery Administration. When the dollar was devalued, howevery, the New Deal lost a friend and gained a persistent critic.

Early in 1937 Mr. Sloan encountered one of the major crises of his business life when newly organized workers in General Motors plants staged a 44-day sitdown strike to obtain union recognition.

The industrialist haughtily refused to deal with the strikers while they "continue to hold our plants unlawfully." He joined the chorus of those assailing John L. Lewis, head of the Committee for Industrial Organization, as seeking to dominate the motor industry. President Roosevelt rebuked him, public sympathy ran against him and he beat a retreat, which was signalized when Gov. Frank Murphy of Michigan brought labor and management together.

Mr. Sloan, however, did not carry on the negotiations personally. He remained in New York, delegating the distasteful job to William S. Knudsen, then vice president in charge of operations, and other executives. A few months later he turned over the company presidency to Mr. Knudsen and became chairman of the board.

A month later, in June, 1937, Mr. Sloan was in the headlines again when Treasury experts reported to a Congressional committee that he and his wife had avoided payment of $1,921,587 in income taxes over a three-year period through personal holding companies.

Although there was no Government charge that this means of tax avoidance was illegal, the implications were so unpleasant that Mr. Sloan issued a statement denying that he ever sought to evade a just share of the tax burden. He said that he and his wife had received in 1936 income totaling $2,876,310. Their Federal and state income taxes, he asserted, ate up $1,725,790, and the remainder—$1,150,520—was divided evenly between charity and themselves.

Toward the end of the year Mr. Sloan made a substantial foray into philanthropy by endowing the Alfred P. Sloan Foundation with $10-million. In announcing the benefaction, he said:

"Having been connected with industry during my entire life, it seems eminently proper that I should turn back, in part, the proceeds of that activity with the hope of promoting a broader as well as a better understanding of the economic principles and national policies which have characterized American enterprise down through the years."

Mr. Sloan, in 1942, with Charles F. Kettering, director of General Motors research laboratory, who developed the electric self starter shown here. It was the first successful one, introduced in 1912. In 1945 the two men sponsored Sloan-Kettering Institute for Cancer Research.

Up to 1966 the value of Mr. Sloan's gifts to the foundation and those of his wife, Irene, totaled $305-million, of which about $130-million has been given away. The gifts have not been restricted to economic studies.

One of the foundation's first large benefactions was in 1945—provision of $2.56-million for the establishment of the Sloan-Kettering Institute for Cancer Research in New York, a component of the Memorial Cancer Center. Grants of $300,000 annually were also made at the same time to help finance research. Charles F. Kettering, the co-sponsor of the institute, was a close friend of Mr. Sloan's and director of the General Motors Research Laboratory. Until his death he was an institute trustee.

Additional funds were given the institute over the years, and it and the hospital were eventually reorganized as the Memorial Sloan-Kettering Cancer Center, with a medical and scientific staff of 1,500 persons.

Another recipient of Mr. Sloan's benefactions was M.I.T., his alma mater. These included a laboratory for study of automotive and aircraft engines and aeronautical engineering problems. In 1945 he gave $350,000 for an industrial management professorship and four years later he donated $1-million for a metals processing laboratory.

In 1950 the Sloan Foundation gave M.I.T. $5.25-million for a School of Industrial Management, subsequently named the Alfred P. Sloan School of Management. Mr. Sloan gave the school $1-million for management research in 1952.

The foundation also gave M.I.T. $5-million to establish a Center for Advanced Engineering Study, whose students are practicing engineers and professors of engineering.

Two years ago Mr. Sloan established the Alfred P. Sloan Fund for Basic Research in the Physical Sciences at M.I.T. The fund included a personal gift of $5-million from Mr. Sloan and an equal amount from his foundation. Last year a similar fund was established at the California Institute of Technology.

As a further venture into education, the Sloan Foundation in 1953 established a program under which four-year scholarships are awarded to outstanding college students. Forty-five institutions now participate in the project, in which 600 students are enrolled.

In an official biographical sketch issued by Mr. Sloan's office in 1966, his attitude toward philanthropy was outlined. "As chairman of the Alfred P. Sloan Foundation," the sketch said, "Mr. Sloan has the responsibility of establishing the fact that every proposed grant is a sound investment in some area of human need, and not in any sense of the word a 'give-away'; further, that adequate responsibility exists to administer the program intelligently. Here is Mr. Sloan's description of what a foundation should be — a well-organized, efficiently managed business enterprise with a wholesome respect for every dollar at its disposal."

A friend once put it more directly, saying, "He's no Scrooge, but he still knows the value of a dollar."

In World War II General Motors, under Mr. Sloan's direction, converted its automotive plants to the manufacture of armaments. A total of 102 plants was involved, and from February, 1942, to September, 1945, no automobiles were produced. Reconversion was a back-breaking process, but it was accomplished more smoothly than many observers had predicted, for virtually all G.M. lines were back in civilian production by the end of 1945.

After the war General Motors expanded its activities in the household appliance field and in diesel motors. The company also developed overseas plants and outlets.

In 1946 Mr. Sloan stepped down as the company's chief executive officer after 25 years in that post. He remained as chairman of the board until 1956, when he was elected honorary chairman, a position he held until his death.

Held Corporate Posts

Although Mr. Sloan's business life was centered on General Motors, he was a director of E. I. du Pont de Nemours & Co., the Pullman Company, J. P. Morgan & Co., the Kennecott Copper Corporation, the Johns Manville Corporation and the Braden Copper Company.

In retirement, Mr. Sloan turned his mind to writing a book. "My Years With General Motors" was published in 1964 by Doubleday. A documented insider's story of the management of General Motors. It sold more than 50,000 hard-cover copies.

In it, he told why one management is successful and another is not. "The causes of success or failure are deep and complex," he wrote, "and chance plays a part. Experience has convinced me, however, that for those who are responsible for a business, two important factors are motivation and opportunity. The former is supplied in good part by incentive compensation, the latter by decentralization."

Mr. Sloan also took time to reply to critics of General Motors and its success. "General Motors has become what it is because of its people and the way they work together, and because of the opportunity afforded those people to participate in an enterprise which combined their activities efficiently.

"The field was open to all; technical knowledge flows from a common storehouse of scientific progress; the techniques of production are an open book, and the related instruments of production are available to all. The market is world-wide, and there are no favorites except those chosen by the customers."

Also in retirement, Mr. Sloan devoted himself to his foundation. He maintained daily hours at its offices, 630 Fifth Avenue. On days when he had no luncheon engagement, he ate in his paneled office. His fare was a homemade sandwich, which he had brought with him, neatly wrapped in paper, in his coat pocket.

The office was always brightened by fresh flowers and it contained a portrait of his wife, the former Irene Jackson, whom he married in 1898. She died in 1956. They had no children.

In addition to Raymond, Mr. Sloan is survived by two other brothers, Harold S. and Clifford A., both of New York, and a sister, Mrs. Katherine Sloan Pratt of Syossett, L. I.

A funeral service will be held tomorrow at 11 A.M. in Christ Church Methodist, 520 Park Avenue. There will be no pallbeorers. Until the funeral, his body will be at Frank E. Campbell's, Madison Avenue at 81st Street.

Burial will be private at St. John's Cemetery, Cold Spring Harbor, L. I.

February 18, 1966

The Making Of a (Corporation) President

By ANDREW HACKER

AMONG the many offices filled at inauguration ceremonies during the opening weeks of this year, the half-dozen most important were probably those assumed by Ronald Reagan, Lester Maddox, Lurleen Wallace, Otto Miller, Gordon Metcalf and Haakon Ingolf Romnes.

While the first three obviously need no introduction or identification, it is also safe to suppose that the last three require a good deal of both. Virtually nothing is known about the men who just took over as presiding officers of Standard Oil of California, Sears, Roebuck and the American Telephone and Telegraph Corporation. Yet Messrs. Miller, Metcalf and Romnes sit at the apexes of corporate edifices that employ over a million people, with five times the combined payrolls of California, Georgia and Alabama, the states governed by Reagan, Maddox and Mrs. Wallace, respectively. Their companies sell goods and services to the annual tune of $20-billion, whereas together the three states collect only $4-billion in taxes each year.

Though these men are representative of America's industrial and financial leadership, the curiosity is that the holders of such pervasive power and influence should remain anonymous—even invisible to the public eye. This is not due to any conspiracy of silence; on the contrary, most companies have public relations departments working overtime to publicize the performance and personalities of their top men. Nevertheless, these efforts are largely in vain. The American preference is for glamour or controversy, characteristics not usually associated with corporation executives. Still, sooner or later we will have to face up to the fact that a Frederic Donner of General Motors is a more potent figure than a John Lindsay, that a David Rockefeller at Chase Manhattan Plaza has a greater ultimate impact on our lives than does his brother in Albany.

THE top men in the top companies are symbolic of a new breed of American. Their distinction lies in having passed the stringent series of tests set by our society to determine who will rise to its heights and who will be left behind. Every modern organization has such multiple hurdles, and the route to the top for an archbishop, a four-star general or a university chancellor has a great deal in common with that traveled by a corporation president. Career success nowadays is based more on talent than on birth or background, and what is especially rewarded is an ability and a willingness to devote those talents to goals decided upon not by oneself but by others.

The future corporation president can emerge from anywhere in the generous bosom of the American middle class. All that companies ask, in their initial recruitment of potential executives, is that a young man possess a college diploma. It doesn't matter where you went to school, and in most cases no one cares who your father was or what he did for a living. Among the top executives of today there are actually more products of the Big 10 than of the Ivy League, and in the corporate circles of the future it is clear that graduates of Purdue will far outnumber those from Princeton.

The president of Boeing Aircraft was born in Lolo, Mont. (population 235) and went on to Montana State University. Itasca, Tex., Walton, Ky., Hattiesburg, Miss., and Shelby, Neb., produced local boys who ultimately made it to the top ranks of Gulf Oil, North American Aviation, Texaco and the Ford Motor Company. Very few went to private preparatory schools and hardly more than three or four out of 100 are listed in the metropolitan Social Registers.

In a way, this is altogether plausible, for the majority of companies

ANDREW HACKER teaches in the department of government at Cornell.

'A David Rockefeller has a greater ultimate impact on our lives than does his brother in Albany.' Why, then, are corporation heads practically Invisible Men?

now do most of their promoting from within, and they draw on the pool of management talent that is subsequently discovered among the college graduates they originally recruited for specialized jobs. Thus, a large corporation will hire as many as 1,000 graduates each year, and the assumption is that out of this legion of engineers and scientists and accountants will eventually emerge enough individuals with executive potentialities.

It is worth noting, therefore, that only a minor fraction of the men who make it to the top have liberal arts degrees. This preference for the practical persists despite the pronouncements of sundry corporate chairmen that business needs more people with backgrounds in the humane disciplines. History and philosophy majors should be warned against taking such assurances too seriously, however. The story is told of the head of a large chemical company who sang the praises of liberal learning in the course of receiving an honorary degree at a Midwestern university, while at that very moment a recruiter from his own company was in the school's placement office with requests for seven chemical engineers, three electrical engineers, two mathematicians and an accountant.

THE open-eyed young man, first taken on as a technician of one sort or another, soon discovers what is wanted if he is to distinguish himself from his classmates. This is the comprehension and conviction that he is, above all else, working in and for a business. "It's remarkable how many of the young fellows we take in go along for years without realizing that their real job is to make money for the company," one executive remarked.

The up-and-comer, however, soon learns to think first and foremost in business terms: the specialized skills he was taught at college are only useful if they can be applied to augmenting the firm's earnings. At a certain point he may have to compromise with professional standards in making or promoting a profitable but less-than-quality product. How he reacts to this challenge will be noted by his superiors.

By the time he is in his early 30's, the man-on-the-way-up will have left his old friends behind at their account books and drafting boards. He is now a manager, of either a large department or perhaps a branch plant. The best indication of his early success is that he now has as his subordinates men older than himself; not only has he passed his peers but he has bypassed people who were once ahead of him. "Anyone can head a department staffed with a lot of youngsters or working stiffs," admitted one executive. "The big step is the one that takes you over people like yourself."

The 10 years between the ages of 35 and 45 are the critical ones. It is here that a junior executive can stop at $20,000—a title on the door but no carpet on the floor—or go on to $100,000. What is required now is the top-management look. This is usually achieved by emulating the appearance and outlook of one's immediate and remote superiors. It is generally an air of taciturn tough-mindedness, an impression of deliberate decisiveness. Those who best manage such a transformation do so not self-consciously but as a responsive adaptation to unwritten codes and customs. However, the change should not take place too suddenly; the trick is to show all the sound sense of middle age without sacrificing one's boyish vitality.

THE executive personality, let it be said, can probably be mastered more easily by the boy from Itasca than by the graduate of Groton. The corporate graces are, on the whole, those represented by the middle-class life of Detroit or Chicago. In contrast to his European counterparts, the American executive does not have to know wines and is actually a step ahead if he prefers his steak without *sauce Béarnaise*. In this, our top men undoubtedly have more in common with Soviet managers than they do with those of France or Britain.

One of the specific lessons to be learned is to be moderate and open-minded in one's politics and to avoid ideological dogmatism of any sort. The potential president will register as a Republican but will refrain from taking positions that are too off-base or far-out. The man who comes out foursquare for Barry Goldwater will probably find himself spending the rest of his career in the Denver office. In fact, it is best to opt out of politics altogether.

A social scientist who has done a good deal of consulting for executive-development programs, often living with these young men for a week or more, has remarked: "It's not that they're afraid to have opinions on touchy subjects like Vietnam or civil rights. They simply don't have any views at all and they don't want to have any. One reason for this may be that they know that policies change and they don't want to be caught out having been on the wrong side."

But what is needed most in these years is ambition, drive and a willingness to make company business the center of your life. The real difficulty is that this test comes at just the wrong time. Your children are in high school and faced with all the problems of adolescence; your wife is beginning to feel the passing of the years and starts to wonder just where she stands in your diffused affections. This is just the period when an attaché-caseful of work must be brought home every night—except those nights you are off traveling to a trade association meeting in San Francisco, to a Congressional hearing in Washington, to merger negotiations in Chicago, or simply to see what has gone wrong at the subassembly plant in Shreveport.

No one can assert with complete confidence that the 14-hour day is absolutely necessary for high-quality executive performance. Walter Bagehot once observed that businessmen work much too hard for their own good; the result is that they make a lot of money in the morning and then, instead of stopping when they're ahead, proceed to lose half of it in the afternoon. However, if the sheep are to be separated from the goats, certain rituals must be enforced and observed. In the academic world it is the writing of a Ph.D. thesis that no one will ever read; with psychoanalysts it is four years of medical schooling. For the rising executive it is being on company time all the time. One corporation chairman calls frequent Sunday morning meetings just to see which of his vice presidents grumble over intrusions into what more mortal men might consider to be the private hours of life.

Quite obviously, not everyone is willing to consent to such a regimen, and not a few who had once set their sights on the top suite now get off the A-train. One such deserter was Tom Rath, the man in Sloan Wilson's gray flannel suit, who had reached the $20,000 level and was on deck for better things. But as he pondered over the state of his stomach and the perils of absentee-husbandhood he decided to climb no further. The reaction of his boss sums up the view from the top: "Somebody has to do the big jobs. This world was built by men like me. To really do a job, you have to live it body and soul. You people who just give half your mind to your work are riding on our backs!" It is here, indeed, that there is a parting of the ways between the organization men and the company men.

DURING this period, also, a presidential contender will have to become something of a philosopher. The theoretical underpinnings of American business have actually not changed much since the days of Adam Smith, although there is a curious materialist overlay that has a lot in common with a brand of thinking that had better not be mentioned here. Thus, the need to affirm that the economy is the central institution of the society, that business profit is the prime mover in the nation's life.

"Our economy, our standard of living, our society result from the success of business in making profits," said the president of the Aluminum Corporation of America in a recent full-page advertisement. "Wages, payments for goods and services, taxes and contributions - all stemming from profits—are what makes the world go 'round."

Other, more spiritual, philosophers have been pondering for centuries in an attempt to discover just what it is that turns our globe on its axis. The on-the-rise executive will display no such perplexity.

He will, moreover, come to believe that whatever it is his company produces is absolutely necessary for the well-being of the American citizen-consumer. He must take the view—and this attitude cannot be faked—that the six-sided frozen French-fried potato is an asset to the nation's dinner table; that automobile exhaust is not really responsible for air pollution; that his firm is doing all it can to give jobs to Negroes and school drop-outs. For only if such sentiments are uttered with a ring of inner conviction will you be adjudged a true company man who can be relied upon in all crises and circumstances.

As a candidate approaches 45, and if no mishaps have occurred, he will be a $75,000 vice president and waiting for the final move upward. His competition will have been narrowed down to three or four brother vice presidents, all about his age and all aspiring to the executive vice presidency that is the grooming position for the top job in the company. The problem is that everyone in the final heat has pretty much the same qualities and abilities: energy and ambition, the right look and outlook, judgment and decisiveness and dedication.

At this point the incumbent president and chairman will make the decision — sometimes easy, sometimes agonizing—as to who will be their heir apparent. And it is not possible for an outsider to generalize about how they go about making up their minds. There are occasions when the choice has actually been settled on many years in advance. Thus, an observer at Standard Oil of California said of Otto Miller, the recently elected chairman: "You could see 20 years ago that the right hand of God was on Otto's shoulder." But such predestination is rare in the career service of corporate America.

A large corporation will hire as many as 1,000 graduates a year, on the theory that from this legion will emerge some with executive ability.

Just what constitutes "executive ability," especially at the higher reaches, is a difficult and perhaps even impossible question to answer. Companies themselves have expensive management "development" programs, and not a few corporations send the more promising of their men to special courses at such places as Harvard and M.I.T., where it is hoped that some insights on business leadership will be obtained. Indeed, the whole puzzle of what-makes-an-effective-executive has become a minor industry in itself, producing endless shelves of self-help books and hint-filled articles in business magazines. (One such piece even went so far as to portray the successful "executive face." The chin was very important.)

All this scurrying after definitions and definitiveness suggests that you know executive ability when you see it but that it is not something you can describe without a specific example to point to.

What *can* be said is that the ascent of a corporation vice president is frequently aided by a specific "record" he has acquired, most usually by taking on a very tough assignment and doing well at it. For example, he may have raised the sales of one line of the company's products from a quite average showing to new and unexpected heights. He may have introduced a new set of procedures and made them work despite the forecasts of doom and disaster from more cautious quarters. In short, a man's ability is best known by his tangible accomplishments; he is tabbed as "the man who . . ." Gordon Metcalf's promotion to the top job at Sears Roebuck was in large measure due to his identification with the fabulously successful Midwest division of the company.

Another—less predictable—consideration has to do with the fact that every executive tends to be earmarked as having some "strength" in a particular field. Thus, a man's fate can be shaped by whether the special area of interest he developed many years ago turns out to be a critical one for the corporation at the time when the penultimate promotions are being made.

A director who serves on several boards put it this way: "Immediately after World War II, the need was to get civilian production rolling again as fast and as efficiently as possible. So, the big emphasis was on production and the men from the manufacturing end were put in the top slot. After a few years it became a buyers' market, so the stress was on sales and you found a lot of salesmen heading companies." This principle was well illustrated at General Motors, where Charles E. Wilson ("Engine Charlie") was succeeded by Harlow Curtice ("Sales - Curve Curtice").

Interestingly, the men picked as presidents in the last few years have come up largely on the financial side of the business. The current presidents at Chrysler, General Telephone and Electronics, Caterpillar Tractor, Consolidated Edison and International Business Machines all held the position of company controller at an earlier stage in their careers. Their elevation may be symbolic of the current importance of budgetary controls, internal economies, interest rates and minimizing the tax bites.

There appears, then, to be a semideterministic Law of Strategic Talents, accelerating the rise of individuals who have skills that unexpectedly take on central significance. Nevertheless, it would be a mistake to counsel an ambitious young man, now entering college, on how to equip himself for the semifinals of 1995. Any advice that he prepare himself for computerized investment programing or psychoanalytic labor relations could well be an act of misguidance. For just when he is ready for the final round the company may discover that consumer resistance has returned and the top job will be given to an old-fashioned sales type who has the unscientific knack of making people want to take out their checkbooks. There are, as the sages keep telling us, some things that just can't be planned. Had Robert McNamara been born 10 years earlier he would probably still be processing payroll vouchers at Ford instead of having been whizzed up to its presidency.

THE final step to the top takes place in a man's early or middle 50's, and he can expect to serve as the company's president for four to five years and then another three or four as its chairman. (In most companies the chairman is now the No. 1 man, with the president as his heir presumptive. But there are still some firms which follow the older pattern of the president as chief executive officer while the chairmanship is a semihonorary post for an ex-president. In a few corporations the two jobs are separate and each has its own line of succession.)

During his tenure his annual salary will be between $200,000 and $300,000, with stock options that permit building up a personal fortune of a few million dollars. He will visit the White House, attend meetings of the prestigious Business Council at Hot Springs and receive a handful of honorary degrees. While his picture will not be in every office, his name will be treated with great respect in the corporate corridors. (This is in marked contrast to at least one other corner of American life. Walk onto any campus and ask any random group of professors what they think of their university's president. The ensuing comments, readily made even to visitors, would be considered high treason in a corporation.)

It is also worth noting, if only in passing, that most corporation executives do not become *multi*millionaires. When Charles E. Wilson stepped down after many years in the higher echelons of General Motors, he had amassed only $3.5-million. Robert McNamara left the Ford presidency for the Pentagon with only $1-million. And lesser executives, and those in smaller companies, retire with even smaller estates.

This is not to shed a tear for today's impecunious tycoons but simply to point out that the progeny of our executive élite will not be a new leisured class. A recent Wall Street Journal study of presidential sons showed that virtually all of these young men were hard at work, with most of them in business (but only a fraction in their fathers' firms).

THE vice president who loses out may well be given as consolation prize an executive vice presidency, and in all likelihood he will remain in that position until his retirement. He may scout around for the presidency of a smaller company, but the chances are increasingly against this.

Yet, there are not a few large corporations where the No. 2 spot is as far as any career man can go. In a significant number of corporations family succession still operates. There is a Ford still in charge at Ford, a Douglas at Douglas, a Grace at Grace and a Zellerbach at Crown Zellerbach. This is surprising because the stock ownership in these firms is now widely diffused and the founding families no longer have a majority vote. Nevertheless, a tendency persists to reserve the top position for a scion of the original founder.

In recent years, Lammot du Pont Copeland, Samuel Johnson and Robert Sarnoff were all elevated to the No. 1 jobs at the Wilmington, Racine and Radio City enterprises which have long been their families' preserves. Another noteworthy case is Armco Steel, which was presided over by its founder, George Verity, for 30 years and which, on his retirement, came under the management of salaried executives. However, just a few months ago the company chose George's grandson, Calvin, as its new president, even though the Verity clan owns only one-tenth of 1 per cent of Armco's stock.

The only explanation is that some American corporations, like some American voters, are attracted by the monarchical principle: tradition, continuity and memories of past glories. The consequence is that red-blooded executives must content themselves with second-rung jobs, and not a few make a judicious move to another company when they hear that Junior is homeward bound from the Harvard Business School. The prospect for the career man is becoming brighter, though, in some firms where royalty once reigned. At I.B.M. it seems that the Watson succession is coming to an end, and there is every indication that the next chief at Ford will not be a Ford.

The typical corporation president will have had almost 30 years of service with the company prior to his final elevation, and the great majority of firms seems content with the promotion-from-within principle. Accusations of in-breeding, conformity and complacency do not seem to bother them, for most large businesses can point to a record of expanding sales and earnings over the past decades. "Something has to be terribly wrong if you have to go outside," one bank director explained. "A company will have at least a half-dozen decent men in the top ranks and to admit that there isn't a single able candidate among them is a pretty sad commentary on the whole outfit."

Even if there is the feeling that a company's management has grown soft, the preferred recipe for shaking it up is to promote a vigorous younger executive over the heads of senior men who have been waiting in line. "Bringing in an outsider is bad for morale," another director indicated. "He will arouse resentments and suspicions, and good people who are coming along further down the line may get the idea that their own prospects for advancement are limited." In fact, if an outsider is chosen as president he will probably insist on bringing in his own circle of executives with him, if only to insure that the new broom he sets in motion will not bump into

A good executive comes to believe that what his company produces is essential to the well-being of the American citizen-consumer.

"Many of the young fellows we take in," said one executive, "go along for years without realizing that their real job is to make money for the company."

sloth or sabotage from aggrieved old-timers.

There are rare occasions when a giant firm will run into financial trouble and undergo the humiliating experience of having a new chief executive forced on it, in the expectation that a transfusion of new blood and ideas will set things to rights. A recent example of such a beleaguered leviathan was Trans World Airlines which, owing to the erratic superintendency of Howard Hughes, was virtually taken into custody by a consortium consisting of two insurance companies and 15 banks. Their terms for renewing a series of loans was T.W.A.'s acceptance of a new president, Charles Tillinghast from the Bendix Corporation. The moral of this story has not been lost on other companies, and it helps to explain the general preference for remaining financially independent.

ALL things considered, the American corporation has become a self-selecting, self-contained civil service. The men at the top of corporate America undergo far less criticism than the average Senator or Governor, in part because they don't have to face popular elections and in part because the ideology of private property insulates them from public scrutiny.

It may well be that the time has come to alter outdated assumptions about the presumed "private" character of our major corporations. By any reasonable measure Haakon Romnes's A.T.&T. is as important an institution in American society as the state of Alabama, and the presiding officer of that company clearly deserves as much attention as Mrs. Lurleen Wallace. The difficulty, when all is said and done, is that corporation executives are not very interesting people. And not the least reason for their blandness is the sort of individuals they have to become in order to get where they do.

The more one watches the men being chosen for the top jobs, the more one is impressed with a certain air of reserve, indeed caution, they possess about themselves and the world in which they travel. However, it would be wrong to call them conservatives, for once again the conventional language of ideology does not apply here. Many of the decisions they make, whether so intended or not, have revolutionary consequences for all of society. The technological and marketing transformations they have effected have served to give a new shape to postwar America, and the plans they are making for the nineteen-seventies may alter the face of the nation beyond recognition.

If an appreciable proportion of executives abandoned Goldwater, it was in the belief that he simply did not understand the new world of corporate business. Even the ideology-bound National Association of Manufacturers is looked upon as out-of-date and ill-equipped to serve as a spokesman. "They're just a bunch of top-drawer guys in their ivory tower, stewing in their own juice and issuing feudal and futile pronouncements," one executive remarked recently.

Both Henry Ford 2d and David Rockefeller have come out for establishing trade ties with Communist China; after all, there is money to be made by having branch banks in Shanghai and clogging the streets of Canton with Mustangs. To be sure, not all corporation chiefs are as secure as Ford and Rockefeller, but most tend to share their view that the world is best regarded as a marketplace rather than as a political arena.

OVER a century ago, Alexis de Tocqueville observed that "a man who raises himself by degrees of wealth and power, contracts, in the course of this protracted labor, habits of prudence and restraint he cannot afterwards shake off. A man cannot gradually enlarge his mind as he does his house."

This judgment on the bootstrap entrepreneurs of the Jacksonian age has not a little relevance to the career servants of our own time. The men who preside over American corporations are chiefly of unpretentious origins, and they have got ahead by passing the tests and following the rules in a race where there is room at the finish line for only a few. At no time in these trials are they expected to display humane learning, any more than a philosophy professor is asked to show a profit for his department.

"We chief executives are just employes like the others these days," one of them said. And the job of an employe is to protect the interests of his employer, even if that employer is an abstract association of assets called a corporation. Most corporation presidents nowadays would not even belabor the theory that what is good for General Electric or General Dynamics is good for the country. Their job, for which they are paid, is to look out for the good of their company.

There are, of course, important exceptions. But it is interesting to note that displays of new and different

The rising executive must be on company time all the time.

qualities of personality usually appear after an executive has departed from the corporate precincts. That Robert McNamara and Charles E. Wilson were willing and able to become public figures deserves recognition, especially in light of the popular criticism that Secretaries of Defense have to undergo. Charles Percy and George Romney are two examples of executives who have left corporate havens for the political rough-and-tumble. However, the fact remains that apart from these four it is hard to think of many corporation presidents who have demonstrated abilities that proved applicable to other sectors of our national life.

This should not be construed as criticism. Most of these men have invested their energies and emotions in a particular line of endeavor. To expect that our corporations will somehow produce an aristocratic echelon is, in fact, to misunderstand important conditions that have accompanied recent changes in the structure of American life.

There is not much point, then, in musing about how nice it would be if our corporate managers underwent more instruction in moral philosophy or modern sociology. The simple fact is that they are busy men, on the way up during most of their formative years, and the exigencies of the climb compel them to think of themselves rather than for themselves. This is an inevitable consequence of opening careers to the talented, of breaking down the barriers that once prevented men of inauspicious backgrounds from rising to the top. These men are, more than anything else, products of an open and a democratic society.

Yet it may well be that these men are less important than the oversized machines at whose controls they temporarily sit. It may be that a Ronald Reagan's impress on the State of California will be greater than the imprint that a Gordon Metcalf can leave on a Sears, Roebuck. "Organization replaces individual authority and no individual is powerful enough to do much damage," John Kenneth Galbraith has written. "Were it otherwise, the stock market would pay close attention to retirements, deaths and replacements in the executive ranks of large corporations. In fact, it ignores such details in tacit recognition that the organization is independent of any individual." If this is so, then the personality is subordinate to the position and we should study the chair rather than the men who sit in it.

Obviously, there is something a bit terrifying about a self-running machine, especially one of great power and influence. Nevertheless, this condition is becoming increasingly evident throughout our entire society. Not only corporations but universities and medical centers, foundations and research institutes, government agencies and the military establishment are recruiting and shaping individuals to serve their needs and eventually fill their top positions. The making of a corporation president is more than a success story. Its greater significance is as part of the natural history of our times, wherein men perceive the personalities that are wanted of them and then pattern their lives to meet those specifications. ■

April 2, 1967

Where Money Grows On Decision Trees

By RICHARD TODD

CAMBRIDGE, Mass.

THE Harvard Business School stands on the west bank of the Charles, across the river from the college. The golden domes of the rest of the university, the bookstores and miniskirt emporiums and the chic, disaffected nomads who roam through Harvard Square seem remote; as everyone at the business school quickly admits, the Charles represents "more than a physical gulf."

The business-school campus is quiet and self-contained, a sort of campus of the imagination. Georgian buildings covered with ivy face a curved avenue lined with elms. Secretaries of the Treasury—Hamilton, Gallatin, Dillon and others—along with such donors as Aldrich and Kresge have given their names to the buildings. Students move about in pin stripes and tweeds. They are shorn. They carry books, but more often attaché cases, and though they talk absorbedly they do not raise their voices. The feeling, just walking around, is mildly anachronistic, and in the eyes of the rest of Harvard the "B School" is apt to seem something worse. "Across the river," one business student shrugs, "they just assume we're all a bunch of robber barons."

After some recent visits, I came to think that this air of remove helped define the school. But in certain obvious ways it is only a deceit. The Harvard Business School, if it stands apart from the university, is intimately in touch with another world. Each year it sends about 700 young men (and an occasional woman) to the outside with degrees as masters of business administration, and they are destined for unusual influence and success; at the moment, nearly 2,000 alumni are corporation presidents or board chairmen.

In addition to M.B.A.'s, the school awards doctoral degrees in business administration and offers an intense Advanced Management Program. The "A.M.P.'s" are older businessmen being groomed for top management jobs, men "who've moved vertically and now face horizontal problems." The school also gives courses for "middle management" people, even one for trade unionists. A faculty of 275 conducts about a million dollars' worth of research (largely endowed by industry) into business problems each year and spends a good portion of its time consulting for corporations. The faculty has lately been so much in demand outside the United States that the school has set up pilot programs in several countries to train teachers in business-school techniques. "Around the world," Dean George Baker remarks, "when you hear someone say 'Harvard,' the chances are 3 to 1 that he means the business school."

The M.B.A.'s, though, are the heart of the school, and—at least

RICHARD TODD is a freelance writer and an editor for a Boston publishing house.

STRICTLY BUSINESS—Before a blackboard showing one of the commandments of U.S. business—"Thou shalt not price fix"—Prof. C. Roland Christensen leads a discussion of "The Electrical Industry and Price Fixing," title of a case history of an actual business problem, which exemplifies the Harvard Business School's method of teaching tyro tycoons.

so far as money suggests esteem—they are among the most valued young men in our society. A man graduating with an M.B.A. from Harvard and without previous experience can expect to take his first job at $12,500 a year. That was the median salary for last year's class, and, as one student said, "Everybody wants at least that." In fact, they are likely to earn more; starting salaries have increased by about $1,000 for each of the last four years. Last spring some M.B.A.'s, most of them in aerospace and investment, began at more than $20,000.

There is an impulse to ask if they are worth it. "No," says John Steele, the school's placement officer. "But companies aren't hiring them for what they can do now, but what they can do five years from now. Some of what these men are taught won't even be used in business for five years."

Personnel men may agree with a New York bank official who called the M.B.A.'s "damn prima donnas," but with a few exceptions* the recruiters hire them nevertheless, and indeed compete for them, often at the urging of those above, for whom Harvard M.B.A.'s on the junior staff are especially pleasing ornaments. "Baker Scholars," the top 5 per cent of the class, are subject to an even more rarefied competition, so intense that a few students keep the honor off their resumés. More than 300 companies pay $75 for the right to look through these resumés, collected and sent out in crimson boxes, as part of the "Job Campaign." Here they read such Algeresque stories as: "Raised by widowed mother. Awarded best trainee in platoon, Parris Island. Winner of 'Meritorious Mast.' Sold ice cream, various other summer jobs . . . Health: excellent."

OTHER business schools produce M.B.A.'s, of course, and at Harvard you hear nothing but kindnesses about such places as Columbia, Stanford, Wharton and the University of Chicago. But refer to "The Business School" and Harvard is understood. It has by far the best reputation; and it promises, along with the education itself, the finishing-school polish of two years "at Harvard." Students

---

*Some companies refuse to consider them, some "wait for the first bounce"; among other things, M.B.A.'s on the job are noted for restlessness.

cherish stories of their potential worth. A Southern boy spoke of an investment firm "down home": "I asked them if I should go to Harvard or Wharton and they said there's no choice — 'We'll hire nothing but Harvard M.B.A.'s.'"

"Partly it's a matter of fashion," said one business-school professor in explaining the desirability of Harvard M.B.A.'s; the other part of the explanation is implicit: they know something that business feels it needs.

"We give a man a certain way of making a decision," Dean Baker remarks. Harvard's rather famous "case method" is the engine for teaching decision-makers their craft. Under the case method, almost nothing is taught abstractly; techniques are derived from case histories of real-world business problems. During their two years, students consider about a thousand cases, each presented in a thick mimeographed pamphlet in which facts, charts and graphs are packed without excessive order; one of the most valuable skills to develop is the art of pulling the relevant figure from the mass of inessential ones.

Classes meet in sections of 100 in horseshoe-shaped, tiered amphitheaters that facilitate the discussions central to the case method. The students sit about like delegates, white name cards in front of them, attaché cases open, cups of coffee at hand. The rule, not always honored, is a decision by the end of every class.

A case-method class typically begins with an eloquent temporizer, a nonvolunteer chosen in preference to the hands in the air. I watched an earnest-eyed fellow open a class about protection for the steel industry: "In essence I would tend to think that I would testify against tariffs and quotas, although I would sympathize with big steel in their need for some protection. . ."

Equivocation earns a quick rebuttal, either from the class or the professor. In this case, Prof. Paul Cherington said, "Doesn't seem as if your testimony would carry much weight, Mr. M. You can always *refuse* to testify, you know. . . . Mr. M. have you ever seen a man *cut up* on the stand?"

It is one of the characteristics of the business school that the students tolerate and even seem to like this sometimes acerbic teaching style, which, of course, is out of fashion in the arts and sciences across the river and elsewhere. ("You're leading me by the hand, but I don't know where we're going," one student said.) Public embarrassment is expected and seems essential to the style of the school. Inflicted by an instructor, it is known as "sawing off," leading a man out on an untenable limb. "A little sawing off is felt to be good for the soul," Professor Cherington told me later.

Following the initial destruction, things move quickly—theories and countertheories in the air—until one cool operative, laying well off the pace until now, extracts some crucial numbers and the case begins to get refined.

Despite an undeniable sense of movement in these sessions, the case method has some detractors. Some say it holds back the bright and confuses the slow. And others point out that it can develop into a game in which the skillful player learns just how often to contribute and acquires the subtle ability to nudge the discussion in a direction of the instructor's choice: everyone playing for private stakes. (The response to this argument is: "And how do you think real business meetings work?")

The case method, however, most impressively *involves* the students, who try on the language and assume the feelings of businessmen—in this instance, Roger Blough, chairman of the board of U.S. Steel. "If I were in Mr. Blough's shoes," a student argued, "I'd realize we've got a whole new ball game. My previous track record in getting selective price increases just isn't in the cards any more. I'd recognize we'd better get hot on R and D and we'd better start studying diversification, and we better face up to the fact that we may need subsidies, too. Then, uh, I'd go home and have a stiff drink."

His classmates laughed; they unembarrassedly liked playing captain of industry. This analysis had the additional strength of including two of a handful of quintessential business-school terms: "R and D" and "diversification." Others are "multinational" and "synergy," the happy state in which everything you do enhances everything else you do.

"Everybody's always talking about this synergy business," said a student in a case on farm problems. "Well, here it is. We take advantage of the cultural lags around the world. Sell your old designs to Europe, sell whatever they can use in India—hoes, if you have to—to build up brand identification. . ."

I ACTUALLY heard an excited student in one class refer to "the whole ball of wax," but the jargon, the role-playing and the general headiness of these sessions disguise some of the techniques being learned. The business-school curriculum was revised at the start of the sixties to anticipate "business in the seventies." It was decided that two disciplines—the social sciences and mathematics—would probably be most influential. Accordingly, all students take an introductory course called Human Behavior in Organizations ("Hobo"), which attempts to attune them to the psychological complications lurking in every managerial act, down to water-cooler placement. In the second year they may study Freudian theory and participate in "T groups," the business version of group therapy, designed to increase sensitivity. But what is newest, most sophisticated and probably most important at the business school is the study of mathematical decision-making.

We need a symbol here. The characteristic doodle at the business school, I think, stands for a great

deal of what is going on. I saw this scratched on several pads:

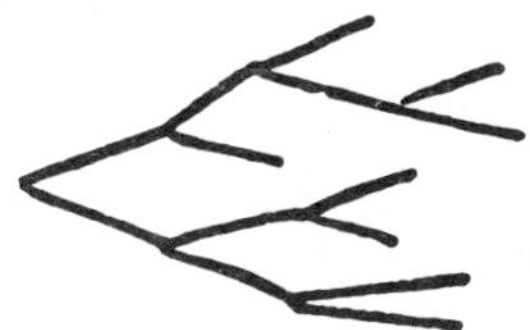

That is a rough sketch of a "decision tree," which is a schematic device for representing the implications of an act and the possibilities for action. It is a map of "options." If you face a decision you may represent your situation by a point, your options by lines emanating from it. This was explained to me step-by-step by a patient student one midnight. Use a square, he said, for the point of decision:

Following out the options leads to fresh situations, new events that may go one way or another. Represent these points with circles. They are called "event forks."

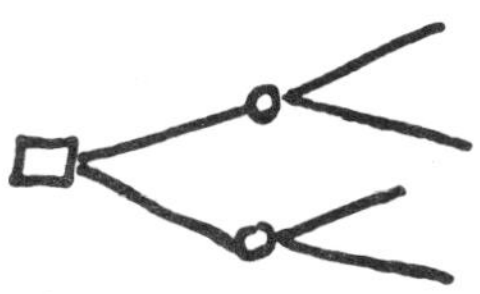

These new situations call for new decisions, leading to new possibilities and so forth, indefinitely:

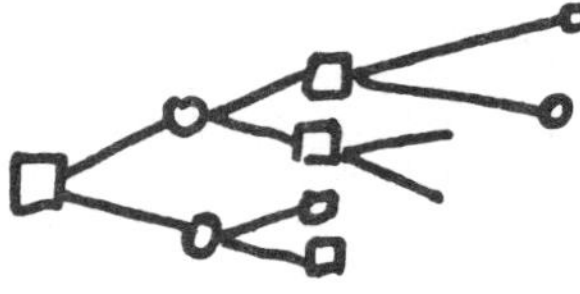

Of course, the trees are only a "handy device," and they are accompanied by numbers that make things more complex. By assigning probabilities to various events, costs to various options, it is possible to calculate the "expected value" of any course of action at a given moment.

The mathematical source of this method is called "decision theory." Courses in decision theory itself are doctoral subjects, but the theory informs one of the central required courses of first-year students, Managerial Economics, Reporting and Control ("Merc"). Harvard has been an innovator in decision theory and stresses it more than any other school. Students learn to draw decision trees in their first three weeks and they never stop.

Decision theory, as it is taught—and, to some extent, created — at the business school, rests on the concept of "subjective probabilities," which allows for the decision-maker's attitude toward risk. Through a device called "the preference curve" (which assesses, say, how much it stings a man to lose $50,000 on a chance of gaining $275,000) this attitude may be translated into numbers and incorporated into decision-tree calculations.

Even without numbers, the decision tree has some function. "Essentially," one student said, "it makes you see the problem in terms of the options open to you." It simplifies, too, by showing that one option can be ruled out because of a weak branch far down the tree. "Divide and conquer, divide and conquer, that's the whole idea," said John Hammond, a young faculty member specializing in decision theory.

As a model, the decision tree suggests a certain way of looking at problems, indeed at experience, that perhaps already has affected our language and thought. Its bias is toward creating alternatives, working with possibilities, facing uncertainty and guiding one's actions by the rational assessment of probabilities. The style of thought is best embodied in the ubiquitous "options," that word popularized by the business school's most famous graduate, Robert McNamara. (Of McNamara and the war, they say at the business school: "He didn't draw his trees out far enough.") "Options" is a favored word at the school, and it finds itself in unlikely circumstances. "Let me give you some options," one professor responded when asked for a phone number, and another referred to his position at the moment as "an option-widening thing."

The techniques of formal decision analysis are only beginning to be felt in business, though they have been used in the Pentagon and in "think tanks" for some time. Often they are introduced through business-school professors doing consulting; often they bubble up from newly hired M.B.A.'s. Scientific decision-making doesn't always sit well with experienced "line managers." "It's all hogwash," said an executive at du Pont, where the new methods are being tried out. What managers resent is not so much the theory as the mathematical evangelism of self-confident M.B.A.'s who seem to disregard personal feelings, to disdain industry's grit and to heed only the computer's print-out. Businessmen may argue that decision theory is no substitute for a seasoned gambler's instincts, and the M.B.A.'s may counter with a preference-curve analysis that shows the boss to be "highly risk-averse." The "B School's" professors are aware that managers mistrust some of their theories, and at least one is careful to caution his "young lions" not to get arrogant in the face of their elders' intuitive ways.

Professor Hammond says: "It's almost a C.P. Snow, two-cultures level of problem between the managers and the operations analyst." This is a frequent experience for business-school consulters, one of whom described the love-hate relationship between the school and industry as "the courting of whooping cranes; you know, one step forward and two steps backward." But when the techniques work,

HELP WANTED — A business-school student notes some job interviews posted in Baker Library. Harvard M.B.A.'s are valued men; last year's median starting salary was $12,500 — and the price keeps rising.

resistance begins to melt, even if it sometimes means temporary embarrassment for oldtimers. A doctoral candidate this year calculated a "probability budget" for a transportation company that accurately foretold a profit half the size of the one the company's comptroller was predicting. "Now that boy is golden," his professor said.

DESPITE the glittering prospects that await them on the outside, the young rationalists of the business school often lead dreary lives. In fact, there is a certain inverse pride over the Spartanness of things. John Seiler, dean of the M.B.A. program, describes it as "a lot like boot camp."

First-year students take 10 courses, all of them required, and, though the class is broken into sections, they study identical cases. Almost everyone is doing exactly the same thing at every moment. Cases become the substance of experience and almost all overheard conversations at the business school seem to be extensions of the classroom. The hothouse atmosphere is intensified by living conditions. Students are urged to live in the dormitories on campus, and most of the unmarried men do. The school is self-sufficient, with its own library, eating facilities, a melancholy basement store that resembles a training post PX (shaving cream and Fritos) and even a bar, "The Gallatin Pub." The Wall Street Journal arrives in every mailbox.

I asked one first-year student how often he went to Cambridge and he said, "Never." It is not at all unusual for students to stay on campus Monday through Saturday, anyway, even though the varieties of Cambridge life begin only a couple of hundred yards across the river.

Students at the business school work hard. Their classes run from 8:10 A.M. until about 2:00 in the afternoon and most of them study straight through until around midnight. It is customary for them to shift at 10 into what is called "a can group" or "head group" (so named because it's made up of men who share a bathroom), to discuss the next day's cases. Students use the meeting as a means of self-protection, a way to test out ideas before a small audience. Fear of embarrassment is the great motivator: "There're a hundred people there and they can *annihilate* you in those classes. You don't want to look like a yo-yo in front of a hundred guys."

The schedule allows little respite. A boy just out of Dartmouth remarked as he headed for bed, "I watched the Johnny Carson show the other night. I know I shouldn't have. I was dragging in class the next day." Tension builds up as the term goes on, leaving 85 per cent of the students worried that they will flunk out during the first year. In fact, only about 5 per cent leave for any reason.

The pressure slackens abruptly in the second year, and a former Harvard undergraduate dismissed it as imaginary: "It's all a myth, just like the myth of the college. The hard thing is getting in; it takes a pretty belligerent attitude to flunk out." In the second year only one course is required, classes are smaller, students feel less competitive and the "Job Campaign" begins.

PARTLY because of their absorption with cases, business-school students are strikingly apolitical compared to their counterparts across the river or almost anywhere. (They were Rockefeller supporters last spring and an "unenthusiastic majority" was for Nixon just before the election.) I mentioned the war to a head group one night. Of the four students there, one had been in Vietnam with the 101st Airborne, and another had commanded a Navy patrol craft in the Mekong Delta. Although they had been studying together every day, neither had known until that moment that the other was a veteran. "I saw the bird on his arm," the Navy man said of the former paratrooper's 'screaming eagle' tattoo, "but I just never thought about it. We don't talk about the war."

About a third of the class are married. They escape the single-mindedness of the dormitory for the Harvard high-rise, Peabody Terrace, or other apartments across the river, but of course they must keep the same schedule the bachelors do, a condition that causes a great malcontent among their wives. One of the frequent rumors at the school puts the divorce rate at appallingly high percentages: "Thirty per cent of all marriages break up by the end of the first summer after graduation," I was told. Recently, the school has encouraged the founding of a "Business School Wives Club," which sponsors such activities as "Slimnastics," a "New Brides' Party" and a singing group, "Executive Sweets."

A glimpse inside a business school student's apartment suggests the sense of estrangement that most of them feel from Cambridge life. The butler's table, the silken slip covers, the matching lamps, the gilt-framed hunting prints on the wall, the silver Revere bowls full of chocolate kisses: all longing, it seems, to be moved to Bloomfield Hills. Walking along Harvard Street after a study group in this setting, I asked a student how he liked living in Cambridge. "Let's put it this way," he said. "It's close to the school and we've got a good building. But most of us just aren't used to living around so many beards, and 'unwashed masses.'"

Not everyone feels that way. Some lament the distance between business school and community and look for ways to reduce it. The student paper, protesting the near impossibility of attending classes across the river (the schedules conflict), editorialized:

". . . Many of tomorrow's top businessmen will continue to isolate themselves in the penthouse world of The Executive Suite, paying no more than lip service to society's problems and consequently being distrusted by that society. Of how many will it be claimed that this attitude became an ingrained habit during their two years in the not-so-splendid isolation of a certain well-known Eastern business school?"

“'Learning things is a waste of time,' says a first-year student. 'Making money is not a waste of time.'”

The men of the business school—their eye-fixing gazes, their close attention to an interlocuter's name—are peculiarly vulnerable to stereotyping, and some of them are sensitive about it. One referred to himself and his classmates as "B-School dulls," a phrase borrowed pre-emptively from the Radcliffe girls who created it.

FOR its part, the school officially strives for a more diverse class, but it faces some difficulties. Nothing like the sort of financial aid other graduate students receive from foundations is available for business students. Only 75 entering students receive fellowships and so most of the student body is likely to be well-to-do. (The school points out that it operates $1,500 in the red for every student, though there is a bootstraps air to its attitude, too: students are reminded that they are expected to borrow on their life insurance before seeking aid.) Costs for a year at the school run to a minimum of $4,600, and the total investment is generally thought of by students as "ten thou."

Last spring, the student newspaper, Harbus News, disclosed that there had only been 24 Negro graduates of the Harvard Business School since World War II. A short time later, the school increased its recruiting activities, and this year's entering class included 28 Negroes. "We had to work like hell to get them," one administrator said. Most of the Negroes were assisted by larger than usual fellowships to cover their full expenses.

About 40 per cent of the students are engineers or scientists, a percentage that the admissions committee struggles to hold down: the combination of a technical degree and an M.B.A. is an almost unbeatable preparation for early wealth. Many of the other students were economics majors, though the committee smiles on B.A.'s in English or philosophy.

Those admitted come "mostly" from the top quarter of the class—though this is far less likely to be true of the third who come from Ivy League or other prestigious New England schools. (Yale and "The College" provide about 100 men in every class.)

The admissions department prizes business experience or some demonstration of social achievement above grades and test scores. On an eight-page form, applicants are asked, for example, to "Give a candid evaluation of yourself as a person . . . Briefly describe what you believe to be your three most substantial accomplishments. . . ."

"We don't get the major intellects," Dean Seiler remarked. And the young dean of admissions, Richard Nohl, added: "I'm not sure we want magnas from the college. This is tricky, but the abilities the college values — scholarship and research—are not necessarily those that make a man able to deal with the pragmatics of administration. We'd like the man who could do both, but if we get him it's usually after he's been out of school a couple of years."

The 3,000 people who apply to the business school each year are likely to be a rather homogeneous group. To aspire to the school, after all, a young man must have consciously rejected the implicit, insistent lesson of most undergraduate education: business is vulgar, business is dull, business is for fourth-raters, business will take away your soul. And he must also have ignored the dizzy choice of routes to self-realization open to him at the moment. In choosing business he opts for the one thing most of his contemporaries scorn. In their eyes, he is judged on a scale ranging from irrelevant to villainous.

WHAT his commitment involves is often assumed to be simply cash. A young wife of a recent Harvard Business School alumnus spoke about a reunion dinner they'd attended: "They have something in common all right. What they have in common is rank, gross greed."

There is evidence of all sorts for this idea. I think of a student whose name began with "S" and who printed that letter on his desk plate with two vertical lines running through it. At The Gallatin Pub, a former Yalie with a relaxed jaw said: "What you're selling when you get out is not what you can do but where you've been. You get your union card here."

And a first-year student who has spent a couple of years in a brokerage put it as plainly as possible: "I'm here for what this can do for me in the long run. Right now I'm wasting my time. Learning things is a waste of time and making money is not a waste of time. I'd rather be out in the real world, playing real games instead of paper games."

BUT one professor warns, "They're not all cold-blooded profit-maximizers," and of course it is true. In a corridor hung with the Karsh-of-Ottawa portraits of senior professors, I talked to the least typical business-school student in sight, a pretty girl in a blue miniskirt and giant hoop earrings, a Radcliffe graduate with a degree in English. (Girls have been admitted to the school since 1963, and about 40 study there now. Beginning in 1969, they will live on campus.) She had worked at the school the year before reading papers and tests. "I decided I had a synthesizing mind," she said, "and that I could do this. I want to learn administrative techniques — not necessarily for business but for education or city planning. A woman, of course, can't always have the choice of where she is; so I'll have something I can use. I suppose I'm not so—well up tight as some of the others because I know the place. Most men come here because they feel it will make them more important — in their own eyes or the world's —and to get money and power. And possibly to take part in a system they believe in. Mainly they're goal-oriented."

If there is a trend at the business school it is away from an automatic homage to big business. Michael Harrington's criticism of the "social-industrial complex," for example, recently found some enthusiasts in a second-year course called "Business, Society and the Individual," which

BUSINESS BEFORE PLEASURE—Business-school students on the way to lunch. Their first class is at 8:10 A.M., and most of them study straight through until midnight. The schedule allows little respite.

attracts the more liberal students. Some 25 per cent of the graduating class now rejects the corporate recruiters and looks for small businesses, as opposed to 10 per cent only a few years ago. There is a questioning over the school's responsiblity to the community. Negro students are decidedly not Tomming; one said: "The white man's reward of the big house, swimming pool and two cars for staying out of the fight must be resisted." Recently some 40 students and faculty members have organized the Unity Bank, which loans money to borderline business risks in Roxbury, Boston's black community.

"Five years ago you wouldn't have seen a single beard around here," a professor remarked. Now there are an intrepid four or five, and they are symbols of some significance to people who hope for a more ecumenical school. I talked to the owner of a luxuriant one, who said he'd been warned that his "placement chances" would be affected by the beard. "What they don't realize," he said, "is I wouldn't work for any company that wouldn't hire me because of a beard." The spirit of this mild liberalism is echoed by a student who presumably spoke for at least a few others when he suggested that by insuring his future, the school had broadened his views: "Without the need to worry about making a buck, I feel a lot different. I guess you could say my sense of social responsibility has grown here."

Almost anyone at the business school, cynic or temperate idealist, is defined by a certain faith in the essential rightness of things and a belief in the ability of problem-solving and decision-making to move a life ever further ahead: if only you draw your trees out far enough something sublime will come to you. One afternoon, leaving the business school, I was reminded of an essay by the French sociologist Michael Crozier, whose book "The Bureaucratic Phenomenon," had been mentioned earlier in the day. On a recent visit to the United States, Crozier wrote that he had found it markedly changed in just a few years, a change expressed by the epithet "The Last Frontier of Reason." He argued that the society was ruled by its trust in the science of decision-making, "the rigorous capacity to calculate the adjustment of means to ends." At the same time he noted the opposition this power had spawned:

"This wave of rational decision-making . . . this belief in the omnipotence of reason, is in sharp contrast to the existential anguish of the hippies and the Negro revolt. But the two movements are the opposite faces of America's transformation, of its passage, as it were, to a new form of society."

Walking from the Harvard Business School over the Anderson Bridge into the existential bazaar of Harvard Square, one cannot miss the aptness of this model, though in Cambridge the odds usually seem to be reversed. On the level of visible energies, anyway, the thrust of life in and around the university favors the forces of revolt. For seasoning, while I was visiting the business school, I stopped by a couple of S.D.S. meetings across the river, lively crowds of 700 to 900 people. At the largest of them, touring Mark Rudd told his audience (in that curious language borrowed, like a field jacket, from the Establishment): "There is no meaningful work in this society, no social option equal to the problems we face. . . ."

An idea that most young people of a Harvard stamp

“Out in the world, the business-school graduate expects to take his place with another elite.”

have at least entertained. This sense of the meaninglessness of the system is, though, the one thing that a Harvard Business School student cannot allow, whether he rejects it from a black faith in the salvation of $200,000 a year and a Lear jet, or from an honest hope that what rewards is not always selfish. Among the grooving throngs of the square and amid the infinite varieties of hipness in Cambridge, he is a stranger and a tailored alien. But Cambridge is not the whole world, and out there he expects to take his place with another élite. ■

November 10, 1968

Industry Seeks Executives in Military

By LEONARD SLOANE

Spurred partially by the growing unrest at campus recruiting centers and partially by the need to hire more young professional and technical employes, corporations are increasingly turning to the military as a source of new executives.

As a result, junior officers with college degrees are being wooed with almost frenetic intensity. Agencies have been created to bring together companies and men being separated from the service.

Among major concerns using this method of recruitment are the Chase Manhattan Bank, Armco Steel Corporation, Continental Can Company, Johnson & Johnson and International Business Machines Corporation.

"We've reduced our campus recruiting activity 25 per cent this year to get at the large number of junior officers getting out of the service," says Albert H. Barlow, a second vice president of the Chase bank. "And these junior officers are going to have a terrific impact on the labor market in the future."

"We find this an excellent source of employes," adds Joseph K. Harrison, coordinator of management and technical recruiting at Armco. "They're more mature individuals, they're more serious about their careers and our attrition rate with these men is extremely low."

One recruiter, remaining anonymous, observes, "It's a great delight to talk to applicants who have haircuts."

Recruiting of new engineers, accountants and other professionals at colleges has long been an important part of corporate employment programs. But, within the last few years, disturbances on some campuses have developed when these recruiters appear. Such disturbances began with protests against the Dow Chemical Company for its manufacture of napalm. They have spread more recently to many big companies for a variety of reasons.

At the same time, the needs of industrial and financial concerns for more new people have broadened. And junior officers, released from the military, must find jobs in the civilian sector.

The agencies that specialize in matching young officers with both big and small interested companies have developed a format that has proved successful in many cases. They hold "career weekends" or "career conferences" in cities throughout the country where they introduce potential employers, help set up interview appointments and hope that the chemistry works.

Lendman Associates, one such agency in Norfolk, Va., held a meeting over the weekend in Washington, D. C. It was attended by 300 officers and 20 companies.

Meeting Set Here

A similar conference for 200 men and 16 companies, under the sponsorship of the Gilbert Lane Personnel Agency of New York, will take place Friday and Saturday at the Summit Hotel here.

"We're holding 45 career weekends in six cities this year, and we have 2,800 junior officers in our active file right now," says Steven M. Campbell, executive vice president of Lendman. "Our percentage of placement is 42 per cent." (Campus recruiters usually count on a 25 per cent ratio of acceptances to offers.)

"We obtain the names of applicants through national advertising, through project officers on the posts and through field recruiting trips by our staff," says Mrs. Irene Redleaf, conference director of Gilbert Lane. "These junior officers are about five or six years older than college graduates, they've usually been in some sort of supervisory position and they've already shown some type of leadership potential."

Companies Pay Fee

At these two-day and three-day recruiting weekends, the junior officers pay no fees and are either guests of the agencies or are charged a reduced rate for their expenses. The companies typically pay the agencies a fee of $500 to participate in each session with pre-screened young officers plus 10 per cent of the starting annual salary for each new man employed.

"This has been our most effective source, as far as agency recruiting is concerned," points out Wayne Snyder, supervisor of organization development and training for the Continental Can Company's paperboard and kraft paper division. "These men have their goals set and they've got this boyish, kiddish, green thing out of the way. They're ready to go to work."

Corporate recruiters indicate that the over-all cost of hiring through these weekends is less than it would cost through the regular on-campus sessions. In addition, they cite the greater seriousness of the candidates and their interest in other-than-monetary rewards in a total compensation package.

Therefore, many companies have stepped up their participation in these conferences for officers in the armed services and have made such activities a regular, rather than a supplementary, part of their recruiting programs.

The progress of junior officer recruiting can be measured both by the large number of returning companies and the expansion of the agencies. For example, Lendman—established by Ernest Lendman, a former seaman who wound up hiring a couple of retired admirals to work for him—began specializing in military recruiting about three years ago. Today it employs 50 people, has branch offices in San Diego, Calif., and Washington and boasts a growth rate of 400 per cent annually in the last two years.

March 17, 1969

For Roche of G.M. Happiness is a 10% Surcharge

By WILLIAM SERRIN

DETROIT.

LIKE the rest of Detroit's automobile men, James M. Roche of General Motors has always been a free trader. The industry's managers are adamantly opposed—in principle—to governmental interference in business. Earlier this year Roche himself said that he did not believe wage-price controls would work.

Auto executives also oppose protectionism, knowing that it is a double-edged sword that can cut against, as well as for, Detroit. They have traditionally been aggressive and confident men who are certain that they can compete with any country in the manufacture of automobiles.

But Roche, G.M.'s chairman, has lamented for months that the industry was imperiled by a grave "crisis of cost." The price of everything was up, materials, parts, labor—particularly labor, he complained. Foreign manufacturers were plundering the American market, this in the land that gave the world the automobile. Like the rest of American industry, Roche said, the car makers were being forced to price themselves out of world markets.

American manufacturers were reeling from foreign imports, true, but what Roche failed to note was that a lot of this was their own fault. The industry dislikes small cars, simply because there is little, if any, profit in them. Big cars are what Detroit likes, with lots of chrome, steel and profitable options. And while it sat back and built these cars, convinced that only big cars were what the consumer wanted, a sixth of the market was seized by the foreigners.

And who is trying to bail the industry out of this dilemma of its own making? The Federal Government, which the industry has always insisted stay clear of its operations. President Nixon's new economic policy freezing wages and prices for 90 days gives the automobile industry a special bonanza: a 10 per cent surcharge on imports plus an end to the 7 per cent auto excise tax.

And what industry is the Government turning to in its attempt to spur the economy? The automobile industry, whose products create a major share of the pollution in the nation and which, a growing number of critics (some of them in the Government) point out, is responsible for other social ills as well, from highway deaths, to urban congestion and the paving of the countryside.

ROCHE is now a happy man. "Nobody likes wage and price controls," he says, but "under the circumstances something had to be done. The President's economic program should go far to accelerate the recovery pace, while establishing a base for greater price stability." And he adds: "It will mean sacrifice for everyone, but everyone will ultimately gain."

According to Roche, the policy should bring a boost of 5 to 10 per cent in Detroit's domestic sales for 1972—an increase of between 425,000 and 850,000 vehicles over the 8.5 million the industry expects to sell this year. But that, he notes, is a rough guess. The surcharge, he predicts, will certainly make the American subcompacts, G.M.'s Vega and Ford's Pinto, more competitive with the imports, led by the Germans with their Volkswagens and the particularly prolific Japanese with their Datsuns and Toyotas. He foresees a reduction of foreign auto sales in the U.S., but declines to predict the number.

It would be a mistake, however, to expect any quick jump in employment in the auto industry because of the President's programs. While officials at all the companies say employment will rise, no one will say when, or predict the size of the increase. The companies are just now beginning production of 1972 models and thus have yet to meet full production schedules.

Industry analysts say that if the expected growth in demand for cars occurs, it will be late this month or early October before the companies increase production, and even then, that increase will probably be met by more overtime, not additional hiring.

General Motors takes its responsibilities to America very seriously. In the wake of the freeze, the company declared that it was rolling

---

WILLIAM SERRIN is a reporter for The Detroit Free Press. His book on the 1970 United Automobile Workers strike at General Motors will be published early next year.

back the 1972 price increases which it had announced in early August. With a flourish that befits the industry leader, G.M. proclaimed that it would "cooperate fully with President Nixon's declaration of a national emergency to strengthen the U.S. international economic position." Ford, Chrysler and American Motors had no choice but to follow suit.

DESPITE its evident cooperation with a policy of Government intervention in the economy, G.M. did not emerge from the historic week without criticism. Four days after the company rolled back prices, its most effective and persistent critic, Ralph Nader, was again condemning G.M. Nader suggested it was possible that the company had advance knowledge of the freeze and that before it was announced G.M. had sent its new models out to dealers—to be placed on sale at the higher 1972 prices—in order to "slide in under the deadline."

Nader noted that Treasury Secretary John Connally admitted he had talked to Roche before the freeze was implemented. Connally insisted that he telephoned Roche only to obtain "details of their pricing," in an attempt to gain "some facts" about the industry. From such a conversation, Nader said, "you can pretty well tell what is coming." He conceded that he had only circumstantial evidence to support his contention. He said that "everything I can get indicates" that Nixon's statement that each 100,000 additional automobiles sold means 25,000 jobs was obtained from the manufacturers.

At a hearing of the Senate-House economic committee, Senator William Proxmire said Nader had made a "very, very serious charge." Could Nader document the accusation? No, he said, adding that "the burden of proof is on the Treasury."

Once again there must have been scurrying back at the General Motors Building in Detroit. Once again men were on the telephones or walking briskly in the halls; the elevator traffic between the 11th floor, the public relations floor, and the 14th floor, the executive floor, was heavy. Roche directed a statement be released: "General Motors had absolutely no advance knowledge of the President's economic program. Mr. Nader's allegations are false."

Connally had called him, Roche says, but on Sunday afternoon just a few hours before Nixon's announcement. He believed, as a result of that conversation, that some action might be coming out of Washington and, when he heard that Nixon was to make a television address at 8 that night, he expected something. Roche says that when he heard of the freeze he was, like millions of Americans, at home with his son and grandchildren, watching the President on TV.

JAMES M. ROCHE, chairman of the world's largest industrial corporation, a man about whom, characteristically, little is known despite the position he holds and the criticism he has received, is the very model of a General Motors man. In his route to becoming one of the nation's highest-paid industrialists.* Roche embodies that particularly American myth that if one works hard, if one plugs away, he will make it to the top. He is a man, as Peter F. Drucker has said of the modern corporation man, to whom the corporation is both servant and master.

He reaches 65 this December, the mandatory retirement age at G.M. His successor seems almost certain to be 61-year-old Richard Gerstenberg, now company vice chairman and a finance specialist whose particular experience is needed at the helm, it is believed, because of the problems of costs and profits that are certain to confront the corporation in coming years. Gerstenberg, who joined General Motors a few months after his graduation from the University of Michigan in 1931, has remained with the company all his life. Like Roche, he is a G.M. man through and through. In his dealings with the corporation's critics and his reactions to social pressures, he is likely to be conservative.

Acting under some of the same pressures in his four years as chairman, Roche displeased many people both within and outside the corporation. While he opened some new avenues for General Motors, he was the target of more vilification than any chairman since Alfred P. Sloan, who was attacked during the tumultuous union organizing days of the nineteen-thirties. Robert Townsend, author of the bestselling "Up the Organization," has called Roche an "idiot" who "lost his guts years ago." Richard Ottinger, the former New York Congressman who now heads an organization called Grassroots Action, described him as the "leading Neanderthal man of the business world," and accused him of "leading the corporation down a path that will certainly spell its own destruction and endanger the very system he claims to be championing." Michael Hamlin, a revolutionary black union leader in Detroit, calls Roche "the Jay Gould of the 20th century."

Nader describes him as the "perfect organization man for the turmoil General Motors has gone through in the last five years; he gives the demeanor of a venerable deacon. He doesn't alienate people . . . he's very dedicated; he's got a personal life above reproach; he's religious, and so on." But, Nader insists: "You've seen those people in charge of concentration camps—by that I mean personal qualities have nothing to do with a man's ability to assume an organizational ethic which is very cruel and very fraudulent in its impact upon people."

In the opinion of many people within G.M., on the other hand—from the short-haired, middle-class young men it recruits as low-level white-collar workers, to the top managers—Roche has been too soft with the critics and, what is more, must accept, as chairman, the blame for an eroded profit picture. There are men within the company who today still wonder why Roche did it—why he went to Washington in March, 1966, to apologize before the nation for the corporation's hiring of private detectives to trail Nader, a man whom at least one G.M. executive considers a Communist and a fascist. Roche, they insist, made Ralph Nader and, in so doing, made the safety issue, the pollution issue, the consumer movement. That spectacle of Roche humbling himself, humbling the corporation, sickens them to this day.

Nevertheless, it can be argued that Roche, directing the corporation through one of its most perilous eras, a time of unprecedented attack, has done a masterful job in de-

*With stock options, Roche's pay in a good year approaches $800,000. In 1969, he made $250,000 in salary and fees, plus a $405,000 bonus. He took a cut of probably $400,000 in income last year when, as a result of the new U.A.W. contract, the company eliminated all bonuses. He also owns 17,077 shares of G.M. stock.

fending the corporation against its enemies. Some say he has blunted the criticism by half measures, others that he is a genuinely concerned man who has begun to move the corporation, however reluctantly and slowly.

For example, under his leadership, the number of blacks employed by the corporation rose noticeably. Minority-group workers (most of them black) now make up 15.3 per cent of the work force, compared to 13.3 just before Roche took over in 1967. There are about 5,000 black white-collar employes, 3 per cent of the total in this category. There are 15 black dealers, compared to two before Roche. There is even a black on the corporation's board of directors, Dr. Leon Sullivan. Under Roche, G.M. has also donated funds to build low-cost housing and placed money in black banks.

All this may not sound too impressive, until one examines the corporation's previous record. Dr. David Lewis, once a highly regarded publicity man for G.M. and now a professor of business history at the University of Michigan, recalls that in the early nineteen-sixties there were only a handful of blacks employed by General Motors at its headquarters, among some 3,500 workers. Lewis says that "Ralph Bunche could literally not have gotten a job as a janitor in those days." He recalls attending a seminar at the University of Wisconsin on problems that would occur during the decade; one problem, the men at the seminar said, would be a rise in black aspirations. Lewis says he returned to General Motors and in a conversation with a vice president asked what would happen if Ebony or Jet magazine sent a reporter to Detroit to probe black employment at General Motors. He recalls that the vice president said, "We'll just have to get some of the boys over in public relations to put on blackface and put on a damn good minstrel show." Behind this joke, Lewis says, was the management's attitude that "G.M. is a white man's corporation, and it's going to stay a white man's corporation."

THERE seems to be an immutable law about General Motors: it does not change. It gives the appearance of change, makes superficial changes, bends with the winds of change (as Roche says, "in line with the change that has occurred in this country"). But on fundamental, meaningful issues, it does not change at all. The critics who want such fundamental change, Roche says, are misguided and dangerous. "Many of the critics have the professed aim to alter the role and influence of corporations and corporate management in and upon American society," he says. "Their philosophy is antagonistic to our American ideas of private property and individual responsibility."

Roche wisely refuses to single out the critics he is talking about. Quite obviously he includes the young men and women of "Campaign G.M.," who demanded an increased shareholder voice in the running of the corporation. He also means the people who demand that General Motors close down its assembly plant and manufacturing operations in the apartheid nation of South Africa, Ralph Nader, the other critics he has helped spawn and all the many people far to the left of Nader.

When critics demand greater public participation in the management of General Motors or any business enterprise, Roche says that if America allows public groups "to operate our private enterprises . . . then we're really talking about a different philosophy of government." The demands of the enemies of the corporation, he says, "have to be opposed to the best of our ability."

ROCHE was born in 1906 in Elgin, Ill., a quiet, tree-shaded Midwestern town some 50 miles west of Chicago, a town straight out of the writings of William Inge or Sherwood Anderson. As a boy, he peddled the local paper, worked in a notions store after school and on Saturdays, and mowed lawns, all to make extra money for the family. This work he considers a valuable experience, and he says that today, when so many young people have so much given to them, "I feel very sorry for any kid who finishes high school and is sent off to college without having had some kind of job."

In 1918, when he was 11, a calamity struck the family; his father, an undertaker, died in the terrible flu epidemic that swept America. His mother, a teacher, took over support of the family; they worked hard and got by, and to this day people in Elgin remember the courage of the Roche family.

Young Jim was a good, but not a gifted student; perseverance, not brilliance, won him good grades. When he was graduated in 1923 from Elgin High School, the yearbook, the Maroon, inexplicably called him "the sheik of '23." Because of the loss of his father, he could not attend college, and when he left high school he accepted a position as a clerk with the gas and electric company in Aurora 22 miles away. At night he studied accounting and economics by correspondence from LaSalle University.

The automobile business was booming in America, and in 1927, at the age of 21, he obtained a new position as a statistician with the Cadillac Motor Division in Chicago. Within a year he was named assistant Chicago branch manager. Soon he was recognized as an expert on business management. He was given positions in Boston and New York, and, in 1932, at the depth of the Great Depression, was brought to the Cadillac home office in Detroit.

These were perhaps Cadillac's toughest years, for, as men with the company at the time recall with some laughter, Cadillacs did not sell well during the Depression. The top General Motors management, it is said, wanted to shut the division down, but the hard-working division manager, Nicholas Dreystadt, convinced the central staff executives to keep Cadillac open. For 11 months Cadillac built no cars at all. Dreystadt directed a retooling at the Cadillac factory; the new model sold well and saved the division.

Roche worked in sales during the Depression and early war years. Then in May 1943, with the division building up its work force as it increased its defense production, Roche was named to the new and important post of director of personnel, with responsibilities that included negotiating with the new union the corporation had recognized, the U.A.W.

Roche performed admirably, a reserved, gentlemanly man who, within the corporation's definition, wished the best possible conditions for the workers. To many union

Sayings of Chairman Roche

Chairman James Roche did nothing for General Motors' reputation as a bastion of white conservatives last May when he was caught in a slip of the tongue at the company's annual meeting.

A young minister from Dayton, Ohio, asked him from the floor why the corporation had not sent representatives to explain on a Dayton television program G.M.'s opposition to the demands of a reformist stockholder group, Campaign G.M.

Roche said the corporation was not interested in television debates. Why not? the minister asked. Wasn't G.M. interested in taking its case before the public? Wasn't G.M. a public corporation?

"We are a public corporation," Roche declared, "owned by free, white . . ."

People gasped. Laughter spread through the audience. "Right on!" some of the critics cried.

Then Roche continued: "*Umm* . . . and . . . and . . . and black and yellow people all over the world."

Though Roche seems to have been trapped by a familiar racist expression, he later said he had been referring to the company's worldwide operations and had stumbled when the audience laughed. Few people believed him, of course. While not accusing Roche of being a racist, Joseph Onek, a member of Campaign G.M., observed that the slip was typical of the "country club mentality" at G.M.—W. S.

men used to tough, unbending company men, Roche was a welcome change; Leonard Woodcock, president of the U.A.W., recalls, "Jim Roche was highly regarded by our people when he was at Cadillac. . . . He is a thoroughly decent man."* At Cadillac, Roche became upset by separate drinking fountains, this in F.D.R.'s arsenal of democracy, and by the refusal of whites to eat with blacks. If they had to eat with blacks, or if blacks were promoted above them, the whites said, they would strike. The union was little help in this matter, but Roche went ahead on his own, risking trouble with the workers, and he succeeded in bringing some integration to the Cadillac plants.

Opinion differs on whether Roche in those years seemed destined for high corporate office. Drucker remembers Roche, whom he met while studying the corporation at its request during World War II, as a "very junior man, very junior." Then in his late thirties, Roche seemed to Drucker a man ticketed for only staff work, a man who lacked the forcefulness and directness necessary for command. "Nobody was more surprised than I was when Jim Roche emerged as the chief operating officer," Drucker says. But Donald E. Ahrens, a Cadillac executive of the time who was to go on to become Cadillac division manager himself, says he always saw in Roche a man destined for the general managership and perhaps a job on the central staff at the General Motors Building. "Whenever another job came up," Ahrens said, "you always picked Jim."

Roche rose steadily, although not quickly. In 1949, he was made director of public relations, as well as head of personnel, at Cadillac. In 1950 he became general sales manager and directed the division to its first 100,000-vehicle year. In 1955, when the automobile industry set a record of 7.9 million in sales, —this was the era of the tailfin and of American chrome —Cadillac sold 143,000 units, a record that was to stand until the nineteen-sixties. Roche was named Cadillac general manager and a General Motors vice president in 1957. He was promoted to the corporate staff in 1960—after 33 years with Cadillac—as vice president of what is now the marketing staff, with responsibilities for sales, marketing, service, advertising, parts and dealer relationships.

By now Roche was a protégé of Frederic Donner, the General Motors chairman, who, while he is remembered by many others as a most acerbic, steely man, is remembered by Roche, understandably, as one of the warmest, most friendly men Roche has ever met.

IN 1962, Roche was jumped over a number of senior men and named executive vice president in charge of overseas operations. Three years later, tapped by Donner, he was elevated to the General Motors presidency. Perhaps Roche would have been merely one of the presidents listed in the corporation archives, his picture in a long row of executives' portraits on the walls of board rooms—a level he could be proud to have achieved, but still an anonymous man—were it not for an intense young lawyer educated at Princeton and Harvard, Ralph Nader.

In Washington, Nader had finished a book on the automobile industry, working feverishly and turning it out in 10 weeks. General Motors runs as excellent intelligence system and knew the book was coming out. They knew something of Nader too, that he was a foe of the auto makers and had written articles against the industry.

In November, 1965, before Nader's "Unsafe at Any Speed" was published, Aloysius F. Power, the head of G.M.'s legal department, ordered an investigation into Nader's background. A New York detective, Vincent Gillen, a former F.B.I. agent, was retained for the investigation, for which General Motors ultimately paid $6,700. Power later said he had ordered the inquiry because Nader was a "mystery man" and because, although he was a lawyer, he did not maintain a law office. He also said that the corporation wanted to find out whether Nader was connected with lawyers pushing cases against General Motors. It was, it can be said, simply a normal action.

But Nader began to report that he was receiving anonymous phones calls and that he was being tailed.

The landlady at his northwest Washington apartment, his stockbroker and an old law professor at Harvard were all visited by apparent private detectives A New Hampshire lawyer who had been injured in an auto crash, and to whom Nader dedicated his book, was visited by Gillen himself. The lawyer said Gillen asked whether Nader had a driver's license, whether he had left-wing political affiliations and whether he was anti-Semitic. Why had Nader never married?

One day while Nader was in a drugstore a few blocks from his apartment, he was approached by a pretty young brunette, who asked him to speak to some friends of hers who often gathered to discuss foreign affairs. Nader refused. Another time, when Nader stopped in a Safeway grocery store to buy a package of cookies, a young girl asked him to come to her apartment to help her move heavy furniture. He refused, and the girl left, asking no one else in the store to help her, although there were a number of people there.

In early March, 1966, stories broke saying that Nader was being investigated by private detectives. Industry men, including two at General Motors, denied they had taken any part in the investigation. Then, the night of March 8, as lights burned late in the General Motors Building and yet another denial was being drafted, a corporation man contacted Roche, who was staying late to handle this important matter.

"The corporation Roche directs is a wonderfully fascinating institution, almost incomprehensibly large, exceedingly powerful, rich, secretive, inbred, smug, full of politics and personalities, as worthy of study as the Kremlin, Peking or the Catholic Church, all of which, in ways, it resembles."

"There is somehing you must know," he said. "We did have detectives investigating Nader."

The next night, shortly before 11 P.M., after the first editions of morning newspapers were on the streets, the company released a statement written at Roche's direction: General Motors, it said, had conducted a "routine investigation through a reputable law firm to determine whether Ralph Nader was acting on behalf of litigants or their attorneys in Corvair-design cases pending against General Motors." Such investigations, the statement continued, were "a well-known and accepted practice in the legal profession."

THIS was a long, dark night for General Motors, one of the most difficult moments in its history. Donner was away, visiting New Zealand and Australia, a most comfortable spot for him to be. Some of the top men in the corporation wanted to somehow camouflage what General Motors had done. Others, particularly men in the legal department whose necks were on the line, wanted to attack, to say, yes, the corporation had conducted the investigation, but this was what any corporation would do under similar circumstances.

Roche listened to all this advice. Finally, he said there was only one course of action: *"We must go to Washington and apologize."*

Many of the men were shocked. We must not apologize, they said. General Mo-

---

*Last November, when G.M. negotiators refused to meet the U.A.W.'s demands to end the union's strike at the corporation—and it seemed that the strike might drag into December and perhaps through the Christmas and New Year's holidays — Woodcock made a secret trip to see Roche and spell out exactly what he believed the union needed to end the strike. After their 20-minute talk, Roche directed the company to meet Woodcock's needs: a 51-cent average wage increase, an unlimited cost-of-living escalator, the start of a $500-a-month pension program. That package set the pattern for the large settlements in the aluminum, can and steel industries this year, which, in turn, were a major reason the Nixon Administration resorted to a wage-price freeze.

tors must never apologize.

"Goddamit," Roche said. *"What the hell do you want me to do? This is the only thing that can be done."*

Two weeks later, on March 22, Roche appeared before a Congressional subcommittee headed by Senator Abraham Ribicoff that was conducting hearings on auto safety. "This investigation [of Nader] was initiated, conducted and completed without my knowledge or consent, and without the knowledge or consent of any member of our governing committee," he said. Such an act, he said, was unworthy of General Motors. "To the extent that G.M. bears responsibility," Roche concluded, "I want to apologize here and now to the members of the subcommittee and Mr. Nader. I sincerely hope that these apologies will be accepted."

It was a fine performance. Ribicoff praised Roche. Nader, who later settled a $26-million lawsuit out of court for $425,000 over the incident, himself concedes that Roche was the perfect man to make the apology—a "kindly, grandfather figure."

BUT Roche did not enjoy that moment. Even today, he cannot erase it. Last March, when a reporter said to Roche, "I guess it is about five years this month since you were put in the position of going to Washington to testify before the Ribicoff subcommittee regarding Mr. Nader," Roche said. "It's been five years ago March 22, 10 A.M."

Roche handled himself well in the months that followed the Nader incident, a difficult period which brought new attacks on the corporation and the automobile industry and passage of the Highway Safety Act in May, 1966. He had made no enemies within the corporation, and few critics said any harsh words about him. As Donner and other top men looked ahead, sure that the pressures on the corporation would only mount, it was apparently clear that they could be best be met by the gentlemanly Roche. In November, 1967, when Donner stepped down, the board, at Donner's request, named Roche to replace him.

In appearance, Roche is an unlikely man for his job, a soft-looking man with soft hands and soft face, somewhat soft now, too, in the neck and stomach, with a bad leg due to varicose veins. He is a soft-talking man whose voice sometimes breaks into stutters, causing impolite people to laugh, and whose hands, when he is nervous, tremble like summer leaves. On television, even the stanchest corporation men admit, he resembles a wooden dummy; he knows this, but he is a game man, and he makes such appearances as a matter of duty, just as, at the 1970 annual meeting, he stood for seven hours confronting the critics from Campaign G.M., refusing a stool or a glass of water, believing that it was his responsibility to face the enemies of the corporation.

He "looks like an undertaker," says a man who used to work for him, but "underneath he is hard as nails, the mailed-fist-in-the-velvet-glove sort of thing." It is said he has never forgotten a name or missed an appointment. Another former employe says, "I think Jim has been very much maligned by calling him a cold fish. Jim is a very warm individual when you get to know him. Very human. He has saved many individuals and actually saved some marriages, saved some families, by some of the things he has done. But he never wants anybody to know about it." About Roche's talents, this man adds: "He's the most brilliant man I know. He can scan a row of figures when you're going over budgets—just run down them and say, here's a mistake."

While in background so much like those who reach the top at General Motors—a self-made man from small-town America—Roche is personally unlike his predecessors. Sloan was aloof and impersonal. Hard of hearing, he was embarrassed and uncomfortable in the presence of men he had not known for years; he would not talk to people he did not know. Harlow Curtice was cold and tough, a man who liked to chop people up, and enjoyed, it is said, making the unemotional decisions that businessmen so often make. Frederic Donner, according to a former G.M. executive, was flinty and demanding, a man who liked to obtain information on his subordinates and tuck the information away for when it might be needed. In retirement he still plays a dominant role in corporate affairs.

If Roche resembles any of the former leaders in personality, he probably is most like William Knudsen, the old General Motors president who was an eminently pleasant fellow (although Roche is a much finer administrator), or perhaps Charles E. Wilson, a more likable man than he is remembered to have been, a man who, when he first went to Washington as Secretary of Defense called Senators "you men," and who is remembered for saying, "What's good for General Motors is good for the country." (He was a victim of sloppy reporting. What he really said was, "For years I thought what was good for the country was good for General Motors and vice versa.")

Each of the top men at General Motors has, it seems, been admirably suited to lead the corporation at the particular time he took over. Sloan was a genius at organization and marketing at a time when the corporation needed an organizational plan so that unprofitable operations could be shut down and a chain of command established, and at a time when the corporation needed to put together a product line that would take full advantage of consumer tastes. Knudsen was a production man in an era when the corporation needed to redesign the Chevrolet and establish new plants to overtake Henry Ford's Model T. Wilson was an engineer at a time—World War II and the postwar years—when engineering talents

TOP BRASS—At the 1970 stockholders' meeting, Roche, right, lines up with vice chairman Richard Gerstenberg, center, the man who is expected to succeed him as chairman when he retires, and president Edward N. Cole.

were needed, first to direct retooling for defense production and then for the creation of the postwar line. Curtice was a master salesman, this in the nineteen-fifties, the time of American chrome, the big-selling years when a salesman's talents were needed. Donner was a finance expert, well-suited to lead when money was tight and, afterward, when the corporation, making money easily, was expanding its overseas markets.

THE corporation Roche directs is a wonderfully fascinating institution, almost incomprehensibly large, exceedingly powerful, rich, secretive, inbred, smug, full of politics, and personalities, as worthy of study, it may be argued, as the Kremlin, Peking or the Catholic Church, all of which, in ways, it resembles.

The men who run General Motors conceive of themselves as the kind of men who built America, the kind of men responsible for the good, abundant American life. They are Middle-Western, friendly, likable, the kind of men who make fine fishing and golf companions; civilized men, men with whom it is pleasant to drink one or two Scotches or to see a baseball game. Yet, they are insulated men, cut off from contemporary currents of thought.

They came out of high school in the nineteen-twenties or thirties and joined the corporation; often it was their first job. Like Roche, some of them did not attend college. They remember the Depression, but most of the executives kept their jobs in that period; for them the Depression is not the horrible scar that it is for the men on the assembly lines. They have worked, every working day of their lives, 10, 12, 14 hours a day, rising early in the morning, 5 or 6 o'clock, sliding into their huge cars and driving down the freeways from their Bloomfield Hills, Southfield, Birmingham, or Grosse Pointe homes to their offices in the General Motors Building often arriving as early as 7. They stay in their offices all day, many times leaving only for lunch in the executive dining room on the 14th floor or in the basement cafeteria (if they want a quiet, nonalcoholic meal), or across the street at Eckner's Chop House or the private Recess Club, or downtown at the Detroit Athletic Club or Detroit Club. Some men who have not forgotten their backgrounds stay at their desks, eating, say, a sandwich and an apple. Then, when the day ends—for most of them this is between 6 and 7, perhaps later—they take the elevator downstairs, walk to their cars and speed back down the freeways to their homes. Many of the wives are active in charity work. Few of their sons enter the automobile industry. Both of Roche's sons are attorneys, though his daughter is the wife of a Florida Chevrolet dealer.

The G.M. bureaucracy is not unlike the Army. There are formalities, uniforms (blue or gray suits, usually white shirts and a dark, narrow tie), military-like courtesies and chains of command. Not surprisingly, many of the men become fawning in manner.

Dr. David Lewis recalls the day in his years as a G.M. publicity man when he was sitting on a toilet in the men's room on the 11th floor of the G.M. headquarters. A colleague burst in, apparently glanced down the row of stalls until he spied a pair of shoes beneath the half door, and cried, "Is that you, Dave?" Lewis said that it was, and the colleague declared that he was wanted on the 14th floor, the executive floor. Lewis emerged at normal speed, and found the man staring at him excitedly, holding his coat. "You're wanted on the *14th floor*," the colleague cried. Lewis says, "Everybody's always talking about the worker's dignity. Well, hell, what about my dignity?"

Once when Harlow Curtice was president, a story goes, a General Motors public-relations man, having discovered that Curtice had a fondness for smoked oysters, followed him for an hour or more through a Bloomfield Hills cocktail party, carrying a tray of smoked oysters—always a step behind and two to the right, like a general's aide, so that Curtice, without looking, could select a tasty oyster when he wished. Lewis says it astonished him in his years at General Motors to see 40- and 50-year-old men, when they received a request to report to an executive on the 14th floor, "dogtrotting" down the corridor, out the door to the elevators, like Western Union boys.

A man who worked for the corporation during the time when Roche went to Washington to apologize to Nader, says, "I found them very smug, very suspicious and hostile, very self-contained and quite impenetrable. A new idea was very difficult to get discussed and received, much less adopted." He says, "There used to be an expression at General Motors, especially about the P.R. operation, that you were part of the Mafia, the mob. And there was something to it. Because if you questioned the group, goddamn it, you'd get your arms cut off . . . . I've seen very good men, who should have known better, who were independent-minded and bright, really just louse up."

In the late nineteen-sixties, a small group of young, middle-echelon executives met for a time in New York and drew up a reform program which they hoped to present to like-minded employes and, eventually, take to the top men in an attempt to promote minority hiring, financial assistance to black capitalist groups and diligence in combating safety and pollution problems. The reformers failed. One of them, Ken Christy, who edited the old house organ called General Motors World, recalls:

"We fell flat. . . . We would show this to hand-selected people that we knew . . . we sat around and picked a few to widen the circle a bit, but we didn't pick up anyone. They were afraid to tie their name to such a radical, frightening thing as a reform group. And that taught us really how futile it all can be and how sad that state of affairs is. It [the corporation] had taken what we thought were fairly liberal, socially conscious, responsible people with some brains and scared them into submission."

Ultimately, Dr. Lewis adds, "the nonconformists either leave or compromise."

INTERESTINGLY, a man who has many kind words for General Motors is Drucker, who, it can be argued, has a more historical perspective from which to judge the corporation than many of its critics.

"This idea that G.M. is insensitive, it just isn't true," Drucker says. Sloan, he says, "was deeply concerned about the unemployed, about training. The General Motors Institute [the corporation's training school at Flint, Mich.] was Sloan's creation: now that is not the idea of a man who did not have responsibility." Drucker says that G.M. "single-handedly developed the standards for safer highways" and that its actions in the nineteen-twenties in supplying capital to its dealers predated the philosophy of the Small Business Administration. "Look," he adds, "nobody has pointed out that when it comes to blacks, G.M. has probably done the pioneering work in industry. G.M. was the first one to tackle minority employment—and fight its own foremen on the issue. And has anybody mentioned that? No."

The fact is, as Drucker notes, "One does not get promoted at General Motors for good intentions." Roche's primary duty is maximization of profits. "Profits, of course," says a vice president of another auto firm. "That's what it's all about."

Nader, however, with consuming contempt for the corporation, is relentless in his criticism. What is needed, he says, is a change in the men who lead the corporation, but he says that he has searched the corporation's junior and upper-middle management for far-sighted, progressive men and found few of them.

"There is absolutely nobody on the horizon who shows a different stance, a different attitude, a different philosophy. The organizational impact on people in the company is really phenomenal. And you know it comes from the fact that you don't argue with success. It's the whole philosophy of General Motors Institute, which teaches the students the industry way. It's the whole philosophy of not supporting a graduate degree program, say, or research programs in automobile engineering. If you ever see anybody with an automotive Ph.D., you know he was educated in Europe."

Nader sees victory for his consumer movement. Looking back at the other institution that is, at times, critical of General Motors, the U.A.W., Nader says: "All labor wanted was a larger piece of the pie. And G.M. could give labor a large piece of the pie if it took it from the consumer, by

INCIDENT—Ralph Nader denounces the auto industry before a Senate subcommittee in 1966. He became such a gadfly that G.M. hired detectives to investigate him. Subsequently, Roche (right, with attorney Theodore Sorensen) apologized to the committee.

monopolizing, parallel pricing, inadequate bumpers—all the things it uses to jack up prices. The worker has, in effect, been squeezing more and more out of the corporation, which has been squeezing more and more out of the consumer—which is often the worker himself, which is why wage levels don't often mean as much as they should."

He argues that G.M., by saying it is concerned with safety, the environment, consumer protection, is following a "flank strategy" of trying to steal issues from the consumer movement. But he insists this strategy will fail, because there is no "centralized leadership" in the movement, and so no bureaucracy can develop that will become too entwined with management.

MANY critics suggest that the automobile industry is, at best, no longer a growth industry, and, at worst, is a dying industry. Drucker says that General Motors is the "last monument to yesterday . . . you in Detroit are as obsolete as the English midlands." And Nader says that G.M. as an organization is right now "where the Yankees were in 1963."

Roche, of course, rejects these contentions:

"Some people are referring to the end of the 'love affair' between Americans and the automobile. I don't think that the public's love affair with the automobile is over. But I do think it has matured to the point where the utility value [of the auto] is given more consideration today perhaps than any time in the past, primarily because of the many different uses to which the automobile is being put today.

"The fact remains that the average American likes the personal mobility of an automobile. We're going to have to find different ways of handling some phases of the problem. For example, the parking facilities, the flow of traffic, things like that. But I think the automobile is going to be with us for a long time."

Cars are becoming safer all the time, he contends, and soon the automobile will be almost pollution-free. But all this, he says, takes time, and the costs must be borne by the consumer. Some critics "think we can wave a magic wand and come up with an electric car or steam car and improve the internal-combustion engine. If we knew how to do it, we'd do it and get it behind us, believe me."

In the 75th year of automobile production in America, the car makers are wary as they talk of the future.

Before increasing capital investment or bringing in additional workers, the companies will want to be sure that the President's new policies are causing a real sales boom, not just a spurt. And it might take the entire 90-day period of the freeze to give them the picture they need to make that decision. Thus, any new hiring might not begin until almost December and perhaps after the first of the year.

While the Nixon Administration says that each 100,000 domestic cars means 25,000 jobs, these jobs are not solely automobile jobs, but include almost every conceivable position of employment linked to the auto industry—from the farmer whose cotton is used in the manufacture of seats to the carhop at the drive-in restaurant. G.M. simply cannot say, for example, how many new jobs might be created at the company if it makes an additional 100,000 cars in 1972. Perhaps none.

G.M. president Edward N. Cole points out that the company could build 300,000 to 400,000 additional units in 1972 by overtime alone, and certainly this figure would represent a substantial part, if not all, of G.M.'s increased production.

Auto analysts point out, additionally, that it would be foolish to expect any long-term employment gains in the industry. Traditionally, they point out, the producers have worked to cut labor costs by reducing the work force; more cars are being built today with fewer workers than a decade ago, they say, and this trend is certain to continue, and probably increase, in the next decade.

Roche says that following the freeze probably "some kind of mechanism"—he says a wage-price review board is one possibility—must be created to continue restraint on wages and prices. "We have started down this road to try to contain inflation," he says, "and I hope we don't get sidetracked."

While Roche declines to say whether the corporation intends to raise prices after the freeze — if it can — certainly higher prices can be expected, the highest that the industry can push through. Roche points out that the 90-day freeze prohibits the corporation from recovering money lost from the higher cost of tooling and manufacturing 1972 autos (although it is likely that most of the costs of the 1970 settlement with the U.A.W. were recovered in the 1971 increases).

Within a week of the start of the wage-price freeze, Roche told a reporter that stringent air-pollution-control regulations in California — 25 per cent of the 1972 models sold in the state must undergo emission control tests on the assembly line—would mean that California cars would cost the company more than cars sold elsewhere, and that the company intended to recover these costs by increased prices. "There is nothing" in the freeze, Roche said, "that requires us to add equipment at no increase."

NOT long ago Roche was asked what he wanted to be remembered for. What would he want to have inscribed on a plaque in the lobby of the General Motors Building when he is gone?

"We do not erect plaques," he said.

But surely, he was asked, he will want his work recalled? Surely he wants to be remembered?

Yes, he said, when he retires he will want the "satisfaction of having had the responsibility for guiding the corporation through this difficult period." And hopefully will be given some credit for "having recognized some of these problems and doing something about them."

There is no sacrifice that cannot be made, Alfred P. Sloan Jr. said years ago, no demand that cannot be met, if one is to fully serve the corporation. In both Sloan's terms and his own, Roche has fulfilled his responsibilities as a family head, an American and a General Motors man. ■

September 12, 1971

Humanizing Executives: A Low Priority

Concerns Put Little Stress On Problem

By WILLIAM D. SMITH

"It made everyone seem so human; as if we all had interests in common."

The speaker was a secretary who had been working for 12 years for the Standard Oil Company (New Jersey). She had just left a meeting called by the company's management to announce to employes that the company's name was being changed to the Exxon Corporation.

The meeting, attended by more than 2,000 of the giant concern's New York-based employes, had opened in an atmosphere of suspicion. It ended with the dominant mood one of fellowship and apparent community of purpose.

The catalytic agent had been almost two hours of frank face-to-face exchange between J. K. Jamieson, Jersey Standard's chairman; Milo Brisco, its president, and the employes. It was an exchange that included a little self-deprecating humor, candid insights into the decision-making process, hints that not all management decisions are *ex cathedra* and pleas for support.

In short, as the girl said, the two men "seemed so human."

Sociologists, management experts and behavioral scientists have urged greater efforts to humanize American industry, including ways of improving the nature of jobs and rekindling human relationships between executives and workers.

Nonetheless, with regard to corporate efforts to humanize executives, a New York Times survey of 30 large corporations indicated a very low priority for the concept. Not one of the companies in the survey had a program dealing with the matter.

Only one concern, Swift & Co., said it had any kind of policy statement. In a management booklet urging managers to have family day parties and open houses it states, "When we learn to know each other, each other's jobs, each other's ideas, each other's families, then we can build a spirit of cooperation and friendship which will help us all do a better job and have a sense of pleasure and satisfaction in doing it."

Many companies said they were aware of the need for creating personal interfaces between executives and workers but that they worked at the matter informally. Some of these companies indicated that it all depended on the individual personality of the executive.

Several companies indicated things were "just fine." The spokesman of one observed: "Our management even rides in the same elevator with employes."

A number of companies gave management conferences and seminars as examples of humanizing programs. The Bethlehem Steel Corporation and E. I. duPont de Nemours & Co. are active in this regard. Many of these companies, however, do not have any programs for executives to come together with the lower-level employes who make up the bulk of the average corporation's work force.

"In a company with more than 60,000 employes you can't expect an important executive to spend his time with the workers," one company spokesman commented. The spokesmen of several other companies had similar explanations.

This apparent corporate apathy is occurring despite increasing evidence of worker alienation and growing public contempt for business. "Big corporations face the worst attitude climate in a decade," the Opinion Research Corporation reported a few weeks ago.

There are indications, however, that pressure to humanize the work environment, of which humanizing executives is only a part, is increasing, according to some experts interviewed.

"The blue-collar revolt, alienated middle management and other social influences on lack of productivity are making companies increasingly aware of facing up to the human element," according to Larry E. Greiner, associate professor of organizational behavior at the

---

The Office Party

In their book "The Imperial Animal," Lionel Tiger and Robin Fox, the highly respected sociologists and anthropologists, call attention to the deep, inherently inescapable need of human beings in large bureaucratic organizations such as corporations to see their leaders, at least occasionally, as fellow human beings rather than as faceless commanders of everyone's destiny. They write:

"Officials spend considerable time protecting themselves as persons against those with whom they interact as office holders. Hence the rule book, and hence the justified charge that systems are more important than the very people whom the systems are alleged to cater....

"The office party is a revealing event, not simply in its apparent aphrodisiac effect; it is a ritual that makes an ironic statement of these strains of being one kind of officer or another. Here are all these people full of valances and antipathies, normally controlled by their rules of work and etiquette of organization; yet the party offers that possibility of reversal which anthropologists describe; The Day of the Lords of Misrule, The Day when the King is Mocked, when the 'officers' serve the 'men.'

"But there is an even deeper reversal going on too: the structure is overturned or mixed up. For a careful, limited few hours the bosses are just people; employes just men and women with rights to the same full grasp of a human occasion as anyone else; particularly the bosses."

Harvard Graduate School of Business Administration.

Arch R. Dooley, the Jesse Philips Professor of Manufacturing at the Harvard Business School, noted that "the need to personalize is definitely coming back into management."

Many companies consider personalizing or humanizing top management as part of the over-all corporate communications effort. As such, the chief and sometimes only method used is through corporate publications such as annual reports, employe newsletters and in-house magazines. Some companies indicated that they thought this effort was sufficient. One company spokesman said, "Well, it isn't much, but hell, it's all we do."

Another common example of a humanizing effort is plant visits and tours by executives. Again, however, the emphasis often seems to be on communicating with local management rather than the workers. "Local management will pass on to the hourly workers anything of importance," was one comment.

Nonetheless, top management will often physically tour plants, stopping to talk with workers. This can have a positive effect, according to social scientists. But many times the chairman or president is accompanied by a retinue of middle management who shield him physically and emotionally from the work force.

Industries that are reported to be particularly hard hit by worker and public alienation, such as automobiles, steel and oil, according to answers to the survey do not appear to be particularly concerned about creating management-worker interfaces. In each industry, however, there were major exceptions.

In the automobile industry, for the last year and a half workers in many of the Chrysler Corporation's 32 plants have been meeting with their foremen, engineers and production managers to exchange ideas, solve problems and make suggestions about jobs.

Videotape is becoming an important tool in bringing management to the workers in a more or less human fashion. A number of companies have top executives give a videotape presentation on major issues followed by a live question-and-answer period handled by local management.

The effectiveness of any program depends upon the credibility built up through the years by any management, according to Prof. Ivar Berg of the Columbia University Graduate School of Business. "A one-shot effort to make the big man real, no matter how polished, won't work," Professor Berg warned, "unless he has demonstrated through the years an honest effort to relate to the employes."

A number of apparently successful programs are simply the result of company tradition. At the Goodyear Tire and Rubber Company, Russell DeYoung, the present chief executive officer, tours a plant almost every day. A spokesman commented, "The first boss at Goodyear was Frank Sieberling who started the company in his garage. Keeping in contact with the plant and the workers was part and parcel of his running the company. We have only had three executives since and each has simply followed the example set by Sieberling. There is probably not a Goodyear employe in Akron that has not spoken personally to DeYoung. His biggest single contact is the annual Christmas party for employes and their families. Russ doesn't play Santa Claus, but he is there to greet some 5,000 to 10,000 people every Christmas."

Top management's association with workers at all levels is also a tradition at Eli Lilly & Co., a spokesman for the company said. "Personal association with employes is near the top of the list of management duties. Several times outside people have suggested that too much executive time is being taken up by employe relations. But the pattern was set by Mr. Lilly and that is the way it has continued."

Professor Greiner of Harvard would extend the importance of this type of experience even farther. "Top executives have to become aware of the symbolic effects of their behavior. They should realize that they are similar to the father figure in the family and that the example they set is quickly picked up and filtered down the line for good or bad," he said, adding, "My impression is that most executives strongly desire to be seen as understanding humans, but the problem is finding ways of showing it especially in big organizations."

He believes that a major task today is to find structured, rather than informal, ways to bring people, workers and executives together within the framework of their common labor.

Social scientists point out the relative ease with which leaders of large groups, whether Government or business, can become isolated from the masses. If the present reports of worker alienation are valid there would appear to be a corporate Czar Nicholas in a number of corporate boardrooms.

July 16, 1972

Executive Blues

The Failure Of the Successful

Success is "to be who I am." It's "doing your own thing."

"Some people still believe that money is success. I don't believe that anymore."

Success is "living the life of Christ in these present day times."

•

Much has been made recently of "blue collar" worker dissatisfaction and youth disaffection, both by gloomy critics who see America's economic vitality sapped by a crisis of values and by those who herald that crisis as signalling a long overdue revaluation of our moral and ethical framework.

But the definitions of success above are not offered by assembly-line workers, by soul-searching students or by Jesus freaks. They are a significant sample of the responses of the 2,800 businessmen and corporation executives questioned by the American Management Association about their attitudes to work, achievement and success.

The findings in "The Changing Success Ethic" indicate that job alienation "has not merely spread to, but may even thrive in, the managerial suites of American business." The executive, in fact, may be as dissatisfied as the men who work for him.

For just as the weekly paycheck and what it can buy no longer compensates factory workers for what have been increasingly recognized by concerned management and labor leaders as legitimate feelings of boredom and dehumanization, material wealth and the badges of corporate achievement are no longer enough for their bosses. They too question the quality of their lives.

Absenteeism, high turnover rates, and isolated acts of sabotage forced attention to the blue-collar blues. "Work in America," a massive Health Education and Welfare Department study issued late last year, hinted at middle management discontent. But it concentrated on what the more progressive industries already know—job enrichment, job retraining, and worker participation in decision-making are critical not only for the workers' psychic wellbeing but for continuing productivity. And many firms, among them General Foods, American Telephone and Telegraph and General Electric, are experimenting with new work conditions designed to attack on-the-job boredom and alienation.

The symptoms and possible cures for executive malaise are more elusive.

In "Death of a Salesman," Willie Loman felt himself to be a personal failure for not succeeding in business. Eighty-three per cent of the businessmen responding to the A.M.A. questionnaire this year don't define success in terms of business at all: 49 per cent say for them success is doing meaningful work, no matter what the business rewards; and 34 per cent say it means the realization of goals which may have little or no relation to career advancement. Nearly 4 out of 10 are not even sure that the organizations for which they work will provide them with opportunities to realize their personal goals.

In lower and middle management—tomorrow's captains of industry—62 per cent don't look to the work they do for a living for realization of their life aspirations. And two-thirds of them don't think the organizations they work for are interested in or even aware of those aspirations.

The expression of such attitudes cannot help but cause controversy in a community that has traditionally found fulfillment on the job, has extolled the competitive spirit and has claimed loyalty to the company as the highest ideal. An overwhelming 83 per cent of the businessmen the A.M.A. interviewed agreed that their attitudes to achievement and success are changing. And most of them feel that their basic life objectives are personal, private, and family centered.

There is less agreement about the causes and the value of the change. The A.M.A. report places the blame on Cotton Mather and Dale Carnegie, on the gap between the social fiction—the Puritan stress on good works and the public relations promise of rewards for charm—and the social fact—urban decay, youth revolt and political and social inequity. The Puritan ethic and the Personality Cult, the report's findings suggest, are out of sync with the realities of human experience in the sixties and seventies.

Whether and how the corporations themselves will respond is an open question. But one implication is clear to Dale Tarnowieski, author of the A.M.A. report: "Organizations that do not serve first the interests of people may experience increased difficulty in finding qualified people interested in serving them."

A 1972 study of youth values and attitudes conducted by Daniel Yankelovich, Inc., an attitude research firm, found America's college students asking the same questions about their life and career goals as men already in business. More surprising is the fact that they came up with similar answers. "Four out of five students believe that a meaningful career is important, but students rank 'the opportunity to make a contribution,' 'job challenge,' 'the ability to find self-expression,' and 'free time for outside interests' as the most important influences on their career choices."

Ironically, relatively few of the businessmen surveyed feel their personal ideas of success differ greatly from those of their peers, while 60 per cent believe there's no great similarity between the younger generations' idea of success and their own. What's more, most of them blame young people's attitudes on "permissiveness."

The tensions in the American dream are obvious. What isn't so obvious is how they might be resolved.

—CAROLINE RAND HERRON

June 3, 1973

Management

Scrutinizing the Corporate Boardroom

Juanita Kreps of Duke University is an outside director on 13 boards, both corporate and nonprofit. At Eastman Kodak's recent annual meeting, a stockholder questioned how much time she could expend on each directorship.

By MARYLIN BENDER

In the world of corporate management, it's pretty easy to locate the fastest game in town. Just follow the invitations to the conferences and count the reports written on a given theme.

Right now the action seems centered in the boardroom. The mammoth bankruptcies, political payoffs and bribes of recent years—of which corporate directors were either unaware or expediently unheeding—and several court decisions holding directors liable for such lack of vigilance have made the vulnerability of boards of directors both a hot topic and a source of confusion.

The current fashion is for a university to undertake a study of the subject with a management consulting or auditing firm paying the cost. The Northwestern University Graduate School of Management and McKinsey & Company are paired in one such effort. The Touche Ross Foundation provided the money for a recent day-long conference at Carnegie-Mellon University's Graduate School of Industrial Management.

Korn/Ferry International, the executive search firm, made a grant to the University of Pennsylvania Law School for a report, recently issued, on the role and responsibility of outside directors.

•

America's largest corporations have been increasing both the size of their boards and the use of outsiders as directors. The composition of boards has been altered slightly, too, with the requisite female, ethnic minority representative and an academic or religious figure taking a place in the once all white male congregation.

The ideal candidate for a director's seat in recent years has been a black female, but this year a couple of giants in heavily regulated industries let it be known they were on the lookout for a woman who just happened to be Jewish.

•

A survey by Korn/Ferry—apart form the University of Pennsylvania Law School report—indicates that only 4.2 percent of the 407 largest corporations use executive searchers to discover outsiders for their boards. Nearly 81 percent make their selections based on recommendations of someone known to the chairman.

That might be one explanation for the overuse of some directors. Take Juanita Kreps, an economist at Duke University who is also a vice president of the school. At the recent annual meeting of the Eastman Kodak Company, a stockholder objected to the election of Dr. Kreps to the Kodak board. Quoting a survey that outside directors spend an average of 99.6 hours a year on board meetings and homework, the stockholder pointed out that Dr. Kreps is a member of 13 boards (six corporate, the others nonprofit) and that it would not be humanly possible for her to discharge her director duties efficiently.

Dr. Kreps unintentionally corroborated the stockholder's point by failing to be present at the Kodak meeting.

At least two of Kodak's male directors were also cited in the same context. Robert S. Hatfield, chairman and chief executive officer of Continental Can, serves on five corporate boards besides his own. Donald S. Perkins, chairman and chief executive of the Jewel Companies, is a director of four corportions other than his own and its affiliates.

Both Mr. Perkins and Dr. Kreps are also members of Kodak's audit committee of the board, a watchdog responsibility being assigned more and more to outsiders and one that presumably should further tax their energies and time.

Another board nomination likely to strengthen the impression of clubbiness at the corporate summit will be made by the General Motors Corporation at its annual meeting on May 21. G.M. is enlarging its board by one member to 24 and asking stockholders to elect John D. deButts as the new director.

Mr. deButts is chairman of American Telephone and Telegraph Company as well as a director of Citicorp, the United States Steel Corporation and the Kraftco Corporation. On the G.M. board he will meet Catherine B. Cleary, a fellow director of Kraftco and of his own A.T. & T. board. Mr. deButts will also recognize Mr. Hatfield, whom he knows from the Citicorp board.

•

It is not only the desire to make a contribution, as the saying goes, that motivates superachievers to join boards. The pay is good and getting better.

According to the Korn/Ferry survey, the average compensation for directors last year was $8,930. G.M. gives its outside directors a flat fee of $10,000, with additional amounts from $7,000 to $15,000 for service on standing committees and an extra fee of $250 for each board meeting attended. Texas Instruments pays as much as $30,000 a year to some of its directors.

On the other hand, Warner Communications Inc., whose chairman, Steven J. Ross, received a $100,000 raise in salary to $487,320 last year, pays its directors $3,000 each.

May 14, 1976

The Gamesman—Tom Sawyer in the Executive Suite

He's Happiest Competing—And Vulnerable In Middle Age

By MICHAEL MACCOBY

A new type of man is taking over leadership of the most technically advanced companies in America. In contrast to the jungle-fighter industrialists of the past, he is driven not to build or to preside over empires, but to organize winning teams. Unlike the security-seeking organization man, he is excited by the chance to cut deals and to gamble. Although more cooperative and less hardened than the autocratic empire builder and less dependent than the organization man, he is more detached and emotionally inaccessible than either. And he is troubled by it: the new industrial leader can recognize that his work develops his head but not his heart.

During the late 19th and 20th centuries, the gamesman took a minor role in large organizations, which were run by autocratic jungle fighters like Carnegie and Frick. In the organizational world of the 1950's, the gamesman was too independent and irreverent to reach the top of the largest corporations.

But the modern gamesman fits the changing leadership needs of organizations based on:

¶Competition—internal, national, international.

¶Innovation—continual creation of new products or projects.

¶Interdependent teams—experts who must discover, develop, and market the product.

¶Fast-moving flexibility—the need to meet the changing schedules and deadlines, requiring a manager who can motivate a team of craftsmen and company men to move at a faster pace.

These factors also describe modern political teams, which increasingly are also led by gamesmen.

The modern gamesman's character is a collection of paradoxes. He is cooperative but competitive; detached and playful but compulsively driven to succeed; a team player but a would-be superstar; a team leader but often a rebel against bureaucratic hierarchy; fair and unprejudiced but contemptuous of weakness; tough and dominating but not destructive.

Unlike other business types, he is energized to compete not because he wants to build an empire, not for riches, but rather for fame, glory, the exhilaration of running his team and of gaining victories. His main goal is to be known as a winner, and his deepest fear is to be labeled a loser.

In American folklore, Tom Sawyer was a prototype gamesman-manager motivating others to do his work for him, manipulating them, but at the same time making the boring work seem enjoyable.

Bedazzled by the perpetually adolescent charm of the gamesman, our society romanticizes him. The gamesman is our favorite anti-hero. In the most popular motion picture of 1974, The Sting, Johnny Hooker and Henry Gondoroff (Robert Redford and Paul Newman), confuse and conquer the hated boss of a large gangster organization, dazzling him with a fake reality created by the fast-moving teamwork of many specialists using technology and sleight-of-hand. Like a modern morality play, The Sting presents the gamesman versus the old-style jungle fighter who built the organization.

Boysh and unprejudiced (black and white work together), the informal gamesmen have the audiences' full support because they are fighting killers. One quickly forgets that they started the trouble by ripping off the organization. One tends to forget that these "heroes" are amoral, manipulative confidence men, lonely hustlers who drift apart after the game is over.

Big business resembles aggressive-competitive games in many ways, but it cannot be classified as a game since it fashions realities that determine our daily life. Yet business increasingly takes the form of interrelated games—money game, the marketing game, the research and development game—all requiring specialized players. Many businessmen can make sense of their crisis life-style world only in gamelike metaphors. They will speak of the game plan. They will say "Let's try an end around and see if we can corner a few more yards of the market." They will test out a new man by "giving him the ball and letting him run with it."

In the most dynamic operations corporations, managerial meetings have a lockerroom atmosphere, where discussion of game strategy is punctuated with mildly sadistic humor, employed by the superior to keep the inferior in his place. These little put-downs can be called "Homeopathic doses of humiliation" necessary to maintain a minimum of hierarchy to show who is boss without having to humiliate the subordinate definitively by, for example, having him eat in another dining room or calling his boss "Mr. Jones" rather than "Jack." (Women who have reached top corporate positions have said that getting used to such joking is one of the hardest hurdles.)

The semiconductor components industry is an example of an industry run by cool and daring gamesmen. Here we find executives who are highly imaginative gamblers. They sell vast quantities of their products (one company president called them "jellybeans") to relatively few customers, mainly those making computers, televisions, and radios (200 customers account for 70 percent of the business, according to this president). This produces fierce competition.

The top executive must constantly

weigh two variables that determine success or disaster. One is the level of design sophistication and the other is the capacity to produce large numbers of components.

I asked the president of one semiconductor company what kind of people succeeded at this work and he said, "It has attracted an enormous number of bright people, but it's like Truman's kitchen, there are many dropouts and crack-ups."

In the electronics industry, they discuss one another in game terms, measuring their opponents as John Kennedy probably did when he saw himself up against Krushchev or Castro. They say, "He tends to bluff in this kind of situation" or "He's going to think he'll get a scientific advantage in this here and so he's not going to produce in time, and I'm going to cut in here and zap him."

The gamesman's emotional attitude has meshed perfectly with the corporation's need for managers who could be turned on by the technical challenges of the post-Sputnik era.

For the gamesman, a high salary is important mainly because this is the way the game is scored. He sees his salary not in absolute terms of becoming rich, but in comparative terms of staying ahead of others in his peer group.

The gamesman is not easily evaluated by traditional moral categories. In contrast to the authoritarian boss of the past, he tends to be unbigoted, nonideological, and liberal. He believes that everybody who is good should be allowed to play, and that race, sex, religion, or anything else has no bearing besides contributing to the team. Nor is he hostile. ("Nastiness and vindictiveness mean that person has already shown himself a loser," one gamesman told us.) Unlike the jungle fighter, he takes no pleasure in another man's defeat. But this does not imply that he is senstive to others' feelings or sympathetic about their special needs.

Unlike softer or more loyal company men, he is ready to replace a player as soon as he feels that person weakens the team. "The word 'loyalty' is too emotional," said one gamesman, "and empathy or generosity get in the way of work."

Many gamesmen operate well while young managers, but fail to resolve middle-age and middle-management crises.

The typical gamesman's mid-career crisis exposes the weaknesses in his character. His strengths are those of adolescence; he is playful, industrious, fair, enthusiastic, and open to new ideas. He has the adolescent's yearning for independence and ideals, but the problem of facing his limitations. Imaginative gamesmen tend to create a new reality, less limiting than normal, everyday reality. Like many adolescents, they seem to crave a more romantic, fast-paced, semifantasy life, and this need puts them in danger of losing touch with reality and of unconsciously lying.

Even such a gifted gamesman as Henry Kissinger imagines himself in an unreal, romantic fantasy. Ignoring the fact that he never travels without an entourage of his aides and the press, he tells an interviewer that he is like "the cowboy entering a city or village alone on his horse. Without even a pistol, maybe, because he doesn't go in for shooting."

The gamesmen's yearnings for autonomy and their fear of being controlled contribute to a common mid-career uneasiness. Even the most successful feel a kind of self-contempt that they are giving in, performing for others rather than developing their own goals. A number of gamesmen respond ingeniously; some try to skirt authority to create their own organizations within the larger company.

Fred Gordon [pseudonyms are used to identify participants in the study] is 36 years old and manages 4,000 people in a division of a multinational corporation. As a young marketing manager, Gordon figured out that the way to the top was to get a relationship with a powerful customer to use against the company. "You need a very big customer who is always in trouble and demands changes from the company," he said. "That way you automatically have power within the company, and with the customer, too. I like to keep my options open."

Gamesmen like Gordon, in gaining their "autonomy", may threaten the whole organization. Such gamesmen may create a successful project and even energize a whole company for a while, but over the long pull, some lack the patience and commitment to people and principles necessary to maintain a dynamic organization.

The fatal danger for gamesmen is to be trapped in perpetual adolescence, never outgrowing the self-centered compulsion to score, never confronting their deep boredom with life when it is not a game, never developing a sense of meaning that requires more of them and allows others to trust them.

An old and tiring gamesman is a pathetic figure, especially after he has lost a few contests, and with them, his confidence. He finds himself starkly alone. His attitude has kept him from deep friendship and intimacy. Nor has he sufficiently developed abilities that would strengthen the self, so that he might gain satisfaction from understanding (science) or creating (invention, art).

Tom Lundberg is now 46. Seven years ago, he was on top, the manager of a project that gained great profits for his corporation. He was a winner. Tall and blond, with an air of command, he had come to the company from the Air Force, where he was a pilot. "I never wanted security," he said. "I felt we were all good racehorses and we'd be allowed to run. I wanted to be part of the winning team. The corporation had begun to take off. It was wide open." Now, he has failed twice, and has become an alcoholic. "I don't fear vague responsibilities. His superiors worry about what to do with him. He has become an alcholic. "I don't fear death now," he said, "but I fear discomfort. Hard knocks grind your ego down."

Those who avoid middle-aged disintegration are the ones who have commited themselves to something beyond just winning games.

At the age of 50, John Price, a gamesman with a company man's quasi-religious identification with the organization, became chief executive of a corporation. Price told me his strength was solving problems with others. "No one knows everything. An executive needs to be able to assess people and to be able to listen to what they say and evaluate it."

"What is central here," he told me, "is that the idea that what we are doing is not only technologically important but socially important. We are doing much more than selling soap. We are at the cutting edge of society."

Price's Rorschach responses indicated that he is sparked, energized by the competition. He played football in high school and intramural sports in college. He loves puzzles and problem-solving, and welcomes the variety of problems at work. He likes to be where the action is, at the center.

Price is also motivated by the fear of failure. "I have always felt I must either move up the ladder or quit," he said. He knows he must keep on being promoted to keep his place. His pride is maintained both by the respect of peers and by a sense (or illusion) of independence which compensates for by unconscious feelings of being like an insignificant insect or small animal scurrying for food (images expressed by Price on the Rorschach).

Gamesmen who have reached the very top take pride in their problem-solving abilities and coolness under stress (control) rather than their power (machismo). They do not try to be glamorous. (In contrast to younger gamesmen on their way up, with young and glamorous secretaries, the executive type invariably picks a plain, nononsense type.)

I have asked gamesmen like Price what they mean when they describe a successful manager as "tough," because while they seem to me detached, they also appear sensitive about hurting anyone's feelings. They lack the jungle fighter's willingness to destroy competitors or even to fire incompetents. (The executives of elite corporations hardly ever fire someone, unless they believe he is harming the company.)

The toughness seems to be within the rules of the game. One top executive told me, "A tough guy genuinely induces fear in others. He has an aura of power, of being right. It is a strength of character, a winning attitude."

Perhaps another reason why executives become tough and even subtly sadistic is because they have to accept constant humiliations.

The Rorschach responses of executives suggested that one of their most repressed feelings is humiliation. Unlike the farmer or craftsman, the manager always remains in some way the schoolboy who is being judged on his performance. In this regard, it is interesting that the executive almost invariably mentions one of his superiors among the people he most admires, even when he complains about this man's treatment of him ("but if he weren't tough, we would not be where we are"). Rather than submit abjectly, he identifies with the aggressor.

The gamesmen save themselves by placing his primary value on fine-tuned control. Control has become as much an end as a means. The cost is dampened passion, emotional castration, and depression. More dependent on the organization than they realize for their life's meaning, their efforts at self-development make them valuable tools for the company. Outside the company, they have little social function or individual purpose. More than anyone else, they have exploited themselves.

The gamesman's wife is, in his terms, "flexible and supportive." Usually she is as intelligent, as energetic, and as competent at any activity she takes on as her husband. She spends time sitting on committees and performing civic duties that enhance both her own image and the corporation's as socially responsible.

The executive wives we interviewed are women who like men. Most of them enjoyed close relationships with fathers. Although they support the women's movement, they disapprove of the "extremists" who hate men or practice lesbianism. They feel at home in a world dominated by men and they admire their husbands.

The gamesman is less likely than more authoritarian jungle fighters or insecure company men to surround himself with yes men. He enjoys the give-and-take, the competitive problem-solving, the trial by combat to assess good ideas and select comers.

So long as the corporation's relative standing is not threatened, the gamesman chief executive will favor programs that make the corporation more attractive to the brightest young people, and that will likely provide more chance for initiative and individual challenge. But here as elsewhere he will wait to respond to pressures.

The gamesman will not initiate social programs that leave his company in an unfavorable competitive position. Nor will he pass up a chance for a big win in the market. He will trade anywhere he can, whether or not he approves of a given regime. He will pollute the environment, even when he privately supports environmentalists. He will produce and advertise anything he can sell unless food and drug laws or other legislation stops him.

Even when he believes that the Government spends too much on weapons, he will make them. Even though he values privacy and is outraged by illegal intrusion of the state in the individual's affairs, he will build the technology that makes this possible.

But the new type of executive is ready and willing to play by the rules. One told me, "Society can make any rules it wants as long as they are clear-cut, the same for everyone. We can win at any game society can invent."

From "The Gamesman" by Michael Maccoby. Copyright 1976 by Michael Maccoby. Reprinted by permission of Simon & Schuster Inc.

January 23, 1977

Management

The Double Standard on Loyalty

By ELIZABETH M. FOWLER

"When I started in this business 10 years ago, the books on management I read advised that I could become chairman of a company if I stuck to it," said Roger M. Kenny. "This is false. It's a timeworn adage."

Mr. Kenny, senior vice president of Spencer Stuart & Associates, a management recruiting firm, asserted that, although upward and sideward mobility was the name of the game these days, many companies still clung to a double standard regarding executive job movement.

The policy of one-way corporate loyalty, he maintained in a recent telephone interview, needs to be seriously questioned by more companies and their attitudes changed to improve management relationships, which have been hurt by the practice.

The double standard involves expectation that an executive's loyalty to a company is greater than the company's loyalty to him.

• • •

"When a company wants to replace a top executive, it initiates a search to find a replacement, usually without notifying him," Mr. Kenny pointed out in explaining how the double standard worked. This behind-the-back-operation is carried on as a standard operating procedure by the personnel department, often working with a recruiter or employment agency, he added.

The unwitting executive is usually shocked to learn that his job is gone.

At the other end of the spectrum, another executive in the company growing increasingly unhappy on his job is in a quandary. He does not dare announce publicly that he wants another job for fear his boss might learn of his plans and dismiss him on the spot, according to Mr. Kenny.

The unhappy executive has to be discreet when talking to management recruiters or employment agencies over the telephone, glancing warily around to make sure no one, especially his secretary, overhears, Mr. Kenny maintained. He also has to hold interviews on the sly or during lunch hours.

• • •

At the very least, "if an executive is found to be considering moving—in effect an extracorporate affair—he is accused of disloyalty," Mr. Kenny said.

Some years ago, it was widely known that Merrill Lynch, Pierce, Fenner & Smith, the world's largest brokerage house, had a policy of immediately dismissing anyone found to be negotiating for a job outside the firm. Once he announced he was leaving, the executive was expected to depart the next day, not even staying on long enough to complete a project or train a successor. Merrill now has a more enlightened policy.

On the other hand, General Electric was cited by Mr. Kenny, as a company that encourages executives to be aware of options outside the comany. International Paper, the world's top papermaker, also has an enlightened approach about wanting its managers to know about opportuities, according to Mr. Kenny.

"In 85 percent of the job changes I see, the basic problem is a failure of the relationship between immediate superior and subordinate," Mr. Kenny said. Executives, fearful of the one-way loyalty tradition, are reluctant to discuss difficulties with their superior.

The solution to the problem, Mr. Kenny believes, is a redefinition of loyalty to include candor, whereby a company should tell an executive when it is dissatisfied with his performance.

At the same time, an unhappy executive should be able to talk frankly with his superiors.

Finally, top management must make it clear that it will not consider an executive disloyal if he discloses a possible job change.

Another management recruiter, Carl Menk, president of Boyden Associates Inc., said he believed that most successful companies these days recognize the need for enlightened personnel practices.

Such companies, he asserted in a telephone interview, "encourage employees who feel that their career paths are thwarted to discuss career plans with senior management, often the corporate personnel executive". This might involve trying to place the individual in another position within the company while at the same time encouraging him to search outside. Also, Mr. Menk believes that progressive managements felt the responsibility to tell managers when they were not performing well.

September 9, 1977

Chapter 3

Corporations and the Social order

Ralph Nader on Capitol Hill.

NYT Pictures/George Tames

CREDIT MOBILIER.

Report of the Poland Committee—Expulsion of Oakes Ames and James Brooks Unanimously Recommended.

WASHINGTON, Feb. 18.—The Special Committee appointed under the following resolutions of the House, to-wit:

Whereas, Accusations have been made in the public Press, founded on alleged letters of Oakes Ames, a Representative from Massachusetts, and upon the alleged affidavits of Henry S. McComb, a citizen of Wilmington, in the State of Delaware, to the effect that members of this House were bribed by Oakes Ames to perform certain legislative acts for the benefit of the Union Pacific Railroad Company, by presents of stock in the Credit Mobilier of America, or by presents of a valuable character derived therefrom, therefore

Resolved, That a special committee of five members be appointed by the Speaker pro tem., whose duty it shall be to investigate whether any member of this house was bribed by Oakes Ames or any other person or corporation in any matter touching his legislative duty.

Resolved, Further, that the committee have the right to employ a stenographer, and that they be empowered to send for persons and papers.

Beg leave to make the following report:

In order to come to a clear understanding of the facts hereinafter stated as to contracts and dealings, in reference to stock of the Credit Mobilier of America, between Mr. Ames and others and members of Congress, it is necessary to make a preliminary statement of the connection of that company with the Union Pacific Railroad, and their relations with each other.

HISTORY OF THE CREDIT MOBILIER.

The company called "The Credit Mobilier of America" was incorporated by the Legislature of Pennsylvania, and in 1864 the control of its charter and franchises had been obtained by certain persons interested in the Union Pacific Railroad Company, for the purpose of using it as a construction company to build the Union Pacific Road. In September, 1864, a contract was entered into between the Union Pacific Company and H. W. Hoxie for the building by said Hoxie of 100 miles of said road, from Omaha west. This contract was at once assigned by Hoxie to the Credit Mobilier Company, as it was expected to be when made. Under this contract and extensions of it some two or three hundred miles of road was built by the Credit Mobilier Company, but no considerable profit appear to have been realized therefrom. The enterprise of building a railroad to the Pacific was of such vast magnitude, and was beset by so many hazards and risks, that the capitalists of the country were generally averse to investing in it, and, notwithstanding the liberal aid granted by the Government, it seemed likely to fail of completion.

OAKES AMES AND OLIVER AMES.

In 1865 or 1866, Mr. Oakes Ames, then and now a member of the House from the State of Massachusetts, and his brother Oliver Ames, became interested in the Union Pacific Company, and also in the Credit Mobilier Company, as the agent for the construction of the road. The Messrs. Ames were men of very large capital, and of known character and integrity in business. By their example and credit and the personal efforts of Mr. Oakes Ames, many men of capital were induced to embark in the enterprise, and to take stock in the Union Pacific Company, and also in the Credit Mobilier Company. Among them were the firm of S. Hooper & Co., of Boston, the leading member of which, Mr. Samuel Hooper, was then and is now a member of the House; Mr. John B. Alley, then a member of the House from Massachusetts; and Mr. Grimes, then a Senator from the State of Iowa. Notwithstanding the vigorous efforts of Mr. Ames, and others interested with him, great difficulty was experienced in procuring the required capital. In the Spring of 1867 the Credit Mobilier Company voted to add fifty per cent. to their capital stock, which was then $2,500,000, and to cause it to be readily taken each subscriber to it was entitled to receive as a bonus an equal amount of first mortgage bonds of the Union Pacific Company. The old stockholders were entitled to take this increase, but even the favorable terms offered did not induce all the old stockholders to take it, and the stock of the Credit Mobilier Company was never considered worth its par value until after the execution of the Oakes Ames' contract hereinafter mentioned. On the 16th day of August, 1867, a contract was executed between the Union Pacific Railroad and Oakes Ames, by which Mr. Ames contracted to build 667 miles of the Union Pacific Road at prices ranging from $42,000 to $96,000 per mile, amounting in the aggregate to $47,000,000. Before the contract was entered into it was understood that Mr. Ames was to transfer it to seven trustees, who were to execute it, and the profits of the contract were to be divided among the stockholders in the Credit Mobilier Company, who should comply with certain conditions set out in the instrument transferring the contract to the trustees. The Ames contract and the transfer to trustees are incorporated in the evidence submitted, and, therefore, further recital of their terms is not deemed necessary.

THE STOCK IMPROVES.

Substantially all the stockholders of the Credit Mobilier Company complied with the conditions named in the transfer, and thus became entitled to share in any profits said trustees might make in executing the contract. All the large stockholders in the Union Pacific were also stockholders in the Credit Mobilier, and the Ames contract and its transfer to trustees were ratified by the Union Pacific and received the assent of the great body of the stockholders, but not of all. After the Ames contract had been executed, it was expected by those interested that, by reason of the enormous prices agreed to be paid for the work, very large profits would be derived from building the road; and very soon the stock of the Credit Mobilier was understood to be worth much more than its par value. The stock was not in the market and had no fixed market value, but the holders of it, December, 1867, considered it worth at least double the par value, and in January or February, 1868, three or four times the par value; but it does not appear that these facts were generally or publicly known, or that the holders of the stock desired they should be. The foregoing statement, the committee thinks, gives enough of the historic details and condition and value of the stock to make the following detailed facts intelligible:

AMES BEGINS TO DISTRIBUTE.

Mr. Oakes Ames was then a member of the House of Representatives, and came to Washington at the commencement of the session—about the beginning of December, 1867. During that month Mr. Ames entered into contracts with a considerable number of members of Congress, both Senators and Representatives, to let them have shares of stock in the Credit Mobilier Company at par, with interest thereon, from the 1st day of the previous July. It does not appear that in any instance he asked any of these persons to pay a higher price than the par value and interest, nor that Mr. Ames used any special effort or urgency to get these persons to take it. In all these negotiations Mr. Ames did not enter into any details as to the value of the stock or the amount of dividend that might be expected upon it, but stated generally that it would be good stock, and in several instances said he would guarantee that they should get at least ten per cent. on their money. Some of these gentlemen, in their conversations with Mr. Ames, raised the question, whether, becoming holders of this stock, would bring them into any embarrassment as members of Congress in their legislative action. Mr. Ames quieted such suggestions by saying it could not, for the Union Pacific had received from Congress all the grants and legislation it wanted, and they should ask for nothing more. In some instances those members who contracted for stock paid to Mr. Ames the money for the price of the stock, par and interest, in others where they had not the money, Mr. Ames agreed to "carry" the stock for them until they could get the money or it should be met by the dividends. Mr. Ames was at this time a large stockholder in the Credit Mobilier, but he did not intend any of those transactions to be sales of his own stock, but intended to fulfill all these contracts from stock belonging to the company.

AMES, DURANT AND M'COMB.

At this time there were about 650 shares of the stock of the company which had for some reason been placed in the name of Mr. T. C. Durant, one of the leading and active men of the concern. Mr. Ames claimed that a portion of this stock should be assigned to him, to enable him to fulfill engagements he had made for stock. Mr. Durant claimed that he had made similar engagements, that he should be allowed stock to fulfill: Mr. McComb, who was present at the time, claimed that he had also made engagements for stock which he should have stock given him to carry out. This claim of McComb was refused, but after the stock was assigned to Mr. Ames, McComb insisted that Mr. Ames should distribute some of the stock to his (McComb's) friends, and named Senators Bayard and Fowler, and Representatives Allison and Wilson, of Iowa. It was finally arranged that 343 shares of the stock of the company should be transferred to Mr. Ames to enable him to perform his engagements, and that number of shares were set over on the books of the company to Oakes Ames, trustee, to distinguish it from the stock held by him before. Mr. Ames, at the time, paid to the company the par of the stock and interest from the July previous, and this stock still stands on the books in the name of Oakes Ames, trustee, except thirteen shares which have been transferred to parties in no way connected with Congress. The committee does not find that Mr. Ames had any negotiation whatever with any of these members of Congress on the subject of this stock, prior to the commencement of the session of December, 1867, except Mr. Scofield, of Pennsylvania, and it was not claimed that any obligation existed from Mr. Ames to him as the result of it.

AMES' MOTIVE.

In relation to the purpose and motive of Mr. Ames in contracting to let members of Congress have Credit Mobilier stock at par, which he and all other owners of it considered worth at least double that sum, the committee, upon the evidence taken by them and submitted to the House, cannot entertain doubt. When he said he did not suppose the Union Pacific Company would ask or need further legislation, he stated what he believed to be true, but he feared the interests of the road might suffer by adverse legislation, and what he desired to accomplish was to enlist strength and friends in Congress who would resist any encroachment upon or interference with the rights and privileges already secured, and to that end wished to create in them an interest identical with his own. This purpose is clearly avowed in his letters to McComb, copied in the evidence, where he says he intends to place the stock "where it will do the most good to us;" and again "We want more friends in this Congress." In his letter to McComb, and also in his statement prepared by counsel, he gives the philosophy of his action, to wit: That he has found there is no difficulty in getting men to look after their own property. The committee are also satisfied that Mr. Ames entertained a fear that when the true relations between the Credit Mobilier Company and the Union Pacific became generally known, and the means by which the great profits expected to be made were fully understood, there was danger that Congressional investigation and action would be invoked. The members of Congress with whom he dealt were generally those who had been friendly and favorable to a Pacific Railroad, and Mr. Ames did not fear or expect to find them favorable to movements hostile to it, but he desired to stimulate their activity and watchfulness in opposition to any unfavorable action, by giving them a personal interest in the success of the enterprise, especially so far as it affected the interest of the Credit Mobilier Company.

THE "WASHBURN MOVEMENT."

On the 9th day of December, 1867, Mr. C. C. Washburn, of Wisconsin, introduced in the House a bill to regulate by law the rates of transportation over the Pacific Railroads. Mr. Ames, as well as others interested in the Union Pacific Road, were opposed to this, and desired to defeat it. Other measures apparently hostile to that company were subsequently introduced into the House by Mr. Washburn, of Wisconsin, and Mr. Washburn, of Illinois. The committee believe that Mr. Ames, in his distribution of the stock, had specially in mind hostile efforts of the Messrs. Washburn, and desired to gain strength to secure their defeat. The reference, in one of his letters, to Washburn's move makes this quite apparent.

THE CONGRESSMEN.

The foregoing is deemed by the committee a sufficient statement of facts as to Mr. Ames, taken in connection with what will be subsequently stated of his transactions with particular persons. Mr. Ames made some contracts for stock in the Credit Mobilier with members of the Senate. In public discussions of this subject, the names of members of both Houses have been connected, and all these transactions were so nearly simultaneous that the committee deemed it their duty to obtain all evidences in their power as to all persons then members of either House, and to report the same to the House. Having done this, and the House having directed that evidence transmitted to the Senate the committee consider their own power and duty, as well as that of the House, fully performed, as far as members of the Senate are concerned. Some of Mr. Ames' contracts to sell stock were with gentlemen who were then members of the House but are not members of the present Congress. The committee have sought for and taken all the evidence within their reach as to those gentlemen, and reported the same to the House. As the House has ceased to have jurisdiction over them as members, the committee have not deemed it their duty to make any special finding of facts as to each, leaving the House and the country to their own conclusions upon the testimony. In regard to each of the members of the present House, the committee deem it their duty to state specially the facts they find proved by the evidence, which, in some instances, is painfully conflicting.

MR. JAMES G. BLAINE, OF MAINE.

Mr. James G. Blaine, of Maine, is among those who have in the public Press been charged with improper participation in Credit Mobilier stock, is the present Speaker, and it was Mr. Blaine who moved the resolution for this investigation. The committee have, therefore taken evidence in regard to him. They find from it that Mr. Ames had conversation with Mr. Blaine in regard to taking ten shares of the stock, and recommended it as a good investment. Upon consideration Mr. Blaine concluded not to take that stock or stock of the Union Pacific Railroad Company, and never did take it, and never paid or received anything on account of it.

MR. HENRY L. DAWES, OF MASSACHUSETTS.

Mr. Dawes had, prior to December, 1867, made some small investments in railroad bonds through Mr. Ames. In December, 1867, Mr.

Dawes applied to Mr. Ames to purchase a $1,000 bond of the Cedar Rapids Road, in Iowa. Mr. Ames informed him that he had sold them all, but that he would let him have for his $1,000 ten shares of Credit Mobilier stock, which he thought was better than the railroad bonds. In answer to inquiry by Mr. Dawes, Mr. Ames said the Credit Mobilier Company had the contract to build the Union Pacific Road, and thought they would make money out of it, and that it would be a good thing; that he would guarantee that he should get ten per cent. on his money, and that if at any time Mr. Dawes did not want the stock, he would pay back his money, with ten per cent. interest. Mr. Dawes made some further inquiry in relation to the stock of Mr. John B. Alley, who said he thought it was good stock, but not as good as Mr. Ames thought; but that Mr. Ames' guarantee would make it a perfectly safe investment. Mr. Dawes thereupon concluded to purchase the ten shares, and on the 11th of January he paid Mr. Ames $800, and in a few days thereafter the balance of the price of the stock at par, and interest from the July previous. In June, 1868, Mr. Ames received a dividend of sixty per cent. in money on his stock, and of it paid to Mr. Dawes $400, and applied the balance of $200 upon accounts between them. This $400 was all that was paid over to Mr. Dawes as a dividend upon this stock. At some time prior to December, 1868, Mr. Dawes was informed that a suit had been commenced in the courts of Pennsylvania by the former owners of the charter of the Credit Mobilier, claiming that those then claiming and using it had no right to do so. Mr. Dawes thereupon informed Mr. Ames that as there was a litigation about the matter, he did not desire to keep the stock. On the 9th of December, 1868, Mr. Ames and Mr. Dawes had a settlement of these matters, in which Mr. Dawes was allowed for the money he paid for the stock, with ten per cent. interest upon it, and accounted to Mr. Ames for the $400 he had received as a dividend. Mr. Dawes received no other benefit under the contract than to get ten per cent. upon his money, and after the settlement had no further interest in the stock.

MR. GLENNI W. SCOFIELD, OF PENNSYLVANIA.

In 1866, Mr. Scofield purchased some Cedar Rapids bonds of Mr. Ames, and in that year they had conversation about Mr. Scofield taking stock in the Credit Mobilier Company, but no contract was consummated. In December, 1867, Mr. Scofield applied to Mr. Ames to purchase more Cedar Rapids bonds, when Mr. Ames suggested that he should purchase some Credit Mobilier stock, and explained generally that it was a contracting company to build the Union Pacific Road; that, as it was a Pennsylvania corporation, he would like to have some Pennsylvanian in it; that he would sell it to him at par and interest, and that he would guarantee he should get eight per cent. if Mr. Scofield would give him half the dividends above that. Mr. Scofield said he thought he would take $1,000 of the stock, but before anything further was done Mr. Scofield was called home by sickness in his family. On his return, in the latter part of January, 1868, he spoke to Mr. Ames about the stock, when Mr. Ames said he thought it was all sold, but he would take his money and give him a receipt and get the stock for him if he could. Mr. Scofield therefore paid Mr. Ames $104, and took his receipt therefor. Not long after Mr. Ames informed Mr. Scofield he could have the stock, but could not give him a certificate for it until he could get a larger certificate dividend. Mr. Scofield received the bond dividend of eighty per cent., which was payable Jan. 3, 1868, taking a bond for $1,000, and paying Mr. Ames the difference. Mr. Ames received the sixty per cent. cash dividend on the stock in June, 1868, and paid over to Mr. Scofield $600, the amount of it. Before the close of that session of Congress, which was toward the end of July, Mr. Scofield became, for some reason, disinclined to take the stock, and a settlement was made between them, by which Mr. Ames was to retain the Credit Mobilier stock and Mr. Scofield took $1,000 Union Pacific stock. The precise basis of the settlement does not appear, neither Mr. Ames nor Mr. Scofield having any full data in reference to it. Mr. Scofield thinks that he only received back his money and interest upon it, while Mr. Ames states that he thinks Mr. Scofield had ten shares of Union Pacific stock in addition. The committee do not deem it specially important to settle this difference of recollection. Since that settlement Mr. Scofield has had no interest in the Credit Mobilier stock, and derived no benefit therefrom.

MR. JOHN BINGHAM, OF OHIO.

In December, 1867, Mr. Ames advised Mr. Bingham to invest in the stock of the Credit Mobilier, assuring him that it would return him his money with profitable dividends. Mr. Bingham agreed to take twenty shares, and about the 1st of January, 1868, paid to Mr. Ames the par value of the stock, for which Mr. Ames executed to him some receipt or agreement. Mr. Ames received all the dividends on the stock or money. Some were delivered, to Mr. Bingham, and some retained by Mr. Ames. The matter was not finally adjusted between them until February, 1872, when it was settled by Mr. Ames retaining the thirty shares of Credit Mobilier stock, and accounting to Mr. Bingham for such dividends upon it as Mr. Bingham had not already received. Mr. Bingham was treated as the real owner of the stock from the time of the agreement to take it in December, 1867, to the settlement in February, 1872, and had the benefit of all the dividends upon it. Neither Mr. Ames or Mr. Bingham had such records of their dealing as to be able to give the precise amount of these dividends.

MR. WILLIAM D. KELLEY, OF PENNSYLVANIA.

They can find from the evidence that in the early part of the second session of the Fortieth Congress, and probably in December, 1867, Mr. Ames agreed with Mr. Kelley to sell him ten shares of Credit Mobilier stock at par and interest from July 1, 1867. Mr. Kelley was not then prepared to pay for the stock, and Mr. Ames agreed to carry the stock for him until he could pay for it. On the 3d day of January, 1868, there was a dividend of eighty per cent. on Credit Mobilier stock in Union Pacific bonds. Mr. Ames received the bonds, as the stock stood in his name, and sold them for ninety-seven per cent. of their face. In June, 1868, there was a cash dividend of sixty per cent., which Mr. Ames also received. The proceeds of the bonds sold and the cash dividends received by Mr. Ames amounted to $1,376. The par value of the stock and interest thereon from the previous July amounted to $1 047, so that after paying for the stock there was a balance of dividends due Mr. Kelley of $329. On the 23d day of June, 1868, Mr. Ames gave Mr. Kelley a check for that sum on the Sergeant-at-Arms of the House of Representatives, and Mr. Kelley received the money thereon. The committee find that Mr. Kelley understood that the money he thus received was a balance of dividends due him after paying for the stock. All the subsequent dividends upon the stock were either in Union Pacific stock or bonds, and they were all received from Mr. Ames. In September, 1868, Mr. Kelley received from Mr. Ames $750, the money which was understood between them to be an advance to be paid out of dividends. There has never been any adjustment of the matter between them, and there is now an entire variance in the testimony of the two men as to what the transaction between them was, but the committee are unanimous in finding the facts above stated. The evidence reported to the House gives some subsequent conversations and negotiations between Mr. Kelley and Mr. Ames on the subject. The committee do not deem it material to refer to it in their report.

MR. JAMES A. GARFIELD, OF OHIO.

The facts in regard to Mr. Garfield, as found by the committee, are identical with the case of Mr. Kelley to the point of reception of the check for $329. He agreed with Mr. Ames to take ten shares of Credit Mobilier stock, but did not pay for the same. Mr. Ames received the eighty per cent. dividend in bonds, and sold them for ninety-seven per cent., and also received the sixty per cent. cash dividend, which, together with the price of the stock and interest, left a balance of $329. This sum was paid over to Mr. Garfield by a check on the Sergeant-at-Arms. Mr. Ames received all the subsequent dividends, and the committee do not find that since the payment of the $329 there has been any communication between Mr. Ames and Mr. Garfield on the subject, until this investigation began. Some correspondence between Mr. Garfield and Mr. Ames, and some conversation between them during this investigation, will be found in the reported testimony.

CONCLUSIONS AS TO THE PRECEDING GENTLEMEN.

The committee do not find that Mr. Ames, in his negotiations with the parties above named, entered into any detail of the relations between the Credit Mobilier Company and the Union Pacific Company, or gave them any specific information as to the amount of dividends they would be likely to receive, further than has already been stated. They all knew from him, or otherwise, that the Credit Mobilier was a contracting company to build the Union Pacific Road, but it does not appear that any of them knew that the profits or dividends were to be in stock or bonds of that company. The Credit Mobilier was a State corporation, not subject to Congressional legislation, and the fact that its profits were expected to be derived from building the Union Pacific Railroad did not apparently create such an interest in that Company as to disqualify the holder of Credit Mobilier stock from participating in any legislation affecting the railroad company. In his negotiations with these members of Congress, Mr. Ames made no suggestion that he desired to secure their favorable influence in Congress in favor of the railroad company, and whenever the question was raised as to whether the ownership of this stock would in any way interfere with or embarrass them in their action as members of Congress, he assured them it would not. The committee, therefore, do not find as to the members of the present House, above named, that they were aware of the object of Mr. Ames, or that they had any other purpose in taking this stock than to make a profitable investment. It is apparent that those who advanced their money to pay for their stock present more the appearance of ordinary investors than those who did not, but the committee do not feel at liberty to find any corrupt purpose or knowledge founded upon the fact of non-payment alone. It ought also to be observed that those gentlemen who surrendered their stock to Mr. Ames, before there was any public excitement upon the subject, do not profess to have done so upon any idea of impropriety in holding it, but for reasons affecting the value and security of the investment. But the committee believe that they must have felt that there was something so out of the ordinary course of business in the extraordinary dividends they were receiving as to render the investment itself suspicious, and that this was one of the motives of their action. The committee have not been able to find that any of these members of Congress have been affected in their official action in consequence of their interest in Credit Mobilier stock. It has been suggested that the fact that none of this stock was transferred to those with whom Mr. Ames contracted was a circumstance from which a sense of impropriety, if not of corruption, was to be inferred. The Committee believe this is capable of explanation without such inference. The profits of building the road under the Ames contract were only to be divided among such holders of Credit Mobilier stock as should come in and become parties to certain conditions set out in the contract of transfer to the trustees, so that a transfer from Mr. Ames to new holders would cut off the right to dividends from the trustees, unless they became parties to the agreement, and this the Committee believe to be the true reason why no transfers were made. The committee are also of opinion that there was also a satisfactory reason for delay on Mr. Ames' part to close settlements with some of the gentlemen for stocks and bonds he had received as dividends upon the stock contracted to them. In the Fall of 1868, Mr. McComb commenced a suit against the Credit Mobilier Company and others, claiming to be entitled to 250 shares of the Credit Mobilier stock upon a subscription for stock to that amount. That suit is still pending. If McComb prevailed in that suit, Mr. Ames might be compelled to surrender so much of the stock assigned to him as trustee, and he was not, therefore, anxious to have the stock go out of his hands until that suit was terminated. It ought also to be stated that no one of the present members of the House above named appear to have had any knowledge of the dealings of Mr. Ames with other members. The committee do not find that either of the above-named gentlemen, in contracting with Mr. Ames, had any corrupt motive or purpose himself, or was aware that Mr. Ames had any; nor did either of them suppose he was guilty of any impropriety, or even indelicacy, in becoming a purchaser of this stock. Had it appeared that these gentlemen were aware of the enormous dividends upon this stock, and how they were to be earned, we could not acquit them; and here, as well as anywhere, the committee may allude to that subject.

THE ENORMOUS DIVIDENDS A FRAUD.

Congress had chartered the Union Pacific road, given to it a liberal grant of lands, and promised a liberal loan of Government bonds to be delivered as fast as sections of the road were completed; as these alone might not be sufficient, Congress authorized the Company to issue their own bonds for the deficit, and secure them by a mortgage upon the road which should be a lien prior to that of the Government. Congress never intended that the owners of the road should execute a mortgage on the road, prior to that of the Government, to raise money to put into their own pockets, but only to build the road. The men who controlled the Union Pacific seem to have adopted as the basis of their action the right to encumber the road by a mortgage, prior to that of the Government, to the full extent, whether the money was needed for the construction of the road or not. It was clear enough they could not do this directly and in terms, and therefore they resorted to the device of contracting with themselves to build the road and fix a price high enough to require the issue of bonds to the full extent, and then divide the bonds or the proceeds of them under the name of profits on the contract. All those acting in the matter seem to have been fully aware of this, and that this was to be the effect of the transaction. The sudden rise of value of Credit Mobilier stock was the result of the adoption of this scheme. Any undue and unreasonable profits thus made by themselves was as much a fraud upon the Government as if they had sold their bonds and divided the money without going through the form of denominating them profits on the building of the road. Now, had these facts been known to these gentlemen, and had they understood they were to share in the proceeds of the scheme, they would have deserved the severest censure. Had they known only that the profits were to be paid in stock and bonds of the Union Pacific Company, and so make them interested in it, we cannot agree to the doctrine which has been urged before us and elsewhere, that it was perfectly legitimate for members of Congress to invest in a corporation deriving all its rights from and subject at all times to the action of Congress. In such case the rule of the House, as well as the rules of decency, would require such member to abstain from voting on any question affecting his interest. But after accepting the position of a member of Congress, we do not think he has the right to disqualify himself from acting upon subjects likely to come before Congress, without some higher and more urgent motive than merely to make a profitable investment. But it is not so much to be feared that in such a case an interested member would vote, as that he would exercise his influence by personal appeal to his fellow-members, and by other modes which method often is far more potent than a silent vote. We do not think any member ought to feel so confident of his own strength as to allow himself to be brought into this temptation. We think Mr. Ames judges shrewdly in saying that a man is much more likely to be watchful of his own interests than those of other people. But there is a broader view still which we think ought to be taken.

PERNICIOUS INFLUENCE OF CORPORATIONS.

This country is fast becoming filled with gigantic corporations wielding and controlling immense aggregations of money, and thereby commanding great influence and power. It is notorious in many State Legislatures that these influences are often controlling, so that in effect they become the ruling power of the State. Within a few years Congress has to some extent been brought within similar influence and the knowledge of the public on that subject has brought great discredit upon the body, far more believed than there were facts to justify. But such is the tendency of the time, and the belief is far too general that all men can be ruled with money, and that the use of such means to carry public measures are legitimate and proper. No member of Congress ought to place himself in circumstances of suspicion so that any discredit to the body shall arise on his account. It is of the highest importance that the national Legislature should be free of all taint of corruption, and it is of almost equal necessity that the people should feel confident that it is so. In a free Government like ours we cannot expect the people will long respect the laws if they lose respect for the law-makers. For these reasons we think it behooves every man in Congress, or in any public position, to hold himself aloof, as far as possible, from all such influences, that he may not only be enabled to look at every public question with an eye only to the public good, but that his conduct and motives be not suspected or questioned.

A RECOMMENDATION TO READ MR. BAYARD'S LETTER.

The only criticism the committee feel competent to make on the action of these members in taking this stock is, that they were not sufficiently careful in ascertaining what they were getting, and that, in their judgment, the assurance of a good investment was all the assurance they needed. We commend to them, and to all men, the letter of the venerable Senator Bayard in response to an offer of some of this stock, found on Page 74 of the testimony. The committee find nothing in the conduct of either of these members in taking this stock that calls for any recommendation by the committee.

MR. JAMES BROOKS, OF NEW-YORK.

The case of Mr. Brooks stands upon a different state of facts from any of those already given. The committee find from the evidence as follows:

Mr. Brooks had been a warm advocate of a Pacific railroad, both in Congress and the public Press. After persons interested in the Union Pacific Road had obtained control of the Credit Mobilier charter, and organized under it for the purpose of making it a construction company to build the road, Dr. Durant, who was then the leading man in the enterprise, made great efforts to get the stock of the Credit Mobilier taken. Mr. Brooks was a friend of Dr. Durant, and he made some effort to aid Dr. Durant in getting subscriptions for the stock. He introduced the matter to some capitalists in New-York, but his efforts were not crowned with success. During this period Mr. Brooks had talked with Dr. Durant about taking some of the stock for himself, and had spoken of taking $15,000 or $20,000 of it, but no definite contract was made between them, and Mr. Brooks was under no legal obligation to take the stock or Durant to give it to him. In October, 1867, Mr. Brooks was appointed by the President one of the Government directors of the Union Pacific Road. In December, 1867, after the stock of the Credit Mobilier was understood by those familiar with the affairs between the Union Pacific and the Credit Mobilier to be worth very much more than par, Mr. Brooks applied to Dr. Durant and claimed that he should have 200 shares of Credit Mobilier stock. It does not appear that Mr. Brooks claimed he had any legal contract for the stock that he could enforce, or that Durant considered himself in any way legally bound to let him have any; but still, on account of what had been said, and the efforts of Mr. Brooks to aid him, he considered himself under obligation to satisfy Mr. Brooks in the matter. The stock had been so far taken up and was then in such demand that Durant could not well comply with Mr. Brooks' demand for 200 shares. After considerable negotiation it was finally adjusted between them by Durant agreeing to let Brooks have 100 shares of Credit Mobilier stock and giving him with it $5,000 of Union Pacific bonds and $20,000 of Union Pacific stock. Dr. Durant testified that he then considered Credit Mobilier stock worth double the par value, and that the bonds and stock he was to give Mr. Brooks worth $9,000, so that he saved about $1,000 by not giving Brooks the additional 100 shares he claimed. After the negotiation had been concluded between Mr. Brooks and Dr. Durant, Mr. Brooks said that as he was a Government director of the Union Pacific Road, and as the law provided such directors should not be stockholders in the company, he would not hold this stock, and directed Dr. Durant to transfer it to his son-in-law, Chas. H. Neilson. The whole negotiation with Durant was conducted by Mr. Brooks himself, and Neilson had nothing to with the transaction, except to receive the transfer. The $10,000 to pay for the 100 shares was paid by Mr. Brooks, and he received the $5,000 of Pacific bonds which came with the stock. The certificate of transfer of the 100 shares from Durant to Neilson is dated Dec. 26, 1867. On the 3d of July, 1868, there was a dividend of eighty per cent. Union Pacific bonds paid on the Credit Mobilier stock. The bonds were received by Neilson, but passed over at once to Mr. Brooks. It is claimed, both by Mr. Brooks and Neilson, that the $10,000 paid by Mr. Brooks was a loan of that sum by him to Neilson, and that the bonds received from Durant, and those received from the dividend, were delivered and held by him as collateral security for the loan. No note or obligation was given for the money by Neilson, nor, so far as we can learn from either Brooks or Neilson, was any account or memorandum of the transaction kept by either of them. At the time of the agreement or settlement above spoken of between Brooks and Durant, there was nothing said about Mr. Brooks being entitled to have fifty per cent. more stock by virtue of his ownership of the 100 shares. Neither Mr. Brooks nor Durant thought of any such thing. Some time after the transfer of the shares to Neilson, Mr. Brooks called on Sidney Dillon, then the President of the Credit Mobilier, and claimed that he or Neilson was entitled to fifty additional shares of the stock by virtue of the purchase of the 100 shares of Durant. This was claimed by Mr. Brooks as his right by virtue of the fifty per cent. increase of the stock hereinbefore described. Mr. Dillon said he did not know how that was, but he would consult the leading stockholders, and be governed by them. Mr. Dillon, in order to justify himself in the transaction, got up a paper authorizing the issue of fifty shares of the stock to Mr. Brooks, and procured it to be signed by most of the principal shareholders. After this had been done, an entry of fifty shares was made on the stock ledger to some person other than Neilson. The name in two places on the book had been erased, and the name of Neilson inserted. The committee are satisfied that the stock was first entered on the books in Mr. Brooks' name. Mr. Neilson soon after called for the certificate for the fifty shares, and on the 29th of February, 1868, the certificate was issued to him, and the entry on the stock-book was changed to Neilson. Mr. Neilson procured Mr. Dillon to advance the money to pay for the stock, and at the same delivered to Dillon $1,000 Union Pacific bonds and fifty shares of Union Pacific stock as collateral security. These bonds and stock were a portion of dividends received at the time, as he was allowed to receive the same per cents of dividends on these fifty shares that had previously been paid on the 100. This matter has never been adjusted between Neilson and Dillon. Messrs. Brooks and Neilson both testify they never paid Dillon, and Dillon thinks he has received his pay, as he has not now the collaterals in his possession. If he has been paid, it is probable it was from the collaterals in some form. The subject has never been named between Dillon and Neilson since Dillon advanced the money, and no one connected with the transaction seems able to give any further light upon it. The whole business by which these fifty shares were procured was done by Mr. Brooks. Neilson knew nothing of any right to have them, and only went for the certificate when told to do so by Mr. Brooks. The committee find that no such right to fifty shares additional stock passed by the transfer of the one hundred, and from Mr. Brooks' familiarity with the affairs of the company, the committee believe he must have known his claim to them was unfounded. The question naturally arises, how was he able to procure them. The stock at this time, by the stockholders, was considered worth three or four times its par value. Neilson sustained no relation to any of these people that commanded any favor, and if he could have used any influence he did not attempt it. If he had this right he was unaware of it till told by Mr. Brooks, and left the whole matter in his hands. It is clear that the shares were procured by the sole efforts of Mr. Brooks, and, as the stockholders who consented to it supposed, for the benefit of Mr. Brooks. What power had Mr. Brooks to enforce an unfounded claim to have for $5,000 stock worth $15,000 or $20,000? Mr. McComb swears that he had heard a conversation between Mr. Brooks and Mr. John B. Alley, a large stockholder and one of the Executive Committee, in which Mr. Brooks urged that he should have the additional fifty shares because he was, or would procure himself to be, made a Government director, and also that, being a Member of Congress he would take care of the Democratic side of the House. Mr. Brooks and Mr. Alley both deny having had any such conversation, or that Mr. Brooks ever made such a statement to Mr. Alley. If, therefore, this matter rested wholly upon the testimony of Mr. McComb, the Committee would not feel justified in finding that Mr. Brooks procured the stock by such use of his position; but all the circumstances seem to point exactly in that direction, and we can find no other satisfactory solution of the above question propounded. Whatever claim Mr. Brooks had to the stock, either legal or moral had been adjusted and satisfied by Dr. Durant. Whether he was getting for himself or to give to his son-in-law, we believe from the circumstances attending the whole transaction that he obtained it knowing that it was yielded to his official position and influence, and with the intent to secure his favor and influence in such positions. Mr. Brooks claims that he has no interest in this stock whatever; that the benefit and advantages of his right to have it he gave to Mr. Neilson, his son-in-law, and that he had had all the dividends upon it. The committee are unable to find this to be the case, for in their judgment all the facts and circumstances show Mr. Brooks to be the real and substantial owner, and that Neilson's ownership is merely nominal and colorable. In June, 1868, there was a cash dividend of $9,000 upon this 150 shares of stock. Neilson received it, of course, as the stock was in his name, but on the same day it was paid over to Mr. Brooks (as Neilson says) to pay so much of the $10,000 advanced by Mr. Brooks to pay for the stock. This then repaid all but the $1,000 of the loan, but Mr. Brooks continued to hold $11,000 of the Union Pacific bonds, which Neilson says he gave him as collateral security, and to draw the interest upon all but $5,000. The interest upon the others, Neilson says, he was permitted to draw and retain. But at one time in his testimony he spoke of the amount he was allowed as being Christmas and New-Year's presents. Mr. Neilson says that during the last Summer he borrowed $14,000 of Mr. Brooks, and now he owes Mr. Brooks nearly as much as the collaterals; but according to his testimony, Mr. Brooks for four years held $16,000 in bonds as security for $1,000, and received the interest on $11,000 of the collaterals. No accounts appear to have been kept between Mr. Brooks and Mr. Neilson; and doubtless what sums he has received from Mr. Brooks out of the dividends were intended as presents rather than the delivering of money belonging to him. Mr. Brooks' efforts procured the stock and his money paid for it. All the cash dividend he has received, and he holds all the bonds except those Dillon received, which seem to have been applied toward paying for the fifty shares. Without further comment upon the evidence, the Committee find that the 150 shares of the stock appearing on the books of the Credit Mobilier in the name of Neilson were really the stock of Mr. Brooks, and subject to his control, and that it was understood by both parties. Mr. Brooks had taken such an interest in the Credit Mobilier Company, and was so connected with Dr. Durant, that he must be regarded as having full knowledge of the relation between that Company and the Railroad Company, and of the contracts between them. He must have known the cause of the sudden increase in value of the Credit Mobilier stock, and how the large expected profits were to be made. We have already expressed our view of the propriety of a member of Congress becoming the owner of stock possessing the knowledge. But Mr. Brooks was not only a member of Congress, but he was a Government director in the Union Pacific Company. As such it was his duty to guard and watch over the interests of the Government in the road, and to see that they were protected and preserved. To insure such faithfulness on the part of Government directors, Congress very wisely provided that they should not be stockholders in the road. Mr. Brooks readily saw that though becoming a stockholder in the Credit Mobilier was not forbidden by the letter of the law, yet it was a violation of the spirit and essence, and therefore had the stock placed in the name of his son-in-law. The transfer of the Oakes Ames contract to the trustees to the building of the road under the contract, from which the enormous dividends were all derived, was all during Mr. Brooks' official life as a Government Director, must have been within his knowledge, and yet passed without the slightest opposition from him. The committee believe this could not have been done without an entire disregard of his official obligations and duty, and that while appointed to guard the public interests in the road, he joined himself with the promoters of a scheme whereby the Government was to be defrauded, and shared in the spoil. In the conclusions of fact upon the evidence the committee are entirely agreed.

In considering what action we ought to recommend to the House, upon these facts, the committee encounter a question which has been much debated: Has this House power and jurisdiction to inquire concerning offenses committed by its members prior to their election and to punish them by censure or expulsion. The committee are unanimous upon the right of jurisdiction of this House over the cases of Mr. Ames and Mr. Brooks upon the facts found in regard to them.

AS TO JURISDICTION.

Upon the question of jurisdiction, the committee present the following views: The Constitution in the fifth section of the first article, defines the power of either House as follows: "Each House may determine the rules of its proceedings, punish its members for disorderly behavior, and with the concurrence of two-thirds may expel a member." It will be observed that there is no qualification of the power, but there is an important qualification of the manner of its exercise. It must be done with the concurrence of two-thirds. The close analogy between this power and the power of impeachment is deserving of consideration. The great purpose of the power of impeachment is to remove an unfit and unworthy incumbent from office; and though a judgment of impeachment may, to some extent, operate as a punishment, that is not its principal object. Members of Congress are not subject to be impeached, but may be expelled; and the principal purpose of expulsion is not as punishment, but to remove a member whose character and conduct shows that he is an unfit man to participate in the deliberations and decisions of the body, and whose presence in it tends to bring the body into contempt and disgrace. In both cases it is a power of purgation and purification to be exercised for the public safety, and in the case of expulsion, for the protection and character of the House. The Constitution defines the causes of impeachment, to wit, treason, bribery, or other high crimes or misdemeanors. The office of the power of expulsion is so much the same as that of the power to impeach, that we think it may be safely assumed that whatever would be a good cause of impeachment would also be a good cause of expulsion. It has never been contended that the power to impeach for any of the causes enumerated was intended to be restricted to those which might occur after appointment to a civil office, so that a civil officer who had secretly committed such offense before his appointment should not be subject, upon detection and exposure, to be convicted and removed from office. Every consideration of justice and sound policy would seem to require that the public interests be secured, and those chosen to be their guardians be free from the pollution of high crimes, no matter at what time that pollution had attached. If this be so in regard to other civil officers under institutions which rest upon the intelligence and virtue of the people, can it well be claimed that the law-making Representative may be vile and criminal with impunity, provided the evidences of his corruption are found to ante-date his election? In the report made to the Senate by John Quincy Adams, in December, 1807, upon the case of John Smith, of Ohio, the following language is used: "The power of expelling a member for misconduct results, on the principles of common sense, from the interests of the nation, that the high trust of legislation shall be invested in pure hands. When the trust is elective, it is not to be presumed that the constituent body will commit the deposit to the keeping of worthless characters. But when a man whom his fellow-citizens have honored with their confidence in a pledge of a spotless reputation has degraded himself by the commission of infamous crimes, which become suddenly and unexpectedly revealed to the world, defective, indeed, would that institution be which should be impotent to discard from its bosom the contagion of such a member, which should have no remedy of amputation to apply until the poison had reached the heart."

The case of Smith was that of a Senator who, after his election, but not during a session of the Senate, had been involved in the treasonable conspiracy of Aaron Burr. Yet the reasoning is general, and was to antagonize some positions which had been taken in the case of Marshall, a Senator from Kentucky, the Senate in that case having, among other reasons, declined to take jurisdiction of the charge, for the reason that the alleged offense had been committed prior to the Senator's election, and was a matter cognizable by the criminal courts of Kentucky. None of the commentators upon the Constitution, or upon parliamentary law assign any such limitation as to the time of the commission of the offense, or the nature of it, which shall contest and limit the power of expulsion. On the contrary, they all assert that the power, in its very nature, is a discretionary one, to be exercised, of course, with grave circumspection at all times and only for good cause. Story, Kent, and Sergeant all seem to accept and rely upon the exposition of Mr. Adams in the Smith case as sound. May, in his *Parliamentary Practice*, page 59, enumerates the causes for expulsion from Parliament, but he nowhere intimates that the offense must have been committed subsequent to the election. When it is remembered that the framers of our Constitution were familiar with the Parliamentary law of England, and must have had in mind the then recent contest of the Wilkes case, it is impossible to conclude that they meant to limit the discretion of the Houses as to the causes of expulsion. It is a received principle of construction that the Constitution is to be interpreted according to the known rules of law at the time of its adoption, and, therefore, when we find them dealing with a recognized subject of legislative authority, and while studiously qualifying and restricting the manner of its exercise, assigning no limitation to the subject matter itself, they must be assumed to have intended to leave that to be determined according to established principles as a high prerogative power to be exercised according to the sound discretion of the body. It was not to be apprehended that two-thirds of the Representatives of the people would ever exercise this power in any capricious or arbitrary manner, or trifle with or trample upon constitutional rights. At the same time it could not be foreseen what necessities for self-preservation or self-purification might arise in the legislative body. Therefore, it was, that they did not, and would not undertake to limit or define the boundaries of those necessities. The doctrine that the jurisdiction of the House over the members is exclusively confined to matters arising subsequent to their election, and that the body is bound to retain the vilest criminal as a member, if his criminal secret was kept until his election was secured, has been supposed by many to have been established and declared in the famous case of John Wilkes before alluded to.

A short statement of that case will show how fallacious is that supposition. Wilkes had been elected a member of Parliament from Middlesex, and in 1764 was expelled for having published a libel of the ministry. He was again elected, and again expelled for a similar offense, on the 3d of February, 1769. Being again elected on the 17th of February, 1769, the Commons passed the following resolution:

That John Wilkes, Esq., having been on this session of Parliament expelled from this House, was, and is, incapable of being elected a member to serve in this present Parliament.

Wilkes was again elected, but the House of Commons declared the seat vacant and ordered a new election. At this election Wilkes was again elected by 1,143 votes, against 296 for his competitor, Luttrell. On the 15th of April, 1769, the House decided that, by the previous action of Wilkes he had become ineligible, and that the votes given for him were void and could not be counted, and gave the seat to Luttrell. Subsequently, in 1783, the House of Commons declared the resolution of Feb. 17, 1769, which had asserted the incapacity of an expelled member to be re-elected to the same Parliament, to be subversive of the rights of the electors, and expunged it from the journal. It will be seen from this concise statement of the Wilkes case that the question was not raised as to the power of the House to expel a member for offenses committed prior to his election. The point decided and afterward most properly expunged was, that expulsion *per se* rendered the expelled member legally ineligible, and that votes cast for him could not be counted. The Wilkes offense was of a purely political character, not involving moral turpitude. He had attacked the Ministry in the Press, and the proceedings against him in Parliament were then claimed to be a partisan political prosecution, subversive of the rights of the people and of the liberty of the Press. These proceedings in the Wilkes case took place during the appearance of the famous "Junius" letters, and several of them are devoted to the discussion of them. The doctrine that expulsion creates ineligibility was attacked and exposed by him with great force, but he concedes that if the cause of expulsion be one that renders a man unfit and unworthy to be a member, he may be expelled for that cause as often as he shall be elected.

The case of Matteson, in the House of Representatives, has also often been quoted as a precedent for this limitation of jurisdiction. In the proceedings and debates of the House upon that case, it will be seen that this was one among many grounds taken in the debate, but as the whole subject was ended by being laid on the table, it is quite impossible to say what was decided by the House. It appeared, however, in that case, that the charge against Matteson had become public, and his letter, upon which the whole charge rested, had been published and circulated through his district during the canvass preceding his election. This fact, we judge, had a most important influence in determining the action of the House in his case.

The committee have no occasion in this report to discuss the question as to the power or duty of the House in a case where a constituency, with a full knowledge of the objectionable character of the man, have selected him to be their representative. It is hardly a case to be supposed that any constituency with a full knowledge that a man had been guilty of an offense involving moral turpitude would elect him. The majority of the committee are not prepared to concede that such a man could be forced upon the House, and would not consider the expulsion of such a man any violation of the rights of the electors. For, while the electors have rights that should be respected, the House as a body has rights also that should be respected and preserved. But that in such case the judgment of the constituency would be entitled to the greatest consideration, and that this should form an important element in its determination is readily admitted. It is universally conceded, as we believe, that the House has ample jurisdiction to punish or expel a member for an offense committed during his term as a member, though committed during a vacation of Congress and in no way connected with his duties as a member. Upon what principle is it that such a jurisdiction can be maintained? It must be upon one or the other or both of the following:

That the offense shows him to be an unworthy and improper man to be a member, or that his conduct brings odium and reproach upon the body. But suppose the offense has been committed prior to his election, but comes to light afterward, is the effect upon own character or the reproach and disgrace upon the body, if they allow him to be a member, any less? We can see no difference in principle in the two cases, and to attempt any would be to create a purely technical and arbitrary distinction, having no just foundation. In our judgment the time is not at all material, except it be coupled with the further fact that he was re-elected with the knowledge on the part of his constituents of what he had been guilty of, and, in such event, we have given our views of the effect. It seems to us absurd to say that an election has given a man political absolution for an offense which was unknown to his constituents. If it be urged again, as it has sometimes been, that this view of the power of the House and the true ground of its proper exercise may be laid hold of and used improperly, it may be answered that no rule known, however narrow and limited, that may be adopted can prevent it. If two-thirds of the House shall see fit to expel a man because they do not like his political or religious principles, or without any reason at all, they have the power. Such exercise of the power would be wrongful and in violation of the principles of the Constitution; but we see no encouragement of such wrong in the views we hold. It is the duty of each House to exercise its rightful functions upon appropriate occasions, and to trust that those who come after them will be no less faithful to duty, and no less zealous for the rights of free, popular representation than themselves. It will be quite time to square other cases with right, reason, and principle when they arise. Perhaps the best way to prevent them will be to maintain strictly public integrity and public honor in all cases as they present themselves. Nor do we imagine that the people of the United States will charge servants with invading their privileges where they conform themselves to the preservation of a standard of official integrity, which the common instincts of humanity recognize as essential to all social order and good government.

APPLICATION IN THE PRESENT CASES.

The foregoing are the views which we deem proper to submit upon the general question of the jurisdiction of the House over its members. But apart from these general views the committee are of the opinion that the facts found in the present cases, amply justify the taking jurisdiction over them for the following reasons:

The subject matter upon which the action of members was intended to be influenced was of a continuous character, and was as likely to be a subject of Congressional action in future Congresses as in the Fortieth. The influences brought to bear on members were as likely to be operative upon them in the future as in the present, and were so intended. Mr. Ames and Mr. Brooks have both continued members of the House to the present time, and so have most of the members upon whom these influences were sought to be exerted. The committee are, therefore, of the opinion that the acts of these men should very properly be treated as offenses against the present House, and so within its jurisdiction upon the most limited rule. Two members of the committee, Messrs. Niblack and McCrary, prefer to express no opinion on the general jurisdictional questions discussed in the report and their judgment on the ground just stated.

AMES.

In relation to Mr. Ames, he sold to several members of Congress stock of the Credit Mobilier Company at par when it was worth double that amount or more, with the purpose and intent thereby to influence their votes and decisions upon matters to come before Congress.

BROOKS.

The facts found in the report as to Mr. Brooks show that he used this influence of his official position as member of Congress and Government Director of the Union Pacific Railroad Company to get fifty shares of the stock of the Credit Mobilier Company at par when it was worth three or four times that sum, knowing that it was given to him with intent to influence his votes and decisions in Congress and his action as a Government director. The sixth section of the act of Feb. 26, 1853, (10 Stat. U. S. 7) is in the following words:

If any person or persons shall directly or indirectly promise, offer or give or cause or procure to be promised, offered or given, any money, goods, right in action, bribe, present or reward, or any promise, contract, undertaking, obligation or annuity for the payment or delivery of any money, goods, right in action, bribe, present or reward, or any other valuable thing whatever, to any member of the Senate or House of Representatives of the United States, after his election as such member, and either before or after he shall have qualified and taken his seat, or to any officers of the United States or persons holding any place of trust or profit, or discharging any official function under or in connection with any department of the Government of the United States after the passage of this act, with intent to influence his vote or decision on any question, matter, cause, or proceeding, which may then be pending, or may by law or under the Constitution of the United States, be brought before him in his official capacity, or in his place of trust or profit, and shall thereof be convicted, such person or persons so offering, promising or giving, or causing or procuring to be promised, offered, or given any such money, goods, right in action, bribe, present, or reward, or any promise, contract, undertaking, obligation, or security for the payment or delivery of any money, goods, right in action, bribe, present, or reward, or other valuable thing whatever, and the member, officer, or person who shall in anywise accept or receive the same, or any part thereof, shall be liable to indictment as for a high crime and misdemeanor, in any of the Courts of the United States having jurisdiction for the trial of crimes and misdemeanors, and shall, upon conviction thereof, be fined not exceeding ten times the amount so offered, promised, or given, and imprisoned in a penitentiary not exceeding ten years; and the person convicted of so accepting or receiving the same, or any part thereof, if an officer or any person holding any such place of trust or profit as aforesaid, shall forfeit his office or place; and any person so convicted under this section shall forever be disqualified to hold any office of honor, trust, or profit under the United States.

In the judgment of the committee, the fact reported in regard to Mr. Ames and Mr. Brooks would have justified their conviction under the above recited statute, and subject them to the penalties therein provided.

The committee need not enlarge upon the dangerous character of these offenses. The sense of Congress is shown by the severe penalty denounced by the statute itself. The offenses are not a violation of private right, but were against the very life of a constitutional government by poisoning the fountain of legislation.

The duty devolved upon the committee has been of a most painful and delicate character. They have performed it to the best of their ability. They have proceeded with the greatest care and deliberation; for, while they desired to do their full duty to the House and the country, they were most anxious not to do injustice to any man. In forming these conclusions they have intended to be entirely cool and dispassionate; not to allow themselves to be swerved by any popular favor on the one hand, or any feeling of personal favor and sympathy on the other.

EXPULSION.

The committee submit to the House and recommend the adoption of the following resolutions:

1. *Whereas*, Mr. Oakes Ames, Representative in this House from the State of Massachusetts, has been guilty of selling to members of Congress shares of stock in the Credit Mobilier of America for prices much below the true value of such stock, with intent thereby to influence the votes and decisions of such members in matters to be brought before Congress for action; therefore

Resolved, That Mr. Oakes Ames be and is hereby expelled from his seat as a member of this House.

2. *Whereas*, Mr. James Brooks, a representative in this House from the State of New-York, did procure the Credit Mobilier Company to issue and deliver to Mr. Charles H. Neilson, for the use and benefit of said Brooks, fifty shares of the stock of said company at a price much below its real value, well knowing that the same was so issued and delivered with intent to influence the vote and decision of said Brooks as a member of the House on matters to be brought before Congress for action, and also to influence the action of said Brooks as a Government director in the Union Pacific Railroad Company; therefore,

Resolved, That Mr. James Brooks be and is hereby expelled from his seat as a member of this House.

February 19, 1873

GLEANINGS FROM THE MAILS

JAY GOULDISM GENERALLY.

SENTIMENTS OF A WESTERN NEWSPAPER THAT WILL BE APPLAUDED EVERYWHERE.

From the Omaha Bee.

The excitement in New-York over the discovery that Jay Gould is endeavoring to capture the Governorship of that State with a view to blocking unfriendly legislation against the corporations which he controls, is natural and gratifying. It is proof that the people of the Empire State are becoming aroused to the dangers which threaten our political institutions through the corrupting influences of corporate monopolies. These designs, if unchecked, threaten to wreck the foundations of the Republic and erect upon its ruins an autocracy whose power is derived from bribery and corruption, and whose authority is based upon wealth and plunder.

It is not at all surprising that Mr. Gould is endeavoring to play the same game in New-York which has been so successful in other portions of the country. Pennsylvania, Ohio, Delaware, and New-Jersey in the East, and every State and Territory west of the Missouri River have felt the corrupting influences of the corporations in politics. In our own State, which for some years Mr. Gould considered as his personal property, the monopolies have taken a leading part in making and unmaking laws, in packing our primaries and conventions, and in elevating their paid tools and attorneys to positions of honor and representative trust. California is now wrestling with the monopoly anaconda which has fastened itself around every industry and holds the Legislature and courts in its slimy grasp. The revolt in New-Jersey against the railroad empire which has been built up at the expense of prosperous cities, growing communities, and the good name of the State, began last Spring, when the bribing of officials and the control of the Legislature by corporation tools was clearly proved to the public. In a score of States public sentiment, so long blinded to the dangers which threatened good government and local prosperity, is arousing itself to demand that the people and not the corporations shall rule the country, and the cry of anti-monopoly is issuing from thousands who five years ago were unable to see in the present management of the railroads anything but a blessing to the Nation and a benefit to the State.

The railroads have no one but themselves to blame if a spirit of bitter antagonism has sprung up between their managers and the people whom they propose to serve. No nation on the globe has so eagerly fostered internal communication as our own. Grants of lands and subsidies of money, State and local bonds, invaluable franchises and privileges have been freely granted to corporations as inducements to build their lines and carry on the business of common carriers for the public. But whatever else they have given up, the people never intended to yield their right of self-government. They never contemplated that the monopolies would ever become their masters, or that corporations after securing every avenue of transportation would also assume to lay hands on the avenue of legislation and Government. The entry of the corporations into politics has been followed by a debauchery and corruption to which our legislative halls were formerly strangers. Our law makers have been bribed and our officials purchased. The will of the people has been made subservient to the caprices of the monopolies, while the aid of the law has been called in to glaze over the schemes of robbery and plunder, which needed the thin covering of a purchased legality to accomplish the wishes of their promoters.

The corporations have never engaged in politics for any good end. In general the object has been to secure positions of trust, which, if held by honest men, would constantly be used to block their dishonest plans of public robbery. In our own State, in New-Jersey, and as events have proved, in New-York, the aim has been to shirk a rightful burden of taxation upon the shoulders of an already overtaxed people. In a hundred cases cited, the object was to control local legislative machinery to further schemes for extorting money from the public in the shape of subsidies and bonds. In every instance their influence has been demoralizing in the extreme. It has fostered corruption, pandered to representative treachery to constituents, wrecked hard-won reputations, and played havoc with character.

The development of the lobby is another result of corporation politics. Our State-houses and the national Capitol have swarmed with the paid advocates of the monopolies, who brazenly boast of the means at their command, and barter the money and favor of their masters for votes and influence.

The people are beginning to cry "hands off." They have listened too long to the demand "hands up." They insist that the corporations shall confine their attention to their business, regulated by the laws and obedient to the restrictions which they have placed upon the common carriers. And they are determined that the machinery of the Government and the law-making and the law-interpreting branches, and the officials who are sworn to carry those laws into effect, shall no longer be controlled by unscrupulous highwaymen or captured by dishonest and designing corporation tricksters.

August 29, 1882

HOW TO BUILD A RAILROAD

THE LITTLE SCHEME THAT IS WORKED ON CAPITALISTS.

HOW THE SIMPLE-MINDED MEN OF MONEY ARE MADE TO PAY FOR ROADS WHICH THE MAN OF WITS OWNS.

It is the easiest thing in the world—on paper. You take a map of the existing railways in any State or States; it looks like an exagerated cob-web; you note when you think another strand is needed in the web, or at least where it looks as if it were needed, it is the some-thing for your purpose. A clever engineer will then draw you a special map of the road you propose to work and you visit that part of the country, where you are surprised with what unanimity the farmers and villages wand, nay, must have, a railroad through their land, and they willingly agree to give free, or for a nominal sum or other consideration, the right of way necessary. Do not get too much of this, as it is a mine you can work by and by. Then make arrangements with a few pot-house politicians or small local bankers in a few of the more important towns along the route, and get them to call a meeting of the citizens. This is sure of good attendance where the admittance is free; a good talker leads off, some resolutions are offered and passed before any one has time to digest them, the local reporters is "seen," and the thing is done—that town is declared auanimously in favor of the new railroad, and has (apparently) pledged itself for, say, $10,000 to $20,000 of the stock or bonds. With a few such resolutions and some clippings from the local newspapers you are prepared to come to New-York and lay your scheme before the capitalists there.

You must now secure the co-operation of one or two shrewd, unscrupulous men—the skirmishers of Wall-street—men who occupy the debatable land between honesty and dishonesty, tricky and doubtful subjects, but whose schemes, through being sometimes successful, are listened to by moneyed men, "making haste to be rich" and eager for investment. The road must have name—call it the Gotham, Oshkosh and Chicago—no matter that it does not start from Gotham, does not go near Oshkesh, or ever reaches Chicago, it is a good name and sounds well. You form one company to build the road and call it the G., O. & C. Construction Company, and another company to take the road when built, and call it the G., O. & C. Railway Company. The same people form both companies, but with different officers, only be careful to have the majority of the officers and Directors on your side, and appoint the Treasurer of the construction company to be the chief engineer of the railway company, so that the monthly estimates of expenditures will be sure to be correct! Appoint a first-class, leading man to be Trustee of the mortgage, but he must be a very busy man, with no time to examine things too closely. His name, however, will carry great weight and have its influence on subscribers. A well-printed prospectus and a handsomely engraged stock certificate have their influence, slight, perhaps, but everything counts. The construction company's stock carries with it a big bonus of, say, dollar for dollar in certificates of first mortgage bonds of the railroad company—these are like faith, "an evidence of things not seen," but hoped for. It is understood that subscriptions will only be called for up to 50 cents on the dollar: of course you do not propose to limit it to that figure, but somebody promises something to that effect; perhaps it is your Treasurer; anyhow, the effect is produced, as it is a curious fact that many very shrewd men think it safer and better to own 100 half-paid shares for $5,000 than 50 full-paid shares for same amount. Of course, you open the lists with a big subscription from yourself and your associates, on which, of course, your Treasurer makes the necessary entries to cover moneys you do not pay in.

When the money begins to come in steadily you make your contract for the building of the road with a friend at good figures, and he sub-lets to the real builders at lesser figures , and as your Treasurer is also chief engineer the measurements on each month's estimate are, of course, correct! You and your double-officer "divvy" with this friend, and, if you are wise with the wisdom of the serpent, you also select some outside railway man and give him an interest in the contract, not that he has done anything for it, but you can work it so that some day his opinion as an expert will be asked by the capitalists, and thus to them assurance is made doubly sure. In the process of time you will put him on the Board of Directors, where, if any awkward questions are asked, he will be a power on your side. The railroad man is a big factor in your scheme. He is probably one of those who come to the surface from time to time and who again sink into oblivion, where they properly belong. While at the surface they cut a big figure; diamond breast-pin and fast horses, broad-cloth suit, loud, vulgar manner; insist on being classed as "gentleman;" house furnished by contract, library for the bindings and pictures by the yard; they do not know a cyclopedia by the yard; they do not know a cyclopedia from an autobiography, but they do know how to buy up engineers and do other dirty work. For the time-being they are eminently respectable, as they have probably made a good thing out of their last contract and can show some ready money. This man as soon as he is on the board take the lead, as a practical man, in all discussions as to the working or building expenses. As the capitalist is, as a rule, ignorant as to details, you can have your engineering and right of was expenses made anything in reason, and as to the cost of grading, bridging, and labor generally, your capitalist is helpless in your hands backed up by our railroad contractor. You yourself stand pretty high in the community, or think you do. You are either an ex-General or an ex-Judge, but your handle sticks to you and lends dignity to the enterprise, and is, of course, worth money, so you sell it to the company under the name of "charter and previous contracts for right of way, entry into Oshkosh," & c- for $100,000, which is divided with your associates—"pals" the vulger call them. After a few months you work your right of way, your agent makes a bargain with a farmer for $15 per acre; a "naught" is added; you pay the bill and "divvy." Perhaps the farmer sues for damages and claims say $5,000; you compromise with great difficulty (!) for $2,000; the farmer gets $200 or ¢300, and again a "divvy," and so on *ad infinitum*.

Though at this rate your money be soon exhausted, yet as the capitalist is in he must keep on to save what he has to put up. Then begins a gentle and judicious "milking" process; you give out that a few thousand dollars more is all that is necessary to finish the road to a certain point, from which it can be put on a paying basis, and then when the market (that elastic term!) is better you will be able to place your railway bonds at a good figure and with the proceeds go on with the work. Meantime you tell them you are negotiating with a trunk line, to whom your "lay-out" is an absolute necessity. A few indefinite interviews with this same trunk line seems to confirm this statement, and the needful funds are raised. The prime movers need put up nothing, you having honestly put in your all(?) already, but not to be outdone in generosity you give up your salaries (you, of course, all had salaries) and agree to go on for nothing. An outsider feels like exclaiming, "Generous men! they bravely determine to work hard day in and day out for a year or two for absolutely nothing, and all they ask is the Divine approval and the consciousness of having done their duty. Is it possible that the board will listen to the counsels of one or two wicked men and begin to suspect that this is too diaphanous? Are these good, disinterested men to have a slight cast on their motives by the suggestion that possibly their nests are already lined? Perish the thought! Let us have an investigation, we insist upon it: only give our Treasurer time to arrange his books and accounts; he possibly finds that his cash-book is blotted, scratched, and looks dirty, and a clean (?) copy must be made; his stock account is a little mixed from so many transfers having been made, and he may not be sure if it tallies; his bond account also requires arranging(?) by reason of the carelessness of clerks and so you manage to get him a month or two to "fix" matters all right. Meantime you get up a quarrel(?) with your own associates, and half of you resign indignantly or are removed; the other half, and especially our railroad friend, must remain with the enemy. An expert is called in, and you quitely and unobtrusively throw every possible obstacle in his way while apparently assisting him in his inquiries. He states clearly and concisely what he finds, but the very enormity of it is too much for human credulity. It cannot be true, you indignantly protest, and besides, if it is true, how ridiculous it makes the enemy. What! to have all New-York made aware of how easily a set of its shrewdest, sharpest men have been guiled: to have these man made a laughing-stock of Wall-Street! it will never do; rather keep it quiet and try to save what is possible. And what good will it do to make it public; will it give back the money? In other words, it won't pay these moneyed men to quarrel with you; their money is in, and they must either face the music and go on or pocket the loss quietly and retire. Many, of course, choose the latter alternative, and it is with those that remain that your railroad friend comes in handy. He too, has put up his money, perhaps inadvertently, a great deal more than he has so far made out of you, and so with virtuous indignation he sides with the enemy. Insinuates all sort of evil against you, but quietly keeps you posted on every movement of the enemy till you and he together gradually get things your own way again, the expert's statements are shelved, suspicion is lulled to sleep for a time and you again proceed to "milk" the capitalist. Meantime, you remain filled with a conscious rectitude of purpose and a little nest egg, while the capitalists have a railroad 10 miles long, beginning and ending nowhere, and which cost half a million dollars in cash and has over half a million in bonds put against it. *"Dum Vivimus Vivamus!"*

October 14, 1883

HIT BACK AT ANTI-PASS RULE.

Pittsburg Newspapers Abolish Favors to the Pennsylvania Lines.

Special to The New York Times.

PITTSBURG, Dec. 27.—The Pennsylvania Railroad having ordered that all advertising be paid for in cash and cut off all transportation to newspapers, the Pittsburg Newspaper Publishers' Association took action to-day.

A resolution was passed to bar from the newspapers all complimentary notices relating to the Pennsylvania Railroad or its officers. All railroad wrecks are to be reported in detail, taking care that the railroads are not favored.

December 28, 1905

PASSLESS LAWMAKERS ACT.

Special to The New York Times.

OMAHA, Jan. 4.—Railroads in this State have failed to send passes, good within the boundaries of Nebraska, to the members of the State Legislature. Curiously a flood of anti-railroad bills has been brought before that body for passage, and men around the State House are now saying that every anti-railroad bill introduced will be passed. Should passes be given perhaps they would reconsider.

January 5, 1907

FINDING THE INDIVIDUAL.

Dr. WILSON'S baccalaureate returns to his favorite theme, that corporations have no moral quality, and that the true solution of corporate abuses is to find the individual responsible for them or to make some individual responsible for acts done by corporations, but which it is impossible to punish the corporation for doing without also punishing innocent shareholders. Dr. WILSON applies his theories to "societies, unions, brotherhoods, leagues, alliances, corporations, and trusts." This is comprehensive, but to our mind stops when it begins to be interesting. Why should not Legislatures be included? The idea that Legislatures can do no wrong is no longer tenable, for we have had the acts of several Legislatures condemned judicially not only as unconstitutional, but as offensive to ordinary morality, and even civilization.

We have also had examples as conspicuous, but a little finer in their application, respecting single officials, whose personality could not be divided, but whose official acts were inconsistent with any view of individual morality, or even with the repute of the officials as gentlemen. In the last analysis it may be asserted that each of us is responsible for all the acts which accord with public opinions and standards, although in conflict with laws. Whoever has admired or envied Captains of Industry is responsible for a distributive share of the acts of the Captains, for our Captains are what we have made them. They are more responsive to public opinion than to legislation, as is proved by the fact that they contest the laws, but bow to the opinion of their fellow-citizens. Thus in the last analysis the person who is to blame for widespread evils is not the corporation officer, nor the arbitrary and oppressive official, but the Average Man.

June 9, 1908

SEARS-ROEBUCK CURBED.

Chicago Firm Is Ordered to Alter Its Methods of Advertising.

WASHINGTON, June 30.—Sears, Roebusk & Co. of Chicago today was ordered by the Federal Trade Commission to desist from certain unfair methods of competition, including the circulation of false and misleading advertisements which the company admitted had been practiced.

Sales of sugar at less than cost, conditioned on the purchase of other groceries on which a sufficient price was received to give a profit on the combined sale, was one of the practices disapproved by the commission. The company also was ordered to stop advertising that its representative supervised the picking of tea offered for sale; that all of its coffees were purchased direct from the best plantations in the world, and that competitors of the company did not deal honestly with their customers.

July 1, 1918

ASSAILS BUSINESS ETHICS.

Rabbi Wise Says They Are to Blame for Oil Scandal.

Rabbi Stephen S. Wise, preaching yesterday on "The Shame of the Republic," at the Free Synogague, declared that low standards in business life were responsible for the conditions disclosed by the Senate oil investigation and criticised those who called for business in government.

"Apparently the bigger the business," he said, "the lower the standards. This is responsible for the shame of the Republic. It corrupts political life. When the captains of big business want something they get it. I look upon the men of the President's Cabinet who had part in the oil negotiations as hired tools of the world of industry, which has and makes its own standards.

"We have come to look upon politics as a business, a trade, not a calling. I deny the validity of transferring the methods and manners of the business world to political life. In business a man sets out for personal gain; in politics it is his duty to serve the people. America isn't setting out to make money.

"We'll hear it, not in 1924, but in 1928 and in 1948, that what the country needs is a business administration. Well, we have it now. The cries will go up 'Let's have an end to the college teachers.' Well, we've got the business administration they'll be clamoring for. Don't you feel like using a million dollars worth of insecticide on the verminous condition?

"A business administration means instead of business being subordinate to Government the big business demons have the opportunity to sell out the honor of the republic. They care nothing for honor and are prepared to take in their hands every weapon of dishonor and shame."

Referring to those who have "trifled and paltered with the honor of the country," Dr. Wise said that he did not mean "the Dohenys and the Sinclairs," but the "Government officials, servants of the republic, who put themselves first, and who betrayed a public trust."

President Coolidge, in the opinion of the clergyman, "is as free from stain as any person in the country." Dr. Wise asserted that one way of preventing further scandals in Government would be to form a third political party.

March 10, 1924

YOUNG SAYS MORALS SHAPE BIG BUSINESS

Financier, in Park Av. Baptist Pulpit, Declares Honesty Is Increasing Requisite.

SEES CONFIDENCE GAINED

Huge Industries, Such as Auto, Now Accepted as Servants of Public, Dawes Plan Aide Holds.

Taking as a parallel the development during the last quarter century of the automobile and the readjustment of modern life to it, Owen D. Young, speaking last night in the pulpit of the Park Avenue Baptist Church, voiced his belief in the aims and development of "big business" and its growing moral aspects and forces.

Even such an abstract and apparently strictly financial question as the bank rate, he said, "bristles with moral problems." Dishonesty in business, he argued, is exploited in the press because it is unusual, so that the dishonest man is less to be feared than the honest man who makes mistakes in judgment. On the other hand, uprightness must exist in the great business organizations of the day "on the simple ground of expediency," while modern industry has made its managers trustees, responsible not only for its material welfare but for its moral conduct as well.

Mr. Young was introduced by the Rev. Harry Emerson Fosdick to an overflowing congregation as on the eve of departure to attend the committee meeting of experts about to consider revision of the Dawes plan. The talk came in a Sunday night course on, "What Is Right With the World?" and was entitled "What is Right With Business?"

Anecdote of Early Auto Days.

"It was on a lovely, crisp October day in 1905," said Mr. Young, "when my old friend David Shaver in his one-horse lumber wagon was driving down the single street in the village of Van Hornesville where I was born. David was 75, and his horse nearly so. Standing on the bottom boards of his wagon, which had no seat, with his beard flying in the wind, David was a striking figure.

"All at once there came round a corner a big red motor car—big, that is, for those days. The old horse caught sight of the motor, heard its roar, and went over the stone wall into a little hollow. David and the wagon followed, in a great mix-up. The driver, who was a gentleman, stopped and asked David if he could do anything for him.

"'No,' said David, 'I think you've done enough for today.'"

His old friend, Mr. Young pointed out, didn't like motor cars and it was ten years before he was prevailed upon to ride in one. When he got out, however, the old man said, "This is the greatest ride of my life," Mr. Young recounted.

"Now in 1905 there was another thing coming round the bend that people didn't like, a thing known as Big Business. The roads weren't fitted for it. The drivers were quite unskilled. The horses didn't like the new device, nor the drivers. The parallel is quite applicable.

Says Big Business Is Servant.

"Dire prophecies were indulged in as to what would happen if large business units were to be permitted. It was said the masses of the people would become enslaved. But in fact it has turned out that these big organizations have become the servants of the masses—not their masters. The business machines have become better adjusted through a quarter of a century. The drivers of them have become skilled. They are, in a sense, people trained for the job, like motor-car drivers. And while we still have some reckless and irresponsible ones who are a menace to the road, by and large we move motor cars by the millions with amazing skill and safety.

"So our big business is no longer feared by the people. Exploiters no longer own the big concerns. Bankers no longer own them. Their shares are spread from one end of the country to the other. Broadly speaking, the vast organizations are in skilled hands and the road is reasonably safe."

"Now when we think of what is right or wrong in business we must take account of the conditions under which such impressions are formed. Everything was wrong with business or especially big business in the common opinion of 1905. Such prejudices which exist against it today are much more largely due to the recollections of the old days than to real complaints in this day. Just as the driver today is less considerate and less careful on the highway so it is likely to be true that the smaller units of business, not the larger ones, are less considerate and less careful.

"We have had to go through the process of adjustment, however. We have had to change our rules and practices in business and our laws governing it in the last quarter of a century, just as we have had to change our rules and practices on the highway. We have had to extend government control over business by way of regulation in the interest of all, just as we have had to compel the carrying of lights and license plates on motor cars. We have to see further ahead, and so we put strong headlights on our cars to show the road, just as we put research laboratories and long-time budgets and surveys onto our machines of business."

The danger today, Mr. Young proceeded, comes not from bad men or bad principles, but from "the difficulty of applying right principles to increasingly complicated situations. Our greatest risk is in the mistaken judgment of good drivers where the traffic is heavy and the signals are complicated."

Moral Aspects of Bank Note.

Mr. Young mentioned the discount rate of the Federal Reserve Bank as an instance.

"Do you say," he demanded, "that there is no question of right or wrong in the moral sense in the fixing of the bank rate—that it is a financial matter? I am here to tell you that I know of no act in business which bristles with more moral problems than the fixing of the bank rate. I do not mean problems in the sense that the men who fix the rate are likely to act in bad faith. Not at all. I mean in the sense that men may fail to apply correctly the sound moral principles which they recognize to a difficult and complicated business problem."

The speaker described the situation when he received a member of the German labor party during the hearings of the Reparations Committee in 1924. The mark had been tumbling rapidly. The answer the German made to Mr. Young's question as to what he could do was, "Give us a stable currency." He cited to M. Young the impossibility of German wage earners to perform their "moral obligations" with a tobogganing mark.

"In principle," Mr. Young pointed out, the Golden Rule is all that a business man needs. "Yet if you ask me to apply the Golden Rule to a bank rate, I find it amazingly difficult to do. It is like telling me to apply the multiplication table to the design and manufacture of a steam turbine. What is right in business requires that the Golden Rule be applied by men of great understanding and knowledge as well as conscience in highly complicated situations. They must be as highly skilled as the turbine engineer who makes the connection between the multiplication table and the modern high pressure turbine.

"I purposely omit from this discussion the immoral things done in business by weak and dishonorable men. Whenever these occur they are exploited in the headlines of the newspapers, not because they are the common thing but because they are the unusual thing.

Finds "Sharpness" Disappearing.

"During the last thirty years the moral standards of business have advanced. A certain amount of astuteness and cleverness and sharpness of the earlier day has disappeared. They would not work very well in large business.

"A storekeeper might short-measure or short-change his customer. He might even induce his clerk to short-weigh and short-measure. But he could not organize a vast department store on that basis. Either his employes are honest people who would refuse or he would soon have as employes a vast organization of crooks who would beat each other and soon ruin the proprietor himself. Big business does not lend itself readily to dishonesty and crookedness."

Mr. Young pointed out that while a few years ago the owners of business were responsible for it, that is not so today where shares of stock are distributed among so many thousand people. "In our modern organizations we have completely divorced ownership from responsibility. And as a result we have developed managers of business, chairmen and presidents and vast executive organizations. They alone know the business. They must be held responsible not only for its material welfare but for its moral conduct."

In the early days of big business, Mr. Young said, the tendency was to appoint lawyers as heads of corporations because lawyers seemed to be the only persons who could manage such affairs and keep inside the law. "While that was the purpose of appointing lawyers," he continued, "the result was quite different from that anticipated.

"If there is one thing a lawyer is taught it is knowledge of trusteeship and the sacredness of that position. Very soon he saw rising a notion that managers were no longer attorneys for stockholders; they were becoming trustees of an institution.

Outlines His Attitude Toward Job.

"If you will pardon me for being personal," Mr. Young proceeded, "it makes a great difference in my attitude toward my job as an executive officer of the General Electric Company whether I am a trustee of the institution or an attorney for the investor. If I am a trustee, who are the beneficiaries of the trust? To whom do I owe my obligations?

"My conception of it is this: That there are three groups of people who have an interest in that institution. One is the group of fifty-odd thousand people who have put their capital in the company, namely, its stockholders. Another is a group of well toward 100,000 people who are putting their labor and their lives into the business of the company. The third group is of customers and the general public.

"Customers have a right to demand that a concern so large shall not only do its business honestly and properly, but, further, that it shall meet its public obligations and perform its public duties—in a word, vast as it is, that it should be a good citizen.

First Safeguards Capital.

"Now, I conceive my trust first to be to see to it that the capital which is put into this concern is safe, honestly and wisely used, and paid a fair rate of return. Otherwise we cannot get capital. The worker will have no tools.

"Second, that the people who put their labor and lives into this concern get fair wages, continuity of employment and a recognition of their right to their jobs where they have educated themselves to highly skilled and specialized work.

"Third, that the customers get a product which is as represented and that the price is such as is consistent with the obligations to the people who put their capital and labor in.

"Last, that the public has a concern functioning in the public interest and performing its duties as a great and good citizen should.

"I think what is right in business is influenced very largely by the growing sense of trusteeship which I have described. One no longer feels the obligation to take from labor for the benefit of capital, nor to take from the public for the benefit of both, but rather to administer wisely and fairly in the interest of all.

"It is no easy matter to determine right and wrong, even as between the groups which I have indicated. To protect capital one must build up reserves against bad years or unforeseen contingencies. To grant fair wages or high wages and adequately reimburse employes means adjusting the price so as to provide income adequate to do it.

"To try to increase price for the sake of labor without regard to whether your labor is efficient, productive and progressive would be to take the road to ruin. It would destroy continuity of employment because one morning we would wake up and find our business gone; our prices too high; a product not good enough; employes discharged."

"Just what is right in all cases we cannot foresee. We make mistakes. We learn from our mistakes. We try to correct them. By and large, looking over the quarter century with which I have been familiar I am pleased with the rapid progress which we are making toward the right in business. We are not perfect and never shall be, but we are training young men with a sense of these great responsibilities, and we are providing them experience from our own mistakes.

"As time goes on I feel that the right in business will more and more prevail. The larger business becomes, the more scrupulously careful the administration of it will be. We have had much difficulty with questions of technical competence and moral responsibility in the offices of Aldermen, but we have had practically none in the great office of President of the United States. Somehow, as responsibility increases, men are found big enough to meet adequately the great questions of right and wrong which come to them. So I welcome big business and big responsibilities, not in the fear that it will make business wrong, but in the hope and belief that it will make business right."

January 21, 1929

GIFFORD WILL SCAN A. T. & T. 'LOBBYING'

At FCC Hearing He Says He Will Investigate Need for Any Reform in Practices

WASHINGTON, April 2 (AP).—A hope that the Communications Commission would do nothing "to unfairly injure the reputation of the A. T. & T." was coupled by President Walter S. Gifford today with a promise to scan the utility's "lobbying" practices to determine whether they should be reformed.

Testifying in the commission's $750,000 investigation of the American Telephone and Telegraph Company as Samuel Becker, special FCC counsel, introduced more than a score of exhibits detailing what he said were A. T. & T. "legislative" activities in Washington and in a dozen States, Mr. Gifford described the "legislative practices" of the A. T. & T. as "very high."

He added that he would re-examine them in the light of FCC disclosures to see whether they could be raised "any higher."

Among other things, he continued, he would study reports that A. T. & T. agents met the trains of new members of Congress to aid them in finding quarters and procuring telephone installations.

"It had never occurred to me there was anything wrong with that," the telephone head remarked. "But that is one of the things I shall consider. I am not sure now that it is such a good thing."

April 3, 1936

5 BIG STORES FINED IN PRICE-FIXING SUIT

Top Ones in Philadelphia and 9 Officials Deny Plot, Cite 'Keenest Competition'

By WILLIAM G. WEART

Special to THE NEW YORK TIMES.

PHILADELPHIA, Jan. 9—This city's five largest department stores — Wanamaker's, Gimbels, Snellenburg's, Lit's and Strawbridge & Clothier—were fined $2,500 each today for conspiring to fix prices in violation of the Sherman Anti-Trust Law.

Like the mid-city establishments, nine top executives of the companies also pleaded nolo contendere (no defense) to the same charge. United States District Court Judge Guy K. Bard suspended sentence on the store officials.

Six lawyers representing the stores and the executives entered the no-defense pleas late this afternoon immediately after the one-count "conspiracy" indictment was returned by a Federal grand jury of ten women and six men on information supplied by the United States Department of Justice.

The indictment charged that the defendants, in violation of the Sherman Act, agreed among themselves to eliminate price differences within certain narrow ranges.

Explanation by the Stores

Maurice Bower Saul, counsel for the John Wanamaker Company, acted as spokesman for all the attorneys. He said that the price increases amounted to only $80,000 for the year, while general price reductions totaled $1,630,000.

The defendants, Mr. Saul said, were willing to enter no-defense pleas because the practice was discontinued last November.

"We see no advantage in fighting out a little problem in court when we have ceased doing what the Government claims was a violation of the law, but which we do not believe it was," he told the court.

The stores are separately owned and "in keenest competition" and there never was any agreement "to sell any particular item at any particular price level," he declared, and added:

"When our clients were advised of the Government view in the fall of 1949, they immediately took steps to insure full compliance with that view. The fullest co-operation was extended by our clients to the Government in its consideration of the practices complained of."

In an outline of the case, George W. Jansen, chief of the Middle Atlantic Office of the Anti-Trust Division of the Department of Justice, told Judge Bard that the "combination and conspiracy" began last February or March. It had the effect, he said, of increasing prices, as follows:

When an article was to be sold for less than $1 it was not to be sold at any price between 90 and 97 cents. When it was to be sold for more than $1 but less than $10, all price endings between 86 and 97 cents were to be eliminated. If the price was more than $10, all price endings between 50 and 94 cents were eliminated.

This, the Government contended, raised prices that were formerly between 90 to 97 cents to a uniform 98 cents; prices that formerly ran from 85 cents to $9.85 to a uniform $1.98 to $9.98; and tags that were formerly $10.50, $11.50, and the like, to a uniform $10.94, $11.94, and so on.

The conspiracy charged by the Government began early in 1949, when the defendants met to devise ways to offset declining prices, Mr. Jansen declared. The method decided upon, he said, resulted in "suppressing and eliminating price competition." Also, he asserted, it "arbitrarily and unreasonably" increased the prices of "more than 5,000,000 items of merchandise sold by the stores." Agents of his department, he added, found "there were no downward changes."

After hearing counsel for both sides, Judge Bard cut Mr. Jansen's suggested fines on the companies in half and inflicted none at all on the individual defendants. The latter are:

John E. Raasch, president of John Wanamaker; Arthur C. Kaufmann, vice president and executive head of Gimbel Brothers; Gustavus Gidley, Gimbel's general merchandising manager; Richard C. Bond, executive vice president of Wanamaker's; Harold W. Brightman, president of Lit Brothers; Dwight G. Perkins, president, Strawbridge and Clothier; Max Robb, merchandising manager, Lit Brothers; Nathan J. Snellenberg, vice president, N. Snellenberg & Co., and James A. Waterfield, merchandising manager of Strawbridge's.

In Washington, Attorney General McGrath said that the price-fixing "was designed to increase the prices of these items and to prevent their return to normal levels in a declining market."

Assistant Attorney General Herbert A. Bergson, in charge of anti-trust cases, had this to say:

"This case should constitute a warning to retailers generally that their customers have a right to the benefits that flow from free competition. Customers of department stores are as much entitled to the protections and salutary effects of the anti-trust laws as any other group of purchasers."

January 10, 1950

BIG CONCERNS SAID TO HIRE CALL GIRLS

Murrow Broadcast Charges That Some Companies Keep Prostitutes on Payroll

By GEORGE BARRETT

Prostitution has become such a standard cost item for big business concerns in this country, a radio program contended last night, that some companies now keep call girls on their payrolls to please customers.

Statements were made by unidentified participants that prostitutes were hired, for example, to help persuade bank presidents to make loans and buyers to make purchases in large lots. It was said that the use of girls-for-hire had become so prevalent that some madams submitted monthly bills to companies instead of demanding separate payments for each date.

The descriptions of the alleged use of prostitutes by business concerns were presented on the Columbia Broadcasting System's radio network program "The Business of Sex." The fifty-five-minute program was a production of the Public Affairs Department of C.B.S. News. Edward R. Murrow, who was the narrator, told the radio audience that the program was "recommended for adult listening only."

Mr. Murrow said that call girls interviewed by reporters for the program had remarked that their assignments brought them "in contact with the highest levels of business."

Madam Is Described

The voice of an unidentified man, described by Mr. Murrow as a person who was "often approached to provide the services of top call girls," declared:

"There's a very famous madam in New York who takes care of your multi-millionaire only. She is a famous name in New York. She puts out a book every year, pictures of the girls she has working for her. And sends this book to her very, very exclusive clients. Now this woman is one who really works with big business; you know, when big corporations have a party, they'll contact this woman. She'll make a flat fee, $3,000, $5,000, all according to how many girls they want. And she'll send them a book, they'll pick out the girls. There's no guesswork here. And she deals with the largest corporations in the United States."

In some cases, according to the program, top executives were directly involved in the sex-entertainment arrangements, giving instructions on the type and the extent that the company would provide.

Make $25,000 a Year

Girls who were described as prostitutes said they made $25,000 a year and more through their deals with companies and did not have to pay income taxes. One girl said: "I don't feel as though the Government's entitled to anything, because these men are all legitimate business men. They deduct you at the end of the year."

Mr. Murrow introduced a man he described as the president of a large international company, who said there was "absolutely no doubt that prostitution per se does help business."

"This is the fastest way that I know of to have an intimate relationship established with a buyer," the executive declared. "It's an experience which has been shared, whether it's together or not makes no difference. The point is, that I know that the buyer has spent the night with a prostitute that I have provided. In the second place, in most cases the buyers are married, with families. It sort of gives me a slight edge; well, we will not call it exactly blackmail, but it is a subconscious edge over the buyer."

One girl described the technique of closing business deals. She said that business conferences were "usually conducted" at the end of the evening.

"After quite a bit of liquor has been consumed, and in this case the fee is $100, she said, "I will first be invited out to dinner. The man who is doing the entertainment will get tickets for whatever shows the buyer requests, and then I will go back to the hotel with the man and usually we'll spend till 2 o'clock in the morning with him. He will often give a verbal agreement, subject to confirmation the next morning."

January 20, 1959

7 Electrical Officials Get Jail Terms in Trust Case

G. E. and Westinghouse Vice Presidents Must Serve 30 Days—$931,500 in Fines Imposed for Bid Rigging

By ANTHONY LEWIS
Special to The New York Times.

PHILADELPHIA, Feb. 6—Seven executives of the country's leading electrical manufacturing companies received jail sentences today for violating the antitrust laws. Federal District Judge J. Cullen Ganey sent each to jail for thirty days.

No appeals from the jail sentences are possible, because all the men had pleaded guilty or no defense.

In addition, Judge Ganey imposed fines totaling $931,500 on individuals and corporations in what the Government has called the largest of all criminal antitrust cases.

It was a long day in Judge Ganey's courtroom. It took from 10 A. M. to 4:30 P. M. to pass sentences in six of twenty pending indictments. The fourteen others are scheduled to be disposed of tomorrow.

Among those drawing prison terms were vice presidents of the General Electric Company and the Westinghouse Electric Corporation—the two largest companies in the industry. Aside from those going to jail, twenty men drew suspended prison sentences.

The charges to which all the defendants had pleaded guilty or no defense were fixing of prices and rigging of bids on heavy electrical equipment, such as power transformers. Sales of the products involved totaled $1,750,000,000 a year.

But the real drama in the courtroom today arose not from the money or the corporations involved. It lay with the men who stood before Judge Ganey to hear their fate.

They were typical business men in appearance, men who would never be taken for lawbreakers. Over and over their lawyers described them as pillars of their communities.

Several were deacons or vestrymen of their churches. One was president of his local Chamber of Commerce, another a hospital board member, another chief fund raiser for the Community Chest, another a bank director, another director of the taxpayer's association, another an organizer of the local Little League.

Judge Scores Companies

Lawyer after lawyer said his client was "an honorable man"—a victim of corporate morality, not its creator. To a degree Judge Ganey agreed.

"The real blame," the judge said in an opening statement, "is to be laid at the doorstep of the corporate defendants and those who guide and direct their policy."

Judge Ganey said the typical individual defendant was "the organization or the company man, the conformist, who goes along with his superiors and finds balm for his conscience in additional comforts and the security of his place in the corporate set-up."

Judge Ganey imposed jail sentences only on men he thought were high enough in their companies to make policy. Jail sentences of any kind are unusual, though not unprecedented, in antitrust cases.

Approximately fifty jail sentences have been imposed under the Sherman Antitrust Act since it was passed in 1890. A recent example was the sentencing of three defendants in a linen antitrust case to ninety days each by Federal District Judge Edmud L. Palmieri of New York. The cases are now on appeal.

Today's sentences were below the statutory maximums — a $50,000 fine on each count and a year in jail for the individual defendants. Most were also below Justice Department recommendations, which were for the most part short of the maximums.

Robert Kennedy Acts

The recommendations were sent to Judge Ganey Jan. 19, the day before the new Administration took office. But the acting chief of the department's antitrust division, W. Wallace Kirkpatrick, read the court a statement by the new Attorney General, Robert F. Kennedy.

Mr. Kennedy said he had reviewed the cases and considered the crimes "so willful and flagrant that even more severe sentences would have been appropriate." He suggested, "under the circumstances," that "sentences at least as severe as those recommended be imposed."

Forty-five individuals and twenty-nine corporations were named as defendants in the package of twenty indictments.

Today sentence was imposed on thirty-six men and twenty-one companies. Some of the same defendants figure in the cases to be handled tomorrow.

The corporate defendants today drew a total of $822,500 in fines. The largest figures were $185,000 for General Electric, in five cases, and $180,000 for Westinghouse, in six.

All of the individual defendants also drew fines, ranging from $1,000 to $12,500. The total for them was $109,000.

These were the seven men who drew prison terms, listed

J. H. Chiles Jr.

W. S. Ginn

Lewis J. Burger

E. R. Jung

in the order they were sentenced:

J. H. Chiles Jr., Westinghouse vice president and division manager.

W. S. Ginn, General Electric vice president and division manager.

Lewis J. Burger, General Electric division manager.

George E. Burens, General Electric vice president and division manager.

C. I. Mauntel, Westinghouse division sales manager.

J. M. Cook, vice president of Cutler-Hammer, Inc.

E. R. Jung, vice president, Clark Controller Company.

Judge Ganey said he had suspended the sentences of some other defendants "reluctantly," and only because of their age or bad health.

He repeatedly rejected pleas by counsel to the effect that their clients were not deeply involved. He would cut in crisply to remark that the defendant had been an "aggressive competitor" in a shocking case.

The formal charge in all the cases was violation of the Sherman Antitrust Act, which prohibits conspiracies in restraint of trade. That is a common charge, but the Government said these conspiracies were unusually elaborate and damaging.

The defendants were said to have held frequent secret meetings, and used codes. They allegedly parceled out Government contracts among each other, submitting low bids in rotation under a scheme called "the phase of the moon."

Some of the customers for this heavy electrical machinery are now expected to bring civil suits for treble damages. The Justice Department has prepared such suits for overcharges to the Federal Government, and states and municipalities and utilities may be next to sue.

The six indictments were handled in turn today, and the drama built slowly in the court room. Government lawyers read their recommendations aloud in each case, and then counsel for the defendants had a chance to plead for mercy, as some called it, or leniency.

Gerhard A. Gesell of Washington, counsel for G. E., took vigorous exception to Judge Ganey's comment about corporate responsibility for the violations.

He noted that G. E. had a company rule, known as Regulation 20.5, directing strict obedience to the antitrust laws. And he observed that the company had demoted all officials involved before any indictments were brought.

"It is simply not a fact that there was a way of life at General Electric that permitted, tolerated or winked at these violations," Mr. Gesell said. "The company abhors, sought to prevent and punished this conduct."

But Judge Ganey disagreed with Mr. Gesell. He said he thought General Electric's Rule 20.5 "was honored in its breach rather than its observance."

Mr. Chiles was the first individual defendant called. A small man with gold-rimmed glasses, he stood with head slightly bowed as his attorney, Philip H. Strubing of Philadelphia, sought leniency.

"No further punishment is needed to keep these men from doing what they have done, again," Mr. Strubing said.

"These men are not grasping, greedy, cut-throat competitors. They devote much of their time and substance to ther communities."

Mr. Strubing listed Mr. Chiles' activities—senior warden of his church, benefactor of charities for crippled children and cancer victims, fellow of an engineering society.

Led Off by Marshal

When Judge Ganey imposed the jail sentence, Mr. Chiles turned to go back to his seat in the courtroom. Then, suddenly, a marshal appeared, grabbed him by the elbow and led him off.

Next was Mr. Ginn, tall and distinguished in appearance. His attorney, Henry T. Reath of Philadelphia, also made a general attack on the Government's demand for jail terms.

He said Government lawyers were "cold-blooded" and did not understand what it would do to a man like Mr. Ginn to "put him behind bars" with "common criminals who have been convicted of embezzlement and other serious crimes."

In contrast to Mr. Gesell, Mr. Reath insisted that Mr. Ginn had had only followed long-established company policy by getting together with supposed competitors to arrange their business.

Mr. Reath said Mr. Ginn was chairman of the building fund for a new Jesuit novitiate in Lenox, Mass.; a director of the Schenectady, N. Y. boys' club and a member of Governor Rockefeller's Temporary State Committee on Economic Expansion.

"It would be a great personal tragedy for this fine man" to go to jail, Mr. Reath concluded. Judge Ganey took only a few seconds to mark Mr. Ginn down for thirty days in prison.

And so it went. Lawyers spoke of their clients' long years with one company, of their daughters in prominent colleges, of the shame that publicity had already caused.

Judge Ganey ordered the seven who were given jail sentences to begin their terms Monday at 10 A. M.

February 7, 1961

Ethics Issue Stirs Business Colleges

By PETER BART

The recent conviction of several leading electrical companies on charges of price-fixing and bid-rigging raised some serious questions about the ethics of big business.

These questions are being debated with special intensity at the nation's business schools — the institutions whose responsibility it is to train tomorrow's business leaders.

The business school professors are wondering whether the price-fixing case and others like it indicate, in part, a failure of their institutions to devote sufficient attention to the complex area of business ethics. They are worried that their schools are placing too much emphasis on the tools of business—accounting, marketing and so forth—and too little on the intellectual and moral development of the future business men. The debate may result in some far-reaching changes in the curriculums of business schools and other executive training programs.

Business school professors agree that the price-fixing case, which resulted in the jailing of several executives of the General Electric Company, the Westinghouse Electric Corporation and other concerns, has had a greater impact on their students than any other incident in recent years.

'Feeling of Shock'

"The case has generated a feeling of shock and surprise

here," noted a professor at the Harvard University Graduate School of Business Administration. "I think it marks a real setback in the confidence of many of our students in the larger corporations." An editorial in the school's student newspaper, The Harbus News, expressed concern about executives "placed by society and the pressures of capitalist conformity in a position where they can succeed in their careers only by violating the laws."

Said Dr. Karl Hill, dean of the Amos Tuck School of Business Administration at Dartmouth College: "Many of our students are quite disturbed about this case. The affair has sparked a great deal of discussion about the whole question of the business executive's social responsibilities."

Many business school professors at different universities believe their institutions must deal more effectively with moral questions, but they disagree on how this should be done. Some favor a general reorientation of the curriculum to downgrade "vocational" courses and emphasize courses more in line with the goals of a liberal education.

Ethics Courses Urged

Other professors, however, propose that courses on business ethics be introduced directly into the present curriculums. One such course was started this semester at New York University's Graduate School of Business Administration. Its instructor, James W. Bunting, is a full-time consultant at General Electric.

Harvard incorporates ethics in a more general course called Business, Society and the Individual. Started three years ago with an enrollment of sixty students, the optional course has about 100 this semester. Its instructor, Professor George Albert Smith Jr. hopes his course helps to "develop a feeling among the students that to attain a position of business leadership represents an opportunity not just for personal gain but for personal service as well."

To many business school faculty members, however, the sensitive issue of business ethics is one that can best be treated not in a single course but throughout the curriculum.

Said Dr. Ernest M. Fisher, a professor at the Columbia University Graduate School of Business: "The function of a business school should be to turn out educated men, not merely business managers. Accordingly, our aim should be to develop a student's intellectual potential and to provide him with the scholarly habits needed to realize that potential."

Dr. Fisher believes that a business school curriculum must encompass the more profound questions involving the relationship between business men and their social environment. According to Dr. Fisher's blueprint, the nation's business schools would be a place to go not just to learn accounting or marketing, but rather to add depth to one's liberal education.

Dr. Fisher's argument draws support from many officials who run corporate executive training programs.

According to James M. Shipton, manager of General Electric's Advanced Business Courses Service at Crotonville, N. Y.: "The main problem with business ethics is that so little is known about how to teach the subject. My suspicion is that this is something you absorb by osmosis over a long period of time and not a subject you can fruitfully take up in a cram course."

At Dr. Shipton's Crotonville Institute, G. E.'s managers usually discuss business ethics for one day during their nine-week seminars. However, the question of how to teach business ethics now is coming under a complete review at the G. E. Institute in line with plans to establish a new "follow-up" program—a sort of "postgraduate course"—for those who have completed the advanced management seminar. G. E. officials now are designing the curriculum for this program.

To be sure, few educators believe that any course or any curriculum can completely transform a potential executive's ethical code. But all hope that if their students do some more thinking—and reading—about questions of ethics, they will be better prepared to meet the stresses and strains of a competitive society.

March 12, 1961

IDENTICAL PRICES A GROWING WORRY

Government Views Causing Anxiety to Business Men

By ROBERT METZ

A man in business reportedly once said, "We lose money on every sale, but we make it up in volume."

Successful business men say that the remark suggests that the man either was legendary or hell-bent for insolvency. And yet, the story has a peculiar relevance today. For, many business men are concerned as to whether a rational pricing policy is possible if their companies are to operate both within the law and within the black.

There is no doubt that some companies have engaged in illegal price-fixing, and recently men have gone to jail for it. On the other hand, a review of events of the last few weeks tends to explain the concern over what is both legal and prudent.

On May 19, Mark W. Cresap Jr., president of Westinghouse Electric Corporation, told the Senate Antitrust Committee that in the electrical equipment industry the necessity of meeting the lowest price in the market place and not collusion was what caused identical pricing.

Collusion and Copying

Senator Estes Kefauver, Democrat of Tennessee, indicated that in his view as far as the Government, the public and price competition were concerned, there would appear to be no difference between actual price collusion and merely copying prices out of competitor's catalogues.

Business men who produce standard items are among those who worry about this point of view. They wonder what a safe response would be to a customer who argued "I got a lower quote from your competitor, why should I pay you more for identical merchandise?"

On June 19, Senator Kefauver said in a television interview that a pattern of identical or similar bids on Government contracts should create a legal presumption of collusion and that bidders should be required to prove otherwise. He went on to say that corporate officials should be made personally responsible for price-fixing practices coming to their attention.

Business men are wondering whether they would be able to defend themselves against this presumption, if it should become law, when marketing forces tended to narrow the spread on competing bids for business.

On June 1, a Federal judge sitting in Hammond, Ind., upheld the conviction of eleven major oil companies on gasoline price-fixing charges. Fines came to $425,000. The judge said a 7-cent-a-gallon increase in gasoline prices in the Mishawaka, Ind., area alone had cost consumers $250,000 a month.

In defense of the similar gasoline prices, Merwin Bristol, general counsel for Standard Oil Company (Indiana), a defendant, said:

"We believe that a fair appraisal of the facts will establish that the long retail price war ended in May, 1957 [the time at which the price began to rise] because of independent action by competing oil companies without any agreement or understanding between them."

On June 15, four major electrical equipment makers agreed to sign an order against sales at "unreasonably low prices" that might lessen competition and tend to create a monopoly.

General Electric Company refused to sign, saying that it preferred to fight a threatened Department of Justice suit for divestment of part of its property rather than sign a decree that it considered foolhardy and impossible of fulfillment. G. E. felt it might be in contempt of court the moment its officials signed the document.

Competitive Injury?

Some of those concerned felt that if a small producer lost a single contract to G. E. or Westinghouse, a court might reasonably rule that the smaller company had suffered a competitive injury through the giant corporation's lower bid.

While General Electric and other major companies weigh the consequences in price-fixing cases, smaller companies, most of them as yet untouched by the controversy, are sitting tight and hoping for the best. Meanwhile, Westinghouse has prepared a defense of identical pricing so far as these pricing policies relate to standard items. Westinghouse begins with a 1925 statement from the Supreme Court:

"In the case of a standardized product sold wholesale to fully informed professional buyers * * * uniformity of price will inevitably result from active, free, and unrestrained competition."

Noting that it produced "thousands of types of standard products," Westinghouse said that they were identified and ordered by catalogue or style number and priced from catalogues, which were sent to thousands of customers and anyone else who wishes to be put on the mailing list.

Standards Adopted

The company said that customers normally purchased standard pieces of electrical equipment simply by specifying that the piece meet minimum engineering standards, which are adopted by national engineering societies.

"The customer's only requirement is that the product meet the specifications, and these can be met by all manufacturers who produce acceptable products for the desired function. Even though the manufacturer offers a product which does more than meet the minimum specifications, the customer seldom makes a further evaluation and seldom exercises a preference for any one brand. He is concerned only with the lowest total cost to him, including transportation cost."

Westinghouse illustrates the point with an item culled from "a recent report in the press" that several companies, including Westinghouse, had submitted to the Tennessee Valley Authority identical bids of $2,508.48 for three 73,000-volt standard station-type lightning arrestors. The company says that it sells hundreds of arresters every year. The $836.16 price of a single arrestor is listed in a published catalogue, which is in the hands of about 7,000 customers, including T. V. A., the company says.

"But our catalogue comes in many parts, because we have

more than half a million products or variations of products in our price lists for industrial equipment alone. Physically, these price lists make up a catalogue which is more than six feet thick. . . . Based on our best estimate, we receive from 1,500 to 2,000 orders for these standard products each day; we probably quote prices 6,000 to 8,000 times a day. The sheer volume of business makes essential a standard pricing system."

The company goes on to say that the cost of business would be prohibitive if on each order someone had to determine the extent of a price difference in favor of a particular customer. The company notes that price discrimination can violate provisions of the Robinson-Patman Act and the Federal Trade Commission Act.

The company says that if it received a report from a local office that a competitor was quoting a lower price on a particular product, it would have to decide whether to meet the price and remain competitive. "Generally, in these standard products, any seller knows that a lower price will be quickly matched by his competitors. So, ordinarily we do not deviate from our catalogue price unless [we are] prepared to accept a lower price level for that product in the entire market."

'Confidential' Prices

The company says that in the case of sealed bids, the lowest bid could be expected to become a new national price. "Experience has shown that prices in informal quotations, even though confidential, also become quickly known."

Westinghouse says that it constantly strives to give its products features that will give them brand preference. In one such instance, the company, certain that its product was superior, held the line against a general price reduction. The competitor was quoting a 30-cent advantage. "It soon became apparent that we had lost a great deal of business because of our 30 cent higher price. Despite the fact that we thought, and still think, our product was substantially superior, we had to meet our competitor's price.

But identical pricing is not restricted to standard items and many manufacturers of machinery and equipment find that their customers remove price considerations from the competitive equation by insisting that each seller meet the lowest bid.

The result is that companies allow their prices to become identical, choosing to compete on the basis of their machinery's output, its long life and its low upkeep—the relatively small amount of "down time" required to keep their machine running.

July 16, 1961

'I Spy' Becomes Big Business

By LAWRENCE STESSIN

INDUSTRIAL espionage — "I.E.," as it is called in executive suites—has become a standard part of the strategy of business, like the doings of the cloak-and-dagger set in international politics. In a Harvard Business School study, 200 executives admitted that competitive intelligence—and counterintelligence—is the way of business life and its indulgence ranges from the ethical (an oil company flies a helicopter over drilling operations of a competitor to photograph an oil strike) to the downright criminal (a firm plants a confederate in a rival's plant to ferret out manufacturing information). Recently, I.E. became front-page news when a young business executive pleaded guilty to an attempt to sell a sales-campaign plan devised by Procter & Gamble, his former employer, to the rival Colgate-Palmolive Company. Although he subsequently received a suspended sentence because of his clean record, he could have been jailed for 10 years and fined $10,000

Norman Jaspan, the "Sherlock Holmes" of business and head of Norman Jaspan Associates, counterespionage agency whose 500 full-time employes are officially listed as "management engineers," has estimated that several hundred white-collar thieves are caught and convicted of filching company secrets every year and that five times that number are not tried because management prefers not to court the publicity involved in pressing a prosecution.

The quarry of the business spy may be a sample of a new soap destined for the half-billion-dollar "kitchen sink" market or a pinch of a germ culture, the base of a successful antibiotic that took 10 years and $20 million to develop. It may be a piece of scrap paper from an executive's wastebasket on which he doodled the company's bid on a huge government contract or a tape of a hotel-room conversation about a projected merger.

IT is the bitter competition of the marketplace that spurs the executive to be on the alert to maneuvers in the "enemy" camp, for too often he has seen a single product shoot up from nowhere and dominate a market. There are, of course, many legitimate ways of finding out what the competition is up to. Comparison shopping has long been an established medium for competitive intelligence. So have been salesmen reports, trade magazines, newsletters and low-key questioning of suppliers. In Detroit, every new part is tested, X-rayed and disassembled by the competition. When Chevrolet comes out with a new model, its first customer is sure to be Ford and vice versa.

But among the auto makers this is where innocent sniffing ends. It has long been an open secret that Detroit is the center of the most sophisticated industrial spying apparatus in the country. It is not uncommon to see a man in shirt-sleeves, with blueprints under his arm, being escorted not too gently out of, say, a Chrysler plant because he is a Lincoln stylist. The Dearborn Inn has no trouble renting its terrace suites to General Motors men with field glasses in their luggage. These rooms overlook the Ford proving grounds.

Guards with telescopes patrol the roofs of auto plants to watch for intruders. In Ford styling offices the wastebaskets are equipped with electric paper shredders and the contents are dumped into a special chute that leads to a furnace. At some G.M. buildings, the locks can be switched in an hour if a key is stolen or lost, and the company's new technical center has a listening device to draw all the curtains at the approach of a helicopter or an airplane.

Spying is so well organized among the auto companies that if a freelance were to proffer a stolen secret, he would be immediately reported to the police. Spying in Detroit is strictly a professional pursuit; amateurs are discouraged from trying to crack the Establishment.

In other industries, however, the industrial informer is usually not a member of a professional élite. There is no Mafia specializing in corporate confidences (although several years ago Lederle Laboratories did discover that there was an Italian syndicate which stole the formula for aureomycin and sold it to several European pharmaceutical houses). For this reason, most companies do not maintain a regular staff of counterespionage agents. Management's attitude is that if a company successfully develops a spirit of loyalty, the employes themselves will report security indiscretions and then outside investigators can be called in to gather evidence.

BY and large, a trade secret is peddled by an employe with a fractured ego. Like the man who worked for the Minnesota Mining and Manufacturing Company and had access to the process for making Scotch Tape. Attributing his lack of progress to corporate indifference, he approached a competitor with the precious information which had made

ON THE MOVE—Spy bouncing is a commonplace in Detroit's fiercely competitive automobile plants.

LAWRENCE STESSIN is a professor of industrial relations at Hofstra University.

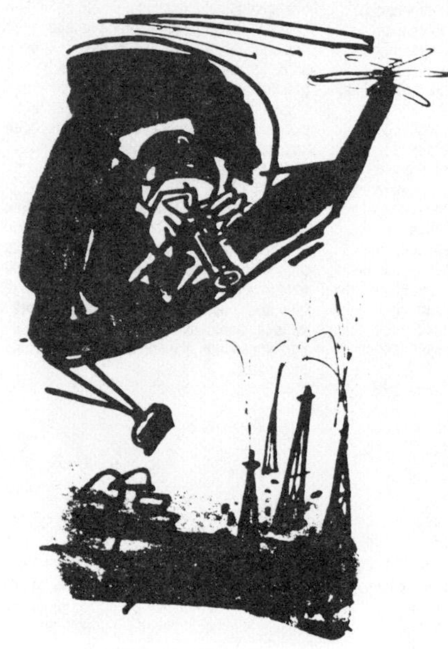

In the growing practice of industrial espionage, scouting a rival oil company by air to photograph a strike is S.O.P.

3M's cellophane and masking tape the undisputed market leaders.

He was hired, and 3M did not discover the conspiracy until a new product "Tuck No. 120 Masking Tape" became a big seller. Conducting some counterespionage of its own, 3M gathered evidence, started suit, and was awarded an injunction, damages and an accounting of the profits from the outfit that had bought man and secret.

The trades-information pilferer is not necessarily an underpaid drone sulking in a routine job. When the Federal Bureau of Investigation arrested the former Procter & Gamble employe it was not surprised tc find that his salary had been in five figures and that his position had definitely entitled him to a key to the executive washroom. In his attache case was the confidential budget of a P. & G. sales campaign to launch a new toothpaste in the New York area, a plan involving $9 million of complex market testing; the price asked for safe delivery to Colgate-Palmolive, according to the F.B.I., was $20,000.

Over 70 per cent of the trade-secret thefts are the work of supervisors, highly trained technicians, scientists and executives, according to Norman Jaspan, an estimate confirmed by other I.E. organizations.

WHEN management suspects that foul play may be afoot, it does not hire the stereotype of the private eye. Its counterintelligence work calls for a sleuth who can spot a doctored blueprint, detect a chink in a machine tool, program a computer to learn whether someone is deliberately feeding wrong information into the machine or decipher a mathematician's notebook for stolen formulas.

This new kind of agent, long on brains and short on brawn, looks more like an accountant than an investigator, and he has the social graces to fit easily into any slot in the decision-making structure of an industrial organization.

If he is a Jaspan man, he is a college graduate with a degree in accounting, engineering or business administration. Or he may have put in several years in a research laboratory before being recruited for undercover work. One of Jaspan's principal competitors, Fidelifacts, is a cooperative of 400 ex-F.B.I. and Secret Service agents throughout the country. Rates for industrial sleuthing run between $100 and $200 a day per man, plus expenses.

Many of Jaspan's employes have permanent jobs in prime companies to watch that trade secrets are not leaked to the outside. Only recently a Jaspan man assigned to a chemical laboratory cosied up to a chemist who, he found, was leaving his job every day at 4 P.M. and going down to the corner drugstore to make an out-of-town call.

Management was already disturbed because it could not seem to get the jump on its competition with new products on which it had spent fortunes to develop. A six-months head start is all that most consumer companies hope for before imitators begin to cut in on the market, and this firm was not getting even that short lead.

Investigation proved that the chemist who telephoned every day from the corner drugstore was in touch with a college professor in a university a hundred miles away. The professor had developed a lucrative consulting business. His clients, who paid him well, marveled at his accurate insight into what was going on in the trade. He had, it turned out, a payroll of six associates in chemical labs around the country.

TRADE secrets are the subject of continuous court battles. One company has 40 lawyers who do nothing ut litigate invasions of such secrets. Most legal fights revolve around attempts of management to stop employes from working for the competition or to prohibit them from going into business with a product line similar to that of their former employers.

Recently, the Time-O-Matic Company started a suit against two former employes who had once enjoyed such management confidence that they had access to the blueprints and drawings of the company's best-selling product, an automatic circuit breaker used widely in display signs. Although the circuit breaker was not original enough for patenting, its mechanism still was sufficiently novel to be closely guarded.

Knowing that the lack of a patent made it possible for anyone to manufacture the product, the two employes decided to go into direct competition. However, they knew it would be illegal to make copies of the blueprints. So they decided to memorize every line and calculation. One assigned to himself one section of the blueprints; the other committed to memory the rest of the diagrams. This took a full year. Then the employes quit and soon had a successful circuit breaker on the market.

In the ensuing suit, their defense was that they could not be enjoined because they had taken away nothing but "a mental picture." The judge, however, ruled that "these mental pictures were obtained while in Time-O-Matic's employ, and to carry them away in this manner was a violation of a confidence," just as if copies or photographs had been carried away.

This, he added, enabled the former employes "to compete with Time-O-Matic on equal terms by sparing them the necessity of spending time and money in acquiring the 'know-how.' "

A not too infrequent victim of industrial spying is the small company with a good product. There was, for example, Paul Steiner, whose electric steam iron was the talk of the trade. When a big company offered to produce his product under a licensing agreement, Steiner was interested, for he was having production problems and profits were nil. When the big outfit's representatives came to the plant, Steiner showed them around and encouraged his aides to talk freely.

Negotiations for the licensing agreement continued briskly and then ground to a halt. Later, Steiner discovered that his iron had a competitor lower in price and wider in distribution. He sued the giant and won.

I.E. is not solely a big-company practice by any means. There is the corner grocer who bribes a printer with a $10-bill for an advance look at the announcements of the A.&P's specials. There are hundreds of small electronic firms which run want ads for engineers without having any intention of hiring. The interviewing is conducted not by personnel

TWO-WAY—Intelligence work in industry has, naturally, called forth another phenomenon, counterintelligence.

men but by product managers and technicians, who pump the applicants for trade secrets.

THEN there is the dishonest partner. One small fur-dying firm did a thriving business with a concoction the two partners had developed after years of experimentation, using the bathtub as their laboratory. Only they knew the formula.

One day, one of the partners discovered that two five-gallon cans of dye were missing. The next week another two were gone. In panic the discoverer of the theft called Jaspan for help. Proof came quickly that the other partner was stealing the cans and planning to go into business for himself. His objective was to accumulate 100 gallons of the formula; with these he could set up his own business and raise capital to manufacture the secret dye himself.

Jaspan suggested a fast arrest, but the partner who had ordered the investigation demurred. "Let's ruin him," he said, and asked Jaspan to find a chemist who could create a fluid that would duplicate the dyestuff in color and smell but, when used on furs, would eat the skin right off.

The desired compound was devised and poured into the stolen cans. The dishonest partner broke away from the firm, advertised his new business, gathered over $200,000 worth of orders (at lower prices)—and within two weeks filed suit for bankruptcy as irate customers sued to collect on their ruined merchandise.

November 28, 1965

AIDE REPORTS I.T.T. SHREDDED PAPERS

Tells Senators Data Were Destroyed After Report Columnist Got Memo

By FRED P. GRAHAM

Special to The New York Times

WASHINGTON, March 16—The general counsel to the International Telephone and Telegraph Corporation testified today that "many sacks of papers" from files of the corporation's Washington office were destroyed the day after Jack Anderson, the columnist, informed the corporation that he had obtained a memorandum written by its Washington lobbyist, Mrs. Dita D. Beard.

The Senate Judiciary Committee was told that the primary reason for feeding the papers into a shredder on Feb. 24 was to destroy documents that might cause "unwarranted embarrassment" to individuals mentioned in them in the event that Mr. Anderson "misused and misconstrued" them in his syndicated column.

Papers were also destroyed because they were outdated or unneeded, Howard J. Aibel, general counsel and a senior vice president of International Telephone, told the committee.

He said that none of the employes in the office knew of any destroyed documents that linked the company's pledge of up to $200,000 toward the expenses of the Republican National Convention with the Justice Department's settlement of three antitrust suits against the concern.

Mrs. Beard's memorandum did link the two events of last summer, saying, "Our noble commitment has gone a long way toward our negotiations on the mergers." Its publication by Mr. Anderson on Feb. 29 led to the current hearings.

Mr. Aibel disclosed that some of the shredded documents did pertain to the San Diego convention and others concerned the antitrust settlements. He said that the San Diego material included tourist brochures and statistics on facilities, which could be replaced, and that the antitrust papers were copies of documents preserved in files elsewhere.

Senator John V. Tunney, Democrat of California, declared, "This looks bad on its face." He added that International Telephone employes could hardly be expected to acknowledge now that documents already destroyed had linked the corporation's convention pledge and the antitrust settlements.

Mr. Aibel testified together with the corporation's president, Harold S. Geneen, who promised the committee yesterday to report today on the document-shredding incident, which was first disclosed in Mr. Anderson's column.

Interim Report Made

An "interim report" was filed with the committee, based upon an inquiry into the shredding incident by four lawyers retained by the corporation. One of the four, John S. Martin Jr. of New York, testified that the lawyers had been assigned to "give separate and distinct advice" to International Telephone's employes about any legal liabilities they might have incurred by destroying the papers.

Mr. Aibel's report said that, shortly after an investigator for Mr. Anderson went to the corporation's Washington office on Feb. 23 to verify the authenticity of Mrs. Beard's memorandum, company headquarters in New York were asked to dispatch a security officer to check out the Washington office's security. Russell Tagliareni, a security official, was sent to Washington that afternoon.

The next morning the Washington office's 25-member staff was told that "our files were an open sieve." According to Mr. Aibel's report, the employes were instructed to destroy unneeded or embarrassing papers. He said that none had been shredded by the security official and there had been no intention to thwart any governmental investigation, as reported by Mr. Anderson. No records required by the internal revenue laws were destroyed, the report said.

Terms Office Lax

Mr. Martin said that John E. Ryan, deputy chief of the Washington office, had gone through Mrs. Beard's files with her to select those to be shredded. No copy of the memorandum that touched off the controversy was found.

Mr. Aibel told the Senators that many of the shredded papers had simply been old documents that had not been routinely destroyed because the Washington office had been lax in following the corporation's "document retention program" for disposing of old papers.

He gave the committee copies of memorandums establishing a three-tier security classification system reminiscent of the secrecy system employed by the Government.

Classified documents are stamped "system confidential," "legal confidential" or "personal and confidential." The last classification, which applied to Mrs. Beard's memorandum, is used for "information of an embarrassing nature," "controversy within or between headquarter staffs, group and/ or I.T.T. unit personnel," and "psychological assessment reports."

In his testimony, Mr. Geneen, the company president, said that he knew of no International Telephone executive who had asked Mrs. Beard to "get out of town" after publication of her memorandum, as reported by Mr. Anderson.

Mr. Geneen also said that the Sheraton Corporation of America, the International Telephone subsidiary that pledged the $200,000 to the Republican convention as a "promotional expense," had not contributed any money to the Democratic National Convention in Miami Beach, although there are two Sheraton hotels there. The difference, he said, is that Sheraton has three hotels in San Diego, including a new one where president Nixon's headquarters will be located.

After the session today, the hearing here was recessed until next Wednesday so that a subcommittee can take Mrs. Beard's testimony on Monday and Tuesday in her hospital room in Denver, where she is confined because of a heart ailment.

The Judiciary Committee chairman, Senator James O. Eastland, Democrat of Mississippi, added Quentin N. Burdick, Democrat of North Dakota, to the subcommittee today. The other members are Philip A. Hart of Michigan, chairman; Edward M. Kennedy of Massachusetts and Mr. Tunney, all Democrats; and Marlow W. Cook of Kentucky, Charles McC. Mathias Jr., of Maryland and Edward J. Gurney of Florida, Republicans.

Says He Was 'Imprecise'

Jerris Leonard, former chief of the Justice Department's Civil Rights Division, said today that he was "imprecise" when he wrote a 1970 memorandum. Mr. Leonard ordered negotiation of a recommended suit against a Southern California real estate company because John N. Mitchell, then the Attorney General, "knows some of the top people" in the company.

In a statement today, Mr. Leonard said that Mr. Mitchell had actually said he understood that the company, Coldwell-Banker & Co., "was a large company and he could not believe it was official company policy to discriminate" against Negroes, as a Justice Department investigation had determined. Mr. Mitchell testified yesterday that he knew nothing about the company except that it had many advertising signs in Southern California and must be a large concern.

The incident was brought into the hearings because the company is a client of the Los Angeles law firm of Herbert W. Kalmbach, President Nixon's personal attorney in California, who has helped arrange financing for the San Diego convention. In the racial discrimination case, which was settled out of court last month, the Coldwell company was represented by O'Melveny & Meyers, another Los Angeles law firm.

March 17, 1972

I. T. T.:

A Private Little Foreign Policy

WASHINGTON—In 1916 Gen. Smedley Butler of the United States Marines led his troops ashore in the Dominican Republic—to make that country safe, as he put it, "for the boys of the National City Bank." The little Caribbean nation had defaulted on loan payments and other obligations, and the United States had decided to intervene militarily to restore order.

In 1970, according to material made public by the syndicated columnist Jack Anderson last week, a vice president of the International Telephone and Telegraph Corporation wrote the White House urging action to make Chile, in effect, safe for I.T.T. The Chileans had elected a Socialist, Salvador Allende Gossens, as President, and the New York-based corporation felt that his inauguration should be prevented so as to safeguard I.T.T. and other United States investments in Chile and other Latin American countries.

Corporation executives have as much right as anyone to lobby the Government for their interests, but the boldness of I.T.T.'s purported venture in persuasion, with its evocation of the heyday of United States interventionism in the hemisphere, created a stir in Washington—and, not surprisingly, in Latin-American capitals as well. Though the State Department stated that "any ideas of thwarting the Chilean constitutional process following the election of 1970 were firmly rejected by this Administration," the Senate Foreign Relations Committee scheduled hearings on the influence of multinational United States corporations on foreign policy.

In recent decades, according to one Senator, these corporations have grown so big as to acquire their own "arrogance of power." The I.T.T. is only the ninth largest corporation in the United States but its resources and access to levers of power are formidable.

The United States Government's defense and intelligence activities are importantly linked to I.T.T.'s technology and know-how in space and satellite communications. I.T.T. has a space division working on top-secret contracts for the Defense Department. But I.T.T. in the past 10 years has acquired 101 corporations in the United States and 67 foreign countries. Its present interests, valued at $6-billion, range far beyond communications—to fire insurance, hotel chains (Sheraton), food industries, housing, car rentals (Avis) and book publishing.

I.T.T., in fact, often acts and sounds more like a government than a private company. It employs former American diplomats and former foreign correspondents, including a Pulitzer Prize winner. In recent years it has established its own foreign-policy and foreign-intelligence units. To assist its president, Harold Geneen, I.T.T. has a star-studded board of directors, including the former head of the Central Intelligence Agency, John A. McCone, and a number of well-connected international bakers.

Employing more than 350,000 persons in the United States and about 200,000 in its affiliates abroad, I.T.T. has its own international communications network, its own fleet of jetliners and its own counterespionage operation. A system of periodic "sweeps" checks its offices for bugs and wiretaps. The company's shredders destroy unwanted or compromising documents. Yet all its precautions have been unable to protect it from that latest governmental phenomenon, the leak.

First, earlier this month, came the material leaked to Mr. Anderson suggesting a possible link between a generous I.T.T. contribution to the Republican party and the dropping of antitrust action against the corporation. Last week came the "Chilean papers." On Tuesday, after Mr. Anderson's first column on them was published, I.T.T. denied that it had sought to interfere in Chilean internal affairs. As more papers were published, I.T.T. clammed up. State Department officials said privately there wasn't much doubt that the material was authentic.

Mr. Allende was elected in September, 1970, on a platform of nationalizing much of Chilean industry, domestic and foreign-owned. The alleged I.T.T. documents suggested that the company, with close to $200-million in diversified investments in Chile, had sought a species of "protective reaction" for its Chilean interests.

For example, a letter from the I.T.T. vice president to Henry A. Kissinger, the White House foreign-policy adviser, suggested—in a style befitting a foreign ministry—that "the present moment is a most expedient time to reappraise and strengthen U. S. policy in Latin America." Other letters and memorandums from the company's top echelon officers, Washington lobbyists and Latin-American field operatives sought to convey the message to the Nixon Administration in blunter terms: that Mr. Allende's inauguration would spell disaster for private investors in the hemisphere.

Some alleged I.T.T. memorandums described purported dealings with the C.I.A. on the possibility of promoting an anti-Allende coup. One I.T.T. official in Washington was said to have reported to his superiors that he had informed the White House that the corporation would provide financial assistance "in seven figures" to help prevent Mr. Allende's inauguration in November, 1970.

What influence I.T.T. has on the making of foreign policy is debatable. Some observers found it curious that with all its denials in the Chilean case last week, the State Department would neither confirm nor deny the substance of an I.T.T. memorandum alleging that 10 days after Mr. Allende's election the United States Ambassador to Chile, Edward M. Korry, received the "green light" from the State Department to do everything possible short of military intervention "to keep Allende from taking power." What is clear thus far is that the new disclosures have embarrassed both I.T.T. and the Nixon Administration and proved a political windfall for President Allende, who had always claimed that "the Yankees are out to get us."

—TAD SZULC

March 26, 1972

In the Name Of Profit

By Robert L. Heilbroner, Morton Mintz, Colman McCarthy, Sanford J. Ungar, Kermit Vandivier, Saul Friedman, James Boyd.
273 pp. New York: Doubleday & Co. $6.95.

By ROBERT TOWNSEND

"Most persons think that a state in order to be happy ought to be large; but even if they are right, they have no idea of what is a large and what is a small state. . . . To the size of states there is a limit, as there is to other things, plants, animals, implements; for none of these retain their natural power when they are too large or too small, but they either wholly lose their nature, or are spoiled." —Aristotle, 322 B.C.

If you think that Dita Beard, Harold Geneen and the other weaselly wafflers in the I.T.T. affair are somehow unusual, read this book. Here are six well-documented cases of corporate conspiracy against the public good. Each is a parable of

Drawing by Jan Faust.

evil, and together they give us a picture of misbehavior that is more the rule today than the exception.

"Like My Lai," writes Robert Heilbroner, "the incidents in this book are atrocities."

In the first half, able reporters from several newspapers write short and highly readable stories on who did what inside the private governments of six monster companies. The reports fulfill their stated purpose: "that readers might understand corporate irresponsibility better if it were presented in terms of human beings rather than of economic institutions acting impersonally." While some of the men have surrendered so much of their manhood as to lose their human status, they are all recognizable types. I know several dozens of each.

In the second half, Heilbroner (Norman Thomas Professor of Economics at the New School in New York) analyzes the economic background and summarizes the various solutions at our disposal. To make corporate organizations our servants rather than our masters, he rightly insists, is the urgent business of the day. He brushes aside the fake solutions—self - policing, nationalization, government regulation—which lead only to higher power concentrations.

But Heilbroner, like Kenneth Galbraith before him, has become unduly discouraged, I believe, just when the prospects are most promising.

Robert Townsend is the author of "Up the Organization."

The mundane, guilt-dodging fatcats who infest this book will be no match for Ralph Nader and the thousands of dedicated young investigators in his wake. Nor will the populist rage now lighting up the political landscape be put out by the foam oozing out of the White House.

Here are what the six cases tell us:

The G.M. school bus case—"deciding to cheapen the product"—informs us that you don't have to buy a Lordsville Vega to get a shoddy product out of the world's biggest corporation. In describing what happened to a man who bought three new G.M. buses, Colman McCarthy's report also illustrates a fundamental weakness of supersize. Instead of helping customers, such companies build legal departments who tell them not to do anything for one they won't do for all, and then to please their lawyers they create huge nothing departments designed to make sure no customer gets any real help at all when he needs it.

The Susquehanna Corporation case hangs out Wall Street's laundry in a blatant example of conglomeration for its own sake. But it is an ordinary basket of Monday dirties. No one who has ever listened for half an hour to Disque Deane, one of the Lazard Frères partners, will be surprised either by the amorality of the sniffing for legal loopholes or by the arrogant confidence that loopholes will be found and kept open by regulatory authorities despite the most determined legal challenges—along with standard semantic deodorizers. James Boyd, the author of this case, reminds us that Jim Fisk did this sort of thing in the 19th century; once, when escaping with the loot intact from an enraged mob of swindled stockholders, he summed up things for his heirs in Susquehanna: "Nothing lost, save honor."

Saul Friedman's Dow Chemical-Napalm story illustrates Gunnar Myrdal's observation that "privileged groups in society invariably display an extraordinary selectivity with regard to what they 'know' about it." As the $249,000-a-year Dow president, Herbert (Ted) Doan could say: "We don't feel that we should put pressure on the Government in areas we do not understand. We really don't know what the [Vietnam] objectives are, and the tactics and strategies." In this depressing yarn, you may rejoice to one encouraging note: Mr. Doan's decision to retire from the Dow presidency at age 48.

In the Colonial Pipeline Company case Morton Mintz documents the bribery of the Woodbridge, N. J., mayor and his crony by the officials of a greater power, an oil company. No one familiar with the oil industry's success in persuading Messrs. Nixon, Mitchell and Flanigan to betray the American consum— —in the oil-import quota outrage of 1969—will be shocked by the petty larceny at Woodbridge.

The next two cases are more impressive. Sanford J. Ungar tells how Richardson- *(Continued)*

Merrell, Inc., doctored its research in order to sell MER/29, an anti-cholesterol drug. What got lost in the greedy rush was mounting evidence that MER/29 tended to make your hair fall out and to start cataracts in your eyes. Kermit Vandiver, who worked with B. F. Goodrich before he blew the whistle on them, describes how that company deliberately cooked the figures in a qualification report so as to deliver an unsafe airbrake on time to a new Air Force plane.

The lessons are all here: Honesty does not pay; keep your mouth shut and follow orders; the respectable corporate crooks get promoted for being loyal; the whistle-blowers get fired for being honest; even when convicted, no higher-up gets more than a wrist-slap. It's an old, old story: Although underling heads rolled, nobody drawing over $40,000 got fired at American Express over the salad-oil scandal. The same was true at R.C.A. after the computer division disaster produced the largest loss in corporate history. And when Life magazine fell on evil days, while working editors had to hit the street, the "Zeppelin pilots," Time Inc.'s squadron of obsolete executives, keep right on living high on their overstuffed perquisites.

In my opinion, the monthly board meeting as a common cause of corporate criminality is illuminated inferentially by the Richardson - Merrell and Goodrich tales. To appreciate these silly but accident-provoking shams, consider the customary attitude of the big company chief executive. Having brown-nosed or inherited his way to the pinnacle of privilege, he devotes all his power to one goal—staying there. To be sure, this means dodging practical risks or decisions for which he may be held responsible. But what is safe to discuss? Sales and profit trends are undetectable month-to-month, and risky: If he elaborates on the 20 per cent increase in March, some director may ask embarrassing questions about the 10 per cent drop in April.

In this framework, every chief executive has felt the constant pressure to come up with something new for every monthly agenda—something to show that he's not just stamping out brushfires and holding his organization together with the thin mucilage of promises nobody believes he's going to keep.

His quest for something new each month leads to widespread corporate premature ejaculation. Half-baked plans and untested products are accelerated to the boardroom and served up predigested and oversimplified. Board members, anxious to believe the best of their host, snap up these offerings and later ask for progress reports.

Then the pressure starts from the top and expands as it pushes down the echelons. "The old man's neck is way out on this one . . . make it happen . . . damn the cost . . . to hell with the research . . . do it, no matter how you do it." Next comes the filtering of information: nobody reports bad news upward. "Armies and corporations alike have ways of sweetening the news as it ascends the hierarchy of command," notes Heilbroner.

These absurdities are the by-product of excessive size and monopoly power. But in Part Two of "In the Name of Profit," Heilbroner cites two studies from the nineteen - fifties to diminish, if not dismiss, the over-all cost of monopoly. I suspect that Heilbroner, long a popular author, has not kept up on more recent research in this special field of economics. In 1964, D. R. Kamerschen estimated our annual costs from monopoly distortion of the market at $48-billion, and in 1970 F. M. Scherer raised the ante to $60-billion. In "The Closed Enterprise System" [also reviewed in this issue on Page 4], Mark J. Green provides a useful updating for those of us who have fallen behind.

Worse yet, Heilbroner throws in the towel on serious antitrust efforts, "the simple expedient of breaking great companies into much smaller units." His logic is a terrifying tour of despair: "First, it is clearly beyond the limits of any realistic economic reform. It . . . seems certain to encounter such a barrage of business opposition that its chances for political passage are nil. . . . [Second] the power of the corporation to work social good or evil would not be lessened by fragmenting it. . . . The big corporation is no longer a special case of business power and organization; it is the normal form. . . . Moreover, the extent and presence of that power has been growing irresistibly. . . . In 1968, the 100 biggest industrial firms owned roughly half the total assets of the nation's 1.5 million corporations. This was the same percentage that the biggest 200 owned only twenty years before."

I find it sad and ironic that great old war horses like Galbraith and Heilbroner should go snuffling back into the barn just as the only real battle of their lives on this issue has begun. "You can't get discouraged now," is the way Ralph Nader put it to this reviewer. "Suppose the Dallas Cowboys had had no opposition for years: running up and down the field, scoring as many points as they wanted. *That* was discouraging. But now all of a sudden there is somebody on the other side of the 50-yard line. Sure it may look like a ragtag bunch of kids in tennis shoes and sweatsuits; and sure they're getting killed. But they are *there*. And there are thousands more on the sidelines waiting to get in the game. And they get better equipped and more experienced every day. How can anybody be discouraged *now*?"

Look at it this way. America is run largely by and for about 5,000 people who are actively supported by 50,000 beavers eager to take their places. I arrive at the round figure this way: maybe 2,500 megacorporation executives, 500 politicians, lobbyists and Congressional committee chairmen, 500 investment bankers, 500 commercial bankers, 500 partners in major accounting firms, 500 labor brokers. If you don't like my figures, make up your own. We won't be far apart in the context of a country with 210-million people. The 5,000 appoint their own successors, are responsible to nobody. They treat this nation as an exclusive whorehouse especially designed for their comfort and kicks. The President of these United States, in their private view, is head towel boy. They prefer clever flunkies who, like most of the present White House gang, are so slippery they can enter a telephone booth and leave by the side door.

For most of us, the 210-million, the result is a tearing frustration. Frustration with unemployment, inequity, taxes and prices, to be sure, but under it all a rage at the giant, impregnable, impenetrable, anonymous, unaccountable, irresponsible, immoveable bastions of power. And now, through the Naderites, through the blizzard of shredded documents at I.T.T. —and through books such as this one—we get our noses rubbed in the whole sick operation of decadent power blocks.

The time has come to have dreams, hopes as tangible as an A.P. dateline and not far off. Samples:

WASHINGTON, Dec. 3, 1972 (AP) — President-elect George McGovern announced the appointment of Mark J. Green, of Ralph Nader's Corporate Accountability Research Group, as United States Attorney General. "It's about time," said the President-elect, "to find out if our laws, properly enforced, are adequate to deal with crime in the suites."

WASHINGTON, Jan. 23, 1973 (AP)—President George McGovern today demanded an end to taxation based on special privilege. He called for the elimination of *all* deductions, exemptions and special provisions, and a fresh start in income taxation with one provision—everybody gets the first $5,000 tax free. "This will provide more money for the Federal Government," said the President, "with the burden falling on those who are clearly able to pay."

At the same time the President called for an end to the corporate income tax along with legislation requiring all corporations to pay out in dividends to their shareholders *all* their earnings over $5 million. "Federal tax receipts will go up," said the President, "because 75 per cent of all corporate stock is owned by 2 per cent of the families, and this income will now be reported and taxed in higher brackets. Inflationary pressure in the country should be lessened," he added, "because income taxes to a corporation are just another cost to be added to the price the consumer pays, when this cost is removed, prices can be lowered."

President McGovern promised to report progress to the American people every 100 days: "I'll give you the names of Congressmen and lobbyists who are blocking these proposals as well as those who are supporting them, so each citizen will be able to exert pressure in whatever direction he thinks is right. Power must be taken from the few and distributed to the many if social democracy and freedom are to survive on this planet."

O.K., so maybe you don't yet buy McGovern. But to me "In the Name of Profit" is an accidental McGovern campaign document. Consider his position. He has had no help from the fat 5,000. He is beholden only to his conscience and the voters. He is too independent to be bossed, too honest to be bought, and too wise to be bamboozled. I have a strong hunch that McGovern is the man that Heilbroner and Galbraith have despaired of ever seeing in the White House—and that they are going to see him there.

"The creation of a responsive and responsible corporation," concludes Heilbroner, "becomes an indispensable step in the creation of a responsive and responsible state—perhaps the central social problem of our age."

I agree. John Ise, early Kansas radical, once said, "The modern corporation is a legal individual without an ass to kick or a soul to save." If McGovern gets in the White House there will be a corporate ass-kicking festival to gladden the hearts of about 209,945,000 Americans. And who will deny the possibility that when the dust clears from the ass-kicking, we may discover that somehow in the process our own souls have been saved? ■

April 30, 1972

The Corporate Political Squeeze

Illegal Contributions Raise Morality Issue

By MICHAEL C. JENSEN

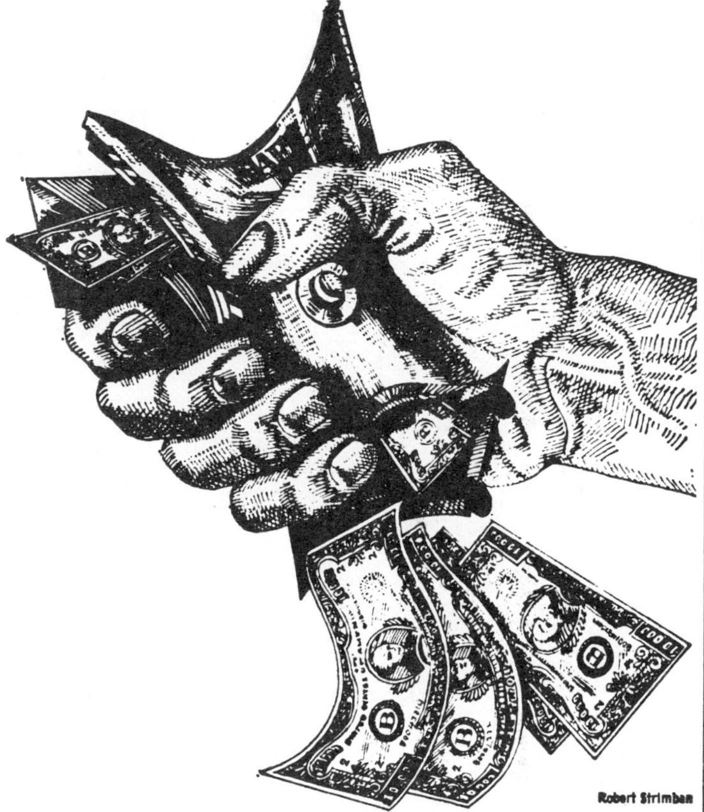

Robert Strimban

During the last two months, seven blue-chip companies with household names such as American Airlines, Gulf Oil and Goodyear Tire and Rubber have admitted in rapid sequence that they illegally contributed almost half a million dollars to President Nixon's 1972 re-election campaign.

Public reaction to the disclosures has ranged from outrage to indifference. But many observers, both inside and outside the business world, agree that confidence in big business, already at a low ebb, has been dealt another blow and that sweeping reform of outmoded campaign-funding practices is a necessity.

Some people show an unwillingness to blame business for conditons that have been forced upon it, but others damn both corporate morality and the public for allowing companies to break the law.

"If a public official had to admit to this kind of thing, he'd be in a hell of a lot of trouble," said Raymond D. Horton, a professor at Columbia University's school of business. "What amazes me is that there isn't more of an outcry. They seem to be getting away with it."

Whether they are getting away with it, of course, remains to be seen. Archibald Cox, the Watergate special prosecutor, has amassed evidence of the contributions and is planning legal action against the corporations.

However, by Mr. Cox's own admission companies that have confessed their sins may be treated more gently than those that are discovered by his investigators.

The shock waves created in corporate circles over the illegal contributions have led to widespread discussion among directors and company officers about preventing such activity. Indeed, some observers believe that the disclosures could have a cleansing effect and help to forestall future abuses.

Most campaign financing experts believe that illegal corporate donations are far from a new phenomenon, but many of them say the practice accelerated during the last election.

At the heart of the problem, many people contend, is an archaic and unjust system of financing political campaigns with massive private gifts. Aggressive solicitation of campaign funds conducted under a political system that gives the Federal Government enormous power over corporations can put severe strains upon corporate morality, they say.

What does a corporate official do when he is approached for more money than he and his colleagues can or want to give legally out of their own personal funds?

During the 1972 Presidential campaign the seven self-confessed illegal contributors, and a number of additional unnamed companies, decided to take a chance and donate corporate funds, an action clearly forbidden by Federal law and punishable by fines and jail sentences.

Many of the company's officials were asked to donate by two of President Nixon's close associates, Maurice H. Stans, formerly Secretary of Commerce, and Herbert Kalmbach, the President's personal lawyer.

"I was solicited by Mr. Herbert W. Kalmbach, who said that we were among those from whom **$100,000 was expected," said George A. Spater, chairman of American Airlines, in explaining why his company gave $55,000 in corporate funds.**

"I knew Mr. Kalmbach to be both the President's personal counsel and counsel for our major competitor [United Airlines]. I believe that such pressures have been regularly applied by campaign solicitors, and that contributions made by corporate officers and employes are directly or indirectly financed out of corporate funds to an extent that creates a significant national problem."

John W. Gardner, head of Common Cause, the citizens' lobbying group, who has talked to dozens of businessmen about the corporate gifts, said, "What Stans and Kalmbach did was demonstrate how a real vacuum cleaner could work."

Many businessmen, he added, felt they had been "shaken down" by Administration fund raisers and were bitter about it.

Why don't the corporate leaders speak out now?

"They're still intimidated," Mr. Gardner said. "You don't want to get on the wrong side of something as powerful as the Federal Government."

Two authorities on campaign funding, both lawyers, said their discussions with corporate executives indicated several reasons why they might have given illegally out of corporate funds.

One, they said, was the long-standing practice of corporate campaign giving. Although such gifts are forbidden, the law has been so loosely enforced that it has hardly acted as a deterrent.

Also, by many accounts, there was extraordinary pressure to donate especially large sums during the 1972 campaign. Braniff Airways, for example, said its chairman, Harding L. Lawrence, at first gave $10,000 to the Nixon campaign from his own personal funds.

"The chairman of the committee who received the first contribution solicited a substantial further contribution," Braniff said," and in response to this solicitation, moneys were made available in the amount of $40,000 out of corporate funds."

"It's the only campaign I'm aware of," one of the Washington lawyers said, "in which officials this high [Mr. Stans and Mr. Kalmbach] went around to companies and said: 'We expect you to give $100,000.'"

Another reason why the corporations were induced to violate the law, according to the lawyers, was that almost every large company in the country has constant dealings with Government agencies and regulatory bodies.

Although instances of a corporation's blatantly trying to buy a favorable decision are rare, many companies were said to believe that they must give generously to prevent unfavorable action against them. In other words, the money must be donated just to get an even shake.

Ironically, many of the recent major Government actions that have affected some of the self-admitted illegal givers seem to have gone against the companies.

At the time it donated $55,000, American Airlines had pending before the Civil Aeronautics Board a plan for a merger with Western Airlines. The merger request was denied on July 28, 1972.

Gulf, along with other oil companies, was under investigation by the Federal Trade Commission when it donated. In July, Gulf and seven other oil companies were accused by the F.T.C. of conspiring to monopolize the refining of petroleum products.

Goodyear, which gave $40,000 to the Nixon campaign, was accused by the Justice Department in early August, along with the Firestone Tire and Rubber Company, its competitor, of trying to gain a monopoly of the direct sale of tires to consumers.

Phillips Petroleum, which gave $100,000 to the Nixon campaign, was accused last November by the F.T.C. of anticompetitive and unfair practices.

In each case, public disclosure of the company's illegal contribution came after a visit to the Watergate special prosecutor, Archibald Cox, and in most instances a stylized pattern was followed.

First, a lawyer representing the company would visit Mr. Cox's office and admit that the corporation had made an illegal contribution. He would then visit the offices of the Finance Committee to Re-elect the President to ask for the company's money back.

Finally, late on a Friday afternoon, which sometimes but not always was the same day the Washington activity had taken place, the company would issue a press release spelling out what it had done.

Most of the press releases were timed for minimum impact — released at 5 P.M. or 6 P.M., after the stock market was closed, and at a time when many newspaper staffs had scattered for the weekend. The stories that did appear were in Saturday editions, which generally have a much lower circulation than on weekdays.

The Boardroom Seven

The seven companies that have publicly disclosed making illegal contributions to President Nixon's re-election campaign and the amounts of their contributions are:

American Airlines	$ 55,000
Ashland Oil	100,000
Gulf Oil	100,000
Goodyear Tire and Rubber	40,000
Minnesota Mining and Manufacturing	30,000
Phillips Petroleum	100,000
Braniff Airways	40,000

The first company to announce was American Airlines.

On Friday, July 6, Mr. Spater, American's chairman, voiced an attitude that other businessmen shared but often left unspoken — illegal contributions often were given not in the expectation of some specific favor but out of fear for what might happen if they were not given.

Two weeks passed, and on Friday, July 20, Ashland Oil, in a terse, five-sentence statement, said one of its unidentified subsidiaries had made an illegal $100,000 cash donation.

For three weeks there was no further word of illegal contributions. Then, on Friday, Aug. 10, late in the day, both Gulf Oil and Goodyear announced that they, too, had been to see Mr. Cox.

Citing "enormous pressure" and "persistent requests" to its Washington lobbyist from the President's fund raisers, Gulf said it had given $100,000 in corporate funds. Goodyear's brief, five-sentence statement said it had made a $40,000 cash contribution out of corporate funds.

Exactly a week after the Gulf and Goodyear disclosures, two more giant corporations announced that they also had made illegal contributions.

At 6 P.M. New York time, Minnesota Mining and Manufacturing said it had contributed $30,000 in corporate funds to the Nixon campaign. A half-hour later, Phillips Petroleum said it had made a $100,000 cash contribution to the President's campaign.

After the first six public announcements of illegal corporate contributions, rumors persisted in Washington that at least four additional companies had visited Mr. Cox but had decided not to publicly disclose their visits.

Finally, on Thursday, Aug. 23, after persistent inquiries from The New York Times, Braniff Airways admitted that it had informed the Cox staff that it had made $40,000 in corporate contributions.

Of course, not all the companies that were approached gave money to the Nixon campaign. In fact, a New York Times survey of major corporations, conducted in mid-July, found that a number of corporate executives had turned down appeals or large contributions.

Among them were officials of the Union Oil Company and the Allied Chemical Corporation. Others donated, but they did so legally, by means of personal, unreimbursed contributions.

Some observers feel that the public outcry over the illegal donations is muted because it is part of the American ethos to shave corners to earn a profit.

"One of the reasons why there isn't more outrage is that we're all out to make a buck," said William Gray, an Episcopal priest at Trinity Church in lower Manhattan. "Everything has a price tag. That five shares of I.T.T. may not pay off if you really get upset."

Whatever the reason, many Americans clearly have a low opinion of business behavior.

The latest Gallup survey of public attitudes toward big business, conducted in mid-1973, found that of the eight institutions ranked in terms of respect and confidence, business rated dead last. Only 26 per cent of the 1,531 persons surveyed said they viewed big business with either a great deal or quite a lot of respect and confidence, while 60 per cent said they had only some, very little or none.

In another sounding of public attitudes, the Opinion Research Corporation last year found that the ranks of the strongest supporters of big business were only half what they were in the mid-nineteen-sixties.

Thomas W. Benham, president of Opinion Research, summed up the situation by saying that there had been a "general disillusionment with business."

In the aftermath of the financing scandal, many corporate officials say they would be happy to see campaign-financing reform.

Lawrence E. Fouraker, dean of Harvard University's Graduate School of Business Administration, said: "I can understand how it happened in some cases because we have a problem that hasn't been resolved—financing of campaigns. Reform is needed to ease these pressures. But I can't say that justifies in any way the misuse of corporate funds."

E. Douglas Kenna, president of the National Association of Manufacturers, agreed.

"Financing reform is under intensive study to eliminate the potential for such abuses," he said. "I was surprised, and other corporate leaders were surprised [at the abuses]. I certainly don't think it's general practice by any means — either the contributions or the pressure to make contributions."

Mr. Gardner, who favors campaign financing by the general public, summed up by observing that he resists formulating the question in terms of morality.

"If you get on that theme, then somebody is sure to say you can't legislate morality," he said. "I feel very strongly that we are operating under a set of arrangements which virtually force these departures from morality.

"A politician doesn't want to be beholden, and a corporation doesn't necessarily want to give. We've simply got to change the arrangements."

September 16, 1973

Ford Signs Antitrust Bill

By JOHN HERBERS

Special to The New York Times

VAIL, Colo., Dec. 23—President Ford signed today legislation designed to strengthen the national antitrust laws and give the Government more authority to act against companies with inflationary policies.

Mr. Ford also vetoed two bills that he described as in excess of his budget and thus inflationary—one to expand Federal health service programs and one to provide Government payment for pollution-control facilities on the Tennessee Valley Authority's electric generators.

According to the President, the two bills would have increased Federal outlays by almost $1.5-billion.

President Ford acted today on 17 bills passed by the recently adjourned 93d Congress, signing 15 and vetoing the two. In his less than five months in office, Mr. Ford has vetoed 18 bills.

Mr. Ford hailed the new Antitrust Procedures and Penalties Act as the first major reform of the nation's antitrust laws in almost 20 years.

The legislation changes some antitrust violations such as price fixing from misdemeanors to felonies. It increases the maximum sentence from one to three years. It raises maximum allowable fines from $50,000 to $1-million for corporations and from $50,000 to $100,00 for individuals.

"The time is long overdue for making violations of the Sherman Act a serious crime, because of the extremely adverse effect which they have on the country and its economy," Mr. Ford said.

He further said that the legislation "will provide a significant deterrent to potential violators and give the courts sufficient flexibility to impose meaningful sanctions."

In linking the fight against inflation to the antitrust legislation, the President appeared to imply that the new law would help prevent large corporations from taking advantage of limited competition to make unwarranted price increases. This could have an anti-inflationary effect.

President Ford said he had decided to veto the health services bill because it conflicted "with my strong commitment to the American taxpayers to hold Federal spending to essential purposes."

"The bill authorizes appropriations of more than $1-billion over my recommendations, and I cannot, in good conscience, approve it," he said. "These appropriation authorizations are almost double the funding levels I recommended for fiscal year 1975 and almost triple the levels that I believe would be appropriate for 1976."

The legislation would have extended and expanded a number of Federal health services programs. Among the programs that would have been increased were those for health education and consultation, rape prevention, hemophilia treatment, blood separation centers and home health services. It would also have set up a number of special study groups on particular diseases.

Mr. Ford said he had vetoed the T.V.A. measure because it would have allowed the authority, a public agency, to write off as much as $430-million that T.V.A. customers otherwise would have had to pay for installing pollution control facilities recent legislation requires.

Mr. Ford acted on the legislation in about four hours of work before and after he skied for three and a half hours on Vail Mountain.

"The snow was excellent," he said after one of the runs. "It was 10 below there. It was just a beautiful day for skiing, an ideal day. I got my legs in shape."

Ron Nessen, the White House press secretary, said Mr. Ford was trying to get in a full schedule of skiing during his 10-day vacation here without disrupting the other vacationers, who swarmed the hills this morning in bright sunlight and again this afternoon in a light snowfall.

Mr. Ford intermingled with the other skiers without attracting much attention, accompanied only by a party of several Secret Service agents and members of his family.

December 24, 1974

The Ugly Corporation

By JOHN M. LeE

IT'S easy to be cynical about businessmen and politicians. Caveat emptor dates from the Romans and doubtless there was also a Latin phrase for, "He's just playing politics." Thus it is hard to know how to react to the unprecedented disclosures of corporate corruption in the form of illegal political contributions at home and secret payoffs abroad.

For some months now, we have been treated to the sorry spectacle of one blue-chip corporation after another being forced by Government monitors to step forward like naughty schoolboys and confess publicly what they have done. The rollcall has included names like United Brands, Northrop, Gulf Oil, Ashland Oil, Phillips Petroleum, Goodyear Tire, Minnesota Mining & Manufacturing, American Airlines, Braniff Airways and American Ship Building.

The confessed sins include $4-million in secret payments by Gulf to the campaign chest of the Government party in South Korea, a $1.25-million bribe by United Brands to reduce the banana export tax in Honduras, payoffs by Northrop to win aircraft contracts abroad and a political slush fund maintained by Braniff from falsified records for airline ticket sales. Some sins were obviously greater than others and technical factors may or may not make certain activities illegal.

The punishment has often entailed the mildest slap on the wrist in the form of a consent decree, in which the defendant agrees to stop any wrongdoing. Or there has been a modest fine. The $150,000 imposed on American Airlines last week was exceptionally large.

What's interesting is that with the exception of United Brands, all the cases arose from the investigations of the Watergate prosecutor into the financing of the 1972 Presidential campaign. As investigators probed deeper, they found the abscess had spread far further than had been thought. Northrop, for example, after first confessing to an illegal campaign contribution, later disclosed it had maintained a political slush fund since 1961 and had made secret payments to representatives abroad totaling $30-million.

Several questions come to mind. One is whether we have seen only the tip of the iceberg. Are the companies who engage in such dubious practices only those who gave corporate funds to the Committee to Re-Elect the President? Or are there large numbers of corporations who escaped by chance the Watergate dragnet and whose improper behavior awaits disclosure?

This raises a second point. Is such behavior typical of American corporations in general? Here we have two possible reactions.

One school says such behavior is not typical, that American businessmen on the whole carry on their activities honorably, ethically and with moral courage. In this view, the ugly corporations are the exception, and we might speculate why a Gulf Oil yielded to extortionate demands when other companies active in South Korea say they are clean.

The other interpretation is that there's nothing new in what businessmen have been doing. The only thing new, some say, is that Government agencies, notably the Securities and Exchange Commission, and Congress are compelling businessmen to disclose it publicly.

Another argument is that petty and not-so-petty bribes and payoffs are such an established part of doing business in Asia, Latin America, the Mediterranean and the Middle East that Americans, to stay in business and compete and thrive, must do as the Romans do. You can't be a Boy Scout when you're dealing with a bunch of pirates, the argument runs. Besides, some say, what harm does it do?

Some businessmen have suggested it is mostly a case of politicians calling the kettle black, of wanting to drag everyone down to the mud-splashed Watergate level. The public might be tempted to cry a pox on both houses

What then are we to think of it all? Clearly the recent disclosures haven't done business any good. But have they really harmed it, any more than price-fixing convictions against General Electric and others did in the 1950's or the attacks on Dow Chemical as the napalm manufacturer did in the 1960's? We would say they have, particularly at a time of ongoing attacks on business as being unresponsive to genuine public concerns. Others may have a different view.

At the least, some new ammunition has been supplied to critics who would impute sinister influences to multinational corporations. The tiresome old examples of International Telephone and Telegraph's behavior in Chile can now be supplemented by fresh tales of United Brands (née United Fruit) in Honduras and Gulf in South Korea.

The business community, it would seem to us, has a real responsibility to make its own views known or accept the tar brush. As for the corporations implicated, the contrite heart is very much in evidence.

"I don't know any matter in my 30-odd years with this company that has caused this company more concern and more grief and more sorrow," said Bob R. Dorsey, the chairman of Gulf.

"We have paid dearly for this mistake," Raymond H. Herzog, chairman of 3M said at the annual meeting. But he consoled stockholders by continuing:

"There are good signs that we are not paying a terribly great price in the marketplace. Most of our customers remain loyal to 3M and surveys show that our reputation in the business community continues to be a strong and good one."

June 1, 1975

Watergate Donors Still Riding High

Convictions Leave Most Financially Unaffected

By MICHAEL C. JENSEN

One might expect them to be the pariahs of the business world. Tarnished by public exposure as illegal campaign contributors during the Watergate scandal, surely they must have slunk away in disgrace to an ignominious retirement—shunned by former friends and an embarrassment to old business associates. At least a few of them must have paid debilitating fines or be serving long sentences in Federal prison.

Guess again. The fact is that most of the 21 business executives who admitted their guilt to the Watergate Special Prosecutor in 1973 and 1974 — especially those from large corporations—are still presiding over their companies. Either that or they are living the good life in semi-retirement on their country estates.

Only two went to jail. They served a few months and were freed. Most are still ensconced in their paneled corporate offices with platoons of lawyers and public relations men at their disposal. They are entertaining friends in their homes, playing golf and tennis at their clubs and mingling with political associates and civic leaders.

Furthermore, the fines of $1,000 or $2,000 that most of the contributors of illegal funds had to pay have not made much of a dent in their style of living.

Harding L. Lawrence, chairman of the Braniff International Corporation, for example, still takes home a paycheck totaling $335,000 a year. Orin E. Atkins, chairman of Ashland Oil, Inc., still makes $314,000. And H. Everett Olson, chairman of the Carnation Company, still earns $212,500.

Even those executives who retired, some of them under fire, are hardly roughing it. Russell DeYoung stepped down as chief executive of the Goodyear Tire and Rubber Company in 1973, but he still is a consultant with the big tire company and heads two of its most important committees.

As a result, he was paid $360,000 last year by Goodyear. He also started collecting a pension estimated at $144,000 a year. His Goodyear stock is worth about 3.6-million.

Claude C. Wild Jr., a Gulf Oil Corporation vice president who resigned at the height of the scandals, was quietly hired back as a consultant a few months later and earned nearly $90,000 in seven months before he again left the payroll.

What Messrs. Lawrence, Atkins, Olson, DeYoung and Wild—and their counterparts at such famous and powerful

Convicted Contributors

Company	Name	Fine/Prison	Current Status
American Ship Building	George M. Steinbrenner 3d	$15,000	Still chairman at $50,000/yr.
	John H. Melcher Jr.	$2,500	Discharged. Practicing law in Cleveland.
Ashland Oil	Orin E. Atkins*	$1,000	Still chairman at $314,000/yr.
Associated Milk Producers	Harold S. Nelson	4-months prison $10,000	Resigned. Now in commodities experts.
	David L. Parr	4-months prison $10,000	Resigned.
	Stuart H. Russell	2-years prison**	Resigned. Now in private law practice.
Braniff International	Harding L. Lawrence	$1,000	Still chairman at $335,000/yr.
Carnation	H. Everett Olson	$1,000	Still chairman at $212,500/yr.
Diamond International	Ray Dubrowin	$1,000	Still V.P. for public affairs.
Goodyear Tire & Rubber	Russell DeYoung	$1,000	Still chairman of 2 committees at $306,000/yr. Also collecting pension of $144,000/yr.
Gulf Oil	Claude C. Wild Jr.	$1,000	Consultant in Washington, D. C.
HMS Electric	Charles N. Huseman	$1,000	Still president.
LBC&W Inc.	William G. Lyles Sr.	$2,000	Still chairman.
Lehigh Valley Cooperative Farmers	Richard L. Allison	Suspended Fine of $1,000	Discharged.
3M	Harry Heltzer	$500	Retired as chairman, but does special projects at $100,000/yr.
Northrop	Thomas V. Jones	$5,000	Still chief executive at $286,000/yr.
	James Allen	$1,000	Retired as V.P. with pension est. at $36,000/yr.
Phillips Petroleum	William W. Keeler	$1,000	Retired with pension est. at $201,742/yr.
Ratrie, Robbins & Schweitzer	Harry Ratrie	1-month probation	Still president
	Augustus Robbins 3d	1-month probation	Still Exec. V.P.
Time Oil	Raymond Abendroth	$2,000	Still president.

*Pleaded no contest

**Under appeal

companies as Northrop, Minnesota Mining and Manufacturing, Phillips Petroleum and American Ship Building — have in common is that they were caught giving, conspiring to give, or otherwise participating in the funneling of corporate fnds to politicians at the national level. That's illegal in the United States.

Most of the businessmen were allowed to plead guilty to a misdemeanor charge, asserting that their violations were 'non-willful."

However, five of them were convicted of "willful" violations — a felony. They were George M. Steinbrenner 3d, chairman of the American Ship Building Company and majority owner of the New York Yankees baseball team; Thomas V. Jones, chief executive of the Northrop Corporation, and three former officials of Associated Milk Producers Inc., a milk cooperative.

Few of the executives seem contrite. Many believe they were unfairly (or unluckily) singled out and prosecuted for doing what other executives had been doing without penalty for years.

Most of them declined to discuss the aftermath of Watergate, although officials of some of the smaller companies talked more freely than did the high-salaried executives of major corporations who responded—sometimes angrily—through public relations spokesmen.

One of these company spokesmen said: "World War III is over and you won. But The New York Times and The Washington Post are so busy doing anniversary stories that they don't know it."

Nevertheless, one conclusion can be drawn from an analysis of the ordeal. For most of the executives, a lifetime of accumulating wealth and power was scarcely upset by the Watergate events. Virtually all the wealth and much of the power remains, even though most of the executives paid their own fines, some have repaid their companies for legal expenses and, in some cases, the money illegally donated has been restored.

Consider the Northrop Corporation, probably the most widely publicized of the corporate bribers, and its chief executive.

•

"Mr. Jones is still running this company vigorously," said a Northrop spokesman who has spent much of his time in recent months fielding questions about the company's payoffs to foreign officials.

Mr. Jones's case is instructive because he was at the forefront of the illegal activities of his company. A special committee of Northrop's board recently recommended

Thomas V. Jones
Northrop

George M. Steinbrenner 3d
American Ship Building

Russell DeYoung
Goodyear Tire & Rubber

Claude C. Wild Jr.
Gulf

William W. Keeler
Phillips Petroleum

Harry Heltzer
3M

that he be stripped of his title of chairman, an action that has been taken.

Despite such moves, Mr. Jones at age 55 is hardly ready for retirement and is fighting to retain his leadership role. (Last year he earned $286,000. and his estimated retirement benefits would be $120,000 a year.)

Although Mr. Jones continues at Northrop's helm, perhaps precariously, another of the company's executives who figured prominently in illegal activities has retired. He is James Allen, a $60,000-a-year vice president who stepped out last December at age 67 with a pension of $36,000 a year.

Although Mr. Allen's pension might be considered sizable, it is clearly not in the same league as William W. Keeler's. Mr. Keeler, former chairman of the Phillips Petroleum Company pleaded guilty on Dec. 4, 1973, to contributing illegally to the Nixon campaign and was fined $1,000.

At the beginning of 1973, Mr. Keeler had resigned as chief executive officer and subsequently stepped down as chairman in April when he turned 65. Following the exposure of his activities, he returned $1,000 to Phillips—the amount he had received in cash reimbursement for tickets he bought to a political fund-raising dinner. He later repaid $82,000 to the company for the fine, legal expenses and loss of interest that resulted from $495,000 in illegal contributions.

Apparently he could afford it. During his last full year as chief executive, Mr. Keeler was paid $300,000 by Phillips. His holdings of the company's stock (at today's price) were worth $3.4-million. And his retirement benefits are estimated by the company at $201,742 a year.

Another big-company executive who is surviving financially is Harry Heltzer of the Minnesota Mining and Manufacturing Company.

Mr. Heltzer resigned as chairman of 3M at age 63, about a year and a half after he had pleaded guilty to charges of making illegal political contributions and had been fined $500. His total compensation from the company in 1974 was $428,000 and his accumulated retirement benefits at age 65 will be about $125,[illegible] a year.

Meanwhile, [illegible] still occupies his [illegible] office on the 14th [illegible] of 3M headquarters in St. Paul, and he is being paid at the rate of $100,000 a year for carrying out special troubleshooting assignments.

Mr. Steinbrenner of American Ship Building is another executive whose power seems little eroded. Although Baseball Commissioner Bowie Kuhn suspended him from participating in professional baseball for two years, Mr. Steinbrenner continues to oversee the activities of American Ship Building, a Cleveland company, from his office in Tampa, Fla.

He says he voluntarily cut his salary from last year's level of $139,500 to about $50,000 and has brought a new chief executive into the company. But associates wonder how much of the real power he will relinquish, and they point out that he still cultivates his political friends at fund-raising dinners.

Mr. Steinbrenner's former associate, John H. Melcher Jr., who was the $70,000-a-year vice president and general counsel at American Ship Building, was not been so lucky. After he pleaded guilty to charges of being an accessory after the fact to an illegal campaign contribution and was fined $2,500, he was discharged by the company.

Mr. Steinbrenner, who says he has largely given up day-to-day control of American Ship Building, tends to be philosophical these days about the problems involved in running a big company.

"Being chief executive officer of a publicly held company," he said in a telephone interview, "is like being a baseball manager with four sore-armed pitchers. It's very hazardous."

Mr. Melcher has been representing some small clients in Cleveland. He is planning legal action against American Ship Building to recover salary he claims he deserved after he was fired.

An investigation into the whereabouts and financial status of the 21 executives involved in illegal contributions leads to a conclusion that the higher the position, the more cushioned the fall—if indeed there was a fall.

Mr. Lawrence of Braniff, for example, not only continues as chairman of his company but improved his financial arrangement with Braniff after he pleaded guilty to misdemeanor charges in 1973 and paid a $1,000 fine.

His new contract calls for continued employment by Braniff until mid-1980 at no less than $250,000 a year, which is $30,000 a year more than the amount specified by his pre-Watergate agreement. The new contract, like the old one, also calls for a consultant fee of $80,000 a year from 1980 to 1990, on top of retirement benefits currently estimated at $85,000 a year.

Some of the corporate executives acknowledge distress about their involvement in illegal political contributions. Mr. Heltzer, for example, said he regretted his "error" as well as his "mistake in judgment." Others, however, tend to be argumentative.

Others have become bitter about their experience. Mr. Wild of Gulf Oil, asked what Watergate had meant to his life, said wryly, "It hasn't been a source of great satisfaction."

"I'm a consultant here in Washington with several clients, and I'm trying to represent them to the best of my ability," Mr. Wild said. "But potential clients don't necessarily want to do business with somebody they read about in the newspapers every day. It's been a disruption of my personal life and my career."

On the other hand, Ray Dubrowin, vice president of public affairs for the Diamond International Corporation, the big match-producing company, is still operating, apparently without disruption, out of his office on Manhattan's Third Avenue.

"We got caught up in this innocently," he said. "It's over and done with. I'd just as soon forget it."

Others are similarly anxious to put such matters behind them. Charles N. Huseman, president of the HMS Electric Corporation, told the sentencing judge in Washington last December after he was fined $1,000, "I did this thing, and I realize I was wrong."

Mr. Huseman added that the resulting publicity had little impact on either his personal life or his business.

A few others, however, were not so fortunate. William G. Lyles Sr., who was president and chairman of LBC&W, Inc., an architectural and engineering company in Columbia, S. C., said the Watergate-related case had been a "horrendous and unfair episode."

"With a professional person his integrity is his life's blood," he said. "This has had an extremely adverse effect on us."

He said he subsequently lost business and had to cut his 350-person staff "significantly." He also said he had relinquished the presidency of the company to his son, Robert. "Nothing could even remotely approach this in unfairness," he said. "We were a victim of circumstances."

•

A similar theme was sounded by Harry Ratrie, president of the Baltimore construction concern of Ratrie, Robbins & Schweizter, Inc. Mr. Ratrie and Augustus Robbins 3d, its executive vice president, both pleaded guilty last January to making an illegal $5,000 contribution to the Nixon campaign. They were placed on probation for one month.

"We didn't even know we were in violation until the doggone thing had occurred," Mr. Ratrie said. "It seems unfortunate that people in business can't support the people they want without involving their personal finances. Unions can funnel millions into these campaigns, but business is handcuffed."

The most serious impact of the Watergate prosecutions was felt by three officials of the Associated Milk Producers, Inc., the nation's largest dairy farmer cooperative. All were convicted of felonies.

Harold S. Nelson, former $100,000-a-year general manager of the organization, and David L. Parr, his chief assistant, were sentenced to four months in prison, and fined $10,000 each, in cases growing out of massive illegal campaign payments aimed at influencing the White House and Congress on milk price decisions.

The sentencing judge said he was meting out jail sentences to deter others. Both officials were released from prison in February with a few weeks off for good behavior.

"I like to think I took it in stride," said Mr. Nelson. "It's a thing I regret. But it's not something I feel wounded over, and I don't want to nurse it. Financially, it's been a very severe blow."

Stuart Russell, a former counsel to the same dairy cooperative, was sentenced earlier this month to two years in prison, with immediate parole possible. He was charged with acting illegally as a conduit to funnel corporate funds into political campaigns.

Mr. Russell said he had appealed and in the meantime was practicing law in Oklahoma City.

"Two years of harassment by five different Government agencies have ruined my health," he said. "I'm insolvent and if my creditors didn't trust me, I'd be in bankruptcy."

Although the Watergate Special Prosecutor's office has completed most of its investigations, its task force on campaign contributions is still active and is expected to seek several additional indictments before going out of business at the end of September.

Meanwhile, most of the subjects of its earlier actions are still going about their business—sometimes sadder, generally wiser and in only a few cases significantly poorer.

August 24, 1975

Gulf Oil and Its Millions for Politicians

By MICHAEL C. JENSEN

Depositions and documents filed in a Washington court in the last few weeks reveal a pattern of illegal domestic political activity by the Gulf Oil Corporation that overshadows anything yet uncovered at other companies, according to Federal investigators.

The documents, filed in connection with a Securities and Exchange Commission lawsuit, chronicle the distribution of millions of dollars in company funds to politicians across the country. The documents have become available even as Gulf waits for the completion of a detailed report by a committee of its outside directors (those who are not Gulf officers) on the company's illegal activities.

The report, scheduled for release by Dec. 15, is expected to contain specific recommendations for Gulf's management, although there is no indication whether it will address itself to the future of individual Gulf executives or directors.

Particularly interesting to investigators and analysts is whether management changes at Gulf will be recommended. Bob R. Dorsey, Gulf's chairman, has been mentioned a number of times in one of the depositions filed recently by the S.E.C.

Among the myriad allegations about other officials in the recently released depositions, some of them reminiscent of the Watergate scandals, are these:

¶A secret letter, written by Gulf's top lobbyist and earmarked for opening if something "happened" to him, was first stored in a company safe and then put through an electric shredder.

¶Gulf acceded to a personal request from Charles Colson, a Presidential aide in the Nixon White House, to finance a rebroadcast of the wedding of Tricia Nixon and Edward Cox. The company said it proceeded with the rebroadcast against its better judgment.

¶A Gulf official said the company was asked in 1972 by the Government of Kuwait, a leading Middle Eastern oil producer and supplier of most of Gulf's crude oil, to make a campaign contribution of $10,000 earmarked for Senator Mark Hatfield, Republican of Oregon.

Bob R. Dorsey, left, Gulf Oil chairman, and Claude C. Wild Jr., former chief lobbyist for the corporation, were mentioned in documents filed in Federal court.

¶A Gulf lobbyist began his career with the company by delivering $50,000 to Lyndon B. Johnson, then the Vice President.

Basically, the depositions and documents indicate that, for more than a decade, Gulf lobbyists and operatives crisscrossed the nation, handing over to politicians cash drawn from a secret and admittedly illegal $10.3 million fund known as "Bahama Ex." Starting in 1970, some contributions also were made from a legal fund known as the Good Government Fund. This fund's purpose was to channel contributions from individuals at Gulf to political candidates.

According to the allegations, sealed envelopes were discreetly passed out by Gulf—once in a motel washroom in Indianapolis, once behind a barn in New Mexico and on other occasions at equally private but less bizarre locations.

The S.E.C. has previously charged that in all Gulf had doled out more than $5.4 million in largely illegal payments in the United States since the early 1960's.

In addition to Mr. Johnson, some of the nation's top political leaders have been mentioned in the documents, including former President Richard M. Nixon and Senator Hugh Scott, Republican of Pennsylvania.

An analysis of more than 500 pages of testimony and documents contained in a court file of the S.E.C. case—which is being heard by Federal Judge John Sirica in Washington—indicates that Gulf at times believed it was under extreme pressure to contribute funds to politicians and to otherwise accommodate them and that the company occasionally resisted such pressures.

In one instance, a Gulf lawyer said, the company rebuffed an appeal from Mr. Colson of the White House staff to retain a Washington public relations firm because it considered the matter essentially related to a job previously performed by the firm for Mr. Colson.

Although the payments by Gulf appeared to be primarily designed to maintain relations with influential members of Congress and the executive branch in Washington, there also were foreign considerations.

In 1972, for example, a Gulf official said, the company was asked by the Government of Kuwait to contribute $10,000, to be earmarked for Senator Hatfield, to the Republican Party's national campaign committee.

Studies Pressed

A spokesman for Mr. Hatfield, asked about the alleged contribution, said the money would have lost its identity after it was given to the committee. He added that the Senator was a friend of the Kuwaiti Ambassador and that any request to Gulf might have been made on that basis.

Gulf's activities are being studied by the Securities and Exchange Commission, the Watergate Special Prosecutor and the Internal Revenue Service, as evidenced by requests from the various agencies for company documents and records an dfor court files. The other investigation by the special committee of Gulf's outside directors, is headed by John J. McCloy, a New York lawyer and former president of the World Bank. Mr. McCloy, who is 80, is not a director of Gulf.

In the S.E.C. case, Gulf has already signed a consent agreement in which it neither admits nor denies the agency's charges about illegal payments. But Claude C. Wild Jr., a former Gulf executive, is contesting the charges.

Implications Seen

The current investigations hold serious implications for Gulf Oil and some of its executives. Mr. Wild, the company's former chief lobbyist, who is 52 and now retired, is said to have retained Edward Bennett Williams, the Washington criminal lawyer.

"I thought Mr. Wild should be represented by a lawyer who had expertise in criminal law," said Leo T. Kissam in a deposition. Mr. Kissam, of Kissam & Halpin, is Mr. Wild's New York lawyer. He added that Mr. Wild had retained Mr. Williams "for the purpose of representation in the criminal aspect of this case being handled by the Watergate Special Prosecution Force."

An attempt yesterday to discuss Mr. Wild's case with Mr. Williams was unsuccessful. A secretary in Mr. Williams's office said he was busy on the telephone and that he did not represent Mr. Wild. A question about whether he had previously represented the former Gulf lobbyist was not answered.

Another indication of the direction the case may be taking is the fact that the S.E.C. has told witnesses in its investigation that the Gulf files have been referred to the Justice Department for possible criminal prosecution, without recommendation as to any specific defendant.

Mr. Dorsey, Gulf's 63-year-old chairman, has indicated that the company will hold a special election of new directors if the McCloy committee uncovers information that would make such an action desirable.

Various Names

In addition, Mr. Dorsey's own role in relation to the company's illegal activities is apparently being scrutinized by investigators who have access to the testimony in court documents.

In one such document, Thomas D. Wright, a 37-year-old Pittsburgh lawyer who serves as an outside counsel for Gulf, reconstructed for S.E.C. investigators Mr. Wild's account of a meeting allegedly held at Gulf's Washington office in late 1963, at which a request for $40,000 from Senator Russell Long, Democrat of Louisiana, was discussed by Mr. Wild and others.

Mr. Wright said the names of several Gulf executives who had supposedly attended the meeting came up, with Mr. Dorsey's name among them.

Mr. Wright said Mr. Wild had subsequently asserted that he could not actually recall any particular meeting with such a group and "could not say that Mr. Dorsey was involved in making any decision or telling him anything on this particular occasion."

In another reference, Mr. Dorsey was said to have discussed political contributions in 1972, but that was after the company had started its legal Good Government Fund.

Mr. Wright also told S.E.C. investigators that Mr. Wild did not "identify" any current Gulf executives as being aware of illegal contributions.

At another point, Mr. Wild was said to have indicated that he reported directly to Gulf's chairman of the board, although he stressed that he was merely citing his "line responsibility" in the chain of command and not stating that he reported on illegal political funding activities to the chairman.

The current disclosures about Gulf come on top of earlier revelations. In 1973 it was disclosed that Gulf had illegally given $100,000 to the Nixon campaign, $10,000 to the campaign of Senator Henry M. Jackson of Washington and $15,000 to the campaign of Representative Wilbur D. Mills of Arkansas. Mr. Jackson and Mr. Mills were Democratic Presidential hopefuls, and Mr. Jackson still is.

Gulf and Mr. Wild were charged with having violated Federal laws. They pleaded guilty. The company was fined $5,000, and Mr. Wild was fined $1,000.

Later, as a result of the lawsuit by the S.E.C. and hearings before a Senate subcommittee it was disclosed that Gulf had funneled large amounts of money out of the country, had contributed $4 million to the party in power in South Korea and had given smaller amounts elsewhere.

According to Mr. Wright's deposition, most of the funds that Gulf used for political contributions came from the Bahamas Exploration Company, a Gulf appendage that was liquidated at the end of 1972.

Bahamas Exploration received its funds from Gulf Petroleum, S.A., which was described as being "in essence the [company's] banker in the Caribbean area."

Carrying of Cash

Mr. Wright said he had been told by William C. Viglia, a 70-year-old former Gulf executive who headed Bahamas Exploration, that funds were periodically transferred by Bahamas Ex (as the appendage was called) to a branch of the Bank of Nova Scotia in Nassau, Bahamas.

Mr. Viglia removed $25,000 or so at a time from the bank, Mr. Wright said, withdrawing the money about every three weeks for delivery to Mr. Wild.

Mr. Wright quoted Mr. Viglia as having said that the bank statement and checks drawn on the account were destroyed as soon as they had been reviewed for accuracy "so he would have no record with respect to this bank account."

Mr. Viglia was also quoted as having said that he had made deliveries of cash to Mr. Wild in Miami, Washington and Houston and that the airline tickets he used were destroyed after the trips.

As for the cash itself, according to Mr. Wright's account, Mr. Viglia "carried it on his person, often in his pocket." Mr. Wright continued:

"And he told us that, as a result of his frequent trips in and out of the country, he had become friends of the customs people, to the extent that nobody checked his baggage or person to determine if he had anything like cash."

Mr. Wright said it appeared that about $5 million had moved through the special Bahamas fund between 1960 and the end of 1972, most of it to Mr. Wild. He said $400,000 was a typical annual budget for distribution by Mr. Wild since the mid-1960's, although it was $300,000 for a "couple of years."

The money was kept by Mr. Wild in his personal safety deposit box, according to Mr. Wright, "in bills—fives, tens, twenties, fifties and hundreds."

Mr. Wild's "Governmental Relations" operation for Gulf was said to have employed a staff of 40 to 45 people, including 24 or 25 in the Washington office, with an operating budget of about $2 million a year, exclusive of the cash from the secret fund.

An account of how Gulf money may have been delivered to politicians was provided to the S.E.C. by Frederick A. Myers, Gulf's former "coordinator of legislation" in Washington.

Mr. Myers said in a deposition that he made 20 trips outside Washington, starting in 1961, to deliver sealed envelopes to various individuals on behalf of Mr. Wild. In most instances, he said, there was little conversation. In a number of cases, the envelopes were reportedly given to other Gulf employees

In 1964, Mr. Myers said, he went to Oklahoma City to deliver an envelope to Fred Harris, who was running for the Senate. He said he called Mr. Harris, "and he came to the hotel" with his wife and perhaps two or three other men to collect the envelope. Mr. Harris has denied ever "knowingly" accepting an illegal contribution.

In another instance, Mr. Myers, 66, said he traveled to Albuquerque, N.M., and was flown to a nearby ranch where he met D. Edwin Mechem, the former United States Senator, and handed him an envelope. "I delivered it to him behind a barn at the ranch," he said.

Trip to Indiana

Then, in 1970, Mr. Myers said, he flew to Indianapolis to deliver an envelope to former Representative Richard L. Roudebush at a Holiday Inn. He said Mr. Roudebush invited him to "adjourn" to a washroom, where the envelope changed hands.

Mr. Roudebush, who is now head of the Veterans Administration, says he has no recollection of the incident or the contribution. Gulf's Good Government Fund shows a $2,000 contribution to "Hoosiers for Roudebush" on the date when Mr. Myers said he made the trip.

In addition to such trips around the country, Mr. Myers said he made a "great number of deliveries of envelopes" in Washington, D.C. "Mr. Wild may have asked me to take something up to the Hill maybe four or five or six times a year," he said.

In only two instances, Mr. Myers said, were envelopes opened in his presence, and both times they contained cash.

One sidelight relating to Mr. Wild's activities involved a letter that was kept in a Gulf office safe in Washington. The letter was described for investigators by Eleanor Webster, a former secretary to Royce H. Savage, Gulf's 71-year-old retired general counsel.

According to Mrs. Webster, Mr. Savage gave her a sealed envelope a day after Mr. Wild had left the office. The envelope bore Mr. Wild's handwriting, she said, and had Mr. Savage's name on it.

She said the letter was "to be kept by him [Mr. Savage] and opened in the event anything happened to Mr. Wild."

Mrs. Webster said she put the envelope into the office safe, where it remained until early 1971, when she put it in an electric shredder and destroyed it along with some other personal papers of Mr. Savage, who had by then retired. She said she took the action on her own authority and never knew what the envelope contained.

According to Mr. Wright, Mr. Wild's career in making payments to politicians on Gulf's behalf began with Lyndon B. Johnson. Mr. Wild was quoted as having said that David Searls, Gulf's former general counsel, gave him $50,000 in the early 1960's to deliver to Mr. Johnson, who was then the Vice President.

"This was his first assignment at Gulf Oil," Mr. Wright said. "He did not know where the funds came from. And, secondly, he did not know anything about the arrangement or why these funds were being delivered."

Testimony has been confused at times. During one portion of Mr. Wright's statement to the S.E.C. about notes he had taken during discussions of gifts by Gulf, he said: "The next item I am talking about is 1971, and I can't read it. I have 'gift' in the left-hand margin, and it looks like 'Sinatra' —but I can't believe it is Sinatra, because I would have remembered it if it were."

The handling of large sums of cash also apparently led to some unusual incidents. Mr. Wright quoted Mr. Wild as having said that in 1970, while he was in Los Angeles, $25,000 that he had just received from another Gulf executive was stolen from his hotel room. The sum was simply accounted for as "L.A.—stolen," Mr. Wright said.

At one point, Mr. Wright observed that his notes from a session with Mr. Wild contained this statement: "All Senators on Watergate except Ervin."

Mr. Wright added that there was no indication of what this meant "except there was some reference in some way [that] Mr. Wild had assisted all of the Senators in Watergate except Senator [Sam J.] Ervin. Mr. Ervin, a North Carolina Democrat, was chairman of the Senate committee that conducted televised hearings on the Watergate affair in 1973.

Later Mr. Wright commented that a number of members of the Senate Watergate committee "show up as being recipients" of Gulf's legal Good Government Fund.

In one of the items allegedly discussed by Gulf executives, Mr. Wright quoted Mr. Wild as having said that Mr. Scott, the Senate Republican leader, was given $5,000 each spring and another $5,000 each fall out of corporate funds.

Practice Described

"We were told by Mr. Wild that Gulf had an arrangement in prior years, whereby Senator Hugh Scott was on a retainer—either him or his law firm. My notes actually refer to the law firm being on a retainer of $20,000 a year," Mr. Wright said.

The practice was altered, Mr.

Wild was quoted as having said, because Mr. Savage, then Gulf's general counsel, objected to it. Consequently, for "many years," he had been following the practice of giving Senator Scott $5,000 twice a year.

"My recollection of the events surrounding that are that first the funds were always made available to the Senator after he described to Mr. Wild his need for money for a personal matter or for some office matter—never in connection with political contribution matters," Mr. Wright said. "And, further, that Mr. Wild gave these funds as a gift for unrestricted use without regard to political campaigns, et cetera."

Senator Scott has said he never knowingly accepted political contributions from corporations. Other alleged recipients of Gulf contributions have made similar statements.

As for the company, observers are watching to see if Gulf's directors take any action, as a result of the current investigations, at their board meeting scheduled for Dec. 9. For the moment, the company is saying nothing, citing the impending release of the McCloy report.

November 26, 1975

JAPAN RIGHTIST GOT $7 MILLION FROM LOCKHEED

Senate Reveals Pattern of Payments Made Abroad to Help Airplane Sales

By ROBERT M. SMITH
Special to The New York Times

WASHINGTON, Feb. 4—The Lockheed Aircraft Corporation paid $7 million to a powerful Japanese rightist, who had both political influence and ties to the Tokyo underworld, to help the company sell its airplanes in Japan, a Senate subcommittee said today.

The subcommittee on multinational corporations—the accidental recipient of some information from Lockheed's independent auditors—also disclosed payments by the company to Italian politicians, "gifts" in Turkey, lobbying in West Germany and the purchase of industrial intelligence from European airline officials.

Details Guarded

Lockheed has previously admitted paying at least $22 million in bribes overseas. However, it has resisted making public the names of the recipients of its bribes (or even the countries where they were paid) on the ground that disclosure would jeopardize the officials involved, the company's contracts and perhaps its corporate existence.

The documents released today add two elements to what was already known. They provide specifics—sometimes in Lockheed's own words—and they present a corporate pattern of influence buying in Western Europe, the Middle East and the Far East.

Senator Frank Church, the Idaho Democrat who heads the subcommittee, said the most disturbing fact the panel had come upon was the employment of Yoshio Kodama as Lockheed's "secret agent" in Japan. The Senator described Mr. Kodama as "a prominent leader of the ultraright-wing militarist political faction in Japan."

2 Foreign Policies

Senator Church said: "In effect, we have had a foreign policy of the United States Government which has vigorously opposed this political line in Japan and a Lockheed foreign policy which has helped to keep it alive through large financial subsidies in support of the company's sales efforts.

"We had better make up our minds whether we are going to have a United States or a corporate foreign policy."

Senator Church also said the subcommittee had discovered an account totaling nearly $600,000 in 1973 that Lockheed had maintained in Paris without recording it on its books.

The fund was maintained first in a trust account of Coudert Brothers, a prominent New York law firm with a Paris office on the Champs-Elysées. Later the trust account was con verted into currency and put in a safe deposit box in Paris.

Coudert Brothers paid money out of the account, according to a subcommittee staff member, at the direction of Lockheed's president, A. Carl Kotchian, and other company officers.

According to a document prepared by Arthur Young & Company, Lockheed's independent auditors, $85,000 from the safe deposit box went to "an official of a customer airline" and two other payments totalling $45,000 went to a marketing consultant "for reasons that are not clear."

The managing partner of Coudert Brothers in New York, John E. Devine, was asked by The New York Times about his firm's handling of the trust account and the money in the safe deposit box.

Amount of Money

Specifically, Mr. Devine was asked whether such a transaction on behalf of a client was not unusual and whether — given the amount of money involved—it might not have put the firm under an obligation to inquire what was taking place.

Mr. Devine said he would check with his colleagues and call back if he had anything to say on the firm's behalf. He did not call today.

The subcommittee was rebuffed last summer by both Lockheed and Arthur Young & Company when it issued subpoenas for information about Lockheed's sales of civilian aircraft. According to a staff member, the accounting firm appeared to have decided not to provide the data.

When information from Arthur Young that supposedly related to Lockheed's military sales was delivered, however, the boxes were found to contain information on all sales.

According to the subcommittee staff member, Arthur Young—one of this country's "big eight" major accounting firms—and its law firm, White & Case, requested that the civilian sales information be returned. The subcommittee refused and began to analyze the data, some of which it made public today.

Names Withheld

In response to Lockheed's plans, the subcommittee decided in closed session to delete the names of the foreign government officials involved. According to subcommittee sources, there has been a division among the Senators on how vigorously to proceed and how much to make public.

Senator Charles H. Percy, Republican of Illinois, is reported to have taken a more conservative stance on public disclosure.

Today Senator Church and the subcommittee's counsel, Jerome I. Levinson, pressed William G. Findley of Arthur Young on why Lockheed would have used its Swiss subsidiary as the cources of some of the cash it paid Mr. Kodama. The reason, they suggested, was that Swiss law made information from the subsidiary's books unavailable to American investigators.

Senator Percy intervened to point out that the Swiss unit was not a "Shell," or company devoid of actual functions. He also said: "Switzerland is a good friend of ours. It's a good place to do business. The United Nations uses it frequently."

The payments to Mr. Kodama were made with money packed in shipping crates. Later, they were made by bearer check—a check cashable by the holder.

The documents that the subcommittee released today show that "more than 85 percent" of $1.68 million in "promotional expenses" that Lockheed scheduled in 1970 in Italy were for a particular minister's political party.

In a handwritten letter from the Grand Hotel in Rome, a Lockheed European employe wrote to Lockheed in Georgia about "compensation to third persons."

He apologized for his handwriting, saying that he could not dictate because "I am in no position to disclose to local third persons the contents hereof."

Kodama's Background

Mr. Kodama, who was named in the Lockheed report, is regarded as one of the most powerful men in Japan. Now 65 years old, he was instrumental in founding Japan's governing Liberal-Democratic Party and has had a hand in naming several prime ministers. He has settled many disputes among businessmen and commands the loyalty of the ultraright wing in Japan.

He also has strong influence over underworld elements in that country. He was imprisoned after World War II as a war criminal but was never brought to trial.

February 5, 1976

Business Morality Has Not Deteriorated—Society Has Changed

The year 1976 was one in which the ethics of business were called into question as never before in recent history. Disclosures of bribery and payoffs at home and abroad tumbled forth almost daily, with charges of wrongdoing spilling from business to government and back again. The issue became heated enough to make it one of the first priorities for President-elect Jimmy Carter. Last week, Mr. Carter issued broad guidelines designed to limit any conflicts of interest that members of his Administration might find themselves involved in.

Among those signing letters of intent to abide by the guidelines was W. Michael Blumenthal, the chief executive officer of the Bendix Corporation who is Mr. Carter's choice as Secretary of the Treasury. The following article was excerpted from a piece written by Mr. Blumenthal prior to his Treasury appointment that is to appear in the Jan. 17 issue of The Advanced Management Journal, a publication of Amacon, a division of the American Management Associations.

Michael Blumenthal, going from Bendix to the Treasury, feels executive prerogatives have been circumscribed.

By W. MICHAEL BLUMENTHAL

The rash of disclosures of corporate bribes and other illegal payments here and abroad has provoked a chorus of questions about ethics, morality, and the modern corporate executive.

In fact, our entire economic system is being scrutinized as never before. Some people have been quick to conclude that the incidence of corporate misconduct is reason enough for a major overhaul of the system. They argue that the process of distributing goods and services in society, since it inevitably involves society's larger goals, is too important to be entrusted to decision-makers in large corporations.

Therefore, the contention is made that big corporations should be fractionalized into smaller, more socially manageable pieces. Others would go even further. For them, nothing less than the removal of the profit motive is necessary to minimize the occasion of corporate sin. So we hear renewed calls to put the entire system under direct government control.

But neither more government control of business nor the breakup of big corporations will lead automatically to a higher standard of morality in business. After all, there is no evidence that government bureaucrats or the proprietors of smaller businesses are any more or less ethical, if you will, than the executives of big corporations.

Furthermore, our economic system works better than any other that has been devised. Consider the various attempts that have been made throughout history to replace the profit motive—from the utopian systems of an earlier age to the centrally planned economies in the Communist and Socialist countries today. None have worked well.

It seems to me that the root causes of the questionable and illegal corporate activities that have come to light recently are to be found in factors other than the profit motive or the structure of modern business. They can be traced to the sweeping changes that have taken place in our society and throughout the world and to the unwillingness of many in business to recognize or adjust to these changes.

All of us have been overtaken by events to one degree or another. To some extent, our priorities have been reordered and now encompass demands that were once considered beyond the traditional scope of business. Changes have also taken place in the standards of moral behavior that now apply to business. Activities once considered as normal practices are now unacceptable. It is in these changes that we will find what is really behind today's headlines.

All of this suggests that the skill to anticipate social change is becoming increasingly critical in business. It is almost impossible to talk about United States business today without talking about the world at large. So great has been the growth in international trade and investment in recent years that the economies of many nations of the world have become interdependent. In addition, corporations have increased in size and complexity. At Bendix, we employ more than 80,000 people. Obviously, it is impossible for us to know for sure whether all of our employees are observing the operating procedures and minimum standards of proper conduct that have been promulgated in the higher councils of our company. We must work through other people. Therefore, the ability to select the right people has become increasingly important.

Employees today are much better educated than their predecessors. They have to be in order to cope with the complexities of a modern business. But employees also have vastly different expectations about their lives and the role of their jobs in fulfilling these expectations. A regular paycheck is still important, but other factors are now regarded as equally important. Employees want to be involved in decision making. They are highly mobile and, therefore, less willing than their predecessors to remain tied to a job or to a company.

The communities in which businesses operate have also changed. Management today must consider what effect a plant closing, for example, will have on a community, particularly if that decision involves the loss of an important source of local employment.

Accompanying the notion of the "socially responsible" company has been a more militant interpretation of the public's right to know how the activities of business are affecting people's lives.

To these changes, we must also add the larger role being played by government in regulating business and in gathering information to make sure that corporate activities are carried out in line with public policies. Entire sections of our corporate staff exist primarily to provide reports to government agencies at the Federal, state, and local levels.

The decision-making process in business, then, has become far more complicated than it used to be. Just as important, many of yesterday's executive prerogatives have been circumscribed.

Some people have interpreted the recent disclosures of bribes and kickbacks as conclusive evidence that business morality has deteriorated. This isn't true. Certain practices that were once acceptable are no longer considered proper because the rules and expectations of society have changed.

In fact, American industry has created many of the changes, yet its tradition of adaptability does not seem to be transferable to certain aspects of corporate behavior. The lavish entertainment of customers is considered a normal and accepted marketing practice in the United States. It does not seem to occur to many executives that there is an important distinction between this practice and outright bribery.

This failure to make important distinctions in business practice shows up in other areas as well—employment activities, for example. In the past, business established its own rules for hiring and firing. This led to personal prejudices becoming an important, if not dominant, factor in employment matters. All this has changed. Today, the executive who permits unfair employment practices will not only find his company in serious trouble with the government but also learn, from the adverse publicity its actions receive, that it is out of step with society's standards of fair and ethical conduct.

It is entirely possible to operate a successful business, fulfilling society's requirements while maintaining the highest standards of morality. I have never had to make a decision at any level of responsibility in business that involved an unbridgeable conflict between market considerations and what is fair and humane. Indeed, it seems to me the way to achieve this equilibrium of considerations is to do in business what one does in personal pursuits.

At Bendix, we decided sometime ago that we would not seek business in a foreign country if it were necessary to compromise our policies to succeed. This policy has not hurt us a bit.

From our experiences, I have drawn some conclusions about how business executives can respond to the current concern about corrupt business practices and also increase their adaptability to the changing conditions that are the root causes of the present predicament.

First, it should be business executives, not outsiders, who are the most vocal in condemning improper conduct. After all, it is the reputation of business that is at stake. But even before speaking out, we should see that our own houses are thoroughly in order. We should get together and organize a national board or council that will monitor the behavior of corporations, provide a forum for resolving issues of morality, and write a code of ethics that will deal with some of the more vexing questions about corporate behavior. And there are many more of them than the public suspects—where "the right thing to do" is not immediately clear.

Just defining what constitutes a payoff is not as easy as it may appear to be at first glance. In many countries, for legal or cultural reasons, it is essential to engage a national as a local representative or agent. The universal custom is to pay the agent a commission on the basis of the sales that are generated. What if the agent uses a portion of the fee to bribe someone? Is that being done in your name? I would treat it as an action being taken by an employee and, therefore, forbid it. But on these and other questions, honest people can differ.

People in business have not suddenly become immoral. What has changed are the contexts in which corporate decisions are made, the demands that are being made on business, and the nature of what is considered proper corporate conduct. Corporation executives today are held accountable to many different constituents and overseers—the board of directors, other members of management, shareholders, customers, employees, the news media, and others. In short, business has become everybody's business.

January 9, 1977

Files of S.E.C. Show Slush Funds In Use Decades Before Watergate

By ROBERT D. HERSHEY Jr.

Special to The New York Times

WASHINGTON, May 17 — American companies began creating slush funds from which they made political contributions and other secret payments decades before the practice was exposed during the Watergate scandal, according to Securities and Exchange Commission files made public today.

American Airlines, for example, was running an unrecorded fund in Mexico in the early 1940's and Ashland Oil Inc. appears to have made a corporate contribution to the Presidential campaign of John F. Kennedy in 1960.

The material on nine companies was released by the S.E.C. in response to Freedom of Information Act requests by news organizations.

Shortly after the arri[illegible] of Harold M. Williams, its new chairman, the commission last month voted to make investigatory files public as soon as it marks the cases closed. This new policy, which the agency regards as required under the information act, might cause a major change in business-Government relations, on Mr. Williams fears may make businessmen more reluctant to share confidences while seeking advice or cooperation with investigators.

Today's material consisted of the initial files of five companies—American Airlines, the American Ship Building Company, Braniff Airways, E. I. du Pont de Nemours & Company and the Butler National Corporation—and additions to files of Ashland Oil, the Minnesota Mining and Manufacturing Company, the Phillips Petroleum Company and Waste Management Inc. that were supplied earlier.

Among the highlights were these:

¶Besides a contribution to the Kennedy campaign, which Ashland's chairman, Orin E. Atkins, told the S.E.C. might have come from the personal resources of the company founder, Paul Blazer, Ashland contributed $12,000 to Louie B. Nunn's Kentucky gubernatorial campaign in 1967. It also used a slush fund to pay directors of its Indian unit, who were restricted in taking money out of their country, and to pay $40,000 a year to John Paul LeGrande, a Parisian oil consultant with a Swiss bank account. Ashland previously admitted making almost $500,000 in questionable payments to Government officials and consultants in Nigeria, Gabon, the Dominican Republic and Libya.

¶Phillips Petroleum, according to a memorandum used to prepare for a conference with the S.E.C., had four unrecorded funds that contained $200,000 when they were discontinued a few years ago. Money in these accounts was generated abroad—in part from rebates from an unidentified foreign airline on tickets bought by Phillips employees—but none was used in this country. Phillips and its former board chairman, William W. Keeler, had previously pleaded guilty to illegally contributing $100,000 to President Richard M. Nixon's re-election campaign and the company also admitted contributions to dozens of Congressional candidates, including Gerald R. Ford.

Butler National, a tiny Kansas company that makes aeronautical equipment, identified the foreign agent who received 30 percent sales commissions totaling $102,500 as Roberto Kobeh Gonzalez, an employee of the Mexican agency that bought navigational gear from Butler. The company's lawyers argued last year that the competitive consequences of this disclosure might be "mortal" to the company but they failed to prevent the commission from bringing a suit, which contained general allegations. Gerald R. Smith, Butler's president, said today the company had not done any business in Mexico since the S.E.C. went to court and that it was still losing money. Mr. Smith said the company could not afford to seek an order barring today's disclosure, which he said would probably be futile in the end.

The files on Minnesota Mining, whose political contributions became widely publicized as various executives lost their jobs after admitting their roles in dispensing some $489,000, provided some detail of a $30,000 transaction. Wilbur M. Bennett, civil affairs director, told the S.E.C. in 1974 that he gave Maurice H. Stans, head of the Committee to Re-elect the President, $30,000 at a brunch for Mr. Stans at the Twin Cities Hilton. He said the money was in $100 bills because "it seemed the simplest way to do it."

The American Airlines files disclosed that it had a company slush fund even before the formation of its Mexican subsidiary in 1942. According to testimony of its former chairman, C. R. Smith, the company paid $5,000 to $6,000 a year between 1934 and 1942.

Mr. Smith said he could not remember where the money came from then. "That's so long ago, and besides we didn't take political problems very seriously in those days," he said. "We had very few demands for money."

The former chairman, referring to the 1934-42 period, added, "I think you would find that American Airlines, outside of the regional services, probably gave less money to politicians than any other company . . . of its size. We had an excellent reputation for being chintzy."

May 18, 1977

CORPORATE SOCIAL RESPONSIBILITY

THE BEST USE OF GREAT WEALTH.

In the Department of Political Economy at Yale, of which Prof. HADLEY, the newly elected President of the university, has been the head, the new Socialism has obtained no foothold. They teach hard common sense in that department if we may judge from the recent utterances of one of its professors upon a question that is much discussed nowadays in this country.

Soon after the publication of the report that Mr. ANDREW CARNEGIE had sold his business interests to his partners for one hundred million dollars, Mr. CARNEGIE was quoted as saying that he did not care to keep on making money to the end of his life; he proposed now to do good with the wealth he had accumulated. A discussion has been going on at Yale as to the way in which Mr. CARNEGIE could do the most good with his hundred millions. To this discussion Prof. J. C. SCHWAB of the Department of Political Economy makes a contribution so sound and sensible that it leaves nothing more to be said:

Probably the best thing that Mr. CARNEGIE could do with his money would be to employ it actively in business; that is, he should build factories and railroads and employ his money productively. If that is out of the question, let him do as he has been doing, establish libraries and similar institutions. The least advantageous way for the disposition of the Carnegie millions would be to establish so-called charitable institutions.

That brief statement is worth a great deal of money to Yale University as an advertisement. Men are willing to send their sons to be educated at a college where political economy of that kind is taught; they are willing by gifts and bequests to increase its power and extend its usefulness.

The doctrine that wealth is best employed when it is put to productive use, when it becomes active capital, paying the wages of labor, performing public services or turning raw material into salable merchandise, ought to be implanted in the belief and understanding of every undergraduate. There is urgent need of such teaching now as a corrective of and defense against the Socialistic demagogues who go about preaching that wealth is culpable and the capitalist a public enemy.

Prof. SCHWAB is right about the best employment of Mr. CARNEGIE's millions. But the ranting, roaring demagogues are doing their utmost and worst to drive him and his millions out of the country, to drive everybody out of the country or out of business who has money to invest and a desire to employ it in productive industries.

Under the leadership of W. J. BRYAN and the addlepates who are clustered about him the Democratic Party is preparing to make its campaign next year on the proposition that Mr. CARNEGIE should be indicted and his millions taken away from him if he tries to do business anywhere in the United States on a larger scale than is approved of by the people of Waco, Texas, or Little Rock, Ark., or by methods to which the captains of industry in those communities are unaccustomed.

Are Prof. SCHWAB's engagements of such a nature that he would be able to take the stump next year, if his services were required in the campaign?

June 6, 1899

ROCKEFELLER, JR.'S, LIFE TO BENEVOLENCE

John D. Rockefeller, Jr., has decided, as it was announced at the Standard Oil offices yesterday, to retire from the many financial concerns in which he is interested to devote the rest of his life to the management and distribution of the great wealth his father has accumulated.

Less than twenty-four hours after the bill for the incorporation of the Rockefeller Foundation was presented in Congress on Wednesday it was announced here that Mr. Rockefeller, Jr., had retired on Jan. 11 last from the Directorate of the Standard Oil Company. Several days ago his withdrawal from the Directorate of the United States Steel Corporation was made public, leaving but two large business corporations with which he is now connected, the American Linseed Company and the Delaware, Lackawanna & Western Railway Company. While no confirmation of the report that he is soon to give up these could be obtained at his office yesterday those in his confidence thought it likely. He is to devote all his time to the management of his private business and to philanthropy, represented by the General Education Board, Chicago University, and above all, the Foundation which bears his and his father's name, and is intended to be the family monument.

Standard Oil Board Reduced.

It was denied at the Standard Oil offices that any effort had been made to conceal Mr. Rockefeller's retirement from that company. It had not become known earlier simply because no one had expected such a thing, it was said. It was announced that the size of the Standard Oil board had been, by special provision, reduced from fifteen to fourteen, so there would be no successor to him. These now comprise the board: John D. Rockefeller, Sr., William Rockefeller, Henry M. Flagler, John D. Archbold, C. M. Pratt, C. W. Harkness, E. T. Bedford, Oliver H. Payne, Walter Jennings, A. C. Bedford, J. A. Moffett, H. C. Folger, Jr., W. C. Teagle, and H. M. Tilford.

When young Mr. Rockefeller was graduated from Brown University and entered the Standard Oil offices a few years ago, it was predicted that he was to follow in his father's footsteps as a business man, continuing the process of piling up the family fortune. He was almost at once elected to the directorates of the Standard Oil, United States Steel Corporation, Missouri Pacific Railroad, Colorado Fuel and Iron Company, Federal Mining and Smelting Company, American Linseed Company, and the Delaware, Lackawanna & Western Railroad, besides several big banks in which the Standard Oil was largely interested.

For a few years he devoted himself to business, but it soon became evident to himself, if not to others, it is said, that he was more interested in the cause of human progress and the mitigation of suffering than in the increase of his fortune. As he became more deeply versed in the work of the General Education Board in almost every conceivable form of education, particularly in the South, and in the Chicago University, his interest in business waned. A friend said for him yesterday that he was too honest to stay in the Standard Oil Board as a Director, when he did not make any serious effort to supervise its affairs, and so overcame every argument against his resignation.

Young Mr. Rockefeller was at his office in the Standard Oil Building much of yesterday. His father has a suite on the fourteenth floor of the building in the rear. Here are the offices also of Starr J. Murphy, the elder Mr. Rockefeller's personal counsel, and Frederick T. Gates, his confidant and adviser in his benevolences. The younger Mr. Rockefeller will retain his office here, it was said yesterday, though no longer having official connection with the company. When reporters sent a note to him in the afternoon, asking for a statement regarding his connection with the Foundation, he sent word that Mr. Gates and Mr. Murphy would tell all that he could on that matter.

But all efforts to get from Mr. Gates and Mr. Murphy confirmation or denial of the report that young Mr. Rockefeller was to be the working head of the Foundation were fruitless. Mr. Gates said there was nothing to conceal, and that as soon as anything happened it would be promptly announced, but not before. Though definite statements on this score were thus lacking, J. I. C. Clarke, the press representative of the Standard Oil Company, said he thought Mr. Rockefeller was retiring from all business to lead the new philanthropic enterprise, and the same opinion was expressed by several close friends of Mr. Rockefeller who have been associated with him in the General Education Board and in business. It is certain that he is to be the chief force in the Foundation, if not nominally its President.

Endowment Not Yet Announced.

Nor could any statement be obtained as to the amount which Mr. Rockefeller, Sr., would put at the Foundation's disposal in the beginning. A few millions may be given until the work is started, as in the case of the Education Board, but eventually, according to Mr. Gates, it is to be the basket into which a great part of Mr. Rockefeller's wealth will find its way. Mr. Gates said, however, that the estimate that the sum would reach $500,000,000 was much exaggerated. It is expected, however, that the fund, which is to be Mr. Rockefeller's final and greatest philanthropy, embracing all others, will have much more than the Education Board's $53,000,000.

Mr. Gates, who was later described by a friend as having the same aptitude for philanthropy that Mr. Rockefeller, Sr., has for business, explained the foundation in great detail, giving a far better idea of its vast scope and perpetual beneficence than was indicated on Wednesday night.

"The fact is," said he, "the newspapers came near missing the chief point of the matter. This plan by which Mr. Rockefeller hopes to benefit humanity through all coming time has been under consideration for two years. He and his advisers have learned something from experience, something from observation, about the guidance of large gifts to philanthropy by a 'dead hand.' When a man gives or bequeaths a large sum of money for this and that object, specifying just how it shall be used, it is likely to happen, as it has happened so many times in this country, in Italy, in France, England, and elsewhere, that in half a century or less one of two things will have taken place. The charity or philanthropy to which the money had been given will not need it or not deserve it, but it had the money still with either nothing to do with it for the benefit of humanity or is abusing it and the original giver's purpose. Much of the time of the British Parliament is taken up in undoing just such bequests, but in this country there is no remedy.

"Mr. Rockefeller has endeavored to avoid such a situation by giving his money, whatever sum it may be, to the keeping of a self-perpetuating corporation which shall have power to use it for whatever advances the human race. It can give to a cause, educational, medical, or what not, as long as the money is needed, or good use is made of it. Then it can take it away. The bill has been drawn so broad that it will be able to contribute to causes and institutions 400 or 500 years from now, which perhaps have never been conceived of. Conditions are continually changing and the needs of humanity with them. Suppose a man in the fourteenth century had left a large amount to be used for a specific purpose in the twentieth century. It might not, and the chances are that it would not, be of any use at all because of the change of conditions and needs.

To Avoid Control by a "Dead Hand."

"What Mr. Rockefeller purposes is for his money to be used in all the times to come as the then existing conditions may require, the determination of those conditions and needs being committed not to a 'dead hand,' but to the men living in those times."

Mr. Gates explained that this was a subject upon which Mr. Rockefeller had been thinking many months, and the outcome was that the Foundation would be something absolutely new in philanthropy. Here Mr. Gates injected a remark to the effect that if the newspapers made the general scheme of the Foundation and its management plain, it would set wealthy men to thinking on the subject and might do good in revolutionizing the character of large bequests to public enterprises.

Mr. Gates gave an illustration of the flexibility of the Foundation's powers. "Suppose," said he, "there is a great earthquake somewhere, with tens of thousands of persons suffering. The Directors of the Foundation could vote any sum thought necessary for the relief of the afflicted and continue this help as long as required, withdrawing it when not needed. This could not be done with an ordinary gift or bequest."

Mr. Gates said that the Foundation was conceived as the means by which Mr. Rockefeller was to dispose of his wealth not only before but at his death. He said that when the framers of the Gallinger bill used the expression "advance the civilization of the peoples of the United States, &c.," they had in mind civilization as expressed in six phases. They were: "Means of subsistence, progress in Government, language and literature, philosophy and science, art and refinement, and morals and religion."

By the terms of the Foundation incorporation act the corporation would be able, and was in fact designed, to advance all of these, beginning first in the United States, and finally encompassing the human race, Mr. Gates said. The benefits of the foundation, he said, would be distributed by preference in the order named, the United States, its dependencies, and finally all the world. As proof of the fact that Mr. Rockefeller has for many months been thinking of this plan of philanthropy, attention was called yesterday to a statement of his made a year ago. He then said:

"I have always held the hope that during my life I should be able to establish efficiency in giving, so that wealth may be of greater use to present and future generations."

A friend of his said he was seeking in the foundation to establish a trust of philanthropy as he had founded an oil trust, and that he hoped eventually to lessen duplication and dissipation of effort in giving, and the opinion was even expressed that the day would come when there would be at least a working agreement among the Rockefeller, Sage, and Carnegie Foundations, if not an actual combination of them.

March 4, 1910

Letters to The Times

Corporation Directors

Are Not Guardians of Public Interest, It Is Said

The writer of the following letter is an attorney in the Department of Justice. He was formerly with the State Department.

TO THE EDITOR OF THE NEW YORK TIMES:

There is a growing tendency in this country to regard the directors of private business corporations as the guardians of what is called the public interest. This theory is basically unsound and, if it is commonly accepted, our whole free enterprise system may be jeopardized.

Congress alone has the responsibility of determining and declaring what the public interest is at any particular time, and with respect to any particular subject, as, for instance, the rise in steel prices. The characteristic feature of a democratic government is that it is the guardian, and the only guardian, of the interests of the people as a whole.

When Congress acts its laws should be scrupulously observed by all of us, including corporate directors. Congress has a perfect right to pass a law controlling prices of commodities; presumably Congress could also declare a corporation like the United States Steel Company a public utility, or could even go so far as to socialize the steel industry. But Congress has done none of these things. Obviously, Congress either does not know what the public interest requires with respect to commodity prices, or else it does not deem it wise to legislate on the subject at this time.

No Responsibility

In the absence of such legislation, corporate directors, even if they were all in agreement as to what is best for the people as a whole, have no responsibility in the matter whatever, unless the private interests of their stockholders are involved, as to which the directors of each corporation are the sole judge.

According to reliable estimates, there are between 400,000 and 500,000 private manufacturing corporations in the United States. These corporations have about ten million stockholders and are now doing a gross business at the rate of over $150,000,000,000 a year, which is close to 95 per cent of all the manufacturing business of the country. This corporate business and the private interests of these ten million stockholders, as such, are in no small degree the basis of our free enterprise and capitalistic system, and cannot be ignored.

Generally speaking, the sole guardians of these vast, highly important and wholly legitimate private interests are the corporate directors. Their only proper end objective is to serve the private long-term interests of their stockholders. This means that they should conduct the affairs of the corporation in such a manner as will result in maximum long-term profits and dividends.

Observance of Laws

In this process, of course, all public laws, federal or state, should be carefully observed. Furthermore, every conscientious, intelligent director knows that their end objective of maximum long-term profits and dividends cannot be achieved without a clear recognition of the true value of good-will, satisfactory labor relations, a good product and satisfied customers.

It should be clearly understood, however, first, that all of these things, however worthy in themselves, are but means to the end objective and, second, that scrupulous observers of the laws of Congress and, of course, the common law, fulfill the entire responsibility of the directors to the American people for serving the public interest.

The erroneous theory that directors have a duty to serve the public interest, according to some purely private definition, and in the absence of a public law on the subject, seems to be the result of an equally erroneous assumption that there is something sordid and ignoble in the profit motive as the basis for corporate action. This evidences a certain lack of faith in our whole free enterprise system, and tends to encourage its enemies, who aim to

We Americans loudly proclaim an enthusiasm for our free enterprise system, and, yet, at times, we seem to be ashamed of what is necessarily involved. It is highly desirable, in this critical contest between capitalism and communism, that we give to the world more convincing evidence of positive faith in our economic way of life. To do this we must first acquire a better understanding of the true function and high value of the American type of private business corporation, which has served us so well through the years, and which has accounted, in such large measure, for our unparalleled prosperity and material greatness.

A. BARR COMSTOCK.
Washington, D. C., March 25, 1948.

April 4, 1948

CORPORATE GIFTS TRACED BY SURVEY

Social Work Conference Hears 'Giants' Gave $239,000,000 in '48—Current Donations Rise

By LUCY FREEMAN
Special to THE NEW YORK TIMES.

CHICAGO, May 26—A new "giant" roams the field of American philanthropy—the corporation. Corporations gave $239,000,000 in 1948 and an equal amount in 1950 and are giving even more this year, F. Emerson Andrews, one of the nation's leading research authorities in the welfare field, reported today.

Mr. Andrews, director of publications for the Russell Sage Foundation of New York, made public for the first time an advance report of the findings of a comprehensive survey on "Corporation Giving," which he directed and which is to be published shortly by the foundation. He addressed the National Conference of Social Work.

In 1951 and 1952, he explained, "a substantial upturn appears to have occurred," because of high dollar profits, increased tax rates with a new excess profits tax and the clarification of the legal situation that had induced many executives to reconsider their policies on contributions.

Individuals donated fifteen times as much as corporations in 1948, Mr. Andrews said, with most of the individual contributions going to churches and "to causes with 'heart appeal' that have mass collection methods."

Corporation contributions averaged $30,000,000 annually from 1936 to 1939, rose sharply during the war years, reaching a record of $266,000,000 in 1945, and dropped in 1946 when the excess profits tax was abolished, Mr. Andrews said.

Breaking down the overall figure in 1950, he reported that in the sample studied, corporations had contributed more than a third of the money to Community Chests, and an additional 8 per cent to other welfare agencies, totaling 44 per cent or nearly half of every dollar.

Health accounted for 27 cents out of every dollar, and of this sum, 15 cents went directly to hospitals, which also received some of the money given for Community Chest budgets. National health agencies, including Red Cross, Polio, Heart and other groups, received another 10 cents and miscellaneous health, the remaining 2 cents.

Education received slightly less than health, or 21 cents of the gift dollar, and religious agencies received 4 per cent of the over-all corporate gifts, although nearly half of all individual contributions go to religious agencies, Mr. Andrews asserted.

May 27, 1952

Washington: The Big Business Progressives

By JAMES RESTON

WASHINGTON, Oct. 11—On Election Day the heart of American big business still belongs to the Republican party, but the rest of the time, despite occasional tiffs with President Johnson, big business support of the Administration's social programs is surprisingly strong.

For example, John A. McCone, California investment banker and former head of the Central Intelligence Agency, who recently came out for Republican Ronald Reagan for Governor of California, has startled his conservative friends by talking about a $100-million program to deal with the Los Angeles Negro ghetto of Watts.

The other day, Sol M. Linowitz, 52, of Rochester, gave up his job as chairman of Xerox International, Inc., to accept an appointment as President Johnson's Ambassador to the Organization of American States.

The Kaiser Lobby

And this week 22 chief executives of major American corporations, under the leadership of Edgar F. Kaiser, president of Kaiser Industries, issued a public statement for the Administration's demonstration cities bill that sounded as if it had been written by Walter Reuther of the A.F.L.-C.I.O. It was signed, among others, by David Rockefeller, president of the Chase Manhattan Bank, Henry Ford 2d, chairman of the board of the Ford Motor Company, Thomas J. Watson Jr., chairman of International Business Machines Corporation, and Thomas S. Gates Jr., chairman of the board of the Morgan Guaranty Trust Company and former Secretary of Defense under President Eisenhower.

There seems to be a growing difference these days between how the big business leaders vote and how they talk and act. Henry Ford recently announced that he wouldn't vote for Democrat G. Mennen Williams "for dog-catcher of Grosse Point," but he has been one of the most enthusiastic backers of what is almost a big business lobby to save Mr. Johnson's $900-million demonstration cities bill in the House.

On the whole, the big business executives have opposed Mr. Johnson's bill to suspend the 7 per cent credit for machinery and equipment, but even on this controversial legislation three prominent business leaders testified here for it: Frederick R. Kappel, chairman of the board of A.T.&T.; W. B. Murphy, president of the Campbell Soup Company and chairman of the Business Council, and Stuart Saunders, chairman of the board of the Pennsylvania Railroad.

The Holdouts

In these days when there is much talk about reaction against the war in Vietnam, against inflation, against some of the Great Society programs and against the pace of racial integration, this evidence of a rising social consciousness by big business leaders is worth noting.

The trend is not general in the entire business community. Outside of the small farmer, the small businessman is still probably the most conservative element in American society, but much of big business is different. It is increasingly directed by men in their forties and early fifties who were well educated, use modern economists in their businesses, and who came to maturity during or after the New Deal. Big business is more and more involved, with its international subsidiaries, in the welfare state and planned economies of other industrial countries, and its progressive attitudes are now expanding well beyond the factory gates.

Maybe these attitudes would change in less prosperous times, but for the time being the old conservative ideological (though not voting) patterns have given way to a new concept that big business is not likely to flourish if large segments of the population are living in poverty and misery.

"Our cities are being submerged," the Kaiser statement said, "by a rising tide of confluent forces—disease and despair, joblessness and hopelessness, excessive dependence on welfare payments, and the grim threats of crime, disorder and delinquency. . . . America needs the demonstration cities act."

To Assure Enactment

Twenty years ago the progressive Committee for Economic Development was bold for its time. But the predecessors at the head of these 22 large corporations would certainly not have endorsed such views. In fact the Kaiser Committee not only issued the statement but asked the White House in advance if the statement would be useful, and is now working on their Congressmen to try to assure the necessary votes.

Something is going on here and this is only fair. Big business has clearly made its contribution to the ugliness and slums of America's cities, but a new generation of corporate leaders is obviously trying to make amends.

October 12, 1966

When Big Business Makes Gifts (Tax-Deductible)

By ANDREW HACKER

EASTERN AIR LINES' recent gift of $500,000 to the Metropolitan Opera for a new production of Wagner's "The Ring" cycle raises an interesting question: What do our major corporations do with their spare cash?

Charitable contributions from corporate treasuries will approach $900-million this year and, if current trends continue, the annual figure will exceed $1-billion before 1970. This is more than simply a great deal of money. For these checks, and the names of the recipients imprinted on them, represent American business's thinking about the social and cultural life of the nation. Moreover, in view of the increasing talk of a new dawn of "industrial statesmanship," an examination of corporate America's philanthropic balance sheet is one way to test the claim that our leading firms are assuming a measure of responsibility for the quality of the country's public life.

One of the first questions that might reasonably be raised is whether companies are giving enough. Under Federal law they are permitted to

ANDREW HACKER teaches in the Department of Government at Cornell.

OUT OF EACH $1 given by corporations, 40 cents goes to health and welfare, 40 cents to education and the rest to culture.

contribute up to 5 per cent of their pretax profits. The 1967 figure of $900-million, however, comes to only 1.2 per cent of the permissible total, for annual net corporate profits now exceed $75-billion. In other words, company donations could theoretically reach $3.4-billion, and it is tempting to argue that the business sector of our affluent society can easily afford to give on a more generous scale.

A quite different line of approach can also be taken, however. It can be argued that the entire conception of corporate giving is misplaced, both in principle and in practice, and that the nation loses more than it gains by permitting executives to play the philanthropist. Indeed, I will suggest here that the corporation money which is now earmarked for gifts could and should be going elsewhere: to stockholders (as increased dividends) or to consumers (in reduced prices), to government (as taxes) or even to the general taxpayer (whose own rates might be lower were the business tax yield greater). Hence, it is legitimate to ask whether corporate contributions make the best use of this pool of money or whether other individuals and agencies might deploy these funds more effectively.

ONE of the unexamined assumptions of our society is that we are a generous people and that our already exemplary record of voluntary giving should be further encouraged —especially by the tax laws. However, corporate cash is rather different in character from personal income. A corporation being what it is, salaried managers have a great deal of discretion when it comes to making donations, even though the money they give away is not really their own. Thus when, say, Metropolitan Life Insurance writes out a check to Radio Free Europe or Yale University, it is not clear just *whose* generosity is being expressed.

The chief categories of corporate giving are straightforward enough: about 40 cents of every donated dollar goes to health and welfare causes, a like amount to education and the remaining 20 cents largely to civic and cultural activities.

On the health-welfare front, the chief recipients are the thousands of United Funds situated in cities where companies have their plants and offices. These once-a-year omnibus drives have become the most efficient way of raising money for local agencies even though, as one executive put it, "they do take some of the heart out of giving." (All-in-one campaigns also save a lot of administrative bother for corporate givers: "We don't even look at individual diseases," a company contributor said.)

There is a good deal of evidence, however, that United Fund and Red Feather drives have traditionally favored established groups, ranging from the Boy Scouts and the Y.M.C.A. to the Salvation Army and the S.P.C.A. They are particularly chary of supporting new endeavors, especially "community-action" programs that threaten to disrupt existing social patterns. This is not surprising, considering the composition of the committees which preside over these drives.

Usual company practice is to write an annual check and let the locals decide on the distribution of donations. "To refuse to meet your community obligations," a steel executive said, "will create ill-will out of all proportion to the cost of conforming to community sentiment." But what needs to be added is that "community sentiment" is not so much overall public opinion as it is the attitudes and outlooks of the local gentry Most large companies are shrewd enough to remain on good terms with Main Street bankers and businessmen, realizing that token displays of deference can pay off when larger issues are at stake.

BUT local managers of national enterprises have very little discretion about giving. For all the rhetoric about decentralized decision-making within large corporations, philanthropy is still one area where control remains in the head office. Only a very few firms allow their on-the-spot people complete independence when it comes to donations of over a few hundred dollars. "It may seem strange," one headquarters official said, "that we permit a plant manager to use his head when it comes to buying $1-million-worth of chemicals but don't trust him with a $500 contribution." The reason, revealingly, is that while a company may have faith in its supervisors' technical competence, it is not willing to rely on their social or political sophistication.

"There are just too many traps in this giving business," a home-office-based giver explained, "and without the right experience even the most intelligent guy could embarrass the hell out of the company with an ill-advised pledge." For this reason, more than a few firms make a point of automatically referring to the Attorney General's list since, as one executive warned, "the names of many subversive organizations are highly misleading." Perhaps they are. Among the 633 cited groups presumed to be bent on the Government's violent overthrow are such booby-traps as the Actors' Laboratory, the American Rescue Ship Mission and the Association of Interns and Medical Students.

FOR the past several years, the chief focus and fashion in company giving at the national level has been higher education. In 1964-65, the last year for which complete figures are available, businesses gave $175-million to colleges and universities. While this, as has been indicated, is about 40 per cent of all corporate contributions, it amounts to less than 15 per cent of the total gifts received by educational institutions.

One has only to spend a short time in the executive suites of Park Avenue or Rockefeller Center to see that more and more corporation executives are getting a good deal of enjoyment out of seeing themselves as honorary trustees. Eastman Kodak gives over $2-million each year to education, and the General Motors scholarship programs pay out more than $5-million annually. U. S. Steel gives regularly to 250 selected small colleges as well as to every member of the Association of American Universities.

Corporations may give up to 5 per cent of their pretax profits to charity. This year donations amount to $900-million. Good or bad?

As might be expected, big corporations prefer the company of big universities. In a sense, Stanford University (which received $5.5-million in corporate money) stands in an ambassadorial relation to Standard Oil of California. Harvard, Columbia, Chicago, Cornell and M.I.T. get over $2-million each from corporations each year. (So do less prestigeful Northwestern and N.Y.U., which shows the advantage of living next door to corporate headquarters.)

There is much to be said for supporting the country's leading institutions, for the entire educational system profits from a hierarchical arrangement of wealth and quality; but any such hierarchy must be reasonably strong in its middle reaches, and it is here that the impact of corporate giving is weakest. There are almost 1,400 private colleges and universities in the United

Drawings by James Flora.

NEW YORK'S LINCOLN CENTER is the most visible example of "corporate involvement with high culture." Eastern Air Lines gave $500,000 for a production of Wagner's "The Ring"; Texaco $450,000 for general purposes, and 33 other firms donated at least $100,000 each.

States, and the distribution of business dollars to them is bound to be diffused.

Bennington College's total receipts from corporate coffers, for instance, amounted to only $5,127 at last reporting, and even a better known Haverford got less than $35,000. Smith College managed to come away with a little over $100,000, but even that fairly impressive figure amounted to only $42 for each of her 2,400 students—at least a few of whom will end up as corporation wives.

THE fact is that corporations cannot be the salvation of private schools. There are just too many of them. What is more, less than a third of corporate contributions are unrestricted funds (and much of this is for matching the gifts of alumni-employes). Company chairmen, no less than the entrepreneurial rich of an earlier day, like to enumerate the ways in which the money will be spent. The Shell Oil Company, for example, by-passes college presidents and distributes $500 to deserving professors for "creative projects." The Esso Education Foundation requires applications for grants, making its own decisions as to which projects warrant support. (These have ranged from "new techniques for theme construction" at Bard College to "group counseling for under-achievers" at the Illinois Institute of Technology.)

Companies plainly enjoy

RELUCTANT PATRON— Were shareholders to be asked if they preferred higher dividends or grand opera, there is little doubt how most would vote.

their relations with colleges and universities, and not simply on economic grounds. Most corporate donations are not made with any direct *quid pro quo* in mind. Institutions of higher learning still bear some of the stamp of disinterested authority, and corporations seem to think that a portion of that legitimacy may rub off on them if they foot part of the bills. About the closest approximation to gifts-for-services-rendered is Bethlehem Steel's policy of giving $4,000 to colleges for each live management-trainee they supply to the company.

BUT perhaps the best test of the aristocratic element in corporate giving lies in the amount and proportion of donations going to the arts. For theater, opera, ballet, serious music and the fine arts have only limited appeal among even the middle-class population, and a company runs no great risk of widespread criticism if it declines to support a symphony orchestra or an art museum. Indeed, a recent Rockefeller Brothers report showed that fully half of the corporations they studied gave nothing at all to cultural endeavors.

The 540 large companies reporting to the National Industrial Conference Board last year gave less than $6-million to cultural activities, which averages out to 78 cents for each of their employes. Even the big Pittsburgh enterprises —among them U. S. Steel, Gulf Oil, Westinghouse and Aluminum Corporation of America—could only manage a $125,000 subvention for their city's orchestra. ("They're all trapshooters," was one characterization of leisure-time preferences among Golden Triangle executives.)

Probably the best touchstone of corporate involvement with high culture is New York's Lincoln Center. It is clearly the most visible enterprise in this area, and it has been as successful in fund-raising as any arts activity can hope to be. On the success side, the center has obtained not only Eastern Air Lines' $500,000 for "The Ring" but also a $450,000 general-purpose grant from Texaco. Another 33 firms have given at least $100,000 apiece—ranging from the predictable I.B.M. to the not-so-predictable Reader's Digest. An inspection of the record shows that Lincoln Center has fared best with what might be called "clean" industries: banking, insurance, investment houses and oil companies. (The last are very antiseptic indeed nowadays: hardly an employe of Shell or Mobil ever sees the stuff anymore.) Businesses in which most of the employes do not dirty their hands are apparently more likely to be appreciative of the performing arts.

Yet of the 600 corporations approached by Lincoln Center, more than 200 did not reply with contributions; and a quarter of the 50 largest firms based in the New York area declined to make even token donations. In addition, less than 20 firms headquartered outside New York gave gifts. All in all, corporate money amounted to less than 8 per cent of the donations received by the center.

THE suspicion arises that only a minority of top management are themselves patrons of the arts. While they are not Philistines or illiterates, they simply live apart from the world of high culture. Hence the occasional impetus to voice the economic argument: "If there are no arts in cities where plants are located," one vice president recently claimed, "engineering and scientific people won't come."

Whether a company-subsidized little theater in Bartlesville, Okla., would actually attract a mathematician who might otherwise have got away cannot really be proved (corporate computers have yet to spell out the factors that induce one man to sign on while another goes elsewhere). Not much more convincing were American Export Lines' announced reasons for financing a Metropolitan production of "Aida" several years ago: "Our line carries opera stars and other artists who spend a great part of their time in travel."

The day has apparently yet to arrive when hard-headed executives can underwrite cultural endeavors without feeling obliged to devise theories about how ballet and opera will sell more electric blankets or attract elusive electrical engineers.

OPERA, theater and the fine arts probably mark the farthest frontiers of business generosity. No one expects General Motors to emulate the Ford Foundation by giving $175,000 to the Detroit branch of CORE, and it would be surprising were Du Pont to be found on S.N.C.C.'s list of contributors. Corporations even shy away from the tax-deductible Legal Defense Fund of the N.A.A.C.P. But in light of all the recent talk about the growing sophistication—indeed, the enhanced social awareness — of corporate thinking, it might be presumed that an agency such as the Urban League would be a ready-made recipient for business money. It is, after all, terribly respectable (too much so for many Negroes, who call it "lily-black") and it makes every effort to accept the facts and values of the economic status quo.

But apparently not. Of the 750 largest companies, only 180 have given $1,000 or more to the Urban League. Another 140 have given less than $1,000; but the majority of the 750 contribute nothing at all. There is some bitterness in Urban League circles about this less than token performance. "Companies will send a man to a dinner to hear Whitney Young," one fund-raiser remarked, "but his firm gives you the run-around when you follow it up with a request for a contribution." Total corporate gifts to the league in 1966 were under $900,000—less than a fifth of what companies gave to Harvard University.

IF even an agency such as the Urban League is "controversial," it is instructive, then, to examine the directions that are taken when some corporations channel their contributions in less orthodox ways.

Several million dollars go each year to organizations that devote themselves to "economic education" or to groups dedicated to the elimination of internal and international subversion. These range from the Foundation for Economic Education (which has doubts about the propriety of a Government-owned post office) to the American Security Council (which urges unalloyed opposition to all shades of Communism). Richfield Oil and Schick Razor have aided Dr. Fred Schwarz's crusades, and various companies underwrite the hyperpatriotic programs of Clarence Manion and Facts Forum.

What needs to be said here is that most blue-chip companies shy away from the ultraconservative organizations. The most generous givers are firms where the top man has a special affinity for ideological causes. A notable example is Patrick Frawley Jr., Eversharp and Technicolor, who recently financed a $100,000 essay contest to muster ideas on how businesses might "meet their responsibilities in the world conflict with Communism." Other firms whose chief executives have shown similar concerns are Motorola, Stewart-Warner and the Illinois Central and Louisville & Nashville Railroads.

A fact requiring some emphasis is that if businessmen feel called upon to assume statesmanlike responsibilities, then the rest of us will have to accept their personal conceptions of what constitutes the public good. The essence of statesmanship, after all, requires turning a deaf ear to the clamor of criticism; it calls for the courage and vision to do the right thing—as you see it—even if the public is against you. If statesmanlike power is what is wanted, whether in the corporate or the political world, then outsiders cannot properly ask to have a say in how it is exercised.

Those who want to give three cheers to Texaco's support for Lincoln Center should not cavil when Richfield Oil subsidizes Dr. Schwarz's Americanism crusades in the Hollywood Bowl. To ask for some kind of "democracy" here is not only self-contradictory but also ill-advised. Were the shareholders of Eastern Air Lines to be consulted on whether they preferred higher dividends or grand opera, there is little doubt as to how most of them would vote.

WHEN all is said and done, the great majority of firms have no real policy, let alone a philosophy, on corporate philanthropy. Companies give because they have money available, and the common approach is to play the game fairly quietly rather than as a full-blown public relations effort. No corporation actually publishes a full list of the amounts it has donated to various causes. "Letting people find out indirectly is the best way," a Koppers vice president remarked. "It is better not to toot your own horn."

Not the least reason for this reticence is that no corporation wants to get the reputation of being a bottomless cornucopia. As matters now stand, companies like International Harvester and Standard Oil of New Jersey get over 5,000 requests for funds every year, and in Jersey's case, more than 700 supplicants annually make personal visits to Rockefeller Center. Hence the comment of an American Cyanamid official: "Any broad publicity is an extremely dangerous thing because it would open the floodgates with appeals."

The problem has come to such a head that a Chicago management consultant advises his clients on how to say no, even supplying sample turn-down letters. ("Your request has been carefully considered by our Committee on Contributions and we regret . . ."; "Priority is given to local projects . . ."; "Current policies of our Board of Directors force us to restrict . . .")

WHETHER corporations should be called generous is a matter of interpretation and opinion. Each year the people of America donate about 2.5 per cent of their personal incomes to charities. (Whether *that* percentage constitutes "generosity" is also a matter for some thought.) Corporations give 1.2 per cent of their disposable income, or less than half the rate for the general citizenry. While it is difficult to draw comparisons between business firms and individual households, both do attempt to live within budgets and both are customarily expected to employ at least a portion of their spare cash in charitable directions.

"A company runs no great risk of widespread criticism if it declines to support a symphony orchestra or an art museum."

Nor is it easy to decide whether companies can "afford" to give more. The key question is how much of current corporate budgets is going for luxuries that serve no discernible business purpose. It has been argued that jet travel and expense-account entertaining, prestige office buildings and conferences at distant resorts are all costly amenities having no real effects on sales or efficiency. Many corporations do indeed have quite a bit of money in their tills, and they spend much of it in making life

FAVORED FEW—"Big corporations prefer big universities;" the nearly 1,400 private colleges and universities have a thinner time.

pleasant and comfortable for those who inhabit their precincts. Yet even if this is so, it is not clear whether the general public—or even an informed special public—should demand that our business enterprises cut down on their high living so that more money will be available for philanthropic causes.

“Were no business philanthropy permitted, 48 per cent of the money going for gifts would go to the Government.”

It should be obvious that all of us are helping to foot the bills. A New York-Washington shuttle flight costs just a little bit more because Eastern supports the opera, and Kodak's dividends are somewhat less than they would be were the company not helping to underwrite the University of Rochester. Indeed, were no business philanthropy to be permitted at all, then 48 per cent of the money now going for gifts would automatically be taken by the Federal Government in corporation taxes. Were that percentage, which will exceed $400-million this year, to be sent to Washington then taxpayers might expect—or at least make a claim for—a lightening of their own April 15 load.

THE point is that corporate donations are independent decisions of management supported by both fiscal and legal blessings. It is assumed that company executives will make as good (or perhaps better) use of these funds than would either the consumers of their goods or the holders of their stock or even the Government itself. Indeed, the implicit theory behind the 5 per cent allowance is that corporations should be encouraged to give away several billions of dollars each year to causes their managers deem worthy.

The charm of this theory is that it rests on none of the major ideological premises of our time. Conservatives who adhere to the strictures of a free-market place have always been wary of corporate benevolence; better to distribute the enterprise's earnings to its owners and let *them* make their own choices about the relative merits of personal comfort and public charity. Those of a more social frame of mind wonder about a Government's willful decision to deprive itself of much-needed tax revenues by permitting businessmen to play the philanthropist: better to have the elected representatives of the people decide on the priorities and problems of our time.

At issue is not whether our corporations' choices of charities are imaginative or inspired; for the most part, they are not. The committees that decide on donations are composed of cautious career men, and it is idle to expect them to enter areas that threaten to be disruptive or controversial. At the same time it is impossible to claim that the conventional targets of corporate gifts are actually undeserving. Even respectable, established and middle-class recipients like Lincoln Center, Cornell University and the Lenox Hill Hospital continue to perform useful services. What can be predicted, however, is that even if business giving were to undergo an appreciable rise the same sorts of agencies as are now being supported would continue to be the major beneficiaries.

THE dilemma we face is that personal philanthropy and government programs are either not willing or not able to cope with the most pressing domestic problems of American society. Most citizens are reluctant to lower their own standards of life to alleviate the suffering of individuals who have been left out or behind in an otherwise affluent generation. Not the least consequence of tax-free business giving is the preservation of the popular illusion that needy causes are taken care of through corporate generosity.

Conservatives are clearly correct in protesting that individuals are ceasing to feel themselves responsible for the condition of the society of which they are a part. One way to test this conservative indictment would be to pay out full dividends to stockholders—just to see what they did with the extra money. If individuals made more charitable contributions and took fewer Caribbean vacations, then the theory would be shown to have some validity. If they didn't, then at least we would have learned some interesting facts about ourselves.

At the same time, it is clear that more and more government agencies are showing themselves to be surprisingly venturesome. It may well be that 50 cents in tax money spent in a birth-control clinic in Bedford-Stuyvesant will do the nation far more good than a whole tax-free dollar that a corporation contributes to Williams College. Given the record thus far, there is reason to question whether business philanthropy has been doing much more than subsidizing primarily middle-class agencies and organizations which could well be made to find alternative sources of support.

No matter how much they may protest their comparative poverty, most opera-lovers and the parents of most college students are quite well off and can afford to pay substantially more than they now do for tickets and tuition. Calls for education and culture at subsidized rates ill become individuals who cheerfully pay the full price for color television sets and air-conditioned automobiles. It is simply a matter of getting one's priorities in order.

The critical and pressing fact is that only well-financed programs on the part of government agencies will begin to make effective inroads into the tensions and deprivations that scar the part of America not blessed with middle-class incomes. The absence of any significant business contribution in this area, coupled with the apparent paucity of tax revenues, suggests the need for a serious review of just how the nation's discretionary dollars are being spent and who ought to be spending them. ■

November 12, 1967

G.M. Acknowledges Investigating Critic

By WALTER RUGABER

Special to The New York Times

DETROIT, March 9—The General Motors Corporation said tonight that it had undertaken an investigation of Ralph Nader, a Washington lawyer whose sharp criticism sparked much of the current controversy over automobile safety.

Mr. Nader, the author of a book entitled "Unsafe at Any Speed," complained last week that he had been followed and harassed and that private detectives had questioned acquaintances about his private life.

General Motors said it "initiated a routine investigation through a reputable law firm" and denied this investigation had included "any of the alleged harassment or intimidation recently reported in the press."

One of the investigators involved, Vincent Gillen of New York, confirmed in a telephone interview last week that he had conducted an inquiry into Mr. Nader's background. The detective refused to name his client.

In Washington yesterday two Senators called on the Justice Department to conduct an investigation of what was termed an apparent attempt to harass and intimidate Mr. Nader.

The legislators were Senators Abraham A. Ribicoff, Democrat of Connecticut and chairman of a subcommittee that investigated auto safety, and Gaylord Nelson, Democrat of Wisconsin.

A Major Witness

Mr. Nader was a major witness before the Ribicoff panel. The young author testified on unsafe vehicle design during an appearance on Feb. 10. He later charged that some of the harassment occurred during that week.

Mr. Ribicoff pointed out on the floor of the Senate that Federal law allows a five-year prison term and a $5,000 fine for anyone who attempts to intimidate a Congressional witness.

The unusual late-evening statement by General Motors came after other automobile manufacturers had denied involvement in any investigation of the safety critic.

John S. Bagas, a vice president and director of the Ford Motor Company, sent a telegram to Mr. Ribicoff. The text was issued by a Ford public relations officials earlier in the evening. The telegram said:

"Ford Motor Company has not been nor is it now directly or indirectly involved in any alleged investigation or harassment of Mr. Nader, nor has it any knowledge of or connection with the alleged incidents concerning him."

The General Motors comment was understood to have been made at the direct order of.

James M. Roche, the company president. There were indications that Mr. Roche learned of the investigation late in the afternoon.

The General Motors statement said the corporation "initiated a routine investigation through a reputable law firm to determine whether Ralph Nader was acting on behalf of litigants or their attorneys in Corvair design cases against General Motors."

Mr. Nader and other critics have charged that the 1960-63 model Corvair automobiles were among the most inherently unsafe cars ever produced in Detroit.

Mainly, it was charged that the early model Corvair's rear suspension system was unstable and could cause the car to go out of control on turns at certain speeds.

The wheel would suddenly "tuck-under" when the Corvair was exposed even to fairly limited lateral forces, critics charged, and the car would abruptly flip over.

After a number of accidents, at least 100 damage suits were filed against General Motors. In the design cases alone, the concern has won two and settled a third.

Basically, General Motors has argued that its controversial car is as stable as most others built at that time and has charged that Mr. Nader's criticisms are "unsupported and repudiated."

The G.M. statement said:

"The investigation was prompted by Mr. Nader's extreme criticism of the Corvair in his writings, press conferences, TV and other public appearances. Mr. Nader's statements coincided with similar publicity by some attorneys handling such litigation.

"It is a well known and accepted practice in the legal profession to investigate claims and persons making claims in the product liability field, such as in the pending Corvair design cases.

"The investigation was limited only to Mr. Nader's qualifications, background, expertise and association with such attorneys. It did not include any of the alleged harassment or intimidation recently reported in the press."

A spokesman for General Motors identified the law firm as Alvord and Alvord of Washington. A partner, Richard G. Danner, was reached at home tonight but declined comment.

General Motors said Mr. Nader's continued attacks on the Corvair lend support to its belief "that there is a connection between Mr. Nader and plaintiff's counsel in pending Corvair design litigation."

The author said tonight he has never represented "any clients involved in the Corvair litigation."

He said he had been questioned by lawyers about the Corvair because "I am one of the few attorneys with any knowledge of automobile products liability."

But he denied he had received any fees and said he had in fact left his active law practice "in order to pursue the cause of safer designed automobiles for the motoring public."

Mr. Nader demanded that General Motors admit its investigation had turned up "not a shred of evidence" to link him with the lawyers in the Corvair cases.

A G.M. spokesman had been asked about results of the company's investigation but said he wasn't familiar with the results.

March 10, 1966

Ralph Nader, Crusader; Or, the Rise of A Self-Appointed Lobbyist

By PATRICK ANDERSON

WASHINGTON.

WHEN Ralph Nader came to Washington in 1964 and began a one-man crusade for automobile safety he was widely regarded as a high-minded crackpot. After he emerged triumphant from his celebrated David-and-Goliath clash with General Motors early last year, Nader advanced in the Washington cosmos from crackpot to celebrity. Today, as he moves quietly about town as a self-appointed lobbyist for the public interest, he shows signs of becoming an institution. For at 33, Nader is settling in for the long haul. He says he will make a career of opposing those centers of power—corporations, unions, government or whatever—he believes are infringing upon the public interest. Whether Nader can maintain his present momentum for very long is anybody's guess. But he has already proved himself to be one of the most shrewd, controversial and enigmatic players to mount the political stage in many a year.

Nader's current activities include the following:

He continues as watchdog and critic of the National Traffic Safety Bureau, the Federal agency which administers the auto-safety bill that he helped pass last year. In so doing, he demonstrates his belief that effective reform must be a continuing process: public exposure, then legislative action, then administrative follow-up.

"His bout with General Motors gave him a priceless image"

He is conducting a once-a-week seminar on corporations at his alma mater, Princeton University; lecturing two or three times a month to various student and professional groups, and writing frequent magazine articles on corporate abuses, mostly for The New Republic.

He is openly active — as lobbyist, witness, writer, investigator and strategist — in three much-disputed issues now before Congressional committees: proposals to fix Federal safety standards for gas pipelines and for X-ray machines, and to extend the Meat Inspection Act to cover intrastate packagers and processors.

He is at work behind the scenes in many other issues, such as opposition to the International Telephone & Telegraph Corporation's proposed merger with the American Broadcasting Company and the campaign to require automobile tire-makers to recall defective tires, led by Senator Gaylord Nelson, Democrat of Wisconsin.

Neither in his personal nor political life does Nader fit any familiar Washington pattern. His go-it-alone operational style often annoys allies as much as it outrages enemies. In a city which respects the fine art of compromise, Nader is determined, as he puts it, "to stake out an area in which there is no compromise." In a city which reveres status symbols and institutional ties, Nader has divested himself of both as a means of reducing vulnerability to outside pressures.

Nader lives in an $80-a-month furnished room, owns no car, eats in cheap restaurants, dresses plainly, works a 100-hour week, has almost no social life and considers marriage at present incompatible with his career. He has an unlisted business

PATRICK ANDERSON, Washington political writer, is at work on a book about the roles of White House staffs in recent Administrations.

telephone number, maintains a secret office in downtown Washington and gives interviews (when he gives them) in out-of-the-way restaurants and hotel lobbies. All this lends a certain semicomic, cloak-and-dagger aura to Nader's activities, yet behind it all is the inescapable reality of a bitterly waged struggle with some of the most powerful and sophisticated economic-political interests in America.

WHY would a young man choose to lead such a life? Why, particularly, when he could open a lucrative law practice or launch a promising political career? (Nader says he has been asked to consider running for the House or the Senate from his native Connecticut, but he would rather continue what he is doing.)

To begin with, Nader is not like you and me. Most of us tune out society's problems and concentrate on our own. Nader has chosen to make society's problems his problems and as a result he exists in a state of constant, barely controlled outrage. He is outraged, for example, that B. F. Goodrich, General Tire, Gates Rubber and Lee Tire have refused to give Senator Nelson information on defective tires. He is outraged that General Electric produced some 150,000 color television sets which emit dangerous levels of radiation and then, in Nader's opinion, was slow about recalling or repairing them. He is outraged that intrastate meat packagers use new antibiotics and preservatives to doctor diseased meat and make it appear normal. He is concerned, though not yet outraged, by many new sociopolitical questions that are just now gathering on the technological horizon. For example, he asks: "Who gets artificial hearts? When? Under what conditions and warranties? At what price?"

The list of Nader's concerns could be extended indefinitely. It stems from the social consciousness of an ultra-individualistic lawyer who, since his teens, has been instinctively opposed to any action he views as an arbitrary exercise of power against the individual. It happened, in the course of his law school studies, that the first issue in which he immersed himself was auto safety. The subject led him to focus on the nation's biggest corporations and today, a decade later, corporate abuses remain his chief concern. But he can be equally critical of unions, government, churches, the military or any group he thinks is suppressing individual rights.

"In Russia," Nader says, "the enemy would be the government." In this country, he feels, the corporate giants have emerged as "private governments" exercising virtually unchecked power over consumers and over the political process. In one speech he declared:

"What we do about corporate air and water pollution, corporate soil and food contamination, corporate-bred trauma on our highways, corporate lack of innovation or suppression of innovation, corporate misallocation of resources, corporate inflationary pricing, corporate domination over local, state and Federal agencies and corporate distortions of political campaigning—to illustrate a few issues—will decide our quality of life."

Two basic fears underlie Nader's wide-ranging criticisms of corporations.

The first is his fear that modern science and technology are more often used against the consumer than for him. The auto industry's preoccupation with styling and its minimal concern with safety—documented in Nader's book, "Unsafe at Any Speed"—is a classic instance. Another, Nader says, is air pollution: "The question is not whether we can build a car that won't pollute the air; the question is whether we can overcome the resistance of the auto industry and the oil industry to get it built."

Nader's second concern goes beyond the way the corporations deal with the public to the way they deal with their own employees. As Nader sees it, when an engineer or lawyer or scientist goes to work for a corporation, he in effect loses his constitutional right of free speech. Nader became interested in this subject when he was investigating auto safety and found that assembly line workers would freely give him information, confident their unions would protect them, but that engineers were afraid to let their names be used, lest they lose their jobs.

Many others have shared his dim view of corporate America, from Louis Brandeis to Paul Goodman, and have expressed their doubts in more detail and more persuasively. What sets Nader apart is that he has moved beyond social criticism to effective political action.

AS a political operator, Nader has shown high intelligence and rare versatility. He has variously functioned in Washington as lawyer, legislative draftsman, author and magazine writer, investigator, public speaker, press agent and political strategist.

Much of Nader's strength rests upon his close ties with the press and with key Congressional aides. And he has won their support because he has made himself one of the best-informed men in Washington, a kind of one-man C.I.A. Nader could have been a brilliant investigative reporter. He learned early that a great deal of valuable intelligence can be gleaned from public sources, and he spends many hours each week skimming through newspapers, magazines, press releases, Federal agency reports, technical journals and similar documents.

Senate hearings last summer on the dangers of overexposure to X-rays resulted directly from this sort of research by Nader. Early this year he came across a report in a medical journal on the dangers of ionizing radiation from medical diagnosis, written by Dr. Karl Z. Morgan, director of the Health Physics Division of the Oak Ridge (Tenn.) National Laboratory. Nader wrote to Dr. Morgan and asked for more information. Next, he sought more data from Federal and state health agencies, as well as from companies that manufacture X-ray machines.

When Nader was convinced that a legitimate issue was at stake, he wrote a lawyer's brief, in effect, arguing why there should be a Congressional inquiry into the subject. He knew that Senator E. L. Bartlett, Democrat of Alaska, was already concerned about radioactive fallout and assumed that Bartlett would be interested in the related question of X-ray emissions.

Nader took his information to one of Bartlett's aides. The immediate result was a well-publicized Senate Commerce Committee hearing. Senator Bartlett chaired it, Dr. Morgan was the star witness and Nader drummed up additional interest by writing a piece on X-ray hazards for The New Republic. Nor has interest died. Earlier this month Dr. Morgan testified again, before the Health and Safety subcommittee of the Commerce Committee, on the perils of unnecessary X-ray exposure in medical diagnoses.

If Nader's voluminous reading is his primary source of information, the countless phone calls and letters he receives are an important secondary source. People somehow get his phone number and address. They send him pieces of a tire that blew out or a shattered windshield. A judge in California sent him an emergency brake along with a note: "It's come off twice—you keep it." Once, a woman in France called at 4 A.M. to report that her Porsche was a lemon.

Many callers want Nader to handle their lawsuits against corporations and won't believe that he doesn't take cases. It was to escape the calls and letters, and to have some privacy to do his work, that he took a hideaway office in downtown Washington. Yet, despite the fact that most calls and letters are a waste of time, Nader continues to read each letter and take each call because now and then one contains a nugget of useful intelligence from a reliable source.

It was such a piece of unsolicited information that led Nader into his current crusade for Federal safety standards governing natural gas pipelines. A professor of engineering approached Nader at an engineering conference early last year and urged him to look into the subject.

"He gave me a few names and outlined the problem," Nader recalls. "Then I went to work. I found some Government reports and some people at the Federal Power Commission who were concerned about pipeline safety; they'd been trying to get Congressional hearings on it for 10 years. I began going through the technical journals and finding pieces of information. One article discussed pipeline corrosion. Another mentioned an explosion or a lawsuit. Then I'd go to the people involved and the thing began to fill out."

As it happened, Senator Warren Magnuson, Democrat of Washington, who is chairman of the Senate Commerce Committee and a leading advocate of consumer protection, was also becoming interested in the question of pipeline safety and had asked the F.P.C. to prepare a report for him. Nader first spoke out on the subject in June, 1966, in a well-publicized speech before the Washington chapter of the American Society of Safety Engineers. Thereafter, Senator Magnuson announced hearings on pipeline safety and last Aug. 1 Nader was a witness.

In recent weeks, Nader has been working with the Commerce Committee staff in drafting the proposed pipeline safety bill. It is standard procedure for committee staffs to consult lobbyists from both sides of an issue—one side generally consisting of Government lawyers — when trying to write legislative language. A good example of the practice was the last hectic moments in the writing of the auto-safety bill last year when Nader was in one Senate anteroom, Lloyd Cutler, a Washington lawyer-lobbyist representing the auto industry, was in another, while Senate aides raced back and forth between them.

66A judge in California sent him an emergency brake along with a note: 'It's come off twice—you keep it.'99

A third example of Nader's role on Capitol Hill is his fight for strong amendments to the Meat Inspection Act. Nader had nothing to do with initiating the issue, but once it came to a head in the House this year he threw himself into the controversy.

Since 1961, Congressman Neal Smith, Democrat of Iowa, has been seeking expanded Federal meat inspection authority to include the intrastate packagers and processors, who now handle about 15 per cent of the commercially slaughtered animals and 25 per cent of the commercially processed meat products in the U.S. each year. Congressman Smith has declared: "Some of the uninspected plants merely cut the eye out of the cancer-eyed cow, like you would cut the core out of an apple, and go ahead and use the rest of the carcass. These uninspected plants, which also process sausages and prepared products, can further reduce their cost per pound by including blood, lungs, detergents, hair, hides, antibiotics and excessive amounts of flour and water, without having to label them in such a manner that the consumer would know what he is buying."

Despite such abuses, pressures from the meat industry on the House Agriculture Committee kept Smith from even getting a hearing until this year and industry lobbyists were confident that the proposed legislation could be killed in committee. Nader's role, which Smith's aides say has been crucial to their effort, has been threefold.

First, he obtained from the Department of Agriculture a little-known, state-by-state study of conditions in intrastate meat-processing plants. By securing and making public this report, which contained many gruesome accounts of unsanitary conditions, Nader focused newspaper attention on the issue. Second, in a meeting with several consumer organizations, he helped spark a nationwide letter-writing campaign that caused many Congressmen to give the subject a second look. Third, Nader wrote several hard-hitting articles for The New Republic which further popularized the cause. At present, supporters of the meat inspection legislation are hopeful of a favorable vote if it reaches the House floor in this session.

OBVIOUSLY, much of Nader's impact is the result of his ability to popularize other men's ideas. Nader's encounter with General Motors made him something of a popular hero — a news-maker — and when he makes a statement, it is guaranteed an audience it might not command if someone else had said it. Realizing the fact, Nader has tried to be a middleman between ideas originating in scientific and academic circles and those journalists and legislators who can translate the ideas into political action.

Nader also works behind the scenes. During the proposed I.T.T.-A.B.C. merger, at a point at which the deal had received little public attention and seemed destined to attain the necessary Federal approval, Nader showed up in key newspaper offices with well-documented, not-for-attribution arguments against it. Articles began to appear that examined and questioned the merger, followed by charges that I.T.T.'s public relations men had harassed reporters who wrote them.

As the public outcry grew louder, the Justice Department took court action in July to block the deal, which is now stalled, perhaps indefinitely. Many close observers of the episode believe the Justice Department would not have acted but for the rash of newspaper publicity which created a favorable climate for anti-merger action.

Nader's role in the affair should not be overestimated. He apparently was working closely with several Senators who also opposed the merger and had he not been available someone else would have been used to stir up public resistance to the deal. But probably no one else would have been a more effective press agent.

There are two main reasons why Nader sometimes remains out of sight. First, it may be necessary to insure that a particular Senator or Congressman gets all the credit for a particular issue. "A reformer can't afford to have an ego," Nader says. "That's not modesty, just tactics." Second, each time Nader publicly takes on another industry he not only mobilizes a new wave of counter-lobbyists, he creates new demands on his time. And the central problem in Nader's life today is that he is already

66The question is whether his operation could stand the transition from Ralph Nader, Crusader, to Ralph Nader, Inc.99

stretched about as far as he can go.

Consequently, he tries to pick his issues carefully. For example, he feels strongly about the health hazards of cigarettes, but he has not taken up the cause because he feels that other people are already doing a good job of publicizing the peril and seeking reform. Similarly, he is personally opposed to the war in Vietnam, but has declined offers to add his name to anti-war protests lest he spread himself too thin.

It would be naive to think that Nader's corporate opponents would shrink from any prudent means of halting his attacks. Yet adversaries must keep in mind General Motors' experience when it tried to swat the young gadfly two years ago. General Motors, it will be recalled, employed a private detective to conduct what G.M. said was a routine investigation of Nader. The detective, Vincent Gillen, said he was assigned to probe Nader's politics, his religion and his sex life to find something that could be used to shut him up.

In either event, the strategy backfired rather spectacularly. It led to public humiliation of G.M., passage of the auto-safety bill, and a $26-million invasion-of-privacy suit by Nader against the corporation, which now awaits trial.

Nader's current adversaries seem to be following a more cautious policy which combines watchful waiting with some not too subtle attempts to discredit him. The watchful waiting is based on the assumption that Nader will eventually make a personal or political slip, espouse an unpopular cause or otherwise expose himself to effective counterattack. The attempts to discredit Nader center on three oft-repeated charges: that he is careless with his facts; that he is enriching himself by his crusades; and that he is a moralistic, intolerant, and otherwise unpleasant fellow.

When representatives of the automobile and pipeline industries were interviewed, they stressed that Nader doesn't get his facts straight. But when asked for examples, those cited were invariably matters of opinion, not matters of fact. The evidence indicates that Nader, who is acutely aware that his every word is scrutinized, is highly cautious with his facts. He says: "The one thing I have that the lobbyists don't often have is credibility. They say, 'Oh, Nader can make wild charges; he has no responsibility.' The opposite is true. I can't make any mistakes. An institution can blur accountability for its errors. I can't."

Upon examination, Nader's allegations almost always prove to be based on government reports (the intrastate meat abuses) or on expert opinion (the X-ray issue). He may disseminate a minority view—Dr. Morgan's opinion on the dangers of X-rays, for example—but it is nonetheless a reputable opinion. What Nader does do, having hit upon an issue, is to dramatize it with the flamboyant language of a muckraker. Pipeline explosions, he said, "may incinerate hundreds or thousands of people in a roaring inferno."

THE charge that Nader's motive is money is made in numerous ways. The pipeline industry's spokesman wondered aloud if Nader might be receiving a retainer from the Oil, Chemical and Atomic Workers International Union. The auto spokesman casually mentioned that he understood Nader has been getting $1,500 lecture fees. Lobbyists have circulated the rumor on Capitol Hill that Nader refers consumer injury cases to—and gets kickbacks from—a private law firm. Another version is that Nader plans to open a law firm specializing in consumer cases.

Such stories do not always fall upon deaf ears, for, as one Congressional observer says, "This is a cynical town—nobody can believe anybody is not out for a buck." Nader himself is not above spreading a rumor or two.

One argument he used against the I.T.T.-A.B.C. merger in his talks with reporters was that the membership of various corporate officials in the President's Club — the $1,000 donors to the Democratic party—was a factor in determining the Administration's early policy on the merger.

The various rumors and charges about Nader's money-making remain unproved. Nader says he has no income except from writing, lectures and the course he gives at Princeton. "Unsafe at Any Speed" was a best-seller (60,000 hardback and 400,000 paperback copies) and will bring him about $50,000 before taxes. He says the most he ever received for a lecture is $1,000 and that often he speaks for free or for a few hundred dollars.

"The corporations strangle the public for profits," he says, "and then they try to hang me because I sold a few books. I'd get $5,000 a lecture, if I could. But if they can prove I've spent one dime on personal luxuries, I'll quit."

Nader says most of his income goes back into his work. His expenses include a massive telephone bill, office rental, travel, subscriptions to dozens of publications and payments to law students he sometimes employs to conduct research.

Nader's operation is not a model of administrative efficiency. He has no secretary or answering service. Friends on Capitol Hill let him use their mimeograph machines to run off his speeches. It is sometimes impossible to reach him. The telephone in his rooming house is in the hall outside his room and is shared with other men who live there. When I called one recent morning the phone was answered by an irate young man with a foreign accent, who declared, "I'm sick of taking messages for that guy!" and refused to take another.

THE criticism that perhaps strikes nearest the mark is that Nader is self-righteous and intolerant. One industry critic says: "Like Martin Luther, Nader is a moralist who is uncharitable about other people's behavior. He arrogates all virtue to himself." Another critic insists: "Mr. Nader doesn't believe there's any integrity in anybody but Mr. Nader."

These are overstatements, but the fact remains that Nader is a moralist and is sometimes intolerant of people who do not measure up to his exacting standards.

His greatest scorn is reserved for lawyers who represent the corporate interests he opposes. He has denounced them as men whose "agility of mind is surpassed only by their viscosity of conscience."

Similarly, he has characterized the American engineer as a "minion to corporate management or other allegiances to which he is chattel," and pictured business executives as "stifled men walking around corporate halls in invisible chains."

Such uncompromising remarks can hurt him on Capitol Hill as well as create enemies in the corporate world. One Congressional observer said Nader "makes some politicians uncomfortable. He doesn't fit the pattern. He's not interested in money. And he doesn't play the game. There are people who lobby for the right side but protect their friends. One criticism made of Nader—I'm not saying it's true—is that he'll turn on his friends."

The charge that Nader will undercut his friends stems from several columns by Drew Pearson which attacked various Congressmen and Administration officials for allegedly trying to sell out the auto-safety and pipeline bills. It was rumored that Nader had leaked the stories to Pearson in order to put some heat on his wavering allies.

Nader denies the accusation, but concedes that he has little use for political alliances. Alliances lead to compromise and, "once you begin to compromise, you erode yourself."

The necessity to resist compromise, both political and social, both internal and external, is a recurring theme in Nader's [illegible] conversations —not so much because he is self-obsessed but because, like an athlete, he feels compelled to know exactly what his strengths and weaknesses are.

He says of several nationally famous lawyers: "They leave. They go off to the jet set—fast cars, fast planes, fast women. Being a celebrity can ruin your value system. I could have gone off. I got all the invitations. But I don't want that. One of the reasons I can do what I do is that I've reduced my vulnerabilities. They can't get at me through any institution, or through saying someone's paying me off, or through a wife and children."

IN THE CAPITOL—Nader, 33, has harassed Congress on car safety, tires, meat inspection, gas pipelines, X-rays.

Nader's social life is minimal and is really an extension of his political life. It consists mainly of dinner or evenings of conversation with what he calls "issue-oriented" people, mainly journalists and Congressional aides. Before he came to Washington he enjoyed an occasional game of chess or basketball but he no longer has the time for either. Nor, apparently, is there time for romance. Once, an attractive female journalist told one of Nader's friends she would be interested in seeing Nader socially. The friend passed the word along and Nader replied very seriously that it wouldn't be fair for him to encourage the girl because he couldn't consider marriage.

Nader realizes that his ascetic life causes many people to dismiss him as a fanatic. "I don't consider myself abnormal," he replies. "I consider the auto industry abnormal—people who, for great profit, sell cars with built-in defects that they know will kill people. That, to me, is real abnormality."

NADER arrived at his present state of normality—or abnormality, as the case may be —within a classic pattern: the immigrant's son who made good. Nader's parents came to this country from Lebanon, and Nader, tall, lean, with dark skin, jet-black hair, flashing brown eyes and slender hands that slap the air excitedly as he talks, very much shows his Lebanese ancestry. His parents settled in Winsted, Conn., where they converted a rundown diner into one of the city's best restaurants.

He was born on Feb. 27, 1934, grew up speaking Arabic as well as English, and has since learned Chinese, Russian, Spanish and Portuguese. As far back as he can remember, his father encouraged him to become a lawyer. Nader credits his parents with instilling in him the sense of justice and civic duty that directed him toward his present career.

There seems to be no tidy textbook explanation for Nader's rare single-mindedness. His father was not run out of business by the A&P store, nor his mother struck down by a defective Buick, nor anything like that. Rather, his seems to be the case of an intense, intelligent, individualistic young man whose instinctive resentment of arbitrary authority led him not to withdraw from society, in the manner of his Beat Generation contemporaries, but to use his talent and legal training to challenge authority.

After Princeton, Nader attended Harvard Law School, and at both schools he was scornful of what struck him as the sheeplike conformity of his fellow students. Nader refused to wear the white buckskin shoes that were part of the undergraduate uniform at Princeton. He was offended by the rigidity of its curriculum and took the most flexible possible course, majoring in Oriental studies. At both places he was angered by the arbitrary power exercised by the administration; students were expelled, he says, with no right of appeal. But when he tried to interest classmates in the issue of due process for students, they were indifferent.

It was in law school that he chanced upon the subject of auto safety. While studying auto injury cases Nader visited the engineering departments of Harvard and M.I.T. to gather data on automotive technology, and became convinced that the law unjustly put all the emphasis on the driver's faults and none on the faults of his car.

After graduating from law school and serving a six-month Army hitch, Nader began practicing law in Hartford in 1960. His obsession with auto safety continued. He wrote magazine articles on the subject and spoke to civic groups. He testified before committees of the Connecticut and Massachusetts Legislatures on auto safety, and still remembers a Bay State legislator who ascertained that Nader was from Connecticut, then asked: "Well, what the hell are you doing in Massachusetts?"

In early 1964, convinced of the futility of fighting for auto safety on the local level, Nader made the crucial decision to carry his crusade to Washington. "I had watched years go by and nothing had happened," Nader says. "Before that, decades had gone by. I decided that what it took was total combat."

An earlier magazine piece by Nader in The Nation on auto safety had appeared at about the same time that a similar one by Daniel P. Moynihan was published by The Reporter, and the two men had corresponded. Now, five years later, Moynihan, who had become an Assistant Secretary of Labor, hired Nader as a consultant to write a report on what the Government should do about auto safety.

Nader began the assignment in April, 1964. He worked at the job for a year, and during that time a number of other forces were converging that would at last make auto safety a national issue. The Democratic landslide of 1964 promised a new Congress primed for social action. Connecticut Democrat Abe Ribicoff, who had won a reputation for cracking down on highway speeders as Governor, announced in mid-February, 1965, that he would open Senate hearings on the "fantastic carnage" taking place on highways. Senator Warren Magnuson said in May he would hold Commerce Committee hearings on Gaylord Nelson's tire-safety bill.

Nader, meanwhile had left the Government and was holed up in his furnished room writing a book on auto safety. When he wasn't writing he was on Capitol Hill, feeding ideas and issues to Senate aides conducting the auto safety hearings. The publication of "Unsafe at Any Speed," which made front-page news across the country, further improved the climate for reform. Early in January, 1966, President Johnson's one-sentence mention of highway safety in his State of the Union Message received almost as much publicity as anything else in the speech, a fact widely noted by politicians at both ends of Pennsylvania Avenue.

Momentum was building—yet passage of an auto safety bill was by no means a certainty. Unfortunately, Congressional passage of consumer-protection legislation must almost always be triggered by some horrible event that mobilizes public opinion. In 1937 it took the deaths of 108 persons caused by a mixture called "elixir sulfanilamide" to secure passage of the Food, Drug and Cosmetic Act which F.D.R.'s adviser, Rexford G. Tugwell, had introduced in 1933. The thalidomide tragedies of 1962 were needed to pass Senator Estes Kefauver's bill to tighten Federal control over the drug industry.

The dramatic event that tipped the balance for auto safety reform in 1966 was not a tragedy but a fiasco: General Motors' crude use of private detectives to harass Nader. Nader prefers to think that auto safety legislation was on the way in any event and that his run-in with G.M. only speeded the process. But many on Capitol Hill agree with the Senator who said of the bill's passage: "Everybody was outraged that a great corporation was out to clobber a guy because he wrote critically about them. At that point everybody said, 'The hell with them.'"

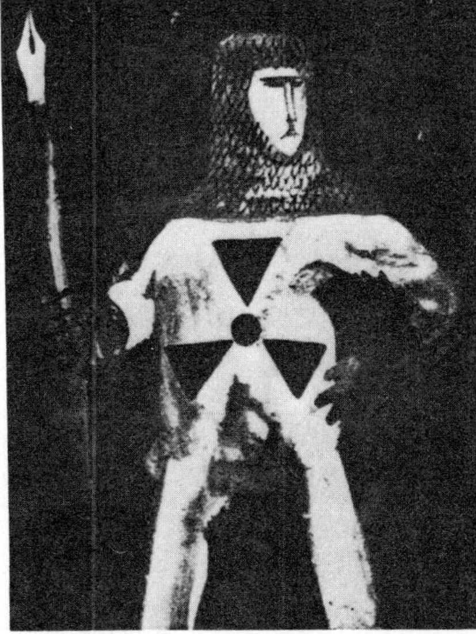

With full credit to Nader's intelligence and energy, the fact remains that much of his effectiveness has stemmed from the priceless image he acquired during the episode with G.M. Nader was instantly fixed in the popular imagination as a lone crusader, a battler against overwhelming odds. The image is accurate enough, as images go, and is one that American romanticism finds irresistible.

The trouble is, Nader is not a romantic. An idealist, yes—but not a romantic. Nader has no special fondness for fighting against overwhelming odds. He would like to be, if not a Goliath, at least a bigger, stronger, more effective David. That is why he is now thinking of a crucial, perhaps dangerous, change in his style of operation.

Nader would like to obtain private funds for a law firm to do what he is doing now, on a bigger scale. He believes that the best young lawyers in America would come to work for his firm at modest salaries. They could "add a new dimension to the legal profession," he says. The firm would handle no individual cases but would, as Nader has been doing, gather information on issues affecting the public interest, work with Congressional committees and appear before regulatory agencies. It would be Nader's aim to represent the public interest in Washington with legal services fully equal to those private interests are already receiving from leading law firms.

Nader has sought no funds nor, prior to this disclosure, made any public announcement of his plan for a public-interest law firm. He hopes that on the basis of his performance during the last two years someone will come to him with the money, and it does not seem inconceivable that some foundation or other private source would finance such an undertaking.

Perhaps the more interesting question is whether, if he gets the money, his operation could withstand the transition from Ralph Nader, Crusader, to Ralph Nader, Inc. First, there is the matter of image. Would Nader continue to intrigue the press and the public if he ceased to be a lone wolf and acquired an office, a staff, secretaries and all the other trappings of normality? Also, there is the question whether Nader can adapt to a quasi-administrative role,

accountable not only for his own conduct and accuracy but for that of others.

Nader is aware of these and other dangers in his proposed plan, but, continually frustrated by the distance between what he wants to do and what he can do as one man, he is willing to take the chance.

It will be interesting to observe Nader's progress. At any given moment the world contains a very small number of practicing reformers and a very large number of ex-reformers. Ex-reformers generally fall into two categories: those who sold out and those who slowed down. People who know Nader don't think he will sell out, but slowing down is a peril that all flesh is heir to.

BEYOND his impact on specific legislation, Nader has exerted another kind of influence on Capitol Hill. As an influential aide to an influential member of Congress explained:

"Ralph has pricked the conscience of many Congressional staff members. He has had almost a religious influence on us, and I use the word carefully. I hate to call myself a convert, but today I'm more inclined to look at whether or not a piece of legislation serves the public interest. In large part, this is because Ralph has time after time raised the moral issues involved in the bills that come before us.

"It's very easy for Congressmen and their staffs to succumb to the Washington milieu. The industry lobbyists are chosen because they are charming and persuasive men. The Senator or Representative knows that consumer protection isn't good politics; the private interests are organized and the public interest isn't. It's easy to go along. What Ralph has done is force a lot of people to face facts, and to remember that they're here to represent the people."

As this suggests, the reformer has a hard way to go in Washington, for all the pressures are toward accommodation with the status quo. No one has put the matter better than Woodrow Wilson when he said: "Things get very lonesome in Washington sometimes. The real voice of the great people of America sometimes sounds faint and distant in that strange city."

Nader deserves to be judged by his own high standards, and he insists: "I haven't even begun my work yet." Still, he has begun. He has added new dimensions to the public interest lobbyist's role in Washington. He has dramatized the fact that consumer protection must be extended beyond helpful hints to the housewife. He has raised issues and set standards. If Nader quit tomorrow, he would have earned a footnote in this decade's history. If he doesn't quit, he may in time accomplish a great deal more. ■

October 29, 1967

AID TO CONSUMERS CALLED UNNEEDED

Retired General Foods Head Assails Political Efforts to Furnish Protections

SCORES FUROR ON CARS

Business Council Is Urged to Unite in a Campaign to Educate Buying Public

Special to The New York Times

HOT SPRINGS, Va., May 12—The recently retired head of General Foods Corporation called upon other big business executives today to unite in a battle against "consumerism." He described this as the efforts of self-serving politicians to give consumers protections they do not need.

Charles G. Mortimer, who is still the chairman of the executive committee of General Foods, said in a speech before the Business Council here that businessmen were losing out in the fight against politicians and "social theorists" because they did not pay sufficient attention to each other's problems.

He said that the food industry, for example, had reacted with "apathy" last year when "the automotive safety slap was staged in circus-like Congressional hearings."

Similarly, he said, there were "few ripples in Detroit" when the National Commission on Food Marketing issued a report "castigating the food industry."

Finds Injury to Economy

Mr. Mortimer chose the auto safety issue as a prime example of the injury that he said could be done to business and the economy by "consumerism."

Mr. Mortimer charged that the book written by Ralph Nader "Unsafe at Any Speed," plus the comments of various members of Congress had left the public with what Mr. Mortimer said was an erroneous impression that most accidents were directly attributable to unsafe cars, rather than unsafe drivers.

The result, he said, was that public confidence in automobiles "eroded to an extent almost beyond belief."

"Automobile sales began falling off immediately," he said.

"Mr. Nader's personal gain from the slap will undoubtedly be appreciable. But the loss to the automobile industry, its investors and the national economy has been several thousand-fold his gain."

Sees Education Needed

Mr. Mortimer spoke at the semi-annual meeting at the Homestead here of the Business Council, of which he is a member. The council is composed of 120 men, most of them presidents or board chairmen of major corporations.

He said that public education was needed if business was to withstand the "rising tide of proposals to interpose the Government between buyer and seller in the market place."

He said that there was no need for either the truth-in-packaging bill that was passed by Congress last year nor for the truth-in-lending bill that is getting serious attention from Congress this year—"thanks, most likely, to a plug from the President in this year's special consumer message."

The lending bill would require a statement of the rate of interest being charged on all consumer loans. The packaging bill mainly required more detailed and explicit disclosure of sizes and contents on packaged products sold to consumers.

May 13, 1967

New Annual-Meeting Note: Social Protest

By DAVID DWORSKY

Stockholders were rocked this spring by the winds of social protest as they made their way to annual meetings across the country.

The protests were not the familiar ones of skimpy dividends, low earnings and high executive sales, as articulated in recent years by a small but highly vocal group of professional stockholders, but of creeping Communism, involvement in the war in Vietnam and racial discrimination.

While only about five of the 1,500 corporations that held their annual meetings in March, April and May fell prey to pickets and demonstrators, they are among the country's most important and affluent companies.

They are the Chase Manhattan Bank, the General Motors Corporation, the Eastman Kodak Company, the Xerox Corporation and the R. J. Reynolds Tobacco Company.

Significantly, observers now feel that social objectors have discovered a heretofore untapped stage for dissent, and one to which they will return next year in large numbers.

A group in opposition to the Chase Manhattan Bank's lending policy in South Africa picketed its meeting, which was held on March 28 in New York. Several of the 30 pickets carried signs which read: "Apartheid has a friend in Chase Manhattan," an intentional distortion of the bank's advertising slogan, which says "You Have a Friend at Chase Manhattan."

In rebuttal, David Rockefeller, president, told stockholders that "none of us at Chase Manhattan holds any brief for the South African Government's policy of separation of the races."

He explained that Chase Manhattan felt no obligation to endorse the polical or economic policies of countries in which it conducts business.

When protests against similar involvement were raised by pickets at the annual meeting of General Motors in Detroit, Frederic G. Donner, chairman, retorted that G.M. runs its South African plant "in its usual nondiscriminatory manner within the laws of the country."

Angry Negro members of a militant organization known by its initials of FIGHT, descended on sleepy Flemington, N. J., on April 25 to demand that the Eastman Kodak Company honor an alleged agreement to hire and train 600 unemployed Negroes.

Kodak claimed it had been made a party to the agreement in question by an assistant vice president who had exceeded his authority.

The Xerox Corporation, which like Eastman Kodak, is based in Rochester, also encountered members of "Freedom, Integration, God, Honor—Today," at its annual meeting here on May 19, but with vastly dissimilar results.

A speaker who identified himself as the Rev. Herbert C. Shankle, vice president of FIGHT, read a telegram from his organization congratulating Xerox on its "willingness to shoulder community and social responsibility in tackling the

United Press International

Demonstrators, demanding Eastman Kodak honor its agreement to hire 600 unemployed Negroes, in Flemington, N. J., where concern held stockholders' meeting.

The Rev. Herbert C. Shankel of Rochester praising the Xerox Corporation at concern's annual meeting for "tackling the hard core unemployment problem."

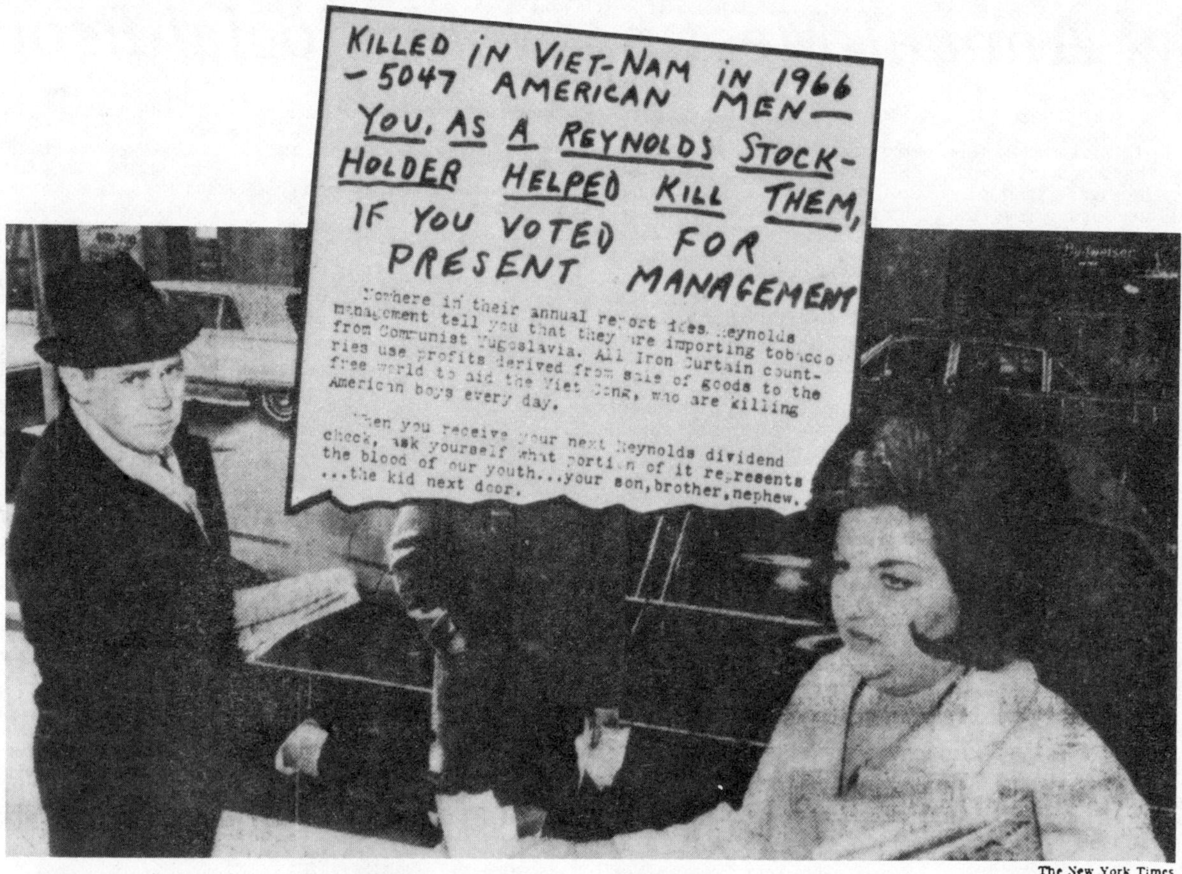

The New York Times

Pickets from the Peter Fechter Brigade greet a shareholder in Jersey City during the R. J. Reynolds Company meeting in April. Anti-Communist group, named after a young East German killed trying to flee over Berlin Wall, charged that company used some Yugoslav tobacco in manufacture of its cigarettes.

hard core unemployment problem."

On April 12, in Jersey City, members of the Peter Fechter Brigade distributed to stockholders arriving for the meeting of the R. J. Reynolds Tobacco Company literature protesting the use in cigarettes of tobacco imported from Communist Yugoslavia.

The Brigade was described by a member as an anti-Communist group formed in 1962 to protest the death of Peter Fechter, a young German who was killed by East German guards while attempting to cross the Berlin Wall to the West.

Its literature further contended that "all Iron Curtain countries use profits derived from the sale of goods to the Free World to aid the Viet Cong, who are killing American boys every day."

Endorsed by Administration

Bowman Gray, chairman of R. J. Reynolds, asserted that the company bought less than one per cent of its tobacco from Yugoslavia, and that the practice was emulated by other cigarette producers and endorsed by the Johnson Administration.

What exactly do protests and demonstrations at stockholder meetings mean? Many observers feel nothing will be gained by those who are demonstrating, or by those against whom the demonstrations are directed.

To Sidney J. Weinberg Sr., an outspoken critic of unbusiness-like conduct at annual meetings, the protests and demonstrations mean little.

Mr. Weinberg, a partner in the investment banking firm of Goldman, Sachs & Co., said such disruptions are "isolated."

He asserted, however, that "I don't think the annual meeting is the proper forum for such protests to be raised."

Adolph A. Berle is equally opposed to the use of stockholder's meetings for organized protests, but feels they are not so easily dismissed.

"When you combine politics and business," he warned, "you are in dangerous waters. We ought not to mix drinks."

Mr. Berle, a professor at Columbia University's Graduate School of Business, and a writer on corporate affairs, anticipates an increase in such proceedings.

Joseph Livingston, author of "The American Stockholder," believes it is useles sto demonstrate before small stockholders because they are powerless to influence the policies and decisions of the corporation.

"Only major shareowners have the power to change corporate policy," he said, "and I don't think they are going to be influenced by such demonstrations."

Philosophical Nature

In a chapter of his book devoted to "Shareholder Inter-Comunication," he writes that "The Securities and Exchange Commission will permit the management to omit proposals of a political or philosophical nature."

The book adds that "a resolution that the Greyhound Corporation do away with segregation in its buses in the South was excluded on the theory that a corporation is run for the profit of shareholders, not for social reform."

Lewis D. Gilbert, who attends about 150 stockholder meetings each year, said, "management should expect social protests and prepare for them."

He thinks many demonstrators stage their protests to gain publicity, and have little hope of accomplishing their goals.

He predicts that protests will continue "for as long as The New York Times writes about them."

Clearly then, these unprecedented intrusions were among the most important developments to emerge from the spring meeting season just ended.

What follows will be a summer, fall and winter of contemplation, and, perhaps, concern, for Lewis D. Gilbert, his brother John, Mrs. Wilma Soss, Mrs. Evelyn Y. Davis and other professional stockholders who clock considerable mileage on the annual meeting circuit.

It appears likely that the conduct of this group has so alienated the country's 22 million shareowners that clamps may be placed on their future activities.

This growing animosity was generated largely through the snarling reluctance of professional stockholders to surrender the floor to others, costumes that diverted attention from the proceedings and many questions of special interest that prolonged routine meetings into lengthy sessions.

At the annual meeting of the International Business Machines Corporation, the first hour was consumed by questions from two women stockholders.

Questions from two minority shareowners sent the meeting of the Hotel Corporation of America into extra innings. Hungry stockholders demanded the meeting be adjourned after three and a half hours of questions on the efficiency of the hotel chain's coat rooms, restaurants, air-conditioning system and cigarette girls.

Corporate managements once schemed and plotted to silence such persistent stockholders in the hope of diluting their impact on the meeting. But such tactics led to charges of railroading.

Management has now learned to avoid this accusation by trusting impatient stockholders to boo and hoot noisy minority stockholders into silent submission.

DOW AIDE DEFENDS SALE OF NAPALM

Tells Students Vietnam War Is Not a Moral Issue

By STEVEN V. ROBERTS

A representative of the Dow Chemical Company said in a campus debate yesterday that the war in Vietnam was not, "on the whole," a moral question and that the use of napalm there was justified because the war was justified.

The representative, Dean Wakefield, spoke before several hundred students in an auditorium on the Washington Heights campus of New York University.

Recruiters for Dow Chemical, a major supplier of napalm, have been the targets of vociferous and occasionally violent protests on campuses throughout the country.

A recruiter who appeared at N.Y.U. yesterday conducted a full schedule of job interviews and was not disturbed, although about 100 students picketed in front of the Gould Student Center during the morning.

The debate was held "to make the Dow people confront us as they go about their work," said Nicholas Gordon, an English instructor, who opposed Mr. Wakefield in the debate. "We are trying to convince them that they are wrong. We call on all employes to stop making napalm and soliders to stop using it. We want to stop the war in whatever way possible."

Invited by Students

Mr. Wakefield, Dow's public-relations director for the Eastern region, said he had appeared because he had been invited by the students, and because he though he could "contribute to the educational process." Dow representatives have appeared in several debates on the West Coast, but this was the first one in this area, he said.

Mr. Wakefield said that he had no way of knowing whether the demonstrations had harmed the company, but that the students "have the capacity to hurt us."

In his opening remarks Mr. Wakefield reiterated a recent policy statement by Dow:

"The United States is involved in Vietnam, and as long as we are involved we believe in fulfilling our responsibility to this national commitment of a democratic society. And we do this because we believe in the long-term goals of our country."

Napalm, he added, is used "in direct confrontation warfare with the enemy" and is no more reprehensible than "dozens of other weapons."

Mr. Gordon said napalm was "especially horrible because it especially affects the civilian population." He quoted numerous newspaper reports that asserted that napalm and other weapons had caused many thousands of civilian casualties each year.

'Commitment' Cited

Mr. Gordon and many members of the audience seemed particularly disturbed at Mr. Wakefield's statement that the war was not a moral question and that Dow felt a responsibility to support the "national commitment" of the United States in Vietnam.

Mr. Gordon said: "You must examine the moral question of what we are doing there. What does pacification mean? Does it mean telling people what to do when they don't agree with us?"

He added, "The debate had limited value. Wakefield was unable to cope with the questions. But maybe he won't be able to rationalize his support of the war so easily any more."

Mr. Wakefield replied by quoting Dr. Howard A. Rusk, who wrote in The New York Times last March that he had not encountered one napalm victim in 20 hospitals he visited in South Vietnam.

Napalm is a jellied gasoline that burns rapidly and is particularly effective in fighting guerrillas in bunkers. Mr. Wakefield noted that was very simple to produce and could be made by the Army if Dow refused to make it.

Mr.Wakefield replied that he had, in fact, made a "conscious, rational decision" to work for Dow and would stick by it.

He was asked what he thought about the Krupp family, which had made munitions for Nazi Germany. "The Krupps were bad people," Mr. Wakefield replied.

A faculty member then asked him to define "what standards you apply in making moral judgments on companies." Mr. Wakefield replied that he drew his moral standards "from history."

The answer drew jeers from the audience, and Mr. Gordon accused him of "ducking the question."

Many of the students seemed pleased that the debate had taken place, but disappointed in the results.

"We reflected what a peaceful demonstration could do," said Robert Burkett, a senior history major who helped organize the event.

November 28, 1967

From Overalls to the Attache Case

By ROBERT A. WRIGHT

BUSINESS is stepping up its involvement with social problems, especially those concerned with the black community.

For example, the JOBS program of the National Alliance of Businessmen, headed by Leo C. Beebe, an aggressive executive salesman on loan from the Ford Motor Company, exceeded its goal of hiring, by July, 1969, 100,000 hard-core unemployed. As of late last month, more than 12,000 companies had pledged 172,153 jobs. The latest figures on hirings totaled 118,411, of which 80,460 were still on the job.

Judging from the JOBS program, speeches by executives and participation by businessmen in hundreds of conferences with themes such as "Business and the Urban Crisis," a growing number of businessmen are convinced of the need for corporate involvement in the nation's social problems.

On the other hand, Howard J. Samuels, a businessman now serving as administrator of the Small Business Administration, has warned repeatedly against "trying to turn our social problems over to private enterprise as if it had some magic formula for success."

Mr. Samuels praises the concept of a business-government partnership to provide jobs, housing and other social needs. But he contends that government must still provide the "leadership and financial backing."

Nixon's Views Awaited

With these views in mind, many businessmen and local officials are anxiously awaiting the priorities of the Nixon Administration. President-elect Richard M. Nixon has appointed a socially aware liberal, Daniel Patrick Moynihan, as chairman of the Cabinet-level Council on Urban Affairs.

But his campaign stressed Government economy and tax incentives to foster "black capitalism," apparently to the neglect of major Federal spending programs. And the Democratic 91st Congress appears unlikely to go along with tax incentives.

Speaking about the model-cities program at the National League of Cities annual meeting in New Orleans, Mayor Jerome P. Cavanagh of Detroit noted, "The new Administration can't dismantle it, but there is always a way to starve any program to death."

Whatever the thrust of the domestic effort, most participants are convinced that it will take time to alleviate the deprivation of most Negroes. Meanwhile, the black community is impatient. As Detroit is learning, jobs — even if they are auto assembly-line jobs at $3.50 an hour to start — are not enough.

As one Negro in the auto industry said: "They don't want to be busting their backs for nothing. They don't want to be wearing overalls. Their symbol of success is the attaché case."

Kind of Job Counts

It is the kind of job that counts with black men these days, another Detroit man observed. "Negroes want the kind of jobs everyone else has, meaning everyone you see on television."

It cannot be said that corporations have plunged into the effort.

The majority of Mayors rate business cooperation as only fair in a survey of 114 cities by the National Industrial Conference Board. Municipal officials said they were encouraged by increasing business involvement, the board's report said, but "believe the urban challenge to be of such magnitude that a much greater corporate commitment is called for."

The Mayor of a West Coast city is quoted in the report: "While some progress has been made by certain industries in the area, it must be understood that much of the industry in the community has not yet been involved, and it would be erroneous to surmise that permanent solutions have been found or even that substantial progress has been made."

Another Mayor told the board: "We feel that there has been no particular way in which business has cooperated with us in the solving of our urban problems. On the contrary, a number of businesses have moved out of the area because of the high percentage of Negroes who live here.

"No large business has moved into the area since the change in the racial composition, which started to take place about 20 years ago."

Finding out how successful a project is can also be difficult. Max Fisher, chairman of New Detroit, Inc., that city's businessman-led urban coalition, asks: "How the devil can you measure the progress of a group of citizens in one year for a problem we've had for 200 years? We may not be able to see the scratches on the surface of our real problems for another five years at least."

Still, the list of real contributions is long. A few of them follow:

¶In Boston, about 40 companies are working with a Small Business Development Corporation funded by the Department of Commerce to train black managers and act as a catalyst in transferring white businesses to black owners.

In New York, F. W. Woolworth, in a sale and lease-back arrangement, is transferring ownership of one of its major stores in Harlem to Negroes. Employes of the Chase Manhattan Bank, with bank approval, devote off-duty hours to advising potential businessmen from minority groups in financial, marketing, planning and other areas.

¶Twenty-five businesess are participating in a Department of Labor training program for hard-core unemployed. Two hundred men have been trained and placed, another 600 are expected to be placed.

¶In St. Louis, The Brown Shoe Company and the Eldger Manufacturing Company announced plans to take their operations into the city's near north side Negro community to provide jobs. Thirty savings and loan associations established a $15-million fund to help finance rehabilitation and purchase of inner-city residential property. The Savings Service Corporation has a program to acquire single-family structures and remodel them for occupancy under a no-downpayment financing subsidized by the Federal Government.

¶In Los Angeles, the Commonwealth United Corporation formed Action Industries, Inc., which will be funded by a stock issue. It is aimed at forming businesses to be managed and operated by the disadvantaged residents of Venice, Calif.

¶Training programs are being operated in several cities. In Columbus, Ohio, the Timken Roller Bearing Company donated a machine shop to the Columbus Area Development and Training School and is supplying an instructor. In Winston-Salem, N. C., the Western Electric Company, R. J. Reynolds Tobacco Company, Fairchild-Hiller Corporation, AMP Corporation and Hanes Corporation are cooperating in a varied training program. In New Jersey, the four Bell System Companies in the state trained and hired 550 hard-core unemployed and in Detroit, the Chrysler Corporation "adopted" one high school, the Michigan Consolidated Gas Company another, to provide students with job training and advice.

¶In Detroit an Economic Development Corporation, organized by executives, raised $1.4-million to funnel into a Negro business group that will give management assistance and technical aid to blacks.

¶In Cleveland, the Warner & Swasey Co. established the Hough Manufacturing Company in the Hough Negro ghetto, eventually to be owned and operated by blacks, to make a variety of industrial products.

¶In Atlanta, the Celotex Corporation is developing a $2.3-million 13.5-acre low and middle-income housing project in Atlanta's University Center Urban Redevelopment Area.

¶In Chicago, Hodge, La., Hopewell, Va., and New York, the Continental Can Company, without Government aid, has opened programed education centers for reading and arithmetic courses. The Radio Corporation of America, under a Labor Department contract, is training hard-core jobless in television repair in Camden, N. J., Newark, Chicago and Los Angeles.

But most businessmen and municipal officials probably believe that whatever projects are undertaken by business, massive infusions of Federal money will be required before urban problems can be solved.

Warren A. Billings, acting director of the New York City region of the National Alliance of Businessmen, said in November that one of the things the group had learned in nine months of operations was that "the assimilation of the hard-core unemployed into a productive work role is generally more effective when employers are assisted by Department of Labor funding."

January 6, 1969

Door to Executive Suite Opens Wider to Working Girls

Last Barriers Are Toppling in Business

By MARYLIN BENDER

Everyone knows it. Even male supremacists concede it. But no one can prove it by statistics.

It's just a realization—one could call it female intuition if so many men weren't asserting it—that women are going places at last in American business and industry.

Within the next decade, newspapers will no longer be recording female firsts. The first women to have been seated on the major stock exchanges, to have moved into the presidential suites of leading corporations on their own and not just because they inherited the stock, will be history rather than news.

Making a million, marrying the client (then losing his account), and finding new worlds to conquer will be the reasonable expectation of any dazzling blonde.

•

On the other hand, male executives need not fear being turned out to the kitchen. Given equality in business, women are unlikely to respond in droves. A majority will still prefer the reflected glory of their husbands.

Women have been playing an increasingly important role in the labor force since World War II. The number of working woman has doubled in the last 25 years. The greater part of them are women over 35 who take jobs for money rather than identity. One out of three married women is working.

But these figures do not hint at the notable progress that women have begun to make in executive positions. The elevation of 64 women to key positions by the First National City Bank is more indicative.

They include four assistant vice presidents, such as Mar-

The New York Times
Judith Chadwick, executive assistant to the executive vice president of Moore-McCormack Lines, at office here.

The New York Times
Marian Schappel, an assistant vice president of First National City Bank, at her desk in branch at 399 Park Ave.

ian Schappel, a branch manager, and Diana Greer, a senior analyst in the investment research department. Miss Greer is one of the Harvard Business School's first three women graduates (class of 1960).

Christopher Rodgers, vice president for personnel administration for the bank, says:

"We're doing some active recruiting in women's colleges, looking for women trained in the computer sciences, which evolves into systems analyst and programmer, but also on the professional banking and investment side."

Mr. Rodgers believes "it's a logical step" for the bank to have a woman vice president in the not-too-distant future.

Though the Harvard Business Review has stopped surveying executive opportunities for career women because "the barriers are so great that there is scarcely anything to study," the Harvard Business School has one of its 1965 graduates, Judith Chadwick, recruiting women.

Miss Chadwick is executive assistant to the executive vice president and director of Moore-McCormack Lines, a middle management post she has just attained after two promotions in two years.

When she talks to college seniors, she points up the increasing number of opportunities for women holding the M.B.A. degree, "which opens many doors." As for a woman's chances of reaching top management, Miss Chadwick says:

"If she has the ability, if she is in a unique situation—this is going to sound like hedging, I know—and if she is working with a unique group of men and has a lot of luck, I think she can make it."

Miss Chadwick and James Foley, assistant dean for external affairs at the Harvard Business School, also hedge somewhat when they interpret discrimination against women in the light of starting salaries for the school's graduates.

The most recent of its 75 women graduates have, as a rule, been offered $11,500. The median salary for a graduate with one year's business experience (which most of the women don't have) has been $12,500. The median for graduates with engineering degrees (which most women don't have either) is $13,000.

This year's entering class of 780 enrolled 31 women. The women in the next class will be the first to live on campus.

There have not, however, been women in the Advanced Management Program or the newer, 16-week Program for Management Development (middle managers), both of which require co-sponsorship by the student's company. "How many companies are going to invest $3,000 tuition plus salary and fringes in a woman rather than a man?" Mr. Foley asked.

J. Fredric Way, director of placement for the Columbia Graduate School of Business, where the number of women in this year's entering class doubled to bring the female component of the school to 4 per cent, believes that companies have begun to realize that women may be able to manage as well as men.

"It may have taken the Fair Employment Practices Act to do it, but many more areas have opened up in the last few years," he said. Banks, accounting firms, even oil companies now see women in the same executive trainee category as men.

"Nobody says, 'We'll see men only,' and if they did, I'd raise merry hell," Mr. Way declared. "This is the start. A company officer finds himself talking to a woman, and discovers she's very qualified."

William Carothers, director of industrial relations for the chemical division of F.M.C., a diversified producer of chemicals, fibers, films and machinery, puts the situation this way:

"When we're looking for chemists, it's talent against talent. We recruit at 90 schools and the jobs are open to anybody in the disciplines we need."

But Mr. Carothers says few women "rush to us when we look for chemical engineers."

Mrs. Hilda Kahne, an economist and research associate of the Radcliffe Institute, finds that women "are not entering the fast-growing engineering and scientific professional categories at the same rate as men, with the exception of mechanical engineering, where the number is too small to be significant."

Only in medicine and law are their ranks multiplying faster than men. Women mathematicians, economists and psychologists are also proliferating, a fact that jibes with their presence in the marketing and analytical areas of industry and finance.

Two years ago, Betty Friedan, author of "The Feminine

Mystique," organized NOW (an acronym for National Organization for Women), a women's rights movement that has campaigned to put teeth into Title VII of the Civil Rights Act of 1964, which outlawed sex discrimination in employment.

The integration of male-female w[illegible]t ads in newspapers is viewed as one of those small achievements with great potential.

Discrimination against women in many of the clubs often considered vital to advancement is one roadblock in the path of business. Another is the refusal of women to take advantage of their new opportunities.

For the last thre[illegible] years Barnard College has participated in recruitment interviews on the Columbia University campus. But last year, only 56 girls from a class of 440 crossed the street to be interviewed, according to Mrs. Jane Schwartz, Barnard's placement director.

"A woman is actually unde[illegible] less pressure to be a success,' says Martha Peterson, Barnard's president. "Today's students want self-actualization for women as well as men, but whether it will lead to more top executive positions for women. I have my do[illegible]bts. I think they will cut out their worthy pieces of work and do them. Maybe they will be leaders in innovation."

January 6, 1969

BUSINESSMEN CALL FOR SELF-REFORM

Action Is Termed Necessary to Meet the Challenge of 'a New Consumerism'

By JOHN D. MORRIS

Special to The New York Times

WASHINGTON, Nov. 12—An advisory group of the United States Chamber of Commerce has drafted a broad program of voluntary business reforms to meet the challenge of what it called "a new consumerism."

The program, embracing unit pricing and some other measures long advocated by leaders of the consumer movement, was outlined in a report by the chamber's Council on Trends and Perspective.

The report will be submitted to the chamber's board of directors tomorrow for possible guidance in policy-making decisions.

In a frank analysis of the performance of American business in satisfying "the changing needs of consumers," the advisory council of 32 business leaders, said:

"Current consumer activism, which has gone beyond protest to the formulation of legislative reform programs, represents a 'new consumerism,' much as the civil rights movement of the fifties sought redress through programs and policies designed to stimulate Government action."

New initiatives by business, the group said, are needed "to minimize ill-conceived legislation and to offset the impact of new Federal regulatory programs which could impose onerous burdens on industry."

"The tardiness of business in responding constructively" to consumers' criticisms, the council said, is a factor in the rise of the consumer movement. The council advised managers to reexamine their practices, particularly in marketing and advertising, "to reflect a greater awareness and sensitivity to the public's evolving ethical values and nonmaterialistic aspirations."

"But whatever the causes," it said, "it is of paramount importance to recognize that the consumer movement is well-established and is likely to gain strength in coming years."

In advocating unit pricing—the listing of the price per ounce or other unit of packaged products—the council said sellers should adopt such a system "wherever possible" as an aid to consumers.

It said sellers should also provide more information on safety, performance and durability of products, both at the point of sale and through "a workable feed-back system for customer complaints and inquiries."

Other recommendations included:

The recasting of local Better Business Bureaus "as a consumer ombudsman to coordinate and strengthen manufacturer-seller-customer complaint, information and warranty performance communications systems."

¶Simplification and modernization of manufacturers' warranties and improvement in the quality and speed of repairs and other warranty services.

¶Better training programs for sales and service personnel "with particular emphasis on informing sales personnel of product capabilities and limitations to avoid overselling the product with consequent adverse customer reactions."

¶Serious consideration of such mechanisms as Federal certification of voluntary product safety standards as well as notification and recall systems for defective products.

¶More forthright and effective action by business against fraud and deception, particularly in sales to low-income consumers.

¶Intensification of efforts, in the development of products, to anticipate social consequences of their use and forestall consumer complaints about "environmental pollution congestion, public safety, health and public morality effects."

The council made no specific recommendation on advertising practices but observed:

"Business will need to become more attuned to the changing values of a better-educated younger generation which is quite critical of orthodox business practices, such as product 'puffing' in advertising."

The council's chairman is F. Ritter Shumway of Rochester, N. Y., chairman of the Sybron Corporation, which manufactures medical and hospital equipment.

November 13, 1969

NADER TO PRESS FOR G.M. REFORM

Opens a Campaign to Make Company 'Responsible'

By RICHARD HALLORAN

Special to The New York Times

WASHINGTON, Feb. 7—Ralph Nader, the advocate of consumer interests and critic of the automobile industry, announced today the opening of a national Campaign to Make General Motors Responsible.

Mr. Nader, speaking at a news conference in the Mayflower Hotel, accused the nation's largest corporation of contributing 35 per cent of the country's air pollution, of collusion in design and marketing praactices, of violating air pollution and safety laws and of manufacturing shoddy cars that cause rocketing repair bills.

Several of Mr. Nader's colleagues, mostly young lawyers, have formed the Project on Corporate Responsibility to conduct the campaign. The project has purchased 12 of G.M.'s 285 million shares of stock to give it a voice in the company's business affairs.

The project sent a letter to the company yesterday recommending three resolutions to be included in the company's proxy statement to shareholders in April. The project coordinators also intend to bring the resolutions up for discussion at the company's annual meeting May 22.

Mr. Nader said that at the meeting, "G.M. may be the host for a great public debate on the role of this giant corporation in American society rather than a wooden recital of aggregate financial data."

He suggested that campaign tactics at that time might resemble the sit-ins of the civil rights and student movements if the company did not respond favorably to the project's demands.

One of the resolutions calls for expanding the corporation's board of directors from 24 to 27 members to include three representatives of the public. The project named as its candidates Betty Furness, President Johnson's adviser on consumer affairs, who is now a columnist for McCalls magazine; René Dubos, a biologist at Rockefeller University, who is a winner of the Lasker Award in Public Health and the Pulitzer Prize and is also a member of President Nixon's Citizen's Advisory Committee on Environmental Quality, and the Rev. Channing Phillips, president of the Housing and Development Corporation here, who is a Democratic national committeeman.

The second resolution would have the company undertake no business activity that "is detrimental to the health, safety, or welfare of the citizens of the United States." In a supporting statement, the project said that "the corporation should take the initiative in creating products that are fully consistent with the health and safety of its consumers and of the nation as a whole."

Shareholders' Committee

The third resolution would establish a shareholders' committee for corporate responsibility. It would have full access to the company's files and employes, would examine the entire range of its activities and would report to the shareholders during the 1971 annual meeting.

Members of the committee would come from management, the United Automobile Workers, conservative groups, consumers, the academic community, civil rights groups, the scientific community, religious and social service groups and small shareholders.

A spokesman for General Motors, reached by telephone in Detroit, said the company had not yet received the letter and resolutions.

"Our procedure is to review submissions from stockholders as they are received," he said. "We follow procedures for handling these resolutions as specified by the S.E.C."

The Securities and Exchange Commission sets the rules for the exercise of stockholders' rights.

Mr. Nader said: "The basic thrust of the campaign will be to alert and inform the public about their omnipresent neighbor, General Motors, and how it behaves. It will ask citizens to make their views known to both shareholders and management."

"It will go to institutions that own G.M. stock," Mr. Nader continued, "and, if they decline to respond, to the constituents of those institutions who will be contacted."

"The campaign will reach to the universities and their students and faculty, to the banks and their depositors and fiduciaries, to churches and their congregations, to insurance companies and their policyholders, to union and company pension funds and their membership and to other investors, he said.

Mr. Nader named the Massachusetts Institute of Technology, Princeton University, Yale, Harvard, and the University of Chicago as owners of G.M. shares.

Mr. Nader said he would have no formal part in the campaign.

It will be run by four young lawyers, Philip W. Moore, a staff counsel to Businessmen for the Public Interest; Geoffrey Cowan of the Center for Law and Social Policy; Joseph N. Onek, assistant counsel for the Senate Subcommittee on Administrative Practice and Procedure, and John Esposito, a Washington lawyer.

February 8, 1970

G.M. TOLD TO PUT CONSUMER MOVES TO STOCKHOLDERS

S.E.C. Orders Vote on Two Nader-Backed Resolutions on Voice in Management

By JERRY M. FLINT

Special to The New York Times

DETROIT, March 19—The Securities and Exchange Commission told the General Motors Corporation today to take two consumer-oriented resolutions directly to its stockholders.

The resolutions are sponsored by the Project on Corporate Responsibility, a group of young Washington lawyers backed by Ralph Nader, the consumer advocate.

The action could lead to efforts to put consumer or environmental issues before the stockholders of other industries, such as the railroads, power companies, gasoline companies or pesticide manufacturers.

Proxy Statement

General Motors said it would include the two motions in its proxy statement — a booklet that is mailed to all stockholders and that contains proposals for stockholder voting.

The resolutions, which will be voted on at the auto maker's May 22 annual meeting, call for placing three new members on the board of directors to represent the public interest and for establishing a General Motors Shareholders' Committee for Corporate Responsibility.

The company's directors will ask the stockholders to vote against the proposals. No such stockholder proposal, opposed by the company, has been passed at G.M. in a quarter-century.

Seven other proposals backed by the young lawyers were not supported in the Government regulatory body's order. These included resolutions calling for the hiring of dealers and managers from racial minority groups and for improved automobile safety design.

Company Will Not Fight

General Motors said that its lawyers believed that all nine resolutions were illegal and that stockholders should not vote on such issues. But the company said it would not fight the commission's order involving the two proposals.

General Motors said that while it "is deeply concerned about the problems of our environment and our urban society, this does not make them proper subjects for a corporation proxy statement."

"We have, however, constantly studied them and have made substantial progress in finding solutions. We are confident we will make further progress in the immediate future," the company said.

In the pollution field in recent months, General Motors has pledged that its car engines will be clean-burning by 1975; that all its engines will be able by this fall to use gasoline that produces less pollution, even if this means sacrificing some engine power and economy, and that it will make available for $20 in a few months a conversion kit to reduce air pollution from old cars.

In the safety field, General Motors engineers have developed the collapsing steering column and a guard rail system in car doors for protection in side crashes.

The company said today: "Anyone who has attended a General Motors stockholders' meeting will attest that there is a full and frank discussion of all matters relating to the corporation which are of interest to stockholders, whether or not they are included in the proxy. We will listen and give factual answers to the questions raised at our meeting. It is our hope that representatives of the project also will listen."

The Securities and Exchange Commission said that the proposal to set up the stockholder committee must note that committee should have only "reasonable amounts" of money to spend, as determined by the General Motors board of directors, and that the information the committee would get would be restricted.

The lawyers' group had asked that the proposed committee receive whatever money and information it needed. The group said today it wanted to negotiate the new S.E.C.-ordered wording with General Motors.

A Corporate First

It is not unusual for the commission to order certain issues placed before a company's stockholders, but this marks the first time that consumer matters are to be put before stockholders.

The commission's move could open the way for a variety of groups to put issues involving the public interest before the owners of American business

The goal, said Geoffrey Cowan, one of the directors of the Washington lawyers' group, is "to make the corporations accountable," to expand business law and make new use of traditional business procedures, and to raise issues such as desegregation, pollution and product safety.

Mr. Cowan's group purchased 12 of G.M.'s estimated total of 290 million shares to obtain stockholders' voting rights.

The group has announced that its nominees for the board of directors would be Rene Dubos, a biologist on President Nixon's Environmental Advisory Committee; Betty Furness, who was President Johnson's adviser on consumer affairs, and the Rev. Channing Phillips, a Negro who is the Democratic national committeeman from Washington.

March 20, 1970

CRITICS DOMINATE MEETING OF G.M.

They Lose on 2 Proposals, but Assail Management

By AGIS SALPUKAS

Special to The New York Times

DETROIT, May 22 — Critics of the giant General Motors Corporation received only miniscule support from shareholders for their proposals today, but they used the annual meeting here to stir debate on pollution control, car safety and minority hiring.

The leaders of the effort — called Campaign G.M. — directed a barrage of questions at five of the top officers of the world's largest industrial corporation, who sat on a blue dias before 3,000 stockholders.

But they were handily defeated on two proposals designed to make the corporation more responsive to the general public. The proposals would have added three more members to the 23-member G.M. board and set up a committee drawn from management, the United Auto Workers and civic groups to report on how the corporation was dealing with such issues as pollution, safety and mass transportation.

The result of the vote on the proposal to create a Committee of Corporate Responsibility was 6.7 million shares, or 2.7 per cent, in favor and 227 million shares against. Thhe proposal to expand the board by three members resulted in 5.7 million shares, or 2.4 per cent, in favor and 228 million shares in opposition. In past meetings proposals brought by stockholders have resulted in 2 to 7 per cent of the shares in favor.

The five-hour meeting was taken up mainly with criticisms of the corporation, but the tension was broken often. At one point, for example, a young Detroit student arose to nominate a friend to the board and said to James M. Roche, the General Motors chairman who conducted the meeting: "How are you today?"

"Seen better," Mr. Roche shot back.

Unexpected Criticism

Criticism of the corporation also came from an unexpected source. Stuart Rawlings Mott, the son of Charles S. Mott, who is the oldest member on the General Motors board and the owner of 86,659 G.M. shares, criticized the General Motors management on grounds that it had not spoken out against the Indochina war and had not dealt with the problem of population explosion.

Mr. Mott, who owns 2,000 shares and is also the beneficiary of trust funds that hold about 700,000 shares, said that the directors of G.M. had the responsibility to speak out "about the disastrous directions of our nation's military policies."

After the meeting Mr. Roche said: "When even a small fraction of our stockholders —even if only one — is not convinced of our record of responsibility then we are concerned. General Motors and those of its critics who are sincere in their desire for a future better than today are really united in purpose."

Mr. Roche, who answered all the questions during the meeting, was complimented by the leaders of Campaign G.M. for his courtesy and stamina.

Mr. Roche, in a news conference after the meeting, reciprocated the compliment and said that the critics had conducted themselves in an orderly manner and had done their homework.

"We're going to search for new ways to communicate with the interests that we heard," he said.

The vote on the two proposals of Campaign G.M. was anticlimactic. The campaign came into the meeting with 330,000 of the 285-million shares in the corporation committed publicly to it.

The first proposal would have added to the board the Rev. Channing Phillips, a civil rights leader; Betty Furness, special assistant for consumer affairs under President Johnson, and Rene Dubos, a biologist at Rockefeller University.

The second proposal would have set up a 15-to-25 person unit called the Committee for Corporate Responsibility.

General Motors waged a wide publicity campaign against the proposals and in a proxy statements sent to its 1.35-million stockholders it denounced the campaign as an attempt to harass the corporation.

The leaders of the campaign did not see the vote as a defeat but as a victory because of the wide debate their effort had created on corporate responsibility throughout the nation.

Supporters Hold Parley

Before the meeting, which began at 2 P.M., the leaders of Campaign G.M. fired up about 300 supporters in a strategy meeting in one of the large rooms in the cavernous Cobo Hall. Many of the supporters wore red and white buttons saying "Tame G.M."

Students with long hair and with peace buttons pinned to their blue denim shirts sat next to housewives dressed in bright flowered print dresses. There were also ministers, businessmen, college professors and presidents. They applauded loudly when Dr. George Wald, professor of biology at Harvard University and a 1967 winner of the Nobel Prize for Medicine, was asked to take a bow.

Jerome Kretchmer, the Environment Protection Administrator for New York City, said that he was representing Mayor Lindsay on behalf of all the cities in the country where the automobile had become the No. 1 enemy to the environment. "We believe that corporations should provide a decent style of life instead of only profits," he said.

Robert Townsend, the former president of Avis Rent a Car Corporation and author of the best seller, "Up the Organization," told the supporters that they were on the right track.

"But to really have an effect," he said, "just don't buy any more of their products. Don't buy any car from G.M. until they produce a clean one."

From the beginning when Campaign G.M. was announced at a news conference in Washington early in February, it was aimed at winning the support of the general public rather than rounding up votes for the proposals presented at the annual meeting.

Joel Kramer, director of research for the campaign, said in an interview, "We chose G.M. because it was a widely held company. They are the general public. All we had going for us was the publicity that we were able to get."

The staff of 10 permanent people, mostly young lawyers and 30 volunteers, mostly students from the colleges, supported themselves through a $30,000 grant made by the foundation connected with Philip Stern, a philanthropist in Washington.

May 23, 1970

G.M. Names 5 Directors As Public-Issue Advisers

By AGIS SALPUKAS

Special to The New York Times

DETROIT, Aug. 31 — The General Motors Corporation announced today the establishment of a "public policy committee" to advise the giant concern on matters that affect the general public.

General Motors, the world's largest industrial corporation, has become a major target of leaders of environmental and consumer movements. The committee is designed to give the board of directors expert advice on how to deal with such issues as pollution and safety.

The committee is made up of five members of the 23-member board of directors of G.M., four of whom are not officers in the company and one of whom is a former vice chairman of the corporation.

James M. Roche, chairman of the board of directors, said the five men "have a broad and diverse background reflecting their deep interest in social, environmental and other concerns." He added that this combination would enable the committee "to act in the best interest of our stockholders as well as the broader community in which we operate."

"General Motors," Mr. Roche added in a statement, "has a long and outstanding record of community action and corporate citizenship. In establishing the public policy committee, the board has given these matters of broad national concern a permanent place on the highest level of management."

The members of the committee are:

John A. Mayer, chairman of the committee. He is also chairman of the Mellon National Bank and Trust Company of Pittsburgh and a trustee of Carnegie - Mellon University, the Carnegie Institute and the University of Pennsylvania.

James R. Killian, chairman of the corporation of the Massachusetts Institute of Technology and former United States Presidential Assistant for science and technology.

John T. Connor, chairman of the Allied Chemical Corporation and former Secretary of Commerce.

George Russell, former vice chairman of General Motors and a trustee and national campaign director for Meharry Medical College in Nashville.

Gerald A. Sivage, president of Marshall Field & Co. of Chicago and a trustee of Northwestern University at Carroll College.

The committee, which will report directly to the board of directors, is G.M.'s apparent answer to demands made by a group of critics at the last stockholder meeting on May 22. The critics, organized in a group called Campaign G.M., had submitted two proposals to make the corporation more responsive to the general public.

One proposal would have added three more members to the board of directors to represent the public interest. The other would have set up a committee of "corporate responsibility" drawn from management, the United Automobile Workers Union and civic groups to report on how the company was dealing with such issues as pollution, safety and mass transportation. The two proposals were overwhelmingly defeated in the proxy balloting, getting less than 3 per cent of the votes.

Ralph Nader, the consumer advocate who helped start Campaign G.M. but did not directly involve himself in the effort, said in an interview that the new committee was "genuinely preposterous."

"The fact that they couldn't go outside of the company for the men is an indication of G.M.'s insecurity. It's so ridiculous that it will backfire on them."

Mr. Nader added that Mr. Connor could not possibly deal fairly with such problems as pollution because he said Mr. Connor's company, Allied Chemical, was one of the biggest polluters in the nation.

'Parochialism' Charged

Philip Moore, executive secretary of Campaign G.M., said: "While we wish the committee well and will do everything in our power to assist its efforts, we are dismayed to observe that it suffers from the same parochialism as the board itself."

He said the committee had no Negroes, women, consumer representatives or environmentalists.

"Indeed, Mr. Morose said, the chairman of the new committee represents financial interests which appear directly to contradict the announced purpose of the committee. As chairman of the Mellon National Bank & Trust Company, John Mayer represents financial interests of the Mellon family, which controls more than 27 per cent of the Gulf Oil Company."

September 1, 1970

A Friedman doctrine—

The Social Responsibility Of Business Is to Increase Its Profits

By MILTON FRIEDMAN

WHEN I hear businessmen speak eloquently about the "social responsibilities of business in a free-enterprise system," I am reminded of the wonderful line about the Frenchman who discovered at the age of 70 that he had been speaking prose all his life. The businessmen believe that they are defending free enterprise when they declaim that business is not concerned "merely" with profit but also with promoting desirable "social" ends; that business has a "social conscience" and takes seriously its responsibilities for providing employment, eliminating discrimination, avoiding pollution and whatever else may be the catchwords of the contemporary crop of reformers. In fact they are—or would be if they or anyone else took them seriously—preaching pure and unadulterated socialism. Businessmen who talk this way are unwitting puppets of the intellectual forces that have been undermining the basis of a free society these past decades.

The discussions of the "social responsibilities of business" are notable for their analytical looseness and lack of rigor. What does it mean to say that "business" has responsibilities? Only people can have responsibilities. A corporation is an artificial person and in this sense may have artificial responsibilities, but "business" as a whole cannot be said to have responsibilities, even in this vague sense. The first step toward clarity in examining the doctrine of the social responsibility of business is to ask precisely what it implies for whom.

Presumably, the individuals who are to be responsible are businessmen, which means individual proprietors or corporate executives. Most of the discussion of social responsibility is directed at corporations, so in what follows I shall mostly neglect the individual proprietor and speak of corporate executives.

IN a free-enterprise, private-property system, a corporate executive is an employe of the owners of the business. He has direct responsibility to his employers. That responsibility is to conduct the business in accordance with their desires, which generally will be to make as much money as possible while conforming to the basic rules of the society, both those embodied in law and those embodied in ethical custom. Of course, in some cases his employers may have a different objective. A group of persons might establish a corporation for an eleemosynary purpose—for example, a hospital or a school. The manager of such a corporation will not have money profit as his objective but the rendering of certain services.

In either case, the key point is that, in his capacity as a corporate executive, the manager is the agent of the individuals who own the corporation or establish the eleemosynary institution, and his primary responsibility is to them.

Needless to say, this does not mean that it is easy to judge how well he is performing his task. But at least the criterion of performance is straightforward, and the persons among whom a voluntary contractual arrangement exists are clearly defined.

Of course, the corporate executive is also a person in his own right. As a person, he may have many other responsibilities that he recognizes or assumes voluntarily—to his family, his conscience, his feelings of charity, his church, his clubs, his city, his country. He may feel impelled by these responsibilities to devote part of his income to causes he regards as worthy, to refuse to work for particular corporations, even to leave his job, for example, to join his country's armed forces. If we wish, we may refer to some of these responsibilities as "social responsibilities." But in these respects he is acting as a principal, not an agent; he is spending his own money or time or energy, not the money of his employers or the time or energy he has contracted to devote to their purposes. If these are "social responsibilities," they are the social responsibilities of individuals, not of business.

What does it mean to say that the corporate executive has a "social responsibility" in his capacity as busi-

---

MILTON FRIEDMAN is a professor of economics at the University of Chicago.

nessman? If this statement is not pure rhetoric, it must mean that he is to act in some way that is not in the interest of his employers. For example, that he is to refrain from increasing the price of the product in order to contribute to the social objective of preventing inflation, even though a price increase would be in the best interests of the corporation. Or that he is to make expenditures on reducing pollution beyond the amount that is in the best interests of the corporation or that is required by law in order to contribute to the social objective of improving the environment. Or that, at the expense of corporate profits, he is to hire "hard-core" unemployed instead of better-qualified available workmen to contribute to the social objective of reducing poverty.

In each of these cases, the corporate executive would be spending someone else's money for a general social interest. Insofar as his actions in accord with his "social responsibility" reduce returns to stockholders, he is spending their money. Insofar as his actions raise the price to customers, he is spending the customers' money. Insofar as his actions lower the wages of some employes, he is spending their money.

The stockholders or the customers or the employes could separately spend their own money on the particular action if they wished to do so. The executive is exercising a distinct "social responsibility," rather than serving as an agent of the stockholders or the customers or the employes, only if he spends the money in a different way than they would have spent it.

But if he does this, he is in effect imposing taxes, on the one hand, and deciding how the tax proceeds shall be spent, on the other.

This process raised political questions on two levels of principle and consequences. On the level of political principle, the imposition of taxes and the expenditure of tax proceeds are governmental functions. We have established elaborate constitutional, parliamentary and judicial provisions to control these functions, to assure that taxes are imposed so far as possible in accordance with the preferences and desires of the public—after all, "taxation without representation" was one of the battle cries of the American Revolution. We have a system of checks and balances to separate the legislative function of imposing taxes and enacting expenditures from the executive function of collecting taxes and administering expenditure programs and from the judicial function of mediating disputes and interpreting the law.

Here the businessman—self-selected or appointed directly or indirectly by stockholders—is to be simultaneously legislator, executive and jurist. He is to decide whom to tax by how much and for what purpose, and he is to spend the proceeds—all this guided only by general exhortations from on high to restrain inflation, improve the environment, fight poverty and so on and on.

> **"The conflict of interest is clear when union officials are asked to subordinate the interest of their members to some more general social purpose."**

The whole justification for permitting the corporate executive to be selected by the stockholders is that the executive is an agent serving the interests of his principal. This justification disappears when the corporate executive imposes taxes and spends the proceeds for "social" purposes. He becomes in effect a public employe, a civil servant, even though he remains in name an employe of a private enterprise. On grounds of political principle, it is intolerable that such civil servants—insofar as their actions in the name of social responsibility are real and not just window-dressing—should be selected as they are now. If they are to be civil servants, then they must be selected through a political process. If they are to impose taxes and make expenditures to foster "social" objectives, then political machinery must be set up to guide the assessment of taxes and to determine through a political process the objectives to be served.

This is the basic reason why the doctrine of "social responsibility" involves the acceptance of the socialist view that political mechanisms, not market mechanisms, are the appropriate way to determine the allocation of scarce resources to alternative uses.

ON the grounds of consequences, can the corporate executive in fact discharge his alleged "social responsibilities"? On the one hand, suppose he could get away with spending the stockholders' or customers' or employes' money. How is he to know how to spend it? He is told that he must contribute to fighting inflation. How is he to know what action of his will contribute to that end? He is presumably an expert in running his company—in producing a product or selling it or financing it. But nothing about his selection makes him an expert on inflation. Will his holding down the price of his product reduce inflationary pressure? Or, by leaving more spending power in the hands of his customers, simply divert it elsewhere? Or, by forcing him to produce less because of the lower price, will it simply contribute to shortages? Even if he could answer these questions, how much cost is he justified in imposing on his stockholders, customers and employes for this social purpose? What is his appropriate share and what is the appropriate share of others?

And, whether he wants to or not, can he get away with spending his stockholders', customers' or employes' money? Will not the stockholders fire him? (Either the present ones or those who take over when his actions in the name of social responsibility have reduced the corporation's profits and the price of its stock.) His customers and his employes can desert him for other producers and employers less scrupulous in exercising their social responsibilities.

This facet of "social responsibility" doctrine is brought into sharp relief when the doctrine is used to justify wage restraint by trade unions. The conflict of interest is naked and clear when union officials are asked to subordinate the interest of their members to some more general social purpose. If the union officials try to enforce wage restraint, the consequence is likely to be wildcat strikes, rank-and-file revolts and the emergence of strong competitors for their jobs. We thus have the ironic phenomenon that union leaders—at least in the U.S. —have objected to Government interference with the market far more consistently and courageously than have business leaders.

The difficulty of exercising "social responsibility" illustrates, of course, the great virtue of private competitive enterprise — it forces people to be responsible for their own actions and makes it difficult for them to "exploit" other people for either selfish or unselfish purposes. They can do good—but only at their own expense.

Many a reader who has followed the argument this far may be tempted to remonstrate that it is all well and good to speak of government's having the responsibility to impose taxes and determine expenditures for such "social" purposes as controlling pollution or training the hard-core unemployed, but that the problems are too urgent to wait on the slow course of political processes, that the exercise of social responsibility by businessmen is a quicker and surer way to solve pressing current problems.

Aside from the question of fact—I

DEMAND—A demonstration in New York. The doctrine of "social responsibility," says the author, would require an executive "to make expenditures on reducing pollution beyond the amount that is in the best interests of his corporation or required by law."

share Adam Smith's skepticism about the benefits that can be expected from "those who affected to trade for the public good"—this argument must be rejected on grounds of principle. What it amounts to is an assertion that those who favor the taxes and expenditures in question have failed to persuade a majority of their fellow citizens to be of like mind and that they are seeking to attain by undemocratic procedures what they cannot attain by democratic procedures. In a free society, it is hard for "good" people to do "good," but that is a small price to pay for making it hard for "evil" people to do "evil," especially since one man's good is another's evil.

I HAVE, for simplicity, concentrated on the special case of the corporate executive, except only for the brief digression on trade unions. But precisely the same argument applies to the newer phenomenon of calling upon stockholders to require corporations to exercise social responsibility (the recent G.M. crusade, for example). In most of these cases, what is in effect involved is some stockholders trying to get other stockholders (or customers or employes) to contribute against their will to "social" causes favored by the activists. Insofar as they succeed, they are again imposing taxes and spending the proceeds.

The situation of the individual proprietor is somewhat different. If he acts to reduce the returns of his enterprise in order to exercise his "social responsibility," he is spending his own money, not someone else's. If he wishes to spend his money on such purposes, that is his right, and I cannot see that there is any objection to his doing so. In the process, he, too, may impose costs on employes and customers. However, because he is far less likely than a large corporation or union to have monopolistic power, any such side effects will tend to be minor.

Of course, in practice the doctrine of social responsibility is frequently a cloak for actions that are justified on other grounds rather than a reason for those actions.

To illustrate, it may well be in the long-run interest of a corporation that is a major employer in a small community to devote resources to providing amenities to that community or to improving its government. That may make it easier to attract desirable employes, it may reduce the wage bill or lessen losses from pilferage and sabotage or have other worthwhile effects. Or it may be that, given the laws about the deductibility of corporate charitable contributions, the stockholders can contribute more to charities they favor by having the corporation make the gift than by doing it themselves, since they can in that way contribute an amount that would otherwise have been paid as corporate taxes.

In each of these—and many similar—cases, there is a strong temptation to rationalize these actions as an exercise of "social responsibility." In the present climate of opinion, with its widespread aversion to "capitalism," "profits," the "soulless corporation" and so on, this is one way for a corporation to generate goodwill as a by-product of expenditures that are entirely justified in its own self-interest.

It would be inconsistent of me to call on corporate executives to refrain from this hypocritical window-dressing because it harms the foundations of a free society. That would be to call on them to exercise a "social responsibility"! If our institutions, and the attitudes of the public make it in their self-interest to cloak their actions in this way, I cannot summon much indignation to denounce them. At the same time, I can express admiration for those individual proprietors or owners of closely held corporations or stockholders of more broadly held corporations who disdain such tactics as approaching fraud.

WHETHER blameworthy or not, the use of the cloak of social responsibility, and the nonsense spoken in its name by influential and prestigious businessmen, does clearly harm the foundations of a free society. I have been impressed time and again by the schizophrenic character of many businessmen. They are capable of being extremely far-sighted and clear-headed in matters that are internal to their businesses. They are incredibly short-sighted and muddle-headed in matters that are outside their businesses but affect the possible survival of business in general. This short-sightedness is strikingly exemplified in the calls from many businessmen for wage and price guidelines or controls or incomes policies. There is nothing that could do more in a brief period to destroy a market system and replace it by a centrally controlled system than effective governmental control of prices and wages.

The short-sightedness is also exemplified in speeches by businessmen on social responsibility. This may gain them kudos in the short run. But it helps to strengthen the already too prevalent view that the pursuit of profits is wicked and immoral and must be curbed and controlled by external forces. Once this view is adopted, the external forces that curb the market will not be the social consciences, however highly developed, of the pontificating executives; it will be the iron fist of Government bureaucrats. Here, as with price and wage controls, businessmen seem to me to reveal a suicidal impulse.

The political principle that underlies the market mechanism is unanimity. In an ideal free market resting on private property, no individual can coerce any other, all cooperation is voluntary, all parties to such cooperation benefit or they need not participate. There are no "social" values, no "social" responsibilities in any sense other than the shared values and responsibilities of individuals. Society is a collection of individuals and of the various groups they voluntarily form.

The political principle that underlies the political mechanism is conformity. The individual must serve a more general social interest—whether that be determined by a church or a dictator or a majority. The individual may have a vote and a say in what is to be done, but if he is overruled, he must conform. It is appropriate for some to require others to contribute to a general social purpose whether they wish to or not.

Unfortunately, unanimity is not always feasible. There are some respects in which conformity appears unavoidable, so I do not see how one can avoid the use of the political mechanism altogether.

But the doctrine of "social responsibility" taken seriously would extend the scope of the political mechanism to every human activity. It does not differ in philosophy from the most explicitly collectivist doctrine. It differs only by professing to believe that collectivist ends can be attained without collectivist means. That is why, in my book "Capitalism and Freedom," I have called it a "fundamentally subversive doctrine" in a free society, and have said that in such a society, "there is one and only one social responsibility of business—to use its resources and engage in activities designed to increase its profits so long as it stays within the rules of the game, which is to say, engages in open and free competition without deception or fraud." ■

September 13, 1970

Letters

THE "FRIEDMAN DOCTRINE"

To the Editor:

I would like to take exception to the underlying assumption of the "Friedman doctrine" ("The Social Responsibility of Business Is to Increase Its Profits," by Milton Friedman, Sept. 13) that the only demand upon the businessman by the stockholder "generally will be to make as much money as possible. . . ."

I speak not only as an investor in American corporations, but also as a "stockholder" in other institutions: my Government, my community, my family, my society. As multiple stockholders, we all make complex and sometimes conflicting demands upon these institutions. When we demand that automobiles be designed so as not to foul the air, we are weighing a 1 per cent reduction in corporate profits against a 10 per cent increase in the cost of remaining healthy. When we applaud efforts to hire the "hard-core unemployed," we are mindful as much of the staggering economic and social costs of welfare and urban renewal as we are of the horrifying plight of many of these individuals. Stockholders seek not to incapacitate the corporate mechanism, but to maximize our over-all economic and social portfolio. This I do not believe to be "pure unadulterated socialism."

TIMOTHY MELLON.
Guilford, Conn.

Drawing by Handelsman; ©1970 The New Yorker Magazine, Inc.

"All I can say is that if being a leading manufacturer means being a leading polluter, so be it."

●

To the Editor:

Milton Friedman's defense of pure Adam Smith is like Billy Graham's defense of the literal truth of Genesis. To believe that a laissez-faire economic theory offers any hope of promoting a viable society, is as naive as the belief that Adam and Eve were the first man and woman.

C. W. GRIFFIN.
Denville, N. J.

To the Editor:

Thanks to Dr. Friedman. His logic is the perfect example of the thinking which has brought this country, its business and its people to where we are now. We can turn to Dr. Friedman as a symbol of the mind which continues to propagate the *status quo*, ignoring the ever clearer handwriting on the wall.

DAVID A. GARDNER,
Harvard University
Graduate School of
Business Administration.
Cambridge, Mass.

●

To the Editor:

Milton Friedman clearly indicates why there is a need for vigorous Government taxation and regulation of industry's environmental pollution, for if it is the objective of each business organization to maximize profits, each can readily do so by forcing society at large to absorb the costs of environmental pollution, rather than internalizing such costs and thereby reducing net profits.

It is incumbent upon the

Government to use its taxation authority (an authority which, according to Friedman, must be respected and obeyed by the corporate executive) to levy effluent taxes that will make it financially irresponsible and disadvantageous to pollute our skies and water, and which will force individual companies to internalize the costs of combating their pollution, rather than passing such costs on to those individuals residing downwind and downstream from them.

RICHARD A. LIROFF,
Graduate Student,
Department of Political Science,
Northwestern University.
Evanston, Ill.

•

TO THE EDITOR:

Here is the key fallacy in Milton Friedman's "What's good for General Motors is good for America" argument. It is becoming quite apparent that all will not necessarily be well with the world just because each man honestly pursues his own private gain. It is becoming apparent that with the best of intentions, and scrupulously observing all laws, a corporate executive may do harm to people.

The corporate executives whose industries have poured harmful ingredients into our lakes have usually done so without violating laws, and in conscientious efforts to maximize profits. Likewise, those men have poisoned our air.

Mr. Friedman certainly makes a strong case that the executive who spends money for social responsibility, takes from the stockholders without their consent. But by the same token, the executive who pollutes the streams takes from the public without *their* consent. Between the alternatives of imposing on his own stockholders and imposing on the public, the executive should lean toward the former because he is still in a position to generate for them a net gain. After all, if Mr. Friedman is to argue that an executive has no right to involve the corporation in activities that are *for* the public, it would follow that he has no right to act *against* that same public.

YALE ROE.
Winnetka, Ill.

•

TO THE EDITOR:

In his denial of the social responsibility of business, Milton Friedman decries business making "expenditures on reducing pollution beyond the amount . . . required by law." He also concludes that profits are a company's most important objective "so long as it . . . engages in open and free competition without deception or fraud." But, laws on pollution and fraud don't just happen; most of them are unable to stem either one of them, all too often as a result of direct business pressure when the laws are written. Differential enforcement of even these laws in the various states and localities has long been recognized as one of our main problems, but business opposes Federal standards on principle.

"Self-regulation" is the usual answer of business spokesmen (including Friedman himself), but how can that work when he says that business has no such social responsibility?

JOHN E. ULLMANN,
Chairman and Professor,
Management, Marketing and Business Statistics,
Hofstra University.
Hempstead, L. I.

October 4, 1970

Letters

IN DEFENSE OF THE "FRIEDMAN DOCTRINE"

TO THE EDITOR:

I know that Dr. Milton Friedman does not need me to defend him or his ideas but, since you printed no reply from him to the six letters, all critical, in your Oct. 4 Letters column, it is not unfitting that I should point out one obvious fact: None of your correspondents read the subject article very carefully or, having read it, understood the rather obvious point. Simply stated, it is up to the Government to set standards for safety, pollution, etc., so that *all* rivals and competitors are under identical restraint or identical compulsion.

For Company A to spend stockholders' money for pollution-control and/or safety equipment the public is under no compulsion to buy and, probably, doesn't care very much for anyway, while its competitors are able to undercut Company A by ignoring these factors, would not promote either safety or a good environment nearly so much as they would ensure the failure of good, civic-minded old A, and, therefore, an abuse of discretion. If air-pollution control devices on automobiles cost money to install, reduce performance and adversely affect gas mileage, for any one of the automobile manufacturers to install such devices on its own would be tantamount to committing suicide. It would have died in a good cause, but try to explain that to the stockholders, the workmen, the suppliers, the community that lived off its wages, and the tax collectors on whose *largesse*, no doubt, a fair percentage of the letter writers depend to some degree.

Considering that one of your correspondents is a graduate student in Political Science, another somehow connected with the Harvard Graduate School of Business Administration and a third the Chairman and Professor of Management, Marketing and Business Statistics at a third university, I despair for higher education.

STANLEY UNGAR.
New York.

October 25, 1970

G.M. Elects First Negro As Member of Its Board

By AGIS SALPUKAS
Special to The New York Times

DETROIT, Jan. 4 — Dr. Leon Howard Sullivan, a black minister from Philadelphia who has been a pioneer in helping Negroes find better jobs in industry, was elected today to the board of directors of the General Motors Corporation.

In announcing the appointment of the first black man to the board of the world's largest industrial corporation, James M. Roche, the board's chairman, said that Dr. Sullivan "is the type of person who can bring to our board the benefit of his knowledge and expertise in areas of public concern."

The leaders of the "Campaign to Make General Motors Responsible," an antimanagement campaign, who at the last stockholders meeting last spring attacked G.M.'s record of hiring of minorities, interpreted the appointment as another victory in their attempt to make the corporation more responsible to social problems and the environment movement.

Phillip W. Moore, the coordinator of Campaign G.M., said in an interview: "We consider the appointment a victory and hope it is just a beginning of a new direction for the corporation."

At the last meeting, Mr. Moore and other leaders of Campaign G.M. criticized the corporation for having no blacks on its board of directors, for having only 11 black automobile dealers out of 1,300 and for not revealing what type of jobs were held by black workers. About 15 per cent of the 800,000 workers at G.M. are black.

Mr. Moore, who plans to present new demands on the corporation at its next stockholders meeting, said that he hoped Dr. Sullivan would work toward getting more blacks into dealerships and management jobs.

Dr. Sullivan, pastor of the Zion Baptist Church, the largest Protestant congregation in the city, began his attempts to provide better employment opportunities for blacks in 1961 by leading 400 ministers in a boycott against some of Philadelphia's largest companies.

However, as the white businessmen began to open up jobs, Dr. Sullivan found few Negroes had the training to accept them.

In 1964, he set up a job-training program called Opportunities Industrialization Centers, which now has training centers in 70 cities and which in 1968 had 35,000 trainees, mainly women high school dropouts.

Although the program is now mostly funded through the Office of Economic Opportunity, Dr. Sullivan insisted that the initial support come from black people.

The 6-foot, 5-inch minister, a highly persuasive speaker, said he had persuaded 200 of his congregation to contribute $10 a month for 36 months for an investment pool.

Besides starting the training program, the funds were used as seed money to finance a 17-store shopping center in North Philadelphia and Progress Aerospace, Inc., the nation's first Negro-owned and managed aerospace-component concern.

In a recent interview he said that the black man must be given a share in the American economy but that blacks should joint the free-enterprise system and not strive for separation.

For G.M., this is the second attempt to placate its critics. Last August, the corporation established a public-policy committee made up of five members of the 23-member board of directors to advise on such issues as pollution and safety.

Mr. Moore and his supporters will be back at the next shareholder meeting next spring with new proposals. They will ask to permit shareholders to nominate directors and vote on them and require management to disclose in its annual report what it has done about air pollution, minority hiring and auto safety during the last year.

January 5, 1971

Watchdogs From Within

The New York Times/Jack Manning

RCA: Herbert T. Brunn, left, the head of RCA's consumer affairs, with Benjamin I. French.

The New York Times/Don Hogan Charles

Chase Manhattan: Marjorie Meares displays data sheet to members of the Chase Manhattan consumer team.

Corporate Ombudsmen Respond to Consumers

By LEONARD SLOANE

An idea for a new greeting card was working its way through the Kansas City headquarters of Hallmark Cards, Inc., recently when it came to an official who pointed out that it might be offensive to the women's liberation movement. The project was scrapped.

A young man stranded in Montreal was desperately awaiting funds from the Chase Manhattan Bank in New York to fly to his father's funeral in Paris. After a call to one person at Chase, the money was wired to a Canadian bank and he was on his way that evening.

A customer of the Michigan Bell Telephone Company in a rural area outside of Detroit was upset because his newly installed telephone wire, placed above ground because of the winter freeze, had broken four times. One man in the company took time to investigate, found that the break had been caused by local boys who snipped the wire and had the line placed in a tree to keep that circuit open until the ground thawed.

In each of these cases the individual with the solution was a new type of executive at American companies. Typically called consumer affairs officers or ombudsmen (om-BOODS-men), their assigned role is to guard consumer interests within their corporations and to show an awareness of and concern for the problems related to their

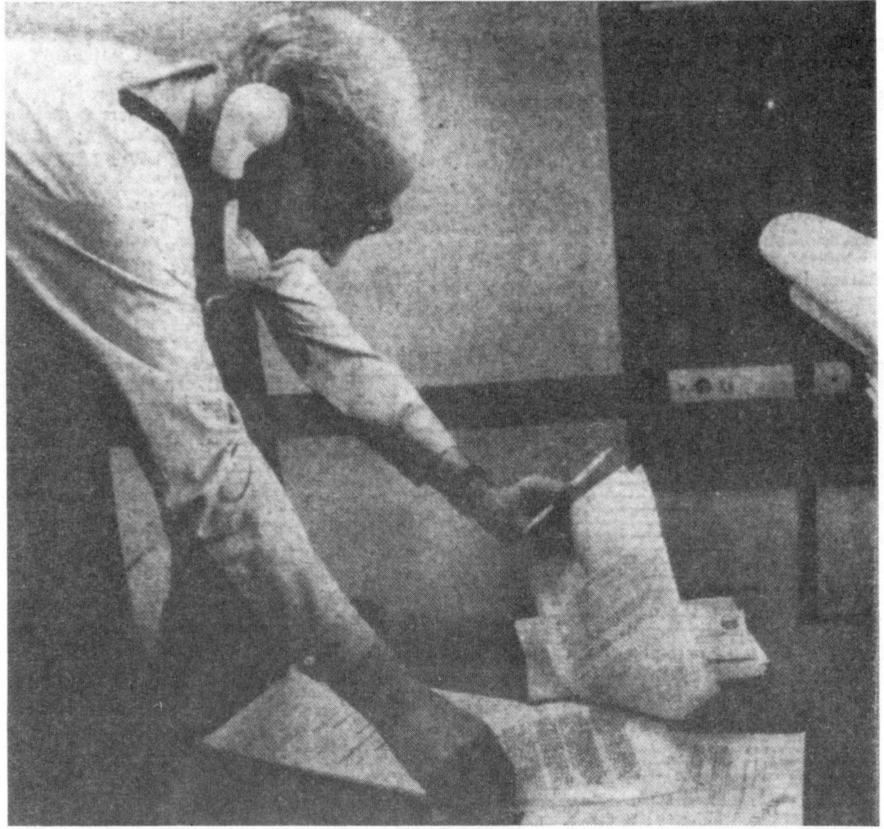

The New York Times/Meyer Liebowitz

Pan American: John M. Barnes, head of consumer affairs department for Pan American, in his office.

The New York Times/Frank Lodge

Chrysler: Byron J. Nichols, lf, Chrysler's new ombudsman(and an assistant, S. L. Noble, in Detroit.

products and services.

As originally envisioned by the Swedes more than 160 years ago, the ombudsman—which means agent, representative or deputy — was to be a disinterested watchdog to ride herd on public officials and investigate citizens' complaints. In recent years some states and local bodies have adopted the concept to move the government closer to the people.

Now as consumerism has become discussed and feared in corporate board rooms, companies are also adopting the ombudsman approach. A number of concerns established this office in 1970 and within the last month alone, two major corporations — Pan American World Airways and the Chrysler Corporation—instituted consumer departments with a flurry.

But there is a degree of skepticism as to the effectiveness of the company ombudsmen. The skeptics see the development as largely a public relations gesture with more rhetoric than substance.

"It's obvious that because these people are within the corporation, their jobs are dependent upon the corporation's goodwill," said Peter Petkas, an associate of Ralph Nadler's Public Interest Research Group and its specialist on consumer complaints.

"It's a step in the right direction, no doubt about it, but I wonder what kind of access we are going to have to the information they're getting. It's their burden to show us in any specific case that it works."

Proponents of the corporate ombudsman idea bristle at the suggestion that the new function is no more than a glorified complaint department. They cite the added dimensions of the role as indicative of the power and prestige it often has.

To begin with, the new consumer affairs officers are usually veteran employes with broad qualifications and knowledge of their companies. For instance, Byron J. Nichols, who was put in charge of such a program at the Chrysler Corporation as vice president-consumer affairs, has been with the automaker 30 years, including 13 as a vice president. Besides filling many important marketing positions at the company, he spent the last year as president of the prestigious National Alliance of Businessmen.

Secondly, the modern corporate ombudsman is a high-level officer who generally is responsible to the president or chairman of his company. As John M. Barnes, a staff vice president of Pan

American who heads its office of consumer action noted, "We report directly to the chief executive rather than the marketing department. Our first point of contact is the head of the department concerned, but in the ultimate resort we can always act directly out of the president's office."

In addition, the model of a modern consumer affairs official is an independent person with the ability and right to cross departmental lines in order to investigate and attempt to solve problems in any part of the company. The old-fashioned complaint man, in contrast, usually is a lower-level employe in the sales or marketing department.

As a man close to Herbert T. Brunn, appointed a year ago to the new post of vice president - consumer affairs by the RCA Corporation, pointed out, "He's great at cutting through red tape and getting to the bottom of a problem. He can even turn off the assembly line any place if he finds it necessary."

Mr. Brunn's five-man consumer relations section receives about 2,000 letters and telephone calls a month. According to his tally, only 15 per cent are complaints, with most of the remainder requests for information and compliments to employes.

"It's very helpful if people let the manufacturer know when they have a problem," he observed. "So frequently a customer gets into a hassle with a dealer or local service agency and the next thing you know he's writing to Virginia Knauer [Special Assistant to President Nixon for Consumer Affairs] or the local Better Business Bureau. The manufacturer is just sitting there and just wishes the customer would let him know."

Mr. Barnes of Pan American envisions his department as a catalyst in making necessary changes. "We are becoming totally visible and accessible in public," he asserted, "and we will open a public office in the lobby of the Pan Am Building [alongside Grand Central Station] next month where we can be seen.

"I don't want to mislead anybody, though, into thinking that we're going to change the airline tomorrow. As every month passes, we're going to be able to change a thing, two things, three things and so, by evolution, be responsive to what is put to us."

The new Chrysler program, called "Your Man in Detroit," evolved from an experiment begun in June 1970 by the Dodge division. This expediting of complaints about dealer service through the intervention of an official at the home office proved so successful that it has been expanded into an important corporate activity.

An extensive advertising and promotion campaign is being waged by Chrysler, to get the word across that the man with whom to speak is Mr. Nichols. "I have enough experience in the corporation to know exactly whom to call," he said, "and by handling our customers" problems well, it will have a good psychological effect." Other companies woth ombudsmen are waging similar campaigns.

Another such man in Detroit is James S. Richards, general commercial manager of Michigan Bell, who is in charge of its 80-man special action forces. "They're responsible for relating the company to the customer and the customer to the company," he said.

Jay T. Boehm began working as director of consumer affairs for Hallmark last September and was charged with looking at the company from a consumer perspective "to pick up things you wouldn't otherwise." He feels that the major part of his job is not reacting to complaints after they occur, but rather preventing them from happening.

"We get about 500 letters a month from consumers with about 5 to 10 per cent on social issues and the rest dealing with where our products can be bought or problems that arise," he remarked. "We answer all the letters here, even if we have to get information from other departments. We're in the social expression business, and if we can't answer letters, who can?"

The ombudsman, or more properly, obmudswoman, at Chase is Miss Marjorie P. Meares, who was quietly named consumer affairs officer in February, 1970. If anyone is the depositor's friend at Chase, it's probably Miss Meares or one of her two assistants as they try to answer the questions posed in the 150 letters and innumerable telephone calls they receive each month.

"The problems we handle deal with everything from why the bank closed a subway entrance to a deposit situation overseas," she said. "We investigate and find out the proper party to send an answer as politely and quickly as possible."

Miss Meares recognizes that her position is to some extent a result of the inroads on the American scene made by the highly articulate consumer advocates and their followers. "I would say that we hit it at the right time," she added. "Our whole object is to improve the service here, and if I find that by doing so I'm going out of business, I'd be very happy."

March 21, 1971

New Names in the Board Room

Ethnic Groups Receiving Recognition

By MARYLIN BENDER

Iacocca of Ford, Riccardo of Chrysler, DeNunzio of Kidder, Peabody (and chairman of the board of governors of the New York Stock Exchange), Halaby of Pan Am, Tavoulareas of Mobil Oil, Krysiak of National Tea, Piore of International Business Machines, Goldman of Xerox. Just a handful of names, but they stand out in ethnic solitude on the canvas of big business' power élite.

"The White Anglo Saxon Protestant, or WASPish mold of corporations, is being cracked and discarded," Bob Rawls Dorsey, the president of Gulf Oil, told a management conference last month. As yet he is unable to offer much supporting evidence from his own industry.

In a year when a Polish American named Muskie thinks he might make it to the White House, a Greek American named Agnew is a heartbeat away from the Presidency, an Italian American named Volpe sits in the Cabinet as Secretary of Transportation and another named Siciliano was just named to the Pay Board, it seems appropriate to wonder whether the corporate world is now opening its top executive suites to similar newcomers.

Some think it not entirely coincidental that General Motors picked its first Irish Catholic chairman in James M. Roche after John F. Kennedy settled that issue for the Presidency.

•

Skeptics may argue that men of Mediterranean or Slavic extraction or avowed Catholic and Jewish religious affiliation have long been in command of some of America's mightiest industrial corporations and financial institutions. But those like Skouras, Sarnoff, Giannini, Rosenwald, Block, Paley, Lazarus and Lehman either created their own empires or muscled their way into others by buying financial control.

In the most recent era of conglomerates, aggressive banking and multinational corporations, names like Palevsky of computer wizardry, Hubshman of the factoring family and Merszei the first Hungarian-Canadian on Dow Chemical's board, have established their places in the sun by having their companies acquired (by Xerox and First National City Bank) or by possessing international expertise.

But now evidence is building, however spottily, that a professional manager with nothing but education and ability, can lift himself to the top of the corporate structure even though he lacks membership or ties in the traditional leadership class.

Lee Iacocca, a son of Italian immigrants, had two engineering degrees and salesmanship when Ford needed it. William Tavoulareas, of Greek and Italian parentage, moved up through Mobil's accounting department. Russian-born Emanuel Piore and Yeshiva graduate Jacob Goldman, both Jews, were physicists whose research brilliance was indispensable to brain-capitalizing companies like I.B.M. and Xerox.

Looking to lower levels of executive hierarchy such as the vice presidencies or division chiefs of the auto com-

Richard Bennett

panies or the assistant secretaries and assistant treasurers of the New York banks, one detects a sprinkle of Italian, Slavic and occasionally Jewish names among the Anglo-Saxon, German, Scandinavian and Irish ones.

•

Scanning the last two years' rosters of such corporation-sponsored management training programs at Columbia's Graduate School of Business and the Harvard Business School, the same scattering of Carbones and Merianskis among the field of Clarks, Barretts and Regans is apparent. Slight perhaps, but more than five years ago when there were none.

"I have the impression that these executive programs are not nearly as homogenious as they used to be," said Eli Ginzberg, professor of economics and manpower resources scholar at the Columbia Graduate School of Business.

Prof. Lewis B. Ward of the Harvard Business School has a similar hunch, although, like Professor Ginzberg, he regrets the lack of statistical support.

"I think there has been a steady shift away from some of the kinds of barriers to the executive suite that used to exist," says Professor Ward, who concluded in a study six years ago that social discrimination (specifically religion as well as race and sex) was keeping minorities from careers in management.

His research suggested that companies that were "limited in kinds of hiring tended to be conservative, stodgy and not forward-looking. There seems to be some improvement," he said, and "if the process continues, there will be less tendency for companies to reproduce their old patterns of the well-rounded men having other well-rounded men around to hire well-rounded men."

Richard Thain, placement director of the University of Chicago Graduate School of Business, believes that "the disadvantages of ethnicity, if we take WASP as nonethnic, have washed out to the point where I don't see it as a handicap in larger business. I'm not positive about smaller business, which tends to have a family cast."

In the small-business category, which can be quite large, he added, are the investment banking houses. "They used to have a major ethnic cast, they used to be WASP or Jewish. But now when I hear from Kuhn, Loeb, I hear from Ken Rich," he said, referring to a black alumnus in the firm's buying department.

"Even in the sacred preserves, the old school tie and the old name are not so terribly important. There's been some real recognition that ingrowness did them no good," he said.

Mr. Thain admitted that 20 years ago, "any fellow with a pronounced ethnic name would have been wise to change it or shorten it. But now having a reasonably exotic name is a lot of fun as long as it isn't unpronounceable."

"I was just talking to a student named Caruso," he continued. "Now I think that name is going to be an asset to him. It reminds you of Enrico, the singer. It's kind of romantic. It's better than Johnston."

•

Mr. Thain mentioned two influences widely recognized as prodding business to a more open-door policy. One is what sociologists Peter and Brigitte Berger have called the bluing of America.

If the college-educated children of the upper middle-class that now runs the technological society are revolting against it, as Prof. Charles Reich of Yale maintained in his book, "The Greening of America," then, say the Bergers, the newly college-educated children of working class ethnics and Southern Baptists will take it over.

Or as Mr. Thain says, "In a sense, a guy with a Polish name from the West Side of Chicago will be more eager to be chief partner in an accounting firm than the WASP partner's son from the North Shore who doesn't understand why dad knocked himself out all these years."

Then there is the black issue, which, as Mr. Thain views it, created so high a barrier between racial minorities and whites that business now tends to lump all whites together. Or as Eli Ginzberg says, "The black issue merged all the others."

Seen from another side, black consciousness has stirred other ethnic awareness. Melvin H. King, former director of the Boston Urban League now directing an urban affairs program at the Massachusetts Institute of Technology, asserts that "one of the things we all understand is that if the power structure closes opportunities for some, they develop mechanisms for closing it to others."

From a random survey of the board memberships of New York banks and various universities, Mr. King decided that the "power structure is pretty WASP. They could easily appoint folks from other ethnic groups," he says, meaning Italians, Poles and Jews as well as blacks.

The concept of mutual aid in sensitizing business by different ethnic groups that feel excluded from the executive suite is spreading. Italians and Poles in Buffalo and Chicago have been openly adopting the formulas of the American Jewish Committee, a crusader against corporate bias.

•

For more than a decade, the A.J.C., through its Executive Suite Program, has used intensive research, convincing statistics and volunteer cadres of Jewish business leaders exerting low-key persuasion on major companies and industries.

It has pressed against the doors of social clubs used by the business community to drop their entrenched religious restrictions.

The A.J.C. has also given research and advice to black groups trying to enter executive ranks. In 1968, the A.J.C., with Ford Foundation financing, established a National Project on Ethnic America to focus attention on the frustrations of minority groups other than blacks and Jews and to try to cool tensions between them and blacks.

The William Paca Society of Buffalo (named after a signer of the Declaration of Independence who was of Italian descent) surveyed Buffalo's social clubs and bank management and found them noticeably lacking in Italian Americans.

"Our group is a respected group of judges, bankers and lawyers," said one of the society's former chairmen, Joseph Mattina of the Erie County Court. "We organized because we didn't want undesirables in our ethnic category taking advantage of the swelling pride and frustration of Italian Americans in Buffalo." About 15 to 20 per cent of Erie County's population is of Italian origin, he estimates.

"We've taken subtle action," Judge Mattina said, crediting it to "the philosophy of the A.J.C." Paca Society members have met informally with business leaders conveying a message that Judge Mattina describes as "give us a chance, us who are qualified, give us a chance to prove it."

"The picture is much brighter now," he said, alluding to the presence of Joseph Brocato, vice president of the Manufacturers & Traders Trust Co., which named Robert Millonzi, a lawyer, to its board, and to John Nasca, also a lawyer, to the board of Liberty National Bank. "The breakthrough is being made," he said.

"I was on a program recently where we were talking about people you look up to. Twenty years ago, I would have said Rocky Graziano, Perry Como. But today I point to Lee Iacocca, John Riccardo, Governor Volpe. These men are reflections of our pride shifting to business," he declared.

Last year, the Joint Civic Committee of Italian Americans in the Chicago area, conducted its "Executive Suite Study." Using the 1970 list of Fortune's 500 Corporations and the A. G. Becker Guide to Publicly Held Corporations in the Chicago area, the committee calculated the number of Italians in top management positions (as officers or directors) of Chicago-based institutions.

•

The percentages were minute as, for example, no officers and one director in the four leading banks, 11 out of 440 officers, 12 out of 457 directors in the industrial companies, three out of 71 officers and one out of 83 directors in the transportation companies.

The committee then set up a program of calling on the companies. "We run into this, 'Oh goodness gracious, we're not prejudiced,'" said Anthony Fornelli, a lawyer who directed the study. "They give us a list of people with Italian names on their payroll but these are lower level management. In time, maybe they will go higher but we wonder how long a time it's going to be."

"We're not looking for a showcase or to push people just because they are Italian," Mr. Fornelli emphasized. "The answer is to move men up regardless of their nationality. Don't hold them back because of it."

Mr. Fornelli indicated that his group was scrutinizing related institutions such as clubs and universities. He said:

"We've had a few of our men turned down and others were able to get into very exclusive clubs. You've got **to keep a little pressure on in a nice way and not fall into the trap of the rabble rousers."**

"Now, how many Italian boys are there in the fine Eastern schools and professional schools," he asked. "I find nothing wrong in a man from the old school giving a man from that school a job. Unfortunately, that man has never been Italian. We have to permeate the entire structure."

The Illinois chapter of the Polish American Congress named its poll, "Opening the Door to the Executive Suite."

According to Mitchell P. Kobelinski, president of the chapter and vice chairman of the Parkway Bank, "one and a half per cent maximum" was the number of Polish American officers and directors in Chicago-based companies. One sixth of the population of the Chicago area is of Polish heritage, by his reckoning.

•

Since the study, the congress has organized a committee to coordinate efforts with Italian groups to fight "discrimination based on peculiar-sounding names." The committee has notified the University of Chicago, civic and political commissions and major banks that their hiring practices and board appointments have been examined and found wanting. "Without response from the financial institutions," Mr. Kobelinski noted.

"These companies just are unwilling to blemish their stationery with a strange-sounding name," he said. "We think everyone should learn to pronounce American names. Wojciechowski is a fine American name."

Mr. Kobelinski said that Polish Americans have attained responsible positions in accounting and engineering departments, "but when it comes to the executive suite, where policy decisions are made, they are not represented."

"We want to be included because we feel we have so much to offer. These big national corporations suffered a management drought because they were no longer drawing from the total available pool of talent."

•

Meanwhile, the American Jewish Committee has tailored some of its efforts to the recession. According to Samuel Freedman, acting director of its National Business and Industry Committee, a program of affirmative action had been worked out last year with several airlines that had no Jews in middle and top management except in legal or industrial relations slots.

An A.J.C. affirmative action program is one in which a company admits "there is a problem of lack of Jews in middle management" and agrees to redirect its executive trainee hiring.

"But the bottom dropped out of the airline picture," he said. Airlines have been laying off rather than hiring.

The A.J.C. intends to keep the agreement alive pending an upturn for the industry.

In the last two years, its joint programs with the Jewish Vocational Service in cities like Cleveland and Los Angeles have been geared toward Jewish junior executives and middle managers who suffered in the general layoffs of technology industries.

•

Acknowledging that "there had never been a problem in the aircraft industry, at least with hiring engineers, as there was in petrochemicals," Mr. Freedman said that "now we're concerned that we still get a piece of the action because even during a cutback there still is some hiring."

The A.J.C. is updating its 1963 study of the utilities industry. Then, eight out of 1,000 senior operating executives were Jewish and four of those were lawyers.

A second updating will concentrate on banking. Five years ago, the A.J.C. found that one of 100 middle to senior management officers in commercial banks were Jewish.

"We will be looking to the pipeline, toward the trainees and junior management because banks promote from within," he said.

The pipeline is where most observers are looking for genuine signs of ethnic infusion. "Assistant treasurer is about where they are," Richard Thain said. "As yet we haven't seen all of this filtering way up."

Ethnic Study

Just eight years ago, in their study of New York's ethnic groups titled "Beyond the Melting Pot," Nathan Glazer and Daniel P. Moynihan wrote, "But just what will happen when Italians join Jews in large numbers in attempting to enter the desirable places in American business is hard to predict.

"Perhaps by that time the American corporation will see itself, as its propaganda so often pictures it, as a truly public institution bound to the same criteria of selection that today affect the government service—freedom from bias, and the requirement at the same time to represent and reflect all parts of the American population."

A Code for Professional Integrity

By RALPH NADER

WASHINGTON — At what point should corporate or government scientists, engineers or other professionals dissent openly from their employer-organization's policy? If the professional does dissent, what is there to protect or defend his decision to place his professional conscience over what he believes is his organization's illegal, hazardous or unconscionable behavior?

These are important questions and they are rarely answered in the context of controversies such as the defoliation of Vietnam or the standards for constructing nuclear power plants. "Duty," said Alfred North Whitehead, "arises from our potential control over the course of events." Staying silent in the face of a professional duty, almost invariably articulated in the profession's canons of ethics, has direct impact on the level of consumer and environmental hazards. This awareness has done little to upset the slavish adherence to "following company orders."

Employed professionals are among the first to know about industrial dumping of mercury or fluoride sludge into waterways, defectively designed automobiles, undisclosed adverse effects of prescription drugs and pesticides. They are first to grasp the technical capabilities to prevent existing product or pollution hazards. But they are very often the last to speak out, much less refuse to be recruited for acts of corporate or governmental negligence or predation.

The twenty-year collusion by the domestic automobile companies against development and marketing of exhaust control systems is a tragedy, among other things, for engineers who, minion-like, programmed the technical artifices of the industry's defiance. Settling the antitrust case brought by the Justice Department against such collusion did nothing to confront the question of subverted engineering integrity.

Three Basic Changes To End the Silence In Organizational Life

A prime foundation for professionalism is sufficient independence to pursue a mission that could save lives, secure rights, or preserve property unjustly imperiled by the employer-organization. The overriding ethic of the professional is to foresee and forestall the risks to which he is privy by his superior access and knowledge, regardless of vested interests. Physicians should strive first to prevent disease; lawyers should apply the law to prevent auto casualties; economists should try to clarify product and service characteristics in the context of quality competition; engineers should make technology more humane as a condition of its use; scientists should anticipate the harmful uses of their genius.

All these ideal missions unfortunately possess neither the outside career roles for their advancement nor the barest of independence for the organizationally employed professional to exert his conscience in practice beyond that of the employer's dictates. The multiple pressures and sanctions of corporate and government employers are very effective to daunt the application of professional integrity. When on occasion such integrity breaks through these restraints, the impact is powerful, which might explain the organization's determined policy of prior restraint.

During the past half dozen years of disclosures about corporate and government injustices, the initiators have largely been laymen or experts who were outsiders to the system exposed. The list is legion—black lung, brown lung, DDT, mercury contamination, enzymes, phosphates and NTA in detergents, SST hazards . . . MER-29, and nerve gas storage and disposal. Inside the systems, however, mum's the word.

Three basic changes are needed as a start.

First, Congress should enact legislation providing for safeguards against arbitrary treatment by corporations against employes who exercise their constitutional rights in a lawful manner. At a minimum, such an act would help Congress obtain expert witnesses for its hearings and authorize the courts to protect a professional's "skill rights" in a far more defined manner.

Second, employed professionals should organize to provide a solid constituency for the adoption by management of the requisite due process procedures, which the professional can appeal to or enforce in the courts.

Third, professional societies should clearly stake out their readiness to defend their colleagues when they are arbitrarily treated for invoking their professional ethics toward the corporate or government activity in which they were involved. Most of the established professional societies or associations never challenge corporate or governmental treatment of lawyers, engineers, scientists, or physicians as the American Association of University Professors has done on occasion for university teachers denied academic freedom. And where there is no willingness to challenge, there is less willingness for the employe to dissent.

To require an act of courage for stating perceived truth is to foster a system of self-censorship and the demise of individual conscience against the organization.

Ralph Nader, the consumer advocate, is author of "Unsafe at Any Speed."

January 15, 1971

A U.S. Irony

Critics Hit At Heart Of Free Enterprise

By JAMES M. ROCHE

America is the envy and the aspiration of the world, but there are those who maintain our economic system is not the best, and ask is there not a better way.

Some who question our society and its achivements are young. Some are well-intentioned. Some are sincere.

But there are others. Their final objectives are not what they first profess. Their beliefs, their purposes, run contrary to the principles of the majority of our people. They question many of our institutions, including our economic system. They crusade for radical changes in our system of corporate ownership, changes so drastic that they would all but destroy free enterprise as we know it. Deliberately or not, they are also weakening our free competitive system.

Many observers have noted the recent growth of a group of critics who have launched, and have pressed, an assault on the reputation of America. They have already diminished the idea of America in the eyes of many people, at home and abroad. The damage they do is greatest among our young, who are no longer even given the time to judge our system by their own experience. Instead, their ideals are aborted, at an age and often in a place—in our schools—where ideals ought to be instilled rather than destroyed.

The current disparagement of America holds many ironies. One is that the country is criticized for the relatively narrow area of shortcomings without credit for the broad range of achievement.

The nation is credited less with a superior system of public higher education than it is criticized for not making it freely available to all, even the unqualified. The nation is credited less with an incomparable transportation system than it is faulted for its traffic jams. The nation is credited less with having two-thirds of its families own their own homes than it is condemned for its slums.

Another irony is that many of today's problems are an outgrowth of yesterday's progress. They are marks of a society that, on the whole, has had extraordinary success in meeting the aspirations of earlier generations. Yet some who criticize our system would substitute other systems that have fallen far short of ours.

•

To the extent that doubt and disparagement are directed toward free enterprise, they are of direct and immediate concern to us as businessmen. And it is all too evident that, in too many cases, the climate of criticism is highly adverse to free enterprise. The equating of profit with immorality is spreading a cloud of suspicion and distrust over all we have achieved and hope to achieve.

Much of the modern criticism of free enterprise is by no means idle, nor is it intended to be. Many of the critics have the professed aim to alter "the role and influence of corporations and corporate management in and upon American society." Their philosophy is antagonistic to our American ideas of private property and individual responsibility.

Their ultimate aim is to alienate the American consumer from business, to tear down long-established relationships that have served both so well. They tell the consumer he is being victimized. New products are being foisted upon him, whether he wants them or not. These products are not as good as they should be—that is, they are less than perfect. Businessmen are greedy and uncaring. Corporations are beyond reach and above response to the consumer's needs. Advertising is false. Prices are padded. Labels are inaccurate. Therefore, the consumer, many would have us believe, is helpless and unprotected when he shops, and is really not responsible for what he buys.

•

This delusion—that the consumer cannot trust his own free choice—strikes at the very heart of our free competitive system. The system is founded on the conviction that in the long run the consumer is the best judge of his own welfare. The entire success of free enterprise can be traced to the vitality it gains by competitive striving to satisfy the discriminating customer. To destroy the concept of consumer supremacy is to destroy free enterprise. If the consumer can be convinced that he really does not know what is good for him—and this is what the critics try to do—then freedom leaves free enterprise.

Every unwise impairment of free enterprise carries some additional costs to 200 million Americans. It carries other great collective costs to the extent that it further reduces the ability of American industry to compete in the markets of the world.

Business today is expected to respond to the new aspirations of the society it serves. This broad public expectation must be recognized, and these new challenges must be accepted. The costs of many are not prohibitive. For example, the costs of providing greater job opportunities, particularly for minorities, can usually be absorbed in the normal course of business.

The same is true of the cost of supporting community and educational activities—business' traditional citizenship role. And for these, we do get value. However, in other areas, for example in the control of pollution, costs are usually substantial. To the extent that they cannot be absorbed, they will raise the price of the product and in turn the over-all level of prices is our economy.

As a nation we must be mature enough to face up to the costs involved in meeting our new aspirations. It can mean a weakened competitive position in the world. It can mean higher prices for the consumer and higher taxes for the citizen. This is no dire forecast. This is already a fact. We are weaker abroad. We have experienced higher prices and higher taxes.

Yet we must not allow this to slow our nation's progress toward the fulfillment of our social aspirations. Our task is to achieve our national social objectives at the least possible cost to our society, to assure full value for the dollars that must be spent, to mount an efficient effort. This is clearly a job where business, and businessmen, have much to contribute. Society must define its objectives and establish priorities.

•

In the end, management must be responsive to the wishes of the stockholders. Management is obliged to inform the stockholders as to the problems and the short-term costs as well as the potential long-range benefits of a greater and more direct involvement in social objectives. Then, management must abide by the owners' decision. Through his proxy, every stockholder has that right to decide and must exercise it. After that has been done, management has the responsibility to manage, to preserve and protect the business while leading it in the directions pointed by the stockholders.

Having pitted consumer against producer, some critics are now busy eroding another support of free enterprise—the loyalty of a management team, with its unifying values of cooperative work. Some of the enemies of business now encourage an employe to be disloyal to the enterprise. They want to create suspicion and disharmony and pry into the proprietary interests of the business. However this is labeled—industrial espionage, whistle blowing or professional responsibility—it is another tactic for spreading disunity and creating conflict.

The dull cloud of pessimism and distrust that some have cast over free enterprise is impairing the ability of business to meet its basic economic responsibilities—not to mention its capacity to take on newer ones. This, as much as any other factor, makes it urgent that those of us who are in business, who have made business our career, who are justifiably proud of our profession, that we stand up and be counted. It is up to us to reaffirm our belief in free enterprise.

Mr. Roche is chairman of the General Motors Corporation. His remarks are excepts from a recent speech to the Executive Club of Chicago.

April 11, 1971

Concerns in Many Cities Leaving for the Suburbs

By RICHARD REEVES

When the General Dynamics Corporation announced two months ago that it was moving its national headquarters out of the city, New York . loss appeared to be St. Louis's gain as the company announced:

"St. Louis is well-located, offers excellent facilities at reasonable cost and provides major living advantages for our people."

But St. Louis gained almost nothing.

General Dynamics has since decided to move to Clayton, Mo., a St. Louis suburb of 16,000 people that has been pulling business out of the Missouri city for 10 years, just as Greenwich, Conn., has pulled business from New York and as Southfield, Mich., has pulled business from Detroit.

The exodus of business from downtown to suburb—a subject much discussed here because of corporate moves in recent months—is not a New York phenomenon, but a national pattern, according to reports from correspondents of The New York Times in 10 cities.

In fact, in Detroit the exodus has reached such proportions that two prime symbols of civic identity, the Detroit Lions football team and The Detroit News, are moving out, the Lions to a new stadium in Pontiac and The News to a new satellite printing plant in Sterling Heights.

With that, a banner at the last banquet of the Detroit Press Club facetiously made one request: "Will the last company to leave Detroit please turn off the lights?"

In St. Louis, which like other cities has a local group—Downtown St. Louis, Inc.—trying to hold or expand downtown business, the number of merchant licenses has decreased from 6,302 in 1969 to 5,608 this year, and manufacturing licenses from 1,270 last year to 1,210 this year.

The suburban business exodus has—and not surprisingly—hit the older cities of the North hardest—cities like Detroit, plagued by older buildings, racial tensions, strikes, school problems, crime and tax increases.

Until the last few years the effects of the suburban moves were mitigated somewhat by expansion of the national economy and growth of many corporations that remained in the cities. New York, for example, was losing hundreds of manufacturing companies and dozens of corporate headquarters, but it was still producing enough jobs to fill new office towers rising all over Manhattan.

The same thing happened in other cities, including St. Louis, which invested hundreds of millions of dollars to rebuild its downtown section. But now, in both New York and St. Louis, businessmen are wondering whether those shiny new towers will be filled with desks and clerks for long.

Some Gains Reported

There are also major breaks in the business-to-the-suburbs pattern, particularly in the newer cities of the West Coast and Southwest. Los Angeles, Portland, Ore., and Houston, are much different places than New York, and their economic development agencies issue glowing reports.

"We are still bringing industry in," said Howard Chappell, president of the Los Angeles Economic Development Board. And John Kenward, executive secretary of the Portland Development Commission, added: "We just have a freshness and vitality in the central city that is refreshing when compared to the Midwest and East."

Kansas City, Mo., has also managed to hold its position as the unchallenged business center of its area, by extending city boundaries into unincorporated suburbs. The area of the city has grown from 60 square miles to 317 in the last 25 years.

Thus, at the moment, Kansas City has something that the Mayors of New York or Detroit will never have again—100 square miles of undeveloped land.

The need for land to expand is a primary factor that drives corporate offices, manfacturing and assembly plants, and even athletic teams, out of central cities.

Space and Costs Cited

"We've contacted firms and asked why they moved," said a spokesman for the Boston Economic Development Industrial Commission. "The prime reason is lack of space and the high cost of space. Only a handful—less than 10 per cent—even list crime, vandalism, congestion or taxes."

But, in other cities—particularly Detroit — city officials and businessmen do tend to talk about the spectrum of urban problems. The vice president of a Detroit insurance company who asked not to be identified, said several major moves had been based on insidious institutional racism."

The insurance executive reported:

"A vice president of [he named a prominent organization] told me that they wanted to move for one reason—to get rid of low-echelon workers, like file clerks and typists. These days in Detroit those workers have to be black."

Some urban spokesmen—New York's Economic Development Administrator, Ken Patton, is one—believe the decisions of companies to move to the suburbs often reflect the feelings of one or two men at the top of the business.

They point to the General Dynamics move and the fact that the company's new chairman, Donald S. Lewis, is moving the headquarters a few minutes driving time from his home near Clayton. When he resigned as president of McDonnell-Douglas, Inc., in St. Louis last year to join General Dynamics in New York, Mr. Lewis's family stayed in the St. Louis suburbs, and now he will be rejoining them.

Clayton itself is an example of what older downtown areas, with all their problems, are competing with. The St. Louis suburb, which calls itself "the Executive City," has aggressively recruited business to its grassy land since World War II. It now has offices with jobs for more than 40,000 people, and its 16,000 residents have not had local taxes increased since 1954. The business that has left St. Louis pays the tax bill.

How It Looks Elsewhere

The situation in other cities surveyed by correspondents of The New York Times follows:

NEW ORLEANS

"This is a very serious problem for us, if for no other reason than because it reduces our city sales-tax collection," says Robert E. Develle, the city's Finance Director.

New Orleans does not compile statistics on its suburban exodus, but it has lost the Elmer Candy Company, the Diebert-Bancroft Machinery Works, automobile dealers and numerous distributors of national products. Most companies have moved to Tangipahoa Parish, which offers tax-exempt bonding for industrial construction.

ATLANTA

Despite the construction of 10 million square feet of office space in downtown Atlanta in the last 10 years, the city has lost many major corporate offices to suburban office parks, including Sinclair Oil, Shell Oil, the Continental Can Company, Avon Cosmetics, the Piedmont Life Insurance Company, and Monsanto Chemical Company.

CHICAGO

"A lot of industries have moved out, but they've been replaced with commercial-type businesses," says Dever Scholes, director of research of the Chicago Association of Commerce and Industry.

The association compiles industrial and commercial development statistics, which show that the number of new industrial projects and industrial expansions have steadily decreased in the city and now total only 24 per cent of similar suburban projects.

But office-building, warehouse and financial-institution projects have increased in Chicago in recent years, and are now growing at about the same rate as similar suburban projects.

BOSTON

The Mayor's Economic Development Industrial Commission reports business loss is a "seious, but manageable, problem." As in many other cities, Boston officials say that they are losing small and medium-sized manufacturing concerns—perhaps 100 in the last five years—but that new office jobs have helped the city "weather the storm."

MILWAUKEE

"We've lost very few companies to the suburbs," says Harvey Hohl, chief economist of the Division of Milwaukee Development. "When we lose them, they normally go to the South or West; they pull out altogether."

Mr. Hohl estimates that his city has gained as much business as it has lost, even though the Jos. Schlitz Brewing Company and other major local companies are building new facilities in the suburbs, because they have run out of space to expand their city operations.

April 28, 1971

No Lack of Social Commitment

But Bars Remain To Major Business Aid Soon

By ALLAN LUKS

The public is being misled into believing that big help in solving the nation's social problems should be coming from business soon. It is not.

The misconception arises because the heavy coverage of business' social efforts by the news media continues to concentrate on the company that has declared it must maintain social programs, the executive who argues that profits should be his only interest and the groups pressing companies to adopt policies reflecting a greater social concern.

The overwhelming majority of the nation's major corporations have social involvement programs. Getting the corporate sector to declare itself committed is not what is now hindering and even stopping social efforts by business.

The declarations have been made. The real blocks are now more mundane and complicated. They arise out of the very foundation of American corporate structure.

It is the company president, for example, who decides to commit the firm socially. He then turns the daily running of the program over to a middle manager, a person competing to rise in the corporate structure.

How willing will the middle manager be to allocate these funds to risky (financially or to the corporate image), limited-profit ventures? Yet, among the choices available, these projects might be the socially neediest. And these social purpose funds normally form a small part of the middle manager's responsibility in the company. How much increased internal corporate recognition will he earn from the way he chooses to allocate these monies?

But these questions, and the others touched on here, are the surface problems. Their source, the answers, arise out of corporate orientation, purpose—essence.

The middle manager's reluctance, for example, is due in large part to specialization, one of the main roots of corporate strength. But just as specialization tends to narrow the individual mind, its limiting effect is far greater on the corporation that only thinks and is alive during working hours.

Then how does a company begin to change the values on which it bases recognition, salary, advancement? To what extent can this reorienting be done without hindering the goals upon which the company's existence depends?

Or consider corporate competition, which will quickly place a company at a disadvantage if its social expenditures — grants, loans, employment training, etc.—exceed those of competing companies. At present, industrywide social programs are few. And until competitors are able to put pressure on each other into accepting equal commitment levels, there is going to be a reluctance and holding back among companies on their social declarations. But if companies are eventually forced into publicly putting pressure on each other, this would change the most basic rules of how, what and why business advertises.

And how does a company determine its commitment amount? Should the company choose a percentage of assets or cash flow based on what it feels it can afford? But is this its proper share? Too much?

If a company adopts a specific dollar pledge, what happens if the concern experiences financial problems and can't fulfill it? Is the company's responsibility to cut back on its social efforts first, or only as a last resort? But without the public pressure generated by a specific pledge, won't efforts wither with each company's financial problems, personnel changes, loss of interest and frustration in dealing with social ills?

And in what problem areas should a company involve its social efforts? What expertise does business have to make these choices? Should a company follow the pressures of public interest groups? But their interests — urban, minority business, investment priorities—seem to change every year.

Does a democracy require that a company allocate its social commitment according to the priorities determined by representative government? This would mean, for example, that private lenders would continue, as now, to finance new or completely rehabilitated low-and moderate-income housing developments, since these loans are federally insured, but not finance riskier moderate rehabilitation, which loans the Government refuses to guarantee and which is vitally needed to stop the ever increasing rate of abandonment and deterioration in the central cities.

Business needs government at all levels, to reorder its priorities and eliminate waste and inefficiency or the nation's social resource gap will never be filled—no matter what private enterprise does. Also, the social efforts of business cannot be truly successful without government aid through legislation, supporting programs, guarantees, tax credits and subsidies. But wouldn't the corporate sector's daily courting of politicians for its own vital purposes be sharply hindered if business began putting pressure on these politicians on social matters?

●

These are the types of questions now blocking social efforts by business. They concern, simply, the techniques companies are now finding they must choose to implement their social declarations. The techniques eventually decided upon will determine how much the corporate sector will be generating into the country's desperate social resource gap, and when.

The New York Times/Robert Walker

Allan Luks at building on East 119th Street. Upper Park Avenue Community Association is sponsoring renovation. Life Insurance Association of America is financing work.

Public pressure will continue to mount on private enterprise to decide on its techniques (and to choose certain ones) as the nation's social ills worsen and government not only pleads that it lacks the resources to solve these problems but also cuts back on many of its admittedly inadequate programs. And this pressure is healthy both for society and business.

But once made these choices can affect the very basis of corporate structure and the basic role private enterprise plays in society. And the public and politicians must begin to realize that because of this it will take time for business to resolve these questions, and to begin generating significant amounts to help solve the nation's social problems.

Mr. Luks is assistant director of the Urban Affairs Department of the Life Insurance Association of America. The Department coordinates the industry's $2-billion social investment program.

May 30, 1971

The Corporate Conscience

The Xerox Corporation, by inaugurating a program that will grant employes extended leaves at full pay to allow them to engage in social action programs, has opened a new chapter for the corporate role in modern society. Though anathema to conservative economists, who see efficient production with a view to maximum profits as a corporation's only legitimate function, the Xerox viewpoint is entirely in tune with the emerging legal interpretation of the corporate conscience.

A historic step in that direction was taken by the Standard Oil Company of New Jersey in 1953 when it instigated a test suit to establish the right of a corporation to donate funds to colleges and universities. In a landmark opinion, the New Jersey Superior Court ruled at the time that such benefactions in fact responded to a "sacred duty" and that "what promotes the general good inescapably advances the corporate weal."

The new Xerox program, at an annual cost of $500,000, takes that concept a considerable step further, not only into public service but also into potential controversy. While the plan properly rules out involvement in partisan politics or illegal acts, it deliberately and courageously opens the door to the kind of social action, such as civil rights, which may to some stockholders appear radical or heretical.

Such risks are well worth taking. They should be measured against the program's potential as an answer to young people's disaffection with a corporate life that many consider a callous withdrawal from a society in crying need of service and reform. In the long run, American corporations will surely be the gainers if they can persuade new generations that economic success and social concern can be full partners.

September 19, 1971

Fund Leaders Reject Bid For Social-Policy Rules

Special to The New York Times

WASHINGTON, Oct. 14—**Leaders of the mutual fund industry largely rejected today a proposal that they establish rules requiring mutual funds to take into account the** social policies of corporations in which they invest shareholders' money.

The board of governors of the Investment Company Institute, which is the trade association of the mutual fund industry, adopted some guidelines on social policy that it said mutual funds ought to think about before making investment decisions.

But the board asserted that "the primary responsibility of the investment company and its management is to produce for its shareholders the optimum financial return . . ."

At the same time, the board sought to minimize the conflict between consideration of social issues and the objective of achieving a maximum return for the shareholders.

Long-Term Interests

It said that since "enlightened corporate responsibility goes hand-in-hand with long-term interests of shareholders, then it follows that there is no fundamental conflict between the investment company's investment responsibility and its approach to issues of corporate responsibility."

Philip Moore, executive director of the project on corporate responsibility, expressed disappointment with the action of the I.C.I. board.

Mr. Moore was one of several public-interest lawyers here who had asked the trade group to set up standards and procedures under which mutual funds could bring pressure on corporations to follow what he considered to be more socially responsible policies.

Mr. Moore said that the I.C.I. had "left these matters of corporate responsibility in the hands of the investment companies."

As a result, he said, his organization would "pursue on a company-by-company basis, our efforts to require mutual funds to try to compel their portfolio companies to be more responsive, particularly in the areas of of minority hiring and the environment."

Mr. Moore had wanted the I.C.I. to compel mutual funds at the least to require more information from corporations in these areas, for example, the statistics on the number and classifications of jobs held by blacks, women and other groups.

The trade association's board did list seven subjects that mutual funds should examine before investing.

They were:

Lawsuits relating to compliance with Government environmental social and economic standards; corporate spending to comply with such standards; fair employment practices; investments in certain foreign countries; product safety records; advertising practices and procedures for nominating corporate directors.

The statement approved by the I.C.I. board recommended strongly that mutual funds not attempt to evade responsibility for the policies of their portfolio companies by failing to vote at stockholder meetings or splitting their votes.

A mutual fund, as the legal owner of corporate shares "has the responsibility for voting its shares," the statement said. "Any delegation of this responsibility appears highly questionable . . . in our judgment, most investment company shareholdwers expect their management to deal with proxy proposals."

October 15, 1971

Many Environment Ads Held 'Blatantly False'

By GLADWIN HILL

Some of the nation's largest corporate advertisers have leapt so eagerly for the environmental bandwagon that they have ended by sprawling in the dust, a business research organization reported yesterday.

The Council on Economic Priorities said an extensive study of the recent spate of corporate environmental advertising indicated that much of the material was misleading and some of it "blatantly false."

Some companies have incurred so much criticism that they have dropped environmental pitches entirely, and some executives have been bluntly admonishing the corporate world to stick to candor and eschew hyperbole, the organization said.

The council is a New York-based nonprofit organization that produces reports on various aspects of corporate performance for the guidance of investors and the business world generally.

Among examples of "falsity" cited were a Southern California Edison company ad depicting as a contented resident of power-plant water waste, a lobster said to have come "from nowhere near the plant"; a Standard oil of California ad representing the Palm Springs courthouse as a company research center; and a widely criticized Potlatch Forests, Inc., ad depicting, as an example of company pollution abatement, an attractive stretch of Idaho's Clearwater River unrelated to the concern's operation.

Of 289 pages of advertising, costing about $6-million, in 1970 issues of Time, Newsweek and Business Week magazines, researchers found that more than half was from the five industries pinpointed in independent studies as having the most pollution cleanup work to do—electric utilities, steel, oil, paper and chemicals.

As examples of misleading material, the council cited:

¶A boasting ad about pollution abatement by the Armco Steel Corporation, defendant in five air and water pollution suits, one by the Federal Government;

¶An ad saying "Texaco prohibits the discharge of oil into the sea anywhere in the world"—although a Texaco refinery spilled 200,000 gallons of diesel oil into Puget Sound at Anacortes, Wash., last April.

¶An International Paper Company ad announcing "a $101-million, four-year plan to combat pollution."

"The ad omits as much as it includes," the council commented. "International Paper has been among the last paper companies to recognize its responsibilities. . . . Nor does it place the $101-million expenditure in any frame of reference.

"The reader does not know that Weyerhaeuser, with less than half the pulp production and fewer mills, has already spent $125-million. Or that Scott [the Scott Paper Company] with one-quarter the pulp production of International Paper, plans to spend $85-million."

Spokesmen for the companies taxed with "falsity" acknowledged technical inaccuracies in the ads but suggested that they did not impugn the validity of the advertising messages.

A spokesman for Southern California Edison said the lobster depicted was "identical in size, specie and apparent satisfaction" with lobsters dwelling in large numbers near one of its power plant's cooling-water discharge points.

November 5, 1971

Study Assails Work of Agricultural Colleges

By WILLIAM ROBBINS

Special to The New York Times

WASHINGTON, May 31 — **The big agriculture and technical universities of the United States have strayed so far from their original research mission of aiding consumers and rural communities that they injure the people they were intended to serve, a study by a public-interest research organ**ization has found.

As a result, the group said in a report released today, those institutions have been largely responsible for troubles in rural areas that have generated major problems in the cities.

The group, the Agribusiness Accountability Project, said that the big universities had focused on research that favored big, agriculture-oriented corporations and the biggest producers while neglecting the more numerous small farmers, farm workers and others in rural communities and nearly ignoring the interests of consumers.

A Six-Month Study

About a million displaced people a year are pouring into the cities as "the waste products of an agricultural revolution designed within the land-grant [college] complex," the report said, adding:

"Today's urban crisis is a consequence of failure in rural America. The land-grant complex cannot shoulder all the blame for that failure, but no single institution — private or public—has played a more crucial role."

At a news conference on the report called today by the research team, Henry Fortmann, northeast regional coordinator for the universities' experiment stations, rose to deplore the study, which he charged derided serious and dedicated researchers. He said, however, that he had not read the report.

Meanwhile, a spokesman for the National Association of State Universities and Land Grant Colleges, which represents the institutions studied, said: "The association believes the report requires careful study and it intends to analyze its contents fully before responding to them in detail." He issued a preliminary statement for the association saying:

"Great agricultural achievements are not accomplished without some side-effects, and the accusation that the land-grant colleges and universities have been taken over by the great food conglomerates and have driven the little farmer out of business tends to overlook the dazzling array of abundant foods this cooperation has made available."

The report, titled "Hard Tomatoes, Hard Times," documents the findings of a six-month study. It will be the basis of a lawsuit planned by the Agribusiness Accountability Project against public and educational officials involved. It will also be the subject of hearings called today by Senator Adlai E. Stevenson 3d, Democrat of Illinois, who is chairman of the Senate Labor Committee's Subcommittee on Migratory Labor.

The study was made by a team of 12 researchers headed by James Hightower, who is the director of the project and the author of the report.

The research group is a Washington-based organization financed by the Field Foundation and sponsored by the Center for Community Change, which in turn is financed by the Ford Foundation. It is often mistaken for efforts started by Ralph Nader, the consumer advocate, but they are unrelated even though their aims and techniques are similar.

Following are the major charges contained in the report:

¶The land-grant institutions' research has focused on projects that primarily aid agribusiness and the biggest producers, such as a two-story factory at Cornell that tests manufacturing methods for processors and, elsewhere, the development of big and costly planting and harvesting machinery.

¶A "cozy" relationship exists between land-grant researchers and big companies like the Chemagro Corporation, which was cited as obtaining a university study of one of its chemical products for a contribution of $500,000. The report said corporate benefits to land-grant personnel such as consultant fees raised serious questions of conflict of interest.

¶The institutions abuse the consumer by breeding crops primarily for easier harvest by the big machines, with little regard for quality or food value. It cited the "hard" tomato, developed by the University of Florida for mechanical picking.

¶Many projects, called "research of the absurd," are merely frivolous, such as a mechanical test to calibrate how hard shoppers should squeeze a grapefruit to determine its firmness and texture.

The concept of land grant colleges—schools endowed with public lands or the monetary equivalent and offering an opportunity for an education of the children of 19th-century farm and factory workers — originated in the Morrill Act of 1862. But the major provisions for research were made in the Hatch Act of 1887.

The Hatch Act provided for "researches basic to the problems of agriculture in the broadest aspects, and such investigations as have their purpose the development and improvement of the rural home and rural life and the maximum contribution by agriculture to the welfare of the consumer."

That is where the land grant system has failed, the research group charges. "It has abandoned that historic mission," the report said, continuing:

"In fact, consumer interests are considered secondarily, if at all, and in many cases the complex works directly against the consumer. Rural people, including the vast majority of farmers, farm workers, small town businessmen and residents, and the rural poor, are ignored or directly abused by the land-grant effort."

The report acknowledges: "American agriculture is enormously productive, largely due to research conducted through the land grant college complex." But it adds: "The question is whether the achievements outweigh the failures, whether benefits are overwhelmed by costs."

The report, though it makes frequent disclaimers of suspicion about the motives of its subjects, often uses harsh terms and makes severe judgments.

There has been little effort to develop machinery that small farmers—the vast majority—could afford to buy and use on limited acreage, it said.

And it reserved a large portion of criticism for the fact that only 5 per cent of the institutions' 6,000 man-years of research annually is devoted to "people-oriented" projects, such as plans to improve the quality of rural life.

$750-Million Expense

Citing $750-million a year in public funds — Federal, state and county—going to the agricultural divisions of the colleges and to related experiment stations and research facilities, the research group asserted:

"The public has a right to expect that those intellectual and scientific resources be more than a subsidy for corporate agribusiness."

The report urged a new look at the priorities of the land-grant institutions, with a view toward redirecting energies and resources. It said more emphasis should be put on ways to help people stay in their rural homes and to improve their circumstances.

It also urged legislation to prohibit private business from earmarking contributions for projects that would primarily serve their own interests and to prohibit professors and university officials from accepting fees or outside jobs that might create conflicts of interest.

The research team documented its charges with findings from a study of research reports from the universities themselves as well as with the results of interviews and investigations on several campuses.

Among projects that primarily serve big producers, the report cited those designed to mechanize the harvest of 25 food crops, from apples to tomatoes, with efforts often duplicated at several campuses. Five institutions, for example—the Universities of Arkansas and Illinois and Iowa State, Louisiana State and Ohio State — are at work on mechanizing the harvest of strawberries, it said.

Cornell, in addition to building its factory to test methods of production for food processors, studied, in cooperation with the National Association of Food Chains, the profitability of members' operations, the report said.

Similarly, it went on, Ohio State tested plastic-coated cartons for dairy products; Virginia Polytechnic Institute studied factors affecting the shelf life of sweet-potato flakes, and the University of Wisconsin developed a fast process to produce mozarella cheese that was "mild but satisfactory for normal uses."

"To a large extent," the report said, "agribusiness firms bought their way into the [land-grant] community." The researchers cited substantial totals of contributions, such as $227,158 in 1970 by chemical, oil and drug companies for research at the University of Florida's Institute of Food and Agricultural Sciences.

The individual grants found were usually small, but they apparently bought valuable research, such as the Chemagro Corporation test — also at the University of Florida — of "Chemagro 7375," an experimental nematacide or roundworm killer.

Along with projects like the test for correct methods of squeezing a grapefruit, the report grouped efforts such as attempts at Michigan State University to breed a seedless cucumber and to cross broccoli with the white cauliflower to produce a green cauliflower. It could find little utility in either product.

In the same category it classed a Cornell study, made with a grant from Superior Pet Products, Inc., on the cleaning of dogs' teeth.

And of a number of studies on the development and care of golf course grasses and athletic-field turfs, including two on "the heat-retaining properties of artificial turf," the report said:

"These researchers are playing around with games while rural America falls apart."

Even among projects apparently aimed at aiding rural people, the report found first appearances often illusory. Among rural housing studies, for example, it found such projects as a test at Iowa State on the effect of foot traffic on wood floors. Most such studies, it said, proved on close examination to be a service to agribusiness.

The New Environmental Executives

Companies Are Adding Specialists These Days

The recent advent of environmentalism in the United States has often brought about a negative reaction from corporate management. But in some companies it has created a new breed of corporate officer whose function is to deal solely with environmental-control issues.

Skeptics are quick to note that the creation of new titles is a long way from accomplishments and that many companies are attempting to counter environmental moves.

The General Motors Corporation, for instance, told the Environmental Protection Agency last week that it could not meet the agency's 1975 deadline on auto-exhaust emissions. The Ford Motor Company and the Chrysler Corporation both backed G.M. in asking for a one-year extension of the E. P. A.'s deadline.

Neil C. Elphick of the FMC Corporation noted last week that "industrial society responds to pressure" and that while "the better managed companies are responding to this pressure in orderly, timely fashion, a lot of them are being dragged, kicking and screaming environmentally into the 20th century."

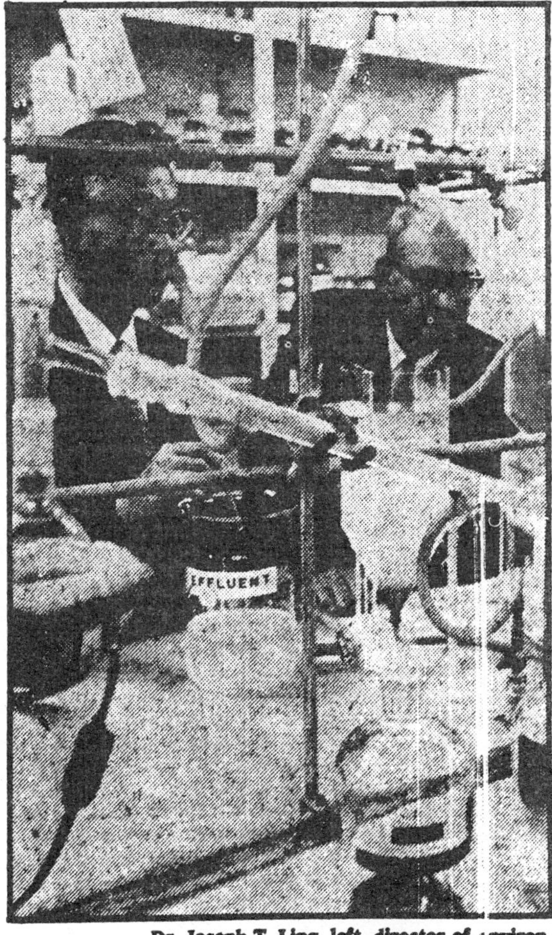

Dr. Joseph T. Ling, left, director of environmental engineering, experimenting in the 3M Company's laboratories in St. Paul. Donald Guthrie, vice president, is with him.

Houston

James M. Quigley, a lawyer by training, joined Champion International in 1968 as vice president-environmental quality. Prior to coming to the company he was a Deputy Attorney General of Pennsylvania, a two-term United States Representative from Pennsylvania, an Assistant Secretary of Health, Education and Welfare and, in 1966, the first Commissioner of the Federal Water Pollution Control Administration.

His background leads him to play a large role before Government agencies. Last week, for instance, he conferred with staffers at the Federal Power Commission in connection with an environmental impact statement and a right-of-way matter involving a new plywood facility planned in South Carolina.

Of his job, Mr. Quigley noted: "We're trying to understand what the Government and public are demanding and to make that understandable to line managers."

Mr. Quigley, like many of the corporate officers who deal with environmental matters, spends a good deal of time traveling. Much of his time this year has been spent at Champion's pulp and paper mill in Pasadena, Tex.

Located on Houston's severely polluted ship channel, Champion's existing waste-water treatment facilities have recently become the nucleus of a joint undertaking with Air Products and Chemicals, Inc.; the Atlantic Richfield Company; the Crown Central Petroleum Corporation, and the Petro-Tex Chemical Corporation.

The five companies, each with plants in the area, have agreed to send industrial waste water to a central treatment facility that will be built to utilize Champion's present installation. The new facility will be built by the Gulf Coast Waste Disposal Authority, which was established by the Texas Legislature in 1969. The agency deals with pollution-control problems in a three-county area.

Wilmington

Richard E. Chaddock, who holds a doctorate in chemical engineering from the University of Michigan, has been executive coordinator of environmental health for Hercules, Inc., since 1968.

In corporate circles some of his sentiments might be regarded as heresy. At a seminar last week at Valley Forge, Pa., Dr. Chaddock declared:

"It has become a privilege rather than a right to operate plants. More importantly, this privilege may be taken away if plants do not comply with pollution-control laws.

"It is also becoming obvious that even more stringent rules will be in force in the future. Most of the Federal and state legislation was needed and some of it should have been enacted even earlier than it was."

Dr. Chaddock, who cocoordinates the activities of the 10-member environmental health committee at Hercules in Wilmington, Del., also keeps abreast of the work and problems encountered by pollution coordinators at each of the company's 48 plants in the United States. He describes his function as seeing to it that the operating departments carry out Hercules's policy on pollution control.

New York

Neil E. Elphick, who holds a bachelor's degree in chemistry from Clemson University and is a graduate of the Advanced Management Program at the Harvard Business School, has been directly involved with environmental matters since 1970 at the FMC Corporation. His formal title is director of the environmental planning department of the company's chemical, fiber and film departments.

Noting that "the problems are out there," Mr. Elphick outlined his itinerary for last week, which included stops in Philadelphia; Charleston, W. Va.; Denver; Modesto, Calif.; Pocatello, Idaho, and Front Royal, Va.

In his view, environmental matters are "now a full-fledged function with all reasonably well managed companies." He added that business is maturing in this respect; it is beginning to recognize that environmental control is a function that can be managed."

Mr. Elphick believes that a maturation process is taking place in the Federal and state bureaucracies, but that "if we have our way, we're going to mature first."

He explained that one of the current objectives in the environmental area is to reach the point "where managers can anticipate where the problems are going to be."

Minneapolis

Joseph T. Ling, who holds the first Ph.D. degree in sanitary engineering granted by the University of Minnesota, is director of the environmental engineering and pollution control department at the Minnesota Mining and Manufacturing Company. He is a nominee of the United States Chamber of Commerce for one of five Presidential appointments to a 15-member commission that will undertake a three-year study of the 1972 Federal Water Quality Act.

Dr. Ling supervises a staff of 38 men and women whose major assignment is to anticipate pollution problems and search for solutions.

His feeling is that "we must be one step ahead of the law." To do so, Dr. Ling's department annually makes a five-year forecast on environmental matters for each of 3M's 30 divisions. The forecast includes budget recommendations covering anticipated environmental problems and an estimated cost of their solution.

DOUGLAS W. CRAY

March 18, 1973

The Selling of the Energy Crisis

By PHILIP H. DOUGHERTY

Probably no public issue since the end of World War II has generated as much corporate advertising as the energy crisis.

With the exception of the coal industry, associations of fuel producers and their individual members have been paying for messages of concern just as public utility associations and their member companies have.

The message has apparently gotten across. One indication is that the American Petroleum Institute has narrowed the thrust of its campaign from all of the United States to just its thought leaders.

The deluge of advertising from the various associations and companies has talked about depleting fuel supplies; the need for new exploration and facilities; how to conserve energy, and pollution.

And it has infuriated some consumerists and environmentalists who complain that the power companies are urging the conservation of energy at the same time that they are promoting its use.

"They create a public issue and a public climate and use it to try to do things they've been unable to do in the past," said Samuel Buffone of the Stern Community Law Firm in Washington. He went on to mention such areas of interest as import quotas, oil-depletion allowances and the environment.

"We watch this advertising with growing horror, with the way they're trying to mislead the American public into a crisis attitude," said George Alderson, legislative director of the Friends of the Earth Foundation.

As recently as 1969 the American Petroleum Institute, an association of the nation's oil companies, was involved in the Discover America program to increase gasoline consumption. Nevertheless, just two years ago with the Leo Burnett Company, the A.P.I. launched a massive $4-million television and newspaper campaign with its new theme, "A country that runs on oil can't afford to run short."

With the help of such advertising and the press coverage the energy crisis is getting, according to a Burnett executive, "knowledge of the crisis has become universal." He said he based this statement on judgment rather than research.

Now the A.P.I. in its 1973 campaign is zeroing in on community and business leaders and opinion molders. This is a smaller and therefore less expensive target to reach and will cost $2.5-million.

The institute is using the three newsweeklies, Sports Illustrated, Harper's and Atlantic, The New Yorker and National Geographic. It is also using two publications one seldom sees on media schedules for corporate campaigns — Editor & Publisher and Broadcasting, the trade magazines of the newspaper and broadcasting industries.

The first two spreads (one of which has run and the other which is about to run are headlined "How Can America Head Off Energy Shortages" and "Can America Have Enough Energy and a Clean Environment?"

The A.P.I. offers three booklets on the subject in the ads, and, according to the agency, after only one ad the institute received 3,000 requests for 7,000 booklets.

The American Gas Association, with 150 members, has been doing its advertising through J. Walter Thompson for the last six years. Using TV entertainment and information specials and magazines, its efforts are aimed at general as well as business and industrial users.

Its current budget is just under $6-million but, according to Thomas H. Lane, a vice president at Thompson, "We are outspent 6 to 1 by all who advertise electricity and its competitive uses."

The association's present advertising extols the attributes of gas, instructs on ways to conserve it and tells what the industry is doing to insure an adequate supply.

About 35 to 40 per cent of

the advertising, Mr. Lane said, is aimed at "maintaining the residential market."

"But," he added, "we are not seeking new load; we're working entirely on a replacement basis."

The gas group's major competitors, the investor-owned electric light and power companies, have been advertising through N. W. Ayer & Son since 1941, originally promoting their type of operation over Government-owned utilities.

More recently, however, the Electric Companies' Advertising Program advertising in news and business publications has heralded the wonders of electricity and the needs of its suppliers.

The 1971 and 1972 campaigns stumped for new generator facilities. The 1973 campaign is seeking higher rates, noting:

"All of this building and research requires larger investments than have ever been needed before. We must earn enough to attract billions of dollars in new money from investors. At the same time, virtually all the costs of providing you with electricity keep rising. This combination of circumstances inevitably means increases in electric rates."

Meanwhile in Washington, Carl Bagge, spokesman for the National Coal Association, noted somewhat sadly, "Long before our energy peers "thought it was fashionable, we were trying to get a national energy policy. No, we don't have an advertising budget, the industry doesn't have that kind of money."

That certainly would not seem to be the case of the individual utility companies, almost all of which are advertising on the subject, the Electric Energy Association reports.

This has stuck in the craw of many consumer groups, apparently because news reports are constantly coming from around the country of protests of one kind or another against the consumer ending up paying for the advertising of something that is a necessity and at the same time in short supply.

And if there is an energy shortage, why is there so much gasoline brand advertising?

"They are merely trying to switch brand preference, not to increase consumption," answered an ad agency executive.

A number of oil companies touch frequently on the energy crisis and its ramifications in their corporate advertising campaigns or run single — and hopefully educational — broadsides.

One of the more notable efforts has been by the Mobil Oil Company, which has touched on every facet of the problem in the one-quarter page ads it runs every Thursday on the Op-Ed Page of The New York Times.

The company has also run ads in The Washington Post, The Los Angeles Times, The Chicago Tribune and The Wall Street Journal and once ran a series of energy commercials on radio in three markets.

Last November and December in newspapers, consumer and trade magazines, the Continental Oil Company made a major— and what it considers a successful — corporate commitment.

It blanketed the nation with an ad headed "Energy & America." The copy for the ad was excerpted from a speech by John G. McLean, the Conoco chairman and chief executive, who is also chairman of the National Petroleum Council's Committee on U. S. Energy Outlook.

More than 70,000 copies of the full text of the speech — which was offered in the ad — have been requested of the company and Ruddick C. Lawrence, vice president for public relations and public affairs, noted that "Cronkite displayed the ad on his news show; four more services carried stories about it abroad; all levels of government have asked for copies; The Associated Press and trade paper columnists devoted their columns to it. It was in every sense a blockbuster."

Mr. Lawrence, who headed up the A.P.I. committee that launched the institute's ad program three years ago, feels that perhaps 20 per cent of the population were aware of the energy crisis a year ago, but "now, with the shortages on us, it would be hard to believe that 100 per cent don't know."

Among the more active critics of some of the energy-crisis advertising is the Media Access Project, a one-and-a half-year-old public interest law firm that has taken legal action in a number of states in behalf of clients who would like to air conflicting opinions on some of the matters raised.

"We don't generally believe they're outright liars," said Thomas R. Asher, the executive director, "but we do believe there is another view to be heard."

April 1, 1973

Corporate-Responsibility Groups Broaden Tactics

By MARYLIN BENDER

Public interest groups are pressing a record number of proposals for corporate action at the annual stockholder meetings that are now beginning. But at the same time the corporate social-responsibility movement is broadening its tactics.

As specialized public-interest groups proliferate, coalesce and sometimes bicker, corporate challenges are increasingly taking a legalistic turn. Lawsuits are being filed. Petitions are being made to government agencies that regulate corporations and industries.

Last week, for example, a Federal district court held the directors and officers of the New York Telephone Company personally liable for a $50,000 contribution from corporate funds to a state bond issue referendum in violation of the state election law.

The suit against the company had originally been filed by the Project on Corporate Responsibility, a Washington-based organization that conducted Campaign G.M. in 1970 and 1971.

•

Though that proxy contest against the auto maker stimulated the interest of college students and institutional investors on their shareholder-voting duties, none of its proposals received more than two per cent of total vote.

"The near impossibility of actually winning a shareholder campaign coupled with the complexity of filing an acceptable proposal have convinced many groups that other tactics may be more effective," notes the Council on Economic Priorities in its forthcoming report on the corporate-responsibility movement.

C.E.P., a non-profit, New York-based research group has itself joined with others in a case involving advertising claims made by Standard Oil of California for its F310 gasoline additive.

Ironically, the Project on Corporate Responsibility may resort to legal action to save its own life.

For the last two and a half years, the Washington-based organization of lawyers and researchers has been seeking tax-exempt status as a public interest law firm and research center. Currently, some $500,000 in foundation grants are tied up pending approval by the United States Treasury for such tax-exemption.

Last week, Philip C. Sorensen, chairman and a founder of the organization, said he had been advised by his attorney to expect a negative ruling soon from the chief counsel of the Internal Revenue Service despite earlier indications of approval from the staff of the I.R.S. exempt organization bureau. The I.R.S. confers such exemptions if it views a public interest law firm as engaging in educational or charitable activities.

Asserting that "these actions indicate political interference," Mr. Sorensen said that if the tax-exemption is denied, "we would go to Federal court and seek some sort of injunctive relief to permit us to survive while the issue of the tax-exemption was litigated. Otherwise, the whole question becomes moot. With these grants outstanding, they can delay us right out of existence."

Application Amended

He pointed out that last June, the tax-exemption application was amended to sever the Project's shareholder proxy activities from its litigation and research because word had been received "that the I.R.S. says proxy fights are not tax exempt."

A spokesman for the Internal Revenue Service, declining comment on the status of the application said last week that there had been no published ruling on the tax-exempt standing of proxy challenges but that applications for tax-exempt status are subject to varying degrees of interpretation and scrutiny.

Mr. Sorenson and his associates argue that proxy fights like Campaign G.M. are educational. However, they did reorganize their activities.

In the reorganization, the original name—Project on Corporate Responsibility—was assigned to proxy challenges, and the Center on Corporate Responsibility was set up to pursue research and shareholder litigation. The Project has submitted three proposals to seven corporations for this year's annual meetings.

The International Business Machines Corporation, Levi Strauss & Co. and the Xerox Corporation are being asked to establish procedures for shareholder nominations to the boards of directors that would appear on the corporate proxies.

Two other proposals on political influence were directed at the Eastman Kodak Company, the General Motors Corporation, the Union Oil Company and the International Telephone and Telegraph Company. One proposal would require disclosures about political contributions. The other, aimed at corporate lobbying efforts, asks the companies to describe how they communicated their positions "concerning any matter of unusual significance to the corporation" to the Federal Government as well as the names of corporate and Government officials involved in its news release, the project linked the proposal "to the I.T.T. affair as an example of the kind of 'impropriety' and damage to the corporation's reputation the disclosures called for in this proposal can prevent."

Although the proposals will not appear on any of the corporate proxy statements (except possibly General Motors, which is still being processed) because the Securities and Exchange Commission ruled them ineligible on a technical point, they will be submitted from the floor at the annual meetings.

As the C.E.P. report comments, "Many groups raising them (proxy proposals) feel the first step to reform is forcing investors to consider them."

All told, some 20 groups are submitting at least three dozen proposals to as many major corporations this year. They confront operations in Southern Africa, military contracts and conversion to peacetime production, the environment, consumerism, minority employment, political influence and reform of the corporate structure.

Nearly half of the proposals emanate from church groups who seem to be carrying the ball on the Southern Africa and military-industrial issues. A coalition of churches has asked for disclosure of operations in Southern Africa from eight corporations.

Resolutions Withdrawn

Several of them — the Burroughs Corporation, I.T.T., Texaco, Xerox and, last week, Ford—subsequently agreed to supply the information, and the resolutions were withdrawn.

The proposal drew only 1.03 per cent of the vote at the First National City Bank meeting last week, well below the S.E.C.'s 3 per cent requirement for submission again within five years.

The church-sponsored resolution on Exxon relates to exploration for oil off the shore of the Portuguese territory of Angola. Exxon has applied for an exploration license. The churches, want a broad-based committee to study the implications of this venture and to report on it.

Continental Oil and Phillips Petroleum are being asked to wind up operations in Namibia (another group of Episcopal churchmen are asking the same of American Metal Climax and Newmont Mining) while Mobil Oil and Newmont have been requested to initiate equality of job opportunity in their operations in countries that practice racial discrimination.

Clergy and Laity Concerned, an antiwar group, have filed resolutions with Honeywell, General Electric and Exxon asking these corporations to stop producing anti-personnel weapons, to suspend military contracts with Government agencies related to the war in Southeast Asia and to establish committees to study conversion to civilian-oriented production.

Environmental resolutions have been filed by Episcopal churchmen against American Metal Climax and by the Field Foundation against the Pittston Company. A Nader-related group of senior citizens is asking the American Telephone and Telegraph Company and Illinois Bell for special rates.

Those long-time corporate critics, the brothers Lewis and John Gilbert and Mrs. Wilma Soss will persist in presenting their resolutions on corporate procedural reform, which would strengthen the power of minority shareholders and their financial interests.

The C.E.P. report observes that "with expansion and diversification and the definition of broad common areas of interest also comes discord and disagreement." Allusion is made to the contradictory resolutions from two church groups within the Protestant coalition filed with one company, Newmont Mining, one urging the company to leave Namibia, the other to practice equal job opportunity there.

Competition Exists

There has also been both cooperation and competition between the research groups established to help institutional investors make up their minds on voting their proxies.

The Investor Responsibility Research Center, Inc., established in Washington last December and funded by the Ford and Rockefeller Foundations and the Carnegie Corporation has enrolled 52 subscribers, the majority of them universities and foundations, and has thus far given them detailed analyses of half a dozen proposals.

Partly because of the existence of the I.R.R.C., interest in the second institutional-investors conference planned for this month by the Center on Corporate Responsibility was so slight that it was canceled.

"One of the basic things we're after are more fundamental questions than appear on the resolutions," Mr. Sorenson said. "We're disappointed if institutions think everything's resolved by subscribing to the Investor Research group. These are the surface issues."

The Center on Corporate Responsibility is undertaking extensive research projects on such topics as corporations whose business is based primarily on women and the plight of hotel employes. The aims of the research program, says Susan Gross, director of research and education, "is to produce exposés to pressure corporations to change policies" and to inform other advocacy groups such as black or feminist organizations "of the need to focus more on corporations."

The chief difference between the Center and the loosely constructed Nader movement is the former's single-minded emphasis on corporations where some of the Nader groups and other public interest law firms and research organizations are looking toward government agencies and other aspects of consumer issues.

'Crowding' Is Cited

"The field is getting a little bit crowded but so far not overcrowded," said John Simon, a Yale law professor and coauthor of "The Ethical Investor," a study, of the problems universities face in making social decisions about their investment portfolios.

Professor Simon is also chairman of Yale University's Advisory Committee on Investor Responsibility, appointed last year to make recommendations on how the university should vote its proxies. An open meeting recently called by the committee drew an audience of 10, half of them committee members. Similr signs of massive indifference were noticed at a hearing by Harvard's committee for the same purpose. Last year, black students staged a sit-in at Harvard asking the university to sell its stock in Gulf Oil, which operates in Angola.

Nevertheless, Professor Simon does not believe that corporate responsibility is withering away. "Corporate gadflies will keep it alive even if students aren't beating up the flames so institutions will have to deal with it," he said.

Last week, Exxon sent several representatives to tell institutional investors at a forum sponsored by the Africa Policy Information Institute why they should vote no on the church-sponsored resolution on Exxon's exploration of Angola.

The Exxon people stressed their belief that the primary corporate mission was to develop energy resources. But they said that international and domestic public opinion were also a genuine concern, and that if public opinion and Government policy were ever jelled in opposition to Exxon's activity in Southern Africa, it might be dropped.

April 2, 1973

Spreading the Word About Good Works

By ERNEST HOLSENDOLPH

Almost everyone has at least a line about it. In many instances, there is a whole page devoted to it. "Corporate social responsibility" has become the watchword in company annual reports this season. But what it means depends on what report is read.

Many companies talk a lot about the money they spend on pollution control, efforts at hiring and promoting women and minorities and on consumer protection, usually concluding that it is good and in the public interest.

In most cases the reader would have to learn elsewhere that these moves, for the most part, are mandated by Federal, state and local laws that came into force despite the best efforts of some businesses.

On the other hand, corporations describe a wide variety of community projects, educational funding and other pursuits that are incidental to their normal operations but that flow from the feeling by many executives that good works also pay dividends.

Eli Goldston, president of Eastern Gas and Fuel Associates in Boston, has been one of the most persistent advocates of corporate responsibility. A four-page insert into his company's 1972 annual report is one of the most detailed discussions of corporate performance in this area.

Called "Toward Social Accounting," the piece attempts to analyze with figures the internal performance of Eastern Gas and Fuel with respect to industrial safety, minority employment, charitable giving and pensions.

Mr. Goldston said he had selected the areas because they could be quantified more easily than others.

•

"We need a new kind of social accounting that goes beyond G.N.P. for the nation," Mr. Goldston said, "and goes beyond net profit for the firm."

The figures were not startling, but Mr. Goldston includes a reply card to his shareholders asking them to check off in boxes their reaction to the statistics and to recommend where priorities should be placed in improving them.

Along the same lines, the Connecticut-based Scovill Manufacturing Company carries a kind of social balance sheet in its report, discussing its involvement in employment opportunity programs, environmental control, community activities and consumerism.

For instance, listed as "assets" in the employment area are the fact that minority employment has increased from 6 per cent in 1963 to 19 per cent in 1972 and that women constitute 40 per cent of the work force.

"Liabilities" in the employment area include the problem of fluctuating employment at various plants and the need to upgrade minority and female employes.

John R. Bunting, chairman of First Pennsylvania Corporation, writes as a prologue to his company's annual report:

"If we are to continue to make progress in our recognition of the worth and dignity of each individual human being, then business must acknowledge its role as the lodestar of all social advancement.

"And if business fails in this responsibility, the entire fabric of our industrial society will be torn apart."

On this ominous note, the book opens withh a color picture of five rusting cans floating in a polluted pond followed by a picture of two wrists—one black and one white — handcuffed together over a copy of the Constitution.

The entire body of the annual report, except for performance figures for last year, is a set of eight interviews with various public figures on social concerns.

Among the interviews, conducted by Mr. Bunting, are sessions with Ralph Nader, the consumer advocate, Carl B. Stokes, former Mayor of Cleveland and now an N.B.C. news commentator, and Barbara Hackman Franklin, a White House assistant who recruits women for high positions in the Administration.

One company has taken a step to broaden its communications, and give a lesson in business. Macmillan, Inc., the book publisher that produces a variety of educational materials, has turned out a children's edition of its annual report, written on a fifth-grade reading level.

Most other annual reports are not so preoccupied with social responsibility, but many deal with the subject.

Jones & Laughlin still spends most of its time making steel, but the company chairman, William R. Roesch, spends a third of his letter to shareholders talking about new plants that will meet pollution-emission standards, charitable contributions and equal-opportunity hiring efforts.

On a full page devoted to "social responsibility," the Atlantic Richfield Company said it had removed 1,000 billboard signs in 36 states because "overcommunicating can be deleterious." The company also said it would increase to $1-million its deposits in minority-owned banks.

The Monsanto Company, the diversified multinational chemical company, used part of its social-concerns space to warn against the threat of major legislation to curb foreign operations of American-based companies. Such measures would "limit the use of technology in other countries," among other things, Monsanto argued.

Some companies, such as General Telephone and Electronics and CPC International, tried to underline equality in hiring practices by printing a page of employe pictures showing various races and colors.

Evidently the new consciousness of companies affected aesthetics as well. The RCA Corporation, depicting an engineer on its cover, used an engineer who looks the part and not a studio model.

The Graniteville Company, a textile manufacturer, has a male model on its cover strutting down the runway, with women looking on.

Most companies have struggled beyond the pictures of pretty bikini-clad girls modeling the latest wrench or widget. Also, evidently few continue to believe that pictures of sweating blacks digging ditches persuade the reader that the company provides equal employment opportunity.

Not all of the companies were captured by the fever, of course. The General Motors Corporation, the world's largest industrial company, continues to voice its opposition to emission-control standards as now set up.

Saying it expects to spend $1-billion this year trying to meet the standards, G.M. adds: "To the extent that their benefits to society fall short of their costs, the standards in effect mandate a waste of productive resources."

April 8, 1973

Stockholder Dissent

Activists' Issues Win Support of Institutions

By MARYLIN BENDER

The frail and colicky movement to reform the American corporation through stockholder action seems to be emerging into a state of cantankerous health.

Corporations have learned that they will continue to be called to account for their social conduct at least at annual meeting time—and not only by the perennial gadflys who make it their business to criticize corporate management.

Institutional shareholders such as universities, pension funds and foundations have decisively broken the "Wall Street rule" as it is called by investor responsibility activists. The rule holds that institutional stockholders automatically vote proxy proposals in favor of management or, if dissatisfied with management, sell their stock.

According to a survey of the voting on shareholder resolutions this year undertaken by the Investor Responsibility Research Center, only one-fourth of the institutions voted their shares with management across the board. The survey, which is being issued today, found that the rest either abstained from voting or voted against the management of some two dozen major corporations on a range of proposals.

These had to do with operations in South Africa, corporate political activities, mine safety, environmental protection and candidates for corporate boards of directors.

•

The shareholder advocates of increased corporate responsibility "achieved more success this year than in the past both in votes and in terms of corporate reaction," observed Elliott J. Weiss, executive director of I.R.R.C., which in the acronym-prone world of public-interest activism is pronounced "irk."

The center was founded last December under the prodding of Stephen B. Farber, assistant to the president of Harvard University, to provide impartial analysis of corporate social responsibility issues for institutional investors and thereby help them do their annual meeting homework. I.R.R.C. was funded by the Ford and Rockefeller Foundations and the Carnegie Corporation. It has 56 subscribers who pay $500 to $5,000 a year for its services.

The survey was based on questionnaires sent to 112 institutions (its own subscribers and 56 other large investors). "Substantive responses" were received from 42 institutions, more than half of which asked that their replies be kept confidential.

By I.R.R.C.'s tabulation, seven of the resolutions received enough votes to make it likely they will appear on next year's proxies. According to Rule 14a-8 of the Securities and Exchange Commission, a corporation can omit a resolution if it did not receive 3 per cent of the vote the first time it was voted on, 6 per cent the second time and 10 per cent on subsequent presentations.

•

Shareholder proposals in large and widely held companies that are the target of activists precisely because of their size and symbolic value, regularly go down to resounding defeat. They usually receive less than 2 per cent of the vote. The reformers expect to be routed. They chose the proxy proposal as a vehicle for attracting public attention and a method of registering concern by ballot.

All the more noteworthy then is the 8.6 per cent vote for a resolution by a women's division of the United Methodist Church asking the Caterpillar Tractor Company to disclose information about its activities in South Africa and the 6.13 per cent vote for a proposal by two individual stockholders asking the United States Steel Corporation to affirm its "political nonpartisanship."

A proposal by the Project on Corporate Responsibility asking Levi Strauss & Co. to establish a procedure whereby shareholders may submit candidates for the board of directors received 9.48 per cent of the votes cast.

Four other resolutions that won enough votes to be resubmitted next year involve the Continental Oil Company and the Phillips Petroleum Company (suggesting they withdraw from South-West Africa); The RCA Corporation (a political nonpartisanship proposal) and the Pittston Company (asked to investigate its mine safety and environmental programs).

The I.R.R.C. report noted also "inroads behind the scenes that were not reflected in the results of the votes." Some corporations voluntarily complied with the proposals, which were then withdrawn from the proxies.

The Burroughs Corporation, the Eastman Kodak Company, the Ford Motor Company, the International Telephone and Telegraph Corporation, the Minnesota Mining and Manufacturing Company, Texaco, Inc., and the Xerox Corporation all agreed to disclose details of their South African operations as a coalition of Protestant churches had asked.

•

In another instance, Walter A. Haas Jr., chairman of Levi Strauss, met with members of the Project on Corporate Responsibility two weeks ago in Washington to discuss feasible ways that ordinary stockholders might make nonfrivolous nominations to the board of directors.

Mr. Weiss of I.R.R.C. also stressed that "institutions are at least thinking about these problems and considering these resolutions separately and seriously."

"The first phase of the investor responsibility movement was telling them they had to face these problems. They are facing them, but not everyone is happy with the way they are facing them," he added.

Though he did not mention it, some activists find it ironic that major institutions have eagerly turned over their research to I.R.R.C. while the Project on Corporate Responsibility, the maverick instigator of corporate reform (it conducted the two pioneer stockholder campaigns against the General Motors Corporation in 1970 and 1971), had to struggle for financial support. It is currently sidelined as it contests the denial of its tax-exempt status by the Internal Revenue Service.

•

Last Thursday, Federal District Judge Charles R. Richey in the District of Columbia held hearings on the denial, which the Project charged was politically motivated.

Mr. Weiss also defined as "a major second generation problem of the investor responsibility movement" the misunderstanding between institutions and activists over the voting of the issues.

Many institutional investors didn't vote for resolutions they supported in principle on the ground the resolutions were poorly drafted. Those who drafted them contended that principle should be the overriding consideration since there was no hope of commanding a majority vote anyway.

"With some of those proposals you may agree with the idea but the way they're written up you have to be against them or abstain," said Peter Liberante, a merchandise manager for the Phillips-Van Heusen Corporation and co-chairman of its employe committee for corporate responsibility.

The committee was appointed last year to recommend how the stock proxies in the company's $12-million pension funds should be voted. It voted against management on seven proposals and abstained on two.

Nearly half of the shareholder proposals submitted this year were made by Protestant church groups.

"Three years ago, investor responsibility was a somewhat controversial issue within the church but more and more it's seen as the responsible thing to be in," said Timothy Smith, executive secretary of the Interfaith Committee on Social Responsibility in Investments, a coalition that drew cooperation from Roman Catholic groups for the first time this year on the issue of disclosure of military contracts and conversion to peacetime production for companies like General Electric.

Regional church groups are increasingly setting up investor responsibility committees and the church coalitions are building alliances with other groups such as labor organizations, he said.

July 8, 1973

Charity

Corporations are becoming less charitable these days.

Although corporate giving increased between 1970 and 1972, corporate profits increased more, and the percentage of pretax income given away decreased to 0.73 per cent from 0.82 per cent. The Conference Board surveyed 443 companies, which gave $323-million to charity, or one-third of all corporate donations.

Health and welfare were the largest beneficiaries of corporate generosity, receiving 42 per cent of the gifts.

Smaller corporations — those with fewer than 250 employes — had the highest rate of giving, 2.4 per cent of pretax income.

November 18, 1973

The Limits of Corporate Responsibility

By Neil W. Chamberlain. 236 pp. New York: Basic Books. $10.

Corporate Power and Social Change

The Politics of the Life Insurance Industry. 232 pp. Baltimore: Johns Hopkins University Press. $10.

Corporate Power and Social Responsibility

By Neil H. Jacoby. 282 pp. New York: The Macmillan Publishing Co. $10.

By STEPHEN B. SHEPARD

In the wake of the traumatic riots that shook American cities in the 1960's, many businessmen suddenly began sounding like social activists. They stumped the ghetto to recruit the hard-core unemployed, launched training programs for dropouts, and started to counsel and fund minority-owned businesses. Hardly a week passed without a speech by a blue-chip executive on "corporate responsibility" or the "new social contract." Then came 1970, a year of recession *cum* inflation, and many of the companies quickly retreated to the sanctuary of their balance sheets. Scores of voluntary social programs were phased out, like outmoded factories, and many of the hard-core trainees found themselves back on the street. Today, though some gains have been made, black capitalism is little more than a slogan and corporate programs have scarcely dented urban problems.

None of this surprises Neil Chamberlain, who teaches at the Columbia Business School. In "The Limits of Corporate Responsibility," he argues that corporations can do "remarkably little" about social problems—from urban and environmental ills to worker alienation and unsafe products. Constrained by the need to profit and grow, he says, companies are "trapped" in the business system they helped create.

Thus, the rise of national and multinational corporations means that business operates with little concern for the needs of any single community. If conditions worsen in a city, many companies simply move, like frightened residents fleeing a decaying neighborhood. Worse, he says, the values of the business culture — autonomy, materialism and competition—have discouraged development of public institutions capable of handling urban woes.

Moreover, the mass-consumption society that feeds business has created a mass-production technology that inevitably results in shoddy goods and unhappy workers, he says. Any major effort to stress product quality or end the boredom of the assembly line will be doomed by the dictates of mass consumption. Similarly for environmental control. "When the costs of achieving more stringent standards of air and water pollution drastically affect the price of consumer goods," he writes, "we can expect public resistance."

In sum, "we cannot rely on big business for social reform." All we will get are "modest concessions," "incremental changes" and "a public relations program designed to reassure worried segments of the public that their concerns are not being ignored." Chamberlain has presented a persuasive case, especially for business impotence in the face of staggering urban ills, which he regards as the greatest threat to the corporate order. But he overdraws some other problems to fit his thesis, especially the conflict between environmental and economic needs.

Environmental control is a special type of corporate responsibility. For one thing, pollution standards are not voluntary, the way hiring policies still largely are. For another, pollution is amenable to technological solutions. We know how to purge sulfur oxides from utility stacks at reasonable cost, for example, yet we are not remotely close to eliminating racial prejudice or providing decent education for the disadvantaged. I'm not suggesting a technological fix exists for every environmental problem or that pollution can be curbed without economic dislocation. But Chamberlain overestimates the costs, underestimates the public's willingness to pay, and erroneously identifies all consumption with severe environmental degradation. He has seriously misjudged the environment movement's force, necessity and progress.

Nonetheless, the capability of corporate America does appear limited in other social areas. On urban problems, Chamberlain's pessimism is supported by "Corporate Power and Social Change," a scholarly study by Karen Orren that reveals how the life-insurance industry invests its money. Focusing on Illinois, she finds the industry consistently discriminates against blacks seeking housing mortgages. "Until 1955, black tracts were virtually cut off" from industry funds, she reports, and even today blacks still lag far behind whites. Though companies claim that most blacks are too poor to qualify for mortgages and ghetto investments are too risky, Orren's data show otherwise. She finds, for example, that blacks receive less financing than whites even at the same level of family income. Her conclusion: the industry is tainted by "institutional racism" resulting from the way companies determine "safe loans" and from the biases many underwriters hold about "property values."

In 1967, the industry announced, with considerable fanfare, a nationwide program to invest $2-billion (0.6 per cent of assets) in the inner city. The program did funnel some money to moderate-income families in Chicago's mixed neighborhoods, she finds, but it barely reached the city's blighted core. Like Chamberlain, Orren believes that corporate preoccupation with autonomy and profit will limit all such voluntary ventures.

A third book on the subject, a naive and bland work called "Corporate Power and Social Responsibility," offers little new perspective. Never fully grasping the issues, educator Neil Jacoby sketches the criticism of business in the weakest way, rather like a defense attorney presenting the prosecutor's case. In the end, he offers a "social environment model" for corporate behavior, which holds that a company "must become socially involved to maximize its profits." But this P.R. pap ignores what happens when social goals conflict sharply with corporate profits.

The large corporation, though still primarily a private economic entity, has such vast social impact (where it locates, whom it hires, what technology it pursues) that it has become a public trust with a communal constituency. It would be nice to believe that corporations will voluntarily respond to what Oliver Wendell Holmes called the "felt necessities" of our time. But public needs must generally be shaped by citizen action or law. The progress of the last few years in environmental control and nondiscriminatory hiring, for example, owes less to corporate responsibility than to citizen protest and the legal clout of the Environmental Protection Agency and the Equal Employment Opportunity Commission.

The lesson is clear. Because meaningful social action usually takes money from corporate coffers or requires drastic changes in executive attitudes, voluntarism is rarely more than a marginal response by a handful of companies. Sustained progress requires effective legislation or direct pressure to institutionalize environmental control, minority hiring and the like into the workaday world. And since regulators have a nasty habit of becoming the captives of those they are supposed to regulate, the government's own performance must be open to citizen participation and monitoring—as has been done, successfully I think, with environmental regulation.

Does that leave corporate responsibility as so much blather? Not really. All corporations are constrained by the same laws and the same profit imperative, yet some respond better than others to social problems. Thus, Owens-Illinois has a better pollution control record than its competitors; Manufacturers Hanover has a higher proportion of minorities and women in key positions than other banks; U.S. Steel (a notorious polluter) operates safer coal mines than any other company. The reasons for the differences vary but this varied response to the letter and spirit of the law defines corporate responsibility. It is a rather limited definition, I admit. But unlike the overblown rhetoric of the past, it has the great virtue of not promising more than it can deliver. ■

Stephen B. Shepard is environment editor at Business Week.

NOTE. The name of the author of "Corporate Power and Social Change," Karen Orren, was inadvertently omitted.

Against 'Naderism'

By Anthony Harrigan

NASHVILLE—America is experiencing an antibusiness binge in which every corporate mistake or imperfection, from a defective can of tuna to a single oil spill off the California coast, becomes an excuse for slowing technological development, proposing new economic controls and urging nationalization of private enterprise.

This shrill crusade against business is as absurd and unfair as it is hurtful to the public. The deficiencies of business are nothing as compared to the excesses of unions with their monopolistic power used to paralyze cities and transportation systems.

Yet business is increasingly subjected to smear attacks and to near-totalitarian demands such as Senator Henry M. Jackson's call for placement of Government representatives on the boards of energy companies. In the view of the critics of business, everyone has rights except the corporation.

The current Naderized antibusiness atmosphere has produced proposals for radical change in the United States economic system, including demands for Federal chartering of business, deconcentration of large corporations, mandatory placement of union representatives on boards of directors, and switching authority to Government for location of plants, choice of products and control of advertising. In effect, there would be a take-over of stockholder rights without due process.

No evidence has been produced indicating that a shift to a socialist or maximum-regulation society would make the American people any wealthier. To replace big business with big government is hardly a progressive step. In country after country, economic controls and nationalization have been a disaster.

It is dismaying that the antibusiness big lie finds any acceptance. The increases of wealth in this country have been the result of activity by individuals and corporations, not Government. The managerial failures of the Federal Government are notorious. The Postal Service can't deliver mail with dispatch; how can anyone believe that bureaucrats could do a better job developing oil resources than companies with decades of experience and global expertise?

Antibusiness groups have proliferated in recent years. They would strip business management of the right to manage. They regard profit as a dirty word. Congress has responded with a barrage of regulations covering numerous industries. Thus, today, we have a condition of regulatory overkill.

Where business has gone wrong is in failing to stand up for its rights against those who seek totalitarian controls over private property. Unhappily, many large companies have sought to appease the enemies of free enterprise.

They have resorted to soft public-relations campaigns instead of battling against Naderism with the most important weapon, truth. These instances of corporate cowardice have only produced more extreme attacks on business.

Ironically, some of the big oil companies that have been drawn and quartered in public long have been among the most tame and meek corporations. They have engaged in ecology-fad advertising and substituted lyrical humbug for tough talk about the disastrous effects of excessive Government regulation.

The foes of a free economy set out several years ago to create a crisis of confidence in capitalism. That's the meaning of the Nader movement. Using sensational charges against business, they have endeavored to create hostility toward the economic system that has enriched our nation. In considerable measure, they have succeeded. If economic freedom is to survive in this country, businessmen must fight back in the forum of public opinion.

Anthony Harrigan is executive vice president of the United States Industrial Council, a nationwide association of conservative businessmen.

April 17, 1974

HIGH COURT CURBS SUITS ON BEHALF OF LARGE GROUPS

Ruling on Class Actions Will Limit Key Legal Weapon of Consumers and Others

Special to The New York Times

WASHINGTON, May 28 — The Supreme Court ruled today that a class action on behalf of a large group of people must be thrown out of court unless all those people who can be identified receive notice of the lawsuit and the person who brings it pays for that notice.

The decision will almost certainly make it more difficult to use the class action, a relatively new legal weapon for people with a small individual stake in a large important issue common to many others.

The ruling, which was unanimous as to its general conclusions, adds significantly to restrictions in effect since 1969, when the high court held that the individual claims of a class could not be pooled to meet the $10,000 minimum claim required before Federal courts would hear a class-action suit. Today's decision applies to antitrust actions, which are exempt from the $10,000 minimum that each member of a class must meet, as well as to consumer, environmental and other actions subject to the $10,000 rule.

The majority held that Federal court rules clearly required notifying all identifiable parties to a class action, so that each of them can bring in his own attorney or drop out if he prefers not to be bound by the outcome.

'Odd Lot' Stock Deals

The case dismissed was a class action brought eight years ago by a group of stocktraders who buy less than 100 shares at a time. They charged that two brokers who handle virtually all this "odd-lot" business were violating the antitrust laws and charging excessive fees.

The vote on the case was 6 to 3, with Justices William O. Douglas, William J. Brennan Jr. and Thurgood Marshall signing a partial dissent. Their quarrel with the majority was relatively small, however, centering on an argument that the particular case could be reshaped rather than dismissed.

The lawsuit was brought by Morton Eisen, who contended only that he had lost $70 through excessive odd-lot brokerage fees, but sued on behalf of a class of some six million other small investors, of whom at least 2.25 million were directly reachable through mailing lists.

Federal District Court estimated that it would cost about $225,000 to notify all these people, and one of the principal issues in the case became the question of who was responsible for this expense, Mr. Eisen or the two brokerage houses—Carlisle & Jacquelin and Decoppe & Doremus—or perhaps all three of them.

Writing for the majority, Justice Lewis F. Powell Jr. said that "the express language and intent" of the applicable rule of procedure "leave no doubt that individual notice must be provided to those class members who are identifiable through reasonable effort."

Justice Powell also declared that Mr. Eisen must bear the full cost of such notice "as part of the ordinary burden of financing his own suit." Federal District Court had shifted 90 per cent of a much more restricted notice procedure to the brokers being sued.

In his dissent, Justice Douglas argued that the case should be sent back to district court to have the class of plaintiffs divided into a smaller, more manageable group, rather than dismissing it altogether.

"The class action is one of the few legal remedies the small claimant has against those who command the status quo," Mr. Douglas said. "I would strengthen his hand with the view of creating a system of law that dispenses justice to the lowly as well as to those liberally endowed with power and wealth."

Today's decision will not affect just class action suits brought in the Federal Courts, for a number of states have rules patterned after the Federal requirement. The Federal rule sustained in the Eisen Case was actually transmitted to Congress by the Supreme Court in 1966 and became effective automatically when the lawmakers did not move to revise it.

As part of its decision, the majority also held that district courts do not have any authority to hold preliminary hearings into the merits of a lawsuit to determine whether it may be maintained as a class action, as was done in the Elsen case.

No one could say precisely as a result of today's decision that some particular class action would be ruled out in the future as too expensive while another would prove practical because of a smaller class involved or a smaller group of identifiable members. The decision cannot be used to reopen past class actions.

In another decision, the Justices dismissed a challenge to a 1972 Washington statute that requires disclosure of a wide variety of financial information, including the incomes of public officials and candidates, spending by lobbyists and details of campaign finance.

The Court said that opponents of the law had not raised any substantial Federal question.

The Washington law was attacked by four public officials receiving no salary or only a nominal amount who contended that requiring them to list their assets and those of their wives was an invasion of privacy. In a second case, a lobbyist argued that some of the reports he was required to file were burdensome and impractical.

May 29, 1974

INDUSTRY RESISTS CAR-SAFETY COSTS

Companies Feel Consumers Will Support Their Fight Against New Standards

By WALTER RUGABER
Special to The New York Times

WASHINGTON, April 5 — The contest between advocates of safer, cleaner automobiles and cost-conscious, style-conscious manufacturers is entering a new phase. After 10 years on the defensive, Detroit is striking back.

Its representatives believe consumers are less attached these days, when many are less affluent and more cost-conscious, to improvements such as strong bumpers, complex braking systems and sophisticated antipollution gear.

The car companies—arguing that Federal guidelines are helping drive up prices at a time of economic hardship—are demanding relief from some existing Government regulations together with a five-year moratorium on any new safety and emissions standards.

Opposing interests, ranging from Ralph Nader to many of the big insurance companies, are defending some or all of the requirements as economical and sensible. They face increasing skepticism and doubt, however.

President Ford seems sympathetic to the industry's cries of distress; the bureaucracy is divided. The internal conflict, the lobbying by both sides, the slow process of making decisions—in many ways they are as interesting as the issues themselves.

The stakes are very high. Pending Federal rules would cost consumers billions of dollars a year—the exact figures are in dispute—while saving thousands of lives and preventing hundreds of thousands of injuries.

Air bags designed to cushion motorists in crashes—a central issue in the current debate—would by themselves raise car prices by about $100 to $250. Proponents say motorists could expect benefits several times as great, however.

During the last six months or so, the argument has taken on a new edge, honed by numerous signs that Federal regulation of the automobile may be undergoing stresses more fundamental than any in the last decade.

For one thing, a proposal to require air bags on 1977 cars has been delayed for several reasons, and Federal officials concede privately that they now would have to issue a new proposal for 1978 models or later.

Detroit on Defensive

The safety push began with the publication in 1965 of Mr. Nader's best-selling book, "Unsafe at Any Speed," and with the passage by Congress in 1966 of the National Traffic and Motor Vehicles Safety Act.

Detroit had lost the political initiative. It was able to weaken and sometimes delay the controls Washington began to impose, but it was forced steadily in the direction safety advocates wanted it to go.

The costs were not insignificant, and the industry passed them along in higher car prices, but in the go-go markets of the late 'sixties and early seventies, consumers paid them cheerfully—or at least indifferently.

Through the 1974 models, according to evaluations by the Bureau of Labor Statistics, safety features added $224 to prices and pollution controls meant $71 additional—a total advance of $295.

The industry's estimates through '74 models are higher. The Ford Motor Company has put the total mandated price increase at $325, the Chrysler Corporation at $344, and the General Motors Corporation [which counted voluntary improvements] at $428.

When the 1975 models went on sale last fall, Government figures showed, new safety devices had pushed up prices by another $10.70 and emissions equipment had added $119.20. By then, buyers were neither cheerful nor indifferent.

The Regulatory Impact

But, as has been the case all along, inflation and changes by the manufacturers are even more significant. The regulatory impact on this year's increase, for example, is barely

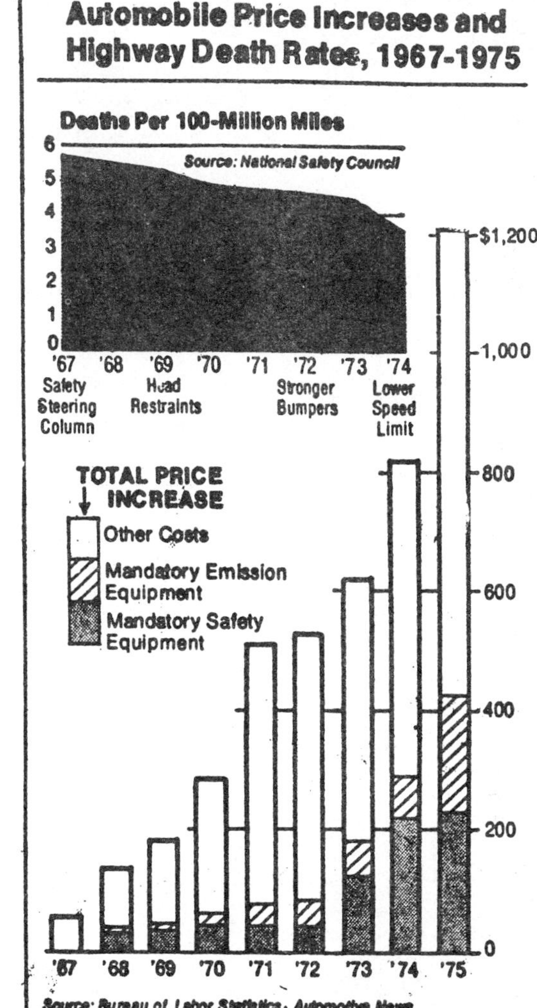

The New York Times/April 6, 1975

a third of the $386 total rise.

Anyway, consumer spokesmen insist, the price increases are more than worth it in the long run, and industry, if it was not so woefully, even willfully inefficient, could do what the Government asks for much less money.

Defenders of the safety program point out that the death rate has dropped steadily in the United States since 1966, when it was 5.7 for each 100 million miles of travel. It was 3.6 last year.

In addition to such benefits, a spokesman for the insurance companies asserted last month that stronger bumper standards alone would save motorists $6-billion in premium payments and repair costs.

At the same time, consumer advocates protest that Detroit squanders huge sums on styling changes while producing safety designs that are often calculated to generate irritation among motorists.

The makers reply they are spending less than in the past on cosmetic improvements, that they are investing billions in smaller and thus more efficient cars, and that Government rules are often inherently inefficient.

Behind these very intricate arguments are the visceral ones

of production and employment. Auto sales fell from 9.66-million in 1973 to 7.44-million last year, the sharpest slump since 1958.

Sharp Drop in Profits

Profits dropped 60 per cent at both General Motors [it was replaced as the world's largest industrial enterprise] and Ford, and the Chrysler Corporation suffered a net loss of $52-million.

And as the earnings reports were being issued, the politically sensitive layoffs continued. More than 200,000 auto workers are now without jobs, and for many unemployment benefits are running low.

While the economic decline is the principal reason for the intensified debate over safety and emissions, there are other factors involved, including the following:

¶The Government is mandating increasingly sophisticated equipment. Ford spent just $5 on each car to meet requirements on its 1969 models, but it has said the new bumpers alone will cost each buyer $208 over the 10-year life of the cars.

¶It is hard to persuade some Americans they should pay more for safety and antipollution equipment at a time when, because of the fuel problem, they are traveling less and at lower speeds.

¶Government regulation in general is coming under closer scrutiny in Washington, with critics blaming it for inefficiencies, anticompetitive tendencies, and a certain amount of inflation.

The National Highway Traffic Safety Administration, a unit of the Department of Transportation established under the 1966 law, regulates the performance of passenger cars old in the United States in about 15 functional areas.

To meet its standards, the manufacturers have installed scores of features, including backup lights and warning flashers, breakaway rearview mirrors, padded dashboards, energy absorbing steering columns, and stronger sides.

Nothing, however, has involved as much effort and concern as Motor Vehicle Safety Standard No. 208, "occupant crash protection," which started with seat belts in 1968 and grew progressively more ambitious.

It has produced frequent controversy—buzzers and ignition interlocks are among the more recent issues—and while it may not be a typical guideline it does offer specific insights into the safety battle.

Under a frequently proposed version of standard 208, motorists doing nothing to protect themselves would have to be able to drive at 30 miles an hour into a fixed barrier and emerge without serious injury.

The companies would be allowed to provide this "passive" restraint in any way they wished, and a few of them, notably Volkswagen, have been experimenting with systems that wrap motorists in straps automatically.

But for most engineers, Standard 208 would mean the air bag, that extensively debated, widely misunderstood device designed to prevent the so-called "second" collision between people and the hard interiors of their autos.

The bags inflate explosively, cushion front seat passengers before they can reach a more unyielding surface, and deflate, all in a couple of seconds. The bags are out of the way before most people realize they have fired.

Early Interlock Advocates

The safety administration believes that this system, if it was installed on all cars, would save 11,600 lives and prevent 620,000 injuries each year and, in all, return to the average motorist more than four times its cost.

But opponents of the air bag contend that people who use their lap and shoulder belts are protected just as well, and in some ways better, and ask why they should be forced to buy a much more expensive restraint.

Because, the air bag advocates reply, most people will not use the cheaper system. The Government estimates that about three motorists in every four wear no resraint of any kind,

Thus pressed, critics of the air bag have come up with some alternatives. One was the ignition interlock, which required the occupants of a car to fasten their belts and harnesses before the vehicle could be started.

Two leading opponents of the bag, Ford and the American Safety Belt Council, were among the earliest proponents of the interlock. The Government agreed to require it on all 1974 models.

The device did result in a dramatic increase in belt use, and it did contribute to the decline in accident death rates, but consumer resistence was intense, and last fall Congress ordered the interlock requirement repealed.

General Motors is the only company that produces a passive system. It began offering the air bag as a $300 option on its 1974 Buicks, Oldsmobiles, and Cadillacs, and so far it has made about 10,000 with the feature.

A lot of the technical doubts have been resolved, but critics of the air bag continue to believe there is insufficient experience to be certain of satisfactory performance when mass-produced for all cars.

That is really only a side argument, however, compared to some of the questions that have been raised over the last several months. There is, for example, a renewed philosophical clash over how far the Government should go to protect people.

Some believe that the Government should order safety improvements on the ground of public health, but others think some of the devices ought to be left to individual choice.

Equally divisive is the economic question. Requiring the Government to appraise the costs and benefits of its rules has become popular in Washington, with far-reaching potential effects.

President Ford issued an Executive order in November requiring legislative proposals and administrative regulations to carry "a statement which certifies that the inflationary impact of the proposal has been evaluated."

The air bag has been the subject of several elaborate cost-benefit analyses, in which experts have made allegedly unbiased judgments on whether the equipment makes financial sense. Completely different conclusions have been reached.

This is in part because no one can agree on how much air bags would cost if mass-produced and in part because of intangibles inherent in calculating the value of an injury or a death.

The disagreement over benefits is even greater. The Government thinks air bags and a simple lap belt would save 8,900 lives and 482,000 injuries a year more than the present belt arrangement.

A principal critic, Economics and Science Planning, Inc., a consulting firm that has made studies for the American Automobile Association and the Federal Council on Wage and Price Stability, forecasts a saving of 3,185 lives and 129,400 injuries.

But while the Government values each death at $242,000 and each injury at $7,000, the conuslting firm put their cost at $189,000 and $3,027 respectively.

The result of these and other important differences is that the safety administration believes the air bag would return 4.2 times its cost while Economics and Science Planning expects a benefit of only 1.1 times cost (against 2.9 times for the present belt equipment).

In the current battle over regulation, one of the principal participants is the Ford Motor Company, and one of the earliest shots was fired on Oct. 1 by the company's charismatic president, Lee A. Iacocca. He said:

"Current and proposed new safety, emissions, and damageability standards for the 1976, 1977 and 1978 model cars would add about $750 per car or $8-billion a year to consumer expenditures, if we could meet them all.

". . . I believe we should have a five-year moratorium on new safety, damageability and emissions standards starting Jan. 1."

On Dec. 9, before members of the Newspaper Advertising Bureau, gathered at the Amer- at the Americana New York, Mr. Iacocca delivered his "Pinto speech," which has acquired a measure of fame as a detailed attack on rules, and on the same day Henry Ford 2d called at the White House.

In his New York speech, Mr. Iacocca asserted that Government standards had increased the price of his company's small car, the Pinto, $284 by 1975 and could be expected to add $847 more by 1978.

Mr. Ford, the company chairman, was accompanied to the White House by his chief representative in Washington, Rodney W. Markley Jr., a golf-playing friend of the President for 25 years.

Other Lobbying Examples

"The discussion centered almost exclusively on the problems caused by present and proposed Government standards of all kinds," Mr. Markley declared. These were said to be "placing an intolerable burden on the economy."

Representatives of the entire industry met with the President a few days later and made essentially the same arguments.

Supporters of the air bag and other devices regard these and other meetings with considerable suspicion. Ralph Nader doesn't get called in for cozy chats with the President, they observe acidly, and one safety advocate said he couldn't even get a letter directly to Mr. Ford.

Industry and White House sources deny there is anything sinister about these contacts. Examples of other sessions cited by both the auto lobbyists and Government officials seem straightforward, even mundane.

For instance, on Oct. 30, several General Motors officials met in a small hearing room on the third floor of the Rayburn House Office Building with staff members of the House and Senate Commerce Committees.

Their listeners included Edward B. Cohen, a professional staff member of the Senate panel, and Michael R. Lemov, counsel to the House Subcommittee on Commerce and Finance.

One of the aides, an air bag proponent who asked not to be quoted by name, described the meeting as unremarkable but useful in that it generated questions he and his colleagues could later throw at the safety agency.

Resistance to the anti-air bag campaign is formidable. Officials of the safety agency are strongly, and in some cases zealously, in favor of requiring the system, so much so that they no longer appear to be seriously lobbied.

Their supporters include a wide range of consumer groups, led by the Center for Auto Safety, a Nader spin-off, and a number of consumer-oriented legislators.

These include Senators Warren G. Magnuson of Washington, Vance Hartke of Indiana and Frank E. Moss of Utah and Representative John E. Moss of California, all Democrats.

With frequent hearings and letters on safety issues, they

try to bolster the safety administration, promising, for example, to "resist efforts to undermine the purpose and intent of the Motor Vehicle Safety Act by this current assault on Federal regulatory activity."

The lawmakers have been joined, in an interesting confrontation within the business community, by insurance companies convinced that equipment like air bags and strong bumpers reduces their losses.

On Feb. 18, two executives of the Allstate Insurance Company, John S. Trees and Michael McCabe, had lunch at Paul Young's, a restaurant on Connecticut Avenue here, with three officials of the Council on Wage and Price Stability.

The Council, part of the Executive Office of the President, views the air bag with great skepticism, as does the powerful Office of Management and Budget. This has caused considerable tension within the bureaucracy.

The council's assistant director for Government operations and research, George Eads, contended in a recent memorandum that there was enough doubt about the air bag "to justify a delay in full-scale implementation."

The new air bag standard, if there is one, will be issued by James B. Gregory, a research chemist for the Union Oil Company of California for more than 20 years before he became the Government Safety chief.

Dr. Gregory has to remain officially neutral until a decision is reached, but there is not much doubt that he continues to feel passive restraints ought to be made mandatory.

Dr. Gregory is certain to consult with the new Secretary of Transportation, William T. Coleman Jr., who has impressed several advocates of the air bag as being favorably disposed.

But most observers believe the Government's policy will originate in the White House and be communicated to Mr. Coleman in some quiet session with Gerald R. Ford. For he, as Dr. Gregory said recently, "is still the boss."

April 6, 1975

Elections Panel to Allow Companies to Raise Funds

BY WARREN WEAVER Jr.

Special to The New York Times

WASHINGTON, Nov. 18—The Federal Election Commission cleared the way today for corporations to invest millions of dollars in contributions from their stockholders and employees in the political campaigns of candidates regarded as friendly to business.

In a ruling that is expected to inject large amounts of money from conservatives into the 1976 Presidential and Congressional elections, the commission split 4 to 2 in deciding that operating expenses of political action programs could be financed from corporation treasuries.

While the commission's advisory opinion specifically authorized the Sun Oil Company to collect voluntary contributions from its shareholders and employees and distribute the money among candidates as it saw fit, it also gave a green light to hundreds of other corporations and business associations to do likewise.

With the new campaign law imposing limits of $1,000 for individuals and $5,000 for committees on political contributions next year, the proliferation of corporate political action committees should ease fund-raising for many Republicans and help to counter the powerful support of organized labor for many Democrats.

Neil Staebler, a Democrat, joined all three Republican members—the chairman, Thomas B. Curtis, Vernon O. Thomson and Joan D. Aikens—in support of the ruling. The dissenters were Democrats, former Representative Robert O. Tiernan and Thomas E. Harris, former associate general counsel of the A.F.L.-C.I.O.

The labor federation and the United Auto Workers had urged the commission to restrict the solicitation of political contributions by corporate committees to stockholders, thus excluding employees.

In some cases, extending a corporation's political solicitation to its employees may make a relatively small numerical difference. The Sun Oil Company, for example, has 126,000 stockholders and 28,000 employees, more than 12,000 of whom are stockholders and would thus be solicted away.

Labor unions have a comparable legal right, upheld by the Supreme Court, to set up a segregated campaign fund, solicit voluntary contributions from members and then pass along the proceeds to favored candidates, with the union paying the expenses of the program from its treasury.

Under the 1971 campaign law, only corporations without Government contracts—a small number—could operate political action committees. Under the 1974 law, all corporations became eligible, and the resulting activity, aimed at the 1976 election, has been considerable. There has been no court test of the law.

Panel Approves Plan

The commission also approved today a plan designed to plug a loophole that Congress left in the new campaign law.

The law does not set any ceiling on the amount that a candidate for delegate to a national nominating convention can spend on his campaign or the amount that a contributor can give him.

Responding to a request by two party state committees, the commission ruled that delegates specifically authorized to represent a Presidential candidate were not subject to individual limits, but that their spending must come within their candidate's state and national ceiling.

A delegate pledged to a candidate but not authorized by him cannot spend more than $1,000 for his campaign, the advisory opinion held, the same limit applied to an independent citizen spending money on behalf of a candidate without contributing it to his organization.

A survey by the United States Chamber of Comerce indicates that 75 corporations, 37 banks, insurance companies and brokerage houses; 102 business associations, and 19 financial institution associations set up political action committees as of Oct. 20.

Among the corporate committees that have registered with the Federal Election Commission the last two months are those sponsored by the American Cyanamid Company, Anaconda Corporation, General Electric Company, General Telephone and Electronics, Lockheed Aircraft Company, Pacific Gas and Electric Company and United States Steel.

In an effort to encourage this trend, the Chamber of Commerce has held 13 seminars, attended by more than 1,000 corporation executives, to provide instructions on setting up political action committees. A dozen more are scheduled in the next month, with more tentatively scheduled for early next year.

Overriding the same two-member minority and its general counsel, John G. Murphy Jr., the commission also voted approval of a second Sun Oil program under which contributions earmarked for a candidate, committee or party may be collected by a political committee and simply passed along to the beneficiary.

The operating expenses of this committee would also come from corporate funds, and Mr. Harris, supported by Mr. Murphy, maintained that this constituted corporate expenditure that was illegal, because it would be made "in connection with a Federal election."

Today's decision conformed with a statement by the Justice Department two weeks ago that the two types of committees proposed by Sun Oil were legal under the campaign law. The statement was submitted by Assistant Attorney General Richard L. Thornburgh.

The long advisory opinion approved by the commission today after an hour and a half of debate does the following things:

¶Permits Sun Oil—and, presumably, any other corporation that follows the same guidelines—to spend its money to set up and operate Sun Pac, its political committee, and solicit voluntary contributions from both stockholders and employees of the corporation.

¶Allows the corporation to "direct the disbursement" of these funds among such candidates and campaign committees as it chooses, subject to the contribution ceilings already in the statute.

¶Recommends guidelines to minimize the possibility that employees could be coerced into making contributions to Sun Pac by pressure from their superiors.

¶Prohibits any public reports identifying contributors to the earmarked campaign fund or recipients of their contributions, because that might constitute "the exercise of direction and control over future contributions."

Association Set Up

Typical of the new political action committees that are springing up throughout the business community is the Association for Responsible Government Fund, which was established a year ago by the Manufacturers Hanover Trust Company in New York.

It is still a small operation, with $16,000 contributed by executives and employees of the bank in the first nine months of this year with $14,000 passed along to 30 political committees and clubs.

Three dozen Manufacturers Hanover officers made contributions totaling $6,000, ranging from $625 from Gabriel Hauge, chairman of the board, down to $100. An additional $10,000 in contributions of less than $100 was not identified as to donor, pursuant to the law. Most of the fund's contributions went to Republican groups. $9,500 as against $2,400 to Democrats. Major Republican gifts were $3,000 to the New York Republican State Committee and $2,875 to the Nassau County Republican Committee.

The largest Democratic contributions were $500 each to the Bronx and Westchester County committees.

The Association for Responsible Government is a mixed fund, including earmarked contributions, given with assurance that they will be passed on to a given candidate or committee, and general contributions, distributed by an eight-member committee in what its members regard as the political interests of the bank.

November 19, 1975

Velvet Ghettos

By Frances Lear

LOS ANGELES—The submergence of the Federal Equal Employment Opportunity Commission under tons of bureaucratic Bumbledom has left women and ethnic minorities without an operative enforcement agency in the work place.

In earlier days, lawsuits with this troubled agency as co-plaintiff, against companies with discriminatory hiring and promotion practices brought some results. Not nearly enough, to be sure, and sometimes threats of such suits were totally ignored.

I sat in the chrome and shocking-blue office of an oil-company vice president who confided in me, "The E.E.O.C. is going to bring a big Title VII sex discrimination case against one of the oil companies. Hell, it could even be us."

Hell! The E.E.O.C. didn't alarm enough companies enough, but it did give women and minorities some clout as well as a focus for their grievances. The hiring process for these men and women not only continues to be discriminatory, but now there is a new variety of discrimination applied to them *after* being hired.

A black woman, a semicelebrity, told me that she had a new job with a giant corporation.

"Good, tell me about it."

"I have a wonderful opportunity to work in ways that are important to me."

"What department?"

"Public affairs."

"Oh."

Public affairs is evolving into a woman's ghetto. So are equal employment opportunity departments, but this ghetto includes men as well. Men and women divide affirmative-action positions between them, although minority men have begun to take a commanding lead. Virtually all jobs held by women and minorities are in "ghettos." An especially pervasive ghetto exists in retailing.

At one time, women were authorized to write huge orders for merchandise. With their "big pencils," they were queens of the hill! Not so today. Today, merchandise men are usurping the buyers' turf, thereby turning this generation of buyers into powerless order-takers.

The oldest, biggest and most debilitating ghetto of them all is secretarial, and even though this ghetto has undergone some remodeling it remains escape-proof.

When numbers of secretaries were promoted to "administrative assistants" in the early 1970's in an attempt to adhere to equal-employment laws, the ghetto did not open a door and let some women out; it merely expanded in order to house the new administrative assistants who had moved in title and pay but stayed exactly where they were in scope and career opportunity.

Lately, as a result of industry's need, bright women and minorities have been let in as economists or certified public accountants or financial analysts; rarely are they corporate controllers or, rarer still, vice presidents and treasurers. Men put money management in the hands of gifted women who, because they have no other option, allow the real decision-making to be done by men.

Increasingly, I have become aware of still another ghetto. It is the cushiest one of all and belongs to a mere handful of women superstars whose careers are championed by presidents or chairmen of the board—a customary business practice, heretofore reserved for men. Each woman enjoys a status-space in either planning or something called "corporate responsibility," reporting directly to her sponsor. Where would she go if her sponsor moved? Very likely with him.

I am not suggesting that any president or chairman of the board is knowingly putting his star into a ghetto. But that is exactly what is happening. Men, in similar positions of favor, go into line management where corporate princes are crowned.

Fully half of the top corporate women in America are in communications/public and consumer affairs and finance/money management. While it is relatively easy to understand the former, the reason why they go into finance bears re-examining. Is it the land of golden opportunity it is perceived to be, or has the financial community developed a system of discrimination that lets in the talents of women while continuing to deny them any real power?

This negative viewpoint of opportunity in the workplace may be difficult for successful professional women and minority friends to accept; it takes time for people in velvet ghettos to know they are there. Unfortunately, the proliferation of corporate ghettos, with their built-in inequities and fresh stereotypes, won't wait.

Frances Lear is head of an executive-search firm.

September 18, 1976

Long Road Ahead for Black Executives

By WILLIAM M. YOUNG

"They come out of college with a degree, a kit of tools, and they're put at a desk beside the Harvard M.B.A. whose father knows the chairman at Pepsi-Cola, and there's this feeling that, 'I'm not going to do it—there's too much working against me.' "

That was the comment of a black bank executive during a survey on the supply of minority managers conducted for the graduate school of management at Northwestern University. That executive was a minority within a minority: a black who had succeeded in big business.

For despite all the talk about equal opportunity and government pressure for employment for members of minority groups, blacks have been almost totally excluded from important positions of responsibility within big business today.

When some large corporation adds a black clergyman to its board of directors, that's window dressing. Offering a select few blacks, newly born executive titles such as "director of urban affairs," or "vice president of consumer concerns," does little to affect black life in general.

The fact is that blacks hold few top positions of authority in any corporation other than those few black-owned ones. And American businessmen seem little concerned. The attitude of the typical senior management executive in this country, as expressed to us numerous times, usually with a sigh, is: "We're doing all this for blacks in the United States, and we're still being criticized."

Although blacks represent 12 percent of the American population, and thus theoretically should occupy 12 percent of management jobs, the actual number is much less than 1 percent. In Chicago more than 40 large companies were surveyed and a senior black executive could scarecely be found.

In making the survey, it was hoped to determine what percentage of companies had minority managers, how high they were, and whether there was much improvement in equal opportunity at the executive level in the last five years.

So few top black executives were found that statistics were almost meaningless—except to say they weren't there.

Those few uncovered in middle management did not seem optimistic about their opportunities to break through into senior management. "I'm perceived as a token black," one such executive told us, "and that bothers me personally, because I'm as good as, or better than, other people."

Another executive described the whites in his organization running around before one important meeting with a black financial company, placing Afro picks in the executive john so nobody would get offended. "That's naive," the executive said. "The mere fact that they made such a big to-do over something like that indicated there was a certain amount of uneasiness with black people."

Another black said: "They talk about special training programs for black people, but we're getting tired of 'special programs.' If there was true equal opportunity, there wouldn't be a need for that."

Blacks typically are employed on three levels in industry—at the entry level, at lower echelons of management and as window dressing. Many companies offered such employment opportunities amid the idealism of the 1960's, suggesting this was merely a stop-gap measure and that eventually more black Americans would be phased into corporate management.

That has not occurred. In fact, senior executives, often isolated in their offices and social clubs, rarely know what the problem is. In talking to the presidents of dozens of large corporations about the problem of minority promotion, few sensitive individuals were found. The general reaction was: "I worked hard and did it. Everybody else can too."

The one significant finding in the survey for Northwestern was that even those few blacks at the so-called senior level did not feel they encountered equal opportunities. They felt this way despite indications that the Federal Government may look at how companies employ minority members at their top management levels. United Airlines recently settled an excutive discrimination lawsuit for $1.5 million. Merrill Lynch was required to pay more than $2 million in back pay in a similar case. The Government is moving slowly into the area of executive discrimination. Many companies will be caught short.

Blacks in big business, meanwhile, sometimes suffer an identity crisis because of their few numbers. They ask themselves: "Am I here because I'm black, or am I here because I'm qualified?" They sometimes are seen as threatening imposters by whites and as having sold out by other minority members. "One has to be prepared to walk a lonely road at times, recognizing one is trusted by neither community," one black said.

Unfortunately, few blacks seem even ready to occupy middle management positions. Business simply is not a primary career choice among minority groups, especially those of highest potential. Most black youths lack a basic understanding of business, simply

A Few Who Have Succeeded

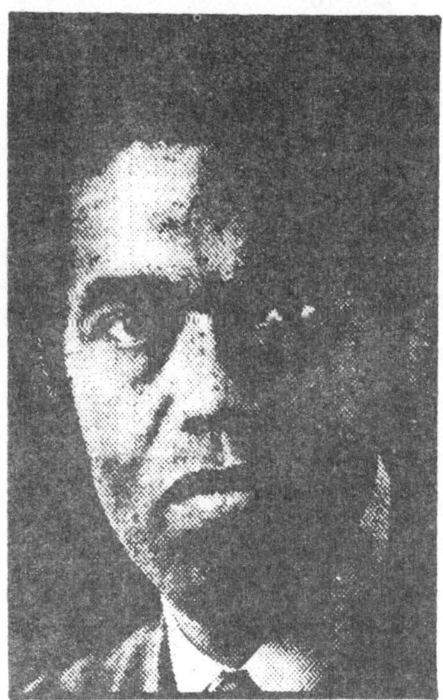

Gilroye A. Griffin, former executive at Bristol-Myers and Kenyon & Eckhardt, is vice president, corporate staff services, at CBS Inc.

Paul G. Gibson, recently New York Deputy Mayor, has returned to American Airlines as vice president for marketing projects.

James A. Joseph (left) and Ulric Haynes Jr. have moved from the Cummins Engine Company to the Government. Mr. Joseph, who was vice president for corporate action at Cummins, is Under Secretary of the Interior. Mr. Haynes, vice president for the Mideast and Africa at Cummins, is Ambassador to Algeria.

because their families are not part of the business world. Their fathers do not know the chairman at Pepsi-Cola. Educated blacks from previous generations entered the traditional fields of preachin', teachin', and healin'. Career education in the secondary schools, which could guide blacks toward business careers, often is inadequate.

As a result, the number of minority students enrolled in graduate business programs is small. Throughout the United States, only 2,000 black students are working toward their masters in business arts.

What is worse, application levels are nearly static.

What is the solution? Here are some suggestions, based on what was learned in the survey:

¶Companies need to establish data banks containing career inventory information, including education, salary, and skills. The record should be updated yearly and, as vacancies occur, this data bank could be searched for current eligible employees, particularly minority members.

¶Career education must receive more attention, since youngsters, particularly black youngsters, have such a limited exposure to business. The Office of Education has a program called Career Education, a curriculum innovation, which makes the world of work the focus of instruction in the elementary and secondary schools.

¶Educational routes other than those offering only the standard college degree need to be established leading toward jobs in business. Businesses could offer classes to develop the competency of their employees. Training programs do occur in industry, but usually only to help people do their jobs better, not to move them into better jobs. A few companies provide courses in business law and English, but these courses are optional and not integrated into a program that could be a business-based alternative to college.

¶Better human relations programs are needed, not merely for middle management but for top management. During the late 1960's and early 1970's, sensitivity programs provided by companies for their employees became almost a fad. By the middle 1970's, however, sensitivity training faded away. Human relations programs could move into this gap, centering on the problems that arise when different groups work together.

Perhaps more important, in addition to these four suggestions, senior executives must make a commitment to employ blacks at the top.

Seeds must be planted early. School programs need to be started to attract blacks to business careers. Individuals interested in business must be identified and enabled to go to college and move into the management pipeline. Once there, they should be promoted.

William M. Young, former dean of education at Chicago State University, is head of William M. Young & Associates of Oak Park, Ill., a consulting firm. short.

July 10, 1977

Wanted: A 9-to-5 Bill of Rights

By DAVID W. EWING

For nearly two centuries Americans have enjoyed freedom of press, speech and assembly, due process of law, privacy, freedom of conscience and other important rights — in their homes, churches, political forums and social and cultural life. But Americans have not enjoyed these civil liberties in most companies, government agencies and other organizations where they work. Once a United States citizen steps through the plant or office door at 9 A.M. he or she is nearly rightless until 5 P.M., Monday through Friday.

To this generalization there are important exceptions. In some organizations, generous managements have seen fit to assure free speech, privacy, due process and other concerns as privileges. But there is no guarantee the privileges will survive the next change of chief executive. As former Attorney General Ramsey Clark once said, "A right is not what someone gives you; it's what no one can take from you." Defined in this manner, rights are rare in business and public organizations.

Rightlessness is most conspicuous for employees who do not belong to unions —for most engineers, scientists, technicians, accountants, sales people, secretaries, managers, administrative assistants and people in related categories. These nonunionized employees make up the great majority of nongovernment workers—about 50 million of the 72 million total.

Union members are not much better off, as a rule. In general, the unions seem to have been far more interested in the material conditions of work life —pay, hours, safety, cleanliness, seniority—than in civil liberties. In fact, these powerful bureaucracies seem to be not much different from the corporate organizations they joust with as far as employee rights are concerned.

Eugene Mihaesco

What about government? Here there is a little more light but not much. A series of Federal court decisions beginning in 1968 appears to have removed the gag from many public employees, but as yet few civil servants have paid much attention to these decisions on speech or even know about them. As for such other rights as privacy, due process and conscience, government employees are in the same ghetto as corporate employees.

In recent years the press has noted numerous casualties of free speech in the Pentagon, Food and Drug Administration, Atomic Energy Commission and other Federal agencies as well as in state and city governments. Occasionally an especially determined dissident will return in triumph, as A. Ernest Fitzgerald, a Pentagon employee, did after testifying against his superiors' wishes about cost overruns on the Lockheed C5A. But most of the dissidents have been buried.

In effect, therefore, United States society is a paradox. The Constitution and Bill of Rights light up the sky over political campaigners, legislators, civic leaders, families, church people and artists. But not over employees.

Speech

In many private and public organizations there is a well oiled machinery for providing relief to an employee who is discharged because of his or her race, religion or sex. But we have no mechanisms for granting similar relief to an employee who is discharged for exercising the right of free speech. Of course, discharge is only the extreme weapon. Many steps short of discharge may work well enough—loss of a raise in pay, demotion, assignment to the boondocks, or perhaps simply a cutback of normal and expected benefits.

Consider the case of a 35-year-old business executive whom I shall call "Mike Z," a respected research manager in a large company. He believed that his company was making only superficial efforts to comply with newly enacted pollution laws. In a management meeting and later in social groups he spoke critically of top management's attitude.

First, his place in the company parking lot was canceled. Then his name was "accidentally" removed from the office building directory inside the main entrance. Soon routine requests he made to attend professional meetings began to get snarled up in red tape or were "lost." Next he found himself harassed by directives to rewrite routine reports. Then his budget for clerical service was cut, followed by a drastic slash in his research budget.

When he tried to protest this treatment, he met a wall of top management silence. Rather than see his staff suffer further for his dissidence, he quit his job and moved his family to another city.

The press

Except for organizations where there are union newspapers and journals, there is no freedom of press in American organization. In the corporate earth here and there an underground press survives. Reportedly, such publications as A.T.&T. Express, The Stranded Oiler (Standard Oil Company of California) and the now-expired Met Lifer (Metropolitan Life Insurance Company) have sought to expose racist and sexist company policies as well as alleged violations of the law. An underground newsletter at the Department of Housing and Urban Development tunnels to the surface of public attention sometimes.

The circulation of underground journals has been low, their publication frequency sporadic, and their editorial quality seedy. Yet the threat of management retaliation is omnipresent, and their editors remain anonymous in order to survive.

Conscientious objection

There is very little protection in industry for employees who object to carrying out immoral, unethical or illegal orders from their superiors. If the employee doesn't like what he or she is asked to do, the remedy is to pack up and leave. This remedy seems to presuppose an ideal economy, where there is another company down the street with openings for jobs like the one the employee left.

In 1970 Shirley Zinman served as a secretary in a Philadelphia employment agency called LIB Services. One day she was instructed by her bosses to record all telephone conversations she might have with prospective clients. This was to be done for "training purposes," she was told, although the callers were not to be told that their words were being taped. The office manager would monitor the conversations on an extension in her office. Miss Zinman refused to play along with this game, not only because it was unethical, in her view, but illegal as well—the telephone company's regulations forbade such unannounced telephone recordings.

So Miss Zinman had to resign. She sought unemployment compensation. The state unemployment pay board refused her application. It reasoned that her resignation was not "compelling and necessitous." She appealed, and three years later the Pennsylvania Commonwealth Court reversed the pay board.

Yet resignation continues to be the accepted response for the objecting employee. Within the organization itself, an employee is expected to sit at the feet of the boss's conscience.

Security and privacy

When employees are in their homes, before and after working hours, they enjoy well-established rights of privacy and to protection from arbitrary search and seizure of their papers and possessions. But no such rights protect them in the average company, government agency or other organization. Their superiors need only the flimsiest pretext to search their lockers, desks, and files.

The boss can rummage through an employee's letters, memoranda and tapes looking for evidence that (let us say) he or she is about to "rat" on the company. "Ratting" might include reporting a violation of safety standards to the Occupational Safety and Health Administration (which is provided for by law) or telling Ralph Nader about a product defect or giving the Mayor's office requested information about a violation of energy-use regulations.

It doesn't matter that employees may be right about the facts or that it may be the superiors, not the employees, who are disloyal to the stockholders.

Outside activities

In practice, most business employees enjoy no right to work after hours for the political, social and community organizations of their choice. To be sure, in many companies an enlightened management will encourage as much diversity of choice in outside activities as employees can make. As noted earlier, however, this is an indulgence which can disappear any time, for most states do not mandate such rights. And, even in those that do, the rights are poorly protected. An employee who gets fired for his or her choice of outside activities can expect no damages for his loss even if he or she wins a suit against the employer.

Ironically, however, a company cannot discriminate against people whose politics it dislikes when it hires them. It has to wait a few days before it can exercise its prerogatives.

In the Federal Government, freedom of choice of outside activities seems to be well recognized.

Due process

"Accidents will occur in the best-regulated families," said Mr. Micawber in "David Copperfield." Similarly, accidents of administration occur even in the best-managed companies, with neurotic, inept or distracted supervisors inflicting needless harm on subordinates. Many a subordinate who goes to such a boss to protest would be well-advised to keep one foot in the stirrups, for he is likely to be shown the open country for his efforts.

This generalization does not hold for civil service employees in the Federal Government, who can resort to a grievance process. Nor does it hold for unionized companies, which also have grievance procedures. But it holds for most other organizations.

In numerous ways sizable corporations, public agencies, and university administrations qualify as "minigovernments." They pay salaries and costs. They have medical plans. They provide for retirement income. They offer recreational facilities. They maintain cafeterias. They may assist an employee with housing, educational loans, personal training, and vacation plans. They schedule numerous social functions. They have "laws," conduct codes and other rules. A few even keep chaplains on the payroll or maintain facilities for religious worship.

In some ways, these minigovernments of today have closer control over an employee than any state did when the Bill of Rights was enacted in George Washington's first term as President. Most employees work at close quarters under careful supervision. Their work and talk may be monitored, and in any event their performance is measured qualitatively and quantitatively.

On the other hand, two centuries ago many Virginians, Pennsylvanians, New Yorkers and other colonists lived off in the woods and fields somewhere, seeing more of their horses than of town, state, or national officials.

Accordingly, it seems foolish to dismiss minigovernments as possible subjects of rights or to exclude employees from discussions of civil liberties. We have assumed that rights are not as important for employees as for political citizens. Our assumption is in error.

David W. Ewing is a member of the faculty of the Harvard Graduate School of Business Administration. This article is extracted from his book, "Freedom Inside the Organization," published by E. P. Dutton. Copyright © 1977 by David W. Ewing.

October 2, 1977

The American Corporate Presence in South Africa

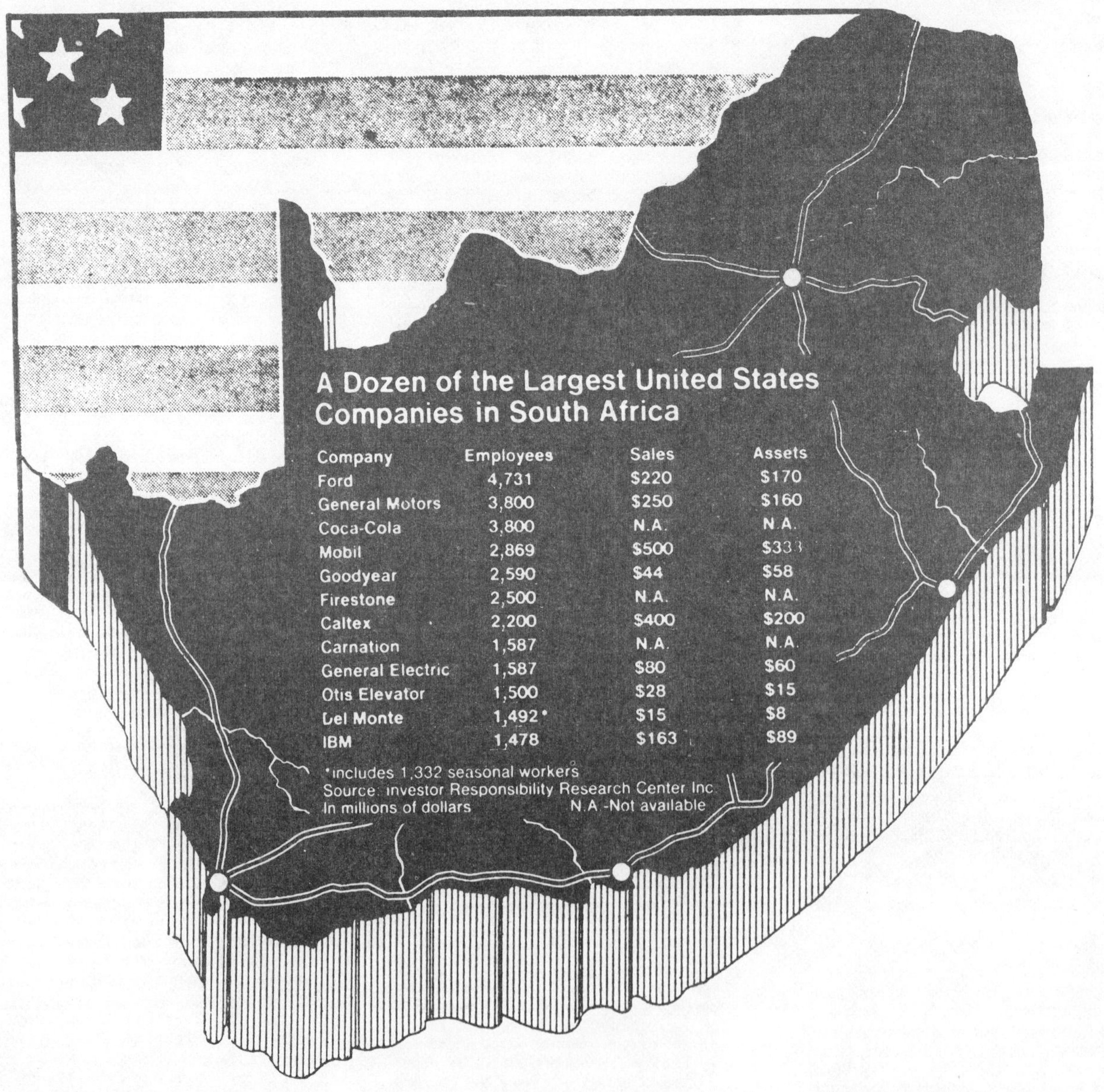

A Dozen of the Largest United States Companies in South Africa

Company	Employees	Sales	Assets
Ford	4,731	$220	$170
General Motors	3,800	$250	$160
Coca-Cola	3,800	N.A.	N.A.
Mobil	2,869	$500	$333
Goodyear	2,590	$44	$58
Firestone	2,500	N.A.	N.A.
Caltex	2,200	$400	$200
Carnation	1,587	N.A.	N.A.
General Electric	1,587	$80	$60
Otis Elevator	1,500	$28	$15
Del Monte	1,492*	$15	$8
IBM	1,478	$163	$89

*includes 1,332 seasonal workers
Source: Investor Responsibility Research Center Inc.
In millions of dollars N.A.-Not available

By MICHAEL C. JENSEN

Dozens of America's most prestigious corporations, under mounting attack for manufacturing and selling products from computers to Cokes in South Africa, are digging in their heels.

"We've been there over 50 years, and we plan to be there for a long time to come," said a spokesman for the General Motors Corporation, which last year sold more than $200 million worth of cars and trucks in South Africa.

About 350 American companies, composing a virtual Who's Who of American business, operate in South Africa, with an aggregate direct investment of nearly $1.7 billion—an estimated 17 percent of the total foreign investment there. United States banks, including the nation's three largest, have outstanding loans and credits of at least $2.2 billion in South Africa, much of it with Government entities. By some estimates, the American banks have supplied, either directly or indirectly, as much as one-third of the money borrowed from any source by Government bodies and corporations in South Africa.

Some unions and universities, charging that the big American companies and banks are supporting apartheid by their presence in South Africa, have sold their stocks in these companies and have withdrawn their money from the banks. A handful of companies operating there have pulled up stakes, though usually, they say, for business reasons. And many of the remaining American companies and banks have issued public statements attacking apartheid, South Africa's discriminatory racial policy, in broad terms. But there are few signs that the companies plan to retrench. In fact, quite the contrary:

- The American business community in South Africa inaugurated a new

American Chamber of Commerce in Johannesburg last month. The executives in leadership positions come from such companies as Esso Standard Oil of South Africa (an Exxon Corporation subsidiary) and the Colgate-Palmolive Company.

•The Caltex Petroleum Corporation, which is owned 50-50 by Texaco Inc. and the Standard Oil Company of California, is spending $134 million to increase its refining capacity in South Africa. "We're doing it because of an expanding market," said a Caltex representative in New York.

•A week after David Rockefeller, chairman of the Chase Manhattan

U. S. critics have called upon them to leave, but the companies are standing pat—or upping the ante.

Bank, told its shareholders that Chase would not make loans that tended to support apartheid, Stephen Pryke, Chase's senior official in South Africa, told a Johannesburg newspaper: "We're just carrying on as before, and we'll shortly be moving to bigger premises."

"Most of the American companies are standing pat," said James Green, international management specialist for the Conference Board, a research organization supported by United States corporations. "They feel that whatever political entity survives will want them there."

To reinforce such resolve, the South African Government has accelerated its lobbying and public relations program in the United States, which is South Africa's second largest trading partner (after Britain). The South Africans are planning to add a fourth information office in Chicago; such offices are already functioning in New York, Washington and Los Angeles.

And the South African Government recently raised its annual payments to Sydney S. Baron & Company, a New York publicity and lobbying firm, from $365,000 to $650,000. Part of the money has been earmarked for visits by American businessmen to South Africa and for promoting business opportunities in that country.

Interviews with dozens of American businessmen indicate that most of them still consider South Africa to be an excellent market for their products and a prime source of raw materials.

An official of the Goodyear Tire and Rubber Company, which employs 2,590 South Africans, said he could foresee "nothing that would lead us" to withdraw from South Africa.

The General Electric Company, which has extensive operations in South Africa, said its presence there could be influenced by a number of things—a change in United States Government policy, for example, or a change in worldwide markets. But one thing would not influence it, a G.E. spokesman said: the requests of activist groups "to get out because they say our presence supports apartheid."

Echoing a theme sounded by virtually every company that does business in South Africa, G.E. said it felt it could do more for its black employees in that country by remaining than by leaving. Jobs for blacks mean money in their pockets and a higher standard of living than they would otherwise enjoy, according to the corporate argument.

Since recent violence in South Africa, a number of American companies and banks that do business there have publicly deplored the repressive nature of the Vorster Government and have vowed not to support apartheid. The Polaroid Corporation halted all sales in South Africa two weeks ago following disclosures that its distributor there was selling film to the Government in violation of a 1971 agreement. But Polaroid was only a bit player in the South African economic game. It did not manufacture products in South Africa or even maintain a sales office of its own.

In March 1977, under the guidance of Leon Sullivan, a black minister who sits on the board of the General Motors Corporation, 12 major American companies agreed to support a set of six principles aimed at promoting fair employment practices at their plants in South Africa. Today the list of companies has grown to 56.

But critics of the American companies are not impressed. For example, Jennifer Davis of the American Committee on Africa calls the principles "an exercise in triviality."

Says Timothy H. Smith, director of the Interfaith Center on Corporate Responsibility, "Many of the signatories of the principles act in ways that directly assist and strengthen the powers of South Africa's white rulers. Citibank has loaned $300 million directly to the South African Government; I.B.M. still provides computers to that Government for any purpose, however repressive. Caltex and Mobil are major suppliers of oil to the South African military, and through South Africa they are the oil lifeline to Rhodesia. Union Carbide assists apartheid by investing in and on the borders of Bantustans. Caltex is in the midst of a $134 million expansion that acts as an economic vote of confidence in white South Africa's future. The list goes on."

Just as no American companies with substantial operations have pulled out entirely, so none of the big American banks have flatly stated that they will not lend money to any borrowers in South Africa.

For one thing, such giants as the Bank of America, Citibank and Chase Manhattan have long-standing relationships with South African banking institutions. For another, many of the big United States banks still have large loans outstanding in South Africa.

In 1976, for example, Citibank reportedly participated as a syndicate member in an estimated $500 million worth of loans that involved South African projects, including a $200 million loan to the country's Electricity Supply Corporation. Other participants in that loan were said to include Chase Manhattan, the Morgan Guaranty Trust Company and the Manufacturers Hanover Trust Company.

Citibank and Morgan Guaranty also were reportedly involved last year in a $110 million loan to the South African Government, and Citibank and Chase Manhattan were said to have participated in an $80 million loan to the country's Iron and Steel Corporation.

No big syndicate loans have been reported this year. Analysts point out that the economy in South Africa has been sluggish, but they do not entirely dismiss the effect of adverse publicity and chanting pickets.

"Overseas investors are continuing to pump money into South Africa," said one American banker who recently returned from Johannesburg. "But the United States institutions are trying to avoid 'press risk.' They don't want to have their names in headlines in The New York Times or The Wall Street Journal because they aren't willing to be seen as supportive of the regime there."

Another international banker said: "What you're getting is a net reduction in exposure. Some banks are playing the game of 'Let's not make them a 10-year loan, but we'll give them a one-year loan.'"

The banks, even more than the American industrial companies, talk cautiously, if at all, about South Africa. Nevertheless, inquiries to the leading banks that lend money to South Africa have elicited some significant differences in their attitudes.

Morgan Guaranty, for instance, simply said that it would continue to make "creditworthy" loans "anywhere in the world we are permitted to." Chase Manhattan, Manufacturers Hanover and the Continental Illinois National Bank indicated that they would not currently make loans that supported apartheid but that they would still consider making loans of—in Chase's words—a "productive nature."

Others talked of specific actions. The First National Bank of Boston said it had reduced the terms of prospective loans to South Africa from five years to three. And Citibank said it would "continue to moderate" its business involvement with South Africa.

William J. McDonough, an executive vice president and head of the international banking department of the First National Bank of Chicago, said recent events in South Africa had "adversely affected" that country's creditworthiness "in a substantial way." For the time being, he said, loans to the Government or its related agencies were out of the question, while loans to the private sector would be "very carefully studied."

South Africans, however, say that they have little trouble attracting outside capital and that, as long as the Government is stable, bankers somewhere in the world will undoubtedly lend it money.

"We aren't as concerned with the capital situation as we are with attracting technology," said Theo Vorster of the South African Consulate General, who contended that his country was relatively self-sufficient from a capital point of view.

He and his colleagues also expressed indignation over what they viewed as the hypocrisy of critics of their Government. "Blacks in the United States may have political equality, but they don't have economic equality," said Mr. Vorster (who is not related to South Africa's chief of Government). "Which is more important: to have the right to vote or to have something to eat?"

There has been some movement out of South Africa by American companies, but most of them say such activity is for business reasons. Last May Weyerhaeuser International, a subsidiary of the Weyerhaeuser Company, sold its interest in four shipping container plants in South Africa to a former partner, Barlow Rand Ltd. Weyerhaeuser said its operations in South Africa lacked "growth potential."

Late last year the Chrysler Corporation merged what was described in some reports as its "ailing subsidiary" into a South African company, but Chrysler kept 25 percent of the voting stock of the new company.

Last June the International Telephone and Telegraph Corporation sold its South African telephone company to a local electronics concern but retained a 36 percent interest. And this year the Phelps Dodge Corporation sold 51 percent of a previously wholly owned subsidiary, the Black Mountain Mineral Development Company, to Gold Fields of South Africa.

The overall condition, however, is still one of relative stability, an impression that is encouraged by South African lobbyists in the United States.

Until a few months ago, Andrew T. Hatcher, former assistant press secretary for Presidents John F. Kennedy and Lyndon B. Johnson, ran the South African account for the Sydney S. Baron firm. As a black man representing a racist regime, Mr. Hatcher encountered considerable criticism. George M. Houser, a white who is executive director of the American Committee on Africa, said that seeing a black man defending South Africa for money was "not unlike seeing a Jew hired by Nazis."

Mr. Hatcher left the account—not, he says, because of any trouble with ideology but because of differences within the Baron firm over how to accomplish the goals most effectively. Of the criticism, he says: "In the public relations business, every account can't be Disney World." Mr. Hatcher is now operating his own business and promoting an international track meet in Dubai.

Protests about corporate or bank involvement in the South African economy have had some effect.

December 4, 1977

THE BUSINESS IMAGE

A MULTI-MILLIONAIRE'S EXPERIENCE.

There are several aspects in which Mr. JOHN D. ROCKEFELLER's little address to his son's Bible class in the Fifth Avenue Baptist Church may profitably be considered. One is the purely human aspect, emphasized by the subsequent remarks of young Mr. ROCKEFELLER, indicating that the father had made the address to please the son. This is altogether attractive and winning, and must tend to conciliate a good many people to whom it may be news that the domestic affections are, or may be, as strong in multi-millionaires as in other people.

The second is like unto it. If a multi-millionaire can find nothing more amusing, or urgent, or attractive, to do than to address the Bible class of a Baptist church, it is evident that he is not, on that account, a proper object of envy. Because evidently this particular pastime or duty is within the reach of the humblest, or at least the humblest Baptist.

But what is mainly calculated to arrest attention and provoke reflection in Mr. ROCKEFELLER's remarks is his averment that, during his business career, he and his associates have dispensed between six and seven hundred millions in wages. Their own united fortunes, great as they may be, cannot amount to any such figure as that. In fact, a "Captain of Industy" is essentially a man who opens new avenues of profitable employment to those who could not have opened such for themselves. That is a consideration which ought to "diminish envy" among all men who work with their hands.

May 2, 1901

MR. ROCKEFELLER AND LABOR.

To the Editor of The New York Times:

Your editorial this morning entitled "A Multi-Millionaire's Experience" is quite delicious. Why do you suppose that it is more commendable in Mr. John D. Rockefeller to make a speech to a Bible class than it would be in anybody else? Who do you think envies him for that? Is it his "cheek" that is envied?

You appear to think it extremely commendable that Mr. Rockefeller and his associates "have dispensed between six and seven hundred millions in wages" in thirty years, especially as "their own united fortunes, great as they may be, cannot amount to any such figure as that." You say they have also opened "new avenues of profitable employment to those who could not have opened them for themselves." You would have the workingmen think that they are greatly indebted to Mr. Rockefeller.

But they will not think so, Mr. Editor, for they are not such fools. Mr. Rockefeller is indebted to them; not they to him. They made him; not he them. The wealth he enjoys they created, and if they had not created it he would not have it. They would have found employment without him, but he could not have accumulated his vast, his inordinate, his outrageous wealth without them. Don't you imagine that the American workingman feels like dropping on his knees and thanking the multi-millionaire for "giving" him work, for he does not. For every dollar paid him he has given a full equivalent in hard, honest work—Rockefeller and his ilk always make sure of that. They pay him as little as they can.

CLERK.

New York, May 2, 1901.

May 5, 1901

MISS TARBELL'S BOOK.

A Glance at the Widely Advertised History of the Standard Oil Company.*

As readable as any "story," and with rather more of romance than the average "business novel," is this history of the rise, development, and ultimate success of the Standard Oil Company. Incidentally, too, it is a history of the petroleum oil business from its first discovery and use as a "patent medicine" to its present position as fourth in the list of exports from this country—a business that enlists the use of something like $500,000,000 of capital. That the telling of this story should have been undertaken by a woman seems strange, perhaps, but Miss Tarbell was born in the Pennsylvania oil regions, and in her girlhood days was in the centre of the sphere of agitation that has existed from the time of the discovery of oil up to the present between the oil producer and the oil refiner. Her people were oil people.

Honest the writer has tried to be to both sides to the various controversies. Her records of these are digested from an enormous mass of statistics contained in almost numberless lawsuits, investigations by Congressional and Legislative Committees, records of hearings brought about by investigation of charges against the Standard Oil Company of combination in restraint of trade and of securing special favors from transportation companies. Indeed, nearly a third of the volumes is given over to documents and records on which are based the facts of her story.

Her text is what she alleges to be an oft-repeated assertion by Mr. Rockefeller that "the oil business and its regulation belonged by right to them"—the Standard Oil Company, of which he was President.

> John D. Rockefeller's one irreconcilable enemy in the oil business has been the oil producer. * * * Whenever he had the chance he sought to persuade the producers to do what he would have done had he owned the oilfields—keep the supply of crude oil short.

It was to this position—controlling markets—after Mr. Rockefeller came into the field, that most of his energies were directed. Had he been successful, Miss Tarbell asserts, it would undoubtedly have been to the advantage of the oil producer from a financial viewpoint, whatever it may have been to the consumer, who, after all, has had to pay all the expenses for the conduct of the various wars that were waged until the supremacy of the Standard Oil Company was firmly established.

Beginning with the discovery of crude petroleum floating on the surface of Oil Creek by Samuel M. Kier, and his exploitation of it as a cure-all about 1850, following with the belief of George H. Bissell that petroleum was a possible illuminant and lubricant, and the confirmation of that belief by the analyses of the late Prof. Silliman of Yale and the subsequent development of the fields through the experimental borings of Edwin L. Drake in 1858, the history rapidly traces the slow growth until the oil fever was at its height in Western Pennsylvania. Then things came rapidly.

At that time there was in business in Cleveland a commission firm known as Clark & Rockefeller. They had but little capital, but Mr. Rockefeller saw the great possibilities in refining petroleum, then being carried on in that city in a primitive fashion. He took in Samuel Andrews as a partner. They improved the methods of refining, as Andrews was a mechanical genius, and later Henry M. Flagler, Stephen V. Harkness, and William Rockefeller were brought into the business. These men in 1870 established the first Standard Oil Company, with a capital of $1,000,000. This was a couple of years after John D. Rockefeller had discovered the possibility and value of railroad rebates and had secured them from the railroads that were hauling his crude oil from the fields and carrying his refined oils to the seaboard. It was that discovery that was the secret of Mr. Rockefeller's success as a refiner, and one that others in the business never were able to get the full advantage of, as was repeatedly shown at hearings instituted to find out how Rockefeller was able to prosper more materially than did others in the same business. That matter of cheap transportation, the writer asserts, was the keynote to the success that Mr. Rockefeller achieved.

While there was a row over this question of rates Mr. Rockefeller found an old charter for the South Improvement Company which granted practically limitless business powers. This he had resuscitated and under a secret arrangement got a lot of his competitors to go into the "trust" business under its provisions—the first thing of the kind ever established in this country. **The producers found out about the company of refiners that had been banded together to limit and control refining of oil, and after a series of suits and legislative investigations succeeded in having the company's charter revoked. But before this was done Mr. Rockefeller had managed to get most of the twenty-five Cleveland refineries under his control, and thus became the greatest of producers and shippers in the West. The railroads were after his trade and got it by rebates that no one else could get, though freely promising similar rebates to others who would ship as much oil as Rockefeller did. This none of them could do, even in combination. All sorts of methods were tried for years to put a stop to these rebates, but under one subterfuge or another the Standard Oil Company managed to get them, and so materially limit successful competition. The oil producers raged and stormed and held meetings and had railroads investigated and tried legislative action—all equally in vain.**

Then came the method of transporting oil from the fields to the refineries in pipe lines. This promised to put all refiners on an equable basis. Then the Standard Oil by devious ways got control of the pipe lines and once more had the producers on the hip. More investigations; decrees that the pipe lines were common carriers and must accept oil from all producers and for delivery to all producers at a common rate to all; acceptance by the Standard Oil; discovery that in spite of these decrees the Standard Oil was still a competitor that no one could meet; finally the unearthing of an agreement with the roads which showed that the Standard Oil Company was not only receiving the same rebate that others were, but that it also received a rebate on all oil that its rivals were shipping, a fact that then Vice President Cassatt of the Pennsylvania Railroad admitted when State and United States investigators, at the request of oil producers, took the matter up.

Yet in spite of the revelations the Standard Oil managed to keep up the advantage it had over its rivals.

With the discovery of a means of pumping oil over the mountains from the fields to the tidewater refineries, oil producers were sure they had found a way to destroy the domination of the Sandard Oil Company over the business. Railroads tried in every way to block the building of the pipe lines, and a dozen local "wars" resulted. But when Mr. Rockefeller was convinced that both crude and refined oils could be piped to the seaboard he took the one way out of the difficulty. **Agents bought out rival refineries in New York, Philadelphia, and Baltimore. All the seaboard terminal and refining facilities that were worth anything were acquired. And when the pipe lines, built with the money of the producers, were completed and in good working order, they found they had no purchasers for their goods except the Standard Oil, which had now spread out to control the markets of the world by building huge tank steamers to transport oil in bulk. There was nothing to do but get discouraged and sell the pipe lines to Mr. Rockefeller and his associates. This they did.**

Meantime, "unwilling that there should be any middleman in handling oil anywhere between the oil fields and the very lamp in which it was burned in the home of the consumers," the Standard established local agencies in every State in the Union to handle its products directly and even built wagons which should distribute the oil by the gallon to the tenement dwellers who were unable to buy in any greater quantities. This system was so perfected that today the company in this way handles 80 per cent. of the entire oil trade of the country, says Miss Tarbell.

Goaded to desperation at the baffling of all their plans, the producers now attacked the very life of the Standard Oil Company, maintaining that all its business was illegally in the hands of nine Trustees, although it included the business of more than a score of companies chartered under the laws of a dozen States. Suits brought in Ohio proved successful, and the trust was ordered dissolved. Producers thought they saw in this an opening of the door to free competition. Mr. Rockefeller thought differently. He had secured a charter in New Jersey for another Standard Oil Company under which business could be carried on as secretly as ever, and he merely smiled when the old trust was dissolved, and kept consolidating his interests and extending their scope under the Jersey charter until they are more firmly intrenched than ever.

And there this story leaves them, probably the most perfect business machine in the world, with a world-wide practical control of the refining and distribution of the cheapest illuminant and lubricating material on earth.

One of Miss Tarbell's conclusions is that "the personal quality of William Rockefeller was and always has been the strongest asset of the Standard Oil Company. * * * There was no obstacle too great for him to overcome, no difficulty but he was ready to meet and conquer, and always by the safest and surest route."

---

*THE HISTORY OF THE STANDARD OIL COMPANY. By Ida M. Tarbell, Author of "The Life of Abraham Lincoln," "The Life of Napoleon Bonaparte," and "Mme. Roland: A Biographical Study." With Portraits, Pictures, and Diagrams. In two volumes. Vol. I.—Pp. xx.-406; Vol. II.—Pp. xiii-469. Cloth, 8vo. New York: McClure, Phillips & Co. $5 net.

December 31, 1904

Wants a Rockefeller Page.

To the Editor of The New York Times:

As a regular reader of THE NEW YORK TIMES, I have noticed with increasing pleasure the strict impartiality with which you give publicity to both kicks and praise. I am therefore emboldened to address you on a little matter which comes within one of those descriptions, I hardly know which. Why not a Rockefeller page in THE NEW YORK TIMES? A Rockefeller Section, or a Rockefeller Department—anything save a Rockefeller Column, which would be altogether too insignificant for a subject, which THE TIMES evidently regards as so urgently important. The taste for reading of Rockefeller daily constantly increases, and your daily doles seem to grow woefully insufficient. The fever for it is upon us—give us more Rockefeller, and let us intoxicate ourselves with the quantity you will furnish. Give us a page of him every day. ARTHUR A. PENN.

New York, Oct. 4, 1905.

October 7, 1905

THE CONFESSIONS OF J. D. ROCKEFELLER.

We are inclined to believe that the people who keep writing to us to protest against the amount of space which we give to the utterances of Mr. JOHN D. ROCKEFELLER, at prayer meetings, receptions, and the other kinds of assemblages which pass with him for social functions, must be friends of his. At least they must be friends of old age and prosperity. Their mental attitude must be that of the sons of NOAH, who regretted and to the best of their ability repaired the indiscretions of the old man.

Such persons may read THE TIMES's reports of Mr. ROCKEFELLER's doings and sayings with their "faces backward." But why anybody who disapproves of the venerable financier should also disapprove of the amount of space which we give to his automatic disclosures is what we fail to see. Of course there is an almost unlimited number of old asses, and even a considerable number of old Midases, who make feeble and platitudinous addresses to Sunday schools in this country every Sunday in the year. We do not report them all. If we did, THE TIMES would not contain the things that would be reported. If we make an exception in favor of Mr. ROCKEFELLER the reason is plain. He is the only billionaire in the lot who makes Sunday school addresses. He is the richest man in America. And it cannot but be wholesome as well as interesting for the youth of America to be able to judge, from his own authentic utterances, what kind of man is the American who has most amply attained the kind of success which is perhaps increasingly coming to be accounted the only kind of success that is worth having.

Nor is the Rockefellerian eloquence entirely beneath contempt, even on its intrinsic merits. The description which the venerable billionaire gave of himself last Sunday as having formerly been a sponge, but being at present a pump, is really felicitous, the more because so many persons are visibly attempting to get hold of the handle. But we admit that his attempt to portray himself as an amiable patriarch is not altogether a success. Readers of DICKENS will remember, in "Little Dorrit," that old fraud Casby, who managed to pose as an amiable patriarch until the irate Pancks cut off his flowing locks. It was only then that he was exposed as what his creator describes as a "goggle-eyed booby," or words to that effect. It is superfluous to observe that Mr. ROCKEFELLER is already devoid of these adjuncts to the patriarchal make-up, and therefore cannot be deprived of them. Our readers who think that we make too much of Mr. ROCKEFELLER ought really to consider that what we are doing is to give him the public opportunity of showing how little he makes of himself.

October 10, 1905

"GREAT FORTUNES FROM RAILROADS"

THIS BOOK* is one of a numerous class whose appearance is a sign of our times. Nothing is more characteristic of our politics and legislation than the interest in other people's money and profits. The idea seems to be that the majority are poor because the minority are rich. It avails nothing that, as this book and others like it show, some of our richest men have made themselves so by their own exertions, and that others may imitate them if they wish to and have the ability. It avails nothing that the accumulators of the great railway fortunes in particular have made more money for others than for themselves. There are less than twenty billions of railway securities altogether, and that is a small figure compared with the land values created and sustained by the railways. Farm lands alone yield an income of eight or nine billions annually—the income on a capital value of, say, twenty-five times that sum.

We could not feed or clothe ourselves, or produce or distribute our manufactures without our railways. If it were true that the Vanderbilt and Gould fortunes—the ones particularly described by Mr. Myers—were altogether the fruit of robbery and worse, with no alleviating circumstances, it would be better for the country, in a material sense, that it should be so, than that the country should be deprived of its railways. Doubtless it would be better yet if the railways had been built with fewer regrettable incidents, whose existence it is in no way sought to shirk or palliate. But the fact is that the railway builders were part and parcel of their times, no better and no worse.

As matters stood, the railways had to be built as they were, or not be built at all in that generation. The moralities suffered, and that is always lamentable; but the world is advanced, even morally, farther than it would have been but for the strenuosity of our railway builders, however wicked they were.

The justification of these trite remarks is that the author shows no per-

* *HISTORY OF THE GREAT AMERICAN FORTUNES. By Gustavus Myers, Vols. II, III Great Fortunes from Railroads, Charles H. Kerr & Co.*

ception of their truth. Not only are the railway builders whose fortunes he describes bad men—they are altogether bad. The account, as he keeps it, has debit entries only. He does not even confine himself to facts, of which a superfluity lay ready to his hand, according to his own account. He knows why all these bad things were done, and does not hesitate to describe motives as though he were a mind-reader, and an instrument of Divine justice as well, commissioned to punish these rascals vicariously through their descendants. It is late in the day for any new villainy to be discovered or disclosed in connection with the great American railway fortunes. The manner of their accumulation has been adequately described before, but never with such wealth of insinuation adapted to set class against class and arouse social unrest. In this lies the novelty and the harm of the book. It is superfluous to worry about the dead millionaires, or about the inheritors of their wealth, whom not even Mr. Myers would hold responsible for the acts of their ancestors. It is the low and unveracious point of view which is reprehensible.

In order to do no injustice to Mr. Myers it will be best to set this out in his own words. The railway men he describes, as has been indicated, but in the course of his narrative it becomes necessary for him to characterize the incidents connected with the throwing of the bombs which killed and wounded some scores of Chicago police in 1886. The actors in those events were "sincere, self-sacrificing, intellectual, burning with compassion and noble ideals for suffering humanity." Roosevelt's career was starting about those troublous times, and of him Mr. Myers has this to say: "The Republican Party nominated a verbose, pushful, self-glorifying young man, a remarkable character whose pugnacious disposition, indifference to political conventionalities, capacity for exhortation, and bold political shrewdness were mistaken for greatness of personality." No exception would need to be taken to this, if it were a contemporaneous characterization; but it is a present-time utterance. These two passages—the indulgence toward bomb throwers and the belittling of such a character as Roosevelt—suffice to indicate the reliance which can be placed upon the author as a leader of the morality of his times. If it is desired to promote among us a social revolution—something very different from social reform—there could be no surer way than to allow prints like these to pass unrebuked.

One other fact about the book may be mentioned for the judgment of the dispassionate reader. Its text is the badness of our own times, and yet worse is alleged of the times before ours. Captain General the Earl of Bellomont in 1700 reported a whole sheaf of briberies within his personal knowledge, with assertions of others before his term. Our briberies are not to be extenuated, but they are neither worse nor more numerous than were those of two centuries ago. One century ago a Boston syndicate corruptly procured five million acres of land from the Georgia legislature. The land scandals of succeeding generations rivaled anything in the history of the steam or traction franchises. These deeds are all of the same quality, and are characteristic of no one time or people. Two wrongs do not make a right, and no wrong is condoned because of a previous wrong. We are growing rather better than worse. If we were bad through and through, the muckrakers could never have had such a tremendous vogue. The revulsion from wrong is proof of essential morality. Mr. Myers's book proves too much for his own case, and leaves such a bad taste in the mouth that readers may be cordially advised to read something else.

July 30, 1910

TELEPHONE COMPANY TO INCREASE PUBLICITY

New Vice President to Have Charge of Public Relations—Takes Office at Once.

The American Telephone and Telegraph Company is to inaugurate a new policy in respect to public relations, it was learned yesterday. Hitherto it has been conservative in making the course of its affairs public, but it proposes to place questions of public relations and publicity in the hands of a Vice President.

Arthur Wilson Page, who resigned recently as a Vice President of Doubleday, Page & Co. and editor of World's Work to become a Vice President of the telephone company, is to be in charge of the new department. He took up his quarters in the A. T. and T. Building at 195 Broadway yesterday and formal announcement of his appointment and duties is expected to be made after the company's Excutive Committee meets tomorrow.

January 4, 1927

MONEY AND THE AMERICAN SCENE

The Part the Great Capitalists Have Played in Our History

THE ROBBER BARONS. By Matthew Josephson. 474 pp. New York: Harcourt, Brace & Co. $3.

By *HENRY HAZLITT*

"To draw the American scene as it unfolded between 1865 and the end of the century," wrote the Beards in "The Rise of American Civilization," without such figures as the Goulds, Vanderbilts, Rockefellers and Morgans looming in the foreground, "is to make a shadow picture; to put in the Presidents and the leading Senators—to say nothing of transitory politicians of minor rank—and leave out such prime factors in the drama is to show scant respect for the substance of life."

It is this passage which seems to have inspired Matthew Josephson to undertake the present work—a history of the great American capitalists from 1861 to 1901. And the success with which his work has been done puts the importance of the Beards' observation beyond dispute. One rises, indeed, from a reading of "The Robber Barons" with the feeling that if, instead of political histories with at best only incidental references to the great capitalists, most of us had been brought up on histories of the great capitalists with only incidental references to the political scene, we would understand our country much better than we do.

It is in the period from the beginning of the Civil War to the end of the nineteenth century that the foundations of most of the great American fortunes were laid. When Lincoln issued his first call for volunteers, Jay Gould, Jim Fisk, J. P. Morgan, Philip Armour, Andrew Carnegie, James J. Hill and John D. Rockefeller were all in their early twenties; Collis Huntington and Leland Stanford were over thirty; Jay Cooke was not yet forty. Nearly all of these men, with an occasional exception like J. P. Morgan, the son of a banker, grew up in poverty; and most of them left their homes early in youth, to wander alone and make their own way. Jim Fisk as a boy traveled all the roads of Vermont in the wagon of his father, a tin peddler. Collis Huntington "secured his freedom from his father when 14 years old by promising to support himself," and wandered about for ten years as a peddler of watch findings. Jay Gould's childhood "was passed in a kind of naked poverty, which he remembered afterward with horror." He had to plead with his father to be permitted even to attend the village school. Andrew Carnegie was brought to America in 1848 as the child of poor and rebellious Scottish weavers; at the age of 14 he was set to work here as a bobbin-boy in a cloth mill and spent twelve hours a day in a dank cellar. Rockefeller's father was a wandering vendor of quack medicine who rarely supported his family and was sometimes a fugitive from the law; the young Rockefeller would work in his youth, by his own account, hoeing potatoes for a neighboring farmer from morning to night for 37 cents a day.

How did these men build their fortunes? Rarely, like Thomas Edison, did they grow rich by important inventions or discoveries. Nearly always their fortunes were laid or expanded by some daring or brilliant stroke in bargaining, in outwitting their rivals or in speculation. The system and conditions under which they grew up permitted them to become rich in one of three ways: by actions which increased the national wealth; by actions which tended in some respects to increase the national wealth but were anti-social in others, and finally by actions that were almost completely anti-social, which either created nothing or actually retarded the country's growth.

The last course was represented, almost in its purest form, in the career of Jay Gould. At 16, when employed as a clerk by the village storekeeper, he learned that his master was negotiating for a good property in the neighborhood which happened to be in chancery, and had offered $2,000 for it. Gould quickly made some investigations of his own, got a loan of $2,500 from his father, bought the property himself and in two weeks had sold it out for $4,000. His employer, incensed at what he saw as trickery and duplicity, dismissed him.

Arrived in New York, Gould made the acquaintance of the aged Zadoc Pratt, a wealthy tanner, who was so impressed with him that he furnished him with nearly all the capital necessary—about $120,000—to found a large tannery. The tannery, which was set up in "Gouldsboro," Pennsylvania, did a lively trade, but no profits ensued. Pratt, seized with suspicions, descended

A Cartoon by Thomas Nast in Harper's Weekly, Oct. 11, 1873.

upon Gouldsboro and found the books in such strange disorder, with heavy speculative commitments by Gould, that in alarm he offered to sell his business to Gould for half the sum he had invested. Gould found a new patron in Charles Leupp of the leather firm of Leupp & Lee. Leupp, too, after a brief season, found the Gouldsboro tannery strangely mismanaged, as if with design. Its capital was completely exhausted by Gould in 1857 in an attempt to create a corner in hides; the panic of that year brought ruin, and Leupp shot himself. Lee, his partner, acting for himself and for Leupp's heirs, finally moved after futile negotiations with Gould to take possession of the plant; but Gould gathered up a mixed crowd of laborers and thugs, filled them with oysters and whisky, and marched them on the tannery, which was attacked, stormed and captured in a moderately bloody clash. Ultimately, after long delays, Gould was ousted by the forces of the law.

In his next phase we find Gould working in collusion with the speculators Daniel Drew and Jim Fisk. Vanderbilt, owner of the New York Central, had determined to buy control of the Erie, and imagined that he had the secret cooperation of Drew, its president. But as he bought more and more shares of the road, Vanderbilt found the supply coming in steadily, "as if flowing from a concealed underground stream." He then discovered that Drew, Gould and Fisk had bought a small railroad, as a private transaction of their own, for $250,000; had issued $2,000,000 of bonds against this asset, and leased it to the Erie system for 499 years in consideration of the Erie's taking over this bonded indebtedness for $2,000,000 of its own convertible bonds. These bonds had been taken by Drew, Gould and Fisk, and they proceeded to convert them into the stock which they were selling in the market to Vanderbilt.

Vanderbilt put a stop to this, but finally made peace with the trio. Soon, however, in resuming his buying campaign, he found again that the flow of stock was unending, and that the executive committee of Drew, Fisk and Gould, the "Erie ring," had secretly authorized the issuance of $10,000,000 more convertible bonds. So he got the obliging Judge Barnard of the New York State Supreme Court to enjoin the Erie directors from further issues of securities, and to order them to return to the road's treasury one-fourth of the shares recently issued as well as $3,000,000 of convertible bonds. But while Judge Barnard kept firing injunctions against them, Gould uncovered another State Supreme Court Judge at Binghamton who obligingly sent forth counter-injunctions. Fisk captured the forbidden shares, anyway, and threw them on the market, and trading was suspended in Erie on the Stock Exchange.

Vanderbilt finally called on Judge Barnard for an order for the arrest of Drew, Gould and Fisk. The three directors, at the railroad's headquarters in West Street, quickly gathered all the funds received from the stock-market transactions, all cash in banks or in the company's treasury, all securities, documents and incriminating evidence, and cramming a great bundle of six millions in greenbacks into a valise, threw themselves into a hack and rode at top speed to the Jersey City Ferry. Arrived in New Jersey, they established their main offices in a hotel known as Taylor's Castle, renamed it "Fort Taylor," threw armed guards about the place and mounted three twelve-pound cannon on the piers. After a few weeks of this exile Gould suddenly departed for Albany with a valise containing $500,000 in greenbacks and, in the words of Charles F. Adams, "assiduously cultivated a thorough understanding between himself and the Legislature." He lobbied for a measure which would legalize the new issues of Erie. Vanderbilt met these tactics with similar ones, but he did not spend with so lavish a hand; the Legislature passed Gould's bill, and the Governor, also believed to have been "assiduously cultivated," signed it.

Gould's further adventures—his systematic pillaging of the Erie and the Union Pacific, his use of the same methods in Washington that he had used in Albany, his seizure of the Western Union, the Manhattan Elevated and the New York Elevated Railway, his treachery toward his closest colleagues and partners—it is impossible to describe here in detail. But Gould's career illustrates more glaringly than that of any other figure whose story Mr. Josephson records, not only the level to which public morality had sunk in America in the Gilded Age, but something of perhaps more permanent significance—the possibilities for accumulating immense wealth under capitalism by a policy not of building but of ruin.

John D. Rockefeller was in many ways as ruthless as Gould; he obtained from the railroads secret rebates on freight rates which enabled him to undersell his competitors and drive them out of business; he even arranged with the railroads that they were to charge his competitors more and pay his companies part of the increase; and with this weapon he was able to buy up competing companies for a half or a third of their value. But Rockefeller incidentally stabilized the oil business and effected economies through larger units and better methods. And James J. Hill, the railroad man, made his wealth principally because he knew railroading and was a real builder. "It is our best interest," he wrote to one of his partners, "to give low rates and do all we can to develop the country and create business." This was one way, as Hill proved, of making money; unfortunately, the Goulds found other ways that seemed faster.

Mr. Josephson has told his story of "The Robber Barons" with great verve and a fine sense of its dramatic values. What he has written is not a mere series of biographies but a genuine history, with the stories of the great American capitalists skillfully interwoven, and with an eye always on the broader social background. He has digested an immense mass of material, and he is particularly to be congratulated upon the lucidity with which he sets forth the complex financial transactions and the uncanny legerdemain by which most of the barons built up their fortunes. True, under the influence of Veblen and Marx, he often paints his figures and their actions in darker colors than are quite necessary, and he is sometimes guilty of carelessness and inaccuracy. Thus, for example, he asserts on page 58 that Secretary Chase's national banking legislation "taxed State banks out of existence," when what was taxed out of existence was not the banks but simply their notes. On the same page he remarks that gold rose to "a premium above 250"; but, as the highest price of a dollar in gold in terms of greenbacks was $2.85, the premium on gold was never higher than 185 per cent. Again, on page 178, he refers to "the resumption of specie payments after 1875"; but 1875 was merely the year of the passage of the Specie Resumption Act; it was not until 1879 that specie payments were actually resumed. Yet these examples of carelessness do not detract substantially from the solid merits of Mr. Josephson's absorbing volume. "The Robber Barons" ought to be read by every one who wants a genuine insight into our national history. Readers who have learned about the Vanderbilts, the Goulds, the Fisks and the Rockefellers will not be too greatly astonished at what is currently revealed about the Insulls, the Mitchells and the Wiggins.

March 4, 1934

IVY LEE DIES AT 57 OF BRAIN AILMENT

Public Relations Counsel for Rockefellers Had Been Ill Since Oct. 29.

SERVED FOREIGN NATIONS

He Was Pioneer in Advising Big Business on Publicity—Started as Reporter.

Ivy Lee, who served as public relations counsel for the Rockefellers and for large corporations and foreign governments, died at 3:45 P. M. yesterday at St. Luke's Hospital. A brain tumor was the cause of death. Mr. Lee was 57 years old.

He had been ill only since Oct. 29, when he entered the hospital. A few days ago it became apparent that his condition was grave, but as recently as last Monday he dictated letters to his secretary. No operation was performed, the physicians who took part in a consultation having decided that it would be futile.

At the bedside when he died were his wife, his two sons, James Wideman Lee 2d and Ivy Lee Jr.; his daughter, Mrs. Chandler Cudlipp; his mother, Mrs. James Wideman Lee; a sister, Mrs. Wilbur T. Trueblood and a brother, Lewis H. Lee.

Started as Reporter.

Mr. Lee, who started his career as a newspaper reporter, probably did as much as any man to turn the gathering of news into a matter of collecting prepared statements from news sources. But no statement had been prepared by his office against his death. There was no obituary ready in the files of the vast organization he directed; his associates hurriedly assembled one and it was run off on the multigraph machine which in recent years has been the source of much information about the Rockefellers and Mr. Lee's corporation clients.

The full list of Lee publicity clients never has been made public, and the senior partner, T. J. Ross, declined yesterday to name the persons and organizations Mr. Lee had served, explaining that the relationship was confidential.

Among those known to have used his service, however, were the vast Rockefeller interests—the various Standard Oil units and the Socony-Vacuum Oil Company—and the members of the Rockefeller family, for whom he acted as spokesman; the interborough Rapid Transit Company, the governments of Rumania and Poland, the Pennsylvania Railroad, Armour & Co., Princeton University and the German dye trust.

Denied Soviet Retainer.

It was widely reported over a period of years that Mr. Lee had been in the employ of the Soviet Government. These rumors were based in part on the fact that more than eight years ago he became a consistent advocate of Soviet recognition by the United States. On several occasions, however, he denied that he had been retained by the Moscow government, and Mr. Ross said yesterday that his interest had been wholly personal.

A few months ago Mr. Lee's connection with the German dye trust received considerable public notice. The Congressional committee investigating un-American activities brought out that his work had consisted of giving advice to officials of the trust, covering the relations between Germany and the American people. Mr. Lee admitted that it was intended that this advice ultimately should reach officials of the government.

Mr. Lee brought something new to the business of publicity. When he was a young New York newspaper man thirty-odd years ago, there were numerous press agents in town who promoted theatres and stage stars, but there was no specialist in publicity who conferred on terms of equality with the boards of directors of great corporations. His life spanned that change, and he had much to do with the change.

Born in Georgia.

On July 16, 1877, Ivy Ledbetter Lee was born at Cedartown, Ga., the son of Emma Eufaula Ledbetter Lee and the Rev. Dr. James Wildman Lee. His father, a Methodist clergyman, is now dead.

After attending Emory College, in Georgia, Mr. Lee went to Princeton, where he was graduated in 1898. Subsequently he did post-graduate work at Harvard and Columbia.

One of the stories told of his youth is to the effect that when he arrived in New York to make his way he had a diploma, a raincoat and $5. He got a job as a beginning reporter on The New York American, then known as The Morning Journal.

Subsequently he worked on THE NEW YORK TIMES and The New York World, but he soon decided that he would be happier out of newspaper work. Already he had seen the place for a publicity organization that would serve big business, and he quit his reporter's job to try it.

First there was a tangential experience as publicity manager for the Citizens Union in the election of Seth Low as Mayor. After that he sent notices to the editors that he was the spokesman for several corporations. One of these was the Pennsylvania Railroad, and within a short time that important client asked him to forget about the rest of his business and become its employe solely.

From 1910 to 1912 Mr. Lee was in Europe as general European manager for Harris, Winthrop & Co., a banking firm. He took this position because he wished to increase his knowledge of world affairs, and while he was abroad he lectured at the London School of Economics.

Returning to the United States, he again became associated with the Pennsylvania Railroad as executive assistant. The reputation he made in this connection was largely instrumental in bringing about his association with the Rockefellers.

National attention was centred on the Colorado Fuel and Iron Company at that time. One of the most famous industrial wars in the history of the nation was brewing. Tension increased with the massacre at Ludlow, Col., and in New York City police broke up angry crowds assembled before the Rockefeller offices.

From that time on Mr. Lee devoted himself to bettering the relations between the public and the Rockefellers. He was an important adviser in the Rockefeller charities, which soon became known throughout the world. Within a few years John D. Rockefeller Sr. was giving away dimes—but Mr. Lee always denied that that was an idea of his.

Set Up First Office Here.

In 1916 Mr. Lee established his first office in New York City—he had maintained headquarters in Philadelphia—and soon his business had broadened to take in many corporations, banks business associations and philanthropic institutions.

In the war he served as publicity director, and later assistant to the chairman, of the American Red Cross.

Mr. Lee's connection with the Polish Government, an associate explained yesterday, was through the Bank of Poland and involved the flotation of a Polish loan. The details of his work for Rumania were not explained, but it was said that the services of the Lee company were for a specific purpose and the company was retained for only a brief time.

November 10, 1934

Advertising News

The National Association of Manufacturers will launch today an advertising campaign to carry the story of American industry to the people, C. M. Chester, president, announced yesterday. The first of a series of five full-page advertisements will appear in Chicago newspapers and will be run over the next few weeks in cities throughout the country, the financing to be done by individual manufacturers in each community.

This campaign will be the first paid advertising sponsored by the association since the turn of the century and the first coordinated effort of industry to publicize through advertising its concrete achievements. At various times, individual industries have carried on cooperative campaigns, generally to promote their products, and the recent advertising of General Motors has been of an institutional nature, pointing out American progress through the advancement in business methods.

In the past the manufacturers association has relied upon free publicity in newspapers, such as cartoons, articles, &c., supplied by it to get across its ideas and, consequently, the paid campaign is a departure. The subjects of the campaigns are: What is your American System All About?; Machines and Employment, Taxation, Americans Standards, and America's Tomorrows. Lord & Thomas is directing the account, with Edgar Kobak as executive.

"Industry's silence in the face of continued criticism against the American business system has been misunderstood," Mr. Chester said, in commenting on the campaign, "The National Association of Manufacturers, as the representative of industry, feels that the time has arrived to provide the public with the real facts about the American system."

August 7, 1936

HISTORIANS RECORD SAGA OF BUSINESS

Growth of U. S. Enterprise Is Traced in Universities From Old Records

By WILL LISSNER

Th· American business man and the individual enterprises he built that helped to make this country the most powerful industrial nation in the worl˙ have been discovered by the historians. In more than a dozen American colleges and universities the saga of American enterprise is being recorded from dusty archives and long-neglected records in projects well under way.

Th· movement to preserve the facts about the rise and growth of American enterprise sprang from professional historians. Several years ago, dismayed at the destruction and loss of valuable historical materials, they began seeking the cooperation of business executives in making their records a ailable for historical research.

This movement is now bearing fruit in studies supported by leading foundations and institutions at American colleges and universities. Among the institutions where the histories of old established enterprises or of enterprise-builders are being carried on are the following:

Harvard, New York, Northwestern, Pennsylvania, Missouri, Wyoming and Chicago Universities; Wheaton, Smith, Dartmouth, Northland Colleges; the State Museum of Denver.

Enterprises whose histories are being written include the Pepperell Manufacturing Company, the Saco-Lowell Shops, the Whitin Machine Works, the Pabst Brewing Company, the Scoville Manufacturing Company, the Washburn-Crosby Company and Western Range Cattle Industry.

Business men have welcomed the movement. Prof. N. S. B. Gras of Harvard University, reports that he and his staff have had more requests to write histories of companies than they could handle. General Motors and other corporations are taking part. The chemical industry has set up a non-profit history committee to aid researchers. The Newcomen Society, an organization composed largely of corporation officers, has set up a Research Policy Committee to forward such studies.

Banks, which once shrouded their records in mystery, have begun to open their files, excepting those concerning confidential relations with clients, to scholars. Among the institutions which have given welcome to members of the Economic History Association are the National City Bank and J. P. Morgan & Co., in New York and banks in Philadelphia and Baltimore.

Among the business leaders active in the movement's behalf are Ralph Budd of the Burlington Lines, and Henry S. Dennison of the Dennison Manufacturing Company. Through Mr. Budd's interest, the Burlington Railroad has made available 900 feet of shelves of its records. The Illinois Central Railroad has opened its files and the Denver, Rio Grande & Western has had its records minutely catalogued.

Most of the projects deal with large-scale enterprises, but the smaller ones and the lesser-known enterprisers are not being neglected. What can be done with the daybooks, letter files, payroll books and real estate records of a smaller company was shown by H. David Condron in his history of the Knapheide Manufacturing Company of Quincy, Ill., already published by The Journal of Economic History.

Mr. Condron traced the growth of the company from the little two-story wagon-maker's shop that Henry Knapheide opened on State Street, Quincy, in 1848, through its competition in 1905, with ten other carriage and wagon-making factories in Quincy that no longer exist, to the present concern, which produces automobile truck and trailer bodies.

Among the enterprisers now engaging the historians are Thomas H. Perkins, John M. Forbes, Fred S. Pearson, Cadwallader C. Washburn and Charles E. Perkins.

Studies of enterprises and enterprisers appeared occasionally in the past, but few were written from corporation records. The present movement received its impetus from the founding of the Economic History Association in 1940 and the establishment of the Committee on Research in Economic History by the Social Science Research Council.

One of the centers of these studies is at the Harvard Graduate School of Business Administration under the direction of Professor Gras. Histories being completed there are the one on the Pepperell company by Mrs. Evelyn H. Knowlton, one on the Saco-Lowell Shops from 1824 by George S. Gibb and one on the Whitin works from 1831 to 1946 by Thomas R. Navin.

The New York University Graduate School of Business Administration will start a business history series next year with the publication of a history of the Pabst company by Prof. Thomas C. Cochran, joint editor of The Journal of Economic History. The Council of Industrial Studies of Smith College is scheduling for publication next year studies in the evolution of machine tools and of mass production methods in precision manufacturing in the Connecticut Valley from 1775 to 1870 and a study of cutlery making there. These are by Felicia Johnson Deyrup and Martha Van Heusen Taber.

The University of Chicago received this year from the social science division of the Rockefeller Foundation a three-year grant for a history of Sears, Roebuck, to be produced under the direction of Dr. Boris Emmet.

The Rockefeller Foundation made a five-year grant for a study of the Western range cattle industry. The humanities division of this foundation and the University of Missouri provided grants under which the Western historical manuscripts collection of the university was set up under W. Francis English. Mr. English is soliciting the help of business men and others in preserving and collecting old records of enterprise in the Missouri and the central Mississippi Valley.

December 8, 194

SUCCESS POLL WON BY 5 BUSINESS MEN

The traditional American success story—in the manner of the Horatio Alger heroes—is symbolized best by five business leaders, according to a nation-wide poll of college students and faculty members.

Kenneth J. Beebe, president of the American Schools and Colleges Association, 30 Rockefeller Plaza, which conducted the survey among its 800 member institutions, said yesterday that the business men were selected as "symbolizing the American tradition of starting from scratch."

The men chosen in the poll were Walter S. Mack, president of the Pepsi-Cola Company; Grover Whalen, chairman of Coty's; I. J. Fox, president of I. J. Fox, Inc.; Charles Wilson, president of the General Electric Company, and Robert R. Young, president of the Chesapeake & Ohio Railroad.

Mr. Beebe pointed out that Mr. Mack started as a textile salesman, Mr. Whalen came from the lower East Side of New York City, Mr. Fox "started business with one fur coat" after returning from World War I, Mr. Wilson once worked for $4 a week and Mr. Young once cut rifle powder in a du Pont plant and lost out in several business ventures before becoming successful.

The poll reflected the general belief, Mr. Beebe said, that American business men "are successful because they take their joust for success as a game in the face of competition." He added that "this sportsmanlike approach, plus courage and ingenuity, accounts for the fact that there are more successful business men in America, in proportion to our population, than in any other country in the world."

Among the runners-up in the poll were Earl Bunting, a farm boy who became president of the O'Sullivan Rubber Company; Walter Hoving, president of the Hoving Corporation, who started as a $20-a-week linoleum salesman; Mayor O'Dwyer, who landed in New York with $25 and worked as a handyman, later becoming a policeman, and Paul Hoffman, president of the Studebaker Corporation, who has been a porter and a car salesman.

July 3, 1947

BIG BUSINESS FOUND FAVORED BY PUBLIC

Three-quarters of the people do not share the Government's fear of large companies or support the Government in trying to break up large organizations such as the Great Atlantic and Pacific Tea Company. This is revealed in a study by the Psychological Corporation, which showed also that most people believe large companies should be encouraged or let alone.

Practically all income groups and all educational groups gave much the same answers. Forty-eight per cent said large companies should be encouraged; 25 per cent, that they should be let alone; 11 per cent that they should be watched; 2 per cent that they were dangerous and should be broken up, and 14 per cent were uncertain.

There was no difference between the answers given by union and non-union families, according to the study. Both overwhelmingly believed that large companies should be encouraged or let alone.

December 23, 1950

Exit 'Robber Baron & Co.'

By EDWARD N. SAVETH

THE traditional historical estimate, revised mainly in the last fifteen years, of the business man and his contribution to American civilization, is a rags to riches story. The industrialist of the nineteenth century, once characterized as a robber baron, is—in terms borrowed from Joseph Schumpeter and Arnold Toynbee—described presently as making a "creative response" to his era. Episodes in the growth of our large corporations, traditionally given a bad historical press (replete with references to price-cutting, pooling and rebating) are now regarded as chapters in industrial statesmanship. Free enterprise, which once left the historical profession chilly, has become a prime determinant in the growth of nineteenth-century political democracy. Thorstein Veblen's predatory captain of industry, all tooth and claw, is almost unrecognizable in the portraits of the industrialist as philanthropist.

Mr. Saveth is the editor of a forthcoming book, "Understanding the American Past."

These contrasts are, perhaps, a little exaggerated. Primarily it is the emphasis which has shifted, since very few historians write entirely in one key. But the altered emphasis is none the less real and important. Allan Nevins, twice winner of the Pulitzer Prize in biography, author of a life of John D. Rockefeller Sr. and of a history of the Ford Motor Company, has called for a thorough revision in historical viewpoint.

According to Mr. Nevins, "our writers in general—for the historians but followed the poets, the novelists, and the dramatists—intimated that America had grown too fast, too coarsely, too muscularly. * * * Without denying that some accompaniments of our swift industrialization were atrociously bad we can now assert that this historical attitude was in part erroneous * * *. Rockefeller and his successors were guiltless of many of the charges flung at them, and in organizing the incredibly chaotic oil business performed a work not destructive, but essentially constructive. Andrew Carnegie, who did so much to build the nation's steel industry, cannot be dismissed with the term 'robber baron.' Nor can James J. Hill, whose Great Northern contributed so much to Northwestern growth. Nor can Henry Ford, who lowered prices, raised wages * * *"

HERE we have a great shift from the point of view maintained by Gustavus Myers in his famous "History of the Great American Fortunes" (1910), a history from which a whole generation of critics of American business drew material and argument.

The Nevins call for revisionism is by no means uncontested. Not a few are convinced that a rewrite is unnecessary; others seem to be saying: "Let the evidence pile up and *then* we shall see about revisionism." What adds zest as well as importance to the controversy is the feeling deep down in the bones of professional historians that the discovery of the business man at this particular juncture reflects a conservative trend throughout the nation.

Business history first began receiving systematic attention when N. S. B. Gras was appointed to a chair in the subject at Harvard in 1927. The attention of the historical profession, as well as of the general public, was then focused elsewhere—mainly upon the provocative syntheses of Charles and Mary Beard and Vernon L. Parrington. The Beards' "Rise of American Civilization" and Parrington's "Main Currents in American Thought" were critical of business practices and the values of a business civilization. The kind of plodding histories of individual businesses that Gras wanted written at Harvard seemed monumentally dull in comparison. The economic depression of the Thirties scarcely contributed to the popularity of business history. The title of Matthew Josephson's "The Robber Barons" reflected the prevailing attitude toward business.

Thorstein Veblen.

THE returning prosperity of the Nineteen Forties created a

climate more favorable to the study of business history. In 1940 appeared Allan Nevins' "John D. Rockefeller," Louis Hacker's "Triumph of American Capitalism" and Thomas Cochran's article on the "Social History of the Corporation." These seem, in retrospect, to have been harbingers of better times. Also, the increased interest of the historian in the business man at this time, should be related to the searchings, mainly by liberals, after new values to replace those made obsolete by American entrance into World War II.

After Hitler's blitz hit France, Archibald MacLeish assailed "irresponsible" writers for failure to develop those aspects of the American tradition which were antithetical to facism. Carl Becker was among those who deplored the "art for art's sake" formulations of the Nineteen Twenties and the class-oriented approach of the Nineteen Thirties and suggested that books be written about the good rather than bad features of American civilization. American liberalism was shifting its traditional orientation from isolationism and economic determinism, typified by Beard and Parrington, to internationalism and a kind of moralism essential to fighting a war in which business and liberalism were allied against fascism.

The intellectual's interest in business was long overdue. Given the intellectual atmosphere of the Nineteen Forties, one wonders that the business man was not discovered sooner and by a greater number of people. The success of Cameron Hawley's recent novel, "Executive Suite," with its favorable portrayal of business characters, and of Stewart Holbrook's by no means first-rate "Age of the Moguls," is indicative of how starved the public has been for books about business that go beneath the surface.

From portrait by Bernard J. Rosenmeyer. Owned by Mrs. Myers.
Gustavus Myers.

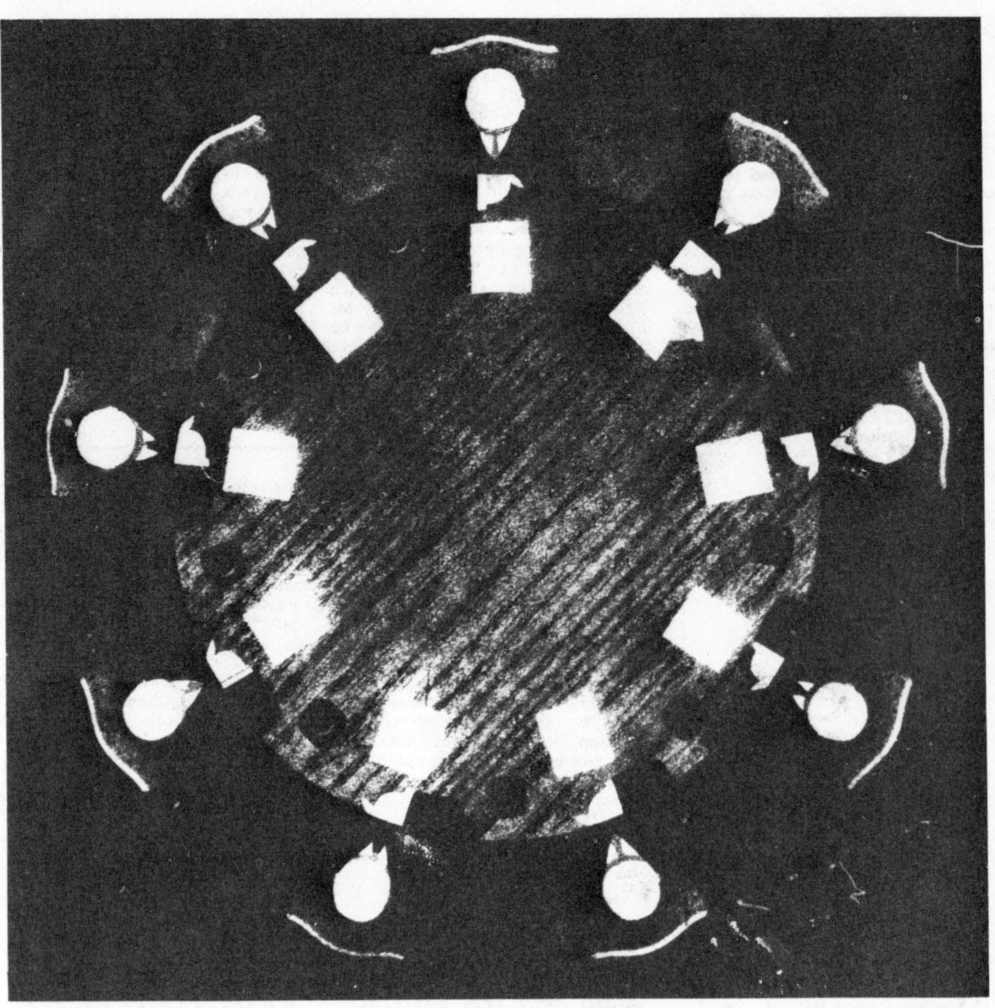

Painting by A. Petrucelli.

". . . performing a work essentially constructive."

QUITE clearly the recent interest in the business man is a product of the shifting liberal intellectual orientation brought on by World War II. One must, then, disagree with those who believe that the kind of revisionism Mr. Nevins calls for is related to a "reactionary complex" fastening itself upon America. Actually, many of the business historians are liberals. Moreover, to lump business history and the business historians with conservatism, is to imply that we can sort out the elements of the liberal and conservative traditions. How entangled our traditions and political heritages have become was illustrated in November, 1952. One historian called for the defeat of the Democratic party in the name of Thomas Jefferson's opposition to big government; meanwhile partisans of the welfare state were deriving increased comfort from the mercantilist practice of Hamilton.

Liberals who would give over the business man and his traditions to the conservatives and reactionaries, must reckon with the findings by Richard Hofstadter, Joseph Dorfman and Bray Hammond. Those findings were that business and the free enterprise spirit of the business community were motive forces in the rise of Jacksonian democracy. These same forces, it has been shown, were responsible for the expansion of political democracy in the later nineteenth century. The entire conception of revisionism as advanced by Mr. Nevins is not a reactionary doctrine but an explanation of how American material strength was forged to the end that democratic values be preserved.

The prevailing pattern of research into business history reflects no particular political orientation. Investigation has followed along these main lines. (1) Corporation and company histories like Ralph Hidy's forthcoming multi - volume treatment of Standard Oil of New Jersey. (2) Studies in entrepreneurial history conducted by the Research Center in Entrepreneurial History at Harvard. (Inspired by the theories of the late Joseph Schumpeter and with some indebtedness to Arnold Toynbee, the Center focuses upon the entrepreneur's response to environmental challenge in the milieu in which it occurred. An outstanding example of this type of investigation is Thomas Cochran's perceptive study of "Railroad Leaders 1845-1890: The Business Mind in Action," which attempts "to establish some norms of thought and attitude for the American railroad president of the period".) (3) Studies of the relationship between business and Government throughout American history such as those sponsored by the Social Science Research Council. (4) Broad syntheses of American history having business as a central theme, like Thomas Cochran and William Miller's, "The Age of Enterprise." (5) Studies of the behavior of men in business situations like the collection edited by William Miller entitled "Men in Business." (6) Studies of the relationship between business and specific phases of American life such as the chapter, "Business and the Life of the Mind" in Merle

Curti's "Growth of American Thought," and Edward C. Kirkland's slender volume, "Business in the Gilded Age."

Along these paths and without reference to readings of the political compass, the historian is making forays into the relatively unknown field of American business history. As a result, the balance of the business man's reputation has improved. This does not mean that spoilers like Jim Fisk, Jay Gould and Daniel Drew are to be honored as "industrial statesmen." The implication is, rather, that the impact of business upon our society is being written in terms of the actual business record and its ramifications.

In the process a better understanding of American life is emerging based upon a truer portrayal of our industrial leadership. Not the least important of the results of revisionism is the reduction of misunderstandings between the business and the intellectual community. That is bound to have a strong influence upon our present and future society.

July 4, 1954

Topics

Eggheads and Business

Widespread use of economists from the college campus by both recent Presidential candidates points up the growing rapprochement between the so-called eggheads and the business community. Not too long ago there seemed to be something almost Pavlovian about the intellectual's response to capitalism and business men generally. He either showed a strong anti-business bias or at best remained aloof from management problems. A cursory glance at the daily newspaper shows how things have changed. A recent meeting of the American Psychological Association included the comments of Dr. Burleigh Gardner, the social anthropologist, on consumer attitudes toward compact cars. A report from Ann Arbor discloses the University of Michigan's Survey Research Center findings of continued "hesitancy" on the part of consumers.

The Social Sciences

These are not isolated instances. A directory of the Advertising Research Foundation lists 150 social scientists available to do research for business. Leading American corporations as well as top Madison Avenue agencies are staffed with specialists in the social sciences. Voluminous grants from the business community to colleges and universities create projects that provide work for additional scholars. In face of this trend, some intellectuals deplore the commitment of the behavioral sciences to management. Its defenders reply that by applying the techniques of the social sciences, academicians have helped put management on a more "scientific" basis and have enabled our economy to move its goods more efficiently.

Why People Buy

Whatever the pros and cons, the point about expediting the flow of goods seems indisputable. After World War II, American business was faced with the huge task of finding customers to absorb the vastly increased productive capacity of the country. The response was development of what became known as motivational research—the attempt to get at the "why" of consumer behavior by depth interviews, sentence-completion tests and the other technical paraphernalia of clinical psychology, psychoanalysis and sociology. Out of early M. R. studies came many promotional and marketing coups, such as that of the black eye-patch that turned an obscure shirt into a whirlwind seller. Above all else, motivational research clearly demonstrated that the man or woman in the street does not buy products for rational reasons alone but for reasons of status, prestige and a multiplicity of other factors.

The Hidden Persuaders

In the last few years a new muckraking literature has devoted itself, among other things, to demolishing the claims of "the hidden persuaders," who are seen as an insidious force preying on the public's fears and anxieties. But the National Industrial Conference Board, a nonprofit business group, recently issued a study saying that while motivational research is hardly a universal panacea for business, it is, when properly used with more conventional methods, a useful tool for management. It found particular merit in M. R. as a source of hunches and new ideas and also stressed its value in pre-testing advertising, the equivalent of the technique known on Broadway of trying out shows on the road.

Nooks and Crannies

Far from the battlefield, meanwhile, undaunted motivational researchers peer into every nook and cranny of American life, turning up findings that often result in major corporate about-faces. Philip Morris, for example, recently changed the package of one of its filter brands when investigation showed that the package was favored by women as against men, whereas men smokers outnumber women by two to one. Social Research, Inc., conducted a study for a staid Wall Street brokerage house that brought on a complete change in its advertising and public relations and resulted in opening a street-level board room on Park Avenue.

A Permanent Wedding

Other studies in the burgeoning fields of communications research and operations research suggest that the scholar may be permanently wedded to business. Nor does it promise to be a one-sided union. If the intellectuals have donated their expertise to business, business has reciprocated by sending its bright young men into the academic groves to find out how the egghead lives. Indeed, it is perhaps the replacement of George Babbitt as the archetypical business man by the new sophisticated executive with a public service flair that has helped the egghead accommodate himself to the business community.

November 16, 1960

When Business Sits for Its Portrait

By JOHN BROOKS

Successful corporations, like successful men, sooner or later find themselves having their portraits painted. When they pay for the portrait (and they sometimes pay sums comprising six figures), they generally want to be painted pretty—prettier, in fact, than they really are. If, on the other hand, the portraitist is financially independent of them, they tend to be wary, suspecting him of being a sardonic Hogarth or Daumier, and often refuse to sit for him at all. The result is that most of the information and opinion that the public gets in book form about corporations—those so crucial institutions in all of our lives—is either tainted or fragmentary.

Mr. Brooks, a New Yorker staff writer, published two books in the business field during the past year, "Business Adventures" and "Once in Golconda."

Perhaps everyone but a really diehard proponent of corporation privilege will agree that the situation is deplorable. What can be done about it?

An authorized, or commissioned, book about a company is a work of history or journalism that is paid for and therefore owned by its subject. Such a book starts out with the obvious advantage that, being written with the cooperation of the subject, it is likely to contain much useful and accurate information not otherwise available. Corporations often open up to their chosen biographers all sorts of facts not normally distributed through the usual publicity channels.

Some notable books have been created under such circumstances. Allan Nevins's and Frank E. Hill's history of the Ford company **Ford** (Scribner's, 3 vols., $30), published between 1954 and 1963, manages to rise so far above the realm of corporate puffery that in places it approaches the tragic sense, a sense of the corporate drama as that of man against his fate—and all in spite of having been done with the full cooperation of the company.

Robert T. Elson's **Time Inc.** (Atheneum, $10), written and researched by people on the Time Inc. payroll, presents such a free-wheeling and even devastating picture of the company it describes (if you choose to read it that way) that anyone wanting to write a muckraking tract on the same subject need scarcely go farther for his source material. Why it was done quite that way remains a puzzling question. Was it the rigorous consciences of Luce and his men, or was it simply that Time Inc. had been in the habit of deftly getting the needle into others for so long that it couldn't change its habits when it got around to itself as a subject? I choose to think it was the former.

In any case, these are exceptions. Much more often, the scenario goes differently. At the outset, a corporation, in commissioning a book about itself, highly resolves that it will be enlightened and high-minded; that, having chosen a writer of reputation, it will encourage him to tell the story as he sees it, let the chips fall where they may. The writer is given the run of the company files. After a long period of breathless waiting on the company's part, he hands in his manuscript. It is eagerly combed, not only by the top corporate brass but also by platoons of lawyers and public-relations men who are trained—and paid—not to see that historical truth is served but that the practical interests of the corporations are.

It is hard to be high-minded by committee, and the bigger the committee, the harder. So the high resolves fall by the wayside. Wouldn't it perhaps be possible, the author is asked, to tone down the part about the Founder's mistresses? The current president, the Founder's son, did seem to have some slight feeling about that. And that chapter about the 1945 antitrust suit—well, after all, that's ancient history, why not just skip it? The tone of these requests is at first diffident, then cajoling, finally importunate. The changes are made; the book that is published ends up not quite the author's book, after all.

Well, fair enough. It was bought and paid for, wasn't it? Moreover, in wanting the warts taken off its portrait the corporation has shown the human trait of vanity; corporations should be encouraged to show human traits.

Realizing the trouble they may be in for, shrewd writers who undertake corporate commissions (and have sufficient bargaining power) have devised special contract provisions to protect their professional integrity and reputation. For example, the late Marquis James took on such commissions only with the agreement that should any changes be made in his manuscript, his name would not appear on the work when it was published.

But, clearly, more is at stake than the writer's reputation. There is also the matter of the reader's right to the whole truth—and, one would think, the book publisher's wish to be something more than an adjunct of the corporation's public-relations department. A commissioned book that has been doctored or censored by the subject and is then offered for sale at a stiff price over the imprint of a well-known publisher is something of a fraud. Yet the most reputable of publishing firms, including university presses, have repeatedly participated in such frauds.

Only a minority of commissioned business books are labeled as such. I recently came upon one of them—**Out of the Cracker Barrel,** by William Cahn (Simon & Schuster, $8.95), on the copyright page of which appears the admirably simple declarative sentence, "This book was commissioned by the National Biscuit Company." There ought to be, if not a law, at least a custom among reputable publishers calling for precisely such disclosure in every case.

All too commonly, the only hint to the circumstances of a company book's origin and the conditions of its production that is to be found between its covers is a line in the author's acknowledgments thanking the corporation and its officers for their cooperation. (I do not recall a case where he thanked them for their money, gracious as such a gesture might be.) Very often, there is not even such a hint as that. The innocent reader has nothing to go on except the text itself. Is the picture of the company that emerges all too flattering, indeed a little saccharine in spots? Does the *(Continued)* treatment of the current top officers border on the unctuous? For example, does the historian give intimations of captivity by incessantly calling them "Mister"? From such clues, the paying customer is left to guess—as in three-card monte at a county fair—whether he is being had.

On the face of the matter, the unauthorized company book is obviously more promising from the customer's point of view. Yet the difficulties that stand in the way of its creation are formidable.

In the first place, the writer does not have all that corporation gold to sustain him through the throes of creation. All he has is a publisher's advance—probably a modest one, since few company books are considered to be potential best sellers — and, if he is lucky, a foundation grant, to last him through a task that may take two years or more if he is to do it right.

In the second place, the company may well make his job as difficult as it can. Getting even simple facts may turn out to be like pulling teeth. Consider the case of William Rodgers, author of the recently published, uncommissioned **Think: A Biography of the Watsons and I.B.M.** (Stein & Day, $7.95). Early in the project—Rodgers reports in his Acknowledgments — a vice president of I.B.M. visited him after having learned what he was up to from a newspaper report. The vice president told Rodgers that the company felt one book about I.B.M. and Watson was enough—there already existed a more or less authorized book, **The Lengthening Shadow** by Thomas G. and Marva R. Belden (Little, Brown, $6.50)—and that it was only fair to warn Rodgers that he "would need the help of the company and that it would not be forthcoming." Rodgers, undaunted, decided to go ahead anyway, relying for sources on what he could get: published material, interviews with former I.B.M. employes, and routine information obtained through token ownership of I.B.M. stock.

The resulting book is unpopular in I.B.M. executive circles, the chief complaint being that it is based so largely on hearsay and gossip. One can only ask: Under the circumstances, what did they expect it to be based on?

Thus the very standard the "unauthorized" business writer sets himself—that of remaining financially independent of his subject—may specifically increase the difficulty of his task. The hair shirt he wears doesn't just hurt, it impedes his freedom of movement too. It would be nice to be able to say that this high moral posture invariably or even frequently produces high literary results. Unfortunately, it does not. Many unauthorized books about corporations are terrible—slipshod, slapdash, half-baked, inaccurate, unannotated, useless for reference—and, paradoxical as it may seem, more sedulous in their kowtowing to their subjects than any self-respecting chairman of the board would allow in a book he was paying for.

Exactly why these unauthorized quickies are cranked out is something of a mystery. Possibly the writer hopes the subject corporation will be pleased with the result and will buy up some copies; or possibly in a few cases he is just bucking for a job in the company's p.r. department. At any rate, neither history nor journalism is served as well by such productions as it is by the better commissioned books.

From the foregoing, it must be obvious that a serious writer who seriously undertakes an unauthorized book-length study of a corporation is probably slightly mad. Indeed, the best of such books do seem to result from obsessions, often those of former employes. Alan Harrington's **Life in the Crystal Palace** (Knopf, $4.50; Avon, paper, 95 cents), a first-rate study of the mores of a huge corporation that is never identified, seems to have been written at least partly as an act of exorcism.

A more recent book, **Robert R. Young, the Populist of Wall Street** by Joseph Borkin (Harper & Row, $6.95), is a partial biography of the late financier by one of his former lawyers, who writes of Young's many legal battles as an outright Young partisan but with the charming air of desperation of a lawyer who can't control his client. Books arising out of such circumstances are often interesting but rather specialized, lacking the sweep and scope of full-scale biographical works. Indeed, the full-scale, wholly independent study of a corporation, written for the general public, is a publishing rarity and no wonder.

All of which leads to the question of the corporation's responsibility in the matter of unauthorized book projects. Has it the right—assuming that it occupies the quasi-public position of having thousands of stockholders and perhaps millions of customers—to choose which writers it will cooperate with and which it will not? I believe that, in general, it has no such right. To be reasonable, there are some projects—because of their nature—for which more than perfunctory cooperation cannot and should not be expected. Sidney Fine's recent **Sitdown: The General Motors Strike of 1936-1937** (University of Michigan Press, $12.50), would seem to me to be one such project. My own investigation for a magazine piece on Ford's Edsel fiasco, undertaken immediately after it happened and republished in my **Business Adventures** (Weybright & Talley, $10), is another. (I recall that when I was out in Dearborn having some marvelously incoherent conversations, nominally about the Edsel, with Ford people, one of them offered me the loan of a Mercury to ride around in while I was there. If they had dredged up a leftover Edsel and offered that, I would have been tempted.)

But the ordinary project—the one where a reputable writer announces that he wants to take a broad view of the company as a whole—is a different matter. When Booton Herndon approached Henry Ford II in connection with research on his recent **Ford: An Unconventional Biography of the Men and Their Times** (Weybright & Talley, $8.95), Ford proposed that he himself write a preface that would read, in full, "I'm not interested in this damn book. I'm only cooperating because I've been asked to. I don't care if anybody reads it or not. Signed, Henry Ford II."

Now that seems to me the model attitude for a corporate boss to take, provided he is as good as his word about cooperating. The lordly Pierpont Morgan, who always refused to meet magazine or newspaper writers, used to grumble to his colleagues that the things appearing about him in the press were produced by writers who had no firsthand knowledge of their subject. The day for such gloriously arrogant illogic is long past. Yet the complaints of corporation heads about what appears in books by authors to whom they have closed their doors sound very similar.

So here are two suggestions aimed at clearing the presently rather murky air, and at promoting better recording of corporate affairs:

1) Every book commissioned by a corporation ought to be so identified on the copyright page. This is the publisher's responsibility.

2) A corporation has a social duty to offer cooperation to any well-qualified and not obviously biased writer. As a corollary to that, any corporation that refused such cooperation deserves what it gets, within the bounds of decency and law, in the resulting book. ■

January 18, 1970

Big Business as Everyman's Villain

By MARK J. GREEN

From Alexander Hamilton to William Simon, business has been our reigning private institution. The robber barons and the Depression pushed the theory and practice of capitalist enterprise to its breaking point, but most Americans still retained a faith in the large corporation as our provider, a faith not without some foundation: in the last forty years, the real per-capita income of American citizens has tripled; in the past 30 years, technological breakthroughs from computerization to penicillin have enriched our lives. This corporate cornucopia seemed so beneficial that author-economist Robert Heilbroner said in 1966 that he believed major corporations had attained such legitimacy as to be immune from successful attack.

But by Watergate 1974, this long-time faith in American business had been severely eroded. "America is experiencing an anti-business binge," observed a conservative corporate executive, and the evidence supports him. In 1965 only 37 per cent of the public thought giant corporations ought to be broken down into smaller units; today, reports the Opinion Research Corp., 53 per cent think so. Nine years ago, 55 per cent hàd "great confidence" in major companies; by 1972 this had fallen to 27 per cent. Whereas a decade ago it was major news in business journals if a shareholder gadfly attended an annual meeting, today corporate executives are buffeted daily by angry environmentalists, local, state and Federal consumer agencies and scores of sophisticated shareholder proposals on social issues.

What accounts for this fall from grace?

•*Corruption*. Business has been a key component of Watergate. Thirteen corporations, such as Gulf Oil, American Airlines and 3M, have pleaded guilty to illegally contributing campaign monies varying in amounts from $24,000 to $150,000. (These convictions may damage popularity but not necessarily income: since the average fine was $4,000 and the average company's gross was $20,000 a minute, it took each about 12 seconds to pay their debt to society.)

Watergate is only the most obvious example of business malpractice. Congressional hearings have

The New York Times/Don Hogan Charles

documented varieties of wrongdoing, as in the drug industry for example, where companies ship billions of doses of amphetamines knowing that medical needs require only a few thousand doses. In addition, in a survey of the presidents of 1,000 companies, 60 per cent of the 110 respondents agreed that "many [corporations] price-fix," which is a crime under the Sherman Act.

• *Profits and Prices.* "God damn Standard Oil," bellowed a character in Eugene O'Neill's *A Moon for the Misbegotten* in 1952. As gasoline prices rose an average of 19.7 per cent and oil industry profits 59 per cent in 1973, many consumers would probably agree with this sentiment. The industry asserted that profits seemed so outrageous only because 1972 was such a poor year by comparison and that in any case high profits were needed to finance new drilling and refining. Yet first quarter 1974 profits rose 80 per cent over the equivalent quarter of 1973.

The drug and auto industries, to take two examples over recent years, each earn a 20 per cent return on equity. This is owing in large measure, many believe, to, respectively, patent restrictions on drugs and the fact that the domestic auto market is concentrated in a few companies.

• *Inefficiency.* Whether revered or reviled, American companies have long been regarded as at least efficient engines of production. Even that verity, however, has come under attack. Although in past years major products have failed (the Edsel and corfam shoes are the most cited examples), recently entire corporations have failed or have encountered serious financial difficulties (Penn Central, Lockheed, Con Ed, LTV, the Franklin National Bank).

Unwieldy Management

Conglomerates and the energy shortage, in the eyes of some, also expose business inefficiency. The diversifying conglomerateurs of the late 1960's have become the divesting conglomerateurs of the early 1970's, as their stock prices plummeted. They came to appreciate the structural limitations of the dinosaur, whose small brain simply could not manage its large body. Not the least of their problems was, as pioneer economist Joe Bain pointed out in his work on corporate size and efficiency, the "diseconomies" of unwieldy management. And the energy shortage revealed how, contrary to economic theory, business does not invariably "maximize profits" by cutting costs. DuPont has said that most corporations could cut their energy use by at least 15 per cent without any sacrifice in productivity.

•*Social Responsibility*. How have corporations responded to social problems like employment discrimination and pollution? In the last year, the Equal Employment Opportunities Commission has moved against nine of the largest 25 firms in the nation for alleged discrimination against black and/or female employes.

Industrial pollution accounts for one-third of all solid waste, one-half of all air pollution and more than half of total water pollution. Industry did spend $2.5-billion in 1970 for air and water pollution control, and General Motors has named a vice-president for environmental activities. But the problem seems far from solved. The Environmental Protection Agency estimates that if the best available technology were applied to sources of particulate emissions, they would decline by 95 per cent.

•*White Collar Blues*—Corporate managers are earning more (their compensation has risen 27 per cent over the last two years), but they may be enjoying it less. For example, John DeLorean at age 48 and with a $550,000 salary and a shot at the presidency of General Motors, suddenly quit. He complained that one simply couldn't be an innovator, a planner on the 14th floor of the G.M. building in Detroit. "You were too harassed and oppressed by committee meetings and paperwork . . . G.M. has gotten to be a total insulation from the realities of the world." The Wall Street Journal has run a series of articles on executive dropouts and Business Week writes frequently about executives under stress.

The American corporation may now be in disfavor, but it still has an impressive impact on our lives. Because it decides where it will invest, whom it will hire, and what the quality and price of its products will be, the corporation intimately affects residents, workers and shoppers. Those who insist on regarding such companies as mere private concerns operating in a laissez-faire market system are indulging in a romantic fiction. When the size of the company is considered—a G.M. employing 800,000 people, an I.T.T. with plants in every state, an I.B.M. whose business product is becoming a *sine qua non* to all other businesses—the power and influence of big business is obvious.

Its accountability, however, is not. The roles of shareholders, directors and state charters, most analysts agree, have become essentially ceremonial —form over function. Today, economist Carl Kaysen has said, "the power of corporate management is, in the political sense, irresponsible power, answerable ultimately to itself."

Mr. Green, author of "The Closed Enterprise System," writes on business and legal matters.

June 30, 1974

CLUB WITHDRAWS BOOK ON DU PONTS

Prentice-Hall Links Fortune Action to Executive's Call

A sober but unflattering book on the du Pont enterprises and the du Pont family has been withdrawn by the Fortune Book Club after a telephone call from a du Pont company executive.

An official of the Book-of-the-Month Club, owner of the Fortune club, denied that the call had influenced its action. And the du Pont executive said his call did not constitute a threat.

However, the book's publisher, Prentice-Hall, said the book club "knuckled under to pressure." Gerard Colb Zilg, author of "Du Pont: Behind the Nylon Curtain," said the corporation was "trying to limit the book's promotion and circulation."

The book, a 623-page account of the development of du Pont, was written after five years of research, according to Mr. Zilg, a former public-school teacher in Wilmington, Del. It carries an endorsement from Leon H. Keyserling, former chairman of the Council of Economic Advisers, who described it as "a fascinating account of all the main ramifications of concentrated and gigantic industrial power."

Optioned Last April

The book, commissioned in 1972 for an advance of just under $10,000, according to Peter Grenquist, head of Prentice-Hall's trade-book division, was optioned to Fortune last April for $5,000 as its selection for November, 1974.

Last July, when the book was in galley, Harold G. Brown Jr., a spokesman for E. I. du Pont de Nemours & Co., telephoned F. Harry Brown, executive vice president and treasurer of the Book-of-the-Month Club. Mr. Brown, of du Pont later said he had informed the club's Mr. Brown that du Pont considered the book "scurrilous and unfair." He denied that this characterization carried any implication of legal action.

The club's Mr. Brown recalled that he had read the book in galley "and found it unpleasant." "I advised against the book," he continued. He contended, however, that his judgment had not been influenced by the du Pont call.

Al Silverman, vice president and editorial director of the Book-of-the-Month Club, said he could not recall a book having been withdrawn under similar circumstances. He said the decision to kill the choice of the book was "collective."

Minor Factual Errors

The club canceled its option and forfeited its $5,000.

Asserting that the club had "knuckled under to pressure," William J. Daly, Prentice-Hall's secretary and general counsel, said he had read the book early last July for possible libel and invasion of privacy. He said he had detected four minor factual errors and had questioned "one or two" adjectives. His suggested revisions, he said, were adopted, and in his opinion the book merited publication.

"Subsequently," Mr. Daly said yesterday, "I talked with Harold Brown of du Pont who told me that the company and members of the family considered the manuscript copy they had read 'scurrilous and actionable.' I assured him that I had read the galleys and that any factual inaccuracies had been corrected. And when I heard of the B.O.M.C.'s action I wrote Mr. Brown in protest."

Mr. Zilg's book was published last Nov. 14. It has received about two dozen reviews, all but two in its praise. Prentice-Hall has 10,000 copies in print and has ordered a printing of 3,000 more.

January 21, 1975

The Major Novelists View the American Businessman

By ROBERT F. LUCID

From one point of view, talking about the figure of the businessman in the annals of American literature is as idle and merely predictable an activity as talking about the figure of the black in antebellum Southern fiction. One figure is as much a stereotype as the other, and a reasonable reaction, at least from the point of view of the businessman and the black, is that most of the time the writers don't know what they're talking about.

But it is one thing to talk about the general view of reality to be found circulating among most literary people, the fashions and popular attitudes that prevail at any given moment, and it is another to talk about the way major writers envision the world in their work. Minor writers, seeking a fashion to follow, may praise or blame various groups pretty much according to which way the wind is blowing, but the work of a writer like Ernest Hemingway, most people would agree, goes its own way, not so much free of prejudice as transcendent of it.

Hemingway, in fact, is a good example to start with here, because, at first glance anyway, he appears to have created a fictional world in which the only business institutions to be found are hotels and bars, the only businessmen waiters, bartenders and room clerks.

But his work reminds us that it is possible to envision a society in a microcosmic way, and the microcosm he uses to symbolize all of our social institutions is the military. For him the military is a perfect symbol, revealing the essence of institutionality, for it acknowledges candidly what most institutions — including industry, of course—often cover up. It acknowledges that, by comparison with the welfare of the institution, the welfare of the individual doesn't matter.

Of course, not all major writers of this century envisioned society in a microcosmic way, and a fair number of them addressed the business figure directly. Theodore Dreiser's Frank Cowperwood, the hero of "The Financier," "The Titan" and "The Stoic," became the prototype of the swashbuckling, robber baron businessman for the period and is the figure that many readers remember.

But Dreises's George Hurstwood, in "Sister Carrie," the manager of a small business far removed from high financial adventure, may be the more truly memorable figure, illustrating as he does what can happen to the individual in our society when he forgets how perilously balanced he is between security and ruin.

There is a largeness and an invitation to self-identification built into both of Dreiser's characterizations and they serve as proof that from the earliest days of the century the businessman can properly be identified as a candidate for heroism in the imagination of the American artist.

What was true for Dreiser and the other naturalists was to an important degree true as well for our more psychologically oriented novelists and neither F. Scott Fitzgerald nor William Faulkner fought particularly shy of the businessman in their fiction.

Indeed for most of our major writers up to World War II the relationship between the individual and the business institution in which he is engaged results, as often as not, in the individual either commanding that institution or at least holding his own against its subsumptive powers, and the ability to do that was the only real test employed to separate the admirable people in society from the villains.

When one turns, however, to the American literature that has appeared since the Second World War and examines the work of our major writers, it is to discover that the figure of the institutional manager has undergone a change. If we accept the anthropological hypothesis that the major literature of a society reflects the working of that society's imagination, then we must conclude that the postwar American imagination began to envision the businessman as either a villain or a weakling, and sometimes as both.

How was the vision expressed? To answer that we must turn to the books. Why did the change come about? Perhaps the books can help us to answer that question as well.

Joseph Heller's "Catch-22" has clearly established itself as one of our most influential postwar novels and its author, like Hemingway, uses the military as a microcosm for all social institutions. But in Heller's military a crucial distinction is drawn between those individuals, officers or enlisted men, who are involved with the institutions simply because they have no choice, and those other people who work for that institution, drawing their vitality and indeed their identity from their managerial roles.

At the center of the first group is Yossarian, the novel's hero, and surrounding him are the rest of the sympathetic figures in the book: Dunbar, Nately, Chaplain Tappman, the masterly Orr and the others. But the people who are allied with the institution form a group that is essentially a rogues gallery, and to a striking degree their moral corruption is delineated for us in terms drawn from the world of business.

The old line military men, like General Dreedle, have a certain simple charm, but the new breed, represented by career officers such as General Peckem, ex-marketing executive Colonel Cargill and his twin Colonel Cathcart, the sinister Colonel Korn, and the entrepreneurs par excellence Milo Minderbinder and ex-Pfc. Wintergreen are all thinly disguised businessmen.

They have all substituted one of several concepts of success for the goal of self-realization and as extensions of the institutional arm they see as their natural enemies all of those individuals who have failed to embrace the institution as the redeemer.

Heller's novel is funny, of course, but bitterly so, and it unqualifiedly associates the destructive element in our society with the success-hunting, profit-taking, soul-selling business executive.

In "Invisible Man" Ralph Ellison avoids the device of setting up a single institution as microcosmic, and in fact is ambitious to achieve the illusion that the action in his novel is so wide-ranging as to encompass the whole macrocosm of our society. His nameless hero traverses a gamut of adversity that begins with the hostility of his small Southern community, continues through his college and the painful experiencing of New York City, extends further through his manipulation by business executives, labor unions, hospitals and revolutionaries both black and white, and ends finally with the hole in the ground where he is deposited.

The vision, clearly, is one in which the seeking individual finds himself in a state of total alienation within his culture and his enemies are legion, but prominent among them is the influential man of business.

The worlds of both Ellison and Heller are, after all, represented to us as insane, and in both of them a primary cause for the derangement of society is discovered in a relationship between institutions and their minions —a relationship indentified as that of the executive to his business establishment.

Most postwar writers are less prepared than either Heller or Ellison to discover the causes of our distress in the external architecture of our social institutions and artists like J. D. Salinger and Saul Bellow, Norman Mailer and Philip Roth are more inclined to discover the individual's enemy residing deep within the individual himself. Even so, when that enemy comes up from the dark to be identified he frequently is found to resemble, in many of his aspects, what might best be termed the institutional man.

To an important degree it is this identity that Holden Caulfield flees in "The Catcher in the Rye," rejecting a commercial value system that, seems to him not simply inadequate but in some way representative of internal obscenity, and Salinger's search for a redemptive religion in his shorter fiction is surely a part of the same rejection.

Saul Bellow is more pointed still and his hero in "Henderson, The Rain King" can usefully be identified as a magically grown-up Holden Caulfield whose adult discovery is that the institutional men have succumbed to a relationship that turned them into pygmies.

Norman Mailer began his career in 1948, of course, with "The Naked and the Dead" and the huge novel, again somewhat in the fashion of Hemingway, offers the Army as a microcosm of our whole social institutional system. Unlike Hemingway, however, Mailer presents his Army people in the most withering of lights, and General Cummings, as the institution's ultimate manager, is so far from the hero as to be virtually the antihero of this novel, perverse, malevolent and despicable.

In the years following, Mailer went on to excoriate, in "The Deer Park" and "Advertisements for Myself," the managers of both the film industry and the publishing industry for what they had done to exploit the art of the cinema and the novel, but he was to reserve his most direct and unqualified characterization of the business manager to two later novels: "An American Dream" and "Why Are We In Vietnam?"

Taken together, the novels present us with the two alternate identities that the postwar artist is prepared to allow the businessman and they remind us powerfully of the great change that has been wrought in those literary identities since the earlier period in the century.

Philip Roth, finally, offers us in his work a glimpse of a world which might help explain the shift between our prewar and postwar bodies of imaginative writing. In "Goodbye Columbus" and again in "Portnoy's Complaint" an angry and bewildered young hero looks at the corruption that a commercial society has generated from within and, in the second book, he then very significantly looks backward, recalling a time in his life when this seemed to him not to have been true.

Portnoy remembers the world that he knew in his prewar childhood, remembers "the men" whom he had admired so, small-business men for the most part who played softball every weekend and served as models for the little boy in the grandstand. Grown up and acting as an investigator of business dealings in New York City, he tells his psychiatrist what he now finds:

"The things that other men do—and get away with! And with never a second thought! To inflict a wound upon a defenseless person makes them smile, for Christ's sake, gives a little lift to their day! The lying, the scheming, the bribing, the thieving—the larceny, Doctor, conducted without batting an eye. The indifference! The total moral indifference!"

What Roth provides here may be a clue to the cause of the shift in vision that we have marked in the work of all the writers discussed so far. If, as amateur anthropologists, we hypothesize that the imaginative writing of the major artists in a culture is a reflection of the cultural imagination itself, we must of course conclude that the figure of the businessman seems to our imagination to have changed. But further investigation would quickly show that all "figures" and all significant institutional activities seem to our postwar imagination to have changed.

The fact is that there is something arbitrary about our focusing in on the figure of the businessman—present though he frequently is in our fiction—and what we need centrally to focus upon is the distress and anger and alarm of the individual in our postwar American society.

Our artists would seem to be telling us that something happened to us in the fairly recent past and that we have come now to believe ourselves capable of stooping to things we would never have imagined ourselves sinking to before. If that is the burden of what postwar American literature is saying, and a strong case can be made to prove that it is, then we should not be surprised that the figure of the businessman, when he happens to appear, is represented in grim and unsympathetic terms.

Dr. Lucid is chairman of the graduate group in the University of Pennsylvania's department of English. This article is excerpted from the Wharton Quarterly, a review published by the Wharton School of the University of Pennsylvania.

June 29, 1975

BUSINESS AND SOCIETY

A Country Called Corporate America

By ANDREW HACKER

PROBLEMS like poverty, civil rights and juvenile delinquency may have been "discovered" only in the past few years, but such can hardly be said about the issue of bigness in American business. On and off, for the last three-quarters of a century, the question has been raised whether the nation's large corporations have reached the point where they can cut a swath through society without having to account for the consequences of their actions.

Allusions to "the trusts," "robber barons" and even "Wall Street" may have an archaic ring. Nevertheless, the frequency and magnitude of recent corporate mergers, the high level of profits despite the persistence of poverty and the latest furor over safety in the country's leading industry are bringing renewed life to a debate that has as much importance for 1966 as it did for 1896, 1912 and 1932.

Our large corporations are very large indeed. General Motors, for example, employs more than 600,000 people, a figure exceeding the combined payrolls of the state Governments of New York, California, Illinois, Pennsylvania, Texas and Ohio. The annual sales of Standard Oil of New Jersey are over $10 billion, more than the total tax collections of Wisconsin, Connecticut and Massachusetts, in addition to the six states just mentioned. In fact, our 50 largest companies have almost three times as many people working for them as our 50 states, and their combined sales are over five times greater than the taxes the states collect.

ANDREW HACKER teaches in the department of government at Cornell.

YET here, as elsewhere, statistics can be made to tell several stories. For example, is big business getting bigger? Between 1957 and 1965, nonagricultural employment in the United States rose by about 10 per cent. But during that same period the number of persons employed by the nation's largest industrial companies went up by 15 per cent. Measured in this way, the big corporations seem to be taking three steps for every two taken by the economy as a whole.

At the same time it must be acknowledged that corporate America is by no means the fastest-growing sector in the country. Government employment, especially at the local level, is increasing at a higher rate; from 1957 to 1965 the public payroll, excluding the military, rose by 25 per cent. Even higher was the percentage increase in service industries. Enterprises like boatyards, car washes and carry-out restaurants—many of them small and locally based—have come to constitute the most vital area of economic growth.

Moreover, the advent of automated processes in large-scale production has actually cut down corporate employment in several dominant industries. At the outset of 1965, for instance, such companies as General Electric and Gulf Oil and United States Steel actually had *fewer* people working for them than they had eight years earlier. While these firms are not yet typical, they may be harbingers of things to come—the apparent ability of corporations to increase their sales, production and profits with a decreasing work force.

IF corporate size has a variety of yardsticks, corporate power is beyond precise measurement. It is not an overstatement to say that we know too much about the economics of big business and not nearly enough about the social impact of these institutions. Professional economists tend to focus on the freedom of large firms to set or manage prices, with the result that attention is deflected from the broader but less tangible role played by corporations in the society as a whole.

By the same token it is all too easy to expose egregious defects in consumer products or advertising or packaging. Congressional hearings make good forums for periodic charges of "irresponsibility," whether the target of the year happens to be automobiles or pharmaceuticals or cigarettes. It is true that the buyer is often stung — and sometimes laid to rest—by the products of even the most prestigeful of corporations. But the quality of merchandise, like the ability to fix prices, is only a secondary aspect of corporate power.

What calls for a good deal more thought and discussion is the general and pervasive influence of the large corporate entity in and on the society. For the decisions made in the names of these huge companies guide and govern, directly and indirectly, all of our lives.

THE large corporations shape the material contours of the nation's life. While original ideas for new products may come from a variety of sources, it is the big companies that have the resources to bring these goods to the public. The argument that the consumer has "free will," deciding what he will and will not buy, can be taken just so far. (Too much can be made of the poor old Edsel.) For in actual fact we *do* buy much or even most of what the large corporations put on the shelves or in the showrooms for us.

To be sure, companies are not unsophisticated and have a fair idea of what the consumer will be willing to purchase. But the general rule, with fewer exceptions than we would like to think, is that if they make it we will buy it. Thus we air-condition our bedrooms, watch color television in our living rooms, brush our teeth electrically in the bathroom and cook at eye-level in the kitchen. It is time for frankness on this score: the American consumer is not notable for his imagination and does not know what he "wants." Thus he waits for corporate America to develop new products and, on hearing of them, discovers a long-felt "need" he never knew he had.

And more than any other single force in society, the large corporations govern the character and quality of the nation's labor market. The most visible example of this process has been the decision of companies to introduce computers into the world of work, bringing in train an unmistakable message to those who must earn a living. Millions of Americans are told, in so many words, what skills they will have to possess if they are to fill the jobs that will be available. A company has the freedom to decide *how* it will produce its goods and services, whether its product happens to be power mowers or life insurance or air transportation. And having made this decision, it establishes its recruiting patterns accordingly. Individuals, in short, must tailor themselves to the job if they want to work at all. Most of us and all of our children, will find ourselves adjusting to new styles of work whether we want to or not.

The impact of corporate organization and technology on the American educational system deserves far closer attention than it has been given. Whether we are talking of a vocational high school in Los Angeles or an engineering college in Milwaukee or a law school in New Haven, the shape of the curriculum is most largely determined by the job needs of our corporate enterprises. The message goes out that certain kinds of people having certain kinds of knowledge are needed. All

American education, in a significant sense, is vocational. Liberal-arts students may enjoy a period of insulation but they are well aware that they will eventually have to find niches for themselves in offices or laboratories.

While many college graduates go into non-corporate or non-business employment, the fact remains that much of their educational tune is still being determined by corporate overtures. Even the liberal-arts college in which I teach has recently voted to establish within its precincts a department of "computer science." It is abundantly clear that while I.B.M. and Sperry Rand did not command Cornell to set up such a department, the university cannot afford to be insensitive to the changing character of the job market.

OUR large firms both have and exercise the power to decide where they will build their new factories and offices. And these decisions, in their turn, determine which regions of the country will prosper and which will stagnate. The new face of the South is, in largest measure, the result of corporate choices to open new facilities in what was hitherto a blighted area. Not only has this brought new money to the region, but new kinds of jobs and new styles of work have served to transform the Southern mentality. The transition to the 20th century has been most rapid in the communities where national corporations have settled. You cannot remain an unrepentant Confederate and expect to get on in Du Pont.

By the same token the regions which have not prospered in postwar years have been those where corporations have opted not to situate. Too much can be made of the New England "ghost towns." Actually corporations have "pulled out" of very few places; more critical has been their failure to establish or expand facilities in selected parts of the country. Thus patterns of migration—from the countryside to the city and from the city to the suburb—are reflections of corporation decisions on plant and office location. If men adjust to machines, they also move their bodies to where the jobs are.

Related to this have been the corporate decisions to rear their headquarters in the center of our largest cities, especially the East Side of New York. Leaving aside the architectural transformation and the esthetic investment with which we will have to live for many years, the very existence of these prestige-palaces has had the effect of drawing hundreds of thousands of people into metropolitan areas not equipped to handle them. Thus not only the traffic snarls and the commuter crush, but also the burgeoning of suburbs for the young-marrieds of management and the thin-walled apartments for others in their twenties, fifties and sixties.

MUCH—perhaps too much—has been made of ours being an age of "organization men." Yet there is more than a germ of truth in this depiction of the new white-collar class which is rapidly becoming the largest segment of the American population. The great corporations created this type of individual, and the habits and style of life of corporate employment continue to play a key role in setting values and aspirations for the population as a whole. Working for a large organization has a subtle but no less inevitable effect on a person's character. It calls for the virtues of adaptability, sociability, and that certain caution necessary when one knows one is forever being judged.

The types of success represented by the man who has become a senior engineer at Western Electric or a branch manager for Metropolitan Life are now models for millions. Not only does the prestige of the corporation rub off on the employe, but he seems to be affixed to an escalator that can only move in an upward direction. Too much has been made of the alleged "repudiation" of business and the corporate life by the current generation of college students. This may be the case at Swarthmore, Oberlin and in certain Ivied circles. But in actual fact, the great majority of undergraduates, who are after all at places like Penn State and Purdue, would like nothing better than a good berth in Ford or Texaco. Indeed, they are even now priming themselves to become the sort of person that those companies will want them to be.

THE pervasive influence of the large corporations, in these and other areas, derives less from how many people they employ and far more from their possession of great wealth. Our largest firms are very well-off indeed, and they have a good deal of spare cash to spend as and where they like. These companies make profits almost automatically every year, and they find it necessary to give only a fraction of those earnings back to their stockholders in the form of dividends.

(If the largest companies are "competitive" it is only really in the sense that we all are: all of us have to keep working at our jobs if we are to survive as viable members of the society. Quite clearly the biggest corporations stand no risk of going out of business. Of the firms ranking among the top 40 a dozen years ago all but two are still in preeminent positions. And the pair that slipped—Douglas Aircraft and Wilson meat-packing—continue to remain in the top 100.)

Thus the big firms have had the money to create millions of new white-collar jobs. Department heads in the large companies ask for and are assigned additional assistants, coordinators, planners and programmers who fill up new acres of office space every year. What is ironic, considering that this is the business world, is that attempts are hardly ever made to discover whether these desk-occupiers actually enhance the profitability or the productivity of the company. But everyone keeps busy enough: attending meetings and conferences, flying around the country, and writing and reading and amending memoranda.

White-collar featherbedding is endemic in the large corporation, and the spacious amenities accompanying such employment make work an altogether pleasant experience. The travel and the transfers and the credit-card way of life turn work into half-play and bring with them membership in a cosmopolitan world. That a large proportion of these employes are not necessary was illustrated about 10 years ago when the Chrysler Corporation had its back to the wall and was forced to take the unprecedented step of firing one-third of its white-collar force. Yet the wholesale departure of these clerks and executives, as it turned out, had no effect on the company's production and sales. Nevertheless, Chrysler was not one to show that an empire could function half-clothed, and it hired back the office workers it did not need just as soon as the cash was again available.

If all this sounds a bit Alice-in-Wonderland, it would be well to ponder on what the consequences would be were all of our major corporations to cut their white-collar staffs to only those who were actually needed. Could the nation bear the resulting unemployment, especially involving so many people who have been conditioned to believe that they possess special talents and qualities of character?

CORPORATE wealth, then, is spent as a corporation wishes. If General Motors wants to tear down the Savoy-Plaza and erect a corporate headquarters for itself at Fifth Avenue and 59th Street, it will go ahead and do so. Quite obviously an office building could, at a quarter of the cost, have been located on Eleventh Avenue and 17th Street. But why should cost be the prime consideration? After all, the stockholders have been paid their dividends, new production facilities have been put into operation, and there is still plenty of money left over. Nor is such a superfluity of spare cash limited to the very largest concerns. Ford, which is generally thought of as General Motors' poor sister, was sufficiently well-heeled to drop a quarter of a billion dollars on its Edsel and still not miss a dividend.

If our large corporations are using their power to reshape American society, indeed to reconstruct the American personality, the general public's thinking about such concentrated influence still remains ambiguous.

There persists, for example, the ideology of anti-trust and the fond place in American hearts still occupied by small business. Thus politicians can count on striking a resonant chord when they call for more vigorous prosecutions under the Sherman Law and for greater appropriations for the Small Business Administration. Most Americans, from time to time, do agree that our largest companies are too big and should somehow or other be broken up into smaller units. But just how strong or enduring this sentiment is is hard to say. No one really expects that Mobil Oil or Bethlehem Steel can or will be "busted" into 10 or a dozen entirely new and independent companies. Thus, if the ideology that bigness equals badness lingers on, there is no serious impetus to translate that outlook into action.

PART of the problem is that if Americans are suspicious of bigness, they are not really clear about just what it is about large corporations that troubles them. Despite the periodic exposures of defective brake cylinders or profiteering on polio vaccine, the big story is not really one of callous exploitation or crass irresponsibility. Given the American system of values, it is difficult to mount a thoroughgoing critique of capitalism or to be "anti-business" in an unequivocal way. The result is that our commentaries in this area are piecemeal and sporadic in character. We have the vocabularies for criticizing both "big government" and "big labor" but the image of the large corporation is a hazy one, and despite its everyday presence in our midst our reaction to its very existence is uncertain.

Take the question of who owns our big enterprises. In terms of legal title the owners are the stockholders, and management is accountable to that amorphous group. But it is well known that in most cases a company's shares are so widely dispersed that the managers of a corporation can run the firm pretty well as they please. Yet even assuming that the executives are acting with the tacit consent of their company's theoretical owners, it is worth inquiring just who these stockholders are.

Interestingly, a rising proportion of the stockholders are not people at all but rather investing institutions. Among these non-people are pension funds, insurance companies, brokerage houses, foundations and universities. Thus some of the most significant "voters" at the annual meetings of the big companies are the Rockefeller Foundation, Prudential Life and Princeton University. And these institutions, out of habit and prudence, automatically ratify management decisions.

It is instructive that the corporations' own public-relations departments have just about given up trying to persuade us that these stockholder gatherings are just another version of the local town meeting. The last report I saw that did this was filled with photographs showing average-citizen stockholders rising to question the board of directors on all manner of company policies. "A sizable number of shareholders participated in the lively discussion periods," the reader is told. "Many more spoke individually with directors and other executives about the affairs of the company." However, in small type in the back of the report is an accounting of the five votes that were actually taken at the meeting. In no case did the management receive less than 96 per cent of the ballots (i.e., shares) that were cast.

From these observations at least one answer is possible: yes, there is a "power élite" presiding over corporate America. Yet the problem with this term is that the "élite" in question consists not so much of identifiable personalities—how many of the presidents of our 20 largest corporations can any of us name? — but rather of the chairs in the top offices.

The typical corporation head stays at his desk for only about seven years. The power he exercises is less discretionary than we would like to believe, and the range of decisions that can be called uniquely his own is severely limited. (It is only in the small companies on the way up, such as the Romney days at American Motors, that the top men impress their personalities on the enterprise.) John Kenneth Galbraith once noted that when a corporation president retires and his successor is named, the price of the company's stock, presumably a barometer of informed opinion, does not experience a perceptible change.

Unfortunately it is far easier to think in terms of actual individuals than of impersonal institutions. Therefore it must be underlined that the so-called "élite" consists not of Frederic Donner and Frederick Kappel and Fred Borch but rather of *whatever* person happens to be sitting in the top seat at General Motors and A.T.&T. and General Electric. We are reaching the point where corporate power is a force in its own right, for all intents and purposes independent of the men who in its name make the decisions.

The modern corporation is not and cannot be expected to be a "responsible" institution in our society. For all the self-congratulatory handouts depicting the large firm as a "good citizen," the fact remains that a business enterprise exists purely and simply to make more profits—a large proportion of which it proceeds to pour back into itself. (True, the big companies do not seek to "maximize" their profits: their toleration of make-work and high living is enough evidence for this.)

But corporations, like all businesses whether large or small, are in the primary busi-

"And so, in the words of Tiny Tim, God bless us every one."

ness of making money; indeed, they do not even exist to produce certain goods or services that may prove useful or necessary to society. If Eli Lilly or Searle and the other drug companies discovered that they could chalk up larger profits by getting out of vaccines and manufacturing frozen orange juice instead, they would have no qualms or hesitation about taking such a step.

A corporation, then, cannot be expected to shoulder the aristocratic mantle. No one should be surprised that in the areas of civil rights and civil liberties our large companies have failed to take any significant initiative. The men who preside over them are not philosopher-kings, and no expectation should be held out that they may become so. At best they can be counted on to give some well-publicized dollars to local community chests and university scholarships. But after those checks are written (and the handing-over of them has been photographed) it is time to get back to business.

And this is as it should be. Corporate power is great —in fact, far more impressive than corporation executives are willing to admit—and were large corporations to become "social-minded," their impact would be a very mixed blessing. For then the rest of us would have to let corporate management define just what constitutes "good citizenship," and we would have to accept such benefactions without an excuse for comment or criticism.

Therefore, when corporations, in the course of doing their business, create social dislocations there is no point in chiding or exhorting them to more enlightened ways. It would be wrong, of course, to lay the blame for all of our social ills at the doorsteps of the large firms. If the drug companies manufacture cheap and effective birth control pills it is a trifle presumptuous to take them to task for whatever promiscuity occurs as a consequence.

Nevertheless, the American corporation, in the course of creating and marketing new merchandise, presents us with temptations — ranging from fast cars to color television — to which we sooner or later succumb. There is nothing intrinsically wrong with color television. It is, rather, that the money we spend for a new set is money that can no longer be put aside for the college education of our children. (Thus, no one should be surprised when, 15 years from now, there is a demand for full Federal scholarships for college students. Not the least reason for such a demand will be that we were buying color TV back in 1966.)

SPECIFIC questions can be framed easily enough. It is the answers that are far from clear. We have unemployment: how far is it because corporations have not been willing or able to create enough jobs for the sorts of people who need them? We have a civil rights problem: how far is it because corporations have been reluctant to hire and train Negroes as they have whites? We have a shortage of nurses: how far is it because corporations outbid and undercut the hospitals by offering girls secretarial jobs at higher pay for less work? We have whole waves of unwanted and unneeded immigrants pouring into our large cities: how far is it because corporations have decided to locate in Ventura County in California rather than Woodruff County in Arkansas?

Questions like these may suggest differing answers but they do add up to the fact that a good measure of laissez-faire continues to exist in our corporate economy. For all their ritual protestations over Government intervention and regulation, our large companies are still remarkably free: free to make and sell what they want, free to hire the people they want for the jobs they have created, free to locate where they choose, free to dispose of their earnings as they like — and free to compel the society to provide the raw materials, human and otherwise, necessary for their ongoing needs.

The task of picking up the pieces left by the wayside belongs to Government. This is the ancient and implicit contract of a society committed to freedom of enterprise. But whether the agencies of Government have the resources or the public support to smooth out the dislocations that have been caused to our economy and society is not at all clear. Negro unemployment, the pollution of the Great Lakes, the architectural massacre of Park Avenue and the wasteland of television seem to be beyond the power and imagination of a Government that has traditionally understood its secondary and complementary role.

Corporate America, with its double-edged benefactions and its unplanned disruptions, is in fact creating new problems at a rate faster than our Governmental bureaus can possibly cope with them. Given that the articulate segments of the American public seem at times to show more confidence in United States Steel than in the United States Senate, the prognosis must be that the effective majority today prefers a mild but apparently bearable chaos to the prospect of serious Government allocation and planning.

The American commitment to private property means, at least for the foreseeable future, that we will be living with the large corporation. On the whole, Americans seem vaguely contented with this development, unanticipated as it may have been. In light of this stolidity, the order of the day — to reverse Karl Marx's dictum — is to understand our world rather than change it; to identify, with as much clarity and precision as is possible, the extent to which a hundred or so giant firms are shaping the contours of our contemporary and future society. Only if we engage in such an enterprise will we be able to make any kind of considered judgment concerning the kind of nation in which we wish to live and the sort of people we want to be.

July 3, 1966

The Shape of Things

THE NEW INDUSTRIAL STATE. By John Kenneth Galbraith. 427 pp. Boston: Houghton Mifflin Company. $6.95.

By RAYMOND J. SAULNIER

OF his new book, John K. Galbraith says that it stands in relation to "The Affluent Society" as a house to a window, an apt and useful contrast. The 1958 volume afforded a view of consumption as one aspect of American life; "The New Industrial State," on the other hand, deals with the whole structure of American society, centering on its economic institutions, and Mr. Galbraith argues a theory of how it has come to be what it is.

This is a tightly organized, closely reasoned book, notable for what it says about the dynamics of institutional change and for certain qualities of its author: a sardonic wit, exercised liberally at the expense of conservatives, and unusual perception. That the latter in fact produces slightly out-of-focus images of reality (the key to understanding Mr. Galbraith) makes it, in a way, all the more interesting.

Although the book's theoretical structure is formidable, its architecture is not particularly novel. It is strongly reminiscent of, among American writings, Thorstein Veblen's "The Engineers and the Price System" (1921); among contemporary writers, Robert Heilbroner and Daniel Bell come to mind as social scientists exploring the same range of problems and coming to broadly similar conclusions.

But novelty isn't everything: one can make a decent case for the proposition that it is more important to be right than different. The critical question is whether Galbraith's building-blocks are sufficiently strong to support his structure. This reader thinks they are not. It is not that what he says on specific issues is completely wrong. Rather, what he says is just true enough to be plausible, but not true enough to make a convincing case. In the end, what Mr. Galbraith presents is a shaky edifice.

Briefly, his theory of social change is technological determinism. As he sees it, modern technology has two principal effects. First, it is so intricate as a process that it can be practiced only by highly specialized professionals operating primarily in groups, their individuality largely submerged in a world of committees within committees. They constitute what he calls the "technostructure" and have a counterpart in government. After the technostructure, the second major creation of modern technology is the "mature corpora-

MR. SAULNIER, professor of economics at Barnard College, is a former chairman of the Council of Economic Advisers.

tion," which comes into being because it is the only entity able to supply the organization of effort and the large amounts of capital required to make technology work. In this context, the antitrust laws lose their meaning. Such commitments of specialized professional personnel and capital make planning by industry an absolute requirement of survival; because so much is at stake, the mature corporation can take no chances. The security of the technostructure, made increasingly precarious by specialization, requires that things be arranged in advance.

What remains for Galbraith to explain—and this constitutes the major part of his book—is how the mature corporation, in an increasingly intimate alliance with government, arranges things so they come out as the technostructure wants and needs them to come out. It will be no surprise to those familiar with his views that Galbraith sees not the slightest chance of accomplishing this by the simple expedient of being informed of consumer wants and organizing to supply them. The market is not reliable; demand and supply must be managed. Advertising takes care very nicely of the consumer's specific choices in spending income; and the possibility that over-all purchasing power might be inadequate—a calamity the technostructure, as such, would be powerless to prevent—is eliminated by fiscal and monetary policies under which government maintains aggregate demand at all times at appropriate levels.

Next, the mature corporation has achieved security against two additional industrial risks: the need to rely on capital markets for financing, with all that that means in accountability to outsiders, and the pressure of trade union demands. As Galbraith sees it, internally generated funds free the mature corporation from dependency on bankers; and a benign state, more and more seen by industry as a partner in its affairs, has largely neutralized trade union power through wage guideposts. Whatever remains of what Galbraith once regarded as the countervailing power of trade unionism is being eliminated by technology, which tends to ally the worker more and more with the technostructure.

Finally, through large military and space expenditures—also useful for maintaining aggregate demand—government underwrites research and development that goes beyond the resources of even the mature corporation, e.g., the supersonic transport, but which is essential to the full flowering of the technostructure. All in all, a pretty tidy world.

Galbraith gives relatively little attention to the question of where this is leading us, but from what he says, and from what is implied by his dialectic, I judge that what might emerge is a kind of "corporative state." In any case, he sees the technostructure of business and government tending to merge into a single technocratic class and pretty much taking charge of things. The one group capable of humanizing the institutional change technology is propelling, and of keeping it on a democratic path, is the "educational and scientific estate." If Galbraith has heroes, they are here.

So much for the essentials of the theory. The crucial question in evaluating it is whether corporate enterprise and government have in fact achieved the degree of control he attributes to them. It is not enough to say they have achieved important control; the question is whether the process has gone far enough to have produced the institutional transformation his theory implies.

In the first place, is the consumer the manipulated, accurately forecastable, somehow faceless figure he is pictured as being, buying what he is told to buy at prices and in amounts that suit the convenience and security of the technostructure? Without meaning to underrate the adman's successes, I suggest that there is little in experience or logic to support this view. If advertising had the power here alleged, would a product ever lose its market position, let alone fail altogether? But the record is full of fatalities; indeed it is rare that a product, design or style, no matter how much advertising money is spent, does not at some point fall from favor. By some beneficent law of nature, admen consume admen.

Second, there is no evidence that corporate enterprise has achieved meaningful financial independence. In the years 1960-65, corporations went to market for one-third of their capital requirements; and last summer a good many treasurers got a quick course of instruction in the virtues of liquidity.

Third, the familiar concept of separation of corporate ownership from control, a piece of now-conventional wisdom that is a key building-block in Galbraith's structure, is actually quite obsolete. It misses entirely the hawk-eye surveillance of corporate management by institutional investors and security analysts, all surrogates of the individual shareholder and, Galbraith notwithstanding, still very much interested in profit maximization. As for comfortable independence, it would be difficult to name a figure on the American scene, political personages not excepted, more closely monitored than the head of a large corporation.

Fourth, contrary to what Galbraith states or implies, there is no convincing empirical evidence of a trend toward greater concentration in markets (for example, in the findings of the Senate Judiciary subcommittee that recently studied this question); there is no basis for asserting that a market with only a few large suppliers (an oligopoly) cannot be intensely competitive, and no *a priori* reason why oligopoly cannot be economically efficient.

Finally, is the technostructure, through its alliance with government, protected against cost increases, and assured of never-failing aggregate demand? Was not 1966 the year the wage guideposts collapsed? And has it not been demonstrated in the past nine months that even with military expenditures approaching $75-billion a year, there is still a risk of recession? It is part of the now-conventional wisdom that the state can prevent such mishaps, but there they are—accompanied, moreover, by budget deficits that could exceed $25 billion a year and a payments imbalance that threatens both the international monetary system and the nation's gold supply.

What it all comes to is that the U. S. economy is not as neatly buttoned-up as Mr. Galbraith's book would lead one to believe. He disarms potential critics with occasional displays of modesty: "Truth is never strengthened by exaggeration" (p. 165) and "I argue only for a complex two-way flow of influence" (p. 317). But his argument is basically dogmatic. Its elements are sufficiently out of focus to produce a distorted over-all picture.

This is not to deny there is a risk that our economy, in its relation to government, will evolve into the near-monolithic shape implied by Galbraith's theory. But if it does, I doubt it will do so by the route he has sketched. Unfortunately, there is more than one road to the monolithic society. A possibility altogether too likely is that basically inflationary fiscal and monetary policies will be persisted in, will invite more and more pervasive regulation of prices and profits and will in the end amount to a suppression of private undertakings.

THERE is an extremely important difference between these two possible roads to statism: there is a certain inevitability implied in Galbraith's (basically, the evolution is propelled by the invisible hand of modern technology) but no parallel inevitability about the second (in which man-made decisions are decisive). Moreover, as a theory of institutional change, the second has three notable merits: it is a better fit to the facts; it places responsibility where responsibility belongs; and it provides more basis for hope that genuinely democratic institutions can be preserved.

But this is another story; for the moment, it is pertinent only to repeat one's admiration for Mr. Galbraith's considerable intellectual achievement. "The New Industrial State" deserves the widest possible attention and discussion. It will provoke much argument among economists; it may well inspire graduate schools of business to ask new questions about what they are doing; and, hopefully, it will provide a conversation-piece in executive dining rooms. All in all, a constructive result.

June 25, 1967

The Corporation Gap

THE MODERN CORPORATION AND PRIVATE PROPERTY. By Adolf A. Berle and Gardiner C. Means. Revised Edition. 380 pp. New York: Harcourt, Brace & World. $9.75.

By ROBERT LEKACHMAN

TWO tests of a book's classic status in the social sciences are easily passed by "The Modern Corporation and Private Property": its major conclusions have been so generally accepted that their source has been mislaid, and though everybody has heard the title almost no one has recently read the book. In this reissue, separate prefaces by the two authors and a new statistical appendix by Mr. Means have been attached to the unchanged original text. The 36 years since original publication have certainly not diminished the social significance of the large corporation, any more than time has weakened the power of Berle's and Means's analysis of its operations. But the book's major influence has perhaps been in a direction unforeseen by its authors and its earliest readers.

The two authors came to three main conclusions about the American corporation: First, economic power was becoming increasingly concentrated as larger and larger percentages of business wealth fell into fewer and fewer corporate hands. Second, the ownership of these huge corporations was increasingly dispersed among a swelling army of stockholders. Third, the separation of ownership and control had gone very far and was likely to proceed still farther.

Berle, a Columbia Law School professor soon to be a member of Roosevelt's Brain Trust and then of his administration, and Means, a Harvard-trained economist, based their judgments upon an elegantly analyzed body of statistical information revealing the size and ownership characteristics of corporations, and an equally impressive interpretation of the case law applicable to modern business. Little by little, Berle demonstrated, the courts had nibbled at the powers of stockholders over corporations which legal myth if not legal fact entitled them to run in stockholder interests. The judges had simultaneously expanded the discretion of managers who owned little or no stock in the huge institutions over which they exercised something approaching plenary power.

On the whole these empirical findings have stood up well over the years, although economists still amuse themselves by debating whether corporate concentration has or has not increased. The authors were boldest when they came to evaluate the significance of their conclusions. The transformed corporation, by its very success, they declared, had "cleared the way for the claims of a group far wider than either the owners or the control. They have placed the community in a position to demand that the modern corporation serve not alone the owners or the control but all society." The issue was one of legitimacy.

Yet, even though Berle and Means were convinced that "the rise of the modern corporation has brought a concentration of economic power which can compete on equal terms with the modern state — economic power versus political power, each strong in its own field," they did not proceed to a program of nationalization or even extensive public control in the manner of liberal commentators like Stuart Chase, who hailed the book in The New Republic and Ernest Gruening (now the senior

Photograph by Clemens Kalischer

MR. LEKACHMAN is on leave from the State University of New York at Stony Brook as a Fellow in Law and Economics at Harvard Law School.

Senator from Alaska), who praised it in The Nation.

The authors' own somewhat vague and general preferences were for a voluntary reinterpretation of corporate goals by the corporate managers themselves. Their key statement contained an implicit appeal to executive statesmanship:

"When a convincing system of community obligations is worked out and is generally accepted, in that moment the passive property right of today must yield before the larger interests of society. Should the corporate leaders, for example, set forth a program comprising fair wages, security to employees, reasonable service to their public, and stabilization of businesses, all of which would divert a portion of their profits from the owners of passive property, and should the community generally accept such a scheme as a logical and human solution of industrial difficulties, the interests of passive property owners would have to give way. Courts would almost of necessity be forced to recognize the result. . . ."

How faithfully has business followed this prospectus? What impact have Berle and Means had upon academic economics? Although John Kenneth Galbraith has said of "The Modern Corporation and Private Property" that "with Keynes' 'General Theory of Employment, Interest and Money,' [it is] one of the two most important books of the 1930's," Berle and Means did not, as Keynes did, revolutionize economic theory — at least as the theorists practice its mysteries.

Although Berle and Means believed that the logic of profit maximization had been fundamentally altered by the tendencies they documented, most economists continue to believe that managers maximize profits very much as owners do. Corporate officials may aim directly at growth rather than profit and they may even appear to perform the political role of harmonizing the interest groups — labor unions, suppliers, stockholders, customers and the anti-trust division of the Department of Justice — that affect the corporation's environment. But the managers' conduct is or at least can be made to seem consistent with the pursuit of all the profits that can be squeezed out of the market.

For economists, Professor Ben Lewis's 1935 review in the Journal of Political Economy probably stated the case best. It was his judgment that the study "will be productive of more pronounced and sustained results in the field of law and public policy than in the realm of economic theory." One such substantial result was the Securities Exchange legislation whose detailed provisions and regulations rested very heavily indeed upon the analysis of the stockholder's situation in Book Three of "The Modern Corporation and Private Property." Public regulation of the stock exchanges is a large monument to any book.

The comparative freedom from major scandal that the securities industry has enjoyed since the 1930's owes much to the vigilance of the Securities and Exchange Commission. In turn the continuing dispersion of stock ownership, the emergence of "People's Capitalism," and the refurbished reputations of investment bankers and brokers all flow from a new public confidence created by the cleansing of the Augean stables of finance. Berle and Means identified a trend toward stock dispersion. The reforms they stimulated undoubtedly accelerated that trend.

It is time to return to the harder questions Berle and Means posed and, in part, answered. Should corporations as gargantuan as General Motors be allowed to operate without explicit federal supervision? Is Berle's and Means's favorite proposal of corporate self-redefinition feasible? Has it indeed occurred? Should corporations "as the dominant institution of the modern world," be responsible for eliminating poverty, rescuing the cities, restoring the countryside, and placing social welfare on a paying basis? Where is the public consensus that might guide corporate executives in the performance of their new duties?

The mere statement of such questions should remind us what a very short distance has been traveled toward explicit and acceptable redefinition of the corporation's legitimate role. Here is one illustrative puzzle: this summer the steel industry did its very best to raise prices by five per cent, in the wake of a moderately expensive settlement with the steelworkers. Presidential wrath, reinforced by threats to take defense contracts away from the offenders, led to a compromise increase of about half the industry's original change.

Query: by what legal right does a President intervene in the pricing decisions made by private corporations? In fact President Johnson did not have a legal leg to stand upon. Nevertheless, the episode is symbolic of a change in public and even business opinion that dates from President Kennedy's successful showdown five years ago with the leaders of the same industry. The men who run the steel industry have come grudgingly to accept the power, if not the right, of Federal government to oversee steel-pricing policy. What steel does substantially influences other prices and the balance of payments. Therefore steel, in common with other large concentrated industries, is seen to be affected with a public interest.

Or consider another of the role conflicts in which large enterprises get entangled. The major life-insurance companies have committed $1 billion to urban slum investment, at interest rates said to average 1 per cent below the market. One per cent of $1 billion is $10 million annually. A tax of $10 million has been assessed upon the owners of the life-insurance companies without their consent. What entitles the life insurance executives to take such action?

THE still inchoate doctrine of social responsibility upon which Berle and Means rested so much hope is possibly surfacing here. It is obvious, however, how far from general acceptance this doctrine is. Businessmen find it so uncomfortable that they are often constrained to con-

Adolf A. Berle.

Gardiner C. Means.

ceal their good deeds under the cloak of normal greed. A Henry Ford explains his company's serious and costly attempt to recruit hard-core blacks from the Detroit slums with the argument that such action is a protection against a recurrence of last summer's Detroit riots. Now while it is undeniable that the fortunes of Ford and Detroit are connected, it is hard to believe that Ford's action alone will really protect Detroit (and Ford) against the possibility of future riots.

A different sort of redefinition of corporate goals appears more significant, and in it profit retains its traditional primacy. Many alert business leaders seem to have identified social welfare with a new and promising market. Litton and Philco among others have managed job camps. U.S. Gypsum seeks to boom sales of its products by dramatic demonstrations of instant rehabilitation of dilapidated slum structures. Innkeepers enter the nursing home industry, bolstered by medicare benefits to the elderly. Alert plumbing-equipment concerns restyle themselves for the growing anti-pollution market. Businessmen have discovered a new set of public markets.

An important factor in encouraging business commitment to these new ways of making money is the drastic change in old, New Deal ideological animosity between government and business. A sophisticated grasp by each party of the potential benefits of partnerships between business and government made possible the love affair between the Johnson Administration and many of the most prestigious members of the business establishment. Of the varieties of such cooperation there is no end. Major defense contractors like McDonnell Douglas and General Dynamics are almost subdivisions of the Pentagon. Supersonic transport is being developed partly by public and partly by private research and development. One current and fashionable tendency is legislation encouraging business housing and plant investment in the slums by intricate combinations of tax incentives, credit guarantees, and direct subsidies.

The traditional logic of profit maximation is not seriously jarred by slum-investment programs that guarantee returns to private corporations of 12 to 14 per cent. Profit maximization may be a tougher beast, and social responsibility a more distant prospect, than Berle and Means believed.

Berle and Means made a final major contribution in their classic study. Their analysis struck a blow, possibly decisive, at the school which has sought early and late to break up large corporations and restore a regime of atomistic competition. For even in describing desirable corporate reforms, Berle and Means were affirming the legitimacy of the large corporation as very nearly a sovereign economic power.

MODERN critics of the large corporation usually take for granted its inevitability. Galbraith's imaginative analysis of the technostructure that manages the corporations really centers upon increasing its enlightenment and enlarging the government's capacity to supervise it in the interest of objectives the corporations neglect. The anti-trust movement has come on sad days because most Americans and even many economists judge large corporations to be useful, important, efficient, and occasionally even benevolent. For better or for worse, Berle and Means played a large role in the evolution of the corporation's good contemporary reputation.

Somewhat paradoxically, then, the largest influence these two critics of corporate practice have had is their contribution to the legitimacy of the giant corporation. Even political liberals are inclined to accept the giant corporation as an inevitable fact. The more cheerful among them do their best to see the corporation as potentially a powerful engine of social as well as economic progress. The liberals of the 1930's interpreted "The Modern Corporation and Private Property" as a radical tract. As matters have turned out, this book has done as much to promote a healthy capitalism as Keynes's "The General Theory of Employment, Interest and Money." ◆

September 15, 1968

The Cultural Contradiction

By DANIEL BELL

The ultimate support for any social system is the acceptance by the population of a moral justification of authority. The older justifications of bourgeois society lay in the defense of private property. But the "new capitalism" of the twentieth century has lacked such moral grounding.

It is in this context that one can see the weakness of corporate capitalism in trying to deal with some of the major political dilemmas of the century. The issues here are not primarily economic but sociocultural. The traditionalist defends fundamentalist religion, censorship, stricter divorce, and anti-abortion laws; the modernist is for secular rationality, freer personal relations, tolerance of sexual deviance, and the like.

Now, the curious fact is that the "new capitalism" of abundance, which emerged in the 1920's, has never been able to define its view of these cultural-political issues. Given its split character, it could not do so. Its values derive from the traditionalist past, and its language is the archaism of the Protestant Ethic.

The fact that the corporate economy has no unified value system of its own, or still mouthed a flaccid version of Protestant virtues, meant that liberalism could go ideologically unchallenged.

> *"American capitalism has lost its traditional legitimacy which was based on a moral system of reward rooted in a Protestant sanctification of work. It has substituted a hedonism which promises a material ease and luxury."*

But liberalism today is in trouble. Not only in politics, where its pragmatic style has been found wanting, but in an arena where it had joined in support of capitalism—in the economy. The economic philosophy of American liberalism had been rooted in the idea of growth.

The liberal answer to social problems such as poverty was that growth would provide the resources to raise the incomes of the poor. The thesis that growth was necessary to finance public services was the center of John Kenneth Galbraith's book "The Affluent Society."

And yet, paradoxically, it is the very idea of economic growth that is now coming under attack—and from liberals. Affluence is no longer seen as an answer. Growth is held responsible for the spoliation of the environment, the voracious use of natural resources, the crowding in the recreation areas, the densities in the city, and the like. One finds, startlingly, the idea of zero economic growth—or John Stuart Mill's idea of the "stationary state"—now proposed as a serious goal of government policy.

American society faces a number of crises. Yet these crises, I believe, are manageable (not solvable; what problems are?) if the political leadership is intelligent and determined. The resources are present (or will be, once the Vietnam war is ended) to relieve many of the obvious tensions and to finance the public needs of the society. The great need here is *time*, for the social changes which are required (a decent welfare and income maintenance system for the poor, the reorganization of the universities, the control of the environment) can only be handled within the space of a decade or more.

It is the demand for "instant solutions" which, in this respect, is the source of political trouble.

But the deeper and more lasting crisis is the cultural one. Changes in moral temper and culture—the fusion of imagination and life-styles (now so celebrated by Charles Reich of Yale)—are not amenable to "social engineering" or political control. They derive from the value and moral traditions of the society, and these cannot be "designed" by precept. The ultimate sources are the religious conceptions which undergird a society; the proximate sources are the "reward systems" and "motivations" (and their legitimacy) which derive from the arena of work (the social structure).

American capitalism has lost its traditional legitimacy which was based on a moral system of reward, rooted in a Protestant sanctification of work. It has substituted a hedonism which promises a material ease and luxury, yet shies away from all the historic implications which a "voluptuary system"—and all its social permissiveness and libertinism—implies.

The characteristic style of an industrial society is based on the principles of economics and economizing: on efficiency, least cost, maximization, optimization, and functional rationality. Yet it is at this point that it comes into sharpest conflict with the cultural trends of the day. The one emphasizes functional rationality, technocratic decision-making, and meritocratic rewards. The other, apocalyptic moods and antirational modes of behavior. It is this disjunction which is the historic crisis of Western society. This cultural contradiction, in the long run, is the deepest challenge to the society.

Daniel Bell is Professor of Sociology at Harvard University and co-editor of The Public Interest.

October 27, 1970

The end of the road?

Business Civilization In Decline

By Robert L. Heilbroner. 127 pp. New York: W. W. Norton & Co. Cloth, $6.95. Paper, $2.95.

By LEONARD SILK

Is capitalism dying? Robert L. Heilbroner is sure it is. He expects it to be gone within a century. Yet, although Heilbroner is himself a socialist, the impending demise of capitalism leaves him joyless; for he is full of apprehension about the conditions that are causing capitalism to rot and bringing statist regimes into being. And he fears that personal freedoms and parliamentary political institutions, which he reveres, may die with capitalism.

Thus Heilbroner, who bears the gentle title of Norman Thomas Professor of Economics at the New School for Social Research and who is always willing to contemplate the imperfections and dangers in his own case, exposes himself to the most basic attack of his enemies, the anti-socialists and anti-planners, such as Friedrich von Hayek and Milton Friedman. They argue that capitalism is the necessary condition for individual freedom and that to kill the one is to kill the other.

For these libertarians, the market is the only means of organizing a complex social and economic order without employing the coercive power of the state. Further, they contend the market system, with its superior ability to allocate resources and its powerful incentives, is both more efficient and more dynamic than any state-controlled system.

For Heilbroner, this paean of praise for capitalism is excessive but far from empty; he appreciates, as did Marx, both the freedom and the fecundity of capitalism. "It has been the first to show what man's activity can bring about. It has accomplished wonders far surpassing Egyptian pyramids, Roman aqueducts, and Gothic cathedrals," said the Communist Manifesto of 1848. And Heilbroner writes: "Much as we now inspect Chichén Itzá, the Great Wall, the pyramids, Machu Picchu, so we may some day visit and marvel at the ruins of the great steel works at Sparrows Point, the atomic complex at Hanford, the computer centers at Houston." But the worst of all, in the future we may long for the time when liberties were accorded to "artistic statements, social or sexual habits, political utterances."

Yet Heilbroner cannot bring himself to lament the passing of capitalism. No other civilization has permitted the calculus of self-interest so to dominate its culture. It has transmogrified greed and philistinism into social virtues, and subordinated all values to commercial values. Thus the business civilization combines liberty and selfishness, egalitarianism and extremes of wealth and poverty, vulgarity and democracy, creativity and waste, respect for the unique and autonomous individual and wage slavery, the conquest of space and the destruction of the environment.

This business civilization can't last beyond the lives of our grandchildren or great-grandchildren at the outside, says Heilbroner, because nature sets the limits. Capitalism is dying, he thinks, not, as Marx predicted, because of the growth of the proletariat and its progressive immiserization, or because the downswings of the business cycle cannot be controlled, but rather because of capitalism's very successes, as Joseph Schumpeter argued.

Capitalist affluence creates an anti-capitalist mentality among the intellectuals and among the children of the well-to-do. Affluence liberates the workers from desperate, immediate need and increases their power — thereby breeding chronic inflation. Advanced industrial technology requires the hierarchical organization of work —and hence, hierarchical control, both within corporations and outside them, via the government. But in the end this mighty industrial machine spews forth so much output that it depletes the earth's resources and pollutes its environment, jeopardizing human life.

Economic growth must cease; but growth was the daemon of capitalism, and capitalism cannot survive in a no-growth world. Without continuously increasing real income with which to buy off and pacify the lower classes, the struggle over distribution of income and wealth will intensify, nationally and internationally.

Even if disastrous conflicts are avoided, however, Heilbroner believes the cessation of growth will fatally undermine the spirit of capitalism. The driving capitalist entrepreneurs will give way to the carefully calculating state planners, who will

Leonard Silk, a member of The New York Times editorial board, is the author of "Capitalism: The Moving Target."

forcibly suppress the populace's appetite for material growth. Private property and the market mechanism will then lose both their legitimacy and their functional purposes.

What system will succeed capitalism? Here Heilbroner grows vague. He contends that terms like "fascism" and "socialism" will have little applicability to a society struggling to adapt to a "stringent and demanding" environment, in which the main goal will be survival. He resorts to analogy with the decline and fall of Rome to suggest that the business civilization will not suddenly die as the result of a single dramatic event; as Roman institutions lingered long after Rome was sacked in A.D. 410, capitalist forms and variant social orders will persist for many years. But finally the capitalist institutions and the capitalist spirit will expire, as did the "classical" spirit of Rome.

A crucial element in the transformation of the business system, he feels, will be the rise of a new religion that will play the role that Christianity did in first undermining the old Roman order and later providing the spirit and shaping the institutional forms of the new order in the Western world. What sort of religion will transform capitalism? A "statist" religion, says Heilbroner, that will elevate mankind's "collective and communal destiny" and absolutely subordinate private interests to public requirements.

In principle, freedom of expression might survive in such a "survival-minded" society but in practice, he fears, the centralization and intensification of political authority "make this seem doubtful."

Perhaps someday, on the still more distant horizon, he speculates, there may be dissolution of centralized power and a turn to self-sufficient and "ecologically safe" small-scale communities. But such a world cannot be reached until the massive structures of industrial civilization have been dissassembled, the threat of nuclear obliteration removed, and the administration of economic life internalized and divorced from the "need for external sanction." Such a world, the model of which would apparently be the farms and villages of a couple of centuries ago, is not on the agenda for the coming century, "at least not for the industrial nations of the world."

For the hundreds of millions who now owe their existence to the vast, worldwide interdependent industrial system, it is indeed difficult to imagine how the return to a set of small-scale farms would take place —except in the wake of a ghastly disaster.

Heilbroner's vision of the end of capitalism is grim. But without implying that grimness should be rebuked, I question whether his prophecy is founded on a correct reading of existing trends and does not ignore potentialities that could lead to a less alarming outcome. Are the capitalist societies less productive than the totalitarian societies? Are they incapable of incorporating socialist elements crucial to their survival? Are they more pollution-prone? Are they more disliked by their citizens or subjects? Are they less capable of developing and exploiting science and technology to deal with emerging problems?

In the United States right now, the public mood has turned against big business; but it is also turning against big government, a possibly important shift to which the politicians are now reacting. Meanwhile, less in the United States but increasingly in Europe, the organization of work is becoming less hierarchical, and the administration of economic life is growing more participatory.

Why should a society—which Daniel Bell calls a post-industrial society—that is shifting from the production of goods to services become a more centralized system, rather than the reverse? Admittedly, the provision of some services, such as telephone communications, may have large economies of scale, but others, including education, medicine, the arts and sciences, do not. Even in massive existing corporations, the degree of vertical and horizontal monopoly in the United States today is less obviously a result of economies of scale than of market power, often reinforced by government, which carries its own political dangers. New technology, such as computers, may make small organizations still more efficient.

Heilbroner has drawn an awesome picture of where existing trends might carry us. But his approach strikes me as overly deterministic and unduly limited to the most pessimistic assumptions. ■

March 21, 1976

Suggested Reading

Adams, Charles F. and Henry Adams. *Chapters of Erie.* Ithaca, New York: Cornell University Press, 1956.

Allen, Frederick Lewis. *Lords of Creation.* New York: Quadrangle, 1966.

Arnold, Thurman W. *Bottlenecks of Business.* New York: Da Capo, 1973.

Benson, Lee. *Merchants, Farmers and Railroads.* New York: Russell and Russell, 1969.

Blair, John M. *The Control of Oil.* New York: Pantheon, 1977.

Brandeis, Louis D. *Other People's Money.* Fairfield, N.J.: Augustus M. Kelley, 1932.

Berle, Adolf A. *Twentieth Century Capitalist Revolution.* New York: Harcourt, Brace, Jovanovich, 1954.

Berle, Adolf A. and Gardiner Means. *The Modern Corporation and Private Property.* New York: Harcourt, Brace, Jovanovich, 1968.

Burnham, James. *The Managerial Revolution.* Westport, Conn.: Greenwood, 1960.

Burns, Arthur R. *The Decline of Competition.* New York: McGraw-Hill, 1936.

Chamberlain, John. *Enterprising Americans: A Business History of the United States.* New York: Harper and Row, 1974.

Chandler, Alfred D. *The Visible Hand.* Cambridge, Mass: Harvard University Press, 1977.

Childs, Marquis W. and Douglas Cater. *Ethics in a Business Society.* Westport, Conn: Greenwood, 1973.

Clark, John M. *Social Control of Business.* New York: McGraw-Hill, 1939.

Cochran, Thomas C. *American Business in the 20th Century.* Cambridge, Mass.: Harvard University Press, 1972.

Cochran, Thomas C. *Business in American Life.* New York: McGraw-Hill, 1972.

Cochran, Thomas C. and W. Miller. *The Age of Enterprise.* New York: Harper and Row, 1968.

Danielian, N. *A.T. & T.* New York: Arno, 1974.

Davis, Joseph S. *Essays in the Earlier History of American Corporations.* New York: Russell and Russell, 1965.

Diamond, Sigmund. *The Reputation of the American Businessman.* Cambridge, Mass.: Harvard University Press, 1955.

Drucker, Peter. *The Concept of the Corporation. Briarcliff Manor, New York: Stein and Day,* 1972.

Galbraith, John K. *The New Industrial State.* Boston, Mass.: Houghton Miflin, 1967.

Gras, N.S.B. and H.M. Larson. *Casebook in American Business History.* New York: Irvington, 1939.

Grayson, T.J. *Leaders and Periods of American Finance.* New York: Arno, 1932.

Josephson, Matthew. *The Robber Barons.* New York: Harcourt, Brace, Jovanovich, 1962.

Kaplan, A.D.H. *Big Enterprise in a Competitive System.* Washington, D.C.: The Brookings Institute, 1954.

Kapp, K. William. *The Social Costs in a Private Enterprise.* New York: Schocken, 1971.

Kirkland, Edward C. *Industry Comes of Age.* New York: Quadrangle, 1967.

Larson, Henrietta. *Jay Cooke.* Westport, Conn.: Greenwood, 1969.

Leech, Harper and J.C. Carroll. *Armour and His Times.* New York: Arno, 1938.

Lloyd, Henry D. *Wealth Against Commonwealth.* Westport, Conn.: Greenwood, 1976.

Mahoney, Tom and L. Sloan. *The Great Merchants.* New York: Harper and Row, 1974.

Mason, Edward S. *The Corporation in Modern Society.* Cambridge, Mass.: Harvard University Press, 1959.

Moore, Wilbert E. *The Conduct of the Corporation.* Westport, Conn.: Greenwood, 1975.

Meyer, B.H. *History of the Northern Securities Case.* New York: Da Capo, 1972.

Nutter, G.W. *The Extent of Enterprise Monopoly in the United States.* New York: Columbia University Press, 1969.

Pecora, Ferdinand. *Wall Street Under Oath.* Fairfield, N.J.: Augustus M. Kelley, 1939.

Stocking, George W. and M.W. Watkins, *Monopoly and Free Enterprise.* Westport, Conn.: Greenwood, 1968.

Sward, Keith T. *The Legend of Henry Ford.* New York: Atheneum, 1968.

Tarbell, Ida M. *The Nationalizing of Business.* New York: Franklin Watts, Inc., 1936.

Wiebe, Robert H. *Businessmen and Reform.* New York: Quadrangle, 1968.

Arno Press provides in its collections basic libraries fo survey and advance study. The primary collection on Americar enterprise is "Big Business: Economic Power in a Free Society' edited by Leon Stein, Stuart Bruchey and Thomas C. Cochran Comprised of 51 volumes, it provides, as do other Arno collec tions, primary source books, scholarly studies and persona narratives. "Companies and Men" is a collection edited b Professor Bruchey and Vincent P. Carosso. It provides 3 volumes, each of which is a history of a single company. Pro fessor Bruchey is also the editor of an open-ended collectio which now numbers 63 "Dissertations on American Economi History."

Other Arno collections that the student of Big Business wi find useful and exciting are "American Farmers and the Rise o Agribusiness" 46 volumes; "The Evolution of Capitalism" 3 volumes; "Getting and Spending: the Consumer's Dilemma" 5 volumes; "Technology and Society" 53 volumes; "Wall Stre and the Security Markets" 58 volumes; and "National Burea of Economic Research Publications in Reprint" 57 volumes.

Index